SECOND EDITION

Financial Accounting using IFRS

M. H. FRANCO WONG
University of Toronto

THOMAS R. DYCKMAN
Cornell University

MICHELLE L. HANLON
Massachusetts Institute of Technology

ROBERT P. MAGEE
Northwestern University

GLENN M. PFEIFFER
Chapman University

To my parents, my wife, Eszter, and my daughters, Olivia and Sofi.
—MHFW

To my wife, Ann, and children, Daniel, James, Linda, and David; and to Pete Dukes, a friend who is always there.
—TRD

To my husband, Chris, and to our children, Clark and Josie.
—MLH

To my wife, Peggy, and our family, Paul and Teisha, Michael and Heather, and grandchildren Sage, Caillean, Rhiannon, Corin, Connor, and Harrison.
—RPM

To my wife, Kathie, and my daughter, Jaclyn.
—GMP

Cambridge Business Publishers

FINANCIAL ACCOUNTING USING IFRS, Second Edition, by M.H. Franco Wong, Thomas R. Dyckman, Michelle L. Hanlon, Robert P. Magee, and Glenn M. Pfeiffer.

Student Edition ISBN: 978-1-61853-196-4

Bookstores & Faculty: To order this book, contact the company via email **customerservice@cambridgepub.com**.

Printed in the United States of America
10 9 8 7 6 5 4 3 2

About the Authors

The combined skills and expertise of Franco Wong, Tom Dyckman, Michelle Hanlon, Bob Magee, and Glenn Pfeiffer create the ideal team to author this exciting financial accounting textbook. Their combined experience in award-winning teaching, consulting, and research in the area of financial accounting and analysis provides a powerful foundation for this pioneering textbook.

M.H. Franco Wong is CPA Ontario Professor of Financial Accounting at the Rotman School of Management at the University of Toronto. He earned his Ph.D. degree in accounting from the Wharton School of the University of Pennsylvania and his B.A. and M.A. in economics from the University of Lethbridge and Simon Fraser University, respectively. Professor Wong has also taught at the University of California at Berkeley's Haas School of Business, University of Chicago's Graduate School of Business (now Booth), and INSEAD. During the 2013–2014 academic year, he was president of the Chinese Accounting Professors' Association of North America.

Professor Wong's research focuses on the production and dissemination of accounting information and the use of accounting information for valuation and contracting purposes. He has examined financial reporting issues about derivatives financial instruments, Internet companies, employee stock options, share repurchases, earnings management, real investment effects of accounting, and equity research analysts. His research has appeared in leading academic journals, including *Journal of Accounting and Economics, Journal of Accounting Research, Review of Accounting Studies,* and *The Accounting Review*. Professor Wong has given over 100 presentations at numerous business schools and conferences around the world. Between 2007 and 2013, he co-organised eight academic conferences in Canada, China, and France.

Professor Wong has taught financial accounting and financial statement analysis to undergraduate and MBA students. He has received several awards for teaching excellence at the Haas School of Business and Rotman School of Management.

Thomas R. Dyckman is Ann Whitney Olin Professor Emeritus of Accounting and Quantitative Analysis at Cornell University's Johnson Graduate School of Management. In addition to teaching accounting and quantitative analysis, he has taught in Cornell's Executive Development Program. He earned his doctorate degree from the University of Michigan. He is a former member of the Financial Accounting Standards Board Advisory Committee and the Financial Accounting Foundation, which oversees the FASB. He was president of the American Accounting Association in 1982 and received the association's *Outstanding Educator* Award for the year 1987. He also received the AICPA's *Notable Contributions to Accounting Literature Award* in 1966 and 1978.

Professor Dyckman has extensive industrial experience that includes work with the U.S. Navy and IBM. He has conducted seminars for Cornell Executive Development Program and Managing the Next Generation of Technology, as well as for Ocean Spray, Goodyear, Morgan Guaranty, GTE, Southern New England Telephone, and Goulds Pumps. Professor Dyckman was elected to The Accounting Hall of Fame in 2009.

Professor Dyckman has coauthored eleven books and written over 50 journal articles on topics from financial markets to the application of quantitative and behavioral theory to administrative decision making. He has been a member of the editorial boards of *The Accounting Review, The Journal of Finance and Quantitative Analysis, The Journal of Accounting and Economics, The Journal of Management Accounting Research,* and *The Journal of Accounting Education*.

Michelle L. Hanlon is the Howard W. Johnson Professor at the MIT Sloan School of Management. She earned her doctorate degree at the University of Washington. Prior to joining MIT, she was a faculty member at the University of Michigan. Professor Hanlon has taught financial accounting to undergraduates, MBA students, Executive MBA students, and Masters of Finance students. Professor Hanlon also teaches Taxes and Business Strategy to MBA students. She is the winner of the 2013 Jamieson Prize for Excellence in Teaching at MIT Sloan.

Professor Hanlon's research focuses primarily on the intersection of taxation and financial accounting. Her recent work examines the capital market effects of the accounting for income tax, the reputational effects of corporate tax avoidance, and the economic consequences of U.S. international tax policies for multinational corporations. She has published research studies in the *Journal of Accounting and Economics*, the *Journal of Accounting Research*, *The Accounting Review*, the *Review of Accounting Studies*, the *Journal of Finance*, the *Journal of Financial Economics*, the *Journal of Public Economics*, and others. She has won several awards for her research and has presented her work at numerous universities and conferences. Professor Hanlon has served on several editorial boards and currently serves as an editor at the *Journal of Accounting and Economics*.

Professor Hanlon is a co-author on another textbook, *Taxes and Business Strategy*. She has testified in front of the U.S. Senate Committee on Finance and the U.S. House of Representatives Committee on Ways and Means about the interaction of financial accounting and tax policy. She served as a U.S. delegate to the American-Swiss Young Leaders Conference in 2010 and worked as an Academic Fellow at the U.S. House Ways and Means Committee in 2015.

Robert P. Magee is Keith I. DeLashmutt Professor of Accounting Information and Management at the Kellogg School of Management at Northwestern University. He received his A.B., M.S. and Ph.D. from Cornell University. Prior to joining the Kellogg faculty in 1976, he was a faculty member at the University of Chicago's Graduate School of Business. For academic year 1980-81, he was a visiting faculty member at IMEDE (now IMD) in Lausanne, Switzerland.

Professor Magee's research focuses on the use of accounting information to facilitate decision-making and control within organisations. He has published articles in *The Accounting Review*, the *Journal of Accounting Research*, the *Journal of Accounting and Economics*, and a variety of other journals. He is the author of *Advanced Managerial Accounting* and co-author (with Thomas R. Dyckman and David H. Downes) of *Efficient Capital Markets and Accounting: A Critical Analysis*. The latter book received the Notable Contribution to the Accounting Literature Award from the AICPA in 1978. Professor Magee has served on the editorial boards of *The Accounting Review*, the *Journal of Accounting Research*, the *Journal of Accounting and Economics* and the *Journal of Accounting, Auditing and Finance*. From 1994–96, he served as Editor of *The Accounting Review*, the quarterly research journal of the American Accounting Association. He received the American Accounting Association's Outstanding Accounting Educator Award in 1999 and the Illinois CPA Society Outstanding Educator Award in 2000.

Professor Magee teaches financial accounting to MBA and Executive MBA students. He has received several teaching awards at the Kellogg School, including the Alumni Choice Outstanding Professor Award in 2003.

Glenn M. Pfeiffer is the Warren and Doris Uehlinger Professor of Business and Associate Dean at the George L. Argyros School of Business and Economics at Chapman University. He received his M.S. and Ph.D. from Cornell University after he earned a bachelors degree from Hope College. Prior to joining the faculty at the Argyros School, he held appointments at the University of Washington, Cornell University, the University of Chicago, the University of Arizona, and San Diego State University.

Professor Pfeiffer's research focuses on financial reporting and capital markets. He has investigated issues relating to lease accounting, LIFO inventory liquidation, earnings per share, employee stock options, corporate reorganisation, and technology investments. He has published articles in *The Accounting Review*, the *Financial Analysts Journal*, the *International Journal of Accounting Information Systems*, the *Journal of Applied Business Research*, the *Journal of High Technology Management Research*, the *Journal of Accounting Education*, and several other academic journals. In addition, he has published numerous case studies in financial accounting and reporting.

Professor Pfeiffer teaches financial accounting and financial analysis to undergraduate, MBA, and Law students. He has also taught managerial accounting for MBAs. He has won several teaching awards at both the undergraduate and graduate levels.

Preface

Welcome to the second edition of *Financial Accounting using IFRS*. We wrote this book to equip students with the accounting techniques and insights necessary to succeed in today's global business environment. It reflects our combined experience in teaching financial accounting to students at all levels and in several countries. For anyone who pursues a career in business, the ability to read, analyse, and interpret published financial reports is an essential skill. *Financial Accounting using IFRS* is written for future business leaders who want to understand how financial statements are prepared and how the information in published financial reports is used by investors, creditors, financial analysts, and managers. Our goal is to provide the most engaging, relevant, and accessible textbook available.

TARGET AUDIENCE

Financial Accounting using IFRS is intended for use in the first financial accounting course at either the undergraduate or graduate level at universities that want to teach IFRS (U.S. GAAP is not covered). This book balances the preparation of financial statements with their analysis and interpretation. This book accommodates mini-courses lasting only a few days as well as extended courses lasting a full semester.

Financial Accounting using IFRS is real-world oriented and focuses on the most salient aspects of accounting. It teaches students how to read, analyse, and interpret financial accounting data to make informed business decisions. To that end, it consistently incorporates **real company data**, both in the body of each chapter and throughout the assignment material.

REAL DATA INCORPORATED THROUGHOUT

Today's business students must be skilled in using real financial statements to make business decisions. We feel strongly that the more exposure students get to real financial statements, the more comfortable they become with the variety in financial statements that exists across companies and industries. Through their exposure to various financial statements, students will learn that, while financial statements do not all look the same, they can readily understand and interpret them to make business decisions. Furthermore, today's students must have the skills to go beyond basic financial statements to interpret and apply nonfinancial disclosures, such as footnotes and supplementary reports. We expose students to the analysis and interpretation of real company data and nonfinancial disclosures through the use of focus companies in each chapter, the generous incorporation of footnotes, financial analysis discussions in nearly every chapter, and an abundance of assignments that draw on real company data and disclosures.

Focus Companies for Each Chapter

Each chapter's content is explained through the accounting and reporting activities of real companies. Each chapter incorporates a "focus company" for special emphasis and demonstration. The enhanced instructional value of focus companies comes from the way they engage students in real analysis and interpretation. Focus companies were selected based on student appeal and the diversity of countries and industries.

Chapter 1 Roche (Switzerland)
Chapter 2 Indigo (Canada)
Chapter 3 Indigo (Canada)
Chapter 4 Qantas Airways (Australia)
Chapter 5 Vodafone (United Kingdom)
Chapter 6 TomTom (The Netherlands)
Chapter 7 VTech (Hong Kong)
Chapter 8 Airbus (France and Germany)
Chapter 9 Samsung Electronics (South Korea)
Chapter 10 Unilever (The Netherlands and United Kingdom)
Chapter 11 Thomson Reuters (Canada)
Chapter 12 SMRT (Singapore)

Footnotes and Management Disclosures

We incorporate footnote and other management disclosures, where appropriate, throughout the book. We explain the significance of the footnote and then demonstrate how to use the disclosed information to make managerial inferences and decisions. A representative sample follows.

Footnote Disclosures, and Interpretations

In its balance sheets, **TomTom** reports trade receivables, net of allowance for doubtful receivables of €115,429,000 at December 31, 2013, and €149,834,000 at December 31, 2012. In the note to the financial statements, the company provides the following information.

(€ in thousands)	2013	2012
Gross trade receivables	118,546	151,697
Allowance for doubtful receivables	− 3,117	− 1,863
TRADE RECEIVABLES (NET)	115,429	149,834

We expect to recover all receivables within a year. An allowance has been made for estimated unrecoverable amounts from the sale of goods. The carrying amount of trade receivables approximates their fair value. The group does not hold any collateral over these balances.

The group's exposure to credit risk is influenced mainly by the individual characteristics of each customer. There is some concentration of credit risk with certain of our large custom-

Financial Analysis Discussions

Each chapter includes a financial analysis discussion that introduces key ratios and applies them to the financial statements of the chapter's focus company. By weaving some analysis into each chapter, we try to instill in students a deeper appreciation for the significance of the accounting methods being discussed. One such analysis discussion follows.

ANALYSING FINANCIAL STATEMENTS

LO5 Calculate accounts receivable turnover and average collection period.

Analysis Objective

We want to evaluate a company's management of its receivables.

Analysis Tool Accounts receivable turnover (ART) and average collection period (ACP)

$$\textbf{Accounts receivable turnover (ART)} = \frac{\textbf{Sales revenue}}{\textbf{Average accounts receivable}}$$

Applying the Accounts Receivable Turnover Ratio to TomTom

$$2013\text{ ART} = \frac{\$963,454}{(\$115,429 + \$149,834)/2} = 7.3\text{ times}$$

$$2012\text{ ART} = \frac{\$1,057,134}{(\$149,834 + \$184,939)/2} = 6.3\text{ times}$$

Guidance Accounts receivable turnover measures the number of times each year that accounts receivable is converted into cash. A high turnover ratio suggests that receivables are well managed and that sales revenue quickly leads to cash collected from customers.

A companion measure to accounts receivable turnover is the **average collection period**, also called *days sales outstanding* which is defined as:

$$\textbf{Average collection period (ACP)} = \frac{\textbf{Average accounts receivable}}{\ldots} = \frac{\textbf{365 days}}{\ldots}$$

Assignments that Draw on Real Data

It is essential for students to be able to apply what they have learned to real financial statements. Therefore, we have included an abundance of assignments in each chapter that draw on recent, real data and disclosures. These assignments are readily identified by an icon in the margin that includes the company's name and its country of origin. A representative example follows.

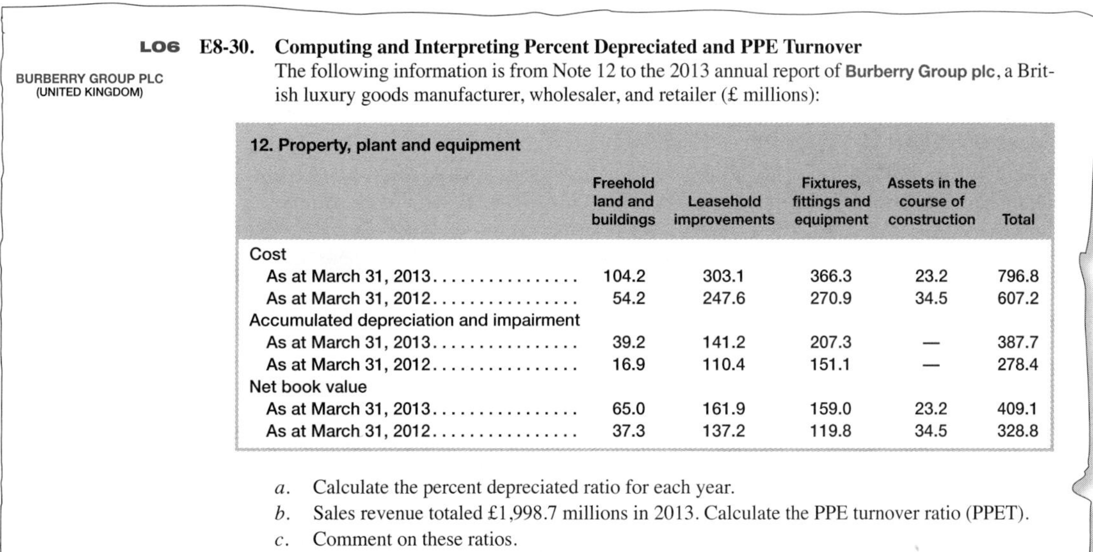

LO6 **E8-30. Computing and Interpreting Percent Depreciated and PPE Turnover**

BURBERRY GROUP PLC (UNITED KINGDOM)

The following information is from Note 12 to the 2013 annual report of Burberry Group plc, a British luxury goods manufacturer, wholesaler, and retailer (£ millions):

12. Property, plant and equipment

	Freehold land and buildings	Leasehold improvements	Fixtures, fittings and equipment	Assets in the course of construction	Total
Cost					
As at March 31, 2013	104.2	303.1	366.3	23.2	796.8
As at March 31, 2012	54.2	247.6	270.9	34.5	607.2
Accumulated depreciation and impairment					
As at March 31, 2013	39.2	141.2	207.3	—	387.7
As at March 31, 2012	16.9	110.4	151.1	—	278.4
Net book value					
As at March 31, 2013	65.0	161.9	159.0	23.2	409.1
As at March 31, 2012	37.3	137.2	119.8	34.5	328.8

a. Calculate the percent depreciated ratio for each year.
b. Sales revenue totaled £1,998.7 millions in 2013. Calculate the PPE turnover ratio (PPET).
c. Comment on these ratios.

BALANCED APPROACH

As instructors of introductory financial accounting, we recognise that the first financial accounting course serves the general business students as well as potential accounting majors. *Financial Accounting* embraces this reality. This book **balances financial reporting, analysis, interpretation**, and **decision making** with the more standard aspects of accounting such as **journal entries**, **T-accounts**, and the **preparation of financial statements**.

3-Step Process: Analyse, Journalise, Post

One technique we use throughout the book to maintain a balanced approach is the incorporation of a 3-step process to analyse and record transactions. **Step 1** analyses the impact of various transactions on the financial statements using the financial statement effects template. **Step 2** records the transaction using journal entries and **Step 3** requires students to post the journal entries to T-accounts.

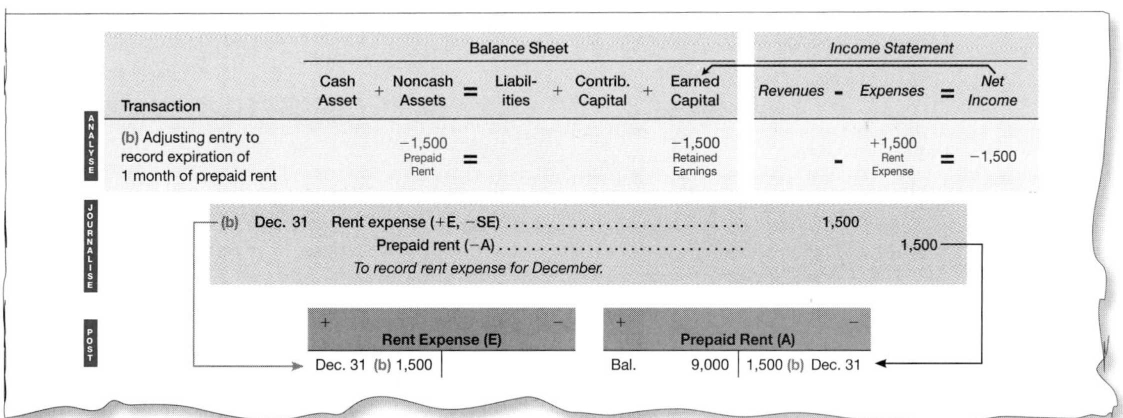

The template captures each transaction's effects on the four financial statements: the balance sheet, income statement, statement of changes in equity, and statement of cash flows. For the balance sheet, we differentiate between cash and noncash assets to identify the cash effects of transactions. Likewise, equity is separated into the contributed and earned capital components (the latter includes retained earnings as its major element). Finally, income statement effects are separated into revenues, expenses, and net income (the updating of retained earnings is denoted with an arrow line running from net income to earned capital). This template provides a convenient means to represent financial accounting transactions and events in a simple, concise manner for assessing their effects on financial statements.

INNOVATIVE PEDAGOGY

Business Insights

Students appreciate and become more engaged when they can see the real-world relevance of what they are learning in the classroom. We have included a generous number of current, real-world examples throughout each chapter in Business Insight boxes. The following is a representative example:

BUSINESS INSIGHT

Investor Beware During fiscal year 2014, the German airline **Lufthansa** increased the useful life of its aircrafts by eight years, leading to a €340 million positive accounting effect. Lufthansa, the world's largest airline by revenue, indicated that the change would put its depreciation policy in line with industry practice. While Lufthansa has a legitimate reason to revise its depreciation assumption, investors should discount any improvement in profit attributed to this one-time accounting change.

Decision Making Orientation

One primary goal of a financial accounting course is to teach students the skills needed to apply their accounting knowledge to solving real business problems. With that goal in mind, **You Make the Call** boxes in each chapter encourage students to apply the material presented to solving actual business scenarios.

YOU MAKE THE CALL

You are the Division Manager You are the division manager for a main operating division of your company. You are concerned that a declining PPE turnover is adversely affecting your division's profitability. What specific actions can you take to increase PPE turnover? [Answers on page 383]

Mid-Chapter and Chapter-End Reviews

Financial accounting can be challenging—especially for students lacking business experience or previous exposure to business courses. To reinforce concepts presented in each chapter and to ensure student comprehension, we include mid-chapter and chapter-end reviews that require students to recall and apply the financial accounting techniques and concepts described in each chapter.

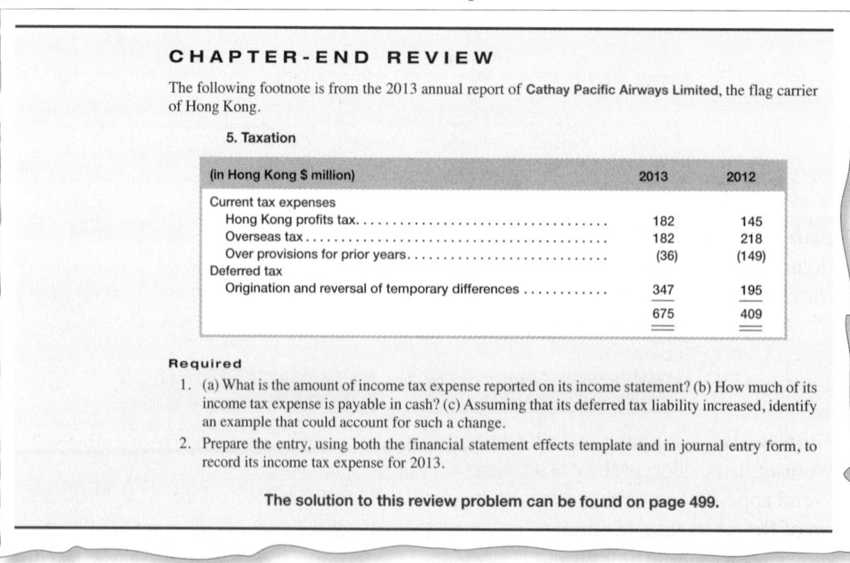

CHAPTER-END REVIEW

The following footnote is from the 2013 annual report of **Cathay Pacific Airways Limited**, the flag carrier of Hong Kong.

5. Taxation

(in Hong Kong $ million)	2013	2012
Current tax expenses		
Hong Kong profits tax	182	145
Overseas tax	182	218
Over provisions for prior years	(36)	(149)
Deferred tax		
Origination and reversal of temporary differences	347	195
	675	409

Required

1. (a) What is the amount of income tax expense reported on its income statement? (b) How much of its income tax expense is payable in cash? (c) Assuming that its deferred tax liability increased, identify an example that could account for such a change.
2. Prepare the entry, using both the financial statement effects template and in journal entry form, to record its income tax expense for 2013.

The solution to this review problem can be found on page 499.

Research Insights for Business Students

Academic research plays an important role in the way business is conducted, accounting is performed, and students are taught. It is important for students to recognise how modern research and modern business practice interact. Therefore, we periodically incorporate relevant research to help students understand the important relation between research and modern business.

RESEARCH INSIGHT

A recent study examines the classification of interest paid, interest received, and dividends received for companies from 13 European countries. It finds that (1) 77% of the firms classify interest paid as operating cash flows and 22% classify it as financing cash flows; (2) 54% of the firms report interest receipts as operating cash flows and 37% report them as investing cash flows; and (3) 49% of the firms classify dividends received as operating cash flows and 48% as investing cash flows. It also documents that over 99% of the firms report taxes paid in operating cash flows and dividends paid in financing cash flows. Source: "Flexibility in cash flow reporting classification choices under IFRS," by E. Gordon, E. Henry, B. Jorgensen, and C. Linthicum.

FLEXIBILITY FOR COURSES OF VARYING LENGTHS

Many instructors have approached us to ask about suggested chapter coverage based on courses of varying length. To that end, we provide the following table of possible course designs:

	15 Week Semester-Course	10 Week Quarter-Course	6 Week Mini-Course	1 Week Intensive-Course
Chapter 1	Week 1	Week 1	Week 1	Day 1
Chapter 2	Week 2 & 3	Week 2	Week 1 & 2	
Chapter 3	Week 3 & 4	Week 3 & 4	Week 2 & 3	Day 2
Chapter 4	Week 5 & 6	Week 4 & 5	Optional	Optional
Chapter 5	Week 6 & 7	Optional	Optional	Optional
Chapter 6	Week 7 & 8	Week 6	Week 3	Day 3
Chapter 7	Week 9	Week 7	Week 4	Day 4
Chapter 8	Week 10	Week 8	Week 5	
Chapter 9	Week 11 & 12	Week 9	Week 6	Day 5
Chapter 10	Week 12 & 13	Week 10	Week 6 (optional)	Skim
Chapter 11	Week 14	Optional	Optional	Optional
Chapter 12	Week 15	Optional	Optional	Optional

NEW IN THE SECOND IFRS EDITION

- **New Co-author:** Michelle Hanlon, the Howard W. Johnson Professor and Professor of Accounting at the MIT Sloan School of Management, joined the 2nd IFRS edition. Michelle has won several awards for her research and is the winner of the 2013 Jamieson Prize for Excellence in Teaching at Sloan where she regularly teaches introductory financial accounting to MBAs. Hanlon recently testified in front of the U.S. Senate Committee on Finance and the U.S. House of Representatives Committee on Ways and Means regarding U.S. tax policy. She brings a wealth of knowledge and expertise to this best-selling author team.
- **Updated Standards:** As appropriate, the text and assignments have been updated to reflect the latest standards. A brief discussion of the pending Revenue Recognition standard is included in Chapter 6 and the chapter-end appendix contains more detailed coverage of the new standard. Chapter 10 now includes a discussion of the new lease standard.

In addition to the chapter-specific changes, there have been several changes that span the entire book. Some of these global changes include: updated numbers for examples, illustrations, and assignments that use real data; updated footnotes and other nonfinancial disclosures; updated excerpts from the business and popular press; and some assignments have been revised or replaced with new assignments.

SUPPLEMENT PACKAGE

Fundamentals of Financial Accounting Tutorial

This interactive tutorial is intended for use in programs that either require or would like to offer a pre-term tutorial that creates a baseline of accounting knowledge for students with little to no prior exposure to financial accounting. Initially developed as a pre-term tutorial for first year MBA students, this product can be used as a warm-up for any introductory level financial accounting course. It is designed as an asynchronous, interactive, self-paced experience for students.

Available Learning Modules (You Select)

1. Introducing Financial Accounting (approximate completion time 2 hours)
2. Constructing Financial Statements (approximate completion time 4 hours)
3. Adjusting Entries and Completing the Accounting Cycle (approximate completion time 4 hours)
4. Reporting and Analysing Cash Flows (approximate completion time 3.5 hours)
5. Analysing and Interpreting Financial Statements (approximate completion time 3.5 hours)

This is a separate, saleable item. Contact your sales representative to receive more information or email customerservice@cambridgepub.com.

Companion Casebook

Cases in Financial Reporting, 8th edition by Michael Drake (Brigham Young University), Ellen Engel (University of Chicago), D. Eric Hirst (University of Texas – Austin), and Mary Lea McAnally (Texas A&M University). This book comprises 27 cases and is a perfect companion book for faculty interested in exposing students to a wide range of real financial statements. The cases are current and cover companies from Canada, France, Austria, the Netherlands, the UK, India, as well as from the U.S. Many of the U.S. companies are major multinationals. Each case deals with a specific financial accounting topic within the context of one (or more) company's financial statements. Each case contains financial statement information and a set of directed questions pertaining to one or two specific financial accounting issues. This is a separate, saleable casebook (**ISBN 978-1-61853-122-3**). Contact your sales representative to receive a desk copy or email customerservice@cambridgepub.com.

For Instructors

- **Solutions Manual:** Created by the authors, the Solutions Manual contains complete solutions to all the assignment material in the text.
- **Test Bank/Computerised Test Bank:** The test bank includes multiple-choice items, matching questions, short-essay questions, and problems. The computerised version of the test bank enables an instructor to add and edit questions; create up to 99 versions of each test; attach graphic files to questions; import and export AsCii files; and select questions based on type or learning objective. It provides password protection for saved tests and question databases and is able to run on a network.
- **PowerPoint:** The PowerPoint slides outline key elements of each chapter.
- **Website:** All instructor materials are accessible via the book's website (password-protected) along with other useful links and marketing information. www.cambridgepub.com

For Students

- **Website:** Practice quizzes and other useful links are available to students free of charge on the book's website.

ACKNOWLEDGMENTS

Special thanks to Eszter Palancz for creating many of the end-of-chapter real-company assignments and for revising Chapter 5. This book has benefited greatly from the valuable feedback of focus group attendees, reviewers, students, and colleagues. We are extremely grateful to them for their help in making this project a success.

Darrin Ambrose, *University of Calgary*
Ben-Hsien Bao, *Hong Kong Polytechnic University*
Jan Barton, *Emory University*
Dan Bens, *INSEAD*
Anne Beyer, *Stanford University*
Mary Ellen Carter, *Boston College*
Judson Caskey, *UCLA*
Paul Chaney, *Vanderbilt University*
Craig Chapman, *Northwestern University*
Travis Chow, *Singapore Management University*
Hans Christensen, *University of Chicago*
John Core, *MIT*
Maria Correia, *London Business School*
Mark DeFond, *University of Southern California*
Ramy Elitzur, *University of Toronto*
Tom Fields, *Washington University*
Yuyan Guan, *City University of Hong Kong*
Wayne Guay, *University of Pennsylvania*
Luzi Hail, *University of Pennsylvania*
Rebecca Hann, *University of Maryland*
Haihong He, *California State University–Los Angeles*
Gilles Hilary, *INSEAD*
Elisabetta Ipino, *Concordia University*
Kim Jae Bum, *Singapore Management University*
Alan Jagolinzer, *University of Colorado—Boulder*
Duane Kennedy, *University of Waterloo*
Jane Kennedy, *University of San Diego*
Edmund Keung, *National University of Singapore*
Irene Kim, *George Washington University*
Gopal Krishnan, *George Mason University*
Benjamin Lansford, *Pennsylvania State University*
Dongyoung Lee, *McGill University*
Na Li, *Singapore Management University*
Xu Li, *University of Hong Kong*
Mingzhi Liu, *University of Manitoba*
Xiaohong Liu, *University of Hong Kong*
Gilad Livne, *University of Exeter*
Ana Marques, *Nova School of Business and Economics*
Greg Miller, *University of Michigan*
James Naughton, *Northwestern University*
Karen Nelson, *Rice University*
Jeff Ng, *Chinese University of Hong Kong*
Christopher Noe, *MIT*
David Oesch, *University of Zurich*
Eszter Palancz, *University of Toronto*
Tharindra Ranasinghe, *Singapore Management University*
Annelies Renders, *Maastricht University*
Gianfranco Siciliano, *Bocconi University*
Sri Sridharan, *Northwestern University*
Dragan Stojanovic, *University of Toronto*
Shyam Sunder, *University of Arizona*
Robert J. Swieringa, *Cornell University*
Ken Trotman, *University of New South Wales*
Ning Zhang, *Queen's University*
Yuping Zhao, *University of Houston*
Zili Zhuang, *Chinese University of Hong Kong*

In addition, we are extremely grateful to George Werthman, Jill Sternard, Katie Jones-Aiello, Jocelyn Mousel, Debbie McQuade, Terry McQuade, and the entire team at Cambridge Business Publishers for their encouragement, enthusiasm, and guidance.

Franco Wong	Thomas R. Dyckman	Michelle L. Hanlon	Robert P. Magee	Glenn M. Pfeiffer
Toronto, ON Canada	*Ithaca, NY U.S.A*	*Cambridge, MA U.S.A.*	*Evanston, IL U.S.A*	*Orange, CA U.S.A*

Brief Contents

Contents

Chapter 3
Adjusting Accounts for Financial Statements 93

Chapter 4
Reporting and Analysing Cash Flows 149

Chapter 5
Analysing and Interpreting Financial Statements 211

Chapter 6
Reporting and Analysing Revenues and Receivables 271

Chapter 9
Reporting and Analysing Liabilities 399

Chapter 10
Reporting and Analysing Leases, Pensions, and Income Taxes 447

Chapter 11
Reporting and Analysing Shareholders' Equity 503

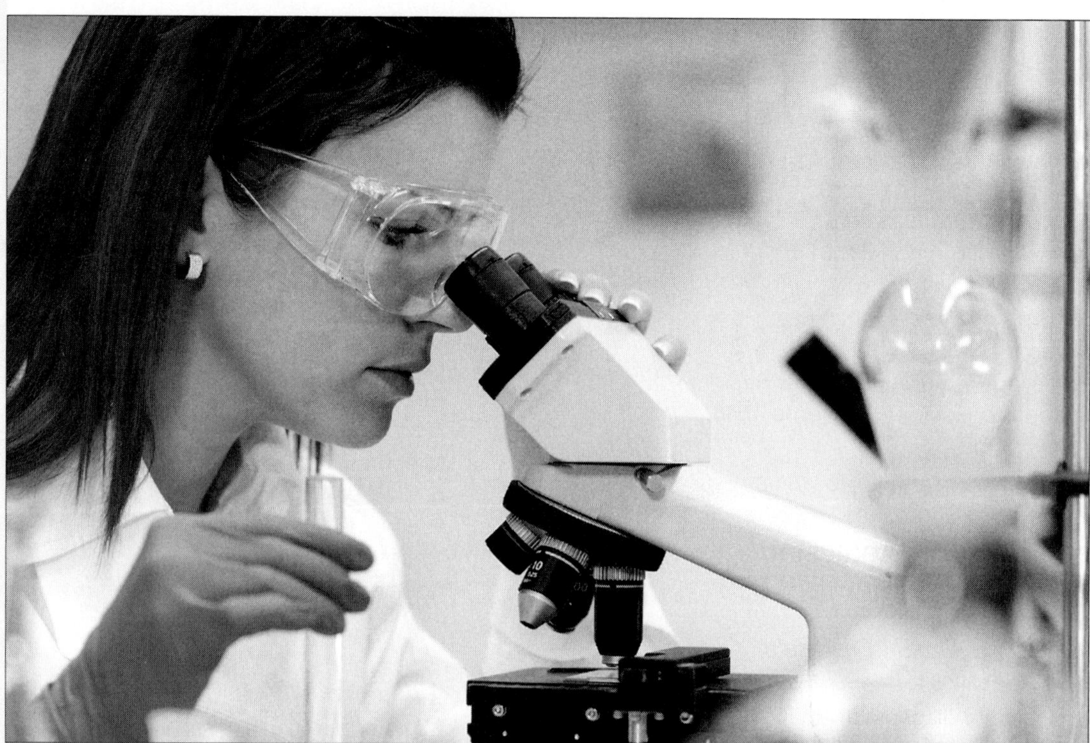

LEARNING OBJECTIVES

1. Identify the users of accounting information and discuss the costs and benefits of disclosure. (p. 4)

2. Describe a company's business activities and explain how these activities are represented by the accounting equation. (p. 7)

3. Introduce the four key financial statements including the balance sheet, income statement, statement of changes in equity, and statement of cash flows. (p. 11)

4. Describe the institutions that regulate financial accounting and their role in establishing generally accepted accounting principles. (p. 17)

5. Compute two key ratios that are commonly used to assess profitability and risk—return on equity and the debt-to-equity ratio. (p. 20)

6. Appendix 1A: Explain the conceptual framework for financial reporting. (p. 24)

CHAPTER

Introducing Financial Accounting

1

Founded in 1896, **Roche** is a global healthcare company based in Basel, Switzerland. Roche markets medicines and diagnostic tests in over 150 countries, produces more than 100 medicines, and operates 26 manufacturing sites in Brazil, China, Germany, Ireland, Italy, Japan, Singapore, Switzerland, the United Kingdom, and the United States. Its holding company, Roche Holding AG, is traded on the SIX Swiss Exchange and the OTCQX market in the United States. In 2013, Roche reported net income of 11.4 billion Swiss francs (CHF) on revenues of 46.8 billion CHF.

ROCHE
www.Roche.com

Roche operates in two sectors. Its pharmaceuticals division discovers, develops and manufactures medicines in oncology, infectious diseases, metabolism, and neuroscience. It is the largest biotechnology company in the world. Its diagnostics division develops and offers products used to test blood and other body fluids and tissue samples for the diagnosis, treatment, and monitoring of diseases. In 2013, pharmaceuticals and diagnostics sales account for 78.2% and 21.8% of Roche's revenues, respectively.

Roche is a science-based healthcare company and invests heavily in innovative research and development. In 2013, it spent 8.7 billion CHF, or 18.6% of its revenues, on research and development. Moreover, Roche expanded its capabilities by acquiring other companies such as Chugai Pharmaceuticals, a leading biotech company in Japan; Ventana, a leader in tissue diagnostics in the United States; and Genentech, a world-class biotech company in the United States. Roche also augments its internal research and development by collaborating with over 150 partners worldwide.

In 2013, Roche had over 30 late-stage (phase III) drug development projects, consisting of over 70 new potential medicines and 20 additional indications for existing medicines. It received approvals from the European Union and United States for three of the compounds and passed phase III trial tests for four other compounds. It also launched three new diagnostics products in 2013.

In 2013, Roche was the 20th largest company in the world and the third largest in Europe by market capitalisation. By 2013, it had increased its dividends for 27 consecutive years. Roche's success is not an accident. Along the way, Roche management made countless decisions that ultimately led the company to where it is today. Each of these decisions involved identifying alternative courses of action and weighing their costs, benefits, and risks in light of the available information.

Accounting is the process of identifying, measuring, and communicating financial information to help people make *economic* decisions. People use financial accounting information to facilitate a wide variety of transactions, including assessing whether, and on what terms, they should invest in a firm,

(continued on next page)

(continued from previous page)

seek employment in a business, or continue purchasing its products. Accounting information is crucial to any successful business, and without it, most businesses would not even exist.

This book explains how to create and analyse *financial statements*, an important source of accounting information prepared by companies to communicate with a variety of users. We begin by introducing transactions between the firm and its investors, creditors, suppliers, employees, and customers. We continue by demonstrating how accounting principles are applied to these transactions to create the financial statements. Then, we "invert" the process and learn how to analyse the firm's financial statements to assess the firm's underlying economic performance. Our philosophy is simple—we believe it is crucial to have a deep understanding of financial accounting to become critical readers and users of financial statements. Financial statements tell a story—a business story. Our goal is to understand that story, and apply the knowledge gleaned from financial statements to make good business decisions.

Source: www.roche.com; Roche 2013 Annual Report; Roche fact sheet 2013.

CHAPTER ORGANISATION

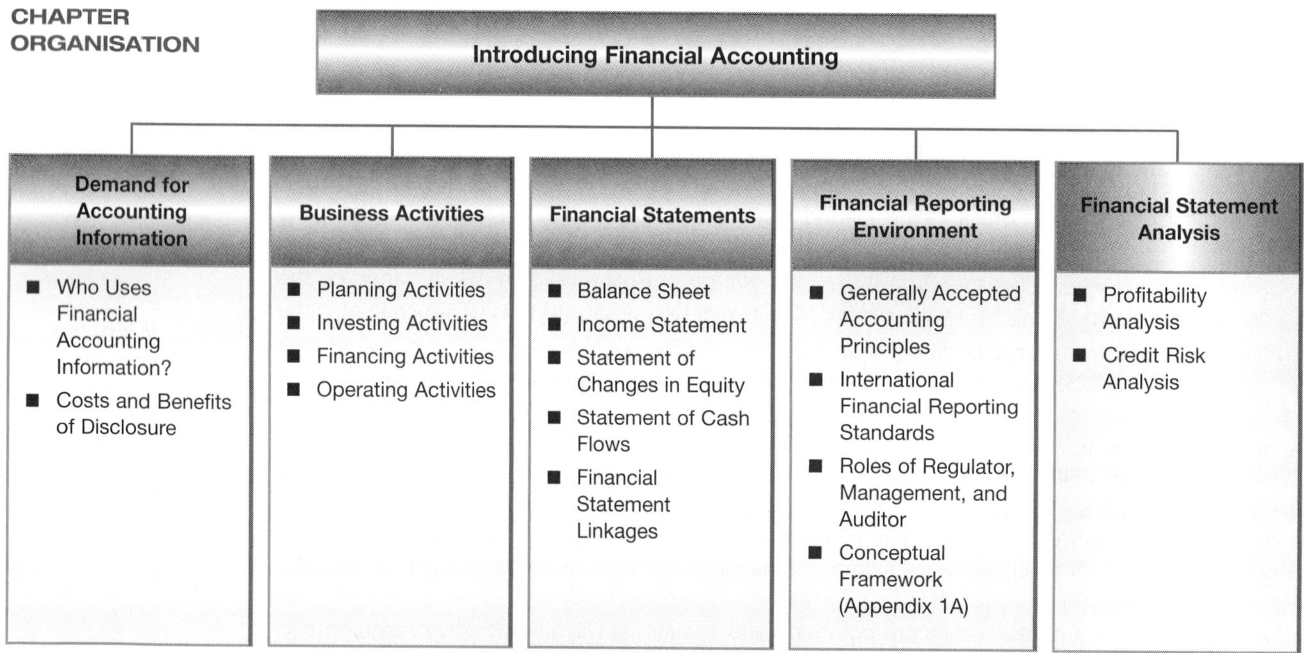

DEMAND FOR ACCOUNTING INFORMATION

LO1 Identify the users of accounting information and discuss the costs and benefits of disclosure.

Accounting can be defined as the process of recording, summarising, and analysing financial transactions. While accounting information attempts to satisfy the needs of a diverse set of users, the accounting information a company produces can be classified into two categories:

- **Financial accounting**—designed primarily for decision makers outside of the company
- **Managerial accounting**—designed primarily for decision makers within the company

Exhibit 1.1 compares and contrasts the information needs of decision makers who use financial and managerial accounting information. Financial accounting reports include information about company profitability and financial health. This information is useful to various economic actors who wish to engage in contracts with the firm, including investors, creditors, employees, customers, and governments. Managerial accounting information is not reported outside of the company because it includes proprietary information about the profitability of specific products, divisions, or customers. Company managers use managerial accounting reports to make decisions such as whether to drop or add products or divisions, or whether to continue serving different types of customers. This text focuses on understanding and analysing financial accounting information.

EXHIBIT 1.1 Information Needs of Decision Makers Who Use Financial and Managerial Accounting

Who Uses Financial Accounting Information?

Demand for financial accounting information derives from numerous users including:

- Shareholders and potential shareholders
- Creditors and suppliers
- Managers and directors
- Financial analysts
- Other users

Shareholders and Potential Shareholders Corporations are the dominant form of business organisation for large companies around the world, and corporate shareholders are one important group of decision makers that have an interest in financial accounting information. A **corporation** is a form of business organisation that is characterised by a large number of owners who are not involved in managing the day-to-day operations of the company.[1] A corporation exists as a legal entity that issues **shares** to its owners in exchange for cash and, therefore, the owners of a corporation are referred to as **shareholders** or **stockholders**.

FYI Shareholders of a corporation are its owners; although managers can own shares in the corporation, most shareholders are not managers.

Because the shareholders are not involved in the day-to-day operations of the business, they rely on the information in financial statements to evaluate management performance and assess the company's financial condition.

In addition to corporations, sole proprietorships and partnerships are also common forms of business ownership. A **sole proprietorship** has a single owner who typically manages the daily operations. Small family-run businesses, such as corner grocery stores, are commonly organised as sole proprietorships. A **partnership** has two or more owners who are also usually involved in managing the business. Many professionals, such as lawyers and accountants, organise their businesses as partnerships.

Most corporations begin as small, privately held businesses (sole proprietorships or partnerships). As their operations expand, they require additional capital to finance their growth. One of the principal advantages of a corporation over sole proprietorships and partnerships is the ability to raise large amounts of cash by issuing (selling) shares and bonds. For example, as Roche grew from a small business into a larger company, it raised the funds needed for expansion by selling its bearer shares to new shareholders in the SIX Swiss Exchange. In many countries,

[1] Corporations are referred to by different names (abbreviations) around the world. For example, firms that are incorporated in the United Kingdom, Ireland, and some Commonwealth countries are referred to as a Limited Company (Ltd.) or Public Limited Company (PLC). Similarly, they are referred to as an Aktiengesellschaft (AG) or Gesellschaft mit beschränkter Haftung (GmbH) in Germany, Austria, and Switzerland; a Sociedad Anónima (SA) in Spain, Brazil, and Portugal; a Naamloze Vennootschap (NV) in the Netherlands and the Dutch-speaking part of Belgium; Société Anonyme (SA) in France, Luxembourg, and the French-speaking parts of Switzerland and Belgium; a Società per Azioni (S.p.A.) in Italy; and Corporation (Corp.) or Incorporated (Inc.) in Canada and the United States.

most corporations can raise funds by issuing shares on organised exchanges. Corporations with shares traded on public exchanges are known as publicly traded corporations or simply public corporations.

Financial statements and the accompanying footnotes provide information on the risk and return associated with owning shares in the corporation, and they reveal how well management has performed. Financial statements also provide valuable insights into future performance by revealing management's plans for new products, new operating procedures, and new strategic directions for the company as well as for their implementation. Corporate management provides this information because the information reduces uncertainty about the company's future prospects which, in turn, increases the market price of its shares and helps the company raise the funds it needs to grow.

FYI Financial statements are typically required when a business requests a bank loan. ■

Creditors and Suppliers Few businesses rely solely on shareholders for the cash needed to operate the company. Instead, most companies borrow from banks or other lenders known as **creditors**. Creditors are interested in the potential borrower's ability to repay. They use financial accounting information to help determine loan terms, loan amounts, interest rates, and collateral. In addition, creditors' loans often include contractual requirements based on information found in the financial statements.

Suppliers use financial information to establish credit sales terms and to determine their long-term commitment to supply-chain relationships. Supplier companies often justify an expansion of *their* businesses based on the growth and financial health of their customers. Both creditors and suppliers rely on information in the financial statements to monitor and adjust their contracts and commitments with a company.

Managers and Directors Financial statements can be thought of as a financial report card for management. A well-managed company earns a good return for its shareholders, and this is reflected in the financial statements. In most companies, management is compensated, at least in part, based on the financial performance of the company. That is, managers often receive cash bonuses, shares of the company, or other *incentive compensation* that is linked directly to the information in the financial statements.

Publicly traded corporations are required by law to have a **board of directors**. Directors are elected by the shareholders to represent shareholder interests and oversee management. The board hires executive management and regularly reviews company operations. Directors use financial accounting information to review the results of operations, evaluate future strategy, and assess management performance.

Both managers and directors use the published financial statements of *other companies* to perform comparative analyses and establish performance benchmarks. For example, managers in some companies are paid a bonus for financial performance that exceeds the industry average.

BUSINESS INSIGHT

Recent court cases involving corporations such as **Enron**, **Nortel**, **Olympus**, **Parmalat**, and **Satyam** have found executives, including several CEOs, guilty of issuing fraudulent financial statements. In some cases, these executives have received substantial fines and long jail sentences. These trials have resulted in widespread loss of reputation and credibility among corporate boards.

Financial Analysts Many decision makers lack the time, resources, or expertise to efficiently and effectively analyse financial statements. Instead, they rely on professional financial analysts, such as credit rating agencies like **Moody's Investors Service**, portfolio managers, and security analysts. Financial analysts play an important role in the dissemination of financial information and often specialise in specific industries. Their analysis helps to identify and assess risk, forecast performance, establish prices for new issues of shares, and make buy or sell recommendations to investors.

Other Users of Financial Accounting Information External decision makers include many users of accounting information in addition to those listed above. For example, ***prospective***

employees often examine the financial statements of an employer to learn about the company before interviewing for or accepting a new job.

Labour unions examine financial statements in order to assess the financial health of firms prior to negotiating labour contracts on behalf of the firms' employees.

Customers use accounting information to assess the ability of a company to deliver products or services and to assess the company's long-term reliability. ***Tax agencies*** use financial accounting to help establish and implement tax policies. Other ***government agencies*** rely on accounting information to develop and enforce regulations, including public protection, price setting, import-export, and various other policies. Timely and reliable information is crucial to effective regulatory policy. Moreover, accounting information is often used to assess penalties for companies that violate various regulations.

Costs and Benefits of Disclosure

The act of providing financial information to external users is called **disclosure**. As with every decision, the benefits of disclosure must be weighed against the costs of providing the information.

One reason companies are motivated to disclose financial information to external decision makers is that it often lowers financing and operating costs. For example, when a company applies for a loan, the bank uses the company's financial statements to help determine the appropriate interest rate. Without adequate financial disclosures in its financial statements, the bank is likely to demand a higher interest rate or perhaps not make the loan at all. Thus, in this setting, a benefit of financial disclosure is that it reduces the company's cost of borrowing.

While there are benefits from disclosing financial information, there are also costs. Besides the obvious cost of hiring accountants and preparing the financial statements, financial disclosures can also result in costs being imposed by competitors. It is common practice for managers to scrutinise the financial statements of competitors to learn about successful products, new strategies, innovative technologies, and changing market conditions. Thus, disclosing too much information can place a company at a competitive disadvantage. Disclosure can also raise investors' expectations about a company's future profitability. If those expectations are not met, they may bring litigation against the managers.

There are also political costs that are potentially associated with accounting disclosure. Highly visible companies, such as defence contractors and oil companies, are often the target of scrutiny by the public and by government officials. When these companies report unusually large accounting profits, they are often the target of additional regulation or increased taxes.

Securities market regulators impose disclosure standards for publicly traded corporations, but the nature and extent of the required disclosures vary substantially across countries. Further, because the requirements set only the minimum level of disclosure, the quantity and quality of information provided by firms will vary. This variation in disclosure ultimately reflects differences among companies in the benefits and costs of disclosing information to the public.

YOU MAKE THE CALL

You are a Product Manager There is often friction between investors' needs for information and a company's desire to safeguard competitive advantages. Assume that you are the product manager for a key department at your company and you are asked for advice on the extent of information to disclose in the annual report on a potentially lucrative new product that your department has test marketed. What considerations affect the advice you provide and why? [Answer on page 28]

BUSINESS ACTIVITIES

LO2 Describe a company's business activities and explain how these activities are represented by the accounting equation.

Businesses produce accounting information to help develop strategies, attract financing, evaluate investment opportunities, manage operations, and measure performance. Before we can attempt to understand the information provided in financial statements, we must understand these business activities. That is, what does a business actually do? For example:

- Where does a company such as Roche find the resources to develop new products and open new retail stores?

- What new products should Roche bring to market?
- How much should Roche spend on product development? On advertising? On executive compensation?
- How does Roche's management determine if a product is a success?

Questions such as these define the activities of Roche and other companies.

Exhibit 1.2 illustrates the activities of a typical business. All businesses *plan* business activities, *finance* those activities, *invest* resources in those activities, and then engage in *operating* activities. Companies conduct all these activities while confronting a variety of *external forces*, including competition from other businesses, government regulation, economic conditions and market forces, and changing preferences of customers. The financial statements provide information that helps us understand and evaluate each of these activities.

EXHIBIT 1.2 Business Activities

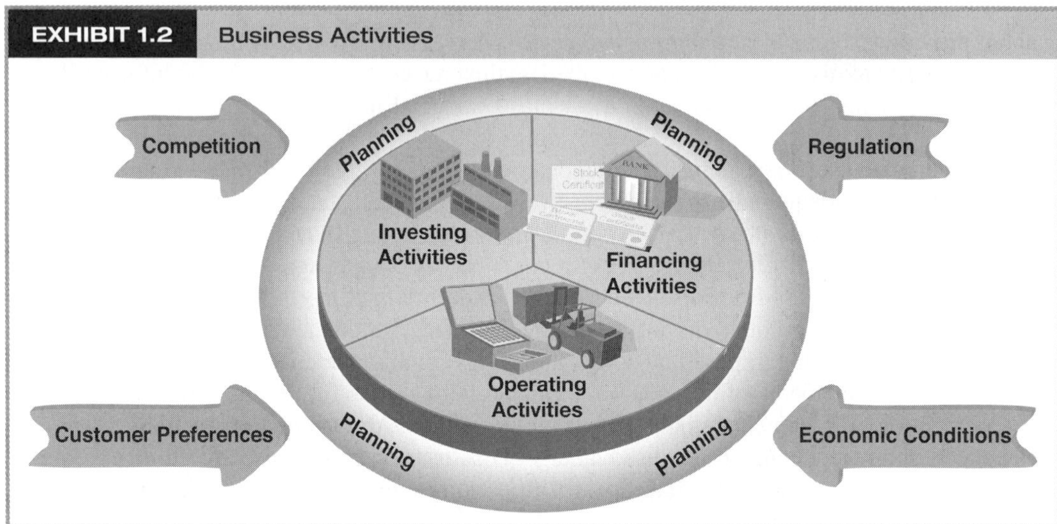

Planning Activities

A company's goals, and the strategies adopted to reach those goals, are the product of its **planning activities**. Roche, for example, states on its website that "Our mission today and tomorrow is to create added value in healthcare by focusing on our expertise in diagnostics and pharmaceuticals."

As is the case with most businesses, Roche's primary goal is to create value for its owners, the shareholders. How the company plans to do so is the company's **strategy**.

A company's *strategic* (or *business*) *plan* describes how it plans to achieve its goals. The plan's success depends on an effective review of market conditions. Specifically, the company must assess both the demand for its products and services, and the supply of its inputs (both labour and capital). The plan must also include competitive analyses, opportunity assessments, and consideration of business threats. The strategic plan specifies both broad management designs that generate company value and tactics to achieve those designs.

Most information in a strategic plan is proprietary and guarded closely by management. However, outsiders can gain insight into planning activities through various channels, including newspapers, magazines, and company publications. Understanding a company's planning activities helps focus accounting analysis and place it in context.

Investing Activities

Investing activities consist of acquiring and disposing of the resources needed to produce and sell a company's products and services. These resources, called **assets**, provide future benefits to the company. Companies differ on the amount and mix of these resources. Some companies require buildings and equipment while others have abandoned "bricks and mortar" to conduct business through the Internet.

Some assets that a company invests in are used quickly. For instance, a retail clothing store hopes to sell its spring and summer merchandise before purchasing more inventory for the fall and winter. Other assets are acquired for long-term use. Buildings are typically used for several decades. The relative proportion of short-term and long-term investments depends on the type of business and the strategic plan that the company adopts.

The graph in Exhibit 1.3 compares the relative proportion of short-term and long-term assets held by Roche and six other companies from different industries and countries, several of which are featured in later chapters. Roche has roughly the same proportions of short-term and long-term assets. **Indigo**, a Canadian bookseller, requires very little investment in long-term resources. In contrast, **Qantas Airways**, **Unilever**, **TomTom**, and **BP** all rely heavily on long-term investments. These companies hold relatively small proportions of short-term assets. This mix of long-term and short-term assets is described in more detail in Chapter 2.

EXHIBIT 1.3 Relative Proportion of Short-term and Long-term Assets

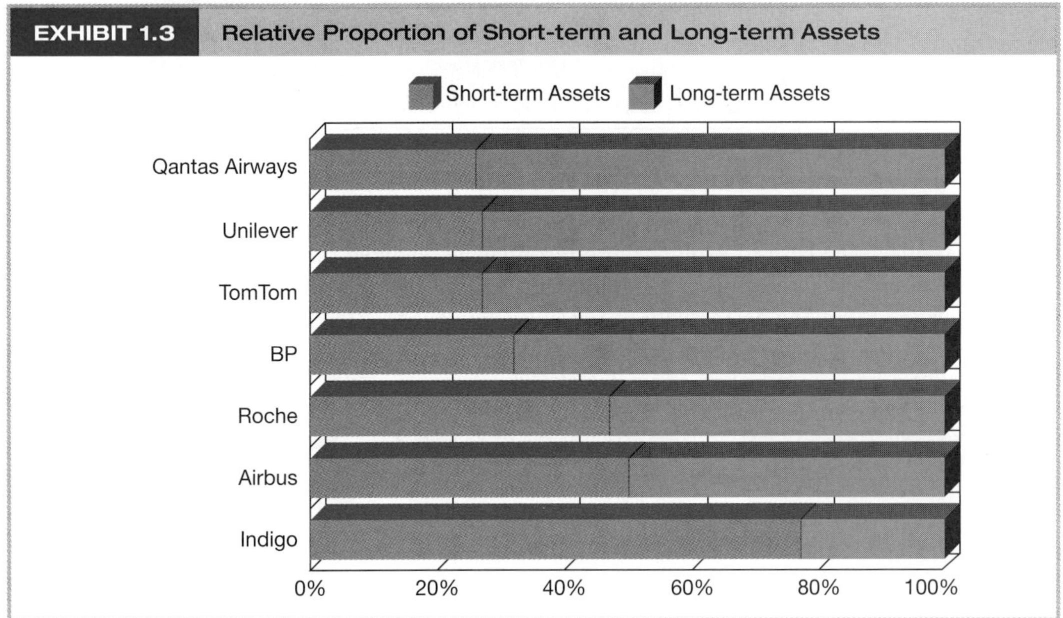

Financing Activities

Investments in resources require funding, and **financing activities** refer to the methods companies use to fund those investments. *Financial management* is the planning of resource needs, including the proper mix of financing sources.

Companies obtain financing from two sources: equity (owner) financing and creditor (non-owner) financing. *Equity financing* refers to the funds contributed to the company by its owners along with any income retained by the company. One form of equity financing is the cash raised from the sale (or issuance) of shares by a corporation. *Creditor* (or debt) *financing* is funds contributed by non-owners, which create *liabilities*. **Liabilities** are obligations the company must repay in the future. One example of a liability is a bank loan. We draw a distinction between equity and creditor financing for an important reason: creditor financing imposes a legal obligation to repay, usually with interest, and failure to repay amounts borrowed can result in adverse legal consequences such as bankruptcy. In contrast, equity financing does not impose an obligation for repayment.

Exhibit 1.4 compares the relative proportion of creditor and equity financing for Roche and other companies. Roche receives 66% of its financing from creditors and 34% from equity holders. In comparison, **Airbus** uses liabilities to finance 88% of its resources and **Indigo** has the lowest proportion of creditor financing in this sample of companies with just 39% of its assets financed by nonowners.

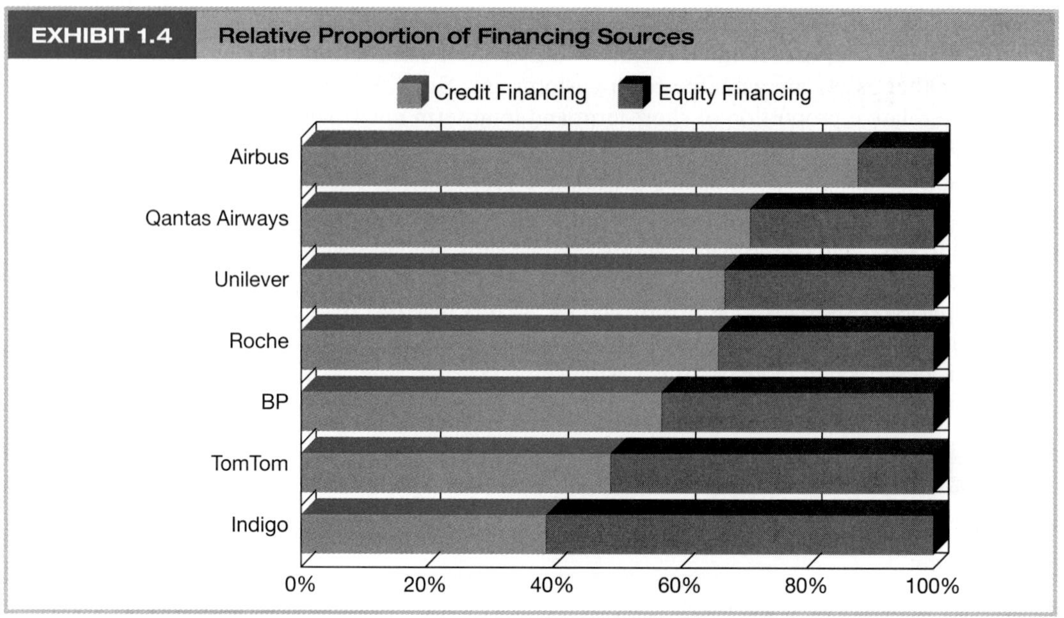

EXHIBIT 1.4 Relative Proportion of Financing Sources

As discussed in the previous section, companies acquire resources, called assets, through investing activities. The cash to acquire these resources is obtained through financing activities, which consist of owner financing, called equity, and creditor financing, called liabilities (or debt). Thus, we have the following basic relation: *investing equals financing*. This equality is called the **accounting equation**, which is expressed as:

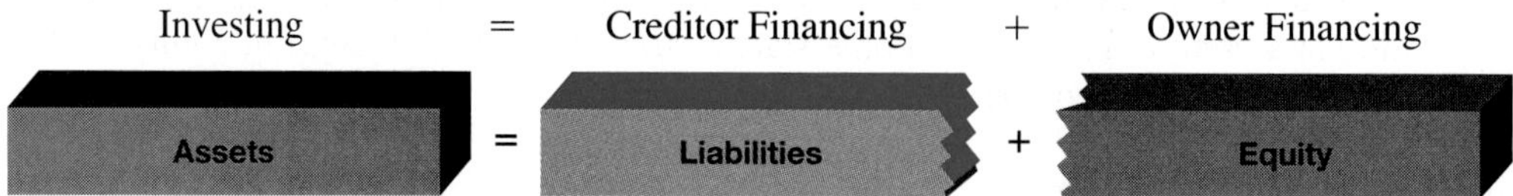

At fiscal year-end 2013, the accounting equation for **Roche** was as follows (Swiss Francs, CHF, in millions):

62,167 CHF = 40,926 CHF + 21,241 CHF

By definition, the accounting equation holds for all companies at all times. This relation is a very powerful tool for analysing and understanding companies, and we will use it often throughout the text.

Operating Activities

Operating activities refer to the production, promotion, and selling of a company's products and services. These activities extend from a company's input markets, involving its suppliers, to its output markets, involving its customers. Input markets generate *operating expenses* (or *costs*) such as inventory, salaries, materials, and logistics. Output markets generate *operating revenues* (or *sales*) from customers. Output markets also generate some operating expenses such as for marketing and distributing products and services to customers. When operating revenues exceed operating expenses, companies report *operating income,* also called *operating profit* or *operating earnings*. When operating expenses exceed operating revenues, companies report operating losses.

Revenue is the increase in equity resulting from the sale of goods and services to customers. The amount of revenue is determined *before* deducting expenses. An **expense** is the cost incurred to generate revenue, including the cost of the goods and services sold to customers as well as the cost of carrying out other business activities. **Income**, also called *net income*, equals revenues minus expenses, and is the net increase in equity from the company's operating activities.

Income = Revenues − Expenses

For fiscal year 2013, Roche reported revenues of 46.8 million CHF and income of 11.4 million CHF.

BUSINESS INSIGHT

Each year, *Financial Times* ranks the 500 largest corporations in the world based on market capitalisation. For 2013, Roche ranked 20th on the *FT Global 500* list with market capitalisation of just over US$201.5 billion, which also made it the third largest company in Europe. The company also ranked 105th in revenues and 37th in profits, with turnover of US$49.7 billion and net income of US$10.4 billion. For comparison, the largest corporation was **Apple**, with market capitalisation of US$415.7 billion, turnover of US$156.5 billion, and net income of US$41.7 billion. (Source: http://www.ft.com/intl/indepth/ft500)

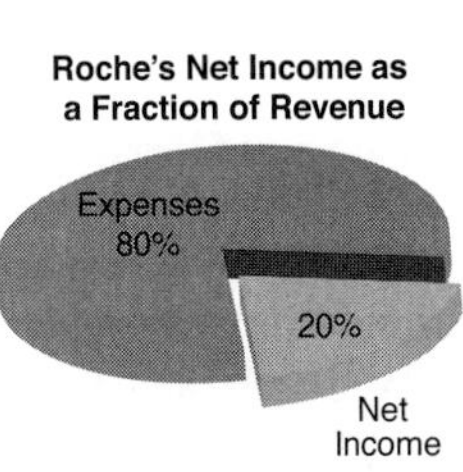

FINANCIAL STATEMENTS

LO3 Introduce the four key financial statements including the balance sheet, income statement, statement of changes in equity, and statement of cash flows.

Four financial statements are used to periodically report on a company's business activities. These statements[2] are:

- **statement of financial position (or balance sheet)**, which lists the company's investments and sources of financing using the accounting equation;
- **income statement**, which reports the results of operations;
- **statement of changes in equity**, which details changes in owner financing;
- **statement of cash flows**, which details the sources and uses of cash.

Exhibit 1.5 shows how these statements are linked across time. A balance sheet reports on a company's position at a *point in time*. The income statement, statement of changes in equity, and the statement of cash flows report on performance over a *period of time*. The three statements in the middle of Exhibit 1.5 (period-of-time statements) link the balance sheet from the beginning of a period to the balance sheet at the end of a period.

EXHIBIT 1.5 Financial Statement Links Across Time

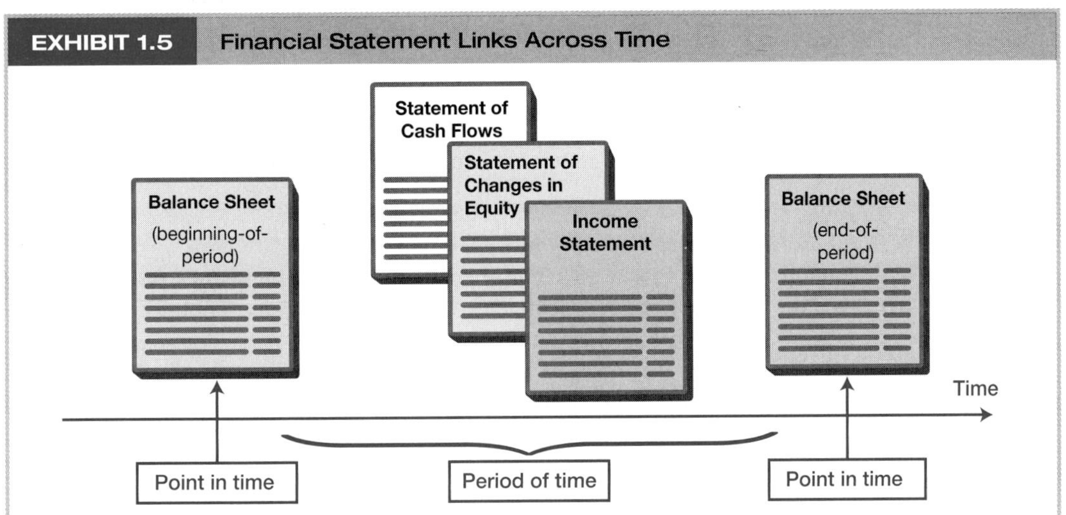

A one-year, or annual, reporting period is common, which is called the *accounting*, or *fiscal year*. Semiannual, quarterly, and monthly reporting periods are also common. *Calendar-year* companies have a reporting period that begins on January 1 and ends on December 31. **Roche**, **Unilever**, and **TomTom** are examples of calendar-year companies. Some companies choose a fiscal

FYI The heading of each financial statement includes who, what, and when. ■

[2] Financial statement notes are an integral part of the financial statements. We illustrate the usefulness of these notes throughout the book.

year ending on a date other than December 31. Seasonal businesses, such as retail stores, often choose a fiscal year that ends when sales and inventories are at their lowest level. For example, **Indigo**, the Canadian bookseller, ends its 52-week fiscal year at the end of March, after the busy holiday season. The heading of each statement identifies the: (1) company name, (2) statement title, and (3) date or time period of the statement.

Balance Sheet

FYI The balance sheet is also known as the statement of financial position and the statement of financial condition. ■

A **balance sheet** reports a company's financial position at a point in time. It summarises the result of the company's investing and financing activities by listing amounts for assets, liabilities, and equity. The balance sheet is based on the accounting equation, also called the *balance sheet equation*: Assets = Liabilities + Equity.

Roche's balance sheet for fiscal year 2013, which ended December 31, 2013, is reproduced in a reduced format in Exhibit 1.6 and reports that assets are 62,167 million CHF, liabilities are 40,926 million CHF, and equity is 21,241 million CHF, where owner financing is the sum of contributed capital of 160 million CHF, retained earnings of 25,643 million CHF, and other equity of −4,562 million CHF. Thus, the balance sheet equation holds true for Roche's balance sheet: assets equal liabilities plus equity.

EXHIBIT 1.6 Balance Sheet (in millions of CHF)

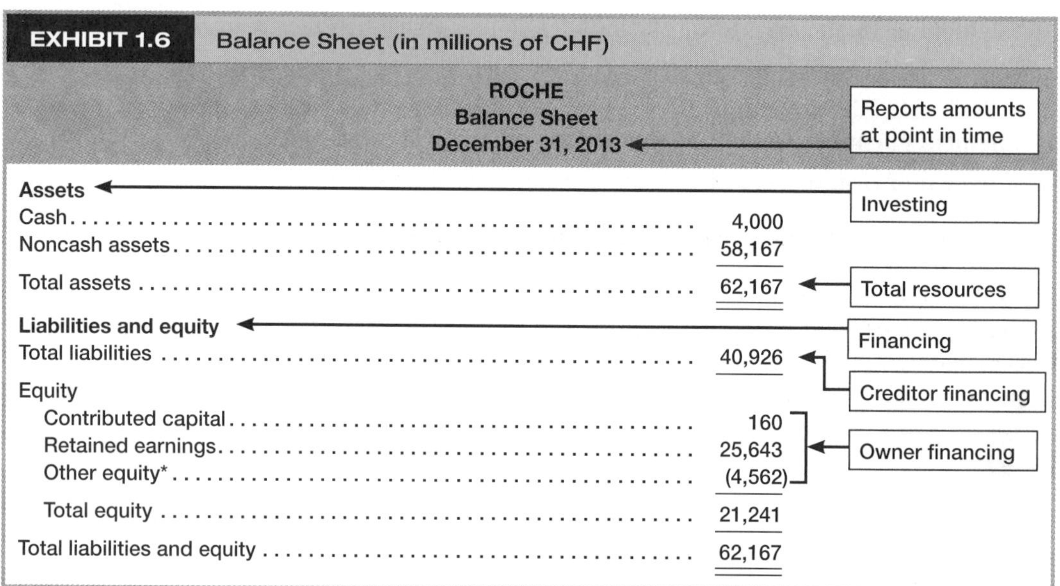

ROCHE
Balance Sheet
December 31, 2013

Assets	
Cash	4,000
Noncash assets	58,167
Total assets	62,167
Liabilities and equity	
Total liabilities	40,926
Equity	
Contributed capital	160
Retained earnings	25,643
Other equity*	(4,562)
Total equity	21,241
Total liabilities and equity	62,167

* Other equity includes accumulated other comprehensive income and non-controlling interests. Other components of equity are discussed in Chapter 11.

Income Statement

FYI The income statement is also known as statement of income, statement of earnings, statement of operations, and statement of profit and loss. ■

The **income statement** reports the results of a company's operating activities over a period of time. It details amounts for revenues and expenses, and the difference between these two amounts is net income. Revenue is the increase in equity that results from selling goods or providing services to customers and expense is the cost incurred to generate revenue. Net income is the increase in equity *after* subtracting expenses from revenues.

An important difference between the income statement and the balance sheet is that the balance sheet presents the company's position at a *point in time*, for instance December 31, 2013, while the income statement presents a summary of activity over a *period of time*, such as January 1, 2013, through December 31, 2013. Because of this difference, the balance sheet reflects the cumulative history of a company's activities. The amounts listed in the balance sheet carry over from the end of one fiscal year to the beginning of the next fiscal year, while the amounts listed in the income statement do not carry over from one year to the next.

Refer to Roche's income statement for the fiscal year ended December 31, 2013, shown in reduced format as Exhibit 1.7. It reports revenues of 48,612 million CHF, expenses of 37,239 million CHF, and net income of 11,373 million CHF. Thus, revenues minus expenses equal net income for Roche.

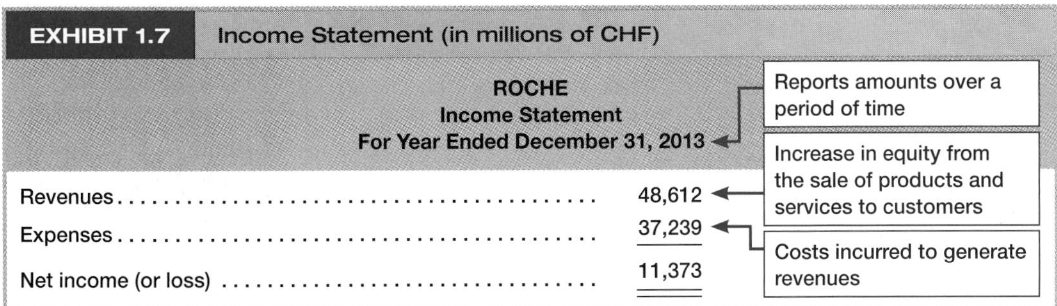
Reports amounts over a period of time
Increase in equity from the sale of products and services to customers
Costs incurred to generate revenues

EXHIBIT 1.7 Income Statement (in millions of CHF)

ROCHE
Income Statement
For Year Ended December 31, 2013

Revenues	48,612
Expenses	37,239
Net income (or loss)	11,373

For manufacturing and merchandising companies, the **cost of goods sold** is an important expense that is typically disclosed separately in the income statement immediately following revenues. It is also common to report a subtotal for gross profit (also called gross margin), which is revenues less the cost of goods sold. The company's remaining expenses are then reported below gross profit. Roche's income statement is presented in this reduced format in Exhibit 1.8:

FYI The term "gross" refers to an amount before subtractions, such as Gross Sales. An exception is made for the term Gross Profit (Gross Margin), defined as Sales less Cost of Goods Sold (Cost of Sales). When items are subtracted from a gross amount, the term "net" is generally used, as in the case of Net Sales (Gross Sales less returns and other items) or Net Income (Sales less all expenses). ■

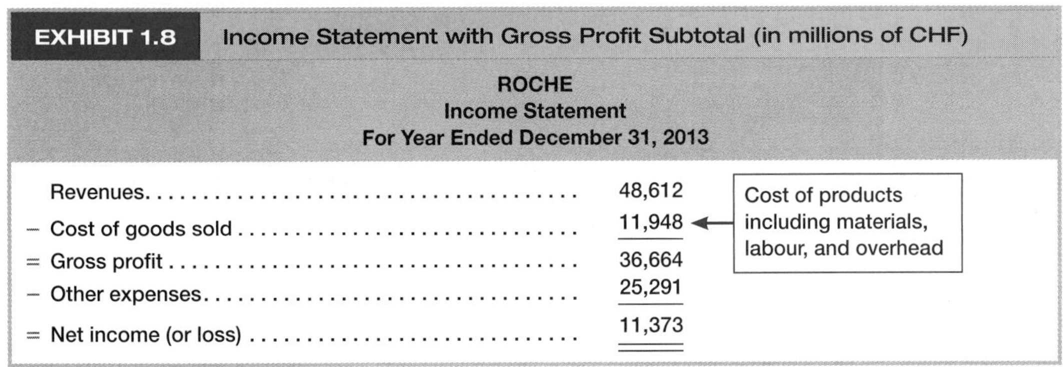
Cost of products including materials, labour, and overhead

EXHIBIT 1.8 Income Statement with Gross Profit Subtotal (in millions of CHF)

ROCHE
Income Statement
For Year Ended December 31, 2013

Revenues	48,612
− Cost of goods sold	11,948
= Gross profit	36,664
− Other expenses	25,291
= Net income (or loss)	11,373

Statement of Changes in Equity

The **statement of changes in equity** reports the changes in the equity accounts over a period of time. Roche's statement of changes in equity for fiscal year ended December 31, 2013, is shown in reduced format as Exhibit 1.9. During the year ended December 31, 2013, Roche's equity changed due to income reinvestment and dividends payment. The exhibit details and classifies these changes into three categories:

- Contributed capital (includes share capital, and contributed surplus)
- Retained earnings (includes cumulative net income or loss, and deducts dividends)
- Other equity

Contributed capital represents the net amount received from issuing shares to shareholders (owners). **Retained earnings** (also called *earned capital*) represents the income the company has earned since its inception, minus the dividends it has paid out to shareholders. Thus, retained earnings equals the amount of income retained in the company. The change in retained earnings links consecutive balance sheets through the income statement. Roche's retained earnings increased from 20,041 million CHF at January 1, 2013, to 25,643 million CHF at December 31, 2013. This increase is explained by net income of 11,373 million CHF, less dividends of 6,238 million CHF and other changes of 467 million CHF. The category titled "other changes" refers to changes in equity that are not recorded in income and is discussed in Chapter 11.

FYI Dividends are reported in the statement of changes in equity, and not in the income statement. ■

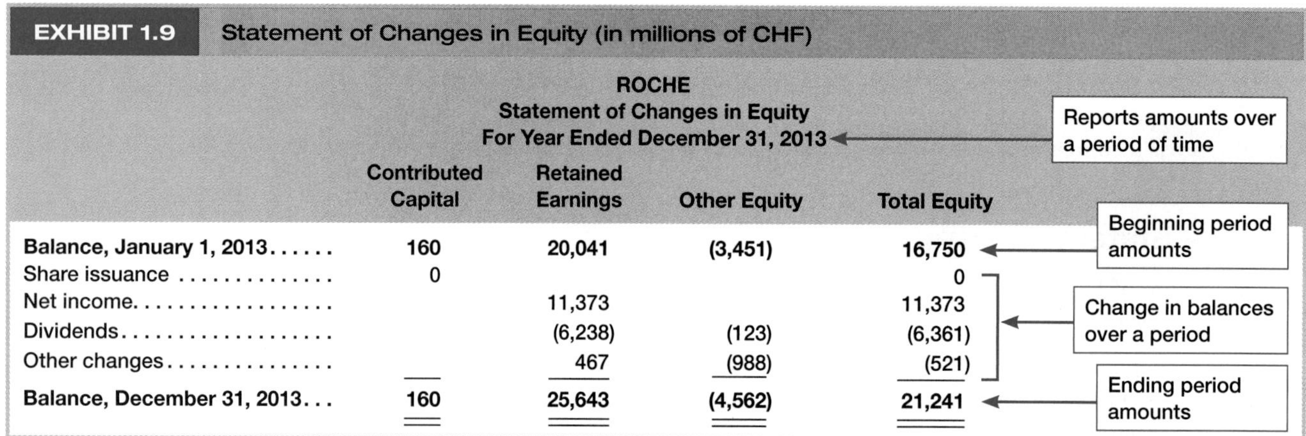

EXHIBIT 1.9 Statement of Changes in Equity (in millions of CHF)

ROCHE
Statement of Changes in Equity
For Year Ended December 31, 2013

	Contributed Capital	Retained Earnings	Other Equity	Total Equity
Balance, January 1, 2013	160	20,041	(3,451)	16,750
Share issuance	0			0
Net income		11,373		11,373
Dividends		(6,238)	(123)	(6,361)
Other changes		467	(988)	(521)
Balance, December 31, 2013	160	25,643	(4,562)	21,241

Statement of Cash Flows

FYI Cash is critical to operations because it is necessary for purchasing resources and paying bills. ■

The **statement of cash flows** reports net cash flows from operating, investing, and financing activities over a period of time. Roche's statement of cash flows for fiscal year ended December 31, 2013, is shown in a reduced format in Exhibit 1.10. The statement reports that the cash balance decreased from 4,530 million CHF to 4,000 million CHF during the fiscal year. Operating activities provided 15,772 million CHF (a cash inflow), investing activities used 1,302 million CHF (a cash outflow), and financing activities used 14,669 million CHF (a cash outflow). The resulting decrease of 530 million CHF brought Roche's ending balance of cash to 4,000 million CHF.

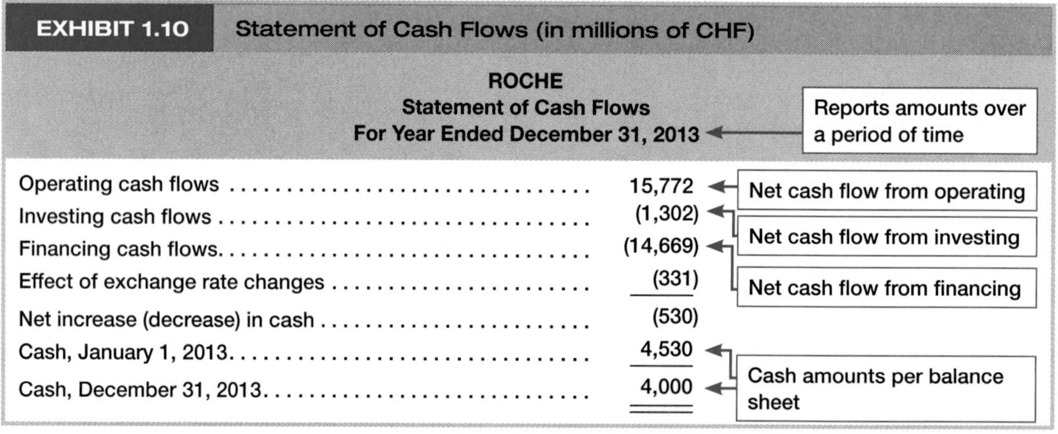

EXHIBIT 1.10 Statement of Cash Flows (in millions of CHF)

ROCHE
Statement of Cash Flows
For Year Ended December 31, 2013

Operating cash flows	15,772
Investing cash flows	(1,302)
Financing cash flows	(14,669)
Effect of exchange rate changes	(331)
Net increase (decrease) in cash	(530)
Cash, January 1, 2013	4,530
Cash, December 31, 2013	4,000

Operating cash flow is the amount of cash generated from operating activities. This amount usually differs from net income due to differences between the time that revenues and expenses are recorded, and the time that the related cash receipts and disbursements occur. For example, a company may report revenues for goods sold to customers this period, but not collect the payment until next period. Consistent with most companies, Roche's operating cash flows of 15,772 million CHF do not equal its net income of 11,373 million.

Both cash flow and net income are important for making business decisions. They each capture different aspects of firm performance and together help financial statement users better understand and assess a company's past, present, and future business activities.

Financial Statement Linkages

A central feature of the accounting system is the linkage among the four primary statements, referred to as the *articulation* of the financial statements. Three of the key linkages are:

- The statement of cash flows links the beginning and ending cash in the balance sheet.
- The income statement links the beginning and ending retained earnings in the statement of changes in equity.
- The statement of changes in equity links the beginning and ending equity in the balance sheet.

Exhibit 1.11 demonstrates these links using Roche's financial statements from Exhibits 1.6 through 1.10. The left side of Exhibit 1.11 presents Roche's beginning-year balance sheet for fiscal year 2013 (which is the same as the balance sheet for the end of fiscal year 2012) and the right side presents Roche's year-end balance sheet for fiscal year 2013. These balance sheets report Roche's investing and financing activities at the beginning and end of the fiscal year, two distinct points in time. The middle column of Exhibit 1.11 presents the three financial statements that report Roche's fiscal year 2013 business activities over time: the statement of cash flows, the income statement, and the statement of changes in equity. The three key linkages shown in Exhibit 1.11 are:

- The statement of cash flows explains how operating, financing, and investing activities decreased the cash balance by 530 million CHF, from the 4,530 million CHF reported in the beginning-year balance sheet, to the 4,000 million CHF reported in the year-end balance sheet.
- The net income of 11,373 million CHF reported in the income statement is added to retained earnings in the statement of changes in equity.
- The statement of changes in equity explains how total equity of 16,750 million CHF, reported in the beginning-year balance sheet, becomes total equity of 21,241 million CHF, reported in the year-end balance sheet.

Information Beyond Financial Statements

Important information about a company is communicated to various decision makers through reports other than financial statements. These reports include the following:

- Management Discussion and Analysis (MD&A)
- Independent Auditor Report
- Financial statement notes
- Regulatory filings, including proxy statements

We describe and explain the usefulness of these additional information sources throughout the book.

FYI An analysis of a firm's activities requires extensive study of its footnotes and the MD&A.

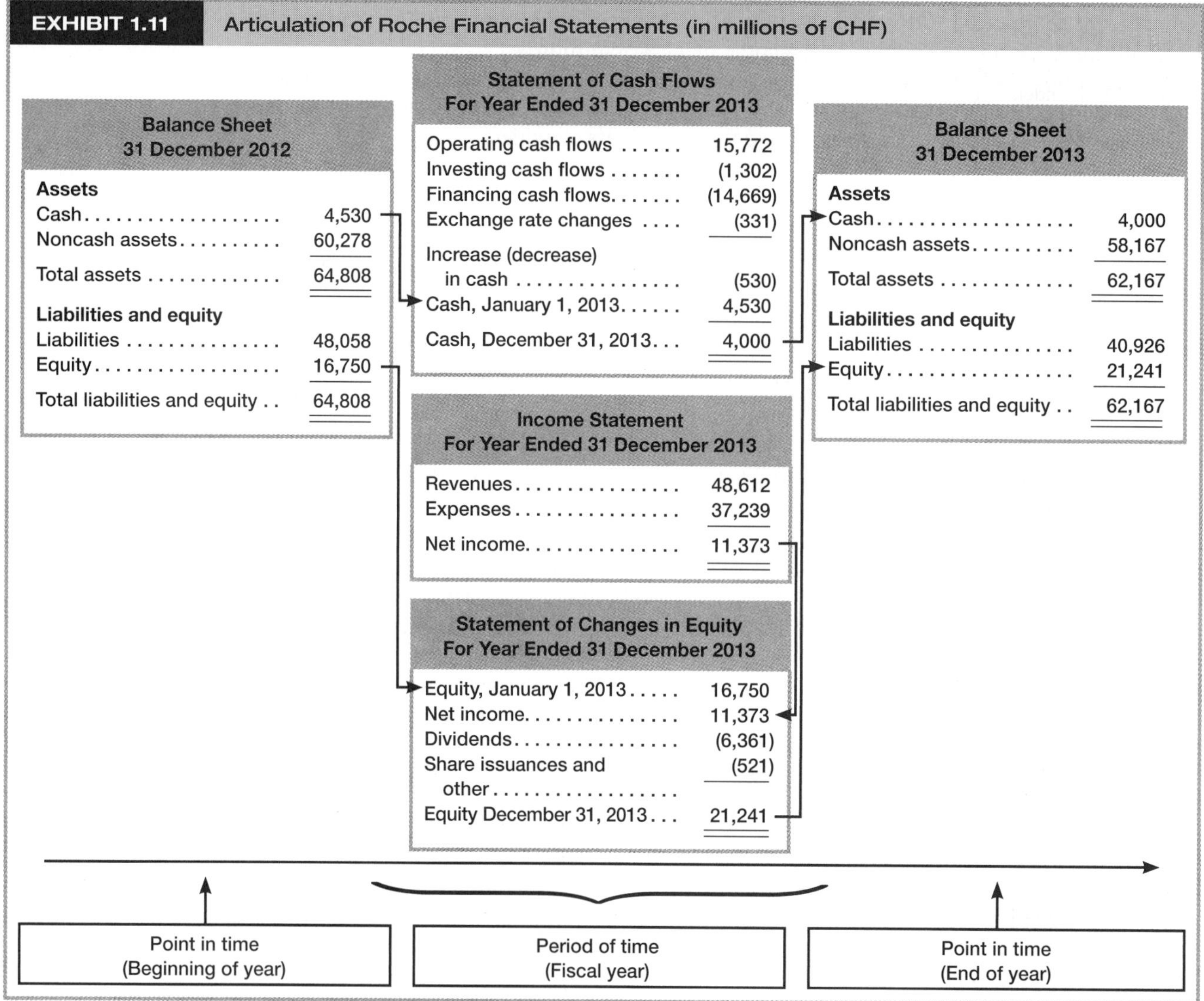

EXHIBIT 1.11 Articulation of Roche Financial Statements (in millions of CHF)

Balance Sheet 31 December 2012

Assets	
Cash	4,530
Noncash assets	60,278
Total assets	64,808
Liabilities and equity	
Liabilities	48,058
Equity	16,750
Total liabilities and equity	64,808

Statement of Cash Flows For Year Ended 31 December 2013

Operating cash flows	15,772
Investing cash flows	(1,302)
Financing cash flows	(14,669)
Exchange rate changes	(331)
Increase (decrease) in cash	(530)
Cash, January 1, 2013	4,530
Cash, December 31, 2013	4,000

Income Statement For Year Ended 31 December 2013

Revenues	48,612
Expenses	37,239
Net income	11,373

Statement of Changes in Equity For Year Ended 31 December 2013

Equity, January 1, 2013	16,750
Net income	11,373
Dividends	(6,361)
Share issuances and other	(521)
Equity December 31, 2013	21,241

Balance Sheet 31 December 2013

Assets	
Cash	4,000
Noncash assets	58,167
Total assets	62,167
Liabilities and equity	
Liabilities	40,926
Equity	21,241
Total liabilities and equity	62,167

MID-CHAPTER REVIEW

TGV S.A. manufactures and markets ski and golf equipment. TGV's financial statements are reported in Euros, the currency of the European Union. The following information is from the company's December 31, 2015, financial statements (€ millions):

	2015
Cash	€ 906
Cash flow from operations	792
Sales revenue	13,344
Equity	5,331
Cost of goods sold	7,000
Cash flow used for financing	(491)
Total liabilities	6,049
Net other expenses	5,674
Noncash assets	10,474
Cash flow used for investing	(566)
Net income	670
Cash, beginning of year	1,156
Effect of exchange rates on cash	€ 15

Required
Prepare TGV's balance sheet at December 31, 2015, and its income statement and cash flow statement for the fiscal year ended December 31, 2015.

The solution to this review problem can be found on pages 36–37.

FINANCIAL REPORTING ENVIRONMENT

LO4 Describe the institutions that regulate financial accounting and their role in establishing generally accepted accounting principles.

Information presented in financial statements is of critical importance to external decision makers. Financial statements affect the prices paid for equity securities and interest rates attached to debt securities. To the extent that financial performance and condition are accurately communicated to business decision makers, debt and equity securities are more accurately priced. By extension, financial reporting plays a crucial role in efficient resource allocation within and across economies. Accounting information contributes to the efficient operation of securities markets, labour markets, commodity markets, and other markets.

To illustrate, imagine the consequences of a breakdown in the integrity of financial reporting. The Sino-Forest Corporation provides a case in point. Founded in 1994 in China, Sino-Forest managed tree plantations and manufactured engineered-wood products. It was headquartered in Mississauga, Ontario, Canada and traded on the Toronto Stock Exchange. On June 2, 2011, Muddy Waters Research published a report alleging that Sino-Forest had been fraudulently inflating its assets and profits. Once it became clear to the capital markets that Sino-Forest had not faithfully and accurately reported its financial condition and performance, its share price plunged 82 percent and its credit rating was downgraded twice in two months. On August 26, the Ontario Securities Commission (OSC), the securities regulator in Ontario, accused Sino-Forest of fraud and suspended the trading of its shares. In March 2012, Sino-Forest filed for bankruptcy protection in Canada. Two months later, the OSC charged Sino-Forest and five of its executives with engaging in misleading and fraudulent activities.

The Sino-Forest case illustrates the importance of reliable financial reporting. Accountants recognise the importance of the information that they produce and, as a profession, they agree to follow a set of standards for the presentation of financial statements and the disclosure of related financial information. In the following paragraphs, we discuss these standards, or *principles*, as well as the institutional and regulatory environment in which accountants operate.

Generally Accepted Accounting Principles/Practice

Decision makers who rely on financial statements expect that all companies follow similar procedures in preparing their statements. In response to these expectations, accountants have developed a set of standards and procedures called **generally accepted accounting principles/practice (GAAP)**. GAAP is not a set of immutable laws. Instead, it is a set of standards and accepted practices, based on underlying principles, that are designed to guide the preparation of the financial statements. GAAP is subject to change as conditions warrant. As a result, specific rules are altered or new practices are formulated to fit changes in underlying economic circumstances or business transactions.

Some people mistakenly assume that financial accounting is an exact discipline—that is, companies select the proper standard to account for a transaction and then follow the rules. The reality is that GAAP allows companies considerable discretion in preparing financial statements. The choice of methods often yields financial statements that are markedly different from one company to another in terms of reported income, assets, liabilities, and equity amounts. In addition, financial statements depend on numerous estimates. Consequently, even though two companies may engage in the same transactions and choose the same accounting methods, their financial statements will differ because their managements have made different estimates about such things as the amount to be collected from customers who buy on credit, the length of time that buildings and equipment will be in use, and the future costs for product warranties.

Accounting standard setters walk a fine line regarding choice in accounting. On one hand, they are concerned that management discretion in preparing financial statements will lead to abuse by those seeking to influence the decisions of those who rely on the statements. On the other hand, they are concerned that companies are too diverse for a "one size fits all" financial accounting system. Ultimately, GAAP attempts to strike a balance by imposing constraints on the choice of accounting procedures, while allowing companies some flexibility within those constraints.

In general, companies prepare financial statements following the GAAP of the country in which they are based or listed. Because countries have a variety of laws and customs, the GAAPs vary considerably from one country to the next, making it difficult to compare the financial statements of companies from one country with those from another country.

YOU MAKE THE CALL

You are a Financial Analyst Accountants, business leaders, and politicians have long debated the importance of considering the **economic consequences** of accounting standards. Should accounting standards be designed to influence behaviour and effect social or economic change considered by, say, a government body or other interested group? Alternatively, should such standards be designed simply to provide relevant and reliable information on which economic decisions can be made by others with a reasonable degree of confidence? What do you believe the objectives of financial reporting should be? [Answers on page 28]

International Financial Reporting Standards

The globalisation of capital markets, combined with the diversity of country-specific GAAPs, has led to an effort to increase the comparability of financial information across countries. In 1973, the International Accounting Standards Committee (IASC) was founded by the nine professional accountancy bodies of the following countries: Australia, Canada, France, Germany, Japan, Mexico, the Netherlands, the United Kingdom and Ireland (Ireland shares financial standards with the United Kingdom), and the United States. The mission of the IASC and its successor is to unify all public companies under "a single set of high quality, understandable, enforceable and globally accepted financial reporting standards based upon clearly articulated principles." By 2000, the IASC had produced 41 International Accounting Standards (IAS), which were endorsed by the International Organisation of Securities Commissions and by the International Federation of Accountants.

In 2001, the **International Accounting Standards Board (IASB)** replaced the IASC. The IASB is an independent standard-setting body with 16 full-time members, overseen by the International Financial Reporting Standards Foundation and a Monitoring Board of public market regulators. Its mandate is further supported by an external advisory council of various stakeholders, an advisory forum of national standard setters, and an Interpretations Committee. The IASB has revised some of the IAS and developed additional standards. These standards, along with numerous interpretations are collectively referred to as the **International Financial Reporting Standards (IFRS)**.

Because it is international in its scope, the IASB and its predecessor have worked with national standard setters to reduce diversity in financial reporting practice. As of December 2015, 116 of the 140 individual jurisdictions surveyed by the IASB had adopted IFRS for publicly traded entities, including Argentina, Australia, Brazil, Canada, all the European Union member states, Hong Kong, Korea, Mexico, Russia, South Africa, and Turkey. Of the remaining 24 jurisdictions, 12 permit IFRS (e.g., India, Japan, and Switzerland), two require IFRS for financial institutions (Saudi Arabia and Uzbekistan), one is in the process of adopting IFRS (Thailand), and eight use their own GAAP (Bolivia, China, Egypt, Guinea-Bissau, Macao, Niger, United States, and Vietnam). While the United States has not adopted IFRS, it has allowed foreign companies with securities traded on its stock exchanges to use IFRS since 2007.

Besides setting standards for financial accounting, the IASB and its predecessor have developed a framework for future discussion of proposed standards and to serve as a guide to accountants for reporting information that is not governed by specific standards. A summary of this *Conceptual Framework* is presented in Appendix 1A at the end of this chapter.

Despite the push for comparability, not everyone is convinced that IFRS will improve the usefulness of accounting information. As one observer put it, "There is a real risk of a veneer of comparability that hides a lot of differences." A number of participating countries have reserved the right to adopt exceptions to IFRS when they deem them to be appropriate.

Roles of Regulator, Management, and Auditor

Each country has its own company and securities laws, which give power to one or more regulators to administer and enforce the laws. In general, the regulators oversee publicly traded corporations, capital markets, and the financial services industry. Most countries have one securities regulator for the whole country, such as the Australian Securities and Investments Commission and the China Securities Regulatory Commission. In Canada, however, securities laws are administered and enforced by provincial regulators. For example, the Ontario Securities Commission regulates the securities industry in Ontario and companies with securities traded on the Toronto Stock Exchange. In the European Union (EU), each member state has its own company and securities laws that are in compliance with the minimum standards set forth in various EU Directives. The European Securities and Markets Authority and its predecessor were established to enhance the harmonisation of financial regulation in the EU. It is overseen by a Board of Supervisors, composed of the heads of 28 EU state regulators, such as the United Kingdom Financial Conduct Authority and the Netherlands Authority for the Financial Markets.

To protect investors and the functioning of the capital markets, securities laws require corporations to disclose financial and other information about securities being offered for public sale and to prohibit deceit, misrepresentation, and other fraud in the sale of securities. While laws and practices vary across countries, the legislation generally requires companies that met certain criteria to submit annual and interim reports, including a complete set of financial statements, to their respective securities and exchange regulator.

What prevents a company from disclosing false or misleading information? For one thing, the Board of Directors (or Supervisory Board) and/or management (or Management Board) are responsible for preparing the financial statements and for maintaining adequate internal control over financial reporting. They attest to the accuracy and completeness of the financial statements, whether due to fraud or error, as well as the effectiveness of the internal control system. Hence, the reputation of the executives and board directors can be severely damaged by false disclosures when subsequent events unfold to refute the information. This situation can adversely affect the firm's ability to compete in capital, labour, and consumer markets. It can also lead to litigation and even criminal charges against management and directors.

To ensure the accuracy and completeness of the financial statements, publicly traded corporations are required to have their annual financial statements **audited** by an *independent audit firm*. The auditors provide an opinion as to whether the statements give a fair view of a company's financial condition and the results of its operations in accordance with the required accounting standards and national laws. In many countries, public corporations are required to have audit committees, established by the Board of Directors or Supervisory Board. The purpose of the audit committee is not to audit but, rather, to appoint the audit firm and assure that what is learned in the audit is disclosed to the firm's directors and shareholders.

The audit opinion is not a guarantee. Auditors only provide reasonable assurance that the financial statements are free of material misstatements. They conduct the audit in accordance with the auditing standards and laws of the respective country. Even so, auditors provide a valuable service. Auditors effectively ensure that the information contained in the financial statements is reliable, thus increasing the confidence of outside decision makers in the information they use to make investment, credit, and other decisions. Therefore, even creditors and shareholders of privately held corporations often demand that the financial statements be audited. In many countries, such as Australia and many European countries, certain private corporations are also required to file audited financial statements with securities regulators.

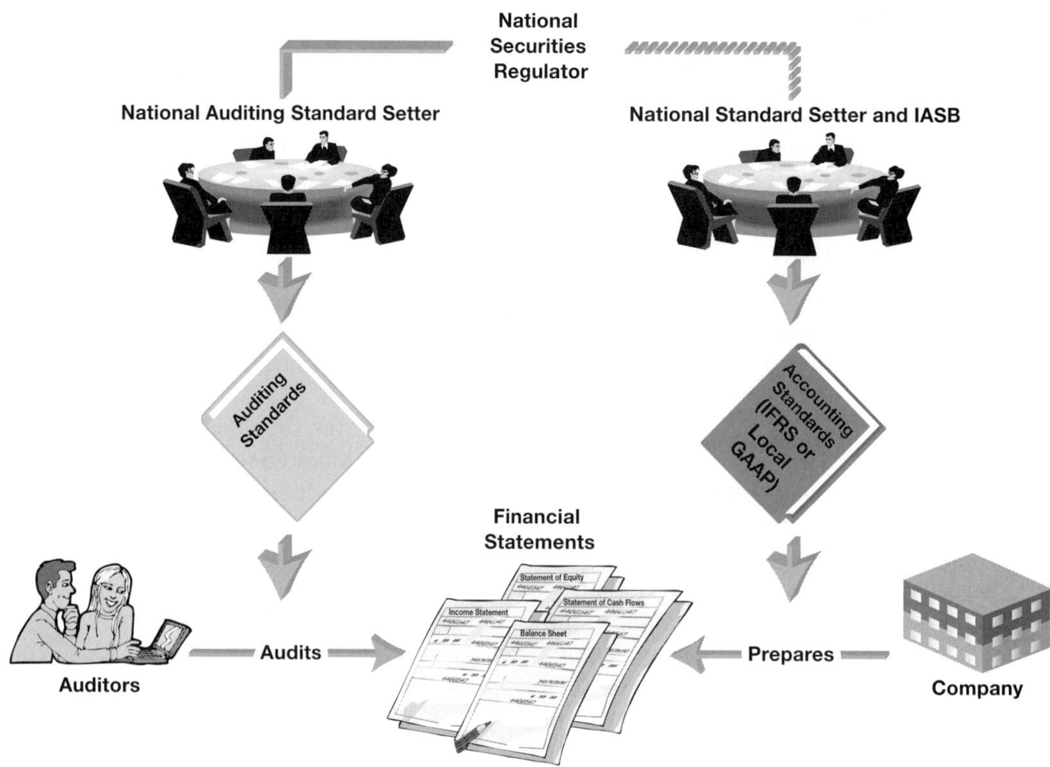

YOU MAKE THE CALL

You are a Member of the Board of Directors Until recently, accounting firms were permitted to earn money for consulting activities performed for clients they audited. Do you see any reason why this might not be an acceptable practice? Do you see any advantage to your firm from allowing such activity? [Answer on page 28]

ANALYSING FINANCIAL STATEMENTS

LO5 Compute two key ratios that are commonly used to assess profitability and risk—return on equity and the debt-to-equity ratio.

The financial statements provide insights into the financial health and performance of a company. However, the accounting data presented in these statements are difficult to interpret in raw form. For example, knowing that Roche's net income was 11.4 billion Swiss francs in 2013 is, by itself, not very useful. Similarly, knowing the dollar amount of liabilities does not tell us whether or not Roche relies too heavily on creditor financing.

Financial analysts use a number of tools to help interpret the information found in the financial statements. They look at trends over time and compare one company to another. They calculate ratios using financial statement information to summarise the data in a form that is easier to interpret. Ratios also allow us to compare the performance and condition of different companies even if the companies being compared are dramatically different in size. Ratios also help analysts spot trends or changes in performance over time.

Throughout the book, we introduce ratios that are commonly used by financial analysts and other users who rely on the financial statements. Our goal is to develop an understanding of how to effectively use the information in the financial statements, as well as to demonstrate how these statements are prepared. In this chapter we introduce one important measure of **profitability** and one measure of financial **risk**.

Profitability Analysis

Profitability reveals whether or not a company is able to bring its product or service to the market in an efficient manner, and whether the market values that product or service. Companies that are consistently unprofitable are unlikely to succeed in the long run.

A key profitability metric for shareholders and other decision makers is company return on equity. This metric compares the level of net income with the amount of equity financing used to generate that income.

Analysis Objective

We are trying to determine Roche's ability to earn a return for its shareholders.

Analysis Tool
Return on Equity

$$\textbf{Return on Equity} = \frac{\textbf{Net Income}}{\textbf{Average Total Equity}}$$

Applying the Return on Equity Ratio to Roche

$$2013 \quad \frac{11{,}373}{[(21{,}241 + 16{,}750)/2]} = 0.599 \text{ or } 59.9\%$$

$$2012 \quad \frac{9{,}660}{[(16{,}750 + 14{,}506)/2]} = 0.618 \text{ or } 61.8\%$$

$$2011 \quad \frac{9{,}544}{[(14{,}506 + 11{,}662)/2]} = 0.729 \text{ or } 72.9\%$$

Guidance Taken over time, ROE ratios that are over 10% and preferably increasing suggest the company is earning reasonable returns. For firms that are in more risky businesses, such as renewable power, even larger returns on equity would be appropriate, while firms in less risky endeavours, such as large food chains, would not be expected to generate as large returns.

Roche in Context

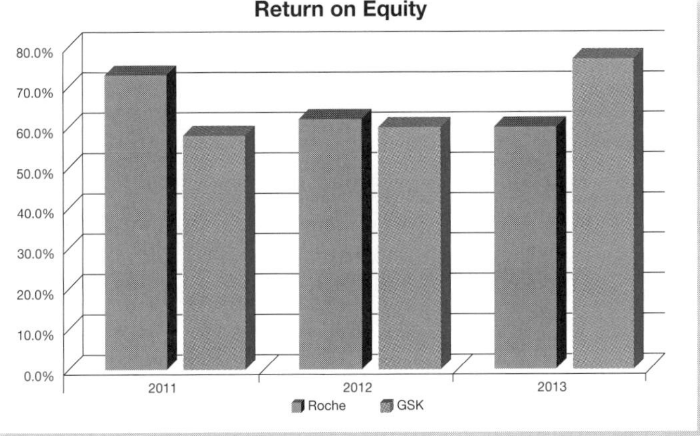

Takeaways Over the 2011–2013 period covered by our calculations and by the graph, it is clear that Roche has done well, earning at least 60% returns for its shareholders. However, the trend in profitability is decreasing, from 73% in 2011 to 60% in 2013. In comparison, its competitor, the UK-based GlaxoSmithKline (GSK), increased its return on equity from 58% to 77% over the same time period. Whether Roche can remain competitive is less clear. Besides GSK, the industry is crowded with companies like Novartis, Pfizer, Merck, Bayer, and AstraZeneca. Roche will need to continue developing new products to preserve its market leadership.

Other Considerations As with all ratios, care in their interpretation is essential. First, we need to be careful that comparisons are reserved to companies that operate in the same product markets. Thus, comparisons with the return ratios of companies in the apparel, accessories, and luxury goods industry can lead to incorrect conclusions.

Second, firms with different customer or supplier demographics can also produce different conclusions. Furthermore, different management policies toward assets and liabilities have their own unique aspects across firms. For example, the conversion of inventories to sales can be subject to slowdowns that affect companies differently, even in the same business.

Third, these measures can be altered by management decisions designed solely for cosmetic effects such as improving current earnings or an important ratio. Thus delaying inventory orders or filling sales orders early can lead to increasing net income and ROE in current periods to the detriment of future periods.

Credit Risk Analysis

FYI Return cannot be evaluated without considering risk; the greater the risk of any decision, the greater the expected return. ■

In addition to measuring profitability, analysts also frequently analyse the level of risk associated with investing in or lending to a given company. The riskier an investment is, the greater the return demanded by investors. For example, a low-risk borrower is likely to be able to borrow money at a lower interest rate than would a high-risk borrower. Similarly, there is a risk-return trade-off in equity returns. Investments in risky companies are expected to earn higher returns than investments in low-risk companies, and company shares are priced accordingly. The higher expected rate of return is compensation for accepting greater uncertainty in returns.

Many factors contribute to the risk a company faces. One important factor is a company's *long-term solvency*. **Solvency** refers to the ability of a company to remain in business and avoid bankruptcy or financial distress. One such measure is the **debt-to-equity (D/E) ratio**.

Analysis Objective

We are interested in determining the ability of a company to make the necessary interest and principal payments on its debt.

Analysis Tool Debt-to-Equity[3]

$$\textbf{Debt-to-Equity Ratio} = \frac{\textbf{Total Liabilities}}{\textbf{Total Equity}}$$

Applying the Debt-to-Equity Ratio to Roche

$$2013 \quad \frac{40{,}926}{21{,}241} = 1.927$$

$$2012 \quad \frac{48{,}058}{16{,}750} = 2.869$$

$$2011 \quad \frac{47{,}074}{14{,}506} = 3.245$$

Guidance Solvency is closely related to the extent a company relies on creditor financing. As the amount of creditor financing increases, the possibility of bankruptcy also increases. Short of bankruptcy, a company that has borrowed too much will occasionally find that the required interest payments are hurting the company's cash flow. The debt-to equity ratio is an important measure used by analysts and others to assess a company's ability to make the necessary interest and principal payments on its debt.

[3] We classify all liabilities as debt. However, the debt-to-equity ratio may also be defined as long-term debt, divided by total equity.

A debt-to equity ratio of one indicates that the company is using equal parts of debt and equity financing. The appropriate D/E ratio level depends on the nature of the business and will differ appreciably as can be seen in the chart below. Typically, firms with large long-term commitments often reflected in fixed assets will find it appropriate to raise more capital through borrowing. The amount of debt relative to equity will also mirror the risk tolerance of the firm's management. If management believes it can earn a return above the debt interest cost, borrowing will increase the expected return to the owners.

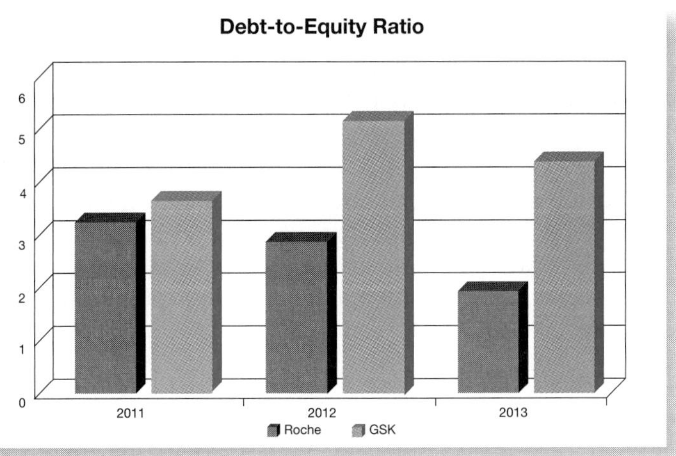

Takeaways Roche's borrowing has consistently been greater than half its assets, resulting in a D/E ratio substantially above one. Over the three years presented, the D/E ratio dropped from 3.245 to 1.927. As shown in the calculations above, the downward trend in D/E is attributed to an increase in equity financing in all three years and a drop in borrowing in 2013. As for GSK, its D/E ratio fluctuated from a low of 3.654 in 2011 to a high of 5.157 in 2012. In calculations not shown above, GSK's total liabilities has remained relatively constant over the three years, but its total equity has fluctuated.

Other Considerations Comparisons with other companies in similar lines of business, such as GSK, are always appropriate. Other competitors, such as Novartis, Merck and AstraZeneca, could also prove insightful to examine in regards to strategic decisions (Pfizer follows U.S. GAAP, making it difficult to compare its financial numbers with those of IFRS companies). In Chapter 9, we will explore the accounting for liabilities in more depth. Balance sheets do not always recognise all obligations of a firm, and a careful reader will examine the footnotes to get a more complete picture of financial health in such comparisons.

There are other measures of profitability and risk that will be introduced in later chapters. Collectively, these ratios, when placed in the context of the company's business activities, help to provide a clear picture of the *drivers* of a company's financial performance and the factors affecting its financial condition. Understanding these performance drivers and their impact on the financial health of a company is key to effectively using the information presented in the financial statements.

ORGANISATION OF THE BOOK

In the pages that follow Chapter 1, we will explore the financial accounting model and how it reflects an organisation's activities and events. Chapters 2 and 3 are focused on building the balance sheet and the income statement from transactions and a set of required adjustments. This process requires a structure for "bookkeeping" and also an understanding of the basic rules of the accounting language. When do we recognise revenue? When do we recognise an asset? We will look at these questions in a relatively simple setting.

In Chapter 4, we will construct the statement of cash flows. The balance sheet, income statement, and statement of cash flows are all built on the same underlying set of information, and they are each designed to give a different perspective on what's going on in the company. Chapter 5 shows how managers and investors organise financial information using ratios and how managers and investors use those ratios to compare companies and to make forecasts of the future.

While the first five chapters build the financial statement structure and its interpretation, the latter seven chapters are more topical. Accounting is not a cut-and-dried process, and financial reports can be affected by a variety of management decisions. So these seven chapters explore more sophisticated settings and analyses. We will find that financial reports rely on management estimates of future events, and that sometimes management has the freedom to choose accounting methods that affect income and assets. And, when accounting practices don't allow reporting discretion, management's choice of transactions can make financial reports look more favourable.

Becoming an effective user of financial information requires an understanding of how the financial reports fit together and a willingness to explore the footnote material to look for useful information. As we progress through *Financial Accounting* together, we will show you how to become a sophisticated reader of financial reports by looking at real companies and real financial statement information.

CHAPTER-END REVIEW

The following information is from TGV's 2015 financial statements:

(millions)	TGV
Net income (loss) (2015)	€ 670
Total equity (2015 year-end)	5,331
Total equity (2014 year-end)	4,623
Total liabilities (2015 year-end)	6,049

Required

a. Calculate the 2015 return on equity (ROE) ratio for TGV.
b. Calculate the 2015 debt-to-equity ratio for TGV.
c. Compare the profitability and risk of TGV to those of its major competitors around the globe. The average ROE and debt-to-equity ratio of its competitors are 11.8% and 1.52, respectively.

The solution to this review problem can be found on page 37.

APPENDIX 1A: Conceptual Framework for Financial Reporting

LO6 Explain the conceptual framework for financial reporting.

Accounting standard setters develop a **conceptual framework** to describe the concepts that underlie the preparation and presentation of financial statements. The framework provides standard setters a structure for developing and revising standards and guides management in areas where standards do not currently exist.

In that regard, the IASB developed the IFRS Conceptual Framework in 2010. The IFRS framework includes, among other items, a statement of the *objective* of financial reporting along with a discussion of the *qualitative characteristics* of useful financial information that are important to users. We discuss this objective and these characteristics in this appendix, along with some of the important assumptions and features underlying the preparation of financial statements.

The Objective of General Purpose Financial Reporting

The objective of general purpose financial reporting is to provide information about the reporting entity that is useful to current and potential investors, lenders, and other creditors in making decisions about investing in equity or debt instruments and providing or settling loans or other forms of credit. These users need information that is useful for assessing the amount, timing, and uncertainty of future cash flows. They also need information for evaluating how effectively and efficiently management and governing boards have discharged their stewardship duties over the entity's resources. To accomplish this objective, financial reporting should provide information about

- an entity's economic resources and financial claims on those resources that might help the users assess the entity's assets and obligations, its liquidity and solvency, and its need and ability to obtain financing. This includes the information in the statement of financial position and any supporting information.
- an entity's financial performance that might help the users assess the entity's past and future ability to generate cash flows. This includes the information in the statement of income, statement of comprehensive income, and any supporting information.
- an entity's cash flows that might help the users assess the entity's generation and use of cash, its borrowing and debt repayments, its cash dividend, etc. This includes the information presented in the statement of cash flows and any supporting information.
- changes in an entity's resources and claims resulting from the issuance of equity instruments or distributions of cash or other assets to shareholders that might help the users assess the total change in the entity's economic resources and claims. This includes the information presented in the statement of changes in equity and any supporting information.

FYI In July 2013, the IASB released a discussion paper addressing possible changes to the IFRS conceptual framework and soliciting comments. Since the end of the comment period in January 2014, the IASB has been working on a draft conceptual framework that will be published for comments from the public.

Qualitative Characteristics of Useful Financial Information

The qualitative characteristics of useful financial information identify the types of information that are likely to be useful to the users. Information must be both relevant and faithfully represented for it to be useful. The usefulness of information is enhanced if it is comparable, verifiable, timely, and understandable. However, these enhancing characteristics cannot make information useful if it is irrelevant or not faithfully represented.

Fundamental Qualitative Characteristics

The fundamental qualitative characteristics of useful financial information are relevance and faithful representation.

Relevance Accounting information must have the ability to make a difference in a decision. Such information may be useful if it has *predictive value, confirmatory value,* or both.

- **Predictive value:** The ability of the information to increase the accuracy of a forecast.
- **Confirmatory value:** The ability of the information to enable users to confirm or change prior expectations.

Materiality Materiality is an entity-specific aspect of relevance based on the nature and/or magnitude of the items. Information is material if its omission or misstatement would influence the judgement of a reasonable decision maker.

Faithful Representation Accounting information should faithfully reflect the underlying economic events it purports to capture. A faithful representation is one that is *complete, neutral* and *free from error*.

- **Complete:** A complete depiction includes all necessary descriptions and explanations for users to understand the item being represented.
- **Neutral:** The selection or presentation of accounting information must be free of any bias intended to attain a predetermined result or to induce a particular mode of behaviour.
- **Free from error:** There are no omissions in the description of the item and no errors in selecting and applying the process used to produce the reported information.

Enhancing Qualitative Characteristics

Comparability, verifiability, timeliness and understandability are qualitative characteristics that enhance the usefulness of information that is relevant and faithfully represented.

Comparability Accounting information should enable users to identify similarities and differences between sets of economic phenomena. For instance, the financial statements of different companies should be presented in a way that allows users to make comparisons across companies concerning their activities, financial condition, and performance. Although management has the flexibility to choose how events are measured and reported, this discretion should not be used to obscure the underlying economic substance of the event. Comparability is enhanced if firms in the same business (industry) use the same, or similar, reporting techniques.

Verifiability This characteristic implies that consensus among measures assures that the information is faithfully represented. Knowledgeable and independent observers should be able to examine the economic phenomena underlying the financial statements and reach conclusions that are similar to those of management concerning how these events are measured and reported.

Timeliness The information must be available to decision makers before it loses its capacity to influence decisions. That is, information that is reported after a decision is made is not timely.

Understandability Accounting information should be presented clearly and concisely so that a knowledgeable reader can understand how it relates to the decision problem at hand. Because different users will require different information, standard setters must tread a fine line between requiring too much or too little information.

Underlying Assumptions and Features

Several assumptions and features underlie the preparation of financial statements. Knowing these assumptions and features is helpful in understanding how the statements are prepared and in interpreting the information reported therein.

Going Concern Companies are assumed to have continuity in that they can be expected to continue in operation over time. This assumption is essential for valuing assets (future benefits) and liabilities (future obligations).

Reporting Frequency While continuity is assumed, company operations must be reported periodically, normally each fiscal year. Interim reporting periods, such as semi-annual or quarterly reports, allow companies to supplement the annual financial statements with more timely information.

Consistency The information supplied to decision makers should exhibit conformity from one reporting period to the next with unchanging policies and procedures. Changes in accounting policies, presentation, and classification should be rare and justifiable as a better means of reporting the organisation's financial condition and performance.

Cost Constraint Cost is a pervasive constraint on the information that can be provided. This characteristic implies that if the benefit to the users does not exceed the cost, the information does not meet the test of usefulness. The need to weigh costs and benefits is an overriding constraint on the financial reporting process.

YOU MAKE THE CALL

You are the Bank Loan Officer Europcar, the rental car firm, has a fleet of relatively new automobiles that it rents to customers for usually short periods. Suppose that Europcar applied to your bank for a loan and offered their fleet of cars as collateral. Would you, as the loan officer, be satisfied with the value shown on Europcar's balance sheet as a measure of the fleet's value? If not, what value would you prefer and how might you estimate that value? [Answers on page 28]

SUMMARY

LO1 Identify the users of accounting information and discuss the costs and benefits of disclosure. (p. 4)

- There are many diverse decision makers who use financial information.
- The benefits of disclosure of credible financial information must exceed the costs of providing the information.

Describe a company's business activities and explain how these activities are represented by the accounting equation. (p. 7) LO2

- To effectively manage a company or infer whether it is well managed, we must understand its activities as well as the competitive and regulatory environment in which it operates.
- All corporations *plan* business activities, *finance* and *invest* in them, and then engage in *operations*.
- Financing is obtained partly from shareholders and partly from creditors, including suppliers and lenders.
- Investing activities involve the acquisition and disposition of the company's productive resources called assets.
- Operating activities include the production of goods or services that create operating revenues (sales) and expenses (costs). Operating profit (income) arises when operating revenues exceed operating expenses.

Introduce the four key financial statements including the balance sheet, income statement, statement of changes in equity, and statement of cash flows. (p. 11) LO3

- The four basic financial statements used to periodically report the company's progress are the balance sheet, the income statement, the statement of changes in equity, and the statement of cash flows. These statements articulate with one another.
- The balance sheet reports the company's financial position *at a point* in time. It lists the company's asset, liability, and equity items, and it typically aggregates similar items.
- The income statement reports the firm's operating activities to determine income earned, and thereby the firm's performance *over a period* of time.
- The changes in equity statement reports the changes in the key equity accounts *over a period* of time.
- The statement of cash flows reports the cash flows into and out of the firm from its operating, investing, and financing sources *over a period* of time.

Describe the institutions that regulate financial accounting and their role in establishing generally accepted accounting principles/practices. (p. 17) LO4

- Generally Accepted Accounting Principles/Practice (GAAP) are established standards and accepted practices designed to guide the preparation of the financial statements. Each country or jurisdiction has its own GAAP.
- International Financial Reporting Standards (IFRS) are set by the International Accounting Standards Board (IASB).
- IFRS are an attempt to achieve a greater degree of commonality in financial reporting across different countries. IFRS has been adopted by many countries and jurisdictions.

Compute two key ratios that are commonly used to assess profitability and risk—return on equity and the debt-to-equity ratio. (p. 20) LO5

- **Return on equity (ROE)**—a measure of profitability that assesses the performance of the firm relative to the investment made by shareholders (equity financing)
- Return on equity (ROE) is an important profitability metric for shareholders.

$$\text{ROE} = \frac{\text{Net income}}{\text{Average total equity}}$$

- **Debt-to-equity ratio**—a measure of long-term solvency that relates the amount of creditor financing to the amount of equity financing
- The debt-to-equity ratio is an important measure of long-term solvency, a determinant of overall company risk.

$$\text{D/E} = \frac{\text{Total liabilities}}{\text{Total equity}}$$

Appendix 1A: Explain the conceptual framework for financial reporting. (p. 24) LO6

- The conceptual framework includes, among other things, a statement of the *objectives* of financial reporting along with a discussion of the *qualitative characteristics* of accounting information that are important to users.

GUIDANCE ANSWERS . . . YOU MAKE THE CALL

You are a Product Manager There are at least two considerations that must be balanced—namely, the disclosure requirements and your company's need to protect its competitive advantages. You must comply with all minimum required disclosures. The extent to which you offer additional disclosures depends on the sensitivity of the information; that is, how beneficial it is to your existing and potential competitors. Another consideration is how the information disclosed will impact your existing and potential investors. Disclosures such as this can be beneficial in that they convey the positive investments that are available to your company. Still, there are many stakeholders impacted by your decision and each must be given due consideration.

You are a Financial Analyst This question has received a lot of discussion from both sides under the title "Economic Consequences." On one side are those who maintain that accounting rules should not only reflect a rule's economic consequences but should be designed to facilitate the attainment of a specific economic goal. One example is the case where the oil industry lobbied for an accounting rule that they and others believed would increase the incentive to explore and develop new oil deposits.

Those on the other side of the argument believe that accounting should try to provide data that are objective, reliable, and free from bias without considering the economic consequences of the decisions to be made. They believe that accounting rule makers have neither the insight nor the public mandate to attempt forecasts of the economic effects of financial reporting. Decisions that will affect the allocation of resources or that affect society's social structure should be made only by our elected representatives. While there are substantive points on both sides, we believe that it is the job of accounting rule makers to work toward the objective of financial reporting that reflects economic reality, subject to practical measurement limitations.

You are a Member of the Board of Directors In order to perform a thorough audit, a company's auditors must gain an intimate knowledge of its operations, its internal controls, and its accounting system. Because of this familiarity, the accounting firm is in a position to provide insights and recommendations that another consulting firm might not be able to provide. However, the independence of the auditor is critical to the credibility of the audit and there is some concern that the desire to retain a profitable consulting engagement might lead the auditors to tailor their audit opinions to "satisfy the customer." Contrary to this concern, however, research finds that there is no evidence that auditors provide more optimistic audit reports for the companies they consult for. Rather, it appears that litigation and/or reputation concerns are reasonably effective in keeping auditors honest. Nevertheless, recent legislation enacted in many countries now prohibits auditors from performing consulting services for their audit clients.

You are the Bank Loan Officer The value shown on Europcar's books will be the purchase price, though perhaps reduced for the time the fleet has been in use. However, the bank would want to know the current market value of the fleet, not its book value, and the bank would then adjust this market value. The current market value of a single car can be found in used-car market quotes. If the bank ultimately becomes the owner of the fleet, it will need to sell the cars, probably a few at a time through wholesalers. Therefore, the adjusted market value and the book value are likely to differ for several reasons, including:

1. Europcar would have been able to buy the fleet at a reduced value due to buying in large volume regularly (market value lower than used-car quotes).
2. Europcar is likely to have kept the cars in better condition than would the average buyer (market value higher than used-car quotes).
3. The bank would reduce the value by some percentage due to the costs associated with disposing of the fleet (including the wholesaler's discount) and the length of the bank loan (reduction to the value as otherwise determined).

KEY RATIOS

$$\text{Return on equity (ROE)} = \frac{\text{Net income}}{\text{Average total equity}}$$

$$\text{Debt-to-equity (D/E)} = \frac{\text{Total liabilities}}{\text{Total equity}}$$

KEY TERMS

Accounting (p. 4)
Accounting equation (p. 10)
Assets (p. 8)
Audited (p. 19)
Balance sheet (p. 11, 12)
Board of directors (p. 6)
Complete (p. 25)
Conceptual framework (p. 24)
Confirmatory value (p. 25)
Corporation (p. 5)
Cost of goods sold (p. 13)
Creditors (p. 6)
Debt-to-equity (D/E) ratio (p. 22)
Disclosure (p. 7)
Economic consequences (p. 18)
Expense (p. 10)
Financial accounting (p. 4)
Financing activities (p. 9)
Free from error (p. 25)
Generally accepted accounting principles/practice (GAAP) (p. 17)
Income (p. 10)
Income statement (p. 11, 12)
International Accounting Standards Board (IASB) (p. 18)
International Financial Reporting Standards (IFRS) (p. 18)
Investing activities (p. 8)
Liabilities (p. 9)
Managerial accounting (p. 4)
Neutral (p. 25)
Operating activities (p. 10)
Partnership (p. 5)
Planning activities (p. 8)
Predictive value (p. 25)
Profitability (p. 20)
Retained earnings (p. 13)
Revenue (p. 10)
Risk (p. 20)
Shareholders (p. 5)
Shares (p. 5)
Sole proprietorship (p. 5)
Solvency (p. 22)
Statement of cash flows (p. 11, 14)
Statement of changes in equity (p. 11, 13)
Stockholders (p. 5)
Strategy (p. 8)
Suppliers (p. 6)

MULTIPLE CHOICE

1. Which of the following is a potential cost of the public disclosure of accounting information?
   a. Loss of competitive advantage caused by revealing information to competitors
   b. Potential increased regulation and taxes due to reporting excessive profits in politically sensitive industries
   c. Raising and then failing to meet the expectations of investors
   d. All of the above are potential costs of disclosure
2. Banks that lend money to corporations are considered
   a. creditors.
   b. shareholders/stockholders.
   c. both *a* and *b* above.
   d. neither *a* nor *b* above.
3. Which of the following financial statements reports the financial condition of a company at a point in time?
   a. The balance sheet
   b. The income statement
   c. The statement of cash flows
   d. The statement of changes in equity
4. Which of the following is *not* one of the four basic financial reports?
   a. The balance sheet
   b. The income statement
   c. The statement of changes in equity
   d. The notes to the financial statements
5. Which of the following expressions is a correct statement of the accounting equation?
   a. Equity + Assets = Liability
   b. Assets − (Liabilities + Equity) = 0
   c. Liabilities − Equity = Assets
   d. Liabilities + Assets = Equity

Multiple Choice Answers
1. d 2. a 3. a 4. d 5. b

Superscript A denotes assignments based on Appendix 1A.

DISCUSSION QUESTIONS

Q1-1. What are the three major business activities of a company that are motivated and shaped by planning activities? Explain each activity.

Q1-2. The accounting equation (Assets = Liabilities + Equity) is a fundamental business concept. Explain what this equation reveals about a company's sources and uses of funds and the claims on company resources.

Q1-3. Companies prepare four primary financial statements. What are those financial statements and what information is typically conveyed in each?

Q1-4. Does a balance sheet report on a period of time or at a point in time? Also, explain the information conveyed in that report. Does an income statement report on a period of time or at a point in time? Also, explain the information conveyed in that report.

Q1-5. Warren Buffett, CEO of Berkshire Hathaway, and known as the "Sage of Omaha" for his investment success, has stated that his firm is not interested in investing in a company whose business model he does not understand through reading their financial statements. Would you agree? Name several information items (3 or 4) reported in financial statements that corporate finance officers would find particularly relevant in considering whether to invest in a firm.

Q1-6. Does a statement of cash flows report on a period of time or at a point in time? Also, explain the information and activities conveyed in that report.

Q1-7. Explain what is meant by the articulation of financial statements.

Q1-8. The trade-off between risk and return is a fundamental business concept. Briefly describe both risk and return and their trade-off. Provide some examples that demonstrate investments of varying risk and the approximate returns that you might expect to earn on those investments.

Q1-9. Why might a company voluntarily disclose more information than is required by IFRS?

Q1-10. Financial statements are used by several interested stakeholders. Develop a listing of three or more potential external users of financial statements and their applications.

Q1-11. What ethical issues might managers face in dealing with confidential information?

Q1-12. Return on equity (ROE) is an important summary measure of financial performance. How is it computed? Describe what this metric reveals about company performance.

Q1-13. Business decision makers external to the company increasingly demand more financial information on business activities of companies. Discuss the reasons why companies have traditionally opposed the efforts of regulatory agencies to require more disclosure.

Q1-14. What are generally accepted accounting principles and how do they aid the decision making process of financial statement users?

Q1-15. What are International Financial Reporting Standards (IFRS)? Why are IFRS needed? What potential issues can you see with requiring all public companies to prepare financial statements using IFRS?

Q1-16. What is the primary function of the auditor? To what does the auditor attest in its opinion?

Q1-17.[A] What are the objectives of financial accounting? Which of the financial statements satisfies each of these objectives?

Q1-18.[A] What are the qualitative characteristics of accounting information? Explain how each characteristic improves the quality of accounting disclosures.

MINI EXERCISES

LO2 **M1-19. Financing and Investing Relations, and Financing Sources**

LOBLAW CO. LTD. (CANADA)

For the year 2013, total assets of Loblaw Companies Limited, the largest Canadian food retailer, equal $20,759 million and its equity is $7,018 million. What is the amount of its liabilities? Does Loblaw receive more financing from its owners or nonowners, and what percentage of financing is provided by its owners?

LO2 **M1-20. Financing and Investing Relations, and Financing Sources**

UNILEVER GROUP (UK AND THE NETHERLANDS)

For the year 2013, total assets of Unilever Group, an Anglo-Dutch multinational consumer goods company, equal €45,513 million and its liabilities equal €30,698 million. What is the amount of its equity? Does Unilever receive more financing from its owners or nonowners, and what percentage of financing is provided by its owners?

M1-21. Applying the Accounting Equation and Computing Financing Proportions LO2

EMBRAER S.A. (BRAZIL)
L'ORÉAL S.A. (FRANCE)
NOKIA OYJ (FINLAND)

Selected 2013 financial information for three companies is given below. Embraer S.A. is a Brazilian aircraft manufacturer. L'Oréal S.A. is a French cosmetic and consumer products company. Nokia Oyj. is a Finnish communications and information technology company. Use the accounting equation to compute the missing financial amounts (a), (b), and (c). Which of these companies is more owner-financed? Which of these companies is more creditor-financed? What may explain the difference in the proportion of owner financing across these three companies?

(Amounts in millions)	Assets	=	Liabilities	+	Equity
Embraer S.A.	$(a)		$6,510.3		$3,632.2
L'Oréal S.A.	€31,298.3		€8,665.5		€(b)
Nokia Oyj.	€25,191		€(c)		€6,660

M1-22. Identifying Key Numbers from Financial Statements LO3

QANTAS AIRWAYS LIMITED (AUSTRALIA)

Access the 2013 annual report for Qantas Airways Limited at the company's website (http://www.qantas.com.au/travel/airlines/investors-annual-reports/global/en). What are Qantas' dollar amounts for assets, liabilities, and equity at 30 June 2013? Confirm that the accounting equation holds in this case. What percent of Qantas' assets is financed from creditor financing sources?

M1-23. Verifying Articulation of Financial Statements LO3

INDITEX S.A. (SPAIN)

Access the 2012 annual report for Inditex S.A. at the company's website (http://www.inditex.com/en/investors/investors_relations/annual_report). Using its consolidated statement of changes in equity, prepare a table similar to Exhibit 1.9 showing the articulation of its retained (reinvested) earnings for the year ended January 31, 2013. Was Inditex more or less profitable in this year?

M1-24. Identifying Financial Statement Line Items and Accounts LO3

Several line items and account titles are listed below. For each, indicate in which of the following financial statement(s) you would likely find the item or account: income statement (IS), balance sheet (BS), statement of changes in equity (SE), or statement of cash flows (SCF).

a. Cash asset
b. Expenses
c. Noncash assets
d. Contributed capital
e. Cash outflow for land
f. Retained earnings
g. Cash inflow for shares issued
h. Cash outflow for dividends
i. Net income

M1-25. Ethical Issues and Accounting Choices LO1

Assume that you are a technology services provider and you must decide whether to record revenue from the instalation of computer software for one of your clients. Your contract calls for acceptance of the software by the client within six months of instalation before payment is due. Although you have not yet received formal acceptance, you are confident that it is forthcoming. Failure to record these revenues will cause your company to miss security analysts' earnings estimates. What stakeholders will be affected by your decision and how might they be affected?

M1-26. Internal Controls and Their Importance LO4

What are internal controls and their purpose? Why do you think it is an important area to monitor and report?

EXERCISES

E1-27. Applying the Accounting Equation and Assessing Financing Contributions LO2

SMRT Corporation is the second-largest public transport operator in Singapore. MTR Corporation is a Hong Kong-based railway operator and property developer. Determine the missing amount from each of the separate situations (a) and (b) below. Which of these companies is more owner-financed? Which of these companies is more creditor-financed?

SMRT CORPORATION (SINGAPORE)
MTR CORPORATION (HONG KONG)

($ millions)	Assets	=	Liabilities	+	Equity
a. SMRT Corp. (in million of Singapore $)	$ 2,073		$(a)		$802
b. MTR Corp. (in million of HK $)	$(b)		$63,121		$152,702

E1-28. Applying the Accounting Equation and Financial Statement Articulation LO2, 3

Answer the following questions. (*Hint*: Apply the accounting equation.)

PRADA S.P.A. (ITALY)
ROGERS COMMUNICATIONS INC. (CANADA)
CARREFOUR S.A. (FRANCE)

a. Prada, an Italian luxury fashion house, had assets equal to €3,888 million and liabilities equal to €1,187 million for January 31, 2014. What was the total equity for Prada's business at year-end?

b. Rogers Communications Inc. is a Canadian communications and media company. At the beginning of 2013, the company's assets were $19,618 million and its equity was $3,768 million. During the year, assets increased $3,983 million and liabilities increased $3,082 million. What was its equity at the end of the year?

c. At the beginning of 2013, Carrefour, a French retailer, reported liabilities of €37,959 (in thousands). During the year, assets decreased by €2,442, and year-end assets equaled €43,564. Liabilities decreased €2,992 during the year. What were its beginning and ending amounts for equity? All numbers are in thousands of Euro.

LO1 **E1-29. Financial Information Users and Uses**

Financial statements have a wide audience of interested stakeholders. Identify two or more financial statement users that are external to the company. Specify two questions for each user identified that could be addressed or aided by use of financial statements.

LO3 **E1-30. Financial Statement Relations to Compute Dividends**

ADIDAS A.G. (GERMANY)

Adidas, a German sporting goods company, reports the following balances in its retained earnings.

(€ millions)	2013	2012
Retained earnings	€4,959	€4,454

During 2013, Adidas reported net income of €790 million.

a. Assume that the only changes affecting retained earnings were net income and dividends. What amount of dividends did Adidas pay to its shareholders in 2013?

b. This dividend amount constituted what percent of its net income?

LO3 **E1-31. Calculating Gross Profit and Preparing an Income Statement**

ADIDAS A.G. (GERMANY)

In 2013, Adidas reported net sales of €14,492 million and cost of sales of €7,352 million. Its net income was €790 million. Calculate gross profit and prepare an income statement using the format illustrated in Exhibit 1.8.

LO2, 5 **E1-32. Applying the Accounting Equation and Calculating Return on Equity and Debt-to-Equity Ratio**

ADIDAS A.G. (GERMANY)

At the end of 2013, Adidas Group reported equity of €5,481 million and total assets of €11,599 million. Its balance in equity at the end of 2012 was €5,291 million. Net income in 2013 was €790 million.

a. Calculate Adidas' return on equity ratio for 2013.

b. Calculate its debt-to-equity ratio as of December 31, 2013. (*Hint:* Apply the accounting equation to determine total liabilities.)

LO1, 4, 6 **E1-33.[A] Accounting in Society**

Financial accounting plays an important role in modern society and business.

a. What role does financial accounting play in the allocation of society's financial resources?

b. What are three aspects of the accounting environment that can create ethical pressure on management?

PROBLEMS

LO2, 5 **P1-34. Applying the Accounting Equation and Calculating Ratios**

The following table contains financial statement information for The P&G Company ($ millions):

Year	Assets	Liabilities	Equity	Net Income
2012	$134,833	$71,451	$?	$13,436
2013	?	66,733	61,439	12,736
2014	138,354	?	68,001	11,797

Required

a. Compute the missing amounts for assets, liabilities, and equity for each year.

b. Compute return on equity for 2013 and 2014. The median ROE for P&G's industry is about 15%. How does P&G compare with this median?

c. Compute the debt-to-equity ratio for 2013 and 2014. The median debt-to-equity ratio for P&G's industry is 1.8. How does P&G compare to this median?

P1-35. Formulating Financial Statements from Raw Data LO2, 3

Following is selected financial information from General Inc., for its fiscal year ended May 29, 2014 ($ millions):

Cash and cash equivalents	$ 619.6
Net cash from operations	1,526.8
Sales	14,880.2
Total equity	6,612.2
Cost of goods sold	8,926.7
Net cash from financing	(865.3)
Total liabilities	12,062.3
Other expenses	4,150.0
Noncash assets	18,054.9
Net cash from investing	(715.1)
Net income	1,803.5
Cash, beginning year	673.2

Required

a. Prepare an income statement, balance sheet, and statement of cash flows for General Inc.

b. What portion of the financing is contributed by owners?

P1-36. Formulating Financial Statements from Raw Data LO2, 3

Following is selected financial information from Fitch Corporation for its fiscal year ended January 29, 2015 ($ millions):

Cash asset	$ 826
Cash flows from operations	392
Sales	3,469
Total equity	1,891
Cost of goods sold	1,257
Cash flows from financing	(143)
Total liabilities	1,050
Other expenses	2,062
Noncash assets	2,115
Cash flows from investing	(93)
Net income	150
Cash, beginning year	670

Required

a. Prepare an income statement, balance sheet, and statement of cash flows for Fitch Corporation.

b. Determine the owner and creditor financing levels.

P1-37. Formulating Financial Statements from Raw Data LO3

FIAT S.P.A. (ITALY)

Following is selected financial information from the Italian auto maker Fiat, for the year ended December 31, 2013 (€ millions):

Cash and cash equivalents	€19,439
Net cash from operations	7,589
Sales	86,816
Total equity	12,584
Cost of sales	74,570
Net cash from financing	2,279
Total liabilities	74,190
Other expenses	10,295
Noncash assets	67,335
Net cash from investing	(8,086)
Net income	1,951
Cash, beginning year	17,657

Required

Prepare an income statement, balance sheet, and statement of cash flows for Fiat.

LO3 **P1-38. Formulating a Statement of Changes in Equity from Raw Data**

Crocker Corporation began calendar-year 2013 with changes in equity of $100,000, consisting of contributed capital of $70,000 and retained earnings of $30,000. During 2013, it issued additional shares for total cash proceeds of $30,000. It also reported $50,000 of net income, of which $25,000 was paid as a cash dividend to shareholders.

Required

Prepare the December 31, 2013 statement of changes in equity for Crocker Corporation.

LO3 **P1-39. Formulating a Statement of Changes in Equity from Raw Data**

DP Systems, Inc., reports the following selected information at December 31, 2013 ($ millions):

Contributed capital, December 31, 2012 and 2013	$ 550
Retained earnings, December 31, 2012	2,437
Cash dividends, 2013	281
Net income, 2013	859

Required

Use this information to prepare its statement of changes in equity for 2013.

LO3, 5 **P1-40. Analysing and Interpreting Return on Equity**

NOKIA OYJ. (FINLAND)

Nokia Oyj. is a communications and information technology company, based in Finland. Total equity for Nokia are €6,660 in 2013 and €9,239 in 2012. In 2013, Nokia reported a loss of €739 on sales of €12,709.

Required

a. What is Nokia's return on equity for 2013?

b. Nokia's total assets were €25,191 at the end of 2013. Compute its debt-to-equity ratio.

c. What are total expenses for Nokia in 2013?

LO3, 5 **P1-41. Presenting an Income Statement and Computing Key Ratios**

Best Co. reported the following amounts in its February 26, 2014, and February 27, 2013, financial statements.

($ millions)	2014	2013
Sales revenue	$49,747	$49,243
Cost of sales	37,197	27,201
Net income	1,277	1,317
Total assets	17,849	18,302
Total equity	7,292	6,964

Required

a. Prepare an income statement for Best Co. for the year ended February 26, 2014, using the format illustrated in Exhibit 1.8.

b. Calculate Best's return on equity for the year ended February 26, 2014.

c. Compute Best's debt-to-equity ratio as of February 26, 2014.

LO3, 5 **P1-42. Presenting an Income Statement and Computing Key Ratios**

NESTLE S.A. (SWITZERLAND)

Nestle, a Swiss food and beverage company, reported the following amounts in its December 31, 2013, and December 31, 2012, financial statements.

(In millions of CHF)	2013	2012
Sales revenue	CHF92,158	CHF89,721
Cost of sales	48,111	47,500
Other operating expenses	33,602	31,544
Total assets	120,442	125,877
Total equity	64,139	62,664

Required

a. Prepare an income statement for Nestle as of December 31, 2013, using the format illustrated in Exhibit 1.8.

b. Calculate Nestle's return on equity for the year ended December 31, 2013.

c. Compute Nestle's debt-to-equity ratio as of December 31, 2013.

CASES AND PROJECTS

C1-43. Computing and Interpreting Key Ratios and Formulating an Income Statement

LO2, 3, 5

HUDSON'S BAY (CANADA)
CANADIAN TIRE (CANADA)

Data from the financial statements of Hudson's Bay and Canadian Tire are presented below. Hudson's Bay, the oldest company in North America, operates a chain of mid-range to upper mid-range department stores in Canada. Canadian Tire operates a chain of general department stores and gasoline stations in Canada.

($ millions of Canadian dollars)	Hudson's Bay	Canadian Tire
Total liabilities, 2013	$5,876.3	$ 8,180.1
Total liabilities, 2012	2,234.6	8,464.3
Total assets, 2013	7,927.0	13,630.0
Total assets, 2012	3,247.6	13,228.6
Revenue, 2013	5,223.4	11,785.6
Cost of goods sold, 2013	3,216.8	8,063.3
Net income, 2013	−258.1	564.4

Required

a. Compute the return on equity ratio for Hudson's Bay and Canadian Tire for 2013. Which company earned the higher return for its shareholders?

b. Compute the debt-to-equity ratio for each company as of 2013. Which company relies more on creditor financing?

c. Prepare a 2013 income statement for each company using the format in Exhibit 1.8. For each firm, compute gross profit as a percentage of sales revenue.

d. Based on your answers to questions *a*, *b*, and *c*, compare these two retail companies. What might be the cause of any differences in the ratios that you computed?

C1-44. Computing and Interpreting Key Ratios

LO5

Data from the financial statements of JB Airways and SW Airlines are presented below.

($ millions)	JB Airways	SW Airlines
Total liabilities, December 31, 2014	$4,939	$ 9,226
Total liabilities, December 31, 2013	5,003	8,815
Total assets, December 31, 2014	6,593	15,463
Total assets, December 31, 2013	6,549	14,269
Revenue, 2014	3,779	12,104
Net income, 2014	97	459

Required

a. Compute the return on equity ratio for JB and SW for 2014. Which company earned the higher return for its shareholders?

b. Compute the debt-to-equity ratio for each company as of December 31, 2014. Which company relies more on creditor financing?

c. For each firm, compute net income as a percentage of revenue in 2014.

d. Based on your answers to questions *a*, *b*, and *c*, compare these two competitors. What might be the cause of any differences in the ratios that you computed?

C1-45. Interpreting Financial Statement Information

LO1, 3, 5

Paula Seale is negotiating the purchase of an extermination firm called Total Pest Control. Seale has been employed by a national pest control service and knows the technical side of the business. However, she knows little about accounting data and financial statements. The sole owner of the firm, Meg Krey, has provided Seale with income statements for the past three years, which show an average net income of $72,000 per year. The latest balance sheet shows total assets of $285,000 and liabilities of $45,000. Seale brings the following matters to your attention and requests advice.

1. Krey is asking $300,000 for the firm. She has told Seale that because the firm has been earning 30% on its investment, the price should be higher than the net assets on the balance sheet.
2. Seale has noticed no salary for Krey on the income statements, even though she worked half-time in the business. Krey explained that because she had other income, the firm only paid $18,000 in cash dividends to Krey (the sole shareholder). If she purchases the firm, Seale will hire a full-time manager for the firm at an annual salary of $36,000.

3. Krey's tax returns for the past 3 years report a lower net income for the firm than the amounts shown in the financial statements. Seale is sceptical about the accounting principles used in preparing the financial statements.

Required

a. How did Krey arrive at the 30% return figure in point 1? If Seale accepts Krey's average annual income figure of $72,000, what would Seale's percentage return be, assuming that the net income remained at the same level and that the firm was purchased for $300,000?

b. Should the dividend to Krey affect the net income reported in the financial statements? What will Seale's percentage return be if she takes into consideration the $36,000 salary she plans to pay a full-time manager?

c. Could there be legitimate reasons for the difference between net income shown in the financial statements and net income reported on the tax returns, as mentioned in point 3? How might Seale obtain additional assurance about the propriety of the financial statements?

LO1, 4 **C1-46. Management, Auditing, and Ethical Behaviour**

Jackie Hardy, an accountant, has a brother, Ted, in the retail clothing business. Ted ran the business as its sole owner for 10 years. During this 10-year period, Jackie helped Ted with various accounting matters. For example, Jackie designed the accounting system for the company, prepared Ted's personal income tax returns (which included financial data about the clothing business), and recommended various cost control procedures. Ted paid Jackie for all these services. A year ago, Ted markedly expanded the business; Ted is president of the corporation and also chairs the corporation's board of directors. The board of directors has overall responsibility for corporate affairs. When the corporation was formed, Ted asked Jackie to serve on its board of directors. Jackie accepted. In addition, Jackie now prepares the corporation's income tax returns and continues to advise her brother on accounting matters.

Recently, the corporation applied for a large bank loan. The bank wants audited financial statements for the corporation before it will decide on the loan request. Ted asked Jackie to perform the audit. Jackie replied that she cannot do the audit because the code of ethics for professional accountants requires that she be independent when providing audit services.

Required

a. Why is it important that an accountant be independent when providing audit services?

b. Which of Jackie's activities or relationships impair her independence?

SOLUTIONS TO REVIEW PROBLEMS

<u>Mid-Chapter Review</u>

Solution

TGV S.A.
Balance Sheet (€ millions)
December 31, 2015

Cash	€ 906	Total liabilities	€ 6,049
Noncash assets	10,474	Total equity	5,331
Total assets	€11,380	Total liabilities and equity	€11,380

TGV S.A.
Income Statement (€ millions)
For Year Ended December 31, 2015

Sales revenue	€13,344
Cost of goods sold	7,000
Gross profit	6,344
Other expenses	5,674
Net income (loss)	€ 670

TGV S.A. Statement of Cash Flows (€ millions) For Year Ended December 31, 2015	
Cash flow from operations	€ 792
Cash flow from investing	(566)
Cash flow from financing	(491)
Effect of exchange rates on cash	15
Net increase (decrease) in cash	(250)
Cash, beginning of year	1,156
Cash, end of year	€ 906

Chapter-End Review

Solution

a. $$\text{ROE} = \frac{€670 \text{ million}}{(€4{,}623 \text{ million} + €5{,}331\text{million})/2} = 0.135 \text{ or } 13.5\%$$

b. $$\text{Debt-to-equity} = \frac{€6{,}049 \text{ million}}{€5{,}331 \text{ million}} = 1.13$$

c. One additional benefit to using ratios to analyse financial information is that ratios can be computed for amounts denominated in any currency. Thus, we can compare TGV with its competitors around the world without translating Euros into other currencies. TGV's ROE of 13.5% is higher than the industry average of 11.8%. This means that TGV is more profitable in that it earned a higher return for its shareholders in 2015.

TGV's debt-to-equity ratio is 1.13 compared to the industry average of 1.52. This means that TGV relies less on debt financing than its average competitor does. The lower debt-to-equity ratio indicates a lower level of risk associated with an investment in TGV than with an investment in a portfolio of its competitors.

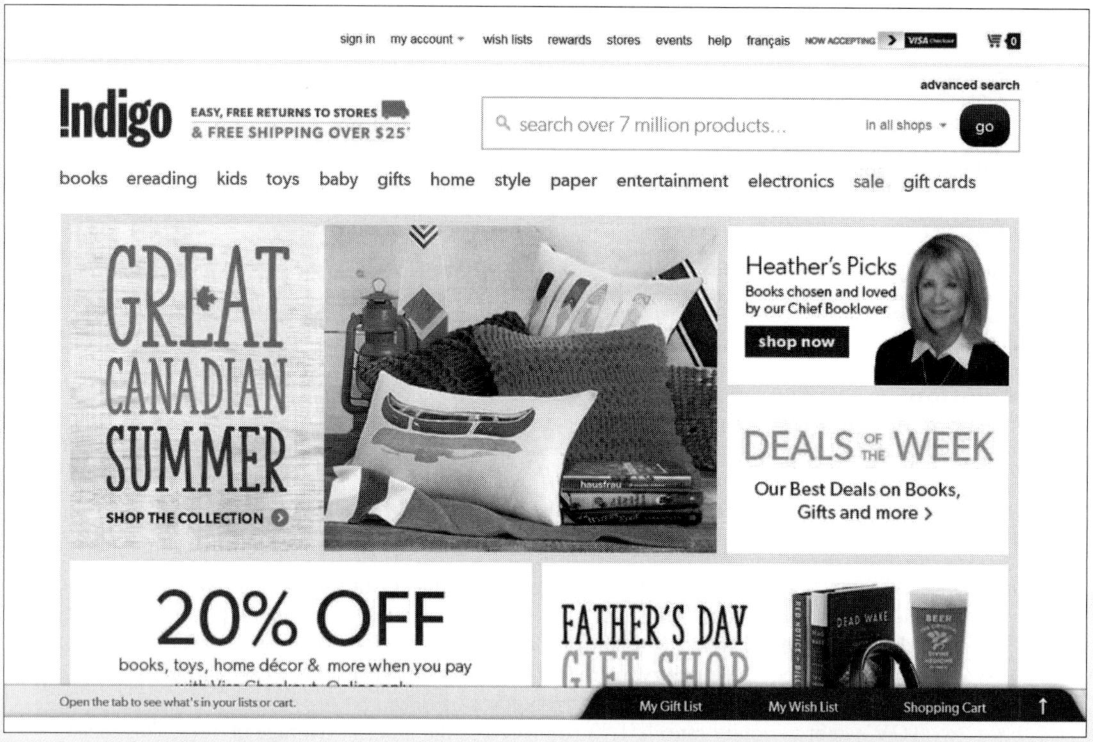

LEARNING OBJECTIVES

1. Describe and construct the balance sheet and understand how it can be used for analysis. (p. 40)
2. Use the financial statement effects template (FSET) to analyse transactions. (p. 45)
3. Describe and construct the income statement and discuss how it can be used to evaluate management performance. (p. 49)
4. Explain revenue recognition, accrual accounting, and their effects on retained earnings. (p. 50)
5. Illustrate equity transactions and the statement of changes in equity. (p. 56)
6. Use journal entries and T-accounts to analyse and record transactions. (p. 57)
7. Compute net working capital, the current ratio, and the quick ratio, and explain how they reflect liquidity. (p. 66)

CHAPTER

Constructing Financial Statements

2

Indigo is Canada's largest book, gift and toy retailer headquartered in Toronto. Heather Reisman (Chair and Chief Executive Officer) founded the company in 1996, and opened the first superstore under the banner "Indigo Books, Music & More" in September 1997. Indigo expanded quickly and became the second largest bookseller in Canada by 2000. In November 2000, Reisman launched a hostile takeover of the largest Canadian bookseller and within a few months successfully acquired a majority stake in Chapters Inc. In August 2001, Indigo merged with Chapters to create the largest bookseller in Canada. As of March 29, 2014, Indigo operated 95 superstores and 131 small-format stores, across all ten Canadian provinces and the Yukon Territory. Indigo also sells online through the www.chapters.indigo.ca website.

INDIGO
www.indigo.ca

Indigo positions itself in a niche segment of the bookselling and retailing industry. Its flagship stores are tastefully furnished and located in premium locations. Indigo emphasises lifestyle books, such as art, home improvement, gardening, travel, and fiction. It complements its books with gifts and home decor items. It also has in-store IndigoKids sections in most of its superstores, while the remaining superstores carry expanded offerings of children's books and specialty toys.

Despite its dominance in the Canadian bookselling market, Indigo faces a number of challenges. First, technological change and globalisation have given consumers access to cheaper alternatives. In particular, the Internet and e-readers have been challenging the business models of traditional booksellers. Second, Indigo has faced increasing competition from Amazon.ca since 2010, when the Department of Canadian Heritage allowed Amazon.ca to operate a book distributing business in Canada, taking away the protection Indigo once received. These factors have caused Indigo to report decreasing sales in the last few years and a loss of $1.21 per share in the most recent fiscal year. Reisman and her management team have been adjusting Indigo's strategy and business plan in light of the changing environment.

As we discovered in Chapter 1, companies like Indigo prepare financial statements annually. These financial statements allow investors and creditors to assess the impact of changing economic conditions on the company's financial health and performance.

This chapter will introduce and explain financial statements using Indigo as its prime example. The chapter also introduces some key accounting procedures such as transaction analysis, journal entries, and posting. The general ledger, key accounting assumptions, and basic accounting definitions are also introduced.

Sources: www.indigo.ca; Indigo 2014 Annual Report; Lorinc, John, February 2000, "The Indigo Way," *Quill & Quire*.

CHAPTER ORGANISATION

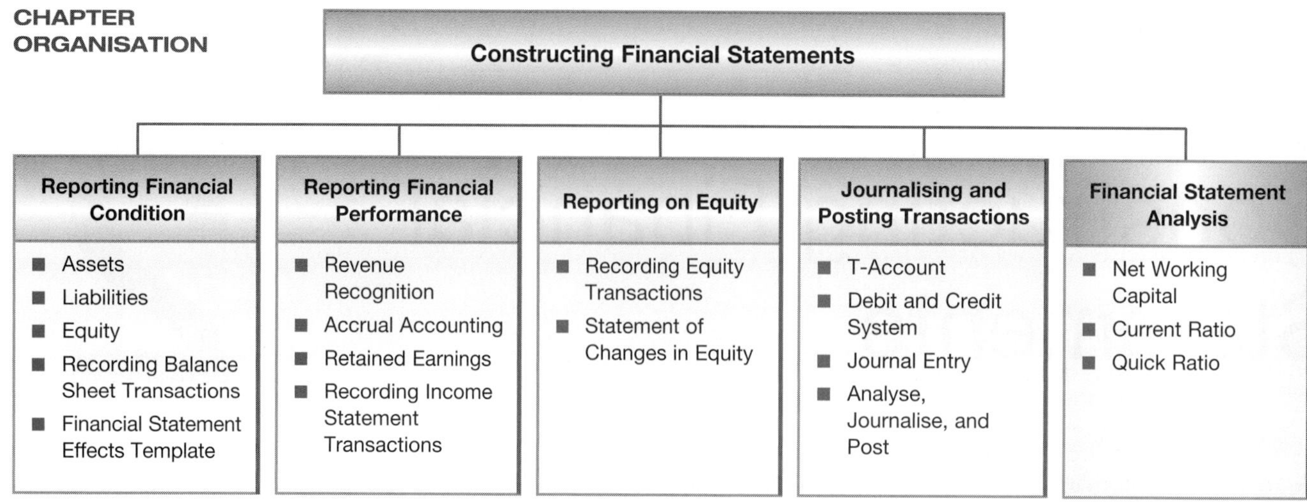

In Chapter 1, we introduced the four financial statements—the balance sheet, the income statement, the cash flow statement, and the statement of changes in equity. In this chapter and in Chapter 3, we turn our attention to how the balance sheet and income statement are prepared. The statement of cash flows is discussed in detail in Chapter 4, and the statement of changes in equity is discussed in detail in Chapter 11.

REPORTING FINANCIAL CONDITION

LO1 Describe and construct the balance sheet and understand how it can be used for analysis.

The statement of financial position (or balance sheet) reports on a company's financial condition and is divided into three components: assets, liabilities, and equity. It provides us with information about the resources available to management and the claims against those resources by creditors and shareholders. At the end of March 29, 2014, Indigo reports total assets of $512,588 thousand, total liabilities of $200,914 thousand, and equity of $311,674 thousand. Drawing on the **accounting equation**, Indigo's balance sheet is summarised as follows (in thousands of Canadian dollars).

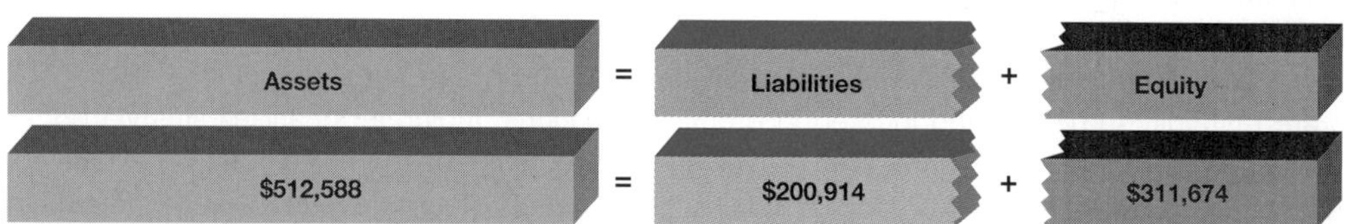

The balance sheet is prepared at a point in time. It is a snapshot of the financial condition of the company at that instant. For Indigo, the above balance sheet amounts were reported at the close of business on March 29, 2014. Balance sheet accounts carry over from one period to the next; that is, the ending balance from one period becomes the beginning balance for the next period.

Indigo's 2014 and 2013 balance sheets are shown in Exhibit 2.1. These balance sheets report the assets and the liabilities and shareholders' equity amounts as of the last Saturday of March, the company's fiscal year-end. Indigo had $569,140 thousand in assets at the end of March 30, 2013, with the same amount reported in liabilities and shareholders' equity. Companies report their audited financial results on a yearly basis.[1] Many companies use the calendar year as their fiscal year. Other companies prefer to prepare their yearly report at a time when business activity is at a low level. Indigo is an example of the latter reporting.

Assets

By definition, an **asset** is a resource controlled by a company as a result of past events and which is expected to provide the company with future economic benefits. The first requirement, that the company must control the asset as a result of past events, implies that the company has the right to

[1] Companies also report semi-annually or quarterly financial statements, and these are reviewed by the independent accountant, but not audited.

use the asset and presumes that the cost to acquire the asset has been incurred, either by paying cash, by trading other assets, or by assuming an obligation to make future payments. The second requirement indicates that the company expects to receive some future benefit from controlling the asset. Benefits can be the expected cash receipts from selling the asset or from selling products produced by the asset. Benefits can also refer to the receipt of other noncash assets, such as accounts receivable or the reduction of a liability (e.g., when assets are given up to settle debts). It should be noted that ownership is not necessary for control and, hence, leased equipment may be an asset.

Finally, an asset is reported on the balance sheet if it satisfies the following two recognition criteria:

1. It is probable that the future economic benefits will flow to the company.
2. It has a cost or value that can be measured reliably.

Companies acquire assets to yield a return for their shareholders. Assets are expected to produce revenues, either directly (e.g., inventory that is sold) or indirectly (e.g., a manufacturing plant that produces inventories for sale). To create shareholder value, assets must yield income that is in excess of the cost of the funds utilised to acquire the assets.

EXHIBIT 2.1 Indigo's Balance Sheets

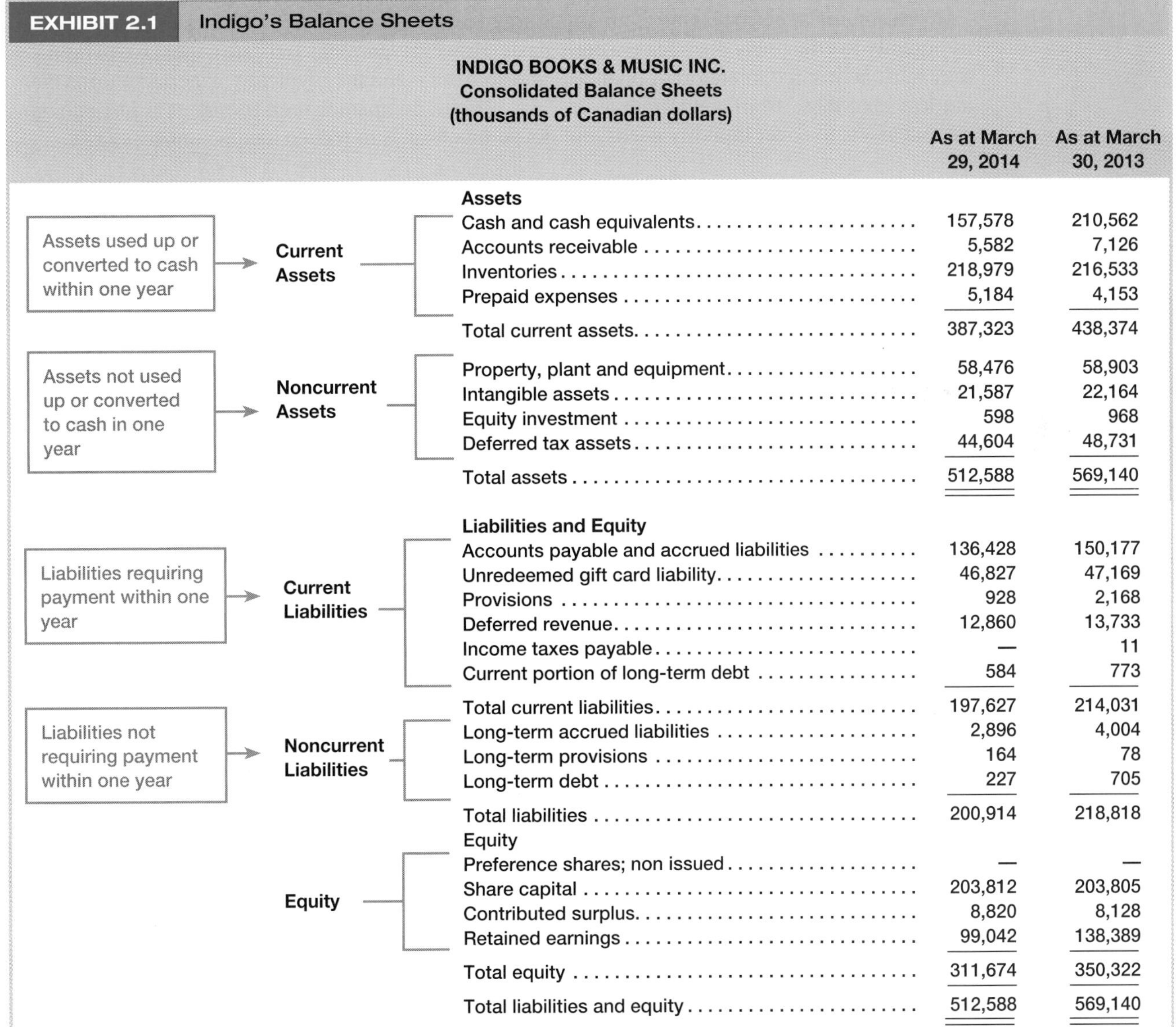

INDIGO BOOKS & MUSIC INC.
Consolidated Balance Sheets
(thousands of Canadian dollars)

			As at March 29, 2014	As at March 30, 2013
		Assets		
Assets used up or converted to cash within one year	Current Assets	Cash and cash equivalents	157,578	210,562
		Accounts receivable	5,582	7,126
		Inventories	218,979	216,533
		Prepaid expenses	5,184	4,153
		Total current assets	387,323	438,374
Assets not used up or converted to cash in one year	Noncurrent Assets	Property, plant and equipment	58,476	58,903
		Intangible assets	21,587	22,164
		Equity investment	598	968
		Deferred tax assets	44,604	48,731
		Total assets	512,588	569,140
		Liabilities and Equity		
Liabilities requiring payment within one year	Current Liabilities	Accounts payable and accrued liabilities	136,428	150,177
		Unredeemed gift card liability	46,827	47,169
		Provisions	928	2,168
		Deferred revenue	12,860	13,733
		Income taxes payable	—	11
		Current portion of long-term debt	584	773
		Total current liabilities	197,627	214,031
Liabilities not requiring payment within one year	Noncurrent Liabilities	Long-term accrued liabilities	2,896	4,004
		Long-term provisions	164	78
		Long-term debt	227	705
		Total liabilities	200,914	218,818
		Equity		
	Equity	Preference shares; non issued	—	—
		Share capital	203,812	203,805
		Contributed surplus	8,820	8,128
		Retained earnings	99,042	138,389
		Total equity	311,674	350,322
		Total liabilities and equity	512,588	569,140

IFRS does not specify the order in which assets are presented on a balance sheet and, hence, practices vary across countries and regions. In Australia, Canada, and the United States, the assets section is usually presented in descending order of **liquidity**, which refers to the ease of converting noncash assets into cash. However, companies in Asia and Europe tend to present the assets section in ascending order of liquidity. The most liquid assets are called **current assets** and the least liquid are called **noncurrent assets**.

Current Assets Current assets are assets expected to be converted into cash or used in operations within the next fiscal year, or within the next operating cycle, whichever is longer. Some typical examples of current assets include the following accounts, which are listed in order of their liquidity:

FYI Cash equivalents are short-term, highly liquid investments that mature in three months or less and can be easily converted to cash. ■

- **Cash**—currency, bank deposits, certificates of deposit, and other *cash equivalents;*
- **Marketable securities**—short-term investments that can be quickly sold to raise cash;
- **Accounts receivable**—amounts due to the company from customers arising from the sale of products or services on credit;
- **Inventory**—goods purchased or produced for sale to customers;
- **Prepaid expenses**—costs paid in advance for rent, insurance, or other services.

The amount of current assets is an important measure of liquidity. Companies require a degree of liquidity to effectively operate on a daily basis. However, current assets are expensive to hold—they must be insured, monitored, financed, and so forth—and they typically generate returns that are less than those from noncurrent assets. As a result, companies seek to maintain just enough current assets to cover liquidity needs, but not so much so as to reduce income unnecessarily.

Noncurrent Assets Noncurrent (long-term) assets are assets not expected to expire or be converted into cash within the next year, or within the next operating cycle. Some typical examples of noncurrent assets are:

- **Long-term financial investments**—investments in debt securities or shares of other firms that management does not intend to sell in the near future;
- **Property, plant, and equipment (PPE)**—includes land, factory buildings, warehouses, office buildings, machinery, office equipment, and other items used in the operations of the company;
- **Intangible and other assets**—includes patents, trademarks, franchise rights, goodwill, and other items that provide future benefits, but do not possess physical substance.

FYI Excluded assets often relate to self-developed, knowledge-based assets, like organisational effectiveness and technology. This is one reason that knowledge-based industries are so difficult to analyse. Yet, excluded assets are presumably reflected in company market values. This fact can explain why the firm's market capitalisation (its share price multiplied by the number of shares) is often greater than the book value shown on the balance sheet. ■

Measuring Assets Assets that are intended to be used, such as inventory and property, plant, and equipment, are reported on the balance sheet at their **historical cost** (with adjustments for depreciation in some cases). Historical cost refers to the original acquisition cost. The use of historical cost to report asset values has the advantage of **reliability**. Historical costs are reliable because the acquisition cost (the amount of cash paid to purchase the asset) can be objectively determined and accurately measured. The disadvantage of historical costs is that some assets can be significantly undervalued on the balance sheet. For example, the Louis Vuitton Building opened on the Champs-Élysées in 1913, was purchased for a mere fraction of its current market value.

Some assets, such as marketable securities, are reported at current market value or **fair value**. The market value of these assets can be easily obtained from online price quotes or from reliable sources such as The Financial Times. Reporting certain assets at fair value increases the **relevance** of the information presented in the balance sheet. Relevance refers to how useful the information is to those who use the financial statements for decision making. For example, marketable securities are intended to be sold for cash when cash is needed by the company to pay its obligations. Therefore, the most relevant value for marketable securities is the amount of cash that the company expects to receive when the securities are sold.

Only those asset values that can be accurately measured are reported on the balance sheet. For this reason, some of a company's most important assets are often not reflected among the reported assets of the company. For example, the well-recognised Indigo logo does not appear as an asset on the company's balance sheet. The image of Mickey Mouse is also absent from The Walt Disney

Company's balance sheet. Each of these items is referred to as an unrecognised intangible asset. These intangible assets and the Coke bottle silhouette, the BMW name, an excellent management team, or a well-designed supply chain, are measured and reported on the balance sheet only when they are purchased from a third party. As a result, *internally created* intangible assets, such as the Mickey Mouse image, are not reported on a balance sheet, even though many of these internally created intangible assets are of enormous value.

Liabilities and Equity

Liabilities and equity represent the sources of capital to the company that are used to finance the acquisition of assets. **Liabilities** represent the firm's obligations for borrowed funds from lenders or bond investors, as well as obligations to pay suppliers, employees, tax authorities, and other parties. These obligations can be interest-bearing or non-interest-bearing. **Equity** represents capital that has been invested by the shareholders, either directly via the purchase of shares, or indirectly in the form of earnings that are reinvested in the business and not paid out as dividends (retained earnings). We discuss liabilities and equity in this section.

The liabilities and equity sections of Indigo's balance sheets for 2014 and 2013 are reproduced in the lower section of Exhibit 2.1. Indigo reports $200,914 thousand of total liabilities and $311,674 thousand of equity as of its 2014 fiscal year-end. The total of liabilities and equity equals $512,588—the same as the total assets—because the shareholders have the residual claim on the company.

By definition, a liability is a present obligation arising from past events. The settlement of the obligation is expected to result in future economic sacrifice. The economic sacrifice can be a future cash payment to a creditor, or it can be an obligation to deliver goods or services to a customer at a future date. A liability must be reported on the balance sheet when the following two recognition criteria are met:

1. The future economic sacrifice is probable.
2. The amount of the obligation can be measured reliably.

When both criteria are satisfied, but the transaction that caused the obligation has not occurred, the obligation is called an **executory contract** and no liability is reported. An example of such an obligation is a purchase order. When a company signs an agreement to purchase materials from a supplier, it commits to making a future cash payment of a known amount. However, the obligation to pay for the materials is not considered a liability until the materials are delivered. Therefore, even though the company is contractually obligated to make the cash payment to the supplier, a liability is not recorded on the balance sheet. However, information about purchase commitments and other executory contracts is useful to investors and creditors, and the obligations, if material, should be disclosed in the notes to the financial statements.

Current Liabilities Liabilities on the balance sheet are listed according to maturity. They are usually presented in ascending order of maturity in Australia, Canada, and the United States, and in descending order of maturity in Asia and Europe. Obligations that are due within one year or within one operating cycle, whichever is longer, are called **current liabilities**. Some examples of common current liabilities include:

- **Accounts payable**—amounts owed to suppliers for goods and services purchased on credit.
- **Accrued liabilities**—obligations for expenses that have been recorded but not yet paid. Examples include accrued compensation payable (wages earned by employees but not yet paid), accrued interest payable (interest on debt that has not been paid), and accrued taxes (taxes due).
- **Short-term borrowings**—short-term debt payable to banks or other creditors.
- **Deferred (unearned) revenues**—an obligation created when the company accepts payment in advance for goods or services it will deliver in the future. Sometimes also called advances from customers or customer deposits.
- **Current maturities of long-term debt**—the current portion of long-term debt that is due to be paid within one year.

Noncurrent Liabilities **Noncurrent liabilities** are obligations to be paid after one year. Examples of noncurrent liabilities include:

FYI Borrowings are often titled **Notes Payable.** When a company borrows money it normally signs a promissory note agreeing to pay the money back—hence, the title notes payable.

- **Long-term debt**—amounts borrowed from creditors that are scheduled to be repaid more than one year in the future. Any portion of long-term debt that is due within one year is reclassified as a current liability called *current maturities of long-term debt.*
- **Other long-term liabilities**—various obligations, such as warranty and deferred compensation liabilities and long-term tax liabilities, that will be satisfied at least a year in the future. These items are discussed in later chapters.

Detailed information about a company's noncurrent liabilities, such as payment schedules, interest rates, and restrictive covenants, are provided in the notes to the financial statements.

BUSINESS INSIGHT

How Much Debt Is Reasonable? In March 2014, **Indigo** reports total assets of $512,588 thousand, liabilities of $200,914 ($197,627 current + $3,287 noncurrent) thousand, and equity of $311,674 thousand. This means that Indigo finances 39% of its assets with borrowed funds and 61% with shareholder investment. Liabilities represent claims for fixed amounts, while shareholders' equity represents a flexible claim (because shareholders have a residual claim). Companies must monitor their financing sources and amounts because borrowing too much increases risk, and investors must recognise that companies may have substantial obligations (like operating lease obligations to be discussed in Chapter 10) that do not appear on the balance sheet.

Equity Equity reflects capital provided by the owners of the company. It is often referred to as a *residual interest*. That is, shareholders have a claim on any assets that are not needed to meet the company's obligations to creditors. The following are examples of items that are typically included in equity:

Contributed Capital

- **Share capital** or **Capital stock**—the capital received from the primary owners of the company. Total share capital is divided into shares. One ordinary share (or common share or common stock) represents the smallest fractional unit of ownership of a company.[2]
- **Contributed surplus** or **Share premium**—amounts received from the primary owners in addition to the par value of the ordinary share.
- **Treasury shares**—the amount paid for its own ordinary shares that the company has reacquired, which reduces contributed capital.

Earned Capital

- **Retained earnings**—the accumulated earnings that have not been distributed to shareholders as dividends.
- **Accumulated other comprehensive income or loss**—accumulated changes in equity that are not reported in the income statement; discussed in Chapters 11 and 12.

The equity section of a balance sheet consists of two basic components: contributed capital and earned capital. **Contributed capital** is the net funding that a company has received from issuing and reacquiring its equity shares. That is, the funds received from issuing shares less any funds paid to repurchase such shares. In 2014, Indigo's equity section reports $311,674 thousand in equity. Its contributed capital is $212,632 thousand ($203,812 in share capital plus $8,820 in contributed surplus and minus $0 in treasury shares). Indigo's shares have no par value. The balance in contributed surplus is attributed to Indigo's granting of deferred shares to its directors. Share-based compensation, including deferred shares and stock options, is discussed in Chapter 11.

Earned capital is the cumulative net income (and losses) retained by the company (not paid out to shareholders as dividends). Earned capital typically includes retained earnings and

[2] Many companies' ordinary shares have a par value, but that value has little economic significance. In most cases, the sum of share capital (at par) and contributed surplus (discussed below) represents the value of shareholders' contributions to the business in exchange for shares. Indigo's shares have no par value.

accumulated other comprehensive income or loss. Indigo's earned capital is $99,042 thousand ($99,042 in retained earnings plus $0 in accumulated other comprehensive income). Other comprehensive income is discussed in Chapters 11 and 12.

RETAINED EARNINGS There is an important relation for retained earnings that reconciles its beginning and ending balances as follows:

	Beginning retained earnings
+	Net income (or − Net loss)
−	Dividends
=	Ending retained earnings

This relation is useful to remember, even though there are other items that sometimes impact retained earnings. We revisit this relation after our discussion of the income statement and show how it links the balance sheet and income statement.

FYI Equity is a term used to describe owners' claims on the company. For corporations, the terms shareholders' equity and stockholders' equity are also used to describe owners' claims. We use all three terms interchangeably. ■

MID-CHAPTER REVIEW 1

Assume Schaefer's Pharmacy, Inc. has the following detailed accounts as part of its accounting system. Enter the letter of the balance sheet category A through E in the space next to the balance sheet items numbered 1 through 20. Enter an **X** in the space if the item is not reported on the balance sheet.

A. Current assets
B. Long-term assets
C. Current liabilities
D. Long-term liabilities
E. Equity

_____ 1. Accounts receivable
_____ 2. Short-term notes payable
_____ 3. Land
_____ 4. Retained earnings
_____ 5. Intangible assets
_____ 6. Share capital
_____ 7. Repairs expense
_____ 8. Equipment
_____ 9. Treasury shares
_____ 10. Investments (noncurrent)
_____ 11. Rent expense
_____ 12. Cash
_____ 13. Buildings
_____ 14. Accounts payable
_____ 15. Prepaid rent
_____ 16. Borrowings (due in 25 years)
_____ 17. Marketable securities
_____ 18. Inventories
_____ 19. Contributed surplus
_____ 20. Unearned revenue

The solution to this review problem can be found on page 88.

Analysing and Recording Transactions for the Balance Sheet

LO2 Use the financial statement effects template (FSET) to analyse transactions.

The balance sheet is the foundation of the accounting system. Every event, or transaction, that is recorded in the accounting system must be recorded so that the following accounting equation is maintained:

Assets = Liabilities + Equity

We use this fundamental relation throughout the book to help us assess the financial impact of transactions. This is our "step 1" when we encounter a transaction. Our "steps 2 and 3" are to journalise those financial impacts and then post them to individual accounts to emphasise the linkage from entries to accounts (steps 2 and 3 are explained later in this chapter).

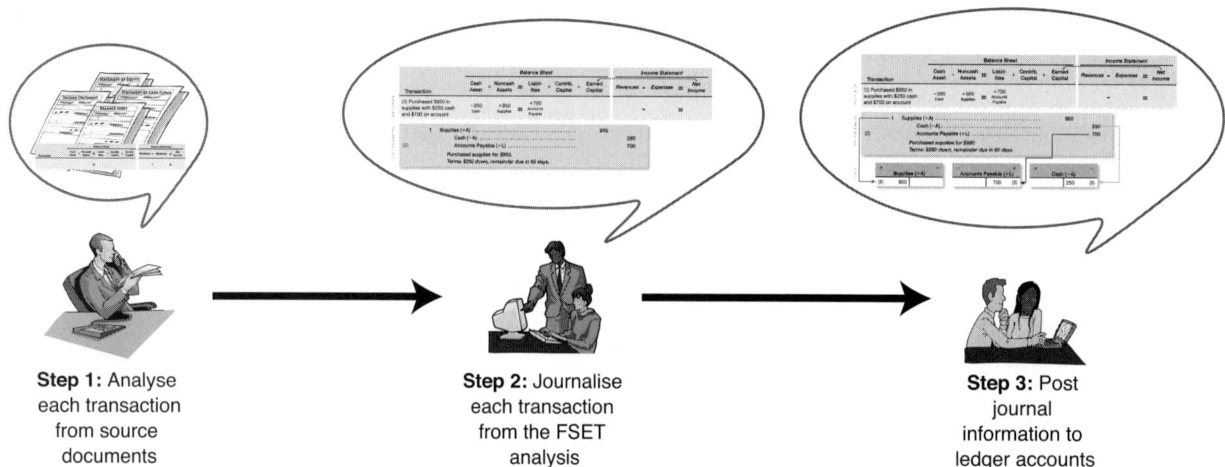
Step 1: Analyse each transaction from source documents
Step 2: Journalise each transaction from the FSET analysis
Step 3: Post journal information to ledger accounts

Financial Statement Effects Template To analyse the financial impacts of transactions, we employ the following **financial statement effects template (FSET)**.

Transaction	Balance Sheet									Income Statement				
	Cash Asset	+	Noncash Assets	=	Liabil-ities	+	Contrib. Capital	+	Earned Capital	Revenues	-	Expenses	=	Net Income
				=							-		=	

The template accomplishes several things. First and foremost, it captures the transaction that must be recorded in the accounting system. That "recording" function is our focus for the next several pages. But accounting is not just recording financial data; it is also the reporting of information that is useful to financial statement readers. So, the template also depicts the effects of the transaction on the four financial statements: balance sheet, income statement, statement of changes in equity, and statement of cash flows. For the balance sheet, we differentiate between cash and noncash assets so as to identify the cash effects of transactions. Likewise, equity is separated into the contributed and earned capital components (the latter includes retained earnings as its major element). Finally, income statement effects are separated into revenues, expenses, and net income (the updating of retained earnings is denoted with an arrow line running from net income to earned capital). This template provides a convenient means to represent financial accounting transactions and events in a simple, concise manner for analysing, journalising, and posting.

The Account An **account** is a mechanism for accumulating the effects of an organisation's transactions and events. For instance, an account labelled "Merchandise Inventory" allows a retailer's accounting system to accumulate information about the receipts of inventory from suppliers and the delivery of inventory to customers.

Before a transaction is recorded, we first analyse the effect of the transaction on the accounting equation by asking the following questions:

- What accounts are affected by the transaction?
- What is the direction and magnitude of each effect?

To maintain the equality of the accounting equation, each transaction must affect (at least) two accounts. For example, a transaction might increase assets and increase equity by equal amounts. Another transaction might increase one asset and decrease another asset, while yet another might decrease an asset and decrease a liability. These *dual effects* are what constitute the **double-entry accounting system**.

The account is a record of increases and decreases for each important asset, liability, equity, revenue, or expense item. The **chart of accounts** is a listing of the titles (and identification codes) of all accounts for a company.[3] Account titles are commonly grouped into five categories: assets, liabilities, equity, revenues, and expenses. The accounts for Natural Beauty Supply, Inc. (introduced below), follow:[4]

Assets	Equity
110 Cash	310 Share Capital
120 Accounts Receivable	320 Retained Earnings
130 Other Receivables	**Revenues and Income**
140 Inventory	410 Sales Revenue
150 Prepaid Insurance	420 Interest Revenue
160 Security Deposit	**Expenses**
170 Fixtures and Equipment	510 Cost of Goods Sold
175 Accumulated Depreciation—Fixtures and Equipment	520 Wages Expense
Liabilities	530 Rent Expense
210 Accounts Payable	540 Advertising Expense
220 Interest Payable	550 Depreciation Expense—Fixtures and Equipment
230 Wages Payable	560 Insurance Expense
240 Taxes Payable	570 Interest Expense
250 Unearned Revenue	580 Tax Expense
260 Notes Payable	

Each transaction entered in the template must maintain the equality of the accounting equation, and the accounts cited must correspond to those in its chart of accounts.

Transaction Analysis Using FSET To illustrate the effect of transactions on the accounting equation and, correspondingly, the financial statements, we consider the business activities of Natural Beauty Supply, Inc. Natural Beauty Supply was established to operate as a retailer of organic beauty and health care products, though the owners hoped that they also would become a wholesale provider of such products to local salons. The company began business on November 1, 2013. The following transactions occurred on the first day of business:

(1) Nov. 1 Investors contributed $20,000 cash to launch Natural Beauty Supply, Inc. (NBS), in exchange for 10,000 shares of NBS.

(2) Nov. 1 NBS borrowed $5,000 cash from a family member of the company's founders by signing a note. The $5,000 must be paid back on November 30 with interest of $50.

(3) Nov. 1 NBS arranged to rent a storefront location and began to use the property. The landlord requires payment of $1,500 at the end of each month. NBS paid a $2,000 security deposit that will be returned at the end of the lease.

(4) Nov. 1 NBS purchased, on account (i.e., to be paid later), and received $17,000 of inventory consisting of natural soaps and beauty products.

Let's begin by analysing the financial statement effects of the first transaction. At the beginning of its life, Natural Beauty Supply has accounts that show no balances, so the financial statements would be filled with zeroes. In the company's very first transaction, shareholders invested $20,000 cash in Natural Beauty Supply, and the company issued 10,000 ordinary shares, which increased equity (contributed capital). This transaction is reflected in the following financial statements effects template.

---

[3] A few countries require their companies to use a national chart of accounts (e.g., Portugal), while some countries provide non-binding guidelines (e.g., France and Sweden). However, most countries allow their companies to choose their own charts of accounts.

[4] Accounting systems at large organisations have much more detail in their account structures than we use here. The account structure's detail allows management to accumulate information by responsibility centre or by product line or by customer.

Transaction	Cash Asset	+	Noncash Assets	=	Liabil-ities	+	Contrib. Capital	+	Earned Capital	Revenues	-	Expenses	=	Net Income
(1) Issue shares for $20,000 cash.	+20,000 Cash			=			+20,000 Share Capital				-		=	

Assets (cash) and equity (share capital) increased by the same amount, and the accounting equation remains in balance (as it always must).

In the second transaction, Natural Beauty Supply borrowed cash by signing a note (loan agreement) with a family member. This transaction increased cash (an asset) and increased notes payable (a liability) by the same amount. The notes payable liability recognises the obligation to repay the family member.

Transaction	Cash Asset	+	Noncash Assets	=	Liabil-ities	+	Contrib. Capital	+	Earned Capital	Revenues	-	Expenses	=	Net Income
(2) Sign a note and receive $5,000 cash.	+5,000 Cash			=	+5,000 Notes Payable						-		=	

At this point, Natural Beauty Supply would not record anything for the interest that will eventually be paid. Interest expense occurs with the passage of time, and at the moment of borrowing on November 1, there is no interest obligation to be recognised.

Also on November 1, 2013, Natural Beauty Supply arranged for rental of a location and paid a security deposit which it expects to be returned at a future date. This transaction decreased cash (an asset) and increased security deposits (another asset). We'll assume that Natural Beauty Supply hopes to move to a more upscale location within a year, so the security deposit is considered a current asset.

Transaction	Cash Asset	+	Noncash Assets	=	Liabil-ities	+	Contrib. Capital	+	Earned Capital	Revenues	-	Expenses	=	Net Income
(3) Sign rental agreement and pay $2,000 security deposit.	−2,000 Cash		+2,000 Security Deposit	=							-		=	

Like the case of interest expense, Natural Beauty Supply would make no entry for rent expense on November 1, because the obligation to pay for the use of the location occurs with the passage of time.

Finally, Natural Beauty Supply purchased and received $17,000 of inventory on credit. This transaction increased inventory (an asset) by $17,000 and increased accounts payable (a liability) by $17,000, recognising the obligation to the supplier. This transaction is recorded as follows:

Transaction	Cash Asset	+	Noncash Assets	=	Liabil-ities	+	Contrib. Capital	+	Earned Capital	Revenues	-	Expenses	=	Net Income
(4) Purchase $17,000 inventory on account.			+17,000 Inventory	=	+17,000 Accounts Payable						-		=	

To summarise, the description of each transaction appears in the first column of the template. Then the financial statement effects of that transaction are recorded with a + or a – in the appropriate columns of the template. Under each number, the account title within that column of the balance sheet or income statement is entered. So far, Natural Beauty Supply's activities have not affected the revenue or expense accounts of the income statement.

After each transaction, the equality of the accounting equation is maintained. If we so choose, we can prepare a balance sheet at any time, reflecting the transactions up to that point in time. At the end of the day on November 1, 2013, Natural Beauty Supply's balance sheet appears as follows:

NATURAL BEAUTY SUPPLY, INC. Balance Sheet November 1, 2013			
Assets		**Liabilities and Equity**	
Cash	$23,000	Notes payable	$ 5,000
Inventory	17,000	Accounts payable	17,000
Security deposit	2,000	Total current liabilities	22,000
Total current assets	42,000	**Equity**	
		Share capital	20,000
Total assets	$42,000	Total liabilities and equity	$42,000

MID-CHAPTER REVIEW 2

Assume that Schaefer's Pharmacy, Inc. enters into the following transactions. Record each of the following transactions in the financial statement effects template.

a. Issued ordinary shares for $20,000 cash.
b. Purchased inventory costing $8,000 on credit.
c. Purchased equipment costing $10,000 for cash.
d. Paid suppliers $3,000 cash for part of the inventory purchased in *b*.

The solution to this review problem can be found on page 88.

REPORTING FINANCIAL PERFORMANCE

LO3 Describe and construct the income statement and discuss how it can be used to evaluate management performance.

While balance sheets provide useful information about the structure of a company's resources and the claims on those resources at a point in time, they provide little sense of recent movement or trajectory. The retained earnings balance represents the amount earned (but not paid out in dividends) over the entire life of the company. Looking at the difference between points in time does not give a clear picture about what happened between those points in time. For that perspective, we need the income statement to see whether our business activities generated more resources than they used. For instance, Indigo's retained earnings decreased by $39,347 thousand over fiscal year 2014, but that amount does not convey the volume of activity that occurred to accomplish it.

Indigo's fiscal years 2014 and 2013 Statements of Earnings (Loss) and Comprehensive Earnings (Loss) are shown in Exhibit 2.2. Indigo reported net loss of $30,999 thousand on revenues of $867,668 thousand, or about $0.045 of each revenue dollar ($30,999/$867,668). Interpretation of this $0.045 loss amount requires further analysis, as shown in Chapter 5, but we can compare it to the previous amount of $0.005 profit in fiscal year 2013.

FYI The income statement is also called the statement of earnings or the statement of operations or the profit and loss statement. Indigo uses all three terms (profit, income and earnings) in Exhibit 2.2. ■

To analyse an income statement, we need to understand some terminology. **Revenues** result from increases in **net assets** (assets minus liabilities) that are caused by the company's operating activities. **Expenses** result from decreases in net assets (assets minus liabilities) that are caused by the company's revenue-generating activities, including costs of products and services sold, operating costs like depreciation, wages and advertising, nonoperating costs like interest on debt and, finally, taxes on income. The difference between revenues and expenses is **net income** when revenues exceed expenses, or **net loss** when expenses exceed revenues. The connection to the balance sheet can be seen in that reporting net income means that revenues exceeded expenses, which in turn means that the company's business activities increased its net assets.

Operating expenses are the usual and customary costs that a company incurs to support its main business activities. These include cost of goods sold, selling expenses, depreciation expense, amortisation expense, and research and development expense. Not all of these expenses are recognised in the period in which cash is disbursed. For example, depreciation expense is recognised in the time period during which the asset is used, not in the period when it was first acquired in exchange for cash. In contrast, other expenses, such as compensation expense, are recognised in the period when the services are performed, which is often before cash is actually paid to employees. Indigo's operating expenses in 2014 were $897,648 thousand ($493,955 thousand + $403,693 thousand).

FYI The terms revenues, sales and turnover are often used interchangeably. ■

EXHIBIT 2.2 Indigo's Statement of Earnings

INDIGO BOOKS & MUSIC INC.
Consolidated Statements of Earnings (Loss)
and Comprehensive Earnings (Loss)

(thousands of Canadian dollars, except per share data)	52-week period ended March 29, 2014	52-week period ended March 30, 2013
Revenues	867,668	878,785
Cost of sales	(493,955)	(495,099)
Gross profit	373,713	383,686
Operating, selling and administrative expenses	(403,693)	(383,319)
Operating profit (loss)	(29,980)	367
Interest on long-term debt and financing charges	(95)	(101)
Interest income on cash and cash equivalents	2,377	2,609
Share of earnings from equity investment	789	1,315
Earnings (loss) before income taxes	(26,909)	4,190
Income tax recovery (expense)		
Current	37	–
Deferred	(4,127)	98
Net earnings (loss) and comprehensive earnings (loss)	(30,999)	4,288
Net earnings (loss) per common share		
Basic	$(1.21)	$0.17
Diluted	$(1.21)	$0.17

Nonoperating revenues and expenses relate to the company's financing and investing activities, and include interest revenue and interest expense. Business decision makers and analysts usually segregate operating and nonoperating activities as they offer different insights into company performance and condition. Indigo's income statement reports net nonoperating income in 2014 of $2,282 thousand ($2,377 thousand − $95 thousand), followed by tax expense of $4,090 thousand ($4,127 thousand − $37 thousand).

It is helpful to distinguish income from continuing operations from nonrecurring items. Many readers of financial statements are interested in forecasting future company performance and focus their analysis on sources of operating income that are expected to *persist* into the future. Nonrecurring revenues and expenses are unlikely to arise in the future and are largely irrelevant to predictions of future performance. Consequently, many decision makers identify transactions and events that are unlikely to recur and separate them from operating income in the income statement. These nonrecurring items are described in greater detail in Chapter 6.

Accrual Accounting for Revenues and Expenses

LO4 Explain revenue recognition, accrual accounting, and their effects on retained earnings.

The income statement's ability to measure a company's periodic performance depends on the proper timing of revenues and expenses. Revenue should be recorded when it is earned, in an amount that reflects how much the company expects to be entitled from the transaction—even if not yet received in cash. Specifically, revenue is earned when the company has transferred goods or services to customers. This is called **revenue recognition**, a topic that receives more attention in Chapter 6. On the other hand, expenses are recorded by matching them with revenues or when incurred in supporting the company's operations—even if not yet paid in cash—as assets are used or liabilities increased. This is called **expense recognition**, a topic to be discussed in Chapter 7. **Accrual accounting** refers to this practice of recognising revenues when earned through the company's operations and recognising expenses as the assets used and obligations incurred in carrying out those operations.

An important consequence of accrual accounting for revenues and expenses is that the balance sheet depicts the resources of the company (besides cash) and the obligations which the company must fulfil in the future. Accrual accounting is required under IFRS because it is considered to be the most useful information for making business decisions and evaluating business performance. (That is not to say that information on cash flows is not important—but it is conveyed by the statement of cash flows discussed in Chapter 4.)

Cost of goods sold (cost of sales) is an expense item in the income statements of manufacturing and merchandising companies. It represents the cost of products that are delivered to customers during the period. The difference between revenues (at selling prices) and cost of goods sold (at purchase price or manufacturing cost) is called **gross profit**. Gross profit for merchandisers and manufacturers is an important number as it represents the remaining income available to cover all of the company's overhead and other expenses (selling, general and administrative expenses, interest, and so on). Indigo's gross profit in 2014 is calculated as total net revenues less cost of sales, which equals $373,713 thousand ($867,668 thousand − $493,955 thousand).

The principles of revenue and expense recognition are crucial to income statement reporting. To illustrate, assume a company purchases inventories for $100,000 cash, which it sells later in that same period for $150,000 cash. The company would record $150,000 in revenue when the inventory is delivered to the customer, because at that point, the company has fulfilled its responsibilities in the exchange with the customer. Also assume that the company pays $20,000 cash for sales employee wages during the period. The income statement is designed to tell how effective the company was at generating more resources than it used, and it would appear as follows (ignoring income taxes for the moment):

Revenues	$150,000
Cost of goods sold	100,000
Gross profit	50,000
Wages expense	20,000
Net income (earnings)	$ 30,000

FYI Purchase of inventories on credit or on account means that the buyer does not pay the seller at the time of purchase. The buyer reports a liability (accounts payable) on its balance sheet that is later removed when payment is made. The seller reports an asset (accounts receivable) on its balance sheet until it is removed when the buyer pays. ■

In this illustration, there is a correspondence between each of the revenues/expenses and a cash inflow/outflow. Net income was $30,000 and the increase in cash was $30,000.

However, that need not be the case under accrual accounting. Suppose that the company sells its product on **credit** (also denoted as *on account*) rather than for cash. Does the seller still report sales revenue? The answer is yes. Under accrual accounting, revenues are reported when a company has earned those sales at delivery. Earned means that the company has done everything required under the sales agreement—no major contingencies remain. The seller reports an accounts receivable asset on its balance sheet, and revenue can be recognised before cash collection.

Credit sales mean that companies can report substantial sales revenue and assets without receiving cash. When such receivables are ultimately collected, no further revenue is recorded because it was recorded earlier when the revenue recognition criteria were met. The collection of a receivable involves the decrease of one asset (accounts receivable) and the increase of another asset (cash), with no resulting increase in net assets.

Next consider a different situation. Assume that the company sells gift cards to customers for $9,500. Should the $9,500 received in cash be recognised as revenue? No. Even though the gift cards were sold and cash was collected, there has been no transfer of goods or services to the customer. The revenue from gift cards is recognised when the product or service is provided. For example, revenue can be recognised when a customer purchases an item of merchandise using the gift card for payment. Hence, the $9,500 is then recorded as an increase in cash and an increase in *unearned revenue*, a liability, with no resulting increase in net assets.

FYI Sales on credit will not always be collected. The potential for uncollectable accounts introduces additional risk to the firm. ■

The proper timing of revenue recognition suggests that the expenses incurred in earning that revenue be recognised in the same fiscal period. Thus, if merchandise inventory is purchased in one period and sold in another, the cost of the merchandise should be retained as an asset until the items are sold. It would not be proper to recognise expense when the inventory was purchased or the cash was paid. Accurate income determination requires the proper timing of revenue and expense recognition, and the exchange of cash is *not* the essential ingredient.

FYI Cash accounting recognises revenues only when received in cash and expenses only when paid in cash. This approach is not acceptable under accrual accounting. ■

We have already seen that when a company incurs a cost to acquire a resource that produces benefits in the future (for example, merchandise inventory for future sale), it recognises an asset. That asset represents costs that are waiting to be recognised as expenses in the future, when these assets are used to produce revenue or to support operations. When inventory is delivered to a customer, we recognise that the asset no longer belongs to the selling company. The inventory asset is decreased, and cost of goods sold is recognised as an expense.

The same principle applies when employees earn wages for work in one period, but are paid in the next period. Wages expense must be recognised when the liability (obligation) is *incurred*, regardless of when they are paid. If the company in the illustration does not pay its employees until the following reporting period, it recognises a wages payable liability of $20,000 and, because this decreases net assets, it would recognise a wage expense of the same amount.

When wages are paid in the next reporting period, both cash and the wages payable liability are decreased. No expense is reported when the wages are paid, because the expense is recognised when the employees worked to generate sales in the prior period.

Accrual accounting principles are crucial for reporting the income statement revenues and expenses in the proper period, and these revenues and expenses provide a more complete view of the inflows and outflows of resources (including cash) for the firm. Was an outflow of cash supposed to produce benefits in the current period or in a future period? Was an inflow of cash the result of past operations or current operations? The accrual accounting model uses the balance sheet and income statement to answer such questions and to enable users of financial statements to make more timely assessments of the firm's economic performance.

However, accrual accounting's timeliness requires management to estimate future events in determining the amount of expenses incurred and revenue earned. The precise amount of cash to be received or disbursed cannot be known until a later date. In the case of wages, the amount of the accrual is known with certainty. In other cases (e.g., incentive bonuses), it may not and thus requires an estimate.

Retained Earnings

Net income for the period is added to the company's retained earnings, which, in turn, is part of equity. The linkage between the income statement and the beginning- and end-of-period balance sheets, which we called articulation in Chapter 1, is achieved by tying net income to retained earnings because net income is, by definition, the *change* in retained earnings resulting from business activities during an accounting period. This link is highlighted by an arrow line running from net income to earned capital at the top of the financial statement effects template (FSET).[5] There are typically other adjustments to retained earnings. The most common adjustment is for dividend payments to shareholders. Exhibit 2.3 provides the annual adjustments to retained earnings for Indigo.

EXHIBIT 2.3 Indigo's Retained Earnings Reconciliation

INDIGO BOOKS & MUSIC INC.
Year Ended March 29, 2014
(thousands of Canadian dollars)

Retained earnings, March 30, 2013	$138,389
Add: Net earnings	(30,999)
Less: Cash dividends declared	(8,348)
Retained earnings, March 29, 2014	$ 99,042

Analysing and Recording Transactions for the Income Statement

Earlier, we introduced the financial statement effects template as a tool to illustrate the effects of transactions on the balance sheet. In this section, we show how this template is used to analyse transactions that may affect the current period's income statement. To do so, we extend our illustration of Natural Beauty Supply (NBS) to reflect the following events in 2013:

(5) Nov. 2 — NBS paid $670 to advertise in the local newspaper for November.

(6) Nov. 18 — NBS paid $13,300 cash to its suppliers in partial payment for the earlier delivery of inventory.

(7) Nov. — — During the month of November, NBS sold products to retail customers. The customers paid $7,000 cash for products that had cost NBS $4,000.

[5] In the FSET, we show that each transaction that affects the income statement also impacts retained earnings. This approach is useful for *analysing* the effect of the transaction on both the income statement and balance sheet. However, the impact of net income on retained earnings is *recorded* only once each accounting period, after all of the revenues and expenses have been recorded. This recording procedure is explained later in this chapter and in Chapter 3.

(8) Nov. — During the month of November, sales to wholesale customers totaled $2,400 for merchandise that had cost $1,700. Instead of paying cash, wholesale customers are required to pay for the merchandise within ten working days.

(9) Nov. — NBS employed a salesperson who earned $1,400 for the month of November and was paid that amount in cash.

(10) Nov. 24 NBS received an order from a wholesale customer to deliver products in December. The agreed price of the products to be delivered is $700 and the cost is $450.

(11) Nov. 25 NBS introduced holiday gift certificates, which entitle the recipient to a one-hour consultation on the use of NBS's products. $300 of gift certificates were sold for cash, but none were redeemed before the end of November.

(12) Nov. 30 NBS received $1,450 in partial payment from customers billed in (8).

(13) Nov. 30 NBS repaid the loan and interest in (2).

(14) Nov. 30 NBS paid $1,680 for a twelve-month fire insurance policy. Coverage begins on December 1.

(15) Nov. 30 NBS paid $1,500 to the landlord for November rent.

In transaction (5), Natural Beauty Supply gave cash in return for advertising for the month of November. This payment does not create a benefit for future periods, so it does not create an asset. Nor does the payment discharge an existing obligation. Therefore, it decreases NBS's net assets (assets minus liabilities). The purpose of this decrease in net assets is to generate revenues for the company, so it is matched by an expense in the income statement.

We begin by entering the decrease in cash and an increase in expenses. (The minus sign in front of expenses insures that the accounting equation still holds.) Recording the expense allows the income statement to keep track of the flows of assets and liabilities that result from the company's operations.

	Balance Sheet										Income Statement				
Transaction	Cash Asset	+	Noncash Assets	=	Liabil-ities	+	Contrib. Capital	+	Earned Capital		Revenues	−	Expenses	=	Net Income
(5) Pay $670 cash for November advertising.	−670 Cash			=								−	+670 Advertising Expense	=	

However, the FSET goes further than recording the accounting entry. It also depicts the effects of the expense on net income and of net income on retained earnings. So, the complete FSET description of transaction (5) is as follows. The FSET uses colour to differentiate between the accounting entry (in blue) and the resulting effect on income and retained earnings (in black).

Transaction	Cash Asset	+	Noncash Assets	=	Liabil-ities	+	Contrib. Capital	+	Earned Capital	Revenues	−	Expenses	=	Net Income
(5) Pay $670 cash for November advertising.	−670 Cash			=					−670 Retained Earnings		−	+670 Advertising Expense	=	−670

In the sixth transaction, Natural Beauty Supply made a partial payment of $13,300 in cash to the suppliers who delivered inventory on November 1. This transaction decreases cash by $13,300 and decreases the accounts payable liability by $13,300. The income statement is not affected by this payment. The cost of merchandise is reflected in the income statement when the merchandise is sold, not when it is paid for (as we will see shortly).

Transaction	Cash Asset	+	Noncash Assets	=	Liabil-ities	+	Contrib. Capital	+	Earned Capital	Revenues	−	Expenses	=	Net Income
(6) Pay $13,300 cash in partial payment to suppliers from transaction (4).	−13,300 Cash			=	−13,300 Accounts Payable						−		=	

In transaction (7), Natural Beauty Supply sold products to customers who paid $7,000 in cash. This cash receipt is an increase in net assets resulting from NBS's revenue-generating activities, so it results in revenue being recognised in the income statement. As in transaction (5), the FSET also depicts the impact of these sales on net income and on the retained earnings balance.

	Balance Sheet					Income Statement		
Transaction	Cash Asset +	Noncash Assets =	Liabil-ities +	Contrib. Capital +	Earned Capital	Revenues −	Expenses =	Net Income
(7a) Sell $7,000 of products for cash.	+7,000 Cash	=			+7,000 Retained Earnings	+7,000 Sales Revenue	−	= +7,000

At the same time, NBS must recognise that these sales transactions involved an exchange, and cash was received while inventory costing $4,000 was delivered. Transaction (7b) recognises that NBS no longer has this inventory and that this decrease in net assets produces an expense called cost of goods sold. In this way, the income statement portrays the increases in net assets (revenues) and the decreases in net assets (expenses like cost of goods sold and advertising) from the company's operating activities. (Again, the minus sign in front of all expenses insures that the accounting equation remains balanced.)

Transaction	Cash Asset	Noncash Assets	Liabilities	Contrib. Capital	Earned Capital	Revenues	Expenses	Net Income
(7b) Record $4,000 for the cost of merchandise sold in transaction (7a).		−4,000 Inventory =			−4,000 Retained Earnings	−	+4,000 Cost of Goods Sold =	−4,000

The eighth transaction is very similar to the previous one, except that Natural Beauty Supply's customers will pay for the products ten days after they were delivered. Should NBS recognise revenue on these sales? The products have been delivered, so the revenue has been earned.[6] Therefore, NBS should recognise that it has a new asset—accounts receivable—equal to $2,400, and that it has earned revenue in the same amount. As above, NBS would also record cost of goods sold to recognise the cost of inventory delivered to the customers.

Transaction	Cash Asset	Noncash Assets	Liabilities	Contrib. Capital	Earned Capital	Revenues	Expenses	Net Income
(8a) Sell $2,400 of products on account.		+2,400 Accounts Receivable =			+2,400 Retained Earnings	+2,400 Sales Revenue −	=	+2,400
(8b) Record $1,700 for the cost of merchandise sold in transaction (8a).		−1,700 Inventory =			−1,700 Retained Earnings	−	+1,700 Cost of Goods Sold =	−1,700

The ninth entry records wage expense. In this case, wages were paid in cash. Cash is decreased by $1,400, and this decrease in net assets results in a recognition of wages expense in the income statement (with resulting decreases in net income and retained earnings).

Transaction	Cash Asset	Noncash Assets	Liabilities	Contrib. Capital	Earned Capital	Revenues	Expenses	Net Income
(9) Record $1,400 in wages to employees.	−1,400 Cash	=			−1,400 Retained Earnings	−	+1,400 Wages Expense =	−1,400

Transaction (10) involves a customer order for products to be delivered in December. This transaction is an example of an *executory contract*, which does not require a journal entry. NBS has not earned revenue, because it has not yet delivered the products.

Transaction	
(10) Receive customer order.	Memorandum entry for customer order

In transaction (11), Natural Beauty Supply sold gift certificates for $300 cash, but none were redeemed. In this case, NBS has received cash, but revenue cannot be recognised because it has not yet been earned. Rather, NBS has accepted an obligation to provide services in the future when the gift certificates are redeemed. This obligation is recognised as a liability titled unearned revenue.

Transaction	Cash Asset	Noncash Assets	Liabilities	Contrib. Capital	Earned Capital	Revenues	Expenses	Net Income
(11) Sell gift certificates for $300 cash.	+300 Cash	=	+300 Unearned Revenue			−	=	

[6] In Chapter 6, we consider the possibility that a customer might not pay the receivable. For the time being, we assume that the receivables' collectability is assured.

In transaction (12), NBS received $1,450 cash as partial payment from customers billed in transaction (8). Cash increases by $1,450 and accounts receivable decreases by $1,450. Recall that revenues are recorded when earned (transaction (8)), not when cash is received.

	Balance Sheet									*Income Statement*				
Transaction	Cash Asset	+	Noncash Assets	=	Liabil-ities	+	Contrib. Capital	+	Earned Capital	*Revenues*	-	*Expenses*	=	*Net Income*
(12) Receive $1,450 cash as partial payment from customers billed in transaction (8).	+1,450 Cash		−1,450 Accounts Receivable	=							-		=	

In transaction (13) on November 30, Natural Beauty Supply paid back the family member who had loaned money to the business. The cash payment was the agreed-upon $5,050 ($5,000 principal and $50 interest). The repayment of the principal does not change the net assets of NBS; cash goes down by $5,000 and the note payable liability goes down an equal amount. However, the payment of $50 interest does cause the net assets to decrease, and this net asset decrease creates an interest expense in the income statement.

Transaction	Cash Asset	+	Noncash Assets	=	Liabil-ities	+	Contrib. Capital	+	Earned Capital	*Revenues*	-	*Expenses*	=	*Net Income*
(13) Pay interest of $50 and repay principal of $5,000.	−5,050 Cash			=	−5,000 Notes Payable				−50 Retained Earnings		-	+50 Interest Expense	=	−50

In the transaction (14), NBS paid an annual insurance premium of $1,680 for coverage beginning December 1. NBS will receive the benefits of the insurance coverage in the future, so insurance expense will be recognised in those future periods. At this time, a noncash asset titled prepaid insurance is increased by $1,680, and cash is decreased by the same amount.

Transaction	Cash Asset	+	Noncash Assets	=	Liabil-ities	+	Contrib. Capital	+	Earned Capital	*Revenues*	-	*Expenses*	=	*Net Income*
(14) Pay $1,680 for one-year insurance policy.	−1,680 Cash		+1,680 Prepaid Insurance	=							-		=	

In the last transaction of the month of November, Natural Beauty Supply paid $1,500 cash to the landlord for November's rent. This $1,500 reduction of net assets is balanced by rent expense in the income statement.

Transaction	Cash Asset	+	Noncash Assets	=	Liabil-ities	+	Contrib. Capital	+	Earned Capital	*Revenues*	-	*Expenses*	=	*Net Income*
(15) Pay $1,500 rent for November.	−1,500 Cash			=					−1,500 Retained Earnings		-	+1,500 Rent Expense	=	−1,500

We can summarise the revenue and expense entries of these transactions to prepare an income statement for Natural Beauty Supply for the month ended November 30, 2013.

NATURAL BEAUTY SUPPLY, INC.
Income Statement
For Month Ended November 30, 2013

Sales revenue	$ 9,400
Cost of goods sold	5,700
Gross profit	3,700
Wages expense	1,400
Rent expense	1,500
Advertising expense	670
Operating income	130
Interest expense	50
Net income	$ 80

REPORTING ON EQUITY

Analysing and Recording Equity Transactions

LO5 Illustrate equity transactions and the statement of changes in equity.

Earlier we recorded the effect of issuing ordinary shares on the balance sheet of Natural Beauty Supply. To complete our illustration, we illustrate one final equity transaction—a dividend payment.

(16) Nov. 30 Natural Beauty Supply paid $50 cash dividend to its shareholders.

To record the dividend payment, we decrease cash and decrease retained earnings.

	Balance Sheet									*Income Statement*				
Transaction	Cash Asset	+	Noncash Assets	=	Liabil-ities	+	Contrib. Capital	+	Earned Capital	*Revenues*	-	*Expenses*	=	*Net Income*
(16) Pay $50 cash dividend to shareholders.	−50 Cash			=					−50 Retained Earnings		-		=	

No revenue or income is recorded from a share issuance. Similarly, no expense is recorded from a dividend. This is always the case. Companies cannot report revenues and expenses from capital transactions (transactions with shareholders' relating to their investment in the company).

The FSET entries can be accumulated by account to determine the ending balances for assets, liabilities and equity. Natural Beauty Supply's balance sheet for November 30, 2013, appears in Exhibit 2.4. The balance in retained earnings is $30 (net income of $80 less the cash dividend of $50).

FYI In Exhibit 2.4, as well as Exhibit 2.1, assets are listed in order of their liquidity and liabilities are presented according to maturity. As pointed out earlier, companies in Asia and Europe list the asset section in reverse order of liquidity and the liability section in reverse order of due dates. ■

EXHIBIT 2.4 Natural Beauty Supply's Balance Sheet

NATURAL BEAUTY SUPPLY, INC.
Balance Sheet
November 30, 2013

Assets		**Liabilities**	
Cash	$ 8,100	Accounts payable	$ 3,700
Accounts receivable	950	Unearned revenue	300
Inventory	11,300	Total current liabilities	4,000
Prepaid insurance	1,680	**Equity**	
Security deposit	2,000	Share capital	20,000
Total current assets	24,030	Retained earnings	30
		Total equity	20,030
Total assets	$24,030	Total liabilities and equity	$24,030

Statement of Changes in Equity

The statement of changes in equity is a reconciliation of the beginning and ending balances of selected equity accounts. The statement of changes in equity for Natural Beauty Supply for the month of November is in Exhibit 2.5.

This statement highlights three main changes to Natural Beauty Supply's equity during November.

1. Natural Beauty raised $20,000 in equity capital during the month.
2. Natural Beauty Supply earned net income of $80. That is, its business activities increased the company's net assets by $80 during the month.
3. Natural Beauty Supply declared a $50 cash dividend.

EXHIBIT 2.5 Natural Beauty Supply's Statement of Changes in Equity

NATURAL BEAUTY SUPPLY, INC.
Statement of Changes in Equity
For Month Ended November 30, 2013

	Contributed Capital	Earned Capital	Total Equity
Balance, November 1, 2013	$ 0	$ 0	$ 0
Ordinary share issued	20,000	—	20,000
Net income	—	80	80
Cash dividends	—	(50)	(50)
Balance, November 30, 2013	$20,000	$30	$20,030

YOU MAKE THE CALL

You are an Analyst Indigo reported a balance in retained earnings of $99,042 thousand at March 29, 2014. This amount compares to $138,389 thousand one year earlier at the end of March 30, 2013. In 2014, Indigo reported net loss of $30,999 thousand. Why did the company's retained earnings go down by more than reported net loss? [Answer on page 69]

MID-CHAPTER REVIEW 3

Part 1. Assume that Schaefer's Pharmacy, Inc.'s records show the following amounts at December 31, 2015. Use this information, as necessary, to prepare its 2015 income statement (ignore income taxes).

Cash	$ 3,000	Cash dividends	$ 1,000
Accounts receivable	12,000	Revenues	25,000
Office equipment	32,250	Rent expense	5,000
Land	36,000	Wages expense	8,000
Accounts payable	7,500	Utilities expense	2,000
Share capital	45,750	Other expenses	4,000

Part 2. Assume that Schaefer's Pharmacy, Inc. reports the following selected financial information for the year ended December 31, 2015.

Retained earnings, Dec. 31, 2015	$30,000	Dividends	$ 1,000
Net income	$ 6,000	Retained earnings, Dec. 31, 2014	$25,000

Prepare the 2015 calendar-year retained earnings reconciliation for this company.

Part 3. Use the listing of accounts and figures reported in part 1 along with the ending retained earnings from part 2 to prepare the December 31, 2015, balance sheet for Schaefer's Pharmacy, Inc.

The solution to this review problem can be found on pages 88–89.

JOURNALISING AND POSTING TRANSACTIONS

LO6 Use journal entries and T-accounts to analyse and record transactions.

The financial statement effects template (step 1) is a useful tool for illustrating the effects of a transaction on the balance sheet, income statement, statement of changes in equity, and statement of cash flows. However, when representing individual transactions or analysing individual accounts, the accounting system records information in journal entries (step 2) that are collected in individual accounts. This section introduces the basics of that system. It also introduces the T-account as a useful tool for learning debits and credits and for representing accounts in the ledger (step 3).

T-Account

Accountants commonly use a graphic representation of an account called a **T-account**, so named because it looks like a large T. The typical form of a T-account is

Account Title	
Debits (Dr.) Always the left side	Credits (Cr.) Always the right side

> **FYI** Recall that an account is a record of increases and decreases in asset, liability, equity, revenue or expense items.

One side of the T-account is used to record increases to the account and the other side is used to record decreases.

Accountants record individual transactions using the journal entry. A **journal entry** is an accounting entry in the financial records (journals) of a company. The journal entry is the *bookkeeping* aspect of accounting. Even if we never make a journal entry for a company, we still interact with accounting and finance professionals who do, and who will use this language. Further, journal entries and T-accounts can help in reconstructing transactions and interpreting their financial effects.

Debit and Credit System

> **FYI** Debit and credit are accounting terms meaning left and right, respectively.

Accountants describe increases and decreases in accounts using the terms **debit** and **credit**. The left side of each account is the debit side (abbreviated Dr.) and the right side of each account is the credit side (abbreviated Cr.). In some accounts, increases are recorded on the debit (left) side of the account and decreases are recorded on the credit (right) side of the account. In other accounts, just the opposite is true—increases are credits and decreases are debits. An easy way to remember what the words debit and credit reflect is to visualise a balance sheet in "T" account form with assets on the left and liabilities and equity on the right as follows:

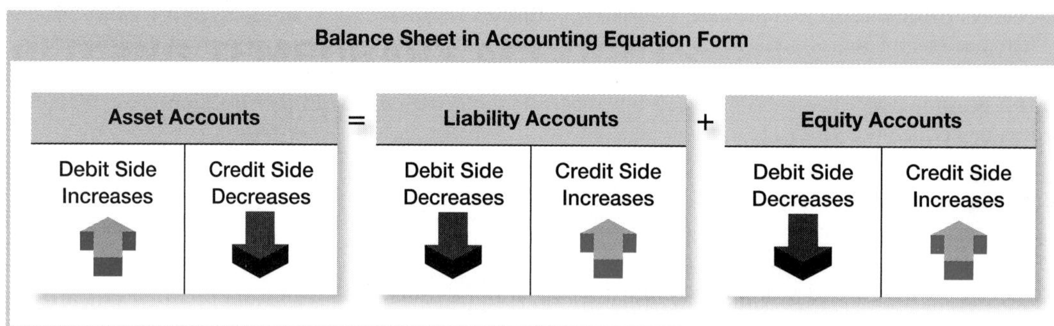

Thus, assets are assigned a *normal debit balance* because they are on the left side. Liabilities and equity are assigned a *normal credit balance* because they are on the right side. So, to reflect an increase in an asset, we debit the asset account. To reflect an increase in a liability or equity account we credit the account. Conversely, to reflect a decrease in an asset account, we credit it. To reflect a decrease in a liability or equity account we debit it. (There are exceptions to these normal balances; one case is accumulated depreciation, which is explained in Chapter 3.)

> **FYI** The rule that total debits equal total credits for each entry is known as double-entry accounting, or the duality of accounting.

The balance sheet must always balance (assets = liabilities + equity). So too must total debits equal total credits in each journal entry. There can, however, be more than one debit and one credit in an entry. These so-called **compound entries** still adhere to the rule: *total debits equal total credits for each entry*. This important relation is extended below to show the *expanded accounting equation* in T-account form with the inclusion of debit (Dr.) and credit (Cr.) rules. Equity is expanded to reflect increases from share issuances and revenues, and to reflect decreases from dividends and expenses.

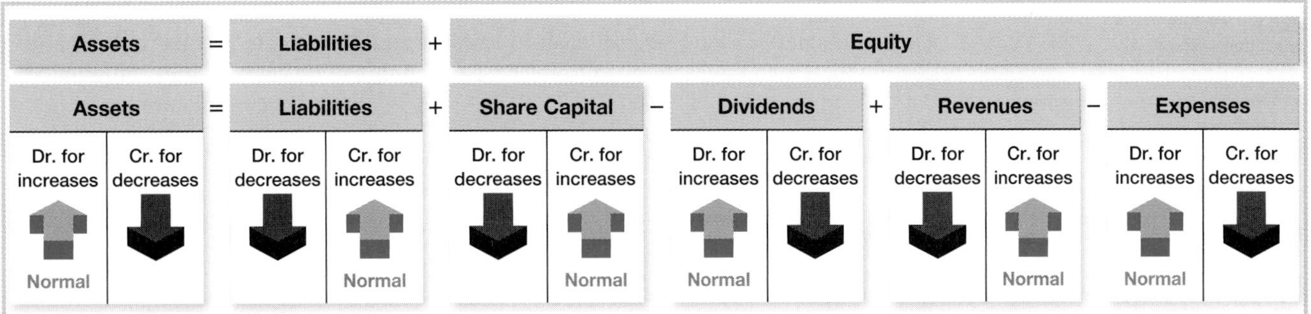

Income (revenues less expenses) feeds directly into retained earnings. Also, anything that increases equity is a credit and anything that decreases equity is a debit. So, to reflect an increase in revenues (which increases retained earnings and, therefore, equity), we credit the revenue account, and to reflect an increase in an expense account (which reduces retained earnings and, therefore, equity), we debit it.

To summarise, the following table reflects the use of the terms debit and credit to reflect increases and decreases to the usual balance sheet and the income statement relations.

FYI The normal balance of any account is on the side on which increases are recorded. ■

Accounting Relation		Debit	Credit
Balance sheet	Assets (A)	Increase	Decrease
	Liabilities (L)	Decrease	Increase
	Equity (SE)	Decrease	Increase
Income statement	Revenue (R)	Decrease	Increase
	Expense (E)	Increase	Decrease

T-Account with Debits and Credits

To illustrate use of debits and credits with a T-account, we use the Cash T-account for NBS transactions (1), (2), (3), and (4) (see page 47). There is a beginning balance of $0 on the left side (which is also the ending balance of the previous period). Increases in cash have been placed on the left side of the Cash T-account and the decreases have been placed on the right side. Transactions (1) and (2) increased the cash balance, while transaction (3) decreased it. Transaction (4) does not involve cash.

The ending balance of cash is $23,000. An account balance is determined by totaling the left side and the right side money columns and entering the difference on the side with the larger total. The T-account is an extremely simple record that can be summarised in terms of four elements: beginning balance, additions, deductions, and the ending balance.

+	Cash (A)		−
Beg. bal.	0		
(1)	20,000	2,000	(3)
(2)	5,000		
End. bal.	23,000		

Dates and other related data are usually omitted in T-accounts, but it is customary to *key* entries with a number or a letter to identify the similarly coded transaction. The number or letter is keyed to the journal entry (discussed next) that identifies the transaction involved. The type and number of accounts used by a business depend on the complexity of its operations and the degree of detail demanded by managers.

The Journal Entry

While the transaction analysis (step 1) illustrates the financial statement effects of a transaction, the journal entry (step 2) records each transaction by summarising the debits and credits. To

FYI We denote the transaction's effect on assets, liabilities, equity, revenues, and expenses in parentheses for each journal entry. ■

illustrate the use of journal entries and T-accounts (step 3), assume that Indigo: (1) Paid employees $1,200 cash wages, and (2) Paid $9,500 cash to acquire equipment. The journal entries and T-accounts reflecting these two transactions follow. The T-accounts can be viewed as an abbreviated representation of the company *ledger,* which is a listing of all accounts and their dollar balances.

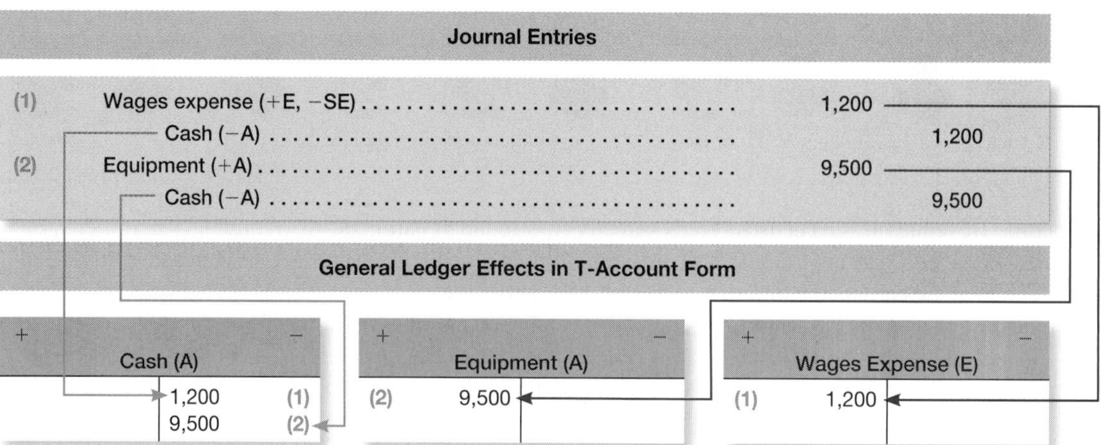

For journal entries, debits are recorded first followed by the credits. Credits are commonly indented. The dollar amounts are entered in both the debit (left) column and credit (right) column. In practice, recordkeepers also enter the date. An alternative presentation is to utilise the abbreviation *Dr* to denote debits and *Cr* to denote credits that precede the account title. We use the first approach in this book.

Analyse, Journalise, and Post

To illustrate the use of journal entries and T-accounts to record transactions, we return to Natural Beauty Supply and reexamine the same transactions recorded earlier in the financial statement effects template (FSET). The following layout illustrates our 3-step accounting process of analysing, journalising, and posting.

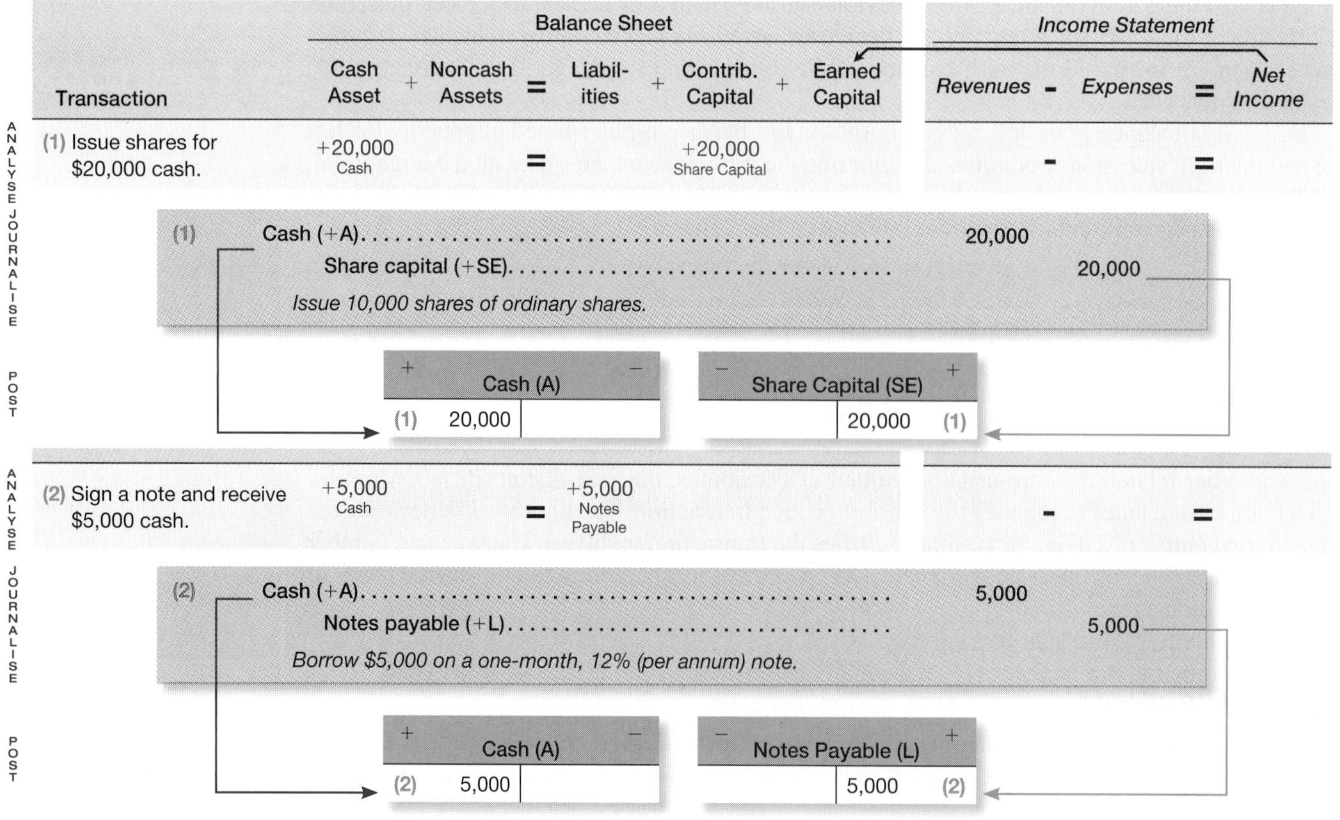

continued

continued from previous page

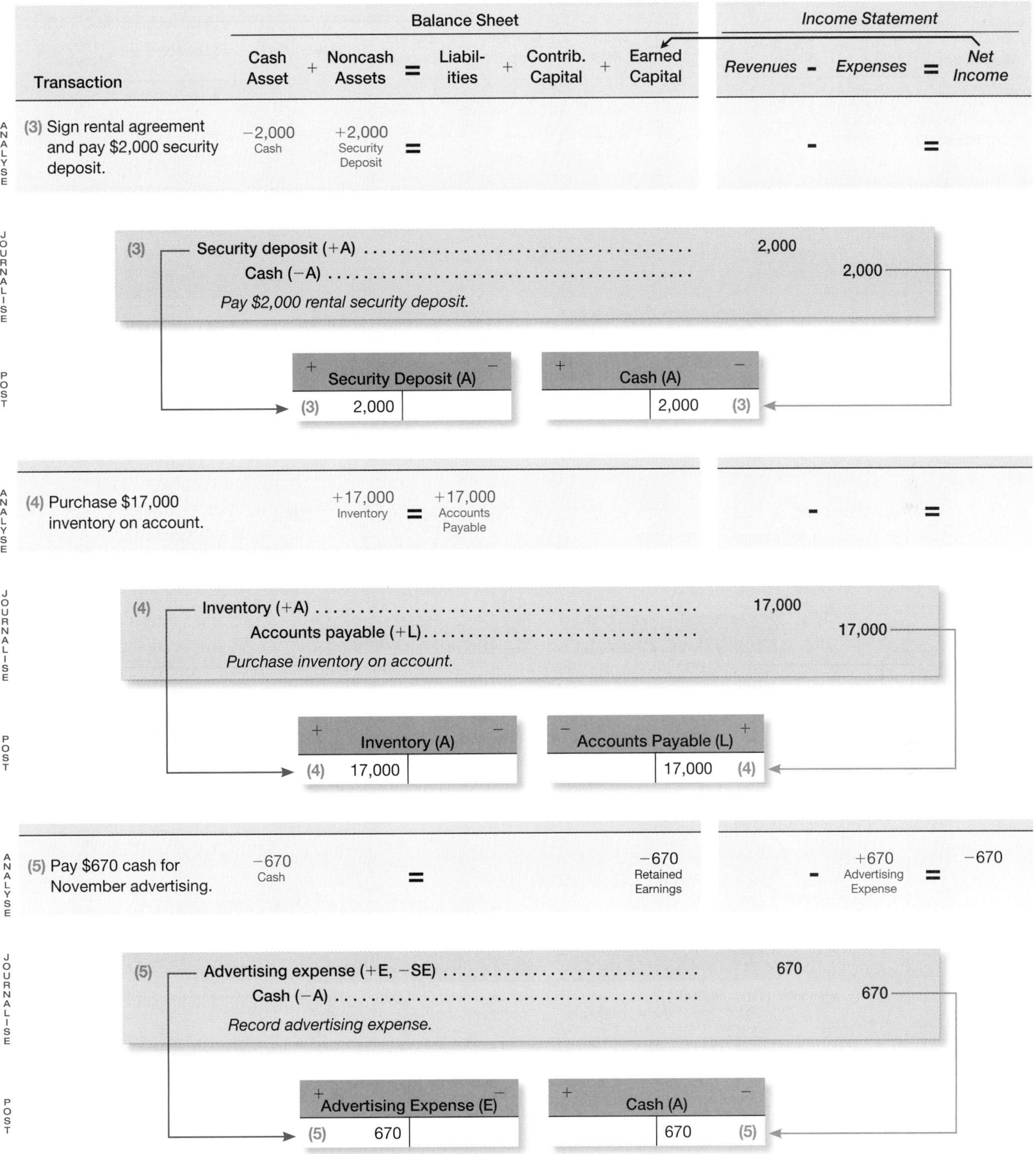

For entries involving income statement accounts, only the transaction itself (**blue type** in the FSET) is recorded in the journal entry and T-account posting. The resulting effects on net income and retained earnings (black font type in the FSET) occur during the closing process (to be discussed in Chapter 3).

continued

continued from previous page

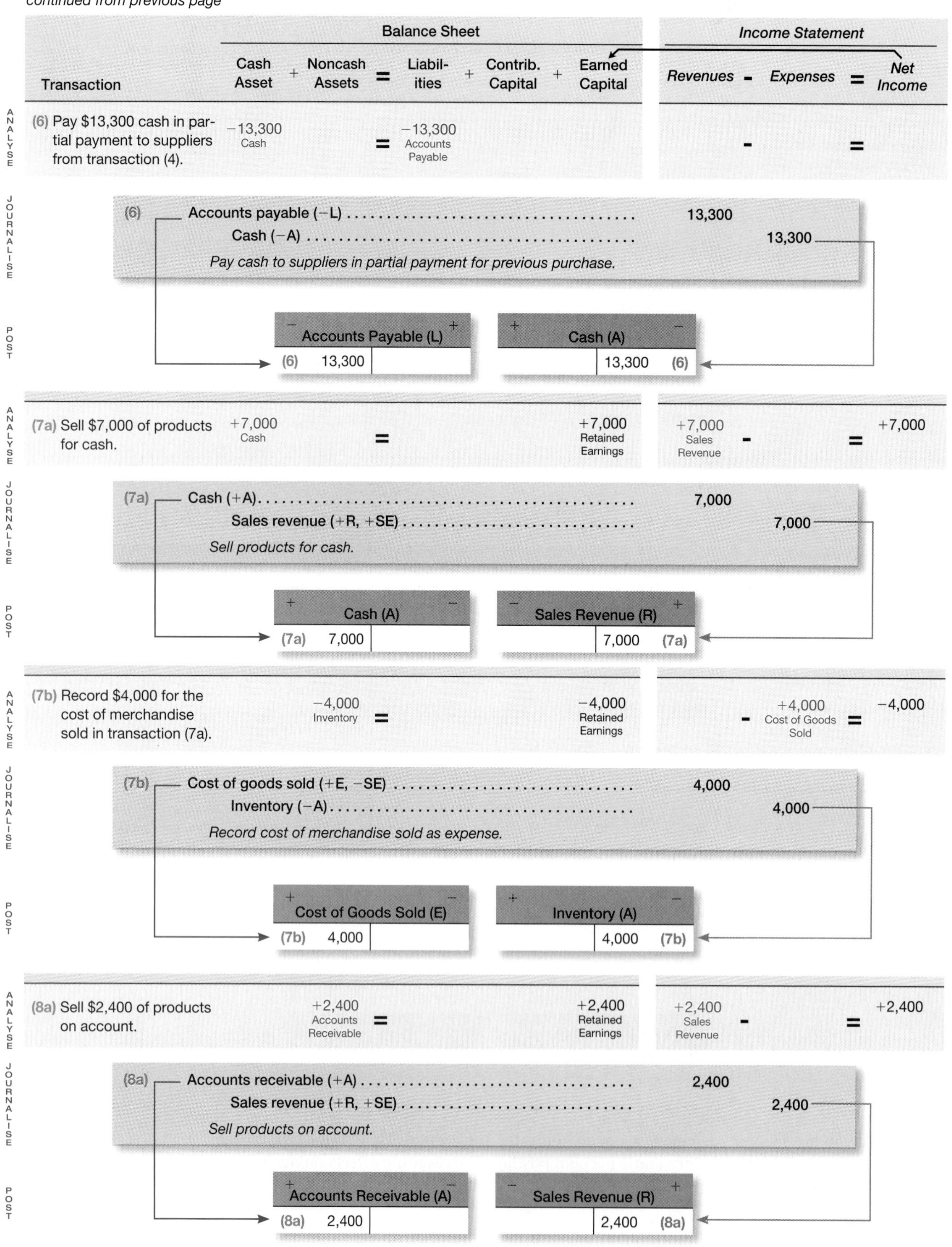

	Balance Sheet										Income Statement				
Transaction	Cash Asset	+	Noncash Assets	=	Liabil-ities	+	Contrib. Capital	+	Earned Capital		*Revenues*	-	*Expenses*	=	*Net Income*
ANALYSE (6) Pay $13,300 cash in partial payment to suppliers from transaction (4).	−13,300 Cash			=	−13,300 Accounts Payable							-		=	
ANALYSE (7a) Sell $7,000 of products for cash.	+7,000 Cash			=					+7,000 Retained Earnings		+7,000 Sales Revenue	-		=	+7,000
ANALYSE (7b) Record $4,000 for the cost of merchandise sold in transaction (7a).			−4,000 Inventory	=					−4,000 Retained Earnings			-	+4,000 Cost of Goods Sold	=	−4,000
ANALYSE (8a) Sell $2,400 of products on account.			+2,400 Accounts Receivable	=					+2,400 Retained Earnings		+2,400 Sales Revenue	-		=	+2,400

JOURNALISE

		Debit	Credit
(6)	Accounts payable (−L)	13,300	
	Cash (−A)		13,300
	Pay cash to suppliers in partial payment for previous purchase.		

POST

− Accounts Payable (L) +	
(6) 13,300	

+ Cash (A) −	
	13,300 (6)

JOURNALISE

		Debit	Credit
(7a)	Cash (+A)	7,000	
	Sales revenue (+R, +SE)		7,000
	Sell products for cash.		

POST

+ Cash (A) −	
(7a) 7,000	

− Sales Revenue (R) +	
	7,000 (7a)

JOURNALISE

		Debit	Credit
(7b)	Cost of goods sold (+E, −SE)	4,000	
	Inventory (−A)		4,000
	Record cost of merchandise sold as expense.		

POST

+ Cost of Goods Sold (E) −	
(7b) 4,000	

+ Inventory (A) −	
	4,000 (7b)

JOURNALISE

		Debit	Credit
(8a)	Accounts receivable (+A)	2,400	
	Sales revenue (+R, +SE)		2,400
	Sell products on account.		

POST

+ Accounts Receivable (A) −	
(8a) 2,400	

− Sales Revenue (R) +	
	2,400 (8a)

continued

Transaction	Cash Asset	+	Noncash Assets	=	Liabil-ities	+	Contrib. Capital	+	Earned Capital	Revenues	-	Expenses	=	Net Income
ANALYSE (8b) Record $1,700 for the cost of merchandise sold in transaction (8a).			−1,700 Inventory	=					−1,700 Retained Earnings		-	+1,700 Cost of Goods Sold	=	−1,700

JOURNALISE

		Dr.	Cr.
(8b)	Cost of goods sold (+E, −SE)	1,700	
	Inventory (−A)		1,700
	Record cost of merchandise sold as expense.		

POST

+ Cost of Goods Sold (E) −	
(8b) 1,700	

+ Inventory (A) −	
	1,700 (8b)

Transaction	Cash Asset	+	Noncash Assets	=	Liabil-ities	+	Contrib. Capital	+	Earned Capital	Revenues	-	Expenses	=	Net Income
ANALYSE (9) Record $1,400 in wages to employees.	−1,400 Cash			=					−1,400 Retained Earnings		-	+1,400 Wages Expense	=	−1,400

JOURNALISE

		Dr.	Cr.
(9)	Wages expense (+E, −SE)	1,400	
	Cash (−A)		1,400
	Pay wages to employees.		

POST

+ Wages Expense (E) −	
(9) 1,400	

+ Cash (A) −	
	1,400 (9)

ANALYSE (10) Receive customer order.

Memorandum entry for customer order

JOURNALISE

No journal entry recorded and no T-accounts affected

Transaction	Cash Asset	+	Noncash Assets	=	Liabil-ities	+	Contrib. Capital	+	Earned Capital	Revenues	-	Expenses	=	Net Income
ANALYSE (11) Sell gift certificates for $300 cash.	+300 Cash			=	+300 Unearned Revenue						-		=	

JOURNALISE

		Dr.	Cr.
(11)	Cash (+A)	300	
	Unearned revenue (+L)		300
	Record unearned revenue from gift certificates.		

POST

+ Cash (A) −	
(11) 300	

− Unearned Revenue (L) +	
	300 (11)

continued

continued from previous page

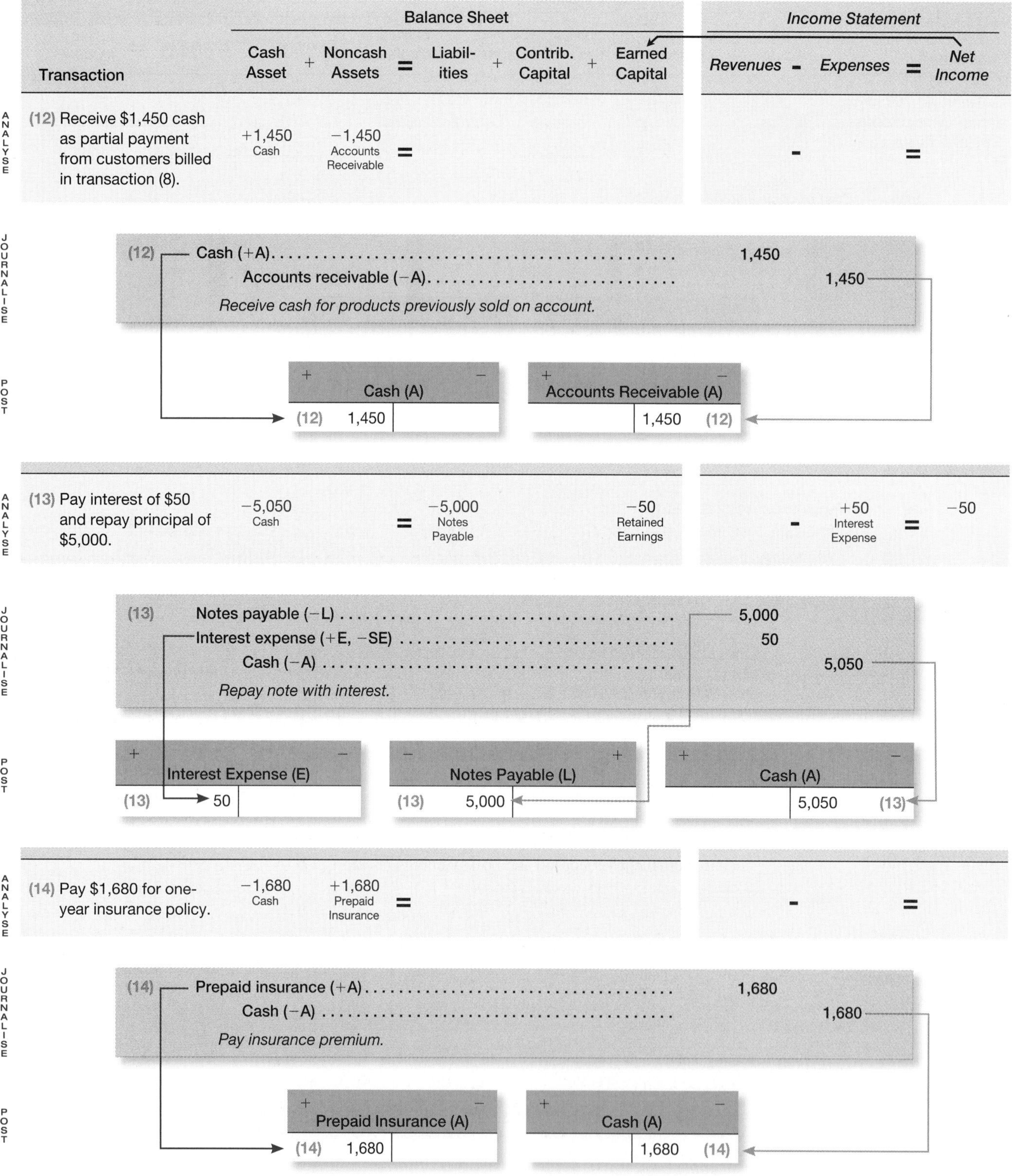

Transaction	Cash Asset	+	Noncash Assets	=	Liabil-ities	+	Contrib. Capital	+	Earned Capital		Revenues	-	Expenses	=	Net Income
(12) Receive $1,450 cash as partial payment from customers billed in transaction (8).	+1,450 Cash		−1,450 Accounts Receivable	=								-		=	
(13) Pay interest of $50 and repay principal of $5,000.	−5,050 Cash			=	−5,000 Notes Payable				−50 Retained Earnings			-	+50 Interest Expense	=	−50
(14) Pay $1,680 for one-year insurance policy.	−1,680 Cash		+1,680 Prepaid Insurance	=								-		=	

continued

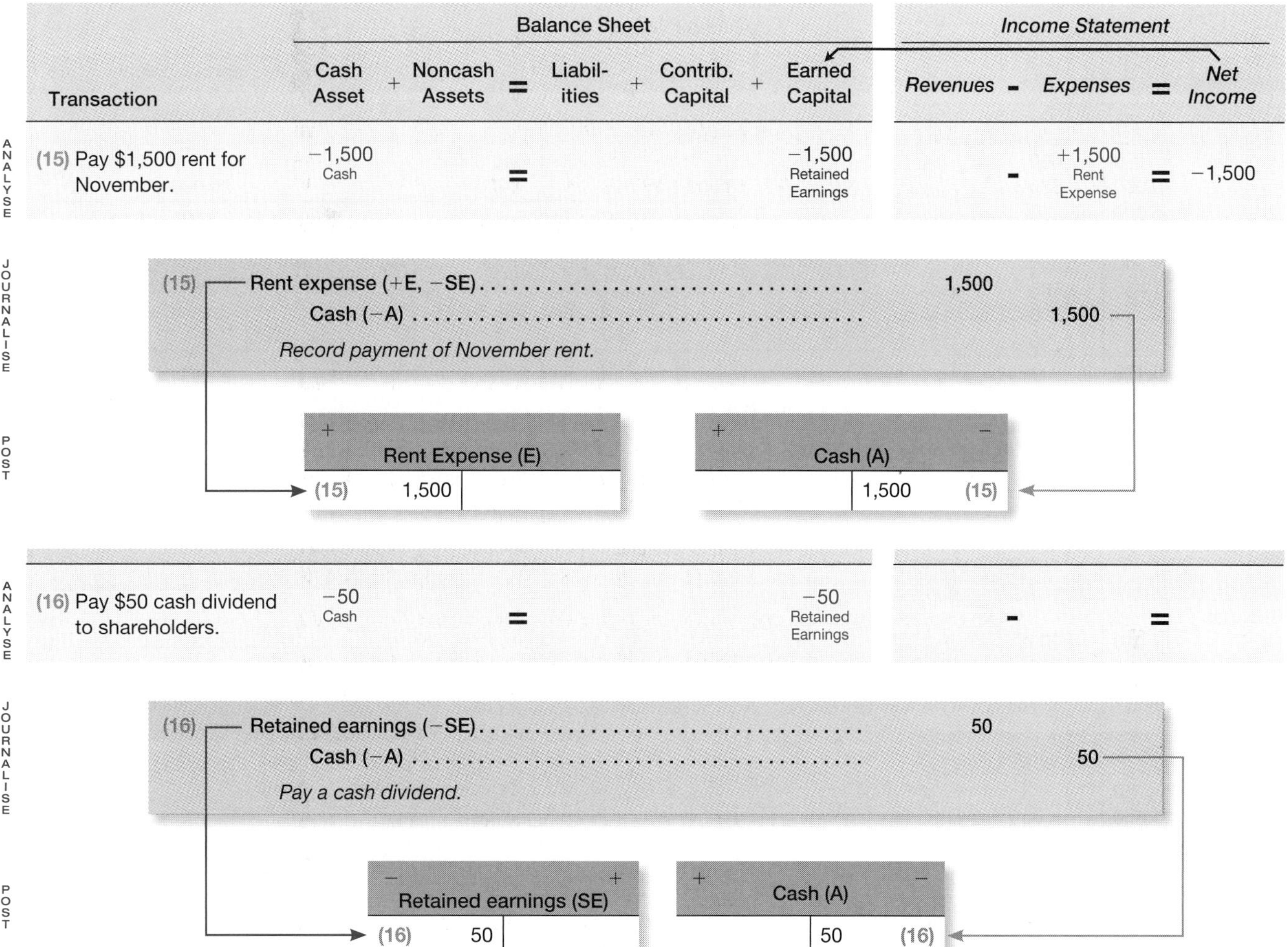

Balance Sheet
Income Statement
Transaction
Cash Asset + Noncash Assets = Liabil-ities + Contrib. Capital + Earned Capital
Revenues - Expenses = Net Income
ANALYSE
(15) Pay $1,500 rent for November.
−1,500 Cash = −1,500 Retained Earnings
- +1,500 Rent Expense = −1,500
JOURNALISE
(15) Rent expense (+E, −SE) 1,500
Cash (−A) 1,500
Record payment of November rent.
POST
Rent Expense (E)
(15) 1,500
Cash (A)
1,500 (15)
ANALYSE
(16) Pay $50 cash dividend to shareholders.
−50 Cash = −50 Retained Earnings
JOURNALISE
(16) Retained earnings (−SE) 50
Cash (−A) 50
Pay a cash dividend.
POST
Retained earnings (SE)
(16) 50
Cash (A)
50 (16)

As shown above, each of the journal entries is posted to the appropriate T-accounts, which represent the general ledger. The complete general ledger reflecting each of these sixteen transactions follows. The dashed line around the six equity accounts indicates those that are reported in the income statement before becoming part of retained earnings. Each balance sheet T-account starts with an opening balance on November 1 (zero in this case), and the ending balances are the starting balances for December. Income statement T-accounts do not have an opening balance, for reasons we explore in Chapter 3.

As always, we see that: Assets = Liabilities + Equity. Specifically, $24,030 assets ($8,100 + $950 + $11,300 + $1,680 + $2,000) = $4,000 liabilities ($3,700 + $300) + $20,030 equity ($20,000 − $50 + $9,400 − $5,700 − $1,400 − $1,500 − $670 − $50).

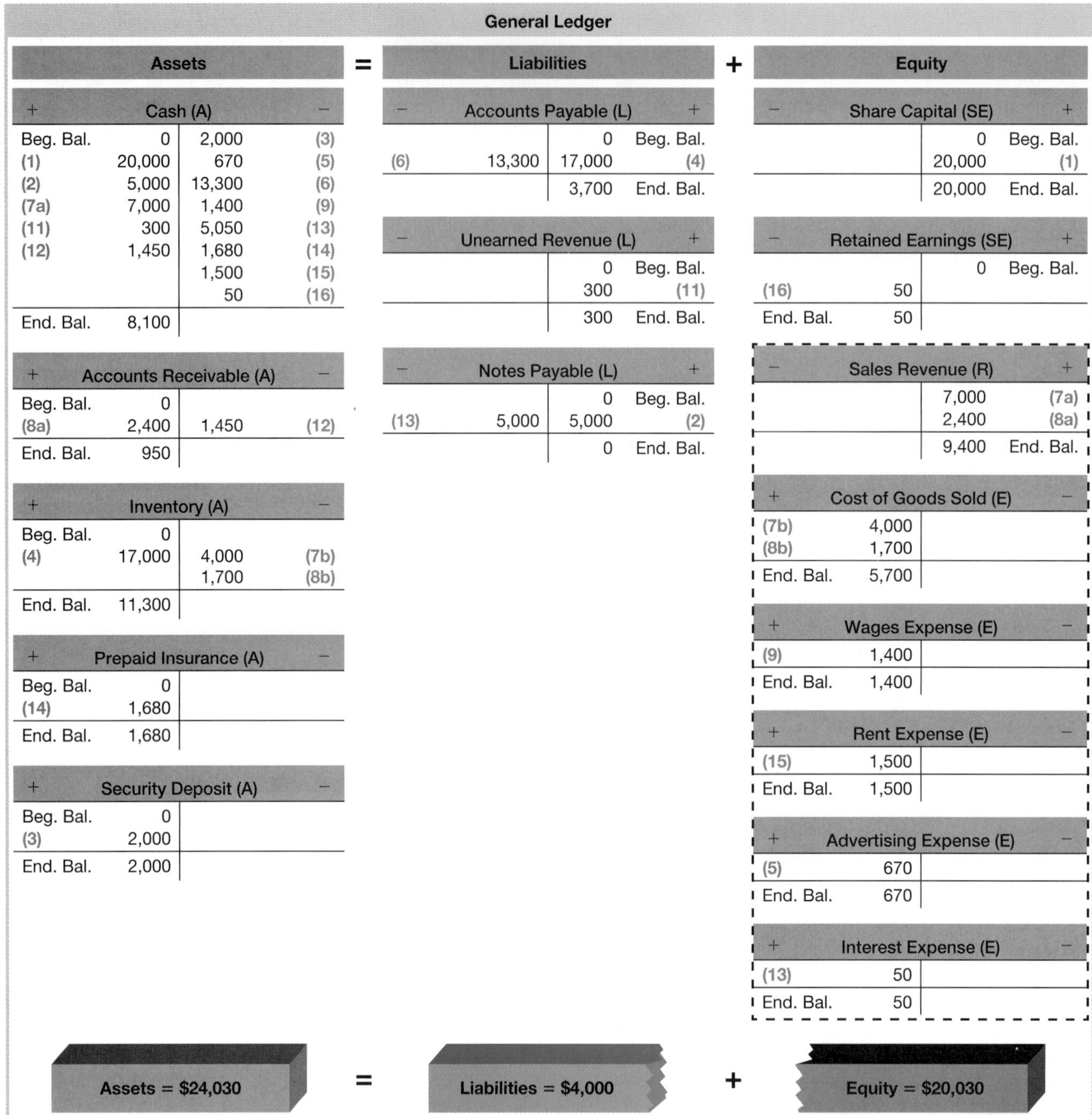

General Ledger
Assets = Liabilities + Equity
+ Cash (A) −
Beg. Bal. 0 | 2,000 (3)
(1) 20,000 | 670 (5)
(2) 5,000 | 13,300 (6)
(7a) 7,000 | 1,400 (9)
(11) 300 | 5,050 (13)
(12) 1,450 | 1,680 (14)
1,500 (15)
50 (16)
End. Bal. 8,100
+ Accounts Receivable (A) −
Beg. Bal. 0
(8a) 2,400 | 1,450 (12)
End. Bal. 950
+ Inventory (A) −
Beg. Bal. 0
(4) 17,000 | 4,000 (7b)
1,700 (8b)
End. Bal. 11,300
+ Prepaid Insurance (A) −
Beg. Bal. 0
(14) 1,680
End. Bal. 1,680
+ Security Deposit (A) −
Beg. Bal. 0
(3) 2,000
End. Bal. 2,000
− Accounts Payable (L) +
0 Beg. Bal.
(6) 13,300 | 17,000 (4)
3,700 End. Bal.
− Unearned Revenue (L) +
0 Beg. Bal.
300 (11)
300 End. Bal.
− Notes Payable (L) +
0 Beg. Bal.
(13) 5,000 | 5,000 (2)
0 End. Bal.
− Share Capital (SE) +
0 Beg. Bal.
20,000 (1)
20,000 End. Bal.
− Retained Earnings (SE) +
0 Beg. Bal.
(16) 50
End. Bal. 50
− Sales Revenue (R) +
7,000 (7a)
2,400 (8a)
9,400 End. Bal.
+ Cost of Goods Sold (E) −
(7b) 4,000
(8b) 1,700
End. Bal. 5,700
+ Wages Expense (E) −
(9) 1,400
End. Bal. 1,400
+ Rent Expense (E) −
(15) 1,500
End. Bal. 1,500
+ Advertising Expense (E) −
(5) 670
End. Bal. 670
+ Interest Expense (E) −
(13) 50
End. Bal. 50
Assets = $24,030 = Liabilities = $4,000 + Equity = $20,030

LO7 Compute net working capital, the current ratio, and the quick ratio, and explain how they reflect liquidity.

ANALYSING FINANCIAL STATEMENTS

Analysis Objective

We are trying to determine if Indigo has sufficient funds to pay their short-term debts as they mature. To accomplish this task, we use several measures of liquidity. We introduce three such measures below to assess liquidity.

Analysis Tool Net Working Capital

$$\textbf{Net working capital} = \textbf{Current assets} - \textbf{Current liabilities}$$

Applying Net Working Capital to Indigo

2014	\$387,323 – \$197,627 = \$189,696
2013	\$438,374 – \$214,031 = \$224,343
2012	\$452,419 – \$228,718 = \$223,701

Guidance A company's net working capital is determined primarily by the time between paying for goods and employee services and the receipt of cash from sales for cash or on credit. This cycle is referred to as the firm's operating cycle (see Exhibit 2.6). The operating cycle can provide additional resources through trade credit financing. For example, inventory is typically bought on credit with terms that allow payment to be deferred for 30 to 90 days without penalty. The delay in payment allows the cash to be invested thereby increasing the cash to be used in the following operating cycle. Of course, the reluctant supplier of the credit strives to reduce this payment delay, for example, through discounts for early payment.

A company's net working capital is a broad measure including all current assets even though some of them—inventories for one—require time to turn them into cash. More conservative measures are useful and available.

EXHIBIT 2.6 Operating Cycle

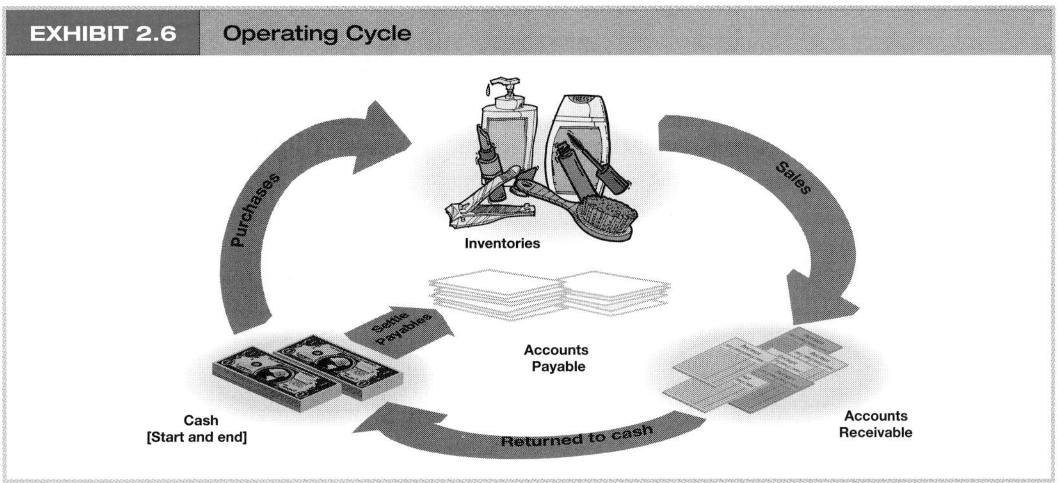

Analysis Tool Current Ratio

$$\text{Current ratio} = \frac{\text{Current assets}}{\text{Current liabilities}}$$

Applying the Current Ratio to Indigo

2014	\$387,323/\$197,627 = 1.96
2013	\$438,374/\$214,031 = 2.05
2012	\$452,419/\$228,718 = 1.98

Guidance The current ratio is just a different form of net working capital and as such simply provides a different viewpoint. Current ratios exceeding one indicate a strong net working capital. However, for firms that find difficulty in predicting sales and collections, a higher current ratio is desirable. Companies generally prefer a current ratio greater than one but less than two. The ratio allows us to discern whether the company is likely to have difficulty meeting its short-term obligations. The current ratio has additional value as a ratio because net working capital does not allow for the size of the company. This is useful when comparing companies as is true below.

Analysis Tool Quick Ratio

$$\textbf{Quick ratio} = \frac{\textbf{Cash + Short-term securities + Accounts receivable}}{\textbf{Current liabilities}}$$

Applying the Quick Ratio to Indigo

2014	($157,578 + $0 + $5,582)/$197,627 = 0.83
2013	($210,562 + $0 + $7,126)/$214,031 = 1.02
2012	($206,718 + $0 + $12,810)/$228,718 = 0.96

Guidance The quick ratio is a more restrictive form of the current ratio in that it excludes inventories. Only those assets that are cash, or near cash, are considered in this liquidity measure, making it a more stringent test of liquidity.

Takeaways Over the three-year period covered by our calculations, we can conclude that Indigo is in a strong position with respect to liquidity. Its net working capital, while declining slightly over the last three years, has remained positive. Its current ratio has been around 2.00 and its quick ratio has been about 1.00.

Other Considerations While the ratios above are fine for booksellers, other companies with different operating cycles are likely to exhibit different values at optimal levels of activity. Thus grocery stores will have few current assets but consistent large operating cash inflows that insure sufficient liquidity despite current ratios less than one. Additionally, companies that efficiently manage inventories, receivables and payables can also operate with current ratios below one. For example, Unilever, a leading consumer goods company, uses its strong market power to extract extended credit terms from suppliers while simultaneously enforcing short payment periods on customers. We can then extend the discussion to conclude that an excessively high current ratio likely reflects inefficient asset use.

CHAPTER-END REVIEW

Assume that the following accounts appear in the ledger of M.E. Carter, a financial consultant to companies in the retail sector. Cash; Accounts Receivable; Office Equipment; Prepaid Subscriptions; Accounts Payable; Share Capital; Retained Earnings; Fees Earned; Salaries Expense; Rent Expense; and Utilities Expense. For each of the following 10 transactions: (a) analyse and enter each into the financial statement effects template, (b) prepare journal entries for each of the transactions, and (c) set up T-accounts for each of the ledger accounts and post the journal entries to those T-accounts—key all entries with the number identifying the transaction. Prepare the general ledger in T-account form, enter the financial effects of all transactions, and determine the ending balance for each account.

(1) M.E. Carter started the firm by contributing $19,500 cash to the business in exchange for ordinary shares.

(2) The firm purchased $10,400 in office equipment on account.

(3) Paid $700 cash for this period's office rent.

(4) Paid $9,600 cash for subscriptions to online financial databases covering the next three periods.

(5) Billed clients $11,300 for services rendered.

(6) Made $6,000 cash payment on account for the equipment purchased in transaction (2).

(7) Paid $2,800 cash for assistant's salary for this period.

(8) Collected $9,400 cash from clients previously billed in transaction (5).

(9) Received $180 invoice for this period's utilities; it is paid early in the next period.

(10) Paid $1,500 cash for dividends to shareholders.

The solution to this review problem can be found on pages 89–91.

SUMMARY

Describe and construct the balance sheet and understand how it can be used for analysis. (p. 40) LO1

- Assets, which reflect investment activities, are reported as current assets (expected to be used typically within a year) and long-term (or plant) assets.
- Assets are reported at their historical cost and not at market values (with few exceptions) and are restricted to those that can be reliably measured.
- Not all assets are reported on the balance sheet; a company's intellectual capital, often one of its more valuable assets, is one example.
- For an asset to be recorded, it must be owned or controlled by the company and carry future economic benefits.
- Liabilities and equity are the sources of company financing.

Use the financial statement effects template (FSET) to analyse transactions. (p. 45) LO2

- The FSET captures the effects of transactions on the balance sheet, income statement, statement of changes in equity, and the statement of cash flows.
- Income statement effects are separated into revenues, expenses, and net income. The updating of retained earnings is denoted with an arrow line running from net income to earned capital.

Describe and construct the income statement and discuss how it can be used to evaluate management performance. (p. 49) LO3

- The income statement presents the revenues, expenses, and net income recognised by the company during the accounting period.
- Net income (or loss) is the increase (decrease) in net assets that results from business activities.
- Net income is determined based on the use of accrual accounting.

Explain revenue recognition, accrual accounting, and their effects on retained earnings. (p. 50) LO4

- Revenues must be recognised only when goods or services have been transferred to the customer.
- Expenses should be recognised as assets are used or liabilities incurred in order to earn revenues or carry out other operating activities.

Illustrate equity transactions and the statement of changes in equity. (p. 56) LO5

- The statement of changes in equity reports transactions resulting in changes in equity accounts during the accounting period.
- Transactions between the company and its owners, such as dividend payments, are not reported in the income statement.

Use journal entries and T-accounts to analyse and record transactions. (p. 57) LO6

- Transactions are recorded in the accounting system using journal entries.
- Journal entries are posted to a general ledger, represented by "T-accounts."
- Accountants use "debits" and "credits" to record transactions in the accounts.

Compute net working capital, the current ratio, and the quick ratio, and explain how they reflect liquidity. (p. 66) LO7

- Net working capital: an indicator of a firm's ability to pay its short-term debts computed as the difference between current assets and current liabilities.
- Current ratio (CR): A measure of solvency indicating the degree of coverage of current liabilities by current assets.
- Quick ratio (QR): A measure of the ability to cover current liabilities using only cash and cash equivalents, such as money market accounts, and accounts receivable.

GUIDANCE ANSWERS . . . YOU MAKE THE CALL

You are an Analyst In 2014, Indigo paid cash dividends of $8,348 thousand. The net income and dividend payments account for the change in retained earnings ($99,042 − $138,389 = −$30,999 − $8,348). On occasion, companies pay dividends in excess of their earnings (or pay dividends even when earning losses, as in this case), resulting in a decrease in retained earnings over the period.

KEY RATIOS

Net working capital = Current assets − Current liabilities

$$\text{Current ratio} = \frac{\text{Current assets}}{\text{Current liabilities}} \qquad \text{Quick ratio} = \frac{\text{Cash} + \text{Short-term securities} + \text{Accounts receivable}}{\text{Current liabilities}}$$

KEY TERMS

Account (p. 46)
Accounting equation (p. 40)
Accounts payable (p. 43)
Accounts receivable (p. 42)
Accrual accounting (p. 50)
Accrued liabilities (p. 43)
Accumulated other comprehensive income or loss (p. 44)
Asset (p. 40)
Cash (p. 42)
Cash accounting (p. 51)
Chart of accounts (p. 46)
Compound entries (p. 58)
Contributed capital (p. 44)
Contributed surplus or Share premium (p. 44)
Cost of goods sold (p. 50)
Credit (p. 51, 58)
Current assets (p. 42)
Current liabilities (p. 43)
Current maturities of long-term debt (p. 43)
Debit (p. 58)
Deferred (unearned) revenues (p. 43)
Double-entry accounting system (p. 46)
Earned capital (p. 44)
Equity (p. 43, 45)
Executory contract (p. 43)
Expense recognition (p. 50)
Expenses (p. 49)
Fair value (p. 42)
Financial statement effects template (FSET) (p. 46)
Gross profit (p. 51)
Historical cost (p. 42)
Intangible and other assets (p. 42)
Inventory (p. 42)
Journal entry (p. 58)
Liabilities (p. 43)
Liquidity (p. 42)
Long-term debt (p. 44)
Long-term financial investments (p. 42)
Marketable securities (p. 42)
Net assets (p. 49)
Net income (p. 49)
Net loss (p. 49)
Noncurrent assets (p. 42)
Noncurrent liabilities (p. 44)
Nonoperating revenues and expenses (p. 50)
Normal balance (p. 59)
Notes payable (p. 44)
Operating expenses (p. 49)
Other long-term liabilities (p. 44)
Prepaid expenses (p. 42)
Property, plant, and equipment (PPE) (p. 42)
Relevance (p. 42)
Reliability (p. 42)
Retained earnings (p. 44)
Revenue recognition (p. 50)
Revenues (p. 49)
Share capital or Capital stock (p. 44)
Shareholders' equity (p. 45)
Short-term borrowings (p. 43)
Stockholders' equity (p. 45)
T-account (p. 58)
Treasury shares (p. 44)
Treasury stock (p. 44)

MULTIPLE CHOICE

Multiple Choice Answers
1. d 2. a 3. c 4. b 5. d

1. Which of the following conditions must exist for an item to be recorded as an asset?
   a. Item is not owned or controlled by the company.
   b. Future benefits from the item cannot be reliably measured.
   c. Item must be a tangible asset.
   d. Item must be expected to yield future benefits.
2. Company assets that are excluded from the company financial statements
   a. are presumably reflected in the company's share price.
   b. include all of the company's intangible assets.
   c. are known as intangible assets.
   d. include investments in other companies.
3. If an asset declines in value, which of the following must be true?
   a. A liability also declines.
   b. Equity also declines.
   c. Either a liability or equity also declines or another asset increases in value.
   d. Neither *a* nor *b* can occur.

4. Which of the following is true about accrual accounting?
   a. Accrual accounting does not require matching.
   b. Accrual accounting is required under IFRS.
   c. Accrual accounting recognises revenue only when cash is received.
   d. Recognition of a prepaid asset (e.g., prepaid rent) is not an example of accrual accounting.

5. Which of the following options accurately identifies the effects a cash sale of a book has on Indigo's accounts?
   a. Accounts receivable increases, sales revenue increases, cost of goods sold increases, and inventory decreases.
   b. Cash increases, sales revenue increases, cost of goods sold decreases, and inventory decreases.
   c. Accounts receivable increases, sales revenue increases, cost of goods sold decreases, and inventory decreases.
   d. Cash increases, sales revenue increases, cost of goods sold increases, and inventory decreases.

DISCUSSION QUESTIONS

Q2-1. The balance sheet consists of assets, liabilities, and equity. Define each category and provide two examples of accounts reported within each category.

Q2-2. Two important concepts that guide income statement reporting are the revenue recognition principle and the matching principle. Define and explain each of these two guiding principles.

Q2-3. IFRS is based on the concept of accrual accounting. Define and describe accrual accounting.

Q2-4. What is the statement of changes in equity? What information is conveyed in that statement?

Q2-5. What are the two essential characteristics of an asset?

Q2-6. What does the concept of liquidity refer to? Explain.

Q2-7. What does the term *current* denote when referring to assets?

Q2-8. Assets are recorded at historical costs even though current market values might, arguably, be more relevant to financial statement readers. Describe the reasoning behind historical cost usage.

Q2-9. Identify three intangible assets that are likely to be excluded from the balance sheet because they cannot be reliably measured.

Q2-10. How does the quick ratio differ from the current ratio?

Q2-11. What three conditions must be satisfied to require reporting of a liability on the balance sheet?

Q2-12. Define net working capital. Explain how increasing the amount of trade credit can reduce the net working capital for a company.

Q2-13. On December 31, 2015, Miller Company had $700,000 in total assets and owed $220,000 to creditors. If this corporation's Share Capital totaled $300,000, what amount of retained earnings is reported on its December 31, 2015, balance sheet?

MINI EXERCISES

M2-14. Determining Retained Earnings and Net Income Using the Balance Sheet LO1

The following information is reported for Kinney Corporation at the end of 2013.

Accounts Receivable	$ 23,000	Retained Earnings	$?
Accounts Payable	11,000	Supplies Inventory	9,000
Cash	8,000	Equipment	138,000
Share Capital	110,000		

a. Compute the amount of retained earnings at the end of 2013.

b. If the amount of retained earnings at the beginning of 2013 was $30,000, and $12,000 in cash dividends were declared and paid during 2013, what was its net income for 2013?

LO1 M2-15. Applying the Accounting Equation to the Balance Sheet
Determine the missing amount in each of the following separate company cases.

	Assets	Liabilities	Equity
a.	$200,000	$85,000	$?
b.	?	32,000	28,000
c.	93,000	?	52,000

LO1 M2-16. Applying the Accounting Equation to the Balance Sheet
Determine the missing amount in each of the following separate company cases.

	Assets	Liabilities	Equity
a.	$375,000	$105,000	$?
b.	?	43,000	11,000
c.	878,000	?	422,000

LO1 M2-17. Applying the Accounting Equation to Determine Unknown Values
Determine the following for each separate company case:

a. The equity of Jensen Corporation, which has assets of $450,000 and liabilities of $326,000.
b. The liabilities of Sloan & Dechow, Inc., which has assets of $618,000 and equity of $165,000.
c. The assets of Clem Corporation, which has liabilities of $400,000, share capital of $200,000, and retained earnings of $185,000.

LO5 M2-18. Analysing Transaction Effects on Equity
Would each of the following transactions increase, decrease, or have no effect on equity?

a. Paid cash to acquire supplies.
b. Paid cash for dividends to shareholders.
c. Paid cash for salaries.
d. Purchased equipment for cash.
e. Shareholders invested cash in business in exchange for ordinary shares.
f. Rendered service to customers on account.
g. Rendered service to customers for cash.

LO1, 3, 5 M2-19. Identifying and Classifying Financial Statement Items
For each of the following items, identify whether they would most likely be reported in the balance sheet (B) or income statement (I).

a. Machinery	____	*e.* Share capital	____	*i.* Taxes expense	____
b. Supplies expense	____	*f.* Factory buildings	____	*j.* Cost of goods sold	____
c. Prepaid advertising	____	*g.* Receivables	____	*k.* Long-term debt	____
d. Advertising expense	____	*h.* Taxes payable	____	*l.* Treasury shares	____

LO2, 3, 4 M2-20. Computing Net Income
Healy Corporation recorded service revenues of $100,000 in 2015, of which $70,000 were for credit and $30,000 were for cash. Moreover, of the $70,000 credit sales for 2015, it collected $20,000 cash on those receivables before year-end 2015. The company also paid $60,000 cash for 2015 wages.

a. Compute the company's net income for 2015.
b. Suppose you discover that employees had earned an additional $10,000 in wages in 2015, but this amount had not been paid. Would 2015 net income change? If so, by how much?

LO1, 3, 5 M2-21. Classifying Items in Financial Statements
Next to each item, indicate whether it would most likely be reported: on the balance sheet (B), the income statement (I), or the statement of changes in equity (SE).

a. Liabilities	____	*d.* Revenues	____	*g.* Assets	____
b. Net income	____	*e.* Share issuance	____	*h.* Expenses	____
c. Cash	____	*f.* Dividends	____	*i.* Equity	____

M2-22. Classifying Items in Financial Statements **LO1, 3, 4, 5**

For each of the following items, indicate whether it is most likely reported on the balance sheet (B), the income statement (I), or the statement of changes in equity (SE).

a.	Accounts receivable	_____	*e.*	Notes payable	_____
b.	Prepaid rent	_____	*f.*	Supplies expense	_____
c.	Net income	_____	*g.*	Land	_____
d.	Equity	_____	*h.*	Supplies	_____

M2-23. Classifying Items in Financial Statements **LO1, 3, 4, 5**

For each of the following items, indicate whether it is most likely reported on the balance sheet (B), the income statement (I), or the statement of changes in equity (SE).

a.	Cash (year-end balance)	_____	*e.*	Dividends	_____
b.	Advertising expense	_____	*f.*	Accounts payable	_____
c.	Share capital	_____	*g.*	Inventory	_____
d.	Printing fees earned	_____	*h.*	Equipment	_____

M2-24. Determining Company Performance and Retained Earnings Using the Accounting Equation **LO4**

Use your knowledge of accounting relations to complete the following table for Silverstrand H.K. Co. (All amounts in $ millions.)

Fiscal year ending	January 29, 2014	January 28, 2015
Beginning retained earnings (deficit)	$2,037	$1,354
Net income (loss).	?	850
Dividends paid.	1,488	?
Increases (decreases) from other retained earnings changes	—	(1,036)
Ending retained earnings (deficit).	?	$ 24

M2-25. Analysing the Effect of Transactions on the Balance Sheet **LO1, 6**

Following the example in *a* below, indicate the effects of transactions *b* through *i* on assets, liabilities, and equity, including identifying the individual accounts affected.

a. Rendered legal services to clients for cash
ANSWER: Increase assets (Cash)
Increase equity (Service Revenues)

b. Purchased office supplies on account

c. Issued additional ordinary shares in exchange for cash

d. Paid amount due on account for office supplies purchased in *b*

e. Borrowed cash (and signed a six-month note) from bank

f. Rendered legal services and billed clients

g. Paid cash to acquire a desk lamp for the office

h. Paid cash to cover interest on note payable to bank

i. Received invoice for this period's utilities

M2-26. Analysing the Effect of Transactions on the Balance Sheet **LO1, 6**

Following the example in *a* below, indicate the effects of transactions *b* through *i* on assets, liabilities, and equity, including identifying the individual accounts affected.

a. Paid cash to acquire a computer for use in office
ANSWER: Increase assets (Office Equipment)
Decrease assets (Cash)

b. Rendered services and billed client

c. Paid cash to cover rent for this period

d. Rendered services to client for cash

e. Received amount due from client in *b*

f. Purchased an office desk on account

g. Paid cash to cover this period's employee salaries

h. Paid cash to cover desk purchased in *f*

i. Declared and paid a cash dividend

LO1, 5 **M2-27. Constructing a Retained Earnings Reconciliation from Financial Data**
Following is financial information from Wynyard Company for the year ended January 1, 2015. Prepare the 2014 fiscal-year retained earnings reconciliation for Wynyard Company ($ millions).

Retained earnings, Jan. 2, 2014	$77,773	Dividends	$6,156
Net earnings	9,672	Retained earnings, Jan. 1, 2015	?
Other retained earnings changes	(38)		

LO3 **M2-28. Analysing Transactions to Compute Net Income**
Guay Corp., a start-up company, provided services that were acceptable to its customers and billed those customers for $350,000 in 2014. However, Guay collected only $280,000 cash in 2014, and the remaining $70,000 of 2014 revenues were collected in 2015. Guay employees earned $200,000 in 2014 wages that were not paid until the first week of 2015. How much net income does Guay report for 2014? For 2015 (assuming no new transactions)?

LO1, 2, 3, 4, 5, 6 **M2-29. Analysing Transactions Using the Financial Statement Effects Template**
Report the effects for each of the following independent transactions using the financial statement effects template provided.

Transaction	Balance Sheet									*Income Statement*				
	Cash Asset	+	Noncash Assets	=	Liabil-ities	+	Contrib. Capital	+	Earned Capital	*Revenues*	-	*Expenses*	=	*Net Income*
a. Issue shares for $1,000 cash.				=							-		=	
b. Purchase inventory for $500 cash.				=							-		=	
c. Sell inventory for $2,000 on credit.				=							-		=	
d. Record $500 for cost of inventory sold in *c.*				=							-		=	
e. Receive $2,000 cash on receivable from *c.*				=							-		=	

LO1, 6 **M2-30. Journalising Business Transactions**
Refer to the transactions in M2-29. Prepare journal entries for each of the transactions *a* through *e*.

LO1, 6 **M2-31. Posting to T-Accounts**
Refer to the transactions in M2-29. Set up T-accounts for each of the accounts referenced by the transactions and post the amounts for each transaction to those T-accounts.

EXERCISES

LO1, 7 **E2-32. Constructing Balance Sheets and Computing Working Capital**
The following balance sheet data are reported for Beaver, Inc., at May 31, 2013.

Accounts Receivable	$18,300	Accounts Payable	$ 5,200
Notes Payable	20,000	Cash	12,200
Equipment	55,000	Share capital	42,500
Supplies	16,400	Retained Earnings	?

Assume that on June 1, 2013, only the following two transactions occurred.

June 1 Purchased additional equipment costing $15,000, giving $2,000 cash and a $13,000 note payable.
Declared and paid a $7,000 cash dividend.

a. Prepare its balance sheet at May 31, 2013.

b. Prepare its balance sheet at June 1, 2013.

c. Calculate its net working capital at June 1, 2013. (Assume that Notes Payable are noncurrent.)

E2-33. Applying the Accounting Equation to Determine Missing Data LO1, 2, 3, 5

For each of the four separate situations *1* through *4* below, compute the unknown amounts referenced by the letters *a* through *d* shown.

	1	2	3	4
Beginning				
Assets	$28,000	$12,000	$28,000	$ (d)
Liabilities	18,600	5,000	19,000	9,000
Ending				
Assets	30,000	26,000	34,000	40,000
Liabilities	17,300	(b)	15,000	19,000
During Year				
Ordinary Share Issued	2,000	4,500	(c)	3,500
Revenues	(a)	28,000	18,000	24,000
Expenses	8,500	21,000	11,000	17,000
Cash Dividends Paid	5,000	1,500	1,000	6,500

E2-34. Preparing Balance Sheets, Computing Income, and Applying the Current and Quick Ratios LO1, 3, 7

Balance sheet information for Lang Services at the end of 2012 and 2013 is:

	December 31, 2013	December 31, 2012
Accounts Receivable	$22,800	$17,500
Notes Payable	1,800	1,600
Cash	10,000	8,000
Equipment	32,000	27,000
Supplies	4,700	4,200
Accounts Payable	25,000	25,000
Equity	?	?

a. Prepare its balance sheet for December 31 of each year.

b. Lang Services raised $5,000 cash through issuing additional ordinary shares early in 2013, and it declared and paid a $17,000 cash dividend in December 2013. Compute its net income or loss for 2013.

c. Calculate the current ratio and quick ratio for 2013.

d. Assume the industry average is 1.5 for the current ratio and 1.0 for the quick ratio. Comment on Lang's current and quick ratios relative to the industry.

E2-35. Constructing Balance Sheets and Determining Income LO1, 3

Following is balance sheet information for Lynch Services at the end of 2012 and 2013.

	December 31, 2013	December 31, 2012
Accounts Payable	$ 6,000	$ 9,000
Cash	23,000	20,000
Accounts Receivable	42,000	33,000
Land	40,000	40,000
Building	250,000	260,000
Equipment	43,000	45,000
Mortgage Payable	90,000	100,000
Supplies	20,000	18,000
Share Capital	220,000	220,000
Retained Earnings	?	?

a. Prepare balance sheets at December 31 of each year.

b. The firm declared and paid a cash dividend of $10,000 in December 2013. Compute its net income for 2013.

LO1, 7 **E2-36. Constructing Balance Sheets and Applying the Current and Quick Ratios**

The following balance sheet data are reported for Brownlee Catering at September 30, 2013.

Accounts Receivable	$17,000	Accounts Payable	$24,000
Notes Payable	12,000	Cash	10,000
Equipment	34,000	Share Capital	27,500
Supplies Inventory	9,000	Retained Earnings	?

Assume that on October 1, 2013, only the following two transactions occurred:

October 1 Purchased additional equipment costing $11,000, giving $3,000 cash and signing an $8,000 note payable.
Declared and paid a cash dividend of $3,000.

Required

a. Prepare Brownlee Catering's balance sheet at September 30, 2013.

b. Prepare the company's balance sheet at the close of business on October 1, 2013.

c. Calculate Brownlee's current and quick ratios on September 30 and October 1. (Assume that Notes Payable are noncurrent.)

d. The October 1, 2013 transactions have decreased Brownlee's current and quick ratios, reflecting a decline in liquidity. Identify two transactions that would increase the company's liquidity.

LO1, 3, 4 **E2-37. Constructing Financial Statements from Transaction Data**

Baiman Corporation commences operations at the beginning of January. It provides its services on credit and bills its customers $30,000 for January sales. Its employees also earn January wages of $12,000 that are not paid until the first of February. Complete the following statements for the month-end of January.

Income Statement		Balance Sheet	
Sales	$	Cash	$ 8,000
Wages expense		Accounts receivable	
Net income (loss)	$	Total assets	$
		Wages payable	$
		Share capital	8,000
		Retained earnings	
		Total liabilities and equity	$

LO1, 3, 4, 7 **E2-38. Classifying Balance Sheet and Income Statement Accounts and Computing Performance and Liquidity Measures**

PHILIPS N.V. (THE NETHERLANDS)

Following are selected accounts for Philips, a Dutch diversified technology company, for December 31, 2013.

(€ millions)	Amount	Classification
Net sales	€23,329	
Income tax expense	466	
Retained earnings	10,415	
Net earnings	1,172	
Property, plant & equipment (net)	2,780	
General & administrative expense	949	
Accounts receivable	4,420	
Total liabilities	15,332	
Equity	11,227	

a. Indicate the appropriate classification of each account as appearing in either its balance sheet (B) or its income statement (I).

b. Using the data, compute its amounts for total assets and for total expenses.

c. Estimate Philips' return on equity (ROE) and its debt-to-equity ratio (ROE and debt-to-equity were defined in Chapter 1).

E2-39. Classifying Balance Sheet and Income Statement Accounts and Computing ROE LO1, 3, 5

Following are selected accounts for Murano S.p.A. at January 29, 2015.

(€ millions)	Amount	Classification
Sales	€67,390	
Depreciation and amortisation	2,084	
Retained earnings	12,698	
Net earnings	2,920	
Property, plant & equipment, net	25,493	
Selling, general & administrative expense	13,469	
Accounts payable	6,625	
Total liabilities and shareholders' investment	43,705	
Total shareholders' investment	15,487	

a. Indicate the appropriate classification of each account as appearing in either its balance sheet (B) or its income statement (I).

b. Using the data, compute Murano's total assets and total expenses.

c. Estimate Murano's return on equity. (ROE was defined in Chapter 1.)

E2-40. Classifying Balance Sheet and Income Statement Accounts and Computing Performance and Liquidity Measures LO1, 3, 7

Following are selected accounts for Jade Asian Ltd. for June 28, 2014.

(Singapore $ millions)	Amount	Classification
Net sales	$2,110	
Interest expense	23	
Retained earnings	1,093	
Net income	24	
Property, plant & equipment, net	329	
Engineering, selling, general & administrative expense	301	
Accounts receivable, net	249	
Total liabilities	928	
Shareholders' investment	738	

a. Indicate the appropriate classification of each account as appearing in either its balance sheet (B) or its income statement (I).

b. Using the data, compute its amounts for total assets and for total expenses.

c. Estimate Jade Asian's return on equity and its debt-to-equity ratio. (ROE and debt-to-equity were defined in Chapter 1.)

E2-41. Classifying Balance Sheet and Income Statement Accounts and Computing Debt-to-Equity LO1, 3, 5

PCCW LIMITED (HONG KONG)

Following are selected accounts for **PCCW Limited**, a Hong Kong telecommunications company, for 2013.

(HK$ millions)	Amount	Classification
Turnover	$27,317	
Cost of sales	13,111	
Retained earnings (accumulated losses)	(9,024)	
Profit for the year	3,055	
Property, plant & equipment, net	15,693	
General & administrative expenses	10,735	
Trade receivables, net	3,501	
Total liabilities	45,304	
Equity	8,633	

a. Indicate the appropriate classification of each account as appearing in either its balance sheet (B) or its income statement (I).

b. Using the data, compute its amounts for total assets and for total expenses.

c. Compute PCCW's debt-to-equity ratio. (Debt-to-equity was defined in Chapter 1.)

LO1, 2 **E2-42. Analysing Transactions Using the Financial Statement Effects Template**
Record the effect of each of the following independent transactions using the financial statements effects template provided. Confirm that Assets = Liabilities + Equity for each transaction.

	Balance Sheet									Income Statement				
Transaction	Cash Asset	+	Noncash Assets	=	Liabil-ities	+	Contrib. Capital	+	Earned Capital	Revenues	-	Expenses	=	Net Income
(1) Receive €50,000 in exchange for ordinary shares.				=							-		=	
(2) Borrow €10,000 from bank.				=							-		=	
(3) Purchase €2,000 of supplies inventory on credit.				=							-		=	
(4) Receive €15,000 cash from customers for services provided.				=							-		=	
(5) Pay €2,000 cash to supplier in transaction (3).				=							-		=	
(6) Receive order for future services with €3,500 advance payment.				=							-		=	
(7) Pay €5,000 cash dividend to shareholders.				=							-		=	
(8) Pay employees €6,000 cash for compensation earned.				=							-		=	
(9) Pay €500 cash for interest on loan in transaction 2.				=							-		=	
Totals				=							-		=	

LO1, 6 **E2-43. Recording Transactions Using Journal Entries and T-Accounts**
Use the information in Exercise 2-42 to complete the following.

a. Prepare journal entries for each of the transactions (1) through (9).
b. Set up T-accounts for each of the accounts used in part *a* and post the journal entries to those T-accounts. (The T-accounts will not have opening balances.)

LO1, 6, 7 **E2-44. Constructing Balance Sheets**
The following balance sheet data are reported for Bettis Contractors at June 30, 2013.

Accounts Payable	$ 8,900	Share Capital	$100,000
Cash	14,700	Retained Earnings	?
Supplies	30,500	Notes Payable	30,000
Equipment	98,000	Accounts Receivable	9,200
Land	25,000		

Assume that during the next two days only the following three transactions occurred:

July 1 Paid $5,000 cash toward the notes payable owed.
2 Purchased equipment for $10,000, paying $2,000 cash and an $8,000 note payable for the remaining balance.
2 Declared and paid a $5,500 cash dividend.

a. Prepare a balance sheet at June 30, 2013.
b. Prepare a balance sheet at July 2, 2013.
c. Calculate its current and quick ratios at June 30, 2013. (Notes Payable is a noncurrent liability.)
d. Assume the industry average is 3.0 for the current ratio and 2.0 for the quick ratio. Comment on Bettis's current and quick ratios relative to the industry.

E2-45. Analysing Transactions Using the Financial Statement Effects Template LO1, 2

Record the effect of each of the following independent transactions using the financial statement effects template provided. Confirm that Assets = Liabilities + Equity.

	Balance Sheet									Income Statement				
Transaction	Cash Asset	+	Noncash Assets	=	Liabil-ities	+	Contrib. Capital	+	Earned Capital	Revenues	-	Expenses	=	Net Income
(1) Receive $20,000 cash in exchange for ordinary shares.				=							-		=	
(2) Purchase $2,000 of inventory on credit.				=							-		=	
(3) Sell inventory for $3,000 on credit.				=							-		=	
(4) Record $2,000 for cost of inventory sold in 3.				=							-		=	
(5) Collect $3,000 cash from transaction 3.				=							-		=	
(6) Acquire $5,000 of equipment by signing a note.				=							-		=	
(7) Pay wages of $1,000 in cash.				=							-		=	
(8) Pay $5,000 on a note payable that came due.				=							-		=	
(9) Pay $2,000 cash dividend.				=							-		=	
Totals				=							-		=	

E2-46. Recording Transactions Using Journal Entries and T-Accounts LO1, 6

Use the information in Exercise 2-45 to complete the following.

a. Prepare journal entries for each of the transactions 1 through 9.
b. Set up T-accounts for each of the accounts used in part *a* and post the journal entries to those T-accounts. (The T-accounts will not have opening balances.)

PROBLEMS

P2-47. Inferring Transactions from Financial Statements LO1, 3

SAMSUNG ELECTRONICS CO. LTD. (SOUTH KOREA)

Samsung Electronics Co. Ltd. is a multinational electronics company with headquarters in Suwon, South Korea and over 200 facilities and offices in 79 countries. Assume that the following transactions have not been recorded (in millions of Korean won):

Revenue	228,692,667
Cost of Sales	137,696,309
Finance costs	7,754,972
Income tax expense	7,889,515

Use the financial statement effects template to record these transactions for Samsung for the fiscal year ended on December 31, 2013.

a. Revenue. Assume that all sales are on credit.
b. Cost of sales.
c. Finance costs. Assume that all costs are paid in cash during the year.
d. Income tax expense. Assume that taxes will be paid the following year.

LO1, 3 **P2-48. Comparing Operating Characteristics Within an Industry**
Selected data from Yin Computer Corp. and Yang Systems, Inc. at October 30, 2015, follow.

($ millions)	Sales	Cost of Goods Sold	Gross Profit	Net Income	Assets	Liabilities	Equity
Yin	$108,249	$64,431	$43,818	$25,922	$116,371	$39,756	$76,615
Yang.........	61,494	50,098	11,396	2,635	38,599	30,833	7,766

Required

a. Compare and discuss the two companies on the basis of how they finance their operations.
b. Which company reports the higher ratio of income to assets (net income/total assets)? Suggest a reason for this result.
c. Which firm has the higher gross margin (gross profit as a percentage of sales)? What factors might account for the difference?

LO1, 3 **P2-49. Comparing Operating Characteristics Within an Industry**

PCCW LIMITED (HONG KONG)
VODAFONE GROUP (UNITED KINGDOM)

Review the following selected income statement and balance sheet data for telecommunications companies PCCW Limited (Hong Kong) and Vodafone Group (United Kingdom) for the year 2013.

(millions)	Sales	Cost of Goods Sold	Gross Profit	Net Income	Assets	Liabilities	Equity
PCCW (HK$ mil.)	27,317	13,111	14,206	3,055	53,937	45,304	8,633
Vodafone (£ mil.)	38,346	27,942	10,404	11,312	121,840	50,059	71,781

Required

a. Using the data above, compare and discuss how PCCW and Vodafone finance their operations.
b. Which company reports the higher ratio of income to assets (net income/total assets)? Suggest a reason for this result.
c. Which company is likely better able to raise capital? Explain.

LO1, 3, 7 **P2-50. Comparing Operating Structure Across Industries**
Review the following selected income statement and balance sheet data from the years 2014 and 2015.

($ millions)	Current Assets	Long-term Assets	Total Assets	Current Liab.	Long-term Liab.	Total Liab.	Equity
Company A*....................	$12,240	$19,376	$ 31,616	$ 5,441	$10,313	$15,754	$15,862
Company B**..................	1,489	1,559	3,048	706	480	1,186	1,862
Company C†....................	44,988	71,383	116,371	27,970	11,786	39,756	76,615

* Manufacturer of consumer and business products
** Retailer of name-brand apparel at premium prices
† Computer company

Required

a. Compare and discuss how these companies finance their operations.
b. Which company has the greatest net working capital? Do you have any concerns about any firm's net working capital position? Explain.

LO1, 3, 5 **P2-51. Preparing a Balance Sheet, Computing Net Income, and Understanding Equity Transactions**
At the beginning of 2013, Barth Company reported the following balance sheet.

Assets		Liabilities	
Cash	$ 4,800	Accounts payable	$12,000
Accounts receivable	14,700	**Equity**	
Equipment	10,000	Share capital	47,500
Land	50,000	Retained earnings	20,000
Total assets	$79,500	Total liabilities and equity	$79,500

Required

a. At the end of 2013, Barth Company reported the following assets and liabilities: Cash, $8,800; Accounts Receivable, $18,400; Equipment, $9,000; Land, $50,000; and Accounts Payable, $7,500. Prepare a year-end balance sheet for Barth. (*Hint:* Report equity as a single total.)

b. Assuming that Barth did not issue any ordinary shares during the year but paid $12,000 cash in dividends, what was its net income or net loss for 2013?

c. Assuming that Barth issued an additional $13,500 ordinary shares early in the year but paid $21,000 cash in dividends before the end of the year, what was its net income or net loss for 2013?

P2-52. Analysing and Interpreting the Financial Performance of Competitors LO1, 3

Air Canada and WestJet Airlines Ltd. are two airlines in Canada. Following are selected data from their fiscal-year ended December 31, 2013, financial statements:

AIR CANADA (CANADA)
WESTJET AIRLINES LTD. (CANADA)

(millions)	Air Canada (Cdn$ mil.)	WestJet (Cdn$ mil.)
Total liabilities and equity	$ 9,470	$4,143
Net income	10	269
Net sales	12,382	3,662
Total liabilities	10,867	2,554
Current assets	3,288	1,526
Current liabilities	3,190	1,406

Required

a. What is the total amount of assets invested in (1) Air Canada and (2) WestJet? What are the total expenses for each company (1) in dollars and (2) as a percentage of sales?

b. What is the net working capital and current ratio for (1) Air Canada and (2) WestJet?

P2-53. Analysing Balance Sheet Numbers from Incomplete Data and Interpreting Liquidity Measures LO1, 3, 4, 6, 7

Selected balance sheet amounts for Gold Coast Company, an Australian manufacturer of consumer and business products, for six recent years follow:

($ millions)	Current Assets	Long-term Assets	Total Assets	Current Liabilities	Long-term Liabilities	Total Liabilities	Total Equity
2009	?	12,348	21,294	7,323	4,012	11,335	?
2010	9,838	14,856	?	?	7,585	12,947	11,747
2011	9,598	15,949	?	5,839	9,829	?	9,879
2012	?	16,455	27,250	4,897	9,051	13,948	?
2013	12,215	17,941	?	6,089	8,050	?	16,017
2014	?	19,376	31,616	5,441	10,313	15,754	?

Required

a. Compute the missing balance sheet amounts for each of the six years shown.

b. What types of accounts would you expect to be included in current assets? In long-term assets?

c. Calculate the current ratio for 2009 and 2014.

d. Assume the industry average is 2.0 for the current ratio. Comment on Gold Coast's current ratio relative to the industry.

P2-54. Analysing and Interpreting Balance Sheet Data and Interpreting Liquidity Measures LO1, 3, 7

Selected balance sheet amounts for Lamma, Inc., a retailer of name-brand apparel at premium prices, for seven recent fiscal years follow.

($ millions)	Current Assets	Long-term Assets	Total Assets	Current Liabilities	Long-term Liabilities	Total Liabilities	Total Equity
2009	947	?	1,790	?	303	795	?
2010	?	1,156	2,248	511	?	843	1,405
2011	1,140	1,428	?	543	406	949	?
2012	1,084	?	2,848	?	553	1,003	1,845
2013	1,236	1,586	?	449	?	994	1,828
2014	1,427	?	2,941	552	498	1,050	1,891
2015	1,489	1,559	?	705	480	?	1,863

Required

a. Compute the missing balance sheet amounts for each of the seven years shown.
b. What asset category would you expect to constitute the majority of its current assets?
c. Has the proportion of current and long-term assets changed markedly over the past seven years? Explain.
d. Does the company appear to be conservatively financed; that is, financed by a greater proportion of equity than of debt? Explain.
e. Calculate the current ratio for 2009 and 2015.
f. Assume the industry average is 2.25 for the current ratio. Comment on the company's current ratio relative to the industry.

LO1, 2, 3, 4 **P2-55. Analysing Transactions Using the Financial Statement Effects Template and Preparing an Income Statement**

On December 1, 2013, R. Lambert formed Lambert Services, which provides career and vocational counselling services to graduating college students. The following transactions took place during December, and company accounts include the following: Cash, Accounts Receivable, Land, Accounts Payable, Notes Payable, Share Capital, Retained Earnings, Counseling Services Revenue, Rent Expense, Advertising Expense, Interest Expense, Salary Expense, and Utilities Expense.

1. Raised $7,000 cash through ordinary share issuance.
2. Paid $750 cash for December rent on its furnished office space.
3. Received $500 invoice for December advertising expenses.
4. Borrowed $15,000 cash from bank and signed note payable for that amount.
5. Received $1,200 cash for counselling services rendered.
6. Billed clients $6,800 for counselling services rendered.
7. Paid $2,200 cash for secretary salary.
8. Paid $370 cash for December utilities.
9. Declared and paid a $900 cash dividend.
10. Purchased land for $13,000 cash to use for its own facilities.
11. Paid $100 cash to bank as December interest expense on note payable.

Required

a. Report the effects for each of the separate transactions 1 through 11 using the financial statement effects template. Total all columns and prove that (1) assets equal liabilities plus equity at December 31, and (2) revenues less expenses equal net income for December.
b. Prepare an income statement for the month of December.

LO6 **P2-56. Recording Transactions in Journal Entries and T-Accounts**

Use the information in Problem 2-55 to complete the following requirements.

Required

a. Prepare journal entries for each of the transactions 1 through 11.
b. Set up T-accounts for each of the accounts used in part *a* and post the journal entries to those T-accounts.

LO1, 3, 4, 6, 7 **P2-57. Analysing and Interpreting Balance Sheet Data and Interpreting Liquidity Measures**

Selected balance sheet amounts for Raffles, Inc., a consumer electronics and computer company, for seven recent fiscal years follow.

($ millions)	Current Assets	Long-term Assets	Total Assets	Current Liabilities	Long-term Liabilities	Total Liabilities	Total Equity
2010	?	2,696	17,205	6,443	?	7,221	?
2011	21,956	?	25,347	?	1,535	10,815	14,532
2012	34,690	4,882	?	14,092	?	18,542	21,030
2013	31,555	?	47,501	11,506	?	15,861	31,640
2014	?	33,505	75,183	20,722	?	27,392	?
2015	44,988	71,383	?	27,970	?	?	76,615

Required

a. Compute the missing balance sheet amounts for each of the six years shown.

b. What asset category would you expect to constitute the majority of the company's current assets? Of its long-term assets?

c. Is the company conservatively financed; that is, is it financed by a greater proportion of equity than of debt?

d. Calculate the current ratio for 2010 and 2015.

e. Assume the industry average is 2.0 for the current ratio. Comment on the company's current ratio relative to the industry.

P2-58. Analysing Balance Sheet Numbers from Incomplete Data and Calculating Working Capital LO1, 3, 4, 6, 7

RONA, INC. (CANADA)

Selected balance sheet amounts for RONA, Inc., a Canadian distributor and retailer of hardware, building materials and home renovation products, for six recent years follow.

($ millions)	Current Assets	Long-term Assets	Total Assets	Current Liabilities	Long-term Liabilities	Total Liabilities	Total Equity
2008	1,064	1,442	2,506	845	?	?	1,493
2009	1,237	1,468	?	433	?	930	1,775
2010	1,301	?	2,922	?	514	1,010	1,912
2011	1,250	1,520	?	519	296	?	1,955
2012	?	1,493	2,797	?	376	914	?
2013	1,036	?	2,343	423	249	?	1,671

Required

a. Compute the missing amounts for each of the six years shown.

b. What asset categories would you expect to be included in its current assets? In its long-term assets?

c. Is the company conservatively financed; that is, is it financed by a greater proportion of equity than of debt? Explain.

d. Calculate net working capital for 2008 and 2013.

P2-59. Analysing and Interpreting Income Statement Data LO1, 3

BILLABONG INTERNATIONAL LTD. (AUSTRALIA)

Selected income statement information for Billabong International Limited, an Australian clothing retailer, for the four recent fiscal years follows.

(A$ '000)	Revenues	Cost of Goods Sold	Gross Profit	Operating Expenses	Operating Income
2011	1,558,459	?	830,161	741,477	?
2012	1,444,079	765,313	?	1,201,431	?
2013	?	541,466	566,026	?	(653,871)
2014	1,125,454	?	?	704,932	(135,236)

Required

a. Compute the missing amounts for each of the four years shown.

b. Compute the gross profit margin (gross profit/sales) for each of the four years. Comment on the company's operating performance, indicating any trends that are evident.

c. What would you expect to be the major cost categories constituting its operating expenses?

LO1, 2, 3, 4 **P2-60. Analysing Transactions Using the Financial Statement Effects Template and Preparing an Income Statement**

On June 1, 2013, a group of pilots in Melbourne, Australia, formed Outback Flights by issuing ordinary shares for $50,000 cash. The group then leased several amphibious aircraft and docking facilities, equipping them to transport campers and hunters to outpost camps owned by various resorts in remote parts of Australia. The following transactions occurred during June 2013, and company accounts include the following: Cash, Accounts Receivable, Prepaid Insurance, Accounts Payable, Share Capital, Retained Earnings, Flight Services Revenue, Rent Expense, Entertainment Expense, Advertising Expense, Insurance Expense, Wages Expense, and Fuel Expense.

1. Issued ordinary shares for $50,000 cash.
2. Paid $4,800 cash for June rent of aircraft, dockage, and dockside office.
3. Received $1,600 invoice for the cost of a reception to entertain resort owners in June.
4. Paid $900 cash for June advertising in various sport magazines.
5. Paid $1,800 cash for insurance premium for July.
6. Rendered flight services for various groups for $22,700 cash.
7. Billed client $2,900 for transporting personnel, and billed various firms for $13,000 in flight services.
8. Paid $1,500 cash to cover accounts payable.
9. Received $13,200 on account from clients in transaction 7.
10. Paid $16,000 cash to cover June wages.
11. Received $3,500 invoice for the cost of fuel used during June.
12. Declared and paid a $3,000 cash dividend.

Required

a. Report the effects for each of the separate transactions 1 through 12 using the financial statement effects template. Total all columns and prove that (1) assets equal liabilities plus equity at June 30, 2013, and (2) revenues less expenses equal net income for June.

b. Prepare an income statement for the month of June.

LO6 **P2-61. Recording Transactions in Journal Entries and T-Accounts**

Use the information in Problem 2-60 to complete the following requirements.

Required

a. Prepare journal entries for each of the transactions 1 through 12.

b. Set up T-accounts for each of the accounts used in part *a* and post the journal entries to those T-accounts.

LO1, 3 **P2-62. Analysing and Interpreting Income Statement Numbers from Incomplete Data**

Selected income statement information for Casa Loma Company, a coffee-related restaurant chain, for seven recent fiscal years follows.

($ millions)	Sales	Cost of Goods Sold	Gross Profit	Operating Expenses	Operating Income	Other Expenses	Net Income
2009	?	2,605	3,764	?	781	287	?
2010	7,787	?	4,608	?	?	329	564
2011	9,412	3,999	?	4,359	1,054	?	673
2012	10,383	?	5,738	?	460	144	316
2013	?	4,325	5,450	4,888	562	171	?
2014	10,707	?	6,248	4,829	?	473	946
2015	11,700	4,949	?	?	1,728	?	1,246

Required

a. Compute the missing amounts for each of the seven years shown.

b. Compute the gross profit margin (gross profit/sales) for each of the seven years and comment on its level and any trends that are evident.

c. What would you expect to be the major cost categories constituting its operating expenses?

LO3 **P2-63. Analysing, Reconstructing, and Interpreting Income Statement Data**

Selected income statement information for Perth Corporation, a department store chain, for seven recent fiscal years follows:

($ millions)	Revenues	Cost of Goods Sold	Gross Profit	Operating Expenses	Operating Income	Other Expenses	Net Income
2009	?	34,927	17,693	?	?	1,915	2,408
2010	59,490	39,399	?	?	5,069	?	2,787
2011	?	41,895	21,472	16,200	5,272	2,423	?
2012	64,948	44,157	?	16,389	4,402	?	2,214
2013	65,357	?	21,295	?	4,673	?	2,488
2014	67,390	45,725	21,665	16,413	5,252	2,332	?
2015	69,865	47,860	?	16,683	5,322	?	2,929

Required

a. Compute the missing amounts for each of the seven years shown.

b. Compute the gross profit margin (gross profit/sales) for each of the seven years and comment on its level and any trends that are evident.

c. What would we expect to be the major cost categories constituting its operating expenses?

P2-64. Preparing the Income Statement, Statement of Changes in Equity, and the Balance Sheet LO1, 3, 4, 5

The records of Geyer, Inc., show the following information after all transactions are recorded for 2013.

Notes Payable	$ 4,000	Supplies	$ 6,100
Service Fees Earned	67,600	Cash	14,800
Supplies Expense	9,700	Advertising Expense	1,700
Insurance Expense	1,500	Salaries Expense	30,000
Miscellaneous Expense	200	Rent Expense	7,500
Share Capital (beg. year)	4,000	Retained Earnings (beg. year)	6,200
Accounts Payable	1,800		

Geyer, Inc., raised $1,400 cash through the issuance of additional ordinary shares during this year and it declared and paid a $13,500 cash dividend near year-end.

Required

a. Prepare its income statement for 2013.

b. Prepare its statement of changes in equity for 2013.

c. Prepare its balance sheet at December 31, 2013.

P2-65. Analysing Transactions Using the Financial Statement Effects Template and Preparing Financial Statements LO1, 2, 3, 4, 5

Schrand Aerobics, Inc., rents studio space (including a sound system) and specialises in offering aerobics classes. On January 1, 2013, its beginning account balances are as follows: Cash, $5,000; Accounts Receivable, $5,200; Equipment, $0; Notes Payable, $2,500; Accounts Payable, $1,000; Share Capital, $5,500; Retained Earnings, $1,200; Services Revenue, $0; Rent Expense, $0; Advertising Expense, $0; Wages Expense, $0; Utilities Expense, $0; Interest Expense, $0. The following transactions occurred during January.

1. Paid $600 cash toward accounts payable.
2. Paid $3,600 cash for January rent.
3. Billed clients $11,500 for January classes.
4. Received $500 invoice from supplier for T-shirts given to January class members as an advertising promotion.
5. Collected $10,000 cash from clients previously billed for services rendered.
6. Paid $2,400 cash for employee wages.
7. Received $680 invoice for January utilities expense.
8. Paid $20 cash to bank as January interest on notes payable.
9. Declared and paid $900 cash dividend to shareholders.
10. Paid $4,000 cash on January 31 to purchase sound equipment to replace the rental system.

Required

a. Using the financial statement effects template, enter January 1 beginning amounts in the appropriate columns of the first row. (*Hint:* Beginning balances for columns can include amounts from more than one account.)

b. Report the effects for each of the separate transactions *1* through *10* in the financial statement effects template set up in part *a*. Total all columns and prove that (1) assets equal liabilities plus equity at January 31, and (2) revenues less expenses equal net income for January.

c. Prepare its income statement for January 2013.

d. Prepare its statement of changes in equity for January 2013.

e. Prepare its balance sheet at January 31, 2013.

LO6 **P2-66. Recording Transactions in Journal Entries and T-Accounts**

Use the information in Problem 2-65 to complete the following requirements.

Required

a. Prepare journal entries for each of the transactions 1 through 10.

b. Set up T-accounts, including beginning balances, for each of the accounts used in part *a*. Post the journal entries to those T-accounts.

LO1, 2, 3, 4, 5 **P2-67. Analysing Transactions Using the Financial Statement Effects Template and Preparing Financial Statements**

Kross, Inc., provides appraisals and feasibility studies. On January 1, 2013, its beginning account balances are as follows: Cash, $6,700; Accounts Receivable, $14,800; Notes Payable, $2,500; Accounts Payable, $600; Retained Earnings, $12,400; and Share Capital, $6,000. The following transactions occurred during January, and company accounts include the following: Cash, Accounts Receivable, Vehicles, Accounts Payable, Notes Payable, Services Revenue, Rent Expense, Interest Expense, Salary Expense, Utilities Expense, Share Capital, and Retained Earnings.

1. Paid $950 cash for January rent.
2. Received $8,800 cash on customers' accounts.
3. Paid $500 cash toward accounts payable.
4. Received $1,600 cash for services performed for customers.
5. Borrowed $5,000 cash from bank and signed note payable for that amount.
6. Billed the city $6,200 for services performed, and billed other credit customers for $1,900 in services.
7. Paid $4,000 cash for salary of assistant.
8. Received $410 invoice for January utilities expense.
9. Declared and paid a $6,000 cash dividend.
10. Paid $9,800 cash to acquire a vehicle (on January 31) for business use.
11. Paid $50 cash to bank for January interest on notes payable.

Required

a. Using the financial statement effects template, enter January 1 beginning amounts in the appropriate columns of the first row. (*Hint:* Beginning balances for columns can include amounts from more than one account.)

b. Report the effects for each of the separate transactions 1 through 11 in the financial statement effects template set up in part *a*. Total all columns and prove that (1) assets equal liabilities plus equity at January 31, and (2) revenues less expenses equal net income for January.

c. Prepare its income statement for January 2013.

d. Prepare its statement of changes in equity for January 2013.

e. Prepare its balance sheet at January 31, 2013.

LO6 **P2-68. Recording Transactions in Journal Entries and T-Accounts**

Use the information in Problem 2-67 to complete the following requirements.

Required

a. Prepare journal entries for each of the transactions 1 through 11.

b. Set up T-accounts, including beginning balances, for each of the accounts used in part *a*. Post the journal entries to those T-accounts.

CASES AND PROJECTS

C2-69. Constructing Financial Statements from Cash Data LO1, 3, 4, 5, 6

Sarah Penney operates the Wildlife Picture Gallery, selling original art and signed prints received on consignment (rather than purchased) from recognised wildlife artists throughout the country. The firm receives a 30% commission on all art sold and remits 70% of the sales price to the artists. All art is sold on a strictly cash basis.

Sarah began the business on March 1, 2013. The business received a $10,000 loan from a relative of Sarah to help her get started; it took on a note payable agreeing to pay the loan back in one year. No interest is being charged on the loan, but the relative does want to receive a set of financial statements each month. On April 1, 2013, Sarah asks for your help in preparing the statements for the first month.

Sarah has carefully kept the firm's checking account up to date and provides you with the following complete listing of the cash receipts and cash disbursements for March 2013.

Cash Receipts	
Original investment by Sarah Penney	$ 6,500
Loan from relative	10,000
Sales of art	95,000
Total cash receipts	111,500
Cash Disbursements	
Payments to artists for sales made	54,000
Payment of March rent for gallery space	900
Payment of March wages to staff	4,900
Payment of airfare for personal vacation of Sarah (vacation will be in April)	500
Total cash disbursements	60,300
Cash balance, March 31, 2013	$ 51,200

Sarah also gives you the following documents she has received:

1. A $350 invoice for March utilities; payment is due by April 15, 2013.
2. A $1,700 invoice from Careful Express for the shipping of artwork sold in March; payment is due by April 10, 2013.
3. Sarah signed a one-year lease for the gallery space; as an incentive to sign the lease, the landlord reduced the first month's rent by 25%; the monthly rent starting in April is $1,200.

In your discussions with Sarah, she tells you that she has been so busy that she is behind in sending artists their share of the sales proceeds. She plans to catch up within the next week.

Required

From the above information, prepare the following financial statements for Wildlife Picture Gallery: (*a*) income statement for the month of March 2013; (*b*) statement of changes in equity for the month of March 2013; and (*c*) balance sheet as of March 31, 2013.

C2-70. Financial Records and Ethical Behaviour LO3

Andrea Frame and her supervisor are sent on an out-of-town assignment by their employer. At the supervisor's suggestion, they stay at the Spartan Inn (across the street from the Luxury Inn). After three days of work, they settle their lodging bills and leave. On the return trip, the supervisor gives Andrea what appears to be a copy of a receipt from the Luxury Inn for three nights of lodging. Actually, the supervisor indicates that he prepared the Luxury Inn receipt on his office computer and plans to complete his expense reimbursement request using the higher lodging costs from the Luxury Inn.

Required

What are the ethical considerations that Andrea faces when she prepares her expense reimbursement request?

SOLUTIONS TO REVIEW PROBLEMS

Mid-Chapter Review 1

Solution

1. A	2. C	3. B	4. E	5. B	6. E	7. X	8. B	9. E	10. B
11. X	12. A	13. B	14. C	15. A	16. D	17. A	18. A	19. E	20. C

Mid-Chapter Review 2

Solution

	Balance Sheet									Income Statement				
Transaction	Cash Asset	+	Noncash Assets	=	Liabil-ities	+	Contrib. Capital	+	Earned Capital	*Revenues*	-	*Expenses*	=	*Net Income*
(a) Issue ordinary shares for $20,000.	+20,000 Cash			=			+20,000 Share Capital				-		=	
(b) Purchase $8,000 of inventory on credit.			+8,000 Inventory	=	+8,000 Accounts Payable						-		=	
(c) Purchase equipment for $10,000 cash.	−10,000 Cash		+10,000 Equipment	=							-		=	
(d) Pay suppliers $3,000 cash.	−3,000 Cash			=	−3,000 Accounts Payable						-		=	
Totals	+7,000		+18,000	=	+5,000		+20,000							
	Assets			=	Liabilities	+	Equity							

Mid-Chapter Review 3

Solution to Part 1

SCHAEFER'S PHARMACY, INC.
Income Statement
For Year Ended December 31, 2015

Revenues		$25,000
Expenses		
Wages expense	$8,000	
Rent expense	5,000	
Utilities expense	2,000	
Other expenses	4,000	
Total expenses		19,000
Net income		$ 6,000

Solution to Part 2

SCHAEFER'S PHARMACY, INC.
Retained Earnings Reconciliation
For Year Ended December 31, 2015

Retained earnings, Dec. 31, 2014	$25,000
Add: Net income	6,000
Less: Dividends	(1,000)
Retained earnings, Dec. 31, 2015	$30,000

Solution to Part 3

SCHAEFER'S PHARMACY, INC. Balance Sheet December 31, 2015			
Cash	$ 3,000	Accounts payable	$ 7,500
Accounts receivable	12,000		
Office equipment	32,250	Share capital	45,750
Land	36,000	Retained earnings	30,000
Total assets	$83,250	Total liabilities and equity	$83,250

Chapter-End Review

Solution

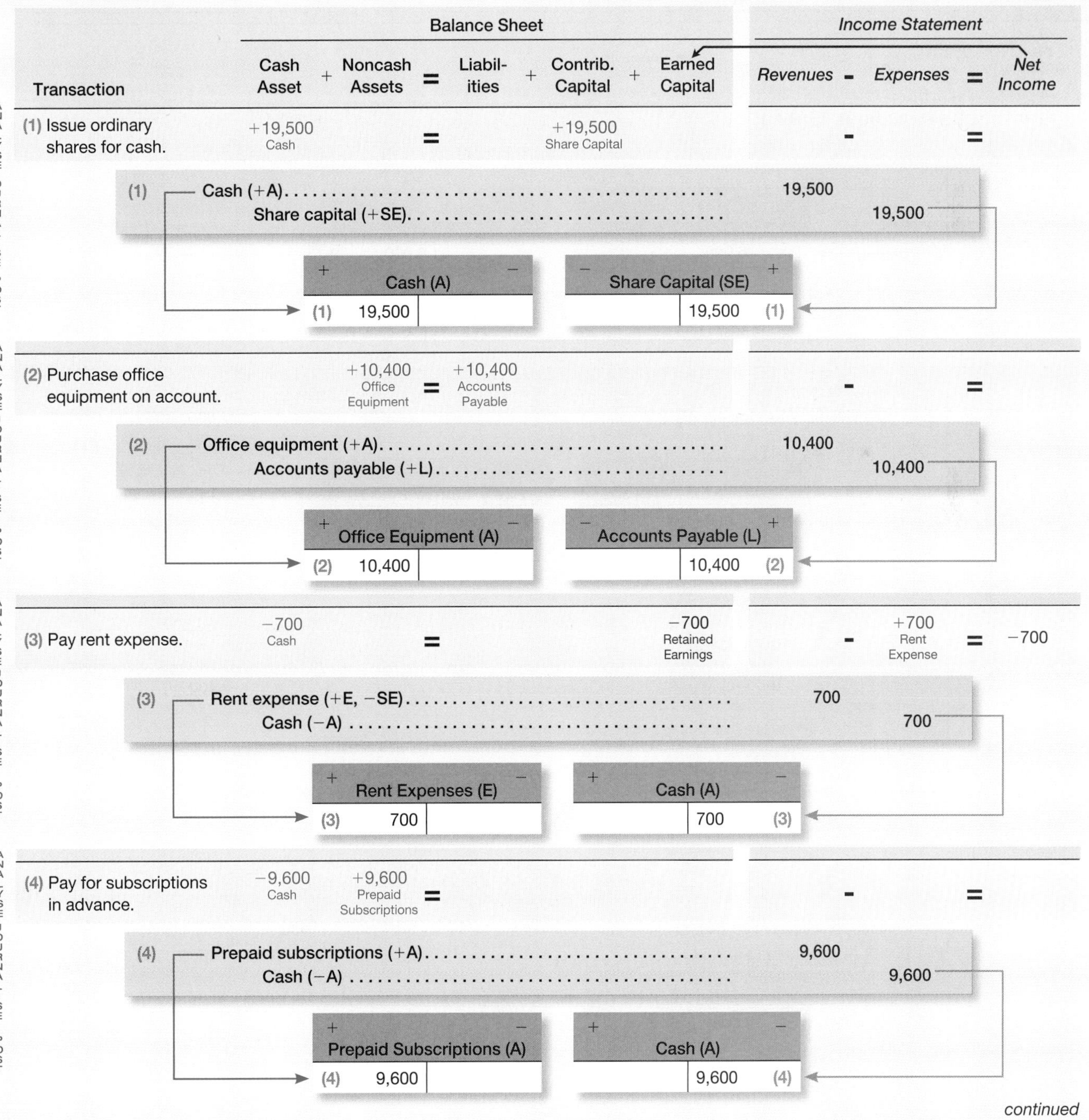

Transaction	Cash Asset	+ Noncash Assets	= Liabilities	+ Contrib. Capital	+ Earned Capital	Revenues	− Expenses	= Net Income
(1) Issue ordinary shares for cash.	+19,500 Cash			+19,500 Share Capital				
(2) Purchase office equipment on account.		+10,400 Office Equipment	+10,400 Accounts Payable					
(3) Pay rent expense.	−700 Cash				−700 Retained Earnings		+700 Rent Expense	−700
(4) Pay for subscriptions in advance.	−9,600 Cash	+9,600 Prepaid Subscriptions						

ANALYSE JOURNALISE POST

(1) Cash (+A) 19,500
Share capital (+SE) 19,500

Cash (A): (1) 19,500 |
Share Capital (SE): | 19,500 (1)

(2) Office equipment (+A) 10,400
Accounts payable (+L) 10,400

Office Equipment (A): (2) 10,400 |
Accounts Payable (L): | 10,400 (2)

(3) Rent expense (+E, −SE) 700
Cash (−A) 700

Rent Expenses (E): (3) 700 |
Cash (A): | 700 (3)

(4) Prepaid subscriptions (+A) 9,600
Cash (−A) 9,600

Prepaid Subscriptions (A): (4) 9,600 |
Cash (A): | 9,600 (4)

continued

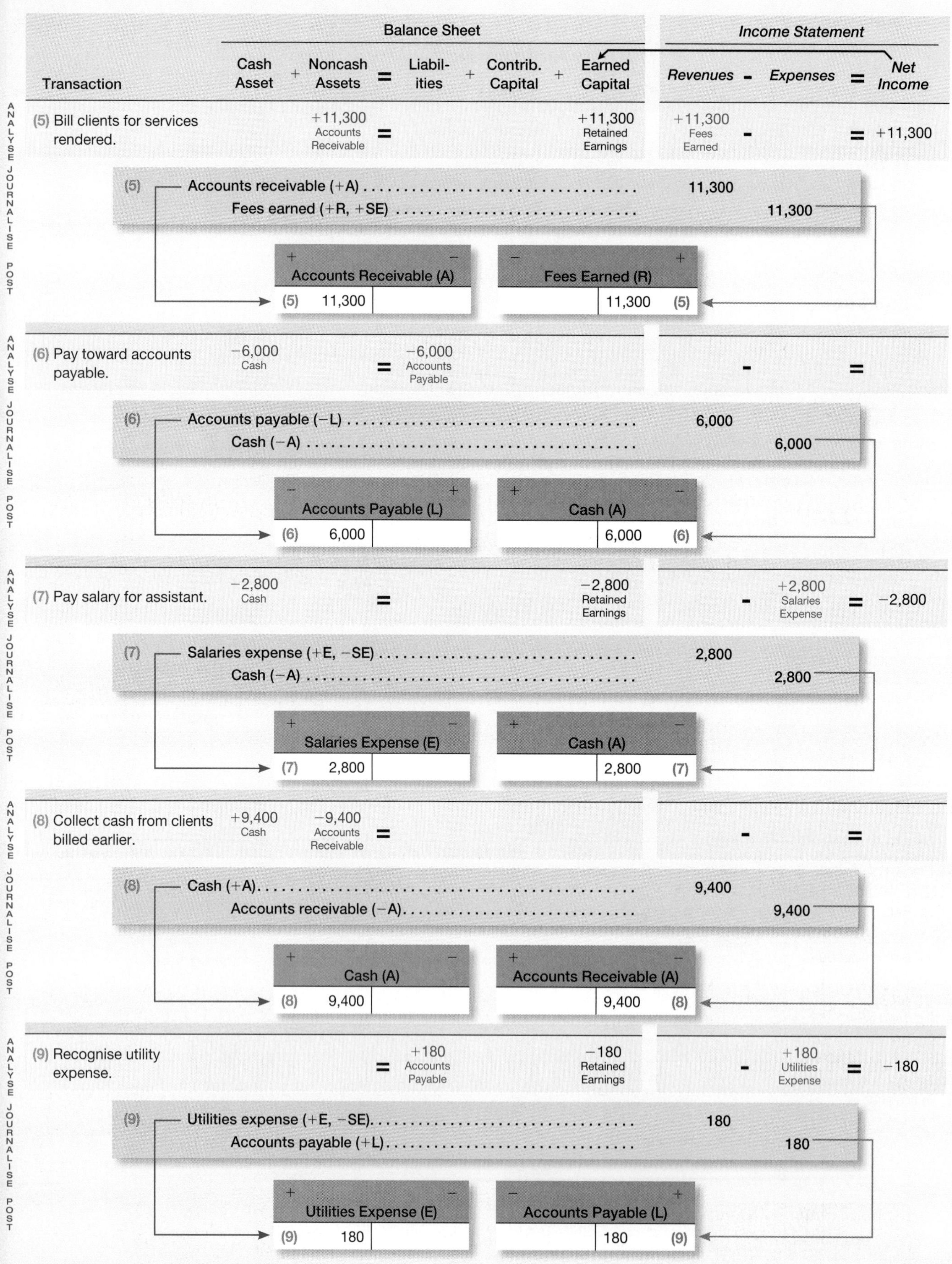
Balance Sheet
Income Statement
Transaction
Cash Asset + Noncash Assets = Liabil-ities + Contrib. Capital + Earned Capital
Revenues - Expenses = Net Income
ANALYSE JOURNALISE POST
(5) Bill clients for services rendered.
+11,300 Accounts Receivable = +11,300 Retained Earnings
+11,300 Fees Earned - = +11,300
(5) Accounts receivable (+A) 11,300
Fees earned (+R, +SE) 11,300
+ Accounts Receivable (A) −
(5) 11,300
− Fees Earned (R) +
11,300 (5)
(6) Pay toward accounts payable.
−6,000 Cash = −6,000 Accounts Payable
- =
(6) Accounts payable (−L) 6,000
Cash (−A) 6,000
− Accounts Payable (L) +
(6) 6,000
+ Cash (A) −
6,000 (6)
(7) Pay salary for assistant.
−2,800 Cash = −2,800 Retained Earnings
- +2,800 Salaries Expense = −2,800
(7) Salaries expense (+E, −SE) 2,800
Cash (−A) 2,800
+ Salaries Expense (E) −
(7) 2,800
+ Cash (A) −
2,800 (7)
(8) Collect cash from clients billed earlier.
+9,400 Cash −9,400 Accounts Receivable =
- =
(8) Cash (+A) 9,400
Accounts receivable (−A) 9,400
+ Cash (A) −
(8) 9,400
+ Accounts Receivable (A) −
9,400 (8)
(9) Recognise utility expense.
= +180 Accounts Payable −180 Retained Earnings
- +180 Utilities Expense = −180
(9) Utilities expense (+E, −SE) 180
Accounts payable (+L) 180
+ Utilities Expense (E) −
(9) 180
− Accounts Payable (L) +
180 (9)

continued

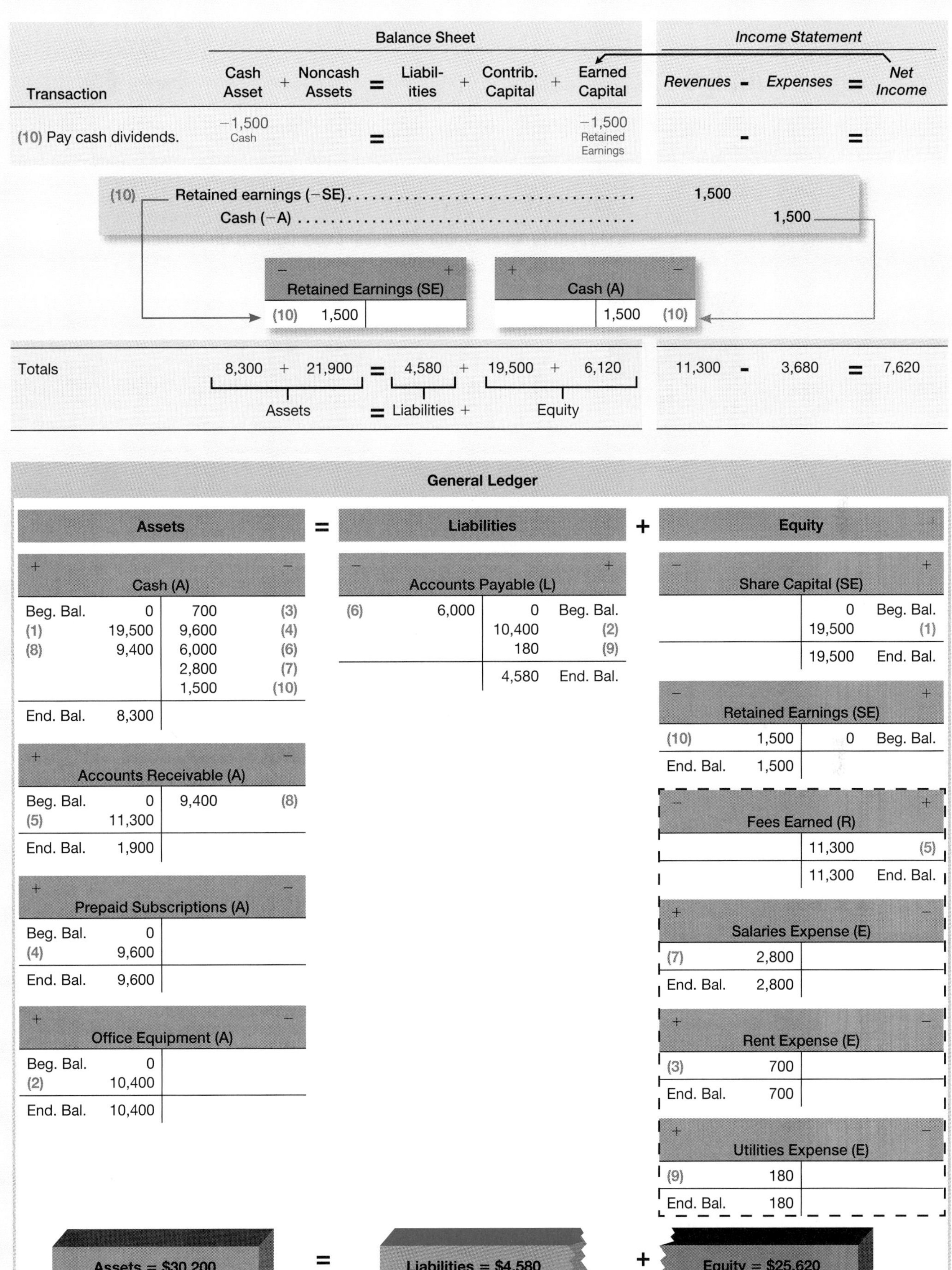

ANALYSE JOURNALISE POST
Balance Sheet
Income Statement
Transaction
Cash Asset + Noncash Assets = Liabil-ities + Contrib. Capital + Earned Capital
Revenues - Expenses = Net Income
(10) Pay cash dividends.
−1,500 Cash
−1,500 Retained Earnings
(10) Retained earnings (−SE) 1,500
Cash (−A) 1,500
Retained Earnings (SE)
(10) 1,500
Cash (A)
1,500 (10)
Totals 8,300 + 21,900 = 4,580 + 19,500 + 6,120
11,300 - 3,680 = 7,620
Assets = Liabilities + Equity
General Ledger
Assets = Liabilities + Equity
Cash (A)
Beg. Bal. 0 | 700 (3)
(1) 19,500 | 9,600 (4)
(8) 9,400 | 6,000 (6)
2,800 (7)
1,500 (10)
End. Bal. 8,300
Accounts Receivable (A)
Beg. Bal. 0 | 9,400 (8)
(5) 11,300
End. Bal. 1,900
Prepaid Subscriptions (A)
Beg. Bal. 0
(4) 9,600
End. Bal. 9,600
Office Equipment (A)
Beg. Bal. 0
(2) 10,400
End. Bal. 10,400
Accounts Payable (L)
(6) 6,000 | 0 Beg. Bal.
10,400 (2)
180 (9)
4,580 End. Bal.
Share Capital (SE)
0 Beg. Bal.
19,500 (1)
19,500 End. Bal.
Retained Earnings (SE)
(10) 1,500 | 0 Beg. Bal.
End. Bal. 1,500
Fees Earned (R)
11,300 (5)
11,300 End. Bal.
Salaries Expense (E)
(7) 2,800
End. Bal. 2,800
Rent Expense (E)
(3) 700
End. Bal. 700
Utilities Expense (E)
(9) 180
End. Bal. 180
Assets = $30,200
Liabilities = $4,580
Equity = $25,620

Note: Income statement T-accounts do not have a beginning balance. More in Chapter 3.

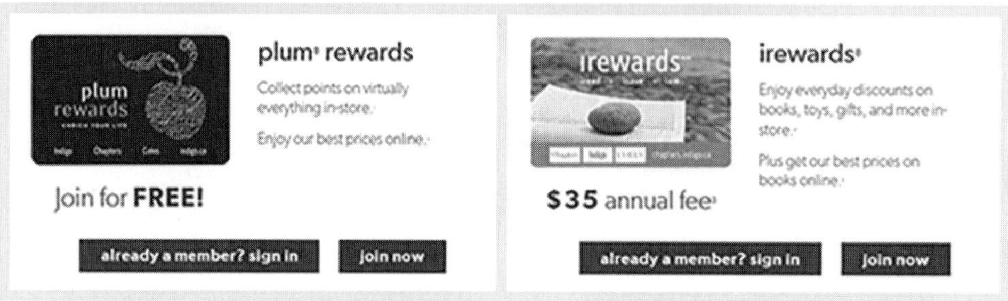

LEARNING OBJECTIVES

1. Identify the major steps in the accounting cycle. (p. 94)
2. Review the process of journalising and posting transactions. (p. 95)
3. Describe the adjusting process and illustrate adjusting entries. (p. 101)
4. Prepare financial statements from adjusted accounts. (p. 110)
5. Describe the process of closing temporary accounts. (p. 114)
6. Analyse changes in balance sheet accounts. (p. 117)

CHAPTER

3

Adjusting Accounts for Financial Statements

INDIGO
www.indigo.ca

Indigo's strategy of growing sales and profits has been to add stores, either through store openings or acquisitions of other booksellers such as Chapters Inc. However, the bookselling and retail industries have undergone dramatic changes. The Internet and mobile devices offer consumers new reading platforms with easy access to a large number of titles, as well as an increased selection of merchandise at a competitive price. As a result, Indigo has experienced decreasing revenues in the last five years and reported losses in three of those five years.

In response to these challenges, founder Heather Reisman has been investing in a process of "reinvention" to establish Indigo as the world's first cultural department store. Specifically, Indigo adapts its physical stores to expand its lifestyle, paper and toy sales, which have been the main growth categories for the company in recent years. To support these growth categories and to enhance margins, Reisman opened a new design office in 2011 to develop proprietary, life-enriching merchandise. Indigo also redesigned its online store and leveraged the synergies across its retail and online channels to enhance the online customer experience. To cut costs, it closed two superstores in fiscal 2014 and reduced the number of small-format stores from 151 in 2010 to 131 in 2014. In sum, Reisman and her management team have been "adjusting" or "updating" their strategy to achieve growth and profitability in light of the challenging environment.

Because the financial statements should reflect the firm's underlying economic reality, Indigo's management will need to "adjust" or "update" its financial statements to reflect the changes in its strategy and performance.

Accounting adjustments are a key part of creating financial statements, and they are central to the difference between accrual and cash accounting. While cash accounting only records transactions that involve cash receipts and disbursements, accrual accounting records revenues when they are earned (even if cash has not yet been received) and expenses as they are incurred (regardless of when the cash disbursement associated with that expense is made). The quality, or lack thereof, of financial statements often hinges on the quality of those adjustments. Thus, understanding how and why accounting adjustments occur is fundamentally important to those who wish to analyse and interpret financial statements.

This chapter describes the need for adjustments, how they are prepared, their financial statement effect, and the need for ethics and oversight in this process. We illustrate how financial statements are prepared from those adjusted accounts. Then, we end the chapter with the closing process for the financial statements. Such "closing of the books" enables firms to report their performance for the year and then "open the books" anew for the next period.

Sources: www.indigo.ca; Indigo 2012 and 2014 Annual Reports.

CHAPTER ORGANISATION

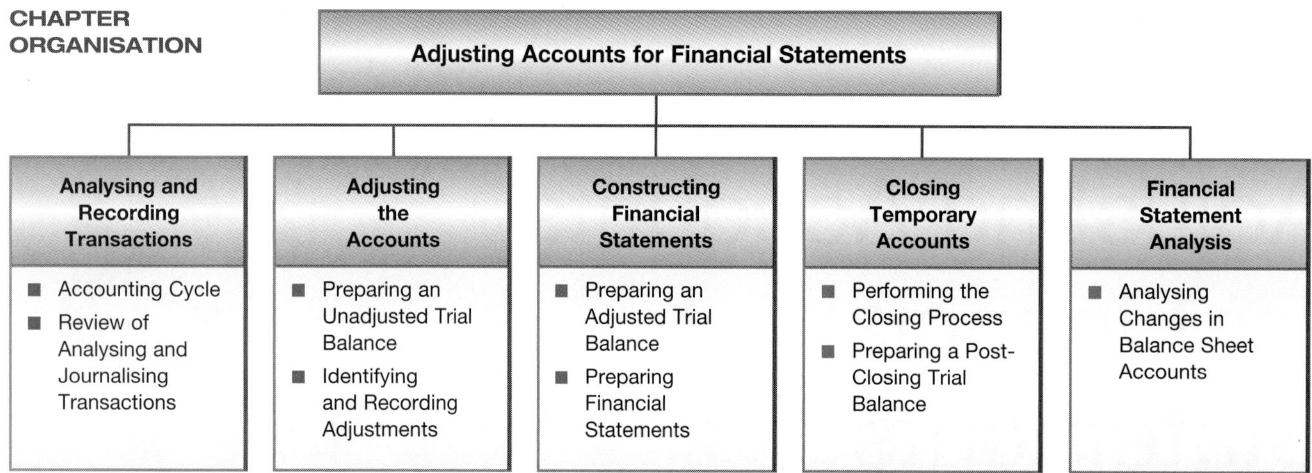

The double-entry accounting system introduced in Chapter 2 provides us with a framework for the analysis of business activities, and we use that framework to record transactions and create financial reports. This chapter describes more fully the procedures companies use to account for the operations of a business during a specific time period. All companies, regardless of size or complexity, perform accounting steps, known as the *accounting cycle*, to accumulate and report their financial information. An important step in the accounting cycle is the *adjusting* process that occurs at the end of every reporting period. This chapter focuses on the accounting cycle with emphasis on the adjusting process.

ACCOUNTING CYCLE

LO1 Identify the major steps in the accounting cycle.

Companies engage in business activities. These activities are analysed for their financial impact, and the results from that analysis are entered into the accounting information system. When management and others want to know where the company stands financially, and what its recent performance tells about future prospects, the financial data often require adjustment prior to financial statements being prepared. At the end of the accounting period, the company *closes the books*. This closing process prepares accounts for the next accounting period.

The process described constitutes the major steps in the **accounting cycle**—a sequence of activities to accumulate and report financial statements. The steps are: analyse, record, adjust, report, and close. Exhibit 3.1 shows the sequence of major steps in the accounting cycle.

EXHIBIT 3.1 Accounting Cycle—Abbreviated

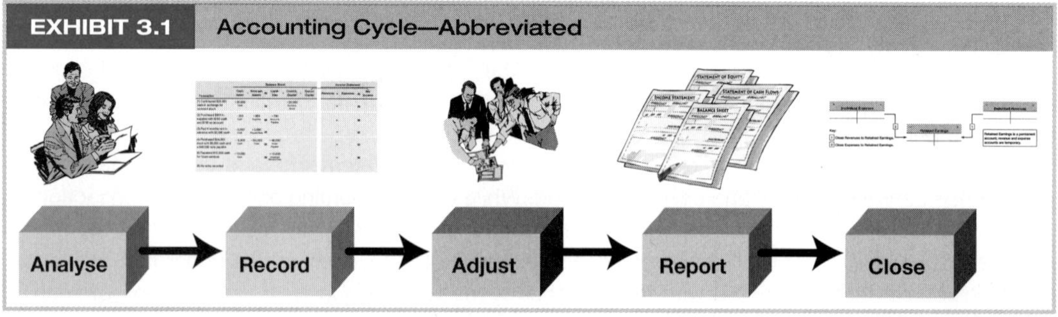

The steps in the accounting cycle do not occur with equal frequency. That is, companies analyse and record daily transactions throughout the accounting period, but they adjust and report only when management requires financial statements, often monthly or quarterly, but at least annually. Closing occurs once during the accounting cycle, at the period-end.

The annual (one-year) accounting period adopted by a company is known as its **fiscal year**. Companies with fiscal year-ends on December 31 are said to be on a **calendar year**. Many companies prefer to have their accounting year coincide with their "natural" year; that is, the fiscal year ends when business is slow. For example, **David Jones Limited**, a specialty retailer in Australia, ends its fiscal year on the last Saturday in July. Fiat SpA, an Italian automobile company and owner of brands such as Ferrari and Maserati, ends its fiscal year on December 31. The British fashion house, Burberry Group plc, ends its fiscal year on March 31.

ANALYSING AND RECORDING TRANSACTIONS

The purpose of this section is to (1) review the analysis and recording of transactions as described in Chapter 2, and (2) to extend the Natural Beauty Supply example to illustrate the process of adjusting and closing accounts in the next section. Natural Beauty Supply's fiscal year-end is December 31.

LO2 Review the process of journalising and posting transactions.

Review of Accounting Procedures

The **chart of accounts** for Natural Beauty Supply is in Exhibit 3.2, and lists the titles and numbers of all accounts found in its general ledger. The account titles are grouped into the five major sections of the general ledger (assets, liabilities, equity, revenues, and expenses). We saw in Chapter 2 that the recording process involves analysing, journalising, and posting. The **general journal**, or *book of original entry*, is a tabular record where business activities are captured in debits and credits and recorded in chronological order before they are posted to the general ledger. The word *journalise* means to record a transaction in a **journal**. Each transaction entered in the journal must be stated in terms of equal dollar amounts of debits and credits—the double-entry system at work. The account titles cited must correspond to those in the general ledger (per the chart of accounts).

EXHIBIT 3.2 Chart of Accounts for Natural Beauty Supply

Assets	Equity
110 Cash	310 Share Capital
120 Accounts Receivable	320 Retained Earnings
130 Other Receivables	
140 Inventory	**Revenues and Income**
150 Prepaid Insurance	410 Sales Revenue
160 Security Deposit	420 Interest Income
170 Fixtures and Equipment	
175 Accumulated Depreciation—Fixtures and Equipment	**Expenses**
	510 Cost of Goods Sold
	520 Wages Expense
Liabilities	530 Rent Expense
210 Accounts Payable	540 Advertising Expense
220 Interest Payable	550 Depreciation Expense—Fixtures and Equipment
230 Wages Payable	560 Insurance Expense
240 Taxes Payable	570 Interest Expense
250 Unearned Revenue	580 Tax Expense
260 Notes Payable	

After transactions are journalised, the debits and credits in each journal entry are transferred to their related general ledger accounts. This transcribing process is called posting to the general ledger, or simply **posting**. Journalising and posting occur simultaneously when recordkeeping is automated. When records are kept manually, posting from the general journal can be done daily, every few days, or at the end of a month. Today, computers are used extensively to perform mechanical accounting tasks such as posting.

FYI Demand for information is often immediate in our fast-paced economy. Accordingly, electronic files of the ledger usually contain up-to-date account balances. ■

Review of Recording Transactions

In Chapter 2, we recorded the November activities of Natural Beauty Supply (NBS) and created the end-of-November financial statements. As NBS continues its activities into the next month, the end-of-November balance sheet provides the starting point for December. Exhibit 3.3 provides a summary of Natural Beauty Supply's December transactions

EXHIBIT 3.3 Transactions for Natural Beauty Supply for December 2013

Event	Date	Description
(17)	Dec. 1	NBS signed a three-year note to borrow $11,000 cash from a financial institution. NBS will pay interest on the first day of every month at the rate of 12% per year or 1% per month. The $11,000 principal is due at the end of three years.
(18)	Dec. 1	NBS purchased and installed improved fixtures and equipment for $18,000 cash.
(19)	Dec. 10	NBS paid $700 to advertise in the local newspaper for December.
(20)	Dec. 20	NBS paid $3,300 cash to its suppliers in partial payment for the delivery of inventory in November.
(21)	Dec. —	During the month of December, NBS sold products costing $5,000 to retail customers for $8,500 cash.
(22)	Dec. —	During the month of December, sales to wholesale customers totaled $4,500 for merchandise that had cost $3,000. Instead of paying cash, wholesale customers are required to pay for the merchandise within ten working days.
(23)	Dec. —	$1,200 of gift certificates were sold during the month of December. Each gift certificate entitles the recipient to a one-hour consultation on the use of NBS' products.
(24)	Dec. —	NBS employed salespersons who were paid $1,625 in cash in December.
(25)	Dec. —	During the month of December, NBS received $3,200 in cash from wholesale customers for products that had been delivered earlier.
(26)	Dec. 28	NBS purchased and received $4,000 of inventory on account.
(27)	Dec. 31	NBS paid $1,500 to the landlord for December rent.
(28)	Dec. 31	NBS paid $50 cash dividend to its shareholders.

Most of these transactions are similar to those that we analysed in Chapter 2. Each of the transactions involves an exchange of some kind. Suppliers provide inventory and employees provide labour services in exchange for cash or the promise of future cash payments. Customers receive products in exchange for cash or a promise to pay cash in the future. For each of these items, we analyse, journalise, and post as shown in Chapter 2.

NBS has the opportunity to secure long-term financing from a financial institution, and signs a note that must be paid back at the end of three years. Cash increases, and a noncurrent liability increases. Interest payments are made at the start of every month, beginning on January 2, 2013, but no entry is made for interest until time passes and an interest obligation is created.

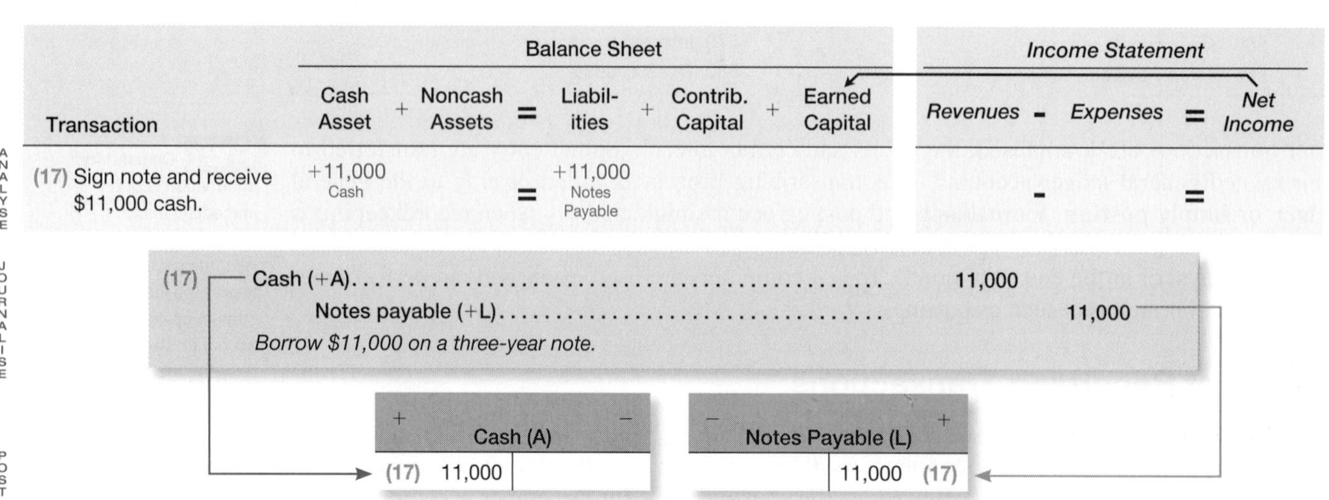

NBS pays $18,000 cash to purchase improved fixtures and equipment for its store location. One asset (cash) decreases, while a noncurrent asset (Fixtures and Equipment) is increased.

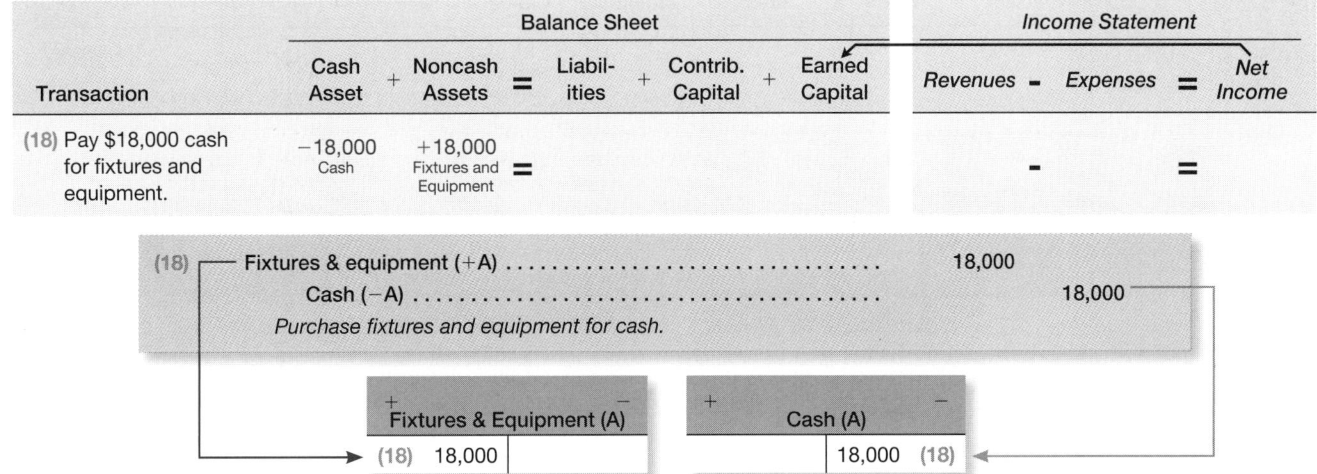

Transactions (19) and (20) are similar to ones that we saw in Chapter 2. The expenditure for advertising results in an expense that decreases net income and ultimately, retained earnings. The payment to suppliers fulfils (in part) an obligation that appeared in the November 30 balance sheet.

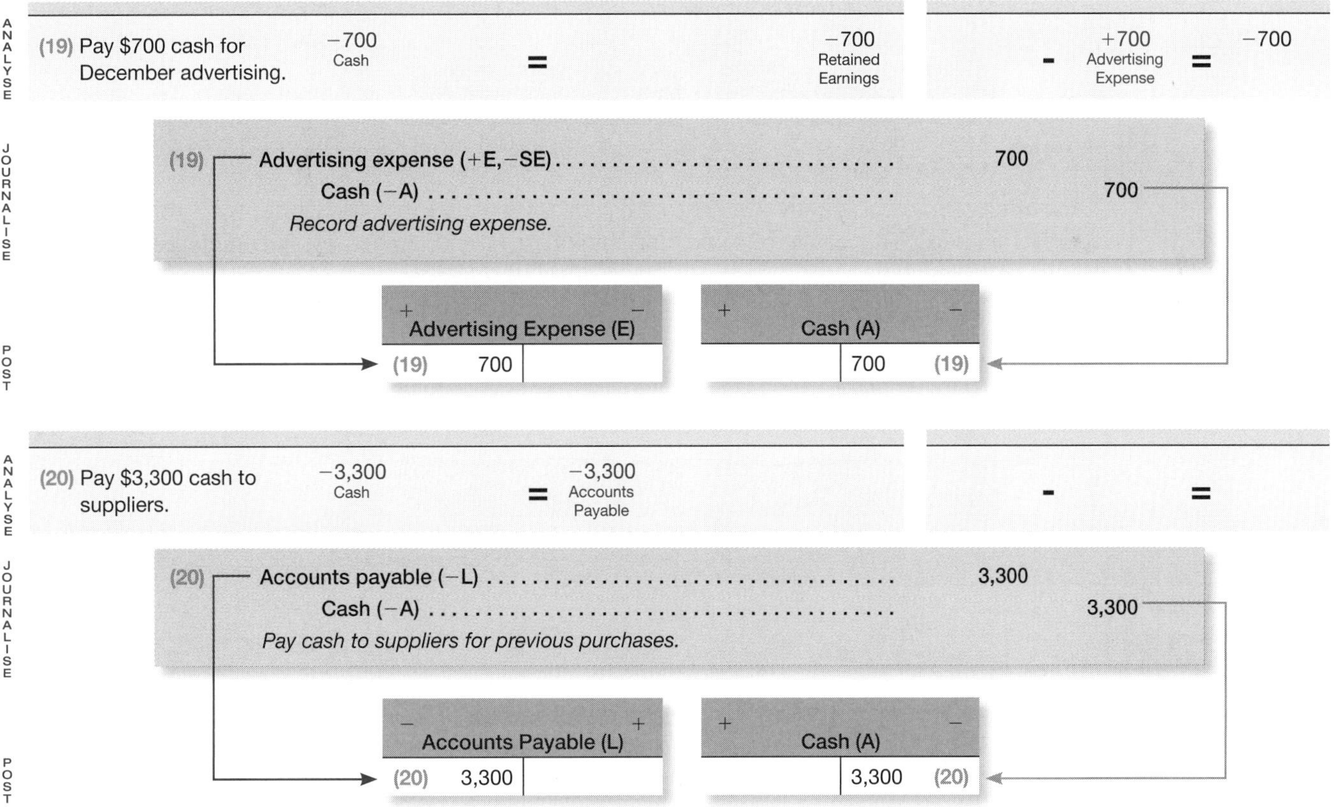

Sales to customers in (21), (22), and (23) are also similar to transactions in Chapter 2, and they are accounted for in similar fashion. Revenue is recognised when products are delivered to customers, rather than when cash is received. When cash is received after delivery, an accounts receivable asset is recognised; when cash is received before delivery, an unearned revenue liability is recognised. Cost of goods sold expense is recognised when the associated revenue is recognised.

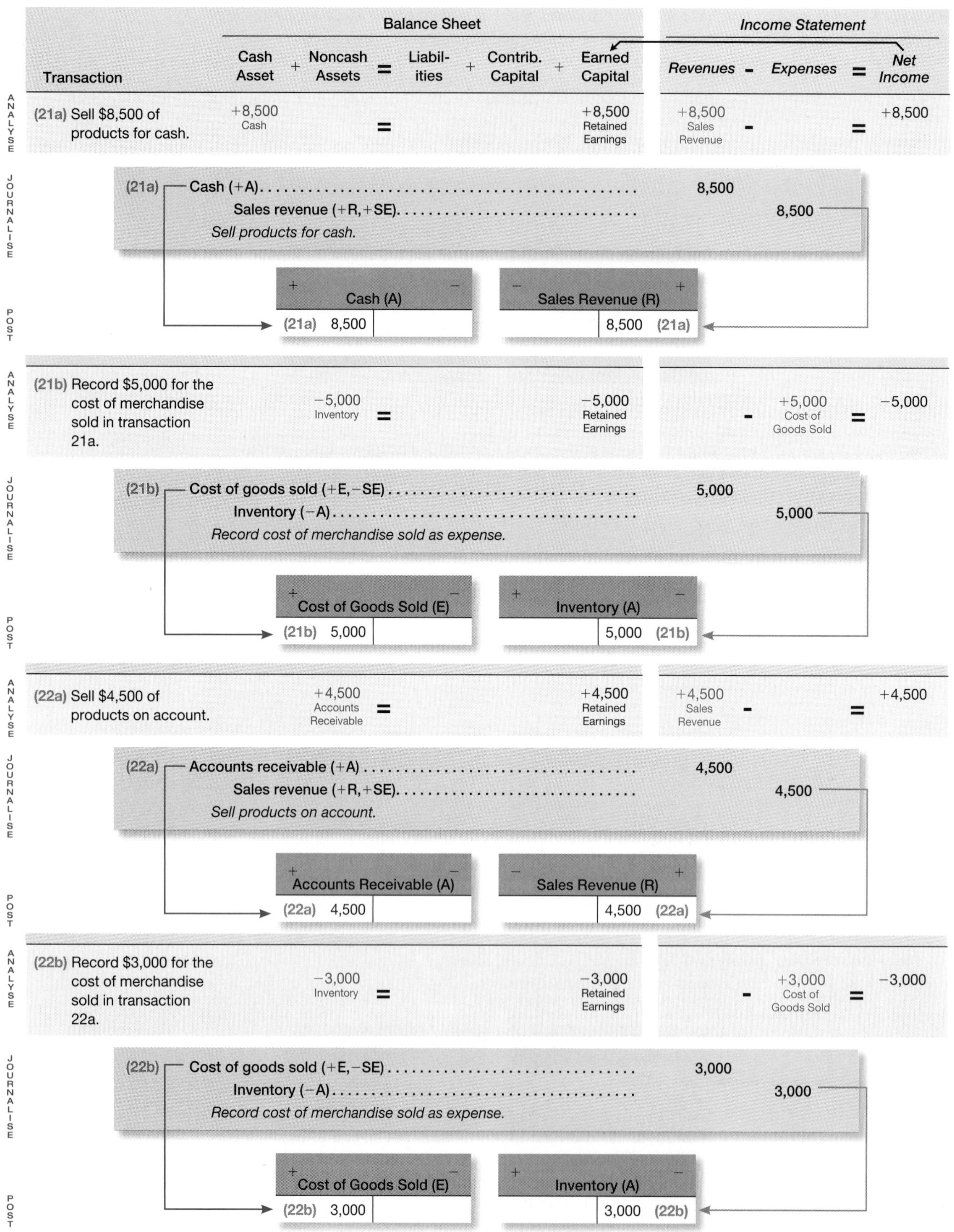
Balance Sheet
Income Statement
Transaction
Cash Asset + Noncash Assets = Liabil-ities + Contrib. Capital + Earned Capital
Revenues - Expenses = Net Income
ANALYSE
(21a) Sell $8,500 of products for cash.
+8,500 Cash = +8,500 Retained Earnings
+8,500 Sales Revenue - = +8,500
JOURNALISE
(21a) Cash (+A) 8,500
Sales revenue (+R, +SE) 8,500
Sell products for cash.
POST
Cash (A)
(21a) 8,500
Sales Revenue (R)
8,500 (21a)
ANALYSE
(21b) Record $5,000 for the cost of merchandise sold in transaction 21a.
−5,000 Inventory = −5,000 Retained Earnings
- +5,000 Cost of Goods Sold = −5,000
JOURNALISE
(21b) Cost of goods sold (+E, −SE) 5,000
Inventory (−A) 5,000
Record cost of merchandise sold as expense.
POST
Cost of Goods Sold (E)
(21b) 5,000
Inventory (A)
5,000 (21b)
ANALYSE
(22a) Sell $4,500 of products on account.
+4,500 Accounts Receivable = +4,500 Retained Earnings
+4,500 Sales Revenue - = +4,500
JOURNALISE
(22a) Accounts receivable (+A) 4,500
Sales revenue (+R, +SE) 4,500
Sell products on account.
POST
Accounts Receivable (A)
(22a) 4,500
Sales Revenue (R)
4,500 (22a)
ANALYSE
(22b) Record $3,000 for the cost of merchandise sold in transaction 22a.
−3,000 Inventory = −3,000 Retained Earnings
- +3,000 Cost of Goods Sold = −3,000
JOURNALISE
(22b) Cost of goods sold (+E, −SE) 3,000
Inventory (−A) 3,000
Record cost of merchandise sold as expense.
POST
Cost of Goods Sold (E)
(22b) 3,000
Inventory (A)
3,000 (22b)

continued

continued from previous page

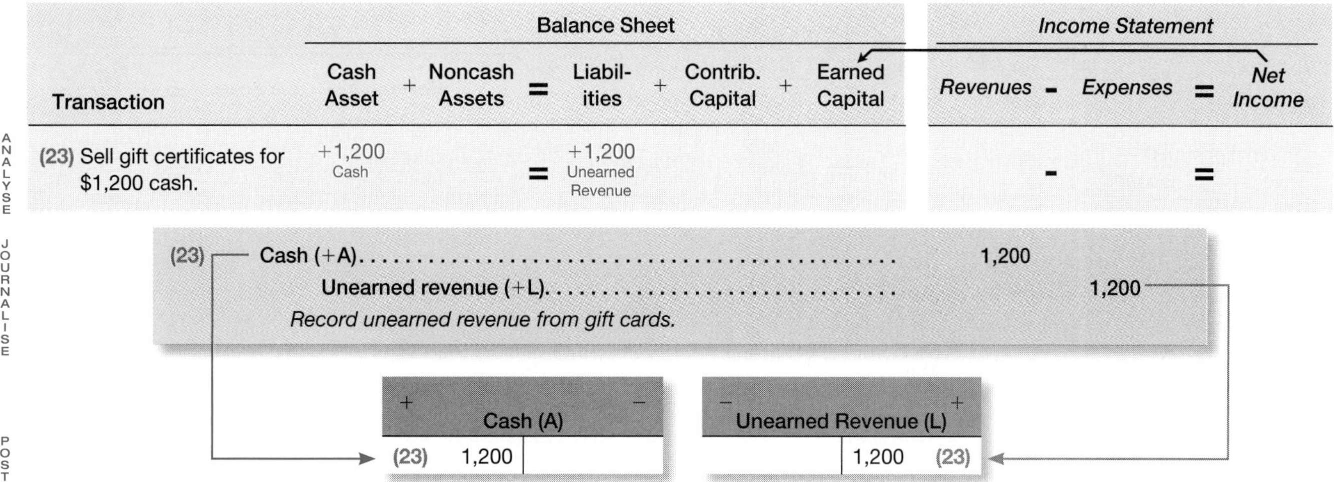

The final five transactions in December also are similar to transactions that NBS had in November. Payment of wages to the employee is reflected in a wage expense. Cash received from wholesale (credit) customers does not cause revenue; rather the increase in cash is balanced by a decrease in accounts receivable. Purchase of inventory on account does not create an expense—the cost of the inventory is held in the inventory asset account until it is purchased by a customer. Payments to the landlord are balanced by a rent expense in the income statement. The cash dividend to shareholders decreases an asset (cash) and equity (retained earnings), but does not affect the income statement.

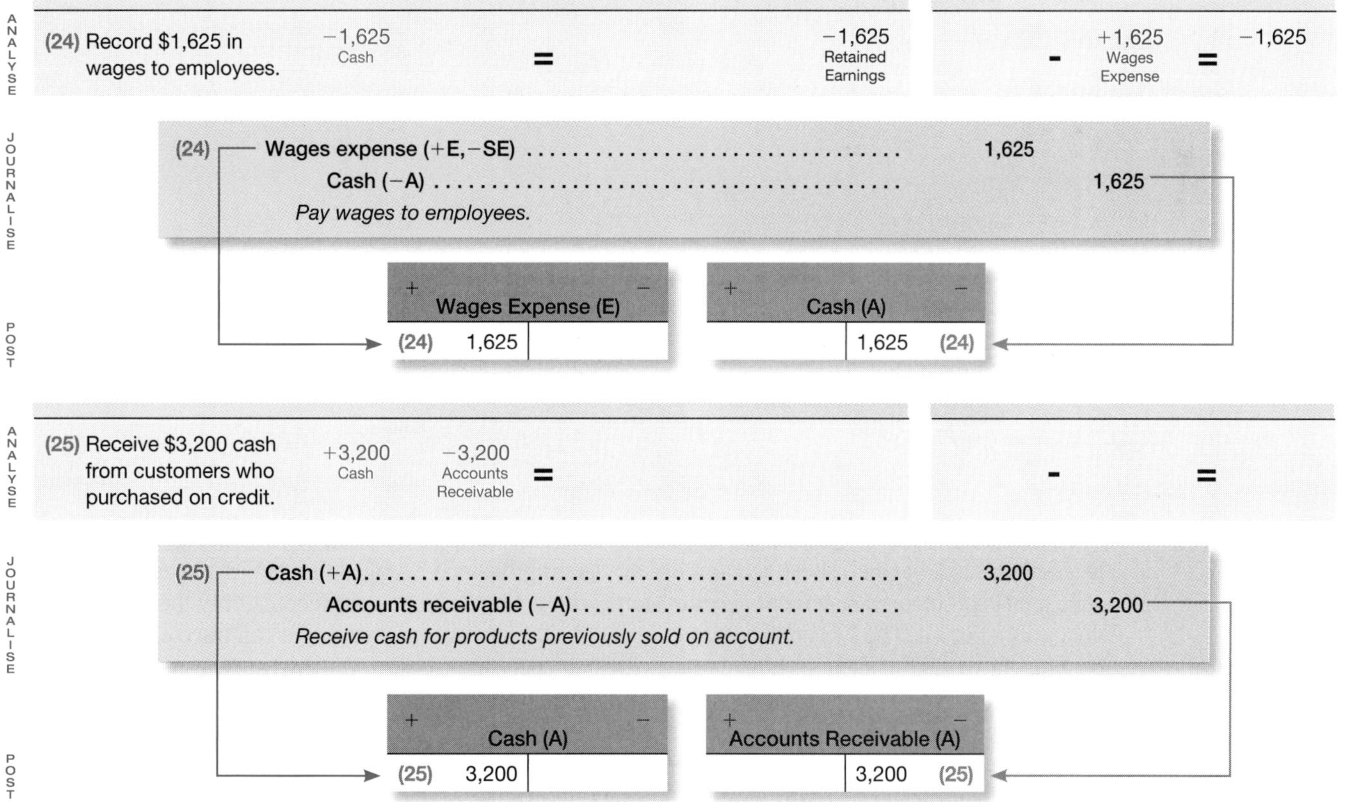

continued

continued from previous page

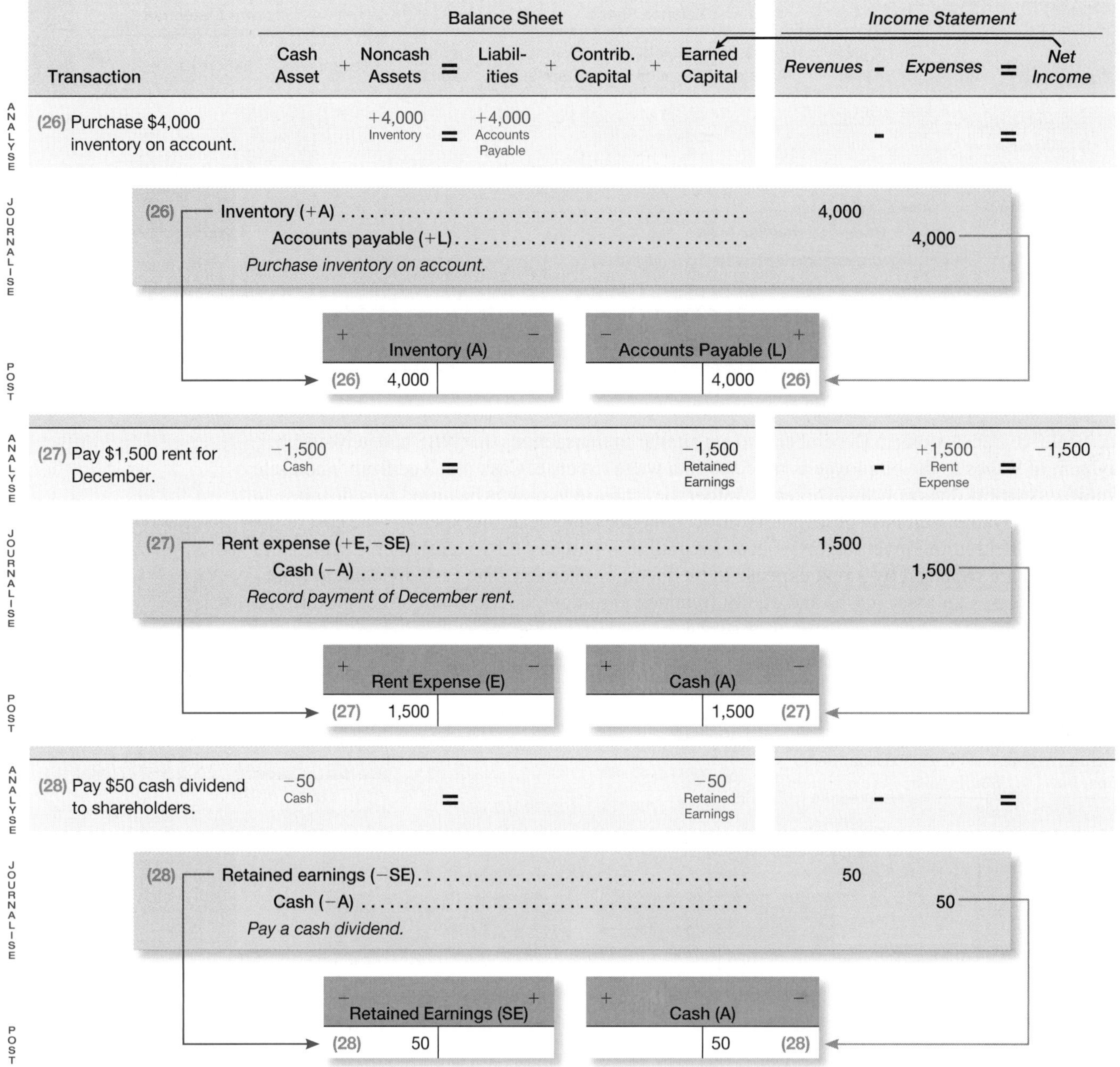

Exhibit 3.4 presents the general ledger accounts of Natural Beauty Supply in T-account form for December. Each balance sheet account has an opening balance equal to the end-of-November balance, and each income statement account starts with a zero balance so it records only the events of the current period. The December transactions (17–28) have been posted. We can trace each of the postings from the transactions above to these ledger accounts.

But the amounts in these accounts are not ready to be assembled into financial reports. There are revenues and expenses and changes in assets and liabilities that occur with the passage of time.[1] Accounting for these items is essential for us to determine how well a company has performed in an accounting period and to assess its financial standing.

[1] Natural Beauty Supply's November activities in Chapter 2 were carefully chosen so we could produce financial statements without adjusting entries. But, as Exhibit 3.1 depicts, the adjusting process is an essential part of the accounting cycle.

EXHIBIT 3.4 General Ledger for Natural Beauty Supply before Adjustments

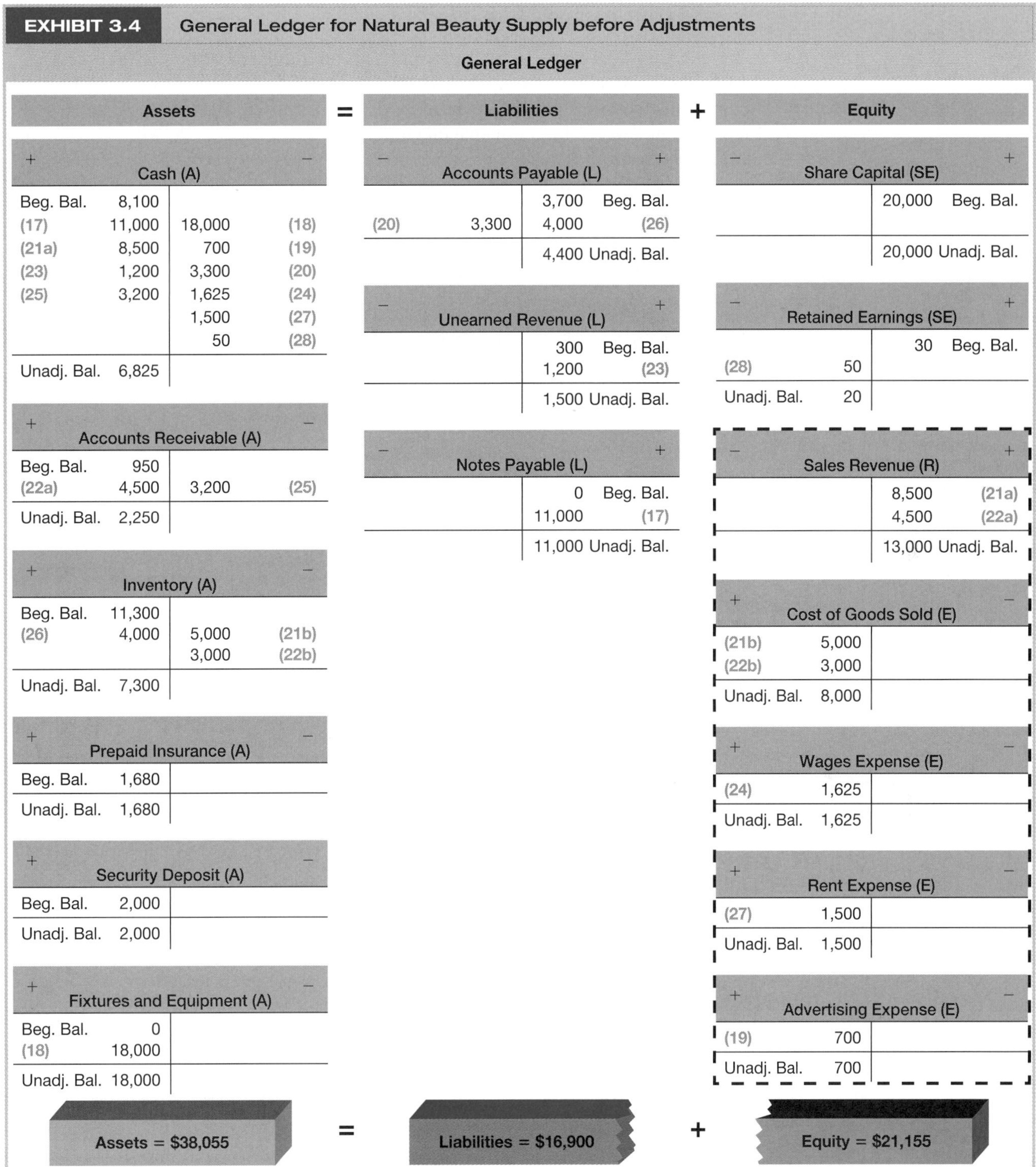

General Ledger
Assets = Liabilities + Equity
+ Cash (A) −
Beg. Bal. 8,100
(17) 11,000 | 18,000 (18)
(21a) 8,500 | 700 (19)
(23) 1,200 | 3,300 (20)
(25) 3,200 | 1,625 (24)
1,500 (27)
50 (28)
Unadj. Bal. 6,825
+ Accounts Receivable (A) −
Beg. Bal. 950
(22a) 4,500 | 3,200 (25)
Unadj. Bal. 2,250
+ Inventory (A) −
Beg. Bal. 11,300
(26) 4,000 | 5,000 (21b)
3,000 (22b)
Unadj. Bal. 7,300
+ Prepaid Insurance (A) −
Beg. Bal. 1,680
Unadj. Bal. 1,680
+ Security Deposit (A) −
Beg. Bal. 2,000
Unadj. Bal. 2,000
+ Fixtures and Equipment (A) −
Beg. Bal. 0
(18) 18,000
Unadj. Bal. 18,000
− Accounts Payable (L) +
3,700 Beg. Bal.
(20) 3,300 | 4,000 (26)
4,400 Unadj. Bal.
− Unearned Revenue (L) +
300 Beg. Bal.
1,200 (23)
1,500 Unadj. Bal.
− Notes Payable (L) +
0 Beg. Bal.
11,000 (17)
11,000 Unadj. Bal.
− Share Capital (SE) +
20,000 Beg. Bal.
20,000 Unadj. Bal.
− Retained Earnings (SE) +
30 Beg. Bal.
(28) 50
Unadj. Bal. 20
− Sales Revenue (R) +
8,500 (21a)
4,500 (22a)
13,000 Unadj. Bal.
+ Cost of Goods Sold (E) −
(21b) 5,000
(22b) 3,000
Unadj. Bal. 8,000
+ Wages Expense (E) −
(24) 1,625
Unadj. Bal. 1,625
+ Rent Expense (E) −
(27) 1,500
Unadj. Bal. 1,500
+ Advertising Expense (E) −
(19) 700
Unadj. Bal. 700
Assets = $38,055 = Liabilities = $16,900 + Equity = $21,155

ADJUSTING THE ACCOUNTS

It is important that accounts in financial statements be properly reported. For many accounts, the balances shown in the general ledger after all transactions are posted are not the proper balances for financial statements. Thus, when it is time to prepare financial statements, management must review account balances and make proper adjustments to these balances. The adjustments required are based on accrual accounting. This section focuses on these issues.

LO3 Describe the adjusting process and illustrate adjusting entries.

Preparing an Unadjusted Trial Balance

The T-accounts in Exhibit 3.4 show balances for each account after recording all transactions, and this set of balances is called an **unadjusted trial balance** because it shows account balances before any adjustments are made. The purpose of an unadjusted trial balance is to be sure the general ledger is in balance before management adjusts the accounts. Showing all general ledger account balances in one place also makes it easier to review accounts and determine which account balances require adjusting. Natural Beauty Supply's unadjusted trial balance at December 31 is shown in Exhibit 3.5.

FYI Even if the unadjusted trial balance shows an equal amount of debits and credits, this does not mean that the general ledger is correct. Journal entries could have been omitted or falsified, or the accounts used or the amounts involved may have been wrong. Thus, the equality of debits and credits is a necessary, but not a sufficient condition for the financial statements to be correct. ■

EXHIBIT 3.5 Unadjusted Trial Balance

NATURAL BEAUTY SUPPLY
Unadjusted Trial Balance
December 31, 2013

	Debit	Credit
Cash	$ 6,825	
Accounts Receivable	2,250	
Inventory	7,300	
Prepaid Insurance	1,680	
Security Deposit	2,000	
Fixtures & Equipment	18,000	
Accounts Payable		$ 4,400
Unearned Revenue		1,500
Notes Payable		11,000
Share Capital		20,000
Retained Earnings	20	
Sales Revenue		13,000
Cost of Goods Sold	8,000	
Wages Expense	1,625	
Rent Expense	1,500	
Advertising Expense	700	
Totals	$49,900	$49,900

Types of Adjustments

Accrual adjustments are caused by a variety of accounting practices. There are some revenues and expenses that arise with the passage of time, rather than in a transaction. There are asset and liability values that change over time or that require estimation based on recent events. All of these require adjustments before proper financial statements can be produced.

Adjusting entries have two common characteristics. First, they occur at the end of a reporting period, just before the construction of financial statements. Second, they (almost) never involve cash. Changes in cash require a transaction, and adjusting entries are not transactions.

Through the course of this book, we will encounter quite a few required adjusting entries, but we will start with four general types of adjustments made at the end of an accounting period.

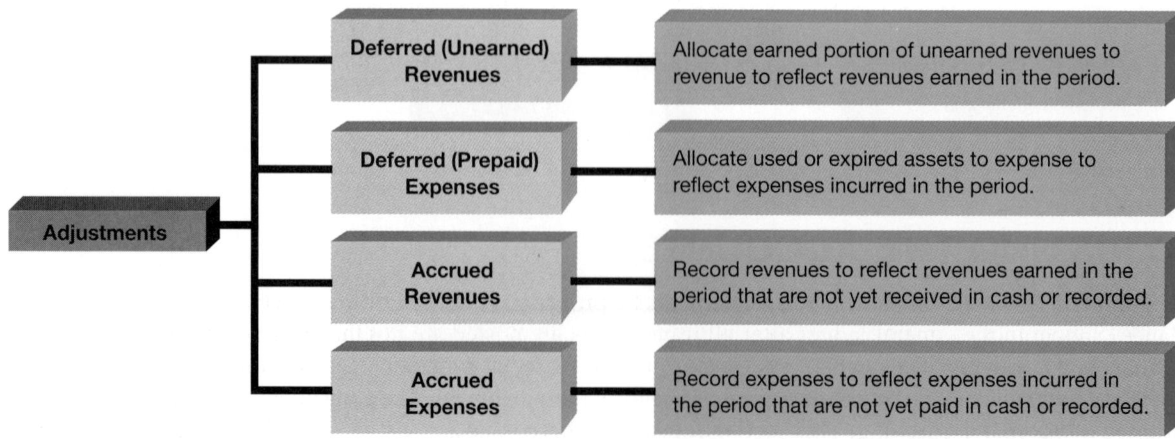

Journal entries made to reflect these adjustments are known as **adjusting entries**. Each adjusting entry usually affects a balance sheet account (an asset or liability account) and an income statement account (an expense or revenue account). The first two types of adjustments—allocating assets to expense and allocating unearned revenues to revenue—are often referred to as **deferrals**. The distinguishing characteristic of a deferral is that the adjustment deals with an amount previously recorded in a balance sheet account; the adjusting entry decreases the balance sheet account and increases an income statement account. The last two types of adjustments—accruing expenses and accruing revenues—are often referred to as **accruals**. The unique characteristic of an accrual is that the adjustment deals with an amount not previously recorded in any account; the type of adjusting entry increases both a balance sheet account and an income statement account. Both accruals and deferrals allow revenue to be recognised when it is earned and realisable and the expenses of the period to be matched against the revenues from that period's operations. Let's consider each of these adjustments in more detail.

Type 1: Deferred Revenue—Allocating Unearned Revenue to Revenue Companies often receive fees for services before services are rendered. Such transactions are recorded by debiting Cash and crediting a liability account for the **unearned revenue**—also referred to as **deferred revenue**. This account reflects the obligation for performing future services. As services are performed, revenue is earned. At period-end, an adjusting entry records the revenue that was earned in the current accounting period and the liability amount that was reduced.

FYI Chapter 2 explained that revenue recognition is key to determining net income under accrual accounting, which recognises revenues when services are performed or when goods are sold and recognises expenses in the period that they help to generate the recorded revenues. ■

DEFERRED REVENUE During November and December, Natural Beauty Supply sold gift certificates that entitled the recipient to a one-hour consultation with a salesperson on the use of natural and organic health and beauty products. When the gift certificates were purchased, NBS recognised an unearned revenue liability that reflected the obligation to provide these services. During the month of December, gift certificates totaling $900 were redeemed. On December 31, Natural Beauty Supply made the adjustment (a) in the following template, journal entry, and T-accounts to recognise the (partial) fulfilment of the obligation and to recognise that $900 of revenue has now been earned. The $900 increase in sales revenue is reflected in net income and carried over to retained earnings.

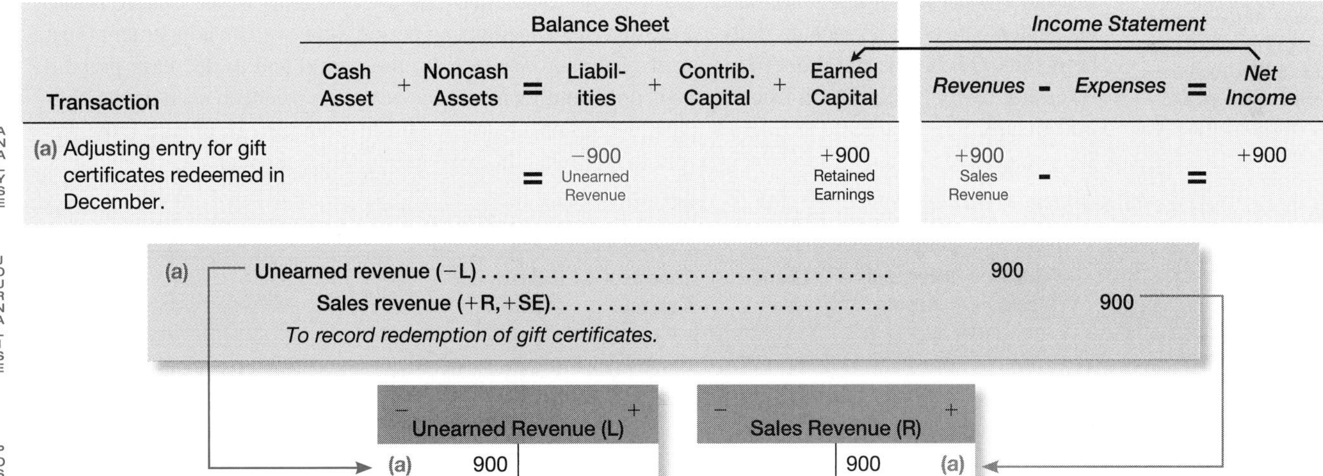

After this entry (a) is posted, the unearned revenue liability account has a balance of $600 for the remaining gift certificates outstanding, and the sales revenue account reflects the $900 earned in December.

In this case, the cost of the salesperson's time has already been recognised as an expense. If Natural Beauty Supply's gift certificates had been redeemable for products, then we would have recognised a cost of goods sold expense for the items purchased with the redeemed certificates.

Other examples of revenues received in advance include gift cards, rental payments received in advance by real estate management companies, insurance premiums received in advance by insurance companies, subscription revenues received in advance by magazine and newspaper publishers, and membership fees received in advance by health clubs. In each case, a liability account is set up when the advance payment is received. Later, an adjusting entry is made to reflect the revenues earned from the services provided or products delivered during the period.

YOU MAKE THE CALL

You are the Chief Accountant REI requires customers of its travel-vacation business to make an initial deposit equal to $400 when the trip is reserved and to make full payment two months before departure. REI's refunding policy is to return the entire deposit if the customer informs REI of the trip's cancellation three or more months in advance of the trip. REI will refund all but $400 of the deposit if the customer cancels between 60 and 90 days prior to the trip or 50% of the deposit if a customer cancels between 30 and 60 days prior to the trip. There is no refund if notification occurs within 30 days of the trip. REI's cancellation rate is very low. How should you account for deposits, and when should revenue be recorded? [Answers on page 120]

Type 2: Prepaid Expenses—Allocating Assets to Expenses Many cash outlays benefit several accounting periods. Examples are purchases of buildings, equipment, and supplies; prepayments of rent and advertising; and payments of insurance premiums covering several periods. These outlays are debited to an asset account when the expenditure occurs. Then at the end of each accounting period, the estimated portion of the outlay that has expired in that period or has benefited that period, is transferred to an expense account.

We can usually see when adjustments of this type are needed by inspecting the unadjusted trial balance for costs that benefit several periods. Looking at the December 31 trial balance of Natural Beauty Supply (Exhibit 3.5), for example, adjustments are required to record the costs of prepaid insurance and the fixtures and equipment for the month of December.

FYI Many transactions reflected in ledger accounts affect net income of more than one period. Likewise, other events that are not yet recorded in accounts affect the current period's income. The adjusting process identifies these situations to record the proper revenues and expenses in the current period. ■

PREPAID INSURANCE On November 30, Natural Beauty Supply paid one year's insurance premium in advance and debited the $1,680 payment to Prepaid Insurance, an asset account. As each day passes and the insurance coverage is being used, insurance expense is being incurred, and the prepaid insurance is decreasing. It is not necessary to record insurance expense on a daily basis because financial statements are not prepared daily. At the end of an accounting period, however, an adjustment must be made to recognise the proper amount of insurance expense for the period and to decrease prepaid insurance by that amount. On December 31, one month's insurance coverage has been used up, so Natural Beauty Supply transfers $140 ($1,680/12 months) from Prepaid Insurance to Insurance Expense. This entry is identified as adjustment (b) in the template, journal entry, and T-accounts.

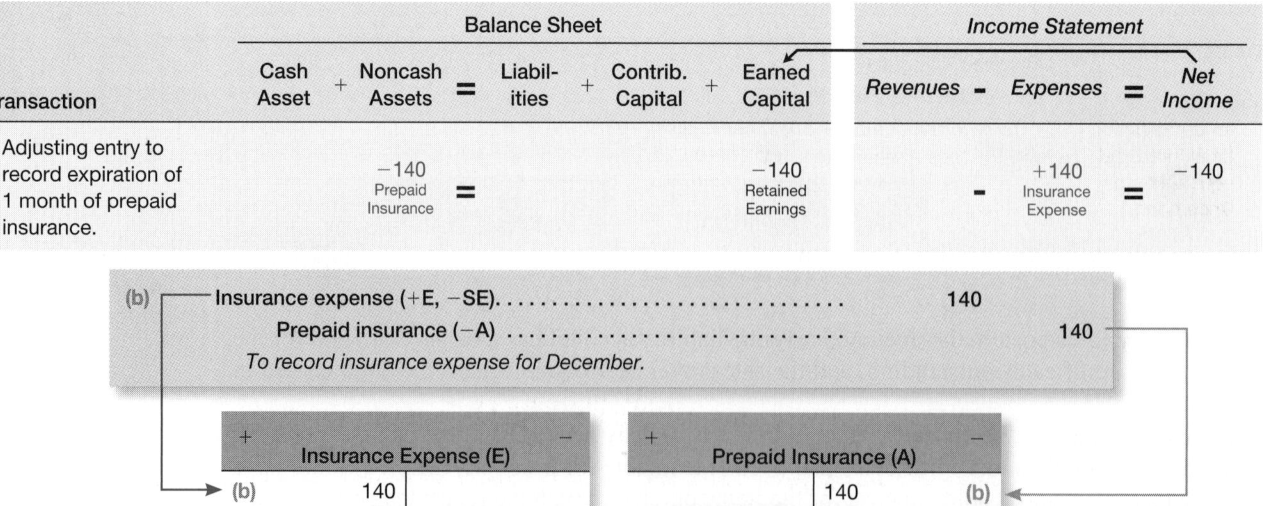

The posting of this adjusting entry creates the proper insurance expense of $140 for December in the Insurance Expense ledger account and reduces the Prepaid Insurance balance to the (eleven-month) amount that is prepaid as of December 31, which is $1,540.

Examples of other prepaid expenses for which similar adjustments are made include prepaid rent and prepaid advertising. When rent payments are made in advance, the amount is debited to a Prepaid Rent asset. At the end of an accounting period, an adjusting entry is made to record the portion of occupancy or usage that expired during the period. Rent Expense is debited and Prepaid Rent is credited. Similarly, when advertising services are purchased in advance, the payment is debited to Prepaid Advertising. At the end of an accounting period, an adjustment is needed to recognise the cost of any of the prepaid advertising used during the period. The adjusting entry debits Advertising Expense and credits Prepaid Advertising.

DEPRECIATION The process of allocating the costs of equipment, vehicles, and buildings to the periods benefiting from their use is called **depreciation**. Each accounting period in which such assets are used must reflect a portion of their cost as expense because these assets helped generate revenue for those periods. This periodic expense is known as *depreciation expense*. Periodic depreciation expense is an estimate. The procedure we use here estimates the annual amount of depreciation expense by dividing the asset cost by its estimated useful life. (We assume that the entire asset cost is depreciated—so-called zero salvage value; later in the book we consider salvage values other than zero.) This method is called **straight-line depreciation** and is the method used by the great majority of companies.

Expenses are recorded when business activities reduce net assets. But when we record depreciation expense, the asset amount is not reduced directly. Instead, the reduction is recorded in a contra account (labelled XA in the journal entries and T-accounts) called *Accumulated Depreciation*. **Contra accounts** are so named because they are used to record reductions in or offsets against a related account. The Accumulated Depreciation account normally has a credit balance and appears in the balance sheet as a deduction from the related asset amount. Use of the contra asset Accumulated Depreciation allows the original cost of the asset to be reported in the balance sheet, followed (and reduced) by the accumulated depreciation. Let's consider an example.

The fixtures and equipment purchased by Natural Beauty Supply for $18,000 are expected to last for four years. Straight-line depreciation recorded on the equipment is $4,500 per year ($18,000/4 years), or $375 per month ($18,000/48 months). At December 31, Natural Beauty Supply makes adjustment (c), as shown in the following template, journal entry, and T-accounts.

The introduction of contra assets requires a new column in the FSET for these accounts.[2] Increases in a contra asset decrease the net balance of the company's long-term assets. The new column is preceded by a minus sign to indicate that increases in contra assets create a decrease in the asset side of the accounting equation.

FYI Contra accounts are used to provide more information to users of financial statements. For example, Accumulated Depreciation is a contra asset reported in the balance sheet, which enables users to estimate asset age. For Natural Beauty Supply, the December 31 balance sheet reveals that its Fixtures and Equipment is nearly new as its accumulated depreciation is only $375, which is 1/48th of the $18,000 original cost. ■

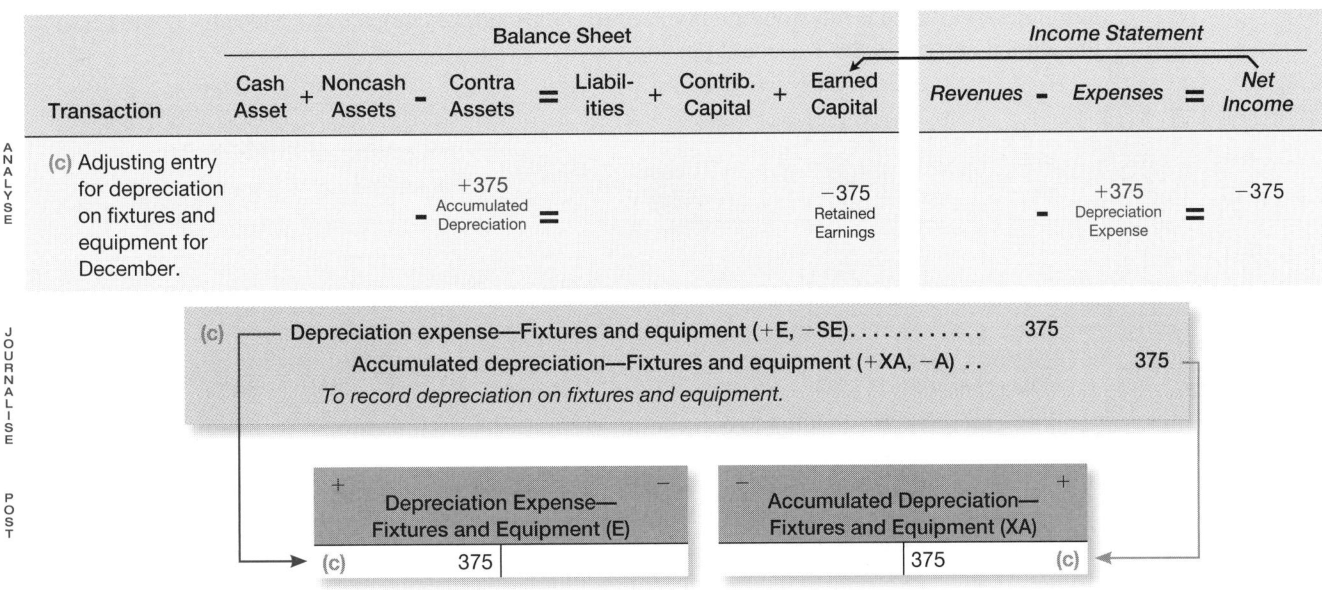

Transaction	Cash Asset	+ Noncash Assets	− Contra Assets	= Liabilities	+ Contrib. Capital	+ Earned Capital	Revenues	− Expenses	= Net Income
(c) Adjusting entry for depreciation on fixtures and equipment for December.			+375 Accumulated Depreciation			−375 Retained Earnings		+375 Depreciation Expense	−375

[2] Our practice is to include a separate FSET column where contra assets are required, but not to do so all the time. As we progress through the topics in this text, we will also see examples of contra liability accounts and contra equity accounts.

When this entry is posted, it properly reflects the cost of using this asset during December, and the $375 depreciation appears in the December income statement. On the balance sheet, the accumulated depreciation is subtracted from the asset amount. The resulting balance (cost less accumulated depreciation), which is the asset's **book value**, represents the unexpired asset cost to be allocated as an expense in future periods. For example, the December 31, 2013, balance sheet reports the equipment with a book value of $17,625, as follows.

FYI An increase in the contra asset account Accumulated Depreciation reduces the book value of the asset. ■

Fixtures and Equipment	$18,000	
Less: Accumulated depreciation	375	
Fixtures and Equipment, net	$17,625	(book value)

In each subsequent month, $375 is recognised as depreciation expense, and the accumulated depreciation contra asset is increased by the same amount (from $375 to $750 to $1,125 and so on). As a result, the book value of the fixtures and equipment is decreased by $375 each month.

Type 3: Accrued Revenues Revenues should be recognised in the period in which they are earned and realisable. Yet a company often provides services or earns income during a period that is neither paid for by clients or customers nor billed at the end of the period. Such values should be included in the firm's current period income statement. To properly account for such transactions, end-of-period adjusting entries are made to reflect any revenues or income for the period that have been earned and realised, but have not been received or billed. Such accumulated revenue is often called **accrued revenue** or **accrued income**.

ACCRUED SALES REVENUE/INCOME At the end of December, Natural Beauty Supply learns that its bank has decided to provide interest on checking accounts for small businesses like NBS. Each month, NBS earns interest income based on the average balance in its checking account. The interest is paid into NBS's checking account on the fifth business day of the following month. Based on its average daily balance, NBS earned $30 in interest during December.

In this instance, Natural Beauty Supply does not receive the interest payment until January. Nevertheless, the company earned interest during the month of December, and it is sure to collect the amount owed. Therefore, it should recognise an interest receivable (or "other receivables") asset and interest income in the income statement. (We could also call this interest revenue, but the term interest income is more commonly used for nonfinancial companies.) The entry in the FSET, the journal entry, and the T-account posting is:

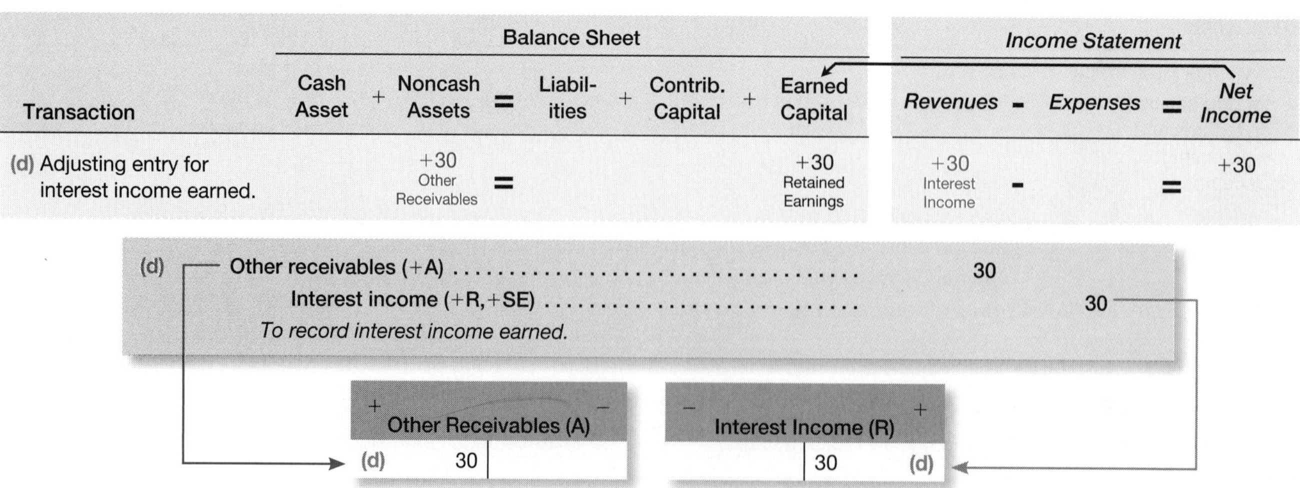

Revenue accruals also occur for landlords who receive rent payments after they are earned and for companies who engage in long-term projects in construction or consulting. In all these cases, revenue has been earned over time without a transaction in which a finished product is delivered to a customer. We look into these issues more closely in Chapter 6.

Type 4: Accrued Expenses Companies often incur expenses before paying for them. Wages, interest, utilities, and taxes are examples of expenses that are incurred before cash payment is made. Usually the payments are made at regular intervals of time, such as weekly, monthly, quarterly, or annually. If the accounting period ends on a date that does not coincide with a scheduled cash payment date, an adjusting entry is required to reflect the expense incurred since the last cash payment. Such an expense is referred to as an **accrued expense**. Natural Beauty Supply has three such required adjustments for December 31; one for wages, one for interest and one for income tax.

ACCRUED WAGES Natural Beauty Supply employees are paid on a weekly basis. Recall that wages of $1,625 were paid during December in transaction 24. However, as of December 31, the company's employees have earned wages of $480 that will be paid in January. Wages expense of $480 must be recorded in the income statement for December because the employees earned those wages, which helped generate revenues for December.

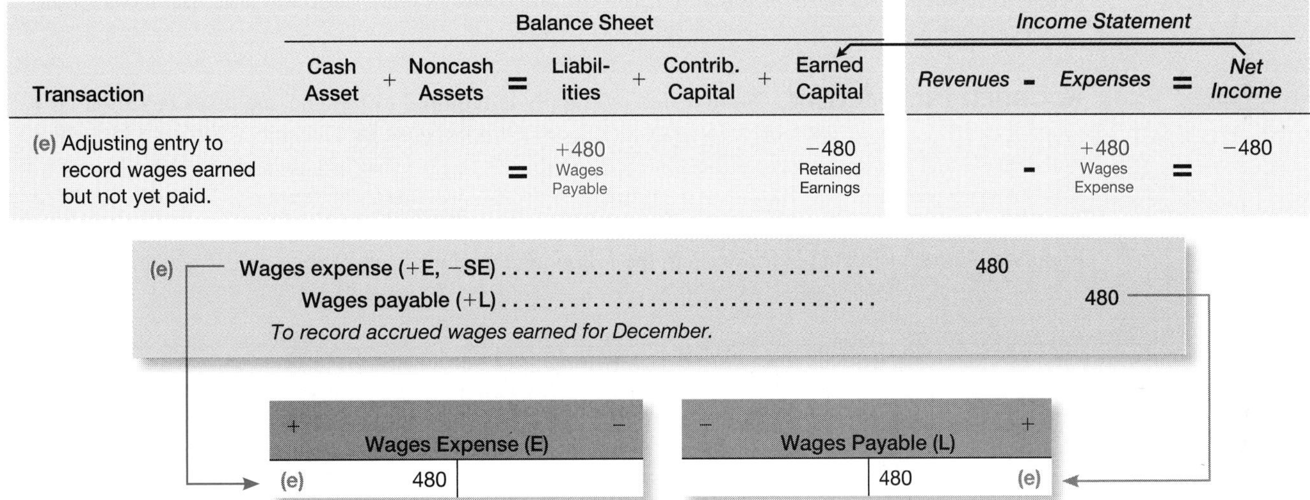

This adjustment enables the firm to reflect as December expense the cost of all wages *incurred* during the month rather than just the wages *paid*. In addition, the balance sheet shows the liability for unpaid wages at the end of the period.

When the employees are paid in January, the following entry is made.

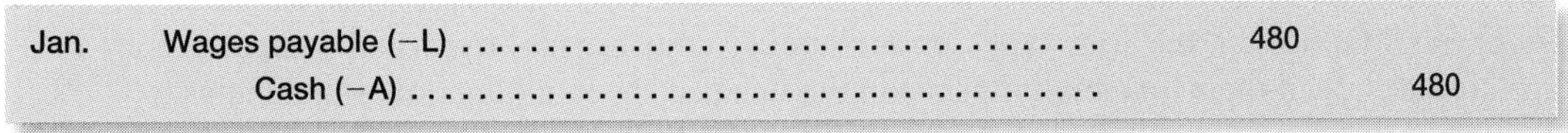

Jan.	Wages payable (−L)	480	
	Cash (−A)		480

This entry eliminates the liability recorded in Wages Payable at the end of December and reduces Cash for the wages paid.

ACCRUED INTEREST On December 1, 2013, Natural Beauty Supply signed a three-year note payable for $11,000. This note has a 12% annual interest rate and requires monthly (interest-only) payments (1% per month), payable on the first day of the following month. (The interest payment for the month of December is due on January 1.) The $11,000 principal on the note is due at the end of three years. An adjusting entry is required at December 31, 2013, to record interest expense for December. December's interest is $110[$11,000 × (12%/12 months)], and at December 31 NBS makes adjustment (f) in the following template, journal entry, and T-accounts.

A N A L Y S E

Transaction	Cash Asset	+	Noncash Assets	=	Liabilities	+	Contrib. Capital	+	Earned Capital		Revenues	−	Expenses	=	Net Income
	Balance Sheet										***Income Statement***				
(f) Adjusting entry to record interest owed but not yet paid.				=	+110 Interest Payable				−110 Retained Earnings			−	+110 Interest Expense	=	−110

J O U R N A L I S E / P O S T

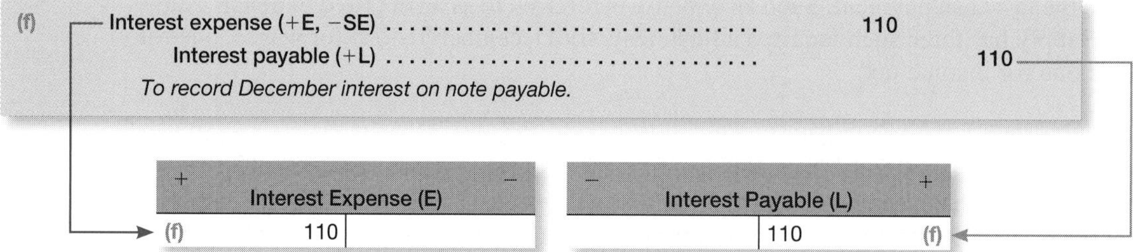

		Dr.	Cr.
(f)	Interest expense (+E, −SE)	110	
	Interest payable (+L)		110
	To record December interest on note payable.		

+ Interest Expense (E) −	
(f) 110	

− Interest Payable (L) +	
	110 (f)

When these entries are posted to the general ledger, the accounts show the correct interest expense for December and the interest liability for one month's interest on the note that has accrued by December 31.

ACCRUED INCOME TAX Natural Beauty Supply is required to pay income taxes based on how much it earns. Using an estimated 35% tax rate, income tax expense for December 2013 is $350, computed as ($13,900 sales revenue + $30 interest income − $8,000 cost of goods sold − $1,500 rent − $2,105 wages expense − $700 advertising expense − $375 depreciation expense − $140 insurance expense − $110 interest expense) × 35%. Taxes are not paid until March 15, 2014. Natural Beauty Supply makes adjustment (g) for taxes in the following template, journal entry, and T-accounts.

A N A L Y S E / J O U R N A L I S E / P O S T

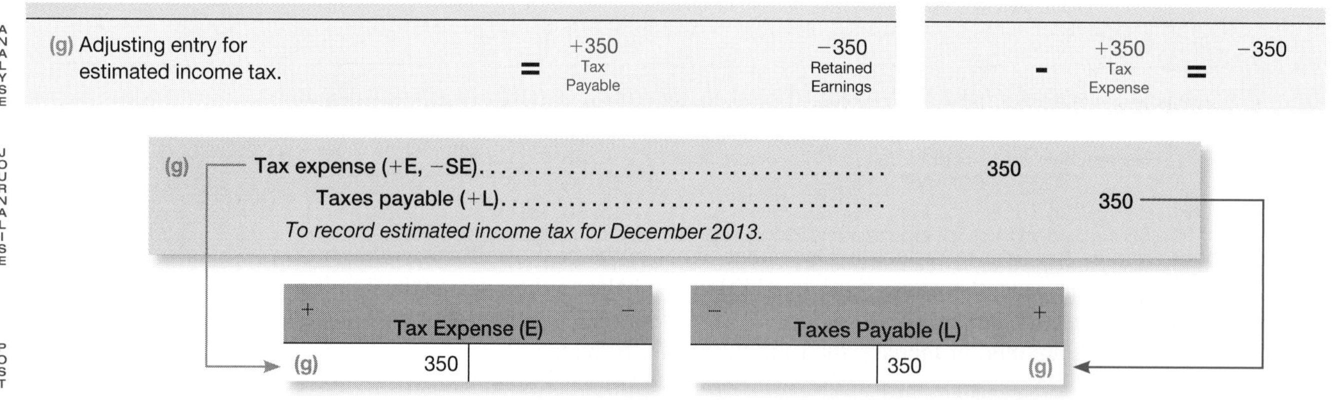

Transaction	Cash Asset	+	Noncash Assets	=	Liabilities	+	Contrib. Capital	+	Earned Capital		Revenues	−	Expenses	=	Net Income
(g) Adjusting entry for estimated income tax.				=	+350 Tax Payable				−350 Retained Earnings			−	+350 Tax Expense	=	−350

		Dr.	Cr.
(g)	Tax expense (+E, −SE)..............................	350	
	Taxes payable (+L)..............................		350
	To record estimated income tax for December 2013.		

+ Tax Expense (E) −	
(g) 350	

− Taxes Payable (L) +	
	350 (g)

Exhibit 3.6 summarises the four types of accounting adjustments, the usual journal entries required for each, and their financial impacts on the balance sheet and income statements.

Ethics and Adjusting Entries

When companies engage in transactions, there is some evidence of the exchange. Cash increases or decreases; asset and liability levels change. Adjusting entries are much more dependent on estimation processes. What was the value of service provided to customers, but not yet billed? What obligations have arisen in the past period without a transaction? What is their value? What is the expected useful life of our depreciable assets?

The usefulness of financial performance measures such as net income depends on these questions being answered to the best of management's ability. However, there often are pressures not to provide the most accurate information. For instance, an estimate might convey information about

EXHIBIT 3.6 Summary of Accounting Adjustments

Accounting Adjustment	Examples	Adjusting Entry	Financial Effects if not Adjusted: Balance Sheet	Financial Effects if not Adjusted: Income Statement
Deferrals:				
Unearned revenues	Delivery on advances from clients, gift cards, and subscribers	Dr. Liability Cr. Revenue	Liability overstated Equity understated	Revenue understated
Prepaid expenses	Expiration of prepaid rent, insurance, and advertising; depreciation of buildings and equipment	Dr. Expense Cr. Asset (or Contra asset)	Asset overstated Equity overstated	Expense understated
Accruals:				
Accrued revenues	Earned but not received service, sales, and interest revenues	Dr. Asset Cr. Revenue	Asset understated Equity understated	Revenue understated
Accrued expenses	Incurred but unpaid wages, interest, and tax expenses	Dr. Expense Cr. Liability	Liability understated Equity overstated	Expense understated

management's strategy that could be used by competitors. Or, for a second example, the financial community has set expectations for performance that management cannot meet by executing its current business plan. In these circumstances, managers are sometimes pressured to use the discretion inherent in the reporting process to meet analysts' expectations or to disguise a planned course of action.

The financial reporting environment described in Chapter 1 imposes significant controls on financial reporting, because that reporting process is important to the health of the economy. Managers who do not report accurately and completely are potentially subject to severe penalties. Moreover, adjusting entry estimates have a "self-correcting" character. Underestimating expenses today means greater expenses tomorrow; overestimating revenues today means lower revenues tomorrow.

MID-CHAPTER REVIEW

The following transactions relate to Lundholm Transport Company.

a. The Supplies and Parts balance on September 30, 2015, the company's accounting year-end, reveals $100,000 available. This amount reflects its beginning-year balance and all purchases for the year. A physical inventory indicates that much of this balance has been used in service operations, leaving supplies valued at $9,000 remaining at year-end September 30, 2015.

b. A $5,000 bill for September and October rent on the warehouse was received on September 29, but has not yet been paid or recorded.

c. A building holding its offices was purchased for $400,000 five years ago. The building's life was estimated at 8 years. Assume the entire asset cost is depreciated over its useful life. No depreciation has been recorded for this fiscal year.

d. An executive was hired on September 15 with a $120,000 annual salary. Payment and work are to start on October 15. No entry has yet been made to record this event.

e. A services contract is signed with the local university on September 1. Lundholm Transport Company received $1,200 cash on September 1 as a retainer for the months of September and October, but it has not yet been recorded. Lundholm Transport Company retains the money whether the university requires its services or not.

f. Employees are paid on the first day of the month following the month in which work is performed. Wages earned in September, but not yet paid or recorded as of September 30, amount to $25,000.

Required

1. For each of the 6 transactions described: (1) enter their effects in the financial statement effects template, and (2) prepare the related journal entries. Lundholm Transport's ledger includes the following ledger accounts and unadjusted normal balances at September 30: Cash $80,000; Accounts Receiv-

able $95,000; Supplies and Parts $100,000; Building $400,000; Accumulated Depreciation—Building $200,000; Land $257,500; Accounts Payable $20,000; Wages Payable $0; Unearned Revenue $0; Share Capital $80,000; Retained Earnings $380,000; Services Revenue $720,000; Rent Expense $27,500; Depreciation Expense $0; Wages Expense $440,000; Supplies and Parts Expense $0.

2. Set up T-accounts for all ledger accounts in part 1 and enter the beginning unadjusted balance, the adjustments from part 1, and the adjusted ending balance.

The solution to this review problem can be found on pages 139–141.

CONSTRUCTING FINANCIAL STATEMENTS FROM ADJUSTED ACCOUNTS

LO4 Prepare financial statements from adjusted accounts.

This section explains the preparation of financial statements from the adjusted financial accounts.

Preparing an Adjusted Trial Balance

After adjustments are recorded and posted, the company prepares an adjusted trial balance. The **adjusted trial balance** lists all the general ledger account balances after adjustments. Much of the content for company financial statements is taken from an adjusted trial balance. Exhibit 3.7 shows the general ledger accounts for Natural Beauty Supply after adjustments, in T-account form.

The adjusted trial balance at December 31 for Natural Beauty Supply is prepared from its general ledger accounts and is in the right-hand two columns of Exhibit 3.8. We show the unadjusted balances along with the adjustments to highlight the adjustment process.

Preparing Financial Statements

A company prepares its financial statements from the adjusted trial balance (and sometimes other supporting information). The set of financial statements consists of (and is prepared in the order of) the income statement, statement of changes in equity, balance sheet, and statement of cash flows. The following diagram summarises this process.

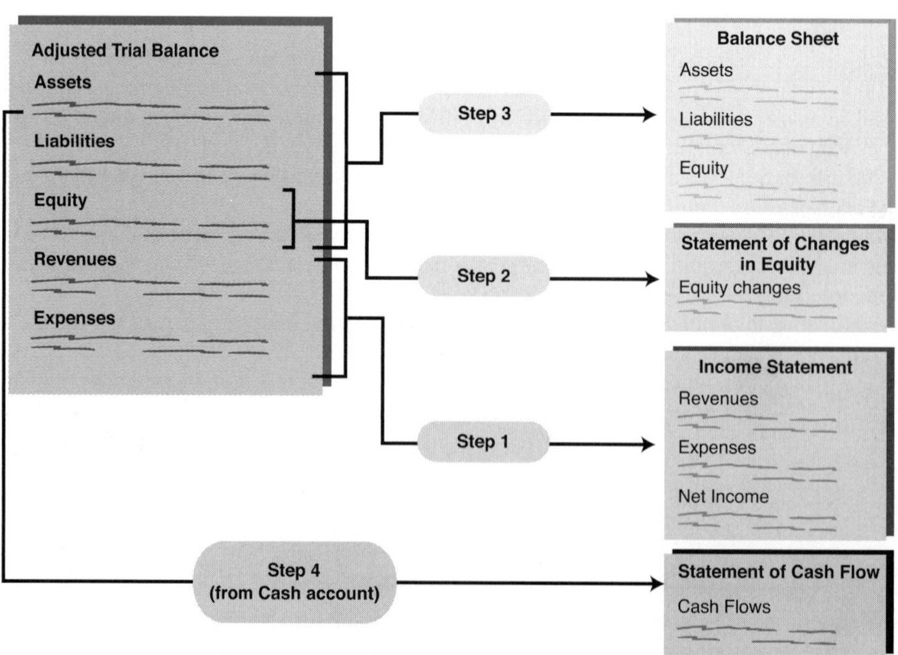

Income Statement The income statement reports a company's revenues and expenses. Natural Beauty Supply's adjusted trial balance contains two revenue/income accounts and eight

EXHIBIT 3.7 General Ledger for Natural Beauty Supply after Adjustments

General Ledger

Assets = Liabilities + Equity

Assets

+ Cash (A) −

Beg. Bal.	8,100		
(17)	11,000	18,000	(18)
(21a)	8,500	700	(19)
(23)	1,200	3,300	(20)
(25)	3,200	1,625	(24)
		1,500	(27)
		50	(28)
Adj. Bal.	6,825		

+ Accounts Receivable (A) −

Beg. Bal.	950		
(22a)	4,500	3,200	(25)
Adj. Bal.	2,250		

+ Other Receivables (A) −

Beg. Bal.	0		
(d)	30		
Adj. Bal.	30		

+ Inventory (A) −

Beg. Bal.	11,300		
(26)	4,000	5,000	(21b)
		3,000	(22b)
Adj. Bal.	7,300		

+ Prepaid Insurance (A) −

Beg. Bal.	1,680	140	(b)
Adj. Bal.	1,540		

+ Security Deposit (A) −

Beg. Bal.	2,000		
Adj. Bal.	2,000		

+ Fixtures and Equipment (A) −

Beg. Bal.	0		
(18)	18,000		
Adj. Bal.	18,000		

− Accumulated Depreciation—Fixtures and Equipment (XA) +

		0	Beg. Bal.
		375	(c)
		375	Adj. Bal.

Liabilities

− Accounts Payable (L) +

		3,700	Beg. Bal.
(20)	3,300	4,000	(26)
		4,400	Adj. Bal.

− Interest Payable (L) +

		0	Beg. Bal.
		110	(f)
		110	Adj. Bal.

− Wages Payable (L) +

		0	Beg. Bal.
		480	(e)
		480	Adj. Bal.

− Taxes Payable (L) +

		0	Beg. Bal.
		350	(g)
		350	Adj. Bal.

− Unearned Revenue (L) +

		300	Beg. Bal.
(a)	900	1,200	(23)
		600	Adj. Bal.

− Notes Payable (L) +

		0	Beg. Bal.
		11,000	(17)
		11,000	Adj. Bal.

Equity

− Share Capital (SE) +

		20,000	Beg. Bal.
		20,000	Adj. Bal.

− Retained Earnings (SE) +

		30	Beg. Bal.
(28)	50		
Adj. Bal.	20		

− Sales Revenue (R) +

		8,500	(21a)
		4,500	(22a)
		900	(a)
		13,900	Adj. Bal.

− Interest Income (R) +

		30	(d)
		30	Adj. Bal.

+ Cost of Goods Sold (E) −

(21b)	5,000		
(22b)	3,000		
Adj. Bal.	8,000		

+ Wages Expense (E) −

(24)	1,625		
(e)	480		
Adj. Bal.	2,105		

+ Rent Expense (E) −

(27)	1,500		
Adj. Bal.	1,500		

+ Advertising Expense (E) −

(19)	700		
Adj. Bal.	700		

+ Depreciation Expense—Fixtures and Equipment (E) −

(c)	375		
Adj. Bal.	375		

+ Insurance Expense (E) −

(b)	140		
Adj. Bal.	140		

+ Interest Expense (E) −

(f)	110		
Adj. Bal.	110		

+ Tax Expense (E) −

(g)	350		
Adj. Bal.	350		

Assets = $37,570 = **Liabilities = $16,940** + **Equity = $20,630**

EXHIBIT 3.8 Unadjusted and Adjusted Trial Balances

NATURAL BEAUTY SUPPLY, INC.
Trial Balance
December 31, 2013

	Unadjusted Trial Balance		Adjustments				Adjusted Trial Balance	
	Debit	Credit		Debit		Credit	Debit	Credit
Cash	$ 6,825						$ 6,825	
Accounts Receivable	2,250						2,250	
Other Receivables			(d)	$ 30			30	
Inventory	7,300						7,300	
Prepaid Insurance	1,680				(b)	$ 140	1,540	
Security Deposit	2,000						2,000	
Fixtures and Equipment	18,000						18,000	
Accumulated Depreciation					(c)	375		$ 375
Accounts Payable		$ 4,400						4,400
Interest Payable					(f)	110		110
Wages Payable					(e)	480		480
Taxes Payable					(g)	350		350
Unearned Revenue		1,500	(a)	900				600
Notes Payable		11,000						11,000
Share Capital		20,000						20,000
Retained Earnings	20						20	
Sales Revenue		13,000			(a)	900		13,900
Interest Income					(d)	30		30
Cost of Goods Sold	8,000						8,000	
Wages Expense	1,625		(e)	480			2,105	
Rent Expense	1,500						1,500	
Advertising Expense	700						700	
Depreciation Expense			(c)	375			375	
Insurance Expense			(b)	140			140	
Interest Expense			(f)	110			110	
Tax Expense			(g)	350			350	
Totals	$49,900	$49,900		$2,385		$2,385	$51,245	$51,245

expense accounts. The revenues and expenses are reported in Natural Beauty Supply's income statement for December as shown in Exhibit 3.9. Its net income for December is $650.

EXHIBIT 3.9 Income Statement

NATURAL BEAUTY SUPPLY, INC.
Income Statement
For Month Ended December 31, 2013

Sales revenue	$13,900
Cost of goods sold	8,000
Gross profit	5,900
Wages expense	2,105
Rent expense	1,500
Advertising expense	700
Depreciation expense	375
Insurance expense	140
Operating income	1,080
Interest income	30
Interest expense	(110)
Income before tax expense	1,000
Tax expense	350
Net income	$ 650

Statement of Changes in Equity The statement of changes in equity reports the events causing the major equity components to change during the accounting period. Exhibit 3.10 shows Natural Beauty Supply's statement of changes in equity for December. A review of its Share

Capital account in the general ledger provides some of the information for this statement; namely, its balance at the beginning of the period and stock issuances during the period. The net income (or net loss) amount comes from the income statement. Dividends during the period are reflected in the retained earnings balance from the adjusted trial balance.

EXHIBIT 3.10 Statement of Changes in Equity

NATURAL BEAUTY SUPPLY, INC.
Statement of Changes in Equity
For Month Ended December 31, 2013

	Contributed Capital	Earned Capital	Total Equity
Balance, November 30, 2013	$20,000	$ 30	$20,030
Net income	—	650	650
Ordinary share issued	—	—	—
Cash dividends	—	(50)	(50)
Balances, December 31, 2013	$20,000	$630	$20,630

FYI Financial statements are most commonly prepared for annual, semiannual and quarterly accounting periods. A request for a bank loan is an example of a situation that can lead to financial statement preparation for a non-accounting period. ■

Balance Sheet The balance sheet reports a company's assets, liabilities, and equity. The assets and liabilities for **Natural Beauty Supply**'s balance sheet at December 31, 2013, shown in Exhibit 3.11, come from the adjusted trial balance in Exhibit 3.8. The amounts reported for Share Capital and Retained Earnings in the balance sheet are taken from the statement of changes in equity for December (Exhibit 3.10).

EXHIBIT 3.11 Balance Sheet

NATURAL BEAUTY SUPPLY, INC.
Balance Sheet
December 31, 2013

Assets			Liabilities	
Cash		$ 6,825	Accounts payable	$ 4,400
Accounts receivable		2,250	Interest payable	110
Other receivables		30	Wages payable	480
Inventory		7,300	Taxes payable	350
Prepaid insurance		1,540	Unearned revenue	600
Security deposit		2,000	Current liabilities	5,940
Current assets		19,945	Notes payable	11,000
Fixtures and Equipment	$18,000		Total liabilities	16,940
Less: Accumulated depreciation	375		**Equity**	
Fixtures and Equipment, net		17,625	Share capital	20,000
			Retained earnings	630
Total assets		$37,570	Total liabilities and equity	$37,570

FYI The income statement, statement of changes in equity, and statement of cash flows report on periods of time. These statements illustrate the accounting period concept—the concept that useful statements can be prepared for arbitrary time periods within a company's life span. The purpose of adjusting entries is to obtain useful statements for specific time periods. ■

Statement of Cash Flows The statement of cash flows is formatted to report cash inflows and outflows by the three primary business activities:

- *Cash flows from operating activities* Cash flows from the company's transactions and events that relate to its primary operations.
- *Cash flows from investing activities* Cash flows from acquisitions and divestitures of investments and long-term assets.
- *Cash flows from financing activities* Cash flows from issuances of and payments toward equity, borrowings, and long-term liabilities.

The net cash flows from these three sections yield the change in cash for the period.

In analysing the statement of cash flows, we should not necessarily conclude that the company is better off if cash increases and worse off if cash decreases. It is not the cash change that is most important, but the reasons for the change. For example, what are the sources of the cash inflows? Are these sources mainly from operating activities? To what uses have cash inflows been put? Such questions (and their answers) are key to properly using the statement of cash flows. In Chapter 4, we examine the statement of cash flows more closely, and we answer these questions. The procedures for preparing a statement of cash flows are discussed in the next chapter. For completeness, we present Natural Beauty Supply's statement of cash flows for December in Exhibit 3.12.

EXHIBIT 3.12 Statement of Cash Flows

NATURAL BEAUTY SUPPLY, INC. Statement of Cash Flows For Month Ended December 31, 2013	
Cash Flows from Operating Activities	
Cash received from customers	$12,900
Cash paid for inventory	(3,300)
Cash paid for wages	(1,625)
Cash paid for rent	(1,500)
Cash paid for advertising	(700)
Net cash provided by operating activities	5,775
Cash Flows from Investing Activities	
Cash paid for fixtures and equipment	(18,000)
Net cash used for investing activities	(18,000)
Cash Flows from Financing Activities	
Cash received from loans	11,000
Cash paid for dividends	(50)
Net cash provided by financing activities	10,950
Net change in cash	(1,275)
Cash balance, November 30, 2013	8,100
Cash balance, December 31, 2013	$ 6,825

CLOSING TEMPORARY ACCOUNTS

LO5 Describe the process of closing temporary accounts.

Temporary accounts consist of revenues and expenses. These accounts accumulate data that relate to a specific accounting period. As such, their balances are reported in period financial statements—the income statement, cash flow statement, and statement of changes in equity. At the end of each accounting period, the balances of these temporary accounts are transferred to a permanent account—the Retained Earnings account. This part of the accounting cycle is referred to as the **closing process**.

A temporary account is *closed* when an entry is made that changes its balance to zero. The entry is equal in amount to the account's balance but is opposite to the balance as a debit or credit. An account that is closed is said to be closed *to* the account that receives the offsetting debit or credit. Thus, a closing entry simply transfers the balance of one account to another account. When closing entries bring temporary account balances to zero, the temporary accounts are then ready to accumulate data for the next accounting period.

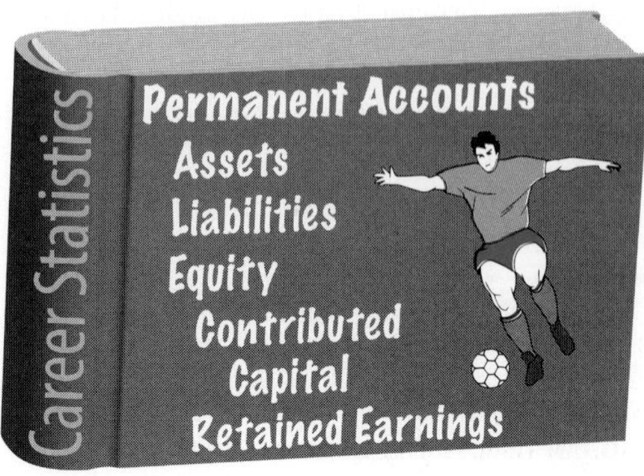

Closing Process

The Retained Earnings account can be used to close the temporary revenue and expense accounts.[3] The entries to close temporary accounts are:

1. **Close revenue accounts**. Debit each revenue account for an amount equal to its balance, and credit Retained Earnings for the total of revenues.
2. **Close expense accounts**. Credit each expense account for an amount equal to its balance, and debit Retained Earnings for the total of expenses.

After these temporary accounts are closed, the difference equals the period's net income (if revenues exceed expenses) or net loss (if expenses exceed revenues) and that difference is now included in retained earnings. The closing process is graphically portrayed as follows.

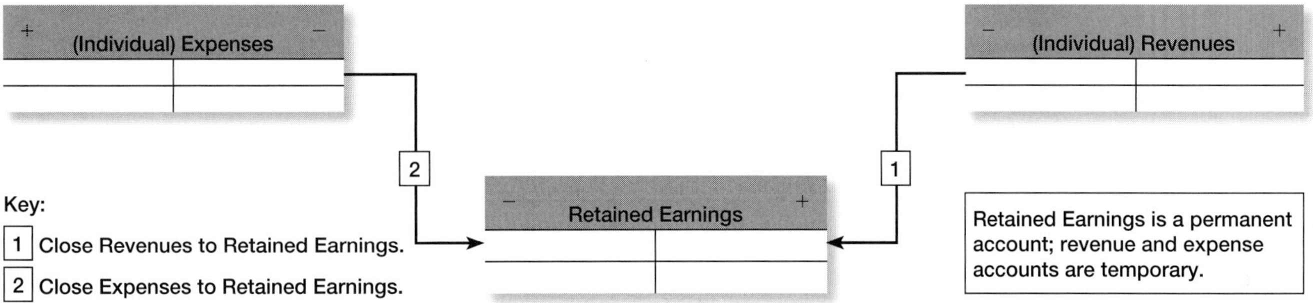

+ (Individual) Expenses −
− (Individual) Revenues +
2
1
Key:
1 Close Revenues to Retained Earnings.
2 Close Expenses to Retained Earnings.
− Retained Earnings +
Retained Earnings is a permanent account; revenue and expense accounts are temporary.

Closing Steps Illustrated

Exhibit 3.13 illustrates the entries for closing revenues and expenses for Natural Beauty Supply. The effects of these entries in T-accounts are shown after the journal entries. (We do not show the financial statement effects template for closing entries because **the template automatically closes revenues and expenses to the Retained Earnings account whenever they occur**—see earlier transactions for examples.)

EXHIBIT 3.13 Closing Revenues and Expenses*

1	Dec. 31	Sales revenue (−R)	13,900	
		Interest income (−R)	30	
		Retained earnings (+SE)		13,930
2	Dec. 31	Retained earnings (−SE)	13,280	
		Cost of goods sold (−E)		8,000
		Wages expense (−E)		2,105
		Rent expense (−E)		1,500
		Advertising expense (−E)		700
		Depreciation expense (−E)		375
		Insurance expense (−E)		140
		Interest expense (−E)		110
		Tax expense (−E)		350

* The two entries in this exhibit can be combined into a single entry where the credit (debit) to retained earnings would be net income (loss).

[3] *All* revenue and expense accounts are temporary accounts, so all revenue and expense accounts are closed to retained earnings at the end of the reporting period. In addition, companies often use a temporary account entitled Dividends Declared to record the amount of shareholder dividends declared during a reporting period. This account would accumulate a debit balance (because it reduces equity), and is closed to retained earnings at the end of the reporting period.

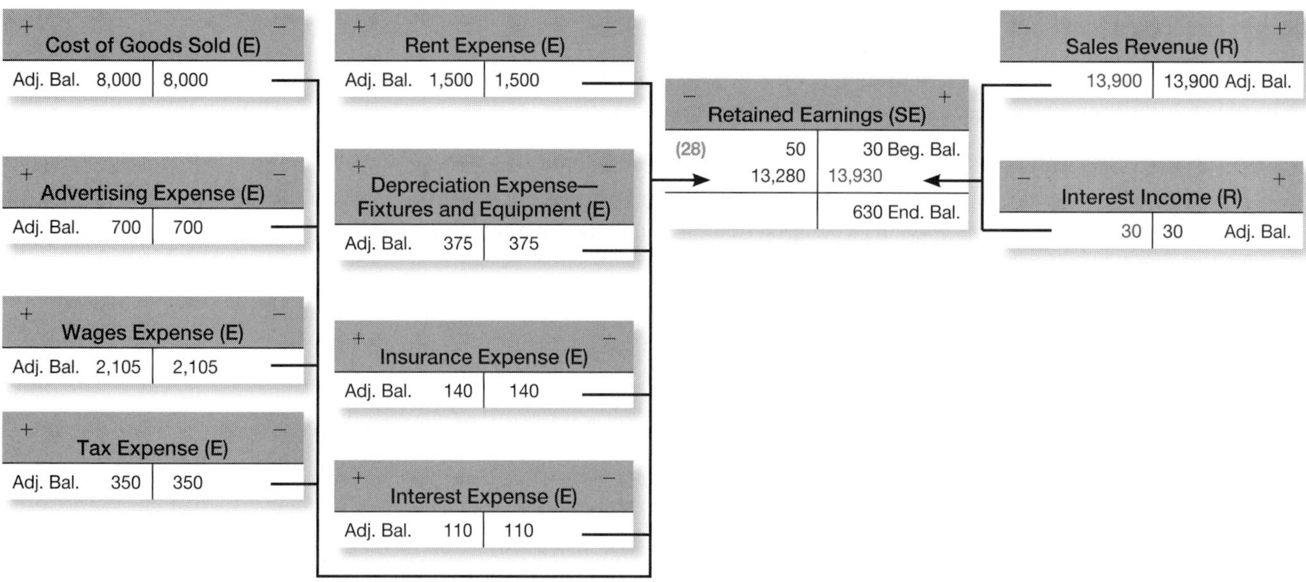

After these two steps, the net adjustment to the Retained Earnings account is a credit equal to the company's net income of $650, computed as $13,930 less $13,280. The Retained Earnings account in this case is increased by $650. We also recall that Natural Beauty Supply paid a cash dividend of $50 (transaction 28), which reduces retained earnings and results in the ending balance of $630.

Preparing a Post-Closing Trial Balance

After closing entries are recorded and posted to the general ledger, all temporary accounts have zero balances. At this point, a **post-closing trial balance** is prepared. A balancing of this trial balance is evidence that an equality of debits and credits has been maintained in the general ledger throughout the adjusting and closing process and that the general ledger is in balance to start the next accounting period. Only balance sheet accounts appear in a post-closing trial balance. The post-closing trial balance for Natural Beauty Supply is shown in Exhibit 3.14.

EXHIBIT 3.14 Post-Closing Trial Balance

NATURAL BEAUTY SUPPLY, INC.
Post-Closing Trial Balance
December 31, 2013

	Debit	Credit
Cash	$ 6,825	
Accounts Receivable	2,250	
Other Receivables	30	
Inventory	7,300	
Prepaid Insurance	1,540	
Security Deposit	2,000	
Fixtures and Equipment	18,000	
Accumulated Depreciation		$ 375
Accounts Payable		4,400
Interest Payable		110
Wages Payable		480
Taxes Payable		350
Unearned Revenue		600
Notes Payable		11,000
Share Capital		20,000
Retained Earnings		630
Totals	$37,945	$37,945

SUMMARISING THE ACCOUNTING CYCLE

The sequence of accounting procedures known as the accounting cycle occurs each fiscal year (period) and represents a systematic process for accumulating and reporting financial data of a company. Exhibit 3.15 expands on Exhibit 3.1 to include descriptions of the five major steps in the accounting cycle.

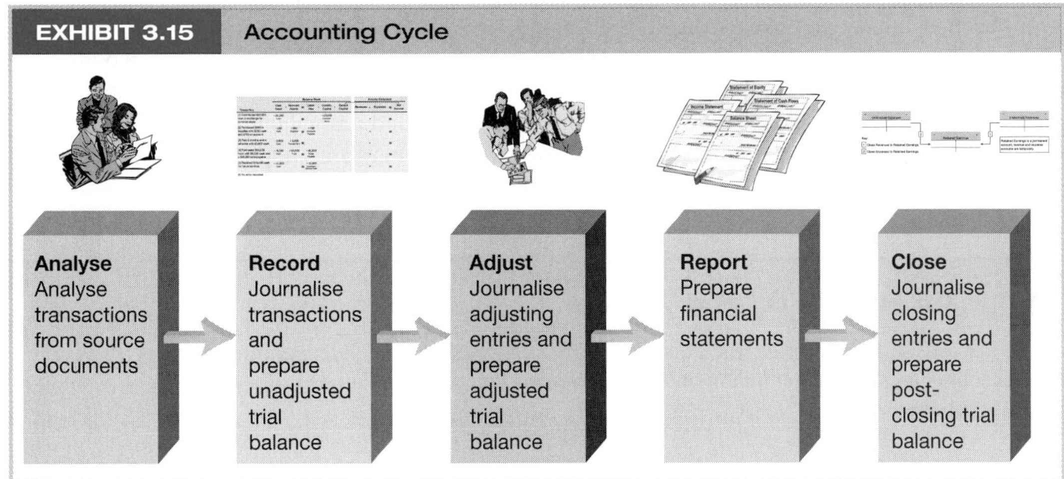
Analyse
Analyse transactions from source documents
Record
Journalise transactions and prepare unadjusted trial balance
Adjust
Journalise adjusting entries and prepare adjusted trial balance
Report
Prepare financial statements
Close
Journalise closing entries and prepare post-closing trial balance

EXHIBIT 3.15 Accounting Cycle

FINANCIAL STATEMENT ANALYSIS

Using Information on Levels and Flows

LO6 Analyse changes in balance sheet accounts.

A careful reader of financial statements must differentiate between those things that depict *levels* and those that depict *flows* or *changes*. The balance sheet portrays levels of resources and claims on those resources at a point in time, and the income statement portrays changes in those levels over a period of time. Knowing how the levels and flows relate to each other can be a very useful tool for analysis.

For instance, suppose that a service business has an inventory of office supplies. On July 1, an inventory count determined that the business has $2,400 of supplies inventory on hand. During the third calendar quarter, there were deliveries of office supplies with a cost of $5,700. And, at the end of the third quarter—on September 30—an inventory count finds $1,900 of supplies on hand. What amount of supplies expense should be recognised for the quarter?

Finding the answer to this question is easier if we recall the transactions that can affect the supplies inventory account, and that these transactions (changes) must lead from the beginning inventory level to the ending inventory level. At present, we know of two such transactions: the purchase of supplies inventory and the usage of supplies inventory.

(a)	Supplies inventory (+A)	5,700	
	Cash (−A) or Accounts payable (+L)		5,700
	Purchase supplies inventory.		
(b)	Supplies expense (+E, −SE)	?	
	Supplies inventory (−A)		?
	Record expense for supplies used.		

The supplies inventory T-account must look like the following:

+	Supplies Inventory (A)		−
Beg. Bal.	2,400		
(a)	5,700	?	(b)
End. Bal.	1,900		

Balancing the account requires that \$2,400 + \$5,700 − ? = \$1,900, and the value that satisfies this condition is \$6,200. That amount would be recorded as supplies expense for the quarter.

This application of the T-account structure is a simple one—in fact, it is used in part *a* of the Mid-Chapter Review. But, suppose that a separate source of information told us that \$5,900 in supplies had been taken from inventory for client service activities. When put into the T-account analysis above, this new fact would imply an additional \$300 in supplies had been removed for reasons such as breakage, obsolescence, or pilferage.

As we progress through the topics in future chapters, we will find that accounting reports do not always provide the information that is most useful for assessment of a company's current performance or standing. In those cases, we can often use T-accounts and journal entries to analyse levels and changes and to develop the numbers that do a better job of answering important questions.

CHAPTER-END REVIEW

Assume that Atwell Laboratories, Inc., operates with an accounting fiscal year ending June 30. The company's accounts are adjusted annually and closed on that date. Its unadjusted trial balance as of June 30, 2015, is as follows.

ATWELL LABORATORIES, INC.
Unadjusted Trial Balance
June 30, 2015

	Debit	Credit
Cash	\$ 1,000	
Accounts Receivable	9,200	
Prepaid Insurance	6,000	
Supplies	31,300	
Equipment	270,000	
Accumulated Depreciation—Equipment		\$ 60,000
Accounts Payable		3,100
Unearned Fees		4,000
Fees Revenue		150,000
Wages Expense	58,000	
Rent Expense	22,000	
Share Capital		120,400
Retained Earnings		60,000
Totals	\$397,500	\$397,500

Additional Information

1. Atwell acquired a two-year insurance policy on January 1, 2015. The policy covers fire and casualty; Atwell had no coverage prior to January 1, 2015.
2. An inventory of supplies was taken on June 30 and the amount available was \$6,300.
3. All equipment was purchased on July 1, 2012, for \$270,000. The equipment's life is estimated at 9 years. Assume the entire asset cost is depreciated over its useful life.
4. Atwell received a \$4,000 cash payment on April 1, 2015, from Beave Clinic for diagnostic work to be provided uniformly over the next 4 months, beginning April 1, 2015. The amount was credited to Unearned Fees. The service was provided per the agreement.
5. Unpaid and unrecorded wages at June 30, 2015, were \$600.
6. Atwell rents facilities for \$2,000 per month. Atwell has not yet made or recorded the payment for June 2015.

Required

1. Show the impact of the adjustments using the FSET, prepare the necessary adjusting journal entries, and enter them in T-accounts. Atwell's ledger includes the following ledger accounts and unadjusted normal balances at June 30: Cash $1,000; Accounts Receivable $9,200; Supplies $31,300; Prepaid Insurance $6,000; Equipment $270,000; Accumulated Depreciation—Equipment $60,000; Accounts Payable $3,100; Wages Payable $0; Rent Payable $0; Unearned Fees $4,000; Share Capital $120,400; Retained Earnings $60,000; Fees Revenue $150,000; Rent Expense $22,000; Insurance Expense $0; Depreciation Expense $0; Wages Expense $58,000; Supplies Expense $0. Use "Unadj. bal." to denote the unadjusted balance in each account when such a balance exists, and use "Adj. bal." to denote the adjusted balance.
2. Prepare its adjusted trial balance.
3. Prepare its closing journal entries and post them to the T-accounts (key the entries).
4. Prepare its balance sheet as of June 30, 2015, and its income statement and statement of changes in equity for the year ended June 30, 2015.

The solution to this review problem can be found on pages 142–146.

SUMMARY

Identify the major steps in the accounting cycle. (p. 94) LO1

- The major steps in the accounting cycle are
  a. Analyse *b.* Record *c.* Adjust *d.* Report *e.* Close

Review the process of journalising and posting transactions. (p. 95) LO2

- Transactions are initially recorded in a journal; the entries are in chronological order, and the journal shows the total effect of each transaction or adjustment.
- Posting is the transfer of information from a journal to the general ledger accounts.

Describe the adjusting process and illustrate adjusting entries. (p. 101) LO3

- Adjusting entries achieve the proper recognition of revenues and the proper matching of expenses with those revenues; adjustments are summarised as follows.

Adjustment	Adjusting Entry
Adjusting prepaid expenses	Increase expense Decrease asset
Adjusting unearned revenues	Decrease liability Increase revenue
Accruing expenses	Increase expense Increase liability
Accruing revenues	Increase asset Increase revenue

Prepare financial statements from adjusted accounts. (p. 110) LO4

- An income statement, statement of changes in equity, balance sheet, and statement of cash flows are prepared from an adjusted trial balance and other information.

LO5 Describe the process of closing temporary accounts. (p. 114)

- *Closing the books* means closing (yielding zero balances) revenues and expenses—that is, all temporary accounts. Revenue and expense account balances are transferred (closed) to the Retained Earnings account.

LO6 Analyse changes in balance sheet accounts. (p. 117)

- The combination of balance sheet levels and income statement flows allows a financial statement reader to infer the effects of transactions and adjustments that are not disclosed directly.

GUIDANCE ANSWERS . . . YOU MAKE THE CALL

You are the Chief Accountant Deposits represent a liability and should be included in REI's current liabilities at the time the cash or cheque is received. The account that would be used may have several names, including advances, trip deposits, and unearned revenues. Revenue should not be recognised until the trip has been completed. It is not unusual for events to occur that result in a refund of some portion or even all of the traveller's total payment. In the present case involving a low cancellation rate, waiting until the trip is over is not only conservative reporting, but is likely more efficient bookkeeping as well.

KEY TERMS

Accounting cycle (p. 94)
Accruals (p. 103)
Accrued expense (p. 107)
Accrued income (p. 106)
Accrued revenue (p. 106)
Adjusted trial balance (p. 110)
Adjusting entries (p. 103)
Book value (p. 106)
Calendar year (p. 94)
Chart of accounts (p. 95)
Close expense accounts (p. 115)
Close revenue accounts (p. 115)
Closing process (p. 114)
Contra accounts (p. 105)
Deferrals (p. 103)
Deferred revenue (p. 103)
Depreciation (p. 105)
Fiscal year (p. 94)
General journal (p. 95)
Journal (p. 95)
Post-closing trial balance (p. 116)
Posting (p. 95)
Straight-line depreciation (p. 105)
Unadjusted trial balance (p. 102)
Unearned revenue (p. 103)

MULTIPLE CHOICE

Multiple Choice Answers
1. d 2. a 3. b 4. c 5. c

1. A journal entry that contains more than two accounts is called
   a. a posted journal entry.
   b. an adjusting journal entry.
   c. an erroneous journal entry.
   d. a compound journal entry.

2. Posting refers to the process whereby journal entry information is transferred from
   a. journal to general ledger accounts.
   b. general ledger accounts to a journal.
   c. source documents to a journal.
   d. a journal to source documents.

3. Which of the following is an example of an adjusting entry?
   a. Recording the purchase of supplies on account
   b. Recording depreciation expense on a truck
   c. Recording cash received from customers for services rendered
   d. Recording the cash payment of wages to employees

4. A piece of equipment was placed in service on January 1, 2013. The cost of the equipment was $20,000, and it is expected to have no value at the end of its eight-year life. Using straight-line depreciation, what amounts will be seen for depreciation expense and accumulated depreciation for fiscal (and calendar) year 2015?

	Fiscal Year 2015 Depreciation Expense	Fiscal Year-end 2015 Accumulated Depreciation
a.	$2,500	$ 2,000
b.	–0–	$20,000
c.	$2,500	$ 7,500
d.	$7,500	$ 7,500

5. When a customer places an order, Custom Cakes requires a deposit equal to the full purchase price. However, Custom Cakes does not recognise revenue until the completed cake is delivered. During the month of November 2013, Custom Cakes received $24,000 in customer deposits. The balance in its unearned revenue liability was $4,000 at the beginning of November and $6,000 at the end of November. How much revenue did Custom Cakes recognise during the month of November?

a. $26,000
b. $24,000
c. $22,000
d. $4,000

DISCUSSION QUESTIONS

Q3-1. What are the five major steps in the accounting cycle? List them in their proper order.

Q3-2. What does the term *fiscal year* mean?

Q3-3. What are three examples of source documents that underlie business transactions?

Q3-4. What is the nature and purpose of a general journal?

Q3-5. Explain the process of posting.

Q3-6. What is a compound journal entry?

Q3-7. What is a chart of accounts? Give an example of a coding system for identifying different types of accounts.

Q3-8. Why is the adjusting step of the accounting cycle necessary?

Q3-9. What four different types of adjustments are frequently necessary at the close of an accounting period? Give examples of each type.

Q3-10. On January 1, Prepaid Insurance was debited with the cost of a two-year premium, $1,872. What adjusting entry should be made on January 31 before financial statements are prepared for the month?

Q3-11. What is a contra account? What contra account is used in reporting the book value of a depreciable asset?

Q3-12. A building was acquired on January 1, 2010, at a cost of $4,000,000, and its depreciation is calculated using the straight-line method. At the end of 2014, the accumulated depreciation contra asset for the building is $800,000. What will be the balance in the building's accumulated depreciation contra asset at the end of 2021? What is the building's book value at that date?

Q3-13. The publisher of *International View*, a monthly magazine, received two-year subscriptions totaling $9,720 on January 1. (a) What entry should be made to record the receipt of the $9,720? (b) What entry should be made at the end of January before financial statements are prepared for the month?

Q3-14. Globe Travel Agency pays an employee $475 in wages each Friday for the five-day workweek ending on that day. The last Friday of January falls on January 27. What adjusting entry should be made on January 31, the fiscal year-end?

Q3-15. The Bayou Company earns interest amounting to $360 per month on its investments. The company receives the interest every six months, on December 31 and June 30. Monthly financial statements are prepared. What adjusting entry should be made on January 31?

Q3-16. Which groups of accounts are closed at the end of the accounting year?

Q3-17. What are the two major steps in the closing process?

Q3-18. What is the purpose of a post-closing trial balance? Which of the following accounts should *not* appear in the post-closing trial balance: Cash; Unearned Revenue; Prepaid Rent; Depreciation Expense; Utilities Payable; Supplies Expense; and Retained Earnings?

Q3-19. Dehning Corporation is an international manufacturer of films and industrial identification products. Included among its prepaid expenses is an account titled Prepaid Catalog Costs; in recent years, this account's size has ranged between $2,500,000 and $4,000,000. The company states that catalogue costs are initially capitalised and then written off over the estimated useful lives of the publications (generally eight months). Identify and briefly discuss the accounting principles that support Dehning Corporation's handling of its catalogue costs.

Q3-20. At the beginning of January, the first month of the accounting year, the Supplies account had a debit balance of $825. During January, purchases of $260 worth of supplies were debited to the account. Although only $630 of supplies were still available at the end of January, the necessary adjusting entry was omitted. How will the omission affect (a) the income statement for January, and (b) the balance sheet prepared at January 31?

MINI EXERCISES

LO2 **M3-21. Journalising Transactions in Template, Journal Entry Form, and T-Accounts**

Creative Designs, a firm providing art services for advertisers, began business on June 1, 2014. The following accounts in its general ledger are needed to record the transactions for June: Cash; Accounts Receivable; Supplies; Office Equipment; Accounts Payable; Share Capital; Retained Earnings; Service Fees Earned; Rent Expense; Utilities Expense; and Salaries Expense. Record the following transactions for June (a) using the financial statement effects template and (b) in journal entry form. (c) Set up T-accounts for each of the ledger accounts and post the entries to them (key the numbers in T-accounts by date).

June 1 Anne Clem invested $12,000 cash to begin the business in exchange for common stock.
2 Paid $950 cash for June rent.
3 Purchased $6,400 of office equipment on account.
6 Purchased $3,800 of art materials and other supplies; paid $1,800 cash with the remainder due within 30 days.
11 Billed clients $4,700 for services rendered.
17 Collected $3,250 cash from clients on their accounts.
19 Paid $3,000 cash toward the account for office equipment suppliers (see June 3).
25 Paid $900 cash for dividends.
30 Paid $350 cash for June utilities.
30 Paid $2,500 cash for June salaries.

LO2 **M3-22. Journalising and Posting Transactions**

Minute Maid, a firm providing housecleaning services, began business on April 1, 2014. The following accounts in its general ledger are *needed* to record the transactions for April: Cash; Accounts Receivable; Supplies; Prepaid Van Lease; Equipment; Notes Payable; Accounts Payable; Share Capital; Retained Earnings; Cleaning Fees Earned; Wages Expense; Advertising Expense; and Van Fuel Expense. Record the following transactions for April (a) using the financial statement effects template and (b) in journal entry form. (c) Set up T-accounts for each of the ledger accounts and post the entries to them (key the numbers in T-accounts by date).

April 1 A. Falcon invested $9,000 cash to begin the business in exchange for common shares.
2 Paid $2,850 cash for six months' lease on van for the business.
3 Borrowed $10,000 cash from bank and signed note payable agreeing to repay it in 1 year plus 10% interest.
3 Purchased $5,500 of cleaning equipment; paid $2,500 cash with the remainder due within 30 days.
4 Paid $4,300 cash for cleaning supplies.
7 Paid $350 cash for advertisements to run in newspaper during April.
21 Billed customers $3,500 for services performed.

23 Paid $3,000 cash on account to cleaning equipment suppliers (see April 3).
28 Collected $2,300 cash from customers on their accounts.
29 Paid $1,000 cash for dividends.
30 Paid $1,750 cash for April wages.
30 Paid $995 cash to service station for gasoline used during April.

M3-23. Journalising Transactions and Adjusting Accounts LO2, 3

Deluxe Building Services offers custodial services on both a contract basis and an hourly basis. On January 1, 2013, Deluxe collected $20,100 in advance on a six-month contract for work to be performed evenly during the next six months.

a. Prepare the entry on January 1 to record the receipt of $20,100 cash for contract work (1) using the financial statements effect template and (2) in journal entry form.

b. Prepare the adjusting entry to be made on January 31, 2013, for the contract work done during January (1) using the financial statements effect template and (2) in journal entry form.

c. At January 31, a total of 30 hours of hourly rate custodial work was unbilled. The billing rate is $19 per hour. Prepare the adjusting entry needed on January 31, 2013, (1) using the financial statements effect template and (2) in journal entry form. (The firm uses the account Fees Receivable to reflect amounts due but not yet billed.)

M3-24. Adjusting Accounts LO3

Selected accounts of Ideal Properties, a real estate management firm, are shown below as of January 31, 2014, before any adjusting entries have been made.

Unadjusted Account Balances	Debits	Credits
Prepaid Insurance	$6,660	
Supplies	1,930	
Office Equipment	5,952	
Unearned Rent Revenue		$ 5,250
Salaries Expense	3,100	
Rent Revenue		15,000

Monthly financial statements are prepared. Using the following information, record the adjusting entries necessary on January 31 (a) using the financial statements effect template and (b) in journal entry form.

1. Prepaid Insurance represents a three-year premium paid on January 1, 2014.
2. Supplies of $850 were still available on January 31.
3. Office equipment is expected to last eight years.
4. On January 1, 2014, Ideal Properties collected six months' rent in advance from a tenant renting space for $875 per month.
5. Accrued employee salaries of $490 are not recorded as of January 31.

M3-25. Inferring Transactions from Financial Statements LO2, 3, 6

CANADIAN TIRE (CANADA)

Canadian Tire, headquartered in Toronto, Ontario is a retailer of auto parts, apparel and sporting goods. For the fiscal year ended December 28, 2013, Canadian Tire purchased merchandise inventory costing $8,041 (in millions). Assume that all purchases were made on account. The following T-accounts reflect information contained in the company's 2012 and 2013 balance sheets (in C$ millions).

+ Inventories (A)	−
12/29/2012 Bal. 1,503	
12/28/2013 Bal. 1,481	

− Accounts Payable (L)	+
	1,631 12/29/2012 Bal.
	1,817 12/28/2013 Bal.

a. Prepare the entry, using the financial statement effects template and in journal entry form, to record its purchases for the 2013 fiscal year.

b. What amount did Canadian Tire pay in cash to its suppliers for fiscal year ended December 28, 2013? Explain. Assume that Accounts Payable is affected only by transactions related to inventory.

c. Prepare the entry, using the financial statement effects template and in journal entry form, to record cost of goods sold for the year ended December 28, 2013.

LO4 M3-26. Preparing a Statement of Changes in Equity

On December 31, 2013, the credit balances of the Share Capital and Retained Earnings accounts were $30,000 and $18,000, respectively, for Architect Services Company. Its stock issuances for 2014 totaled $6,000, and it paid $9,700 cash toward dividends in 2014. For the year ended December 31, 2014, the company had net income of $29,900. Prepare a 2014 statement of changes in equity for Architect Services.

LO5 M3-27. Applying Closing Procedures

Assume you are in the process of closing procedures for Echo Corporation. You have already closed all revenue and expense accounts to the Retained Earnings account. The total debits equal $308,800 and total credits equal $347,400. The Retained Earnings account had a credit balance of $99,000 at the start of this current year. What is the post-closing ending balance of Retained Earnings at the end of this current year?

LO5 M3-28. Preparing Closing Entries Using Journal Entries and T-Accounts

The adjusted trial balance at December 31, 2014, for Smith Company includes the following selected accounts.

Adjusted Account Balances	Debit	Credit
Commissions Revenue		$84,900
Wages Expense	$36,000	
Insurance Expense	1,900	
Utilities Expense	8,200	
Depreciation Expense	9,800	
Retained Earnings		72,100

a. Prepare entries to close these accounts in journal entry form.

b. Set up T-accounts for each of these ledger accounts, enter the balances above, and post the closing entries to them. After these entries are posted, what is the post-closing balance of the Retained Earnings account?

LO2, 3, 6 M3-29. Inferring Transactions from Financial Statements

TIM HORTONS (CANADA)

Tim Hortons Inc. is a Canadian casual restaurant chain known for its coffee and doughnuts. For the year ended December 29, 2013, Tim Hortons' cost of sales was $1,972,903 (in thousands of Canadian dollars). Assume that all purchases were made on account. The following T-accounts reflect information contained in the company's 2012 and 2013 balance sheets (in thousands).

+	Inventories (A)	−
2012 Bal.	107,000	
2013 Bal.	104,326	

−	Accounts Payable (L)	+
	169,762	2012 Bal.
	204,514	2013 Bal.

a. Prepare the entry, using the financial statement effects template and in journal entry form, to record cost of sales for the year ended December 29, 2013.

b. Prepare the entry, using the financial statement effects template and in journal entry form, to record its purchases.

c. What amount did Tim Hortons pay in cash to its suppliers for the year ended December 29, 2013? Explain.

LO2, 3, 5 M3-30. Preparing Entries Across Two Periods

Hatcher Company closes its accounts on December 31 each year. On December 31, 2013, Hatcher accrued $600 of interest income that was earned on an investment but not yet received or recorded (the investment will pay interest of $900 cash on January 31, 2014). On January 31, 2014, the company received the $900 cash as interest on the investment. Prepare journal entries to:

a. Accrue the interest earned on December 31;

b. Close the Interest Income account on December 31 (the account has a year-end balance of $2,400 after adjustments); and

c. Record the cash receipt of interest on January 31, 2014.

EXERCISES

E3-31. Journalising and Posting Closing Entries LO5

The adjusted trial balance as of December 31, 2013, for Brooks Consulting Company contains the following selected accounts.

Adjusted Account Balances	Debit	Credit
Service Fees Earned		$80,300
Rent Expense	$20,800	
Salaries Expense	45,700	
Supplies Expense	5,600	
Depreciation Expense	10,200	
Retained Earnings		67,000

a. Prepare entries to close these accounts in journal entry form.

b. Set up T-accounts for each of the ledger accounts, enter the balances above, and post the closing entries to them. After these entries are posted, what is the post-closing balance of the Retained Earnings account?

E3-32. Preparing and Journalising Adjusting Entries LO3, 6

For each of the following separate situations, prepare the necessary adjustments (a) using the financial statement effects template, and (b) in journal entry form.

1. Unrecorded depreciation on equipment is $610.
2. The Supplies account has an unadjusted balance of $2,990. Supplies still available at the end of the period total $1,100.
3. On the date for preparing financial statements, an estimated utilities expense of $390 has been incurred, but no utility bill has yet been received or paid.
4. On the first day of the current period, rent for four periods was paid and recorded as a $2,800 debit to Prepaid Rent and a $2,800 credit to Cash.
5. Nine months ago, the Hartford Insurance Company sold a one-year policy to a customer and recorded the receipt of the premium by debiting Cash for $624 and crediting Unearned Premium Revenue for $624. No adjusting entries have been prepared during the nine-month period. Hartford's annual financial statements are now being prepared.
6. At the end of the period, employee wages of $965 have been incurred but not yet paid or recorded.
7. At the end of the period, $300 of interest income has been earned but not yet received or recorded.

E3-33. Preparing Adjusting and Closing Entries Across Two Periods LO2, 3, 5

Norton Company closes its accounts on December 31 each year. The company works a five-day work week and pays its employees every two weeks. On December 31, 2013, Norton accrued $4,700 of salaries payable. On January 7, 2014, the company paid salaries of $12,000 cash to employees. Prepare journal entries to:

a. Accrue the salaries payable on December 31;

b. Close the Salaries Expense account on December 31 (the account has a year-end balance of $250,000 after adjustments); and

c. Record the salary payment on January 7.

E3-34. Analysing Accounts Using Adjusted Data LO3, 6

Selected T-account balances for Fields Company are shown below as of January 31, 2014; adjusting entries have already been posted. The firm uses a calendar-year accounting period but prepares *monthly* adjustments.

+	Supplies (A)	−
Jan. 31 Bal.	800	

+	Supplies Expense (E)	−
Jan. 31 Bal.	960	

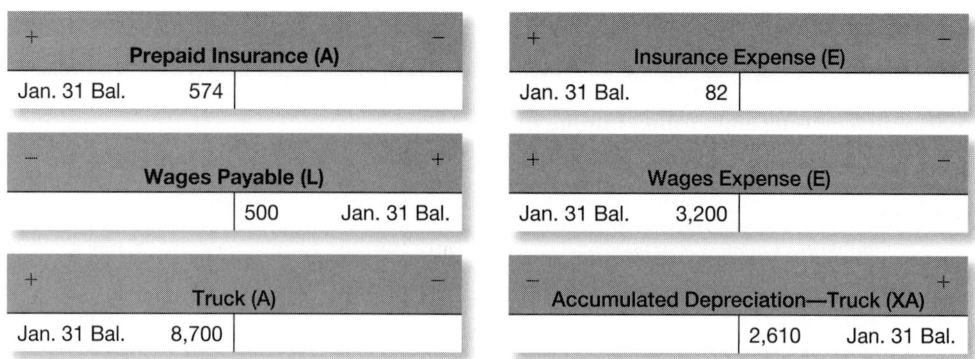

a. If the amount in Supplies Expense represents the January 31 adjustment for the supplies used in January, and $620 worth of supplies were purchased during January, what was the January 1 beginning balance of Supplies?

b. The amount in the Insurance Expense account represents the adjustment made at January 31 for January insurance expense. If the original insurance premium was for one year, what was the amount of the premium and on what date did the insurance policy start?

c. If we assume that no beginning balance existed in Wages Payable or Wages Expense on January 1, how much cash was paid as wages during January?

d. If the truck has a useful life of five years, what is the monthly amount of depreciation expense and how many months has Fields owned the truck?

LO2, 3, 6 **E3-35. Preparing Adjusting Entries**

Jake Thomas began Thomas Refinishing Service on July 1, 2014. Selected accounts are shown below as of July 31, before any adjusting entries have been made.

Unadjusted Account Balances	Debit	Credit
Prepaid Rent	$5,700	
Prepaid Advertising	630	
Supplies	3,000	
Unearned Refinishing Fees		$ 600
Refinishing Fees Revenue		2,500

Using the following information, prepare the adjusting entries necessary on July 31 (a) using the financial statement effects template and (b) in journal entry form. (c) Set up T-accounts for each of the ledger accounts, enter the balances above, and post the adjusting entries to them.

1. On July 1, the firm paid one year's advance rent of $5,700 in cash.
2. On July 1, $630 cash was paid to the local newspaper for an advertisement to run daily for the months of July, August, and September.
3. Supplies still available at July 31 total $1,100.
4. At July 31, refinishing services of $800 have been performed but not yet recorded or billed to customers. The firm uses the account Fees Receivable to reflect amounts due but not yet billed.
5. A customer paid $600 in advance for a refinishing project. At July 31, the project is one-half complete.

LO2, 3, 6 **E3-36. Inferring Transactions from Financial Statements**

Tai Koo Industries Inc. manufactures and sells motor homes as well as retail parts and accessories, throughout the United States and Canada. The following information is taken from Tai Koo's fiscal 2015 annual report. (All amounts in $ thousands.)

Selected Balance Sheet Data	2014	2015
Inventories	$43,526	$69,165
Accrued Compensation	10,529	10,841

a. Tai Koo reported cost of goods sold of $456,664 for its fiscal year 2015. Prepare the entry, using the financial statement effects template and in journal entry form, to record inventory purchases for its fiscal year 2015.

b. Assume that Tai Koo reported compensation expense of $40,000 for its fiscal year 2015. What amount of compensation was paid to its employees for fiscal year 2015?

c. Where would you expect Tai Koo to report its Accrued Compensation?

E3-37. Preparing Closing Procedures LO5

The adjusted trial balance of Parker Corporation, prepared December 31, 2015, contains the following selected accounts.

Adjusted Account Balances	Debit	Credit
Service Fees Earned		$92,500
Interest Income		2,200
Salaries Expense	$41,800	
Advertising Expense	4,300	
Depreciation Expense	8,700	
Income Tax Expense	9,900	
Retained Earnings		42,700

a. Prepare entries to close these accounts in journal entry form.

b. Set up T-accounts for each of the ledger accounts, enter the balances above, and post the closing entries to them. After these entries are posted, what is the post-closing balance of the Retained Earnings account?

E3-38. Preparing Closing Journal Entries LO5

QANTAS AIRLINES (AUSTRALIA)

Qantas Airlines is Australia's largest airline and one of the oldest airlines in the world. Selected accounts of Qantas's adjusted trial balance, prepared June 30, 2014, are given in the table below:

(AUD millions)	Debits	Credits
Total passenger and freight revenue		$15,352
Manpower and staff related	$3,717	
Fuel	4,461	
Aircraft operating variable	3,142	
Depreciation and amortisation	1,422	
Other expenses	6,382	
Finance costs	204	
Income tax benefit	1,133	
Retained earnings		1,172

a. Prepare entries to close these accounts in journal entry form.

b. Set up T-accounts for each of the ledger accounts, enter the balances above, and post the closing entries to them. After these entries are posted, what is the post-closing balance of the Retained Earnings account?

LO4, 5 **E3-39. Preparing Financial Statements and Closing Procedures**
Solomon Corporation's adjusted trial balance for the year ending December 31, 2015, is:

SOLOMON CORPORATION Adjusted Trial Balance December 31, 2015	Debit	Credit
Cash	$ 4,000	
Accounts Receivable	6,500	
Equipment	78,000	
Accumulated Depreciation		$ 14,000
Notes Payable		10,000
Share Capital		43,000
Retained Earnings		12,600
Service Fees Earned		71,000
Rent Expense	18,000	
Salaries Expense	37,100	
Depreciation Expense	7,000	
Totals	$150,600	$150,600

a. Prepare its income statement and statement of changes in equity for the current year, and its balance sheet for the current year-end. Cash dividends were $8,000 and there were no stock issuances or repurchases.

b. Prepare entries to close its temporary accounts in journal entry form.

c. Set up T-accounts for each of the ledger accounts, enter the balances above, and post the closing entries to them. After these entries are posted, what is the post-closing balance of the Retained Earnings account?

PROBLEMS

LO2, 3, 4 **P3-40. Journalising and Posting Transactions, and Preparing a Trial Balance and Adjustments**
B. Lougee opened Lougee Roofing Service on April 1, 2015. Transactions for April are as follows:

Apr. 1 Lougee contributed $11,500 cash to the business in exchange for common shares.
1 Paid $2,880 cash for two-year premium toward liability insurance effective immediately.
2 Paid $6,100 cash for the purchase of a used truck.
2 Purchased $3,100 of ladders and other equipment; paid $1,000 cash, with the balance due in 30 days.
5 Purchased $1,200 of supplies on account.
5 Received an advance of $1,800 cash from a customer for roof repairs to be done during April and May.
12 Billed customers $5,500 for roofing services performed.
18 Collected $4,900 cash from customers on their accounts.
29 Paid $675 cash for truck fuel used in April.
30 Paid $100 cash for April newspaper advertising.
30 Paid $2,500 cash for assistants' wages.
30 Billed customers $4,000 for roofing services performed.

Required

a. Set up a general ledger in T-account form for the following accounts: Cash; Accounts Receivable; Supplies; Prepaid Insurance; Trucks; Accumulated Depreciation—Trucks; Equipment; Accumulated Depreciation—Equipment; Accounts Payable; Unearned Roofing Fees; Share Capital; Roofing Fees Earned; Fuel Expense; Advertising Expense; Wages Expense; Insurance Expense; Supplies Expense; Depreciation Expense—Trucks; and Depreciation Expense—Equipment.

b. Record these transactions for April (1) using the financial statement effects template and (2) in journal entry form. (3) Post these entries to their T-accounts (key numbers in T-accounts by date).

c. Prepare an unadjusted trial balance as of April 30, 2015.

d. Supplies still available on April 30 amount to $400; and depreciation for April was $125 on the truck and $35 on equipment; and one-fourth of the roofing fee received in advance was earned by April 30. Prepare entries to adjust the books for Insurance Expense, Supplies Expense, Depreciation Expense—Trucks, Depreciation Expense—Equipment, and Roofing Fees Earned (1) using the financial statement effects template and (2) in journal entry form. (3) Post adjusting entries to their T-accounts.

P3-41. Preparing an Unadjusted Trial Balance and Adjustments LO2, 3, 4

SnapShot Company, a commercial photography studio, has just completed its first full year of operations on December 31, 2015. General ledger account balances *before* year-end adjustments follow; no adjusting entries have been made to the accounts at any time during the year. Assume that all balances are normal.

Cash	$ 2,150	Accounts Payable	$ 1,910
Accounts Receivable	3,800	Unearned Photography Fees	2,600
Prepaid Rent	12,600	Share Capital	24,000
Prepaid Insurance	2,970	Photography Fees Earned	34,480
Supplies	4,250	Wages Expense	11,000
Equipment	22,800	Utilities Expense	3,420

An analysis of the firm's records discloses the following.

1. Photography services of $925 have been rendered, but customers have not yet paid or been billed. The firm uses the account Fees Receivable to reflect amounts due but not yet billed.
2. Equipment, purchased January 1, 2015, has an estimated life of 10 years.
3. Utilities expense for December is estimated to be $400, but the bill will not arrive or be paid until January of next year.
4. The balance in Prepaid Rent represents the amount paid on January 1, 2015, for a 2-year lease on the studio.
5. In November, customers paid $2,600 cash in advance for photos to be taken for the holiday season. When received, these fees were credited to Unearned Photography Fees. By December 31, all of these fees are earned.
6. A 3-year insurance premium paid on January 1, 2015, was debited to Prepaid Insurance.
7. Supplies available at December 31 are $1,520.
8. At December 31, wages expense of $375 has been incurred but not paid or recorded.

Required

a. Prove that debits equal credits for SnapShot's unadjusted account balances by preparing its unadjusted trial balance at December 31, 2015.

b. Prepare its adjusting entries: (1) using the financial statement effects template, and (2) in journal entry form.

c. Set up T-accounts, enter the balances above, and post the adjusting entries to them.

P3-42. Preparing Adjusting Entries, Financial Statements, and Closing Entries LO2, 3, 4, 5

Murdock Carpet Cleaners ended its first month of operations on June 30, 2015. Monthly financial statements will be prepared. The unadjusted account balances are as follows.

MURDOCK CARPET CLEANERS
Unadjusted Trial Balance
June 30, 2015

	Debit	Credit
Cash	$ 1,180	
Accounts Receivable	450	
Prepaid Rent	3,100	
Supplies	2,520	
Equipment	4,440	
Accounts Payable		$ 760
Share Capital		2,000
Retained Earnings		5,300
Service Fees Earned		4,650
Wages Expense	1,020	
	$12,710	$12,710

The following information is available.

1. The balance in Prepaid Rent was the amount paid on June 1 for the first four months' rent.
2. Supplies available at June 30 were $820.
3. Equipment, purchased June 1, has an estimated life of five years.
4. Unpaid and unrecorded employee wages at June 30 were $210.
5. Utility services used during June were estimated at $300. A bill is expected early in July.
6. Fees earned for services performed but not yet billed on June 30 were $380. The company uses the account Accounts Receivable to reflect amounts due but not yet billed.

Required

a. Prepare its adjusting entries at June 30, 2015: (1) using the financial statement effects template, and (2) in journal entry form.
b. Set up T-accounts, enter the balances above, and post the adjusting entries to them.
c. Prepare its income statement for June and its balance sheet at June 30, 2015.
d. Prepare entries to close its temporary accounts in journal entry form and post the closing entries to the T-accounts.

LO3 P3-43. Preparing Adjusting Entries

The following information relates to the December 31 adjustments for Kwik Print Company. The firm's fiscal year ends on December 31.

1. Weekly employee salaries for a five-day week total $1,800, payable on Fridays. December 31 of the current year is a Tuesday.
2. Kwik Print has $20,000 of notes payable outstanding at December 31. Interest of $200 has accrued on these notes by December 31, but will not be paid until the notes mature next year.
3. During December, Kwik Print provided $900 of printing services to clients who will be billed on January 2. The firm uses the account Fees Receivable to reflect amounts due but not yet billed.
4. Starting December 1, all maintenance work on Kwik Print's equipment is handled by Richardson Repair Company under an agreement whereby Kwik Print pays a fixed monthly charge of $400. Kwik Print paid six months' service charge in advance on December 1, debiting Prepaid Maintenance for $2,400.
5. The firm paid $900 cash on December 15 for a series of radio commercials to run during December and January. One-third of the commercials have aired by December 31. The $900 payment was debited to Prepaid Advertising.
6. Starting December 16, Kwik Print rented 400 square feet of storage space from a neighbouring business. The monthly rent of $0.80 per square foot is due in advance on the first of each month. Nothing was paid in December, however, because the neighbour agreed to add the rent for the one-half of December to the January 1 payment.
7. Kwik Print invested $5,000 cash in securities on December 1 and earned interest of $38 on these securities by December 31. No interest payment will be received until January.
8. Annual depreciation on the firm's equipment is $2,175. No depreciation has been recorded during the year.

Required

Prepare its adjusting entries required at December 31:

a. using the financial statement effects template, and
b. in journal entry form.

P3-44. Preparing Financial Statements and Closing Entries LO4, 5

The following adjusted trial balance is for Trueman Consulting Inc. at December 31, 2015. The company had no stock issuances or repurchases during 2015.

	Debit	Credit
Cash	$ 2,700	
Accounts Receivable	3,270	
Supplies	3,060	
Prepaid Insurance	1,500	
Equipment	6,400	
Accumulated Depreciation—Equipment		$ 1,080
Accounts Payable		845
Long-Term Notes Payable		7,000
Share Capital		1,000
Retained Earnings		3,305
Service Fees Earned		58,400
Rent Expense	12,000	
Salaries Expense	33,400	
Supplies Expense	4,700	
Insurance Expense	3,250	
Depreciation Expense—Equipment	720	
Interest Expense	630	
	$71,630	$71,630

Required

a. Prepare its income statement and statement of changes in equity for 2015 and its balance sheet at December 31, 2015.

b. Prepare entries to close its accounts in journal entry form.

P3-45. Preparing Closing Entries LO5

The following adjusted trial balance is for Wilson Company at December 31, 2015.

	Debit	Credit
Cash	$ 8,500	
Accounts Receivable	8,000	
Prepaid Insurance	3,600	
Equipment	72,000	
Accumulated Depreciation		$ 12,000
Accounts Payable		600
Share Capital		25,000
Retained Earnings		19,100
Service Fees Earned		97,200
Miscellaneous Income		4,200
Salaries Expense	42,800	
Rent Expense	13,400	
Insurance Expense	1,800	
Depreciation Expense	8,000	
Income Tax Expense	8,800	
Income Tax Payable		8,800
	$166,900	$166,900

Required

a. Prepare closing entries in journal entry form.

b. After the firm's closing entries are posted, what is the post-closing balance for the Retained Earnings account?

c. Prepare its post-closing trial balance.

LO2, 3, 5 **P3-46. Preparing Entries Across Two Periods**
The following selected accounts appear in Shaw Company's unadjusted trial balance at December 31, 2015, the end of its fiscal year (all accounts have normal balances).

Prepaid Advertising.	$ 1,200	Unearned Service Fees.	$ 5,400
Wages Expense.	43,800	Service Fees Earned	87,000
Prepaid Insurance	3,420	Rental Income	4,900

Required

a. Prepare its adjusting entries at December 31, 2015, (1) using the financial statement effects template, and (2) in journal entry form using the following additional information.
   1. Prepaid advertising at December 31 is $800.
   2. Unpaid and unrecorded wages earned by employees in December are $1,300.
   3. Prepaid insurance at December 31 is $2,280.
   4. Unearned service fees at December 31 are $3,000.
   5. Rent revenue of $1,000 owed by a tenant is not recorded at December 31.

b. Prepare entries on January 4, 2016, using the financial statement effects template and in journal entry form, to record (1) payment of $2,400 cash in wages, which includes the $1,300 accrued at December 31 and (2) cash receipt of the $1,000 rent revenue owed from the tenant.

LO2, 3, 4 **P3-47. Journalising and Posting Transactions, and Preparing a Trial Balance and Adjustments**
Market-Probe, a market research firm, had the following transactions in June 2014, its first month of operations.

June 1 B. May invested $24,000 cash in the firm in exchange for common shares.
1 The firm purchased the following: office equipment, $11,040; office supplies, $2,840. Terms are $4,400 cash with the remainder due in 60 days. (Make a compound entry requiring two credits.)
2 Paid $875 cash for June rent owed to the landlord.
2 Contracted for 3 months' advertising in a local newspaper at $310 per month and paid for the advertising in advance.
2 Signed a 6-month contract with a customer to provide research consulting services at a rate of $3,200 per month. Received two months' fees in advance. Work on the contract started immediately.
10 Billed various customers $5,800 for services rendered.
12 Paid $3,600 cash for two weeks' salaries (5-day week) to employees.
15 Paid $1,240 cash to employee for travel expenses to conference.
18 Paid $520 cash to post office for bulk mailing of research questionnaire (postage expense).
26 Paid $3,600 cash for two weeks' salaries to employees.
28 Billed various customers $5,200 for services rendered.
30 Collected $7,800 cash from customers on their accounts.
30 Paid $1,500 cash for dividends.

Required

a. Set up a general ledger in T-account form for the following accounts: Cash; Accounts Receivable; Office Supplies; Prepaid Advertising; Office Equipment; Accumulated Depreciation—Office Equipment; Accounts Payable; Salaries Payable; Unearned Service Fees; Share Capital; Retained Earnings; Service Fees Earned; Salaries Expense; Advertising Expense; Supplies Expense; Rent Expense; Travel Expense; Depreciation Expense—Office Equipment; and Postage Expense.

b. Record these transactions (1) using the financial statement effects template, and (2) in journal entry form. (3) Post these entries to their T-accounts (key numbers in T-accounts by date).

c. Prepare an unadjusted trial balance at June 30, 2014.

d. Prepare adjusting entries (1) using the financial statement effects template and (2) in journal entry form, that reflect the following information at June 30, 2014:
   - Office supplies available, $1,530
   - Accrued employee salaries, $725
   - Estimated life of office equipment is 8 years

   Adjusting entries must also be prepared for advertising and service fees per information in the June transactions. (3) Post adjusting entries to their T-accounts.

P3-48. Preparing an Unadjusted Trial Balance and Adjusting Entries LO3

DeliverAll, a mailing service, has just completed its first full year of operations on December 31, 2015. Its general ledger account balances *before* year-end adjustments follow; no adjusting entries have been made to the accounts at any time during the year. Assume that all balances are normal.

Cash	$ 2,300	Accounts Payable	$ 2,700
Accounts Receivable	5,120	Share Capital	9,530
Prepaid Advertising	1,680	Mailing Fees Earned	86,000
Supplies	6,270	Wages Expense	38,800
Equipment	42,240	Rent Expense	6,300
Notes Payable	7,500	Utilities Expense	3,020

An analysis of the firm's records reveals the following.

1. The balance in Prepaid Advertising represents the amount paid for newspaper advertising for one year. The agreement, which calls for the same amount of space and cost each month, covers the period from February 1, 2015, to January 31, 2016. DeliverAll did not advertise during its first month of operations.
2. Equipment, purchased January 1, has an estimated life of eight years.
3. Utilities expense does not include expense for December, estimated at $325. The bill will not arrive until January 2016.
4. At year-end, employees have earned an additional $1,200 in wages that will not be paid or recorded until January.
5. Supplies available at year-end amount to $1,520.
6. At year-end, unpaid interest of $450 has accrued on the notes payable.
7. The firm's lease calls for rent of $525 per month payable on the first of each month, plus an amount equal to 1/2% of annual mailing fees earned. The rental percentage is payable within 15 days after the end of the year.

Required

a. Prove that debits equal credits for its unadjusted account balances by preparing its unadjusted trial balance at December 31, 2015.

b. Prepare its adjusting entries: (1) using the financial statement effects template, and (2) in journal entry form.

c. Set up T-accounts, enter the balances above, and post the adjusting entries to them.

P3-49. Preparing Adjusting Entries LO3, 4, 5

Wheel Place Company began operations on March 1, 2014, to provide automotive wheel alignment and balancing services. On March 31, 2014, the unadjusted balances of the firm's accounts are as follows.

WHEEL PLACE COMPANY
Unadjusted Trial Balance
March 31, 2014

	Debit	Credit
Cash	$ 1,900	
Accounts Receivable	3,820	
Prepaid Rent	4,770	
Supplies	3,700	
Equipment	36,180	
Accounts Payable		$ 2,510
Unearned Service Revenue		1,000
Share Capital		38,400
Service Revenue		12,360
Wages Expense	3,900	
Totals	$54,270	$54,270

The following information is available.

1. The balance in Prepaid Rent was the amount paid on March 1 to cover the first 6 months' rent.
2. Supplies available on March 31 amount to $1,720.

3. Equipment has an estimated life of nine years and a zero salvage value.
4. Unpaid and unrecorded wages at March 31 were $560.
5. Utility services used during March were estimated at $390; a bill is expected early in April.
6. The balance in Unearned Service Revenue was the amount received on March 1 from a car dealer to cover alignment and balancing services on cars sold by the dealer in March and April. The Wheel Place agreed to provide the services at a fixed fee of $500 each month.

Required

a. Prepare its adjusting entries at March 31, 2014, (1) using the financial statement effects template, and (2) in journal entry form.

b. Set up T-accounts, enter the balances above, and post the adjusting entries to them.

c. Prepare its income statement for March and its balance sheet at March 31, 2014.

d. Prepare entries to close its temporary accounts in journal entry form and post the closing entries to the T-accounts.

LO4, 5 **P3-50. Preparing Financial Statements and Closing Entries**

Trails, Inc., publishes magazines for skiers and hikers. The company's adjusted trial balance for the year ending December 31, 2015, is:

	Debit	Credit
Cash	$ 3,400	
Accounts Receivable	8,600	
Supplies	4,200	
Prepaid Insurance	930	
Office Equipment	66,000	
Accumulated Depreciation		$ 11,000
Accounts Payable		2,100
Unearned Subscription Revenue		10,000
Salaries Payable		3,500
Share Capital		25,000
Retained Earnings		23,220
Subscription Revenue		168,300
Advertising Revenue		49,700
Salaries Expense	100,230	
Printing and Mailing Expense	85,600	
Rent Expense	8,800	
Supplies Expense	6,100	
Insurance Expense	1,860	
Depreciation Expense	5,500	
Income Tax Expense	1,600	
Totals	$292,820	$292,820

Required

a. Prepare its income statement and statement of changes in equity for 2015, and its balance sheet at December 31, 2015. There were no cash dividends and no stock issuances or repurchases during the year.

b. Prepare entries to close its accounts in journal entry form.

LO5 **P3-51. Preparing Closing Entries**

The following adjusted trial balance is for Mayflower Moving Service at December 31, 2015.

	Debit	Credit
Cash	$ 3,800	
Accounts Receivable	5,250	
Supplies	2,300	
Prepaid Advertising	3,000	
Trucks	28,300	
Accumulated Depreciation—Trucks		$ 10,000
Equipment	7,600	
Accumulated Depreciation—Equipment		2,100
Accounts Payable		1,200
Unearned Service Fees		2,700

continued

continued from previous page

	Debit	Credit
Share Capital		5,000
Retained Earnings		15,550
Service Fees Earned		72,500
Wages Expense	29,800	
Rent Expense	10,200	
Insurance Expense	2,900	
Supplies Expense	5,100	
Advertising Expense	6,000	
Depreciation Expense—Trucks	4,000	
Depreciation Expense—Equipment	800	
Totals	$109,050	$109,050

Required

a. Prepare closing entries in journal entry form.

b. After its closing entries are posted, what is the post-closing balance for the Retained Earnings account?

c. Prepare Mayflower's post-closing trial balance.

P3-52. Preparing Entries Across Two Periods **LO2, 3, 5**

The following selected accounts appear in Zimmerman Company's unadjusted trial balance at December 31, 2015, the end of its fiscal year (all accounts have normal balances).

Prepaid Maintenance	$2,700	Commission Fees Earned	$84,000
Supplies	8,400	Rent Expense	10,800
Unearned Commission Fees	8,500		

Required

a. Prepare its adjusting entries at December 31, 2015 (1) using the financial statement effects template, and (2) in journal entry form. Additional information is as follows.

1. On September 1, 2015, the company entered into a prepaid equipment maintenance contract. Zimmerman Company paid $2,700 to cover maintenance service for 6 months, beginning September 1, 2015. The $2,700 payment was debited to Prepaid Maintenance.
2. Supplies available on December 31 are $3,200.
3. Unearned commission fees at December 31 are $4,000.
4. Commission fees earned but not yet billed at December 31 are $2,800. (*Hint:* Debit Fees Receivable.)
5. Zimmerman Company's lease calls for rent of $900 per month payable on the first of each month, plus an annual amount equal to 1% of annual commissions earned. This additional rent is payable on January 10 of the following year. (*Hint:* Use the adjusted amount of commissions earned in computing the additional rent.)

b. Prepare entries on January 10, 2016, using both the financial statement effects template and in journal entry form, to record (1) the billing of $4,600 in commissions earned (which includes the $2,800 of commissions earned but not billed at December 31) and (2) the cash payment of the additional rent owed for 2015.

P3-53. Preparing Adjusting Entries, Financial Statements, and Closing Entries **LO3, 4, 5, 6**

Fischer Card Shop is a small retail shop. Fischer's balance sheet at year-end 2013 is as follows. The following information details transactions and adjustments that occurred during 2014.

1. Sales total $145,850 in 2014; all sales were cash sales.
2. Inventory purchases total $76,200 in 2014; at December 31, 2014, inventory totals $14,500. Assume all purchases were made on account.
3. Accounts payable totals $4,100 at December 31, 2014.
4. Annual store rent of $24,000 was paid on March 1, 2014, covering the next 12 months. The balance in prepaid rent at December 31, 2013, was the balance remaining from the advance rent payment in 2013.
5. Wages are paid every other week on Friday; during 2014, Fischer paid $12,500 cash for wages. At December 31, 2014, Fischer owed employees unpaid and unrecorded wages of $350.

6. Depreciation on equipment totals $1,700 in 2014.

FISCHER CARD SHOP Balance Sheet December 31, 2013				
Cash		$ 8,500	Accounts payable	$ 5,200
Inventories		12,000	Wages payable	100
Prepaid rent		3,800	Total current liabilities	5,300
Total current assets		24,300	Total equity (includes retained earnings)	23,500
Equipment	$7,500		Total liabilities and equity	$28,800
Less accumulated depreciation	3,000			
Equipment, net		4,500		
Total Assets		$28,800		

Required

a. Prepare any necessary journal entries for 2014 and adjusting entries at December 31, 2014, (1) using the financial statement effects template, and (2) in journal entry form.

b. Set up T-accounts, enter the balances above, and post the adjusting entries to them.

c. Prepare its income statement for 2014, and its balance sheet at December 31, 2014.

d. Prepare entries to close its temporary accounts in journal entry form and post the closing entries to the T-accounts.

LO2, 3, 4, 5 **P3-54. Applying the Entire Accounting Cycle**

Rhoades Tax Services began business on December 1, 2015. Its December transactions are as follows.

Dec. 1 Rhoades invested $20,000 in the business in exchange for common stock.
2 Paid $1,200 cash for December rent to Bomba Realty.
2 Purchased $1,080 of supplies on account.
3 Purchased $9,500 of office equipment; paying $4,700 cash with the balance due in 30 days.
8 Paid $1,080 cash on account for supplies purchased December 2.
14 Paid $900 cash for assistant's wages for 2 weeks' work.
20 Performed consulting services for $3,000 cash.
28 Paid $900 cash for assistant's wages for 2 weeks' work.
30 Billed clients $7,200 for December consulting services.
31 Paid $1,800 cash for dividends.

Required

a. Set up a general ledger in T-account form for the following accounts: Cash; Fees Receivable; Supplies; Office Equipment; Accumulated Depreciation—Office Equipment; Accounts Payable; Wages Payable; Share Capital; Retained Earnings; Consulting Revenue; Supplies Expense; Wages Expense; Rent Expense; and Depreciation Expense.

b. Record these transactions (1) using the financial statement effects template, and (2) in journal entry form. (3) Post these entries to their T-accounts (key numbers in T-accounts by date).

c. Prepare an unadjusted trial balance at December 31, 2015.

d. Journalise the adjusting entries at December 31 (using both the financial statement effects template and journal entry form), drawing on the following information.

1. Supplies available at December 31 are $710.
2. Accrued wages payable at December 31 are $270.
3. Depreciation for December is $120.
4. Rhoades has spent 30 hours on an involved tax fraud case during December. When completed in January, his work will be billed at $75 per hour. (It uses the account Fees Receivable to reflect amounts earned but not yet billed.)

Then post adjusting entries to their T-accounts.

e. Prepare an adjusted trial balance at December 31, 2015.

f. Prepare a December 2015 income statement and statement of changes in equity, and a December 31, 2015, balance sheet.

g. Record its closing entries in journal entry form. Post these entries to their T-accounts.

h. Prepare a post-closing trial balance at December 31, 2015.

CASES AND PROJECTS

C3-55. Preparing Adjusting Entries, Financial Statements, and Closing Entries LO2, 3, 4, 5

Seaside Surf Shop began operations on July 1, 2014, with an initial investment of $50,000. During the initial 3 months of operations, the following cash transactions were recorded in the firm's checking account.

Cash receipts		Cash payments	
Initial investment by owner	$ 50,000	Rent	$ 24,000
Collected from customers	81,000	Fixtures and equipment	25,000
Borrowed from bank 7/1/2014	10,000	Merchandise inventory	62,000
Total cash receipts	$141,000	Salaries	6,000
		Other expenses	13,000
		Total cash payments	$130,000

Additional information

1. Most sales were for cash, however, the store accepted a limited amount of credit sales; at September 30, 2014, customers owed the store $9,000.
2. Rent was paid on July 1 for six months.
3. Salaries of $3,000 per month are paid on the 1st of each month for salaries earned in the month prior.
4. Inventories are purchased for cash; at September 30, 2014, inventory worth $21,000 was available.
5. Fixtures and equipment were expected to last five years with zero salvage value.
6. The bank charges 12% annual interest (1% per month) on its bank loan.

Required

a. Prepare any necessary adjusting entries at September 30, 2014, (1) using the financial statement effects template, and (2) in journal entry form.

b. Set up T-accounts and post the adjusting entries to them.

c. Prepare its initial three-month income statement for 2014 and its balance sheet at September 30, 2014. (Ignore taxes.)

d. Analyse the statements from part *c* and assess the company's performance over its initial 3 months.

C3-56. Analysing Transactions, Impacts on Financial Ratios, and Loan Covenants LO2, 3, 6

Wyland Consulting, a firm started three years ago by Reyna Wyland, offers consulting services for material handling and plant layout. Its balance sheet at the close of 2015 is as follows.

WYLAND CONSULTING
Balance Sheet
December 31, 2015

Assets			Liabilities	
Cash		$ 3,400	Notes payable	$30,000
Accounts receivable		22,875	Accounts payable	4,200
Supplies		13,200	Unearned consulting fees	11,300
Prepaid insurance		4,500	Wages payable	400
Equipment	$68,500		Total liabilities	45,900
Less: accumulated depreciation	23,975	44,525	**Equity**	
			Share capital	8,000
			Retained earnings	34,600
Total assets		$88,500	Total liabilities and equity	$88,500

Earlier in the year Wyland obtained a bank loan of $30,000 cash for the firm. One of the provisions of the loan is that the year-end debt-to-equity ratio (ratio of total liabilities to total equity) cannot exceed 1.0. Based on the above balance sheet, the ratio at the end of 2015 is 1.08. Wyland is concerned about being in violation of the loan agreement and requests assistance in reviewing the situation. Wyland believes that she might have overlooked some items at year-end. Discussions with Wyland reveal the following.

1. On January 1, 2015, the firm paid a $4,500 insurance premium for 2 years of coverage; the amount in Prepaid Insurance has not yet been adjusted.
2. Depreciation on the equipment should be 10% of cost per year; the company inadvertently recorded 15% for 2015.
3. Interest on the bank loan has been paid through the end of 2015.
4. The firm concluded a major consulting engagement in December, doing a plant layout analysis for a new factory. The $6,000 fee has not been billed or recorded in the accounts.
5. On December 1, 2015, the firm received an $11,300 advance payment from Croy Corporation for consulting services to be rendered over a 2-month period. This payment was credited to the Unearned Consulting Fees account. One-half of this fee was earned by December 31, 2015.
6. Supplies costing $4,800 were available on December 31; the company has made no entry in the accounts.

Required

a. What portion of the company is financed by debt versus equity (called the debt-to-equity ratio and defined in Chapter 1) at December 31, 2015?

b. Is the firm in violation of its loan agreement? Prepare computations to support the correct total liabilities and total equity figures at December 31, 2015.

LO2, 3 C3-57. Ethics, Accounting Adjustments, and Auditors

It is the end of the accounting year for Juliet Javetz, controller of a medium-sized, publicly held corporation specialising in toxic waste cleanup. Within the corporation, only Javetz and the president know that the firm has been negotiating for several months to land a large contract for waste cleanup in Western Europe. The president has hired another firm with excellent contacts in Western Europe to help with negotiations. The outside firm will charge an hourly fee plus expenses, but has agreed not to submit a bill until the negotiations are in their final stages (expected to occur in another 3 to 4 months). Even if the contract falls through, the outside firm is entitled to receive payment for its services. Based upon her discussion with a member of the outside firm, Javetz knows that its charge for services provided to date will be $150,000. This is a material amount for the company.

Javetz knows that the president wants negotiations to remain as secret as possible so that competitors will not learn of the contract the company is pursuing in Europe. In fact, the president recently stated to her, "Now is not the time to reveal our actions in Western Europe to other staff members, our auditors, or the readers of our financial statements; securing this contract is crucial to our future growth." No entry has been made in the accounting records for the cost of contract negotiations. Javetz now faces an uncomfortable situation. The company's outside auditor has just asked her if she knows of any year-end adjustments that have not yet been recorded.

Required

a. What are the ethical considerations that Javetz faces in answering the auditor's question?

b. How should Javetz respond to the auditor's question?

LO2, 3, 4 C3-58. Inferring Adjusting Entries from Financial Statements

Lady G's Fashions, a specialty retailer of women's apparel, markets its products through retail stores and catalogues. Selected information from its 2015 and 2014 balance sheets is as follows.

Selected Balance Sheet Data ($ thousands)	2014	2015
Prepaid catalogue expenses (asset)	$3,894	$4,306
Advertising credits receivable	21	534
Customer deposits	6,108	7,053

The following excerpts are from Lady G's Fashions accompanying footnotes:

- Catalog costs in the direct segment are considered direct response advertising and as such are capitalised as incurred and amortised over the expected sales life of each catalogue, which is generally a period not exceeding six months.

- The Company periodically enters into arrangements with certain national magazine publishers whereby the Company includes magazine subscription cards in its catalogue mailings in exchange for advertising credits or discounts on advertising.

Required

a. Assume that Lady G's Fashions spent $62,550 to design, print, and mail catalogues in 2015. Also assume that it received advertising credits of $849. Prepare the entry, using the financial statement effects template and in journal entry form, that Lady G's Fashions would have recorded when these costs were incurred.

b. Prepare the adjusting entry, using the financial statement effects template and in journal entry form, that would be necessary to record its amortisation of prepaid catalogue costs.

c. How do advertising credits expire? Prepare the adjusting entry, using both the financial statement effects template and in journal entry form, that Lady G's Fashions would record to reflect the change in advertising credits.

d. Assume that Lady G's Fashions sold gift certificates valued at $19,175 in 2015. Prepare the entry, using the financial statement effects template and in journal entry form, that Lady G's Fashions would make to record these sales. Next, prepare the entry, using the financial statement effects template and in journal entry form, that it makes to record merchandise sales to customers who pay with gift certificates.

SOLUTIONS TO REVIEW PROBLEMS

Mid-Chapter Review

Solution to Part 1

a.

	Balance Sheet						Income Statement		
Transaction	Cash Asset	+ Noncash Assets	− Contra Assets	= Liabilities	+ Contrib. Capital	+ Earned Capital	Revenues	− Expenses	= Net Income
(a) Adjusting entry to record supplies and parts used.		−91,000 Supplies and Parts	−	=		−91,000 Retained Earnings		− +91,000 Supplies and Parts Expenses	= −91,000

		Dr.	Cr.
(a)	Supplies and parts expense (+E, −SE)	91,000	
	Supplies and parts (−A)		91,000

b.

Transaction	Cash Asset	+ Noncash Assets	− Contra Assets	= Liabilities	+ Contrib. Capital	+ Earned Capital	Revenues	− Expenses	= Net Income
(b) Adjusting entry to record rent expense accrued but not yet paid.			−	= +2,500 Accounts Payable		−2,500 Retained Earnings		− +2,500 Rent Expense	= −2,500

		Dr.	Cr.
(b)	Rent expense (+E, −SE)	2,500	
	Accounts payable (+L)		2,500

The $2,500 expense for October is not recorded because it is not yet incurred as of September 30.

c.

	Balance Sheet						Income Statement		
Transaction	Cash Asset	+ Noncash Assets	− Contra Assets	= Liabilities	+ Contrib. Capital	+ Earned Capital	*Revenues*	− *Expenses*	= *Net Income*
(c) Adjusting entry to record depreciation on building.			+50,000 Accumulated Depreciation —Building			−50,000 Retained Earnings		+50,000 Depreciation Expense	−50,000

		Debit	Credit
(c)	Depreciation expense (+E, −SE)	50,000	
	Accumulated depreciation—Building (+XA, −A)		50,000

d. No entry required; the executive has not yet begun work and thus no expense is incurred.

e.

Transaction	Cash Asset	+ Noncash Assets	− Contra Assets	= Liabilities	+ Contrib. Capital	+ Earned Capital	Revenues	− Expenses	= Net Income
(e) Adjusting entry to record cash advance, of which a part is earned.	+1,200 Cash			+600 Unearned Revenue		+600 Retained Earnings	+600 Services Revenue		+600

		Debit	Credit
(e)	Cash (+A)	1,200	
	Unearned revenue (+L)		600
	Services revenue (+R, +SE)		600

f.

Transaction	Cash Asset	+ Noncash Assets	− Contra Assets	= Liabilities	+ Contrib. Capital	+ Earned Capital	Revenues	− Expenses	= Net Income
(f) Adjusting entry to record wages earned but not yet paid.				+25,000 Wages Payable		−25,000 Retained Earnings		+25,000 Wages Expense	−25,000

		Debit	Credit
(f)	Wages expense (+E, −SE)	25,000	
	Wages payable (+L)		25,000

Solution to Part 2

General Ledger

Assets = Liabilities + Equity

Assets

Cash (A) (+ / −)

+		−
Unadj. bal.	80,000	
(e)	**1,200**	
Adj. bal.	81,200	

Accounts Receivable (A) (+ / −)

+		−
Unadj. bal.	95,000	
Adj. bal.	95,000	

Supplies & Parts (A) (+ / −)

+		−	
Unadj. bal.	100,000		
		91,000	(a)
Adj. bal.	9,000		

Building (A) (+ / −)

+		−
Unadj. bal.	400,000	
Adj. bal.	400,000	

Accumulated Depreciation—Building (XA) (− / +)

−	+	
	200,000	Unadj. bal.
	50,000	(c)
	250,000	Adj. bal.

Land (A) (+ / −)

+		−
Unadj. bal.	257,500	
Adj. bal.	257,500	

Liabilities

Accounts Payable (L) (− / +)

−	+	
	20,000	Unadj. bal.
	2,500	(b)
	22,500	Adj. bal.

Wages Payable (L) (− / +)

−	+	
	0	Unadj. bal.
	25,000	(f)
	25,000	Adj. bal.

Unearned Revenue (L) (− / +)

−	+	
	0	Unadj. bal.
	600	(e)
	600	Adj. bal.

Equity

Share Capital (SE) (− / +)

−	+	
	80,000	Unadj. bal.
	80,000	Adj. bal.

Retained Earnings (SE) (− / +)

−	+	
	380,000	Unadj. bal.
	380,000	Adj. bal.

Services Revenue (R) (− / +)

−	+	
	720,000	Unadj. bal.
	600	(e)
	720,600	Adj. bal.

Rent Expense (E) (+ / −)

+		−
Unadj. bal.	27,500	
(b)	**2,500**	
Adj. bal.	30,000	

Depreciation Expense (E) (+ / −)

+		−
Unadj. bal.	0	
(c)	**50,000**	
Adj. bal.	50,000	

Wages Expense (E) (+ / −)

+		−
Unadj. bal.	440,000	
(f)	**25,000**	
Adj. bal.	465,000	

Supplies & Parts Expense (E) (+ / −)

+		−
Unadj. bal.	0	
(a)	**91,000**	
Adj. bal.	91,000	

Assets = $592,700 = **Liabilities = $48,100** + **Equity = $544,600**

Chapter-End Review

Solution to Part 1

Transaction	Cash Asset	+ Noncash Assets	− Contra Assets	= Liabil-ities	+ Contrib. Capital	+ Earned Capital	Revenues	− Expenses	= Net Income
	Balance Sheet						Income Statement		
(1) Adjustment to record insurance expense.		−1,500 Prepaid Insurance				−1,500 Retained Earnings		+1,500 Insurance Expense	−1,500
(2) Adjustment to record supplies expense.		−25,000 Supplies				−25,000 Retained Earnings		+25,000 Supplies Expense	−25,000
(3) Adjustment to record depreciation expense.			+30,000 Accumulated Depreciation —Equipment			−30,000 Retained Earnings		+30,000 Depreciation Expense	−30,000
(4) Adjustment to record fees revenue.				−3,000 Unearned Fees		+3,000 Retained Earnings	+3,000 Fees Revenue		+3,000
(5) Adjustment to record wages expense.				+600 Wages Payable		−600 Retained Earnings		+600 Wages Expense	−600

		Dr.	Cr.
(1)	Insurance expense (+E, −SE)...............................	1,500	
	Prepaid insurance (−A)		1,500
	Record insurance expired $6,000 × (6 months/24 months).		

		Dr.	Cr.
(2)	Supplies expense (+E, −SE)	25,000	
	Supplies (−A)		25,000
	Record supplies used ($31,300 − $6,300).		

		Dr.	Cr.
(3)	Depreciation expense (+E, −SE)	30,000	
	Accumulated depreciation—Equipment (+XA, −A)		30,000
	Record depreciation [($270,000 − $0) ÷ 9 years].		

		Dr.	Cr.
(4)	Unearned fees (−L).......................................	3,000	
	Fees revenue (+R, +SE).............................		3,000
	Record fees earned.		

		Dr.	Cr.
(5)	Wages expense (+E, −SE)..................................	600	
	Wages payable (+L).................................		600
	Record employee wages incurred.		

continued

continued from previous page

Transaction	Cash Asset	+	Noncash Assets	-	Contra Assets	=	Liabil-ities	+	Contrib. Capital	+	Earned Capital	Revenues	-	Expenses	=	Net Income
	Balance Sheet											***Income Statement***				
(6) Adjustment to record rent expense.				-		=	+2,000 Rent Payable				−2,000 Retained Earnings		-	+2,000 Rent Expense	=	−2,000

		Debit	Credit
(6)	Rent expense (+E, −SE)	2,000	
	Rent payable (+L)		2,000
	Record rent owed.		

General Ledger

Assets = Liabilities + Equity

Assets

+ Cash (A) −			
Unadj. bal.	1,000		
Adj. bal.	1,000		

+ Accounts Receivable (A) −			
Unadj. bal.	9,200		
Adj. bal.	9,200		

+ Prepaid Insurance (A) −			
Unadj. bal.	6,000	1,500	(1)
Adj. bal.	4,500		

+ Supplies (A) −			
Unadj. bal.	31,300	25,000	(2)
Adj. bal.	6,300		

+ Equipment (A) −			
Unadj. bal.	270,000		
Adj. bal.	270,000		

− Accumulated Depreciation—Equipment (XA) +			
		60,000	Unadj. bal.
		30,000	(3)
		90,000	Adj. bal.

Liabilities

− Accounts Payable (L) +			
		3,100	Unadj. bal.
		3,100	Adj. bal.

− Unearned Fees (L) +			
(4)	3,000	4,000	Unadj. bal.
		1,000	Adj. bal.

− Wages Payable (L) +			
		0	Unadj. bal.
		600	(5)
		600	Adj. bal.

− Rent Payable (L) +			
		0	Unadj. bal.
		2,000	(6)
		2,000	Adj. bal.

Equity

− Share Capital (SE) +			
		120,400	Unadj. bal.
		120,400	Adj. bal.

− Retained Earnings (SE) +			
		60,000	Unadj. bal.
		60,000	Adj. bal.

− Fees Revenue (R) +			
		150,000	Unadj. bal.
		3,000	(4)
		153,000	Adj. bal.

+ Insurance Expense (E) −			
Unadj. bal.	0		
(1)	1,500		
Adj. bal.	1,500		

+ Supplies Expenses (E) −			
Unadj. bal.	0		
(2)	25,000		
Adj. bal.	25,000		

+ Depreciation Expense (E) −			
Unadj. bal.	0		
(3)	30,000		
Adj. bal.	30,000		

+ Rent Expense (E) −			
Unadj. bal.	22,000		
(6)	2,000		
Adj. bal.	24,000		

+ Wages Expense (E) −			
Unadj. bal.	58,000		
(5)	600		
Adj. bal.	58,600		

Assets = $201,000 = Liabilities = $6,700 + Equity = $194,300

Solution to Part 2

ATWELL LABORATORIES, INC. Adjusted Trial Balance June 30, 2015	Debits	Credits
Cash	$ 1,000	
Accounts Receivable	9,200	
Prepaid Insurance	4,500	
Supplies	6,300	
Equipment	270,000	
Accumulated Depreciation—Equipment		$ 90,000
Accounts Payable		3,100
Rent Payable		2,000
Wages Payable		600
Unearned Fees		1,000
Fees Revenue		153,000
Wages Expense	58,600	
Rent Expense	24,000	
Insurance Expense	1,500	
Supplies Expense	25,000	
Depreciation Expense	30,000	
Share Capital		120,400
Retained Earnings		60,000
Totals	$430,100	$430,100

Solution to Part 3

		Debit	Credit
a.	Retained earnings (−SE)	139,100	
	Insurance expense (−E)		1,500
	Supplies expense (−E)		25,000
	Depreciation expense (−E)		30,000
	Rent expense (−E)		24,000
	Wages expense (−E)		58,600

		Debit	Credit
b.	Fees revenue (−R)	153,000	
	Retained earnings (+SE)		153,000

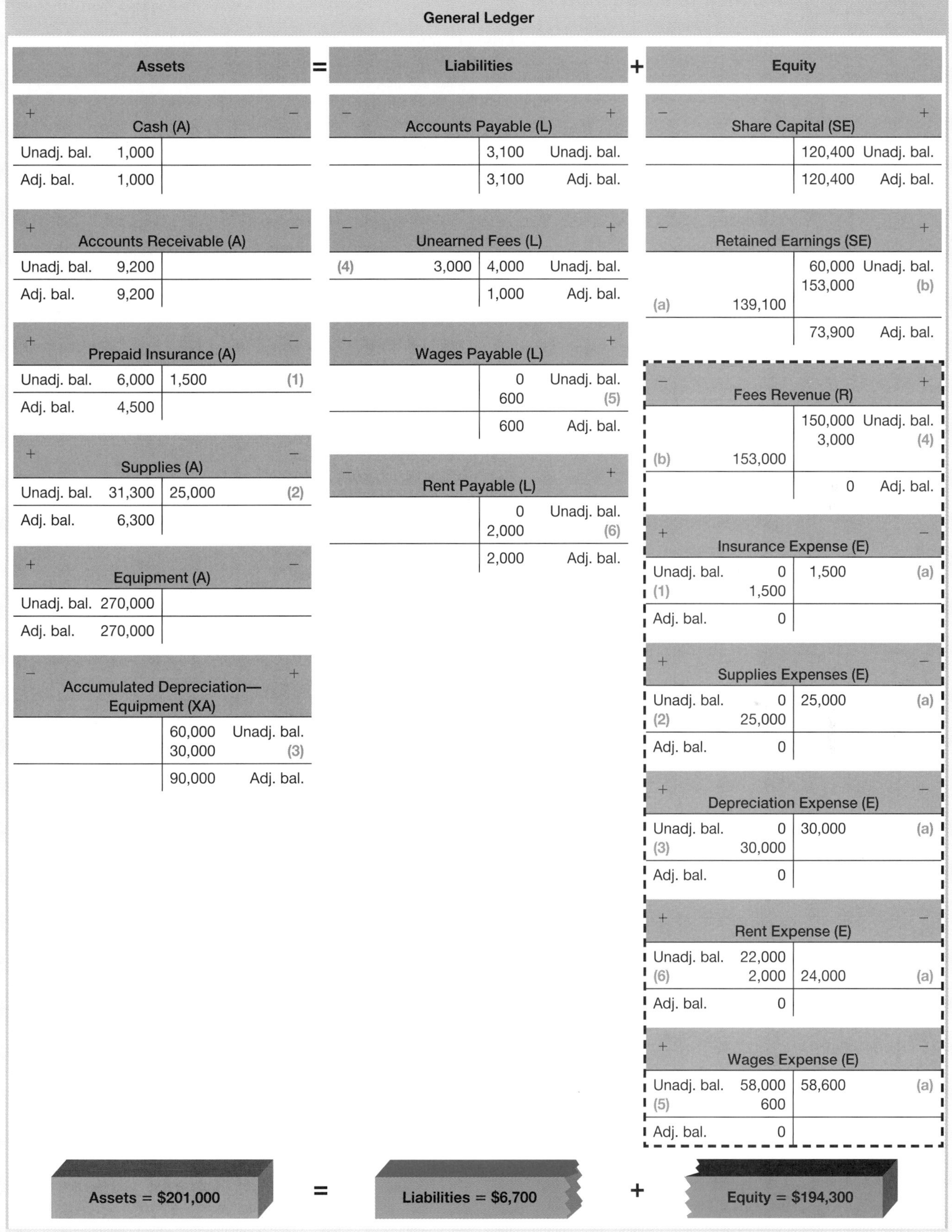
General Ledger
Assets
=
Liabilities
+
Equity
Cash (A)
Unadj. bal. 1,000
Adj. bal. 1,000
Accounts Receivable (A)
Unadj. bal. 9,200
Adj. bal. 9,200
Prepaid Insurance (A)
Unadj. bal. 6,000 | 1,500 (1)
Adj. bal. 4,500
Supplies (A)
Unadj. bal. 31,300 | 25,000 (2)
Adj. bal. 6,300
Equipment (A)
Unadj. bal. 270,000
Adj. bal. 270,000
Accumulated Depreciation—Equipment (XA)
60,000 Unadj. bal.
30,000 (3)
90,000 Adj. bal.
Accounts Payable (L)
3,100 Unadj. bal.
3,100 Adj. bal.
Unearned Fees (L)
(4) 3,000 | 4,000 Unadj. bal.
1,000 Adj. bal.
Wages Payable (L)
0 Unadj. bal.
600 (5)
600 Adj. bal.
Rent Payable (L)
0 Unadj. bal.
2,000 (6)
2,000 Adj. bal.
Share Capital (SE)
120,400 Unadj. bal.
120,400 Adj. bal.
Retained Earnings (SE)
60,000 Unadj. bal.
153,000 (b)
(a) 139,100
73,900 Adj. bal.
Fees Revenue (R)
150,000 Unadj. bal.
3,000 (4)
(b) 153,000
0 Adj. bal.
Insurance Expense (E)
Unadj. bal. 0 | 1,500 (a)
(1) 1,500
Adj. bal. 0
Supplies Expenses (E)
Unadj. bal. 0 | 25,000 (a)
(2) 25,000
Adj. bal. 0
Depreciation Expense (E)
Unadj. bal. 0 | 30,000 (a)
(3) 30,000
Adj. bal. 0
Rent Expense (E)
Unadj. bal. 22,000
(6) 2,000 | 24,000 (a)
Adj. bal. 0
Wages Expense (E)
Unadj. bal. 58,000 | 58,600 (a)
(5) 600
Adj. bal. 0
Assets = $201,000
=
Liabilities = $6,700
+
Equity = $194,300

Solution to Part 4

ATWELL LABORATORIES, INC.
Balance Sheet
June 30, 2015

Assets			Liabilities	
Cash		$ 1,000	Accounts payable	$ 3,100
Accounts receivable		9,200	Unearned fees	1,000
Prepaid insurance		4,500	Wages payable	600
Supplies		6,300	Rent payable	2,000
Total current assets		21,000	Total current liabilities	6,700
Equipment, original cost	$270,000			
Less accumulated depreciation	90,000	180,000	**Equity**	
			Share capital	120,400
			Retained earnings	73,900
Total assets		$201,000	Totals liabilities and equity	$201,000

ATWELL LABORATORIES, INC.
Income Statement
For Year Ended June 30, 2015

Fees revenue		$153,000
Expenses		
Insurance expense	$ 1,500	
Supplies expense	25,000	
Depreciation expense	30,000	
Rent expense	24,000	
Wages expense	58,600	
Total expense		139,100
Net income		$ 13,900

ATWELL LABORATORIES, INC.
Statement of Changes in Equity
For Year Ended June 30, 2015

	Share Capital	Retained Earnings	Total
Balance at June 30, 2014	$120,400	$60,000	$180,400
Net Income	—	13,900	13,900
Balance at June 30, 2015	$120,400	$73,900	$194,300

Atwell's statement of changes in equity is much simpler than the usual statement because we have focused on the adjustment and closing process. In doing so, we did not consider additional activities in which corporations commonly engage, such as paying dividends, issuing stock, and repurchasing stock. (Requirements did not ask for a statement of cash flows. The next chapter is devoted to the statement of cash flows.)

LEARNING OBJECTIVES

1. Explain the purpose of the statement of cash flows and classify cash transactions by type of business activity: operating, investing, or financing. (p. 150)
2. Construct the operating activities section of the statement of cash flows using the direct method. (p. 155)
3. Reconcile cash flows from operations to net income and use the indirect method to compute operating cash flows. (p. 164)
4. Construct the investing and financing activities sections of the statement of cash flows. (p. 166)
5. Compute and interpret ratios that reflect a company's liquidity and solvency using information reported in the statement of cash flows. (p. 174)
6. Appendix 4A: Use a spreadsheet to construct the statement of cash flows. (p. 178)

CHAPTER

Reporting and Analysing Cash Flows

4

Founded in 1920 as "Queensland and Northern Territory Aerial Services (QANTAS)," **Qantas** is Australia's flagship carrier and the oldest continuously operating airline in the world. It is headquartered in Mascot, a suburb of Sydney, and has main hubs located in Sydney, Brisbane, and Melbourne. Its fleet can be easily identified by the Flying Kangaroo logo featured on the tail of the aircraft. Qantas and its subsidiaries serve almost 80 destinations in 20 countries. In 2013, Qantas entered into a partnership with Emirates Airline, thereby opening up 65 destinations across Europe, the Middle East and North Africa. Qantas is also a founding member of the OneWorld global airline alliance.

QANTAS
www.qantas.com.au

Like many of its competitors, Qantas follows a two-brand strategy. Hence, it also owns a low-cost airline, Jetstar Airways. During 2012–2013, Qantas and Jetstar had a 65% share of the Australian domestic market. Qantas has also launched other Jetstar-branded airlines in Asia, by partnering with local investors to meet foreign ownership rules. Specifically, it owns 49% of the Singapore-based Jetstar Asia, 30% of the Vietnam-based Jetstar Pacific, 33.3% of Jetstar Japan, and 33.3% of Jetstar Hong Kong (awaiting regulatory approval).

In his 2013 letter to shareholders, CEO Alan Joyce said that "Qantas is in a period of transformation as we make our business better and stronger." In particular, it has withdrawn from loss-making routes, retired old aircraft, and consolidated operations. In recent years, Qantas has also invested in new aircraft to improve the customer experience and increase operational efficiency. As a result, group-wide comparable unit cost has been reduced by 5% and the average scheduled passenger aircraft age has fallen to 7.9 years—the lowest in two decades. These costs are listed in the company's cash flow statement under investing activities. Over the next three years, Qantas is planning to cut a sixth of its workforce and slow the expansion of Jetstar in Asia.

In addition to making investments to improve operations, Qantas returned $52 million cash to its shareholders by buying back its own stock (treasury shares) and paid down net borrowings. These cash outflows are reported in Qantas's statement of cash flows under financing activities. How does a company with income of $6 million spend over $1 billion in investments and share repurchases? To accomplish its objectives, Qantas must generate positive cash flow from operating activities. Indeed, its operating activities produced cash flows of $1.4 billion in the fiscal year ended 30 June 2013. The company's operations are the engine that produces cash that can be used to grow the business and to provide a return to shareholders.

As we will discover in this chapter, a business must make sure that its cash inflows are adequate to fund new investments, meet obligations to creditors as they come due, and pay dividends to shareholders. Even a profitable company can fail if it does not have a healthy cash flow. We will also discover why it is important to look at the cash flow statement along with the income statement and balance sheet when trying to assess the financial health of a company.

Sources: www.qantas.com.au; Qantas 2013 Annual Report; The Economist, "A giant leap for the flying kangaroo," March 4, 2014.

CHAPTER ORGANISATION

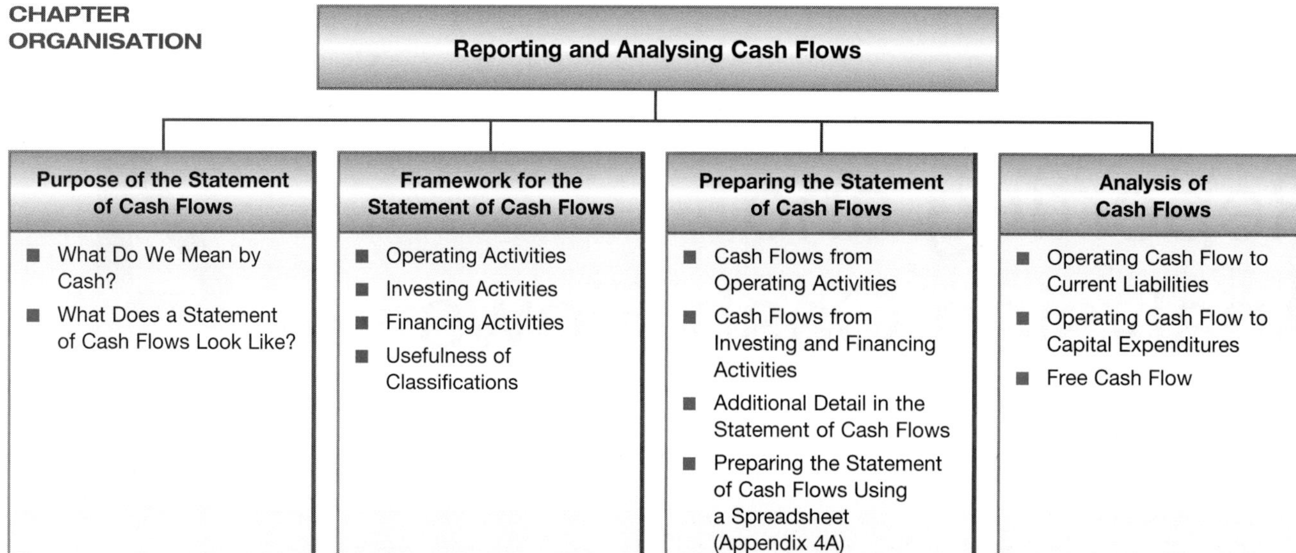

PURPOSE OF THE STATEMENT OF CASH FLOWS

LO1 Explain the purpose of the statement of cash flows and classify cash transactions by type of business activity: operating, investing, or financing.

In addition to the balance sheet and the income statement, corporations are required to report a statement of cash flows. The **statement of cash flows** tells us how a company generated cash (cash inflows) and how it used cash (cash outflows). The statement of cash flows complements the income statement and the balance sheet by providing answers that neither the income statement nor the balance sheet can provide. For instance, slower collection of receivables doesn't affect income, but it does reduce the amount of cash coming into the company.

Understanding the statement of cash flows helps us understand trends in a firm's **liquidity** (ability to pay near-term liabilities and take advantage of investment opportunities), and it helps us assess a firm's **solvency** (ability to pay long-term liabilities). With information about how cash was generated or used, creditors and investors are better able to assess a firm's ability to settle its liabilities and pay dividends to shareholders. A firm's need for outside financing is also better evaluated when using cash flow data. Over time, the statement of cash flows permits users to observe and assess management's investing and financing policies. For example, a business that is not generating enough cash flow internally, i.e., from operations, must get cash from borrowing, issuing shares, or selling off its assets.

The statement of cash flows also provides information about a firm's ability to generate sufficient amounts of cash to respond to unanticipated needs and opportunities. Information about past cash flows, particularly cash flows from operations, helps in assessing a company's financial flexibility. An evaluation of a firm's ability to survive an unexpected drop in demand, for example, should include a review of its past cash flows from operations. The larger these cash flows, the greater is the firm's ability to withstand adverse changes in economic conditions.

So, whether we are a potential investor, loan officer, future employee, supplier, or customer, we greatly benefit from an understanding of the cash inflows and outflows of a company.

What Do We Mean by "CASH"?

FYI A cash equivalent is a short-term, highly liquid investment that is easily converted to a known amount of cash and is subject to little risk of change in value. ■

The statement of cash flows explains the change in a firm's cash *and* cash equivalents. Cash includes cash on hand and demand deposits in the bank. **Cash equivalents** are short-term, highly liquid investments that (1) are easily convertible into a known amount of cash and (2) are subject to an insignificant risk of change in value. Short-term fixed deposits, money market funds, and securities having maturities of three months or less at acquisition are typical examples of cash equivalents.

When preparing a statement of cash flows, the cash and cash equivalents are added together and treated as a single sum. The addition is done because the purchase and sale of investments in cash equivalents are considered to be part of a firm's overall management of cash rather than a source or use of cash. As statement users evaluate and project cash flows, for example, it should not matter whether the cash is readily available in a cash register or safe, deposited in a bank account, or invested in cash equivalents. Consequently, transfers back and forth between a firm's cash on hand, its bank accounts, and its investments in cash equivalents, are not treated as cash inflows and cash outflows in its statement of cash flows. When discussing the statement of cash flows, managers generally use the word *cash* rather than the phrase *cash and cash equivalents*. We will follow the same practice.

What Does a Statement of Cash Flows Look Like?

Exhibit 4.1 reproduces Qantas's cash flow statement for the fiscal year ended on June 30, 2013. During this fiscal year, Qantas generated $1,417 million in cash from its operations. Investing activities used $1,045 million in cash, and financing activities used another $953 million of cash. Over the entire year, the company's cash balance decreased by $581 million and ended the year at $2,829 million on June 30, 2013.

EXHIBIT 4.1 Qantas Cash Flow Statement

QANTAS GROUP
Consolidated Cash Flow Statement
For the Year Ended June 30, 2013

	2013 $A Millions
Cash Flows from Operating Activities	
Cash receipts in the course of operations	16,582
Cash payments in the course of operations	(15,185)
Interest received	110
Interest paid	(229)
Dividends received from associates and jointly controlled entities	142
Income tax paid	(3)
Net cash from operating activities	1,417
Cash Flows from Investing Activities	
Payments for property, plant and equipment and intangible assets	(1,247)
Net payments for aircraft assigned to associates[1]	(12)
Interest paid and capitalised on qualifying assets	(61)
Proceeds from disposal of property, plant and equipment	32
Net proceeds from repayment of loans receivable from jointly controlled entities	125
Proceeds from sale and operating leaseback of non-current assets	8
Proceeds from disposal of controlled entities, net of cash disposed	18
Proceeds from disposal of jointly controlled entities	189
Payments for the acquisition of controlled entities, net of cash acquired	(24)
Payments for investments in associates	(73)
Net cash used in investing activities	(1,045)
Cash Flows from Financing Activities	
Payments for shares bought back[2]	(36)
Payments for treasury shares	(16)
Proceeds from borrowings	846
Repayments of borrowings	(1,494)
Proceeds from sale and finance leaseback of non-current assets	83
Net payments for aircraft security deposits and hedges related to debt	(336)
Net cash used in financing activities	(953)
Net decrease in cash and cash equivalents held	(581)
Cash and cash equivalents at the beginning of the year	3,398
Effects of exchange rate changes on cash and cash equivalents	12
Cash and cash equivalents at the end of the year	2,829

[1] Net payments for aircraft assigned to Jetstar Japan Co., Ltd and Jetstar Hong Kong Airways Limited.

[2] 23,377,832 shares were bought back and cancelled during the year ended June 30, 2013.

FRAMEWORK FOR THE STATEMENT OF CASH FLOWS

The statement of cash flows classifies cash receipts and payments into one of three categories: operating activities, investing activities, or financing activities. Classifying cash flows into these categories identifies the effects on cash of each of the major activities of a firm. The combined effects on cash of all three categories explain the net change in cash for the period. The period's net change in cash is then reconciled with the beginning and ending amounts of cash.

Operating Activities

FYI Cash flows from operating activities (cash flows from operations) refer to cash inflows and outflows directly related to the firm's primary day-to-day business activities. ■

A company's income statement mainly reflects the transactions and events that constitute its operating activities. The cash effects of these operating transactions and events determine the net cash flow from operating activities. The usual focus of a firm's **operating activities** is on selling goods or rendering services, but the activities are defined broadly enough to include any cash receipts or payments that are not classified as investing or financing activities. For example, Qantas reports cash received from customers in the course of operations, as well as from borrowers, associates, and joint ventures. The company paid cash to suppliers and employees in the course of operations, as well as to tax authorities and lenders. Companies are allowed to report interest and dividend receipts as part of either operating activities or investing activities and to classify interest payments as either operating or financing cash flows (as done by Qantas). The following are examples of cash inflows and outflows relating to operating activities.

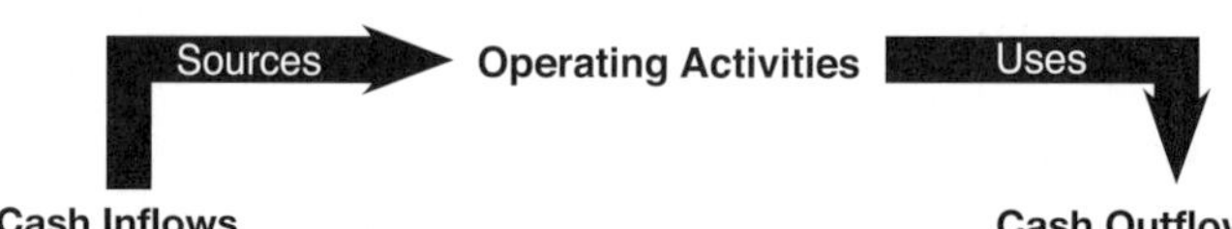

Cash Inflows

1. Cash receipts from customers for sales made or services rendered (or in anticipation of future deliveries of goods or services).
2. Cash receipts of interest and dividends (or reported as investing cash flows).
3. Other cash receipts that are not related to investing or financing activities, such as rentals, lawsuit settlements, and refunds received from suppliers.

Cash Outflows

1. Cash payments to employees or suppliers.
2. Cash payments to purchase inventories.
3. Cash payments of interest to creditors (or reported as financing cash flows).
4. Cash payments of taxes to government.
5. Other cash payments that are not related to investing or financing activities, such as contributions to charity and lawsuit settlements.

Investing Activities

FYI Cash flows from investing activities are cash inflows and outflows related to acquiring or selling productive assets and the investments in securities of other entities. ■

A firm's transactions involving (1) the acquisition and disposal of property, plant, and equipment (PPE) assets and intangible assets (as reported by Qantas), (2) the purchase and sale of government securities and securities of other companies, including stocks, bonds, and other securities that are not classified as cash equivalents, and (3) the lending and subsequent collection of money constitute the basic components of its **investing activities**. The related cash receipts and payments appear in the investing activities section of the statement of cash flows and, if material in amount, inflows and outflows should be reported separately (not as a net amount). Finally, companies can report interest and dividend receipts as part of either operating activities or investing activities. Examples of these cash flows follow:

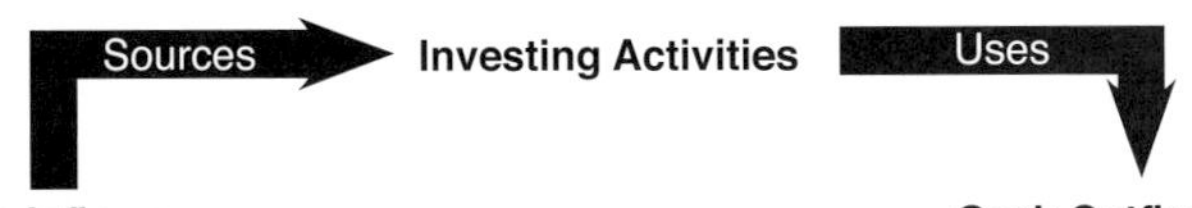

Cash Inflows

1. Cash receipts from sales of property, plant, and equipment (PPE) assets and intangible assets.
2. Cash receipts from sales of investments in government securities and securities of other companies (including divestitures).
3. Cash receipts from repayments of loans by borrowers.
4. Cash receipts of interest and dividends (or reported as operating cash flows).

Cash Outflows

1. Cash payments to purchase property, plant, and equipment (PPE) assets and intangible assets.
2. Cash payments to purchase government securities and securities of other companies (including acquisitions).
3. Cash payments made to lend money to borrowers.

Financing Activities

A firm engages in **financing activities** when it receives cash from shareholders, returns cash to shareholders, borrows from creditors, and repays amounts borrowed. Cash flows related to these transactions are reported in the financing activities section of the statement of cash flows and again, inflows and outflows should be reported separately (not as a net amount) if material. For instance, Qantas reports proceeds from new debt and debt repayments separately, rather than as a net amount. Moreover, companies can classify interest payments as either operating or financing cash flows. Examples of these cash flows follow:

FYI Cash flows from financing activities are cash inflows and outflows related to external sources of financing (owners and nonowners).

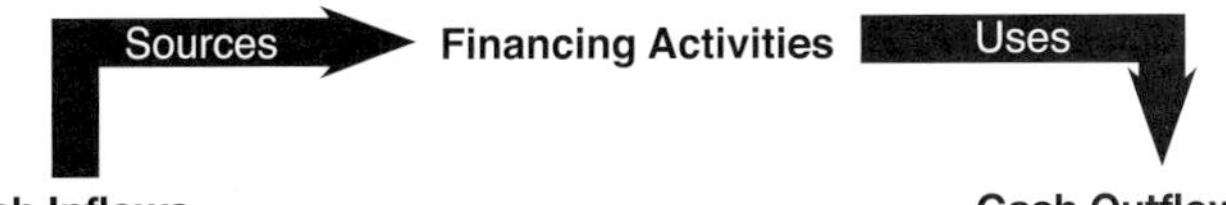

Cash Inflows

1. Cash receipts from issuances of ordinary shares and preferred shares and from sales of treasury shares.
2. Cash receipts from issuances of bonds payable, mortgage notes payable, and other notes payable.

Cash Outflows

1. Cash payments to acquire treasury shares.
2. Cash payments of dividends.
3. Cash payments to settle outstanding bonds payable, mortgage notes payable, and other notes payable.
4. Cash payments of interest to creditors (or reported as operating cash flows).

Paying cash to settle such obligations as accounts payable, wages payable, interest payable, and income tax payable are operating activities, not financing activities because they are related to the daily operations of the company such as buying and selling inventory. Also, cash paid to shareholders as dividends is classified as cash flows from financing activities.

FYI Treasury shares refers to the amount paid by a company to purchase its own ordinary shares.

RESEARCH INSIGHT

A recent study examines the classification of interest paid, interest received, and dividends received for companies from 13 European countries. It finds that (1) 77% of the firms classify interest paid as operating cash flows and 22% classify it as financing cash flows; (2) 54% of the firms report interest receipts as operating cash flows and 37% report them as investing cash flows; and (3) 49% of the firms classify dividends received as operating cash flows and 48% as investing cash flows. It also documents that over 99% of the firms report taxes paid in operating cash flows and dividends paid in financing cash flows. Source: "Flexibility in cash flow reporting classification choices under IFRS," by E. Gordon, E. Henry, B. Jorgensen, and C. Linthicum.

Usefulness of Classifications

The classification of cash flows into three categories of activities helps financial statement users interpret cash flow data. To illustrate, assume that Faultless, Inc., Peerless Co. and Dauntless Ltd.

each reports a $100,000 cash increase during the current year. Information from their current-year statements of cash flows is summarised in Exhibit 4.2.

EXHIBIT 4.2 Summary Information for Three Competitors

	Faultless	Peerless	Dauntless
Net cash provided by operating activities	$100,000	$ 0	$ 0
Cash flows from investing activities			
Sale of property, plant, and equipment	0	100,000	0
Cash flows from financing activities			
Issuance of notes payable	0	0	100,000
Net increase in cash	$100,000	$100,000	$100,000

One of the keys to evaluating a company's worth is estimating its future cash flows based on the information available. Companies that can generate a stream of future cash flows are worth more than a company with a single cash flow. In Exhibit 4.2, each company's net cash increase was the same, but the source of the increase varied by company. This variation affects the analysis of the cash flow data, particularly for potential creditors who must evaluate the likelihood of obtaining repayment in the future for any funds loaned to the company. Based only on these cash flow data, a potential creditor would feel more comfortable lending money to Faultless than to either Peerless or Dauntless. This choice is because Faultless's cash increase came from its operating activities, and operations tend to be continuing. Both Peerless and Dauntless could only break even on their cash flows from operations. Also, Peerless's cash increase came from the sale of property, plant, and equipment (PPE) assets—a source of cash that is not likely to recur regularly. Dauntless's cash increase came entirely from borrowed funds. This means Dauntless faces additional cash burdens in the future when the interest and principal payments on the note payable become due.

BUSINESS INSIGHT

Objectivity of Cash Usefulness of financial statements is enhanced when the underlying data are objective and verifiable. Measuring cash and the changes in cash are among the most objective measurements that accountants make. Thus, the statement of cash flows is arguably the most objective financial statement. This characteristic of the statement of cash flows is welcomed by those investors and creditors interested in evaluating the quality of a firm's income.

MID-CHAPTER REVIEW 1

Assume Qantas executed the following transactions during 2013. Indicate whether the transaction creates a cash inflow (In) or outflow (Out). Next, determine how each item should be classified in the statement of cash flows: an operating activity (O), an investing activity (I), or a financing activity (F). For example: $50,000 cash received for the sale of snack foods. Answer: In/O

1. ____ $250,000 cash paid to purchase a warehouse
2. ____ $120,000 cash paid for interest on a loan
3. ____ $850,000 cash paid to employees as wages
4. ____ $20,000,000 cash raised through the issuance of stock
5. ____ $450,000 cash paid to the government for taxes
6. ____ $350,000 cash received as part of a settlement of a legal case
7. ____ $630,000 cash received from the sale of long-term securities
8. ____ $75,000 cash received from the sale of used office equipment
9. ____ $500,000 cash dividend paid to shareholders
10. ____ $90,000 cash received as interest earned on a government bond

The solution to this review problem can be found on page 206.

PREPARING THE STATEMENT OF CASH FLOWS—OPERATING ACTIVITIES

LO2 Construct the operating activities section of the statement of cash flows using the direct method.

In Chapter 3's Exhibit 3.12, we presented a statement of cash flows for Natural Beauty Supply (hereafter, NBS) for the month of December, 2013. This statement is reproduced in Exhibit 4.3. The statement details how NBS's cash balance decreases by $1,275 in December, from $8,100 to $6,825. The statement was prepared by examining all of the cash transactions that occurred during the month, and then grouping them according to the type of activity each represents—operating, investing, or financing. Transaction (17) was the loan, so that was a financing activity, transaction (18) was the purchase of fixtures and equipment, an investing activity, and so on. These cash transactions can be taken directly from the cash T-account, which is reproduced here:

+	Cash (A)		−
Beg. Bal.	8,100		
(17)	11,000	18,000	(18)
(21)	8,500	700	(19)
(23)	1,200	3,300	(20)
(25)	3,200	1,625	(24)
		1,500	(27)
		50	(28)
End. Bal.	6,825		

This approach to preparing the statement of cash flows is straightforward and doesn't require any additional bookkeeping steps, other than those introduced in Chapters 2 and 3.

EXHIBIT 4.3 NBS Statement of Cash Flows (Direct Method)

NATURAL BEAUTY SUPPLY, INC.
Statement of Cash Flows
For the Month of December, 2013

Cash Flows from Operating Activities		
Cash received from customers (entries 21, 23, 25)	$12,900	
Cash paid for inventory (entry 20)	(3,300)	
Cash paid for wages (entry 24)	(1,625)	
Cash paid for rent (entry 27)	(1,500)	
Cash paid for advertising (entry 19)	(700)	
Net cash provided by operating activities		$ 5,775
Cash Flows from Investing Activities		
Cash paid for fixtures and equipment (entry 18)	(18,000)	
Net cash used for investing activities		(18,000)
Cash Flows from Financing Activities		
Cash received from loans (entry 17)	11,000	
Cash paid for dividends (entry 28)	(50)	
Net cash provided by financing activities		10,950
Net change in cash		(1,275)
Cash balance, November 30, 2013		8,100
Cash balance, December 31, 2013		$ 6,825

However, for many companies, the number and variety of cash transactions that occur each period are so large that such an approach is often impractical. A company with revenues and assets and liabilities in the billions of dollars, like Qantas for example, has thousands of cash transactions each day. It has accounts with several different banks in numerous locations, and regularly transfers cash from one account to another or back and forth between cash accounts and cash equivalents, as needed. For such a company, simply listing the cash transactions is not practical.

An alternative to this approach of compiling a list of cash flows is to reconcile the information in the income statement and balance sheet to prepare the cash flow statement. The statement of cash flows complements the balance sheet and the income statement. The balance sheet details the financial position of the company at a given point in time. Comparing two balance sheets prepared

EXHIBIT 4.4 NBS Income Statement and Comparative Balance Sheet

NATURAL BEAUTY SUPPLY
Income Statement
For the Month of December, 2012

Sales revenue		$13,900
Cost of goods sold		8,000
Gross profit		5,900
Operating expenses:		
Rent	$1,500	
Wages	2,105	
Advertising	700	
Depreciation	375	
Insurance	140	
Total operating expenses		4,820
Operating income		1,080
Interest income		30
Interest expense		(110)
Income before taxes		1,000
Income tax expense		350
Net income		$ 650

NATURAL BEAUTY SUPPLY
Comparative Balance Sheets

	12/31/12	11/30/12
Assets:		
Cash	$ 6,825	$ 8,100
Interest receivable	30	
Accounts receivable	2,250	950
Inventory	7,300	11,300
Prepaid insurance	1,540	1,680
Security deposit	2,000	2,000
Fixtures and equipment	18,000	
Accumulated depreciation	(375)	
Total assets	$37,570	$24,030
Liabilities:		
Accounts payable	$ 4,400	$ 3,700
Unearned revenue	600	300
Wages payable	480	
Interest payable	110	
Income taxes payable	350	
Notes payable	11,000	
Stockholders' equity:		
Share capital	20,000	20,000
Retained earnings	630	30
Total liabilities and equity	$37,570	$24,030

at the beginning and at the end of a period reveals changes that transpired during the accounting period. These changes are explained by the income statement and the statement of cash flows. Both the income statement and the cash flow statement summarise the events and transactions of the business during the accounting period, and as such, provide complementary descriptions of a company's activities. While the cash flow statement provides information that is not explicitly found in either of the other two statements, it must articulate with the balance sheet and income statement to present a complete picture of company activities.

One of the characteristics of the accounting system is that when an entry changes net income without a change in cash, then it must change another account on the balance sheet. And, when an operating cash flow occurs without a change in net income, then there must be a change in some other balance sheet account. Therefore, we can start with information from the income statement and then use the balance sheet (and some additional information) to prepare the statement of cash flows. Exhibit 4.4 presents the income statement and comparative balance sheets for NBS. We will use the data from these financial statements to prepare NBS's reconciliation of net income to cash from operating activities.

Converting Revenues and Expenses to Cash Flows from Operating Activities

We know from Chapter 3 that net income consists of revenues and expenses, gains and losses. We also know that these are often not cash transactions. For example, sales on account will be considered revenue but are not cash flows until collected. Depreciation is an expense, but is not a current-period cash flow (the cash flow presumably occurred when the underlying asset was acquired). We can compute cash flow from operating activities by making adjustments to the revenues and expenses presented in the income statement. The adjustment amounts represent differences between revenues, expenses, gains, and losses recorded under accrual accounting and the related operating cash inflows and outflows. The adjustments are added to or subtracted from net income, depending on whether the related cash flow is more or less than the accrual amount.

Convert Sales Revenues to Cash Received from Customers To illustrate this adjustment procedure for revenues and cash receipts from customers, consider the Chapter 3 transactions and adjusting entry that occurred for NBS in December 2013:

(21) Dec. During the month of December, NBS sold products costing $5,000 to retail customers for $8,500 cash.

(22) Dec. During the month of December, sales to wholesale customers totaled $4,500 for merchandise that had cost $3,000. Instead of paying cash, wholesale customers are required to pay for the merchandise within ten working days.

(23) Dec. $1,200 of gift certificates were sold during the month of December. Each gift certificate entitles the recipient to a one-hour consultation on the use of NBS's products.

(25) Dec. During the month of December, NBS received $3,200 in cash from wholesale customers for products that had been delivered earlier.

(a) Dec. Gift certificates worth $900 were redeemed during the month.

We enter the revenue and cash receipts implications of each of these into the Financial Statement Effects Template (FSET) below. Whenever there is a difference between the revenue recognised and the cash received, that difference affects an operating asset (accounts receivable) or an operating liability (unearned revenue). For instance, in transaction (22a), NBS recognises credit sales revenue. That is, revenue increases, but cash does not, and the accounting equation is kept by increasing accounts receivable, an operating asset. When NBS received cash in advance of revenue recognition, as in transaction (23), the balancing entry is in unearned revenue, an operating liability. We will find that when an operating transaction affects cash or income—but not both—the operating assets and operating liabilities serve as a temporary buffer between the two.

The total of each of these columns is given in the last row, and because each individual entry is balanced, the totals are balanced.

	Balance Sheet										Income Statement				
Transaction	Cash Asset	+	Noncash Assets	=	Liabilities	+	Contrib. Capital	+	Earned Capital		Revenues	-	Expenses	=	Net Income
(21a) Sell $8,500 of products for cash.	+8,500 Cash			=					+8,500 Retained Earnings		+8,500 Sales Revenue	-		=	+8,500
(22a) Sell $4,500 of products on account.			+4,500 Accounts Receivable	=					+4,500 Retained Earnings		+4,500 Sales Revenue	-		=	+4,500
(23) Sell gift certificates for $1,200 cash.	+1,200 Cash			=	+1,200 Unearned Revenue							-		=	
(25) Receive $3,200 cash from customers who purchased on credit.	+3,200 Cash		−3,200 Accounts Receivable	=								-		=	
(a) Adjusting entry for gift certificates redeemed in December.				=	−900 Unearned Revenue				+900 Retained Earnings		+900 Sales Revenue	-		=	+900
Total Changes	+12,900 Cash	+	+1,300 Accounts Receivable	=	+300 Unearned Revenue	+	0	+	+13,900 Retained Earnings		+13,900 Sales Revenue	-	0	=	+13,900

We can see that December's revenue was $13,900, and NBS collected $12,900 from customers during the month. Accounts receivable increased by $1,300 over the month, and unearned revenue increased by $300. The FSET maintains the accounting equation at every entry, so we know that the equality will hold for the totals in the last row.

Cash flow (receipts)	+	**Change in accounts receivable**	=	**Change in unearned revenue**	+	**Net income (Sales revenue)**
$12,900	+	**$1,300**	=	**$300**	+	**$13,900**

And this relationship can be rewritten as the following:

Cash flow =	Net income −	Change in accounts receivable	+	Change in unearned revenue
$12,900 =	$13,900 −	$1,300	+	$300

So, when we start with net income and then subtract the change in accounts receivable and add the change in unearned revenue, we convert the revenues in net income into the cash receipts from customers needed for cash from operations.

Convert Cost of Goods Sold to Cash Paid for Merchandise Purchased As a second illustration, let's examine the December 2013 transactions involving NBS's inventory and its suppliers (Exhibit 3.3 in Chapter 3).

(20) Dec. 20 NBS paid $3,300 cash to its suppliers in partial payment for the delivery of inventory in November.

(21) Dec. During the month of December, NBS sold products costing $5,000 to retail customers for $8,500 cash.

(22) Dec. During the month of December, sales to wholesale customers totaled $4,500 for merchandise that had cost $3,000. Instead of paying cash, wholesale customers are required to pay for the merchandise within ten working days.

(26) Dec. 28 NBS purchased and received $4,000 of inventory on account.

When a company like NBS purchases inventory for future sale, we know that the purchase will be followed by two events in the normal course of business. One event is that NBS will have to pay the supplier in cash according to the terms of the purchase, resulting in a cash outflow. The other event is the sale of that inventory to a customer of NBS, resulting in a cost of goods sold expense on the income statement. But these two events do not necessarily occur at the same point in time. As we enter these events into the FSET, we see that the differences between cash payments for inventory and cost of goods sold expense are buffered by inventory, an operating asset, and accounts payable, an operating liability.

	Balance Sheet									*Income Statement*				
Transaction	Cash Asset	+	Noncash Assets	=	Liabil-ities	+	Contrib. Capital	+	Earned Capital	*Revenues*	−	*Expenses*	=	*Net Income*
(20) Pay $3,300 cash to suppliers.	−3,300 Cash			=	−3,300 Accounts Payable						−		=	
(21b) Record $5,000 for the cost of merchandise sold in transaction 21a.			−5,000 Inventory	=					−5,000 Retained Earnings		−	+5,000 Cost of Goods Sold	=	−5,000
(22b) Record $3,000 for the cost of merchandise sold in transaction 22a.			−3,000 Inventory	=					−3,000 Retained Earnings		−	+3,000 Cost of Goods Sold	=	−3,000
(26) Purchase $4,000 inventory on account.			+4,000 Inventory	=	+4,000 Accounts Payable						−		=	
Total changes	−3,300 Cash	+	−4,000 Inventory	=	+700 Accounts Payable	+	0	+	−8,000 Retained Earnings	0	−	+8,000 Cost of Goods Sold	=	−8,000

Again, the FSET keeps the accounting equation with every entry, so we know that the total changes in the last row must also conform to the accounting equation.

Cash flow (payments)	+	Change in inventory	=	Change in accounts payable	+	Net income (COGS expense)
−$3,300	+	−$4,000	=	+$700	+	−$8,000

And this relationship can be written as the following:

$$\text{Cash flow} = \text{Net income} - \text{Change in inventory} + \text{Change in accounts payable}$$
$$-\$3{,}300 = -\$8{,}000 - (-\$4{,}000) + \$700$$

The change in inventory is negative for NBS during December 2013, so when we subtract the change in inventory above, we must subtract a negative number, making a positive adjustment. (That is, −(−$4,000) = +$4,000.) And, when we subtract the change in inventory from net income and add the change in accounts payable to net income, we convert the (minus) cost of goods sold expense to the (minus) payments to suppliers we need for the cash from operations.

Stepping back to look at the big picture, we begin to see a pattern. The cash flow effect of an item is equal to its income statement effect, minus the change in any associated operating asset(s) plus the change in any associated operating liability(ies). That pattern can be confirmed as we look at the remaining necessary adjustments.

Convert Wages Expense to Cash Paid to Employees To determine the adjustment needed for transactions involving employees, we look at the two entries from Chapter 3 related to the wages earned and paid during the month of December 2013.

	Balance Sheet									Income Statement				
Transaction	Cash Asset	+	Noncash Assets	=	Liabil-ities	+	Contrib. Capital	+	Earned Capital	Revenues	−	Expenses	=	Net Income
(24) Record $1,625 in wages to employees.	−1,625 Cash			=					−1,625 Retained Earnings		−	+1,625 Wages Expense	=	−1,625
(e) Adjusting entry to record wages earned but not yet paid.				=	+480 Wages Payable				−480 Retained Earnings		−	+480 Wages Expense	=	−480
Total changes	−1,625 Cash	+	0	=	+480 Wages Payable	+	0	+	−2,105 Retained Earnings	0	−	+2,105 Wages Expense	=	−2,105

Using the same approach as above, the FSET tells us the following about the totals:

$$\text{Cash flow (payments)} = \text{Change in wages payable} + \text{Net income (wage expense)},$$

which can be rewritten as

$$\text{Cash flow} = \text{Net income} + \text{Change in wages payable}$$
$$-\$1{,}625 = -\$2{,}105 + \$480$$

NBS recorded more wage expense than it paid to its employees, and that additional expense goes into an operating liability—wages payable. If wages payable had decreased over the period, it would imply that NBS had paid more to its employees than they had earned during the period (perhaps because they were owed compensation from a prior period).

Convert Rent Expense to Cash Paid for Rent and Advertising Expense to Cash Paid for Advertising The December 2013 entries for rent and advertising are presented in the FSET below.

Transaction	Cash Asset	+	Noncash Assets	=	Liabilities	+	Contrib. Capital	+	Earned Capital	Revenues	−	Expenses	=	Net Income
(19) Pay $700 cash for December advertising.	−700 Cash			=					−700 Retained Earnings		−	+700 Advertising Expense	=	−700
(27) Pay $1,500 rent for December.	−1,500 Cash			=					−1,500 Retained Earnings		−	+1,500 Rent Expense	=	−1,500
Total changes	−2,200 Cash	+	0	=	0	+	0	+	−2,200 Retained Earnings	0	−	−2,200 Advertising and Rent Expense	=	−2,200

For these items, the amount paid is exactly equal to the amount recorded as expense, so no adjustment is necessary. The amounts included for advertising and rent in the determination of net income are exactly what we want in the cash from operations. If NBS had paid rent in advance or promised to pay later for its advertising, then operating assets and/or liabilities would have been created, and an adjustment would have been necessary (as we see in the case immediately following).

Other Adjustments There are five more items in NBS's income statement that require adjustment to arrive at the amount of cash from operations for the month of December. Four of these items are insurance expense, interest income, interest expense and income tax expense. In this example, we classify interest (and dividends) received and interest paid as cash flows from operating activities. Hence, we need to adjust for interest (and dividend) income and interest expense. These items involved only adjusting entries during the month of December, so there were no cash flows involved, and we present the adjustments in an abbreviated fashion below.

	Balance Sheet										Income Statement				
Transaction	Cash Asset	+	Noncash Assets	=	Liabil-ities	+	Contrib. Capital	+	Earned Capital		*Revenues*	-	*Expenses*	=	*Net Income*
(b) Adjusting entry to record expiration of 1 month of prepaid insurance.			−140 Prepaid insurance	=					−140 Retained Earnings			-	+140 Insurance Expense	=	−140
Total changes	0 Cash	+	−140 Prepaid Insurance	=	0	+	0	+	−140 Retained Earnings		0	-	+140 Insurance Expense	=	−140

Cash flow + Change in prepaid insurance = Net income, or

Cash flow = Net income − Change in prepaid insurance, or
\$0 (zero) = − \$140 − (−\$140)

Transaction	Cash Asset	+	Noncash Assets	=	Liabil-ities	+	Contrib. Capital	+	Earned Capital		Revenues	-	Expenses	=	Net Income
(d) Adjusting entry for interest income earned.			+30 Other Receivables	=					+30 Retained Earnings		+30 Interest Income	-		=	+30
Total changes	0 Cash	+	+30 Other Receivables	=	0	+	0	+	+30 Retained Earnings		+30 Interest Income	-	0	=	+30

Cash flow + Change in other receivables = Net income, or

Cash flow = Net income − Change in other receivables, or
\$0 (zero) = +\$30 − (+\$30)

Transaction	Cash Asset	+	Noncash Assets	=	Liabil-ities	+	Contrib. Capital	+	Earned Capital		Revenues	-	Expenses	=	Net Income
(f) Adjusting entry to record interest owed but not yet paid.				=	+110 Interest Payable				−110 Retained Earnings			-	+110 Interest Expense	=	−110
Total changes	0 Cash	+	0	=	+110 Interest Payable	+	0	+	−110 Retained Earnings		0	-	+110 Interest Expense	=	−110

Cash flow = Change in interest payable + Net income, or

Cash flow = Net income + Change in interest payable, or
\$0 (zero) = −\$110 + (+\$110)

Transaction	Cash Asset	+	Noncash Assets	=	Liabil-ities	+	Contrib. Capital	+	Earned Capital		Revenues	-	Expenses	=	Net Income
(g) Adjusting entry for estimated income tax.				=	+350 Tax Payable				−350 Retained Earnings			-	+350 Tax Expense	=	−350
Total Changes	0 Cash	+	0	=	+350 Tax Payable	+	0	+	−350 Retained Earnings		0	-	+350 Tax Expense	=	−350

Cash flow = Change in tax payable + Net income, or

Cash flow = Net income + Change in tax payable, or

\$0 (zero) = −\$350 + (+\$350)

Each of the above four items involved only an adjusting entry (i.e., an entry at the end of the fiscal period). Adjusting entries rarely involve cash, so the adjustment simply cancels out the item in the income statement. We will see more examples in later chapters (e.g., write-downs of physical or intangible assets, restructuring charges, etc.).

Eliminate Depreciation Expense and Other Noncash Operating Expenses NBS recorded an adjusting entry for depreciation at the end of December 2013 for \$375. That entry into the FSET was the following.

	Balance Sheet											Income Statement				
Transaction	Cash Asset	+	Noncash Assets	−	Contra Assets	=	Liabil-ities	+	Contrib. Capital	+	Earned Capital	Revenues	−	Expenses	=	Net Income
(c) Adjusting entry for depreciation on fixtures and equipment for December.					+375 Accumulated Depreciation	=					−375 Retained Earnings		−	+375 Depreciation Expense	=	−375
Total changes	0	+	0	−	+375 Accumulated Depreciation	=	0	+	0	+	−375 Retained Earnings	0	−	+375 Depreciation Expense	=	−375

We can see that this entry reduced net income by \$375, but it had no effect on cash. When we look at the total impact of this entry on the FSET (in the last row), its effect can be written in the following way.

$$\textbf{Cash flow} - \frac{\textbf{Change in accumulated depreciation}}{\textbf{(for depreciation expense)}} = \textbf{Net income,}$$

or

Cash flow = Net income + Depreciation expense
\$0 (zero) = −\$375 + \$375

So, NBS's net income of \$650 for December 2013 includes a depreciation expense of \$375 that did not involve any cash outflow. When we add back depreciation expense (and similar items like amortisation expense), we move the net income number one step closer to cash from operations.

Would increasing depreciation expense increase the cash flows from operations? That question is more complex than it initially appears. In Chapter 8, we will find that companies use different depreciation methods for tax reporting and financial reporting, and in Chapter 10 we will see how differences between tax and financial reporting are reconciled. Increasing the tax depreciation expense reduces taxable income and the amount of tax that has to be paid. Increasing depreciation expense in financial reports to shareholders has no effect on the amount of taxes paid and, therefore, no effect on the amount of cash generated.

A General Rule . . . with a Note of Caution The relationships illustrated in the above examples suggest a general rule that we can use to prepare the cash flow statement:

> The difference between a revenue or an expense reported in the income statement and a related cash receipt or expenditure reported in the statement of cash flows will be reflected in the balance sheet as a change in one or more balance sheet accounts.

More specifically, all the above reconciliation adjustments for NBS can be summarised in a pattern:

Net income ± Adjustments = Cash from operations

Or, more particularly

$$\textbf{Net income} + \frac{\textbf{Depreciation}}{\textbf{expense}} + \frac{\textbf{Other noncash}}{\textbf{operating expenses}} - \frac{\textbf{Change in}}{\textbf{operating assets}} + \frac{\textbf{Change in}}{\textbf{operating liabilities}} = \frac{\textbf{Cash from}}{\textbf{operations}}$$

By "operating assets," we mean receivables, inventories, prepaid expenses and similar assets. "Operating liabilities" refers to accounts and wages payable, accrued expenses, unearned revenues, taxes payable, interest payable and similar items. Investing assets (like investment securities and property, plant and equipment) and financing liabilities (like notes payable and long-term debt) would not be included in these adjustments.

Exhibit 4.5 summarises the basic adjustments needed to convert the revenues, expenses, gains and losses presented in the income statement to cash receipts and payments presented in the statement of cash flows from operating activities. (The adjustments for non-operating gains and losses will be discussed shortly.)

We have now applied the adjustments to convert each accrual revenue and expense to the corresponding operating cash flow. We use these individual cash inflows and outflows to prepare the operating activities section of the statement of cash flows. The adjustments to convert revenues and expenses to operating cash flows are summarised in Exhibit 4.6, and this information can be used to produce NBS's cash from operating activities by using the information in the income statement and balance sheet.

Like all general rules, this one provides useful insights, but it also has limitations. As we learn more and more about business activities and the accounting for them, we find the need for refinements of this general rule. For instance, in Chapter 12, we will see that operating assets and liabilities can increase from acquisitions (an investing activity) as well as from operations. But for the time-being, the general rule is a useful way to approach the indirect method operating cash flow.

EXHIBIT 4.5 Adjustments to Convert Income Statement Items to Cash Flows From Operating Activities

Net income =	Sales revenue	− Cost of goods sold	− Operating expenses	− Depreciation expense	+ Dividend and Interest income*	− Interest expense*	+ Gains	− Losses	− Income tax expense
Adjustments:									
Add back depreciation expense				+ Depreciation expense					
Subtract (add) non-operating gains (losses)							− Gains	+ Losses	
Subtract the change in operating assets (operating investments)	− change in accounts receivable	− change in inventory	− change in related prepaid expenses		− change in dividend and interest receivable				
Add the change in operating liabilities (operating financing)	+ change in unearned revenue	+ change in accounts payable	+ change in related accrued liabilities			+ change in interest payable			+ change in income tax payable
Cash from operations =	Receipts from customers	− Payments for merchandise	− Payments for expenses	− 0	+ Receipts from dividends and interest	− Payments for interest	+ 0	− 0	− Payments for income tax

* If a firm classifies dividends received, interest received and interest paid as cash flows from operating activities, it needs to adjust for dividend income, interest income and interest expense to convert net income to cash flows from operations.

EXHIBIT 4.6 Converting Revenues and Expenses to Cash Inflows and Outflows from Operating Activity (Natural Beauty Supply)

Net income		Sales revenue		Interest income		Cost of goods sold		Wages expense		Rent expense		Advertising expense		Insurance expense		Interest expense		Depreciation expense		Income tax expense
$ 650	=	$13,900	+	30	−	8,000	−	2,105	−	1,500	−	700	−	140	−	110	−	375	−	350
Adjustments:																				
Add back depreciation expense																		⊕ 375 depreciation expense		
Subtract the change in operating assets (operating investments)		⊖ 1,300 change in accounts receivable		⊖ 30 change in interest receivable		⊖ (−4,000)* change in inventory								⊖ (−140)* change in prepaid insurance						
Add the change in operating liabilities (operating financing)		⊕ 300 change in unearned revenue				⊕ 700 change in accounts payable		⊕ 480 change in wages payable								⊕ 110 change in interest payable				⊕ 350 change in income tax payable
$5,775	=	$12,900	+	0	−	3,300	−	1,625	−	1,500	−	700	−	0	−	0	−	0	−	0
Cash from operations	=	Receipts from customers	+	Receipts for interest	−	Payments for merchandise	−	Payments to employees	−	Payments for rent	−	Payments for advertising	−	Payments for insurance	−	Payments for interest	−	0	−	Payments for income tax

* When the change in an operating asset is negative, subtracting that negative amount results in a positive adjustment.

MID-CHAPTER REVIEW 2

The income statement and comparative balance sheets for Mug Shots, Inc., (a photography studio) are presented below. Use the information in these financial statements and the frameworks in Exhibits 4.5 and 4.6 to compute Mug Shots' cash flow from operating activities using the direct method. Classify interest paid as cash flows from operating activities.

MUG SHOTS, INC.
Income Statement
For Month Ended December 31, 2013

Revenue		
Sales revenue		$31,000
Expenses		
Cost of goods sold	$16,700	
Wages expense	4,700	
Interest expense	300	
Advertising expense	1,800	
Rent expense	1,500	
Depreciation expense	700	
Total expenses		25,700
Income before taxes		5,300
Income tax expense		1,855
Net income		$ 3,445

MUG SHOTS, INC.
Comparative Balance Sheets

	12/31/13	11/30/13
Assets		
Cash	$10,700	$ 5,000
Accounts receivable	2,500	
Inventory	32,300	24,000
Prepaid rent	7,500	9,000
Equipment	30,000	18,000
Accumulated depreciation	(700)	
Total assets	$82,300	$56,000
Liabilities		
Accounts payable	$25,000	$24,000
Interest payable	300	
Wages payable	2,200	
Income tax payable	1,855	
Unearned revenue	500	
Notes payable	30,000	12,000
Equity		
Share capital	20,000	20,000
Retained earnings	2,445	
Total liabilities and equity	$82,300	$56,000

The solution to this review problem can be found on page 206.

Reconciling Net Income and Cash Flow from Operating Activities

LO3 Reconcile cash flows from operations to net income and use the indirect method to compute operating cash flows.

We now have two metrics to consider when examining the operations of a company over a period of time—net income and cash from operations. For December 2013, NBS reported net income of $650 and cash from operations of $5,775. While both net income and cash from operations measure aspects of operations over the same time period, they can sometimes be very far apart, as seen in the following table.

	2013 (amounts in millions)	
	Net Income	**Cash from Operations**
Adidas	€ 790	€ 634
Airbus	€ 1,475	€ 1,931
Burberry	£ 259	£ 425
Carrefour	€ 1,364	€ 1,675
Fiat	€ 1,951	€ 7,589
Indigo	C$ (31)	C$ (17)
Inditex	€ 2,367	€ 3,119
Philips	€ 1,172	€ 1,138
Qantas	A$ 6	A$ 1,417
Roche	CHF 11,371	CHF 15,772
Singapore Airlines	S$ 442	S$ 1,854
TomTom	€ 20	€ 259
Unilever	€ 5,263	€ 6,294

Source: Company annual reports.

It would be natural for a financial statement reader to want to understand the source(s) of the differences between net income and cash from operations. So, companies that present their statement of cash flows like Qantas must also present a reconciliation of net income to cash from operations. The reconciliation for Qantas's fiscal year ending June 30, 2013, is given in Exhibit 4.7.

EXHIBIT 4.7 Qantas Reconciliation

QANTAS GROUP
Consolidated Statement of Cash Flows—Continued
For the Fiscal Year Ended June 30, 2013
Reconciliation of Profit to Net Cash from Operating Activities

	2013 $A Millions
Profit for the year	6
Add: depreciation and amortisation	1,450
Add: dividends received from associates and jointly controlled entities	142
Add: share-based payments	20
Add: net impairment of property, plant and equipment	93
Add: net impairment of goodwill and intangible assets	24
(Less)/add: net gain/(loss) on disposal of property, plant and equipment	(1)
Less: net gain on disposal of investments in jointly controlled entities	(30)
Less: share of net loss/(profit) of associates and jointly controlled entities	39
(Less)/add: other items	(40)
Movements in operating assets and liabilities:	
– Change in receivables	(18)
– Change in inventories	5
– Change in other assets	30
– Change in payables	(41)
– Change in revenue received in advance	(88)
– Change in provisions	(173)
– Change in deferred tax liabilities	(1)
Net cash from operating activities	1,417

This reconciliation leads to exactly the same number that was presented in the operating section of Exhibit 4.1, but in a very different format. How is it produced? It is constructed using exactly the same adjustment process depicted in Exhibits 4.5 and 4.6.

Qantas's reconciliation contains a couple of entries that we did not see for Natural Beauty Supply. A company's income statement may contain gains and losses related to investing or financing activities. Examples include gains and losses from the sale of plant assets and gains and losses from the retirement of bonds payable. Qantas reported a $1 million gain on sale of assets in its income statement. Because these gains and losses are not related to operating activities, Exhibits 4.5 and 4.7 show that we omit them as we convert income statement items to various cash flows from operating activities. The cash flows relating to these gains and losses are reported in the investing activities or financing activities sections of the statement of cash flows. NBS had no gains or losses in December, but Qantas made an adjustment for an investing activity gain in its reconciliation in Exhibit 4.7, and we will see an example of this type of adjustment in a later section.

Exhibit 4.7 shows that Qantas made a $142 million adjustment for dividends received from its associates and joint ventures, and a $39 million adjustment for its share of their net loss. We will cover the accounting for associates and joint ventures in Chapter 12. Qantas also made a $20 million adjustment for share-based payment, which is noncash in nature. The accounting for share-based compensation will be covered in Chapter 11. Qantas also added back to net income $93 million for impairment losses on fixed assets and $24 million for impairment losses on goodwill and intangibles. Asset impairments will be discussed in Chapter 8.

Cash Flow from Operating Activities Using the Indirect Method

Two alternative formats may be used to report the net cash flow from operating activities: the direct method and the indirect method. *Both methods report the same amount of net cash flow from operating activities*. Net cash flows from investing and financing activities are prepared in the same manner under both the indirect and direct methods; only the format for cash flows from operating activities differs.

For Natural Beauty Supply, we computed cash flow from operating activities using the direct method. The **direct method** presents the components of cash flow from operating activities as a list of gross cash receipts and gross cash payments. This format is illustrated in Exhibit 4.3 and by Qantas's statement in Exhibit 4.1.

The direct method is logical and relatively easy to follow. In practice, however, nearly all statements of cash flows are presented using what is called the **indirect method**. Under this method, the reconciliation of net income to operating cash flow (e.g., Exhibit 4.7) is used for the presentation of cash flow from operations. The cash flow from operations section begins with net income and applies a series of adjustments to net income to convert it to net cash flow from operating activities. However, the adjustments to net income are not cash flows themselves, so the indirect method does not report any detail concerning individual operating cash inflows and outflows. In fact, there are no cash flows in the indirect method operating section of the cash flow statement, except the subtotal—cash flow from operations.

IASB has stated a preference for the direct method, but a survey of large firms reporting under IFRS, found that less than 15% used the direct method for cash from operations, so the Qantas presentation is unusual. The indirect method is popular because (1) it is easier and less expensive to prepare than the direct method and (2) companies that use the direct method are required to present a supplemental disclosure showing the reconciliation of net income to cash from operations (thus, essentially requiring the company to report both methods for cash from operations).

The procedure for presenting indirect method cash flows from operations uses the same approach that we applied above to convert income statement items to operating cash flows. In fact, the indirect method can be viewed as a "short-cut" calculation of the process shown in Exhibit 4.6. That is:

Net income ± Adjustments = Cash flow from operating activities

In Exhibit 4.6, revenue and expense components of the income statement are presented in the first row that totals to net income. The following rows list the adjustments, and cash receipts and

FYI Managers can boost declining sales by lengthening credit periods or by lowering credit standards. The resulting increase in accounts receivable can cause net income to outpace operating cash flow. Consequently, many view a large receivables increase as a warning sign. ■

payments are listed in the last row at the bottom. The total of the last row is cash flow from operating activities. The indirect method skips the listing of individual revenues and expenses and starts with net income. After adjustments, we have total cash flow from operating activities, but not individual receipts and payments.

Cash flow from operating activities for NBS is presented using the indirect method in Exhibit 4.8. The calculation begins with the December net income of $650 and ends with cash flow from operating activities, $5,775. The total cash flow from operating activities is the same amount as was computed in Exhibit 4.6 using the direct method. If we compare Exhibit 4.6 and Exhibit 4.8, we see that the two exhibits are very similar. The only difference is that all of the revenues and expenses are listed in the first row at the top of Exhibit 4.6, while Exhibit 4.8 only lists the total—net income. Similarly, the last row at the bottom of Exhibit 4.6 lists all of the cash inflows and outflows, while the bottom line of Exhibit 4.8 only lists the net cash flow from operating activities. In both exhibits, the centre rows list the adjustments.

EXHIBIT 4.8 NBS Cash Flow from Operating Activities—Indirect Method

Net income	$650		
Adjustments:			
Add back depreciation expense		$ 375	
Subtract:			
Change in accounts receivable		(1,300)	
Change in interest receivable		(30)	
Change in inventory		4,000*	
Change in prepaid insurance		140*	
Add:			
Change in unearned revenue		300	
Change in accounts payable		700	
Change in wages payable		480	
Change in interest payable		110	
Change in income tax payable		350	
Total adjustments		$5,125	
Cash flow from operating activities			$5,775

* When the change in an operating asset is negative, subtracting that negative amount results in a positive adjustment.

MID-CHAPTER REVIEW 3

Refer to the financial statements for Mug Shots, Inc. presented in Mid-Chapter Review 2. Compute cash flows from operating activities for Mug Shots, Inc. using the indirect method. Classify interest paid as cash flows from operating activities.

The solution to this review problem can be found on page 207.

PREPARING THE STATEMENT OF CASH FLOWS—INVESTING AND FINANCING ACTIVITIES

LO4 Construct the investing and financing activities sections of the statement of cash flows.

The remaining sections of the statement of cash flows focus on investing and financing activities. Investing activities are concerned with transactions affecting noncurrent (and some current) noncash assets. Financing activities are concerned with raising capital from owners and creditors. The presentation of the cash effects of investing and financing transactions is not affected by the method of presentation (direct or indirect) of cash flows from operating activities.

Accounting standard-setters require that financing and investing items be presented in the statement of cash flows using gross amounts instead of net amounts. In Exhibit 4.1, Qantas reports that it spent $1,247 million cash to acquire property, plant and equipment in 2013, and it received $32 million in cash from the sale of property, plant and equipment. It would not be acceptable to show the net amount—an outflow of $1,215 million—as a single item unless one of the components is consistently immaterial.

Cash Flows from Investing Activities

Investing activities cause changes in noncash asset accounts. Usually the accounts affected (other than cash) are noncurrent operating asset accounts such as property, plant and equipment assets and investing assets like marketable securities and long-term financial investments. Cash paid for acquisitions of other companies would be included as well. To determine the cash flows from investing activities, *we analyse changes in all noncash asset accounts not used in computing net cash flow from operating activities*. Our objective is to identify any investing cash flows related to these changes.

Purchases of noncash assets cause cash outflow. Conversely, a sale of a noncash asset results in cash inflow. This relationship is highlighted in the following decision guide:

Cash flows increase due to:	Cash flows decrease due to:
Sales of assets	Purchases of assets

NBS had only one investing transaction during December—the purchase of fixtures and equipment for $18,000. Any change in the Fixtures and Equipment account in the balance sheet is usually the result of one or both of the following transactions: (1) buying assets, or (2) selling assets.[1] Buying and selling assets are classified as investing transactions. NBS's journal entry to record the purchase of fixtures and equipment for cash is as follows:

(18) Fixtures and equipment (+A)	18,000	
Cash (−A)		18,000

The resulting $18,000 cash outflow is listed in the statement of cash flows under cash flow used for investing activities.

Cash Flows from Financing Activities

Financing activities cause changes in financial liabilities and stockholders' equity accounts. Financial liabilities include current liability items like seasonal bank borrowing and the current portion of long-term debt due within the next year, plus noncurrent items like long-term debt issues and longer term borrowing from financial institutions. Cash receipts from the issuance of these liabilities and cash payments to settle outstanding principal balances are considered cash flows from financing activities. Stockholders' equity accounts include contributed capital (share capital, contributed surplus and treasury shares) and retained earnings. Transactions with shareholders are always considered part of a company's financing activities. This relationship is highlighted in the following decision guide:

Cash flows increase due to:	Cash flows decrease due to:
Taking on a financial liability or issuing shares	Repaying principal on a financial liability or paying dividends to shareholders or making share repurchases

NBS had two financing transactions during December. It borrowed $11,000 on a three-year note, resulting in an increase in cash, and it paid $50 in cash dividends to shareholders. The journal entry to record the $11,000 note is illustrated as:

(17) Cash (+A).	11,000	
Notes payable (+L)		11,000

[1] The Accumulated Depreciation-Fixtures and Equipment contra-asset account is affected by depreciation expense and selling assets.

The resulting $11,000 cash inflow is listed in the statement of cash flows under cash flow from financing activities.

The journal entry to record dividends is illustrated as follows:

(28) Retained earnings (−SE)	50	
Cash (−A)		50

This dividend payment is a financing cash outflow and would be deducted from cash flow from financing activities.

When using the indirect method for the cash flow from operating activities, we should remember that there are some balance sheet accounts that will be affected by more than one type of activity. For instance, the balance in retained earnings will be affected by net income (which is going to appear in the operations section) and shareholder dividends (which will appear in the financing section).

The statement of cash flows lists cash flows from operating activities first (using either the direct or the indirect method), followed by cash flows from investing activities, then cash flows from financing activities. Once all three categories of cash flows have been listed, we total the three amounts to arrive at net cash flow for the period. The final step is to reconcile the cash balance from the beginning of the period to the ending balance. The completed statement of cash flows for NBS using the indirect method for operating cash flows is presented in Exhibit 4.9. We see from this statement that operating activities produced a cash inflow of $5,775, while investing activities resulted in a cash outflow of $18,000, and financing activities resulted in a cash inflow of $10,950. The sum of these three amounts ($5,775 − $18,000 + $10,950) equals the change in cash for December of −$1,275 ($6,825 − $8,100).

FYI The net cash inflow or outflow for the period is the same amount as the increase or decrease in cash and cash equivalents for the period from the balance sheet. ■

EXHIBIT 4.9 NBS Statement of Cash Flows—Indirect Method

NATURAL BEAUTY SUPPLY
Statement of Cash Flows
For the Month of December, 2013

Operating activities:			
Net income	$ 650		
Adjustments:			
Add back Depreciation expense		$ 375	
Subtract:			
Change in accounts receivable		(1,300)	
Change in interest receivable		(30)	
Change in inventory		4,000*	
Change in prepaid insurance		140*	
Add:			
Change in unearned revenue		300	
Change in accounts payable		700	
Change in wages payable		480	
Change in interest payable		110	
Change in income tax payable		350	
Total adjustments		5,125	
Cash flow from operating activities			$5,775
Investing activities:			
Purchase of fixtures and equipment		(18,000)	
Cash flow used for investing activities			(18,000)
Financing activities:			
Bank note		11,000	
Dividends paid		(50)	
Cash flow from financing activities			10,950
Net decrease in cash			(1,275)
Cash, November 30, 2013			8,100
Cash, December 31, 2013			$ 6,825

* When the change in an operating asset is negative, subtracting that negative amount results in a positive adjustment.

MID-CHAPTER REVIEW 4

Refer to the financial statements for Mug Shots, Inc. in Mid-Chapter Review 2. Prepare a complete statement of cash flows for December using the indirect method for cash flows from operating activities. Classify interest paid as cash flows from operating activities. Follow the format used in Exhibit 4.9.

The solution to this review problem can be found on page 207.

ADDITIONAL DETAIL IN THE STATEMENT OF CASH FLOWS

There are two additional types of transactions that we must explore to understand the statement of cash flows. The first of these is the sale of investing assets like equipment or an investment security. The transaction itself is not very complicated, but the use of the indirect method for operating cash flows makes it seem so. And, companies often engage in investing and financing activity that does not involve cash (e.g., acquiring another company through an exchange of stock). This section explores the accounting for these two types of transactions and their effect on the statement of cash flows.

Case Illustration Natural Beauty Supply did not have any disposals of assets or repayments of debt in December 2013, so there is no adjustment to make in this case. However, let's consider the financial statements of One World Café, a coffee shop that is located next door to NBS. The income statement and comparative balance sheet for One World Café are presented in Exhibit 4.10. The cash flow statement is presented in Exhibit 4.11.

EXHIBIT 4.10 One World Café Income Statement and Comparative Balance Sheets

ONE WORLD CAFÉ, INC.
Income Statement
For Year Ended December 31, 2013

Revenue		
Sales revenue		$390,000
Expenses		
Cost of goods sold	$227,000	
Wages expense	82,000	
Advertising expense	9,800	
Depreciation expense	17,000	
Interest expense	200	
Loss on sale of plant assets	2,000	
Total expenses		338,000
Income before taxes		52,000
Income tax expense		17,000
Net income		$ 35,000

ONE WORLD CAFÉ, INC.
Comparative Balance Sheets
At December 31

	2013	2012
Assets		
Cash	$ 8,000	$ 12,000
Accounts receivable	22,000	28,000
Inventory	94,000	66,000
Prepaid advertising	12,000	9,000
Plant assets, at cost	208,000	170,000
Less accumulated depreciation	(72,000)	(61,000)
Total assets	$272,000	$224,000
Liabilities		
Accounts payable	$ 27,000	$ 14,000
Wages payable	6,000	2,500
Income tax payable	3,000	4,500
Notes payable	5,000	—
Equity		
Share capital	134,000	125,000
Retained earnings	97,000	78,000
Total liabilities and equity	$272,000	$224,000

EXHIBIT 4.11 Cash Flow Statement for One World Café

ONE WORLD CAFÉ, INC.
Statement of Cash Flows
For Year Ended December 31, 2013

Cash flows from operating activities		
Net income	$35,000	
Add (deduct) items to convert net income to cash basis		
Add back depreciation	17,000	
Add back loss on sale of plant assets	2,000	
Subtract change in:		
Accounts receivable	6,000*	
Inventory	(28,000)	
Prepaid advertising	(3,000)	
Add change in:		
Accounts payable	13,000	
Wages payable	3,500	
Income tax payable	(1,500)**	
Net cash provided by operating activities		$44,000
Cash flows from investing activities		
Purchase of plant assets	(45,000)	
Proceeds from sale of plant assets	4,000	
Net cash used for investing activities		(41,000)
Cash flows from financing activities		
Issuance of ordinary shares	9,000	
Payment of dividends	(16,000)	
Net cash flows used for financing activities		(7,000)
Net cash decrease		(4,000)
Cash at beginning of year		12,000
Cash at end of year		$ 8,000

* When the change in an operating asset is negative, subtracting that negative amount results in a positive adjustment.
** When the change in an operating liability is negative, adding that negative amount results in a negative adjustment.

For One World Café, creation of the statement of cash flows requires information that cannot be discerned from the income statement and balance sheet. (After all, the statement of cash flows is *supposed* to provide additional information!) In particular, the following events occurred during the year.

- Plant assets were purchased for cash.
- Obsolete plant assets, with original cost of $12,000 and accumulated depreciation of $6,000, were sold for $4,000 cash, resulting in a $2,000 loss.
- Additional ordinary shares were issued for cash.
- Cash dividends of $16,000 were declared and paid during the year.
- One World Café acquired $5,000 of plant assets by issuing notes payable.

Reviewing One World Café's comparative balance sheet, we see that plant assets at cost increased from $170,000 to $208,000, an increase of $38,000. In addition, the accumulated depreciation contra-asset increased by $11,000 from $61,000 to $72,000. However, these are *net* increases, and we need information on the individual components of the increases. Consequently, we need to determine the gross amounts to ensure the statement of cash flows we create properly presents the gross amounts in the investing activities section.

In addition to the changes in plant assets and accumulated depreciation, notes payable increased by $5,000 in 2013. The best way to fully understand what happened to cause the changes in balance sheet accounts during the year, and the impact of these changes on cash flows, is to "work backwards" to reconstruct the investing and financing transactions using journal entries and T-accounts, especially the plant assets and accumulated depreciation accounts.

Gains and Losses on Investing and Financing Activities

The focus of the income statement is on the revenues and expenses that are generated by a company's transactions with customers, suppliers, employees, and other operating activities. But the income statement also contains gains and losses that result from investing or financing transactions. Gains and losses from the sale of investments, property, plant and equipment, or intangible assets result from investing activities, not operating activities. A gain or loss from the retirement of bonds payable is an example of a financing gain or loss. When these transactions occur, the income statement does not show a revenue and an expense, but rather shows only the net amount as a gain or loss.

The full cash flow effect from these types of events is reported in the investing or financing sections of the statement of cash flows. To illustrate, we record the sale of Old World Café's obsolete plant assets at a loss with the following journal entry:

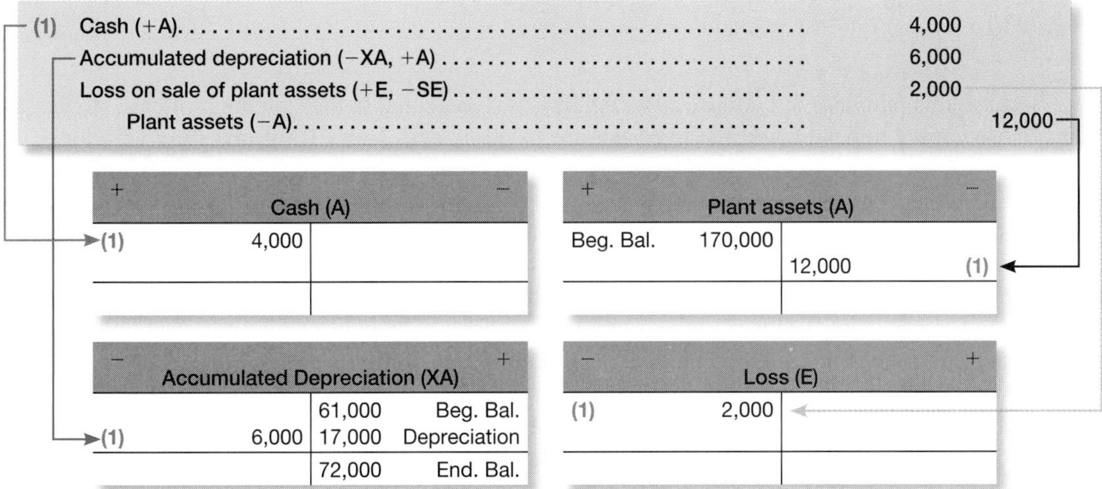

The $4,000 of cash received from this sale should be listed as a cash inflow under cash flows from investing activities, and it can be seen in Exhibit 4.11. The $4,000 cash flow is equal to the $6,000 net book value of the plant assets that were sold ($12,000 − $6,000) less the $2,000 loss on the sale.

If we were using the direct method to report the cash flows from operating activities, we would not need to take any additional steps. But an indirect method operating cash flows starts with net income, and Old World Café's net income includes a $2,000 loss from this investing transaction (Exhibit 4.10). So, when we add back the investing loss to net income (or subtract an investing gain), we remove the effect of this investing transaction from the determination of cash flows from operating activities. It is one more step in the adjustments that are needed to reconcile net income to the cash flows from operating activities.

In Chapter 9, we will find that companies can experience financing gains (losses) from the early retirement of their debt. These gains and losses appear in the income statement, but they result from financing activities. In an indirect method statement of cash flows, the financing gains (losses) must be subtracted from (added to) net income to determine cash flows from operating activities.

We also see that the accumulated depreciation account started with a credit balance of $61,000, and the obsolete asset sale reduced this by $6,000 to $55,000. But the balance sheet in Exhibit 4.10 tells us that the ending (credit) balance is $72,000. The difference is due to $17,000 depreciation expense for the year.

Noncash Investing and Financing Activities

In addition to reporting how cash changed from one balance sheet to the next, cash flow reporting is intended to present summary information about a firm's investing and financing activities. Many of these activities affect cash and are therefore already included in the investing and financing sections of the statement of cash flows. Some significant investing and financing events, however, do not affect current cash flows. Examples of **noncash investing and financing activities** are the issuance of stocks, bonds, or leases in exchange for property, plant, and equipment (PPE) assets or intangible assets; the exchange of long-term assets for other long-term assets; and the conversion of long-term debt into ordinary shares.

To illustrate the effect of noncash transactions on the preparation of the cash flow statement, consider One World Café's purchase of $5,000 of plant assets that was financed with notes payable. The journal entry to record the purchase is as follows:

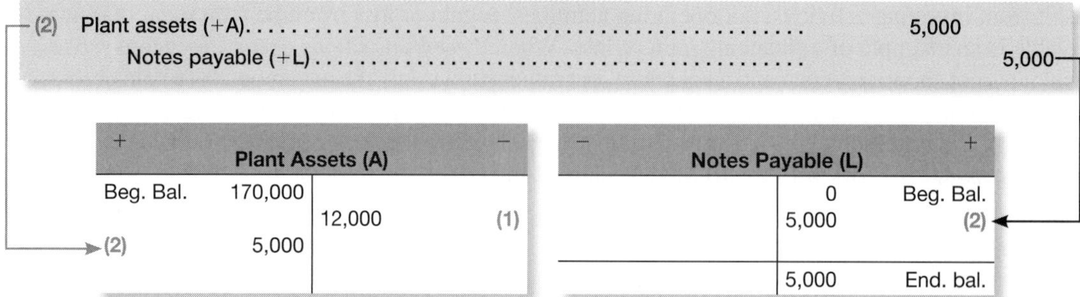

		Debit	Credit
(2)	Plant assets (+A)	5,000	
	Notes payable (+L)		5,000

+	Plant Assets (A)		−
Beg. Bal.	170,000		
		12,000	(1)
(2)	5,000		

−	Notes Payable (L)		+
		0	Beg. Bal.
		5,000	(2)
		5,000	End. bal.

Because this purchase did not use any cash, it is not presented in the statement of cash flows. Only those capital expenditures that use cash are listed as cash flows from investing activities. That is, cash flows from investing activities should reflect the actual amount of cash spent to purchase plant assets or investment assets.

Noncash investing and financing transactions generally do affect *future* cash flows. Issuing notes payable to acquire equipment, for example, requires future cash payments for interest and principal on the notes, and should produce future operating cash flows from the equipment. Alternatively, converting bonds payable into ordinary shares eliminates future cash payments related to the bonds, but may carry the expectation of future cash dividends. Knowledge of these types of events, therefore, is helpful to users of cash flow data who wish to assess a firm's future cash flows.

Information on noncash investing and financing transactions is disclosed in a schedule that is separate from the statement of cash flows. The separate schedule is reported either immediately below the statement of cash flows or among the notes to the financial statements.

Solving for Purchases of Plant Assets The remaining entry affecting plant assets is the purchase of plant assets for cash. The amount of plant assets purchased can be determined by solving for the missing amount in the plant assets T-account:

+	Plant Assets (A)		−
Beg. Bal.	170,000		
		12,000	(1)
(2)	5,000		
(3)	X		
End. Bal.	208,000		

Balancing the account requires that we solve for the unknown amount:

$$\$170{,}000 + \$5{,}000 + X - \$12{,}000 = \$208{,}000$$
$$X = \$45{,}000$$

Thus, plant assets costing $45,000 were purchased for cash. This amount is listed as a cash outflow under cash flows for investing activities.

Examining the cash flow statement for One World Café in Exhibit 4.11, we see that two cash flows are listed under investing activities: (1) a $45,000 cash outflow for the purchase of plant assets, and (2) a $4,000 cash inflow from the sale of plant assets. The purchase of plant assets costing $5,000 by issuing notes payable is not listed; nor is the increase in notes payable listed under financing activities.

Appendix 4A at the end of this chapter introduces a spreadsheet approach that can be used to prepare the statement of cash flows. The appendix uses the One World Café financial statements as the illustration.

MID-CHAPTER REVIEW 5

The balance sheet of Jack's Snacks, Inc. reports the following amounts:

	End-of-year	Beginning-of-year
Property, plant & equipment at cost	$670,000	$600,000
Accumulated depreciation	(150,000)	(140,000)
Property, plant & equipment, net	$520,000	$460,000

Additional information:

During the year, Jack's Snacks disposed of a used piece of equipment. The original cost of the equipment was $80,000 and, at the time of disposal, the accumulated depreciation on the equipment was $60,000. The purchaser of the used piece of equipment paid in cash, and Jack's Snacks reported a gain of $35,000 on the disposal.

All acquisitions of new property, plant and equipment were paid for in cash.

Questions:

1. How much cash did Jack's Snacks receive from the used equipment disposal?
2. How much cash did Jack's Snacks spend to acquire new property, plant and equipment during the year?
3. How much depreciation expense did Jack's Snacks record during the year?

The solution to this review problem can be found on pages 207–208.

The Effects of Foreign Currencies on the Cash Flow Statement

Multinational companies often engage in transactions that involve more than one currency and may hold assets that are denominated in foreign currencies or liabilities that must be repaid in foreign currencies. Also, part of a company's cash balance may be held in various currencies. If the company prepares its financial statements in one currency (the so-called "functional currency), other foreign currency amounts must be converted, or translated, into that currency before preparing the financial statements. The process of translating transactions based in many currencies into one common currency for financial statement presentation is beyond the scope of an introductory text. However, foreign exchange rates fluctuate and these fluctuations can have an effect on the cash flow statement.

The statement of cash flows explains the change in the cash balance during the fiscal year, but part of this change may be due to changes in the value of foreign currencies. This amount is typically small and it is not a cash flow, but it is included in the cash flow statement so that we can accurately reconcile the beginning balance in cash to the ending balance. As an example, the bottom of Exhibit 4.1 shows that the effects of exchange rate changes on Qantas's cash and cash equivalents was $12 million for fiscal year 2013.

Supplemental Disclosures

When the indirect method is used in the statement of cash flows, three separate supplemental disclosures are required: (1) two specific operating cash outflows—cash paid for interest and cash paid for income taxes, (2) a schedule or description of all noncash investing and financing transactions, and (3) the firm's policy for determining which highly liquid, short-term investments are treated as cash equivalents. If the direct method is used, a reconciliation of net income to cash flows from operating activities is also required. A firm's policy regarding cash equivalents is placed in the financial statement notes. The other disclosures are reported either in the notes or at the bottom of the statement of cash flows.

One World Café Case Illustration One World Café incurred $200 of interest expense which was paid in cash. It also reported income tax expense of $17,000 and reported a decrease in income taxes payable of $1,500 ($4,500 − $3,000). Thus, One World Café paid $18,500 ($17,000 + $1,500) in income taxes during 2013. It also had the noncash investment in plant assets costing $5,000, which was financed with notes payable. One World Café would provide the following disclosure:

Supplemental cash flow information	
Cash payments for interest	$ 200
Cash payments for income taxes	18,500
Noncash transaction—investment in plant assets financed with notes payable	5,000

ANALYSING FINANCIAL STATEMENTS

LO5 Compute and interpret ratios that reflect a company's liquidity and solvency.

Cash is a special resource for companies because of its flexibility. At short notice, it can be used to fulfil obligations and to take advantage of investment opportunities. When companies run short of cash, their suppliers may be reluctant to deliver and lenders may be able to take over control of decision making. In Chapter 2, we introduced the current ratio, which compares the level of current assets to the level of current liabilities at a point in time. But the statement of cash flows gives us the opportunity to compare a company's ongoing cash generating activities to its obligations and to its investment opportunities.

Interpreting Indirect Method Cash from Operations

We want to interpret the cash flows from operations presented using the indirect method.

When companies use the indirect method to present their cash flows from operating activities, it is difficult to interpret the numbers presented to adjust net income to cash from operating activities. For instance, in Exhibit 4.11, One World Café reports $6,000 for the change in accounts receivable. Does that mean that the company received cash payments of $6,000 from its customers? It does not! Every item in the reconciliation has to be interpreted relative to the net income at the top. Net income includes revenue of $390,000, and the adjustment addition of $6,000 means that One World Café received payments of $390,000 + $6,000 = $396,000 from its customers.

The $3,500 adjustment for wages payable does not mean that One World Café' received payments of $3,500 from its employees. Rather, the company paid its employees $3,500 less than it recognised as wage expense in determining net income. The adjustment for income tax payable was ($1,500), but that does not mean that One World Café's tax payments totaled $1,500 for the year. Rather, the $35,000 net income already includes tax expense of $17,000, so the adjustment means that One World's payments for income tax totaled $17,000 + $1,500 = $18,500. Depreciation expense is added back not because it increases cash, but because it is an expense that doesn't require a cash outflow.

How should we interpret the changes in operating assets and liabilities? These assets and liabilities are a function of both the scale of the business and the practices of the business. If we're selling to 10% more customers this year, then we would expect an increase in receivables of about 10% over the previous year. If the increase is substantially more than that amount, then there must have been some other change as well. Perhaps increasing sales required that we give more favourable payment terms and customers are taking longer to pay. Such a development could cause an investor to question the "quality" of the company's earnings. If sales are constant and accounts payable are increasing, that may imply that the company is taking longer to pay its suppliers. That change would appear as a positive adjustment in the indirect method cash from operations, but it may indicate an unfavourable development for the company.

The indirect method may also alert us to gains and losses from non-operating transactions. These gains and losses are often in "other income" in the income statement, and therefore it's easy for a financial statement reader to miss them. The fact that gains must be subtracted and losses must be added back in the indirect cash from operations, gives them a prominence that they don't have in the income statement.

Analysis Objective

We are trying to gauge Qantas's generation of cash from its operating activities relative to its average short-term obligations found in the balance sheet.

Analysis Tool Operating Cash Flow to Current Liabilities (OCFCL)

$$\textbf{Operating cash flow to current liabilities} = \frac{\textbf{Operating cash flow}}{\textbf{Average current liabilities}}$$

Applying the Operating Cash Flow to Current Liabilities Ratio to Qantas

$$2013: \frac{1{,}417}{6{,}744} = 0.21 \text{ or } 21\%$$

$$2012: \frac{1{,}810}{6{,}677} = 0.27 \text{ or } 27\%$$

$$2011: \frac{1{,}782}{6{,}238} = 0.29 \text{ or } 29\%$$

Guidance The ability of a company to pay its debts is determined by whether its operations can generate enough cash to cover debt payments. Thus, a higher OCFCL ratio is generally preferred. Qantas's OCFCL has decreased over the last three years, suggesting a deterioration in its ability to meet its obligations. The OCFCL ratio complements the current ratio and quick ratio introduced in Chapter 2.

Qantas in Context

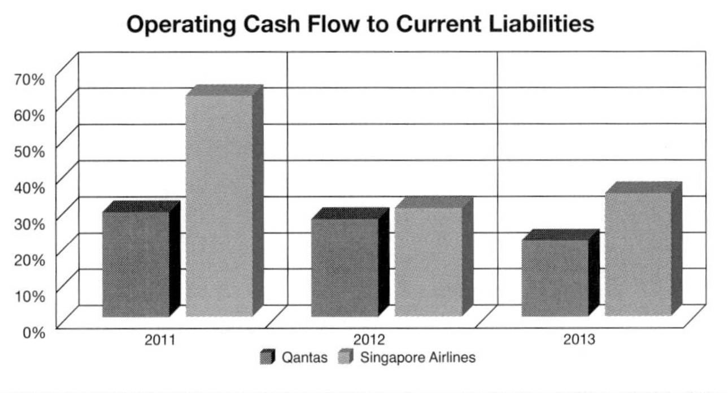

Takeaways We can see considerable reduction in this measure over the last three years, especially for Singapore Airlines. The drop is due to decreasing operating cash flows, as both companies' current liabilities have remained stable over the period. For Singapore Airlines, the big drop in OCFCL is due to an unusually high cash flow from operations in 2011. Qantas's OCFCLs are lower than those of Singapore Airlines over the three years 2011–2013, suggesting that its ability to meet its short-term obligations is lower than that of Singapore Airlines.

Other Considerations There are some transactions that change both the numerator and the denominator, like using cash to pay current operating liabilities. Such a transaction would decrease both the numerator and the denominator, and these changes have an indeterminate effect on the ratio. Paying $100 to a creditor decreases operating cash flow and ending current liabilities by $100, with the average current liabilities decreasing by $50. If the OCFCL is below 2.0 prior to the transaction, it will be even lower after the transaction. If the OCFCL is greater than 2.0 prior to the transaction, it will be even higher after the transaction. Delaying a payment to the creditor would have the opposite effect.

It is also important to take a look at the components of current liabilities. Sometimes there is a large portion of long-term debt that comes due and increases current liabilities for one year. Or, in the case of Qantas, more than 47% of their current liabilities represent unearned revenue from customers who have purchased tickets in advance of travel (like the gift certificates at NBS). For this liability, Qantas does not have to pay someone, they just need to keep flying.

Analysis Objective

We wish to determine Qantas's ability to fund the capital expenditures needed to maintain and grow its operations.

Does Qantas generate enough cash from its operations to make its capital investments? If it does not, then Qantas will have to finance those investments by selling other investments, by borrowing (resulting in future interest costs), by getting cash from shareholders or by reducing cash balances. If it generates more cash than needed for capital expenditures, then the additional cash can be used to grow the business (e.g., by acquisition) or to distribute cash to investors. Two measures may be used in making this assessment. The first of these measures, operating cash flow to capital expenditures, is a ratio that facilitates comparisons with other companies. The second, free cash flow,[2] is a monetary amount that reflects the funds available for investing in new ventures, buying back stock, paying down debt, or returning funds to stockholders in the form of dividends. The concept is also used in mergers and acquisitions to indicate cash that would be available to the acquirer for investment.

Analysis Tools Operating Cash Flow to Capital Expenditures (OCFCX)

$$\textbf{Operating cash flow to capital expenditures} = \frac{\textbf{Operating cash flow}}{\textbf{Annual capital expenditures}}$$

Free Cash Flow (FCF)

Free cash flow = Operating cash flow – Net capital expenditures

Applying the Operating Cash Flow to Capital Expenditures Ratio and Free Cash Flow to Qantas

	OCFCX	FCF
2013:	$\frac{\$1,417}{\$1,247} = 1.14$ or 114%	$1,417 – $1,215 = $202
2012:	$\frac{\$1,810}{\$2,129} = 0.85$ or 85%	$1,810 – $2,075 = $(265)
2011:	$\frac{\$1,782}{\$2,407} = 0.74$ or 74%	$1,782 – $2,321 = $(539)

Guidance Operating cash flows to capital expenditures ratios that exceed 1.0 (or free cash flows that are positive) mean that the company can make its capital investments without obtaining additional financing or reducing its cash balances. The excess cash could be used to reduce borrowing, or it could be returned to shareholders. In both 2011 and 2012, Qantas's cash from operations was lower than its capital expenditures. A principal reason for the higher expenditures in those two years was investment in new aircraft. Because of its fleet modernization program, the average age of Qantas's passenger aircraft fell to the lowest level in two decades. As the modernisation programme ended, Qantas was able to cut down on new investment in 2013, leading to positive free cash flows (or an OCFCX ratio that exceeds 1.0) that year.

[2] Free cash flow can be defined in several ways, but it always includes a measure of the cash resources generated by the company's current operations minus a measure of the cash required to sustain those operations. One of the simpler, more common definitions is presented here.

Qantas in Context

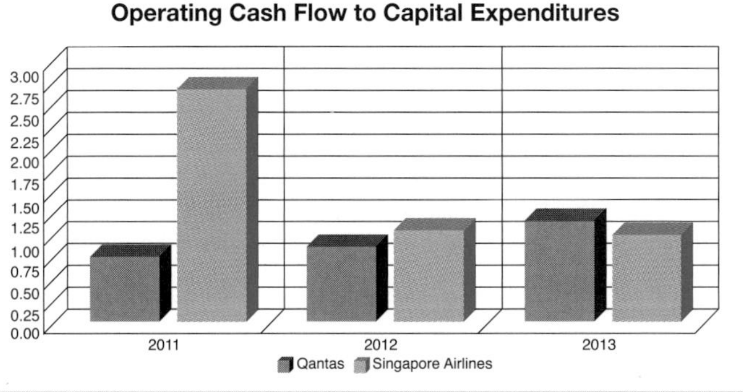

Takeaways OCFCX increased over the last three years for Qantas, but the opposite is true for Singapore Airlines. For Qantas, the improvement in OCFCX in 2013 was due to the end of the fleet modernisation programme. For Singapore Airlines, the high OCFCX in 2011 was due to an unusually high level of operating cash flows and net profit in 2011. In 2012 and 2013, Singapore Airlines generated just enough cash flows from its operations to cover its planned capital expenditures.

Other Considerations Measurement of cash flows is regarded as more objective than measures of income and less dependent on management judgments and estimates. But it may be subject to "lumpy" behaviour from management's decisions, particularly for a smaller company. Capital expenditures may differ significantly from year to year if management takes on large, but infrequent, projects. A series of high values of OCFCX followed by a low value might mean deterioration in cash generating performance, but it might also mean that management has been accumulating cash in anticipation of a major project.

RESEARCH INSIGHT

Is the Cash Flow Statement Useful? Some analysts rely on cash flow forecasts to value ordinary shares. Research shows that both net income and operating cash flows are correlated with stock prices, but that stock prices are more highly correlated with net income than with cash flows. So, do we need both statements? Evidence suggests that by using ***both*** net income and cash flow information, we can improve our forecasts of ***future*** cash flows. Also, net income and cash flow together are more highly correlated with stock prices than either net income or cash flow alone. This result suggests that, for purposes of stock valuation, information from the cash flow statement complements information from the income statement.

CHAPTER-END REVIEW

Refer to One World Café's statement of cash flows and comparative balance sheets from Exhibits 4.10 and 4.11 to complete the following.

Required

1. Calculate the operating cash flow to current liabilities (OCFCL) ratio for One World Café and interpret your findings. Assume that the notes payable are due within the year and are a current liability.
2. Calculate One World Café's operating cash flow to capital expenditures (OCFCX) ratio. What observations can you make about your findings?
3. Calculate the free cash flow for One World Café.

The solution to this review problem can be found on page 208.

APPENDIX 4A: A Spreadsheet Approach to Preparing the Statement of Cash Flows

LO6 Use a spreadsheet to construct the statement of cash flows.

Preparing the statement of cash flows is aided by the use of a spreadsheet. The procedure is somewhat mechanical and is quite easy once someone has mastered the material in the chapter. We illustrate this procedure using the data for One World Café presented in the chapter in Exhibit 4.10. By following the steps presented below, we are able to readily prepare One World Café's cash flow statement for 2013.

To set up the spreadsheet, we list all of the accounts in the balance sheet in the first column of the spreadsheet. We list depreciable assets net of accumulated depreciation. In Column C, we list the most recent balance sheet (the ending balances) followed by the earlier balance sheet (beginning balances) in Column D. There is no need to list totals such as total assets or total current liabilities. See Exhibit 4A.1. We will build the statement of cash flows in columns F, G and H.

EXHIBIT 4A.1 Cash Flow Spreadsheet for One World Café

	A	B	C	D	E	F	G	H	I	J
1						Effect of change on cash flow				
2		O, I or F?	2013	2012	Change	Operating	Investing	Financing	No effect on cash	Total F,G,H,I
3	**Assets**									
4	Cash		8,000	12,000	(4,000)					
5										
6	Accounts receivable	O	22,000	28,000	(6,000)	6,000				6,000
7	Inventory	O	94,000	66,000	28,000	(28,000)				(28,000)
8	Prepaid advertising	O	12,000	9,000	3,000	(3,000)				(3,000)
9	Plant assets, net	O,I	136,000	109,000	27,000					
10	Depreciation expense					17,000				
11	Plant assets purchased						(45,000)		(5,000)	(27,000)
12	Plant assets sold					2,000	4,000			
13										
14	**Liabilities**									
15	Accounts payable	O	27,000	14,000	13,000	13,000				13,000
16	Wages payable	O	6,000	2,500	3,500	3,500				3,500
17	Income tax payable	O	3,000	4,500	(1,500)	(1,500)				(1,500)
18	Notes payable	F	5,000	—	5,000					
19	New borrowing								5,000	5,000
20	Borrowing repayments									
21										
22	**Shareholders' Equity**									
23	Share capital	F	134,000	125,000	9,000					
24	New issue of ordinary shares							9,000		9,000
25	Repurchase of ordinary shares									
26	Retained earnings	O,F	97,000	78,000	19,000					
27	Net income					35,000				19,000
28	Dividends							(16,000)		
29										
30	**Totals**					44,000	(41,000)	(7,000)	—	(4,000)

Step 1: classify the balance sheet accounts. For each of the accounts (other than cash), classify them in column B as Operating (O), Investing (I) or Financing (F) according to where the effect of changes in that account will appear in the statement of cash flows. There are two accounts that have a double classification. Changes in the plant assets, net account can be caused by depreciation expense (which will appear in the indirect method cash from operations) and by investing activities, so we label it as (O, I). Changes in the retained earnings account are caused by net income (which appears in the indirect method cash from operations) and dividends, so we label it as (O, F).

For those rows labelled I or F, insert two rows below: one for increases in the account and one for decreases in the account because we must report increases and decreases separately. For plant assets, net, insert three rows below: one for depreciation expense, one for plant asset acquisitions and one for plant asset sales. For retained earnings, insert two rows below: one for net income and one for dividends.

Step 2: compute the changes in the balance sheet accounts. Subtract the beginning balances in each account from the ending balances and record these in column E. We highlight the change in the cash balance, because this is the amount that we are trying to explain. At this point it is useful to verify that the change in cash is equal to the changes in liabilities plus the changes in stockholders' equity minus the changes in noncash assets:

$$\Delta \text{ Cash} = \Delta\text{Liabilities} + \Delta \text{ Stockholders' Equity} - \Delta \text{ Noncash Assets}$$

In effect, we're going to use changes on the right-hand side of this equation to explain the changes in cash on the left-hand side.

Step 3: handle the accounts that have single classifications. For those accounts that are operating-only assets (accounts receivable, inventory, prepaid expenses, etc.), we enter in column F the *negative* of the value in column E. The 28,000 increase in inventories in column E results in (28,000) for the operating cash flows in column F. Changes in assets have the opposite effect on cash. Increases in assets have a negative effect on cash, while decreases in assets lead to positive adjustments to cash.

For those accounts that are operating only liabilities (accounts payable, wages payable, taxes payables, etc.), we enter in column F the value in column E. The 13,000 increase in accounts payable produces a 13,000 entry in column F.

For those accounts that are financing only (notes payable, share capital), we enter in column H the cash effect(s) of the change in column E. For example, we must be aware that the share capital account could have changed due to both issuing stock for cash and repurchasing stock for cash. For One World Café, there was only a 9,000 inflow due to a new stock issue in column H. (We will deal with the notes payable changes in the next step.)

One World Café has no assets that are investing only, but for such accounts (marketable securities, investments, etc.), we would again make entries for increases and decreases separately. And, since these are assets, the change in the balance sheet has the opposite sign of the entry in the cash flow columns. For instance, if One World Café had invested $10,000 in a financial security, its investments asset would increase, and we would put an entry of ($10,000) in column G.

Step 4: enter the effect of investing/financing transactions that do not involve cash. We know from the information provided about One World Café that it arranged the purchase of $5,000 of plant assets by signing a note payable for the same amount. This transaction affected an investing asset and a financing liability at the same time, and we put the effects into column I. $5,000 is put in the new borrowing row (19), and ($5,000) is put in the plant assets purchased row (11). This transaction will not appear in the cash flow statement in columns F, G and H, but it does explain some of the changes in the company's assets and liabilities.

Step 5: analyse the change in retained earnings. Some accounts require special attention because the change in the account balance involves two types of cash flow effects. For example, the change in retained earnings is actually two changes—net income, which is related to operations, and dividends, which is a financing cash outflow.

One World Café's retained earnings increased by $19,000. It reported net income of $35,000, which is listed as an operating item (because we're using the indirect method), and paid dividends of $16,000, a cash outflow listed under financing activities. For clarity, it is helpful to list each of these changes on a separate line. Thus, we have inserted two lines into the spreadsheet immediately below retained earnings—the first for net income and the second for dividends. The $35,000 inflow and the $16,000 outflow net to $19,000.

Step 6: analyse the change in plant assets. A change in depreciable assets is actually the result of both operating and investing items. The change in plant assets can be explained by looking at the individual transactions that caused the change. As was the case with retained earnings, it is helpful to list each of these transactions in a separate row in the spreadsheet. Thus, we have inserted three rows into the spreadsheet immediately below the change in plant assets. First, we recall that One World Café reported depreciation expense of $17,000, which reduced its plant assets, net. This is listed in the first row under plant assets as a positive adjustment to cash flow from operations because cash flow effects on the asset side have the opposite sign.

In the next row, we list purchases of plant assets. One World Café purchased plant assets for $45,000 in cash, which is listed under investing as a cash outflow in column F. There was also the $5,000 purchase of plant assets that was financed with notes payable. This transaction did not affect cash so it's in column I.

In the third row below plant assets, we list the sale of plant assets. One World Café sold plant assets for $4,000 cash, recognising a loss of $2,000. The loss is listed in the operations column (as a positive adjustment to operating cash flow) and the proceeds from the sale are listed under investing as a cash inflow in column F.

When all of the balance sheet changes have been analysed, the change for each account should add up to the sum of the effect on operating, investing, and financing cash flows, plus the amount in the "no effect" column. That is, for each change listed in the spreadsheet in column E, we can add columns F, G, H and I to get the change in the balance sheet account in column J. For retained earnings: $35,000 − $16,000 =

\$19,000. For assets, the total will be the *negative* of the change. Adding up entries for plant assets: \$17,000 − \$45,000 − \$5,000 + \$2,000 + \$4,000 = −\$27,000, which is minus the amount in column E, row 9.

Step 7: total the columns. We add up the effects listed in columns F, G, H and I to get the cash flow subtotals. One World Café had cash flow from operations of \$44,000, investing cash flows of −\$41,000 and financing cash flows of −\$7,000. The total for the "no effect" column (column I) should be \$0, because the entries in this column had no effect on cash flow. Finally, we add up these totals to make sure that the cash flow effects equal the change in cash: \$44,000 − \$41,000 − \$7,000 − \$0 = −\$4,000. If the totals do not add up to the change in cash, then there must be an error in analysing one or more of the balance sheet changes. For example, if we had forgotten to subtract dividends, then the cash flow effects in columns F, G and H would not add up to the change in retained earnings listed in column E. Likewise, if we had mistakenly omitted the sale of plant assets, then the change in plant assets would not add up correctly. Totaling the columns and rows is a cheque to verify that our analysis is complete and correct.

Step 8: prepare the cash flow statement. Starting with operating cash flows (column F), we list each of the items in the statement of cash flows. We start with net income, and then add depreciation and the loss on the sale of plant assets, then we list the remaining adjustments, starting with the change in accounts receivable and working down the column. Next, we do the same for the items listed in the investing (column G) and financing (column H) sections of the cash flow statement. The resulting statement is identical to the statement presented in Exhibit 4.11.

APPENDIX-END REVIEW

The comparative balance sheets and income statement for Rocky Road Bicycles, Inc., are as follows.

ROCKY ROAD BICYCLES, INC.
Comparative Balance Sheets

At December 31	2013	2012
Assets		
Cash	\$ 106,000	\$ 96,000
Accounts receivable	156,000	224,000
Inventory	752,000	528,000
Prepaid rent	68,000	72,000
Plant assets	1,692,000	1,360,000
Less accumulated depreciation	(562,000)	(488,000)
Total assets	\$2,212,000	\$1,792,000
Liabilities		
Accounts payable	\$ 216,000	\$ 112,000
Wages payable	18,000	20,000
Income tax payable	44,000	36,000
Equity		
Share capital	1,142,000	1,000,000
Retained earnings	792,000	624,000
Total liabilities and equity	\$2,212,000	\$1,792,000

Additional Information:

- Rocky Road reported net income of \$326,000 in 2013.
- Depreciation expense was \$122,000 in 2013.
- Rocky Road sold plant assets during 2013. The plant assets originally cost \$88,000, with accumulated depreciation of \$48,000, and were sold for a gain of \$16,000.
- Rocky Road declared and paid a \$158,000 cash dividend in 2013.

Required
Use a spreadsheet to create a statement of cash flows for Rocky Road Bicycles, Inc.

The solution to this review problem can be found on page 209.

SUMMARY

Explain the purpose of the statement of cash flows and classify cash transactions by type of business activity: operating, investing or financing. (p. 150) LO1

- The statement of cash flows summarises information about the flow of cash into and out of the business.
- Operating cash flow includes any cash transactions related to selling goods or rendering services, as well as interest payments and receipts, tax payments and any transaction not specifically classified as investing or financing.
- Investing cash flow includes acquiring and disposing of plant assets, buying and selling securities, including securities of other companies, and lending and subsequently collecting funds from a borrower.
- Financing cash flow includes all cash received or paid to shareholders, including stock issued or repurchased and dividends paid. In addition, it includes amounts borrowed and repaid to creditors.

Construct the operating activities section of the statement of cash flows using the direct method. (p. 155) LO2

- The direct method presents net cash flow from operating activities by showing the major categories of operating cash receipts and payments.
- The operating cash receipts and payments are usually determined by converting the accrual revenues and expenses to corresponding cash amounts.

Reconcile cash flows from operations to net income and use the indirect method to compute operating cash flows. (p. 166) LO3

- Because operating cash flow differs from net income, a reconciliation of these two amounts helps financial statement users understand the sources of this difference.
- The indirect method reconciles net income and operating cash flows by making adjustments for noncash revenues and expenses and changes in balance sheet accounts related to operations.

Construct the investing and financing activities sections of the statement of cash flows. (p. 164) LO4

- Cash investment outlays are captured in the investing section along with any cash receipts from asset disposals. Because cash receipts include any gain on sale (or reflect any loss), the gain (loss) must be subtracted from (added to) net income in the operating section to avoid double-counting.
- Cash obtained from the issuance of securities or borrowings, and any repayments of debt, are disclosed in the financing section. Cash dividends are also included in this section. Interest payments are included in the operating or financing section of the statement.
- Dividends and interest receipts are included in either the operating or investing section of the statement.
- Some events, for example assets donated to the firm, provide resources to the business that are important but which do not involve cash outlays. These events are disclosed separately, along with the statement of cash flows as supplementary disclosures or in the notes.

Compute and interpret ratios that reflect a company's liquidity and solvency. (p. 174) LO5

- Interpreting indirect method cash from operations requires reference to those items that comprise net income. Each adjustment is intended to modify an income statement item to bring it to cash from operations.
- Two ratios of importance that are based on cash flows include:
  - Operating cash flow to current liabilities—a measure of the adequacy of current operations to cover current liability payments.
  - Operating cash flow to capital expenditures—a reflection of a company's ability to replace or expand its activities based on the level of current operations.
- Free cash flow is defined as: Cash flow from operations − Net capital expenditures.
- Free cash flow is a measure of a company's ability to apply its resources to new endeavours.

Appendix 4A: Use a spreadsheet to construct the statement of cash flows. (p. 178) LO6

- A spreadsheet helps to prepare the statement of cash flows by classifying the effect of each change in the balance sheet as operating, investing, financing, or not affecting cash.
- The spreadsheet approach relies on the key relationship:

  Cash = Liabilities + Stockholders' equity − Noncash assets

KEY RATIOS

$$\text{Operating cash flow to current liabilities} = \frac{\text{Operating cash flow}}{\text{Average current liabilities}}$$

$$\text{Operating cash flow to capital expenditures} = \frac{\text{Operating cash flow}}{\text{Annual capital expenditures}}$$

Free cash flow = Operating cash flow – Net capital expenditures

KEY TERMS

Cash equivalents (p. 150)
Direct method (p. 165)
Financing activities (p. 153)
Indirect method (p. 165)
Investing activities (p. 152)
Liquidity (p. 150)
Noncash investing and financing activities (p. 171)
Operating activities (p. 152)
Solvency (p. 150)
Statement of cash flows (p. 150)
Treasury shares (p. 153)

MULTIPLE CHOICE

Multiple Choice Answers
1. a 2. c 3. d 4. c 5. c

1. Which of the following is not disclosed in a statement of cash flows?
   a. A transfer of cash to a cash equivalent investment
   b. The amount of cash at year-end
   c. Cash outflows from investing activities during the period
   d. Cash inflows from financing activities during the period

2. Which of the following events appears in the cash flows from investing activities section of the statement of cash flows?
   a. Cash received from customers
   b. Cash received from issuance of ordinary shares
   c. Cash purchase of equipment
   d. Cash payment of dividends

3. Which of the following events appears in the cash flows from financing activities section of the statement of cash flows?
   a. Cash purchase of equipment
   b. Cash purchase of bonds issued by another company
   c. Cash received as repayment for funds loaned
   d. Cash purchase of treasury stock

4. Tyler Company has a net income of $49,000 and the following related items:

Depreciation expense	$ 5,000
Accounts receivable increase	2,000
Inventory decrease	10,000
Accounts payable decrease	4,000

   Using the indirect method, what is Tyler's net cash flow from operations?
   a. $42,000
   b. $46,000
   c. $58,000
   d. $38,000

5. Refer to information in Mid-Chapter Review 2. Assume that notes payable are not due within the coming year and are classified as a noncurrent liability. The operating cash flow to current liabilities ratio for Mug Shots, Inc. in December is
   a. 6.4%.
   b. 2.9%.
   c. 2.6%.
   d. impossible to determine from the data provided.

Superscript A denotes assignments based on Appendix 4A.

DISCUSSION QUESTIONS

Q4-1. What is the definition of *cash equivalents*? Give three examples of cash equivalents.

Q4-2. Why are cash equivalents included with cash in a statement of cash flows?

Q4-3. What are the three major types of activities classified on a statement of cash flows? Give an example of a cash inflow and a cash outflow in each classification.

Q4-4. In which of the three activity categories of a statement of cash flows would each of the following items appear? Indicate for each item whether it represents a cash inflow or a cash outflow:

a. Cash purchase of equipment.
b. Cash collection on loans.
c. Cash dividends paid.
d. Cash dividends received.
e. Cash proceeds from issuing stock.
f. Cash receipts from customers.
g. Cash interest paid.
h. Cash interest received.

Q4-5. Traverse Company acquired a $3,000,000 building by issuing $3,000,000 worth of bonds payable. In terms of cash flow reporting, what type of transaction is this? What special disclosure requirements apply to a transaction of this type?

Q4-6. Why are noncash investing and financing transactions disclosed as supplemental information to a statement of cash flows?

Q4-7. Why is a statement of cash flows a useful financial statement?

Q4-8. What is the difference between the direct method and the indirect method of presenting net cash flow from operating activities?

Q4-9. In determining net cash flow from operating activities using the indirect method, why must we add depreciation back to net income? Give an example of another item that is added back to net income under the indirect method.

Q4-10. Vista Company sold for $98,000 cash land originally costing $70,000. The company recorded a gain on the sale of $28,000. How is this event reported in a statement of cash flows using the indirect method?

Q4-11. A firm uses the indirect method. Using the following information, what is its net cash flow from operating activities?

Net income	$88,000
Accounts receivable decrease	13,000
Inventory increase	9,000
Accounts payable decrease	3,500
Income tax payable increase	1,500
Depreciation expense	6,000

Q4-12. What separate disclosures are required for a company that reports a statement of cash flows using the indirect method?

Q4-13. If a business had a net loss for the year, under what circumstances would the statement of cash flows show a positive net cash flow from operating activities?

Q4-14. A firm is converting its accrual revenues to corresponding cash amounts using the direct method. Sales on the income statement are $925,000. Beginning and ending accounts receivable on the balance sheet are $58,000 and $44,000, respectively. What is the amount of cash received from customers?

Q4-15. A firm reports $86,000 wages expense in its income statement. If beginning and ending wages payable are $3,900 and $2,800, respectively, what is the amount of cash paid to employees?

Q4-16. A firm reports $43,000 advertising expense in its income statement. If beginning and ending prepaid advertising are $6,000 and $7,600, respectively, what is the amount of cash paid for advertising?

Q4-17. Rusk Company sold equipment for $5,100 cash that had cost $35,000 and had $29,000 of accumulated depreciation. How is this event reported in a statement of cash flows using the direct method?

Q4-18. What separate disclosures are required for a company that reports a statement of cash flows using the direct method?

Q4-19. How is the operating cash flow to current liabilities ratio calculated? Explain its use.

Q4-20. How is the operating cash flow to capital expenditures ratio calculated? Explain its use.

MINI EXERCISES

LO1, 3 **M4-21. Identifying the Impact of Account Changes on Cash Flow from Operating Activities (Indirect Method)**

The following account information was presented as adjustments to net income in a recent statement of cash flows for Causeway Bay Inc. Determine whether each item would be a positive adjustment or a negative adjustment to net income in determining cash from operations. ($ millions).

a. Operating activities increased accounts payable by $232.
b. Operating activities increased inventories by $322.
c. Operating activities decreased other noncurrent liabilities by $97.
d. Depreciation and amortisation expense was $2,131.
e. Operating activities decreased other noncurrent assets by $43.

LO1, 3 **M4-22. Classifying Cash Flows**

For each of the items below, indicate whether the cash flow relates to an operating activity, an investing activity, or a financing activity.

a. Cash receipts from customers for services rendered.
b. Sale of long-term investments for cash.
c. Acquisition of plant assets for cash.
d. Payment of income taxes.
e. Bonds payable issued for cash.
f. Payment of cash dividends declared in previous year.
g. Purchase of short-term investments (not cash equivalents) for cash.

LO1, 3 **M4-23. Classifying Cash Flow Statement Components**

SINGAPORE TELECOMMUNICATIONS LTD. (SINGAPORE)

The following table presents selected items from the 2013 cash flow statement of **Singapore Telecommunications Limited (Singtel)**. For each item, determine whether the amount would be disclosed in the cash flow statement under operating activities, investing activities, or financing activities. (Singtel uses the indirect method of reporting cash flows from operating activities.)

SINGAPORE TELECOMMUNICATIONS LIMITED Selected Items from its Cash Flow Statement	
1	Repayment of term loans
2	Changes in trade and other receivables
3	Depreciation and amortisation
4	Change in inventories
5	Final dividend paid to shareholders of the Company
6	Other noncash items
7	Proceeds from sale of associates and joint ventures
8	Net income
9	Change in trade and other payables
10	Proceeds from bond issue
11	Payment for purchase of property, plant and equipment

LO1 **M4-24. Classifying Cash Flows**

For each of the items below, indicate whether it is (1) a cash flow from an operating activity, (2) a cash flow from an investing activity, (3) a cash flow from a financing activity, (4) a noncash investing and financing activity, or (5) none of the above.

a. Paid cash to retire bonds payable at a loss.
b. Received cash as settlement of a lawsuit.
c. Acquired a patent in exchange for ordinary shares.
d. Received advance payments from customers on orders for custom-made goods.
e. Gave large cash contribution to local university.
f. Invested cash in 60-day commercial paper (a cash equivalent).

M4-25. Reconciling Net Income and Cash Flow from Operations Using FSET LO2, 3

BEYER GMBH (GERMANY)

For fiscal year 2012, Beyer GMBH had the following summary information available concerning its operating activities. The company had no investing or financing activities this year.

1.	Sales of merchandise to customers on credit	€507,400
2.	Sales of merchandise to customers for cash	91,500
3.	Cost of merchandise sold on credit	320,100
4.	Cost of merchandise sold for cash	63,400
5.	Purchases of merchandise from suppliers on credit	351,600
6.	Purchases of merchandise from suppliers for cash	47,700
7.	Collections from customers on accounts receivable	483,400
8.	Cash payments to suppliers on accounts payable	340,200
9.	Operating expenses (all paid in cash)	172,300

Required

a. Enter the items above into the Financial Statement Effects Template. Under noncash assets, use two separate columns for accounts receivable and inventories. Calculate the totals for each column.

b. What was the company's net income for the year? What was the cash flow from operating activities? (Use the direct method.)

c. Indicate the direction and amounts by which each of the following accounts changed during the year.
1. Accounts receivable
2. Merchandise inventory
3. Accounts payable

d. Using your results above, prepare the operating activities section of the statement of cash flows using the indirect format.

M4-26. Calculating Net Cash Flow from Operating Activities (Indirect Method) LO3

The following information was obtained from Galena Company's comparative balance sheets. Assume that Galena Company's 2013 income statement showed depreciation expense of $8,000, a gain on sale of investments of $9,000, and a net income of $45,000. Calculate the net cash flow from operating activities using the indirect method.

	Dec. 31, 2013	Dec. 31, 2012
Cash	$ 19,000	$ 9,000
Accounts receivable	44,000	35,000
Inventory	55,000	49,000
Prepaid rent	6,000	8,000
Long-term investments	21,000	34,000
Plant assets	150,000	106,000
Accumulated depreciation	40,000	32,000
Accounts payable	24,000	20,000
Income tax payable	4,000	6,000
Share capital	121,000	92,000
Retained earnings	106,000	91,000

M4-27. Reconciling Net Income and Cash Flow from Operations Using FSET LO2, 3

For fiscal year 2015, Riffe Enterprises had the following summary information available concerning its operating activities. The company had no investing or financing activities this year.

1.	Sales of services to customers on credit	$769,200
2.	Sales of services to customers for cash	46,200
3.	Employee compensation earned	526,700
4.	Cash payment in advance to landlord for offices	149,100
5.	Cash paid to employees for compensation	521,600
6.	Rental expense for offices used over the year	117,900
7.	Collections from customers on accounts receivable	724,100
8.	Operating expenses (all paid in cash)	122,800
9.	Depreciation expense	23,000

Required

a. Enter the items above into the Financial Statement Effects Template. Under noncash assets, use three separate columns for accounts receivable and prepaid rent and the accumulated depreciation contra-asset. Calculate the totals for each column.

b. What was the company's net income for the year? What was the cash flow from operating activities? (Use the direct method.)

c. Indicate the direction and amounts by which each of the following accounts changed during the year.

1. Accounts receivable
2. Prepaid rent
3. Accumulated depreciation
4. Wages payable

d. Using your results above, prepare the operating activities section of the statement of cash flows using the indirect format.

LO3 **M4-28. Calculating Net Cash Flow from Operating Activities (Indirect Method)**

Weber Company had a $21,000 net loss from operations for 2013. Depreciation expense for 2013 was $8,600 and a 2013 cash dividend of $6,000 was declared and paid. Balances of the current asset and current liability accounts at the beginning and end of 2013 follow. Did Weber Company's 2013 operating activities provide or use cash? Use the indirect method to determine your answer.

	Ending	Beginning
Cash	$ 3,500	$ 7,000
Accounts receivable	16,000	25,000
Inventory	50,000	53,000
Prepaid expenses	6,000	9,000
Accounts payable	12,000	8,000
Accrued liabilities	5,000	7,600

LO1, 3 **M4-29. Classifying Cash Flow Statement Components and Determining Their Effects**

CHINA MOBILE LIMITED (CHINA)

The following table presents selected items from the 2013 cash flow statement of China Mobile Limited, the world's largest mobile phone operator by subscribers (about 760 million as of July 2013).

a. For each item, determine whether the amount would be disclosed in the cash flow statement under operating activities, investing activities, or financing activities. (China Mobile uses the indirect method of reporting.)

b. For each item, determine whether it will appear as a positive or negative in determining the net increase in cash and cash equivalents.

CHINA MOBILE LIMITED Consolidated Statement of Cash Flows—Selected Items	
1	Increase in accounts receivable
2	Capital expenditures
3	Proceeds from disposal of a joint venture
4	Gain on disposal of property, plant and equipment
5	Repayment of interest bearing borrowings
6	Increase in inventories
7	Increase in prepayments and other current assets
8	Proceeds from issuance of shares under share option scheme
9	Increase in accounts payable
10	Profit before taxation
11	Acquisition of other intangible assets
12	Increase in accrued expenses and other payables
13	Dividends paid to the Company's equity shareholders
14	Depreciation of property, plant and equipment

M4-30. Calculating Operating Cash Flows (Direct Method) LO2

Calculate the cash flow for each of the following cases.

a. Cash paid for rent:

Rent expense	$60,000
Prepaid rent, beginning year	10,000
Prepaid rent, end of year	8,000

b. Cash received as interest (classify interest income as operating cash flow):

Interest income	$16,000
Interest receivable, beginning year	3,000
Interest receivable, end of year	3,700

c. Cash paid for merchandise purchased:

Cost of goods sold	$98,000
Inventory, beginning year	19,000
Inventory, end of year	22,000
Accounts payable, beginning year	11,000
Accounts payable, end of year	7,000

M4-31. Calculating Operating Cash Flows (Direct Method) LO2

Howell Company's current year income statement reports the following:

Sales	$825,000
Cost of goods sold	550,000
Gross profit	$275,000

Howell's comparative balance sheets show the following (accounts payable relate to merchandise purchases):

	End of Year	Beginning of Year
Accounts receivable	$ 71,000	$60,000
Inventory	109,000	96,000
Accounts payable	31,000	37,000

Compute Howell's current-year cash received from customers and cash paid for merchandise purchased.

EXERCISES

E4-32. Comparing Firms Using Ratio Analysis LO5

Consider the following 2011 data for several pharmaceutical firms ($ millions):

	Average current liabilities	Cash from operations	Expenditures on PPE	Proceeds from the sale of PPE
Merck & Co., Inc.	$15,943	$12,383	$1,723	$ 0
Pfizer Inc.	28,353	20,240	1,660	0
Abbott Laboratories	16,371	8,970	1,492	0
Johnson & Johnson	22,942	14,298	2,893	1,342

a. Compute the operating cash flow to current liabilities (OCFCL) ratio for each firm.

b. Compute the free cash flow for each firm.

c. Comment on the results of your computations.

LO5 **E4-33. Comparing Firms Using Ratio Analysis**

DAVID JONES LIMITED (AUSTRALIA)
MELBOURNE IT (AUSTRALIA)

David Jones Limited is a high-end department store chain in Australia. **Melbourne IT** is an Australian Internet company. Consider the following data for these two companies from 2013 (A$'000):

	Average current liabilities	Cash from operations	Expenditures on PPE	Proceeds from the sale of PPE
David Jones Limited.	304,064	180,036	74,890	232
Melbourne IT.	46,354	7,308	1,777	250

a. Compute the operating cash flow to current liabilities (OCFCL) ratio for both firms.
b. Compute the free cash flow for both firms.
c. Comment on the results of your computations.

LO2 **E4-34. Preparing a Statement of Cash Flows (Direct Method)**

Use the following information about the 2013 cash flows of Mason Corporation to prepare a statement of cash flows under the direct method. Classify interest income, interest expense, and dividends income as operating cash flow. Refer to Exhibit 4.3 for the appropriate format.

Cash balance, end of 2013	$ 12,000
Cash paid to employees and suppliers	148,000
Cash received from sale of land.	40,000
Cash paid to acquire treasury stock	10,000
Cash balance, beginning of 2013.	16,000
Cash received as interest	6,000
Cash paid as income taxes.	11,000
Cash paid to purchase equipment.	89,000
Cash received from customers.	194,000
Cash received from issuing bonds payable.	30,000
Cash paid as dividends.	16,000

LO3, 5 **E4-35. Calculating Net Cash Flow from Operating Activities (Indirect Method)**

Lincoln Company owns no plant assets and reported the following income statement for the current year:

Sales		$750,000
Cost of goods sold	$470,000	
Wages expense.	110,000	
Rent expense.	42,000	
Insurance expense	15,000	637,000
Net income.		$113,000

Additional balance sheet information about the company follows:

	End of Year	Beginning of Year
Accounts receivable	$54,000	$49,000
Inventory	60,000	66,000
Prepaid insurance	8,000	7,000
Accounts payable	22,000	18,000
Wages payable	9,000	11,000

Use the information to

a. calculate the net cash flow from operating activities under the indirect method.

Also, compute its

b. operating cash flow to current liabilities (OCFCL) ratio. (Assume current liabilities consist of accounts payable and wages payable.)

E4-36. Accounting Sleuth: Reconstructing Entries LO4

Meubles Fischer SA had the following balances for its property, plant and equipment accounts (in thousands of euros):

	September 30, 2012	September 30, 2013
Property, plant and equipment at cost	€1,000	€1,200
Accumulated depreciation	(350)	(390)
Property, plant and equipment, net	€ 650	€ 810

During fiscal year 2013, Meubles Fischer acquired €100 thousand in property by signing a mortgage, plus another €300 thousand in equipment for cash. The company also received €100 thousand in cash from the sale of used equipment, and its income statement reveals a €20 thousand gain from this transaction.

a. What was the original cost of the used equipment that Meubles Fischer SA sold during fiscal year 2013?

b. How much depreciation had been accumulated on the used equipment at the time it was sold?

c. How much depreciation expense did Meubles Fischer SA recognise in its fiscal year 2013 income statement?

E4-37. Accounting Sleuth: Reconstructing Entries LO4

Kasznik Ltd. had the following balances for its property, plant and equipment accounts (in millions of pounds):

	December 31, 2012	December 31, 2013
Property, plant and equipment at cost	£175	£183
Accumulated depreciation	(78)	(83)
Property, plant and equipment, net	£ 97	£100

During 2013, Kasznik Ltd. paid £28 million in cash to acquire property and equipment, and this amount represents all the acquisitions of property, plant and equipment for the period. The company's income statement reveals depreciation expense of £17 million and a £5 million loss from the disposal of used equipment.

a. What was the original cost of the used equipment that Kasznik Ltd. sold during 2013?

b. How much depreciation had been accumulated on the used equipment at the time it was sold?

c. How much cash did Kasznik Ltd. receive from its disposal of used equipment?

E4-38. Reconciling Changes in Balance Sheet Accounts LO2, 4

METRO INC. (CANADA)

The following table presents selected items from the 2013 and 2012 balance sheets and 2013 income statement of Metro Inc., a food and pharmaceutical retailer and distributor in Quebec and Ontario, Canada.

METRO (CAD$ millions)				
Selected Balance Sheet Data			**Selected Income Statement Data**	
	2013	**2012**		**2013**
Inventories	$ 781.3	$ 784.4	Cost of merchandise sold	$10,581.6
Property and equipment, less accumulated depreciation	1,328.4	1,280.3	Depreciation expense	179.6
Trade accounts payable	1,004.9	1,086.9	Net earnings	721.6
Retained earnings	2,165.9	1,874.4		

a. Compute the cash paid for merchandise inventories in 2013. Assume that trade accounts payable is only for merchandise purchases.

b. Compute the net cost of property acquired in 2013.

c. Compute the cash dividends paid in 2013.

LO1, 4 **E4-39. Analysing Investing and Financing Cash Flows**

During 2013, Paxon Corporation's long-term investments account (at cost) increased $15,000, which was the net result of purchasing stocks costing $80,000 and selling stocks costing $65,000 at a $6,000 loss. Also, its bonds payable account decreased $10,000, the net result of issuing $130,000 of bonds and retiring bonds with a book value of $140,000 at a $9,000 gain. What items and amounts appear in the (a) cash flows from investing activities and (b) cash flows from financing activities sections of its 2013 statement of cash flows?

LO4 **E4-40. Reconciling Changes in Balance Sheet Accounts**

The following table presents selected items from the 2015 and 2014 balance sheets and 2015 income statement of Gastown Enterprises, Inc.

GASTOWN ENTERPRISES, INC.

Selected Balance Sheet Data	2015	2014	Selected Income Statement Data	2015
Property and Equipment, cost . . .	$84,767,771	$80,132,394	Depreciation expense	$3,174,956
Accumulated depreciation	60,121,353	57,852,770	Gain on sale of property and equipment.	79,483
Retained earnings	18,866,264	17,319,003	Net income.	3,014,768

Gastown Enterprises reported expenditures for property and equipment of $5,559,183 in 2015.

a. What was the original cost of the property and equipment that Gastown Enterprises sold during 2011? What was the accumulated depreciation on that property and equipment at the time of sale?

b. Compute the cash proceeds from the sale of property and equipment in 2011.

c. Prepare the journal entry to describe the sale of property and equipment.

d. Determine the cash dividends paid in 2011.

LO2 **E4-41. Calculating Operating Cash Flows (Direct Method)**

Calculate the cash flow for each of the following cases.

a. Cash paid for advertising:

Advertising expense	$62,000
Prepaid advertising, beginning of year	11,000
Prepaid advertising, end of year.	15,000

b. Cash paid for income taxes:

Income tax expense	$29,000
Income tax payable, beginning of year	7,100
Income tax payable, end of year	4,900

c. Cash paid for merchandise purchased:

Cost of goods sold	$180,000
Inventory, beginning of year.	30,000
Inventory, end of year	25,000
Accounts payable, beginning of year.	10,000
Accounts payable, end of year.	12,000

E4-42. Preparing a Statement of Cash Flows (Indirect Method) LO3, 4

The following financial statements were issued by Hoskins Corporation for the fiscal year ended December 31, 2013. All amounts are in millions of U.S. dollars.

Balance Sheets	December 31, 2012		December 31, 2013	
Assets				
Cash		$ 300		$ 550
Accounts receivable		600		1,500
Inventory		400		500
Prepaid expenses		400		150
Current assets		1,700		2,700
Property, plant and equipment at cost	6,200		6,100	
Less accumulated depreciation	(2,100)		(1,750)	
Property, plant and equipment, net		4,100		4,350
Total assets		$5,800		$7,050
Liabilities and Shareholders' Equity				
Accounts payable		$ 400		$ 800
Income tax payable		200		100
Short-term debt		1,200		2,700
Current liabilities		1,800		3,600
Long-term debt		1,000		0
Total liabilities		2,800		3,600
Contributed capital		800		800
Retained earnings		2,200		2,650
Total shareholders' equity		3,000		3,450
Total liabilities and shareholders' equity		$5,800		$7,050

Income Statement	Fiscal year 2013
Sales revenues	$6,500
Cost of goods sold	3,400
Gross profit	3,100
Selling, general and administrative expenses	1,450
Depreciation expense	350
Operating income	1,300
Interest expense	350
Income before income tax expense	950
Income tax expense	250
Net income	$ 700

Additional information:

1. During fiscal year 2013, Hoskins Corporation acquired new equipment for $1,200 in cash. In addition, the company disposed of used equipment that had original cost of $1,300 and accumulated depreciation of $700, receiving $600 in cash from the buyer.
2. During fiscal year 2013, Hoskins Corporation arranged short-term bank financing and borrowed $1,500, using a portion of the cash to repay all of its outstanding long-term debt.
3. During fiscal year 2013, Hoskins Corporation engaged in no transactions involving its ordinary share, though it did declare and pay a $250 cash dividend.

Required

Prepare a statement of cash flows (all three sections) for Hoskins Corporation's fiscal year 2013, using the indirect method for the cash from operations section (classify interest income as operating cash flow).

LO2, 5 **E4-43. Analysing Operating Cash Flows (Direct Method)**
Refer to the information in Exercise 4-35. Calculate the net cash flow from operating activities using the direct method. Show a related cash flow for each revenue and expense. Also, compute its operating cash flow to current liabilities (OCFCL) ratio. (Assume current liabilities consist of accounts payable and wages payable.)

LO2, 3 **E4-44. Interpreting Cash Flow from Operating Activities**
Carter Company's income statement and cash flow from operating activities (indirect method with interest income classified as operating cash flow) are provided as follows ($ thousands):

Income statement	
Revenue	$400
Cost of goods sold	215
Gross profit	185
Operating expenses	110
Operating income	75
Interest expense	25
Income before taxes	50
Income tax expense	15
Net income	$ 35

Cash flow from operating activities	
Net income	$35
Plus depreciation expense	70
Operating asset adjustments	
Less increase in accounts receivable	(25)
Less increase in inventories	(50)
Less increase in prepaid rent	(5)
Plus increase in accounts payable	65
Plus increase in income tax payable	5
Cash flow from operating activities	$95

a. For each of the four statements below, determine whether the statement is true or false.
b. If the statement is false, provide the (underlined) dollar amount that would make it true.
1. Carter collected $375 from customers in the current period.
2. Carter paid $0 interest in the current period.
3. Carter paid $20 in income taxes in the current period.
4. If Carter increased the depreciation expense by $50, it would increase its cash from operations by $50.

PROBLEMS

LO3 **P4-45. Reconciling and Computing Operating Cash Flows from Net Income**
Petroni Company reports the following selected results for its calendar year 2013.

Net income	$135,000
Depreciation expense	25,000
Gain on sale of assets	5,000
Accounts receivable increase	10,000
Accounts payable increase	6,000
Prepaid expenses decrease	3,000
Wages payable decrease	4,000

Required
Prepare the operating section only of Petroni Company's statement of cash flows for 2013 under the indirect method of reporting.

P4-46. Preparing a Statement of Cash Flows (Indirect Method) LO3, 4, 5

Wolff Company's income statement and comparative balance sheets follow.

WOLFF COMPANY Income Statement For Year Ended December 31, 2013		
Sales		$635,000
Cost of goods sold	$430,000	
Wages expense	86,000	
Insurance expense	8,000	
Depreciation expense	17,000	
Interest expense	9,000	
Income tax expense	29,000	579,000
Net income		$ 56,000

WOLFF COMPANY Balance Sheets	Dec. 31, 2013	Dec. 31, 2012
Assets		
Cash	$ 11,000	$ 5,000
Accounts receivable	41,000	32,000
Inventory	90,000	60,000
Prepaid insurance	5,000	7,000
Plant assets	250,000	195,000
Accumulated depreciation	(68,000)	(51,000)
Total assets	$329,000	$248,000
Liabilities and Stockholders' Equity		
Accounts payable	$ 7,000	$ 10,000
Wages payable	9,000	6,000
Income tax payable	7,000	8,000
Bonds payable	130,000	75,000
Share capital	90,000	90,000
Retained earnings	86,000	59,000
Total liabilities and equity	$329,000	$248,000

Cash dividends of $29,000 were declared and paid during 2013. Also in 2013, plant assets were purchased for cash, and bonds payable were issued for cash. Bond interest is paid semiannually on June 30 and December 31. Accounts payable relate to merchandise purchases.

Required

a. Compute the change in cash that occurred during 2013.

b. Prepare a 2013 statement of cash flows using the indirect method (classify interest income as operating cash flow).

c. Compute and interpret Wolff's

(1) operating cash flow to current liabilities ratio, and

(2) operating cash flow to capital expenditures ratio.

LO2 **P4-47. Computing Cash Flow from Operating Activities (Direct Method)**
Refer to the income statement and comparative balance sheets for Wolff Company presented in P4-46.

Required

a. Compute Wolff Company's cash flow from operating activities using the direct method (classify interest income as operating cash flow). Use the format illustrated in Exhibit 4.5 in the chapter.

b. What can we learn from the direct method that may not be readily apparent when reviewing a cash flow statement prepared using the indirect method?

LO3, 4, 5 **P4-48. Preparing a Statement of Cash Flows (Indirect Method)**
Arctic Company's income statement and comparative balance sheets follow.

ARCTIC COMPANY
Income Statement
For Year Ended December 31, 2013

Sales		$728,000
Cost of goods sold	$534,000	
Wages expense	190,000	
Advertising expense	31,000	
Depreciation expense	22,000	
Interest expense	18,000	
Gain on sale of land	(25,000)	770,000
Net loss		$ (42,000)

ARCTIC COMPANY
Balance Sheets

	Dec. 31, 2013	Dec. 31, 2012
Assets		
Cash	$ 49,000	$ 28,000
Accounts receivable	42,000	50,000
Inventory	107,000	113,000
Prepaid advertising	10,000	13,000
Plant assets	360,000	222,000
Accumulated depreciation	(78,000)	(56,000)
Total assets	$490,000	$370,000
Liabilities and Stockholders' Equity		
Accounts payable	$ 17,000	$ 31,000
Interest payable	6,000	—
Bonds payable	200,000	—
Share capital	245,000	245,000
Retained earnings	52,000	94,000
Treasury stock	(30,000)	—
Total liabilities and equity	$490,000	$370,000

During 2013, Arctic sold land for $70,000 cash that had originally cost $45,000. Arctic also purchased equipment for cash, acquired treasury stock for cash, and issued bonds payable for cash in 2013. Accounts payable relate to merchandise purchases.

Required

a. Compute the change in cash that occurred during 2013.

b. Prepare a 2013 statement of cash flows using the indirect method (classify interest income as operating cash flow).

c. Compute and interpret Arctic's
(1) operating cash flow to current liabilities ratio, and
(2) operating cash flow to capital expenditures ratio.

P4-49. Computing Cash Flow from Operating Activities (Direct Method) LO2

Refer to the income statement and comparative balance sheets for Arctic Company presented in P4-48.

Required

a. Compute Arctic Company's cash flow from operating activities using the direct method (classify interest income as operating cash flow). Use the format illustrated in Exhibit 4.5 in the chapter.

b. What can we learn from the direct method that may not be readily apparent when reviewing a cash flow statement prepared using the indirect method?

P4-50. Preparing a Statement of Cash Flows (Indirect Method) LO3, 4, 5

Dair Company's income statement and comparative balance sheets follow.

DAIR COMPANY
Income Statement
For Year Ended December 31, 2013

Sales		$700,000
Cost of goods sold	$440,000	
Wages and other operating expenses	95,000	
Depreciation expense	22,000	
Amortisation expense	7,000	
Interest expense	10,000	
Income tax expense	36,000	
Loss on bond retirement	5,000	615,000
Net income		$ 85,000

DAIR COMPANY
Balance Sheets

	Dec. 31, 2013	Dec. 31, 2012
Assets		
Cash	$ 27,000	$ 18,000
Accounts receivable	53,000	48,000
Inventory	103,000	109,000
Prepaid expenses	12,000	10,000
Plant assets	360,000	336,000
Accumulated depreciation	(87,000)	(84,000)
Intangible assets	43,000	50,000
Total assets	$511,000	$487,000
Liabilities and Shareholders' Equity		
Accounts payable	$ 32,000	$ 26,000
Interest payable	4,000	7,000
Income tax payable	6,000	8,000
Bonds payable	60,000	120,000
Share capital	252,000	228,000
Retained earnings	157,000	98,000
Total liabilities and equity	$511,000	$487,000

During 2013, the company sold for $17,000 cash old equipment that had cost $36,000 and had $19,000 accumulated depreciation. Also in 2013, new equipment worth $60,000 was acquired in exchange for $60,000 of bonds payable, and bonds payable of $120,000 were retired for cash at a loss. A $26,000 cash dividend was declared and paid in 2013. Any stock issuances were for cash.

Required

a. Compute the change in cash that occurred in 2013.

b. Prepare a 2013 statement of cash flows using the indirect method (classify interest income as operating cash flow).

c. Prepare separate schedules showing
(1) cash paid for interest and for income taxes and
(2) noncash investing and financing transactions.

d. Compute its
(1) operating cash flow to current liabilities ratio,
(2) operating cash flow to capital expenditures ratio, and
(3) free cash flow.

LO2, 3, 4 **P4-51. Interpreting the Statement of Cash Flows**

BOMBARDIER INC. (CANADA)

Following is the statement of cash flows of **Bombardier Inc.**, a Canadian multinational aerospace and transportation company, for the year 2013.

BOMBARDIER, INC. (USD million)	Year Ended December 31, 2013
Operating activities	
Net income	$ 572
Noncash items:	
Amortisation	391
Deferred income taxes	74
Gain on disposal of a business	(23)
Share of income of joint ventures and associates	(119)
Share-based expense	11
Dividends received from joint ventures and associates	115
Net change in noncash balances	
Trade and other receivables	(134)
Inventories	(631)
Other financial assets and liabilities, net	(15)
Other assets	(437)
Trade and other payables	749
Provisions	(161)
Advances and progress billings in excess of long-term contract inventories	301
Advances on aerospace programs	334
Retirement benefits liability	(8)
Other liabilities	361
Cash flows from operating activities	1,380
Investing activities	
Additions to PP&E and intangible assets	(2,357)
Proceeds from disposals of PP&E and intangible assets	70
Additions to AFS investments in securities	(122)
Proceeds from disposal of AFS investments in securities	52
Net proceeds from disposal of a business	83
Other	13
Cash flows from investing activities	(2,261)
Financing activities	
Net proceeds from issuance of long-term debt	1,983
Repayments of long-term debt	(51)
Dividends paid	(196)
Other	(13)
Cash flows from financing activities	1,723
Effect of exchange rates on cash and cash equivalents	(2)
Net increase (decrease) in cash and cash equivalents	**840**
Cash and cash equivalents at beginning of year	2,557
Cash and cash equivalents at end of year	**$3,397**

Required

a. Explain why Bombardier adds $391 of amortisation to net income to calculate cash flows from operating activities.

b. Explain why Bombardier subtracts $23 of "gain on disposal of a business" from net income to calculate cash flows from operating activities.

c. How should we interpret the $(134) for trade and other receivables? Explain.

d. How should we interpret the $749 for trade payables under operating activities? Did Bombardier receive $749 for trade payables for the year ended December 31, 2013? Explain.

e. Did the balance of Bombardier's inventories decrease in 2013? Explain.

f. Why does Bombardier list the "effect of exchange rates on cash and cash equivalents" in its cash flow statement? What does this amount represent?

g. Does Bombardier present a "healthy" cash flow picture for the year? How is Bombardier using the cash generated by its operations? Explain.

P4-52. Preparing a Statement of Cash Flows (Indirect Method) LO3, 4, 5

Rainbow Company's income statement and comparative balance sheets follow.

RAINBOW COMPANY Income Statement For Year Ended December 31, 2013		
Sales		$750,000
Dividend income		15,000
Total revenue		765,000
Cost of goods sold	$440,000	
Wages and other operating expenses	130,000	
Depreciation expense	39,000	
Patent amortisation expense	7,000	
Interest expense	13,000	
Income tax expense	44,000	
Loss on sale of equipment	5,000	
Gain on sale of investments	(3,000)	675,000
Net income		$ 90,000

RAINBOW COMPANY Balance Sheets	Dec. 31, 2013	Dec. 31, 2012
Assets		
Cash and cash equivalents	$ 19,000	$ 25,000
Accounts receivable	40,000	30,000
Inventory	103,000	77,000
Prepaid expenses	10,000	6,000
Long-term investments	—	57,000
Land	190,000	100,000
Buildings	445,000	350,000
Accumulated depreciation—Buildings	(91,000)	(75,000)
Equipment	179,000	225,000
Accumulated depreciation—Equipment	(42,000)	(46,000)
Patents	50,000	32,000
Total assets	$903,000	$781,000
Liabilities and Stockholders' Equity		
Accounts payable	$ 20,000	$ 16,000
Interest payable	6,000	5,000
Income tax payable	8,000	10,000
Bonds payable	155,000	125,000
Preferred stock ($100 par value)	100,000	75,000
Share capital ($5 par value)	379,000	364,000
Contributed surplus	133,000	124,000
Retained earnings	102,000	62,000
Total liabilities and equity	$903,000	$781,000

During 2013, the following transactions and events occurred:

1. Sold long-term investments costing $57,000 for $60,000 cash.
2. Purchased land for cash.
3. Capitalised an expenditure made to improve the building.
4. Sold equipment for $14,000 cash that originally cost $46,000 and had $27,000 accumulated depreciation.
5. Issued bonds payable at face value for cash.
6. Acquired a patent with a fair value of $25,000 by issuing 250 shares of preferred stock at par value.
7. Declared and paid a $50,000 cash dividend.
8. Issued 3,000 ordinary shares for cash at $8 per share.
9. Recorded depreciation of $16,000 on buildings and $23,000 on equipment.

Required

a. Compute the change in cash and cash equivalents that occurred during 2013.

b. Prepare a 2013 statement of cash flows using the indirect method (classify interest income as operating cash flow).

c. Prepare separate schedules showing (1) cash paid for interest and for income taxes and (2) noncash investing and financing transactions.

d. Compute its (1) operating cash flow to current liabilities ratio, (2) operating cash flow to capital expenditures ratio, and (3) free cash flow.

LO2, 3, 4 **P4-53. Preparing a Statement of Cash Flows (Direct Method)**

Refer to the data for Rainbow Company in Problem 4-52.

Required

a. Compute the change in cash that occurred in 2013.

b. Prepare a 2013 statement of cash flows using the direct method (classify interest income as operating cash flow). Use one cash outflow for "cash paid for wages and other operating expenses." Accounts payable relate to inventory purchases only.

c. Prepare separate schedules showing (1) a reconciliation of net income to net cash flow from operating activities and (2) noncash investing and financing transactions.

P4-54. Interpreting the Statement of Cash Flows

LO3, 4

ASTRAZENECA PLC (UNITED KINGDOM)

The 2013 consolidated statement of cash flows for AstraZeneca Plc, a British biopharmaceutical company, is given below. All amounts are expressed in millions of U.S. dollars.

Consolidated Statement of Cash Flows For Year Ended December 31	Notes	2013 $m
Cash flows from operating activities		
Profit before tax*		3,267
Finance income and expense*	3	445
Depreciation, amortisation and impairment		4,583
(Increase)/decrease in trade and other receivables		(383)
Decrease/(increase) in inventories		135
Increase/(decrease) in trade and other payables and provisions		414
Profit on disposal of subsidiary	22	—
Non-cash and other movements		258
Cash generated from operations		8,719
Interest paid		(475)
Tax paid		(844)
Net cash inflow from operating activities		7,400
Cash flows from investing activities		
Acquisitions of business operations	22	(1,158)
Movement in short-term investments and fixed deposits		130
Purchase of property, plant and equipment		(742)
Disposal of property, plant and equipment		69
Purchase of intangible assets		(1,316)
Disposal of intangible assets		35
Purchase of non-current asset investments		(91)
Disposal of non-current asset investments		38
Net cash received on disposal of subsidiary	22	—
Dividends received		—
Interest received		114
Payments made by subsidiaries to non-controlling interests		(10)
Payments received by subsidiaries from non-controlling interests		42
Net cash outflow from investing activities		(2,889)
Net cash inflow before financing activities		4,511
Cash flows from financing activities		
Proceeds from issue of share capital		482
Repurchase of shares		—
Repayment of obligations under finance leases		(27)
Issue of loans		—
Repayment of loans		—
Dividends paid		(3,461)
Hedge contracts relating to dividend payments		(36)
Movement in short-term borrowings		(5)
Net cash outflow from financing activities		(3,047)
Net increase/(decrease) in cash and cash equivalents in the period		1,464
Cash and cash equivalents at the beginning of the period		7,596
Exchange rate effects		(65)
Cash and cash equivalents at the end of the period	13	8,995

Required

a. AstraZeneca begins its cash flows from operating activities with profit before taxes, then adds $4,583 million for depreciation, amortisation, and impairment. Why is AstraZeneca adding depreciation, amortisation, and impairment to pre-tax profit in the computation of net cash flow from operating activities?

b. How should we interpret the $(383) for trade and other receivables and the $135 for inventories under cash flows from operating activities? Explain.

c. AstraZeneca shows a positive $414 for trade and other payables and provisions. Does this mean that AstraZeneca received $414 for trade payables in 2013? Explain.

d. What was AstraZeneca's net investment in property and equipment and intangible assets? Was it enough to cover the wear and tear on these assets?

e. How much cash did AstraZeneca return to its shareholders in 2013?

f. Overall, does AstraZeneca generate a healthy cash flow from its operations? How is AstraZeneca using the cash generated by its operations? Explain.

LO5, 6 **P4-55.**[A] **Preparing the Statement of Cash Flows Using a Spreadsheet**

The table below provides the balance sheets for Golden Enterprises, Inc. for the fiscal years ended June 3, 2011 and May 28, 2010.

	Year Ended	
Consolidated Balance Sheets	**June 3, 2011**	**May 28, 2010**
ASSETS		
Cash and cash equivalents	$ 2,721,638	$ 1,443,801
Receivables, net	10,220,220	9,534,542
Inventories	4,995,629	4,900,665
Prepaid expenses	1,803,827	1,573,253
Accrued income taxes	865,467	—
Deferred income taxes	633,370	580,154
Total current assets	21,240,151	18,032,415
Property, plant and equipment at cost	84,767,771	80,132,394
Accumulated depreciation	60,121,353	57,852,770
Property, plant and equipment, net	24,646,418	22,279,624
Cash surrender of life insurance	934,844	1,299,084
Other	1,299,493	1,132,237
Total assets	$48,120,906	$42,743,360
LIABILITIES & STOCKHOLDERS' EQUITY		
Checks outstanding in excess of bank balances	$ 998,386	$ 1,083,512
Accounts payable	6,323,448	6,137,412
Accrued income taxes	—	238,031
Current portion of long-term debt	344,791	350,304
Line of credit outstanding	1,777,567	1,781,996
Other accrued expenses	4,604,603	4,465,977
Salary continuation plan	167,662	154,812
Total current liabilities	14,216,457	14,212,044
Note payable to bank, non-current	6,064,983	3,479,879
Salary continuation plan	1,211,895	1,317,251
Deferred income taxes	2,969,917	1,586,833
Total liabilities	24,463,252	20,596,007
Common stock at par	9,219,195	9,219,195
Additional paid-in capital	6,497,954	6,497,954
Retained earnings	18,866,264	17,319,003
Treasury shares, at cost	(10,925,759)	(10,888,799)
Total stockholders' equity	23,657,654	22,147,353
Total liabilities and stockholders' equity	$48,120,906	$42,743,360

Additional information:

1. Net income for the year ended June 3, 2011 was $3,014,768.
2. Depreciation expense for the year ended June 3, 2011 was $3,174,956.
3. Accounts for the life insurance asset and salary continuation liabilities are operating.
4. Checks outstanding in excess of bank balances should be treated as a financing liability.
5. During the year ended June 3, 2011, Golden Enterprises sold used property, plant and equipment, receiving $96,916 in cash and recognising a gain of $79,483.
6. For the year ended June 3, 2011, debt proceeds (encompassing the liabilities for current portion of long-term debt, line of credit outstanding and note payable to bank, non-current) were $38,903,745 and debt repayments were $36,328,583.

Required

a. Set up a spreadsheet to analyse the changes in Golden Enterprises' comparative balance sheets. Use the format illustrated in Exhibit 4A.1.

b. Prepare a statement of cash flows (including operations, investing and financing) for Golden Enterprises for the year ended June 3, 2011 using the indirect method for the operating section.

c. Using information in the statement of cash flows prepared in part *b*, compute (1) the operating cash flow to current liabilities ratio and (2) the operating cash flow to capital expenditures ratio.

P4-56. Interpreting the Statement of Cash Flows LO3, 4, 5

DAIMLER AG (GERMANY)

The statement of cash flows for **Daimler AG** follows:

DAIMLER AG
Consolidated Statement of Cash Flows

(millions of euros)	Fiscal Year 2011
Profit before income taxes	€ 8,449
Depreciation and amortisation	3,575
Other noncash expense and income	(122)
Gains (–)/losses on disposals of assets	(102)
Change in operating assets and liabilities	
Inventories	(2,328)
Trade receivables	(620)
Trade payables	1,762
Receivables from financial services	(4,526)
Vehicles on operating leases	(2,874)
Other operating assets and liabilities	(1,093)
Income taxes paid	(2,817)
Cash provided by/(used for) operating activities	(696)
Additions to property, plant and equipment	(4,158)
Additions to intangible assets	(1,718)
Proceeds from disposals of property, plant and equipment and intangible assets	252
Investments in share property	(899)
Proceeds from disposals of share property	203
Acquisition of marketable debt securities	(5,478)
Proceeds from sales of marketable debt securities	5,241
Other	20
Cash provided by/(used for) investing activities	(6,537)
Change in short-term financing liabilities	2,589
Additions to long-term financing liabilities	26,037
Repayment of long-term financing liabilities	(20,560)
Dividend paid to shareholders of Daimler AG	(1,971)
Dividends paid to non-controlling interests	(278)
Proceeds from issuance of share capital	71
Acquisition of treasury shares	(28)
Acquisition of non-controlling interests in subsidiaries	(18)
Cash provided by/(used for) financing activities	5,842
Effect of foreign exchange rate changes on cash and cash equivalents	64
Net increase/(decrease) in cash and cash equivalents	(1,327)
Cash and cash equivalents at the beginning of the period	10,903
Cash and cash equivalents at the end of the period	€ 9,576

Required

a. Daimler begins its cash flow statement with net income of €8,449 million, then adds €3,575 million for depreciation and amortisation. Why is Daimler adding depreciation and amortisation to net income in this computation?

b. Why does Daimler subtract €102 million of gains on disposals of assets in its indirect method cash flows from operating activities? If these gains are all created by disposals of property, plant and equipment and intangible assets, what was the book value of the assets Daimler disposed of during fiscal year 2011?

c. Daimler shows a negative €2,328 million for inventories in the statement of cash flows. Does this mean that Daimler paid €2,328 million for inventories in 2011? Explain.

d. Compute Daimler's free cash flow for 2011. How did the company finance its investing activities?

e. Daimler reports a cash outflow from operating activities of €696 million, despite reporting net income of €8,449 million. What principal activities account for this difference? Does this raise concerns about the health of Daimler AG?

CASES AND PROJECTS

LO3, 4 **C4-57. Analysing a Projected Statement of Cash Flows and Loan Covenants**

The President and CFO of Lambert Co. will be meeting with their bankers next week to discuss the short-term financing needs of the company for the next six months. Lambert's controller has provided a projected income statement for the next six-month period, and a current balance sheet along with a projected balance sheet for the end of that six-month period. These statements are presented below ($ millions).

LAMBERT CO.
Projected Six-Month Income Statement

Revenues	$400
Cost of goods sold	200
Gross profit	200
Selling and administrative expense	50
Depreciation expense	120
Income before income taxes	30
Income taxes	12
Net income	$ 18

LAMBERT CO. Current and Projected Six-Month Balance Sheets	Current	6-month projected
Cash	$ 50	$???
Accounts receivable	180	220
Inventory	200	180
Total current assets	430	???
Property, plant & equipment, cost	400	500
Less accumulated depreciation	(150)	(220)
Property, plant & equipment, net	250	280
Total assets	$680	???
Accounts payable	$150	$180
Income taxes payable	20	10
Short-term borrowing	50	???
Long-term debt	200	180
Total liabilities	420	???
Share capital at par	100	125
Retained earnings	160	148
Total liabilities and shareholders' equity	$680	???

Additional Information (already reflected in the projected income statement and balance sheet):

- Lambert's current long-term debt includes $100 that is due within the next six months. During the next six months, the company plans to take advantage of lower interest rates by issuing new long-term debt that will provide $80 in cash proceeds.
- During the next six months, the company plans to dispose of equipment with an original cost of $125 and accumulated depreciation of $50. An appraisal by an equipment broker indicates that Lambert should be able to get $75 in cash for the equipment. In addition, Lambert plans to acquire new equipment at a cost of $225.
- A small issue of ordinary shares for cash ($25) and a cash dividend to shareholders ($30) are planned in the next six months.
- Lambert's outstanding long-term debt imposes a restrictive loan covenant on the company that requires Lambert to maintain a debt-to-equity ratio below 1.75.

Required

The CFO says, "I would like a clear estimate of the amount of short-term borrowing that we will need six months from now. I want you to prepare a forecasted statement of cash flows that we can take to the meeting next week."

Prepare the required statement of cash flows, using the indirect method to compute cash flow from operating activities. The forecasted statement should include the needed amount of short-term borrowing and should be consistent with the projected balance sheet and income statement, as well as the loan covenant restriction.

LO1, 3, 4 **C4-58. Reconstructing Journal Entries and T-Accounts from Completed Financial Statements** Lundholm Company's comparative balance sheets, income statement, and statement of cash flows for July are presented below:

LUNDHOLM COMPANY
Comparative Balance Sheets

	July 1	July 31
Cash	$ 600	$ 1,184
Accounts receivable	6,500	6,800
Inventory	2,400	1,800
Prepaid rent	—	400
Current assets	9,500	10,184
Fixtures and equipment at cost	1,900	2,620
Accumulated depreciation	(800)	(880)
Plant and equipment, net	1,100	1,740
Total assets	$10,600	$11,924
Accounts payable	$ 3,000	$ 3,100
Salaries and wages payable	100	70
Taxes payable	—	374
Bank loan payable	1,600	—
Current liabilities	4,700	3,544
Long-term loan	—	2,000
Share capital	4,600	4,600
Retained earnings	1,300	1,780
Total liabilities and shareholders' equity	$10,600	$11,924

LUNDHOLM COMPANY
Income Statement
Month ended July 31

Revenue		$3,800
Operating expenses:		
Cost of goods sold	$1,800	
Salaries and wages	700	
Rent	200	
Depreciation	150	
Total operating expenses		2,850
Operating income		950
Interest expense		16
Income before taxes		934
Income taxes		374
Net income		$ 560

LUNDHOLM COMPANY Statement of Cash Flows Month ended July 31	
Operating activities:	
Net income	$ 560
Adjustments:	
Depreciation	150
Increase in accounts receivable	(300)
Decrease in inventory	600
Increase in prepaid rent	(400)
Increase in accounts payable	100
Decrease in salaries and wages payable	(30)
Increase in taxes payable	374
Total adjustments	494
Cash flow from operating activities	1,054
Investing activities:	
Proceeds from disposal of fixtures and equipment	10
Purchases of fixtures and equipment	(800)
Cash flow used for investing activities	(790)
Financing activities:	
Loan repayment	(1,600)
Proceeds from new loan	2,000
Dividends paid to shareholders	(80)
Cash flow from financing activities	320
Net increase in cash	584
Cash balance, July 1	600
Cash balance, July 31	$1,184

Required

a. Set up T-accounts and enter beginning and ending balances for each account in Lundholm Company's balance sheet.

b. Provide a set of *summary journal entries* for July that would produce the financial statements presented above. For simplicity, you may assume that all of Lundholm Company's sales are made on account and that all of its purchases are made on account. One such entry is provided as an example.

(1)	Accounts receivable (+A)	3,800	
	Sales revenue (+R, +SE)		3,800

c. Post the journal entries from part *a* to T-accounts and verify ending balances.

SOLUTIONS TO REVIEW PROBLEMS

Mid-Chapter Review 1

Solution

1. Out/I; 2. Out/O or Out/F; 3. Out/O; 4. In/F; 5. Out/O; 6. In/O; 7. In/I; 8. In/I; 9. Out/F; 10. In/O or In/I

Mid-Chapter Review 2

Solution

MUG SHOTS, INC.
Computation of Cash Flow from Operating Activities
For Month Ended December 31, 2013

	Net income $3,445	=	Sales revenue $31,000	−Cost of goods sold −16,700	−Wage expenses −4,700	−Interest expense −300	−Advertising expense −1,800	−Rent expense −1,500	−Depreciation expense −700	−Income tax expense −1,855
Adjustments:										
Add back depreciation expense									+Depreciation expense +700	
Subtract (add) non-operating gains (losses)										
Subtract the change in operating assets (operating investments)			⊖ change in accounts receivable −2,500	⊖ change in inventory −8,300				⊖ change in prepaid rent −(−1,500)		
Add the change in operating liabilities (operating financing)			⊕ change in unearned revenue +500	⊕ change in accounts payable +1,000	⊕ change in wages payable +2,200	⊕ change in interest payable +300				⊕ change in income tax payable +1,855
	Cash from operations $700	=	Receipts from customers $29,000	−Payments for merchandise −24,000	−Payments for Wages −2,500	−Payments for interest 0 (zero)	Payments for advertising −1,800	−Payments for rent 0 (zero)	0 (zero)	−Payments for income tax 0 (zero)

Mid-Chapter Review 3

Solution

MUG SHOTS, INC. Cash Flow from Operating Activities—Indirect Method		
Net income		$3,445
Adjustments:		
Add back depreciation expense	$ 700	
Subtract changes in:		
Accounts receivable	(2,500)	
Inventory	(8,300)	
Prepaid rent	1,500	
Add changes in:		
Unearned revenue	500	
Accounts payable	1,000	
Wages payable	2,200	
Interest payable	300	
Income tax payable	1,855	
Total adjustments		(2,745)
Cash flow from operating activities		$ 700

Mid-Chapter Review 4

Solution

MUG SHOTS, INC. Statement of Cash Flows For Month Ended December 31, 2013		
Cash flow from operating activities		
Net income	$ 3,445	
Add back depreciation	700	
Subtract changes in:		
Accounts receivable	(2,500)	
Inventory	(8,300)	
Prepaid rent	1,500	
Add changes in:		
Accounts payable	1,000	
Unearned revenue	500	
Income tax payable	1,855	
Wages payable	2,200	
Interest payable	300	
Net cash provided by operating activities		$ 700
Cash flow from investing activities		
Purchase of equipment	(12,000)	
Net cash used by investing activities		(12,000)
Cash flow from financing activities		
Bank loan	18,000	
Payment of dividend	(1,000)	
Net cash provided by financing activities		17,000
		5,700
Cash, beginning of period		5,000
Cash, end of period		$10,700

Mid-Chapter Review 5

Solution

There are three entries that affected the balance sheet accounts of Property, plant and equipment at cost and Accumulated Depreciation. We know some of the amounts involved, but not all. Let P be the proceeds on the sale of used equipment, let A be the cash spent to acquire new property, plant and equipment, and let D be the year's depreciation expense. Here are the entries:

1. Disposal:

DR Cash (+A)	P	
DR Accumulated depreciation (−XA, +A)	60,000	
CR Property, plant and equipment at cost (−A)		80,000
CR Gain on equipment disposal (+R, +SE)		35,000

The value of P must be \$55,000, because Jack's Snacks reported a gain of \$35,000 on selling an asset with book value of \$20,000 (= \$80,000 − 60,000).

2. Acquisition:

DR Property, plant and equipment at cost (+A)	A	
CR Cash (−A)		A

We can determine the cost of acquired assets by looking at the T-account for Property, plant and equipment at cost.

+ Property, plant and equipment at cost			−
Beg. Bal.	600,000		
Purchases	A	80,000	Disposal
End. Bal.	670,000		

The value of A, i.e., the amount spent on acquiring PPE must have been \$150,000.

3. Depreciation expense:

DR Depreciation expense (+E, −SE)	D	
CR Accumulated depreciation (+XA, −A)		D

We can determine the depreciation expense by looking at the T-account for the accumulated depreciation contra-asset.

+ Accumulated depreciation			−
		140,000	Beg. Bal.
Disposal	60,000	D	Deprec. Exp.
		150,000	End. Bal.

The depreciation expense for the year, D, must have been \$70,000, because the contra-asset increased by 10,000 even though the disposal decreased it by 60,000.

Chapter-End Review

Solution

1. We assume that One World Café's notes payable are classified as current liabilities. If so, current liabilities are \$41,000 (\$27,000+\$6,000+\$3,000+\$5,000) in 2013 and \$21,000 (\$14,000+\$2,500+\$4,500) in 2012.
   \$44,000 / [(\$41,000 + \$21,000)/2] = 1.42
   One World Café is generating cash flows from operations in excess of its current liabilities. Assuming that this continues, it should have no difficulty meeting its obligations.
2. \$44,000 / \$45,000 = 0.98
   One World Café spent a little more on plant capacity than it generated through operations. However, for a small business, capital expenditures are often irregular. Thus, this ratio is not alarmingly low.
3. \$44,000 – (\$45,000 − \$4,000) = \$3,000.

Appendix-End Review

Solution

Cash Flow Spreadsheet for Rocky Road Bicycles, Inc.

	A	B	C	D	E	F	G	H	I	J
1						Effect of change on cash flow				
2		O, I, or F?	2013	2012	Change	Operating	Investing	Financing	No effect on cash	Total F, G, H, I
3	**Assets**									
4	Cash		106,000	96,000	10,000					
5										
6	Accounts receivable	O	156,000	224,000	(68,000)	68,000				68,000
7	Inventory	O	752,000	528,000	224,000	(224,000)				(224,000)
8	Prepaid rent	O	68,000	72,000	(4,000)	4,000				4,000
9	Plant assets, net	O, I	1,130,000	872,000	258,000					
10	Depreciation expense					122,000				
10	Plant assets purchased						(420,000)			(258,000)
12	Plant assets sold					(16,000)	56,000			
13										
14	**Liabilities**									
15	Accounts payable	O	216,000	112,000	104,000	104,000				104,000
16	Wages payable	O	18,000	20,000	(2,000)	(2,000)				(2,000)
17	Income tax payable	O	44,000	36,000	8,000	8,000				8,000
18	Notes payable	F								
19	New borrowing									—
20	Borrowing repayments									
21										
22	**Shareholders' Equity**									
23	Share capital	F	1,142,000	1,000,000	142,000					
24	New issue of ordinary shares							142,000		142,000
25	Repurchase of ordinary shares									
26	Retained earnings	O, F	792,000	624,000	168,000					
27	Net income					326,000				168,000
28	Dividends							(158,000)		
29										
30	Totals					390,000	(364,000)	(16,000)	—	10,000

$390,000 − $364,000 − $16,000 = $10,000.

ROCKY ROAD BICYCLES, INC.
Statement of Cash Flows
For Year Ended December 31, 2013

Cash flows from operating activities		
Net income	$326,000	
Add (deduct) items to convert net income to cash basis		
Depreciation	122,000	
Gain on sale of plant assets	(16,000)	
Accounts receivable	68,000	
Inventory	(224,000)	
Prepaid rent	4,000	
Accounts payable	104,000	
Wages payable	(2,000)	
Income tax payable	8,000	
Net cash provided by operating activities		$390,000
Cash flows from investing activities		
Purchase of plant assets	(420,000)	
Proceeds from sale of plant assets	56,000	
Net cash used for investing activities		(364,000)
Cash flows from financing activities		
Issuance of ordinary shares	142,000	
Payment of dividends	(158,000)	
Net cash used for financing activities		(16,000)
Net cash increase		10,000
Cash at beginning of year		96,000
Cash at end of year		$106,000

LEARNING OBJECTIVES

1. Prepare and analyse common-size financial statements. (p. 213)

2. Compute and interpret measures of return on investment, including return on equity (ROE), return on assets (ROA), and return on financial leverage (ROFL). (p. 218)

3. Disaggregate ROA into profitability (profit margin) and efficiency (asset turnover) components. (p. 221)

4. Compute and interpret measures of liquidity and solvency. (p. 227)

5. Appendix 5A: Measure and analyse the effect of operating activities on ROE. (p. 234)

6. Appendix 5B: Prepare *pro forma* financial statements. (p. 236)

CHAPTER

5

Analysing and Interpreting Financial Statements

VODAFONE GROUP PLC
www.vodafone.com

Vodafone Group Plc is a mobile telecommunications company based in the United Kingdom. It has mobile operations in 27 countries and partners with mobile networks in 48 other countries. In 2013, Vodafone was ranked second in its industry (behind China Mobile) on the FT Global 500, based on either market capitalisation or revenue.

Because of competitive, regulatory, and macroeconomic pressures in its European operations, Vodafone struggled during 2012 and 2013. It saw revenue drop by 2% in fiscal 2012, and then recover slightly by 0.8% to £38.3 billion in 2013 due to strong growth in its emerging markets businesses. Operating loss increased from £2.2 billion in 2012 to £3.9 billion in 2013, as a result of higher customer costs and higher amortisation. During fiscal 2013, it recorded impairment charges of £6.6 billion relating to the deteriorating economic environment in Germany, Spain, Portugal, the Czech Republic, and Romania. Despite reporting an operating loss in 2013, Vodafone reported a net profit for the year due to a large income tax credit generated from the recognition of deferred tax assets in Luxembourg and Germany.

Furthermore, Vodafone sold its 45% interest in Verizon Wireless to Verizon Communications for £79 billion in 2013. Its share of income from Verizon Wireless and the gain from the sales are classified as profit from discontinued operations, which provided a positive contribution to Vodafone's net profit in both 2012 and 2013. After returning £51 billion of the sales proceed to its shareholders, Vodafone paid down its long-term borrowings, reducing its debt-to-equity ratio from 0.91 in 2012 to 0.70 in 2013.

Vodafone's most recent efforts have included the acceleration of investment in its mobile network, the acquisition of a leading cable operator and other fixed-line businesses in Europe, the introduction of an all-in-one postpaid plan called "Vodafone RED" in its European markets, and the expansion of its mobile-phone-based money transfer service (M-Pesa) to Eastern Europe and other African countries. It is too soon to tell whether these efforts will produce the growth that investors desire. Ultimately, we will be able to assess the success of this initiative by looking at specific measures of Vodafone's performance. In doing so, we seek to answer the question: Can Vodafone achieve a high return on investment and, if so, is that return sustainable?

As is the case in most companies, Vodafone's management employs a number of financial measures to assess the performance and financial condition of its operating units. These measures include ratios related to profitability and asset utilisation as well as return on investment. Outside stakeholders—investors, creditors and financial analysts—use similar measures to evaluate company performance, assess credit risk, and estimate share value.

(continued on next page)

(continued from previous page)

This chapter focuses on the analysis of information reported in the financial statements. We discuss a variety of measures that provide insights into a company's performance to answer questions such as: Is it managed efficiently and profitably? Does it use assets efficiently? Is the performance achieved with an optimal amount of debt? We pay especially close attention to measures of return. Although profitability is important, it is only part of the story. More meaningful insights are gained by comparing the level of profitability with the amount of investment. All return metrics follow the same basic formula—they divide some measure of profit by a measure of investment. In Chapter 1, we introduced one such return metric, namely return on equity (ROE). In this chapter, we review ROE and add another return metric—return on assets (ROA)—which measures the return produced by the company's investment in its assets.

ROE and ROA differ by the use of debt financing, or financial leverage. Companies can increase ROE by borrowing money and using these funds to finance investment in operating assets. However, debt financing can increase company risk and, if not used judiciously, is likely to have a detrimental effect on ROE and even lead to financial distress. In the latter part of this chapter, we examine metrics that measure liquidity and solvency that allow us to assess that risk.

Sources: www.vodafone.com; Vodafone Group Plc 2014 Annual Report; Financial Times 2013 FT Global 500.

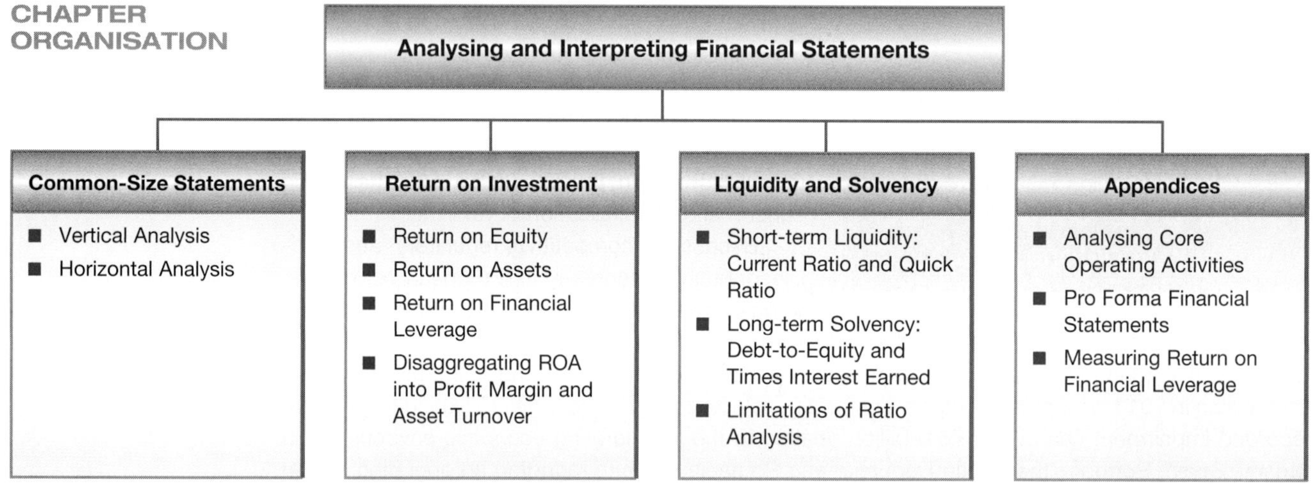

CHAPTER ORGANISATION
Analysing and Interpreting Financial Statements
Common-Size Statements
Vertical Analysis
Horizontal Analysis
Return on Investment
Return on Equity
Return on Assets
Return on Financial Leverage
Disaggregating ROA into Profit Margin and Asset Turnover
Liquidity and Solvency
Short-term Liquidity: Current Ratio and Quick Ratio
Long-term Solvency: Debt-to-Equity and Times Interest Earned
Limitations of Ratio Analysis
Appendices
Analysing Core Operating Activities
Pro Forma Financial Statements
Measuring Return on Financial Leverage

INTRODUCTION

Companies prepare financial statements to be used. These statements are used by investors who rely on financial statement information to assess investment risk, forecast income and dividends, and estimate value. They are used by creditors to assess credit risk and monitor outstanding loans for compliance with debt covenants. And, as the Vodafone example illustrates, they are used by management to evaluate the performance of operating units. **Financial statement analysis** identifies relationships between numbers within the financial statements and trends in these relationships from one period to the next. The goal is to help users such as investors, creditors, and managers interpret the information presented in the financial statements.

Financial statement analysis is all about making comparisons. Accounting information is difficult to interpret when the numbers are viewed in isolation. For example, a company that reports net income of $7 million may have had a good year or a bad year. However, if we know that total sales were $100 million, assets total $90 million, and that the previous year's net income was $6 million, we have a better idea about how well the company performed. If we go a step further and compare these numbers to those of a competing company or to an industry average, we begin to make an assessment about the relative quality of management, the prospects for future growth, overall company risk, and the potential to earn sustainable returns.

Assessing the Business Environment

Financial statement analysis cannot be undertaken in a vacuum. A meaningful interpretation of financial information requires an understanding of the business, its operations, and the environment in which it operates. That is, before we begin crunching the numbers, we must consider the broader business context in which the company operates. This approach requires starting with the Management's Discussion and Analysis section of the financial reports and asking questions about the company and its business environment, including:

- *Life cycle*—At what stage in its life is this company? Is it a start-up, experiencing the growing pains that often result from rapid growth? Is it a mature company, reaping the benefits of its competitive advantages? Is it in decline?
- *Outputs*—What products does it sell? Are its products new, established, or dated? Do its products have substitutes? Are its products protected by patents? How complicated are its products to produce?
- *Customers*—Who are its customers? How often do customers purchase the company's products? What demographic trends are likely to have an effect on future sales?
- *Competition*—Who are the company's competitors? How is it positioned in the market relative to its competition? Is it easy for new competitors to enter the market for its products? Are its products differentiated from competitors' products? Does it have any cost advantages over its competitors?
- *Inputs*—Who are the company's suppliers? Are there multiple supply sources? Does the company depend on one (or a few) key supply sources creating the potential for high input costs?
- *Labour*—Who are the company's managers? How effective are they? Is the company unionised? Does it depend on a skilled or educated workforce?
- *Technology*—What technology does the company employ to produce its products? Does the company outsource production? What transport systems does the company rely on to deliver its products?
- *Capital*—To what extent does the company rely on public markets to raise needed capital? Has it recently gone public? Does it have expansion plans that require large sums of cash to carry out? Is it planning to acquire another company? Is it in danger of defaulting on its debt?
- *Political*—How does the company interact with the communities, states, and countries in which it operates? What government regulations affect the company's operations? Are any proposed regulations likely to have a significant impact on the company?

These are just a few of the questions that we should ask before we begin analysing a company's financial statements. Ultimately, the answers will help us place our numerical analysis in the proper context, so that we can effectively interpret the accounting numbers.

In this chapter, we introduce the tools that are used to analyse and interpret financial statements. These tools include common-size financial statements that are used in vertical and horizontal analysis and ratios that measure return on investment and help to assess liquidity and solvency.

VERTICAL AND HORIZONTAL ANALYSIS

LO1 Prepare and analyse common-size financial statements.

Companies come in all sizes, a fact that presents difficulties when making comparisons between firms and over time. **Vertical analysis** is a method that attempts to overcome this obstacle by restating financial statement information in ratio (or percentage) form. Specifically, it is common to express components of the income statement as a percent of net sales, and balance sheet items as a percent of total assets. This restatement is often referred to as **common-size financial statements** and it facilitates comparisons across companies of different sizes as well as comparisons of accounts within a set of financial statements.

Exhibit 5.1 presents Vodafone's summarised comparative balance sheets for the years ended March 31, 2014 and 2013, referred to as fiscal years 2013 and 2012, respectively. Next to the comparative balance sheets are common-size balance sheets for the same two years. Vertical analysis

EXHIBIT 5.1 Vodafone Comparative Balance Sheets

VODAFONE GROUP PLC
Balance Sheets and Common-Size Balance Sheets
March 31, 2014 and March 31, 2013

			As a Percentage of Total Assets	
£ millions	March 31, 2014 (FY 2013)	March 31, 2013 (FY 2012)	March 31, 2014 (FY 2013)	March 31, 2013 (FY 2012)
Noncurrent assets				
Goodwill	23,315	24,390	19.1%	17.6%
Other intangible assets	23,373	19,749	19.2%	14.3%
Property, plant and equipment	22,851	17,584	18.8%	12.7%
Investments in associates and joint ventures	114	46,447	0.1%	33.6%
Other investments	3,553	773	2.9%	0.6%
Deferred tax assets	20,607	2,848	16.9%	2.1%
Post employment benefits	35	52	0.0%	0.0%
Trade and other receivables	3,270	4,832	2.7%	3.5%
	97,118	116,675	79.7%	84.3%
Current assets				
Inventory	441	353	0.4%	0.3%
Taxation recoverable	808	397	0.7%	0.3%
Trade and other receivables	8,886	8,018	7.3%	5.8%
Other investments	4,419	5,350	3.6%	3.9%
Cash and cash equivalents	10,134	7,531	8.3%	5.4%
Assets held for sale	34	—	0.0%	
	24,722	21,649	20.3%	15.7%
Total assets	121,840	138,324	100.0%	100.0%
Equity				
Called up share capital	3,792	3,866	3.1%	2.8%
Additional paid-in capital	116,973	154,279	96.0%	111.5%
Treasury shares	(7,187)	(9,029)	−5.9%	−6.5%
Accumulated losses	(51,428)	(88,834)	−42.2%	−64.2%
Accumulated other comprehensive income	8,652	11,195	7.1%	8.1%
Total equity shareholders' funds	70,802	71,477	58.1%	51.7%
Non-controlling interests	1,733	1,890	1.4%	1.4%
Put options over non-controlling interests	(754)	(879)	−0.6%	−0.6%
Total non-controlling interests	979	1,011	0.8%	0.7%
Total equity	71,781	72,488	58.9%	52.4%
Noncurrent liabilities				
Long-term borrowings	21,454	27,904	17.6%	20.2%
Taxation liabilities	50	150	0.0%	0.1%
Deferred tax liabilities	747	6,671	0.6%	4.8%
Post employment benefits	584	580	0.5%	0.4%
Provisions	846	855	0.7%	0.6%
Trade and other payables	1,339	1,307	1.1%	0.9%
	25,020	37,467	20.5%	27.1%
Current liabilities				
Short-term borrowings	7,747	11,800	6.4%	8.5%
Taxation liabilities	873	1,922	0.7%	1.4%
Provisions	963	715	0.8%	0.5%
Trade and other payables	15,456	13,932	12.7%	10.1%
	25,039	28,369	20.6%	20.5%
Total equity and liabilities	121,840	138,324	100.0%	100.0%

helps us interpret the composition of the balance sheet. For example, as of the end of fiscal year 2013, 20.3% of Vodafone's assets were current assets and 18.8% were property, plant, and equipment. Intangible assets made up 38.3% of the company's total assets in 2013. In addition, 58.9% of Vodafone's total assets were financed with equity—up from 52.4% in 2012. Short-term and long-term borrowings decreased from 28.7% (= 8.5% + 20.2%) of total assets in fiscal 2012 to 24% (= 6.4% + 17.6%) in fiscal 2013. This significant change in borrowings was largely due to the redemption of US$5.65 billion of bond following the sale of Vodafone's 45% interest in Verizon Wireless, and also to favourable foreign exchange movements. Financial statement analysts should be aware of changes in a company's organisation that produce significant changes in financial statement relationships. It is not uncommon for companies to use debt financing to fund expansion, especially if management believes that low share prices prevent them from issuing shares. However, increasing debt levels are a concern if profits and cash flows are not growing fast enough to cover the rising interest and principal payments.

In Exhibit 5.2, we present Vodafone's summarised comparative income statements for 2013 and 2012, along with common-size income statements for the same years. Vertical analysis reveals that cost of sales was 72.9% of revenues, up from 69.8% in 2012, leading to a decline in the company's gross profit margin from 30.2% to 27.1%. The increase in cost of sales could be due to a number of causes, including unexpected increases in the cost of network infrastructure, supply chain problems, or service inefficiencies. Vodafone reported operating losses for both years. The operating loss increased from 5.8% in 2012 to 10.2% of revenues in 2013, as lower impairment charges were offset by lower revenues, higher customer costs and higher administrative costs. Due to a significant income tax credit related to operations in Luxembourg and Germany, Vodafone reported £11,312 million (29.5% of revenues) in profit from continuing operations in 2013. Furthermore, Vodafone reported an even larger profit of £59,420 million, attributable to selling of assets from discontinued operations. In order to focus on Vodafone's

EXHIBIT 5.2 Vodafone Comparative Income Statements

VODAFONE GROUP PLC
Income Statements and Common-Size Income Statements
Fiscal years ended March 31, 2014 and March 31, 2013

			As a Percentage of Total Revenue	
£ millions	**March 31, 2014 (FY 2013)**	**March 31, 2013 (FY 2012)**	**March 31, 2014 (FY 2013)**	**March 31, 2013 (FY 2012)**
Revenue	38,346	38,041	100.0%	100.0%
Cost of sales	(27,942)	(26,567)	72.9%	69.8%
Gross profit	10,404	11,474	27.1%	30.2%
Selling and distribution expenses	(3,033)	(2,860)	7.9%	7.5%
Administrative expenses	(4,245)	(4,159)	11.1%	10.9%
Share of results of equity accounted associates and joint ventures	278	575	0.7%	1.5%
Impairment losses	(6,600)	(7,700)	17.2%	20.2%
Other income and expense	(717)	468	1.9%	1.2%
Operating (loss)/profit	(3,913)	(2,202)	10.2%	5.8%
Non-operating income and expense	(149)	10	0.4%	0.0%
Investment income	346	305	0.9%	0.8%
Financing costs	(1,554)	(1,596)	4.1%	4.2%
(Loss)/profit before taxation	(5,270)	(3,483)	13.7%	9.2%
Income tax credit/(expense)	16,582	(476)	43.2%	1.3%
Profit/(loss) for the financial year from continuing operations	11,312	(3,959)	29.5%	10.4%
Profit from discontinued operations	48,108	4,616	125.5%	12.1%
Profit for the financial year	59,420	657	155.0%	1.7%

operating performance and make the data across years comparable, our analysis in this chapter will be based on Vodafone's net income from continuing operations. Profit from discontinued operations, a significant non-recurring item, will be disregarded. While further analysis would be necessary to determine the exact causes of any changes in the financial data, common-size financial statements generally reveal a number of contributing factors to the increase or decrease in profit as a percentage of revenues.

Horizontal analysis examines changes in financial data across time. Comparing data across two or more consecutive periods is helpful in analysing company performance and in predicting future performance. Exhibit 5.3 presents a horizontal analysis of a few selected items from Vodafone's income statement—revenue, operating income, and net income from continuing operations. The amounts reported in each year from 2009 through 2013 are shown for each item along with a percentage change for each item. The amount of the change for a given year is computed by subtracting the amount for the prior year from the amount for the current year. The change is then divided by the reported amount for the prior year to get the percentage change. For example, Vodafone's percentage change in net revenue was 0.80% in 2013, computed as follows:

$$0.80\% = \frac{\text{£38,346 million} - \text{£38,041 million}}{\text{£38,041 million}}$$

Exhibit 5.3 highlights some important changes in Vodafone's income statement. During the 5-year period, revenues have fluctuated between £38,041 million in 2012 and £45,884 million 2010, with the largest decline of 15.39% occurring in 2011. As discussed in Vodafone's annual report, the ongoing regulatory pressures in the European operations, the weak macroeconomic environment, and stiff competition all have hindered the company's revenue growth and operating performance. The company exhibited the largest decrease in operating profit and net income in 2012. In 2013, however, the company reported the highest net income in five years, despite a 77.7% decline in operating profit. This suggests that the improvement in net income did not come from the company's operations. Instead, it was attributable to the large income tax credit mentioned earlier in our discussion.

EXHIBIT 5.3 Horizontal Analysis of Selected Income Statement Items

VODAFONE GROUP PLC
Revenue, Operating Income and Net Income
(£ millions and percent changes)

	FY 2013	FY 2012	FY 2011	FY 2010	FY 2009
Revenue	38,346	38,041	38,821	45,884	44,472
	0.80%	−2.01%	−15.39%	3.18%	
Operating profit/(loss)	(3,913)	(2,202)	5,618	5,596	9,480
	−77.70%	−139.20%	0.39%	−40.97%	
Net income/(loss)	11,312	(3,959)	3,439	7,870	8,618
	385.73%	−215.12%	−56.30%	−8.68%	

Horizontal analysis is useful in identifying unusual changes that might not be obvious when looking at the reported numbers alone. At the same time, it is important to look at both the percentage change and the reported amount. If a reported amount is close to $0 in one year, the percentage change will likely be very large the following year, even if the amount reported in that year is small. Similarly, if reported earnings is negative one year and positive the next, the percentage change will be negative even though the earnings increased. To overcome this issue, we use the absolute value of the amount in the denominator to calculate the percentage change in operating profit and net income in 2013.

MID-CHAPTER REVIEW 1

Following are summarised 2013 and 2012 income statements and balance sheets for China Mobile Limited, the world's largest mobile phone operator by market capitalisation or revenue (as of 2013).

Required

Prepare common-size income statements and balance sheets for China Mobile. Comment on any noteworthy relationships that you observe.

CHINA MOBILE LIMITED
Consolidated Statements of Comprehensive Income
for the year ended December 31

(in RMB millions)	2013	2012
Operating revenue (Turnover)		
Revenue from telecommunications services	590,811	560,413
Revenue from sales of products and others	39,366	21,422
	630,177	581,835
Operating expenses		
Leased lines	18,727	9,909
Interconnection	25,998	25,140
Depreciation	104,699	100,848
Personnel	34,376	31,256
Selling expenses	91,834	80,232
Cost of products sold	61,363	41,448
Other operating expenses	157,531	140,272
	494,528	429,105
Profit from operations	135,649	152,730
Non-operating net income	910	615
Interest income	15,289	12,661
Finance costs	(331)	(390)
Share of profit of associates	7,062	5,685
Share of loss of a joint venture	—	(1)
Profit before taxation	158,579	171,300
Taxation	(36,776)	(41,919)
PROFIT FOR THE YEAR	121,803	129,381

CHINA MOBILE LIMITED
Consolidated Balance Sheets
for the year ended December 31

(in RMB millions)	2013	2012
Noncurrent assets		
Property, plant and equipment	479,227	430,509
Construction in progress	85,000	55,507
Land lease prepayments and other prepayments	19,735	14,244
Goodwill	36,894	36,894
Other intangible assets	1,063	924
Interest in associates	53,940	48,343
Interest in a joint venture	—	6
Deferred tax assets	17,401	13,544
Restricted bank deposits	6,816	5,418
Other financial assets	127	127
	700,203	605,516

continued

continued from prior page

(in RMB millions)	2013	2012
Current assets		
Inventories	9,152	7,195
Accounts receivable	13,907	11,722
Other receivables	11,649	8,605
Prepayments and other current assets	11,832	15,913
Amount due from ultimate holding company	94	102
Tax recoverable	647	153
Bank deposits	374,977	331,997
Cash and cash equivalents	44,931	70,906
	467,189	446,593
Total assets	1,167,392	1,052,109
Current liabilities		
Accounts payable	173,157	123,896
Bills payable	1,360	1,159
Deferred revenue	61,789	57,988
Accrued expenses and other payables	125,811	103,774
Amount due to ultimate holding company	22	39
Amount due to immediate holding company	—	16
Obligations under finance leases	68	68
Current taxation	8,706	10,856
	370,913	297,796
Noncurrent liabilities		
Interest-bearing borrowings	4,989	28,619
Deferred revenue, excluding current portion	662	334
Deferred tax liabilities	104	51
	5,755	29,004
Total liabilities	376,668	326,800
Net assets	790,724	725,309
Capital and reserves		
Share capital	2,142	2,142
Reserves	786,631	721,305
Total equity attributable to equity shareholders of the Company	788,773	723,447
Non-controlling interests	1,951	1,862
Total equity	790,724	725,309

The solution to this review problem can be found on pages 264–265.

RETURN ON INVESTMENT

LO2 Compute and interpret measures of return on investment, including return on equity (ROE), return on assets (ROA), and return on financial leverage (ROFL).

Common-size financial statements and percentage changes are useful, but there is a limit to what we can learn from this type of analysis. While vertical and horizontal analysis focuses on relationships within a particular financial statement, either the income statement or the balance sheet, many of the questions that we might ask about a company can be answered only by comparing amounts between statements. For example, return on investment measures are ratios that divide some measure of performance—typically reported in the income statement—by the average amount of investment as reported in the balance sheet.

In this section, we discuss three important return metrics—return on equity (ROE), return on assets (ROA), and return on financial leverage (ROFL). In addition we will examine return on investment in detail by disaggregating ROA into performance drivers that capture profitability and efficiency. It should be noted that several of the financial ratios to be discussed in this chapter can be calculated using slightly different formulas.

Return on Equity (ROE)

Return on equity (ROE) is the primary summary measure of company performance and is defined as:

$$\text{ROE} = \frac{\textbf{Net income}}{\textbf{Average total equity}}$$

ROE relates net income to the average investment by shareholders as measured by total equity from the balance sheet. The net income number in the numerator measures the performance of the firm for a specific period (typically a fiscal year). Therefore, in order to accurately capture the return for that period, we use the average level of total equity for the same period as the denominator. The average is computed by adding the beginning and ending total equity balances and then dividing by two.

FYI Whenever we compare an income statement amount with a balance sheet amount, the balance sheet amount should be the *average* balance for the period (beginning balance plus ending balance divided by 2) rather than the year-end balance.

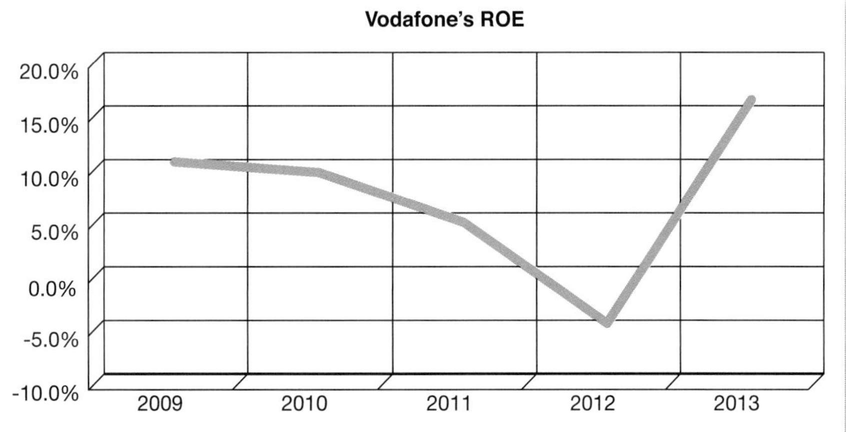

Vodafone's ROE was 15.68% in 2013. This return is computed as £11,312 million/[{£72,488 million + £71,781 million}/2]. Vodafone's ROE fluctuated between 2009 and 2013, ranging from a high of 15.68% in 2013 to a low of −5.25% in 2012.

ROE is widely used by analysts, investors, and managers as a key overall measure of company performance. Billionaire investor Warren Buffett highlights ROE as part of his acquisition criteria: "businesses earning good returns on equity while employing little or no debt." Companies can use debt to increase their return on equity, but too much debt increases risk as the failure to make required debt payments is likely to yield many legal consequences, including bankruptcy. This is one reason why many analysts focus on returns generated by assets used in operations, rather than on returns produced by increasing the amount of debt financing. Next, we discuss each of these sources of return in more detail.

Return on Assets (ROA)

ROE measures the return on the investment made by the firm's shareholders. In contrast, **return on assets (ROA)** measures the return earned on each dollar that the firm invests in assets. By focusing on the asset side of the balance sheet, ROA captures the returns generated by the firm's operating and investing activities, without regard for how those activities are financed. ROA is defined as:

$$\textbf{Return on assets (ROA)} = \frac{\textbf{Earnings without interest expense (EWI)}}{\textbf{Average total assets}}$$

Average total assets is computed in much the same way that we calculated average equity for ROE. We add the beginning and ending balances in total assets and then divide by two. The numerator in this ratio, **earnings without interest expense (EWI)**, is defined to be:

$$\textbf{Earnings without interest expense (EWI)} = \textbf{Net income} + [\textbf{Interest expense} \times (1 - \textbf{Statutory tax rate})]$$

EWI measures the income generated by the firm before taking into account any of its financing costs. Interest costs should be excluded from the ROA calculation so that return is measured without the effect of debt financing. Because interest expense is subtracted when net income is calculated, it must be added back to net income when we compute EWI. However, interest expense is tax deductible and, as such, it reduces the firm's tax obligation. That is, interest expense produces a tax *savings* for the firm. This tax savings is equal to the interest expense times the statutory tax rate. In order to eliminate the full effect of interest cost on EWI, we must add back the interest expense *net* of the resulting tax savings. To accomplish this, we multiply the interest expense by (1 − the statutory tax rate). This amount is then added to net income to get EWI. Thus, we can compute ROA as follows:

$$\textbf{Return on assets (ROA)} = \frac{\textbf{Net income} + [\textbf{Interest expense} \times (1 - \textbf{Statutory tax rate})]}{(\textbf{Beginning total assets} + \textbf{Ending total assets}) / 2}$$

ROA is an important measure of how well a company's management has utilised assets to earn a profit. If ROA is high, the firm can pay its interest costs to creditors and still have sufficient resources left over to distribute to shareholders as a dividend or to reinvest in the firm.

Vodafone's ROA was 9.6% in 2013. Vodafone's return is computed as follows:[1]

$$\textbf{ROA} = \frac{\textbf{£11,312 million} + [\textbf{£1,554 million} \times (1 - 24\%)]}{(\textbf{£138,324 million} + \textbf{£121,840 million})/2} = \textbf{9.6\%}$$

Vodafone's return on assets fluctuated between 2009 and 2013 from a low of −2.01% in 2012 to a high of 9.6% in 2013.

Return on Financial Leverage (ROFL)

The principal difference between ROE and ROA is the effect that liabilities (including debt financing) have on the return measure. ROA is calculated so that it is independent of financing costs, whereas ROE is computed net of the cost of debt financing. **Financial leverage** refers to the effect that liabilities (including debt financing) have on ROE. A firm's management can increase the return to shareholders (ROE) by effectively using financial leverage. On the other hand, too much financial leverage can be risky. To help gauge the effect that financial leverage has on a firm, the **return on financial leverage (ROFL)** is defined as:

$$\textbf{ROFL} = \textbf{ROE} - \textbf{ROA}$$

This return metric captures the amount of ROE that can be attributed to financial leverage. In the case of Vodafone, the ROFL is 6.08% (15.68% − 9.6%). The impact of financial leverage on Vodafone's ROE is illustrated in Exhibit 5.4. The height of each bar in the graph reflects Vodafone's ROE for that year. Each bar is split into two components—ROA for the same year (the lower portion of each bar) and ROFL (the upper portion of each bar).

[1] In 2013, the statutory tax rate for corporations in the UK was 24%.

EXHIBIT 5.4 Contribution of Financial Leverage to Vodafone's ROE

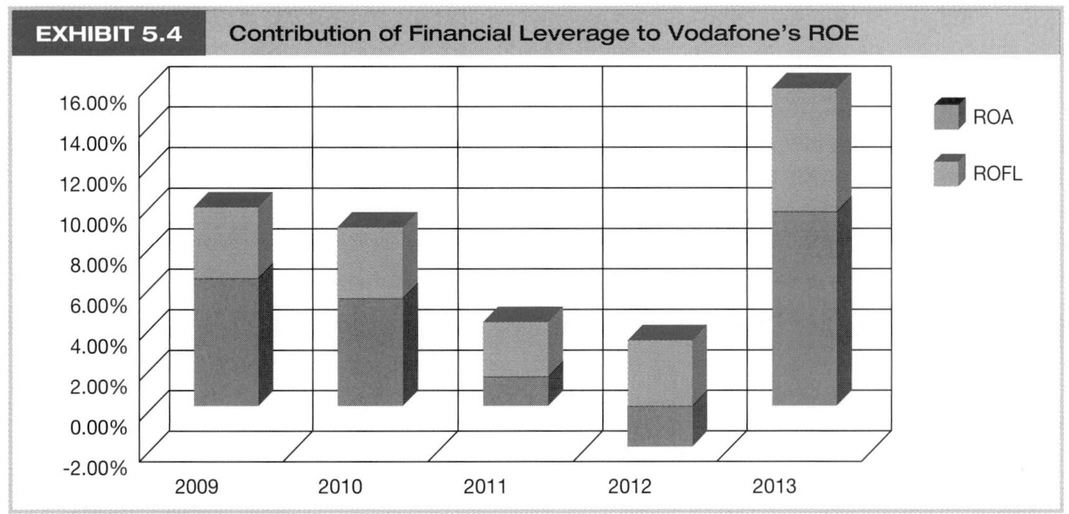

Later in this chapter, we examine the effects of financial leverage more closely and discuss several ratios that measure liquidity and solvency. These ratios help us to evaluate the risk associated with using financial leverage. In Appendix 5C, we present an alternative derivation of ROFL.

MID-CHAPTER REVIEW 2

Required

Refer to the financial statements for **China Mobile Limited** presented in Mid-Chapter Review 1 earlier in this chapter. Calculate China Mobile's ROE, ROA and ROFL for 2013.

The solution to this review problem can be found on page 265.

Disaggregating ROA

LO3 Disaggregate ROA into profitability (profit margin) and efficiency (asset turnover) components.

We can gain further insights into return on investment by disaggregating ROA into performance drivers that capture profitability and efficiency. ROA can be restated as the product of two ratios—profit margin and asset turnover—by simultaneously multiplying and dividing ROA by sales revenue:

$$\text{ROA} = \frac{\textbf{Earnings without interest expense}}{\textbf{Average total assets}} = \underbrace{\frac{\textbf{Earnings without interest expense}}{\textbf{Sales revenue}}}_{\text{Profit Margin}} \times \underbrace{\frac{\textbf{Sales revenue}}{\textbf{Average total assets}}}_{\text{Asset Turnover}}$$

The first ratio on the right-hand side of the above relationship is the **profit margin (PM)**. This ratio measures the profit, without interest expense, that is generated from each dollar of sales revenue. All other things being equal, a higher profit margin is preferable. Profit margin is affected by the level of gross profit that the company earns on its sales (sales revenue minus cost of goods sold), which depends on product prices and the cost of manufacturing or purchasing its product. It is also affected by operating expenses that are required to support sales of products or services. These include wages and salaries, marketing, research and development, as well as depreciation and other **capacity costs**. Finally, profit margin is affected by the level of competition, which affects product pricing, and by the company's operating strategy, which affects operating costs, especially discretionary costs such as advertising and research and development.

In 2013 Vodafone's profit margin ratio was 32.6%, computed as follows (£ millions):

$$\textbf{Profit margin (PM)} = \frac{\textbf{Earnings without interest expense (EWI)}}{\textbf{Sales revenue}} = \frac{\textbf{£11,312} + [\textbf{£1,554} \times (1 - 24\%)]}{\textbf{£38,346}} = \textbf{32.6\%}$$

This ratio indicates that each pound of sales revenue produced 32.6 pence of after-tax profit before financing costs. Vodafone's profit margin for 2013 was up from prior years. In 2009, the company reported a profit margin ratio of 22.0% and experienced a steady decline until 2012, when the profit margin was −7.2%. However, we need to exercise caution when drawing any conclusions based on Vodafone's profitability in 2013. As explained earlier, Vodafone received a large tax credit in 2013, which helped it turn a profit and resulted in an impressive profit margin. It is difficult to tell whether the upward trend in profit margin will continue next year. The profit margin ratio over the period 2009–2013 is graphed in Exhibit 5.5.

EXHIBIT 5.5 Vodafone's Profit Margin Ratio, 2009-2013

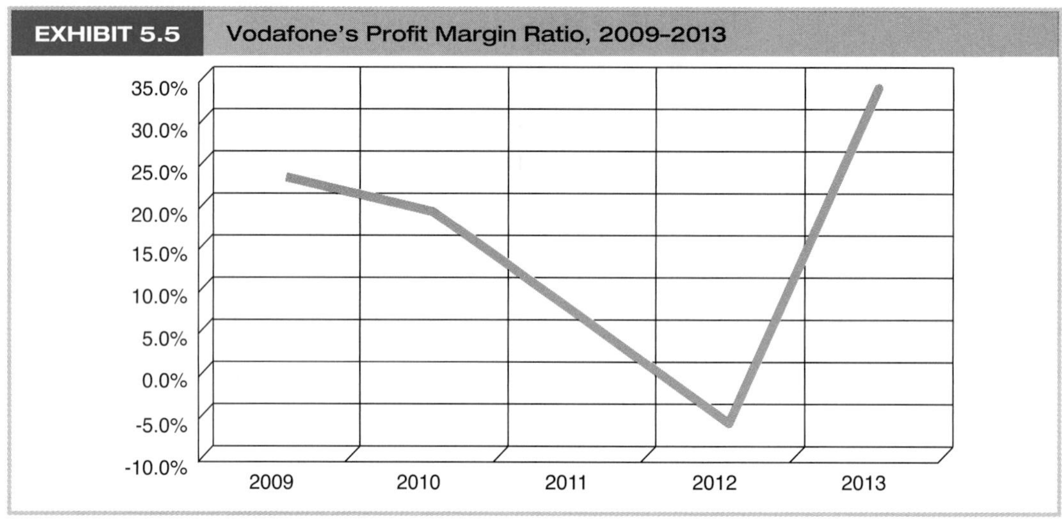

The **asset turnover (AT)** ratio reveals insights into a company's productivity and efficiency. This metric measures the level of sales generated by each dollar that a company invests in assets. A high asset turnover ratio suggests that assets are being used efficiently so, all other things being equal, a high asset turnover ratio is preferable. The ratio is affected by inventory management practices, credit policies, and most of all, the technology employed to produce a company's products or deliver its services.

The asset turnover ratio can be improved by increasing the level of sales for a given level of assets, or by efficiently managing assets. For many companies, efficiently managing working capital—primarily inventories and receivables—is the easiest way to limit investment in assets and increase turnover. On the other hand, it is usually more difficult to increase asset turnover by managing investment in long-term assets. Capital intensive companies, such as those in the communications or energy production industries, tend to have lower asset turnover ratios (often less than 1.0) because the production technology employed by these firms requires a large investment in property, plant and equipment. Retail companies, on the other hand, tend to have a relatively small investment in plant assets. As a result, they tend to have higher asset turnover ratios (sometimes over 3.0). These ratios are also affected by leasing and other methods of using assets that do not appear on the balance sheet. Leasing and other off-balance-sheet financing methods are discussed in Chapter 10.

Vodafone's asset turnover ratio is computed as follows (£ millions):

$$\textbf{Asset turnover (AT)} = \frac{\textbf{Sales revenue}}{\textbf{Average total assets}} = \frac{\textbf{£38,346}}{\textbf{(£138,324 + £121,840)/2}} = \textbf{0.295}$$

The ratio indicates that each pound of assets generated 29.5 pence in sales revenue in 2013. As illustrated by the graphic in Exhibit 5.6, Vodafone reported an asset turnover ratio between 0.27 and 0.30 over the period 2009–2013. There is less than 10% variation in this ratio from year to year, indicating no significant change in the company's efficiency in utilising its assets. Vodafone's low asset turnover ratio is typical of the telecommunications industry.

EXHIBIT 5.6 Vodafone's Asset Turnover Ratio, 2009-2013

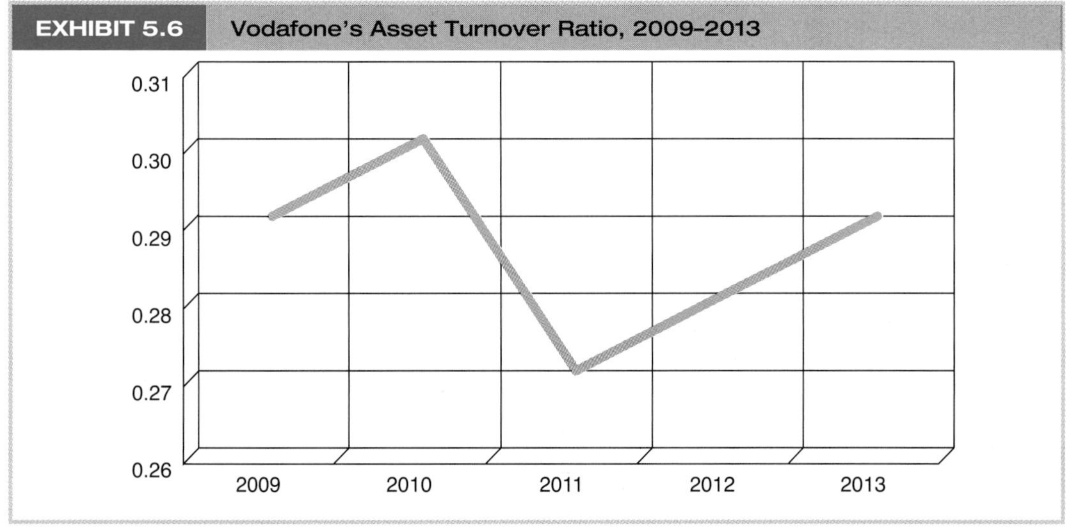

YOU MAKE THE CALL

You are the Entrepreneur You are analysing the performance of your start-up company. Your analysis of ROA reveals the following (industry benchmarks in parentheses): ROA is 16% (10%), PM is 18% (17%), and AT is 0.89 (0.59). What interpretations do you draw that are useful for managing your company? [Answer, page 245]

Trade-Off Between Profit Margin and Asset Turnover ROA is the product of profit margin and asset turnover. By decomposing ROA in this way, we can identify the sources that led to an increase in Vodafone's ROA between 2012 and 2013:

	ROA	=	Profit Margin	×	Asset Turnover
2012:	−2.0%	=	−7.2%	×	0.278
2013:	9.6%	=	32.6%	×	0.295

Between 2012 and 2013, Vodafone's profit margin increased from −7.2% to 32.6%, while asset turnover increased from 0.278 to 0.295. As reported in the company's financial statements, revenues increased slightly and average total assets declined, leading to a higher asset turnover ratio. The increase in revenue was driven by revenue growth in the company's emerging markets, and it was partially offset by revenue declines in Europe. The decline in average total assets was mainly attributable to the sale of the company's 45% interest in Verizon Wireless. Although there were acquisitions as well, average total assets declined by 5% in 2013. As mentioned earlier when we examined Vodafone's common-size income statement, the increase in profit margin was mainly due to a large income tax credit, which may not recur next year. On the other hand, the company experienced increases in cost of sales, in selling and distribution expenses, and in administrative expenses as a percentage of sales revenue. Hence, one of the opportunities for management to increase ROA in the future would be to focus its efforts on increasing profitability by better managing its cost structure.

Basic economics tells us that any successful business must earn an acceptable return on investment if it wants to attract capital from investors and survive. Yet, there are an infinite number of combinations of asset turnover and profit margin that will yield a given ROA. The trade-off between profit margin and asset turnover is heavily influenced by a company's business model. A company can attempt to increase its ROA by targeting higher profit margins, or by increasing its asset turnover. To an extent, this trade-off is the result of strategic decisions made by management. However, to a greater extent, the relative mix of margin and turnover is dictated by the industry in which the company operates. As mentioned earlier, one determinant of a company's profit margin is its competitive environment, while asset turnover is heavily influenced by the production technology employed. For this reason, companies in the same industry tend to exhibit similar combinations of margin and turnover while comparisons between industries can exhibit much greater variation. That is, within a given industry, differences in the mix of profit margin and asset turnover often reflect the specific strategy employed by each individual firm, while variations between industries are caused by differences in the competitive environment and production technology of each industry.

This trade-off is illustrated in Exhibit 5.7. The solid curved line represents the average ROA for all companies over the period from 2012 through 2014. Each point along that curve represents a combination of asset turnover and profit margin that yields the average ROA. Industries that are plotted near the upper left side of the graph are those that achieve their ROA targets by maintaining a high asset turnover. These industries are often characterised by intense competition and low profit margins. On the other hand, industries in the lower right-hand portion of the graph have lower asset turnover ratios because they typically employ capital-intensive production technologies. At the same time, the competitive environment within these industries allows companies to achieve higher profit margins to offset the lower turnover ratios.

EXHIBIT 5.7 Profit Margin and Turnover Across Industries

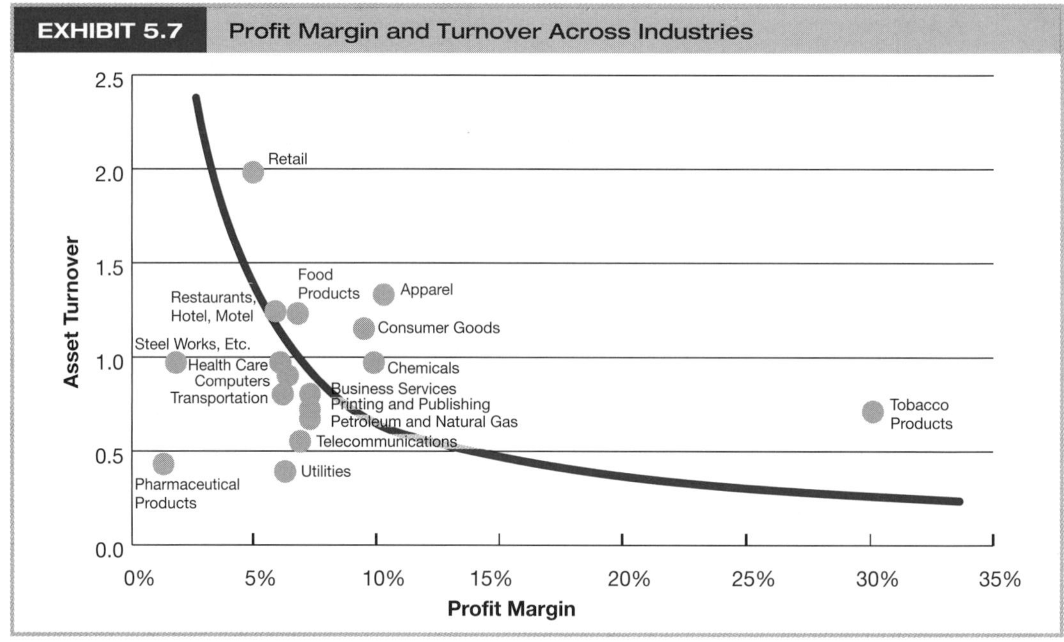

BUSINESS INSIGHT

The DuPont Model Disaggregation of return on equity (ROE) into three components—profitability, turnover, and financial leverage—was initially introduced by the **E.I. DuPont de Nemours and Company** to aid its managers in performance evaluation. DuPont realised that management's focus on profit alone was insufficient because profit can be increased simply by adding investments in low-yielding, but safe, assets. Further, DuPont wanted managers to think like investors and to manage their portfolio of activities using investment principles that allocate scarce investment capital to competing projects based on a goal of maximising return on investment.

The basic DuPont model disaggregates ROE as the product of three ratios as follows:

$$ROE = \underbrace{\frac{\text{Net income}}{\text{Sales}}}_{\text{Net Profit Margin}} \times \underbrace{\frac{\text{Sales}}{\text{Average total assets}}}_{\text{Asset Turnover}} \times \underbrace{\frac{\text{Average total assets}}{\text{Average total equity}}}_{\text{Financial Leverage}}$$

An important limitation of the DuPont model is that net profit margin is measured using net income in the numerator rather than earnings without interest expense (EWI). This means that this measure of profitability is affected by financial leverage—as financial leverage increases, interest expense increases and the net profit margin decreases. As a consequence, the model fails to adequately separate the effects of operating profitability on ROE from the effects of financial leverage. Despite this limitation, the DuPont model is widely used as a simple, straightforward way to disaggregate ROE.

Further Disaggregation of Profit Margin and Asset Turnover While disaggregation of ROA into profit margin and asset turnover yields useful insights into the factors driving company performance, analysts, investors, creditors, and managers often disaggregate these measures even further. The purpose of this analysis is to be more precise about the specific determinants of profitability and efficiency.

To disaggregate profit margin (PM), we examine gross profit on products sold and individual expense accounts that contribute to the total cost of operations. The key ratios include the gross profit margin and expense-to-sales ratios. **Gross profit margin (GPM)** is defined as:

$$\textbf{Gross profit margin (GPM)} = \frac{\textbf{Sales revenue} - \textbf{Cost of goods sold}}{\textbf{Sales revenue}}$$

In 2013, Vodafone's GPM was 27.1% ([£38,346 million − £27,942 million]/£38,346 million). That is, just 27.1 pence of every sales pound was gross profit, while 72.9 pence (72.9%) went to cover the cost of products sold.

Gross profit margin measures the percentage of each sales dollar that is left over after product costs are subtracted. It is easily determined by looking at the common-size income statement. This ratio is discussed in more detail in Chapter 7.

An **expense-to-sales (ETS)** ratio measures the percentage of each sales dollar that goes to cover a specific expense item and is computed by dividing the expense by sales revenue. Expense items that might be examined with ETS ratios include selling, general and administrative (SG&A) expenses, advertising expense, or research and development (R&D) expense, among others. Which specific ETS ratio is appropriate depends on the company being analysed. For instance, advertising expense is an important expense item for a consumer products company, such as **L'Oréal (France)**, while R&D expense is important for an R&D intensive pharmaceutical company, such as **Bayer (Germany)**. Analysts study trends in ETS ratios over time in an effort to uncover clues that might explain changes in profit margin and make predictions about future profitability.

SG&A ETS ratio is computed by dividing selling, distribution, and administrative expenses by net revenue. Vodafone's 2013 SG&A ETS ratio was 19.0% ([£3,033 million + £4,245 million]/£38,346 million). This ratio indicates that 19 pence of every sales pound goes to pay marketing and administrative costs.

To disaggregate asset turnover (AT), we examine individual asset accounts and compare them to sales or cost of goods sold. We focus on three specific turnover ratios—accounts receivable turnover (ART), inventory turnover (INVT), and property, plant and equipment turnover (PPET).

Accounts receivable turnover (ART) is defined as follows:

$$\textbf{Accounts receivable turnover (ART)} = \frac{\textbf{Sales revenue}}{\textbf{Average accounts receivable}}$$

ART measures how many times receivables have been turned (collected) during the period. More turns indicate that accounts receivable are being collected more quickly, while low turnover often indicates difficulty with a company's credit policies. In 2013, Vodafone's ART was 11.11 times (£38,346 million/[{£3,627 million + £3,277 million}/2]). Since Vodafone reports trade and other receivables on its balance sheet, we obtain the amount of accounts receivable from a note to its financial statements. ART is discussed in greater detail in Chapter 6.

Inventory turnover (INVT) is defined as:

$$\textbf{Inventory turnover (INVT)} = \frac{\textbf{Cost of goods sold}}{\textbf{Average inventory}}$$

INVT measures the number of times during a period that total inventory is turned (sold). A high INVT indicates that inventory is managed efficiently. Retail companies, such as **Hudson's Bay (Canada)**, **Tesco (United Kingdom)**, and **Watsons (Hong Kong)** focus a great deal of management attention on maintaining a high INVT ratio. Vodafone's inventory primarily consists of mobile handsets.

In 2013, its INVT was 13.5 times (£5,340 million/[{£441 million + £353 million}/2]).[2] This ratio is discussed further in Chapter 7.

Property, plant and equipment turnover (PPET) measures the sales revenue produced for each dollar of investment in PP&E. It is computed as the ratio of sales to average PP&E assets:

$$\textbf{Property, plant \& equipment turnover (PPET)} = \frac{\textbf{Sales revenue}}{\textbf{Average PP \& E}}$$

PPET provides insights into asset utilisation and how efficiently a company operates given its production technology. In 2013, Vodafone's PPET was 1.9 times (£38,346 million/[{£22,851 million + £17,584 million}/2]). Chapter 8 revisits this ratio.

In the next section, we examine ratios that focus on liquidity and solvency. These ratios help us evaluate the risk associated with debt financing and weigh the costs and benefits of financial leverage. Exhibit 5.8 presents a schematic summary of the disaggregation of ROE. It identifies the two primary components of ROE—ROA and ROFL—and highlights the disaggregation of ROA into profit margin and asset turnover, along with the drivers of these ratios. In addition, the link between ROFL and liquidity and solvency analysis is highlighted.

EXHIBIT 5.8 ROE Disaggregation

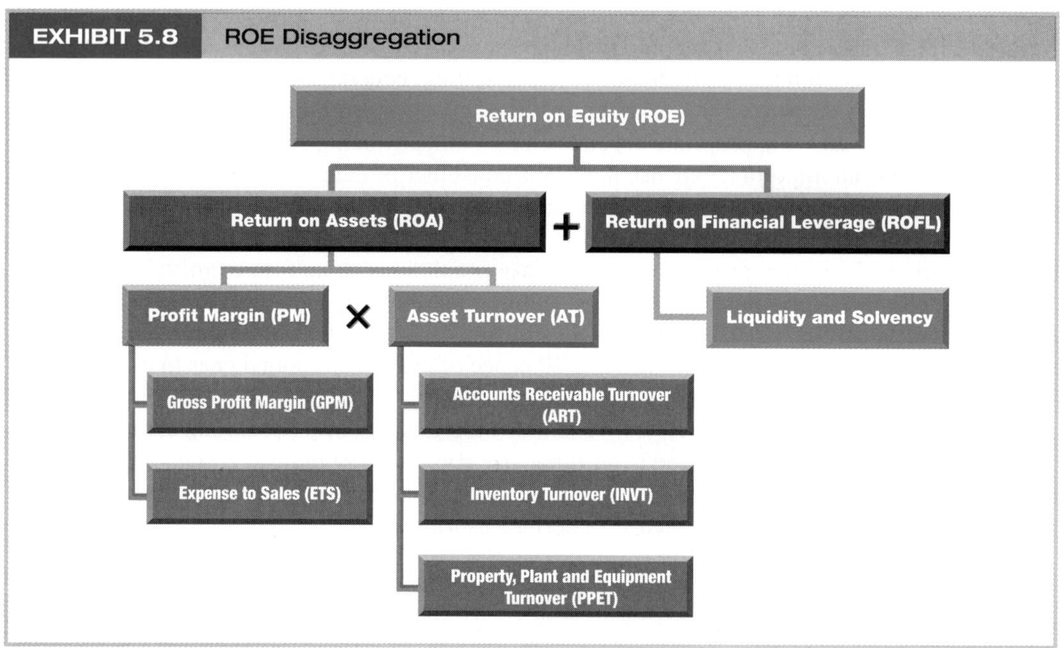

MID-CHAPTER REVIEW 3

Required

Refer to the financial statements for China Mobile Limited presented in Mid-Chapter Review 1 earlier in this chapter.

1. Calculate China Mobile's profit margin (PM) and asset turnover (AT) ratios for 2013.
2. Show that ROA = PM × AT using China Mobile's financial data.
3. Calculate China Mobile's gross profit margin (GPM), accounts receivable turnover (ART), inventory turnover (INVT), and property, plant and equipment turnover (PPET) ratios for 2013.
4. Evaluate China Mobile's ratios in comparison to those of Vodafone.

The solution to this review problem can be found on pages 265–266.

[2] Since Vodafone is also a service provider, the cost of sales reported on the balance sheet only partly relates to the sale of inventory. In order to obtain a true picture of inventory turnover, we use the cost of sales related to inventory (£5,340) available from a note to its financial statements.

LIQUIDITY AND SOLVENCY

LO4 Compute and interpret measures of liquidity and solvency.

Companies can use debt to increase financial leverage and boost ROE. The increase in ROE due to the use of debt is called *return on financial leverage (ROFL)*. The primary advantage of debt financing is that it is typically less costly than equity financing; the cost of debt financing is currently a little over 2%, while equity financing averages about 8%.[3]

Exhibit 5.9 illustrates a comparison between two companies—one (Company A) is financed with 100% equity and the other (Company B) is financed with 50% debt and 50% equity. Both companies have $1,000 in (average) assets and EWI of $100, producing an ROA of 10% ($100/$1,000). Because Company A does not use debt financing, average equity equals average total assets. Also, it reports no interest expense in its income statement so net income equals EWI. Therefore, for Company A, ROE = ROA, and its ROFL = 0%.

EXHIBIT 5.9 The Effect of Debt Financing on ROE (ROA > interest rate)

	Company A	Company B
Assets (average)	$1,000	$1,000
EWI	100	100
ROA (EWI/Assets)	10%	10%
Equity (average)	$1,000	$ 500
Debt	0	500
Interest expense (4% of debt)	0	20
Net income (EWI − interest)	100	80
ROE (Net income/equity)	10%	16%
ROFL (ROE − ROA)	0%	6%

In contrast, Company B has $500 of equity financing and $500 of debt financing. It reports interest expense of $20 ($500 × 4%) leaving net income of $80 ($100 − $20). Company B's ROE is 16% ($80/$500), which means that its ROFL is 6% (16% − 10%). Company B has made effective use of debt financing to increase its ROE. As long as a company's ROA is greater than its cost of debt, its ROFL will be positive.[4]

We might further ask: If a higher ROE is desirable, why don't companies use as much debt financing as possible? The answer is that there are risks associated with debt financing. As the amount of debt in a company's balance sheet increases, so does the burden of interest costs on income and debt payments on cash flows. In the best of times, financial leverage increases returns to shareholders (ROE). In contrast, when earnings are depressed, financial leverage has the effect of making a bad year even worse. In the worst case, too much debt can lead to financial distress and even bankruptcy.

To illustrate how debt financing can reduce shareholder returns, Exhibit 5.10 compares Company A and Company B in a year when reported profits are lower than in the previous example. Both companies have $1,000 in (average) assets and both report EWI of $30, producing an ROA of 3% ($30/$1,000). Company A does not use debt financing, so its ROE = 3%, and its ROFL = 0%. Because Company B has $500 of equity and $500 of debt, it reports interest expense of $20 ($500 × 4%) leaving net income of $10 ($30 − $20). Company B's ROE is 2% ($10/$500), which means that its ROFL is −1% (2% − 3%). That is, for Company B, the use of financial leverage has a negative effect on ROE. As this example illustrates, whenever ROA is less than the interest rate on the debt, debt financing reduces the return to shareholders.

As a general rule, shareholders benefit from increased use of debt financing provided that the assets financed with the debt earn a return that exceeds the cost of the debt. However, increasing levels of debt result in successively higher interest rates charged by creditors. At some point, the cost of debt exceeds the return on assets that a company can expect from the debt financing. Thereafter, further debt financing does not make economic sense. The market, in essence, places a limit on the amount that a company can borrow.

[3] Equity financing is more costly than debt because, in the event that the firm fails, creditors collect their investment first, while shareholders collect the residual. Shareholders, therefore, demand a greater return on investment to compensate for assuming greater risk.

[4] The interest cost on debt is tax deductible. Therefore, the relevant cost of debt to use to compare to ROA is the after-tax interest rate.

EXHIBIT 5.10 The Effect of Debt Financing on ROE (ROA < interest rate)

	Company A	Company B
Assets (average)	$1,000	$1,000
EWI	30	30
ROA (EWI/Assets)	3%	3%
Equity (average)	$1,000	$ 500
Debt	0	500
Interest expense (4% of debt)	0	20
Net income (EWI − interest)	30	10
ROE (Net income/equity)	3%	2%
ROFL (ROE − ROA)	0%	−1%

In addition, creditors usually require a company to execute a loan agreement that places various restrictions on its operating activities. These restrictions, called **covenants**, help safeguard debtholders in the face of increased risk. This occurs because debtholders do not have a voice on the board of directors like shareholders do. These debt covenants impose a "cost" on the company beyond that of the interest rate, and these covenants are more stringent as a company increases its reliance on debt financing.

The median ratio of total liabilities to total equity, which measures the relative use of debt versus equity in a company's capital structure, is just over 1.0 for all publicly traded companies. This means that the typical company relies more on debt financing than on equity. However, the relative use of debt varies considerably across industries as illustrated in Exhibit 5.11.

EXHIBIT 5.11 Median Ratio of Liabilities to Equity for Selected Industries

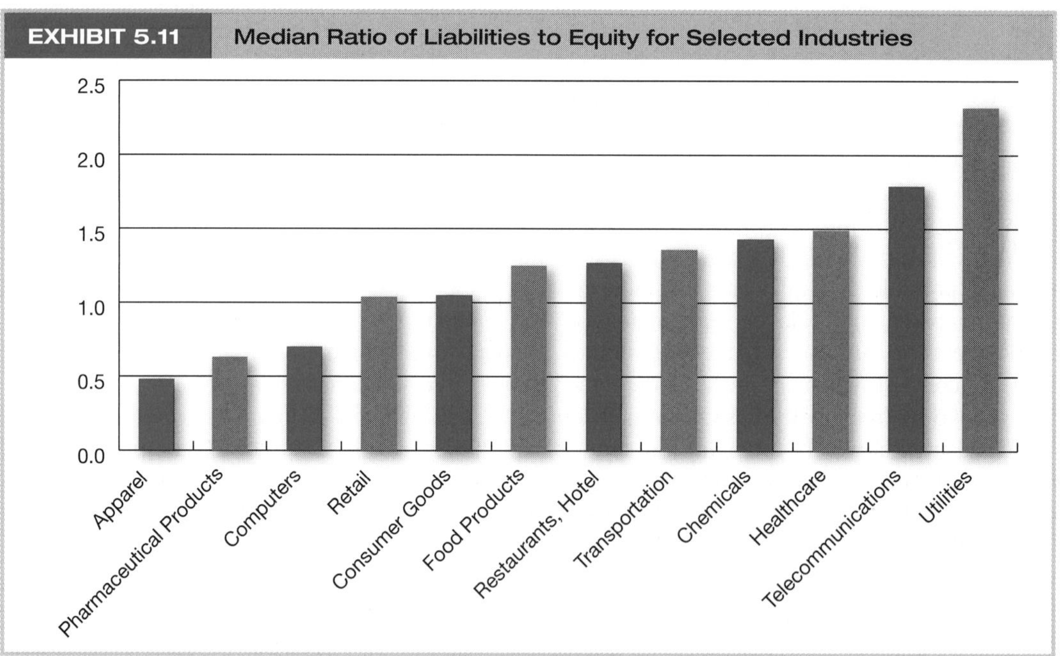

Companies in the utilities industry have relatively high proportions of debt. Because the utilities industry is regulated, profits and cash flows are relatively certain and stable and, as a result, utility companies can support a higher debt level. The healthcare and telecommunications industries also utilise a relatively high proportion of debt. These industries are not regulated, but their heavy investments in property, plant and equipment require significant long-term debt. At the lower end of debt financing are pharmaceuticals and apparel companies. Historically, these industries have been characterised by relatively uncertain profits and cash flows. In addition, success in these industries depends heavily on intellectual property and human resources devoted to research and product development. These "assets" do not appear on the balance sheet and cannot be used as collateral when borrowing funds. Consequently, they use less debt in their capital structures.

To summarise, companies can effectively use debt to increase ROE. Although it reduces financing costs, debt increases **default risk**: the risk that the company will be unable to repay debt when it comes due. Because of this risk, analysts carefully examine a company's financial statements to determine if it is using debt financing effectively and judiciously.

The core of our analysis relating to debt is the examination of a company's ability to generate cash to *service* its debt (that is, to make required debt payments of both interest and principal). Analysts, investors, and creditors are primarily concerned about whether the company has sufficient cash available or, alternatively, whether it is able to generate the required cash in the future to cover its debt obligations. The analysis of available cash is called **liquidity analysis**. The analysis of the company's ability to generate sufficient cash in the future is called **solvency analysis** (so named because a bankrupt company is said to be "insolvent").

Liquidity Analysis

Liquidity refers to cash availability: how much cash a company has, and how much it can raise on short notice. The most common ratios used to assess the degree of liquidity are the current ratio and the quick ratio, which were first introduced in Chapter 2, as well as the operating cash flow to current liabilities ratio, which was introduced in Chapter 4. Each of these ratios links required near-term payments to cash available in the near term.

Current Ratio *Current assets* are those assets that a company expects to convert into cash within the next operating cycle, which is typically a year. *Current liabilities* are those liabilities that come due within the next year. An excess of current assets over current liabilities (Current assets − Current liabilities), is known as *net working capital* or simply **working capital**. Positive working capital implies more expected cash inflows than cash outflows in the short run. The **current ratio** expresses working capital as a ratio and is computed as follows:

$$\textbf{Current ratio} = \frac{\textbf{Current assets}}{\textbf{Current liabilities}}$$

A current ratio greater than 1.0 implies positive working capital. Both working capital and the current ratio consider existing balance sheet data only and ignore cash inflows from future sales or other sources. The current ratio is more commonly used than working capital because ratios allow comparisons across companies of different size. Generally, companies prefer a higher current ratio; however, an excessively high current ratio indicates inefficient asset use. Furthermore, a current ratio less than 1.0 is not always problematic for at least two reasons:

1. A cash-and-carry company (like a grocery store) can have little or no receivables (and a low current ratio), but consistently large operating cash inflows ensure the company will be sufficiently liquid. A company can efficiently manage its working capital by minimising receivables and inventories and maximising payables. **Carrefour (France)** and **Tesco (United Kingdom)**, for example, use their buying power to exact extended credit terms from suppliers. Consequently, because both companies are essentially cash-and-carry companies, their current ratios are less than 1.0 and both are sufficiently liquid.
2. A service company will typically report little or no inventories among its current assets. In addition, some service companies do not report significant accounts receivable. If short-term borrowings and accrued expenses exceed cash and temporary investments, a current ratio of less than 1.0 would result. **Vodafone** is an example of such a firm.

The aim of current-ratio analysis is to discern if a company is having, or is likely to have, difficulty meeting its short-term obligations. If a company cannot cover its short-term debts with cash provided by operations, it may need to liquidate current assets to meet its obligations. In 2013, **Vodafone**'s current ratio was 0.99 (£24,722 million/£25,039 million). At the end of 2012, its current ratio was 0.76 (£21,649 million/£28,369 million).

Quick Ratio The **quick ratio** is a variant of the current ratio. It focuses on quick assets, which are those assets likely to be converted to cash within a relatively short period of time, usually less than 90 days. Specifically, quick assets include cash, marketable securities, and accounts receivable; they exclude inventories and prepaid assets. The quick ratio is defined as follows:

$$\text{Quick ratio} = \frac{\text{Cash} + \text{Short-term securities} + \text{Accounts receivable}}{\text{Current liabilities}}$$

The quick ratio reflects on a company's ability to meet its current liabilities without liquidating inventories that could require markdowns. It is a more stringent test of liquidity than the current ratio and may provide more insight into company liquidity in some cases.

In 2013, Vodafone's quick ratio was 0.73 ([£10,134 million + £4,419 million + £3,627 million]/£25,039 million), which was up from 0.57 in 2012 ([£7,531 million + £5,350 million + £3,277 million]/£28,369 million). Although the current ratio and the quick ratio were less than 1.0, both ratios increased in 2013, indicating improvement in Vodafone's liquidity.

Operating Cash Flow to Current Liabilities The **operating cash flow to current liabilities (OCFCL)** ratio was introduced in Chapter 4 and is defined as follows:

$$\text{Operating cash flow to current liabilities (OCFCL)} = \frac{\text{Cash flow from operations}}{\text{Average current liabilities}}$$

Cash flow from operations is taken directly from the statement of cash flows. It represents the net amount of cash derived from operating activities during the year. Ultimately the ability of a company to pay its debts is determined by whether its operations can generate enough cash to cover debt payments. Thus, a higher OCFCL ratio is generally preferred by analysts.

In 2013, Vodafone reported an OCFCL ratio of 0.23 (£6,227 million/[{£25,039 million + £28,369 million}/2]). Its 2012 OCFCL ratio was 0.35 (£8,824 million/[{£28,369 million + £21,623 million}/2]). Unlike the current and quick ratios, Vodafone's OCFCL ratio decreased from 2012 to 2013, suggesting that the improvement in liquidity was not driven by operations. Instead, the proceeds from the disposal of Verizon Wireless contributed significantly to the company's improving liquidity in 2013. Exhibit 5.12 provides a plot of all three ratios between 2009 and 2013. While the current ratio and quick ratios improved over time, the OCFCL ratio has been declining since 2009 and it should be examined further.

EXHIBIT 5.12 Vodafone's Liquidity Ratios, 2009-2013

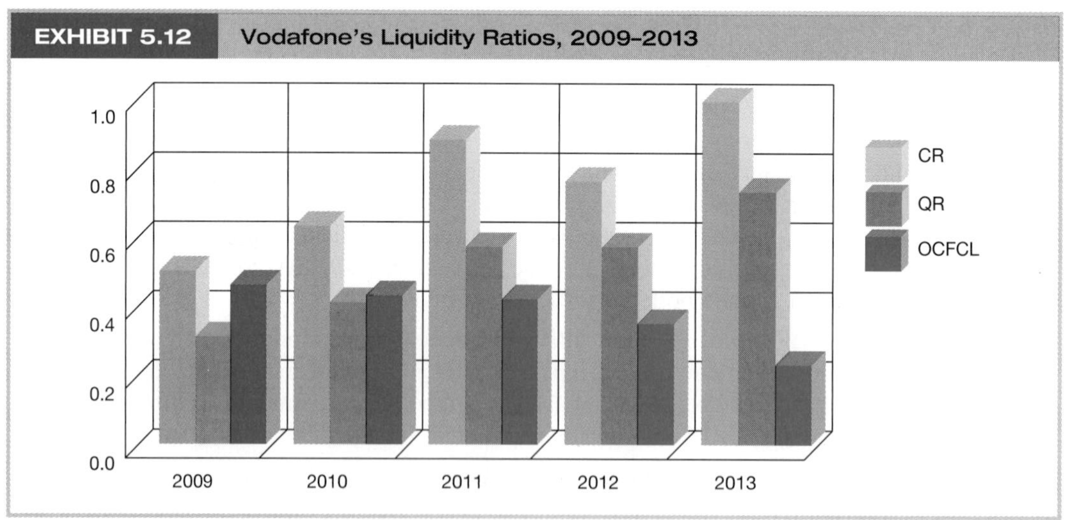

Solvency Analysis

Solvency refers to a company's ability to meet its debt obligations, including both periodic interest payments and the repayment of the principal amount borrowed. Solvency is crucial because an insolvent company is a failed company. There are two general approaches to measuring solvency. The first approach uses balance sheet data and assesses the proportion of capital raised from creditors. The second approach uses income statement data and assesses the profit generated relative to debt payment obligations. We discuss each approach in turn.

Debt-to-Equity The **debt-to-equity ratio**, which was introduced in Chapter 1, is a useful tool for the first type of solvency analysis. It is defined as follows:

$$\textbf{Debt-to-equity ratio} = \frac{\textbf{Total liabilities}}{\textbf{Total equity}}$$

This ratio conveys how reliant a company is on creditor financing (which are fixed claims) compared with equity financing (which are flexible or residual claims). A higher ratio indicates less solvency, and more risk. In 2013 Vodafone's debt-to-equity ratio was 0.70 (£50,059 million/£71,781 million). Compared with the industry average of 1.79 (from Exhibit 5.13), Vodafone's debt-to-equity ratios over the period 2009–2013 were considered low. In 2013, Vodafone further paid down its debt using the cash received from the sale of its interest in Verizon Wireless.

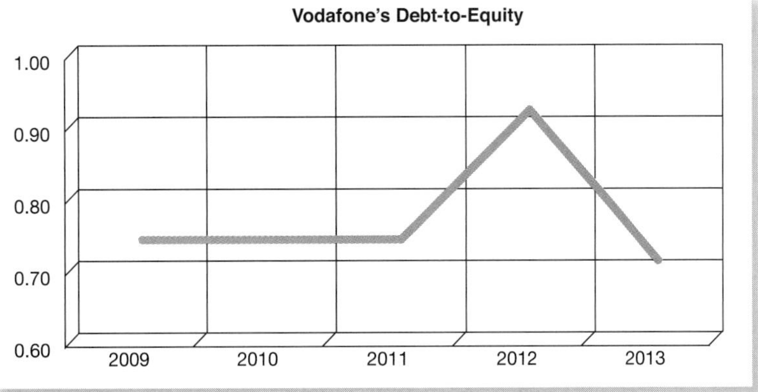

In practice, analysts use a variety of solvency measures that are similar to the debt-to-equity ratio. One variant of this ratio considers a company's *long-term* debt divided by equity. This approach assumes that current liabilities are repaid from current assets (so-called self-liquidating). Thus, it assumes that creditors and shareholders need only focus on the relative proportion of long-term capital.

EXHIBIT 5.13 Industry Ratios: Medians of Companies with Market Capitalisation > $500 Million (2012–2014)

	ROE	ROA	ROFL	PM	GPM	AT	ART	INVT	PPET	DE	TIE	CR	QR	OCFCL
Apparel.	16.3%	9.5%	5.4%	10.3%	50.5%	1.34	9.79	3.20	7.87	0.48	32.36	2.84	1.54	0.75
Business Services.	9.9%	5.0%	3.7%	7.3%	64.7%	0.81	5.64	28.30	10.52	0.83	9.22	1.80	1.62	0.48
Chemicals	18.1%	8.1%	8.6%	9.9%	32.7%	0.98	6.53	5.17	3.13	1.43	8.95	2.18	1.24	0.54
Computers.	9.8%	5.4%	4.0%	6.4%	52.5%	0.91	5.52	7.16	11.00	0.70	12.44	2.07	1.71	0.45
Consumer Goods	13.9%	8.3%	6.7%	9.5%	47.8%	1.16	7.19	5.44	6.67	1.05	14.37	1.70	1.11	0.43
Food Products.	13.3%	7.0%	5.9%	6.8%	32.4%	1.24	12.26	6.29	4.80	1.25	7.48	1.82	0.88	0.52
Healthcare	11.7%	5.9%	5.3%	6.1%	21.9%	0.98	7.39	44.73	4.74	1.49	4.39	1.52	1.16	0.60
Petroleum	8.5%	5.3%	2.9%	7.3%	45.4%	0.68	6.83	15.94	0.44	1.13	3.87	1.26	0.84	1.10
Pharmaceutical	−3.1%	−3.1%	−1.1%	1.3%	62.6%	0.44	5.85	2.39	4.48	0.63	3.50	4.14	3.50	0.11
Printing & Publishing. . .	12.5%	5.7%	7.1%	7.3%	55.5%	0.73	6.58	19.82	7.62	1.52	5.45	1.32	0.91	0.43
Restaurants, Hotel.	14.5%	6.4%	6.7%	5.9%	26.0%	1.25	30.37	55.46	2.37	1.27	6.12	1.02	0.66	0.78
Retail	14.6%	7.5%	6.0%	5.0%	34.0%	1.99	46.25	5.40	6.77	1.04	9.75	1.70	0.63	0.51
Steel.	5.6%	3.4%	1.4%	1.8%	17.5%	0.98	7.68	5.26	2.84	1.19	3.44	2.34	1.22	0.42
Telecommunications. . .	12.1%	6.1%	5.2%	6.9%	51.2%	0.56	7.13	25.51	1.65	1.79	3.38	1.14	0.91	0.69
Tobacco.	13.1%	14.2%	9.0%	30.1%	52.7%	0.72	40.01	3.34	7.84	2.15	9.36	1.02	0.49	0.49
Transportation.	11.1%	5.5%	4.6%	6.2%	30.0%	0.81	10.24	32.27	1.00	1.36	4.22	1.33	1.09	0.69
Utilities.	9.6%	4.1%	5.4%	6.3%	28.9%	0.40	7.47	13.55	0.46	2.32	3.12	0.93	0.59	0.66
Overall	11.0%	5.7%	5.3%	7.1%	34.6%	0.87	7.19	5.48	4.77	1.25	7.35	1.81	1.19	0.48

Times Interest Earned The second type of solvency analysis compares profits to liabilities. This approach assesses how much operating profit is available to cover debt obligations. A common measure for this type of solvency analysis is the **times interest earned (TIE)** or interest coverage ratio (see Chapter 9) defined as follows:

$$\textbf{Times interest earned} = \frac{\textbf{Earnings before interest expense and taxes (EBIT)}}{\textbf{Interest expense}}$$

The times interest earned ratio reflects the operating income available to pay interest expense. The underlying assumption is that only interest needs to be paid because the principal will be refinanced. This ratio is sometimes abbreviated as EBIT/I. The numerator is similar to earnings without interest (EWI), but it is *pretax* instead of after tax.

Management wants the TIE ratio to be sufficiently high so that there is little risk of default. Vodafone's 2013 EBIT, the numerator of the ratio, was calculated by adding the financing costs of £1,554 million (£1,596 million in 2012) to its earnings before taxation. Since the company generated before tax losses of £5,270 million in 2012 and £3,483 million in 2013, its EBIT were negative in both years. Calculating TIE on negative EBIT is not meaningful, because the company cannot service its debt from a loss. However, it is important to keep in mind that it is not necessarily an indication of default. This is because the company can cover its interest payments from sources other than operations. As we might recall, the sale of Vodafone's interest in Verizon Wireless resulted in ample funds, which allowed the company not only to cover its interest payments, but also to reduce its overall debt. In 2011, Vodafone's TIE ratio was 3.34 ([£4,144 million + £1,768 million]/£4,144 million), indicating that its EBIT was sufficient to cover the interest expense 3.34 times.

There are many variations of solvency and liquidity analysis and the ratios used. The basic idea is to construct measures that reflect a company's credit risk exposure. There is not one "best" financial leverage ratio. Instead, as financial statement users, we want to use measures that capture the risk we are most concerned with. It is also important to compute the ratios ourselves to ensure we know what is included and excluded from each ratio.

RESEARCH INSIGHT

Using Ratios to Predict Bankruptcy Several research studies have examined the use of various financial ratios, such as those discussed in this chapter, to predict financial distress of large companies. In a pioneering study, Professor Edward Altman used discriminant analysis to develop a method for scoring a company's credit risk and using that score to predict bankruptcy. Altman's model produced a **Z-score** as follows:

$$\text{Z-score} = 1.2 \times \frac{\text{Working capital}}{\text{Total assets}} + 1.4 \times \frac{\text{Retained earnings}}{\text{Total assets}} + 3.3 \times \frac{\text{EBIT}}{\text{Total assets}} + 0.6 \times \frac{\text{Market value of equity}}{\text{Total liabilities}} + 0.99 \times \frac{\text{Sales}}{\text{Total assets}}$$

The first variable is a measure of liquidity. The second and third variables measure long-term and short-term profitability. The fourth variable captures a company's financial leverage and the last variable is asset turnover. A Z-score greater than 3.0 indicates a healthy company, while a Z-score below 1.8 suggests a high potential for near-term bankruptcy. The model was 95% accurate at predicting bankruptcy one year in advance and 72% accurate two years in advance. Today, credit scoring models like Altman's Z-score are used by nearly all financial institutions and many other businesses to evaluate credit risk. (Altman, E., "Financial Ratios, Discriminant Analysis and the Prediction of Corporate Bankruptcy," *Journal of Finance*, September, 1968.)

Limitations of Ratio Analysis

The quality of financial statement analysis depends on the quality of financial information. We ought not blindly analyse numbers; doing so can lead to faulty conclusions and suboptimal decisions. Instead, we need to acknowledge that current accounting rules (IFRS) have limitations, and be fully aware of the company's environment, its competitive pressures, and any structural and strategic changes. Exhibit 5.13 shows how ratios can differ significantly across industries, so comparisons to companies with similar customers, technologies and competitive pressures will be most meaningful. Even within industries, there may be differences in strategy that create big differences in ratio values. There can be other factors that limit the usefulness of financial accounting information for ratio analysis.

IFRS Limitations Several limitations in IFRS can distort financial ratios. Limitations include:

1. **Measurability**. Financial statements reflect what can be reliably measured. This results in nonrecognition of certain assets, often internally developed assets, the very assets that are most likely to confer a competitive advantage and create value. Examples are brand name, a superior management team, employee skills, and a reliable supply chain.
2. **Non-capitalised costs**. Related to the concept of measurability is the expensing of costs relating to "assets" that cannot be identified with enough precision to warrant capitalisation. Examples are brand equity costs from advertising and other promotional activities, and research costs relating to future products.
3. **Historical costs**. Assets and liabilities are usually recorded at original acquisition or issuance costs. Subsequent increases in value are not recorded until realised, and declines in value are recognised only if deemed permanent.

Thus, IFRS balance sheets omit important and valuable assets. Our analysis of ROE, including that of liquidity and solvency, must consider that assets can be underreported and that ratios can be distorted. We discuss many of these limitations in more detail in later chapters.

Company Changes Many companies regularly undertake mergers, acquire new companies, and divest subsidiaries. Such major operational changes can impair the comparability of company ratios across time. Companies also change strategies, such as product pricing, R&D, and financing. We must understand the effects of such changes on ratios and exercise caution when we compare ratios from one period to the next. Companies also behave differently at different points in their life cycles. For instance, growth companies possess a different profile than do mature companies. Seasonal effects also markedly impact analysis of financial statements at different times of the year. Thus, we must consider life cycle and cyclicality when we compare ratios across companies and over time.

Conglomerate Effects Few companies are pure-play; instead, most companies operate in several businesses or industries. Most publicly traded companies consist of a parent company and multiple subsidiaries, often pursuing different lines of business. Vodafone reports financial information for different geographical and business segments. Most heavy equipment manufacturers have finance subsidiaries (for example, **Fidis S.p.A.** is a wholly owned subsidiary of **Fiat Group Automobiles S.p.A.**). Financial statements of such conglomerates are consolidated and include the financial statements of the parent and its subsidiaries. Consequently, such consolidated statements are challenging to analyse. Typically, analysts break the financials apart into their component businesses and separately analyse each component. Fortunately, companies must report financial information (albeit limited) for major business segments in their annual reports.

Means to an End Ratios reduce, to a single number, the myriad complexities of a company's operations. No one number can accurately capture the qualitative aspect of a company. Ratios cannot hope to capture the innumerable transactions and events that occur each day between a company and various parties. Ratios cannot meaningfully convey a company's marketing and management philosophies, its human resource activities, its financing activities, its strategic initiatives, and its product management. In our analysis we must learn to look through the numbers and ratios to better understand the operational factors that drive financial results. Successful analysis seeks to gain insight into what a company is really about and what the future portends. Our overriding purpose in analysis is to understand the past and present to better predict the future. Computing and examining ratios is just one step in that process.

CHAPTER-END REVIEW

Refer to the income statements and balance sheets for China Mobile Limited presented in Mid-Chapter Review 1 earlier in this chapter.

Required

Compute the following liquidity and solvency ratios for China Mobile and interpret your results in comparison to those of Vodafone.

1. Current ratio
2. Quick ratio.
3. Debt-to-equity ratio.
4. Times interest earned.

The solution to this review problem can be found on page 266.

APPENDIX 5A: Analysing and Interpreting Core Operating Activities

LO5 Measure and analyse the effect of operating activities on ROE.

In Chapter 4, we analysed cash flows by grouping them into three categories—operating, investing, and financing. Similarly, the income statement and balance sheet can be formatted to distinguish between operating and nonoperating (investing and financing) activities. In this appendix, we consider the effect of operating activities on the return on investment. The distinction between returns earned from operating activities and those generated by nonoperating activities is important. Operations provide the primary value drivers for shareholders. It is for this reason that many analysts argue that operating activities must be executed successfully if a company expects to remain profitable in the long run.

Operating activities refer to the core transactions and events of a company. They consist of those activities required to deliver a company's products and services to its customers. A company is engaged in operating activities when it conducts research and development, establishes supply chains, assembles administrative support, produces and markets its products, and follows up with after-sale customer service. Although nonoperating activities, namely investing and financing activities, are important and must be managed well, they are not the primary value drivers for investors and creditors.

Operating returns are measured by the **return on net operating assets (RNOA)**. This return metric is defined as follows:

$$\text{RNOA} = \frac{\textbf{Net operating profit after taxes (NOPAT)}}{\textbf{Average net operating assets (NOA)}}$$

In order to calculate this ratio, we must first classify the income statement and balance sheet accounts into operating and nonoperating components so that we can assess each separately. First we will consider operating components of the income statement and the calculation of NOPAT. Then we consider operating and nonoperating components of the balance sheet and the calculation of NOA.

Reporting Operating Activities in the Income Statement The income statement reports operating activities through accounts such as sales revenue, cost of goods sold, selling, general and administrative (SG&A) expenses, depreciation, rent, insurance, wages, advertising, and R&D expenses. These activities create the most long-lasting effects on profitability and cash flows. Nonoperating items in the income statement include interest expense on borrowed funds and interest and dividend income on investments as well as gains and losses on those investments.

A commonly used measure of operating income is **net operating profit after taxes (NOPAT)**. NOPAT is calculated as:

$$\textbf{NOPAT} = \textbf{Net income} - [(\textbf{Nonoperating revenues} - \textbf{Nonoperating expenses}) \times (1 - \textbf{Marginal tax rate})]$$

NOPAT is an important measure of profitability. It is similar to net income except that NOPAT focuses exclusively on after-tax *operating* performance.

Computation of NOPAT requires that we separate nonoperating revenues and expenses from operating sources of income. Companies often report income from operations as a subtotal (before income taxes) within the income statement. These numbers should be interpreted with caution. Currently, there are no requirements within IFRS that specify which revenue and expense items should be included in operating income.[5] As a consequence, some line items, such as SG&A, might include nonoperating items. For example, a company may have investments in affiliated companies and include income from these investments in its SG&A expense in the income statement. While this income might appear to be nonoperating, most analysts would argue that the amount should be included in the calculation of NOPAT if these operations are part of the core operating activities of the company.

The tax rate used to compute NOPAT is the **marginal tax rate**. This rate is the effective tax rate on nonoperating revenues and expenses. As we have done throughout this chapter, we use the UK statutory tax rate of 24% to approximate the marginal tax rate.[6] Vodafone's NOPAT can be computed using this tax rate:

$$\textbf{NOPAT} = \textbf{£11,312 million} - [(\textbf{£346 million} - \textbf{£1,703 million}) \times (1 - 0.24)] = \textbf{£12,343 million}$$

Vodafone's NOPAT was greater than its earnings from continuing operations of £11,312 million in 2013. The difference between the two figures was the nonoperating income and expenses, including the interest expense on its debt and the interest income on its investments.

Reporting Operating Activities in the Balance Sheet The balance sheet also reflects both operating and nonoperating activities. The asset side of the balance sheet reports resources devoted to operating activities in accounts such as cash, receivables, inventories, property, plant and equipment, and intangible assets. Among liabilities, accounts payable, accrued expenses, and some long-term liabilities such as deferred compensation and pension benefits arise out of operating activities. In addition, accrued and deferred income taxes are generally considered operating liabilities.

Investments in securities of other companies are usually considered nonoperating. The exception is that some equity-type investments are related to operations. Vodafone's investment in its network operators and network infrastructure providers is an example of this type of investment. Equity investments are discussed further in Chapter 12. Among a company's liabilities, short-term and long-term debt accounts are classified as nonoperating. These include accounts such as notes payable, interest payable, current maturities of long-term debt, capital leases, and long-term debt.

Vodafone reported other current investments of £4,419 million in 2013 (£5,350 million in 2012). Other noncurrent investments of £3,553 million in 2013 (£773 million in 2012) also included a number of listed and unlisted investments. These investments were considered nonoperating. The company reported long-term investments in associates and joint ventures of £114 million in 2013 (£46,447 million in 2012). These long-term investments were the aforementioned equity investments in network operators and network infrastructure providers and most analysts would consider them to be part of Vodafone's operations. Vodafone's nonoperating liabilities included short-term debt obligations of £7,747 million in 2013 (£11,800 million in 2012) and long-term debt obligations of £21,454 million in 2013 (£27,904 million in 2012).

By subtracting total operating liabilities from total operating assets, we get **net operating assets (NOA)**.[7] Vodafone's NOA for 2013 and 2012 is calculated as follows (£ millions):

	2013	2012
Operating assets	£121,840 − £4,419 − £3,553 = £113,868	£138,324 − £5,350 − £773 = £132,201
Operating liabilities . . .	£50,059 − £7,747 − £21,454 = £ 20,858	£65,836 − £11,800 − £27,904 = £ 26,132
NOA	£ 93,010	£106,069

Given NOPAT and NOA we can compute Vodafone's RNOA as follows:

$$\textbf{RNOA} = \frac{\textbf{NOPAT}}{\textbf{Average NOA}} = \frac{\textbf{£12,343 million}}{(\textbf{£93,010 million} + \textbf{£106,069 million})/2} = \textbf{12.4\%}$$

Vodafone's ROE was 15.68% in 2013. Its RNOA was 12.4%, which represents about 80% of the total return earned by shareholders.

[5] The IASB and US Financial Accounting Standards Board (FASB) were conducting a joint project on financial statement presentation. Among other things, the objective is to better distinguish operating and nonoperating activities. The project is currently on hold until further notice.

[6] As we argued earlier in this chapter, the statutory tax rate is a reasonable approximation of the marginal tax rate in many instances, including our analysis of Vodafone. However, some nonoperating sources of revenue and expense are not taxed at the statutory tax rate. A detailed analysis of marginal tax rates is beyond the scope of this text. Nevertheless, a thorough analysis of operating return would normally include a close examination of a company's income taxes.

[7] Total operating assets can be computed by subtracting nonoperating assets from total assets. Similarly, we can determine operating liabilities either by adding up the operating items or by subtracting the nonoperating items from total liabilities.

Disaggregating RNOA

We gain further insights into operating returns by disaggregating RNOA into operating profit margin and asset turnover. RNOA can be presented as the product of net operating profit margin (NOPM) and net operating asset turnover (NOAT). We define **net operating profit margin (NOPM)** as the amount of operating profit produced as a percentage of each sales dollar. NOPM is similar to the profit margin (PM) ratio defined in the chapter, except that it excludes all nonoperating revenues and expenses from the calculation. Vodafone's NOPM was 32.19% in 2013, computed as:

$$\text{NOPM} = \frac{\textbf{NOPAT}}{\textbf{Sales revenue}} = \frac{\textbf{£12,343 million}}{\textbf{£38,346 million}} = \textbf{32.19\%}$$

This ratio indicates that each pound of sales revenue generated 32 pence of after-tax operating profit. Vodafone's NOPAT was very close to Vodafone's EWI, because the primary nonoperating item in the company's income statement was interest expense. Thus its NOPM was almost identical to its profit margin of 32.6%.

Net operating asset turnover (NOAT) is defined as the ratio of sales revenue to average net operating assets (NOA). NOAT captures the amount of sales revenue generated by each dollar of net investment in operating assets. Vodafone's NOAT is 0.39 times, computed as:

$$\text{NOAT} = \frac{\textbf{Sales revenue}}{\textbf{Average NOA}} = \frac{\textbf{£38,346 million}}{\textbf{(£93,010 million + £106,069 million)/2}} = \textbf{0.39}$$

This ratio suggests that each pound of investment in net operating assets generated 0.39 pence of sales revenue in 2013. This ratio was higher than Vodafone's asset turnover (AT) ratio of 0.29. This difference is caused by the difference between net operating assets (NOA) and total assets. NOAT is computed using average NOA in the denominator rather than average total assets. Thus, nonoperating assets are excluded, and operating assets are presented net of operating liabilities. The resulting denominator is, therefore, smaller.

Vodafone's RNOA is 12.4%. This return can be disaggregated into the product of NOPM and NOAT as follows:

$$\textbf{RNOA} = \textbf{NOPM} \times \textbf{NOAT}$$
$$\textbf{12.4\%} = \textbf{32.19\%} \times \textbf{0.39}$$

APPENDIX-END REVIEW A

Refer to the financial statements of China Mobile Limited presented in Mid-Chapter Review 1. Calculate China Mobile's return on net operating assets (RNOA) and then disaggregate RNOA into net operating profit margin (NOPM) and net operating asset turnover (NOAT).

The solution to this review problem can be found on page 267.

APPENDIX 5B: Pro Forma Financial Statements

LO6 Prepare *pro forma* financial statements.

The ability to forecast future financial activities is an important aspect of many business decisions. We might, for example, wish to estimate the value of a company's equity before purchasing its shares. Or, we might want to evaluate the creditworthiness of a prospective borrower. We might also be interested in comparing the financial impact of alternative business strategies or tactics. For each of these decision contexts, a forecast of future earnings and cash flows would be relevant to such an evaluation.

Pro forma financial statements are hypothetical statements prepared to reflect specific assumptions about the company and its transactions. The most common type of pro forma statements are those prepared for future periods based on assumptions about the future activities of a business.[8] By varying the assumptions, pro forma statements allow us to ask "what if" questions about the future activities of the company, the answers to which provide the necessary inputs underlying most business decisions.

In this appendix, we present a common, yet simple method for preparing pro forma financial statements. This method proceeds in seven steps:

[8] The term "pro forma financial statements" is a term that is also used to describe *current* period financial statements prepared under alternative assumptions. For example, management might use the term pro forma earnings when referring to earnings computed after excluding a major revenue or expense item, such as restructuring charges or income from discontinued operations. The term can also be used to describe financial statements prepared under a different set of accounting principles.

1. Forecast sales revenue.
2. Forecast operating expenses, such as cost of goods sold and SG&A expenses.
3. Forecast operating assets and liabilities, including accounts receivable, inventory, property, plant and equipment, accounts payable, and prepaid and accrued expenses.
4. Forecast nonoperating assets, liabilities, contributed capital, revenues and expenses.
5. Forecast net income, dividends and retained earnings.
6. Forecast the amount of cash required to balance the balance sheet.
7. Prepare a pro forma cash flow statement based on the pro forma income statement and balance sheet.

Step 1. Forecast Sales Revenue

The sales forecast is the crucial first step in the preparation of pro forma financial statements, because many of the accounts in the pro forma income statement and balance sheet depend on their relation to the sales forecast. The general method for forecasting sales is to assume a revenue growth rate and apply that rate to the current sales revenue amount:

Forecasted revenues = Current revenues × (1 + Revenue growth rate)

A good starting point for estimating the revenue growth rate is the historical rate of sales growth. This is obtained by using data from the horizontal analysis discussed earlier in the chapter. Once we have this historical rate as a starting point, we can then adjust the growth rate up or down based on other relevant information. For example, we might attempt to answer the following questions:

- How will future sales be affected by economic conditions? What will happen in the economy in the coming year? Do we expect economic growth or a recession? How will economic growth vary in various markets, such as Europe, Asia, North America, and Latin America?
- What changes are expected from the company? Are there any new strategic initiatives planned? Is the company planning to open new stores, launch new products, new advertising campaigns, or new pricing tactics? Do we expect any acquisitions of other businesses?
- What changes in the competitive environment do we expect? Are new competitors entering the market? How will existing competitors respond to changes in the company's strategy? How will substitute products affect sales?

To answer each of the above questions, we rely on a variety of information sources, not the least of which is the management's discussion and analysis (MD&A) section of the company's annual report. We can also use publicly available information from competitors, suppliers, customers, industry organisations and government agencies to provide some insight into trends that can have an effect on future revenues. Our objective is to be able to adjust the historical growth rate up or down to reflect the insights we gain from reviewing this additional information.

Based on data from the horizontal analysis, we can conclude that Vodafone experienced a decline in revenues between 2010 and 2012. There was a slight recovery in 2013 with revenue growth of 0.8%. The company's CEO indicated in the annual report that the competitive and macroeconomic pressures in Europe would continue. Nonetheless, the company undertook a series of acquisitions, including Kabel Deutschland in Germany, Ono Spain, and Cable and Wireless Worldwide in the UK, in order to strengthen its strategic position in Europe. These acquisitions are expected to increase Vodafone's market share in fixed services, a large and growing revenue pool across Europe. In the emerging markets, increased mobile data usage and strong performance is expected to continue. Although the revenue outlook is optimistic for Vodafone, we assume a modest overall sales growth rate of 1% until the company demonstrates a trend in revenue growth. This makes the 2014 revenue forecast £38,729 million (£38,346 million × 1.01).

Step 2. Forecast Operating Expenses

Given our forecast of sales revenue, we then turn to forecasting operating expenses. We rely on the common-size income statement as a starting point to identify the relationship between operating expense items and sales revenue. That is, we use the expense-to-sales (ETS) ratio for each operating expense item to compute the forecasted expense:

Forecasted operating expense = Forecasted revenues × ETS ratio

While historical ETS ratios provide a good place to start, we may want to adjust these ratios up or down based on observed trends or any additional information that we might have. For example, when we examined Vodafone's common-size income statements, we learned that cost of goods sold increased to 72.9% of sales in 2013, up from 69.8% in 2012. Will this trend continue into 2014? Or, alternatively, do we anticipate that this expense item will revert to historical levels in relation to sales? Has the company taken any steps to alter the trend in this ETS ratio? As was the case with the sales forecast, there are numerous sources of information that are potentially useful for making adjustments to the historical relationships.

For the purpose of illustration, we assume that the ETS ratios for all operating expense items, except for impairment losses and income from associates and joint ventures, remain the same in 2014 as they were in 2013. For example, we forecast Vodafone's 2014 administrative expenses to be £4,287 million (£38,729 million × 11.07%). We assume no impairment losses and no change in the share of profit from associates and joint ventures. According to the annual report, these impairment charges relate solely to goodwill and are driven by lower than anticipated cash flows in the European region. Since impairment is transitory in nature, we forecast it to be zero in future periods.

Step 3. Forecast Operating Assets and Liabilities

The sales forecast can also be used to forecast operating assets and liabilities. The relationship between operating assets and revenues is based on asset turnover analysis. For example, when we compute accounts receivable turnover (ART), sales revenue is divided by average accounts receivable. When forecasting accounts receivable, we assume a relationship between sales revenue and year-end accounts receivable:

$$\textbf{Forecasted accounts receivable} = \frac{\textbf{Forecasted sales revenue} \times \textbf{Reported accounts receivable}}{\textbf{Reported sales revenue}}$$

In 2013, Vodafone reported short-term trade and other receivables of £8,886 million, which included £3,627 million in trade receivables (according to a financial statement note). This represents 9.5% of the reported sales revenue of £38,346 million. The forecasted accounts receivable for 2014 is, therefore, £3,663 million (£38,729 million × 9.5%).

The same procedure can be used to forecast other operating assets, such as inventories, prepaid expenses and property, plant and equipment, as well as operating liabilities such as accounts payable and accrued expenses.

Step 4. Forecast Nonoperating Assets, Liabilities, Revenues and Expenses

While operating expenses, assets, and liabilities tend to be related to sales revenue, this is typically not the case for nonoperating items. Instead, nonoperating revenues, such as interest and dividend income, tend to be related to investments, while nonoperating expense, namely interest expense, is related to debt financing. As a starting point, we forecast each of these items by assuming no change from the current amounts. For example, Vodafone reported long-term debt of £21,454 million in 2013, along with short-term obligations of £7,747 million. We forecast the same level of debt financing in 2014. Likewise, financing cost should remain the same at £1,554 million.

There may be information in the notes or in the MD&A section of the annual report to suggest other assumptions. For example, the notes typically reveal the amount of long-term debt that will come due in each of the next five years. This information can be used to adjust the balance in short-term obligations, because current maturities of long-term debt would be included under this item. Nevertheless, an assumption of no change is a good place to start.

Step 5. Forecast Net Income, Dividends, and Retained Earnings

Once we have forecasts of sales revenue (from step 1), operating expenses (step 2), and nonoperating revenues and expenses (step 4), we can calculate pretax earnings, income tax expense, and net income. Income tax expense is forecasted by multiplying pretax income by the effective tax rate:

Forecasted income tax expense = Forecasted pretax income × Effective tax rate

The **effective tax rate** is the average tax rate applied to pretax earnings, and is computed by dividing reported income tax expense by reported pretax earnings. In 2013, Vodafone reported a pretax loss of £5,270 million and an income tax credit of £16,582 million. Therefore, it is not meaningful to use these numbers to calculate the effective tax rate. Instead, we apply the 2013 UK statutory tax rate of 24% to the forecasted pretax earnings to compute the 2014 forecasted income taxes. This assumption results in forecasted income taxes of $325 million (£1,354 million × 24%) and forecasted net income of £1,029 million (£1,324 million − £325 million). Vodafone's 2014 pro forma income statement is presented in Exhibit 5B.1 alongside its 2013 reported income statement.

Our forecast of dividends relies on the **dividend payout ratio**, defined as dividend payments divided by net income.

Forecasted dividends = Forecasted net income × Dividend payout ratio

In 2013, Vodafone paid cash dividends of £5,340 million, which was 47.2% of its profit from continuing operations of £11,312 million. Applying the same dividend payout ratio to the 2014 earnings of £1,029 million would result in a dividend forecast of £486 million. However, according to the annual report, the Board of directors considered the ordinary dividend to be the core element of shareholders return, and they also believed in a consistent dividend policy. In 2013, the company raised the dividend per share by 8%. As a reflection of its confidence in the company's future performance, the Board intended to raise the dividend annually thereafter. Hence, instead of relying on the 2013 dividend payout ratio, we assume the same amount of dividends in 2014.

Next, we can forecast retained earnings using the forecasts of net income and dividends:

$$\textbf{Forecasted retained earnings} = \textbf{Beginning retained earnings} + \textbf{Forecasted net income} - \textbf{Forecasted dividends}$$

Throughout this chapter, we have presented Vodafone's equity as a single amount, without separating retained earnings from contributed capital. If we assume no change in contributed capital for 2014, we can forecast total equity using the same method as would normally be used to forecast retained earnings. Thus, Vodafone's forecasted 2014 equity is £67,470 million (£71,781 million + £1,029 million − £5,340 million).

EXHIBIT 5B.1 Vodafone Pro Forma Income Statement

VODAFONE GROUP PLC
2013 Income Statement and 2014 Pro Forma Income Statement

(£ millions)	pro forma FY 2014	as reported FY 2013
Revenue (38,346 × 1.01)	**38,729**	38,346
Cost of sales (38,729 × 72.87%)	(28,221)	(27,942)
Gross profit	**10,508**	10,404
Selling and distribution expenses (38,729 × 7.91%)	(3,063)	(3,033)
Administrative expenses (38,729 × 11.07%)	(4,287)	(4,245)
Share of results of equity accounted associates and joint ventures (no change)	278	278
Impairment losses	—	(6,600)
Other income and expense (38,729 × 1.87%)	(724)	(717)
Operating (loss)/profit	**2,711**	(3,913)
Non-operating income and expense (no change)	(149)	(149)
Investment income (no change)	346	346
Financing costs (no change)	(1,554)	(1,554)
(Loss)/profit before taxation	**1,354**	(5,270)
Income tax credit/(expense) (1,354 × 24%)	(325)	16,582
Profit/(loss) for the financial year from continuing operations	**1,029**	11,312
Profit for the financial year from discontinued operations	—	48,108
Profit for the financial year	1,029	59,420

Step 6. Forecast Cash

If the forecasts of all other components of the balance sheet are in place, we can then forecast the cash balance. This forecast is simply a "plug" amount that makes the balance sheet balance:

$$\textbf{Forecasted cash} = \textbf{Forecasted liabilities} + \textbf{Forecasted equity} - \textbf{Forecasted noncash assets}$$

It is possible that the resulting forecast of cash will be negative or unreasonably small or large. If this occurs, we then revisit steps 4 and 5. If the cash forecast is negative or too low, we adjust our forecast of short-term debt and interest expense to reflect increased borrowing to cover cash needs. If the cash forecast is too large, we can assume that excess cash is invested in marketable securities and increase the amount of interest income. In either case, we then modify our forecast of income taxes, net income, dividends and retained earnings, before recalculating the cash forecast.

Vodafone's 2014 pro forma balance sheet is presented in Exhibit 5B.2, alongside the company's 2013 actual balance sheet. The cash balance is forecasted to decrease by approximately 46.4% (from £10,134 million in 2013 to £5,431 million in 2014). This decrease is significant, and if the cash balance is too low, we may need to adjust our forecast of debt upward, though we do not do so here.

Step 7. Prepare the Pro Forma Cash Flow Statement

Once we have a pro forma income statement and balance sheet, we can prepare a pro forma cash flow statement using the methods illustrated in Chapter 4. To do so, we need a forecast of depreciation expense (if that item is not explicitly listed as an operating expense in the income statement). The procedure for forecasting depreciation expense is the same as was used for other operating expenses—we simply use the depreciation ETS ratio.

EXHIBIT 5B.2 Vodafone Pro Forma Balance Sheet

VODAFONE GROUP PLC
2013 Balance Sheet and 2014 Pro Forma Balance Sheet

(£ millions)	pro forma FY 2014	as reported FY 2013
Noncurrent assets		
Goodwill (no change)	23,315	23,315
Other intangible assets (38,729 × 61%)	23,607	23,373
Property, plant and equipment (38,729 × 59.6%)	23,080	22,851
Investments in associates and joint ventures (no change)	114	114
Other investments (no change)	3,553	3,553
Deferred tax assets (no change)	20,607	20,607
Post employment benefits (no change)	35	35
Trade and other receivables (no change)	3,270	3,270
	97,580	97,118
Current assets		
Inventory (38,729 × 1.2%)	445	441
Taxation recoverable (no change)	808	808
Trade and other receivables (38,729 × 23.2%)	8,975	8,886
Other investments (no change)	4,419	4,419
Cash and cash equivalents (PLUG)	5,431	10,134
Assets held for sale (no change)	34	34
	20,112	24,722
Total assets	117,693	121,840
Total equity	67,470	71,781
Noncurrent liabilities		
Long-term borrowings (no change)	21,454	21,454
Taxation liabilities (no change)	50	50
Deferred tax liabilities (no change)	747	747
Post employment benefits (no change)	584	584
Provisions (no change)	846	846
Trade and other payables (no change)	1,339	1,339
	25,020	25,020
Current liabilities		
Short-term borrowings (no change)	7,747	7,747
Taxation liabilities (no change)	873	873
Provisions (38,729 × 2.5%)	973	963
Trade and other payables (38,729 × 40.3%)	15,611	15,456
	25,203	25,039
Total equity and liabilities	117,693	121,840

In a note to its financial statements, Vodafone reported depreciation and amortization expense of £7,560 million in 2013, which was 19.7% of sales revenue. Using this ETS ratio, we forecast depreciation expense to be £7,636 million in 2014 (£38,729 million × 19.7%). Using this forecast, along with other items forecasted earlier, we prepare the pro forma cash flow statement, which is presented in Exhibit 5B.3.

Additional Considerations

Pro forma financial statements are based on a set of assumptions about the future. Any decisions that are based on pro forma statements are only as good as the quality of these assumptions. Therefore it is important that we appreciate the effect that each assumption has on the forecasted amounts. To this end, it is often helpful to use **sensitivity analysis** to examine the effect of alternative assumptions on the pro forma statements. For example, we might prepare three different pro forma income statements, one using our "most-likely" assumption for the sales forecast, and one each for the "best-case" and "worst-case" scenarios. In some situations, a change in the sales forecast can have a dramatic effect on net income and cash flows. Sensitivity analysis helps to identify these effects before a decision is made so that costly mistakes can be avoided.

It is also important to remember that these statements are predictions about the future and, as such, are bound to be wrong. That is, we expect that there will be **forecast errors**—differences between the forecasted and the actual amounts. The goal of a good forecast is accuracy, which means that we want the forecast errors to be as small as possible. Generating pro forma statements using a computer is relatively easy and the efficiency and precision of spreadsheet software can provide a false sense of confidence in the numbers. Spreadsheets routinely calculate forecasted amounts to the "nth" decimal place whether or not such precision is justified. However, an amount forecasted to the nearest penny may not be useful if the forecast is off by millions of pounds/dollars/euros. It is better to be imprecisely accurate than to be precisely inaccurate.

EXHIBIT 5B.3 Vodafone Pro Forma Cash Flow Statement

VODAFONE GROUP PLC
2014 Pro Forma Cash Flow Statement

(£ millions)	pro forma 2014
Net Income	1,029
Depreciation and amortisation (forecast)	7,636
Increase in inventory	(4)
Increase in trade and other receivables	(89)
Increase in trade and other payables	155
Increase in provisions	10
Net cash flow from operating activities	8,736
Cash flows from investing activities	
Investment in property, plant and equipment and intangible assets, net	(8,098)
Net cash flow from investing activities	(8,098)
Cash flows from financing activities	
Dividends paid	(5,340)
Net cash flow from financing activities	(5,340)
Net cash flow	(4,702)
Cash and cash equivalents at beginning of the financial year	10,134
Exchange (loss)/gain on cash and cash equivalents	0
Cash and cash equivalents at end of the financial year	5,431

APPENDIX-END REVIEW B

Refer to the income statements and balance sheets of China Mobile Limited presented in Mid-Chapter Review 1.

Required

Make the following assumptions:

- 2014 sales revenue is 670,000 RMB.
- Operating expenses increase in 2014 in proportion to sales revenue.
- Operating assets and liabilities increase based on their 2013 relation to sales revenue. Classify other financial assets and obligations under finance leases as non-operating.
- Assume that nonoperating revenues, expenses, assets and liabilities do not change from 2013 to 2014.
- Dividend payout is 60% of net income.
- Assume 25% income tax rate

Prepare a pro forma income statement and balance sheet for 2014.

The solution to this review problem can be found on pages 267–268.

APPENDIX 5C: Measuring Return on Financial Leverage

In this appendix, we present an alternative method for calculating the return on financial leverage (ROFL). ROFL is the effect that debt financing has on ROE. In the chapter, we define ROFL as the difference between ROE and ROA. ROFL can also be computed directly. In order to do so, we first define the **net interest rate (NIR)**, which is the average interest rate after taxes on total liabilities, as follows:[9]

$$\textbf{Net interest rate (NIR)} = \frac{\textbf{Interest expense} \times (1 - \textbf{Statutory tax rate})}{\textbf{Average total liabilities}}$$

The net interest rate (NIR) is the ratio of annual net interest expense to average total liabilities. Because some liabilities, such as accounts payable and accrued expenses, are non-interest-bearing, the NIR is typically lower than prevailing interest rates. Nevertheless, NIR is an important variable that helps us understand the effects of financial leverage. Specifically, whenever ROA is greater than NIR, leverage will increase ROE, thus benefiting the firm. On the other hand, whenever ROA is less than NIR, debt financing will be harmful to the firm as it has the effect of reducing ROE.

Given our definition of the NIR, ROFL can be computed directly, as follows:

$$\textbf{ROFL} = \frac{\textbf{Average total liabilities}}{\textbf{Average total equity}} \times (\textbf{ROA} - \textbf{NIR})$$

The first term on the right-hand side of this equality is the ratio of average total liabilities to average total equity. This ratio is similar to the debt-to-equity ratio that was discussed earlier in the chapter except that the debt-to-equity ratio is computed using liabilities and equity at a point in time (e.g., year-end) while the averages are used here.

The second term on the right-hand side of the equality is the aforementioned difference between ROA and NIR. This difference is called the **spread**. When the spread is positive (ROA > NIR), ROFL is positive and ROE is greater than ROA. When the spread is negative (ROA < NIR), ROFL is negative, which implies that ROE < ROA.

Vodafone's 2013 ROFL was 6.08%, which was the difference between ROE and ROA (15.68% − 9.6%). We obtain the same value for ROFL when it is calculated directly, as follows. First, we calculate Vodafone's NIR (£ millions):

$$\textbf{NIR} = \frac{\textbf{£1,554} \times (1 - 0.24)}{(\textbf{£65,836} + \textbf{£50,059})/2} = \textbf{2.04\%}$$

Using the NIR, we then compute Vodafone's ROFL as (£ millions):

$$\textbf{ROFL} = \frac{(\textbf{£65,836} + \textbf{£50,059})/2}{(\textbf{£72,488} + \textbf{£71,781})/2} \times (\textbf{9.60\%} - \textbf{2.04\%}) = \textbf{6.08\%}$$

APPENDIX-END REVIEW C

Refer to the financial statements for China Mobile presented in Mid-Chapter Review 1. Calculate China Mobile's NIR and ROFL for 2013.

The solution to this review problem can be found on page 268.

SUMMARY

LO1 Prepare and analyse common-size financial statements. (p. 213)

- Vertical analysis restates items in the income statement as a percentage of sales revenue and items in the balance sheet as a percentage of total assets.
- Horizontal analysis examines the percentage change from one year to the next for specific items in the income statement and balance sheet.

[9] The net interest rate (NIR) should not be confused with *net interest* which is a term that is sometimes used in the income statement to refer to interest expense minus interest income.

Compute and interpret measures of return on investment, including return on equity (ROE), return on assets (ROA), and return on financial leverage (ROFL). (p. 218) LO2

- ROE is the primary measure of company performance. It captures the return earned by shareholder investment in the firm.
- ROA measures the return earned on the firm's investment in assets. It is not affected by the way those assets are financed.
- ROFL is the difference between ROE and ROA and measures the effect that financial leverage has on ROE.

Disaggregate ROA into profitability (profit margin) and efficiency (asset turnover) components. (p. 221) LO3

- ROA can be disaggregated as the product of profit margin (PM) and asset turnover (AT).
- PM can be analysed further by examining the gross profit margin and expense-to-sales ratios.
- AT can be analysed further by examining accounts receivable turnover (ART), inventory turnover (INVT), and property, plant and equipment turnover (PPET).
- The trade-off between PM and AT is determined by the company's strategy and its competitive environment.

Compute and interpret measures of liquidity and solvency. (p. 227) LO4

- The current ratio (CR) and quick ratio (QR) measure short-term liquidity by comparing liquid assets to short-term obligations.
- The debt-to-equity ratio (D/E) and times interest earned ratio (TIE) measure long-term solvency by comparing sources of financing and the level of earnings to the cost of debt (interest).

Appendix 5A: Measure and analyse the effect of operating activities on ROE. (p. 234) LO5

- Net operating profit after taxes (NOPAT) measures the portion of income that results from a business' core operating activities.
- Return on net operating assets (RNOA), defined as NOPAT/average net operating assets, measures the return on a company's net investment in operating assets.

Appendix 5B: Prepare *pro forma* financial statements. (p. 236) LO6

- *Pro forma* financial statements are statements prepared for future periods based on assumptions about the future activities of the business.
- *Pro forma* statements can be used to evaluate the effects of alternative actions or assumptions on the financial statements.

KEY RATIOS

RETURN MEASURES

$$\text{Return on equity (ROE)} = \frac{\text{Net income}}{\text{Average total equity}}$$

$$\text{Earnings without interest expense (EWI)} = \text{Net income} + \text{Interest expense} \times (1 - \text{Statutory tax rate})$$

$$\text{Return on assets (ROA)} = \frac{\text{Earnings without interest expense (EWI)}}{\text{Average total assets}}$$

$$\text{Return on financial leverage (ROFL)} = \text{ROE} - \text{ROA}$$

PROFITABILITY RATIOS

$$\text{Profit margin (PM)} = \frac{\text{Earnings without interest expense (EWI)}}{\text{Sales revenue}}$$

$$\text{Gross profit margin (GPM)} = \frac{\text{Sales revenue} - \text{Cost of goods sold}}{\text{Sales revenue}}$$

$$\text{Expense-to-sales (ETS)} = \frac{\text{Individual expense items}}{\text{Sales revenue}}$$

TURNOVER RATIOS

$$\text{Asset turnover (AT)} = \frac{\text{Sales revenue}}{\text{Average total assets}}$$

$$\text{Accounts receivable turnover (ART)} = \frac{\text{Sales revenue}}{\text{Average accounts receivable}}$$

$$\text{Inventory turnover (INVT)} = \frac{\text{Cost of goods sold}}{\text{Average inventory}}$$

$$\text{Property, plant and equipment turnover (PPET)} = \frac{\text{Sales revenue}}{\text{Average PP\&E}}$$

LIQUIDITY RATIOS

$$\text{Current ratio (CR)} = \frac{\text{Current assets}}{\text{Current liabilities}}$$

$$\text{Quick ratio (QR)} = \frac{\text{Cash} + \text{ST investments} + \text{Receivables}}{\text{Current liabilities}}$$

$$\text{Operating cash flow to current liabilities (OCFCL)} = \frac{\text{Operating cash flow}}{\text{Average current liabilities}}$$

SOLVENCY RATIOS

$$\text{Times interest earned (TIE)} = \frac{\text{Earnings before interest expense and taxes (EBIT)}}{\text{Interest expense}}$$

$$\text{Debt-to-equity} = \frac{\text{Total liabilities}}{\text{Total equity}}$$

KEY TERMS

Accounts receivable turnover (ART) (p. 225)
Asset turnover (AT) (p. 222)
Capacity costs (p. 221)
Common-size financial statements (p. 213)
Covenants (p. 228)
Current ratio (p. 229)
Debt-to-equity ratio (p. 231)
Default risk (p. 228)
Dividend payout ratio (p. 238)
Earnings without interest expense (EWI) (p. 220)
Effective tax rate (p. 238)
Expense-to-sales (ETS) (p. 225)
Financial leverage (p. 220)
Financial statement analysis (p. 212)
Forecast error (p. 241)
Gross profit margin (GPM) (p. 225)
Horizontal analysis (p. 216)
Inventory turnover (INVT) (p. 225)
Liquidity (p. 229)
Liquidity analysis (p. 229)
Marginal tax rate (p. 235)
Net interest rate (NIR) (p. 242)
Net operating assets (NOA) (p. 235)
Net operating asset turnover (NOAT) (p. 236)
Net operating profit after taxes (NOPAT) (p. 234)
Net operating profit margin (NOPM) (p. 236)
Operating cash flow to current liabilities (OCFCL) (p. 230)
Profit margin (PM) (p. 221)
Pro forma financial statements (p. 236)
Property, plant and equipment turnover (PPET) (p. 226)
Quick ratio (p. 229)
Return on assets (ROA) (p. 219)
Return on equity (ROE) (p. 219)
Return on financial leverage (ROFL) (p. 220)
Return on net operating assets (RNOA) (p. 234)
Sensitivity analysis (p. 240)
Solvency (p. 230)
Solvency analysis (p. 229)
Spread (p. 242)
Times interest earned (TIE) (p. 232)
Vertical analysis (p. 213)
Working capital (p. 229)

MULTIPLE CHOICE

1. Which of the following ratios would not be affected by an increase in cost of goods sold?
   a. ROA
   b. INVT
   c. Quick ratio
   d. PM

2. A company has the following values: PM = 0.07; EWI = $1,885; Average total assets = $37,400. AT equals
   a. 0.05
   b. 0.72
   c. 0.36
   d. AT is not determinable because its sales are not reported.

3. A company's current ratio is 2 and its quick ratio is 1. What can be said about the sum of the company's cash + marketable securities + accounts receivable?
   a. The sum exceeds the current liabilities.
   b. The sum is equal to the sum of the current liabilities.
   c. The sum is equal to 1⁄2 of the total current liabilities.
   d. None of the above is correct.

4. A company's interest expense is $500,000 and its net income is $14 million. If the company's effective tax rate is 30%, what is the company's times interest earned (TIE) ratio?
   a. 90
   b. 41
   c. 32
   d. 16

5. If a company's ROFL is negative, which of the following is *not* true?
   a. ROA > ROE
   b. The DE ratio is negative.
   c. ROA < net interest rate
   d. The company likely has a low TIE ratio.

Multiple Choice Answers
1. c 2. b 3. b 4. b 5. b

GUIDANCE ANSWERS . . . YOU MAKE THE CALL

You are the Entrepreneur Your company is performing substantially better than its competitors. Namely, your ROA of 16% is markedly superior to competitors' ROA of 10%. However, ROA disaggregation shows that this is mainly attributed to your AT of 0.89 versus competitors' AT of 0.59. Your PM of 18% is essentially identical to competitors' PM of 17%. Accordingly, you will want to maintain your AT as further improvements are probably difficult to achieve. Importantly, you are likely to achieve the greatest benefit with efforts at improving your PM of 18%, which is only marginally better than the industry norm of 17%.

Superscript $^{A(B,C)}$ denotes assignments based on Appendix 5A (5B, 5C).

DISCUSSION QUESTIONS

Q5-1. Explain in general terms the concept of return on investment. Why is this concept important in the analysis of financial performance?

Q5-2. (a) Explain how an increase in financial leverage can increase a company's ROE. (b) Given the potentially positive relation between financial leverage and ROE, why don't we see companies with 100% financial leverage (entirely nonowner financed)?

Q5-3. Gross profit margin [(Sales revenue − Cost of goods sold)/Sales revenue] is an important determinant of profit margin. Identify two factors that can cause gross profit margin to decline. Is a reduction in the gross profit margin always bad news? Explain.

Q5-4. Explain how a reduction in operating expenses as a percentage of sales can produce a short-term gain at the cost of long-term performance.

Q5-5. Describe the concept of asset turnover. What does the concept mean and why is it so important to understanding and interpreting financial performance?

Q5-6. Explain what it means when a company's ROE exceeds its ROA.

Q5-7. What are common-size financial statements? What role do they play in financial statement analysis?

Q5-8. How does a firm go about increasing its AT ratio? What strategies are likely to be most effective?

Q5-9.[A] What is meant by the term "net" in net operating assets (NOA)?

Q5-10. Why is it important to disaggregate ROA into profit margin (PM) and asset turnover (AT)?

Q5-11. What insights do we gain from the graphical relation between profit margin and asset turnover?

Q5-12. Explain the concept of liquidity and why it is crucial to company survival.

Q5-13. Identify at least two factors that limit the usefulness of ratio analysis.

MINI EXERCISES

LO2, 3 **M5-14. Return on Investment, DuPont Analysis and Financial Leverage**

The following table presents selected 2013 financial information for Sunder Company.

SUNDER COMPANY Selected 2013 Financial Data	
Balance Sheet:	
Average total assets	$1,000,000
Average total liabilities	500,000
Average total equity	500,000
Income statement:	
Sales revenue	$1,000,000
Earnings before interest (net of tax)	20,000
Interest expense (net of tax)	15,000
Net income	5,000

a. Compute Sunder's ROE, ROA and ROFL for 2013.

b. Use the DuPont analysis described in the Business Insight on page 224 to disaggregate ROE.

c. How did the use of financial leverage affect Sunder's ROE in 2013? Explain.

LO1 **M5-15. Common-Size Balance Sheets**

Following is the balance sheet for Sentosa Stores, a retailing chain. Prepare Sentosa's common-size balance sheets as of January 28, 2015 and January 29, 2014.

($ millions)	January 28, 2015	January 29, 2014
Assets		
Cash and cash equivalents	$ 794	$ 1,712
Accounts receivable, net	5,927	6,153
Inventory	7,918	7,596
Other current assets	1,810	1,752
Total current assets	16,449	17,213
Property and equipment, net	29,149	25,493
Other noncurrent assets	1,032	999
Total assets	$46,630	$43,705

continued

Liabilities and shareholders' investment		
Accounts payable	$ 6,857	$ 6,625
Accrued liabilities	3,644	3,326
Current portion of long-term debt and notes payable	3,786	119
Total current liabilities	14,287	10,070
Long-term debt	13,697	15,607
Deferred income taxes	1,191	934
Other noncurrent liabilities	1,634	1,607
Total shareholders' investment	15,821	15,487
Total liabilities and shareholders' investment	$46,630	$43,705

M5-16. Common-Size Income Statements LO1

Following is the income statement for Sentosa Stores. Prepare Sentosa's common-size income statement for the fiscal year ended January 28, 2015.

($ millions)	Fiscal year ended January 28, 2015
Sales	$68,466
Net credit card revenues	1,399
Total revenues	69,865
Cost of sales	47,860
Selling, general and administrative expenses	14,106
Credit card expenses	446
Depreciation and amortisation	2,131
Earnings before interest expense and income taxes	5,322
Net interest expense	866
Earnings before income taxes	4,456
Income tax expense	1,527
Net earnings	$ 2,929

M5-17. Compute ROA, Profit Margin, and Asset Turnover LO2, 3

Refer to the financial information for Sentosa Stores, presented in M5-15 and M5-16.

a. Compute its return on assets (ROA) for the fiscal year ending January 28, 2015. Interest income for this year was $3 million, so interest expense was $869 million. The statutory tax rate is 35%.

b. Disaggregate ROA into profit margin (PM) and asset turnover (AT). Confirm that ROA = PM × AT.

M5-18. Analysis and Interpretation of Liquidity and Solvency LO4

Refer to the financial information of Sentosa Stores in M5-15 and M5-16 to answer the following.

a. Compute Sentosa's current ratio and quick ratio for January 2015 and January 2014. Comment on any observed trends.

b. Compute Sentosa's times interest earned for the year ended January 28, 2015, and its debt-to-equity ratios for January 2015 and January 2014. Comment on any trends observed.

c. Summarise your findings in a conclusion about the company's liquidity and solvency. Do you have any concerns about Sentosa's ability to meet its debt obligations?

LO1 **M5-19. Common-Size Balance Sheets**

MOL HUNGARIAN OIL AND GAS PLC (HUNGARY)

Following is the balance sheet for **MOL Hungarian Oil and Gas Plc.** Prepare common-size balance sheets for 2013 and 2012.

MOL HUNGARIAN OIL AND GAS PLC.
Consolidated Balance Sheet

(HUF million)	2013	2012
Assets		
Noncurrent assets		
Intangible assets	323,646	345,950
Property, plant and equipment, net	2,252,927	2,608,375
Investments in associated companies and joint ventures	128,220	123,974
Available-for-sale investments	14,636	20,571
Deferred tax assets	46,314	34,750
Other noncurrent assets	36,899	36,658
Total noncurrent assets	2,802,642	3,170,278
Current assets		
Inventories	494,407	507,151
Trade receivables, net	512,584	570,994
Securities	6,604	29,202
Other current assets	221,034	156,186
Prepaid taxes	39,447	14,742
Cash and cash equivalents	564,170	317,654
Total current assets	1,838,246	1,595,929
Total assets	4,640,888	4,766,207
EQUITY AND LIABILITIES		
Equity attributable to equity holders of the parent		
Share capital	79,215	79,202
Reserves	1,587,082	1,468,430
Profit for the year attributable to equity holders of the parent	21,442	151,484
Equity attributable to equity holders of the parent	1,687,739	1,699,116
Non-controlling interests	473,517	547,205
Total equity	2,161,256	2,246,321
Noncurrent liabilities		
Long-term debt, net of current portion	673,248	674,046
Provisions	303,553	290,860
Deferred tax liabilities	74,877	123,762
Other noncurrent liabilities	27,247	57,646
Total noncurrent liabilities	1,078,925	1,146,314
Current liabilities		
Trade and other payables	1,038,797	913,014
Current tax payable	2,537	2,138
Provisions	49,976	42,452
Short-term debt	211,223	145,838
Current portion of long-term debt	98,174	270,130
Total current liabilities	1,400,707	1,373,572
TOTAL EQUITY AND LIABILITIES	4,640,888	4,766,207

LO1 **M5-20. Common-Size Income Statements**

MOL HUNGARIAN OIL AND GAS PLC (HUNGARY)

Following is the income statement for **MOL Hungarian Oil and Gas Plc.** Prepare common-size income statements for 2013 and 2012.

MOL HUNGARIAN OIL AND GAS PLC. Consolidated Income Statement (HUF million)	2013	2012
Net revenue	5,400,417	5,521,324
Other operating income	75,696	15,662
Total operating income	5,476,113	5,536,986
Raw materials and consumables used	4,418,408	4,424,275
Personnel expenses	259,747	264,741
Depreciation, depletion, amortisation and impairment	539,686	319,375
Other operating expenses	293,727	370,314
Change in inventories of finished goods and work in progress	24,748	(981)
Work performed by the enterprise and capitalised	(41,575)	(46,033)
Total operating expenses	5,494,741	5,331,691
Operating profit	(18,628)	205,295
Financial income	29,385	63,100
Financial expense	87,729	84,493
Financial expense, net	58,344	33,157
Income from associates	20,062	33,608
Profit before tax	(56,910)	205,746
Income tax expense	(37,500)	49,721
Profit for the year	(19,410)	156,025

M5-21. Compute ROA, Profit Margin, and Asset Turnover LO2, 3 MOL HUNGARIAN OIL AND GAS PLC (HUNGARY)

Refer to the balance sheet and income statement information for MOL Hungarian Oil and Gas Plc, presented in M5-19 and M5-20.

a. Compute MOL's 2013 return on assets (ROA). MOL's statutory tax rate was 19% in 2013.

b. Disaggregate ROA into profit margin (PM) and asset turnover (AT). Confirm that ROA = PM × AT.

M5-22. Compute ROA, Profit Margin, and Asset Turnover LO2, 3 BMW GROUP (GERMANY)

Selected balance sheet and income statement information from BMW Group follows.

(€ millions)	2013 Revenues	2013 Earnings before Interest Expense (EWI)	2013 Total Assets	2012 Total Assets
	€76,058	€5,652	€138,368	€131,835

a. Compute BMW's 2013 return on assets (ROA).

b. Disaggregate ROA into profit margin (PM) and asset turnover (AT). Confirm that ROA = PM × AT.

M5-23. Compute and Interpret Liquidity and Solvency Ratios LO4 BMW GROUP (GERMANY)

Selected balance sheet and income statement information from BMW Group follows.

(€ millions)	2013	1012
Current assets	€ 52,174	€ 50,530
Current liabilities	50,043	48,395
Total liabilities	102,725	101,229
Equity	35,643	30,606
Earnings before interest and taxes	8,362	8,178
Interest expense	449	375
Net cash flow from operating activities	3,614	5,076

a. Compute the current ratio for each year and discuss any trend in liquidity. How does BMW's current ratio compare to the median for the telecommunications industry in Exhibit 5.13? What additional information about the numbers used to calculate this ratio might be useful in helping us assess liquidity? Explain.

b. Compute times interest earned, the debt-to-equity, and the operating cash flow to current liabilities ratios for each year and discuss any trends for each. Do you have any concerns about the extent of BMW's financial leverage and the company's ability to meet interest obligations? Explain.

LO2, 3 **M5-24. Computing Turnover Ratios for Companies in Different Industries**

Selected data from recent financial statements of The Procter & Gamble Company, McDonald's Corporation, and Valero Energy Corporation are presented below:

($ millions)	Procter & Gamble	McDonald's	Valero Energy
Sales	$ 83,680	$27,006	$125,987
Cost of sales	42,391	6,167	115,719
Average receivables	6,172	1,257	6,645
Average inventories	7,050	113	5,285
Average PP&E	20,835	22,448	23,923
Average total assets	135,299	32,483	40,202

a. Compute the asset turnover (AT) ratio for each company.

b. Compute the accounts receivable turnover (ART), inventory turnover (INVT), and PP&E turnover (PPET) for each company.

c. Discuss any differences across these three companies in the turnover ratios computed in *a* and *b*.

EXERCISES

LO2, 3 **E5-25. Compute and Interpret ROA, Profit Margin, and Asset Turnover of Competitors**

Selected balance sheet and income statement information for department store retailers Target Corporation and Wal-Mart Stores, Inc., follows.

($ millions)	Sales Revenue	Interest Expense	Net Income	Average Total Assets
Target	$ 69,865	$ 869	$ 2,929	$ 45,168
Wal-Mart	446,950	2,322	16,387	187,094

a. Compute the return on assets (ROA) for each company.

b. Disaggregate ROA into profit margin (PM) and asset turnover (AT) for each company.

c. Discuss any differences in these ratios for each company. Your interpretation should reflect the distinct business strategies of each company.

LO2 **E5-26. Compute ROA, ROE and ROFL and Interpret the Effects of Leverage**

Basic income statement and balance sheet information is given below for six different cases. For each case, the assets are financed with a mix of non-interest-bearing liabilities, 10% interest-bearing liability and equity. In all cases, the income tax rate is 40%.

Case	A	B	C	D	E	F
Assets	1000	1000	1000	1000	1000	1000
Non-interest-bearing liabilities	0	0	0	0	200	200
Interest-bearing liabilities	0	250	500	500	0	300
Shareholders' equity	1000	750	500	500	800	500
Earnings before interest and taxes (EBIT)	120	120	120	80	100	80

a. For each case, calculate the return on equity (ROE), return on assets (ROA) and return on financial leverage (ROFL).

b. Consider cases A, B and C. How does increasing leverage affect the three ratios? Why does the ROE grow from case A to case C?

c. Consider cases C and D. When does leverage work in favour of shareholders? Does that hold for case E?

d. Consider cases A and F. Case F has two types of liabilities. How does ROA compare to the rate on interest-bearing liabilities? Does leverage work in favour of the shareholders? Why?

E5-27. Compute, Disaggregate, and Interpret Competitors' Rates of Return LO2, 3

Selected balance sheet and income statement information for the drug retailers CVS Caremark Corporation and Walgreen Co. follows.

($ millions)	CVS Caremark	Walgreen
Sales revenue—2011	$107,100	$72,184
Interest expense—2011	588	89
Net income—2011	3,457	2,714
Total assets—2011	64,543	27,454
Total assets—2010	62,169	26,275
Total equity—2011	38,051	14,847
Total equity—2010	37,700	14,400

a. Compute the 2011 return on assets (ROA) for each company.

b. Disaggregate ROA into profit margin (PM) and asset turnover (AT) for each company.

c. Compute the 2011 return on equity (ROE) and return on financial leverage (ROFL) for each company.

d. Discuss any differences in these ratios for each company. Identify the factor(s) that drives the differences in ROA observed from your analyses in parts *a* through *c*.

E5-28. Compute, Disaggregate, and Interpret ROE and ROA LO2, 3

AIR NEW ZEALAND (NEW ZEALAND)

Selected balance sheet and income statement information from Air New Zealand for the fiscal year ended June 30, 2014 is given in the following table (NZ$ millions).

Sales 2014	Interest Expense 2014	Net Income 2014	Total Assets 2014	Total Assets 2013	Total Equity 2014	Total Equity 2013
4,663	90	262	5,850	5,596	1,872	1,801

a. Compute the 2014 return on equity (ROE), return on assets (ROA), and return on financial leverage (ROFL). The statutory tax rate in New Zealand is 28%.

b. Disaggregate the ROA from part *a* into profit margin (PM) and asset turnover (AT).

c. What can we learn by comparing PM to AT? What explanation can we offer for the relation between ROE and ROA observed and for Air New Zealand's use of financial leverage?

E5-29. Return on Investment, Financial Leverage, and DuPont Analysis LO2, 3

The following tables provide information from the recent annual reports of Dollarama, Inc., a leading dollar store operator in Canada. Dollarama aims to provide customers with a consistent shopping experience, offering a broad assortment of everyday consumer products and seasonal items at selected fixed price points up to $3.00.

DOLLARAMA, INC. (CANADA)

Balance sheets ($ '000)	2013	2012	2011
Total assets	$1,566,780	$1,453,692	$1,407,741
Total liabilities	702,619	522,202	512,795
Total equity	864,166	931,490	894,946

Income statements ($ '000)	2013	2012
Sales revenue	$2,064,676	$1,858,818
Earnings before interest and income taxes	354,504	315,893
Interest expense	11,673	10,839
Earnings before income taxes	342,831	305,054
Income tax expense	92,737	84,069
Net earnings	$ 250,094	$ 220,985

a. Calculate Dollarama's return on equity (ROE) for fiscal years 2013 and 2012.

b. Calculate Dollarama's return on assets (ROA) and return on financial leverage (ROFL) for both years. The statutory tax rate is 26.7%. Is financial leverage working to the advantage of Dollarama's shareholders?

c. Decompose the ROA computed above into profit margin (PM) and asset turnover (AT). Which of these two factors drives ROA for Dollarama? What inferences do you draw from comparing PM to AT?

LO5 E5-30.[A] Computing and Analysing Operating Returns

DAIMLER AG (GERMANY)

Selected information from the financial statements of **Daimler AG** is provided below:

(€ millions)	2011	2010
Revenue	€106,540	€ 97,761
Operating income	8,690	7,273
Interest expense, net of interest income	514	497
Net income	6,029	4,674
Operating assets	143,844	131,487
Operating liabilities	23,571	21,191

Required

a. Compute Daimler's net operating profit after taxes (NOPAT) for 2011 and 2010.

b. Compute Daimler's net operating profit margin (NOPM) for each year.

c. Compute Daimler's return on net operating assets (RNOA) for 2011.

LO2, 3 E5-31. Compute, Disaggregate and Interpret ROE and ROA

PCCW LIMITED (HONG KONG)

Selected balance sheet and income statement information from **PCCW Limited**, a Hong Kong-based telecommunications and media company, is given in the following table (HK$ millions).

Sales	Interest Expense	Net Income	Total Assets		Total Equity	
2013	2013	2013	2013	2012	2013	2012
$27,317	$1,111	$3,055	$53,937	$49,844	$8,633	$8,138

a. Compute the 2013 return on equity (ROE), return on assets (ROA), and return on financial leverage (ROFL). The statutory tax rate in Hong Kong is 16.5%.

b. Disaggregate the ROA from part *a* into profit margin (PM) and asset turnover (AT).

c. What can we learn by comparing PM to AT? What explanation can we offer for the relation between ROE and ROA observed and for PCCW's use of financial leverage?

LO4 E5-32. Compute and Interpret Liquidity and Solvency Ratios

PCCW LIMITED (HONG KONG)

Selected balance sheet and income statement information from **PCCW Limited** follows (HK$ millions).

	Total Current Assets	Total Current Liabilities	Pretax Income	Interest Expense	Total Liabilities	Total Equity
2011	$14,941	$10,747	$2,318	$1,565	$38,403	$7,447
2012	16,774	19,412	2,797	966	41,706	8,138
2013	17,579	10,658	3,265	1,111	45,304	8,633

a. Compute the current ratio for each year and discuss any trend in liquidity. Do you believe the company is sufficiently liquid? Explain. What additional information about the accounting numbers comprising this ratio might be useful in helping you assess liquidity? Explain.

b. Compute times interest earned and the debt-to-equity ratio for each year and discuss any trends for each.

c. How do PCCW's ratios compare to the medians for the telecommunications industry in Exhibit 5.13?

d. What is your overall assessment of the company's liquidity and solvency from the analyses above? Explain.

E5-33. Compute and Interpret Liquidity and Solvency Ratios LO4

Selected balance sheet and income statement information from Siemens, AG, for 2012 through 2014 follows (€ millions).

	Total Current Assets	Total Current Liabilities	Cash Flow from Operations	Pretax Income	Interest Expense	Total Liabilities	Equity
2012	€52,128	€42,627	€6,923	€6,636	€760	€77,396	€30,855
2013	46,937	37,868	7,186	5,813	784	73,825	28,111
2014	48,076	36,598	7,230	7,427	764	73,925	30,954

SIEMENS AG (GERMANY)

a. Compute the current ratio for each year and discuss any trend in liquidity. Also compute the operating cash flow to current liabilities (OCFCL) ratio for each year. (In 2011, current liabilities totaled €43,560 million.) Do you believe the company is sufficiently liquid? Explain. What additional information about the accounting numbers comprising this ratio might be useful in helping you assess liquidity? Explain.

b. Compute times interest earned and the debt-to-equity ratio for each year and discuss any trends for each.

c. What is your overall assessment of the company's liquidity and solvency from the analyses in *a* and *b*? Explain.

E5-34. Compute, Disaggregate and Interpret ROE and ROA LO2, 3

Income statements for The Gap, Inc., follow, along with selected balance sheet information ($ millions).

THE GAP, INC.
Consolidated Statement of Earnings

Fiscal year ended	Jan. 28, 2012	Jan. 29, 2011
Net sales	$14,549	$14,664
Cost of goods sold and occupancy expenses	9,275	8,775
Gross profit	5,274	5,889
Operating expenses	3,836	3,921
Operating income	1,438	1,968
Interest expense (reversal)	74	(8)
Interest income	(5)	(6)
Income before income taxes	1,369	1,982
Income taxes............	536	778
Net earnings	833	1,204

THE GAP, INC.
Selected Balance Sheet Data

	Jan. 28, 2012	Jan. 29, 2011
Merchandise inventories............	$1,615	$1,620
Total assets............	7,422	7,065
Total equity	2,755	4,080

a. Compute the return on equity (ROE), return on assets (ROA), and return on financial leverage (ROFL) for the fiscal year ended January 28, 2012.

b. Disaggregate ROA into profit margin (PM) and asset turnover (AT).

c. Compute the gross profit margin (GPM) and inventory turnover (INVT) ratios for the fiscal year ended January 28, 2012.

d. Assess the Gap's performance. What are the most important drivers of the Gap's success?

LO1, 6 **E5-35.[B] Common-Size and Pro Forma Income Statements**

Refer to the income statements for The Gap, Inc., presented in E5-34.

a. Prepare common-size income statements for fiscal years 2011 (ending January 28, 2012) and 2010 (ending January 29, 2011). What are the most significant changes between these two income statements?

b. Prepare a pro forma income statement for the fiscal year 2012 (ending January 27, 2013), based on the following assumptions:

- Net sales total $15,000 million.
- Cost of goods sold and occupancy expenses are 64% of sales.
- Operating expenses total 26% of sales.
- Interest income and interest expense are unchanged from the 2011 amounts.
- The Gap's effective tax rate is 39%.

c. Given the Gap's business strategy, what are the factors that ultimately determine the accuracy of the pro forma statement prepared in *b*?

PROBLEMS

LO2, 3 **P5-36. Analysis and Interpretation of Return on Investment for Competitors**

NIKE, INC. (USA)
ADIDAS GROUP (GERMANY)

Balance sheets and income statements for **NIKE, Inc.**, and **Adidas Group** follow. Refer to these financial statements to answer the requirements.

	NIKE, INC. Balance Sheets ($ millions) May 31,		ADIDAS GROUP, AG Balance Sheets (€ millions) December 31,	
	2014	2013	2014	2013
Assets				
Cash and cash equivalents	$ 2,220	$ 3,337	€ 1,683	€ 1,587
Short-term investments	2,922	2,628	403	224
Accounts receivable	3,434	3,117	1,946	1,809
Inventories	3,947	3,484	2,526	2,634
Other current assets	1,173	1,064	789	603
Total current assets	13,696	13,630	7,347	6,857
Property, plant, and equipment	2,834	2,452	1,454	1,238
Intangible assets and goodwill	413	420	2,763	2,787
Long-term investments	—	—	171	150
Other noncurrent assets	1,651	1,043	682	567
Total assets	$18,594	$17,545	€12,417	€11,599
Liabilities and shareholders' equity				
Short-term debt	$ 174	$ 155	€ 288	€ 681
Accounts payable	1,930	1,669	1,652	1,825
Accrued expenses	2,491	2,036	1,249	1,147
Income taxes payable	432	84	294	240
Other current liabilities	—	18	894	839
Total current liabilities	5,027	3,962	4,378	4,732
Long-term debt	1,199	1,210	1,584	653
Other noncurrent liabilities	1,544	1,292	837	733
Total liabilities	7,770	6,464	6,799	6,118
Shareholders' equity	10,824	11,081	5,618	5,481
Total liabilities and shareholders' equity	$18,594	$17,545	€12,417	€11,599

	NIKE, INC. Income Sheets ($ millions) Year ended May 31,		ADIDAS GROUP, AG Income Sheets (€ millions) Year ended December 31,	
	2014	2013	2014	2013
Net sales	$27,799	$25,313	€14,534	€14,203
Cost of sales	15,353	14,279	7,610	7,202
Gross profit	12,446	11,034	6,924	7,001
Operating expenses, net	8,766	7,796	6,041	5,820
Operating profit	3,680	3,238	883	1,181
Interest and other income (expense)	(83)	38	19	26
Interest expense	53	20	67	94
Income before income taxes	3,544	3,256	835	1,113
Income taxes	851	805	271	340
Income from continuing operations	2,693	2,451	564	773
Gain (loss) from discontinued operations	—	21	(68)	17
Net income	$ 2,693	$ 2,472	€ 496	€ 790

Required

a. Compute return on equity (ROE), return on assets (ROA), and return on financial leverage (ROFL) for NIKE and Adidas in 2014. The corporate tax rate in Germany, where Adidas is headquartered, is about 30%.

b. Disaggregate the ROA's computed into profit margin (PM) and asset turnover (AT) components. Which of these factors drives ROA for each company?

c. Compute the gross profit margin (GPM) and operating expense-to-sales ratios for each company. How do these companies' profitability measures compare?

d. Compute the accounts receivable turnover (ART), inventory turnover (INVT), and property, plant, and equipment turnover (PPET) for each company. How do these companies' turnover measures compare?

e. NIKE's fiscal year ends on May 31, 2014, while Adidas's fiscal year ends on December 31, 2014 (a difference of seven months). How does this difference affect your analysis of ROE and ROA for these two companies?

f. NIKE's financial statements are prepared in accordance with U.S. GAAP, while Adidas, a German company, follows IFRS rules. How does this difference in financial reporting standards affect your comparison of these companies' financial statements?

P5-37. Analysis and Interpretation of Liquidity and Solvency for Competitors LO4

NIKE, INC. (USA)
ADIDAS GROUP (GERMANY)

Refer to the financial statements of NIKE and Adidas presented in P5-36.

Required

a. Compute each company's current ratio and quick ratio for each year. Comment on any changes that you observe.

b. Compute each company's times interest earned ratio and debt-to-equity ratio for each year. Comment on any observed changes.

c. Compare these two companies on the basis of liquidity and solvency. Do you have any concerns about either company's ability to meet its debt obligations?

P5-38. Common-Size Financial Statements LO1

NESTLÉ S.A. (SWITZERLAND)

The following are the balance sheets and income statements for Nestlé S.A., the largest food company in the world. Nestlé is headquartered in Vevey, Switzerland.

NESTLÉ S.A.
Consolidated Balance Sheets

December 31, In millions of CHF	2013	2012	2011
Assets			
Current assets			
Cash and cash equivalents	6,415	5,713	4,938
Short-term investments	638	3,583	3,050
Inventories	8,382	8,939	9,255
Trade and other receivable	12,206	13,048	13,340
Prepayments and accrued income	762	821	900
Derivative assets	230	576	731
Current income tax assets	1,151	972	1,094
Assets held for sales	282	368	16
Total current assets	30,066	34,020	33,324
Noncurrent assets			
Property, plant and equipment	26,895	26,576	23,971
Goodwill	31,039	32,688	29,008
Intangible assets	12,673	13,018	9,356
Investments in associates and joint ventures	12,315	11,586	8,629
Financial assets	4,550	4,979	7,161
Employee benefits assets	537	84	127
Current income tax assets	124	27	39
Deferred tax assets	2,243	2,899	2,476
Total noncurrent assets	90,376	91,857	80,767
Total assets	120,442	125,877	114,091
Liabilities and equity			
Current liabilities			
Financial debt	11,380	18,408	16,100
Trade and other payables	16,072	14,627	13,584
Accruals and deferred income	3,185	3,078	2,909
Provisions	523	452	576
Derivative liabilities	381	423	646
Current income tax liabilities	1,276	1,608	1,417
Liabilities directly associated with assets held for sale	100	1	—
Total current liabilities	32,917	38,597	35,232
Noncurrent liabilities			
Financial debt	10,363	9,008	6,207
Employee benefits liabilities	6,279	8,360	7,105
Provisions	2,714	2,827	3,094
Deferred tax liabilities	2,643	2,240	2,060
Other payables	1,387	2,181	2,119
Total noncurrent liabilities	23,386	24,616	20,585
Total liabilities	56,303	63,213	55,817
Equity			
Share capital	322	322	330
Treasure shares	(2,196)	(2,078)	(6,722)
Translation reserve	(20,811)	(17,924)	(16,927)
Retained earnings and other reserves	85,260	80,687	80,116
Total equity attributable to shareholders of the parent	62,575	61,007	56,797
Non-controlling interests	1,564	1,657	1,477
Total equity	64,139	62,664	58,274
Total liabilities and equity	120,442	125,877	114,091

NESTLÉ S.A. Consolidated Income Statements For the year ended December 31, in millions of CHF	2013	2012	2011
Sales	92,158	89,721	83,642
Other revenue	215	210	128
Cost of goods sold	(48,111)	(47,500)	(44,127)
Distribution expenses	(8,156)	(8,017)	(7,602)
Marketing and administration expenses	(19,711)	(19,041)	(17,395)
Research and development costs	(1,503)	(1,413)	(1,423)
Other trading income	120	141	51
Other trading expenses	(965)	(637)	(736)
Trading operating profit	14,047	13,464	12,538
Other operating income	616	146	112
Other operating expenses	(1,595)	(222)	(179)
Operating profit	13,068	13,388	12,471
Financial income	219	120	115
Financial expenses	(850)	(825)	(536)
Profit before taxes, associates and joint ventures	12,437	12,683	12,050
Taxes	(3,256)	(3,259)	(3,112)
Share of result of associates and joint ventures	1,264	1,253	866
Profit for the year	10,445	10,677	9,804
of which attributable to non-controlling interests	430	449	317
of which attributable to shareholders of the parent (Net profit)	10,015	10,228	9,487

Required

a. Prepare common-size income statements for fiscal years 2013 and 2012. What are the most significant changes between these two income statements?

b. Prepare common-size balance sheets for fiscal years 2013 and 2012. What are the most significant changes between these two balance sheets?

P5-39. Analysis and Interpretation of Profitability LO2, 3

NESTLÉ S.A. (SWITZERLAND)

Refer to the financial information of Nestlé S.A. in P5-38 to answer the following requirements for fiscal 2013 and 2012.

Required

a. Compute the company's return on investment, including return on equity (ROE), return on assets (ROA), and return on financial leverage (ROFL). The statutory tax rates in Switzerland were 27.0% in 2013 and 27.3% in 2012. Is financial leverage working to the advantage of the company's shareholders?

b. Decompose the ROA computed above into profit margin (PM) and asset turnover (AT). Which of these two factors drives ROA? What inferences do you draw from comparing PM to AT?

c. Further analyse the company's profitability by calculating the gross profit margin (GPM) and any expense to sales (ETS) ratios that you think might help explain the company's profitability.

d. Further examine the company's efficiency by computing the accounts receivable turnover (ART), inventory turnover (INVT), and property, plant and equipment turnover (PPET) for the company.

P5-40. Analysis and Interpretation of Liquidity and Solvency LO4

NESTLÉ S.A. (SWITZERLAND)

Refer to the financial information of Nestlé S.A. in P5-38 to answer the following requirements for fiscal 2013 and 2012.

Required

a. Compute the company's current ratio (CR) and quick ratio (QR). What additional information about the accounting numbers comprising these ratios might be useful in helping you assess liquidity? Do you believe the company is sufficiently liquid?

b. Compute the company's times interest earned (TIE) and debt-to-equity (D/E) ratios. Do you have any concerns about the company's ability to meet its debt obligations?

LO2, 3 **P5-41. Analysis and Interpretation of Profitability**
Balance sheets and income statements for UPS Business Service, Inc. follow. Refer to these financial statements to answer the following requirements.

UPS BUSINESS SERVICE, INC.
Income Statement

Years Ended December 31 ($ millions)	2015	2014
Revenue	$53,105	$49,545
Operating expenses		
Compensation and benefits	27,575	26,557
Other	19,450	17,347
	47,025	43,904
Operating profit	6,080	5,641
Other income and (expense)		
Investment income	44	3
Interest expense	(348)	(354)
	(304)	(351)
Income before income taxes	5,776	5,290
Income taxes	1,972	1,952
Net income	$ 3,804	$ 3,338

UPS BUSINESS SERVICE, INC.
Balance Sheet

December 31 ($ millions)	2015	2014
Assets		
Cash and cash equivalents	$ 3,034	$ 3,370
Marketable securities	1,241	711
Accounts receivable, net	6,246	5,627
Deferred income taxes	611	659
Other current assets	1,152	1,202
Total current assets	12,284	11,569
Property, plant & equipment—net	17,621	17,387
Goodwill	2,101	2,081
Intangible assets, net	585	599
Noncurrent investments and restricted cash	303	458
Other noncurrent assets	1,807	1,503
Total assets	$34,701	$33,597
Liabilities and shareowners' equity		
Current maturities of long-term debt and commercial paper	$ 33	$ 355
Accounts payable	2,300	1,974
Accrued wages and withholdings	1,843	1,505
Self-insurance reserves	781	725
Other current liabilities	1,557	1,343
Total current liabilities	6,514	5,902
Long-term debt	11,095	10,491
Pension and postretirement obligations	5,505	4,663
Deferred income tax liabilities	1,900	1,870
Other noncurrent liabilities	2,579	2,624
Total liabilities	27,593	25,550
Shareowners' equity	7,108	8,047
Total liabilities and shareowners' equity	$34,701	$33,597

Required

a. Compute ROA and disaggregate it into profit margin (PM) and asset turnover (AT) for 2015 and 2014; total assets is $31,883 million in 2013. Comment on the drivers of the ROA.

b. Compute any expense to sales (ETS) ratios that you think might help explain UPS's profitability.

c. Compute return on equity (ROE) for 2015 and 2014; the 2013 equity is $7,696 million.

d. Comment on the difference between ROE and ROA. What does this relation suggest about UPS's use of debt?

P5-42. Analysis and Interpretation of Liquidity and Solvency LO4

Refer to the financial information of UPS Business Service in P5-41 to answer the following requirements.

Required

a. Compute its current ratio and quick ratio for 2015 and 2014. Comment on any observed trends.

b. Compute its times interest earned and its debt-to-equity ratios for 2015 and 2014. Comment on any trends observed.

c. Summarise your findings in a conclusion about the company's liquidity and solvency. Do you have any concerns about its ability to meet its debt obligations?

P5-43.[A] Computing and Analysing Operating Returns LO5

Refer to the financial statements of UPS Business Service in P5-41 to answer the following requirements.

Required

a. Compute net operating profit after taxes (NOPAT) for 2015 and net operating assets (NOA) for 2014 and 2015.

b. Compute the return on net operating assets (RNOA) for 2015. What percentage of UPS's ROE is generated by operations?

c. Decompose RNOA by computing net operating profit margin (NOPM) and net operating asset turnover (NOAT) for 2015.

d. What can be inferred about UPS from these ratios?

P5-44.[B] Preparing Pro Forma Financial Statements LO6

Refer to the financial statements of UPS Business Service in P5-41 to answer the following requirements. The following assumptions should be useful:

- UPS's sales forecast for 2016 is $57,000 million.
- Operating expenses and operating profits increase in proportion to sales.
- Depreciation and amortisation expense (which is included in other operating expenses) is 3.5% of sales.
- Investment income and interest expense are unchanged in 2016.
- Income taxes are 35% of pretax earnings.
- Marketable securities and short-term investments are unchanged in 2016; all other assets (except cash) increase in proportion to sales.
- Long-term debt and current maturities of long-term debt are unchanged in 2016; all other liabilities increase in proportion to sales.
- Dividends are 50% of net income. Income and dividends are the only changes to equity in 2016.

Required

a. Prepare a pro forma income statement and pro forma balance sheet for 2016.

b. Prepare a pro forma cash flow statement for 2016.

P5-45.[C] Direct Computation of ROFL LO2

Refer to the financial information of UPS Business Service in P5-41 to answer the following requirements.

Required

a. Compute its net interest rate (NIR) and Spread for 2015.

b. Compute UPS's ROFL using the NIR and spread you computed in question *a*.

c. What do your computations in parts *a* and *b* suggest about the company's use of borrowed funds?

LO3 **P5-46. Analysis and Interpretation of Return on Investment in the Apparel Business**

GILDAN ACTIVEWEAR INC. (CANADA)
REITMANS LIMITED (CANADA)

Reitmans Limited is a retailing company, specialising in affordable women's fashion and clothing. Gilan Activewear Inc. is a supplier of quality branded basic family apparel. It owns and operates vertically-integrated, large-scale manufacturing facilities. Balance sheets and income statements for Reitmans Limited and Gildan Activewear Inc. follow.

Refer to these financial statements to answer the requirements.

REITMANS LIMITED
Balance Sheets
Fiscal years ended February 2, 2013 and January 28, 2012

($ thousands)	2013	2012
Assets		
Current assets		
Cash & cash equivalents	$ 97,626	$196,835
Marketable securities	71,630	71,442
Trade and other receivables	3,600	3,033
Derivative financial assets	548	751
Income taxes recoverables	8,709	4,735
Inventory	93,317	93,188
Prepaid expenses	25,944	11,902
Total current assets	301,374	381,886
Noncurrent assets		
Property & equipment	205,131	184,221
Intangible assets	19,224	17,057
Goodwill	42,426	42,426
Deferred income taxes	26,400	23,174
Total noncurrent assets	293,181	266,878
Total assets	594,555	648,764
Liabilities & shareholder equities		
Current liabilities		
Trades and other payables	68,781	78,778
Derivative financial liability	266	1,505
Deferred revenue	16,297	22,278
Current portion of long-term debt	1,570	1,474
Total current liabilities	86,914	104,035
Noncurrent liabilities		
Other payables	11,425	11,110
Deferred lease credits	16,805	17,317
Long-term debt	7,003	8,573
Employee pension liability	17,390	14,877
Total noncurrent liabilities	52,623	51,877
Shareholder's equity		
Share capital	39,227	39,890
Contributed surplus	6,521	5,158
Retained earnings	400,605	439,067
Accumulated other comprehensive income	8,665	8,737
Total shareholder equity	455,018	492,852
Total liability & shareholder equity	$594,555	$648,764

GILDAN ACTIVEWEAR INC.
Balance Sheets
Fiscal years ended September 29, 2013 and September 30, 2012

($ thousands)	2013	2012
Assets		
Current assets		
Cash & cash equivalents	$ 97,368	$ 70,410
Trade and other receivables	255,018	257,595
Income taxes recoverables	700	353
Inventory	595,794	553,068
Prepaid expenses	14,959	14,451
Assets held for sale	5,839	8,029
Other current assets	11,034	8,694
Total current assets	980,712	912,600
Noncurrent assets		
Property, plant & equipment	655,869	552,437
Intangible assets	247,537	259,981
Goodwill	150,099	143,833
Investment in joint venture	—	12,126
Deferred income taxes	1,443	4,471
Other noncurrent assets	7,991	10,989
Total noncurrent assets	1,062,939	983,837
Total assets	2,043,651	1,896,437
Liabilities & shareholder equities		
Current liabilities		
Trades and other payables	289,414	256,442
Total current liabilities	289,414	256,442
Noncurrent liabilities		
Long-term debt	—	181,000
Provisions	16,325	13,042
Employee benefit obligations	18,486	19,612
Total noncurrent liabilities	34,811	213,654
Shareholder's equity		
Share capital	107,867	101,113
Contributed surplus	28,869	25,579
Retained earnings	1,583,346	1,306,724
Accumulated other comprehensive income	(656)	(7,075)
Total shareholder equity	1,719,426	1,426,341
Total liability & shareholder equity	$2,043,651	$1,896,437

REITMANS LIMITED
Income Statements
Fiscal years ended February 2, 2013 and January 28, 2012

($ thousands)	2013	2012
Sales	$1,000,513	$1,019,397
Cost of goods sold	372,135	363,333
Gross profit	628,378	656,064
Selling and distribution expenses	550,165	547,367
Administrative expenses	47,371	46,878
Operating income	30,842	61,819
Finance cost	1,330	1,509
Finance income	5,624	5,562
Earnings before income tax (EBIT)	35,136	65,872
Income tax expense	8,517	18,333
Net earnings	$ 26,619	$ 47,539

GILDAN ACTIVEWEAR INC.
Income Statements
Fiscal years ended September 29, 2013 and September 30, 2012

($ thousands)	2013	2012
Sales	$2,184,303	$1,948,253
Cost of goods sold	1,550,266	1,552,128
Gross profit	634,037	396,125
Selling, general & administrative expenses	282,563	226,035
Restructuring and acquisition-related costs	8,788	14,962
Operating income	342,686	155,128
Financial expenses, net	12,013	11,598
Equity earnings in investment in joint venture	(46)	(597)
Earnings before income taxes (EBIT)	330,719	144,127
Income tax expense (recovery)	10,541	(4,337)
Net earnings	$ 320,178	$ 148,464

Required

a. Compute return on equity (ROE), return on assets (ROA), and return on financial leverage (ROFL) for each company in 2013.

b. Disaggregate the ROA's computed into profit margin (PM) and asset turnover (AT) components. Which of these factors drives ROA for each company?

c. Compute the gross profit margin (GPM) and operating expense-to-sales ratios for each company. How do these companies' profitability measures compare?

d. Compute the accounts receivable turnover (ART), inventory turnover (INVT), and property, plant and equipment turnover (PPET) for each company. How do these companies' turnover measures compare?

e. Compare and evaluate these competitors' performance in 2013.

LO3 **P5-47. Analysis and Interpretation of Liquidity and Solvency for the Apparel Business**

GILDAN ACTIVEWEAR INC. (CANADA)
REITMANS LIMITED (CANADA)

Refer to the financial statements of Reitmans Limited and Gildan Activewear Inc. presented in P5-46.

Required

a. Compute each company's current ratio and quick ratio for each year. Comment on any changes that you observe.

b. Compute each company's times interest earned ratio and debt-to-equity ratio for each year. Comment on any observed changes.

c. Compare these two companies on the basis of liquidity and solvency. Do you have any concerns about either company's ability to meet its debt obligations?

CASES AND PROJECTS

C5-48. Management Application: Gross Profit and Strategic Management LO3

One way to increase overall profitability is to increase gross profit. This can be accomplished by raising prices and/or by reducing manufacturing costs.

Required

a. Will raising prices and/or reducing manufacturing costs unambiguously increase gross profit? Explain.

b. What strategy might you develop as a manager to (i) yield a price increase for your product, or (ii) reduce product manufacturing cost?

C5-49. Management Application: Asset Turnover and Strategic Management LO3

Increasing net operating asset turnover requires some combination of increasing sales and/or decreasing net operating assets. For the latter, many companies consider ways to reduce their investment in working capital (current assets less current liabilities). This can be accomplished by reducing the level of accounts receivable and inventories, or by increasing the level of accounts payable.

Required

a. Develop a list of suggested actions to achieve all three of these objectives as manager.

b. Examine the implications of each. That is, describe the marketing implications of reducing receivables and inventories, and the supplier implications of delaying payment. How can a company achieve working capital reduction without negatively impacting its performance?

C5-50. Ethics and Governance: Earnings Management LO2, 3, 4

Companies are aware that analysts focus on profitability in evaluating financial performance. Managers have historically utilised a number of methods to improve reported profitability that are cosmetic in nature and do not affect "real" operating performance. These are typically subsumed under the general heading of "earnings management." Justification for such actions typically includes the following arguments:

- Increasing share price by managing earnings benefits shareholders; thus, no one is hurt by these actions.
- Earnings management is a temporary fix; such actions will be curtailed once "real" profitability improves, as managers expect.

Required

a. Identify the affected parties in any scheme to manage profits to prop up share price.

b. Do the ends (of earnings management) justify the means? Explain.

c. To what extent are the objectives of managers different from those of shareholders?

d. What governance structure can you envision that might prohibit earnings management?

SOLUTIONS TO REVIEW PROBLEMS

Mid-Chapter Review 1

Solution

CHINA MOBILE LIMITED
Consolidated Balance Sheets
for the year ended December 31

(in RMB million)	2013	2012
Noncurrent assets		
Property, plant and equipment	41.1%	40.9%
Construction in progress	7.3%	5.3%
Land lease prepayments and other prepayments	1.7%	1.4%
Goodwill	3.2%	3.5%
Other intangible assets	0.1%	0.1%
Interest in associates	4.6%	4.6%
Interest in a joint venture	N/A	0.0%
Deferred tax assets	1.5%	1.3%
Restricted bank deposits	0.6%	0.5%
Other financial assets	0.0%	0.0%
	60.0%	57.6%
Current assets		
Inventories	0.8%	0.7%
Accounts receivable	1.2%	1.1%
Other receivables	1.0%	0.8%
Prepayments and other current assets	1.0%	1.5%
Amount due from ultimate holding company	0.0%	0.0%
Tax recoverable	0.1%	0.0%
Bank deposits	32.1%	31.6%
Cash and cash equivalents	3.8%	6.7%
	40.0%	42.4%
Total assets	100.0%	100.0%
Current liabilities		
Accounts payable	14.8%	11.8%
Bills payable	0.1%	0.1%
Deferred revenue	5.3%	5.5%
Accrued expenses and other payables	10.8%	9.9%
Amount due to ultimate holding company	0.0%	0.0%
Amount due to immediate holding company	N/A	0.0%
Obligations under finance leases	0.0%	0.0%
Current taxation	0.7%	1.0%
	31.8%	28.3%
Noncurrent liabilities		
Interest-bearing borrowings	0.4%	2.7%
Deferred revenue, excluding current portion	0.1%	0.0%
Deferred tax liabilities	0.0%	0.0%
	0.5%	2.8%
Total liabilities	32.3%	31.1%
NET ASSETS	67.7%	68.9%
TOTAL EQUITY	67.7%	68.9%

CHINA MOBILE LIMITED Consolidated Statements of Comprehensive Income for the year ended December 31		
(in RMB million)	2013	2012
Operating revenue (Turnover)		
Revenue from telecommunications services	93.8%	96.3%
Revenue from sales of products and others	6.2%	3.7%
	100.0%	100.0%
Operating expenses		
Leased lines	3.0%	1.7%
Interconnection	4.1%	4.3%
Depreciation	16.6%	17.3%
Personnel	5.5%	5.4%
Selling expenses	14.6%	13.8%
Cost of products sold	9.7%	7.1%
Other operating expenses	25.0%	24.1%
	78.5%	73.8%
Profit from operations	21.5%	27.3%
Non-operating net income	0.1%	0.1%
Interest income	2.4%	2.2%
Finance costs	(0.1%)	(0.1%)
Share of profit of associates	1.1%	1.0%
Share of loss of a joint venture	N/A	0.0%
Profit before taxation	25.2%	29.4%
Taxation	(5.8%)	(7.2%)
Profit for the year	19.3%	22.2%

Mid-Chapter Review 2

Solution (RMB millions)

$$ROE = \frac{121{,}803}{(790{,}724 + 725{,}309)/2} = 16.07\%$$

$$ROA = \frac{121{,}803 + 331 \times (1 - 0.25)}{(1{,}167{,}392 + 1{,}052{,}109)/2} = 11.00\%$$

$$ROFL = 16.07\% - 11.00\% = 5.07\%$$

Mid-Chapter Review 3

Solution (RMB millions)

$$PM = \frac{121{,}803 + 331 \times (1 - 0.25)}{630{,}177} = 19.37\%$$

$$AT = \frac{630{,}177}{(1{,}167{,}392 + 1{,}052{,}109)/2} = 0.568$$

$$ROA = 19.37\% \times 0.578 = 11.00\%$$

$$GPM = \frac{630{,}177 - (18{,}727 + 25{,}998 + 61{,}363)}{630{,}177} = 83.2\%$$

Note: The cost of sales is not given in the financial statements. We compute it as the sum of the leased lines expenses, interconnection expenses, and cost of products sold.

$$\text{ART} = \frac{630{,}177}{(13{,}907 + 11{,}722)/2} = 49.18 \text{ times}$$

$$\text{INVT} = \frac{(18{,}727 + 25{,}998 + 61{,}363)}{(9{,}152 + 7{,}195)/2} = 12.98 \text{ times}$$

$$\text{PPET} = \frac{630{,}177}{(479{,}227 + 430{,}509)/2} = 1.385 \text{ times}$$

Vodafone and China Mobile follow similar business models, and both companies achieve attractive returns on the capital invested by their shareholders. In 2013, China Mobile had slightly higher ROE and ROA (16.07% and 11.00%) than Vodafone (15.68% and 9.6%). Both companies relied more on equity financing than debt financing. However, Vodafone had a higher ROFL (6.08%) than China Mobile (5.07%), because it used other liabilities as a source of financing. Vodafone had a higher PM (32.6% versus 19.37%), while China Mobile achieved a higher AT (0.57 versus 0.29). The higher AT may be attributed to the fact that China Mobile had more subscribers than Vodafone (700 million versus 434 million). Further analysis of individual turnover ratios reveals that INVT was similar for the two companies (12.98 vs. 13.5), suggesting similarities in their product mix or inventory management process. On the other hand, ART was significantly higher for China Mobile, implying that the company employed a more stringent credit policy. This difference plays a significant role in China Mobile's superior asset turnover ratio.

Chapter-End Review

Solution (RMB millions)

$$\text{Current Ratio} = \frac{467{,}189}{370{,}913} = 1.26$$

$$\text{Quick Ratio} = \frac{44{,}931 + 374{,}977 + 13{,}907}{370{,}913} = 1.17$$

$$\text{Debt-to-equity ratio} = \frac{376{,}668}{790{,}724} = 0.48$$

$$\text{Times interest earned} = \frac{158{,}579 + 331}{331} = 480.09$$

China Mobile was more liquid than Vodafone, as indicated by a higher current ratio (1.26 vs. 0.99) and a higher quick ratio (1.17 vs. 0.73). The debt-to-equity ratios of both companies were below one, indicating that they rely more on equity financing than debt financing. However, Vodafone was more debt-financed than China Mobile, as shown by their debt-to-equity ratios of 0.70 and 0.48, respectively. This is consistent with Vodafone having a higher ROFL ratio than China Mobile (see Mid-Chapter Review 2). Nevertheless, neither company had issues with solvency. In particular, China Mobile reported a TIE ratio of 480.09, indicating that it had no difficulty meeting its short-term debt obligations. TIE for Vodafone cannot be computed for FY 2013, because its EBIT was negative. However, Vodafone's high cash balance, the reduction of debt outstanding, and the decision to increase dividends in 2013 all suggest that it too had no liquidity problem.

Appendix-End Review A

Solution (RMB millions)

Operating assets:

2013: $1,167,392 - 53,940 - 127 - 94 = 1,113,231$

2012: $1,052,109 - 48,343 - 6 - 127 - 102 = 1,003,531$

Operating liabilities:

2013: $376,668 - 4,989 - 22 = 371,657$

2012: $326,800 - 28,619 - 39 - 16 = 298,126$

Net operating assets (NOA):

2013: $1,113,231 - 371,657 = 741,574$

2012: $1,003,531 - 298,126 = 705,405$

$$\text{NOPAT} = 121,803 - [(23,261 - 331) \times (1 - 25\%)] = 104,606$$

$$\text{RNOA} = \frac{\text{NOPAT}}{\text{Avg. NOA}} = \frac{104,606}{(741,574 + 705,405)/2} = 14.46\%$$

$$\text{NOPM} = \frac{\text{NOPAT}}{\text{Sales revenue}} = \frac{104,606}{630,177} = 16.60\%$$

$$\text{NOAT} = \frac{\text{Sales revenue}}{\text{Avg. NOA}} = \frac{630,177}{(741,574 + 705,405)/2} = 0.87$$

$$\text{RNOA} = \text{NOPM} \times \text{NOAT} = 16.60\% \times 0.87 = 14.46\%$$

Appendix-End Review B

Solution (RMB millions)

CHINA MOBILE LIMITED
Pro Forma Income Statement
(in RMB million)

Year ended December 31	2014	
Operating revenue (Turnover)	670,000	(6.32% growth)
Operating expenses		(6.32% increase)
Leased lines	19,910	
Interconnection	27,641	
Depreciation	111,315	
Personnel	36,548	
Selling expenses	97,637	
Cost of products sold	65,241	
Other operating expenses	167,486	
	525,779	
Profit from operations	144,221	
Non-operating net income (no change)	910	
Interest income (no change)	15,289	
Finance costs (no change)	(331)	
Share of profit of associates (no change)	7,062	
Profit before taxation	167,151	
Taxation @ 25%	(41,788)	
Profit for the year	125,363	

CHINA MOBILE LIMITED Pro Forma Balance Sheet (in RMB million)	
December 31,	**2014**
Noncurrent assets	
Property, plant and equipment (0.76 × 670,000)	509,511
Intangible assets	1,130
Goodwill	39,225
Other long-term assets	187,203
Other financial assets (no change)	6,943
	744,012
Current assets	
Inventories	9,730
Accounts receivable	14,786
Other receivables	12,385
Prepayments and other current assets	13,368
Other financial assets (no change)	374,977
Cash and cash equivalents (plug)	71,762
	497,008
Total assets	1,241,020
Current liabilities	
Accounts payable	184,099
Deferred revenue	65,694
Accrued expenses and other payables	144,487
Obligations under finance lease (no change)	68
	394,348
Noncurrent liabilities	
Interest-bearing borrowings (no change)	4,989
Other long-term liabilities	814
	5,803
Total liabilities	400,151
Net assets	840,869
Total equity	840,869

Appendix-End Review C

Solution (RMB millions)

$$\text{Net Interest Rate (NIR)} = \frac{331 \times (1 - 25\%)}{(326{,}800 + 376{,}668)/2} = 0.07\%$$

$$\text{ROFL} = \frac{(326{,}800 + 376{,}668)/2}{(725{,}309 + 790{,}724)/2} \times (11.00\% - 0.07\%) = 5.07\%$$

LEARNING OBJECTIVES

1. Describe and apply the criteria for determining when revenue is recognised. (p. 274)
2. Illustrate revenue and expense recognition when the transaction involves future deliverables. (p. 276)
3. Illustrate revenue and expense recognition for long-term projects. (p. 279)
4. Estimate and account for uncollectible accounts receivable. (p. 282)
5. Calculate accounts receivable turnover and average collection period. (p. 288)
6. Discuss earnings management and explain how it affects analysis and interpretation of financial statements. (p. 290)
7. Appendix 6A: Describe and illustrate the reporting for nonrecurring items. (p. 291)
8. Appendix 6B: Describe the new standard for revenue recognition and discuss its potential effects. (p. 294)

CHAPTER

6

Reporting and Analysing Revenues and Receivables

TOMTOM
www.tomtom.com

TomTom N.V. is a Dutch provider of Global Positioning System (GPS) navigation devices, software, and content. It is headquartered in Amsterdam, Netherlands, with ordinary shares traded on Euronext. TomTom operates in four business segments. Its Consumer business produces and sells portable navigation devices (PNDs), as well as GPS enabled sports watches. Its Automotive business sells map content, traffic data services, navigation software, and pre-integrated navigation systems to car manufacturers. Its Licensing unit offers navigation software and content to in-dash system vendors and automotive equipment manufacturers. Its Business Solutions provides fleet management solutions to commercial fleets.

In 2013, TomTom owned 51% of the PND market in Europe and 18% in North America. TomTom became the provider of mapping data for Apple's new mobile operating system in 2012 and the provider of real-time traffic data for BlackBerry's customers in 2013. TomTom reported revenue of €963 million in 2013, compared with €1,057 million in 2012. While the gross margin increased from 52% in 2012 to 54% in 2013, higher operating expenses reduced operating income from €70 million in 2012 to €26 million in 2013 (the corresponding operating margin decreased from 7% to 3%).

Profitability is the primary measure by which financial statement users gauge a company's success in efficiently offering products and services that receive a favourable response from customers. In this chapter, we focus on how companies report operating income. Operating income is determined by decisions about how and when to recognise revenues and how expenses are matched against revenues. In addition, the income statement also includes nonrecurring (or transitory) items, such as income or loss from discontinued operations and restructuring charges. Transitory items are often important events reflecting very large dollar amounts and are distinguished by the fact that they are unlikely to recur in subsequent years. Understanding how such nonrecurring items are reported is crucial to interpreting a company's profitability.

TomTom's performance cannot be measured by profits alone. In order to control costs and improve operating profits, TomTom has to effectively manage operating assets. These assets include receivables, inventories, and plant assets. For example, accounts receivable is an important operating asset at TomTom because its sales are all on account. By extending credit to customers on favourable credit terms, TomTom stimulates sales. However, extending credit exposes the company to collectability risk—the risk that some customers will not pay the amounts owed. In addition, accounts receivable do not earn interest, and involve administrative costs associated with billing and collection. Hence, management of receivables is critical to financial success. In addition to discussing operating income, this chapter describes the reporting of receivables. The reporting of other operating assets is covered in subsequent chapters.

Sources: www.tomtom.com; TomTom 2013 Annual Report.

CHAPTER ORGANISATION

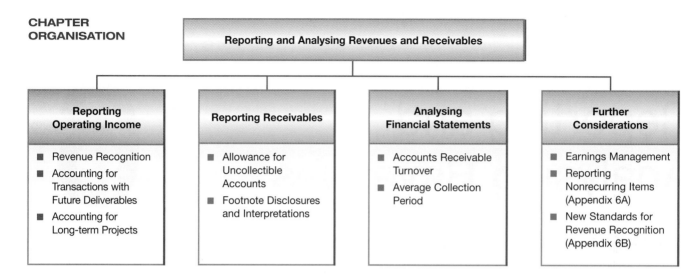

Reporting and Analysing Revenues and Receivables

Reporting Operating Income	Reporting Receivables	Analysing Financial Statements	Further Considerations
■ Revenue Recognition ■ Accounting for Transactions with Future Deliverables ■ Accounting for Long-term Projects	■ Allowance for Uncollectible Accounts ■ Footnote Disclosures and Interpretations	■ Accounts Receivable Turnover ■ Average Collection Period	■ Earnings Management ■ Reporting Nonrecurring Items (Appendix 6A) ■ New Standards for Revenue Recognition (Appendix 6B)

REPORTING OPERATING INCOME

The income statement is the primary source of information about recent company performance. This information is used to predict future performance for investment purposes and to assess the credit-worthiness of a company. The income statement is also used to evaluate the quality of management.

This section describes the information reported in the income statement and its analysis implications. The central questions that the income statement attempts to answer are

- How profitable has the company been recently?
- How did it achieve that profitability?
- Will the current profitability level persist?

To answer these three profitability questions, it is not enough to focus on a company's net income. Rather, we must use the various classifications within the income statement to see how profits were achieved and what the future prospects look like. Exhibit 6.1 provides a schematic of the primary income statement classifications.

EXHIBIT 6.1 Income Statement Classifications

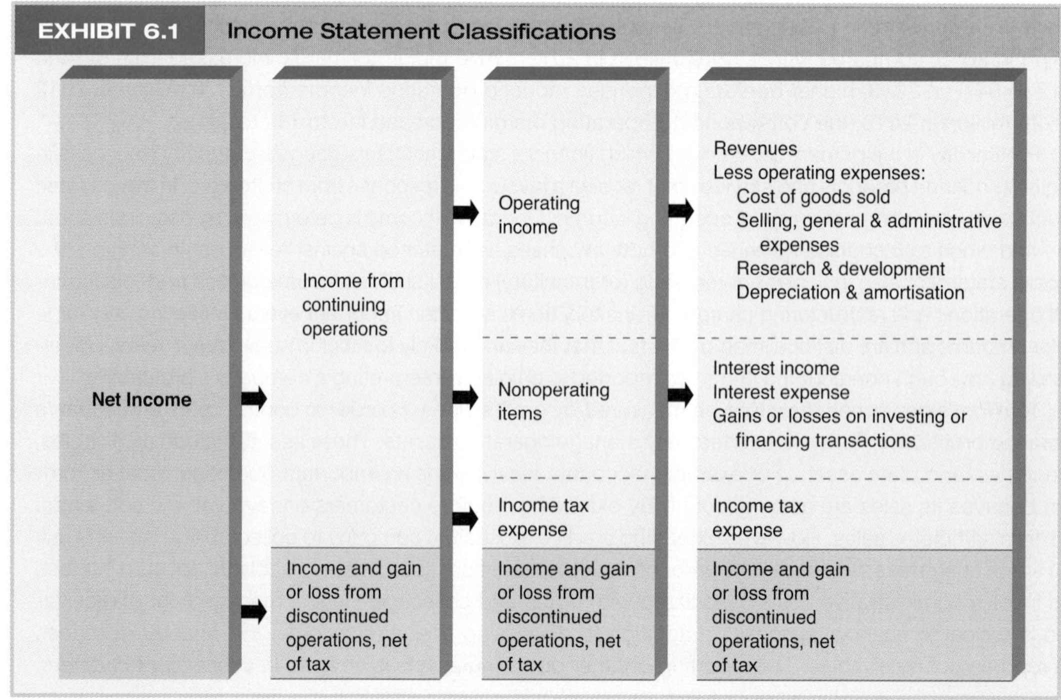

Operating activities refer to the primary transactions and events of a company. These include the purchase of goods from suppliers, the conversion of materials into finished products, the promotion and distribution of goods, the sale of goods and services to customers, and post-sale customer support. Operating activities are reported in the income statement under items such as sales, cost of goods sold, and selling, general, and administrative expenses. They represent a company's primary activities, which must be executed successfully for a company to remain consistently profitable.

Nonoperating activities relate to the financial (borrowing) and securities investment activities of a company. These activities are typically reported in the income statement under items such as interest income and expenses, dividend revenues, and gains and losses on sales of securities. Distinguishing income components by operating versus nonoperating is an important part of effective financial statement analysis because operating activities drive company performance. It is of interest, for example, to know whether company profitability results from operating activities, or whether poorly performing operating activities are being masked by income from nonoperating activities.

FYI When analysing a company's income statement, it is important to distinguish operating activities from nonoperating activities and recurring activities from nonrecurring activities. ■

All the line items in income from continuing operations are presented before taxes, with the final line item being income tax expense. The accounting for income taxes is discussed more fully in Chapter 10.

After income from continuing operations, the income statement may present an item that is considered nonrecurring in nature: income or loss from discontinued operations. When this item is presented, it is always listed after income from continuing operations and net of income tax expense or benefit. Appendix 6A at the end of this chapter provides a detailed description of nonrecurring items. Finally, many large corporations report something called net income attributable to **noncontrolling interests**. Such an amount arises when a company consolidates a subsidiary that it controls, but for which it holds less than 100% ownership. This topic is covered in Chapter 12.

Exhibit 6.2 presents the 2013 and 2012 statements of income (also called statements of operations or income statements) for TomTom. TomTom has no discontinued operations during this time period, so income from continuing operations is the same as net income (or net result, as TomTom calls it). Like many companies, TomTom presents gross result and operating result as subtotals in its income statement. Gross result (or gross profit) is computed by subtracting cost of sales from sale revenue (also called turnover). TomTom's operating result (also called operating profit or operating income) is computed by subtracting its total operating expenses (including research and development; amortisation; marketing; selling, general and administrative; and stock compensation) from gross result. Nonoperating income and expenses, such as interest income and expense, other financial gain and loss, and share of results of associates (discussed in Chapter 12), are added to or deducted from the subtotal for operating result, yielding income before tax. Finally, income tax expense is subtracted from income before tax to compute net income. However, not all of the €20,063,000 net income goes to TomTom's shareholders. This is because TomTom has non-wholly-owned subsidiaries: €19,539,000 of the €20,063,000 net income is attributable to TomTom's shareholders, while the remaining €524,000 is attributable to the minority shareholders of TomTom's non-wholly-owned subsidiaries. The accounting for subsidiaries is discussed in Chapter 12.

IFRS does not have specific rules for classifying revenue and expense items as either operating or nonoperating, so financial statement users must be careful to examine each revenue and expense item to determine if it is appropriately listed as part of operating income. Specifically, sales, cost of goods sold, and most selling, general, and administrative expenses are categorised as operating activities. Alternatively, investment-related income from dividends and interest is nonoperating, as is interest expense. Gains and losses on debt retirements and sales of investments are also nonoperating.[1]

[1] To further complicate matters, the classification of some items in the income statement as nonoperating is not consistent with their classification in the cash flow statement. Specifically, interest and dividend income and interest expense could be classified as operating in the cash flow statement, but nonoperating in most income statements. Of course, the distinction between operating and nonoperating items depends on the company's business. For TomTom, interest income and expense would be classified as nonoperating, but for a financial institution (e.g., a bank), those same items would be considered part of their operations. Purchases and sales of production equipment would be considered nonoperating for TomTom, but operating for a company in the business of buying and selling used equipment.

EXHIBIT 6.2 Distinguishing Operating and Nonoperating Sources of Income

TOMTOM
Consolidated Statements of Income
for the year ended December 31

(€ in thousands)	2013	2012
Revenue	963,454	1,057,134
Cost of sales	442,207	502,398
Gross result	521,247	554,736
Operating expenses		
Research and development expenses	165,408	166,315
Amortisation of technology and databases	81,436	84,011
Marketing expenses	62,577	57,305
Selling, general and administrative expenses	178,300	169,716
Stock compensation expense	7,980	7,140
Total operating expenses	495,701	484,487
Operating result	25,546	70,249
Interest result	(2,945)	(12,084)
Other financial result	(1,619)	1,642
Result of associates	3,091	726
Result before tax	24,073	60,533
Income tax (expense)/income	(4,010)	68,660*
Net result	20,063	129,193
Attributable to:		
Equity holders of the parent	19,539	128,724
Non-controlling interests	524	469
Net result	20,063	129,193
Eernings per share (in €)		
Basic	0.09	0.58
Diluted	0.09	0.58

* Included a one-time tax gain of €80 million related to the settlement of prior years' tax issues with the Dutch tax authorities during 2012.

TomTom also invests in financial assets and has a significant equity stake in other companies, which generate investment income, as well as gain and loss. Furthermore, TomTom finances its operations with borrowings, which incur interest expense. So, making predictions about TomTom's profitability for future years would be improved by separating the results of its product and service operations from those of its investing and financing activities. In addition, operating income is the normal focus of business unit managers in a company—financing activities and investments in financial instruments and tax administration are usually determined at the central corporate level.

Revenue Recognition

LO1 Describe and apply the criteria for determining when revenue is recognised.

Revenue is one of the most important metrics of a company's operating success. The objective of almost all operating activities is to obtain a favourable response from customers, and revenue is a primary indicator of how customers view the company's product and service offerings. Companies can improve profits by reducing costs, but the effects of those improvements are limited unless revenues are increasing. Accordingly, growth in revenue is carefully monitored by management and by investors, as exemplified by the attention given to "same-store sales growth" in the retail industry.

BUSINESS INSIGHT

New Revenue Recognition Standards The IASB and the U.S. Financial Accounting Standards Board (FASB) issued new, converged accounting standards for revenue recognition in May of 2014. The new standard is intended to consolidate the guidance on revenue recognition into one standard, eliminate inconsistencies that currently exist in applying revenue recognition to different transactions and in different industries, and align IFRS and U.S. GAAP on revenue recognition. The new standard generally employs many of the same broad concepts to revenue recognition as the current standards. Revenues will still have to be earned to be recognised, but the determination of when revenues are earned will change in some cases under the new standard. The new standard is effective for publicly traded, calendar year-end companies starting January 1, 2018. Since the effective date is more than two years away at the time of this writing, we do not have examples of companies applying the new revenue standard. We provide an expanded discussion of the new standard and conjecture about implications of the new standard in Appendix 6B at the end of this chapter. We discuss and provide examples of the current standards in the text of the chapter.

Revenue recognition refers to the timing and amount of revenue reported by the company. The decision of when to recognise revenue depends on certain criteria. Determining whether the criteria for revenue recognition are met is often subjective and requires judgement. Therefore, financial statement readers should pay careful attention to companies' revenue recognition, particularly when companies face pressures to meet income targets. Indeed, many enforcement actions against companies for inaccurate, and sometimes fraudulent financial reporting are for improper (usually premature) revenue recognition.

IFRS dictates two **revenue recognition criteria** that must be met for revenue to be recognised (and reported) on the income statement. Revenue is recognised when (1) it is probable that future economic benefits will flow to the entity, and (2) these benefits can be reliably measured. IFRS provides further guidance for three specific categories of revenue. First, revenue from the sale of goods should be recognised when (1) the entity has transferred the significant risks and rewards of ownership to the buyer, (2) the entity retains no managerial involvement and effective control over the goods sold, (3) the amount of revenue can be reliably measured, (4) it is probable that the economic benefits associated with the sale will flow to the entity, and (5) the costs incurred or to be incurred can be reliably measured. Second, revenue from rendering of services should be recognised when the stage of completion of the transaction can be reliably measured and conditions (3) to (5) above are met. Third, interest revenue should be recognised using the effective interest method (discussed in Chapter 9), royalty revenue should be recognised on an accrual basis according to the substance of the transaction, and dividends revenue should be recognised when the shareholder's right to receive payment is established.

Many companies recognise revenues when the product or service is delivered to the customer. For these companies, delivery occurs at the same time, or shortly after, the sale takes place. Complications arise if there is uncertainty about collectibility or when the sale is contingent on product performance, product approval, or similar contingencies. In some industries, it is standard practice to allow customers to return the product within a specified period of time. When the customer retains a **right of return**, it is sometimes inappropriate to recognise revenue at the time of delivery. For many companies, returns are either immaterial in amount or relatively easy to predict based on history of a large number of similar transactions. For these companies, revenue can be recognised when the product is delivered to the customer. The expected returns are estimated and deducted from revenue when reporting the sale in the income statement. However, if the amount of returns is difficult to estimate, revenues should not be recognised until the return period expires.

The term "delivery" does not refer only to transportation to the customer's location, but also the transfer of title and the risks and rewards of ownership. In a **consignment** sale, a *consignor* delivers product to a *consignee*, but retains ownership until the consignee sells the product to the ultimate customer. As long as ownership remains with the consignor, a sale has not taken place. Only when the consignee sells the product should the consignor record the sales revenue.

BUSINESS INSIGHT

Product Returns and Sales Incentives at TomTom Following is an excerpt from TomTom's accounting policies as reported in its 2013 annual report.

> When returns are probable, an estimate is made of the expected financial impact of these returns. The estimate is based upon historical data on the return rates and information on the inventory levels in the distribution channel.
>
> The group reduces revenue for estimates of sales incentives. We offer sales incentives, including channel rebates and end-user rebates for our products. The estimate is based on our historical experience, taking into account future expectations on rebate payments.

TomTom's policy regarding product returns and sales incentives is consistent with IFRS, in that expected returns and rebates are estimated and deducted from revenue at the time the sale is recorded. TomTom makes these estimates by taking into account historical experience and future expectations.

LO2 Illustrate revenue and expense recognition when the transaction involves future deliverables.

Revenue Recognition Subsequent to Customer Purchase There are many businesses in which customers purchase a product or a service prior to its delivery. For instance, a customer may pay for a year's subscription to a periodical. The publisher receives the cash at the start of the subscription, but it earns revenue when it delivers the periodical to the subscriber. Or, a homeowner may pay for the upcoming year's casualty insurance, but the insurance company can only recognise revenue as it provides insurance coverage.

In settings where a company's customers pay for the product or service prior to its delivery, the company must recognise a liability (usually called **unearned revenue** or **deferred revenue**)[2] at the time of the customer's payment. Then this liability is reduced, and revenue recognised, as the product or service is delivered.

Suppose that on January 1, a subscriber pays $36 for an annual subscription to a monthly magazine. At the time of payment, the publisher would make the following entry:

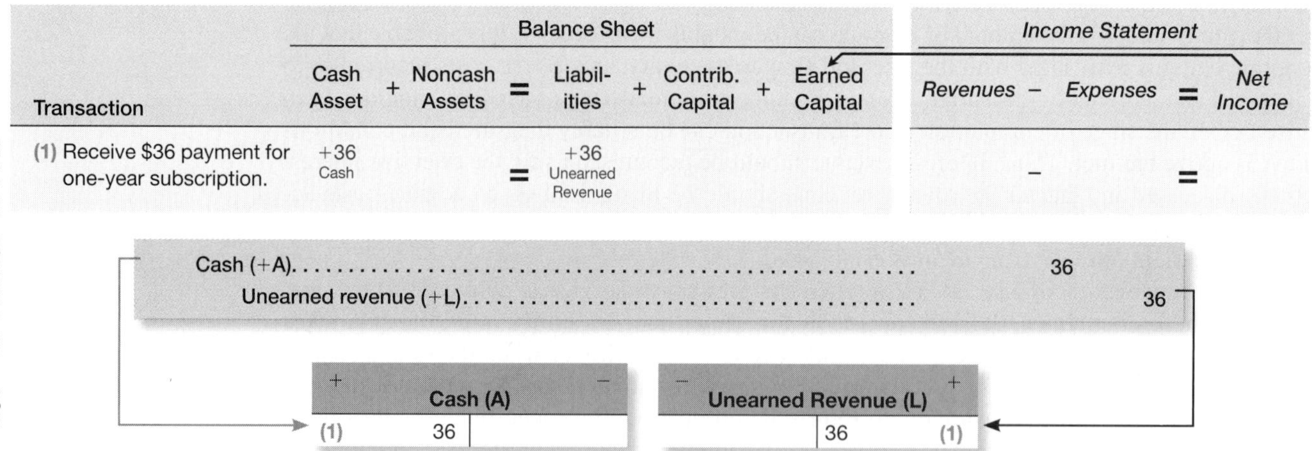

Transaction	Cash Asset	+	Noncash Assets	=	Liabilities	+	Contrib. Capital	+	Earned Capital	Revenues	−	Expenses	=	Net Income
(1) Receive $36 payment for one-year subscription.	+36 Cash			=	+36 Unearned Revenue						−		=	

ANALYSE / JOURNALISE / POST

Cash (+A)	36	
Unearned revenue (+L)		36

+ Cash (A) −	
(1) 36	

− Unearned Revenue (L) +	
	36 (1)

The unearned revenue liability represents the publisher's obligation—not to make a payment, but to provide the promised publication. Most liabilities reflect obligations to make a future payment, but unearned revenue is one of a handful of *deferred performance liabilities* that represent an obligation for future performance.

On March 31, at the end of its first quarter, the publisher would recognise that three magazines had been delivered to the subscriber, and the publisher has earned three times the monthly revenue of $3, or $9. The entry to recognise this revenue is the following.

[2] The term used for unearned revenue may be particular to the company's business. For instance, both **British Airways** and **Singapore Airlines** use Sales in Advance of Carriage to represent customers' purchases of tickets in advance of their flights.

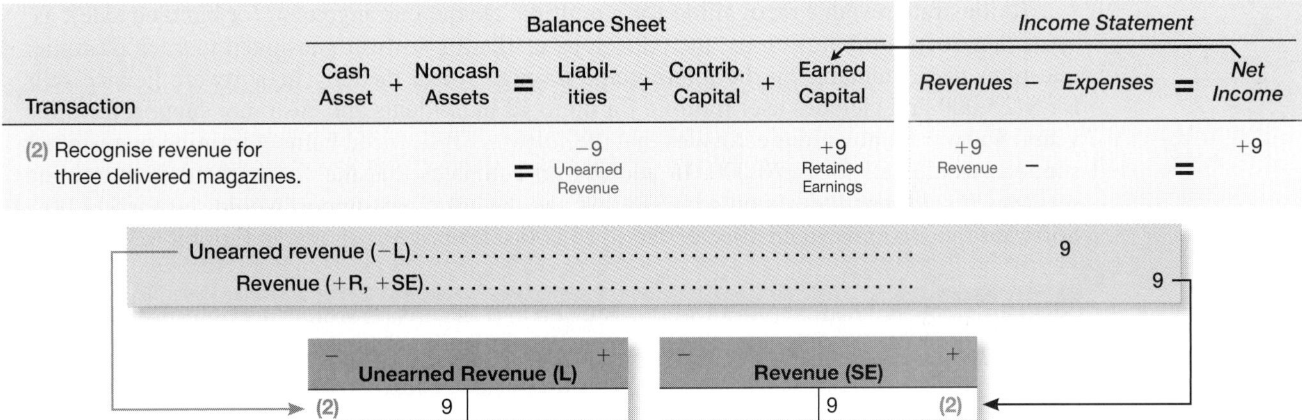

The same entries would be made until the subscription expired. In the March 31 balance sheet, the publisher would have a deferred revenue liability of $27, reflecting the remaining obligation for nine months of subscription delivery. And, the quarter's indirect method operating cash flows would include $9 in revenue (in net income) and the $27 increase in unearned revenue liability which, in total, reflect the $36 received from the customer.

Unearned revenue is seen in a growing number of financial statements as companies increase their promises of future deliveries of products and service due to the changing nature of products and services in the economy and also in an effort to build a continuing relationship with their customers. From the point of view of a financial analyst, one implication of revenue deferral is that the change in revenue from one period to the next is not equal to the change in customer purchases over the same period. In the case of our publisher with one-year subscriptions, quarterly revenue is actually a composite of subscriber purchases over the current quarter plus the last three quarters and, therefore, not an ideal indicator of how current customers are responding to the publisher's offerings. Both the revenue and unearned revenue accounts need to be analysed to obtain a complete picture.

A revenue recognition complication arises when two or more products or services are sold under the same sales agreement for one lump-sum price. These bundled sales are called **multiple element arrangements** and are commonplace in the software industry, where developers sell software, training, maintenance, and customer support in one transaction. In these circumstances, IFRS requires that the sales price be allocated among the various elements of the sale in proportion to their fair value. Revenue allocated to the elements that have not been delivered (such as maintenance and customer support) must be deferred and recognised as the service is rendered in future periods. As shown in the Business Insight box below, TomTom's accounting for multiple element arrangements is consistent with this requirement.

BUSINESS INSIGHT

TomTom's Revenue Recognition Following is an excerpt from TomTom's policies on revenue recognition as reported in notes to its 2013 annual report.

> Revenue on the sale of goods is only recognised when the risks and rewards of ownership of goods are transferred to the customers. . . . The risks and rewards of ownership are generally transferred at the time the product is shipped and delivered to the customer and . . . title and risk have passed to the customer and acceptance of the product . . . has been obtained.
>
> Royalty revenue . . . is recognised on an accrual basis based on the contractual terms and substance of the relevant arrangements with the customers.
>
> Services revenue . . . is recognised over the agreed or estimated service period on a straight-line basis.
>
> The group's product and services offerings include arrangements that require the group to deliver equipment (e.g., navigation hardware) and/or a number of services (e.g., traffic information services) under one agreement, or under a series of agreements that are commercially linked (referred to as 'multiple-element arrangements'). In such multiple-element arrangements, the consideration received is allocated to each separately identifiable element, based on the relative fair values of each identifiable element . . .

TomTom's criteria for revenue recognition mirror IFRS guidance for the three categories of revenue described earlier in this chapter.

To illustrate revenue recognition for a multiple element arrangement (or bundled sale), assume that Software Innovations, Inc., develops marketing software designed to track customer questions and comments on the Internet and through social media. The software licence sells for $125,000 and includes user training for up to 12 individuals and customer support for three years. Software Innovations estimates that the software, if licenced without training or customer support, would sell for $120,000. In addition, it estimates that the value of the user training services, if sold separately, would be $18,000 and the customer support would sell for $12,000. Software Innovations would allocate the $125,000 sales price as shown in Exhibit 6.3.

EXHIBIT 6.3 Allocation of the Sales Price in a Multiple Element Arrangement

Element	Estimated value	Percent of total value		Bundle sales price		Sales price allocated to each element
Software licence	$120,000	80%	×	$125,000	=	$100,000
Training	18,000	12%	×	$125,000	=	15,000
Customer support	12,000	8%	×	$125,000	=	10,000
Total	$150,000	100%				$125,000

The sale would be recorded as revenue for the portion that was allocated to software and as deferred (or unearned) revenue for that portion that was allocated to training and customer support:

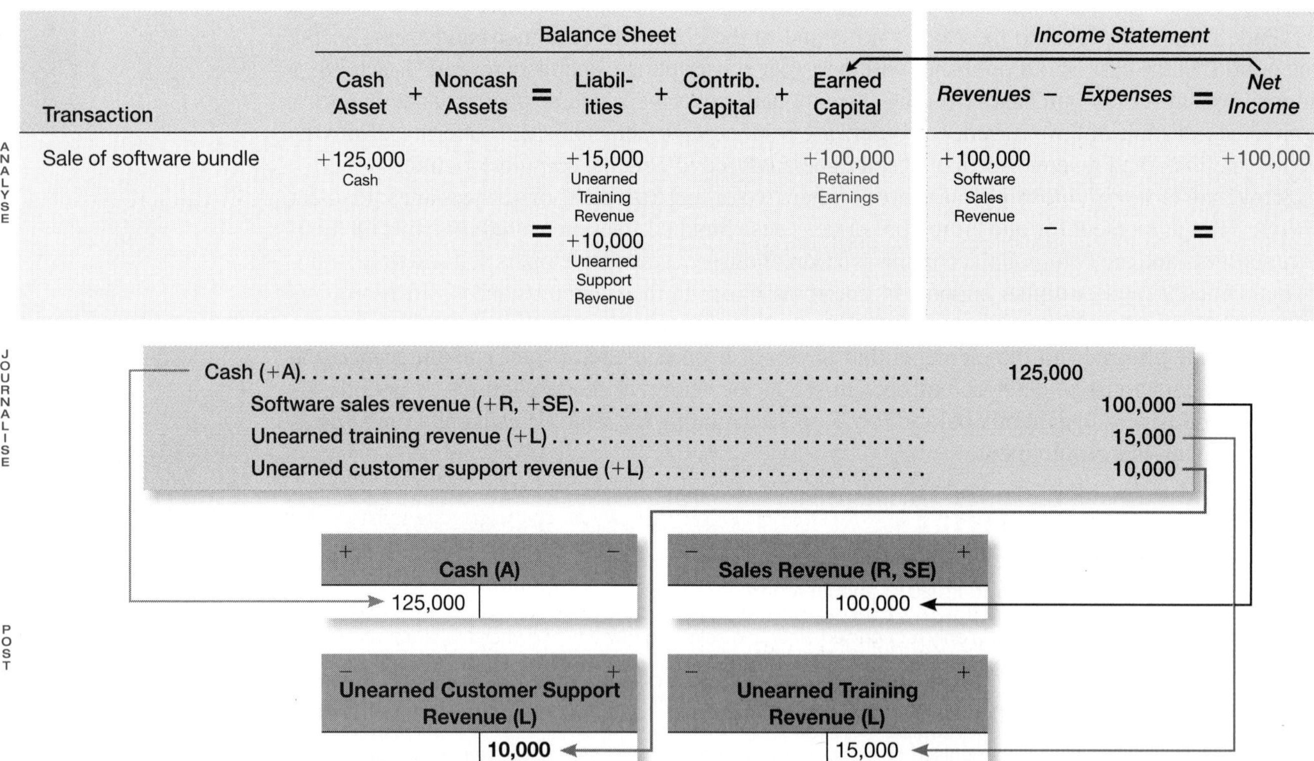

The unearned training revenue would be recognised as training services are provided. Software Innovations might recognise 1/12 of the $15,000, or $1,250 for each individual trained. The unearned customer support revenue would be recognised over time ($10,000/3 = $3,333 each year).

MID-CHAPTER REVIEW 1

The Sage Group plc is a British software company and a leading provider of enterprise resource planning software to small and medium sized companies. When Sage sells a software subscription, it recognises revenue ratably over the term of the subscription contract and it also defers some of the revenue because it will deliver support and upgrades in the future. For instance, in its 2014 annual report, it states

> Subscription contract revenue and maintenance and support revenue is recognised on a straight-line basis over the term of the contract (including non-specified upgrades when included). Revenue relating to future periods is classified as deferred income on the balance sheet.

Information about Sage's revenues from its income statements and deferred income liability from its balance sheets is given below (all amounts in £ millions).

Fiscal year ended September 30	Revenue	Deferred income liability (end of year)
2014	£1,306.8	£402.7
2013	1,376.1	406.8
2012	1,340.2	420.3
2011	1,334.1	404.7

Sage put into the deferred income liability the amount of customer purchases made during a year that were not recognised as revenue at the time of customer purchase, and it took out from the deferred income liability the amounts of revenue recognised during the year that derived from customer purchases made in earlier periods.

Required

1. Calculate the revenue growth rates for fiscal years 2013 and 2014.
2. From the information on revenues and on changes in the unearned revenue liability, determine the amount of customer purchases for fiscal years 2012, 2013, and 2014.
3. Calculate the growth rates in customer purchases for fiscal years 2013 and 2014. Why do these differ from those calculated in part 1?

The solution to this review problem can be found on page 314.

LO3 Illustrate revenue and expense recognition for long-term projects.

Revenue Recognition for Long-term Projects Challenges arise in determining revenue recognition for companies with long-term production processes (spanning more than one reporting period) such as consulting firms, construction companies, and defence contractors. For these companies, revenue is often recognised using the **percentage-of-completion method**, which recognises revenue based on the costs incurred under the contract relative to its total expected costs.[3] In addition to determining when to recognise revenues to properly measure and report a company's performance, we must also decide when to recognise expenses. The **matching principle** was introduced in Chapter 2 and requires that expenses be recognised in the same period that the associated revenue is recognised. In particular, expenses are recognised when assets are diminished (or liabilities increased) as a result of earning revenue or supporting operations, even if there is no immediate decrease in cash. The following illustration demonstrates the appropriate recognition of revenues and expenses using the percentage-of-completion method.

PERCENTAGE-OF-COMPLETION METHOD To illustrate the percentage-of-completion method, assume that Built-Rite Construction signs a $10 million contract to construct a building. The company estimates $7.5 million in construction costs, yielding an expected gross profit of $2.5 million. Further assume that Built-Rite incurs $4.5 million in construction costs during the first year of construction, and the remaining $3 million in costs during the second year. The amount of revenue and gross profit that Built-Rite would report each year is illustrated in Exhibit 6.4.

[3] In some circumstances, a company may use some other indicator of progress, like employee time or the achievement of customer-specified milestones.

EXHIBIT 6.4 Revenue Recognition Using the Percentage-of-Completion Method

Year	Percentage completed	Revenue recognised	Expense recognised	Gross profit
1.	$4,500,000/$7,500,000 = 60%	$10,000,000 × 60% = $ 6,000,000	$4,500,000	$1,500,000
2.	$3,000,000/$7,500,000 = 40%	$10,000,000 × 40% = $ 4,000,000	$3,000,000	$1,000,000
Totals	100%	$10,000,000	$7,500,000	$2,500,000

Using the percentage-of-completion method, Built-Rite would report $1.5 million in gross profit from this project in the first year and $1.0 million in the second year. The timing of revenue and gross profit coincides with the amount of work completed.

FYI IFRS requires use of the percentage-of-completion method for long-term contracts whenever management can reasonably estimate revenues and expenses. ■

The percentage-of-completion method of revenue recognition requires an estimate of total costs. This estimate is made at the beginning of the contract and is typically the one used to initially bid the contract. However, estimates are inherently prone to estimation error. If total construction costs are underestimated, the percentage of completion is overestimated (the denominator is too low) and too much revenue and gross profit are recognised in the early years of the project. The estimation process used in this method has the potential for inaccurate or, even, improper revenue recognition. Estimates of costs to complete projects are also difficult to verify for auditors. This uncertainty adds additional risk to financial statement analysis.

COST-RECOVERY METHOD To justify use of the percentage-of-completion method, a company must have a contract with the customer that specifies a fixed or determinable price. In addition, project costs must be reasonably estimable. When a long-term project fails to meet these criteria, the cost-recovery method should be used instead. Under the **cost-recovery method**, revenue is recognised in an amount equal to the cash collected, and no gross profit is reported until the total cost of the project is fully recovered. Assume that Built-Rite Construction receives cash payments of $4 and $6 million in the first and second years, respectively. In the first year, it would recognise $4 million in revenue and match it with $4 million in expense to report a zero gross profit. In the second year, it should recognise $6 million in revenue and match it with the remaining cost of $3.5 million, resulting in a gross profit of $2.5 million. Exhibit 6.5 provides a comparison of the gross profit calculations using each of these two accounting methods for the Built-Rite Construction contract described earlier.

EXHIBIT 6.5 Comparison of the Percentage-of-Completion and Cost-Recovery Methods

Percentage-of-Completion Method			Cost-Recovery Method		
	Year 1	Year 2		Year 1	Year 2
Revenues.	$6,000,000	$4,000,000	Revenues.	$4,000,000	$6,000,000
Expenses.	4,500,000	3,000,000	Expenses.	4,000,000	3,500,000
Gross profit	$1,500,000	$1,000,000	Gross profit	$ 0	$2,500,000

FYI Application of percentage-of-completion enhances earnings timeliness relative to the cost-recovery method. However, poor or biased estimates for applying percentage-of-completion can reduce or reverse the benefits of that more timely reporting. ■

The total revenue and gross profit across the two years are the same under either revenue recognition method. Likewise, there is no difference in the costs incurred to construct the building. The only difference between the percentage-of-completion method and the cost-recovery method is *when* the revenue and gross profit are reported in the income statement.

It is very likely that Built-Rite would have received some cash payments from the customer during the construction period. However, neither the percentage-of-completion method nor the cost-recovery method is affected by the schedule of cash payments from the customer. It would not make sense for Built-Rite to enter into this contract unless it had a high degree of confidence in the customer's ability and willingness to pay.

MID-CHAPTER REVIEW 2

Following is a footnote from the 2014 annual report of Bruges N.V.

> **Note 2: Revenue Recognition**
> Revenue from long-term government contracts is recognised using the percentage of completion method of accounting. Production costs are capitalised by project and are expensed based on the ratio of current period costs to estimated total contract costs. Revenue from contracts with private organisations is recognised using the cost-recovery method.

Required

1. Speculate as to possible reasons why Bruges uses different revenue recognition policies for long-term government contracts and for contracts with private organisations.
2. Assume that Bruges signed a contract in 2014 for a long-term project at a contract price of €40,000,000. The project is estimated to take three years to complete and cost €30,000,000. The cost incurred in 2014 was €12,000,000, and projected costs in 2015 and 2016 are €13,500,000 and €4,500,000 respectively. Moreover, cash collected from the customer was €10,000,000 in 2013, and Bruges is expected to receive two payments of €15,000,000 in 2014 and 2015, respectively. Compute gross profit for each year assuming that the contract is reported using the
   a. percentage-of-completion method
   b. cost-recovery method
3. Assume that Bruges overestimated the cost of the contract in question 2, such that the actual cost incurred in 2016 was €1,500,000 instead of €4,500,000. What effect would this overestimate have on income in each year?

The solution to this review problem can be found on pages 314–315.

REPORTING ACCOUNTS RECEIVABLE

Receivables are usually a major part of operating working capital. They must be carefully managed as they represent a substantial asset for most companies. IFRS requires companies to report receivables at the amount they expect to collect, necessitating an estimation of uncollectible accounts. These estimates determine the amount of receivables reported on the balance sheet as well as revenues and expenses reported on the income statement. Accordingly, it is important that companies accurately assess uncollectible accounts and report them. It is also necessary that readers of financial reports understand management's accounting choices and the effects of those choices on reported balance sheets and income statements.

FYI The phrase *trade receivables* refers to accounts receivable from customers. ■

When companies sell to other companies, they usually do not expect cash upon delivery as is common with retail customers. Instead, they offer credit terms, and the resulting sales are called **credit sales** or *sales on account*.

FYI Receivables are claims held against customers and others for money, goods, or services. ■

Companies establish credit policies (to determine which customers receive credit) by weighing the expected losses from uncollectible accounts against the expected profits generated by offering credit. Sellers know that some buyers will be unable to pay their accounts when they become due. Buyers, for example, can suffer business downturns that are beyond their control and which limit their cash available to meet liabilities. They must, then, make choices concerning which of their liabilities to pay. Liabilities to government agencies, to banks, and to bondholders are usually paid, as those creditors have enforcement powers and can quickly seize assets and disrupt operations, leading to bankruptcy and eventual liquidation. Buyers also try to cover their payroll, as they cannot exist without employees. Then, if there is cash remaining, these customers will pay suppliers to ensure a continued flow of goods.

When a customer faces financial difficulties, suppliers are often the last creditors to receive payment and are often not paid in full. Consequently, there is risk in the collectibility of accounts receivable. This *collectibility risk* is crucial to analysis of accounts receivable.

Accounts receivable are reported on the balance sheet of the seller at **net realisable value**, which is the net amount that the seller expects to collect. TomTom reports €115,429,000 of trade receivable in the current asset section of its 2013 balance sheet. Its receivables are reported net of allowances for doubtful receivables of €3,117,000. This means that the total amount owed to TomTom by customers is €118,546,000 (€115,429,000 + €3,117,000), but the company estimates that €3,117,000 of these receivables will be uncollectible. Thus, only the net amount that TomTom expects to collect is reported on the balance sheet.

FYI Receivables are classified into three types: (1) current or noncurrent, (2) trade or nontrade, (3) accounts receivable or notes receivable. Notes receivable and notes payable are discussed in Chapter 9. ■

We might ask why TomTom would sell to companies from whom they do not expect to collect the amounts owed. The answer is they would not if they knew beforehand who those companies were. That is, TomTom probably cannot identify those companies that constitute the €3,117,000 in uncollectible accounts as of its balance sheet date. Yet, TomTom knows from past experience that a certain portion of its receivables will prove uncollectible. IFRS requires a company to estimate the dollar amount of uncollectible accounts each time it issues its financial statements (even if it cannot identify specific accounts that are uncollectible), and to report its accounts receivable at the resulting *net realisable value* (total receivables less an **allowance for uncollectible accounts**).

Determining the Allowance for Uncollectible Accounts

LO4 Estimate and account for uncollectible accounts receivable.

The amount of expected uncollectible accounts is usually estimated based on an **ageing analysis**. When ageing the accounts, an analysis of receivables is performed as of the balance sheet date. Specifically, each customer's account balance is categorised by the number of days or months that the related invoices are outstanding. Based on prior experience, assessment of current economic conditions, or on other available statistics, uncollectible (bad debt) percentages are applied to each of these categorised amounts, with larger percentages applied to older accounts. The result of this analysis is a dollar amount for the allowance for uncollectible accounts (also called allowance for doubtful accounts) at the balance sheet date.

To illustrate, Exhibit 6.6 shows an ageing analysis for a seller that began operations this year and is owed $100,000 of accounts receivable at year-end. Those accounts listed as current consist of those outstanding that are still within their original credit period. Accounts listed as 1–60 days past due are those 1 to 60 days past their due date. This classification would include an account that is 45 days outstanding for a net 30-day invoice (i.e., payable within 30 days). This same logic applies to all aged categories.

EXHIBIT 6.6 Ageing of Accounts Receivable

Age of Accounts Receivable	Receivable Balance	Estimated Percent Uncollectible	Accounts Estimated Uncollectible
Current	$ 50,000	2%	$1,000
1–60 days past due	30,000	3	900
61–90 days past due	15,000	4	600
Over 90 days past due	5,000	8	400
Total	$100,000		$2,900

The calculation illustrated in Exhibit 6.6 also reflects the seller's experience with uncollectible accounts, which manifests itself in the uncollectible percentages for each aged category. For example, on average, 3% of buyers' accounts that are 1–60 days past due prove uncollectible for this seller. Hence, it estimates a potential loss of $900 for those $30,000 in receivables for that aged category.

Another means of estimating uncollectible accounts is to use the **percentage of sales**. To illustrate, if our seller reports sales of $100,000 and estimates the uncollectible accounts at 3% of sales, estimated uncollectible accounts would be $3,000. The percentage of sales approach focuses on the amount of potentially uncollectible accounts among current-period sales, whereas the ageing analysis is based on the current balance in accounts receivable. Thus, these two methods nearly always result in different estimates of uncollectible accounts. While the percentage of sales method is arguably simpler, an ageing analysis generally provides more accurate estimates.

Reporting the Allowance for Uncollectible Accounts

How does the accounting system record this estimate? The amount that appears in the balance sheet as accounts receivable represents a collection of individual accounts—one or more receivables for each customer. Because we need to keep track of exactly how much each customer owes us, we cannot simply subtract estimated uncollectibles from accounts receivable.

In Chapter 3, we introduced contra-asset accounts to record accumulated depreciation. A contra-asset account is directly associated with an asset account, but serves to offset the balance of the asset account. To record the estimated uncollectible accounts without disturbing the balance in accounts receivable, we use another contra-asset—the allowance for uncollectible accounts (also called allowance for bad debts or allowance for doubtful accounts).

To illustrate, we use the data from Exhibit 6.6. First the summary journal entry to reflect credit sales follows.

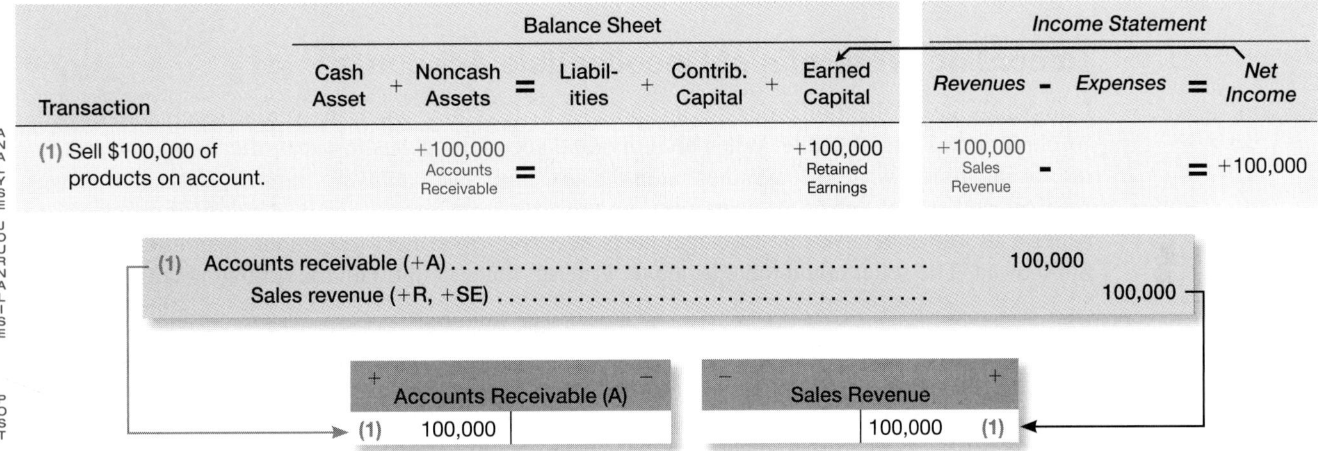

For an adjusting entry at year-end, uncollectible accounts are estimated and recorded as follows as **bad debts expense**. The allowance for uncollectible accounts is a contra-asset account. It offsets (reduces) accounts receivable.

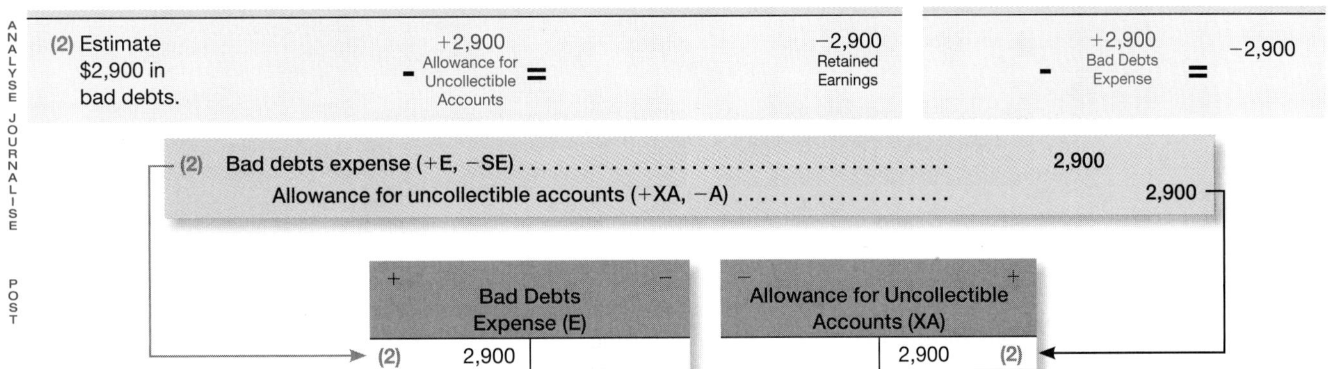

This accounting treatment serves three purposes. First, the balance in accounts receivable is reported in the balance sheet net of estimated uncollectible accounts as follows:

Accounts receivable, net of $2,900 in allowances..........................	$97,100

The $97,100 is the net realisable value of the accounts receivable. Second, the original value of accounts receivable is preserved. The individual accounts that add up to the $100,000 in accounts receivable have not been altered. Third, bad debts expense of $2,900, which is part of the cost of offering credit to customers, is matched against the $100,000 sales generated on credit and reported in the income statement. Bad debts expense is usually included in SG&A expenses.

The allowance for uncollectible accounts is increased by bad debts expense and decreased when an account is written off. Because the allowance for uncollectible accounts is a contra-asset account, credit entries increase its balance. The greater the balance in the contra-asset account, the more the corresponding asset account is offset.

> **BUSINESS INSIGHT**
>
> **Expense or reduction in revenue?** Technically speaking, bad debts expense is not really an expense. It is, instead, a reduction of revenue. Although it is correct under current accounting rule to record this item as a subtraction from sales revenue, companies commonly record bad debts expense as part of selling expenses to emphasise that this amount is a cost of offering credit to customers. (See Appendix 6B for a brief discussion of the accounting for bad debts under the new accounting standard for revenue recognition.)

Recording Write-offs of Uncollectible Accounts

Companies have collection processes and policies to determine when an overdue receivable should be classified as uncollectible. When an individual account reaches that classification, it is written off. To illustrate a write-off, assume that in the next period (Year 2), the company described above receives notice that one of its customers, owing $500 at the time, has declared bankruptcy. The seller's attorneys believe that the legal costs necessary to collect the amount would exceed the $500 owed. The seller could then decide to write off the account with the following entry.

ANALYSE

	Balance Sheet							Income Statement		
Transaction	Cash Asset	+ Noncash Assets	− Contra Asset	= Liabil-ities	+ Contrib. Capital	+ Earned Capital		Revenues	− Expenses	= Net Income
(3) Write off $500 in accounts receivable.*		−500 Accounts Receivable	− −500 Allowance for Uncollectible Accounts	=					−	=

*There is no effect on accounts receivable, net of the allowance for uncollectible accounts. Consequently, there is no *net* effect on the balance sheet.

JOURNALISE / POST

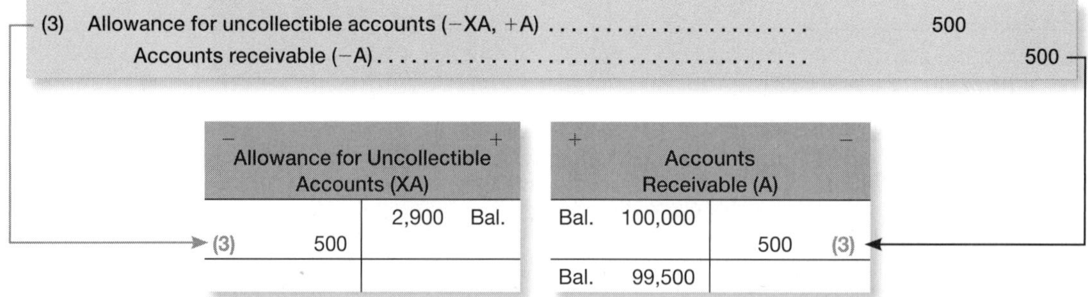

(3) Allowance for uncollectible accounts (−XA, +A) 500
Accounts receivable (−A) 500
− Allowance for Uncollectible Accounts (XA) +
2,900 Bal.
(3) 500
+ Accounts Receivable (A) −
Bal. 100,000
500 (3)
Bal. 99,500

Exhibit 6.7 summarises the effects of this write-off on the individual accounts.

EXHIBIT 6.7 Effects of an Accounts Receivable Write-Off

	Before Write-Off	Effects of Write-Off	After Write-Off
Accounts receivable	$100,000	$ (500)	$99,500
Less: Allowance for uncollectible accounts.	2,900	500	2,400
Accounts receivable, net of allowance.	$ 97,100		$97,100

The net amount of accounts receivable that is reported in the balance sheet after the write-off is the same amount that was reported before the write-off. This is always the case. The individual account receivable was reduced and the contra-asset was reduced by the same amount. Also no entry was made to the income statement. The expense was estimated and recorded in the period when the credit sales were recorded.[4]

To complete the illustration, assume that management's ageing of accounts at the end of Year 2 shows that the ending balance in the allowance account should be $3,000, so another $600 ($3,000 − $2,400) should be added to the allowance account at the end of Year 2. This $600 amount would reflect sales made in Year 2, as well as the seller's experience with collections during Year 2. The entry to record the Year 2 bad debts expense follows.

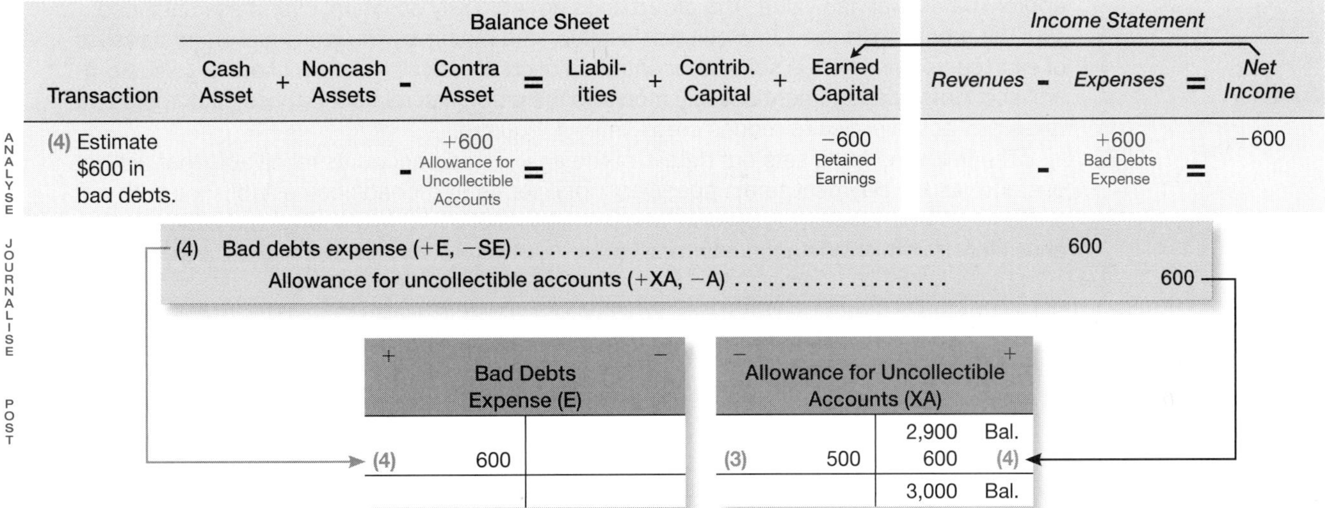

This entry is the same (albeit with a different dollar amount) as the entry made to record the estimate in Year 1. A reconciliation of allowance for uncollectible accounts for the two years follows.

	Year 1	Year 2
Allowance for uncollectible accounts, beginning balance	$ 0	$2,900
Add: bad debts expense..	2,900	600
Subtract: write-offs of uncollectible accounts receivable......................	0	(500)
Allowance for uncollectible accounts, ending balance........................	$2,900	$3,000

To summarise, the *main balance sheet and income statement effects occur when the bad debts expense is made to the allowance for uncollectible accounts*. Accounts receivable (net) is reduced, and that reduction is reflected in the income statement as bad debts expense (usually part of selling, general, and administrative expenses). The net income reduction yields a corresponding equity reduction (via reduced retained earnings). Importantly, the main financial statement effects are at the point of *estimation*, not upon the event of *write-off*. In this way, the net accounts receivable reflects the most up-to-date judgments about future customer payments, and bad debts expense matches the current period's sales and incorporates any changes in management's assessment of the likelihood that customers will pay.

Footnote Disclosures, and Interpretations

In its balance sheets, **TomTom** reports trade receivables, net of allowance for doubtful receivables of €115,429,000 at December 31, 2013, and €149,834,000 at December 31, 2012. In the note to the financial statements, the company provides the following information.

[4] Suppose a previously written off account is unexpectedly paid. If that occurs, the write-off entry (3) is reversed (reinstating the receivable and increasing the allowance), and the payment of this reinstated receivable is accounted for in the usual fashion.

(€ in thousands)	2013	2012
Gross trade receivables	118,546	151,697
Allowance for doubtful receivables	– 3,117	– 1,863
TRADE RECEIVABLES (NET)	115,429	149,834

We expect to recover all receivables within a year. An allowance has been made for estimated unrecoverable amounts from the sale of goods. The carrying amount of trade receivables approximates their fair value. The group does not hold any collateral over these balances.

The group's exposure to credit risk is influenced mainly by the individual characteristics of each customer. There is some concentration of credit risk with certain of our large customers' accounts. Management actively monitors the credit risk related to these customers and takes pro-active action to reduce credit limits if required.

The following table sets out details of the age of trade accounts receivable that are not overdue, as the payment terms specified in the terms and conditions established with our customers have not been exceeded, and an analysis of overdue amounts and related allowances for doubtful trade accounts receivable:

(€ in thousands)	2013	2012
Of which:		
Not overdue	94,883	117,574
Overdue < 3 months	20,594	32,583
3 to 6 months	1,463	299
Over 6 months	1,606	1,241
Less allowance	– 3,117	– 1,863
TRADE RECEIVABLES (NET)	115,429	149,834

The allowances recorded in 2013 and 2012 are mainly related to the overdue amounts.

In the same note, TomTom also discloses the movement in the allowance for doubtful receivables.

(€ in thousands)	2013	2012
Balance as at January 1	– 1,863	– 1,814
Additional receivables impairment	– 2,567	– 1,856
Receivables written off during the year as uncollectible	410	1,163
Unused amounts reversed	654	635
Translation effects	249	9
Balance as at December 31	– 3,117	– 1,863

The reconciliation of TomTom's allowance account provides insight into the level of its bad debts expense relative to its write-offs. In 2013, TomTom wrote off €410,000 in uncollectible accounts while recording a bad debts expense of €2,567,000. Because the expense exceeded the write-offs, the total allowance increased from €1,863,000 in 2012 to €3,117,000 in 2013.

In comparison, TomTom reported bad debts expense of €2,597,000 in 2011 and €379,000 in 2010. The large increase in bad debts expense, both in absolute amount and as a percentage of sales revenue, in the last three years over the 2010 figure could be caused by a number of factors. First, the creditworthiness of TomTom's customers may have deteriorated. This deterioration can be caused by changing economic conditions or a change in TomTom's credit policies (including collection efforts). Second, the company's customer mix may have changed, and it is now selling to a broader set of customers to boost sales.

The footnotes may also disclose whether or not a company has *pledged* its accounts receivable as collateral for a short-term loan. If this is the case, a short-term loan is presented in the liabilities section of the balance sheet and a footnote explains the arrangement. As an alternative to borrowing, a company may *factor* (or sell) its accounts receivable to a bank or other financial institution. If the receivables have been factored, the bank or other financial institution accepts all responsibility for collection. Consequently, the receivables do not appear on the balance sheet of the selling company because they have been sold.

The magnitude of TomTom's uncollectible accounts relative to the company's overall size and profitability makes it an unlikely place for earnings management. But companies in other industries (banking, publishing, retail) often have receivables that require substantial adjustments for expected returns or uncollectible accounts. For instance, the publisher John Wiley & Sons, Inc., reports accounts receivable of $171.6 million in its April 30, 2012, balance sheet, but this amount is net of an allowance for doubtful accounts of $6.9 million and an allowance for sales returns of $48.6 million. So, Wiley only expects to collect about 75% of the amounts it has billed customers. For such companies, modest changes in expectations of returns or collections can have a material effect on reported income.

Experience tells us that many companies have used the allowance for uncollectible accounts to shift income from one period into another. For instance, a company may overestimate its allowance in some years. Such an overestimation may have been unintentional, or it may have been an intentional attempt to manage earnings by building up a reserve (during good years) that can be drawn down in subsequent periods. Alternatively, a company may underestimate its bad debts expense and, hence, allowance in some years. This underestimation may be unintentional, or it may be an attempt to boost earnings to achieve some desired target. Looking at the patterns in the reconciliation of the allowance for uncollectible accounts may provide some indicators of this behaviour.

The MD&A section of a company's annual report often provides insights into changes in company policies, customers, or economic conditions to help explain changes in the allowance account. Further, the amount and timing of the uncollectible allowance is largely controlled by management. Although external auditors assess the reasonableness of the allowance for uncollectible accounts, auditors do not possess the inside knowledge of management and are, therefore, at an information disadvantage, particularly if a dispute arises.

Ultimately, a company makes two representations when reporting accounts receivable (net) in the current asset section of its balance sheet:

1. It expects to collect the asset amount reported on the balance sheet (remember, accounts receivable are reported net of allowance for uncollectible accounts).
2. It expects to collect the asset amount within the next year (implied from its classification as a current asset).

From an analysis viewpoint, we scrutinise the adequacy of a company's allowance for its uncollectible accounts. If the allowance is inadequate, the cash ultimately collected will be less than what the company is reporting as net receivables.

The financial statement effects of uncollectible accounts are at the point of estimation, not at the time of a write-off. Nevertheless, it is important to remember that management sets the size of the allowance, albeit with auditor assurances.

MID-CHAPTER REVIEW 3

At December 31, 2013, Jumbo Kingdom Company had a balance of $770,000 in its Accounts Receivable account and an unused balance of $7,000 in its Allowance for Uncollectible Accounts. The company then analysed and aged its accounts receivable as follows:

Current	$468,000
1–60 days past due	244,000
61–180 days past due	38,000
Over 180 days past due	20,000
Total accounts receivable	$770,000

In the past, the company experienced losses as follows: 1% of current balances, 5% of balances 1–60 days past due, 15% of balances 61–180 days past due, and 40% of balances over 180 days past due. The company bases its allowance for credit losses on the ageing analysis.

Required

1. What amount of uncollectible accounts (bad debts) expense will Jumbo Kingdom report in its 2013 income statement?
2. Show how Accounts Receivable and the Allowance for Uncollectible Accounts appear in its December 31, 2013, balance sheet.
3. Assume that Jumbo Kingdom's allowance for uncollectible accounts has maintained a historical average of 2% of gross accounts receivable. How do you interpret the level of the current allowance percentage?
4. Report the effects for each of the following summary transactions in the financial statement effects template, prepare journal entries, and then post the amounts to the appropriate T-accounts.
   a. Bad debts expense estimated at $23,580.
   b. Write off $5,000 in customer accounts.

The solution to this review problem can be found on pages 315–316.

ANALYSING FINANCIAL STATEMENTS

LO5 Calculate accounts receivable turnover and average collection period.

Analysis Objective

We want to evaluate a company's management of its receivables.

Analysis Tool Accounts receivable turnover (ART) and average collection period (ACP)

$$\textbf{Accounts receivable turnover (ART)} = \frac{\textbf{Sales revenue}}{\textbf{Average accounts receivable}}$$

Applying the Accounts Receivable Turnover Ratio to TomTom

$$\text{2013 ART} = \frac{\$963{,}454}{(\$115{,}429 + \$149{,}834)/2} = 7.3 \text{ times}$$

$$\text{2012 ART} = \frac{\$1{,}057{,}134}{(\$149{,}834 + \$184{,}939)/2} = 6.3 \text{ times}$$

Guidance Accounts receivable turnover measures the number of times each year that accounts receivable is converted into cash. A high turnover ratio suggests that receivables are well managed and that sales revenue quickly leads to cash collected from customers.

A companion measure to accounts receivable turnover is the **average collection period**, also called *days sales outstanding* which is defined as:

$$\textbf{Average collection period (ACP)} = \frac{\textbf{Average accounts receivable}}{\textbf{Average daily sales}} = \frac{\textbf{365 days}}{\textbf{Accounts receivable turnover}}$$

Average daily sales equals annual sales divided by the number of days in the period (for example, 365 for a year). The ACP ratio indicates how many days of sales revenue are invested in accounts receivable, or alternatively, how long, on average, it takes the company to collect cash after the sale. TomTom's ACP is approximately 50 days (365/7.3) in 2013 and 58 days (365/6.3) in 2012, which indicates that the average dollar of sales is collected within 50 days and 58 days of the sale in 2013 and 2012, respectively.

TomTom in Context

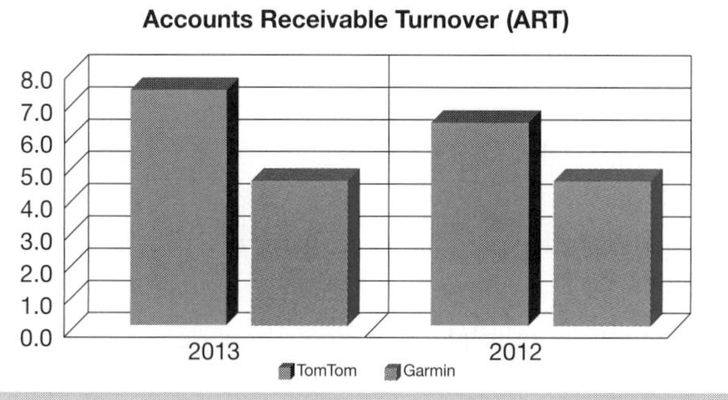

Takeaways The accounts receivable turnover and the average collection period yield valuable insights on at least two dimensions:

1. *Receivables quality* A change in receivables turnover (and collection period) provides insight into accounts receivable quality. If turnover slows (collection period lengthens), the reason could be deterioration in collectibility of receivables. However, before reaching this conclusion, consider at least three alternative explanations:
   a. A seller can extend its credit terms. If the seller is attempting to enter new markets or take market share from competitors, it may extend credit terms to attract buyers.
   b. A seller can take on longer-paying customers. For example, facing increased competition, many computer and automobile companies began leasing their products, thus reducing the cash outlay for customers and stimulating sales. The change in mix away from cash sales and toward leasing had the effect of reducing receivables turnover and increasing the collection period.
   c. The seller can increase the allowance balance. Receivables turnover is often computed using net receivables (after the allowance for uncollectible accounts). Overestimating the allowance balance reduces net receivables and increases turnover.
2. *Asset utilisation* Asset turnover is an important measure of financial performance, both by managers for internal performance goals, as well as by the market in evaluating companies. High performing companies must be both efficient (controlling margins and operating expenses) and productive (getting the most out of their asset base). An increase in receivables ties up cash as the receivables must be financed, and slower-turning receivables carry increased risk of loss. One of the first "low-hanging fruits" that companies pursue in efforts to improve asset utilisation is efficiency in receivables collection.

Other Considerations Accounts receivable are sometimes used by companies to obtain financing. This is done in one of two ways: (1) the company can use accounts receivable as collateral for a short-term loan in a transaction called *securitisation*, or (2) the company can sell its receivables, which is referred to as *factoring*. A thorough discussion of these transactions is beyond the scope of this text. Nonetheless, if a firm uses securitisation or factoring of receivables to obtain short-term financing, the amount of accounts receivable listed on the balance sheet is altered which, in turn, affects the ART ratio.

YOU MAKE THE CALL

You are the Receivables Manager You are analysing your receivables turnover report for the period, and you are concerned that the average collection period is lengthening, causing a drop in cash flow from operations. What specific actions can you take to reduce the average collection period? [Answer on page 297]

EARNINGS MANAGEMENT

LO6 Discuss earnings management and explain how it affects analysis and interpretation of financial statements.

Management choices about transactions, accounting principles, estimates, disclosure, and presentation of income components are an inevitable part of financial reporting. Earnings management occurs when management uses this discretion to mask the underlying economic performance of a company.

There are many motives for earnings management, but these motives generally fall into one of two categories:

1. A desire to mislead some financial statement users about the financial performance of the company to gain economic advantage, or
2. A desire to influence legal contracts that use reported accounting numbers to specify contractual obligations and outcomes.[5]

FYI Earnings management involves earnings quality and management ethics. For the latter, management must consider both legal and personal ethical standards of conduct. ■

Most earnings management cases relate to aggressive revenue or expense recognition practices. However, financial statement presentation can also be a concern. Below, we identify several examples of potentially misleading reporting.

- *Overly optimistic (or overly pessimistic) estimates.* The use of estimates in accrual accounting is extensive. For instance, revenue recognition based on percentage of completion requires estimates of future construction costs. Depreciation expense depends on estimates of useful life, and bad debts expense depends on estimates of future customer payments. Although changes in estimates may be warranted by changes in business conditions, they can have a significant effect on reported net income and, thereby, may provide opportunities for managers to report income that is better (or worse) than it should be.
- *Channel stuffing.* **Channel stuffing** arises when a company uses its market power over customers or distributors to induce them to purchase more goods than necessary to meet their normal needs. Or, the seller may offer significant price reductions to encourage buyers to stock up on their products. Channel stuffing usually occurs immediately before the end of an accounting period and boosts the seller's revenue for that period (while increasing the buyer's inventory). The practice is not illegal and revenue may be recorded, as long as the transactions meet the necessary criteria for a sale.
- *Strategic timing and disclosure of transactions and nonrecurring gains and losses.* Management has some discretion over the timing of transactions that can affect financial statements. If management has an asset (e.g., a tract of land) with book value less than market value, it can choose when to sell the asset to recognise a gain and maintain steady improvements in net income. This practice is known as **income smoothing**. In some cases, these smoothing effects are reported in combination with other items, making it more difficult to separate recurring amounts from nonrecurring amounts. Or, a company could take a **big bath** by recording a nonrecurring loss in a period of already depressed income. Concentrating bad news in a single period reduces the amount of bad news recognised in other periods. Given adequate disclosure, the astute reader of the financial statements will separate nonrecurring income items from persistent operating income, making these income management tactics transparent.
- *Mischaracterising transactions as arm's-length.* Transfers of inventories or other assets to related entities typically are not recorded until later **arm's-length** sales occur. Sometimes sales are disguised as being sold to unrelated entities to inflate income when (1) the buyer is a related party to the seller, (2) financing is provided or guaranteed by the seller, or (3) the buyer is a special-purpose entity that fails to meet independence requirements. This financial reporting practice is not consistent with IFRS and may be fraudulent.

FYI An arm's-length transaction is any transaction between two unrelated parties. ■

The consequence of earnings management is that the usefulness of the information presented in the income statement is compromised. **Quality of earnings** is a term that analysts often use to describe the extent to which reported income reflects the underlying economic performance of a company. Financial statement users must be careful to examine the quality of a company's earnings before using that information to evaluate performance or value its securities.[6]

[5] See Healy, Paul M., and James M. Wahlen, "A Review of Earnings Management Literature and Its Implications for Standard Setting," *Accounting Horizons*, December 1999.

[6] See Dechow, Patricia, Weili Ge, and Catherine Schrand, "Understanding Earnings Quality: A Review of the Proxies, their Determinants, and their Consequences," *Journal of Accounting and Economics*, December, 2010.

YOU MAKE THE CALL

You are the Controller While evaluating the performance of your sales staff, you notice that one of the salespeople consistently meets his quarterly sales quotas but never surpasses his goals by very much. You also discover that his customers often return an unusually large amount of product at the beginning of each quarter. What might be happening here? How would you investigate for potential abuse? [Answer on page 297]

RESEARCH INSIGHT

non-IFRS Income Nonrecurring items in income such as discontinued operations and restructuring charges make it difficult for investors to determine what portion of income is sustainable into the future. The past decade has seen more companies reporting **non-IFRS** or **pro forma income**, which purportedly excludes the effects of nonrecurring or noncash items that companies feel are unimportant for valuation purposes. Research, however, provides no evidence that more exclusions via pro forma income lead to more predictable future cash flows. More important, investors appear to be misled by the exclusions at the time of the non-IFRS income release. Research also finds that companies issuing pro forma income are more likely to be young companies concentrated in technology and business services. Too often, these companies are characterised by below-average sales and income when they choose to report pro forma income. Evidence also shows that the pro forma income can exceed IFRS income by as much as 20 percent.

Critics of non-IFRS income argue that the items excluded by managers from IFRS income are inconsistent across companies and time. They contend that a major motive for pro forma income is to mislead stakeholders. Legendary investor Warren Buffett puts pro forma in context (Berkshire Hathaway, Annual Report): "When companies or investment professionals use terms such as 'EBITDA' and 'pro forma,' they want you to unthinkingly accept concepts that are dangerously flawed."

CHAPTER-END REVIEW

Canadian Tire Corporation operates a chain of general department stores and petrol stations in Canada. It also offers its branded credit cards. Dollarama, Inc. is a leading dollar store operator in Canada. It sells a broad assortment of everyday consumer products and seasonal items at selected fixed price points up to $3.00. The following data were taken from the fiscal 2013 annual reports of the two companies (all amounts in millions of Canadian dollars):

(CDN$ millions)	Canadian Tire	Dollarama
Sales revenue	$11,785.60	$2,064.68
Accounts receivable, net (end-of-year)	758.50	5.80
Accounts receivable, net (beginning-of-year)	750.60	5.96

Required

1. Compute the following for each company:
   a. Accounts receivable turnover (ART).
   b. Average collection period (ACP).
2. Compare these two companies based on the ratios computed in (1). What inferences can you make about these competitors?

The solution to this review problem can be found on page 317.

APPENDIX 6A: Reporting Nonrecurring Items

LO7 Describe and illustrate the reporting for nonrecurring items.

In addition to categorising income statement elements as either operating or nonoperating, it is also useful to separate **recurring** sources of income from those sources that are **nonrecurring**. Isolating nonrecurring earnings is useful for two reasons. First, to evaluate company performance or management quality, it is helpful to make comparisons of current performance with prior years and with other companies facing similar economic circumstances. It is easier to make these comparisons if we focus on recurring income components. Nonrecurring income components are likely to be specific to one company and one accounting period, making them irrelevant for comparative purposes. Second, estimation of company value involves forecasts of income and cash flows. Such forecasts are better when we can identify any nonrecurring effects in income and cash flows and then eliminate them from projections. Recurring earnings and cash flows are more **persistent** and, therefore, more useful in estimating company value.

Accounting standards attempt to distinguish some nonrecurring income components. Two of the most common nonrecurring items are:

- **Discontinued operations**—income related to business units that the company has discontinued and sold or plans to sell.
- **Restructuring charges**—expenses and losses related to significant reorganisation of a company's operations.

Discontinued Operations

Discontinued operations refer to any separately identifiable component of the company that management sells or intends to sell. The income or loss of the discontinued operations (net of tax), and the after-tax gain or loss on sale of the unit, are reported in the income statement below income from continuing operations. The segregation of discontinued operations means that its revenues and expenses are *not* reported with revenues and expenses from continuing operations.

To illustrate, assume that Chapman Company's income statement results were the following.

	Continuing Operations	Discontinued Operations	Total
Revenues	$10,000	$3,000	$13,000
Expenses	7,000	2,000	9,000
Pretax income	3,000	1,000	4,000
Tax expense (40%)	1,200	400	1,600
Net income	$ 1,800	$ 600	$ 2,400

The reported income statement would then appear with the separate disclosure for discontinued operations (shown in bold, separately net of any related taxes) as follows.

Revenues	$10,000
Expenses	7,000
Pretax income	3,000
Tax expense (40%)	1,200
Income from continuing operations	1,800
Income from discontinued operations, net of income taxes	**600**
Net income	$ 2,400

FYI Income, gains, and losses from discontinued operations are reported separately from other items to alert readers to their transitory nature. ■

Revenues and expenses reflect the continuing operations only, and the (persistent) income from continuing operations is reported after deducting the related tax expense. Results from the (transitory) discontinued operations are collapsed into one line item and reported separately net of any related taxes. The same is true for any gain or loss from sale of the discontinued operation's net assets. The net income figure is unchanged by this presentation, but our ability to evaluate and interpret income information is greatly improved.

FYI Management's ability to reduce income from restructuring charges and later reverse some of that charge (creating subsequent period income) reduces earnings quality. IFRS requires disclosures that enable a financial statement reader to track the restructuring activities and to identify any reversals that occur. ■

Restructuring Costs

Restructuring costs are similar to discontinued operations, except that they do not involve the sale of a component of the company with separately identifiable operations and cash flows. These costs typically involve activities such as consolidating production facilities, reorganising sales operations, outsourcing some activities, or discontinuing product lines within a business unit. Restructuring costs are a substantial expense item in many companies' income statements. They tend to be large in magnitude and, as a result, IFRS requires enhanced disclosure, either as a separate line item in the income statement (as a "special item") or in a footnote. These costs are considered transitory because companies do not engage in restructuring activities every year. As such, these costs should be reclassified to a transitory category for analysis purposes even though companies include them in income from continuing operations. The reporting of restructuring costs in the income statement typically consists of two parts:

1. Employee severance costs
2. Asset write-downs

The first of these, **employee severance costs**, represent accrued (estimated) costs for termination of employees as part of a restructuring programme. The second part of restructuring costs consists of **asset write-downs**, also called *write-offs* or *charge-offs*. Restructuring activities usually involve closure or relocation of manufacturing or administrative facilities. This process can require the write-down of long-term assets (such as plant assets), and the write-down of inventories that are no longer salable at current carrying costs.

Roche reported restructuring costs of 163 million CHF in its fiscal 2013 income statement and 2,054 million CHF in its 2012 income statement. These costs were detailed in a note to its 2013 annual report.

During 2013 the Group continued with the implementation of several major global restructuring plans initiated in prior years, notably the reorganisation of research and development in the Pharmaceuticals Division and programmes to address the long-term profitability in the Diabetes Care and former Applied Science businesses in Diagnostics. Additionally, there was income of 531 million Swiss francs from the reversal of previously incurred impairment charges for a bulk drug production unit at the Vacaville site in California.

Global restructuring plans: costs incurred in millions of CHF

Year ended December 31, 2013	**Diagnostics [1]**	**Pharma R&D [2]**	**Other plans [3]**	**Total**
Global restructuring costs				
— Employee-related costs	89	44	132	265
— Site closure costs	48	38	(491)	(405)
— Other reorganisation expenses . . .	83	157	66	306
Total global restructuring costs	220	239	(293)	166
Additional costs				
— Impairment of goodwill.	35	—	—	35
— Impairment of intangible assets. . .	12	—	—	12
— Legal and environmental costs . . .	3	(53)	—	(50)
Total costs	270	186	(293)	163
Year ended December 31, 2012				
Global restructuring costs				
— Employee-related costs	91	188	207	486
— Site closure costs	63	381	125	569
— Other reorganisation expenses . . .	26	27	328	381
Total global restructuring costs	180	596	660	1,436
Additional costs				
— Impairment of goodwill.	187	—	—	187
— Impairment of intangible assets. . .	29	46	112	187
— Legal and environmental costs . . .	—	243	1	244
Total costs	396	885	773	2,054

[1] Includes restructuring of the Diabetes Care and former Applied Science business areas.

[2] Includes closure of the Nutley site and associated infrastructure and environmental remediation costs.

[3] Includes the Operational Excellence programme (Pharmaceuticals and Diagnostics) and in 2012 dalcetrapib (Pharmaceuticals).

Roche's restructuring costs included compensation to employees who were laid off or who elected to take early retirement, site closure costs, reorganisation expenses, write-down (or impairment) of goodwill and other intangible assets, as well as legal and environmental costs.

RESEARCH INSIGHT

Restructuring Costs and Managerial Incentives Research has investigated the circumstances and effects of restructuring costs. Some research finds that stock prices increase upon announcement of a restructuring as if the market appreciates the company's candour. Research also finds that many companies that reduce income through restructuring costs later reverse those costs, resulting in a substantial income boost for the period of reversal. These reversals often occur when their absence would have yielded an earnings decline. Whether or not the market responds favourably to trimming the fat or simply disregards such transitory items as uninformative, managers have incentives to exclude such income-decreasing items from operating income. These incentives are contractually-based, extending from debt covenants and restrictions to managerial bonuses.

YOU MAKE THE CALL

You are the Financial Analyst You are analysing the financial statements of a company that has reported a large restructuring cost, involving both employee severance and asset write-downs, in its income statement. How do you interpret and treat this cost in your analysis of its current and future period profitability? [Answer on page 297]

APPENDIX 6A REVIEW

On April 30, 2013, Singh Corporation decided to close its operations in Fiji. During the first four months of the year (January through April) these operations had reported a loss of $120,000. Singh paid its employees $12,000 in severance pay. The assets of this operation were sold at a loss of $18,000. The tax rate in Fiji is 30%.

Required

a. If this closure is recorded as discontinued operations, how should it be presented in Singh's income statement?

b. If this closure is classified as a restructuring charge, how would it be presented in Singh's income statement?

c. What would determine whether this event should be reported as discontinued operations or a restructuring charge?

The solution to this review problem can be found on page 317.

APPENDIX 6B: NEW STANDARD FOR REVENUE RECOGNITION

LO8 Describe the new standard for revenue recognition and discuss its potential effects.

The IASB and the U.S. Financial Accounting Standards Board (FASB) issued new, converged accounting standards for revenue recognition in May of 2014.[7] The new standard is intended to develop a common revenue standard between IFRS and U.S. GAAP and to consolidate the guidance and rules for revenue recognition into one standard as opposed to the patchwork of standards and sources of guidance that had developed over time for various transactions and industries. In addition, the new standard aims to eliminate inconsistencies that exist across industries and transactions. The new standard employs many of the same overriding concepts to revenue recognition as the current standards. The standard setters intend for the new standard to improve comparability and disclosure for financial statement users.

Publicly traded companies are required to apply the new standard to annual reporting periods beginning after December 15, 2017, including interim reporting periods within that reporting period. Thus, for calendar year-end companies, the effective date for the new standard is January 1, 2018.[8] Since the effective date is more than two years away at the time of the writing of this text, we do not have examples of companies applying the new standard. In this appendix, we discuss the overriding principles of the new standard and conjecture about potential implications of the new standard based on industry reports and company disclosures available at this time.

The new standard's core principle is that an entity should recognise revenue to depict the transfer of goods or services to customers in an amount that reflects the consideration to which the entity expects to be entitled in the exchange for those goods and services. The standard outlines the following five steps in the revenue recognition process:

Step 1. Identify the contract with a customer
Step 2. Identify the performance obligations in the contract
Step 3. Determine the transaction price
Step 4. Allocate the transaction price
Step 5. Recognise revenue when or as the entity satisfies a performance obligation

Collectibility of payment (broadly similar to the idea of realised or realisable discussed as part of the current accounting standards for revenue recognition) continues to be an important issue for revenue recognition.

[7] IASB issued International Financial Reporting Standards 15 and the FASB issued Accounting Standards Update 2014-09, both entitled Revenue from Contracts with Customers.

[8] Early adoption is permitted, but only as of annual reporting periods beginning after December 15, 2016, including interim reporting periods within that reporting period.

Under the new standard, collectibility should be assessed in determining whether a contract exists (i.e., whether the entity has passed Step 1 of the 5-step revenue recognition process listed above).

In general, the new revenue recognition standard does not conceptually change the accounting for bad debts from the current rules. However, the new standard will require more judgment on the part of management in determining whether the expectation of partial payment on a sales contract is 1) evidence that the contract lacks collectibility in which case revenue cannot be recorded, 2) due to a price concession in which case revenue should be recorded but at the expected lower amount, or 3) a bad debt, in which case sales should be recognised in full but with bad debt provision recorded. The additional required judgment about collectibility could lead to uncertainty and potentially significant changes to revenue recognition for some entities. As companies apply the standard in future years, we will be able to observe and discuss more fully the consequences of these changes.

Long-Term Contracts

With respect to the accounting for long-term contracts, the new revenue recognition standard does not use the terms percentage-of-completion method, cost-recovery method, or completed contract method (under U.S. GAAP only). All contracts fall under the 5-step process outlined above and revenue is recognised as performance obligations are satisfied, that is, when control of the good or service transfers to the customer. This can occur either at a point in time or over time. For most long-term contracts, revenue will be recognised over time. Under the new standard, measuring progress toward completion is done using either what is called the input method or the output method. It is likely that for many long-term contracts, such as construction contracts, most performance obligations will be measured over time using the input method. This method of revenue recognition is consistent with the percentage-of-completion method that is often applied under the current standard. Thus, the general overriding principles for revenue recognition are similar between the old and new standards for long-term contracts.

Disclosure

Significant changes in disclosure are required in the new standard. Companies will need to provide both qualitative and quantitative disclosure about contracts with customers including revenues recognised, disaggregation of revenues, contract balances, and performance obligations (including transaction prices allocated to remaining performance obligations). Additional disclosures will also be required about judgments and changes in judgments such as determining the timing of satisfaction of performance obligations (over time or at a point in time) and determining the transaction price and amounts allocated to performance obligations.

Potential Effects of the New Standard

The effects of the new accounting standard for revenue recognition are not entirely clear. At the time of this writing, most companies indicate that they are assessing the impact of adopting the new standard on their financial statements and will determine the adoption date. The new standard calls for enhanced disclosure and additional documentation of internal controls over revenue recognition. In addition, while the overall spirit of the new standards is similar to the current ones, it is likely the new standards will affect the reporting of revenues to some extent for many companies, especially those with multiple element contracts requiring revenue to be deferred and recognised across multiple periods. Some examples of potential and expected impacts are as follows.

- Airline companies may have to change the way they account for loyalty programs (e.g., frequent flier programs). For example, it appears likely that loyalty points will be treated as a revenue element and some portion of the transaction price will have to be allocated to the loyalty element based on the estimated standalone selling price of each performance obligation (Source: E&Y Technical Line, "The New Revenue Recognition Standard—Airlines").
- Companies that provide promotions or "free" goods may have to allocate revenues differently than they do currently. For example, when a wireless carrier sells a service contract and gives a free or discounted phone to the customer, it is likely that under the new standard more revenue will likely be allocated to the sale of the phone, reducing margins on the service contracts. Even a simple retailer that offers a promotion such as buy three and get one free, will have to allocate revenue across the four products under the new standard.
- A panel of experts suggested that companies should be aware of changes to footnote disclosure requirements and should not regard those as an insignificant event. Lynne Triplett, a partner at Grant Thornton, said her greatest concern, "is that companies aren't going to be prepared for the disclosures aspect." (Source: Bloomberg BNA conference entitled, "Inside Revenue Recognition: A Deep Dive into Assessment & Implementation Under the New Revenue Recognition Standard" held on September 17, 2015, reported in Bloomberg BNA on September 22, 2015).

At a high level, the new standard applies many of the same broad principles of revenue recognition as the current standards. However, there will likely be significant changes for many companies in terms of the timing of recognition, the allocation of revenue to transactions, and the disclosures about the revenue recognition process. These changes could have far reaching implications. For example, revenue recognition changes could affect operational decisions and outcomes such as the use of coupons, compensation in the form of sales commissions, and many others. As companies start to apply the new standard, the standard setters may issue additional guidance or clarifications. In future editions of this text, we will incorporate examples from company disclosures as the new standard is applied and will discuss any future updates and guidance from the standard setters.

SUMMARY

LO1 Describe and apply the criteria for determining when revenue is recognised. (p. 274)

- Revenue is recognised when it is probable that future economic benefits will flow to the entity and these benefits can be reliably measured.

LO2 Illustrate revenue and expense recognition when the transaction involves future deliverables. (p. 276)

- When customers pay prior to the delivery of all elements of the product (or service) package, an unearned revenue liability must be recognised.
- When a company recognises an unearned revenue liability, its reported revenue for a period does not coincide with the purchases made by customers in that period.

LO3 Illustrate revenue and expense recognition for long-term projects. (p. 279)

- Long-term contracts are recorded using the percentage-of-completion method when a signed contract exists with a fixed or determinable price, collection is reasonably assured, and the cost of completing the contract can be estimated.
- The cost-recovery method is used when the conditions for using percentage-of-completion are not met.

LO4 Estimate and account for uncollectible accounts receivable. (p. 282)

- Uncollectible accounts are usually estimated by ageing the accounts receivable.
- Estimated uncollectible accounts are recorded as a contra-asset called allowance for uncollectible accounts.
- Write-offs of uncollectible accounts are deducted from accounts receivable and from the allowance account.

LO5 Calculate accounts receivable turnover and average collection period. (p. 288)

- Accounts receivable turnover (ART) and average collection period (ACP) measure the ability of the company to convert receivables into cash through collection.

LO6 Discuss earnings management and explain how it affects analysis and interpretation of financial statements. (p. 290)

- Earnings management occurs when management uses its discretion to mask the underlying economic performance of a company.
- The consequence of earnings management is that the usefulness of the information presented in the income statement is compromised.

LO7 Appendix 6A: Describe and illustrate the reporting for nonrecurring items. (p. 291)

- Income from discontinued operations are transitory (nonrecurring) items that are reported net of income taxes after earnings from continuing operations.
- Restructuring charges include asset write-downs and employee severance costs. Even though these charges are typically reported among earnings from continuing operations, they are classified as transitory for analysis purposes.

LO8 Appendix 6B: Describe the new standard for revenue recognition and discuss its potential effects. (p. 294)

- New standards for revenue recognition were issued to create a common revenue standard between IFRS and U.S. GAAP and to consolidate various rules and industry guidance into one standard.
- The effective date for calendar year companies that are publicly traded is January 1, 2018 and is January 1, 2019 for calendar year companies that are privately held.
- The new revenue standard is, at a high level, conceptually similar to the current standard. However, the timing of revenue recognition will likely change for many companies, especially those with multiple element sales contracts. The new standard also requires much more disclosure about a company's revenue recognition process.

GUIDANCE ANSWERS . . . YOU MAKE THE CALL

You are the Receivables Manager First, you must realise that the extension of credit is an important tool in the marketing of your products, often as important as advertising and promotion. Given that receivables are necessary, there are some methods we can use to speed their collection. (1) We can better screen the customers to whom we extend credit. (2) We can negotiate advance or progress payments from customers. (3) We can use bank letters of credit or other automatic drafting procedures so that billings need not be sent. (4) We can make sure products are sent as ordered to reduce disputes. (5) We can improve administration of past due accounts to provide for more timely notices of delinquencies and better collection procedures.

You are the Controller The salesperson may be channel stuffing or recording sales without a confirmed sales order. The unusual amount of returns suggests that sales revenues are most likely being recognised prematurely. To investigate, you could examine specific sales orders from customers who returned goods early in the following quarter, or contact customers directly. Most companies delay bonuses until after an appropriate return period expires and only credit the sales staff with net sales.

You are the Financial Analyst There are two usual components to a restructuring charge: asset write-downs (such as inventories, property, plant, and goodwill) and severance costs. Write-downs occur when the cash flow generating ability of an asset declines, thus reducing its current market value below its book value reported on the balance sheet. Arguably, this decline in cash flow generating ability did not occur solely in the current year and, most likely, has developed over several periods. Delays in loss recognition, such as write-downs of assets, are not uncommon. Thus, prior period income is arguably not as high as reported, and the current period loss is not as great as is reported. Turning to severance costs, their recognition can be viewed as an investment decision by the company that is expected to increase future cash flows (through decreased wages). If this cost accrual is capitalised on the balance sheet, current period income is increased and future period income would bear the amortisation of this "asset" to match against future cash flow benefits from severance. This implies that current period income is not as low as reported; however, this adjustment is not IFRS as such severance costs cannot be capitalised. Yet, we can make such an adjustment in our analysis.

KEY RATIOS

Accounts receivable turnover (ART)

$$ART = \frac{\text{Sales revenue}}{\text{Average accounts receivable}}$$

Average collection period (ACP)

$$ACP = \frac{\text{Average accounts receivable}}{\text{Average daily sales}} = \frac{365}{\text{Accounts receivable turnover (ART)}}$$

KEY TERMS

MULTIPLE CHOICE

Multiple Choice Answers
1.c 2.b 3.a 4.d 5.a 6.d

1. Which of the following best describes the condition(s) that must be present for the recognition of revenue?
   a. Revenue must be earned and collected.
   b. There are no uncertainties in measurement of income.
   c. It is probable that future economic benefits will flow to the entity and these benefits can be reliably measured.
   d. Expenses must be measurable and directly associated with the revenues.

2. When multiple products or services are bundled and sold for one price, the revenue should be
   a. Recognised when the bundle of products is sold
   b. Allocated among the different elements and recognised as each element is delivered to the customer
   c. Deferred until all elements of the bundle are delivered to the customer.
   d. Recognised when the customer pays cash for the products or services.

3. The percentage-of-completion method is preferable to the cost-recovery method and should be used unless:
   a. There is a lack of dependable estimates or inherent hazards cause forecasts to be doubtful.
   b. Completion rates are certain.
   c. Profits are low.
   d. Projects are more than five years to completion.

4. When management selectively excludes some revenues, expenses, gains, and losses from earnings calculated using generally accepted accounting principles, it is an example of
   a. income smoothing.
   b. big bath accounting.
   c. cookie jar accounting.
   d. pro forma earnings.

5. If bad debts expense is determined by estimating uncollectible accounts receivable, the entry to record the write-off of a specific uncollectible account would decrease
   a. allowance for uncollectible accounts.
   b. net income.
   c. net book value of accounts receivable.
   d. bad debts expense.

6. If management intentionally underestimates bad debts expense, then net income is
   a. overstated and assets are understated.
   b. understated and assets are overstated.
   c. understated and assets are understated.
   d. overstated and assets are overstated.

Superscript ^{A} denotes assignments based on Appendix 6A.

DISCUSSION QUESTIONS

G2000 (HONG KONG)

Q6-1. What are the criteria that guide firms in recognition of revenue? What does each of the criteria mean? How are the criteria met for a company like G2000, a clothing retailer?

Q6-2. How are the criteria met for a construction company that builds offices under long-term contracts with developers?

Q6-3. Why are discontinued operations reported separately from continuing operations in the income statement?

Q6-4. Identify the two typical categories of restructuring costs and their effects on the balance sheet and the income statement. Explain the concept of a *big bath* and why restructuring costs are often identified with this event.

Q6-5. Why might companies want to manage earnings? Describe some of the tactics that some companies use to manage earnings.

Q6-6. What is the concept of *pro forma income* and why has this income measure been criticised?

Q6-7. Why does IFRS allow management to make estimates of amounts that are included in financial statements? Does this improve the usefulness of financial statements? Explain.

Q6-8. How might earnings forecasts that are published by financial analysts encourage companies to manage earnings?

Q6-9. Explain how management can shift income from one period into another by its estimation of uncollectible accounts.

Q6-10. During an examination of Wallace Company's financial statements, you notice that the allowance for uncollectible accounts has decreased as a percentage of accounts receivable. What are the possible explanations for this change?

Q6-11. Under what circumstances would it be correct to say that a company would be better off with more uncollectible accounts?

Q6-12. Estimating the bad debts expense by ageing accounts receivable generally results in smaller errors than the percentage of credit sales approach. Can you explain why?

MINI EXERCISES

M6-13. Computing Percentage-of-Completion Revenues LO3

Bartov Corporation agreed to build a warehouse for $2,500,000. Expected (and actual) costs for the warehouse follow: 2013, $400,000; 2014, $1,000,000; and 2015, $500,000. The company completed the warehouse in 2015. Compute revenues, expenses, and income for each year 2013 through 2015 using the percentage-of-completion method.

M6-14. Assessing Revenue Recognition of Companies LO1

GILDAN ACTIVEWEAR INC. (CANADA)
ROCHE PHARMACEUTICALS (SWITZERLAND)
CNH INDUSTRIAL N.V. (ITALY)
COMMONWEALTH BANK (AUSTRALIA)
SAMSUNG HEAVY INDUSTRIES (SOUTH KOREA)

Identify and explain when each of the following companies should recognise revenue.

a. Gildan Activewear Inc.: Gildan is a Canadian marketer and manufacturer of quality branded basic family apparel.

b. Roche Pharmaceuticals: Roche, founded in Switzerland, engages in the development, manufacturing, and marketing of pharmaceutical products and sells its drugs to retailers in Europe and overseas.

c. CNH Industrial N.V.: Registered in the Netherlands, CNH is an Italian manufacturer of agricultural and construction equipment. It sells equipment to a network of independent distributors, who in turn sell the equipment to customers. CNH provides financing and insurance services both to distributors and customers.

d. Commonwealth Bank: CommBank is an Australian bank and financial services company with headquarters in Sydney. It lends money to individuals and corporations and invests excess funds in marketable securities.

e. Samsung Heavy Industries (SHI): Based in South Korea, SHI is one of the largest shipbuilders in the world. It manufactures products under long-term contracts.

M6-15. Estimating Revenue Recognition with Right of Return LO1

The Unlimited Company offers an unconditional return policy for its retail clothing business. It normally expects 2% of sales at retail selling prices to be returned at some point prior to the expiration of the return period, and returned items cannot be resold. Assuming that it records total sales of $5 million for the current period, how much net revenue would it report for this period?

M6-16. Using Percentage-of-Completion and Cost-Recovery Methods LO3

Shatin Building Company signed a contract to build an office building for $40,000,000. The scheduled construction costs follow.

Year	Cost
2013	$ 9,000,000
2014	15,000,000
2015	6,000,000
Total	$30,000,000

Assume that Shatin receives cash payments of $9,000,000, $15,000,000 and $16,000,000 in 2013, 2014 and 2015 respectively. The building is completed in 2015.

For each year, compute the revenue, expense, and gross profit reported for this construction project using each of the following methods.

a. Percentage-of-completion method
b. Cost-recovery method

LO1, 2 **M6-17. Explaining Revenue Recognition and Bundled Sales**

A.J. Smith Electronics is a retail consumer electronics company that also sells extended warranty contracts for many of the products that it carries. The extended warranty provides coverage for three years beyond expiration of the manufacturer's warranty. In 2013, A.J. Smith sold extended warranties amounting to $1,700,000. The warranty coverage for all of these begins in 2014 and runs through 2016. The total expected cost of providing warranty services on these contracts is $500,000.

a. How should A.J. Smith recognise revenue on the extended warranty contracts?
b. Estimate the revenue, expense, and gross profit reported from these contracts in the year(s) that the revenue is recognised.
c. In 2014, as a special promotion, A.J. Smith sold a digital camera (retail price $300), a digital photograph printer (retail price $125), and an extended warranty contract for each (total retail price $75) as a package for a special price of $399. The extended warranty covers the period from 2015 through 2017. The company sold 200 of these camera–printer packages. Compute the revenue that A.J. Smith should recognise in each year from 2014 through 2017.

LO4 **M6-18. Reporting Uncollectible Accounts and Accounts Receivables**

Mohan Company estimates its uncollectible accounts by ageing its accounts receivable and applying percentages to various aged categories of accounts. Mohan computes a total of $2,100 in estimated losses as of December 31, 2013. Its Accounts Receivable has a balance of $98,000, and its Allowance for Uncollectible Accounts has an unused balance of $500 before adjustment at December 31, 2013.

a. What is the amount of bad debts expense that Mohan will report in 2013?
b. Determine the net amount of accounts receivable reported in current assets at December 31, 2013.
c. Set up T-accounts for both Bad Debt Expense and for Allowance for Uncollectible Accounts. Enter any beginning balances and effects from the information above (including your results from parts *a* and *b*). Explain the numbers for each of your T-accounts.

LO4 **M6-19. Explaining the Allowance Method for Accounts Receivable**

At a recent board of directors meeting of Ascot, Inc., one of the directors expressed concern over the allowance for uncollectible accounts appearing in the company's balance sheet. "I don't understand this account," he said. "Why don't we just show accounts receivable at the amount owed to us and get rid of that allowance?" Respond to that director's question, include in your response (a) an explanation of why the company has an allowance account, (b) what the balance sheet presentation of accounts receivable is intended to show, and (c) how the matching principle relates to the analysis and presentation of accounts receivable.

LO4 **M6-20. Analysing the Allowance for Uncollectible Accounts**

Following is the current asset section from Tate plc, balance sheet:

At December 31 (£ millions)	2014	2013
Cash and cash equivalents	£ 1,974	£ 2,481
Receivables (less allowances of £143 in 2014 and £246 in 2013)	6,361	6,539
Inventories, net	5,706	5,310
Deferred income taxes	912	898
Other current assets	1,249	993
Total current assets	£16,202	£16,221

a. Compute the gross amount of accounts receivable for both 2014 and 2013. Compute the percentage of the allowance for uncollectible accounts relative to the gross amount of accounts receivable for each of these years.

b. How do you interpret the change in the percentage of the allowance for uncollectible accounts relative to total accounts receivable computed in part *a*?

c. Tate reported net sales of £54,365 million in 2014. Compute its accounts receivable turnover and days sales outstanding for that year.

M6-21. Analysing Accounts Receivable Changes LO4

The comparative balance sheets of Sloan Company reveal that accounts receivable (before deducting allowances) increased by $15,000 in 2013. During the same time period, the allowance for uncollectible accounts increased by $2,100. If sales revenue was $120,000 in 2013 and bad debts expense was 2% of sales, how much cash was collected from customers during the year?

M6-22. Evaluating Accounts Receivable Turnover for Competitors LO5

The Procter & Gamble Company and Colgate-Palmolive Company report the following sales and accounts receivable balances ($ millions):

PROCTER & GAMBLE			COLGATE-PALMOLIVE		
Fiscal year	Sales	Accounts Receivable	Fiscal year	Sales	Accounts Receivable
June 30, 2012	$83,680	$6,068	December 31, 2011	$16,734	$1,675
June 30, 2011	81,104	6,275	December 31, 2010	15,564	1,610

a. Compute accounts receivable turnover and average collection period for both companies.

b. Identify and discuss a potential explanation for the difference between these competitors' accounts receivable turnover.

M6-23. Analysing Accounts Receivable Changes LO4

In 2013, Grant Corporation recorded credit sales of $3,200,000 and bad debts expense of $42,000. Write-offs of uncollectible accounts totaled $39,000 and one account, worth $12,000, that had been written off in an earlier year was collected in 2013.

a. Prepare journal entries to record each of these transactions.

b. If net accounts receivable increased by $220,000, how much cash was collected from credit customers during the year? Prepare a journal entry to record cash collections.

c. Set up T-accounts and post each of the transactions in parts *a* and *b* to them.

d. Record each of the above transactions in a financial statement effects template to show the effect of these entries on the balance sheet and income statement.

M6-24. Analysing Unearned Revenue Changes LO2

Finn Publishing Corp. produces a monthly publication aimed at competitive swimmers, with articles profiling current stars of the sport, advice from coaches, and advertising by swimwear companies, training organisations and others. The magazine is distributed through newsstands and bookstores, and by mail to subscribers. The most common subscription is for twelve months. When Finn Publishing receives payment of an annual subscription, it records an Unearned Revenue liability that is reduced by 1/12th each month as publications are provided.

The table below provides four years of revenues from the income statement and unearned revenue from the balance sheet. (All amounts in $ thousands.)

Fiscal year	Revenue	Unearned revenue liability (end of year)
2012	48,000	20,000
2013	55,000	24,000
2014	62,000	26,000
2015	62,000	25,000

a. Calculate the growth in revenue from 2012 to 2013, 2013 to 2014, and from 2014 to 2015.

b. Calculate the amount of customer purchases in 2013, 2014, and 2015. Customer purchases are defined as sales made at newsstands and bookstores, plus the amount paid for new or renewal subscriptions. Again, calculate the growth rates from 2013 to 2014 and from 2014 to 2015.

c. Explain the differences in growth rates between parts *a* and *b* above.

LO2 **M6-25. Applying Revenue Recognition Criteria**

Commtech, Inc., designs and sells cellular phones. The company creates the technical specifications and the software for its products, though it outsources the production of the phones to an overseas contract manufacturer. Commtech has arrangements to sell its phones to the major wireless communications companies who, in turn, sell the phones to end customers packaged with calling plans.

The product life cycle for a phone model is about six months, and Commtech recognises revenue at the time of delivery to the wireless communications company. The product team for the CD924 model has met to consider a possible modification to the phone. The software team has developed an improved global positioning application for a new phone model, and this application works in the CD924. It could be uploaded to existing phones through the wireless networks.

Marketing's analysis of focus groups and customer feedback is that further sales of the CD924 would be enhanced significantly if the new application were made available. The software engineers have demonstrated that the new GPS application can be successfully sent wirelessly to the CD924.

However, the finance manager points out that Commtech's financial statements have been based on the assumption that the company's phones do not involve "multiple deliverables," like upgrades. All revenue is recognised at the point of sale to the wireless communications companies. Like many communications hardware companies, Commtech has been under pressure to demonstrate its financial performance. Offering an upgrade to the CD924's navigation capabilities would probably be viewed as a significant deliverable in terms of customer value, and the finance manager says that "the accounting won't let us do it."

How should the product team proceed?

EXERCISES

LO1 **E6-26. Assessing Revenue Recognition Timing**

MARKS AND SPENCER PLC (UK)
AIRBUS GROUP (FRANCE)
METCASH LIMITED (AUSTRALIA)
TELEVISION BROADCASTS LTD. (HONG KONG)
OCBC BANK (SINGAPORE)
TOYOTA MOTOR CORP. (JAPAN)
LEOPARD PUBLISHING (ITALY)

Discuss and justify when each of the following businesses should recognise revenues:

a. A clothing retailer like Marks and Spencer plc in the United Kingdom.
b. A contractor like Airbus Group that performs work under long-term contracts.
c. An operator of grocery stores like Metcash Limited in Australia.
d. A television broadcaster and producer of television shows, such as Television Broadcasts Limited (TVB) in Hong Kong that syndicates its content to television stations.
e. A Toronto-based residential real estate developer who constructs only speculative apartments and later sells these apartments to buyers.
f. A banking institution like the OCBC Bank in Singapore that lends money for home mortgages.
g. An auto manufacturer like the Toyota Motor Corporation in Japan.
h. A publisher of magazines such as Leopard Publishing in Italy.

LO1, 6 **E6-27. Assessing Revenue Recognition Timing and Income Measurement**

INVESTORS CHRONICLE (UNITED KINGDOM)
OPENTEXT CORPORATION (CANADA)
CATSOFT (AUSTRALIA)
BANDAI NAMCO GAMES INC. (JAPAN)

Discuss and justify when each of the following businesses should recognise revenue and identify any income measurement issues that are likely to arise.

a. Investors Chronicle, a division of The Financial Times Limited, provides investment advice to customers for an up-front fee. It provides these customers with password-protected access to its Web site where customers can download certain investment reports. Investors Chronicle has an obligation to provide updates on its Web site.
b. OpenText Corporation develops general ledger and other business application software that it sells to its customers. The customer pays an up-front fee to gain the right to use the software and a monthly fee for support services.
c. Catsoft develops tax preparation software that it sells to its customers for a flat fee. No further payment is required and the software cannot be returned, only exchanged if defective.
d. Bandai Namco Games Inc. develops computer games and sells its software with a 10-day right of return period during which the software can be returned for a full refund. After the 10-day period has expired, the software cannot be returned.

LO3 **E6-28. Constructing and Assessing Income Statements Using Percentage of Completion**

AGGREKO FRANCE (FRANCE)
THE EDF GROUP (FRANCE)

Assume that Aggreko France agreed in February 2013 to construct an electricity generating facility for the French utility company EDF. The contract price of €500 million is to be paid as follows: €200 million at the time of signing; €100 million on December 31, 2013; and €200 million at completion in May 2014. Aggreko incurred the following costs in constructing the power plant: €100 million in 2013, and €300 million in 2014.

a. Compute the amount of Aggreko's revenue, expense, and income for both 2013 and 2014 under the percentage-of-completion revenue recognition method.

b. Compute the amount of Aggreko's revenue, expense, and income for both 2013 and 2014 using the cost-recovery method.

c. Discuss whether you believe that the percentage of completion method or the cost-recovery method provides a good measure of Aggreko's performance under the contract.

E6-29. Constructing and Assessing Income Statements Using Percentage of Completion **LO3**

On March 15, 2014, Frankel Construction contracted to build a shopping centre at a contract price of $120 million. The schedule of expected (equals actual) cash collections and contract costs follows:

Year	Cash Collections	Cost Incurred
2014	$ 30 million	$15 million
2015	50 million	40 million
2016	40 million	30 million
Total	$120 million	$85 million

a. Calculate the amount of revenue, expense, and income for each of the three years 2014 through 2016 using (1) the percentage-of-completion method, and (2) the cost-recovery method. Which method most closely follows the cash flows produced by this project?

b. Discuss which method you believe provides the best measure of the construction company's performance under this contract.

E6-30. Accounting for Multiple-Element Arrangements **LO2**

Amazon.com, Inc. provides the following description of its revenue recognition policies in its 2011 annual report:

> Revenue arrangements with multiple deliverables are divided into separate units and revenue is allocated using estimated selling prices if we do not have vendor-specific objective evidence or third-party evidence of the selling prices of the deliverables. Sales of our Kindle device are considered arrangements with multiple deliverables, consisting of the device, 3G wireless access and delivery for some models, and software upgrades. We allocate the arrangement price to each of the elements based on the estimated selling prices of each element. Estimated selling prices are management's best estimates of the prices that we would charge our customers if we were to sell the standalone elements separately and include considerations of customer demand, prices charged by us and others for similar deliverables, and the price if largely based on costs. The revenue related to the device, which is the substantial portion of the total sale price, and related costs are recognised upon delivery. Revenue related to 3G wireless access and delivery and software upgrades is amortised over the average life of the device, which is estimated to be three years.

a. What is an "arrangement with multiple deliverables"? How are revenues recognised in such arrangements under IFRS?

b. Assume that Amazon sells a Kindle with 3G wireless access and a commitment for future software upgrades for $190. Also assume that the device, if sold alone, would sell for $170 and that management estimates the selling price of the 3G access and software upgrades would be $30 if they were to be sold separately. What amount of revenue would Amazon recognise in the year of the sale? How would the remaining revenues be recognised?

c. Record the transaction described in *b* using the financial statement effects template and in journal entry form.

E6-31. Analysing Unearned Revenue Transactions and Multiple-Element Arrangements **LO1, 2**

TELUS CORPORATION (CANADA)

TELUS Corporation is a Canadian telecommunications company that provides a wide range of products and services, including wireless, data, Internet, voice, television, entertainment, and video. As of December 31, 2013, the company has 7.8 million wireless subscribers, 3.3 million wireline network access lines, 1.4 million Internet subscribers, and 815,000 television customers. The following are excerpts from the company's annual report concerning its revenue recognition policy.

Revenue Recognition

General

We earn the majority of our revenue (wireless: voice and data; wireline: data (including: Internet protocol; television; hosting, managed information technology and cloud-based services; and healthcare solutions), voice local and voice long distance) from access to, and usage of, our telecommunications infrastructure. The majority of the balance of our revenue (wireless equipment and other) arises from providing services and products facilitating access to, and usage of, our telecommunications infrastructure.

We offer complete and integrated solutions to meet our customers' needs. These solutions may involve the delivery of multiple services and products occurring at different points in time and/or over different periods of time. As appropriate, these multiple element arrangements are separated into their component accounting units, consideration is measured and allocated among the accounting units based upon their relative fair values (derived using company-specific objective evidence) and then our relevant revenue recognition policies are applied to the accounting units. (We estimate that more than two-thirds of our revenues arise from multiple element arrangements.)

Voice and data

We recognise revenues on an accrual basis and include an estimate of revenues earned but unbilled. Wireless and wireline service revenues are recognised based upon access to, and usage of, our telecommunications infrastructure and upon contract fees.

Advance billings are recorded when billing occurs prior to provision of the associated service; such advance billings are recognised as revenue in the period in which the services are provided. Similarly, and as appropriate, upfront customer activation and connection fees are deferred and recognised over the average expected term of the customer relationship.

Required

a. What are "multiple element arrangements"?

b. How does TELUS recognise revenues from sales of multiple element arrangements?

c. Suppose that TELUS sells a smartphone with a 2-year service contract for $300 at the end of the year. If sold separately, the smartphone would sell for $130 and the service contract $220. The smartphone and service contract cost TELUS $50 and $90, respectively. What amount of revenue would TELUS recognise in the year of the sale? How would the remaining revenues be recognised?

d. Assume that TELUS receives $1 billion of upfront activation and connection fees from its customers and it estimates that the average customer contract life is 5 years. How should TELUS record the $1 billion upfront customer activation and connection fees?

LO1, 6 **E6-32. Applying Revenue Recognition Criteria**

Simpyl Technologies, Inc., manufactures electronic equipment used to facilitate control of production processes and tracking of assets using RFID and other technologies. Since its initial public offering in 1996, the company has shown consistent growth in revenue and earnings, and the stock price has reflected that impressive performance.

Operating in a very competitive environment, Simpyl Technologies provides significant bonus incentives to its sales representatives. These representatives sell the company's products directly to end customers, to value-added resellers, and to distributers.

Consider the four situations below. In each case, determine whether Simpyl Technologies can recognise revenue at this time. Describe the reasons for your judgement.

a. When selling directly to the end customer, Simpyl Technologies requires a sales contract with authorised signatures from the customer company. At the end of Simpyl's fiscal year, sales representative A asks to book revenue from a customer. The customer's purchasing manager has confirmed the intention to complete the purchase, but the contract has only one of the two required signatures. The second person is travelling and will return to the office in a few days (but after the end of Simpyl's fiscal year). The inventory to fulfil the order is sitting in Simpyl's warehouse. Can Simpyl recognise revenue at this time?

b. Sales representative B has an approved contract to deliver units that must be customised to meet the customer's specifications. Just prior to the end of the fiscal year, the uncustomised units are shipped to an intermediate staging area where they will be reconfigured to meet the customer's requirements. Can Simpyl recognise revenue on the basic, uncustomised units at this time?

c. Sales representative C has finalised an order from a value-added reseller who regularly purchases significant volumes of Simpyl's products. The products have been delivered to the customer at the beginning of the fiscal year, and Simpyl Technologies has no further responsibilities for the items. However, the sales representative (with the regional sales manager) is still conducting negotiations with the value-added reseller as to the volume discounts that will be offered for the current year. Can Simpyl recognise revenue on the items delivered to the customer?

d. Sales representative D has finalised an order from a distributor, and the items have been delivered. However, an examination of the distributor's financial condition shows that it does not have the resources to pay Simpyl for the items it has purchased. It needs to sell those items, so the resulting proceeds can be used to pay Simpyl. Can Simpyl recognise revenue on the items delivered to the distributor?

E6-33. Reporting Uncollectible Accounts and Accounts Receivable LO4

LaFond Company analyses its accounts receivable at December 31, 2013, and arrives at the aged categories below along with the percentages that are estimated as uncollectible.

Age Group	Accounts Receivable	Estimated Loss %
Current (not past due)	$250,000	0.5%
1–30 days past due	90,000	1
31–60 days past due	20,000	2
61–120 days past due	11,000	5
121–180 days past due	6,000	10
Over 180 days past due	4,000	25
Total accounts receivable	$381,000	

At the beginning of the fourth quarter of 2013, there was a credit balance of $4,350 in the Allowance for Uncollectible Accounts. During the fourth quarter, LaFond Company wrote off $3,830 in receivables as uncollectible.

a. What amount of bad debts expense will LaFond report for 2013?

b. What is the balance of accounts receivable that it reports on its December 31, 2013, balance sheet?

c. Set up T-accounts for both Bad Debts Expense and for the Allowance for Uncollectible Accounts. Enter any unadjusted balances along with the dollar effects of the information described (including your results from parts *a* and *b*). Explain the numbers in each of the T-accounts.

E6-34. Analysis of Accounts Receivable and Allowance for Doubtful Accounts LO4, 5, 6

Ethan Allen Interiors Inc. reported the following amounts in its 2012 and 2011 annual report.

($ thousands)	2012	2011
From the income statement:		
Net sales	$729,373	$678,960
From the balance sheet:		
Accounts receivable, net	14,919	15,036
Customer deposits	65,465	62,649
From the disclosure on Allowance for doubtful accounts:		
Balance at beginning of period	1,171	1,160
Additions (reductions) charged to income	9	11
Adjustments or deductions	70	—
Balance at end of period	1,250	1,171

a. Prepare the journal entry to record accounts receivable written off as uncollectible in 2012. Also prepare the entry to record bad debts expense for 2012. What effect did these entries have on Ethan Allen's income for that year?

b. Calculate Ethan Allen's gross receivables for the years given, and then determine the allowance for doubtful accounts as a percentage of the gross receivables.

c. Calculate Ethan Allen's accounts receivable turnover for 2012. (Use Accounts receivable, net for the calculation.)

d. How much cash did Ethan Allen receive from customers in 2012?

LO4 **E6-35. Analysing and Reporting Receivable Transactions and Uncollectible Accounts (Using Percentage-of-Sales Method)**

At the beginning of 2014, Penman Company had the following (normal) account balances in its financial records:

Accounts Receivable	$122,000
Allowance for Uncollectible Accounts	7,900

During 2014, its credit sales were $1,173,000 and collections on credit sales were $1,150,000. The following additional transactions occurred during the year:

Feb. 17	Wrote off Nissim's account, $3,600.
May 28	Wrote off Weiss's account, $2,400.
Dec. 15	Wrote off Ohlson's account, $900.
Dec. 31	Recorded bad debts expense at 0.8% of credit sales for the year. (*Hint*: The allowance account is increased by 0.8% of credit sales regardless of any prior write-offs.)

Compute and show how accounts receivable and the allowance for uncollectible accounts are reported in its December 31, 2014, balance sheet.

LO4 **E6-36. Estimating Bad Debts Expense and Reporting of Receivables**

At December 31, 2013, Sunil Company had a balance of $375,000 in its accounts receivable and an unused balance of $4,200 in its allowance for uncollectible accounts. The company then aged its accounts as follows:

Current	$304,000
0–60 days past due	44,000
61–180 days past due	18,000
Over 180 days past due	9,000
Total accounts receivable	$375,000

The company has experienced losses as follows: 1% of current balances, 5% of balances 0–60 days past due, 15% of balances 61–180 days past due, and 40% of balances over 180 days past due. The company continues to base its allowance for credit losses on this ageing analysis and percentages.

a. What amount of bad debts expense does Sunil report on its 2013 income statement?

b. Show how accounts receivable and the allowance for uncollectible accounts are reported in its December 31, 2013, balance sheet.

c. Set up T-accounts for both Bad Debts Expense and for the Allowance for Uncollectible Accounts. Enter any unadjusted balances along with the dollar effects of the information described (including your results from parts *a* and *b*). Explain the numbers in each of the T-accounts.

LO4 **E6-37. Estimating Uncollectible Accounts and Reporting Receivables over Multiple Periods**

Barth Company, which has been in business for three years, makes all of its sales on credit and does not offer cash discounts. Its credit sales, customer collections, and write-offs of uncollectible accounts for its first three years follow:

Year	Sales	Collections	Accounts Written Off
2012	$751,000	$733,000	$5,300
2013	876,000	864,000	5,800
2014	972,000	938,000	6,500

a. Barth uses the allowance method of recognising credit losses that provides for such losses at the rate of 1% of sales. (This means the allowance account is increased by 1% of credit sales regardless of any write-offs and unused balances.) What amounts for accounts receivable and the allowance for uncollectible accounts are reported on its balance sheet at the end of 2014? What total amount of bad debts expense appears on its income statement for each of the three years?

b. Comment on the appropriateness of the 1% rate used to provide for bad debts based on your results in part *a*. (*Hint*: T-accounts can help with this analysis.)

E6-38.[A] Identifying Operating and Nonrecurring Income Components

LO7

BOMBARDIER INC. (CANADA)

Following is the income statement of Bombardier Inc., a Canadian multinational aerospace and transportation company, for the year 2013.

BOMBARDIER INC. CONSOLIDATED STATEMENTS OF INCOME For the fiscal years ended December 31 (in millions of U.S. dollars, except per share amounts)	Notes	2013	2012
			restated
Revenues		$18,151	$16,414
Cost of sales	17	15,658	14,053
Gross margin		2,493	2,361
SG&A		1,417	1,442
R&D	7	293	299
Share of income of joint ventures and associates	36	(119)	(153)
Other expense (income)	8	9	(33)
Special items	9	(30)	140
EBIT		923	666
Financing expense	10	271	295
Financing income	10	(119)	(165)
EBT		771	536
Income taxes	12	199	66
Net income		$ 572	$ 470
Attributable to			
Equity holders of Bombardier Inc.		$ 564	$ 460
NCI		8	10
		$ 572	$ 470
EPS (in dollars)	13		
Basic and diluted		$ 0.31	$ 0.25

Required

a. Identify the components in its statement that you would consider operating.

b. Identify the components that you would consider nonrecurring.

E6-39. Interpreting Accounts Receivable and Uncollectible Accounts

LO4, 5

UNILEVER (NETHERLANDS AND U.K.)

Unilever Group is the third largest consumer products company in the world by revenue. It owns more than 400 brands of personal care, home care, refreshment, and foods products that are sold to 2 billion consumers in over 190 countries. Unilever maintained two separate legal parent companies: Unilever NV, headquartered in Rotterdam, and Unilever PLC, headquartered in London. However, it is operating as a single business entity through various agreements between the two parent companies and the same directors sitting on the boards of both companies.

The company provided the following information concerning its receivable account in note 13 of its fiscal 2013 annual report:

Trade and other current receivables	€ million 2013	€ million 2012
Due within one year		
Trade receivables	2,852	2,793
Prepayments and accrued income	516	549
Other receivables	1,463	1,094
	4,831	4,436

Impairment provision for trade receivables—current and non-current impairments	€ million 2013	€ million 2012
1 January	151	145
Charged to income statement	38	33
Reductions/releases	(30)	(23)
Currency retranslation	(10)	(4)
December 31	149	151

Required

a. Prepare journal entries (and post to the related T-accounts) to record bad debts expense and accounts receivable write-offs for 2012 and 2013.

b. Compute the allowance for doubtful accounts as a percentage of accounts receivable for 2012 and 2013. Comment on any observed changes.

c. The company reported revenue of €49,797 in 2013. Calculate the accounts receivable turnover ratio and average collection period for 2013 using net accounts receivable. Recalculate these ratios using total accounts receivable. How do you interpret the difference between these two calculations?

LO2 **E6-40. Accounting for Membership Fees and Rewards Programme**

Costco Wholesale Corporation provides the following description of its revenue recognition policies for membership fees and rewards in its annual report dated September 2, 2012:

Membership fee revenue represents annual membership fees paid by substantially all of the Company's members. The Company accounts for membership fee revenue, net of estimated refunds, on a deferred basis, whereby revenue is recognised ratably over the one-year membership period. The Company's Executive Members qualify for a 2% reward (beginning November, 1, 2011 the reward increased from a maximum of $500 to $750 per year on qualified purchases), which can be redeemed at Costco warehouses. The Company accounts for this reward as a reduction in sales. The sales reduction and corresponding liability are computed after giving effect to the estimated impact of non-redemptions based on historical data. The net reduction in sales was $900, $790, and $688 in 2012, 2011, and 2010, respectively.

The following data were extracted from Costco's 2012 income statement and balance sheet:

	2012	2011
Revenue		
Net sales	$97,062	$87,048
Membership fees	2,075	1,867
Total revenue	99,137	88,915
Current Liabilities		
Accounts payable	$ 7,303	$ 6,544
Current portion of long-term debt	1	900
Accrued salaries and benefits	1,832	1,758
Accrued member rewards	661	602
Accrued sales and other taxes	397	335
Other current liabilities	965	938
Deferred membership fees	1,101	973
Total current liabilities	$12,260	$12,050

a. Explain Costco's accounting for membership fees and rewards programmes.

b. Prepare journal entries to record (1) membership fees collected in cash in fiscal 2012 and (2) membership fee revenue recognised in 2012.

c. Prepare journal entries to record (1) member rewards earned by "executive members" in fiscal 2012 and (2) rewards redeemed during the year.

PROBLEMS

P6-41.[A] Identifying Operating and Nonrecurring Income Components LO7

Following is the Hutong Systems, Inc. income statement.

Required

a. Identify the components in its statement that you would consider operating.

b. Identify those components that you would consider nonrecurring.

(In Renminbi millions) For Year Ended December 31	2014	2013
Net sales	¥53,674	¥44,875
Cost of sales	45,780	39,148
Research and development expenses	1,660	1,492
Selling, general, and administrative expenses	2,609	2,487
Amortisation of intangibles	509	399
Goodwill impairment losses	—	7
Restructuring charges	26	689
Purchased in-process research and development charges	—	7
Acquisition-related expenses	143	166
Litigation-related credit	54	—
Equity in earnings of nonconsolidated affiliates	1,112	630
Sundry income—net	125	891
Interest income	37	39
Interest expense and amortisation of debt discount	1,473	1,571
Income before income taxes	2,802	469
Provision for income taxes	481	(97)
Net income from continuing operations	2,321	566
Discontinued operations	—	110
Net income	¥ 2,321	¥ 676

P6-42. Percentage-of-Completion and Cost-Recovery Methods LO3

Bloor Company signed a three-year contract to provide sales training to the employees of Spadina Company. The contract price is $1,200 per employee and the estimated number of employees to be trained is 400. The expected number to be trained in each year and the expected training costs follow. Payment is made as $150,000, $240,000 and $90,000 in 2013, 2014 and 2015 respectively.

	Number of employees	Training costs incurred
2013	125	$ 60,000
2014	200	75,000
2015	75	40,000
Total	400	$175,000

Required

a. For each year, compute the revenue, expense, and gross profit reported assuming revenue is recognised using the following method.

1. Percentage-of-completion method, where percentage-of-completion is determined by the number of employees trained.
2. Percentage-of-completion method, where percentage-of-completion is determined by the costs incurred.
3. Cost-recovery method.

b. Which method do you believe is most appropriate in this situation? Explain.

P6-43. Incentives for Earnings Management LO6

Harris Corporation pays senior management an annual bonus from a bonus pool. The size of the bonus pool is determined as follows.

Reported net income	Bonus pool
Less than or equal to $10 million	$0
Greater than $10 million, but less than or equal to $20 million.	10% of income in excess of $10 million
Greater than $20 million	$1 million

Required

a. Assume that senior management expects current earnings to be $21 million and next year's earnings to be $18 million. What incentive does management of Harris Corporation have for managing earnings?

b. Assume that senior management expects current earnings to be $17 million and next year's earnings to be $24 million. What incentive does management of Harris Corporation have for managing earnings?

c. Assume that senior management expects current earnings to be $9.5 million and next year's earnings to be $12 million. What incentive does management of Harris Corporation have for managing earnings?

d. How might the bonus plan be structured to minimise the incentives for earnings management?

LO4 **P6-44. Interpreting Accounts Receivable and Uncollectible Accounts**

Orchard Shopping Corp. provided the following information concerning its accounts receivable in note 3 of its 2015 annual report (amounts in millions of Singapore dollars):

NOTE 3: ACCOUNTS RECEIVABLE

The components of accounts receivable are as follows:

	2015	2014
Total credit card receivables.	$2,074	$2,103
Allowance for credit losses.	(115)	(145)
Credit card receivables, net	1,959	1,958
Other accounts receivable	74	68
Accounts receivable, net.	**$2,033**	$2,026

Activity in the allowance for credit losses for the past two fiscal years is as follows:

Fiscal year	2015	2014
Allowance at beginning of year	$145	$190
Bad debt expense.	101	149
Write-offs.	(153)	(211)
Recoveries.	22	17
Allowance at end of year.	**$115**	$145

Credit Quality

The primary indicators of the credit quality of our credit card receivables are ageing and delinquency, particularly the levels of account balances delinquent 30 days or more as these are the accounts most likely to be written off. The following table illustrates the ageing and delinquency status of our credit card receivables:

	2015		2014	
	Balance	% of Total	Balance	% of Total
Current.	$1,928	93.0%	$1,942	92.4%
1–29 days delinquent	92	4.4%	97	4.6%
30+ days delinquent:				
30–59 days delinquent.	20	1.0%	24	1.1%
60–89 days delinquent.	13	0.6%	17	0.8%
90 days or more delinquent.	21	1.0%	23	1.1%
Total 30+ days delinquent.	54	2.6%	64	3.0%
Total credit card receivables.	$2,074	100.0%	$2,103	100.0%

Required:

a. What amount did Orchard report as accounts receivable, net in its 2015 balance sheet?

b. Prepare journal entries to record bad debts expense, write-offs of uncollectible accounts, and recoveries in fiscal 2015. Post these entries to T-accounts. How should Orchard record recoveries?

c. Compute the ratio of allowance for credit losses to total credit card receivables for fiscal 2014 and 2015. Speculate as to what might be the cause of any change that you observe.

d. Orchard reported net sales of $10,497 million in fiscal 2015. Compute its accounts receivable turnover and average collection period for that year.

P6-45. Accounting for Product Returns LO4

In its income statement for fiscal year 2014, Telford Shopping, Inc., reported net sales of $14,549 million and cost of goods sold and occupancy expenses of $9,275 million, resulting in a Gross Profit of $5,274 million. In its footnotes, Telford reports that "Allowances for estimated returns are recorded based on estimated gross profit using our historical return patterns."

When Telford accounts for estimated sales returns, it reduces sales revenue by the returns' expected sales price, reduces cost of goods sold by the returns' expected cost and recognises a sales return allowance as a liability equal to the returns' expected gross profit.

A sales returns allowance of $21 million was reported among Telford's liabilities at the end of fiscal year 2014, and the footnotes report that $634 million in allowance for returns was added to this liability during fiscal year 2014. Actual returns were reported at $635 million and subtracted from the liability.

Required

a. What was the balance in Telford's sales returns allowance liability at the beginning of fiscal year 2014?

b. Suppose Telford sells 100 units of an item for $50 each, and its gross profit on each unit is $20. Further, suppose Telford expects that 10 of the units will be returned. What entries will be made to record the sale of 100 units (for cash) and the expected returns? What entry is made when ten customers subsequently return the items and receive a cash refund? Assume that the units are undamaged and can be sold to other customers.

c. Assume that the gross profit margin (gross profit divided by sales revenue) for returned items is the same as that for those that are not returned. Reconstruct the entry Telford made to account for expected product returns in 2014. What were the 2014 gross sales for Telford? What percentage of its sales does Telford expect to be returned?

d. Suppose Telford entered a new market in which it did not have the ability to predict product returns. How should it deal with the prospect of returns when it sells products to customers?

P6-46. Analysing Unearned Revenue Changes LO2

Belem Interactive S.A. is a developer, marketer, publisher and distributor of video game software and content to be played on a variety of platforms. There is an increasing demand for the ability to play these games in an online environment, and Belem has developed this capability in many of its products. In addition, Belem maintains servers (or arranges for servers) for the online activities of its customers. When customers purchase online subscriptions, revenue is recognised ratably over the subscription period.

Belem treats a significant portion of its software sales as "multiple element arrangements" and—through fiscal 2010—deferred a portion of customer purchases based on the estimated value of the online services offered. Beginning in fiscal 2011, it was not possible to estimate the separate value of the software and the online services, so Belem began to defer all such revenue over a six-month period. In addition, Belem's 2015 annual report states that the company uses the Internet to provide post-purchase updates or additional content to customers, again treating such situations as "multiple element arrangements."

Information from Belem's financial statements is given below. Prior to fiscal year 2009, no revenue was deferred. All amounts are in € millions.

Fiscal year ending March 31	Net revenue	Deferred net revenue (liability)
2008	€3,129	€ 0
2009	2,951	9
2010	3,091	32
2011	3,665	387
2012	4,212	261
2013	3,654	766
2014	3,589	1,005
2015	4,143	1,048

Required

a. Calculate the growth rates in net revenue over the years in the table.

b. What are the purchases by customers in each of these years? What are the growth rates? Why do you think they differ from the growth rates in net revenue?

c. Would you predict a growth in 2016 revenue equal to that in 2015? Why?

CASES AND PROJECTS

LO1, 2 C6-47. Revenue Recognition and Refunds

Groupon, Inc. is an Internet-based marketing company which sells coupons (called "Groupons") for products and services offered by other merchants (merchant partners). Groupon offers a "daily deal" to subscribers. The daily deal provides significant savings on a variety of products and services provided that a minimum number of customers purchase the Groupon for each deal offered. This feature guarantees a sufficient volume of customers to ensure that the deal is profitable to the merchant partner.

When Groupon sells a coupon, it collects the proceeds from the customer (gross billings) and then remits a payment to the merchant partner. These payments are typically paid out over a 60-day period. Groupon's revenue recognition policy is described in its annual report as follows:

Revenue Recognition

The Company recognises revenue from Groupons when the following criteria are met: persuasive evidence of an arrangement exists; delivery has occurred; the selling price is fixed or determinable; and collectability is reasonably assured. These criteria are met when the number of customers who purchase the daily deal exceeds the predetermined threshold, the Groupon has been electronically delivered to the purchaser and a listing of Groupons sold has been made available to the merchant. At that time, the Company's obligations to the merchant, for which it is serving as an agent, are substantially complete. The Company's remaining obligations, which are limited to remitting payment to the merchant and continuing to make available on the Company's website the listing of Groupons previously provided to the merchant, are inconsequential or perfunctory. The Company records the net amount it retains from the sale of Groupons after paying an agreed upon percentage of the purchase price to the featured merchant excluding any applicable taxes. Revenue is recorded on a net basis because the Company is acting as an agent of the merchant in the transaction.

Groupon reported gross billings of $3,985.5 million in 2011, up from $745.3 million in 2010. Its net revenues were $1,610.4 million in 2011 and $312.9 million in 2010. Groupon also reported that it changed its method of revenue recognition during 2011:

The Company restated the Condensed Consolidated Statements of Operations for the three months ended March 31, 2011 to correct for an error in its presentation of revenue. Most significantly, the Company restated its reporting of revenues from Groupons to be net of the amounts related to merchant fees. Historically, the Company reported the gross amounts billed to its subscribers as revenue. The Condensed Consolidated Statement of Operations for the three months ended March 31, 2011, was restated to show the net amount the Company retains after paying the merchant fees. The effect of the correction resulted in a reduction of previously reported revenues and corresponding reductions in cost of revenue in those periods. The change in presentation had no effect on pre-tax loss, net loss or any per share amounts for the period.

Groupon's refund policy is also described in its 2012 annual report:

Our Groupon Promise states that we will provide our customers with a refund of the purchase price of a Groupon if they believe that we have let them down. . . . Our standard agreements with our merchant partners generally limit the time period during which we may seek reimbursement for customer refunds or claims. Our customers may make claims for refunds with respect to which we are unable to seek reimbursement from our merchant partners.

At the time revenue is recorded, we record an allowance for estimated customer refunds. We accrue costs associated with refunds in accrued expenses on the consolidated balance sheets. The cost of refunds where the amount payable to the merchant is recoverable is recorded in the consolidated statements of operations as a reduction to revenue. The cost of refunds when there is no amount recoverable from the merchant are presented as a cost of revenue.

To determine the amount of our refund reserve, we track refund patterns of prior deals, use that data to build a model and apply that model to current deals. Further analysis of our refund activity into 2012 indicated deviations from modelled refund behaviour for deals featured in late 2011, particularly due to a shift in our fourth quarter deal mix and higher price point offers. Accordingly, we updated our refund model to reflect changes in the deal mix and price point of our deals over time and we believe this updated model will enable us to more accurately track and anticipate refund behaviour.

Required

a. Assume that Groupon offers a daily deal that costs $200 per Groupon. It sells 600 of the Groupons and agrees to remit 50% of the gross revenue to the merchant within 60 days. Using journal entries and T-accounts, illustrate how Groupon would record the sale of this Groupon deal.

b. In the first quarter of 2011, Groupon changed its revenue recognition policy. How did this change affect its income statement?

c. Refer to the facts presented in *a* above. Assume that Groupon expects that 10% of the Groupon customers will demand a refund within the first 60 days. How does Groupon record this estimate of returns? How are actual refunds recorded?

d. Now assume that an additional 5% of Groupon's customers demand refunds after the first 60 days. How are these refunds handled?

e. Given the uncertainty surrounding refunds, what alternative accounting approaches might Groupon consider for handling refunds?

C6-48. Interpreting Revenue Recognition Policies and Earnings Management LO1, 2, 6

A *Wall Street Journal* article dated October 31, 2007, reported that an internal investigation at Dell Inc. had uncovered evidence of earnings management. The article states:

An internal investigation found that senior executives and other employees manipulated the company's financial statements to give the appearance of hitting quarterly performance goals.

One of the biggest problems uncovered in the investigation was the way Dell recognised revenue on software products it sells. Dell, a large reseller of other companies' software products, said it historically recognised revenue from software licences at the time that the products were sold. . . . Based on its internal review, it should have deferred more revenue from software sales.

Another issue was product warranties. In some cases, Dell said it improperly recognised revenue associated with [extended] warranties over a shorter period of time than the duration of the contract.

The income statements from Dell's 2007 annual report are presented below, along with the footnote outlining Dell's revenue recognition policies:

	Fiscal Year Ended		
	February 2, 2007	February 3, 2006 As Restated	January 28, 2005 As Restated
Net revenue	$57,420	$55,788	$49,121
Cost of net revenue	47,904	45,897	40,103
Gross margin	9,516	9,891	9,018
Operating expenses:			
Selling, general, and administrative	5,948	5,051	4,352
Research, development, and engineering	498	458	460
Total operating expenses	6,446	5,509	4,812
Operating income	3,070	4,382	4,206
Investment and other income, net	275	226	197
Income before income taxes	3,345	4,608	4,403
Income tax expense	762	1,006	1,385
Net income	$ 2,583	$ 3,602	$ 3,018

Revenue Recognition Net revenue includes sales of hardware, software and peripherals, and services (including extended service contracts and professional services). These products and services are sold either separately or as part of a multiple-element arrangement. Dell allocates revenue from multiple-element arrangements to the elements based on the relative fair value of each element, which is generally based on the relative sales price of each element when sold separately. The allocation of fair value for a multiple-element arrangement involving software is based on vendor specific objective evidence ("VSOE"), or in the absence of VSOE for delivered elements, the residual method. Under the residual method, Dell allocates revenue to software licences at the inception of the licence term when VSOE for all undelivered elements, such as Post Contract Customer Support ("PCS"), exists and all other revenue recognition criteria have been satisfied. In the absence of VSOE for undelivered elements, revenue is deferred and subsequently recognised over the term of the arrangement. For sales of extended warranties with a separate contract price, Dell defers revenue equal to the separately stated price. Revenue associated with undelivered elements is deferred and recorded when delivery occurs. Product revenue is recognised, net of an allowance for estimated returns, when both title and risk of loss transfer to the customer, provided that no significant obligations remain. Revenue from extended warranty and service contracts, for which Dell is obligated to perform, is recorded as deferred revenue and subsequently recognised over the term of the contract or when the service is completed. Revenue from sales of third-party extended warranty and service contracts or software PCS, for which Dell is not obligated to perform, and for which Dell does not meet the criteria for gross revenue recognition under EITF 99-19 is recognised on a net basis. All other revenue is recognised on a gross basis.

Required

a. Explain how Dell accounts for sales of other companies' software products. What are the potential risks of abuse of these accounting policies as a means to manage earnings?

b. Explain how Dell accounts for sales of extended warranty contracts. How did Dell employees manipulate these policies to manage earnings?

c. Discuss the incentives that exist to manage earnings to "give the appearance of hitting quarterly performance goals." How can a company such as Dell prevent earnings management in circumstances such as this?

SOLUTIONS TO REVIEW PROBLEMS

Mid-Chapter Review 1

Solution (all amounts in £ millions)

1.

Fiscal year	Revenue growth rates
2014	(£1,306.8 – £1,376.1)/ £1,376.1 = –5.0%
2013	(£1,376.1 – £1,340.2)/ £1,340.2 = 2.7%

2. To determine the customer purchases during the year, we start with the revenue, then add the change in Deferred Income.

Fiscal year	Revenue	Deferred Income	Change in Deferred Income	Customer Purchases = Revenue + Change in Deferred Income
2014	£1,306.8	£402.7	£–4.1	£1,302.70
2013	1,376.1	406.8	–13.5	1,362.60
2012	1,340.2	420.3	15.6	1,355.80
2011	1,334.1	404.7		

3.

Fiscal year	Growth in Customer Purchases
2014	(£1,302.70 – £1,362.60)/ £1,362.60 = –4.4%
2013	(£1,362.60 – £1,355.80)/ £1,355.80 = 0.5%

When a customer makes a purchase, Sage defers a substantial portion of the amount received and recognises that portion over future periods. Therefore, revenue reported on the income statement is a combination of customer purchases in the current period, plus customer purchases in previous periods.

Mid-Chapter Review 2

Solution

1. The terms of the contract are likely different for government contracts and contracts with private organisations. To justify the use of the percentage-of-completion method, there must be a contract that specifies a fixed or determinable price. The contracts for private organisations might have more ambiguity as far as the pricing is concerned. Alternatively, Bruges most likely has experience that would indicate that government contracts are less likely to be cancelled.

2. The percentage completed in each year is 40% in 2014 (€12,000,000/€30,000,000), 45% in 2015 (€13,500,000/€30,000,000), and 15% in 2016 (€4,500,000/€30,000,000).
   a. Percentage-of-completion method

	2014	2015	2016
Percentage completed	40%	45%	15%
Contract revenue.	€16,000,000	€18,000,000	€6,000,000
(Percentage completed × €40,000,000)			
Contract expense	12,000,000	13,500,000	4,500,000
Gross profit	€ 4,000,000	€ 4,500,000	€1,500,000

   b. Cost-recovery method

	2014	2015	2016
Contract revenue.	€10,000,000	€15,000,000	€15,500,000
Contract expense	10,000,000	15,000,000	5,000,000
Gross profit	€ 0	€ 0	€10,000,000

3. Under the percentage-of-completion method, income would be understated in 2014 and 2015 (since percentages completed were understated), but the difference would be made up in 2016 with higher than expected earnings. The gross profit in 2016 would be €6,000,000 − €1,500,000 = €4,500,000.

   Under the cost-recovery method, gross profits in 2014 and 2015 would remain unchanged at zero, but gross profit in 2016 would increase to €13,000,000 (€15,000,000 − €2,000,000). This is because the total cost of the project was overestimated by €3,000,000 (€4,500,000 − €1,500,000).

Mid-Chapter Review 3

Solution

1. As of December 31, 2013,

Current.	$468,000 × 1%	=	$ 4,680	
1–60 days past due	244,000 × 5%	=	12,200	
61–180 days past due	38,000 × 15%	=	5,700	
Over 180 days past due	20,000 × 40%	=	8,000	
Amount required			$30,580	
Unused allowance balance. . .			7,000	
			$23,580	2013 bad debts expense

2. Current assets section of balance sheet.

Accounts receivable, net of $30,580 in allowances.	$739,420

3. Jumbo Kingdom Company has markedly increased the percentage of the allowance for uncollectible accounts to gross accounts receivable—from the historical 2% to the current 4% ($30,580/$770,000). There are at least two possible interpretations:
   a. The quality of Jumbo Kingdom Company's receivables has declined. Possible causes include the following: (1) sales can stagnate and the company can feel compelled to sell to lower-quality accounts to maintain sales volume; (2) it may have introduced new products for which average credit losses are higher; and (3) its administration of accounts receivable can become lax.
   b. The company has intentionally increased its allowance account above the level needed for expected future losses so as to reduce current period income and "bank" that income for future periods (income shifting).

4. Transaction effects shown in the financial statement effects template.

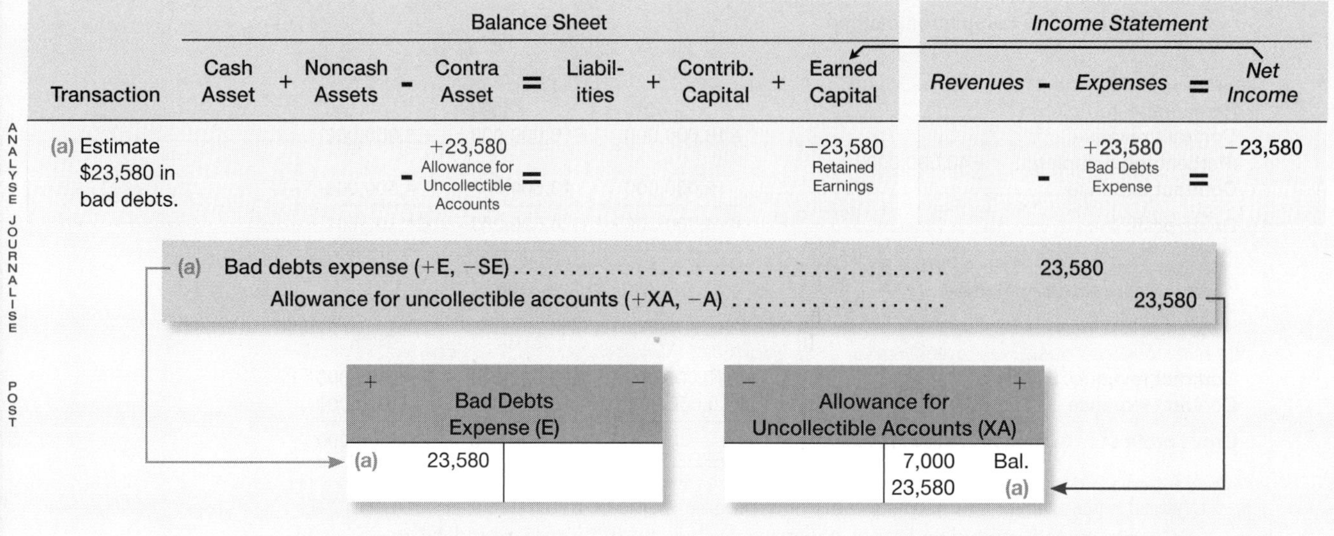

ANALYSE

Transaction	Cash Asset +	Noncash Assets −	Contra Asset =	Liabilities +	Contrib. Capital +	Earned Capital	Revenues −	Expenses =	Net Income
(a) Estimate $23,580 in bad debts.			+23,580 Allowance for Uncollectible Accounts			−23,580 Retained Earnings		+23,580 Bad Debts Expense	−23,580

(Balance Sheet: Cash Asset through Earned Capital; Income Statement: Revenues through Net Income)

JOURNALISE

		Dr	Cr
(a)	Bad debts expense (+E, −SE)	23,580	
	Allowance for uncollectible accounts (+XA, −A)		23,580

POST

+ Bad Debts Expense (E) −	
(a) 23,580	

− Allowance for Uncollectible Accounts (XA) +	
	7,000 Bal.
	23,580 (a)

ANALYSE

Transaction	Cash Asset +	Noncash Assets −	Contra Asset =	Liabilities +	Contrib. Capital +	Earned Capital	Revenues −	Expenses =	Net Income
(b) Write off $5,000 in accounts receivable.*		−5,000 Accounts Receivable	−5,000 Allowance for Uncollectible Accounts						

(Balance Sheet: Cash Asset through Earned Capital; Income Statement: Revenues through Net Income)

* There is no effect on net accounts receivable.

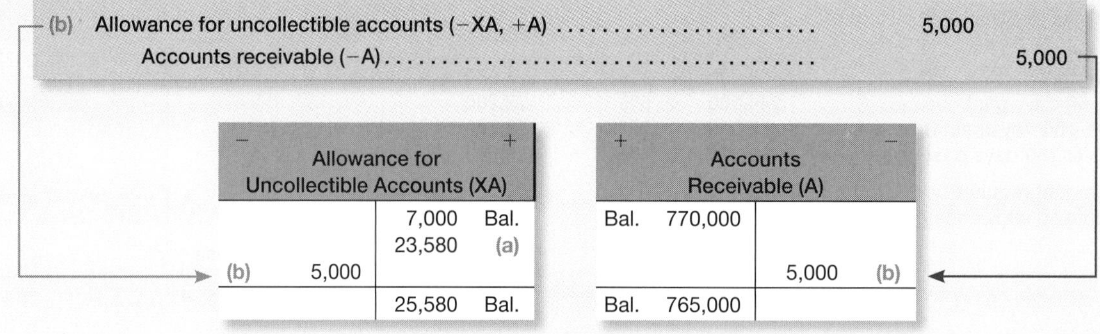

JOURNALISE

		Dr	Cr
(b)	Allowance for uncollectible accounts (−XA, +A)	5,000	
	Accounts receivable (−A)		5,000

POST

− Allowance for Uncollectible Accounts (XA) +	
	7,000 Bal.
	23,580 (a)
(b) 5,000	
	25,580 Bal.

+ Accounts Receivable (A) −	
Bal. 770,000	
	5,000 (b)
Bal. 765,000	

Chapter-End Review

Solution

1.

(CDN$ millions)	Canadian Tire	Dollarama
Accounts receivable turnover.	=$11,785.60/[($758.50 + $750.60)/2] = 15.6	= $2,064.68/[($5.80 + $5.96)/2] = 351.1
Average collection period.	= 365/15.6 = 23.4 days	= 365/351.1 = 1.0 days

2. Canadian Tire turns its receivables 15.6 times per year, for an average collection period (ACP) of 23.4 days. Dollarama, on the other hand, has an accounts receivable turnover (ART) of 351.1 times and an ACP of just 1.0 days. In comparison, the median ART for the retail industry is 90.5. The turnover ratio for Dollarama is high, because of its cash-base business model. For Canadian Tire, its below industry median ART is mainly due to its credit card business, which allows its customers additional time to pay.

Appendix Review

Solution

a. A loss from discontinued operations of $105,000 would be reported below income from continuing operations. The loss is net of tax and is calculated as follows: $105,000 = ($120,000 + $12,000 + $18,000) × (1 − 30%).

b. A restructuring charge of $30,000 ($12,000 + $18,000) would be reported as part of operating income. The loss is before taxes. The tax effect of the restructuring charge would be included in income tax expense.

c. Singh could report this loss as discontinued operations only if the closure represented a separate business unit within the company. Otherwise, it must be reported as a restructuring charge.

LEARNING OBJECTIVES

1. Interpret disclosures of information concerning operating expenses, including manufacturing and retail inventory costs. (p. 320)
2. Account for inventory and cost of goods sold using different costing methods. (p. 325)
3. Apply the lower of cost or market rule to value inventory. (p. 329)
4. Discuss the required financial statement disclosure and how outsiders may use it to analyse a company's inventory management. (p. 331)
5. Define and interpret gross profit margin and inventory turnover ratios. (p. 333)
6. Appendix 7A: Discuss LIFO and adjusting the financial statements to FIFO. (p. 337)

CHAPTER

7

Reporting and Analysing Inventory

VTECH
www.vtech.com

VTech Holdings Ltd. is the world's largest manufacturer of cordless phones, a global leader in electronic learning products, and one of the top 50 contract manufacturing services providers in the world. It is based in Hong Kong and has three manufacturing facilities in China and R&D centres in Canada, Germany, Hong Kong, and China. Its ordinary shares are listed in the Hong Kong Stock Exchange.

The company was founded in Hong Kong in 1976 as a home video game business. In 1980, it launched its first electronic learning products (ELP) and subsequently entered the preschool ELP market in 1989. In 2013, it was the foremost supplier of ELPs from infancy to preschool in the combined market of France, Germany, Spain, United Kingdom, and the United States. VTech entered the cordless customer phone business in 1991 with its fully digital 900MHz cordless phone. In 2000, it acquired Lucent Technologies' consumer phone business and the right to use the AT&T brand to sell its landline phones and accessories in Canada and the United States. It introduced commercial phones in 2009 and hotel phones in 2011. Since 1984, VTech has also provided contract manufacturing services (CMS) to medium sized companies. In 2013, it was ranked 27th among the world's top 50 CMS providers.

As a consumer electronics company, VTech's performance is very sensitive to economic conditions and changing consumer tastes. Despite the slow economic recovery in the United States and the economic uncertainty in Western Europe (these two markets accounted for over 90% of its sales), the company's sales revenue for the year ended March 31, 2013, rose 4.1% to US$1,858.0 million and net profit increased 5.4% to US$202.3 million. The company's net profit margin (net profit divided by sales revenue) increased 0.1% point to 10.9%, reflecting lower material costs offset by higher labour costs and manufacturing overhead.

VTech's competitive strategy is based on product innovation, gains in market share, geographic expansion and operational excellence. Every year, the company has invested 3–4% of its annual sales on R&D and introduced over 100 new products. With its own manufacturing facilities, VTech can better control its operational costs and efficiency. Given its large production volumes, the company can negotiate the best prices for raw materials and key electronic components. As a manufacturer and CMS provider, VTech carries a large amount of inventory (almost 30% of total assets), including raw materials, work in process, and finished goods. Hence, a key element of VTech's operating strategy is inventory management. Ineffective inventory management would adversely affect the cost of goods sold and, hence, reduce operating performance, as measured by gross profit, operating profit, and net profit.

In this chapter, we examine the reporting of inventory and cost of goods sold. For most retail and manufacturing businesses, cost of goods sold and the related inventory management costs represent

(continued on next page)

(continued from previous page)

the largest expenses in the income statement. (Financial and service companies, including banks and insurance, are different.) Carrying large stocks of inventory is costly for any business. The more a business can minimise the amount of resources tied up in merchandise or materials, while still meeting customer demand, the more profitable it will be. Moreover, excessive inventory balances can indicate poor inventory management, obsolete products, and weakening sales. This chapter explores accounting methods designed to measure inventory costs and determine cost of goods sold. We also look at measures that help us assess the effectiveness of inventory management practices for retail and manufacturing companies such as VTech.

Sources: www.vtech.com; VTech 2013 Annual Report.

CHAPTER ORGANISATION

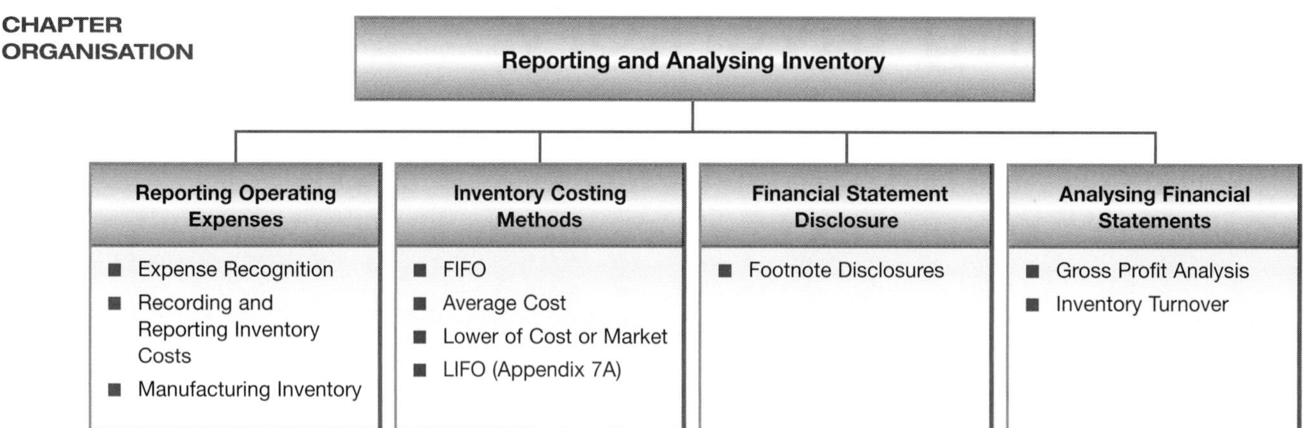

REPORTING OPERATING EXPENSES

LO1 Interpret disclosures of information concerning operating expenses, including manufacturing and retail inventory costs.

In Chapter 6, we introduced the concept of operating income and discussed issues surrounding revenue recognition and how best to measure and report a company's performance. But the amount of revenue from customers must be interpreted relative to the resources that were required to achieve it. Operating expenses include the costs of acquiring the products (and services) that customers purchase, plus the costs of selling efforts, administrative functions, and any other activities that support the operations of the company. Careful examination of these costs allows financial statement users to judge management's performance, to identify emerging problems, and to make predictions of future performance. For instance, we may address the following questions.

- Are the company's costs of providing products increasing or decreasing?
- Is the company able to maintain its margins in the face of changes in costs or competition?
- Does management's ability to judge customer tastes and preferences allow it to avoid overstocks of unpopular inventory and the resulting price discounts that reduce margins?

In this chapter, we begin our examination of operating expenses by studying inventory and cost of goods sold. The reporting of inventory and cost of goods sold is important for three reasons. First, cost of goods sold is often the largest single expense in a company's income statement, and inventory may be one of the largest assets in the balance sheet. Consequently, information about inventory and cost of goods sold is critical for interpreting the financial statements. Second, in order to effectively manage operations and resources, management needs accurate and timely information about inventory quantities and costs. Finally, alternative methods of accounting for inventory and cost of goods sold can distort interpretations of margins and turnovers unless the information in the financial statement footnotes is used.

Expense Recognition Principles

In addition to determining when to recognise revenues to properly measure and report a company's performance, we must also determine when to recognise expenses. The matching principle requires that expenses be recognised in the same period that the associated revenue is recognised. Expense recognition can be generally divided into the following three approaches.

- **Direct association**. Any cost that can be *directly* associated with a specific source of revenue should be recognised as an expense at the same time that the related revenue is recognised. For a merchandising company (a retailer or a wholesaler), an example of direct association is matching cost of goods sold with sales revenue when the product is delivered to the customer. The cost of acquiring the inventory is recorded in the inventory asset account where it remains until the item is sold. At that point, the inventory cost is removed from the inventory asset and transferred to expenses. The future costs of any obligations arising from current revenues should also be estimated and recognised as liabilities and matched as expenses against those revenues. An example of such an expense is expected warranty costs, a topic covered in Chapter 9.

  For a manufacturing company, the accounting system distinguishes between *product costs* and *period costs*. Product costs are incurred to benefit the company's manufacturing activities and include raw materials, production workers and supervisors, depreciation on equipment and facilities, utilities, and so on. Even though some of these costs cannot be directly associated with a unit of production, the accounting system accumulates product costs and assigns them to inventory assets until the unit is sold. All costs not classified as product costs are considered period costs.
- **Immediate recognition**. Many period costs are necessary for generating revenues and income but cannot be directly associated with specific revenues. Some costs can be associated with all of the revenues of an accounting period, but not with any specific sales transaction that occurred during that period. Examples include most administrative and marketing costs. These costs are recognised as expenses in the period when the costs are incurred. Other expense items, such as research expense, are recognised immediately because of IFRS requirements.
- **Systematic allocation**. Costs that benefit more than one accounting period and cannot be associated with specific revenues or assigned to a specific period must be allocated across all of the periods benefited. The most common example is depreciation expense. When an asset is purchased, it is capitalised (recorded in an asset account). The asset cost is then converted into an expense over the duration of its useful life according to a depreciation formula or schedule established by management. Depreciation of long-term assets is discussed in Chapter 8.

Inventory and cost of goods sold expense are important for product companies—manufacturers, wholesalers, and retailers. But before turning to an examination of these accounts at VTech, we should recognise that cost of sales expense is also a critical performance component for many service companies, particularly those who engage in projects for their clients and customers. For fiscal 2014, the consulting firm **Accenture PLC** reports revenues of $31.9 billion and cost of services of $22.2 billion, and **Google Inc.** reported revenue of $66 billion and cost of sales of $25.7 billion. While these companies report no inventory, the relationship of revenues to costs of revenues remains important.

Reporting Inventory Costs in the Financial Statements

To help frame our discussion of inventory, Exhibits 7.1 and 7.2 present information from the current asset section of the balance sheet and the continuing operations section of the income statement for VTech. We highlight stocks (i.e., inventories) in the balance sheet as well as cost of sales in the income statement.

When inventory is purchased or produced, it is capitalised and carried on the balance sheet as an asset until it is sold, at which time its cost is transferred from the balance sheet to the income statement as an expense (cost of goods sold). Cost of goods sold (COGS) is then subtracted from sales revenue to yield **gross profit**:

Gross profit = Sales revenue − Cost of goods sold

The manner in which inventory costs are transferred from the balance sheet to the income statement affects both the level of inventories reported on the balance sheet and the amount of gross profit (and net income) reported on the income statement.

EXHIBIT 7.1 Balance Sheets (Current Assets Only)

VTECH HOLDINGS LTD
Consolidated Balance Sheets (Current Assets Only)
As at March 31

	2013 US$ million	2012 US$ million
Current assets:		
Stocks	$276.9	$239.2
Debtors, deposits and prepayments	259.5	244.2
Taxation recoverable	0.4	0.8
Deposits and cash	308.6	326.5
Total current assets	$845.4	$810.7

EXHIBIT 7.2 Income Statement

VTECH HOLDINGS LTD
Consolidated Income Statements
For the year ended March 31

$ millions	2013 US$ million	2012 US$ million
Revenue	$1,858.0	$1,784.5
Cost of sales	(1,260.2)	(1,213.7)
Gross profit	597.8	570.8
Selling and distribution costs	(260.0)	(255.0)
Administrative and other operating expenses	(56.0)	(49.1)
Research and development expenses	(57.1)	(57.2)
Operating profit	224.7	209.5
Net finance income	1.7	2.1
Profit before taxation	226.4	211.6
Taxation	(24.1)	(19.7)
Profit for the year and attributable to shareholders of the Company	$ 202.3	$ 191.9

Recording Inventory Costs in the Financial Statements

To illustrate the inventory purchasing and selling cycle, assume that a start-up company purchases 800 units of merchandise inventory at a cost of $4 cash per unit. We account for this transaction as follows:

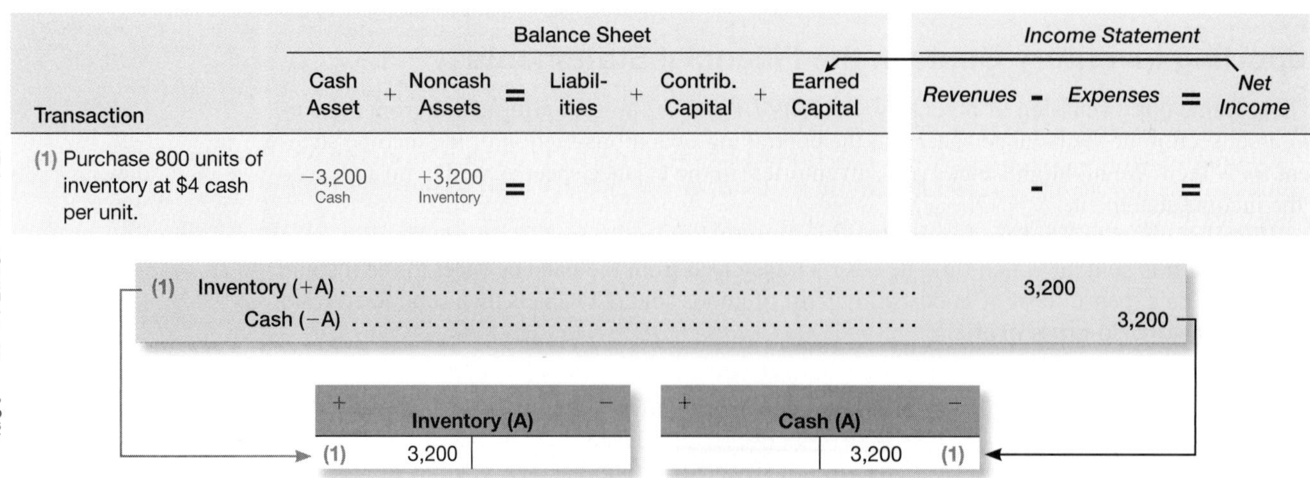

ANALYSE
Balance Sheet
Income Statement
Transaction
Cash Asset + Noncash Assets = Liabilities + Contrib. Capital + Earned Capital
Revenues - Expenses = Net Income
(1) Purchase 800 units of inventory at $4 cash per unit.
−3,200 Cash
+3,200 Inventory
JOURNALISE
(1) Inventory (+A) 3,200
Cash (−A) 3,200
POST
Inventory (A)
(1) 3,200
Cash (A)
3,200 (1)

Next, assume this company sells 500 of those units for $7 cash per unit. The two following entries are required to record (a) the sales revenue and (b) the expense for the cost of the inventory sold.

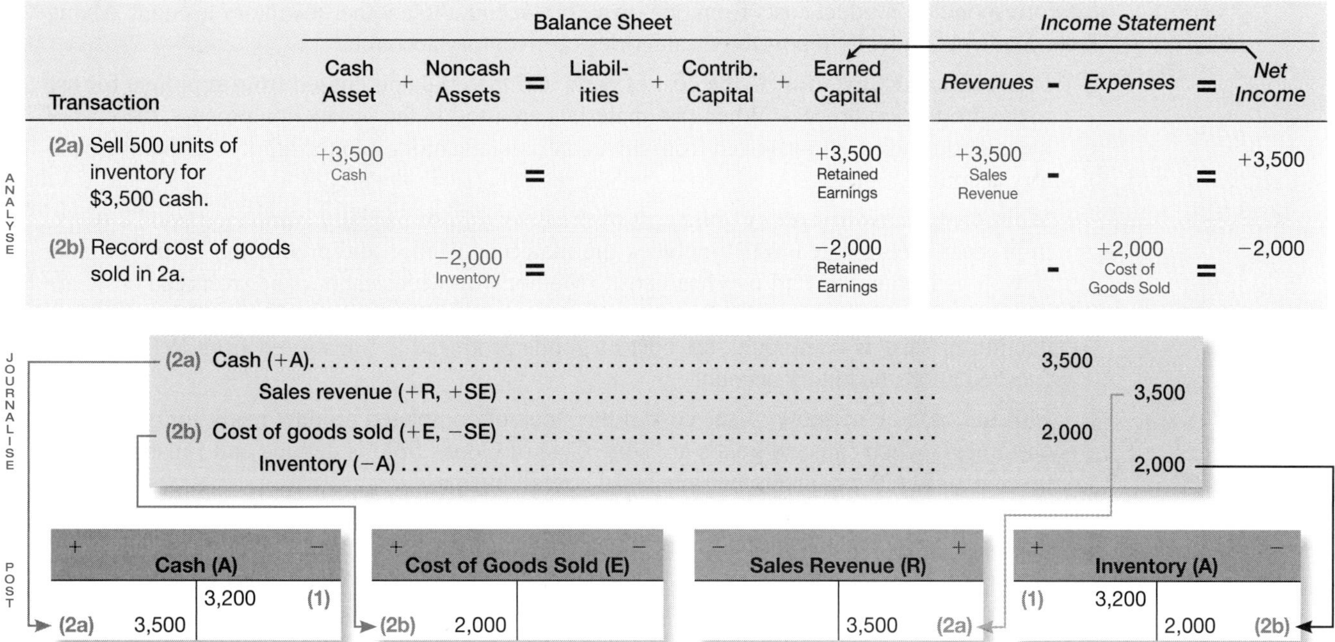

Balance Sheet
Income Statement
Transaction
Cash Asset + Noncash Assets = Liabilities + Contrib. Capital + Earned Capital
Revenues - Expenses = Net Income
ANALYSE
(2a) Sell 500 units of inventory for $3,500 cash.
+3,500 Cash
+3,500 Retained Earnings
+3,500 Sales Revenue
+3,500
(2b) Record cost of goods sold in 2a.
−2,000 Inventory
−2,000 Retained Earnings
+2,000 Cost of Goods Sold
−2,000
JOURNALISE
(2a) Cash (+A) 3,500
Sales revenue (+R, +SE) 3,500
(2b) Cost of goods sold (+E, −SE) 2,000
Inventory (−A) 2,000
POST
Cash (A)
3,200 (1)
(2a) 3,500
Cost of Goods Sold (E)
(2b) 2,000
Sales Revenue (R)
3,500 (2a)
Inventory (A)
(1) 3,200
2,000 (2b)

The gross profit from this sale is $1,500 ($3,500 − $2,000). Also, $1,200 worth of merchandise remains in inventory (300 units × $4 per unit).

Inventory and the Cost of Acquisition

In general, a company should recognise all inventories to which it holds legal title, and that inventory should be recognised at the cost of acquiring the inventory. On occasion, that means that the company will recognise items in inventory that are not on its premises. For instance, if a company purchases inventory from a supplier on an "FOB shipping point" basis, meaning that the purchasing company receives title to the goods as soon as they are shipped by the supplier, the purchasing company should recognise the inventory as soon as it receives notice that the goods have been shipped. A similar situation occurs when a company ships its own products to a customer, but has not yet fulfilled the requirements for recognising revenue on the shipment. In this case, the cost of the products remains in the selling company's inventory account until revenue (and cost of goods sold) can be recognised.

Inventory is reported in the balance sheet at its cost, including any cost to acquire, transport, and prepare goods for sale. In some cases, determining the cost of inventory requires accounting for various incentives that suppliers offer to purchase more or to pay promptly. If a company qualifies for a supplier's volume discount or rebate, it should immediately recognise the effective reduction in the cost of inventory and cost of goods sold. Or, if the company purchases inventory on credit, suppliers often grant **cash discounts** to buyers if payment is made within a specified time period. Cash discounts are usually established as part of the credit terms and stated as a percentage of the purchase price. For example, credit terms of 1/10, n/30 (one-ten, net-thirty) indicate that a 1% cash discount is allowed if the payment is made within 10 days. If the cash discount is not taken, the full purchase price is due in 30 days. Cash discounts are discussed in greater detail in Chapter 9.

> **FYI** The term **FOB ("free on board") shipping point** means that title passes to the purchaser as soon as it is shipped by the seller. **FOB destination** means that the seller retains title until the item arrives at the purchaser's location. ■

Inventory Reporting by Manufacturing Firms

Retail and wholesale businesses purchase merchandise for resale to customers. In contrast, a manufacturing firm produces the goods it sells and, hence, incurs two types of costs:

- **Product costs**—costs directly associated with production. They are recorded on the balance sheet in three categories of inventory account (discussed below) when incurred.
- **Period expenses**—costs not directly associated with production. They are expensed to the income statement in the period incurred.

Inventory accounting for manufacturing firms keeps track of product costs in different stages of the production process. As the production process moves from one stage to the next, we transfer

> **FYI** Only one inventory account appears in the financial statements of a merchandiser. A manufacturer normally has three inventory accounts: Raw Materials, Work-in-Process (or work-in-progress), and Finished Goods. ■

the corresponding product costs from one inventory account to another inventory account. Manufacturing firms typically report three categories of inventory account:

- **Raw materials inventory**—the cost of parts and materials purchased from suppliers for use in the production process. When raw materials are used in the production process, the cost of the materials used is transferred from raw materials inventory into the work-in-process inventory account.
- **Work-in-process inventory**—the cost of the inventory of partially completed goods. Work-in-process (abbreviated WIP) includes the materials used in the production of the product as well as labour cost and overhead cost. (Methods by which labour and overhead costs are assigned to products in the WIP account are a managerial accounting topic.) When the production process is completed, the cost of goods produced is transferred from WIP into the finished goods inventory account.
- **Finished goods inventory**—the cost of the stock of completed product ready for delivery to customers. When finished goods are sold, Cost of Goods Sold is debited and finished goods inventory is credited, much the same as in a retail business.

Illustration A complete illustration of the accounting process for a manufacturing business is beyond the scope of this text. Hence, we will focus on the concept behind it in this example. Assume that the Kiwi Manufacturing Company conducts an inventory count every quarter, and the balances of its inventory accounts for the first quarter of 2014 are summarised in the following table:

	Ending balance	Beginning balance
Raw materials inventory	$43,000	$49,000
Work-in-process inventory	62,000	67,000
Finished goods inventory	84,000	88,000

Further assume that the company incurred the following manufacturing-related costs during the first quarter of 2014:

Raw materials purchased	$400,000
Factory labour services received	200,000
Factory overhead (e.g., rent, utilities, depreciation, etc.) incurred	180,000

Kiwi Manufacturing would record raw materials purchased of $400,000 in its raw materials inventory account. We can compute the cost of raw materials (RM) used during the production process, using the following relationship:

Ending RM Inventories = Beginning RM Inventories + RM Purchased − RM Used.

This means that RM Used = Beginning RM Inventories + RM Purchased − Ending RM Inventories. Therefore, RM Used is $406,000 (= $49,000 + $400,000 − $43,000).

The raw materials used in production are transferred from raw materials inventory into work-in-process (WIP) inventory, rather than expensed to the income statement. Similarly, factory labour and overhead costs incurred during the production process are recorded in WIP inventory, rather than expensed immediately. This is the key difference between inventory accounting for manufacturers and retailers; the latter expense their labour and overhead costs immediately.

When the production process is completed, the cost of goods produced is transferred from the WIP inventory account into finished goods inventory. We can compute the cost of goods produced using the following fact:

$$\textbf{Ending WIP Inventories} = \textbf{Beginning WIP Inventories} + \left(\textbf{RM Used} + \textbf{Factor Labour Services Received} + \textbf{Factory Overhead Incurred}\right) - \textbf{Goods Produced}$$

Therefore, Goods Produced is $791,000 [= $67,000 + ($406,000 + $200,000 + $180,000) − $62,000].

Finally, when finished goods are sold, the cost of goods sold is transferred from finished goods inventory to the income statement, the same as in a retail business. We can use the finished goods (FG) inventory account to compute the cost of goods sold as follows:

Ending FG Inventories = Beginning FG Inventories + Goods Produced − Cost of Goods Sold.

Hence, the Cost of Goods Sold is $795,000 (= $88,000 + $791,000 − $84,000).

It is useful to understand how these inventory accounts are presented in the financial statements of manufacturing firms. In some cases, each of the three categories of inventory is presented in the balance sheet. Usually, however, the balance sheet only presents the combined total of the three accounts, leaving the detail to be presented in the footnotes.

As shown in Exhibit 7.1, VTech reported inventory of $276.9 million in its balance sheet dated March 31, 2013. Exhibit 7.3 details the components of VTech's inventory balance as presented in a note to the financial statements. It shows that finished goods inventory represented the largest portion of the total inventory balance. Exhibit 7.3 is representative of the footnote disclosure provided by many manufacturing companies.

EXHIBIT 7.3 Components of Inventory for VTech

	2013 US$ million	2012 US$ million
Raw materials	89.9	82.1
Work in progress	29.2	35.1
Finished goods	157.8	122.0
	276.9	239.2

BUSINESS INSIGHT

If a manufacturing company has an unexpected buildup of inventory, the interpretation depends on the type of inventory. A larger-than-normal buildup of finished goods would imply that the company was having difficulty getting customers to purchase its products. However, if the buildup is in work-in-process inventory, it might imply a problem with manufacturing processes, particularly if accompanied by a decrease in finished goods inventory.

MID-CHAPTER REVIEW 1

Billabong International Limited is an Australian clothing manufacturer and retailer. The inventory footnote from Billabong's 2013 annual report follows.

Components of Inventory (Australian $'000)	2013	2012
Raw materials and stores	$ 3,640	$ 3,842
Work in progress	12,584	7,734
Finished goods	250,582	281,625
Total	$266,806	$293,201

Billabong reported Cost of Goods Sold of $682,378 in 2013. Compute Billabong's cost of goods produced in 2013.

The solution to this review problem can be found on page 353.

LO2 Account for inventory and cost of goods sold using different costing methods.

INVENTORY COSTING METHODS

The computation of cost of goods sold is important and is shown in Exhibit 7.4.

EXHIBIT 7.4 Cost of Goods Sold Computation

	Beginning inventory value (prior period ending balance sheet)
+	Cost of inventory purchases and/or production
	Cost of goods available for sale
−	Ending inventory value (current period balance sheet)
	Cost of goods sold (current income statement)

The cost of inventory available at the beginning of a period is a carryover from the ending inventory balance of the prior period. The costs of current period purchases of inventory (or costs of newly manufactured inventories) are added to the costs of beginning inventory on the balance sheet, yielding the total cost of goods (inventory) available for sale. Then, the total cost of goods available either ends up in cost of goods sold for the period (reported on the income statement) or is carried forward as inventory to start the next period (reported on the ending balance sheet). This cost flow is schematically shown in Exhibit 7.5.

EXHIBIT 7.5 Inventory Cost Flows to Financial Statements

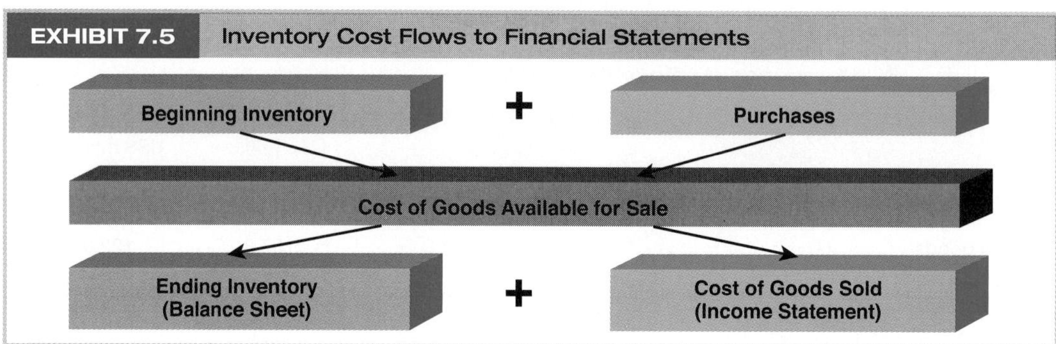

Understanding the flow of inventory costs is important. If the beginning inventory plus all inventory purchased or manufactured during the period is sold, then COGS is equal to the cost of the goods available for sale. However, when inventory remains at the end of a period, companies must identify the cost of those inventories that have been sold and the cost of those inventories that remain.

Most companies will organise the physical flow of their inventories to keep the cost of inventory management low, while minimising the likelihood of spoilage or obsolescence. However, the accounting for inventory and cost of goods sold does not have to follow the physical flow of the units of inventory, so companies may report using a **cost flow assumption** that does not conform to the actual movement of product through the firm.

Illustration To illustrate the possible cost flow assumptions that companies can adopt, assume that Exhibit 7.6 reflects the inventory records of Butler Company.

EXHIBIT 7.6 Summary Inventory Records for Butler Company

		Number of Units	Cost per Unit	Total Cost	Number of Units	Price per Unit	Total Revenue
January 1, 2013	Beginning inventory	500	$100	$ 50,000			
2013	Inventory purchased	200	170	34,000			
	Inventory sold				450	$250	$112,500
2014	Inventory purchased	600	180	108,000			
	Inventory sold				500	255	127,500

Butler Company began the period with inventory consisting of 500 units it purchased at a total cost of $50,000 ($100 each). During the two-year period, the company purchased an additional 200 units costing $34,000 and 600 units costing $108,000. The total cost of goods available for sale for this two-year period equals $192,000.

Tracking the number of units available for sale each year and in inventory at the end of each year is simple. However, the changing cost per unit makes it more complicated to determine the cost of goods sold and the ending inventory. The relationships depicted in Exhibit 7.5 can hold in multiple ways, depending on the cost flow assumption chosen. Two inventory costing methods are acceptable under IFRS.

First-In, First-Out (FIFO)

The **first-in, first-out (FIFO)** inventory costing method transfers costs from inventory in the order that they were initially recorded. That is, FIFO assumes that the first costs recorded in inventory (first-in) are the first costs transferred from inventory (first-out) to cost of goods sold. Conversely, the costs of the last units purchased are the costs that remain in inventory at year-end. Applying FIFO to the data in Exhibit 7.6 means that the costs relating to the 450 units sold are all taken from its *beginning* inventory, which consists of 500 units. The company's 2013 cost of goods sold and gross profit, using FIFO, is computed as follows:

FYI First-in, first-out (FIFO) assumes that goods are used in the order in which they are purchased; the inventory remaining represents the most recent purchases.

Sales	$112,500
COGS (450 @ $100 each)	45,000
Gross profit	$ 67,500

The cost remaining in inventory and reported on its 2013 year-end balance sheet is $39,000 ($50,000 + $34,000 − $45,000; also computed 50 × $100 + 200 × $170).

The same process can be used for 2014, and Exhibit 7.7 depicts the FIFO costing method and shows the resulting financial statement items using FIFO for 2013 and 2014. FIFO cost of goods sold for 2014 is 50 units at $100 each plus 200 units at $170 each plus 250 units at $180 each, or $84,000. Ending inventory for 2014 is 350 units at $180 each, or $63,000. Over the two-year period, the total cost of goods available for sale of $192,000 is either recognised as cost of goods sold ($45,000 + $84,000 = $129,000) or remains in ending inventory ($63,000).

EXHIBIT 7.7 Butler Company using FIFO Inventory Costing

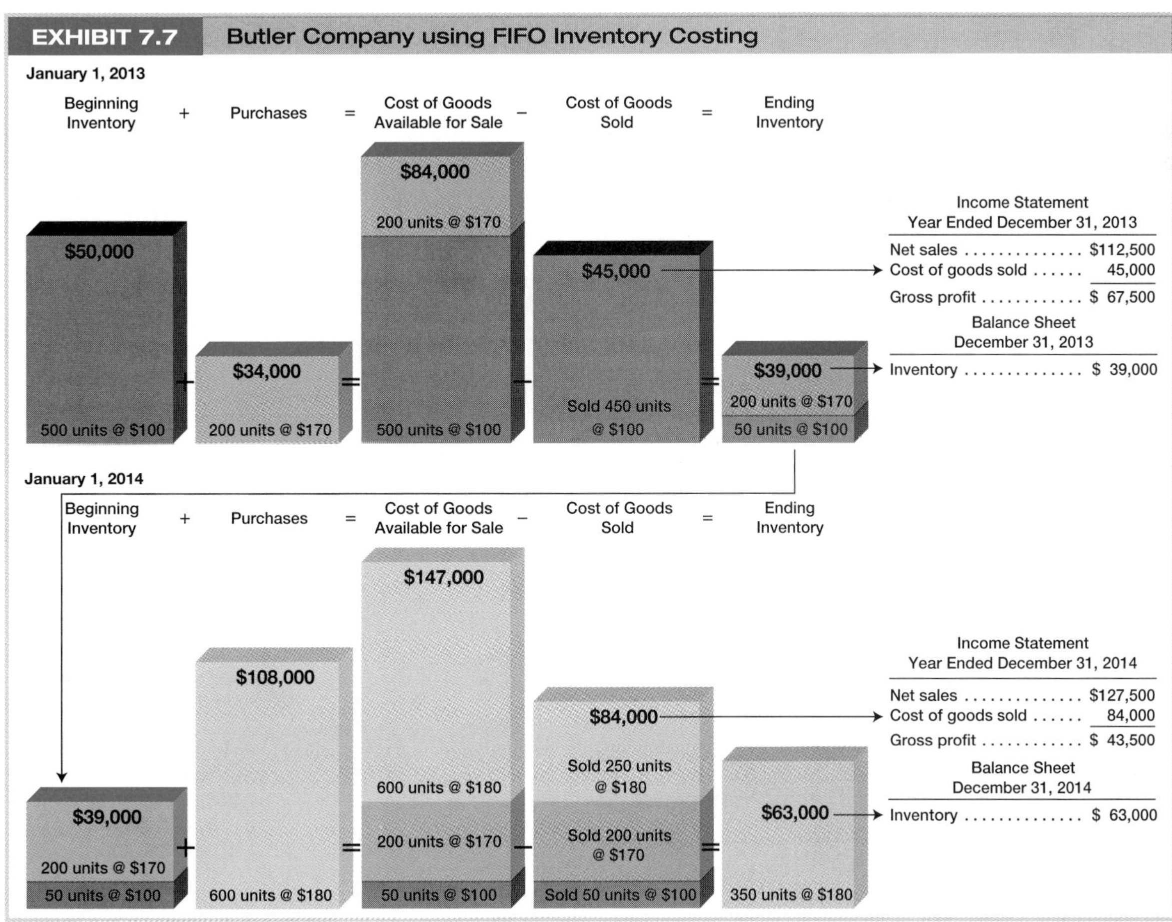

Average Cost (AC)

FYI Average cost values inventory on the basis of the average cost of all similar goods available during the period. ■

The **average cost** (AC) method computes the 2013 cost of goods sold as an average of the cost to purchase all of the inventories that were available for sale during the period as follows:

Sales	$112,500
COGS (450 @ $120 [{$50,000 + $34,000}/700 units] each)	54,000
Gross profit	$ 58,500

The average cost of $120 per unit is determined from the total cost of goods available for sale divided by the number of units available for sale ($84,000/700 units). The cost remaining in inventory and reported on its 2013 balance sheet is $30,000 ($84,000 − $54,000; also computed 250 × $120).

When average cost is applied to the future years, the beginning inventory balance's average cost is again averaged with the inventory acquisitions made during the year. This new average is used to assign costs to that year's ending inventory and cost of goods sold. For the Butler Company, the average cost is $120 for 2013 and $162.35 (rounded) for 2014. The average cost for 2014 is the opening inventory balance plus the period's purchases ($30,000 + $108,000) divided by the total number of units available for sale (250 + 600). So, 2014 cost of goods sold is 500 units at $162.35 each, and ending inventory is 350 units at that same average cost. Exhibit 7.8 depicts the average cost method and shows the resulting financial statement values using average cost for both years.

EXHIBIT 7.8 Butler Company using Average Cost Inventory Costing

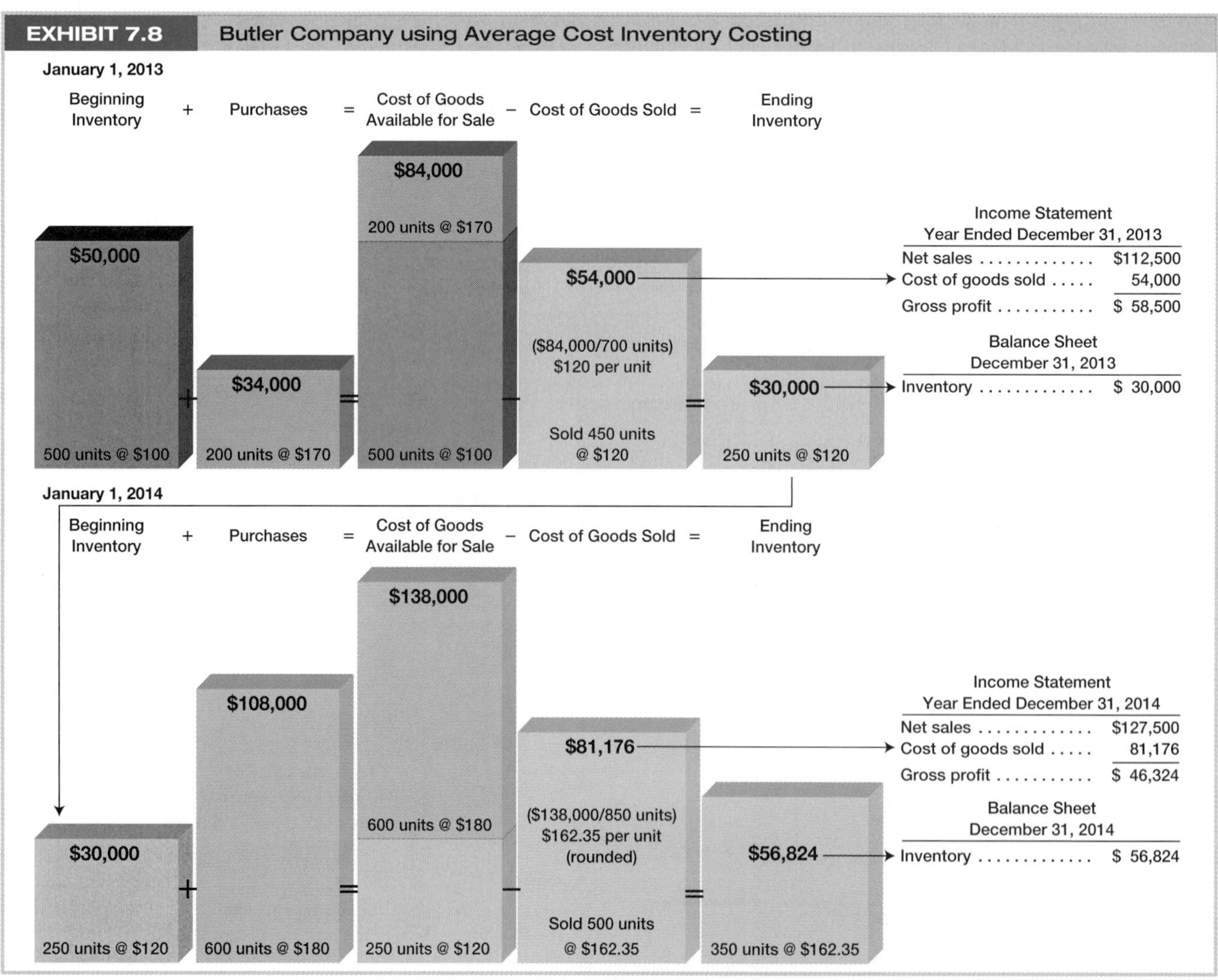

Lower of Cost or Market

LO3 Apply the lower of cost or market rule to value inventory.

Companies are required to write down the carrying amount of inventories on the balance sheet, *if* the reported cost (using FIFO, for example) exceeds the market value (determined by net realisable value). This process is called reporting inventories at the **lower of cost or market (LOCOM)**. Should the net realisable value (market value) be less than reported cost, the inventories must be written down from cost to market value, resulting in the following financial statement effects.

- Inventory book value is written down to current market value (net realisable value), reducing total assets.
- Inventory write-down is reflected as an expense (part of cost of goods sold) on the income statement, reducing current period gross profit, income, and equity.

FYI If inventory declines in value below its original cost, for whatever reason, the inventory is written down to reflect this loss. ■

Inventory write-downs are included in cost of goods sold (or on a separate line item in the income statement). Companies are allowed to reverse the write-down of the inventory up to the acquisition cost if market values warrant. The revaluation results in a debit to inventory and a credit to cost of goods sold (or to the separate line item created for the write-down).

Exhibit 7.9 shows information on VTech's inventory write-down and reversal. The company included both inventory write-down and the reversal of inventory write-down in its cost of goods sold. It wrote down inventories by $5.4 million in 2013 and reported a reversal of write-down of $300,000, resulting in a net increase of $5.1 million in cost of goods sold. VTech attributed the reversal of inventory write-down to an increase in estimated net realisable value of certain products as a result of change in consumer preferences.

EXHIBIT 7.9 Inventory Write-down and Reversal of Write-down at VTech

	2013 US$ million	2012 US$ million
Carrying amount of inventories sold	$1,255.1	$1,214.3
Write-down of inventories	5.4	2.3
Reversal of write-down of inventories	(0.3)	(2.9)
	$1,260.2	$1,213.7

FYI Standards require the consistent application of costing methods from one period to another. ■

Illustration To illustrate the lower of cost or market rule, assume LCM Construction has the following items in its current period ending inventory:

Item	Quantity	Cost per Unit	Market Value (net realisable value)	LOCOM per unit	Total LOCOM
Spools of copper wire	250	$10	$15	$10	250 × $10 = $2,500
Sheets of wood panelling	500	$ 8	$ 6	$ 6	500 × $ 6 = $3,000

A write-down is not necessary for the spools of copper wire because the current market value ($15 per unit) is higher than the acquisition cost ($10 per unit). However, the 500 sheets of wood panelling should be recorded in the current period's ending inventory at the current market value of $6 per unit because it is lower than the acquisition cost of $8 per unit. When the market value (replacement cost) of inventory declines below its acquisition cost, we must record a write-down. Before the write-down, inventory is recorded at cost of $6,500. With the write-down of $1,000, inventory after the write-down is recorded at LOCOM of $5,500. The effects of this write-down and corresponding journal entries follow:

	Balance Sheet					Income Statement		
Transaction	Cash Asset	+ Noncash Assets	= Liabil-ities	+ Contrib. Capital	+ Earned Capital	Revenues	− Expenses	= Net Income
Write-down inventory to lower of cost or market.		−1,000 Inventory	=		−1,000 Retained Earnings		− +1,000 Cost of Goods Sold	= −1,000

ANALYSE JOURNALISE POST

Cost of goods sold (+E, −SE)	1,000	
Inventory (−A)		1,000

+ Inventory (A) −	
	1,000

+ Cost of Goods Sold (E) −	
1,000	

BUSINESS INSIGHT

In September 2013, **Blackberry Limited**, a Canadian smartphone maker, recorded a non-cash, pre-tax inventory charge of approximately US$934 million, which is primarily attributable to its BlackBerry Z10 touch-screen devices introduced that January. Blackberry included the inventory write-down in cost of sales, leading to a gross profit of –US$374 (or gross profit margin of −24%) for that fiscal quarter.

MID-CHAPTER REVIEW 2

Part 1

At the beginning of the current period, Gaudi S.A. holds 1,000 units of its only product with a per-unit cost of €18. A summary of purchases during the current period follows:

	Units	Unit Cost	Cost
Beginning Inventory	1,000	€18.00	€18,000
Purchases: #1	1,800	18.25	32,850
#2	800	18.50	14,800
#3	1,200	19.00	22,800
Goods available for sale	4,800		€88,450

During the current period, Gaudi sells 2,800 units.

Required

1. Assume that Gaudi uses the first-in, first-out (FIFO) method. Compute the cost of goods sold for the current period and the ending inventory balance.
2. Assume that Gaudi uses the average cost (AC) method. Compute the cost of goods sold for the current period and the ending inventory balance.
3. As manager, which one of these two inventory costing methods would you choose to reflect what is probably the physical flow of goods? Explain.
4. Record the effects of each of the following summary transactions *a* and *b* in the financial statement effects template, prepare journal entries, set up T-accounts for each of the accounts used, and post the journal entries to those T-accounts.
   a. Purchased inventory for €70,450 cash.
   b. Sold €50,850 of inventory for €85,000 cash.

continued

Part 2

Covent Garden Limited had the following inventory at December 31, 2014.

	Quantity	Unit Price Cost	Market
Fans			
Model X1	300	£18	£19
Model X2	250	22	24
Model X3	400	29	26
Heaters			
Model B7	500	24	28
Model B8	290	35	32
Model B9	100	41	38

Required

1. Determine ending inventory by applying the lower of cost or market (LOCOM) rule to
   a. Each item of inventory.
   b. Each major category of inventory.
   c. Total inventory.
2. Which of the LOCOM procedures from requirement 1 results in the lowest net income for 2014? Explain.

The solution to this review problem can be found on pages 353–355.

FINANCIAL STATEMENT DISCLOSURE

LO4 Discuss the required financial statement disclosure and how outsiders may use it to analyse a company's inventory management.

IFRS requires note disclosure about inventory to assist users in understanding a company's management of inventory. The required disclosures include (1) the inventory costing methods used (which can differ for different types of inventory), (2) the carrying amount of inventories, (3) the carrying amount of inventories carried at net realisable value, (4) the amount of inventory write-down, (5) the amount of reversal of a write-down and the reasons for the reversal, (6) the carrying amount of inventories pledged, and (7) the cost of goods sold.

To illustrate, VTech reports $276.9 million in stocks (or inventories) on its March 31, 2013, balance sheet as a current asset. The following information was taken from two notes in that annual report:

Stocks

Stocks are stated at the lower of cost and net realisable value. Cost is calculated on the weighted average or the first-in-first-out basis, and comprises materials, direct labour and an appropriate share of production overheads incurred in bringing the inventories to their present location and condition. Net realisable value is the estimated selling price in the ordinary course of business, less estimates of costs of completion and selling expenses.

When stocks are sold, the carrying amount of those stocks is recognised as an expense in the period in which the related revenue is recognised. The amount of any write-down of stocks to net realisable value and all losses of stocks are recognised as an expense in the period the write-down or loss occurs. The amount of any reversal of any write-down of stocks is recognised as a reduction in the amount of stocks as an expense in the period in which the reversal occurs.

(a) Inventories in the consolidated balance sheet comprise:

	2013 US$ million	2012 US$ million
Raw materials	89.9	82.1
Work in progress	29.2	35.1
Finished goods	157.8	122.0
	276.9	239.2

continued

continued from previous page

Stocks carried at net realisable value at March 31, 2013 amounted to US$5.8 million (2012: US$6.7 million).

(b) The analysis of the amount of inventories recognised as an expense and included in the consolidated income statement is as follows:

	2013 US$ million	2012 US$ million
Carrying amount of inventories sold	$1,255.1	$1,214.3
Write-down of inventories..............	5.4	2.3
Reversal of write-down of inventories	(0.3)	(2.9)
	$1,260.2	$1,213.7

The reversal of write-down of inventories arose due to an increase in estimated net realisable value of certain products as a result of change in consumer preferences.

VTech also provides the following supplementary information in the Management Discussion and Analysis section of the annual report:

Stocks as of March 31, 2013 were US$276.9 million, increased from US$239.2 million as of March 31, 2012 . . . The higher stock level was primarily to cater for increased demand for the Group's products in the first quarter of the financial year 2014. Furthermore, we had arranged early production of the Group's products in order to better utilise the Group's production capacities.

As at March 31, 2013 and 2012 All figures are in US$ million	2013	2012
Stocks	276.9	239.2
Average stocks as a percentage of Group revenue	13.9%	13.1%

The above disclosures include several items that would be of interest to financial statement users:

1. VTech uses both the FIFO and average cost methods to determine the cost of its inventory. As permitted by IFRS, many companies use different inventory costing methods for different categories of inventory.
2. Inventory is reported at the lower of cost or market value (net realisable value). The amount of write-down and reversal for the year ended March 31, 2013 were $5.4 million and $0.3 million, respectively, leading to a $5.3 million increase in cost of goods sold. Moreover, $5.8 million of inventories were carried at net realisable value at March 31, 2013.
3. Inventories increased from $239.2 million in 2012 to $276.9 million in 2013. The increase is due to the company preparing for higher demand for its products and utilising its excess manufacturing capacity.

Companies periodically take a physical count of inventory to identify "shrink." Shrink refers to the loss of inventory due to theft, breakage or damage, spoilage (for perishable goods), or other losses, as well as inaccurate records. When businesses adjust inventory balances for shrink, the loss is debited to cost of goods sold. Hence, cost of goods sold expense on the income statement includes the actual cost of products sold during the period plus the loss due to shrink as well as losses resulting from lower of cost or market adjustments and discounts lost.

Why do companies disclose such details on inventory, and why is so much attention paid to inventory in financial statement analysis? First, the magnitude of a company's investment in inventory is often large—impacting both balance sheets and income statements. Second, risks of inventory losses are often high, as they are tied to technical obsolescence and consumer tastes. Third, it can provide insight into future performance—both good and bad. Fourth, high inventory levels result in substantial costs for the company, such as:

- Financing costs to purchase inventories (when not purchased on credit)
- Storage costs of inventories (such as warehousing and related facilities)
- Handling costs of inventories (including wages)
- Insurance costs of inventories

Consequently, companies seek to keep inventories at levels that balance these costs against the cost of insufficient inventory (stock-out and resulting lost sales and delays in production, as machines and employees sit idle awaiting inventories to process).

ANALYSING FINANCIAL STATEMENTS

Analysis Objective

LO5 Define and interpret gross profit margin and inventory turnover ratios.

We are trying to determine whether VTech's sales provide sufficient revenues to cover its operation costs, primarily selling and administrative expenses, after allowing for the costs of manufacturing.

Analysis Tool Gross Profit Margin (GPM) Ratio

$$\text{Gross profit margin} = \frac{\text{Sales revenue} - \text{Cost of goods sold}}{\text{Sales revenue}}$$

Applying the Gross Profit Margin Ratio to VTech

$$2013 \quad \frac{(1{,}858.8 - 1{,}260.2)}{1{,}858.8} = 0.322 \text{ or } 32.2\%$$

$$2012 \quad \frac{(1{,}784.5 - 1{,}213.7)}{1{,}784.5} = 0.320 \text{ or } 32.0\%$$

$$2011 \quad \frac{(1{,}712.8 - 1{,}145.9)}{1{,}712.8} = 0.331 \text{ or } 33.1\%$$

Guidance The gross profit margin is commonly used instead of the dollar amount of gross profit as it allows for comparisons across companies and over time. A decline in GPM is usually cause for concern because it indicates that the company has less ability to pass on to customers increased costs in its products. Because companies try to charge the highest price the market will bear, a decline in GPM is often the result of market forces beyond the company's control. Some possible reasons for a GPM decline are:

- Product line is stale. Perhaps it is out of fashion and the company must resort to markdowns to reduce overstocked inventories. Or, perhaps the product lines have lost their technological edge, yielding reduced demand.
- A change in product mix resulting from a change in buyers' behaviour (more generic brands, more necessities, fewer big-ticket items).
- New competitors enter the market. Perhaps substitute products or new technologies are now available from competitors, yielding increased pressure to reduce selling prices.
- General decline in economic activity. Perhaps an economic downturn reduces product demand.
- Inventory is overstocked. Perhaps the company overproduced goods and finds itself in an overstock position. This can require reduced selling prices to move inventory.

VTech in Context

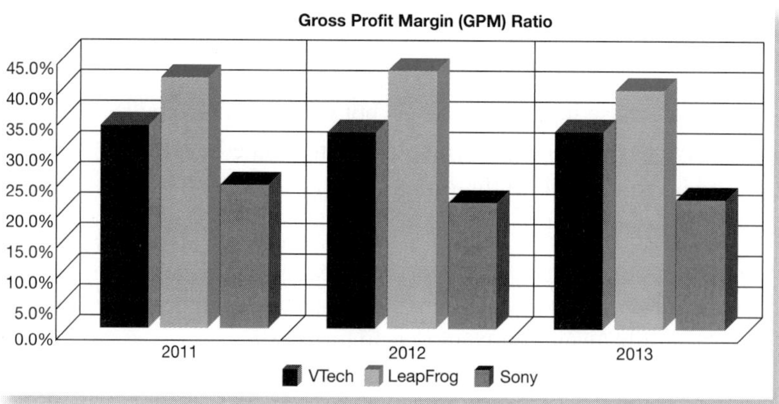

Takeaways Despite the recent decline in the toy market in the U.S. and Western Europe, VTech's sales revenue increased steadily from fiscal year 2011 to fiscal year 2013. The company was successful in maintaining its gross profit margin at around 32%. To properly evaluate gross profit margin, we compare VTech's gross profit margin with those of two companies, LeapFrog Enterprises, Inc. and Sony Corp. LeapFrog is a U.S.-based developer of educational entertainment for children and it reports its inventories using FIFO. Sony is a Japanese conglomerate, with businesses in consumer electronics, game, entertainment, etc. Sony reports inventories using average cost and FIFO.

As the bar graph illustrates, VTech has consistently reported a lower gross profit margin than LeapFrog and a higher gross profit margin than Sony over the 2011–2013 period. While the percentages fluctuate slightly from year to year, the relative level of gross profit percentage remains the same over time, reflecting the fact that product mix is a major determinant of gross profit margin. Specifically, VTech has three lines of business, but LeapFrog is a single-segment company and Sony is a conglomerate. Further analysis (such as segment-level analysis) is needed before we can draw any conclusions regarding their relative performance. In general, a persistent decline in gross profit margin, especially relative to the competition, would signal problems for any company.

Because of competitive pressures, companies rarely have the opportunity to affect gross margin with price increases. (Of course, an astute choice of product offerings is likely to reduce pricing discounts and improve the gross profit margin.) Most improvements in gross margin are the result of better management of supply chains, production processes, or distribution networks. Similarly, a decline in gross profit margin suggests problems or inefficiencies in these processes. Companies that succeed typically do so because of better performance on basic business processes. In its 2013 annual report, VTech indicates that it aims to maintain its gross profit margin next year "with efficiency gains through higher automation, product optimisation and process improvement."

Analysis Objective

We wish to determine how quickly inventory passes through the production process and results in sales.

Analysis Tool Inventory Turnover (INVT) Ratio

$$\textbf{Inventory turnover} = \frac{\textbf{Cost of goods sold}}{\textbf{Average inventory}}$$

Applying Inventory Turnover Ratio to VTech

2013	\$1,260.2/[(\$276.9 + \$239.2)/2] = 4.9 times per year
2012	\$1,213.7/[(\$239.2 + \$229.8)/2] = 5.2 times per year
2011	\$1,145.9/[(\$229.8 + \$159.3)/2] = 5.9 times per year

VTech in Context

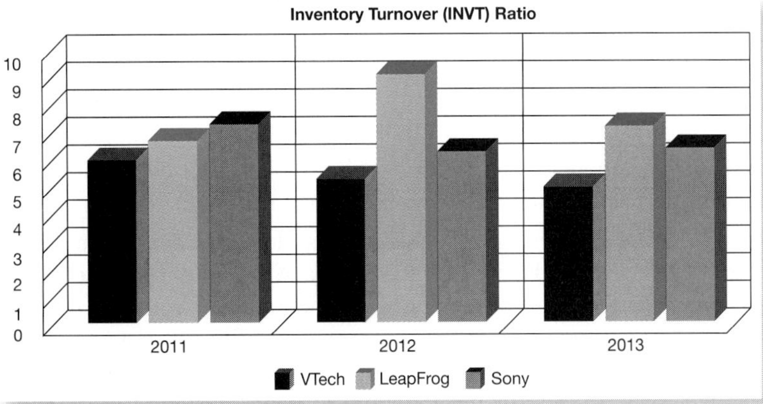

Cost of goods sold is in the numerator because inventory is reported at cost. The denominator is the average of beginning inventory and ending inventory to recognise growth (or decline) in the company's investment in inventory over the period. Inventory turnover indicates how many times inventory turns (is sold) during a period. More turns indicate that inventory is being sold more quickly.

Analysis Tool Average inventory days outstanding (AIDO), also called *days inventory outstanding*:

$$\textbf{Average inventory days outstanding} = \frac{\textbf{Average inventory}}{\textbf{Average daily cost of goods sold}}$$

Applying Average Inventory Days Outstanding Ratio to VTech

2013	[($276.9 + $239.2)/2]/(21,260.2/365) = 75 Days
2012	[($239.2 + $229.8)/2]/(21,213.7/365) = 71 Days
2011	[($229.8 + $159.3)/2]/(21,145.9/365) = 62 Days

VTech in Context

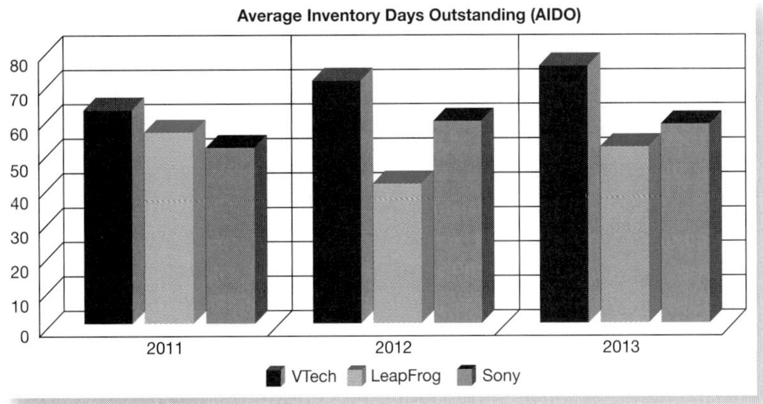

The average daily cost of goods sold equals cost of goods sold divided by the number of days in the period (for our example, 365 for a year).

Average inventory days outstanding indicates how long, on average, inventories are on the shelves or in production before being sold. For example, if a retailer's annual cost of goods sold is $1,200 and average inventories are $300, inventories are turning four times and are on the shelves 91.25 days [$300/($1,200/365)] on average. This performance might be an acceptable turnover for the retail fashion industry where it needs to sell out its inventories each retail selling season, but it would not be acceptable for the grocery industry.

Guidance Analysis of inventory turnover is important for at least two reasons:

1. *Inventory quality*. Inventory turnover can be compared with those of prior periods and competitors. Higher turnover is viewed favourably, implying that products are salable, preferably without undue discounting of selling prices, or that production processes are functioning smoothly. Conversely, lower turnover implies that inventory is on the shelves for a longer period of time, perhaps from excessive purchases or production, missed fashion trends or technological advances, increased competition, and so forth. Our conclusions about higher or lower turnover must consider alternative explanations including:
   a. Company product mix can change to higher-margin, slower-turning inventories or vice-versa. This change can occur from business acquisitions and the resulting consolidated inventories.
   b. A company can change its promotion policies. Increased, effective advertising is likely to increase inventory turnover. Advertising expense is in SG&A, not COGS. Therefore, the cost is in operating expenses, but the benefit is in gross profit and turnover. If the promotion campaign is successful, the positive effects in margin and turnover should offset the promotion cost in SG&A.
   c. A company can realise improvements in manufacturing efficiency and lower investments in direct materials and work-in-process inventories. Such improvements reduce inventory and, consequently, increase inventory turnover. Although positive, such improvements do not yield any information about the desirability of a company's product line.
2. *Asset utilisation*. Companies strive to optimise their inventory investment. Carrying too much inventory is expensive, and too little inventory risks stock-outs and lost sales (current and future). There are operational changes that companies can make to reduce inventory including:
   a. Improved manufacturing processes can eliminate bottlenecks and the consequent build-up of work-in-process inventories.
   b. Just-in-time (JIT) deliveries from suppliers that provide raw materials to the production line when needed can reduce the level of raw materials required.
   c. Demand-pull production, in which raw materials are released into the production process when final goods are demanded by customers instead of producing for estimated demand, can reduce inventory levels. Dell Inc. was founded on a business model that produced for actual, rather than estimated, demand; many of its computers are manufactured after the customer order is received.

   Reducing inventories reduces inventory carrying costs, thus improving profitability and increasing cash flow (asset reduction is reflected as a cash inflow adjustment in the statement of cash flows). However, if inventories get too low, production can be interrupted and sales lost.

There is normal tension between the sales side of a company that argues for depth and breadth of inventory and the finance side that monitors inventory carrying costs and seeks to maximise cash flow. Companies, therefore, seek to *optimise* inventory investment, not *minimise* it.

Takeaways VTech's inventory turnover was lower than those of LeapFrog and Sony over all three years. As mentioned earlier, this difference could be due to differences in product mix. VTech's inventory turnover declined over the last three years, from 5.9 times in 2011 to 4.9 times in 2013 (the corresponding average inventory days outstanding increased from 62 days to 75 days). Sony experienced a similar decline, with its inventory turnover ratio dropping from 7.2 in 2011 to 6.2 in 2012 and 6.3 in 2013. In its 2013 annual report, VTech explains that the decline in its inventory turnover was due to a higher inventory level at the end of fiscal 2013, because it was preparing for increased demand for its products in the coming quarter and it had scheduled early production of some products to better utilise its manufacturing capacities. Furthermore, VTech indicated that its product mix and sales mix have been evolving over time, with electronic learning products becoming its largest product line in 2013.

YOU MAKE THE CALL

You are the Plant Manager You are analysing your inventory turnover report for the month and are concerned that the average inventory days outstanding is lengthening. What actions can you take to reduce average inventory days outstanding? [Answer on page 340]

CHAPTER-END REVIEW

The following table presents sales revenue, cost of goods sold, and inventory amounts for two Canadian companies in the apparel business: Gildan Activewear Inc. and Reitmans Limited.

Gildan Activewear Inc. ($ '000)	2013	2012
Revenues	$2,184,303	$1,948,253
Cost of goods sold	1,550,266	1,552,128
Inventory	595,794	553,068
Reitmans Limited		
Revenues	$1,000,513	$1,019,397
Cost of goods sold	372,135	363,333
Inventory	93,317	93,188

Required

1. Compute the gross profit margin (GPM) for each of these companies for 2013 and 2012.
2. Compute the inventory turnover ratios for 2013 and estimate the 2012 value.
3. What factors might determine the differences among these two companies' ratios?

The solution to this review problem can be found on page 355.

APPENDIX 7A: LIFO

LO6 Discuss LIFO and adjusting the financial statements to FIFO.

Besides FIFO and Average Cost, U.S. GAAP allows the use of the last-in, first-out (LIFO) method for inventory costing. An analyst comparing an IFRS company to a U.S. GAAP company would need to keep an eye on these inventory differences and, when necessary, do the adjustments discussed in this appendix.

Last-In, First-Out (LIFO)

The **last-in, first-out (LIFO)** inventory costing method transfers to cost of goods sold the most recent costs that were recorded in inventory. That is, we assume that the most recent costs recorded in inventory (last-in) are the first costs transferred from inventory (first-out). Conversely, the costs of the first units purchased are the costs that remain in inventory at year-end. Butler Company's 2013 cost of goods sold and gross profit, using LIFO, is computed as follows:

FYI Last-in, first-out (LIFO) matches the cost of the last goods purchased against revenue.

Sales	$112,500
COGS: (200 @ $170 each = $34,000)	
(250 @ $100 each = $25,000)	59,000
Gross profit	$ 53,500

The cost remaining in inventory and reported on its 2013 balance sheet is $25,000 ($50,000 + $34,000 − $59,000; also computed 250 × $100).

The same process can be used for 2014, and Exhibit 7A.1 depicts the LIFO costing method and shows the resulting financial statement values using LIFO for both years. LIFO cost of goods sold for 2014 is 500 units at $180 each, or $90,000. Ending inventory is 250 units at $100 each plus 100 units at $180 each, or $43,000. Again, the two-year total cost of goods available for sale of $192,000 is either recognised as cost of goods sold ($59,000 + $90,000 = $149,000) or remains in inventory ($43,000).

The exhibit shows that **LIFO layers** of inventories added in each year are kept separately. So, the ending inventory in 2014 consists of a pre-2013 layer of 250 units at $100 each plus a 2014 layer of 100 units at $180 each. When unit sales exceed purchases, the first costs carried to cost of goods sold are those purchased in the current year, followed by the most recent layer of LIFO inventory and working down to the oldest layers. So, the 2013 beginning inventory value of $100 per unit remains in LIFO inventory as long as there are 250 units remaining at the end of the year. One aspect of this flow assumption is that reported LIFO inventory values can be significantly lower than the current cost of acquiring the same inventory.

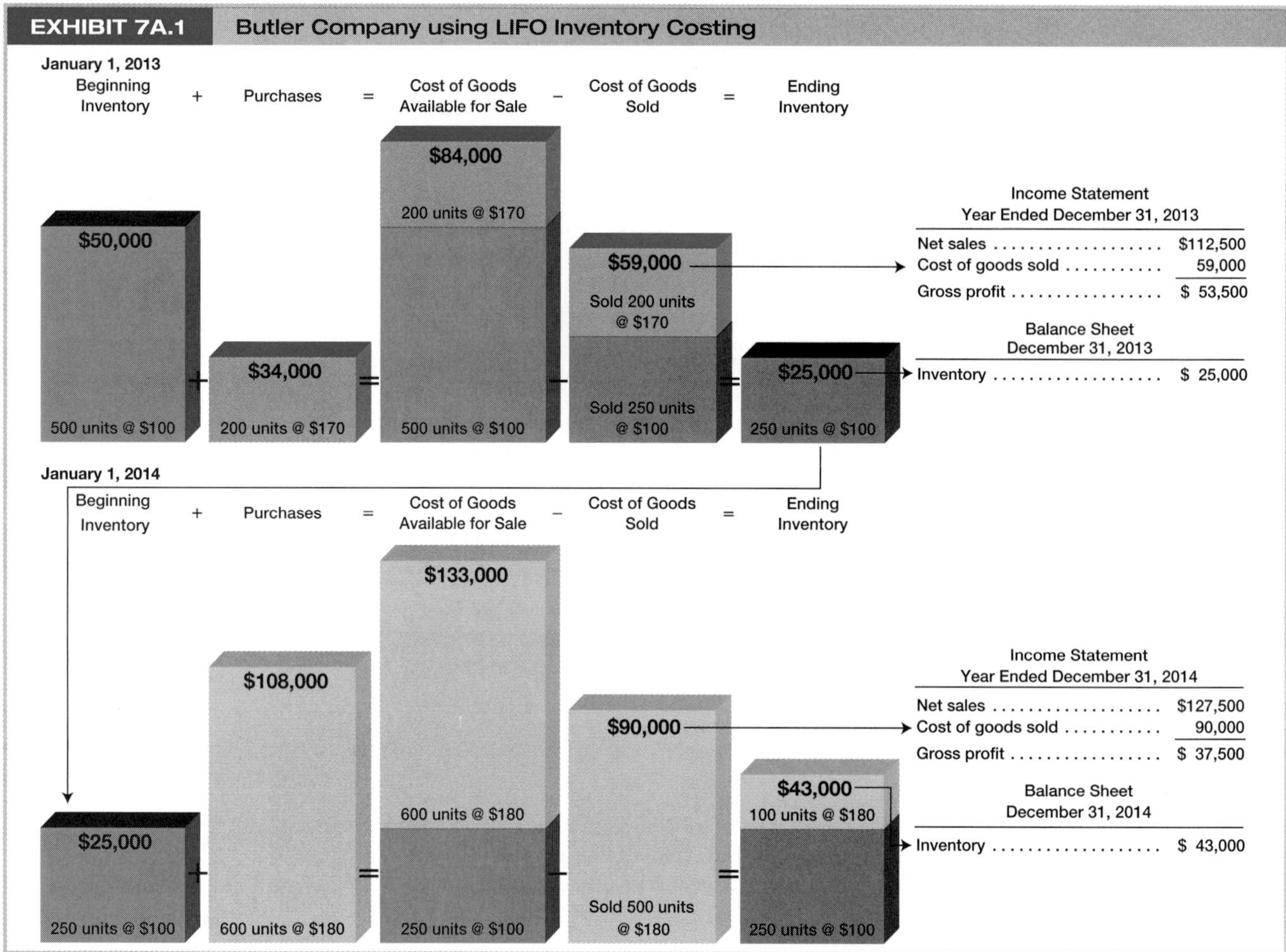

LIFO inventory costing is always applied on a periodic, annual basis. This means that Butler's cost of goods sold and ending inventory for 2014 do not depend on the timing of the sales and purchases within the year. Inventory levels might be drawn down below 250 units *during* the year, but the 250 unit LIFO layer at $100 each remains in ending inventory as long as inventory is built up to 250 units by the *end* of the year.

Using LIFO Reserve to Convert LIFO to FIFO

Under U.S. GAAP, companies using LIFO are required to disclose the **LIFO reserve**, which is the difference between the ending inventory's FIFO cost (or current cost) and LIFO cost. LIFO reserve is also the *cumulative* difference between LIFO and FIFO cost of goods sold. Hence, the change in the LIFO reserve is the difference between LIFO and FIFO cost of goods sold for the current period.

We can estimate what the FIFO inventory cost and FIFO cost of goods sold would have been by using the following two equations:

FIFO inventory cost = LIFO inventory cost + LIFO reserve

FIFO cost of goods sold = LIFO cost of goods sold – Change in the LIFO reserve

For example, Chevron Corporation reported an inventory of $5,543 million using LIFO on its December 31, 2011 balance sheet. It also disclosed that its LIFO reserve was $9,025 and $6,975 on December 31, 2011 and 2010, respectively. To adjust Chevron's inventory from LIFO to FIFO, we add the LIFO reserve to its LIFO inventory. Thus, inventory is increased by $9,025 million to $14,568 million ($5,543 + $9,025). To adjust the income statement from LIFO to FIFO, we use the *change* in the LIFO reserve. For Chevron, the LIFO reserve changed from $6,975 million in 2010 to $9,025 million in 2011, an increase of $2,050 million. To adjust the income statement to FIFO, we subtract $2,050 from the cost of goods sold (reported using LIFO) and add the same amount to the gross profit and pretax income.

We emphasise that, even though the various methods produce different financial statement numbers, the underlying events are the same. That is, different accounting methods can make similar situations seem more different than they really are.

Adjusting Turnover Ratios For a company using the last-in, first-out (LIFO) inventory method, it is advisable to make an adjustment before calculating the inventory turnover ratio. LIFO is most commonly used when management has experienced a trend of rising inventory costs. As a result, LIFO puts higher (newer) costs into cost of goods sold and leaves lower (older) costs in inventory. This creates a potential mismatch between the numerator and denominator of the inventory turnover ratio.

The magnitude of this adjustment can be significant. For instance, Chevron reports that its 2011 expense for "Purchased crude oil and products" was $149,923 million. Chevron's balance sheet totals for inventories were $5,493 at the end of 2010 and $5,543 million at the end of 2011, for an average of $5,518 million. These numbers would give an inventory turnover ratio of $149,923 ÷ $5,518, or 27.2 times, implying that inventory is held less than 14 days on average.

However, we know that the LIFO inventory balances are out of date. Chevron's LIFO reserve disclosure says that the replacement cost of inventories was higher than the reported amounts by $6,975 million at the end of 2010 and $9,025 million at the end of 2011, making the replacement cost of inventories equal to $12,468 million at the end of 2010 and $14,568 million at the end of 2011. The adjusted inventory turnover ratio would be $149,923/[($12,468 + $14,568)/2] = 11.1, implying that inventory is held about 33 days.

Following a similar line of analysis, it would be possible to construct a FIFO inventory turnover for Chevron, which could be useful in making comparisons to another company that uses IFRS in its financial reports.

APPENDIX-END REVIEW

General Electric Company (GE) reports inventory and cost of goods sold using the last-in, first-out (LIFO) costing method for a "significant portion" of U.S. inventory. The table below presents financial information from its 2009, 2010, and 2011 annual reports.

($ millions)	2011	2010	2009
Income Statement:			
Revenue	$147,300	$149,593	$154,438
Cost of goods sold	51,455	46,005	50,580
Cost of services sold	16,823	25,708	25,341
Gross profit	$ 79,022	$ 77,880	$ 78,517
Balance Sheet:			
Inventory	$ 13,792	$ 11,526	$ 11,987
Note (5):			
LIFO reserve	$ 450	$ 404	$ 529

Required

1. Compute the gross profit margin for each year, 2009 through 2011, and the inventory turnover ratio for 2010 and 2011.
2. What amount for cost of goods sold and gross profit would GE report in 2010 and 2011 if FIFO were used to assign costs to inventory and cost of goods sold? (Assume that FIFO cost is equal to the current value of GE's inventory.)
3. Recalculate GE's inventory turnover ratio for 2010 and 2011 assuming that FIFO had been used to value inventory.

The solution to this review problem can be found on pages 355–356.

SUMMARY

Interpret disclosures of information concerning operating expenses, including manufacturing and retail inventory costs. (p. 320) LO1

- Inventory is reported in the balance sheet at its cost, including any cost to acquire, transport and prepare goods for sale.

- Manufacturing inventory consists of raw materials, work in process and finished goods. The cost of manufacturing inventory includes the cost of materials and labour used to produce goods, as well as overhead cost.

LO2 Account for inventory and cost of goods sold using different costing methods. (p. 325)

- FIFO places the cost of the most recent purchases in ending inventory and older costs in the cost of goods sold.
- The average cost method computes an average unit cost, which is used to value inventories *and* cost of goods sold.

LO3 Apply the lower of cost or market rule to value inventory. (p. 329)

- If the market value of inventory falls below its cost, the inventory is written down to market value, thereby reducing total assets.
- The loss is added to cost of goods sold and reported in the income statement (unless it is large enough to warrant separate disclosure).

LO4 Discuss the required financial statement disclosure and how outsiders may use it to analyse a company's inventory management. (p. 331)

- IFRS requires disclosures of the inventory costing methods used, the carrying amount of inventories, and the cost of goods sold.
- Companies also need to disclose the amount of inventory write-down, the amount of reversal of a write-down and the reasons for the reversal, and the carrying amount of inventories carried at net realisable value.
- The carrying amount of inventories pledged as collateral must be disclosed.

LO5 Define and interpret gross profit margin and inventory turnover ratios. (p. 333)

- Gross profit margin (GPM)—a measure of profitability that focuses on the amount of revenue in excess of cost of goods sold as a percentage of revenue
- Gross profit margin is defined as Gross profit/Sales revenue.
- Inventory turnover (INVT)—a measure of the frequency at which the average balance in inventory is sold each year
- Inventory turnover is defined as Cost of goods sold/Average inventory.
- These ratios provide insight into how efficiently the company is managing inventory.

LO6 Appendix 7A: Discuss LIFO and adjusting the financial statements to FIFO. (p. 337)

- One of the important differences in inventory accounting between IFRS and U.S. GAAP is that U.S. GAAP allows LIFO, in addition to FIFO and average costing methods.
- LIFO places the cost of the most recent purchases in cost of goods sold and older costs in inventory. When inventory costs are rising, LIFO costing reports higher cost of goods sold and lower income than either FIFO or average costing.
- LIFO distorts the inventory turnover ratio because inventories are often severely undervalued (relative to current cost of goods sold). Footnote disclosures enable a financial statement reader to determine the up-to-date costs of LIFO inventories, to estimate what cost of goods sold would have been under FIFO, and to compute an inventory turnover ratio that is not subject to distortions.

GUIDANCE ANSWERS . . . YOU MAKE THE CALL

You are the Plant Manager Companies need inventories to avoid lost sales opportunities; however, there are several ways to minimise inventory needs. (1) We can reduce product costs by improving product design to eliminate costly features not valued by customers. (2) We can use more cost-efficient suppliers; possibly including production in lower wage-rate parts of the world. (3) We can reduce raw material inventories with just-in-time delivery from suppliers. (4) We can eliminate bottlenecks in the production process that increase work-in-process inventories. (5) We can manufacture for orders rather than for estimates of demand to reduce finished goods inventories. (6) We can improve warehousing and distribution to reduce duplicate inventories. (7) We can monitor product sales and adjust product mix as demand changes to reduce finished goods inventories.

KEY RATIOS

Gross profit (GP)

GP = Sales revenue – Cost of goods sold

Gross profit margin (GPM)

$$\text{Gross profit margin} = \frac{\text{Sales revenue} - \text{Cost of goods sold}}{\text{Sales revenue}}$$

Inventory turnover (INVT)

$$\text{INVT} = \frac{\text{Cost of goods sold}}{\text{Average inventory}}$$

Average inventory days outstanding (AIDO)

$$\text{AIDO} = \frac{\text{Average inventory}}{\text{Average daily cost of goods sold}}$$

KEY TERMS

Average cost (AC) (p. 328)
Cash discounts (p. 323)
Cost flow assumption (p. 326)
Direct association (p. 321)
Finished goods inventory (p. 324)
First-in, first-out (FIFO) (p. 327)
FOB destination (p. 323)
FOB shipping point (p. 323)
Gross profit (p. 321)
Immediate recognition (p. 321)
Last-in, first-out (LIFO) (p. 337)
LIFO layers (p. 337)
LIFO reserve (p. 338)
Lower of cost or market (LOCOM) (p. 329)
Period expenses (p. 323)
Product costs (p. 323)
Raw materials inventory (p. 324)
Systematic allocation (p. 321)
Work-in-process inventory (p. 324)

Superscript ^{A} denotes assignments based on Appendix 7A.

MULTIPLE CHOICE

1. Which of the following is not normally reported as part of total manufacturing inventory cost?
   a. Work-in-process
   b. Finished goods
   c. Property, plant and equipment
   d. Raw materials

2. When the current year's ending inventory amount is overstated, then the
   a. current year's cost of goods sold is overstated.
   b. current year's total assets are understated.
   c. current year's net income is overstated.
   d. next year's income is overstated.

3.^{A} In a period of rising prices, the inventory cost allocation method that tends to result in the lowest reported net income is
   a. LIFO.
   b. FIFO.
   c. average cost.
   d. specific identification.

4.^{A} Assume that Beyer Corporation has the following initial balance and subsequent purchase of inventory:

Beginning inventory, 2014.	2,000 units @ $50 each	$100,000
Inventory purchased in 2014.	5,000 units @ $75 each	$375,000
Cost of goods available for sale in 2014	7,000 units	$475,000

Multiple Choice Answers
1. c 2. c 3. a 4. d 5. b

During 2014, Beyer Corporation sold 6,000 units. Which of the following is not true?

a. FIFO cost of goods sold would be $400,000.
b. FIFO ending inventory would be $75,000.
c. LIFO cost of goods sold would be $425,000.
d. LIFO ending inventory would be $75,000.

5.[A] Sletten Industries uses the last-in, first-out (LIFO) method of accounting for the inventories of its single product. For fiscal year 2014, the company reported sales revenue of $200 million and cost of goods sold of $135 million. The following table was reported in the financial statement footnotes.

($ millions)	January 1, 2014	December 31, 2014
Inventory value at LIFO	$25	$28
LIFO Reserve	14	22
Inventory value at FIFO	$39	$50

If Sletten Industries had used FIFO to account for its inventory, its 2014 gross profit would be

a. $87 million.
b. $73 million.
c. $57 million.
d. $65 million.

DISCUSSION QUESTIONS

Q7-1. Under what circumstances is it justified to include transportation costs in the value of the inventory purchased?

Q7-2. Why do relatively stable inventory costs reduce the importance of management's choice of an inventory costing method?

Q7-3. What is one explanation for increased gross profit during periods of rising inventory costs when FIFO is used?

Q7-4. What are the three inventory accounts in a typical manufacturing firm?

Q7-5. Do manufacturing firms capitalise both product costs and period costs?

BLACKBERRY LIMITED (CANADA)

Q7-6. In a press release, **Blackberry Limited** made the following announcement in reference to its inventories for the three-month period ended August 31, 2013: "During the second quarter of fiscal 2014, the Company recorded a primarily non-cash, pre-tax charge against inventory and supply commitments of approximately $934 million, $666 million after tax, which is primarily attributable to BlackBerry Z10 devices." What basic accounting principle caused Blackberry to record this $934 million pretax charge? Briefly describe the rationale for this principle.

Q7-7. Under what conditions would each of the inventory costing methods discussed in the chapter produce the same results?

Q7-8. What is inventory "shrink?" How does a company determine the amount of inventory shrink that may have occurred?

Q7-9.[A] If inventory costs are rising, which inventory costing method—first-in, first-out; last-in, first-out; or average cost—yields the (a) lowest ending inventory? (b) lowest net income? (c) largest ending inventory? (d) largest net income? (e) greatest cash flow assuming that method is used for tax purposes?

Q7-10.[A] Even though it does not reflect their physical flow of goods, why might companies adopt last-in, first-out inventory costing in periods when costs are consistently rising?

Q7-11.[A] What is a LIFO reserve? How is the LIFO reserve related to unrealised holding gains?

Q7-12.[A] Analysts claim that it is more difficult to forecast net income for a company that uses LIFO. Why might this be true?

MINI EXERCISES

M7-13. Recording an Inventory Purchase LO1

Shields Company has purchased inventories incurring the following costs: (a) the invoice amount of $500, (b) shipping charges of $30, (c) interest of $10 on the $500 borrowed to finance the purchase, and (d) $5 for the cost of moving the inventory to the company's warehouse.

Required

Determine the cost to be assigned to the inventory and record the purchase using "T" accounts.

M7-14. Recording Inventory Costs LO1

Schrand Inc., a merchandiser, is requesting help in determining what costs ought to be considered as costs when incurred or treated as inventory costs, which are expensed as COGS. The costs include: salespersons' wages, utilities such as heat and light in the store, the floor supervisor's salary, the cost of merchandise to be sold, costs of packaging and shipping to buyers.

Required

Determine the items above that should be included in inventory.

M7-15. Determining Cost of Goods Sold for a Manufacturing Company LO1

Ybarra Products began operations in 2014. During its first year, the company purchased raw materials costing $84,000 and used $63,000 of those materials in the production of its products. The company's manufacturing operations also incurred labour costs of $58,000 and overhead costs of $28,000. At year end 2014, Ybarra had $19,000 of partially completed product in work-in-process inventory and $35,000 in finished goods inventory. What was Ybarra Company's cost of goods sold in 2014?

M7-16. Calculating Gross Profit Margin LO5

Darling Harbour Corp. reported the following revenue and cost of goods sold information in its annual report for 2014, 2013, and 2012.

(Millions of Australian Dollars)	2014	2013	2012
Sales to customers	$65,030	$61,587	$61,897
Cost of products sold	20,360	18,792	18,447

Compute Darling Harbour's gross profit margin for each year.

M7-17. Calculating Effect of Inventory Errors LO1

For each of the following scenarios, determine the effect of the error on income in the current period and in the subsequent period. To answer these questions, rely on the inventory equation:

Beginning inventory + Purchases − Cost of goods sold = Ending inventory

a. Porter Company received a shipment of merchandise costing $32,000 near the end of the fiscal year. The shipment was mistakenly recorded at a cost of $23,000.

b. Chiu, Inc., purchased merchandise costing $16,000. When the shipment was received, it was determined that the merchandise was damaged in shipment. The goods were returned to the supplier, but the accounting department was not notified and the invoice was paid.

c. After taking a physical count of its inventory, Murray Corporation determined that it had "shrink" of $12,500, and the books were adjusted accordingly. However, inventory costing $5,000 was never counted.

M7-18.[A] Calculating LIFO, FIFO, Income and Cash Flows LO2, 4, 6

An acquaintance has proposed the following business plan to you. A local company requires a consistent quantity of a commodity and is looking for a reliable supplier. You could become that reliable supplier.

The cost of the commodity is expected to rise steadily over the foreseeable future, but the company is willing to pay more than the price that is current at the time. All you would need to do is make an investment, purchase the inventory and then deliver inventory to the company over the following year. One complication is that the commodity is available for purchase only seasonally, so at the end of every year you would need to purchase the supply for the following year. The customer pays promptly on delivery.

An initial cash investment of $62,000 would be used to purchase $50,000 of inventory in December 2013. The remaining cash would be held for liquidity needs. In the following year, you would deliver this inventory to the customer. Inventory costs are expected to increase by $10,000 per year, and the customer agrees to pay $15,000 more than the current cost of inventory. So, during 2014, you would deliver inventory that originally cost $50,000, receive payment of $75,000 and pay $60,000 to purchase inventory for the current year. This pattern would continue in future years, but with annually increasing costs of inventory and corresponding increases in the price charged the customer.

If you accept this proposal, your objective would be to receive $9,000 in dividends (about a 15% return on the $62,000 investment) at the end of each year. Assume your business would have an income tax rate of 40%.

a. Construct a projected balance sheet as of the end of December 2013.

b. Construct financial forecasts of income statements, cash flows (direct method) and balance sheets for the next three years (through 2016). Assume that your business would operate in a tax jurisdiction that requires the use of FIFO for inventory. Would this opportunity meet your financial objective?

c. Suppose that your business would operate in a tax jurisdiction that allowed the use of LIFO for inventory. Would this opportunity meet your financial objective? Why?

LO2 M7-19. Computing Cost of Goods Sold and Ending Inventory Under FIFO and Average Cost

Assume that Gode Company reports the following initial balance and subsequent purchase of inventory:

Beginning inventory, 2014.	1,000 units @ $100 each	$100,000
Inventory purchased in 2014.	2,000 units @ $150 each	300,000
Cost of goods available for sale in 2014	3,000 units	$400,000

Assume that 1,700 units are sold during 2014. Compute the cost of goods sold for 2014 and the balance reported as ending inventory on its 2014 balance sheet under the following inventory costing methods:

a. FIFO

b. Average Cost

LO2 M7-20. Inferring Purchases Using Cost of Goods Sold and Inventory Balances

Geiger Corporation, a retail company, reported inventories of $1,320,000 in 2013 and $1,460,000 in 2014. The 2014 income statement reported cost of goods sold of $6,980,000.

a. Compute the amount of inventory purchased during 2014.

b. Prepare journal entries to record (1) purchases, and (2) cost of goods sold.

c. Post the journal entries in part *b* to their respective T-accounts.

d. Record each of the transactions in part *b* in the financial statement effects template to show the effect of these entries on the balance sheet and income statement.

LO2 M7-21. Computing Cost of Goods Sold and Ending Inventory

Bartov Corporation reports the following beginning inventory and purchases for 2014:

Beginning inventory, 2014.	400 units @ $10 each	$ 4,000
Inventory purchased in 2014.	700 units @ $12 each	8,400
Cost of goods available for sale in 2014	1,100 units	$12,400

Bartov sells 600 of these units in 2014. Compute its cost of goods sold for 2014 and the ending inventory reported on its 2014 balance sheet under each of the following inventory costing methods:

a. FIFO

b. Average Cost

LO5 M7-22. Computing and Evaluating Inventory Turnover

Mong Kok Outlets Ltd. and TST Stores, Inc. reported the following in their financial reports:

(HK $ billions)	Mong Kok			TST		
Fiscal Year	Sales	COGS	Inventory	Sales	COGS	Inventory
2014	$444	$335	$40.7	$69.9	$47.9	$7.92
2013	419	315	36.4	67.4	45.7	7.60
2012	405	304	32.7	65.4	44.1	7.18

a. Compute the 2014 and 2013 inventory turnovers for each of these two retailers.
b. Discuss any changes that are evident in inventory turnover across years and companies from part *a*.
c. Describe ways in which a retailer can improve its inventory turnover. Are there ways to increase inventory turnover that are not beneficial to the company's long-term interests?

M7-23. Inferring Purchases Using Cost of Goods Sold and Inventory Balances LO2
Penno Company reported ending inventories of $23,560,000 in 2014 and $25,790,000 in 2013. Cost of goods sold totaled $142,790,000 in 2014.

a. Prepare the journal entry to record cost of goods sold.
b. Set up a T-account for inventory and post the cost of goods sold entry from part *a* to this account.
c. Using the T-account from *b*, determine the amount of inventory that was purchased in 2014. Prepare a journal entry to record those purchases.
d. Using the financial statement effects template, show the effects of the entries in parts *a* and *c* on the balance sheet and income statement.

M7-24. Determining Lower of Cost or Market LO3
The following data refer to Froning Company's ending inventory.

Item Code	Quantity	Unit Cost	Unit Market
LXC.	60	$45	$48
KWT	210	38	34
MOR.	300	22	20
NES	100	27	32

Determine the ending inventory amount by applying the lower of cost or market rule to (*a*) each item of inventory and (*b*) the total inventory.

EXERCISES

E7-25. Calculating Gross Profit Margin LO5
Prada S.p.A, the Italian luxury fashion house reported the following revenue and cost of goods sold information in its annual report for the twelve months ended January 31 in 2014, 2013, and 2012.

PRADA S.P.A (ITALY)

(€ '000)	2014	2013	2012
Net revenues	€3,587,347	€3,297,219	€2,555,606
Cost of goods sold	938,698	920,678	727,581

Compute Prada's gross profit margin for each year.

E7-26. Applying and Analysing Inventory Costing Methods LO2
At the beginning of the current period, Chen carried 1,000 units of its product with a unit cost of $20. A summary of purchases during the current period follows:

	Units	Unit Cost	Cost
Beginning Inventory	1,000	$20	$20,000
Purchases: #1	1,800	22	39,600
#2	800	26	20,800
#3	1,200	29	34,800

During the current period, Chen sold 2,800 units.

a. Assume that Chen uses the first-in, first-out method. Compute its cost of goods sold for the current period and the ending inventory balance.

b. Assume that Chen uses the average cost method. Compute its cost of goods sold for the current period and the ending inventory balance.

c. Which of these two inventory costing methods would you choose to:

1. Reflect what is probably the physical flow of goods? Explain.
2. Report the largest amount of income for the period? Explain.

LO2 **E7-27. Computing Cost of Sales and Ending Inventory**

Stocken Company has the following financial records for the current period:

	Units	Unit Cost
Beginning inventory	100	$46
Purchases: #1	650	42
#2	550	38
#3	200	36

Ending inventory at the end of this period is 350 units. Compute the ending inventory and the cost of goods sold for the current period using (*a*) first-in, first-out and (b) average cost.

LO3 **E7-28. Determining Lower of Cost or Market**

Crane Company had the following inventory at December 31, 2014.

		Unit Price	
	Quantity	Cost	Market
Desks			
Model 9001	70	$190	$210
Model 9002	45	280	268
Model 9003	20	350	360
Cabinets			
Model 7001	120	60	64
Model 7002	80	95	88
Model 7003	50	130	126

a. Determine the ending inventory amount by applying the lower of cost or market rule to

1. Each item of inventory.
2. Each major category of inventory.
3. Total inventory.

b. Which of the LOCOM procedures from requirement *a* results in the lowest net income for 2014? Explain.

LO2, 6 **E7-29.[A] Analysing LIFO Inventory Footnote Disclosure**

GENERAL MOTORS CORPORATION (USA)

General Motors Corporation reported the following information in its annual report:

Inventories at December 31 ($ millions)	2008	2007
Productive material, work in process, and supplies	$ 4,849	$ 6,267
Finished product, service parts, etc.	9,426	10,095
Total inventories at FIFO	14,275	16,362
Less LIFO allowance	(1,233)	(1,423)
Total automotive and other inventories, less allowances	$13,042	$14,939

The company reports its inventory using the LIFO costing method during 2007 and 2008.

a. At what dollar amount are inventories reported on its 2008 balance sheet?

b. At what dollar amount would inventories have been reported in 2008 if FIFO inventory costing had been used?

c. What cumulative effect has the use of LIFO had, as of year-end 2008, on GM's pretax income, compared to the pretax income that would have been reported using the FIFO costing method?

d. Assuming a 35% income tax rate, what is the cumulative effect on GM's tax liability as of year-end 2008?

e. In July 2009, GM changed its inventory accounting to FIFO costs. Why do you suppose GM made that choice?

E7-30.[A] Analysing of LIFO Inventory and Footnote Disclosure

LO2, 6

DEERE & COMPANY (USA)

The inventory footnote from Deere & Company's 2010 annual report follows ($ millions).

At December 31	2010	2009
Raw materials and supplies	$1,201	$ 940
Work in process.	483	387
Finished goods and parts	2,777	2,437
Total FIFO value	4,461	3,764
Less adjustment to LIFO value	$1,398	$1,367

Deere also reports the following footnote to its 2010 annual report:

Inventories: Most inventories owned by Deere & Company and its US equipment subsidiaries are valued at cost, on the "last-in, first-out" (LIFO) basis. Remaining inventories are generally valued at the lower of cost, on the "first-in, first-out" (FIFO) basis, or market. The value of gross inventories on the LIFO basis represented 59 percent of worldwide gross inventories at FIFO value on October 31, 2010 and 2009. If all inventories had been valued on a FIFO basis, estimated inventories by major classification at October 31 in millions of dollars would have been as given in the above table.

We note that not all of Deere's inventories are reported using the same inventory costing method (companies can use different inventory costing methods for different inventory pools).

a. At what dollar amount are Deere's inventories reported on its 2010 balance sheet?

b. At what dollar amount would inventories have been reported on Deere's 2010 balance sheet had it used FIFO inventory costing?

c. What *cumulative* effect has the use of LIFO inventory costing had, as of year-end 2010, on its pretax income compared with the pretax income it would have reported had it used FIFO inventory costing? Explain.

d. Assuming a 35% income tax rate, by what *cumulative* dollar amount has Deere's tax liability been affected by use of LIFO inventory costing as of year-end 2010? Has the use of LIFO inventory costing increased or decreased its cumulative tax liability?

e. What effect has the use of LIFO inventory costing had on Deere's pretax income and tax liability for 2010 (assume a 35% income tax rate)?

E7-31.[A] Analysing Inventories Using LIFO Inventory Footnote

LO2, 5, 6

WHOLE FOODS MARKET, INC. (USA)

The footnote below is from the 2011 annual report of Whole Foods Market, Inc., a Texas-based retail grocery chain.

Inventories We value our inventories at the lower of cost or market. Cost was determined using the last-in, first-out ("LIFO") method for approximately 92.3% and 93.9% of inventories in fiscal years 2011 and 2010, respectively. Under the LIFO method, the cost assigned to items sold is based on the cost of the most recent items purchased. As a result, the costs of the first items purchased remain in inventory and are used to value ending inventory. The excess of estimated current costs over LIFO carrying value, or LIFO reserve, was approximately $29.7 million and $19.4 million at September 25, 2011 and September 26, 2010, respectively. Costs for remaining inventories are determined by the first-in, first-out ("FIFO") method.

Whole Foods operates the world's largest chain of natural and organic food stores. In 2011, Whole Foods reported sales revenue of $10,108 million and cost of goods sold of $6,571 million. The following information was extracted from the company's 2011 and 2010 balance sheets:

($ millions)	2011	2010
Merchandise inventories.	$337	$323

a. Calculate the amount of inventories purchased by Whole Foods in 2011.

b. What amount of gross profit would Whole Foods have reported if the FIFO method had been used to value all inventories?

c. Calculate the gross profit margin (GPM) as reported and assuming that the FIFO method had been used to value all inventories.

LO5 **E7-32. Calculating Gross Profit Margin and Inventory Turnover**

The following table presents sales revenue, cost of goods sold, and inventory amounts for two retailers of fine jewellery, Tangs & Co. and Changi, Inc. (an Internet retailer).

(millions of Singapore Dollars)	2014	2013
Tangs & Co.		
Revenues	$3,643	$3,085
Cost of goods sold	1,492	1,263
Inventory	2,073	1,625
Changi, Inc.		
Revenues	$ 348	$ 333
Cost of goods sold	276	261
Inventory	29	20

a. Compute the gross profit margin (GPM) for each of these companies for 2014 and 2013.

b. Compute the inventory turnover ratios for 2014 and estimate the 2013 value.

c. What factors might determine the differences among these two companies' ratios?

PROBLEMS

LO1 **P7-33. Calculating Manufacturing Costs**

VTECH HOLDING LTD. (HONG KONG)

VTech Holding Ltd. provided the following information detailing the components of its inventory balance in a note to its annual report dates March 31, 2013:

Components of Inventory for VTech (US$ million)	2013	2012
Raw materials	$ 89.9	$ 82.1
Work in progress	29.2	35.1
Finished goods	157.8	122.0
Total	$276.9	$239.2

Furthermore, VTech reported cost of sales of $1,260.2 million in fiscal 2013 and it purchased $500 million in raw materials during fiscal 2013.

Required

a. Compute VTech's cost of goods produced in 2013.

b. Compute VTech's cost of raw materials used in 2013.

c. Compute VTech's labour and overhead costs incurred in 2013.

LO1, 3 **P7-34. Calculating Manufacturing Costs and Analysing the Lower of Cost or Market Rule**

BILLABONG INTERNATIONAL LIMITED (AUSTRALIA)

Billabong International Limited is an Australian clothing manufacturer and retailer. The inventory footnote from Billabong's 2013 annual report follows (Australian $'000).

Note 13. Current assets—Inventories	2013	2012
Raw materials and stores—at cost	$ 3,640	$ 3,842
Work in progress—at cost	12,584	7,734
Finished goods:		
—at cost	226,217	255,821
—at net realisable value	24,365	25,804
	$266,806	$293,201

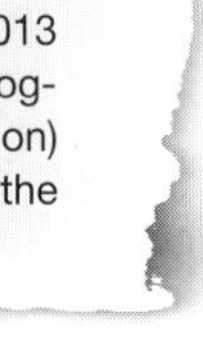

Inventory expense
Inventories recognised as an expense from continuing operations during the year ended June 30, 2013 amounted to $651.4 million (2012: $691.6 million). Write-downs of inventories to net realisable value recognised as an expense during the year ended June 30, 2013 amounted to $31.0 million (2012: $73.7 million) with $7.2 million (2012: $32.9 million) representing inventory realised through sale to customers during the year. The expense has been included in "cost of goods sold" in the income statement.

As indicated in the above note, Billabong recorded Cost of Goods Sold of $682.4 (= $651.4 + $31.0) million in its 2013 Income statements.

Required

a. Compute Billabong's cost of goods produced in 2013.

b. What additional information do we need in order to compute Billabong's cost of raw materials used?

c. Why did Billabong write down some of its inventories in 2012 and 2013?

d. How did the write-down of inventories affect Billabong's Income Statement?

P7-35.[A] **Analysing LIFO Inventory and Its Footnote Disclosure**

LO2, 5, 6

CATERPILLAR INC. (USA)

KOMATSU LTD. (JAPAN)

Caterpillar Inc. and Komatsu Ltd. are international manufacturers of industrial and construction equipment. Caterpillar's headquarters is in the United States, while Komatsu's headquarters is in Japan. The following information comes from their recent financial statements.

Caterpillar—fiscal year ending December 31, 2011 ($ millions)	
Cost of goods sold	$43,578
Beginning inventory	9,587
Ending inventory	14,544
Komatsu—fiscal year ending March 31, 2012 (¥ millions)	
Cost of goods sold	¥1,440,765
Beginning inventory	473,876
Ending inventory	612,359

In its footnotes, Caterpillar also provides the following information:

Inventories are stated at the lower of cost or market. Cost is principally determined using the last-in, first-out (LIFO) method. The value of inventories on the LIFO basis represented about 65% of total inventories at December 31, 2011, and about 70% of total inventories at December 31, 2010 and 2009. If the FIFO (first-in, first-out) method had been in use, inventories would have been $2,422 million, $2,575 million and $3,022 million higher than reported at December 31, 2011, 2010 and 2009, respectively.

Required

a. Calculate the inventory turnover ratios for Caterpillar and Komatsu using the information reported in their financial statements. Describe some operational reasons that companies might have differing inventory turnover ratios, even if they are in the same industry.

b. Did the cost of Caterpillar's acquiring (i.e., producing) products go up or down in 2011?

c. Assuming a 35% income tax rate, by what cumulative dollar amount has Caterpillar's tax liability been affected by use of LIFO inventory costing as of fiscal year-end 2011? Has the use of LIFO inventory costing increased or decreased its cumulative tax liability?

d. What effect has the use of LIFO inventory costing had on Caterpillar's pretax income and tax liability for fiscal year 2011? (Assume a 35% tax rate.)

e. In its footnotes, Komatsu reports that it "determines cost of work in process and finished products using the specific identification method based on actual costs accumulated under a job-order cost system. The cost of finished parts is determined principally using the first-in, first-out method." What effect does this footnote have on your interpretation in question *a* above? Use the information available to make a more appropriate comparison of the two companies' inventory turnover.

LO2, 5, 6 **P7-36.[A] Analysing Inventory Disclosure Comparing LIFO and FIFO**

THE KROGER CO. (USA)

The current asset section of the 2011 and 2012 fiscal year end balance sheets of The Kroger Co. are presented in the accompanying table:

($ millions)	January 28, 2012	January 29, 2011
Current assets		
Cash and temporary cash investments	$ 188	$ 825
Deposits in-transit	786	666
Receivables	949	845
FIFO inventory	6,157	5,793
LIFO credit	(1,043)	(827)
Prepaid and other current assets	288	319
Total current assets	$7,325	$7,621

In addition, Kroger provides the following footnote describing its inventory accounting policy:

> Inventories are stated at the lower of cost (principally on a last-in, first-out "LIFO" basis) or market. In total, approximately 97% of inventories for 2011 and 2010 were valued using the LIFO method. Cost for the balance of the inventories, including substantially all fuel inventories, was determined using the first-in, first-out ("FIFO") method. Replacement cost was higher than the carrying amount by $1,043 at January 28, 2012 and $827 at January 29, 2011. The Company follows the Link-Chain, Dollar-Value LIFO method for purposes of calculating its LIFO charge or credit.

Required

a. At what dollar amount does Kroger report its inventory in its January 28, 2012, balance sheet?

b. What is the cumulative effect (through January 28, 2012) of the use of LIFO on Kroger's pretax earnings?

c. Assuming a 35% tax rate, what is the cumulative (through January 28, 2012) tax effect of the use of LIFO to determine inventory costs?

d. Kroger reported net earnings of $602 million in its fiscal year 2011 income statement. Assuming a 35% tax rate, what amount of net earnings would Kroger report if the company used the FIFO inventory costing method?

e. Kroger reported merchandise costs (cost of goods sold) of $71,494 million in fiscal year 2011. Compute its inventory turnover for the year.

f. How would the inventory turnover ratio differ if the FIFO costing method had been used?

LO5 **P7-37. Calculating Gross Profit and Inventory Turnover**

DELL INC.
HEWLETT-PACKARD COMPANY
APPLE INC. (USA)

The following table presents sales revenue, cost of goods sold, and inventory amounts for three computer/electronics companies, Dell Inc., Hewlett-Packard Company, and Apple Inc.

($ millions)	Fiscal year ending		
Dell Inc.	Feb. 3, 2012	Jan. 28, 2011	Jan. 29, 2010
Revenues	$ 62,071	$ 61,494	$ 52,902
Cost of goods sold	48,260	50,098	43,641
Inventory	1,404	1,301	1,051
Hewlett-Packard Company	Oct. 31, 2011	Oct. 31, 2010	Oct. 31, 2009
Revenues (Products only)	$127,245	$126,033	$114,552
Cost of goods sold	65,167	65,064	56,503
Inventory	7,490	6,466	6,128
Apple Inc.	Sep. 24, 2011	Sep. 25, 2010	Sep. 26, 2009
Revenues	$108,249	$ 65,225	$ 42,905
Cost of goods sold	64,431	39,541	25,683
Inventory	776	1,051	455

Required

a. Compute the gross profit margin (GPM) for each of these companies for all three fiscal years.

b. Compute the inventory turnover ratios for the last two fiscal years. (All three firms use FIFO inventory costing.)

c. What factors might determine the differences among these three companies' ratios?

CASES AND PROJECTS

C7-38. Computing and Evaluating Inventory Turnover for Two Companies LO5

FIAT S.p.A. (ITALY)
HYUNDAI MOTOR COMPANY (SOUTH KOREA)

Fiat S.p.A. is a global automaker for the mass market under the Fiat and Chrysler brands, as well as luxury cars under the Ferrari and Maserati brands. Hyundai Motor Company is a South Korean automaker and it operates the largest integrated automobile manufacturing facility in the world. The following information is taken from the 2013 annual reports of the two companies.

	Fiat (in millions of Euros)			Hyundai (in millions of Korean Won)		
	Sales	Cost of Goods Sold	Inventories	Sales	Cost of Goods Sold	Inventories
2012	€86,816	€74,570	€10,230	₩87,307,636	₩67,859,491	₩7,073,116
2013	83,957	71,701	9,295	84,469,721	64,967,273	6,772,864

Required

a. Compute the 2013 inventory turnover and the 2013 gross profit margin (in %) for each company.

b. How do these companies' inventory turnover measures and gross profit margins compare? Do the differences reflect their respective business models? Explain.

c. What strategy could the companies follow to improve their inventory turnover measures?

C7-39. Analysing Inventory and Margin in a Seasonal Business LO5

West Marine, Inc., opened its first boating supply store in 1975. Since that time, the company has grown to be one of the largest boating supply companies in the world, with fiscal year 2011 revenues in excess of $640 million. The accompanying table provides financial information for two recent years. West Marine's fiscal year is closely aligned with the calendar year. All amounts are in millions.

Time Period	Net Revenues	Cost of Goods Sold	Ending Inventory
Fiscal year 2009	—	—	**$197**
First quarter 2010.	$110	$ 85	243
Second quarter 2010.	233	151	240
Third quarter 2010	173	123	209
Fourth quarter 2010.	107	89	202
Fiscal year 2010	**623**	**448**	**202**
First quarter 2011.	114	89	248
Second quarter 2011	236	151	242
Third quarter 2011	180	126	212
Fourth quarter 2011.	113	93	193
Fiscal year 2011	**643**	**459**	**193**

Required

a. Using the fiscal year (annual) information for 2010 and 2011, calculate the gross profit margin and the inventory turnover ratio.

b. West Marine is in a seasonal business, in which the sales total for the second and third quarters is substantially higher than the sales total for the first and fourth quarters. Calculate the company's gross profit margin by quarter. What do you learn from the seasonal pattern in the gross profit margin?

c. What is the seasonal pattern in inventory balances? What effect does West Marine's choice of fiscal year-end have on the inventory turnover ratio calculated in *a*?

d. Recalculate West Marine's inventory turnover ratios for 2010 and 2011 using a weighted average of the company's inventory investment over the year.

LO2, 5, 6 **C7-40.**[A] **Analysing Effects of LIFO on Inventory Turnover Ratios**

EXXON MOBIL CORPORATION (USA)
BP, PLC (UNITED KINGDOM)

The current assets of **Exxon Mobil Corporation** follow:

(millions)	2011	2010
Current assets		
Cash and cash equivalents	$13,068	$ 8,453
Notes and accounts receivable, less estimated doubtful amounts	38,642	32,284
Inventories:		
Crude oil, products and merchandise	11,665	9,852
Materials and supplies	3,359	3,124
Other current assets	6,229	5,271
Total current assets	$72,963	$58,984

In addition, the following note was provided in its 2011 annual report:

Inventories. Crude oil, products and merchandise inventories are carried at the lower of current market value or cost (generally determined under the last-in, first-out method—LIFO). Inventory costs include expenditures and other charges (including depreciation) directly and indirectly incurred in bringing the inventory to its existing condition and location. Selling expenses and general and administrative expenses are reported as period costs and excluded from inventory cost. Inventories of materials and supplies are valued at cost or less.
The aggregate replacement cost of inventories was estimated to exceed their LIFO carrying values by $25.6 billion and $21.3 billion at December 31, 2011 and 2010, respectively.

Required

a. Exxon Mobil reported pretax earnings of $73,257 million in 2011. What amount of earnings would have been reported by the company if inventory had been reported using the FIFO costing method?

b. Exxon Mobil reported cost of goods sold of $266,534 million in 2011. Compute its inventory turnover ratio for 2011 using total inventories.

c. **BP, p.l.c.** (BP) reports its financial information using IFRS. For fiscal year 2011, BP reported cost of goods sold of $285,618 million, beginning inventory of $26,218 million and ending inventory of $25,661 million. Compute BP's inventory turnover ratio for fiscal year 2011.

d. Compare your answers in parts *b* and *c*. BP can't use LIFO to report under IFRS, so revise your calculations in such a way as to find out which company has faster inventory turnover.

LO2, 6 **C7-41.**[A] **Analysing Effects of Change from LIFO to FIFO Inventory Costing**

HORMEL FOODS CORPORATION (USA)

Hormel Foods Corporation provided the following footnote in its 2006 annual report:

Change in Accounting Principle: In the first quarter of fiscal 2006, the company changed its method of accounting for the materials portion of turkey products and substantially all inventoriable expenses, packages, and supplies that had previously been accounted for utilising the last-in first-out (LIFO) method to the first-in first-out (FIFO) method. As a result, all inventories are now stated at the lower of cost, determined on a FIFO basis, or market. The change is preferable because it provides a more meaningful presentation of the company's financial position as it values inventory in a manner that more closely approximates current cost; it provides a consistent and uniform costing method across the company's operations; FIFO inventory values better represent the underlying commercial substance of selling the oldest products first; it is the prevalent method used by other entities within the company's industry; and it enhances the comparability of the financial statements with those of our industry peers. As required by U.S. generally accepted accounting principles, the change has been reflected in the consolidated statements of financial position, consolidated statements of operations, and consolidated statements of cash flows through retrospective application of the FIFO method. Inventories as of the beginning of fiscal 2005 were increased by the LIFO reserve ($36.7 million), and shareholders' investment was increased by the after-tax effect ($23.0 million). Previously reported net earnings for fiscal years 2005 and 2004 were increased by $1.1 million and $1.9 million, respectively.

Required

a. Hormel's 2005 annual report includes a LIFO reserve in the amount of $38.5 million. What dollar effect did this accounting method change have on total assets? retained earnings? income tax liabilities?

b. What were Hormel's stated reasons for the change?
c. What effect did this change likely have on 2006 net income?
d. Can you think of any possible motivations for this change in accounting method other than those provided by management?

SOLUTIONS TO REVIEW PROBLEMS

Mid-Chapter Review 1

Solution (All amounts in thousands of Australia dollars)
The cost of goods produced is calculated as follows:
Ending Finished Goods (FG) Inventory = Beginning FG Inventory + Cost of Goods Produced − Cost of Goods Sold
i.e., \$250,582 = \$281,625 + Cost of Goods Produced − \$682,378
Hence, Cost of Goods Produced = \$651,335.

Mid-Chapter Review 2 Part 1

Solution
Preliminary computation: Units in ending inventory = 4,800 available − 2,800 sold = 2,000

1. First-in, first-out (FIFO)

Cost of goods sold computation:	Units		Cost		Total
	1,000	@	€18.00	=	€18,000
	1,800	@	€18.25	=	32,850
	2,800				€50,850
Cost of goods available for sale		€88,450			
Less: Cost of goods sold		50,850			
Ending inventory (€22,800 + €14,800)		€37,600			

2. Average cost (AC)

Average unit cost	= €88,450/4,800	= €18.427
Cost of goods sold	= 2,800 × €18.427	= €51,596
Ending inventory	= 2,000 × €18.427	= €36,854

3. FIFO in most circumstances reflects physical flow. For example, FIFO would apply to the physical flow of perishables and to situations where the earlier items acquired are moved out first because of risk of deterioration or obsolescence.
4. Transaction effects shown in the financial statement effects template, journal entries, and T-accounts.

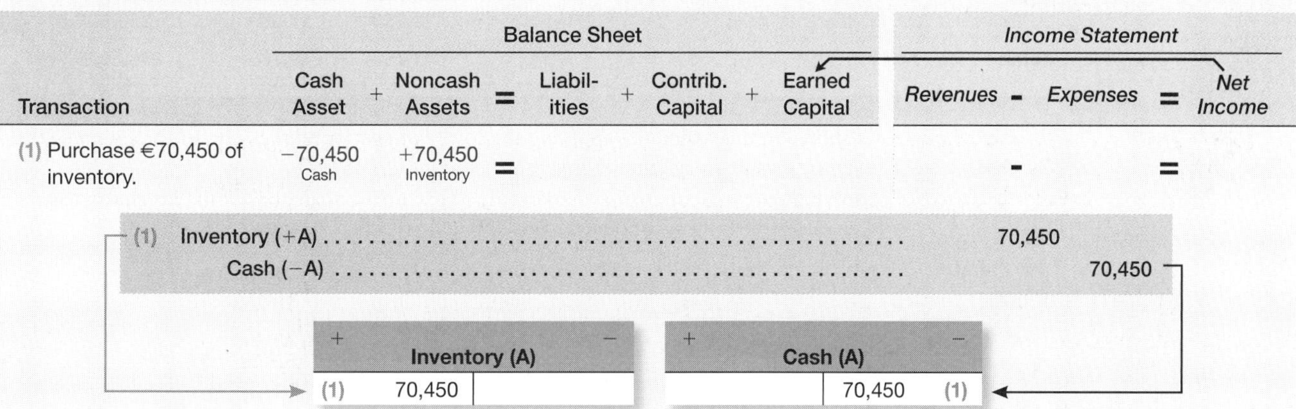

Balance Sheet
Income Statement
Transaction
Cash Asset + Noncash Assets = Liabilities + Contrib. Capital + Earned Capital
Revenues − Expenses = Net Income
(1) Purchase €70,450 of inventory.
−70,450 Cash
+70,450 Inventory
(1) Inventory (+A) 70,450
Cash (−A) 70,450
Inventory (A)
(1) 70,450
Cash (A)
70,450 (1)
ANALYSE JOURNALISE POST

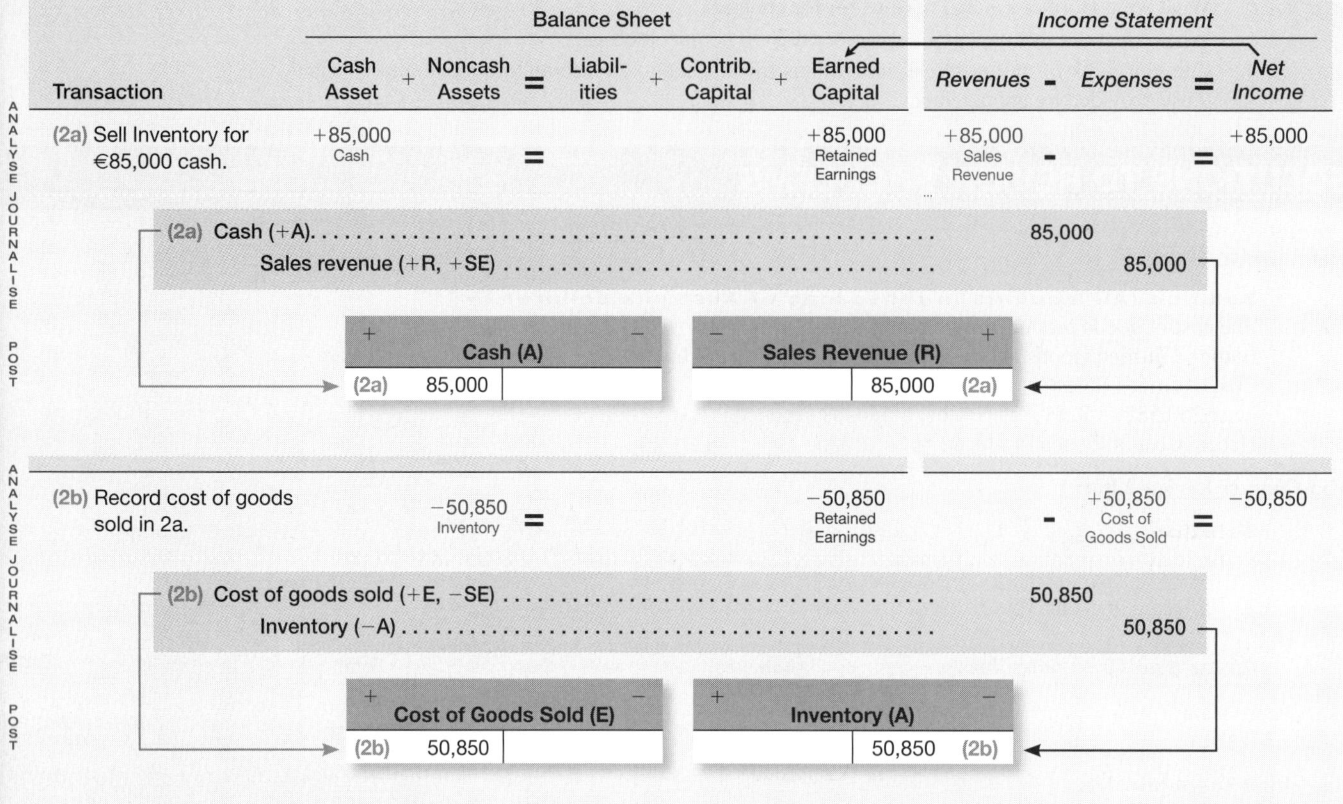

Mid-Chapter Review 2 Part 2

Solution

1.

Item	Quantity	Cost	Market	Inventory Amounts: Cost	Market	LOCOM (by Item)
Fans						
Model X1	300	£18	£19	£ 5,400	£ 5,700	£ 5,400
Model X2	250	22	24	5,500	6,000	5,500
Model X3	400	29	26	11,600	10,400	10,400
Totals				£22,500	£22,100	£21,300
Heaters						
Model B7	500	24	28	£12,000	£14,000	£12,000
Model B8	290	35	32	10,150	9,280	9,280
Model B9	100	41	38	4,100	3,800	3,800
Totals				26,250	27,080	25,080
Totals				£48,750	£49,180	£46,380

a. As shown in this schedule, applying the lower of cost or market rule to each item of the inventory results in an ending inventory amount of £46,380.

b. Applying the lower of cost or market rule to each major category of the inventory results in an ending inventory amount of £48,350, calculated as follows:

Fans	£22,100
Heaters..............................	26,250
	£48,350

c. As shown in this schedule, applying the lower of cost or market rule to the total inventory results in an ending inventory amount of £48,750.

2. The LOCOM procedure that results in the lowest ending inventory amount also results in the lowest net income for the year (the lower the ending inventory amount, the higher the cost of goods sold). Applying the lower of cost or market rule to each item of the inventory results in the lowest net income for the year.

Chapter-End Review

Solution (All amounts in thousands of Canadian dollars)

1. Gross profit margin is calculated as follows:

	Gildan	Reitmans
2013	$\frac{(\$2{,}184{,}303 - \$1{,}550{,}266)}{\$2{,}184{,}303} = 29.03\%$	$\frac{(\$1{,}000{,}513 - \$372{,}135)}{\$1{,}000{,}513} = 62.81\%$
2012	$\frac{(\$1{,}948{,}253 - \$1{,}552{,}128)}{\$1{,}948{,}253} = 20.33\%$	$\frac{(\$1{,}019{,}397^{\circ} - \$363{,}333)}{\$1{,}019{,}397} = 64.36\%$

2. We can use the average inventory to calculate the inventory turnover rate for 2013. Since the 2011 inventory value is not given, we use the 2012 final inventory value only to estimate the 2012 inventory turnover ratio.

	Gildan	Reitmans
2013	$\frac{1{,}550{,}266}{[(553{,}068 + 595{,}794)/2]} = 2.70$	$\frac{372{,}135}{[(93{,}317 + 93{,}188)/2]} = 3.99$
2012 estimate	$\frac{1{,}552{,}128}{553{,}068} = 2.81$	$\frac{363{,}333}{93{,}188} = 3.90$

3. Although both companies are in the apparel business, they represent two different industries. Reitmans is a pure retailer, while Gildan is vertically integrated. Hence, the two businesses have different product mixes and, therefore, their financial ratios are not directly comparable. However, the low inventory turnover ratio exhibited by Gildan may reflect the fact that it manufactures its own products.

Appendix-End Review

Solution

1. GE presents the cost of services sold as a separate expense item in the calculation of gross profit. The gross profit margin is calculated as follows:

Gross profit margin:		
2009:	$78,517/$154,438 =	0.508 (or 50.8%)
2010:	$77,880/$149,593 =	0.521 (or 52.1%)
2011:	$79,022/$147,300 =	0.536 (or 53.6%)
Inventory turnover:		
2010:	$46,005/[($11,526 + $11,987)/2] =	3.91 times
2011:	$51,455/[($13,792 + $11,526)/2] =	4.06 times

2. Cost of goods sold and gross profit must be adjusted by the change in the LIFO reserve to convert to FIFO.

Cost of goods sold		
2010:	$46,005 – ($404 – $529) =	$46,130
2011:	$51,455 – ($450 – $404) =	$51,409
Gross profit		
2010:	$77,880 + ($404 – $529) =	$77,755
2011:	$79,022 + ($450 – $404) =	$79,068

The use of LIFO resulted in a lower cost of goods sold and a higher gross profit in 2011.

3. Restated inventory turnover calculations:

2010:	$46,130/[($11,930 + $12,516)/2] =	3.77 times
2011:	$51,409/[($14,242 + $11,930)/2] =	3.93 times

Because inventory values are higher and cost of goods sold is lower under FIFO, the inventory turnover ratio is slightly lower when FIFO numbers are used.

LEARNING OBJECTIVES

1. Describe and distinguish between tangible and intangible assets. (p. 360)
2. Determine which costs to capitalise and report as assets and which costs to expense. (p. 361)
3. Apply different depreciation methods to allocate the cost of assets over time. (p. 363)
4. Determine the effects of asset sales and impairments on financial statements. (p. 367)
5. Describe the accounting and reporting for intangible assets. (p. 375)
6. Analyse the effects of tangible and intangible assets on key performance measures. (p. 381)

CHAPTER

8

Reporting and Analysing Long-Term Operating Assets

Airbus Group is a leading developer and manufacturer of commercial and military aircrafts, civil and military helicopters, and defence and space products and systems. Airbus Industrie was originally formed as a consortium in 1970, with France's Aerospatiale and Germany's Deutsche Airbus each having a 50% share. The Spanish company CASA and British Aerospace joined the consortium in 1971 and 1979, respectively. In 2000, the partner companies merged to form the European Aeronautic Defence and Space Company (EADS N.V.). It was renamed "Airbus Group" on January 2, 2014, as part of a restructuring of its businesses and to take advantage of the globally recognised name of its Airbus commercial aircraft division.

AIRBUS GROUP
www.airbus-group.com

The company has headquarters in the Netherlands and main offices in France. Currently, it has 16 manufacturing sites in Europe and three final assembly lines in France, Germany, and Spain. It also has a joint venture in Tianjin, China, to assemble single-aisle aircrafts for the Asian region. As a commitment to its American market, the company will open a final assembly line in Mobile, Alabama, in 2015.

Airbus's competitive strategy is to focus on providing value to its customers through innovations that "deliver concrete economic and performance benefits." As a result, in 1974 it launched the world's first twin-engine widebody passenger jet (A300), thereby saving on engine costs. Moreover, it was the first commercial jet manufacturer to use lightweight composite materials to reduce aircraft weight, and it introduced the forward-facing crew cockpit layout to eliminate the need for a flight engineer. In 1984, it brought electronic flight instrument displays and fly-by-wire technology to commercial jetliners (A320). In October 2007, it delivered the world's largest passenger jetliner (A380) to Singapore Airlines. On December 22, 2014, Qatar Airways accepted delivery of Airbus's newest family of super-efficient aircraft, A350 XWB ("extra wide body").

In this chapter, we explore the reporting and analysis of long-term operating assets. In order to maintain growth in sales, income, and cash flows, capital-intensive companies like Airbus must be diligent in managing long-term operating assets. As is the case with Airbus, many companies have made large investments in innovation. These investments are not always reflected adequately in the balance sheet. Management's choices and accounting rules concerning the reporting of long-term operating assets can have a marked impact on the analysis and interpretation of financial statements.

Sources: www.airbus-group.com; Airbus Group 2013 Annual Report.

CHAPTER ORGANISATION

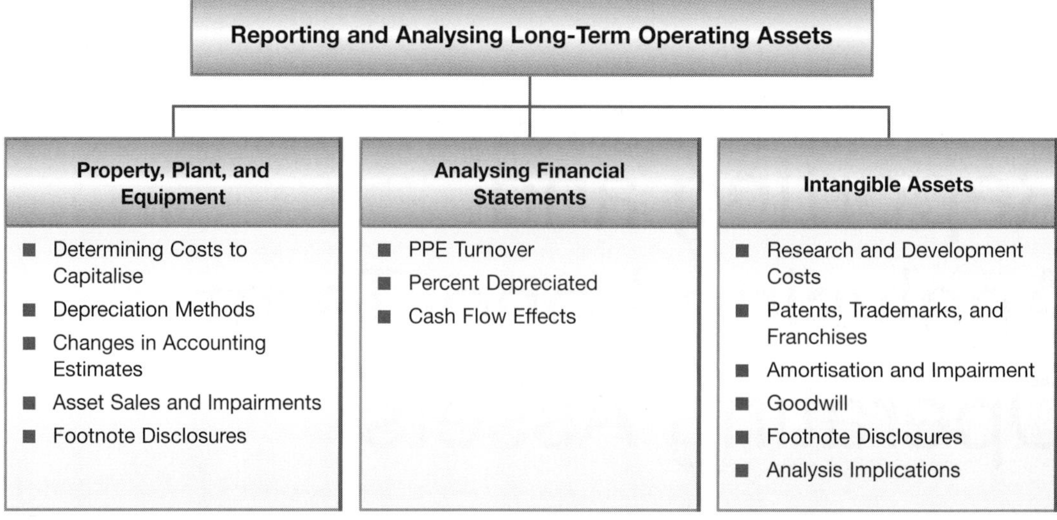

INTRODUCTION

Investments in long-term operating assets often represent the largest component of a company's balance sheet. Effectively managing long-term operating assets is crucial, because these investments affect company performance for several years and are frequently irreversible. To evaluate how well a company is managing operating assets, we need to understand how they are measured and reported.

LO1 Describe and distinguish between tangible and intangible assets.

This chapter describes the accounting, reporting, and analysis of long-term operating assets including tangible and intangible assets. **Tangible assets** are assets that have physical substance. They are frequently included in the balance sheet as *property, plant and equipment*, and include land, buildings, machinery, fixtures, and equipment. **Intangible assets**, such as trademarks and patents, do not have physical substance, but provide the owner with specific rights and privileges.

Long-term operating assets have two common characteristics. First, unlike inventory, these assets are not acquired for resale. Instead, they are necessary to produce and deliver the products and services that generate revenues for the company. Second, these assets help produce revenues for multiple accounting periods. Consequently, accountants focus considerable attention on how they are reported in the balance sheet and how these costs are transferred over time to the income statement as expenses.

To illustrate the size and importance of long-term operating assets, the asset section of Airbus Group's balance sheet is reproduced in Exhibit 8.1. We can see as of the end of Airbus's fiscal year on December 31, 2013, Airbus's net investment in intangible assets and property, plant, and equipment totaled €13,653 million and €15,856 million, respectively. Together, these two categories of assets make up over 60% of Airbus's non-current assets, or 30% of total assets.

This chapter is divided into two main sections. The first section focuses on accounting for tangible property, plant, and equipment and the related depreciation expense that is reported each period in the income statement. The second section examines the measurement and reporting of intangible assets.

PROPERTY, PLANT, AND EQUIPMENT (PPE)

For many companies, the largest category of operating assets is its long-term property, plant, and equipment (PPE) assets. The size and duration of this asset category raises several important questions, including:

- Which costs should be **capitalised** on the balance sheet as assets? Which should be expensed?
- How should capitalised costs be allocated to the accounting periods that benefited from the asset?
- How should asset sales or significant changes in assets' fair value be reported?

This section explains the accounting, reporting, and analysis of PPE assets and related items.

EXHIBIT 8.1 Airbus Group Balance Sheet (assets only)

EADS N.V. (now Airbus Group)
Consolidated Statements of Financial Position (assets only)
at December 31, 2013 and 2012

(in € million)	2013	2012
Assets		
Non-current Assets		
Intangible assets	€13,653	€13,429
Property, plant and equipment	15,856	15,196
Investment property	69	72
Investments in associates accounted for under the equity method	2,902	2,662
Other investments and other long-term financial assets	1,864	2,115
Non-current other financial assets	2,076	1,386
Non-current other assets	1,653	1,415
Deferred tax assets	3,840	4,532
Non-current securities	4,300	5,987
	€46,213	€46,794
Current assets		
Inventories	25,060	23,216
Trade receivables	7,239	6,788
Current portion of other long-term financial assets	181	287
Current other financial assets	1,557	1,448
Current other assets	2,074	2,046
Current tax assets	632	458
Current securities	2,590	2,328
Cash and cash equivalents	7,765	8,756
	47,098	45,327
Total assets	€93,311	€92,121

Determining Costs to Capitalise

LO2 Determine which costs to capitalise and report as assets and which costs to expense.

When a company acquires an asset, it must first decide which portion of the cost should be included among the expenses of the current period and which costs should be capitalised as part of the asset and reported in the balance sheet. Outlays to acquire PPE are called **capital expenditures**. Expenditures that are recorded as an asset must possess each of the following two characteristics:

1. It is probable that the future economic benefits associated with the asset will flow to the entity.
2. The cost of the asset can be measured reliably.

All normal costs incurred to acquire an asset and prepare it for its intended use should be capitalised and reported in the balance sheet. These costs would include the purchase price of the asset plus any of the following: instalation costs, taxes, shipping costs, legal fees, and setup or calibration costs. If owning an asset carries legal obligations at the end of the asset's life (for example, to remove the asset or to perform environmental remediation), the current cost of those obligations should be included in the asset's cost and recognised as a liability (to be discussed in Chapter 9) at the time the asset is acquired. This cost will be included in the subsequent depreciation of the asset.

Determining the specific costs that should be capitalised requires judgement. There are two important considerations to address when deciding which costs to capitalise. First, companies can only capitalise costs that are *directly linked* to future benefits. Incidental costs or costs that would be incurred regardless of whether the asset is purchased should not be capitalised. Second, the costs capitalised as an asset can be no greater than the expected future benefits to be derived from use of the asset. This requirement means that if a company reports a $200 asset, we can reasonably expect that it will derive at least $200 in expected future cash inflows from the use and ultimate disposition of the asset.

Sometimes, companies construct assets for their own use rather than purchasing a similar asset from another company. In this case, all of the costs incurred to construct the asset—including materials, labour, and a reasonable amount of overhead—should be included in the cost that is capitalised. In addition, actual borrowing cost incurred during the construction period is capitalised as part of the asset's cost. This interest is called **capitalised interest**. Capitalising some of a company's borrowing costs as part of the cost of a self-constructed asset reduces interest expense in the current period and increases depreciation expense in future periods when the asset is placed in service.

Once an asset is placed in service, additional costs are often incurred to maintain and improve the asset. Routine repairs and maintenance costs are necessary to realise the full potential benefits of ownership of the asset and should be treated as expenses of the period in which the maintenance is performed. However, if the cost can be considered an *improvement or betterment* of the asset, the cost should be capitalised. An improvement or betterment is an outlay that either enhances the usefulness of the asset or extends the asset's useful life beyond the original expectation.

YOU MAKE THE CALL

You are the Company Accountant Your company has just purchased a plot of land as a building site for an office building. After the purchase, you discover that the building site was once the site of an oil well. Before construction can commence, your company must spend $40,000 to properly cap the oil well and prepare the site to meet current environmental standards. How should you account for the $40,000 cleanup cost? [Answers on page 383]

Depreciation

FYI Depreciation is a systematic allocation of asset cost over the useful life—not a measure of the change in fair value.

Once an asset has been recorded in the balance sheet, the cost must be transferred over time from the balance sheet to the income statement and reported as an expense. The nature of long-term operating assets is that they benefit more than one period. As a consequence, it is impossible to match a specific portion of the cost *directly* to the revenues of a particular period. Accounting principles require that this expense be recognised as equitably as possible over the asset's useful economic life. Therefore, we rely on a *systematic allocation* to assign a portion of the asset's cost to each period benefited. This systematic allocation of cost is called **depreciation**.

The concept of systematic allocation of an asset's cost is important. When depreciation expense is recorded, the reported value of the asset (also called the *book value* or *carrying value*) is reduced. Naturally, it is tempting to infer that the fair value of the asset is lower as a result. However, this reported value does not reflect the fair value of the asset. The fair value of the asset may decline by more or less than the amount of depreciation expense, and can even increase in some periods. Depreciation expense should only be interpreted as an assignment of costs to an accounting period and not a measure of the decline in fair value of the asset.

The amount of cost that is allocated to a given period is recorded as depreciation expense in the income statement with a balancing entry in **accumulated depreciation** in the balance sheet. Accumulated depreciation is a contra-asset account (denoted "XA" in the journal entry). Like all contra-asset accounts, it offsets the balance in the corresponding asset account. To illustrate, assume that Macquarie Company purchases a heavy-duty delivery truck for $100,000 and decides to record $18,000 of depreciation expense in the first year of operation. The following entries would be recorded with a cash outflow reflected in the investing section of the statement of cash flows.

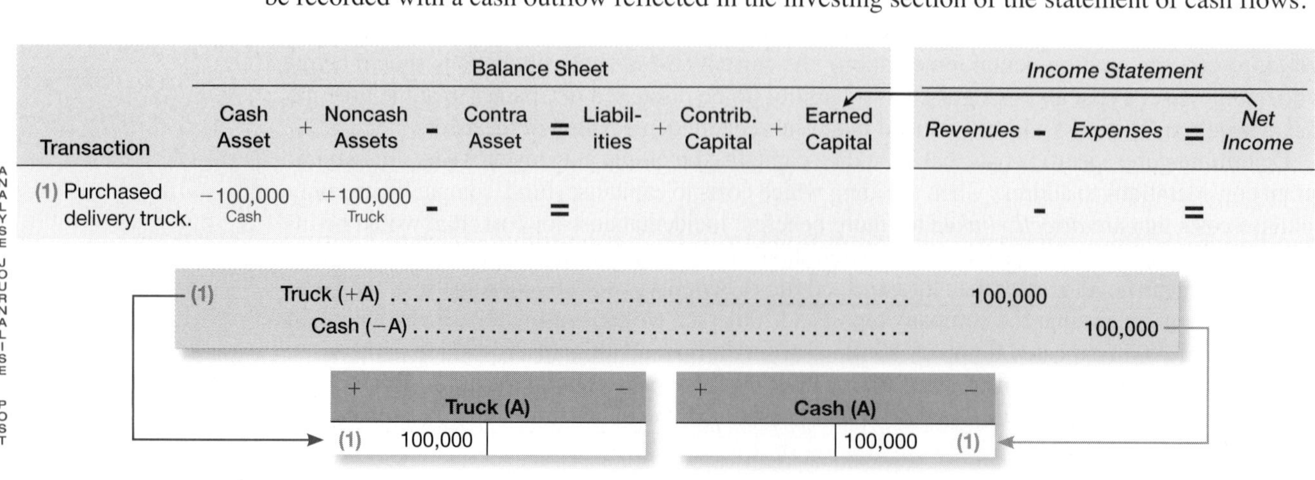

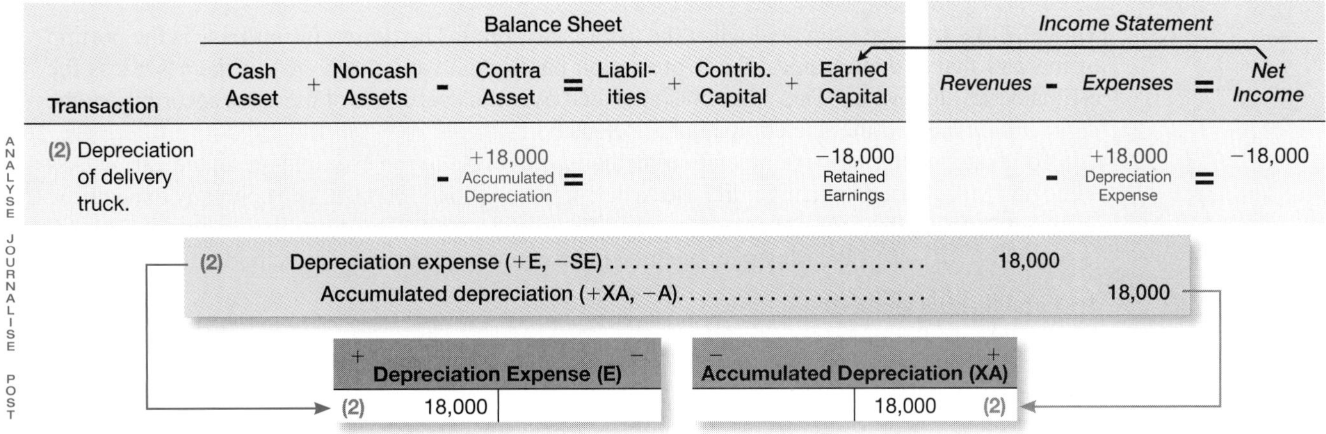

The asset would be presented in the balance sheet at period-end at its net book value.

Delivery truck, at cost	$100,000	
Less accumulated depreciation	18,000	
Delivery truck, net	$ 82,000	(Book Value)

By presenting the information using a contra-asset account, the original acquisition cost of the asset is preserved in the asset account. The balance in the accumulated depreciation account is the sum of the depreciation expense that has been recorded to date. Depreciation expense is included in the income statement as a component of operating income (often included among selling, general, and administrative expenses).[1] The net book value of the asset is presented in the balance sheet and it reflects the acquisition cost less accumulated depreciation and impairment. For example, Airbus Group reports in a note of its 2013 annual report that the original cost of its property, plant and equipment is €32,535 million and the accumulated depreciation and impairment losses as of December 31, 2013, is €16,679 million. The result is a net book value of €15,856 million, as reported on the balance sheet in Exhibit 8.1.

Finally, each significant component of an asset must be depreciated separately. So a company that acquires a building is required to recognise a bundle of assets such as the structure, the roof, the elevators, the electrical system, etc. Each of these components would be depreciated separately over its expected useful life. When a component requires replacement, the cost of replacing the component is capitalised if the recognition criteria are met. The carrying value of the replaced component is removed from the balance sheet.

Depreciation Methods

LO3 Apply different depreciation methods to allocate the cost of assets over time.

Two estimates are required to compute the amount of depreciation expense to record each period.

1. **Useful life**. The useful life is the period of time over which the asset is expected to provide economic benefits to the company. The useful life is not the same as the physical life of the asset. An asset may or may not provide economic benefits to the company for its entire physical life. This useful life should not exceed the period of time that the company intends to use the asset. For example, if a company has a policy of replacing automobiles every two years, the useful life should be set at no longer than two years, even if the automobiles physically last three years or more.
2. **Residual (or salvage) value**. The residual value is the expected realisable value of the asset at the end of its useful life. This value may be the disposal or scrap value, or it may be an estimated resale value for a used asset.

[1] As discussed in Chapter 7, manufacturing-related depreciation, such as that on factory machinery, is capitalised in the work-in-process inventory account. It will flow to finished goods inventory when the products are completed, and to the income statement as cost of sales when the finished products are sold.

These factors must be estimated when the asset is acquired. The **depreciation base** is the portion of the cost that is depreciated. The depreciation base is the capitalised cost of the asset less the estimated residual value. This amount is allocated over the useful life of the asset according to the *depreciation method* that the company has selected.

To illustrate alternative depreciation methods, we return to the example presented earlier. Assume that Macquarie Company purchases a delivery truck for $100,000. The company expects the truck to last five years and estimates a residual value of $10,000. The depreciation base is $90,000 ($100,000 – $10,000). We illustrate the three most common depreciation methods:

1. Straight-line method
2. Double-declining-balance method
3. Units-of-production method

Straight-Line Method Under the **straight-line method**, depreciation expense is recorded evenly over the useful life of the asset. That is, the same amount of depreciation expense is recorded each year. The **depreciation rate** is equal to one divided by the useful life. In our example, 1/5 = 0.2 or 20% per year. The depreciation base and depreciation rate follow.

Depreciation Base	Depreciation Rate
Cost − Salvage value = $100,000 − $10,000 = $90,000	1/Estimated useful life = 1/5 years = 20%

Depreciation expense per year for this asset is $18,000, computed as $90,000 × 20%. For the asset's first full year of usage, $18,000 of depreciation expense is reported in the income statement. At the end of that first year the asset is reported on the balance sheet as shown on the preceding page.

Accumulated depreciation is the sum of all depreciation expense that has been recorded to date. The asset **book value (BV)**, or *net book value* or *carrying value,* is cost less accumulated depreciation. Although the word "value" is used here, it does not refer to fair value. Depreciation is a cost allocation concept (transfer of costs from the balance sheet to the income statement), not a valuation concept.

In the second year of usage, another $18,000 of depreciation expense is recorded in the income statement and the net book value of the asset on the balance sheet follows:

Truck, at cost	$100,000
Less accumulated depreciation	36,000
Truck, net	$ 64,000

Accumulated depreciation now includes the sum of the first and second years' depreciation ($36,000), and the net book value of the asset is now reduced to $64,000. After the fifth year, a total of $90,000 of accumulated depreciation will be recorded, yielding a net book value for the truck of $10,000, its estimated salvage value.

Double-Declining-Balance Method IFRS allows companies to use **accelerated depreciation** methods. Accelerated depreciation methods record more depreciation expense in the early years of an asset's useful life and less expense in the later years. The total depreciation expense recorded *over the entire useful life* of the asset is the same as with straight-line depreciation. The only difference is in the amount of depreciation recorded for *any given year*.

The **double-declining-balance (DDB) method** is an accelerated depreciation method that computes the depreciation rate as twice the straight-line rate. This double rate is then multiplied by the net book value of the asset, which declines each period as accumulated depreciation increases. For Macquarie Company, the depreciation base and the depreciation rate are computed as follows:

Depreciation Base	Depreciation Rate
Net Book Value = Cost − Accumulated Depreciation	2 × SL rate = 2 × 20% = 40%

The depreciation expense for the first year of usage for this asset is $40,000, computed as $100,000 × 40%. At the end of the first full year, $40,000 of depreciation expense is reported on the income statement (compared with $18,000 under the SL method), and the asset is reported on the balance sheet as follows:

Truck, at cost	$100,000
Less accumulated depreciation	40,000
Truck, net	$ 60,000

FYI When calculating DDB depreciation, the depreciation rate is multiplied by the book value; residual value is not subtracted from book value.

In the second year, $24,000 ($60,000 × 40%) of depreciation expense is reported in the income statement and the net book value of the asset on the balance sheet follows:

Truck, at cost	$100,000
Less accumulated depreciation	64,000
Truck, net	$ 36,000

The double-declining-balance method continues to record depreciation expense in this manner until the salvage amount is reached, at which point the depreciation process is discontinued. This leaves a net book value equal to the salvage value as with the straight-line method. The DDB depreciation schedule for the life of this asset is illustrated in Exhibit 8.2.

EXHIBIT 8.2 Double-Declining-Balance Depreciation Schedule

Year	Book Value at Beginning of Year	Depreciation Expense	Book Value at End of Year
1	$100,000	100,000 × 40% = $40,000	$60,000
2	60,000	60,000 × 40% = 24,000	36,000
3	36,000	36,000 × 40% = 14,400	21,600
4	21,600	21,600 × 40% = 8,640	12,960
5	12,960	12,960 − 10,000 = 2,960*	10,000

*The depreciation expense in the fifth year is not calculated as 40% × $12,960 because the resulting depreciation would reduce the net book value below the $10,000 residual value. Instead, the residual value ($10,000) is subtracted from the remaining book value ($12,960), resulting in depreciation expense of $2,960.

Exhibit 8.3 compares the depreciation expense and net book value for both the SL and DDB methods. During the first two years, the DDB method yields higher depreciation expense in comparison with the SL method. Beginning in the third year, this pattern reverses and the SL method produces higher depreciation expense. Over the asset's life, the same $90,000 in total depreciation expense is recorded, leaving a residual value of $10,000 on the balance sheet under both methods.

EXHIBIT 8.3 Comparison of Straight-Line and Double-Declining-Balance Depreciation

	Straight-Line		Double-Declining-Balance	
Year	Depreciation Expense	Book Value at End of Year	Depreciation Expense	Book Value at End of Year
1	$18,000	$82,000	$40,000	$60,000
2	18,000	64,000	24,000	36,000
3	18,000	46,000	14,400	21,600
4	18,000	28,000	8,640	12,960
5	18,000	10,000	2,960	10,000
	$90,000		$90,000	

All depreciation methods yield the same salvage value

Total depreciation over asset life is identical for all methods

Units-of-Production Method Under the **units-of-production method**, the useful life of the asset is defined in terms of the number of units of service provided by the asset. For instance, this could be the number of units produced, the number of hours that a machine is operated, or, as with Macquarie Company's delivery truck, the number of miles driven. To illustrate, assume that Macquarie Company estimates that the delivery truck will provide 150,000 miles of service before it is sold for its residual value of $10,000. The depreciation rate is expressed in terms of a cost per mile driven, computed as follows:

$$\frac{\$100{,}000 - \$10{,}000}{150{,}000 \text{ miles}} = \$0.60 \text{ per mile}$$

If the delivery truck is driven 35,000 miles in year 1, the depreciation expense for that year would be $21,000 (35,000 × $0.60). This method produces an amount of depreciation that varies from year to year as the use of the asset varies.

The units-of-production method is used by companies with natural resources such as oil reserves, mineral deposits, or timberlands. These assets are often referred to as **wasting assets**, because the asset is consumed as it is used. The acquisition cost of a natural resource, plus any costs incurred to prepare the asset for its intended use, should be capitalised and reported among PPE assets in the balance sheet.

When the natural resource is used or extracted, inventory is created. The cost of the resource is transferred from the long-term asset account into inventory and, once the inventory is sold, to the income statement as cost of goods sold. The process of transferring costs from the resource account into inventory is called **depletion**.

Depletion is very much like depreciation of tangible operating assets, except that the amount of depletion recorded each period should reflect the amount of the resource that was actually extracted or used up during that period. As a result, depletion is usually calculated using the units-of-production method. The depletion rate is calculated as follows:

$$\textbf{Depletion rate per unit consumed} = \frac{\textbf{Acquisition cost} - \textbf{Residual value}}{\textbf{Estimated quantity of resource available}}$$

The calculation requires an estimate of the quantity of the resource available, which usually requires the assistance of experts, such as geologists or engineers, who are trained to make these determinations.

Depreciation for Tax Purposes Most companies use the straight-line method for financial reporting purposes and an accelerated depreciation method for tax returns. Governments allow accelerated depreciation, in part, to provide incentives for taxpayers to invest. As a result of the differing depreciation methods used for financial accounting and tax purposes, lower depreciation expense (and higher income) is reported for financial accounting purposes early in the life of an asset relative to tax purposes. Even though this difference reverses in later years, companies prefer to defer the tax payments so that the cash savings can be invested to produce earnings. Further, even with the reversal in the later years of an asset's life, if total depreciable assets are growing at a fast enough rate, the additional first-year depreciation on newly acquired assets more than offsets the lower depreciation expense on older assets, yielding a continuing deferral of taxable income and taxes paid. There are other differences between financial reporting and tax reporting that create issues in determining a company's tax expense. In Chapter 10, we explore these differences further and examine deferred tax liabilities and deferred tax assets.

Changes in Accounting Estimates

The estimates required in the depreciation process are made when the asset is acquired. When necessary, companies can, and do, change these estimates during the useful lives of assets. When either the useful life or residual value estimates change, the change is applied prospectively. That is, companies use the new estimates from the date of the change going forward and do not restate the financial statements of prior periods.

To illustrate, assume that, after three years of straight-line depreciation, Macquarie Company decided to extend the useful life of its truck from 5 years to 6 years. From Exhibit 8.3, the book value of the delivery truck at the end of the third year is \$46,000. The change in estimated useful life would not require a formal accounting entry. Instead, depreciation expense would be recalculated for the remaining three years of the truck's useful life:

$$\frac{\$46{,}000 - \$10{,}000}{3 \text{ years}} = \$12{,}000 \text{ per year}$$

Thus, beginning in year four, depreciation expense of \$12,000 (instead of \$18,000) would be recorded each year.

BUSINESS INSIGHT

Investor Beware During fiscal year 2014, the German airline Lufthansa increased the useful life of its aircrafts by eight years, leading to a €340 million positive accounting effect. Lufthansa, the world's largest airline by revenue, indicated that the change would put its depreciation policy in line with industry practice. While Lufthansa has a legitimate reason to revise its depreciation assumption, investors should discount any improvement in profit attributed to this one-time accounting change.

Asset Sales and Impairments

This section discusses gains and losses from asset sales and computation and disclosure of asset impairments.

LO4 Determine the effects of asset sales and impairments on financial statements.

Gains and Losses on Asset Sales

The gain or loss on the sale (disposition) of a long-term asset is computed as follows:

Gain or loss on asset sale = Proceeds from sale – Book value of asset sold

The book (carrying) value of an asset is its acquisition cost less accumulated depreciation. When an asset is sold, its acquisition cost and related accumulated depreciation are removed from the balance sheet and any gain or loss is reported in income from continuing operations. To illustrate such a transaction, assume that Macquarie Company decided to sell the delivery truck after four years of straight-line depreciation. From Exhibit 8.3, we know that the book value of the truck is \$28,000 (\$100,000 − \$72,000). If the truck is sold for \$30,000, the entry to record the sale follows.

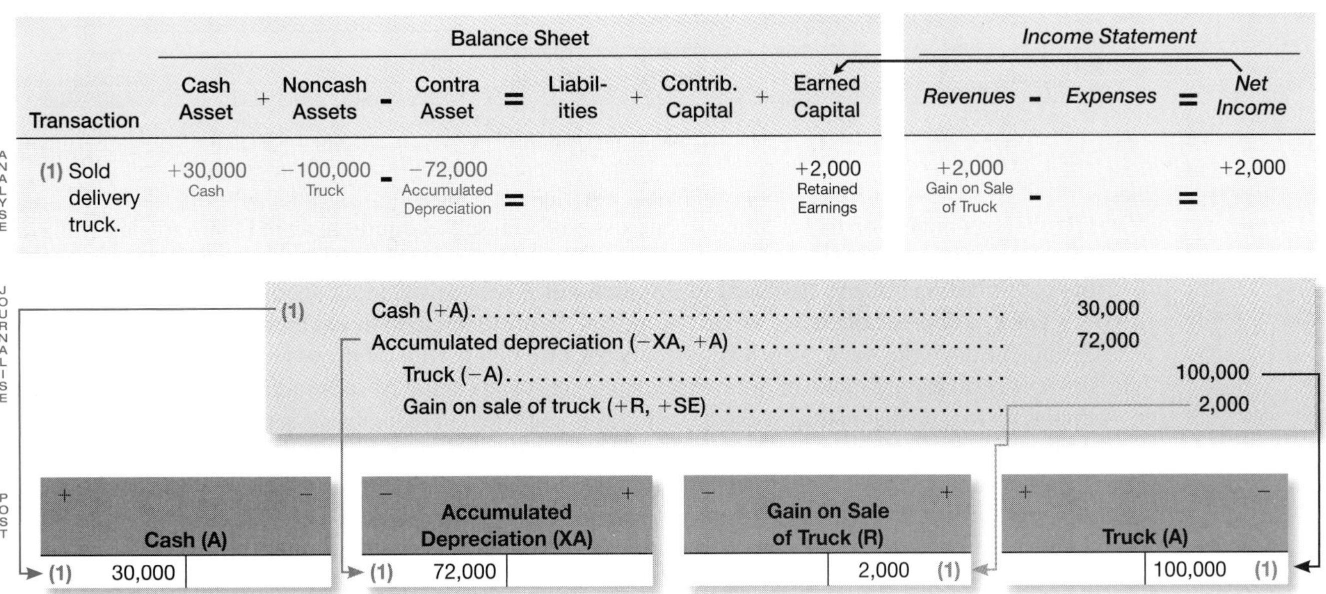

	Balance Sheet							Income Statement		
Transaction	Cash Asset	+ Noncash Assets	− Contra Asset	= Liabilities	+ Contrib. Capital	+ Earned Capital		Revenues	− Expenses	= Net Income
(1) Sold delivery truck.	+30,000 Cash	−100,000 Truck	−72,000 Accumulated Depreciation	=		+2,000 Retained Earnings		+2,000 Gain on Sale of Truck	−	= +2,000

		Dr.	Cr.
(1)	Cash (+A)	30,000	
	Accumulated depreciation (−XA, +A)	72,000	
	Truck (−A)		100,000
	Gain on sale of truck (+R, +SE)		2,000

+ Cash (A) −		− Accumulated Depreciation (XA) +		− Gain on Sale of Truck (R) +		+ Truck (A) −	
(1) 30,000		(1) 72,000			2,000 (1)		100,000 (1)

Gains and losses on asset sales can be large, and analysts must be aware of these nonrecurring operating income components. Further, if the gains are deemed immaterial, companies often include such gains and losses in general line items of the income statement—often as a component of selling, general and administrative expenses. As described in Chapter 4, the $30,000 increase in cash is an investing cash inflow in the statement of cash flows, and the $2,000 gain would be subtracted from net income in an indirect-method statement of cash flows from operating activities.

Asset Impairments Property, plant, and equipment (PPE) assets are reported at their net book values (original cost less accumulated depreciation and impairment). This is the case even if the values of these assets increase subsequent to acquisition. As a result, there can be unrecognised gains hidden in the balance sheet.

However, if the values of PPE assets subsequently decrease—and it can be determined that the asset value is permanently impaired—then companies must recognise impairment losses on those PPE assets. In particular, an asset is subject to an **impairment** test if there is an indication that it may be impaired. Indicators of impairment include a decline in market value; an adverse change in technology, markets, economy, or regulations; the asset is obsolete, damaged, idle, part of restructuring, or held for disposal; etc. If there is a sign that the asset may be impaired, a formal impairment test is conducted by comparing the carrying value (or net book value) of the asset with its **recoverable amount**. Recoverable amount is the higher of the asset's fair value less costs of disposal (the so called "net selling price") or its **value in use** (computed as the present value of expected future cash flows). If the carrying value is lower than the recoverable amount, no impairment is deemed to exist. However, if the carrying value is higher, the asset is deemed impaired and it is written down to its recoverable amount. If necessary, the depreciation assumptions on the impaired asset should be reviewed and adjusted. Exhibit 8.4 depicts this impairment analysis.

When a company records an impairment charge, assets are reduced by the amount of the write-down and the loss is recognised in the income statement, which reduces current period income. These effects are illustrated in Exhibit 8.5. Impairment charges are sometimes included as part of **restructuring costs** along with future costs of workforce reductions. The entry in Exhibit 8.5 reduces net income, but does not affect current cash flows, so the impairment charges would be added back to net income when reporting an indirect-method cash flows from operating activities. Managers often refer to impairment charges as "noncash" items, though it may be important to remember that they did involve cash when the asset was originally acquired.

EXHIBIT 8.5 Financial Statement Effects of Asset Impairment

Balance Sheet										Income Statement				
Cash Asset	+	Noncash Assets	=	Liabil-ities	+	Contrib. Capital	+	Earned Capital		*Revenues*	-	*Expenses*	=	*Net Income*
		Decrease	=					Decrease			-	Increase	=	Decrease

If there is an indication that an impairment loss has been subsequently reversed, the carrying value of the asset is increased to its recoverable amount, but not to exceed what it would have been without the prior impairment. **Reversal of impairment** is recognised in the income statement.

Once a depreciable asset is written down, future depreciation charges are reduced by the amount of the writedown. This result occurs because that portion of the asset's cost that is written down is permanently removed from the balance sheet and cannot be subsequently depreciated. It is important to note that management determines if and when to recognise asset impairments. Write-downs of long-term assets are often recognised in connection with a restructuring programme.

Analysis of asset write-downs presents two potential challenges:

EXHIBIT 8.4 Impairment Analysis of Long-Term Assets

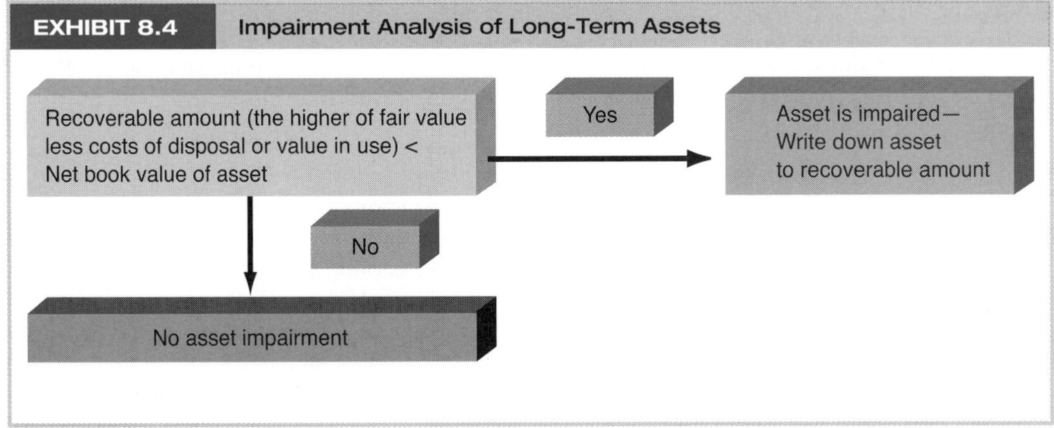

1. *Insufficient write-down*. Assets sometimes are impaired to a larger degree than is recognised. This situation can arise if management is overly optimistic about future prospects or is reluctant to recognise the full loss in income. Underestimation of an impairment causes current income to be overstated and income in future years to be lower.
2. *Aggressive write-down*. This *big bath* scenario can arise if income is currently and severely depressed. Management's view is that the market will not penalise the firm for an extra write-off, and that doing so purges the balance sheet of costs that would otherwise reduce future years' income. This leads to income being overstated for several years after the write-down.

Neither of these cases is condoned under IFRS. Yet, because management is estimating future cash flows for the impairment test and such estimates are difficult to verify, it has some degree of latitude over the timing and amount of the write-off and can use that discretion to manage reported income.

BUSINESS INSIGHT

Asset Writedown at Maersk In July 2014, Maersk Oil, a division of the Danish **A.P. Moller-Maersk Group**, wrote off $1.7 billion of its $2.4 billion investment in three oilfields in Brazil. The company indicated that the writedown was due to the lower than expected amount of oil reserves in the fields and the decline in oil price since it had invested in the oilfields three years ago.

Revaluation Model

The accounting method we discussed above is called the "cost model." Under the cost model, PPE assets are carried at their original cost minus accumulated depreciation and impairment. Companies can also use the "revaluation model" to account for PPE. Under the revaluation model, a PPE asset is reported on a revalued basis, which is its fair value at the date of revaluation minus subsequent depreciation and impairment. If an asset is revalued, the entire class of assets to which that asset belongs is also revalued.

If a revaluation results in an increase in the carrying value of an asset, the "gain" is included in other comprehensive income, and accumulated in equity under the heading "revaluation surplus." However, if the increase represents the reversal of a revaluation decrease of the same asset previously recognised in net income, the gain is recognised in net income. If the revaluation results in a decrease in the asset's carrying value, the "loss" is first used to offset any balance in the revaluation surplus account associated with the asset, with the remaining loss being recognised in net income. When a revalued asset is disposed of, any revaluation surplus is either transferred directly to retained earnings or left in the revaluation surplus.

Footnote Disclosure

Airbus Group provides the following information in note 2 (Summary of Significant Accounting Policies) of its 2013 Annual Report to describe its accounting for PPE assets.

Property, Plant and Equipment—Property, plant and equipment is valued at acquisition or manufacturing costs less accumulated depreciation and impairment losses. Such costs include the estimated cost of replacing, servicing and restoring part of such property, plant and equipment. Items of property, plant and equipment are generally depreciated on a straight-line basis . . .

The following useful lives are assumed: buildings 10 to 50 years; site improvements 6 to 30 years; technical equipment and machinery 3 to 20 years; and other equipment, factory and office equipment 2 to 10 years. The useful lives, depreciation methods and residual values applying to property, plant and equipment are reviewed at least annually and in case they change significantly, depreciation charges for current and future periods are adjusted accordingly.

If the carrying amount of an asset exceeds its recoverable amount an impairment loss is recognised immediately in profit or loss. At each end of the reporting period, it is assessed whether there is any indication that an item of property, plant and equipment may be impaired . . .

Property, plant and equipment is derecognised when it has been disposed of or when the asset is permanently withdrawn from use. The difference between the net disposal proceeds and the carrying amount of such assets is recognised in the Consolidated Income Statement in the period of derecognition.

The note details Airbus's depreciation method (straight-line), the estimated useful lives of various classes of PPE assets, test for impairment, and accounting for the disposal of PPE assets. It also indicates that Airbus uses the cost model, instead of revaluation model, to account for its PPE assets.

RESEARCH INSIGHT

Recent research provides evidence that while IFRS provides a free choice between fair value and historical cost for non-financial assets, most companies using IFRS commit to historical cost accounting for plant and equipment. The evidence is consistent with market demands leading managers to utilise historical cost when the reliability of fair value is lower and when costs of estimating fair value are higher. (Source: Christensen, Hans B., and Valeri V. Nikolaev, "Does fair value accounting for non-financial assets pass the market test?" Review of Accounting Studies, September 2013.)

ANALYSING FINANCIAL STATEMENTS

Most companies produce their financial performance with their long-term operating assets like property, plant and equipment and with their intellectual property. Effective use of these assets represents one of the key components of success for companies. In addition, these assets are acquired with the anticipation that they will provide benefits for an extended period of time. They are often expensive relative to their annual benefit, and most of these assets require replenishment on an ongoing basis.

Analysis Objective

We are trying to gauge the effectiveness of Airbus Group's use of its physical productive assets.

Analysis Tool PPE Turnover (PPET)

$$\textbf{PPE Turnover (PPET)} = \frac{\textbf{Sales revenue}}{\textbf{Average PPE, net}}$$

Applying the PPE Turnover ratio to Airbus Group

$$2013 \quad \frac{59{,}256}{(15{,}856 + 15{,}196)/2} = 3.82$$

$$2012 \quad \frac{56{,}480}{(15{,}196 + 14{,}146)/2} = 3.85$$

$$2011 \quad \frac{49{,}128}{(14{,}146 + 13{,}427)/2} = 3.56$$

Guidance Property, plant & equipment turnovers vary greatly by industry and are affected by companies' manufacturing strategies, so it is difficult to give specific guidance. In general, a higher ratio is preferred, as it is one significant component of the company's return on assets.

Airbus Group in Context

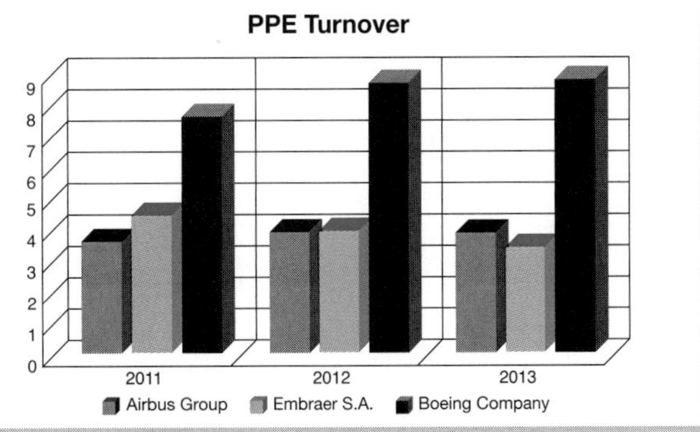

Takeaways Companies prefer that PPET be higher rather than lower, because a higher PPET implies a lower level of capital investment is required to achieve a given level of sales revenue. Airbus improved its PPET from 3.56 in 2011 to over 3.80 in both 2012 and 2013. In comparison, Airbus's PPET was lower than Embraer, a Brazilian aerospace company, in 2011 and 2012, but it surpassed Embraer in 2013. However, Embraer is less than one-tenth the size of Airbus. Boeing is more comparable to Airbus in terms of size and product offerings, but Boeing follows U.S. GAAP. Boeing reported a higher PPET than both Airbus and Embraer over the 2011–2013 period. Like Airbus, Boeing also experienced an upward trend in PPET over those three years. The difference in accounting methods (U.S. GAAP versus IFRS) may partly explain Boeing's high PPET.

Other Considerations Besides effectiveness of asset usage, PPET depends on a number of factors that affect the denominator and that should be taken into account in interpreting the numbers. First, it reflects the company's manufacturing strategy; a company that outsources its production will have a very high PPET. Or, a company that has assets that are more fully depreciated will also report a high PPET. In Chapter 12, we discuss how ratios mixing income statement and balance sheet information can be affected by acquisitions of other companies. Finally, we find in Chapter 10 that there are (at the time of this writing) ways for a company to acquire the use of productive resources that do not appear among its assets, increasing the ratio.

Analysis Objective

We are trying to gauge the age of Airbus Group's long-term tangible operating assets relative to their expected useful lives. Companies that have recently invested in the latest technology have a lower ratio, while those with a high ratio may be approaching a time when substantial capital investments need to be made.

Analysis Tool Percent Depreciated

$$\textbf{Percent depreciated} = \frac{\textbf{Accumulated depreciation}}{\textbf{Cost of depreciable assets}}$$

Applying the Percent Depreciated Ratio to Airbus Group Accumulated depreciation can be seen in the balance sheet or footnotes and the original cost of depreciable assets can be found in the same places (Airbus presented them in the footnote). Two types of PPE assets are not depreciated. First, land is not depreciated because it has an indefinite life. Second, construction in progress is not depreciated until the constructed asset is placed in service. For Airbus, the €32,535 million original cost of PPE assets includes €2,350 million for construction in progress and an unknown amount of land. Hence, we can only remove the €2,350 million of construction in progress from the denominator. While the percent depreciated ratio will be understated, the bias should be small. (The original cost of land is not separately disclosed, indicating that it is immaterial.)

$$2013 \quad \frac{16{,}679}{(32{,}535 - 2{,}350)} = 55.3\%$$

$$2012 \quad \frac{15{,}926}{(31{,}122 - 3{,}441)} = 57.5\%$$

$$2011 \quad \frac{14{,}167}{(28{,}313 - 3{,}011)} = 56.0\%$$

Guidance Percent depreciated depends on a company's age and on the occurrence of disruptive technological shifts in products and production methods. A new company will have a lower ratio, as will a company that has just made substantial investments in new productive facilities. A high ratio could mean that a company's productive resources are nearing the end of their useful lives and that substantial investments will be required in the near future.

Airbus Group in Context

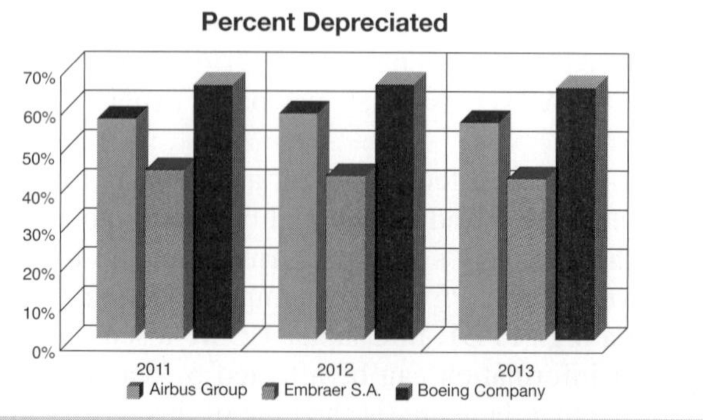

Takeaways Both Airbus and Embraer were formed in the late 1960s, while Boeing launched its commercial jet business in 1958. All three are mature companies experiencing long-term steady growth. They acquire assets on a continuing basis and, as a result, they have some assets that are brand new and others that are reaching the end of their productive lives. Over the 2011–2013 period, Boeing's percent depreciated ratio was approximately 65%, while that of Airbus was slightly above 55%. In contrast, Embraer's ratio was close to 40%, suggesting that it has newer PPE assets than Airbus and Embraer. The higher ratio for Boeing indicates that it may need new investment in PPE soon.

Other Considerations Companies' percent depreciated ratio may differ because they are using different depreciation methods (straight-line or accelerated) or because they have chosen different useful lives for their assets. For instance, one airline depreciates its aircraft over twenty-five years to zero salvage value, while another depreciates its aircraft over fifteen years to ten percent salvage. A percent depreciated ratio of 50% for the first company would mean its average aircraft is 12.5 years old, while the same 50% ratio would imply aircraft that was 8.3 years old for the second company. As a result, it is always advisable to cheque companies' footnotes to insure that the ratios are interpreted correctly.

BUSINESS INSIGHT

Federal authorities in the United States arrested **WorldCom, Inc.**'s CEO, Bernie Ebbers, and chief financial officer, Scott Sullivan, in August 2002 for allegedly conspiring to alter the telecommunications giant's financial statements to meet analyst expectations. They were accused of *cooking the books* so the company would not show a loss for 2001 and subsequent quarters.

Specifically, WorldCom incurred large costs in anticipation of an increase in Internet-related business that did not materialise. The executives shifted these costs to the balance sheet and recorded them as PPE, thereby inflating current profitability. By capitalising these costs (moving them from the income statement to the balance sheet), WorldCom was able to disguise these costs as an asset to be allocated as future costs. Contrary to WorldCom's usual practices and prevailing accounting principles, no support existed for capitalisation.

Although the WorldCom case also involved alleged fraud, an astute analyst would have suspected something was amiss from analysis of WorldCom's long-term asset turnover (Sales/Average long-term assets) as shown below. The decline in turnover reveals that its assets constituted an ever-increasing percent of total sales during 1995 to 2002, by quarter. This finding does not, in itself, imply fraud. It does, however, raise serious questions that should have been answered by WorldCom executives in meetings with analysts.

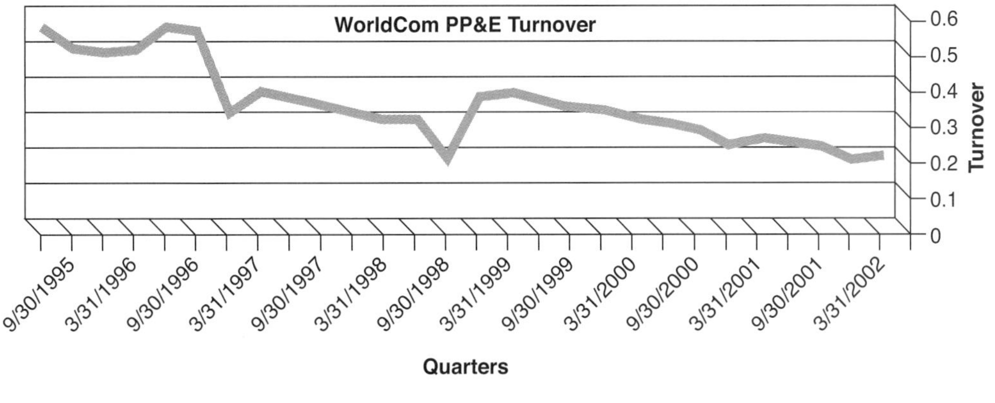

Cash Flow Effects

When cash is involved in the acquisition of plant or equipment, the cash amount is reported as a use of cash in the investment section of the statement of cash flows as discussed in Chapter 4. Any cash received from asset sales is reported as a source of cash. The investing section of Airbus Group's 2013 annual report is shown below.

(In € million)	2013	2012	2011
Investments:			
Purchases of intangible assets, property, plant and equipment.	€(2,949)	€(3,270)	€ (2,197)
Proceeds from disposals of, intangible assets, Property, plant and equipment	60	73	79
Acquisitions of subsidiaries, joint ventures, businesses and non-controlling interests (net of cash)	(16)	(201)	(1,535)
Proceeds from disposals of subsidiaries (net of cash)	0	0	18
Payments for investments in associates, other investments and other long-term financial assets	(292)	(328)	(312)
Proceeds from disposals of associates, other investments and other long-term financial assets	157	232	77
Dividends paid by companies valued at equity.	52	46	50
Payments for investments in securities	(1,401)	(3,237)	(11,091)
Proceeds from disposals of securities.	2,673	6,659	10,713
Change in cash from changes in consolidation.	(26)	0	0
Cash (used for) investing activities.	€(1,742)	€ (26)	€ (4,198)

In 2013, Airbus paid cash of €2,949 million to acquire intangible and PPE assets, and received cash of €60 million on the disposal of intangible assets and PPE. Losses (gains) on these disposal transactions are added (subtracted) as adjustments in the operating section, since the company used the indirect method to present cash flows from operations. Acquisitions and disposals of other companies, as well as purchases and sales of securities, made up the rest of the company's investing activities (to be discussed in Chapter 12).

For the Macquarie Company delivery truck sale described earlier in this chapter, the investing section of the cash flow statement would show $30,000 of cash proceeds. The gain on the sale would be subtracted from net income in the operating section. No receivable was involved in the sale.

YOU MAKE THE CALL

You are the Division Manager You are the division manager for a main operating division of your company. You are concerned that a declining PPE turnover is adversely affecting your division's profitability. What specific actions can you take to increase PPE turnover? [Answers on page 383]

MID-CHAPTER REVIEW

On January 2, Yonge Company purchases equipment for use in fabrication of a part for one of its key products. The equipment costs $95,000, and its estimated useful life is five years, after which it is expected to be sold for $10,000.

Required

1. Compute depreciation expense for each year of the equipment's useful life for each of the following depreciation methods:
   a. Straight-line
   b. Double-declining-balance
2. Assume that Yonge Company uses the straight-line depreciation method. Show the effects of these entries on the balance sheet and the income statement using the financial statement effects template. Prepare journal entries to record the initial purchase of the equipment on January 2 and the year-end depreciation adjustment on December 31, and post the journal entries to T-accounts.
3. Show how the equipment is reported on Yonge's balance sheet at the end of the third year assuming straight-line depreciation.
4. Assume that this is the only depreciable asset the company owns and that it uses straight-line depreciation. Using the depreciation expense computed in 1*a* and the balance sheet presentation from *3*, estimate the percent depreciated for this asset at the end of the third year.

The solution to this review problem can be found on pages 394–395.

INTANGIBLE ASSETS

LO5 Describe the accounting and reporting for intangible assets.

Intangible assets are assets that lack physical substance but provide future benefits to the owner in the form of specific property rights or legal rights. For many companies, these assets have become an important source of competitive advantage and company value.

For financial accounting purposes, intangible assets are classified as either identifiable or not identifiable (i.e., goodwill). An intangible asset is identifiable if it is separable or it arises from contractual or other legal rights. Customer lists, unpatented technologies, formulas, processes, and databases are all examples of intangible assets that are separable from a company and can be sold, transferred, or exchanged. Intangible assets that are the product of contractual or other legal rights include patents, trademarks, copyrights, franchises, licence agreements, broadcast rights, mineral rights, and noncompetition agreements. Goodwill, which cannot be separately transferred and therefore not identifiable, is discussed later in this chapter. Airbus Group reports €13,653 million of intangible assets on its 2013 balance sheet. The corresponding note for intangible assets indicates three main categories of intangibles (€ in millions): Goodwill €10,962; Capitalised development costs €1,626; and Other €1,065.

The issues involved in reporting intangible assets are conceptually similar to those of accounting for property, plant and equipment. We must first decide which costs to capitalise and then we need to determine how and when those costs will be transferred to the income statement. However, intangible assets often pose a particularly difficult problem for accountants. This problem arises because the benefits provided by these assets are often uncertain and difficult to quantify. In addition, the useful life of an intangible asset is often impossible to estimate with confidence.

As was the case with property, plant and equipment, intangible assets are either purchased from another individual or company or internally developed. Like PPE assets, the cost of purchased intangible assets is capitalised. Unlike PPE assets, though, we generally do not capitalise the cost of internally developed intangible assets. Research and advertising costs, and the patents and brands that are created as a result, serve as useful examples.

Research and Development Costs

R&D activities are a major expenditure for most companies, especially for those in technology and pharmaceutical industries where R&D expenses can exceed 10% of revenues. These expenses include employment costs for R&D personnel, R&D-related contract services, and R&D plant asset costs.

Companies invest millions of dollars in R&D because they expect that the future benefits resulting from these activities will eventually exceed the costs. Successful R&D activities create new products that can be sold and new technologies that can be utilised to create and sustain a competitive advantage. Unfortunately, only a fraction of R&D projects reach commercial production, and it is difficult to predict which projects will be successful. Moreover, it is often difficult to predict when the benefits will be realised, even if the project is successful.

Because of the uncertainty surrounding the benefits of R&D, research and some development costs are immediately recognised as an expense, as described in Chapter 7. Development costs are capitalised only after the intangible asset created from the R&D activities has reached technical and commercial feasibility. In particular, the company must be able to demonstrate that it has the intention and the resources to complete the intangible asset and that the intangible asset will generate future economic benefits through use or sale. If the research phase of a project cannot be distinguished from the development phase, the entire costs for that project are treated as if they were incurred in the research phase only. In general, R&D costs include the salaries and wages of personnel engaged in R&D activities, the cost of materials and supplies, and the equipment and facilities used in the project. Should any of the R&D activities prove successful, the benefits should result in higher net income in future periods. Similarly, software development costs (whether for use or sale) are expensed until the technological feasibility of the product is established.

If equipment and facilities are purchased for a specific R&D project, and have no other use, their cost is expensed immediately even though their useful life would typically extend beyond the current period. The expensing of R&D equipment and facilities is in stark contrast to the capitalisation-and-depreciation of non-R&D plant assets. The expensing of R&D plant assets is mandated unless those assets have alternative future uses (in other R&D projects or otherwise). For example, a general research facility housing multi-use lab equipment should be capitalised and depreciated like any other depreciable asset. However, project-directed research buildings and equipment with no alternate uses must be expensed.

BUSINESS INSIGHT

Accounting for Development Costs at Airbus Group In its 2013 annual report, Airbus discloses that it started capitalising development costs for the A350 XWB programme in 2012, when the first aircraft entered the final assembly line. In other words, the company considered the A350 XWB programme technically and commercially feasible at that point.

> The Group has capitalised development costs in the amount of €1,626 million as of 31 December 2013 (€1,365 million as of 31 December 2012) as internally generated intangible assets mainly for the Airbus A380 and A350 XWB programme... Capitalisation for development costs of the A350 XWB programme started in the second quarter 2012 when the first aircraft entered the final assembly line. Since 1 April 2012, a total amount of €720 million was capitalised.

Patents

Successful research and development activity often leads a company to obtain a **patent** for its discoveries. A patent is an exclusive right to produce a product or use a technology. Patents are granted to protect the inventor of the new product or technology by preventing other companies from copying the innovation. The fair value of a patent depends on the commercial success of the product or technology. For example, a patent on the formula for a new drug to treat diabetes could be worth billions of dollars.

If a patent is purchased from the inventor, the purchase price is capitalised and reported in the balance sheet as an intangible asset. On the other hand, if the patent is developed internally, only the legal costs, registration fees, and development costs incurred after the product or technology has reached technical and commercial feasibility are capitalised. The research and development costs incurred before technological feasibility are expensed. This accounting illustrates the marked difference between purchased and internally created intangible assets.

Copyrights

A copyright is an exclusive right granted by a jurisdiction to an individual author, composer, play writer, or similar individual for the life of the creator plus either 50 or 70 years in most jurisdictions. Corporations can also obtain a copyright for varying periods set by law. Copyrights, like patents, can be acquired. The acquisition cost would be capitalised and amortised over the expected remaining economic life.

Trademarks

A **trademark** is a registered name, logo, package design, image, jingle, or slogan that is associated with a product. Many trademarks are easily recognisable, such as Apple's bitten apple, the Flying Kangaroo of Qantas, McDonald's golden arches, and Adidas' three parallel bars. Companies spend millions of dollars developing and protecting trademarks and their value is enhanced by advertising programmes that increase their recognition. If a trademark is purchased from another company, the purchase price is capitalised. However, the cost of internally developed trademarks is expensed as incurred. Likewise, all advertising costs are expensed immediately, even if the value of a trademark is enhanced by the advertisement. For this reason, many trademarks are not presented in the balance sheet.

Franchise Rights

A **franchise** is a contractual agreement that gives a company the right to operate a particular business in an area for a particular period of time. For example, a franchise may give the owner the right to operate a number of fast-food restaurants in a particular geographic region for twenty years. *Operating rights* and *licences* are similar to franchise rights, except that they are typically granted by government agencies. Most franchise rights are purchased and, as a result, the purchase price should be capitalised and presented as an intangible asset in the balance sheet.

Amortisation and Impairment of Identifiable Intangible Assets

When intangible assets are acquired and capitalised, a determination must be made as to whether the asset has a **definite life**. Examples of intangible assets with definite lives include patents and franchise rights. An intangible asset with a definite life must be *amortised* over the expected useful life of the asset. **Amortisation** is the systematic allocation of the cost of an intangible asset to the periods benefited. Like the depreciation of tangible assets, amortisation is motivated by the matching principle.

Amortisation expense is generally recorded using the straight-line method. The expense is included in the income statement as a component of operating income, and is often included among selling, general and administrative expenses. The cost of the intangible asset is presented in the balance sheet net of accumulated amortisation and impairment.

Amortisation To illustrate, assume that Landsman Company spent $100,000 in early 2013 to purchase a patent. The entry to record the capitalisation of this cost follows.

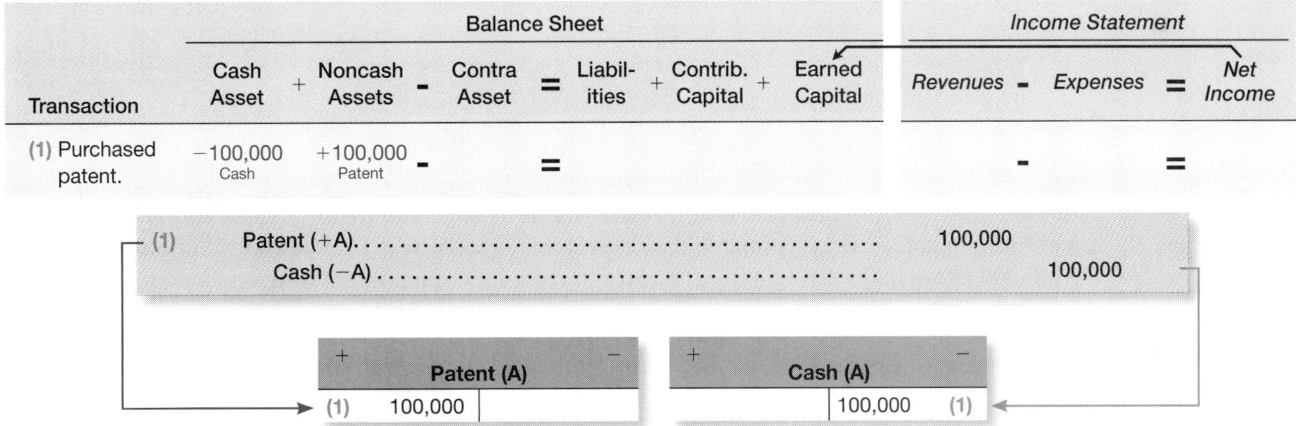

Transaction	Cash Asset	+ Noncash Assets	− Contra Asset	= Liabilities	+ Contrib. Capital	+ Earned Capital	Revenues	− Expenses	= Net Income
(1) Purchased patent.	−100,000 Cash	+100,000 Patent	−	=				−	=

(1) Patent (+A) 100,000
Cash (−A) 100,000

+ Patent (A) −	
(1) 100,000	

+ Cash (A) −	
	100,000 (1)

Although the patent had a remaining legal life of 12 years, Landsman estimated that the useful life of the patent was 5 years. Thus the intangible asset has a definite life of 5 years. The entry to record the annual amortisation expense at the end of 2013 follows.

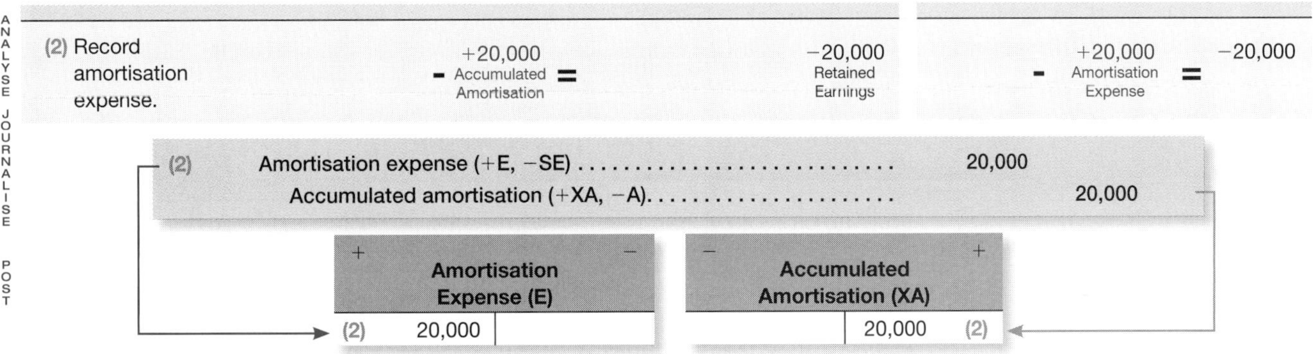

Transaction	Cash Asset	+ Noncash Assets	− Contra Asset	= Liabilities	+ Contrib. Capital	+ Earned Capital	Revenues	− Expenses	= Net Income
(2) Record amortisation expense.			− +20,000 Accumulated Amortisation	=		−20,000 Retained Earnings		− +20,000 Amortisation Expense	= −20,000

(2) Amortisation expense (+E, −SE) 20,000
Accumulated amortisation (+XA, −A) 20,000

+ Amortisation Expense (E) −	
(2) 20,000	

− Accumulated Amortisation (XA) +	
	20,000 (2)

Some transferable intangible assets, such as some trademarks, have indefinite lives. For these assets, the expected useful life extends far enough into the future that it is impossible for management to estimate a useful life. An intangible asset with an indefinite life should not be amortised until the useful life of the asset can be specified. That is, no expense is recorded until management can reasonably estimate the useful life of the asset.

FYI Intangible assets may be reported at a revalued amount, if fair value can be determined from an active market. Since active markets for intangibles rarely exist, this option is not common. See the PPE section above for a description of the revaluation method.

Impairment An intangible asset with a finite useful life is subject to an impairment test if there is an indication that it may be impaired. However, an intangible asset with an indefinite life must be tested for impairment annually. The impairment test is identical to the one used for PPE assets. In particular, the carrying value (original cost minus accumulated amortisation and impairment) of the asset is compared with its recoverable amount (the higher of fair value minus costs of disposal or its value in use). If the carrying value is higher than the recoverable amount, the asset is deemed impaired and it is written down to its recoverable amount. If the carrying value is lower, no impairment is deemed to exist.

To illustrate, assume that Norell Company purchased a trademark in 2009 for $240,000 and determined that the intangible asset had an indefinite life. The entry to record the purchase of the trademark follows.

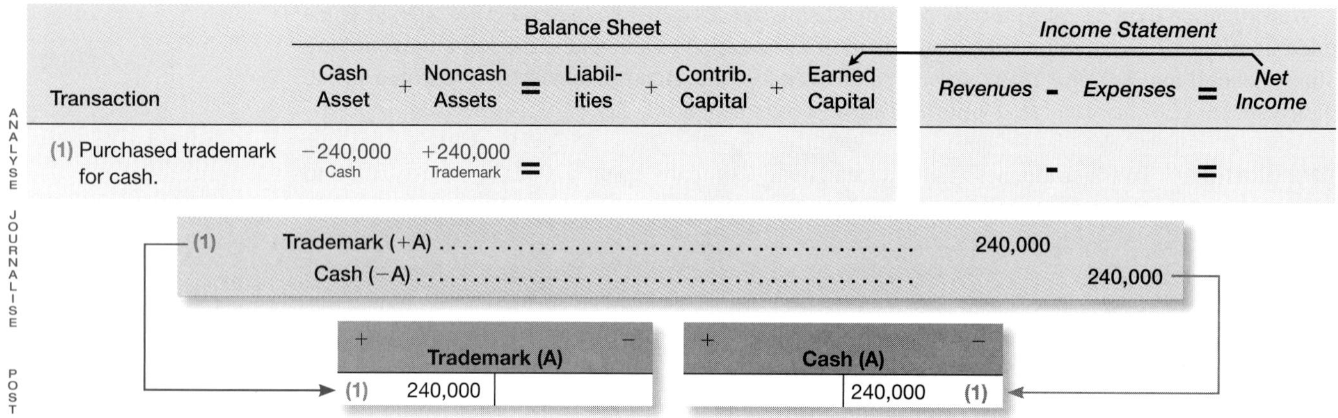

In 2013, changes in consumer taste caused Norell to conclude that the value of the trademark had been impaired. They estimated the recoverable amount was $100,000, resulting in a loss of $140,000 ($240,000 – $100,000). The entry to record the impairment of the trademark would be as follows.

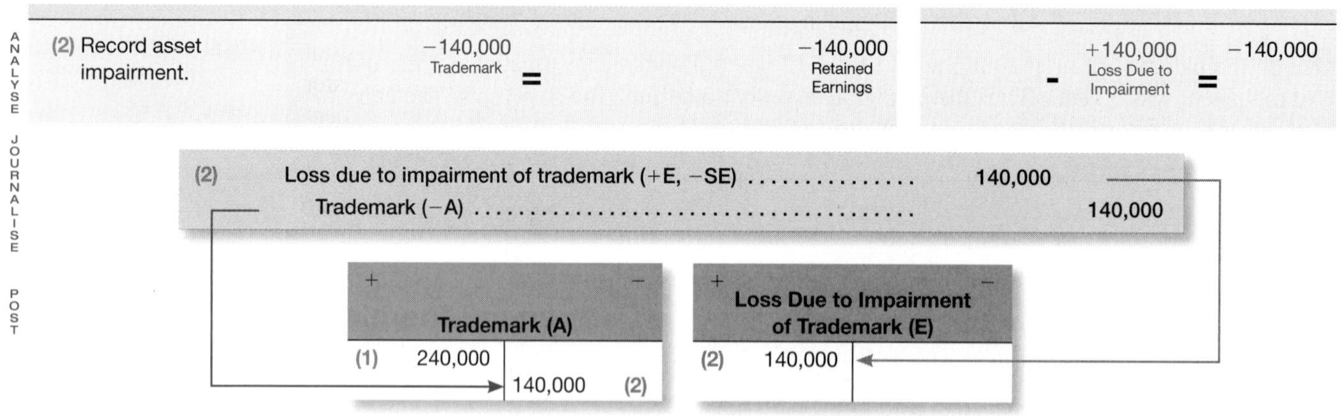

If the value of the trademark subsequently decreases further, additional impairment losses would be recorded. On the other hand, if an impairment loss has subsequently been reversed, the carrying value of the asset is increased to its recoverable amount, up to what it would have been without the prior impairment. Reversal of an impairment loss is recognised in the income statement. Furthermore, if, at any time, Norell determined that the trademark had a definite life, the company would begin amortising the remaining value over the remaining estimated life.

BUSINESS INSIGHT

Intangible Assets and Licences at Rogers Communications Rogers is Canada's leading provider of wireless, cable television, internet, and telephony services. The following excerpts from the company's 2013 annual report describe its accounting for intangible assets, including spectrum and broadcast licences, brands, customer relationships, roaming and marketing agreements, and programme rights.

> **Intangible Assets** We record intangible assets we acquire in business combinations at fair value, and test for impairment as required . . . We do not amortise intangible assets with indefinite lives (spectrum and broadcast licences) because there is no foreseeable limit to the period that these assets are expected to generate net cash inflows for us. We use judgement to determine the indefinite life of these assets, analysing all relevant factors, including the expected usage of the asset, the typical life cycle of the asset and anticipated changes in the market demand for the products and services that the asset helps generate . . .
>
> Brand names, customer relationships, roaming agreements and marketing agreements are all intangible assets with finite lives and we amortise them in depreciation and amortisation expense in the consolidated statements of income. This amounted to $150 million in 2013 (2012–$141 million) . . . We amortise the costs of acquired programme rights over the expected performances of the related programmes, recording them in other external purchases in operating costs in the consolidated statements of income. This amounted to $52 million in 2013 (2012–$64 million).

Goodwill

Goodwill is an intangible asset that is recorded only when one company acquires another company. **Goodwill** is defined as the excess of the purchase price paid for a company over the fair value of its *identifiable* net assets (assets minus the liabilities assumed). The identifiable net assets include any *identifiable intangible assets* acquired in the purchase. Therefore, goodwill can neither be linked to any identifiable source, nor can it be sold or separated from the company. It represents the value of the acquired company above and beyond the specific identifiable assets listed on the balance sheet.

By definition, goodwill has an indefinite life. Once it is recorded in the balance sheet, it is not amortised. Instead, it is subject to an annual impairment test. The detail of the test is beyond the scope of this text. Simply put, goodwill is first allocated to each of the acquirer's **cash-generating units** that are expected to gain from the acquisition. If the carrying amount of a cash-generating unit is higher than the recoverable amount of the unit, the unit and its goodwill are impaired. If this occurs, goodwill is written down to reduce the carrying amount of the unit to its recoverable amount. Finally, unlike PPE and other intangible assets, reversal of an impairment loss for goodwill is not allowed. The goodwill write-down (also called a goodwill write-off) results in the immediate transfer of some or all of a company's goodwill book value from the balance sheet to the income statement as an expense. The book value of the intangible assets is immediately reduced and a corresponding expense is reported in the income statement. Like the impairment write-down of tangible assets, the write-down of goodwill is a discretionary expense whose amount and timing are largely determined by management (with auditor acceptance).

It is commonplace to see goodwill impairment write-downs related to unsuccessful acquisitions, particularly those from the acquisition boom of the late 1990s and the recent recession of 2008–2009. Goodwill write-downs usually represent material amounts. For example, Adidas took a €265 million impairment charge in the fourth quarter of 2013, mainly due to poor sales and lower growth potential at its Reebok brand that it had acquired in 2005. As a result, the carrying value of Adidas's goodwill was cut by 17%. Goodwill write-downs are usually nonrecurring, but are typically reported by companies in income from continuing operations. For analysis purpose we normally classify them as operating and nonrecurring.

Footnote Disclosures

As of December 31, 2013, Airbus reported €13,653 million of intangible assets, compared with €15,856 million of PPE assets. The company provides the following information in note

2 (Summary of Significant Accounting Policies) that describes its accounting for research and development activities and other intangible assets.

Research and development expenses . . . Costs for self-initiated research and development activities are assessed whether they qualify for recognition as internally generated intangible assets. An intangible asset may only be recognised if technical as well as commercial feasibility can be demonstrated and cost can be measured reliably. It must also be probable that the intangible asset will generate future economic benefits and that it is clearly identifiable and allocable to a specific product.

Further to meeting these criteria, only such costs that relate solely to the development phase of a self-initiated project are capitalised. Any costs that are classified as part of the research phase of a self-initiated project are expensed as incurred...

Capitalised development costs are generally amortised over the estimated number of units produced. In case the number of units produced cannot be estimated reliably capitalised development cost are amortised over the estimated useful life of the internally generated intangible asset. Amortisation of capitalised development costs is recognised in cost of sales . . .

Intangible assets—Intangible assets comprise (i) internally generated intangible assets, i.e. internally developed software and other internally generated intangible assets (see above: "Research and development expenses"), (ii) acquired intangible assets, and (iii) goodwill . . .

Separately acquired intangible assets are initially recognised at cost. Intangible assets acquired in a business combination are recognised at their fair value at acquisition date. Acquired intangible assets with finite useful lives are generally amortised on a straight line basis over their respective estimated useful lives (3 to 10 years) to their estimated residual values . . . The amortisation method and the estimate of the useful lives of the separately acquired intangible asset is reviewed at least annually and changed if appropriate.

Intangible assets having an indefinite useful life are not amortised but tested for impairment at the end of each financial year as well as whenever there is an indication that the carrying amount exceeds the recoverable amount of the respective asset (see below "Impairment of non-financial assets"). For such intangible assets the assessment for the indefinite useful life is reviewed annually on whether it remains supportable. A change from indefinite to finite useful life assessment is accounted for as change in estimate . . .

In the same note, Airbus also explains its accounting policy for asset impairment.

Impairment of non-financial assets—The Group assesses at each end of the reporting period whether there is an indication that a non-financial asset may be impaired. In addition, intangible assets with an indefinite useful life, intangible assets not yet available for use and goodwill are tested for impairment in the fourth quarter of each financial year irrespective of whether there is any indication for impairment. An impairment loss is recognised in the amount by which the asset's carrying amount exceeds its recoverable amount . . .

Impairment losses recognised for goodwill are not reversed in future periods. For any other non-financial assets an assessment is made at each end of the reporting period as to whether there is any indication that previously recognised impairment losses may no longer exist or may have decreased. If such indication exists, the Group estimates the asset's or cash-generating unit's recoverable amount. A previously recognised impairment loss is reversed only if there has been a change in the assumptions used to determine the asset's recoverable amount since the last impairment loss was recognised. The reversal is limited so that the carrying amount of the asset does not exceed its recoverable amount, nor exceed the carrying amount that would have been determined, net of depreciation, had no impairment loss been recognised for the asset in prior years. Such a reversal is recognised in the Consolidated Income Statement.

Finally, Airbus provides detailed information on its intangible assets in note 14. Selected information from that note is reproduced below.

14. Intangible Assets

A schedule detailing gross values, accumulated depreciation and impairment and net values of intangible assets as of 31 December is as follows:

(In € million)	2012	2013
Cost		
Goodwill	€12,191	€12,151
Capitalised development costs	1,955	2,323
Other intangible assets	2,729	2,965
Total	€16,875	€17,439
Accumulated Amortisation / Impairment		
Goodwill	€ (1,174)	€ (1,189)
Capitalised development costs	(590)	(697)
Other intangible assets	(1,682)	(1,900)
Total	€ (3,446)	€ (3,786)
Net Book Value		
Goodwill	€11,017	€10,962
Capitalised development costs	1,365	1,626
Other intangible assets	1,047	1,065
Total	€13,429	€13,653

There are several observations that we can make from the above disclosures. First, Airbus Group has purchased a significant amount of intangible assets by acquiring other companies. We can infer this from the large amount of goodwill assets reported (€10,962 million at the end of 2013). Second, the net book value of goodwill decreased from €11,017 million to €10,962 million. Since goodwill is not amortised and the company disclosed no goodwill impairment in 2013, some assets involving goodwill must have been sold during 2013. Third, most of Airbus's identifiable intangible assets are capitalised development costs (€1,626 million). The company indicated in a note (not shown here) that there was impairment of capitalised development costs and other intangible assets during 2013. As a result, the impairment lowers the amount of amortisation expense on these intangible assets in future years. However, investors should be aware that goodwill impairment write-offs could be substantial in any given year.

Analysis Implications

LO6 Analyse the effects of tangible and intangible assets on key performance measures.

Because internally generated intangible assets are not capitalised, an important component of a company's assets is potentially hidden from users of the financial statements. Moreover, differential treatment of purchased and internally created assets makes it difficult to compare companies. If one company generates its patents and trademarks internally, while another company purchases these intangibles, their balance sheets can differ dramatically, even if the two companies are otherwise very similar.

These hidden intangible assets can distort our analysis of the financial statements. For example, when a company expenses R&D costs, especially R&D equipment and facilities that can potentially benefit more than one period, both the income statement and balance sheet are distorted. Net income, assets, and stockholders' equity are all understated.

The income statement effects may be small if a company regularly purchases R&D assets and the amount of purchases is relatively constant from year to year. Specifically, after the average useful life is reached, say in 5 to 10 years, the expensing of current-year purchases will be approximately the same as the depreciation that would have been reported had the assets been capitalised.

Thus, the income statement effect is mitigated. However, the recorded assets and equity are still understated. This accounting produces an upward bias in asset turnover ratios and ROE.

Finally, the statement of cash flows is also affected by the manner in which a company acquires its intellectual assets. A company that generates its patents and trademarks internally recognises the expenditures as part of cash flow from operating activities. However, a company that purchases its patents and trademarks from an independent party or through acquisitions recognises the expenditures as part of cash flow from investing activities.

CHAPTER-END REVIEW

In 2013, Cyberport Technologies, Inc. developed a new production process that significantly reduced the time and cost required to manufacture its product. R&D costs were $120,000. The process was patented on July 1, 2013. Legal costs and fees to acquire the patent totalled $12,500. Cyberport estimated the useful life of the patent at 10 years.

On July 1, 2015, Cyberport sold the nonexclusive right to use the new process to Pok Fu Lum (PFL) Company for $90,000. Because Cyberport retained the patent, the agreement allows PFL to use, but not sell, the new technology for a period of 5 years. Both Cyberport and PFL have December 31 fiscal years.

On July 1, 2017, another competitor obtained a patent on a new process that made Cyberport's patent obsolete.

Required

1. If the process was not economically feasible until the company obtained the patent, how should Cyberport account for the R&D costs and legal costs incurred to obtain the patent? Show the effects of these entries using the financial statement effects template, prepare the appropriate journal entries necessary to account for the costs incurred in 2013, and post the entries to T-accounts.
2. What amount of amortisation expense would Cyberport record each year? Show the effects of these transactions using the financial statement effects template, prepare a journal entry to record amortisation expense on December 31, 2013, and post the entries to T-accounts.
3. How would PFL record the acquisition of the rights to use the new technology? Show the effects of this transaction using the financial statement effects template, prepare a journal entry to record the purchase of the technology rights, and post the entry to T-accounts.
4. What effect would the new patent registered by the other competitor have on Cyberport? On PFL Company? Show the effects of this transaction using the financial statement effects template, prepare a journal entry to record the impairment loss for PFL, and post the entry to T-accounts.

The solution to this review problem can be found on pages 396-397.

SUMMARY

LO1 Describe and distinguish between tangible and intangible assets. (p. 360)

- Tangible assets, including land, buildings, machinery, and equipment are assets with physical substance and are usually classified as property, plant and equipment.
- Intangible assets are long-term assets lacking in physical substance, such as patents, trademarks, franchise rights and goodwill.

LO2 Determine which costs to capitalise and report as assets and which costs to expense. (p. 361)

- All costs incurred to acquire an asset and prepare it for its intended use should be capitalised and reported in the balance sheet.
- The cost of self-constructed assets should include all costs incurred during construction, including the interest cost of financing the construction.

LO3 Apply different depreciation methods to allocate the cost of assets over time. (p. 363)

- Depreciation methods generally fall into three categories:
  (1) Straight-line depreciation
  (2) Accelerated depreciation, such as the double-declining-balance method
  (3) Units-of-production method

Determine the effects of asset sales and impairments on financial statements. (p. 367) LO4

- The sale of a long-term asset will result in a gain or loss if the proceeds from the sale are greater than or less than the book value of the asset.
- If the carrying value of an asset is higher than the recoverable amount, the asset is deemed impaired, and it is written down to its recoverable amount. Recoverable amount is the higher of the asset's fair value less costs of disposal or its value in use (computed as the present value of future cash flows).

Describe the accounting and reporting for intangible assets. (p. 375) LO5

- For the most part, internally generated intangible asserts are not recognised in the balance sheet.
- Intangible assets purchased from other companies are capitalised and presented separately in the balance sheet.
- Intangible assets with definite lives are amortised using the straight-line method.
- Intangible assets with indefinite lives are not amortised.

Analyse the effects of tangible and intangible assets on key performance measures. (p. 381) LO6

- PPE turnover and long-term asset turnover ratios provide insights into the capital intensity of a company and how efficiently the company is utilising these investments.
- The ratio of accumulated depreciation divided by the cost of depreciable assets measures the percent depreciated.

GUIDANCE ANSWERS . . . YOU MAKE THE CALL

You are the Company Accountant Any cost that is necessary in order to bring an asset into service should be capitalised as a part of the cost of the asset. In this case, your company cannot build an office building on this property until the oil well is properly capped. Therefore, the $40,000 cost of capping the oil well should be capitalised as part of the cost of the land.

You are the Division Manager To increase PPE turnover one must either increase sales or reduce PPE assets. The first step is to identify unproductive or inefficiently utilised assets. Unnecessary assets can be sold, and some processes can be outsourced. Also, by reducing down time, effective maintenance practices will increase asset productivity.

KEY RATIOS

$$\text{PPE Turnover (PPET)} = \frac{\text{Sales revenue}}{\text{Average PP\&E}}$$

$$\text{Percent depreciated} = \frac{\text{Accumulated depreciation}}{\text{Cost of depreciable asset}}$$

KEY TERMS

Accelerated depreciation (p. 364)
Accumulated depreciation (p. 362)
Amortisation (p. 377)
Book value (BV) (p. 364)
Capital expenditures (p. 361)
Capitalised (p. 360)
Capitalised interest (p. 362)
Cash-generating unit (p. 379)
Definite life (p. 377)
Depletion (p. 366)
Depreciation (p. 362)
Depreciation base (p. 364)
Depreciation rate (p. 364)
Double-declining-balance (DDB) method (p. 364)
Franchise (p. 376)
Goodwill (p. 379)
Impairment (p. 368)
Intangible assets (p. 360)
Patent (p. 376)
Recoverable amount (p. 368)
Residual (or salvage) value (p. 363)
Restructuring costs (p. 368)
Reversal of impairment (p. 368)
Straight-line method (p. 364)
Tangible assets (p. 360)
Trademark (p. 376)
Units-of-production method (p. 366)
Useful life (p. 363)
Value in use (p. 368)
Wasting assets (p. 366)

MULTIPLE CHOICE

Multiple Choice Answers
1. a 2. b 3. c 4. d 5. c 6. b

1. Burgstahler Corporation bought a lot to construct a new corporate office building. An older building on the lot was razed immediately so that the office building could be constructed. The cost of razing the older building should be
   a. recorded as part of the cost of the land.
   b. written off as a loss in the year of purchase.
   c. written off as an extraordinary item in the year of purchase.
   d. recorded as part of the cost of the new building.

2. The purpose of recording periodic depreciation of long-term PPE assets is to
   a. report declining asset values on the balance sheet.
   b. allocate asset costs over the periods benefited by use of the assets.
   c. account for costs to reflect the change in general price levels.
   d. set aside funds to replace assets when their economic usefulness expires.

3. When the estimate of an asset's useful life is changed,
   a. depreciation expense for all past periods must be recalculated.
   b. there is no change in the amount of depreciation expense recorded for future years.
   c. only depreciation expense for current and future years is affected.
   d. only depreciation expense in the current year is affected.

4. If the sale of a depreciable asset results in a loss, the proceeds from the sale were
   a. less than current fair value.
   b. greater than cost.
   c. greater than book value.
   d. less than book value.

5. Which of the following principles best describes the current method of accounting for research and development costs before the project reaches technical and economical feasibility?
   a. Revenue recognition method
   b. Systematic and rational allocation
   c. Immediate recognition as an expense
   d. Income tax minimisation

6. Goodwill should be recorded in the balance sheet as an intangible asset only when
   a. it is sold to another company.
   b. it is acquired through the purchase of another business.
   c. a company reports above-normal earnings for five or more consecutive years.
   d. it can be established that a definite benefit or advantage has resulted from some item such as an excellent reputation for service.

DISCUSSION QUESTIONS

Q8-1. How should companies account for costs, such as maintenance or improvements, which are incurred after an asset is acquired?

Q8-2. What is the effect of capitalised interest on the income statement in the period that an asset is constructed? What is the effect in future periods?

Q8-3. Why is the recognition of depreciation expense necessary to properly match revenues and expenses?

Q8-4. Why do companies use accelerated depreciation for income tax purposes, when the total depreciation taken over the asset's useful life is identical to straight-line depreciation?

Q8-5. How should a company treat a change in an asset's estimated useful life or residual value? Which period(s)—past, present, or future—is affected by this change?

Q8-6. What factors determine the gain or loss from the sale of a long-term operating asset?

Q8-7. When is a PPE asset considered to be impaired? How is the impairment loss determined?

Q8-8. What is the proper accounting treatment for research and development costs before the project reaches technical and economical feasibility? What is the rationale before this treatment?

Q8-9. Why are some intangible assets amortised while others are not? What is meant by an intangible asset with an "indefinite life"?

Q8-10. Under what circumstances should a company report goodwill in its balance sheet? What is the effect of goodwill on the income statement?

MINI EXERCISES

M8-11. Determining Whether to Capitalise or Expense LO2

For each of the following items, indicate whether the cost should be capitalised or expensed immediately:

a. Paid $1,200 for routine maintenance of machinery
b. Paid $5,400 to rent equipment for two years
c. Paid $2,000 to equip the production line with new instruments that measure quality
d. Paid $20,000 to repair the roof on the building
e. Paid $1,600 to refurbish a machine, thereby extending its useful life
f. Purchased a patent for $5,000

M8-12. Computing Depreciation under Straight-Line and Double-Declining-Balance LO3

A delivery van costing $18,000 is expected to have a $1,500 salvage value at the end of its useful life of 5 years. Assume that the truck was purchased on January 1, 2013. Compute the depreciation expense for 2014 (its second year) under each of the following depreciation methods:

a. Straight-line
b. Double-declining-balance

M8-13. Computing Depreciation under Alternative Methods LO3

Equipment costing $130,000 is expected to have a residual value of $10,000 at the end of its six-year useful life. The equipment is metered so that the number of units processed is counted. The equipment is designed to process 1,000,000 units in its lifetime. In 2013 and 2014, the equipment processed 180,000 units and 140,000 units respectively. Calculate the depreciation expense for 2013 and 2014 using each of the following methods:

a. Straight-line
b. Double-declining-balance
c. Units of production

M8-14. Recording the Sale of PPE Assets LO4

As part of a renovation of its showroom, Thalys Auto Dealership sold furniture and fixtures that were eight years old for €3,500 in cash. The assets had been purchased for €40,000 and had been depreciated using the straight-line method with no residual value and a useful life of ten years.

a. Prepare a journal entry to record this transaction.
b. Show how the sale of the furniture and fixtures affects the balance sheet and income statement using the financial statement effects template.

M8-15. Recording the Sale of PPE Assets LO4

Gaver Company sold machinery that had originally cost $75,000 for $25,000 in cash. The machinery was three years old and had been depreciated using the double-declining-balance method assuming a five-year useful life and a residual value of $5,000.

a. Prepare a journal entry to record this sale.
b. Using the financial statement effects template, show how the sale of the machinery affects the balance sheet and income statement.

M8-16. Computing Depreciation under Straight-Line and Double-Declining-Balance for Partial Years LO3

A machine costing $145,800 is purchased on May 1, 2013. The machine is expected to be obsolete after three years (36 months) and, thereafter, no longer useful to the company. The estimated salvage value is $5,400. Compute depreciation expense for both 2013 and 2014 under each of the following depreciation methods:

a. Straight-line
b. Double-declining-balance

LO1, 2, 5 **M8-17. Accounting for Research and Development**

SIEMENS A.G. (GERMANY)

The following information on Siemens AG's treatment of research and development is extracted from its 2011 financial statements. Siemens AG is an integrated technology company with activities in the fields of industry, energy and healthcare. The company is incorporated under the laws of Germany.

During 2011, Siemens AG recognised impairment of Other intangible assets in the amount of €36 million. Should the amounts capitalised be tested annually for impairment?

Research and development costs—Costs of research activities undertaken with the prospect of gaining new scientific or technical knowledge and understanding are expensed as incurred.

Costs for development activities, whereby research findings are applied to a plan or design for the production of new or substantially improved products and processes, are capitalised if (1) development costs can be measured reliably, the product or process is (2) technically and (3) commercially feasible, (4) future economic benefits are probable and (5) Siemens intends, and (6) has sufficient resources, to complete development and to use or sell the asset. The costs capitalised include the cost of materials, direct labour and other directly attributable expenditure that serves to prepare the asset for use. Such capitalised costs are included in line item Other intangible assets as other internally generated intangible assets, see Note 17 Other intangible assets. Other development costs are expensed as incurred. Capitalised development costs are stated at cost less accumulated amortisation and impairment losses with an amortisation period of generally three to five years.

LO3 **M8-18. Computing Double-Declining-Balance Depreciation**

DeFond Company purchased equipment for $50,000. For each of the following sets of assumptions, prepare a depreciation schedule (all years) for this equipment assuming that DeFond uses the double-declining-balance depreciation method.

Useful life	Residual value
a. Four years	$8,000
b. Five years	$3,000
c. Ten years	$1,000

LO3 **M8-19. Computing and Recording Depletion Expense**

The Nelson Oil Company estimated that the oil reserve that it acquired would produce 4 million barrels of oil. The company extracted 300,000 barrels the first year, 500,000 barrels in 2014, and 600,000 barrels in 2015. Nelson paid $32,000,000 for the oil reserve.

a. Compute the depletion expense for each year—2013, 2014, and 2015.

b. Prepare the journal entries to record (i) the acquisition of the oil reserve, and (ii) the depletion for 2013.

c. Open T-accounts and post the entries from part *b* in the accounts.

LO3 **M8-20. Computing Depreciation and Accounting for a Change of Estimate**

Salzburg Mining A.G. purchased a drill for €11,000 that had an estimated residual value of €1,000 and estimated useful life of 5 years. After 3 years, Salzburg decided that the drill would last 6 more years and that the residual value would be €2,000.

a. Compute depreciation expense for the drill for the first three years using the straight-line method.

b. Compute the net book value of the drill at the end of the third year.

c. Compute the revised deprecation expense.

LO5, 6 **M8-21. Assessing Research and Development Expenses**

Buda KFT reports the following income statement (in partial form):

Year Ended December 31 (In thousands of Hungarian Forint (HUF))	2014
Net sales	HUF38,851,259
Cost of products sold	15,540,580
Research and development	4,801,914
Selling, general and administrative	12,756,817
Total operating cost and expenses	33,099,311
Operating earnings	HUF 5,751,948

a. Compute the percent of net sales that Buda spends on research and development (R&D). How would you assess the appropriateness of its R&D expense level?

b. Using the financial statement effects template, describe how the accounting for R&D expenditures affects Buda's balance sheet and income statement. Assume that all development costs are expensed.

EXERCISES

E8-22. Recording Asset Acquisition, Depreciation, and Disposal LO2, 3, 4

On January 2, 2013, Hutton Company acquired a machine for $85,000. In addition to the purchase price, Hutton spent $2,000 for shipping and instalation, and $2,500 to calibrate the machine prior to use. The company estimates that the machine has a useful life of five years and residual value of $7,000.

a. Prepare journal entries to record the acquisition costs.

b. Calculate the annual depreciation expense using straight-line depreciation and prepare a journal entry to record depreciation expense for 2013.

c. On December 31, 2016, Hutton sold the machine to another company for $12,000. Prepare the necessary journal entry to record the sale.

E8-23. Computing Straight-Line and Double-Declining-Balance Depreciation LO3

On January 2, Haskins Company purchases a laser cutting machine for use in fabrication of a part for one of its key products. The machine cost $80,000, and its estimated useful life is five years, after which the expected salvage value is $5,000. Compute depreciation expense for each year of the machine's useful life under each of the following depreciation methods:

a. Straight-line

b. Double-declining-balance

E8-24. Computing Depreciation, Asset Book Value, and Gain or Loss on Asset Sale LO3, 4

Sloan Company uses its own executive charter plane that originally cost $800,000. It has recorded straight-line depreciation on the plane for six full years, with an $80,000 expected salvage value at the end of its estimated 10-year useful life. Sloan disposes of the plane at the end of the sixth year.

a. At the disposal date, what is the (1) cumulative depreciation expense and (2) net book value of the plane?

b. Prepare a journal entry to record the disposal of the plane assuming that the sales price is

1. Cash equal to the book value of the plane.
2. $195,000 cash.
3. $600,000 cash.

E8-25. Computing Straight-Line and Double-Declining-Balance Depreciation LO3

On January 2, 2015, Tumbalong Company purchases a machine to help manufacture a part for one of its key products. The machine cost $218,700 and is estimated to have a useful life of six years, with an expected salvage value of $23,400.

Compute each year's depreciation expense for 2015 and 2016 for each of the following depreciation methods.

a. Straight-line

b. Double-declining-balance

E8-26. Computing Depreciation, Asset Book Value, and Gain or Loss on Asset Sale LO3, 4

Palepu Company owns and operates a delivery van that originally cost $27,200. Straight-line depreciation on the van has been recorded for three years, with a $2,000 expected salvage value at the end of its estimated six-year useful life. Depreciation was last recorded at the end of the third year, at which time Palepu disposes of this van.

a. Compute the net book value of the van on the sale date.

b. Compute the gain or loss on sale of the van if its sales price is for:

1. Cash equal to book value (of van).
2. $15,000 cash.
3. $12,000 cash.

LO3 **E8-27. Computing Depreciation and Accounting for a Change of Estimate**
Lambert Company acquired machinery costing $110,000 on January 2, 2013. At that time, Lambert estimated that the useful life of the equipment was 6 years and that the residual value would be $15,000 at the end of its useful life. Compute depreciation expense for this asset for 2013, 2014, and 2015 using the

a. straight-line method.
b. double-declining-balance method.
c. Assume that on January 2, 2015, Lambert revised its estimate of the useful life to 7 years and changed its estimate of the residual value to $10,000. What effect would this have on depreciation expense in 2015 for each of the above depreciation methods?

LO3 **E8-28. Computing Depreciation and Accounting for a Change of Estimate**
In January 2015, Sai Kung & Company paid $8,500,000 for land and a building. An appraisal estimated that the land had a fair value of $2,500,000 and the building was worth $6,000,000. Sai Kung & Company estimated that the useful life of the building was 30 years, with no residual value.

a. Calculate annual depreciation expense using the straight-line method.
b. Calculate depreciation for 2015 and 2016 using the double-declining-balance method.
c. Assume that in 2017, Sai Kung & Company changed its estimate of the useful life of the building to 25 years. If the company is using the double-declining-balance method of depreciation, what amount of depreciation expense would Sai Kung & Company record in 2017?

LO6 **E8-29. Estimating the Percent Depreciated**
The property and equipment footnote from the Koala & Company balance sheet follows ($ millions):

PROPERTY AND DEPRECIATION
A summary of property and equipment at October 31, 2015, in millions of Australian dollars follows:

	Useful Lives (Years)	2015
Land		$ 121
Buildings and building equipment	24	2,501
Machinery and equipment	11	4,254
Dies, patterns, tools, etc.	7	1,213
All other	5	770
Construction in progress		649
Total at cost		9,508
Less accumulated depreciation		5,156
Property and equipment—net		$4,352

During 2015, the company reported $516 million of depreciation expense.
Estimate the percent depreciated of Koala's depreciable assets. How do you interpret this figure?

LO6 **E8-30. Computing and Interpreting Percent Depreciated and PPE Turnover**
BURBERRY GROUP PLC (UNITED KINGDOM)
The following information is from Note 12 to the 2013 annual report of **Burberry Group plc**, a British luxury goods manufacturer, wholesaler, and retailer (£ millions):

12. Property, plant and equipment

	Freehold land and buildings	Leasehold improvements	Fixtures, fittings and equipment	Assets in the course of construction	Total
Cost					
As at March 31, 2013	104.2	303.1	366.3	23.2	796.8
As at March 31, 2012	54.2	247.6	270.9	34.5	607.2
Accumulated depreciation and impairment					
As at March 31, 2013	39.2	141.2	207.3	—	387.7
As at March 31, 2012	16.9	110.4	151.1	—	278.4
Net book value					
As at March 31, 2013	65.0	161.9	159.0	23.2	409.1
As at March 31, 2012	37.3	137.2	119.8	34.5	328.8

a. Calculate the percent depreciated ratio for each year.
b. Sales revenue totaled £1,998.7 millions in 2013. Calculate the PPE turnover ratio (PPET).
c. Comment on these ratios.

E8-31. Identifying and Accounting for Intangible Assets LO1, 5

On the first day of 2015, Fontainebleau S.A. acquired the assets of Carnot S.A. including several intangible assets. These include a patent on Carnot's primary product, a device called a plentiscope. Carnot carried the patent on its books for €1,500, but Fontainebleau believes that the fair value is €200,000. The patent expires in seven years, but competitors can be expected to develop competing patents within three years. Fontainebleau believes that, with expected technological improvements, the product is marketable for at least 20 years.

The registration of the trademark for the Carnot name is scheduled to expire in 15 years. However, the Carnot brand name, which Fontainebleau believes is worth €500,000, could be applied to related products for many years beyond that.

As part of the acquisition, Carnot's principal researcher left the company. As part of the acquisition, he signed a five-year noncompetition agreement that prevents him from developing competing products. Fontainebleau paid the scientist €300,000 to sign the agreement.

a. What amount should be capitalised for each of the identifiable intangible assets?
b. What amount of amortisation expense should Fontainebleau record in 2015 for each asset?

E8-32. Computing and Recording Depletion Expense LO3

In 2015, Hyde Mining Company purchased land for $7,200,000 that had a natural resource reserve estimated to be 500,000 tonnes. Development and road construction costs on the land were $420,000, and a building was constructed at a cost of $50,000. When the natural resources are completely extracted, the land has an estimated residual value of $1,200,000. In addition, the cost to restore the property to comply with environmental regulations is estimated to be $800,000. Production in 2015 and 2016 was 60,000 tonnes and 85,000 tonnes, respectively.

a. Compute the depletion charge for 2015 and 2016. (You should include depreciation on the building, if any, as part of the depletion charge.)
b. Prepare a journal entry to record each year's depletion expense as determined in part *a*.

E8-33. Computing and Comparing PPE Turnover for Two Companies LO6

CANADIAN TIRE CORP.
DOLLARAMA, INC.
(CANADA)

Canadian Tire Corporation operates a chain of general department stores and gasoline stations. **Dollarama, Inc.** offers a broad assortment of everyday consumer products at price points up to $3.00. The following data were taken from the fiscal year 2013 annual reports of the two companies (in millions of Canadian dollars):

(CDN$ millions)	Canadian Tire	Dollarama
Sales revenue	$11,785.60	$2,064.68
PPE, net (end-of-year)	3,516.10	197.50
PPE, net (beginning-of-year)	3,343.50	250.60

a. Compute the 2013 PPE turnover for both companies. Comment on any difference you observe.
b. Discuss ways in which retailers like these two companies can increase their PPE turnover.

E8-34. Computing and Assessing Plant Asset Impairment LO4

Ghent Properties N.V. owns and manages a housing complex. At the end of 2014, Ghent's accounting system shows that the acquisition cost and accumulated depreciation of the complex are €20 million and €5 million, respectively. An independent appraiser determines that the fair value of the complex is €12 million and the total cost to sell it is €1 million. Furthermore, the present value of the complex's future cash flows, given its current use, is estimated to be €14 million (i.e., value in use).

Is Ghent's building complex impaired at the end of 2014? If it is impaired, prepare a journal entry to record the loss.

E8-35. Computing and Assessing Plant Asset Impairment LO4

Jurong Company purchases equipment for $225,000 on July 1, 2011, with an estimated useful life of 10 years and expected salvage value of $25,000. Straight-line depreciation is used. On July 1, 2015, economic factors cause the recoverable amount of the equipment to decline to $90,000.

a. Is the equipment impaired at July 1, 2015? Explain.
b. If the equipment is impaired on July 1, 2015, compute the impairment loss and prepare a journal entry to record the loss.
c. What amount of depreciation expense would Jurong record for the 12 months from July 1, 2015 through June 30, 2016? Prepare a journal entry to record this depreciation expense.
d. Using the financial statement effects template, show how the entries in parts *b* and *c* affect Jurong Company's balance sheet and income statement.

PROBLEMS

LO4 **P8-36. Computing and Recording Gain or Loss on Asset Sale**

The following information was provided in the 2015 annual report of Saas Fee A.G.

Note 10: Land, Buildings and Equipment

	June 3, 2015	May 28, 2014
Property, Plant and Equipment, Gross, Total..........	€84,767,771	€80,132,394
Less: Accumulated depreciation	60,121,353	57,852,770
Property, Plant and Equipment, Net, Total............	€24,646,418	€22,279,624

The company's statement of cash flows, including the reconciliation of net income to cash from operations, provided the following information for the year ended June 3, 2015:

- Depreciation expense was €3,174,956.
- Purchases of property, plant and equipment were €5,559,183.
- Proceeds from the sale of property, plant and equipment were €96,916.

Required

Using this information, prepare a journal entry to record the sale of property, plant and equipment.

LO5 **P8-37. Analysing and Assessing Research and Development Expenses**

NOKIA OYJ (FINLAND)

Nokia Oyj, a Finnish communications and information technology company, reports the following information in its 2013 annual report:

Nokia Continuing Operations

The following table sets forth selective line items for the fiscal years 2013, 2012, and 2011.

For year ended December 31 (€ millions)	2013	2012	2011
Net sales	€12,709	€15,400	€15,968
Cost of sales	(7,364)	(9,841)	(10,408)
Gross profit	5,345	5,559	(5,560)
Research and development expenses..............	(2,619)	(3,081)	(3,334)
Selling and marketing expenses...................	(974)	(1,372)	(1,608)
Administrative and general expenses	(697)	(690)	(735)
Impairment expenses	—	—	(1,090)
Other operating income and expenses	(536)	(1,237)	(181)
Operating profit (loss)	€ 519	€ (821)	€(1,388)

Success in the mobile communications industry requires continuous introduction of new products and services and their combinations based on the latest available technology. Consequently, we have made substantial research and development ("R&D") investments in each of the last three years . . . For continuing operations, the R&D expenses were €2,619 million in 2013, €3,081 million in 2012 and €3,334 million in 2011.

Required

a. What percentage of its total net revenue is Nokia spending on research and development?
b. How are its balance sheet and income statement affected by the accounting for R&D costs?
c. What are some possible ways that a company might reduce its R&D intensity and, hence, R&D expenses? What are some of the possible implications for the company?

P8-38. Reporting PPE Transactions and Asset Impairment LO4

The following note information is taken from the 2014 annual report of Rambla Market S.A.

Property and equipment consists of the following:

Euro in thousands	2014	2013
Leasehold improvements	€ 809,239	€ 831,757
Fixtures and equipment	572,155	576,488
Capitalised software	292,424	267,724
Land and buildings	126,061	135,692
Corporate systems projects in progress	56,602	65,989
Construction in progress	1,568	14,905
Corporate aircraft (held for sale)	0	10,029
Total	1,858,049	1,902,584
Accumulated depreciation and amortisation	(1,127,493)	(1,073,557)
Property and equipment—net	€ 730,556	€ 829,027

We review the carrying value of all long-lived assets for impairment, primarily at a store level, whenever events or changes in circumstances indicate that the carrying value of an asset may not be recoverable. We review for impairment all stores for which current or projected cash flows from operations are not sufficient to recover the carrying value of the assets. Impairment results when the carrying value of the assets exceeds the estimated undiscounted future cash flows over the remaining life of the lease. Our estimate of undiscounted future cash flows over the store lease term (generally 5 to 22 years) is based upon our experience, historical operations of the stores and estimates of future store profitability and economic conditions. The future estimates of store profitability and economic conditions require estimating such factors as sales growth, gross margin, employment rates, lease escalations, inflation on operating expenses and the overall economics of the retail industry, and are therefore subject to variability and difficult to predict. If a long-lived asset is found to be impaired, the amount recognised for impairment is equal to the difference between the net carrying value and the asset's fair value.

Moreover, Rambla Market's cash flow statement reported that the company made capital expenditures of €61,906,000 during fiscal 2014, impaired assets of €5,453,000 and recorded depreciation expense of €144,630,000. In addition, the company reported a gain on the disposal of property and equipment of €1,139,000.

Required

Prepare journal entries to record the following for fiscal 2014:

a. Depreciation expense
b. Capital expenditures
c. Impairment of property and equipment (Assume that impairments and write-downs reduce the property and equipment account, rather than increasing accumulated depreciation.)
d. Disposal of property and equipment

P8-39. Reporting PPE Transactions and Asset Impairment LO4

AIR CANADA (CANADA)

Air Canada is Canada's largest airline and a founding member of Star Alliance. It offers direct flights to more than 175 destinations on five continents and serves close to 35 million passengers annually. Following are Note 2(T) and Note 4 from Air Canada's fiscal 2013 annual report, describing the company's property and equipment.

2. BASIS OF PRESENTATION AND SUMMARY OF SIGNIFICANT ACCOUNTING POLICIES
T) PROPERTY AND EQUIPMENT

Property and equipment is recognised using the cost model...

The Corporation allocates the amount initially recognised in respect of an item of property and equipment to its significant components and depreciates separately each component. Property and equipment are depreciated to estimated residual values based on the straight-line method over their estimated service lives. Aircraft and flight equipment are componentised into airframe, engine, and cabin interior equipment and modifications. Airframe and engines are depreciated over 20 to 25 years, with 10% to 20% estimated residual values. Cabin interior equipment and modifications are depreciated over the lesser of 5 years or the remaining useful life of the aircraft... Buildings are depreciated on a straight-line basis over their useful lives not exceeding 50 years... Ground and other equipment is depreciated over 3 to 25 years.

Residual values and useful lives are reviewed at least annually and depreciation rates are adjusted accordingly on a prospective basis. Gains and losses on disposals of property and equipment are determined by comparing the proceeds with the carrying amount of the asset and are included as part of non-operating gains and losses in the consolidated statement of operations.

4. PROPERTY AND EQUIPMENT	Aircraft and flight equipment	Buildings, and leasehold improvements	Ground and other equipment	Purchase deposits, including capitalised interest	Total
Year ended December 31, 2012					
At January 1, 2012.	$4,346	$356	$140	$ 96	$4,938
Additions	86	38	18	282	424
Reclassifications	30	24	—	(54)	—
Disposals	(22)	—	(1)	—	(23)
Depreciation	(571)	(33)	(24)	—	(628)
At December 31, 2012.	$3,869	$385	$133	$324	$4,711
At December 31, 2012					
Cost	$5,991	$662	$311	$324	$7,288
Accumulated depreciation . . .	(2,122)	(277)	(178)	—	(2,577)
	$3,869	$385	$133	$324	$4,711
Year ended December 31, 2013					
At January 1, 2013.	$3,869	$385	$133	$324	$4,711
Additions	736	(4)	27	198	957
Reclassifications	143	3	20	(166)	—
Disposals	(65)	—	—	—	(65)
Depreciation	(445)	(32)	(23)	—	(500)
Impairment.	(30)	—	—	—	(30)
At December 31, 2013.	$4,208	$352	$157	$356	$5,073
At December 31, 2013					
Cost	$6,119	$660	$359	$356	$7,494
Accumulated depreciation . . .	(1,911)	(308)	(202)	-	(2,421)
	$4,208	$352	$157	$356	$5,073

In 2013, an impairment charge of $30 was recorded in Depreciation, amortisation and impairment expense related mainly to four A340-300 aircraft... The impairment charge was based upon the net proceeds expected upon the return or other disposition of these aircraft.

Air Canada's cash flow statement reported disposal proceeds for property and equipment of $70 million.

Required

a. Prepare journal entries to record the following for 2013:
   i. Depreciation expense
   ii. Capital expenditures
   iii. Impairment of property and equipment
   iv. Disposal of property and equipment

b. Describe the impairment test for property and equipment.

LO5 **P8-40. Analysing and Assessing Intangible Assets**

AIR CANADA (CANADA)

The following note is provided in the 2013 annual report of **Air Canada**, the largest airline in Canada.

W) INTANGIBLE ASSETS

Intangible assets are initially recorded at cost. Indefinite life intangible assets are not amortised while assets with finite lives are amortised on a straight line basis over their estimated useful lives.

	Estimated Useful Life	Remaining Amortisation Period as at December 31, 2013
International route rights and slots.	Indefinite	Not applicable
Marketing based trade names	Indefinite	Not applicable
Contract and customer based	10 years	1 year
Technology based (internally developed).	5 years	1 to 5 years

Development costs that are directly attributable to the design, development and testing of identifiable software products are recognised as technology based intangible assets if certain criteria are met, including technical feasibility and intent and ability to develop and use the technology to generate probable future economic benefits; otherwise they are expensed as incurred. Directly attributable costs that are capitalised as part of the technology based intangible assets include software-related, employee and third party development costs and an appropriate portion of relevant overhead. Air Canada has international route and slot rights which enable the Corporation to provide services internationally. The value of the recorded intangible assets relates to the cost of route and slot rights at Tokyo's Narita International Airport, Washington's Reagan National Airport and London's Heathrow Airport. Air Canada expects to provide service to these international locations for an indefinite period.

Air Canada and certain of its subsidiaries have trade names, trademarks, and domain names (collectively, "Trade Names"). These items are marketing based intangible assets as they are primarily used in the selling and promotion of Air Canada's products and services. The Trade Names create brand recognition with customers and potential customers and are capable of contributing to cash flows for an indefinite period of time. Air Canada intends to continuously re-invest and market the Trade Names to support classification as indefinite life intangibles. If there were plans to cease using any of the Trade Names, the specific names would be classified as finite and amortised over the expected remaining useful life.

Required

a. What are technology-based intangible assets? How does Air Canada account for the costs associated with this type of intangible assets?

b. Why does Air Canada not amortise "international route and slot rights" and "marketing based trade names"?

c. Under what condition will Air Canada change its amortisation policy for marketing based trade names?

CASES AND PROJECTS

C8-41. Managing Operating Assets to Improve Performance. A Management Application LO6

Return on a company's net operating assets is commonly used to evaluate financial performance. One way to increase performance is to focus on operating assets.

Required

Indicate how this might be done in relation to the following asset categories. Indicate also any potential problems a given action might create.

a. Receivables

b. Inventories

c. Property, plant, and equipment

d. Intangibles

C8-42. Determining the Effects of Capitalising Versus Expensing Software Development Costs LO4, 5, 6

The following excerpts are taken from the March 31, 2012 annual report of Take-Two Interactive Software, Inc., a maker and distributor of video games. All amounts are in thousands of dollars.

Income Statement Information:	2012	2011
Net sales	$825,823	$1,136,876
Cost of goods sold	528,855	689,381
Operating expenses	381,234	370,353
Income (loss) from operations	$ (84,266)	$ 77,142

Information from the Management Discussion, Balance Sheet and Note 8:

Software Development Costs and Licenses

We capitalise internal software development costs (including stock-based compensation, specifically identifiable employee payroll expense and incentive compensation costs related to the completion and release of titles), third-party production and other content costs, subsequent to establishing technological feasibility of a software title...Amortisation of capitalised software development costs and licences commences when a product is released and is recorded on a title-by-title basis in cost of goods sold. For capitalised software development costs, amortisation is calculated using (1) the proportion of current year revenues to the total revenues expected to be recorded over the life of the title or (2) the straight-line method over the remaining estimated useful life of the title, whichever is greater. For capitalised licences, amortisation is calculated as a ratio of (1) current period revenues to the total revenues expected to be recorded over the remaining life of the title or (2) the contractual royalty rate based on actual net product sales as defined in the licencing agreement, whichever is greater...At each balance sheet date, or earlier if an indicator of impairment exists, we evaluate the recoverability of capitalised software costs, licences and any other unrecognised minimum commitments that have not been paid, using an undiscounted future cash flow analysis...When management determines that the value of a title is unlikely to be recovered by product sales, capitalised costs are charged to cost of goods sold in the period in which such determination is made.

Capitalised Software Development Costs and Licenses	2012	2011
Beginning balance.	$269,996	$253,948
Additions	196,683	159,859
Amortisation and write-downs	(150,700)	(143,811)
Ending balance	$315,979	$269,996

Assume an income tax rate of 35% where necessary.

Required

a. You wish to compare the performance of Take-Two with one of its competitors, Electronic Arts, Inc. However, Electronic Arts does not capitalise any significant amounts of its software development costs. Estimate Take-Two's 2012 Income from operations if it did not capitalise any software development costs. *Briefly* explain your adjustment(s).

b. Is there any indication that Take-Two might have changed its software amortisation estimates from 2011 to 2012? Explain *briefly*.

LO3 **C8-43. Interpreting Changes in Accounting Estimates**

DEUTSCHE LUFTHANSA AG (GERMANY)

Deutsche Lufthansa AG is a German airline and one of the largest airlines in the world. Following is Note 2 from Lufthansa's 2013 annual report, describing its accounting for property and equipment (€ millions).

Property, Plant and Equipment

Until the end of the financial year 2012, new commercial aircraft and reserve engines were depreciated over a period of twelve years to a residual value of 15 percent. Technological developments and the higher demands made of their cost-effectiveness due to increasing competition have resulted in significant changes to the forecast useful economic life of the commercial aircraft and reserve engines used in the Lufthansa Group. In line with the fleet strategy, which takes these aspects into account, as well as with external considerations, commercial aircraft and reserve engines have been depreciated over a period of 20 years to a residual value of five percent since January 1, 2013. The adjustment to their useful lives was made prospectively as a change in an accounting estimate in accordance with IAS 8.32. The change was therefore not made retrospectively for past reporting periods. As a result of the change in the accounting estimate of the useful economic life of these assets, depreciation and amortisation was EUR 68m lower in the financial year 2013 and impairment losses were EUR 76m lower. In future reporting periods, the adjustment to useful lives will reduce depreciation and amortisation by around EUR 340m for the financial year 2014, by EUR 350m for the financial year 2015 and by around EUR 250m p. a. for the five subsequent financial years.

Required

a. What assumptions are used by Lufthansa to depreciate its aircrafts starting from fiscal year 2013?

b. What assumptions were used by Lufthansa to depreciate its aircrafts before fiscal year 2013?

c. How were Lufthansa's balance sheet and income statement affected by the changes in accounting estimates?

SOLUTIONS TO REVIEW PROBLEMS

Mid-Chapter Review

Solution

1*a*. Straight-line Depreciation expense = ($95,000 − $10,000)/5 years = $17,000 per year

1*b*. Double-declining-balance (twice straight-line rate = 2 × (100%/5) = 40%

Year	Book Value × Rate	Depreciation Expense
1.	$95,000 × 0.40 =	$38,000
2.	($95,000 − $38,000) × 0.40 =	22,800
3.	($95,000 − $60,800) × 0.40 =	13,680
4.	($95,000 − $74,480) × 0.40 =	8,208
5.	($95,000 − $82,688) × 0.40	2,312*

*The formula value of $4,925 is not reported because it would depreciate the asset below residual value. Only the $2,312 needed to reach residual value is depreciated.

2*a*.

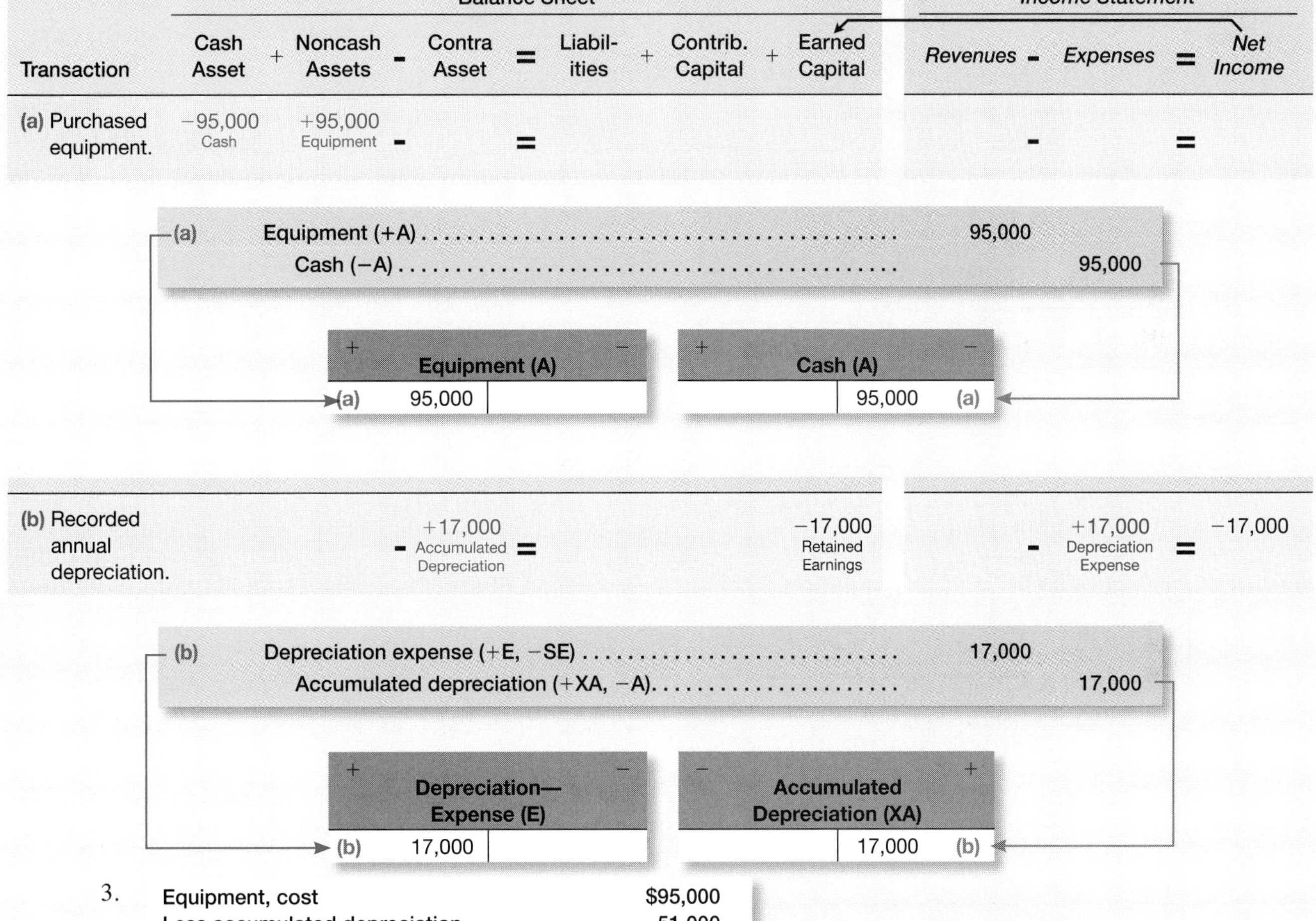

3.

Equipment, cost	$95,000
Less accumulated depreciation	51,000
Equipment, net	$44,000

Equipment is reported on Yonge's balance sheet at its net book value of $44,000.

4. The percent depreciated is computed as: Accumulated Depreciation/Depreciable Asset Cost = $51,000/$95,000 = 53.7%. The equipment is more than one-half depreciated at the end of the third year. Again, the lack of knowledge of salvage value has resulted in an underestimate of the percent depreciated. Still, this estimate is useful in that we know that the company's asset is over one-half depreciated and is likely to require replacement in about 2 years (less than one-half of its useful life of 5 years). This replacement will become a cash outflow or financing need when it arises and should be considered in our projections of future cash flows.

Chapter-End Review

Solution

1. Cyberport Technologies, Inc. would expense the $120,000 in R&D costs in 2013. The $12,500 in legal fees to obtain the patent would be capitalised. As a result, the book value of the patent would be $12,500 on July 1, 2013. The entries to record these costs would be:

Transaction	Cash Asset	Noncash Assets	Contra Asset	Liabilities	Contrib. Capital	Earned Capital	Revenues	Expenses	Net Income
	Balance Sheet						***Income Statement***		
(a) Record R&D costs as R&D expense.	−120,000 Cash					−120,000 Retained Earnings		+120,000 R&D Expense	−120,000

(a) R&D expense (+E, −SE) 120,000
    Cash (−A) 120,000

+ Research & Development Expense (E) −	
(a) 120,000	

+ Cash (A) −	
	120,000 (a)

Transaction	Cash Asset	Noncash Assets	Contra Asset	Liabilities	Contrib. Capital	Earned Capital	Revenues	Expenses	Net Income
(b) Record acquisition of patent.	−12,500 Cash	+12,500 Patent							

(b) Patent (+A). 12,500
    Cash (−A) 12,500

+ Patent (A) −	
(b) 12,500	

+ Cash (A) −	
	120,000 (a)
	12,500 (b)

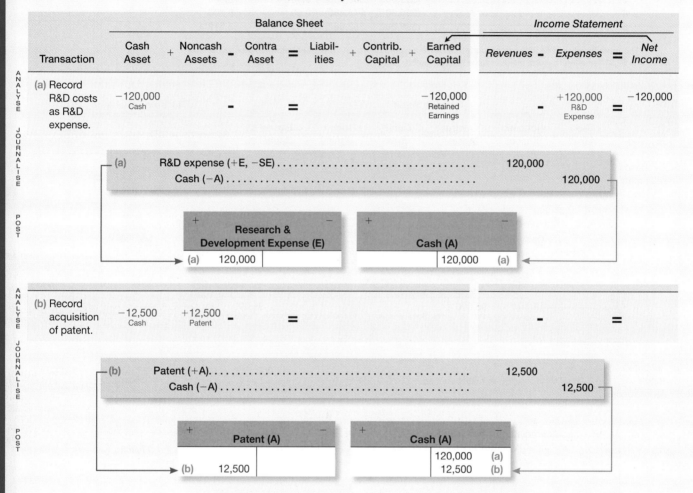

2. Each year, beginning on July 1, 2013, Cyberport would record amortisation expense of $1,250 ($12,500/10). For 2013, six months of amortisation expense, or $625, would be recorded ($1,250/2). The journal entry would be:

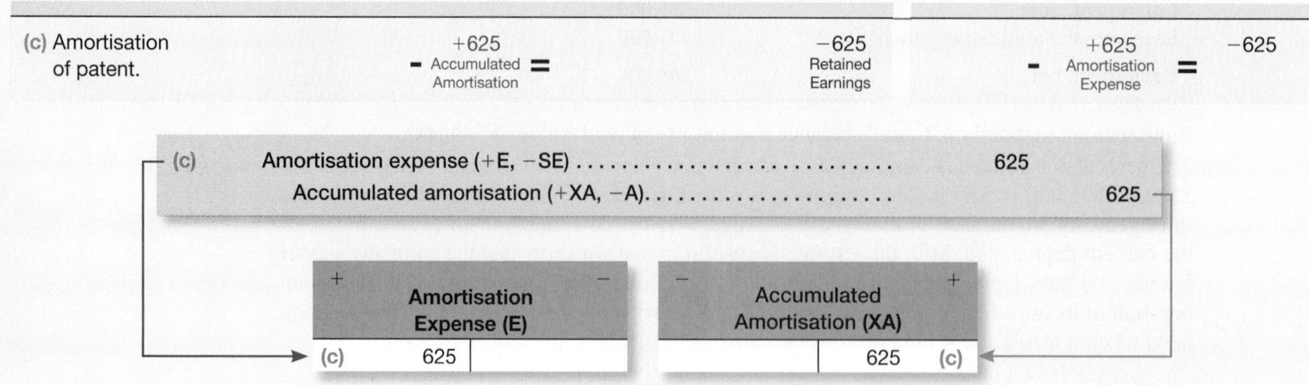

Transaction	Cash Asset	Noncash Assets	Contra Asset	Liabilities	Contrib. Capital	Earned Capital	Revenues	Expenses	Net Income
(c) Amortisation of patent.			+625 Accumulated Amortisation			−625 Retained Earnings		+625 Amortisation Expense	−625

(c) Amortisation expense (+E, −SE) 625
    Accumulated amortisation (+XA, −A). 625

+ Amortisation Expense (E) −	
(c) 625	

− Accumulated Amortisation (XA) +	
	625 (c)

3. Because PFL purchased the right to use the technology, the purchase price can be capitalised as an intangible asset and amortised over the five-year length of the agreement. PFL would record amortisation expense of $18,000 ($90,000/5) each year, beginning July 1, 2015.

(Cyberport would recognise the $90,000 as revenue.) The journal entry that PFL Company would need to record the acquisition of the technology rights would be as follows:

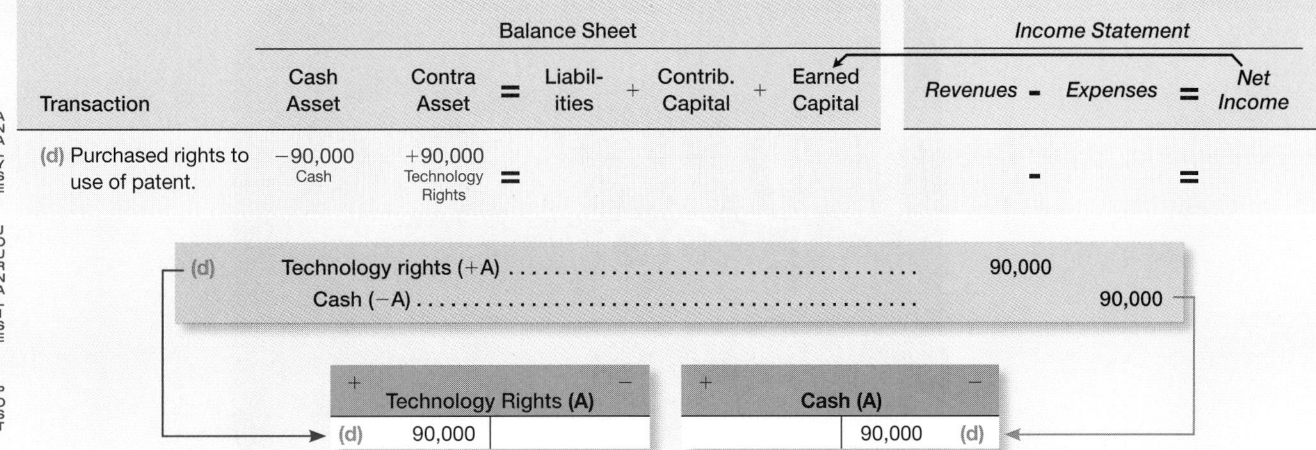

4. Given that the patent is obsolete, both Cyberport Technologies, Inc. and PFL Company would record impairment losses. Cyberport would write off the unamortised balance in the patent account, resulting in a loss of $7,500 [$12,500 − ($1,250 × 4)]. PFL Company would write off the remaining value of the technology agreement, recording an impairment loss of $54,000 [$90,000 − ($18,000 × 2)]. PFL's journal entry would be:

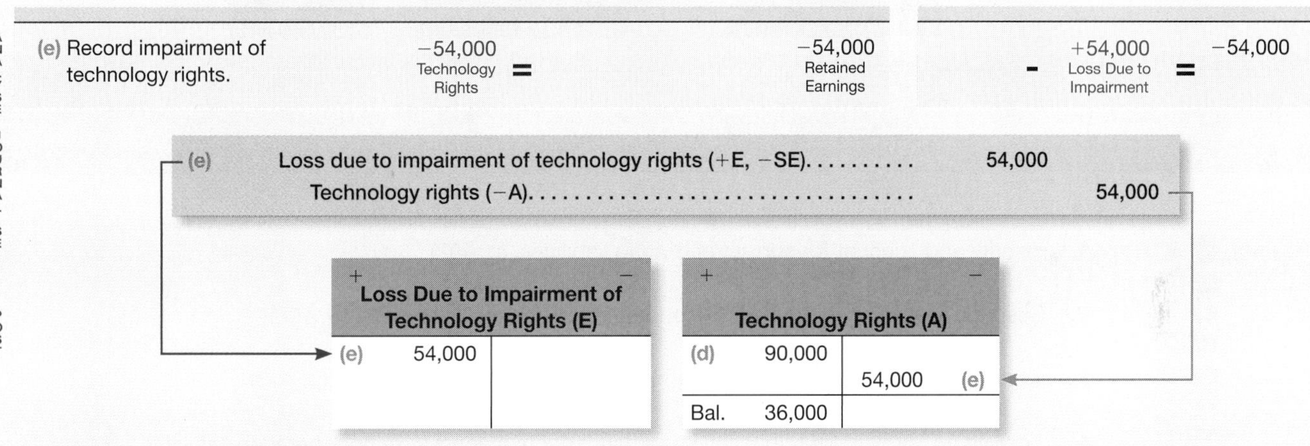

LEARNING OBJECTIVES

1. Identify and account for current operating liabilities. (p. 402)
2. Describe and account for current nonoperating (financial) liabilities. (p. 408)
3. Explain and illustrate the pricing of long-term nonoperating liabilities. (p. 413)
4. Analyse and account for financial statement effects of long-term nonoperating liabilities. (p. 416)
5. Explain how solvency ratios and debt ratings are determined and how they impact the cost of debt. (p. 423)

CHAPTER

9

Reporting and Analysing Liabilities

SAMSUNG ELECTRONICS
www.samsung.com

Samsung Electronics Co. Ltd. (SEC) is the world's largest manufacturer of mobile phones, smartphones, LED panels, and digital TVs. It is headquartered in Suwon, South Korea and has over 200 facilities and offices in 79 countries. Its ordinary shares are traded on the Korea Exchange and London Stock Exchange, and the Samsung Group owns a majority stake in SEC. The company prepares its financial statements using Korean IFRSs, which are identical to IASB's IFRSs except for timing differences for newly published standards. In 2013, SEC reported 228.7 trillion Korean won (USD 216.7 billion) in sales and 30.5 trillion won (USD 28.3 billion) in profit, making it the largest information technology company in the world by revenues.

SEC is recognised as one of the world's top ten global brands. It organises its businesses into three divisions. The consumer electronics division develops and manufactures digital TVs, monitors, printers, digital appliances, and medical equipment. The information technology and mobile communications division includes smartphones, tablet computers, wearable devices, digital cameras, and network equipment. The device solution division designs and manufactures smartphone processors, camera image sensors, flash memories, and LED panels.

The company's goal is to reach USD 400 billion in sales by 2020 and to achieve recognition as one of the most innovative companies in the world. To pursue growth and innovation, SEC operates six design centers and more than 30 R&D centers around the globe. In 2013, it invested 14.8 trillion won (USD 14.0 billion) in R&D. The company will need to continue investing in R&D and capital assets to accomplish its goal. These investments require a significant amount of cash at a time when the company was faced with more than 64 trillion won in total liabilities at the end of fiscal 2013.

Previous chapters focused on the reporting of operating assets, including receivables, inventories, property, plant and equipment, and intangible assets, along with the related expenses. In this chapter and the next two, we turn our attention to the other side of the balance sheet. Chapters 9 and 10 are concerned with reporting liabilities, while Chapter 11 addresses the reporting of shareholders' equity. We discuss how we value liabilities and how debt financing along with the subsequent payment of interest and principal affect the financial statements. We also discuss the required disclosures that enable us to effectively analyse a company's ability to make its liability payments as they mature.

Sources: www.samsung.com; Samsung Electronic 2013 Annual Report; Samsung Group Profile 2013.

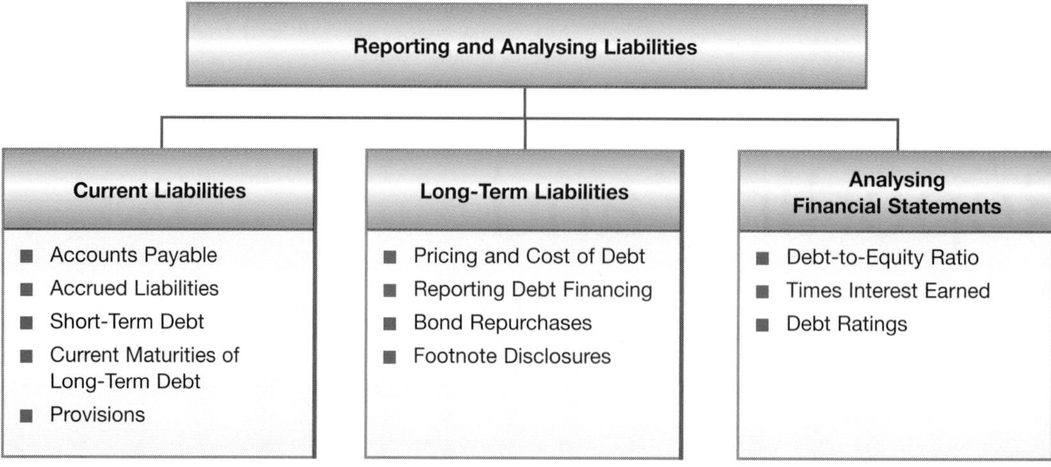

INTRODUCTION

Just as asset disclosures provide us with information on where a company invests its funds, the disclosures concerning liabilities and equity inform us as to how those assets are financed. To be successful, a company must not only invest funds wisely, but must also be astute in the manner in which it finances those investments.

Companies hope to finance their assets at the lowest possible cost. The cost of financing assets with liabilities is the interest charged by the lender. While many liabilities bear explicit interest rates, many other liabilities (such as accounts payable and accrued liabilities) are non-interest-bearing. This fact does not mean that these liabilities are cost-free. For example, while a supplier may appear to offer interest-free credit terms, the cost of that credit is implicitly included in the price it charges for the goods or services it sells.

Samsung's liabilities and equity, as taken from its 2013 annual report, are presented in Exhibit 9.1. Just as assets are classified as either current or non-current, so are liabilities presented in the balance sheet as either current or non-current.

Current liabilities, as the name implies, are short-term in nature, generally requiring payment within the coming year. As a result, they are not a suitable source of funding for long-term assets that generate cash flows over several years. Instead, companies often finance long-term assets with long-term liabilities that require payments over several years, so that the cash outflows required by the financing source match the cash inflows produced by the assets to which they relate.

When a company acquires assets, and finances them with liabilities, its **financial leverage** increases. Because the magnitude of required liability payments increases with the level of liability financing, those larger payments increase the chance of default should a downturn in business occur. Increasing levels of liabilities make the company riskier to creditors who, consequently, demand a higher return on the financing they provide to the company. The assessment of default risk is part of liquidity and solvency analysis.

This chapter, along with Chapter 10, focuses on liabilities that are reported on the balance sheet and the corresponding interest costs reported in the income statement. All such liabilities represent probable, nondiscretionary, future obligations that are the result of events that have already occurred. Chapter 10 also addresses *off-balance sheet financing*, which encompasses future obligations that are reported in the notes, but not on the face of the balance sheet. An understanding of both on-balance sheet and off-balance sheet financing is central to evaluating a company's financial condition and assessing its risk of default.

CURRENT LIABILITIES

Liabilities are separated on the balance sheet into current and non-current. We first focus our attention on current liabilities, which are obligations that must be met (paid) within one year or

EXHIBIT 9.1 Samsung Electronics' Liabilities and Equity

(In millions of Korean won)	December 31, 2013	December 31, 2012
Liabilities and Equity		
Current liabilities		
Trade and other payables	17,633,705	16,889,350
Short-term borrowings	6,438,517	8,443,752
Advances received	1,706,313	1,517,672
Withholdings	1,176,046	966,374
Accrued expenses	11,344,530	9,495,156
Income tax payable	3,386,018	3,222,934
Current portion of long-term borrowings and debentures	2,425,831	999,010
Provisions	6,736,476	5,054,853
Other current liabilities	467,973	343,951
Total current liabilities	**51,315,409**	**46,933,052**
Non-current liabilities		
Long-term trade and other payables	1,053,756	1,165,881
Debentures	1,311,068	1,829,374
Long-term borrowings	985,117	3,623,028
Net defined benefit liabilities	1,854,902	1,729,939
Deferred income tax liabilities	6,012,371	3,429,467
Provisions	460,924	408,529
Other non-current liabilities	1,065,461	472,094
Total liabilities	**64,059,008**	**59,591,364**
Equity attributable to owners of the parent		
Preferred stock	119,467	119,467
Common stock	778,047	778,047
Share premium	4,403,893	4,403,893
Retained earnings	148,600,282	119,985,689
Other components of equity	(9,459,073)	(8,193,044)
Non-controlling interests	**5,573,394**	**4,386,154**
Total equity	**150,016,010**	**121,480,206**
Total liabilities and equity	**214,075,018**	**181,071,570**

one operating cycle, whichever is longer. Most current liabilities such as those related to utilities, wages, insurance, rent, and taxes, generate a corresponding impact on operating expenses.

Samsung reports nine categories of current liabilities: (1) Trade and other payables, (2) short-term borrowings, (3) advances received, (4) withholdings, (5) accrued expenses, (6) income tax payable, (7) current portion of long-term borrowings and debentures, which include long-term obligations that are scheduled for payment in the upcoming year, (8) provisions, and (9) other current liabilities, which consist of miscellaneous short-term obligations too small to list separately.

It is helpful to separate current liabilities into operating and nonoperating components. These two components primarily consist of:

1. Current operating liabilities
   - **Accounts payable** or **trade payable** Obligations to suppliers for amounts owed on purchases of goods and services. These are usually non-interest-bearing.
   - **Accrued liabilities** or **accrued expenses** Obligations for expenses incurred that have not been paid as of the end of the current period. These include, for example, accruals for employee wages earned but yet unpaid, accruals for taxes (usually quarterly) on payroll and current-period profits, and accruals for other liabilities such as rent, utilities, and insurance. Accruals are made to properly reflect the liabilities owed as of the statement date and the expenses incurred in the period. If an item is material, it should be listed

separately, like Samsung does for income tax payable. Each one is journalised by a debit to an expense account and a credit to a related liability.

- **Deferred performance liabilities** Obligations that will be satisfied, not by paying cash, but instead, by providing products or services to customers. Examples of deferred performance liabilities include customer deposits (advances received), unearned gift card revenues for retail companies, and liabilities for frequent flier programmes offered by airlines.

2. Current nonoperating liabilities
   - **Short-term debt** Short-term bank borrowings and notes expected to mature in whole or in part during the upcoming year; including any accrued interest payable on these obligations.
   - **Current maturities of long-term debt** Long-term borrowings and debentures that are scheduled to mature in whole or in part during the upcoming year including any accrued interest for the period on these obligations.

The remainder of this section describes current liabilities.

Accounts or Trade Payable

LO1 Identify and account for current operating liabilities.

Accounts payable, which are part of current operating liabilities, arise from the purchase of goods and services from others on credit. Samsung reports ₩17,633,705 in trade and other payables as of December 31, 2013.

Accounts payable are a non-interest-bearing source of financing. Increased payables reduce the amount of net working capital, because these payables are deducted from current assets in the computation of net working capital. Also, increased payables improves operating cash flow (because inventories were purchased without using cash). An increase in accounts payable also increases profitability because it causes a reduction in the level of interest-bearing debt that is required to finance operating assets. ROE increases when companies make use of this low-cost financing source. However, management must be careful to avoid excessive "**leaning on the trade**" because short-term income and cash flow gains can result in long-term costs such as damaged supply channels.[1]

When a company purchases goods or services on credit, suppliers often grant **cash discounts** to buyers if payment is made within a specified time period. Cash discounts are usually established as part of the credit terms and stated as a percentage of the purchase price. For example, credit terms of 1/10, n/30 (one-ten, net-thirty) indicate that a 1% cash discount is allowed if the payment is made within 10 days. If the cash discount is not taken, the full purchase price is due in 30 days.

Net-of-Discount Method To illustrate a cash discount, assume that a company purchases 1,000 units of merchandise at $4 per unit on terms of 1/10, n/30. The total purchase price is 1,000 × $4 = $4,000. However, if payment is made within 10 days, the net purchase price would then be $3,960 ($4,000 − $40). While this difference seems like a small amount, consider the cost of not taking the discount. If the discount is missed, the buyer is afforded an extra 20 days to pay for the merchandise, for which it pays a penalty of $40, or $2 per day. Two dollars per day is the equivalent of $730 dollars per year which, in turn, is equivalent to paying interest at an annual rate of 18.4% ($730/$3,960).[2]

When cash discounts are offered, the inventory purchase should be recorded at its cost using the **net-of-discount method**. When the net-of-discount method is used, inventory is capitalised at the net cost, assuming that the discount will be taken by the buyer. Continuing with our example, the following entry would be recorded by the buyer at the time of purchase:

---

[1] We must be careful, because excessive delays in the payment of payables can result in suppliers charging a higher price for their goods or, ultimately, refusing to sell to certain buyers. This situation is a hidden "financing" cost that, even though it is not interest, is a real cost.

[2] Compound interest methods (introduced in Appendix A) would arrive at a slightly higher annual rate of interest, about 19.6%.

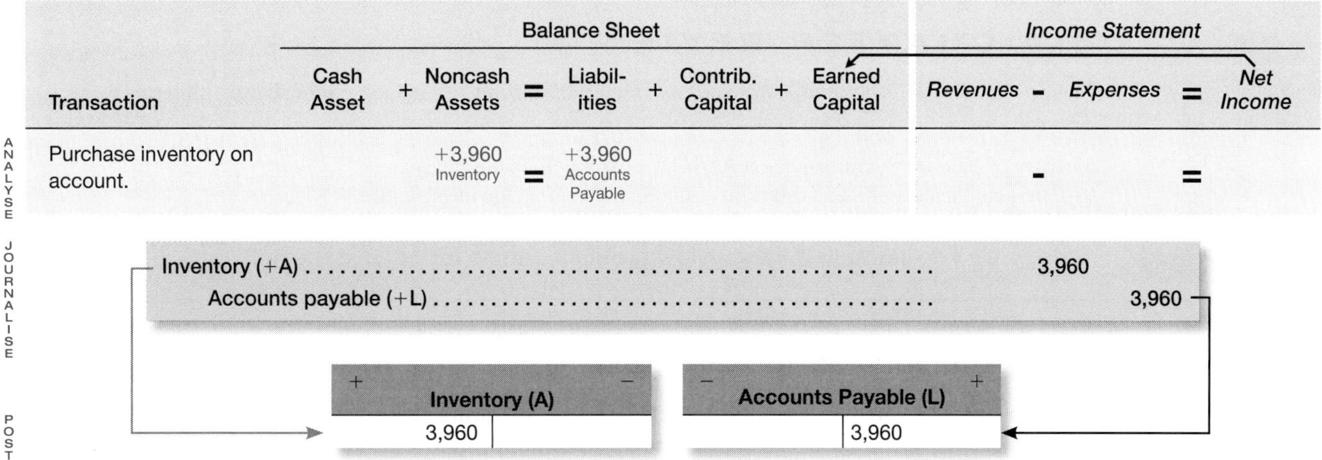

When payment is made within the 10-day discount period, accounts payable is debited and cash is credited:

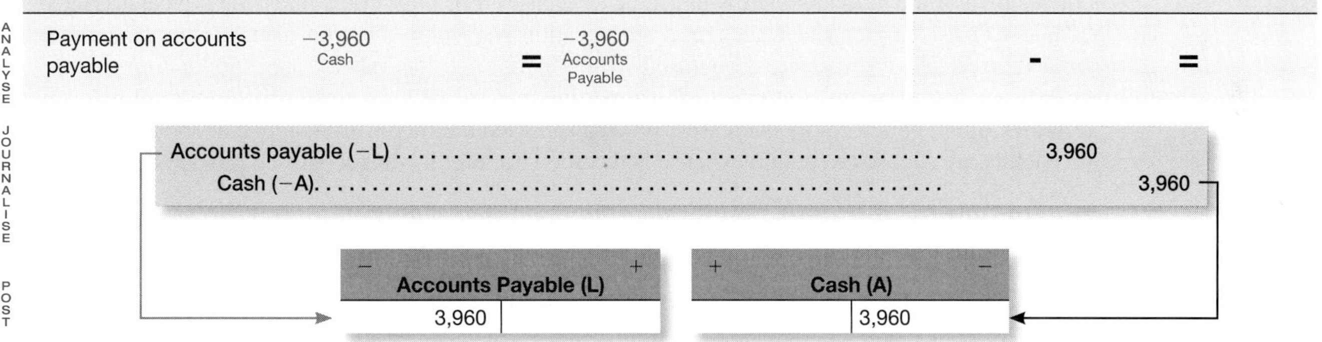

However, when a discount is missed, the lost discount must be recorded. For example, if full payment is made after the 10-day discount period, the payment is recorded as follows:

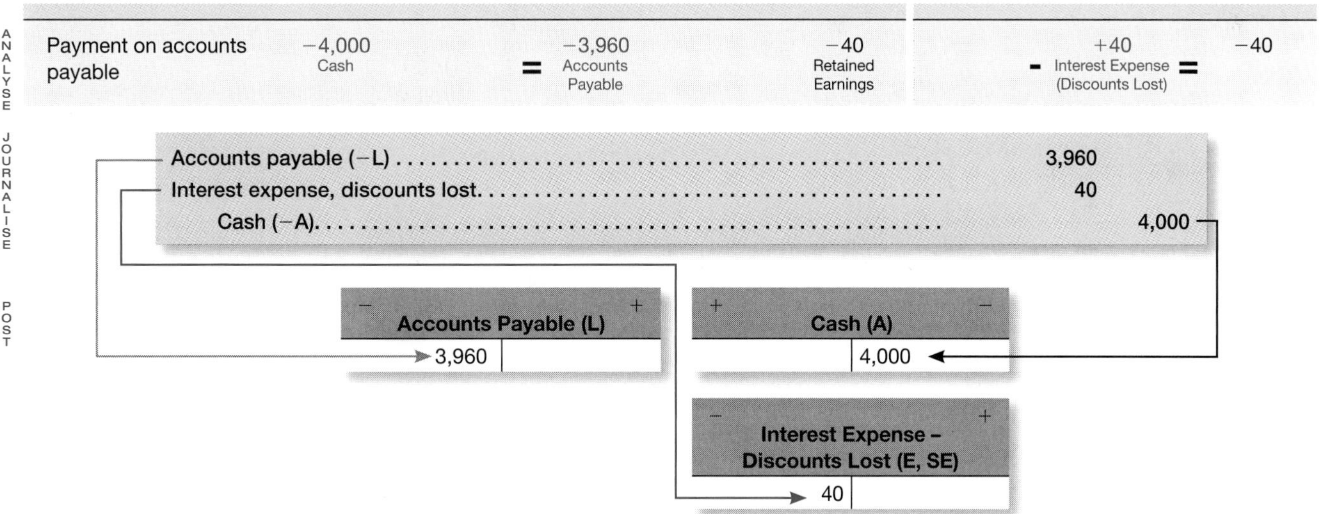

The missed discount is an expense in the period when the discount is lost. This serves two purposes. First, discounts lost are not capitalised as part of inventory and are not added to cost of goods sold. Instead, the lost discounts are treated like a finance charge and recorded as an expense of the period when the discount is missed. Second, the net-of-discount method highlights late payments by explicitly keeping a record of lost discounts. Given the high cost of missed cash discounts, most businesses would likely want to minimise the amount of discounts lost. Thus, keeping a record of discounts lost is useful when it comes to managing cash and accounts payable.

MID-CHAPTER REVIEW 1

On April 12, Bugis Corporation purchased raw materials costing $29,000 on credit. The credit terms were 2/10, n/30.

a. If Bugis paid for the materials on April 19, how much would it pay?
b. Compute the cost of a lost discount as an annual percentage interest rate.

The solution to this review problem can be found on page 443.

Accrued Liabilities

Accrued liabilities are identified at the end of an accounting period to reflect liabilities and expenses that have been incurred during the period but are not yet paid or recognised in financial statements.[3]

As shown in Exhibit 9.1 earlier, Samsung reports ₩11,344,530 million in accrued expenses and ₩3,386,018 million in income tax payable as of December 31, 2013. The company does not provide a breakdown of the individual items in accrued expenses. For most companies, the typical accruals include accrued salaries and wages, accrued vacation pay, interest payable, utilities payable, and accrued taxes. The accruals are recognised with a liability on the balance sheet and a corresponding expense on the income statement. This reporting means that liabilities increase, current income decreases, and reported equity decreases. When an accrued liability is ultimately paid, both cash and the liability are decreased (but no expense is recorded because it was recognised previously).

Accounting for Accrued Liabilities The following entries illustrate the accounting for a typical accrued liability, accrued wages:

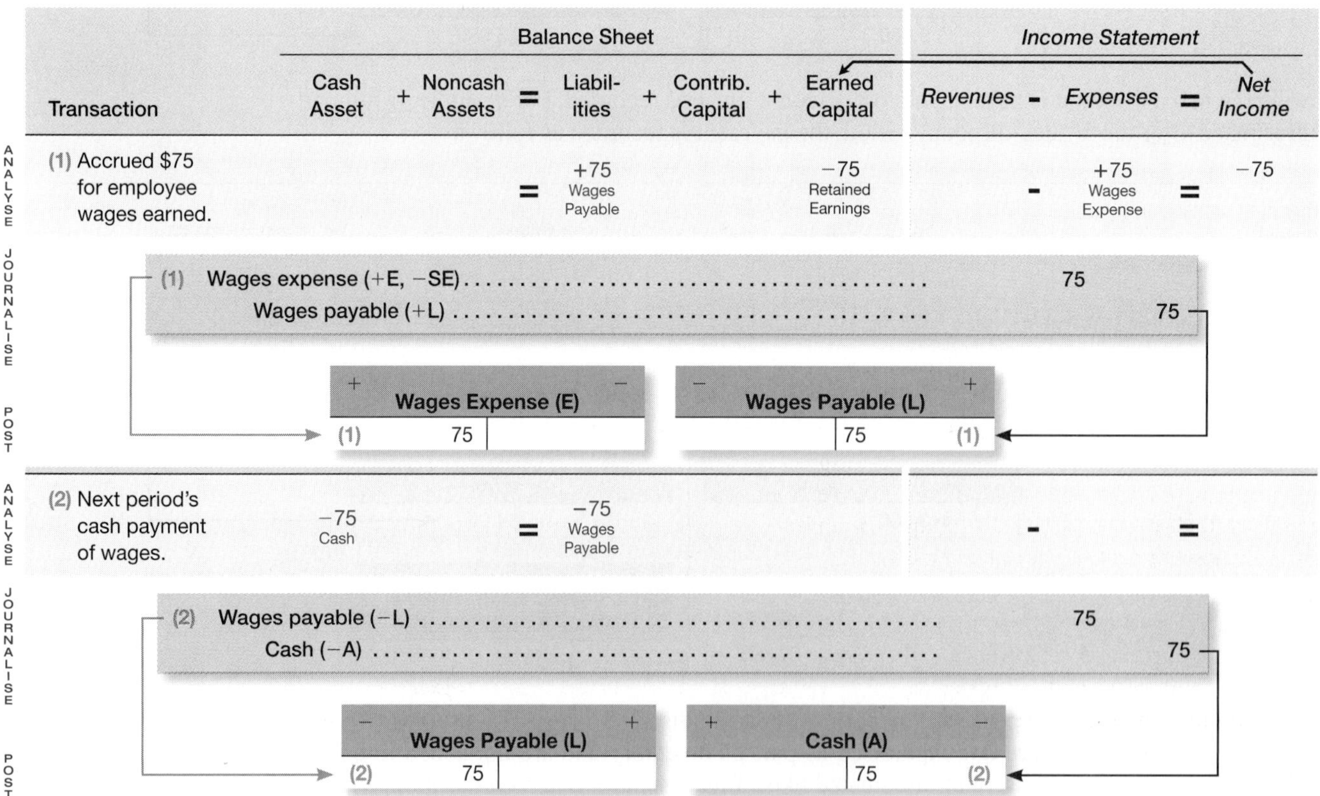

[3] Accruals can also be made for recognition of revenue and a corresponding receivable. An example of this situation would be revenue recognition on a long-term contract that has reached a particular milestone, or for interest earned but not received on an investment in bonds that is still outstanding at period-end.

The following financial statement effects result from this accrual of employee wages:

- Employees have worked during a period and have not yet been paid. The effect of this accrual is to increase wages payable on the balance sheet and to recognise wages expense on the income statement. Failure to recognise this liability and associated expense would understate liabilities on the balance sheet and overstate income.
- Employees are paid in the following period, resulting in a cash decrease and a reduction in wages payable. This payment does not result in expense because the expense was recognised in the prior period when incurred.

Provisions The accrued wages illustration relates to events that are fairly certain. Some accrued liabilities, however, are less certain than others. Consider a company facing a lawsuit. Should it record the possible liability and related expense? The answer depends on the likelihood of occurrence and the ability to estimate the obligation. If it is probable (i.e., with at least a 50% chance) that an outflow of economic benefits will occur and the amount is reasonably estimable, a company will recognise this obligation, called a provision, at the most likely amount. The most likely amount is calculated as the expected value of all the possible amounts.

In note 18 of its 2013 annual report, Samsung reports details of its ₩7,197,400 million provisions on the balance sheet (₩6,736,476 million under current liabilities and ₩460,924 million under non-current liabilities):

18. Provisions

Changes in the provisions for the year ended December 31, 2013, are as follows:

(In millions of Korean won)	Warranty	Royalty expenses	Long-term incentives	Others	Total
Balance as of January 1	₩2,032,817	₩2,773,196	₩576,329	₩81,040	₩5,463,382
Charged (credited) to the statement of income	2,076,633	1,854,900	498,483	(6,862)	4,423,154
Payment	(2,104,019)	(278,961)	(152,964)	(16,636)	(2,552,580)
Others*	(59,439)	(76,465)	—	(652)	(136,556)
Balance as of December 31	₩1,945,992	₩4,272,670	₩921,848	₩56,890	₩7,197,400

* Others include effects of changes in foreign currency exchange rates.

Samsung recognises three specific types of provisions: warranty, royalty expenses, and long-term incentives. The warranty provision covers the obligation to provide future repairs, service, and recalls to customers (see details below). The company makes provisions for the estimated royalty expenses that it is negotiating with counterparties. Finally, Samsung makes a provision for the estimated cost of an executive incentive plan, which is based on performance over the next three years. Other examples include provisions for restructuring, environmental clean up, removal cost, customer refunds, etc.

Warranties Warranty liabilities are an example of a provision, which is a liability of uncertain amount or timing. Warranties are commitments made by manufacturers to their customers to repair or replace defective products within a specified period of time. The expected cost of this commitment usually is reasonably estimated at the time of sale based on past experience. As a result, manufacturers are required to record the expected cost of warranties as a liability, and to record the related expected warranty expense in the income statement to match against the sales revenue reported for that period.[4]

To illustrate, the effects of an accrual of a $1,000 warranty liability are:

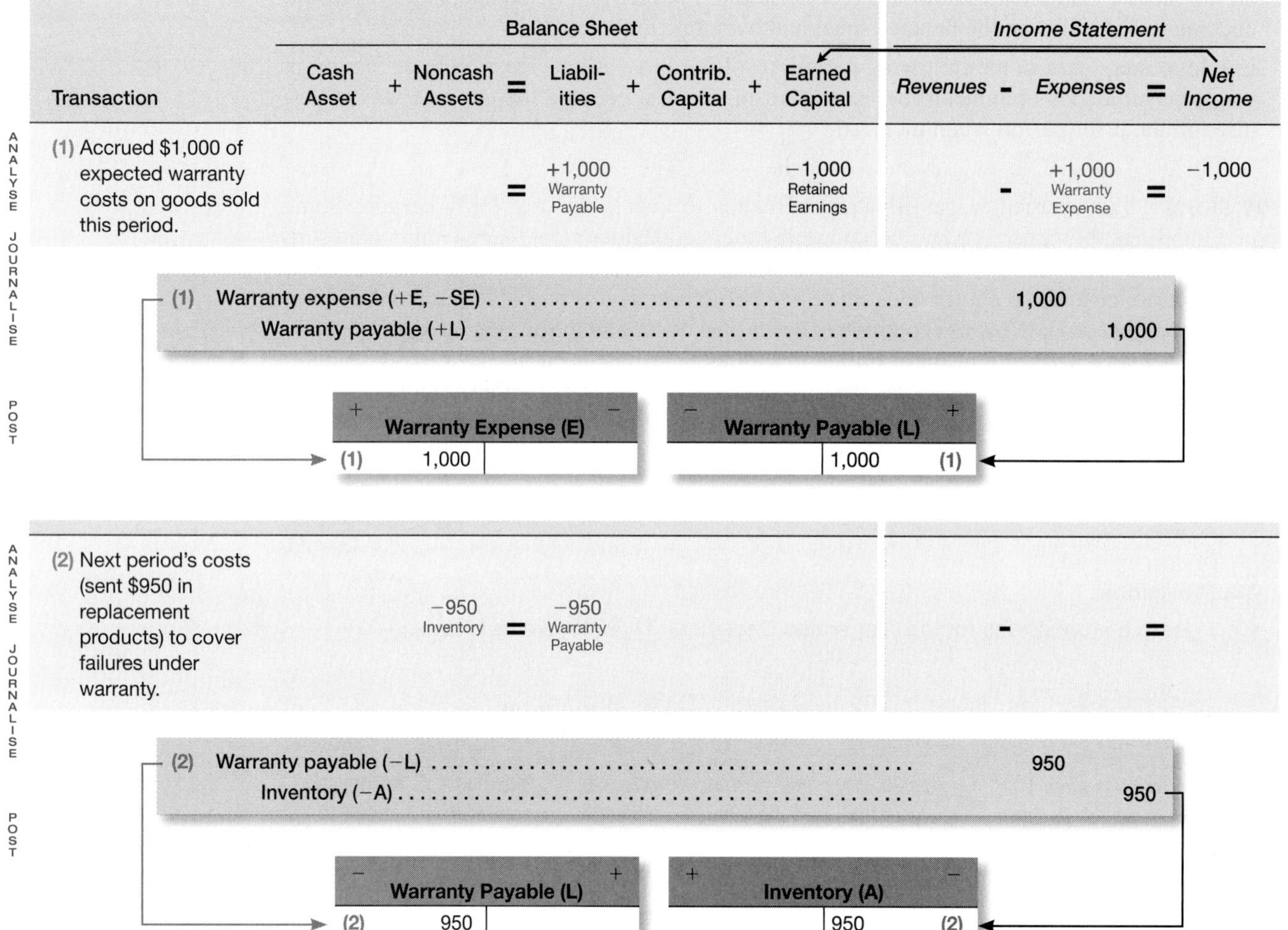

Reporting of warranty liabilities has the same effect on financial statements as does the accrual of wages expense in the previous section. That is, a liability is recorded on the balance sheet and an expense is reported in the income statement, reducing income by the warranty accrual. When the defective product is later replaced (or repaired), the liability is reduced together with the cost of the inventory (or other assets) spent to satisfy the claim. (Only a portion of the products estimated to fail does so in the current period; we expect other product failures in future periods. Management monitors this estimate and adjusts it if failure is higher or lower than expected.) As in the accrual of wages, the expense is reported when it is incurred and the liability is estimated at that time, not when payments are made.

As shown in the previous section, Samsung reported ₩2,032,817 million of warranty liability as of January 1, 2013. During 2013, the company accrued an additional ₩2,076,633 million in new

[4] The new revenue recognition standard discussed in Chapter 6 and Appendix 6B has implications for the accounting for warranty obligations. When a company delivers a product with a warranty, is the warranty simply assurance that the product will function as intended, or should it be considered a separate performance obligation? If it is considered a separate performance obligation, then the company would allocate the purchase price between the product and the warranty and recognise an unearned revenue liability at the time of purchase, as shown in Chapter 6. However, if the warranty is not a separate performance obligation (e.g., it cannot be purchased separately from the product and is intended as assurance that the product will perform as expected), a liability accrual for the warranty obligation must be made at the time of purchase.

warranty liabilities. On the other hand, it incurred ₩2,104,019 million in cost to replace or repair defective products during the year, reducing the liability by this amount. This cost can be in the form of cash paid to customers or to employees as wages, and in the form of parts used for repairs. As a result, the balance in warranty liability was ₩1,945,992 million at the end of fiscal year 2013. It is important to realise that only the increase in the liability resulting from additional accruals affects the income statement, reducing income through the additional warranty expense. Warranty payments reduce the warranty liability but have no impact on the income statement.

IFRS requires that the warranty liability reflect the estimated amount of cost that the company expects to incur as a result of warranty claims. This amount is often difficult to estimate and is prone to error. There is also the possibility that a company might intentionally underestimate its warranty liability to report higher current income, or overestimate it so as to depress current income and create an additional liability on the balance sheet that can be used to absorb future warranty costs without the need to record additional expense. Doing so would shift income from the current period to one or more future periods. Warranty liabilities should be compared with sales levels. Any deviations from the historical relation of the warranty liability to sales may indicate a product quality issue or, alternatively, it may reveal earnings management.

All accrued liabilities result in a liability on the balance sheet and an expense on the income statement. Management has some latitude in determining the amount and timing for accruals. This latitude can lead to misreporting of income and liabilities (unintentional or otherwise). For example, if accruals are underestimated, then liabilities are underestimated, income is overestimated, and retained earnings are overestimated. In subsequent periods when an understated accrued liability is reversed (it is recognised in the account), reported income is lower than it should be; this is because prior period income was higher than it should have been. (The reverse holds for overestimated accruals.) The over- and under-reporting of accruals, therefore, results in the shifting of income from one period into another.

Experience tells us that some accrued liabilities are more prone to misstatement than others. Estimated accruals that are linked with restructuring programmes, including severance accruals and accruals for asset write-downs, are often overstated, as are estimated environmental liabilities. Companies sometimes overestimate these "one-time" accruals, resulting in early recognition of expenses and a corresponding reduction in current period income. This choice, in turn, boosts income in future years when management decides that the accrual can be reversed because it was initially too large. This may suggest that management is conservative and wants to avoid understating liabilities. It can also reflect a desire by management to show earnings growth in the future by shifting current income to future periods. Accrued liabilities set up to smooth income over future periods are called "**reserves**." The terms "clearing the decks" and "taking a big bath" have also been applied to such accounting practices.

Contingent Liabilities A contingent liability is a potential obligation that will arise if some uncertain event occurs in the future (regardless of the company's ability to estimate the amount), or a present obligation but payment is not probable or the amount of payment cannot be reliably estimated. Contingent liability is not reported on the balance sheet. If the liability is considered material, companies should disclose the nature and details of the potential liability in a note to the financial statements.

BUSINESS INSIGHT

BP and the Gulf of Mexico Oil Spill In response to the April 2010 Gulf of Mexico oil spill, the UK-based **BP** recorded US$16.3 billion in **provisions** on its balance sheet as of December 31, 2010. The provisions included amounts to cover environmental expenditures, spill response costs, litigation and claims, and Clean Water Act penalties.

BP further disclosed in its 2010 annual report that it was named as a defendant in about 600 civil lawsuits and was subject to civil fines and penalties from a number of federal and state governmental agencies. It explained that "[g]iven the large number of claims that may be asserted, it is not possible at this time to determine whether and to what extent any such claims would be successful or what penalties or fines would be assessed . . . Any such possible obligations are therefore **contingent liabilities** and, at present, it is not practicable to estimate their magnitude or possible timing of payment . . . "

YOU MAKE THE CALL

You are the Analyst Dow Chemical Company reported accrued environmental liabilities in excess of $706 million in its 2014 balance sheet. What conditions needed to be met before these liabilities could be reported? The company also indicated in a footnote that actual environmental liabilities could be twice this amount. How does this uncertainty potentially affect Dow's balance sheet? [Answers on page 428]

MID-CHAPTER REVIEW 2

The Keukenhof N.V. reported warranty liabilities of €56,934,000 in its 2014 balance sheet. In 2015, it reported a liability of €62,730,000. It recognised €39,570,000 in net warranty expenses during 2015. What amount of cost did Keukenhof N.V. incur to cover warranty claims in 2015? How would these warranty claims be recorded?

The solution to this review problem can be found on page 443.

Current Nonoperating (Financial) Liabilities

LO2 Describe and account for current nonoperating (financial) liabilities.

Current nonoperating (financial) liabilities include short-term bank loans, the accrual of interest on those loans, and the current maturities of long-term debt. Companies generally try to structure their financing so that debt service requirements (payments) of those financing obligations coincide with the cash inflows from the assets financed. This strategy means that current assets are usually financed with current liabilities, and that long-term assets are financed with long-term liability (and equity) sources.

The use of short-term financing is particularly important for companies that have seasonal sales. To illustrate, a seasonal company's investment in current assets tends to fluctuate during the year as depicted in the graphic below:

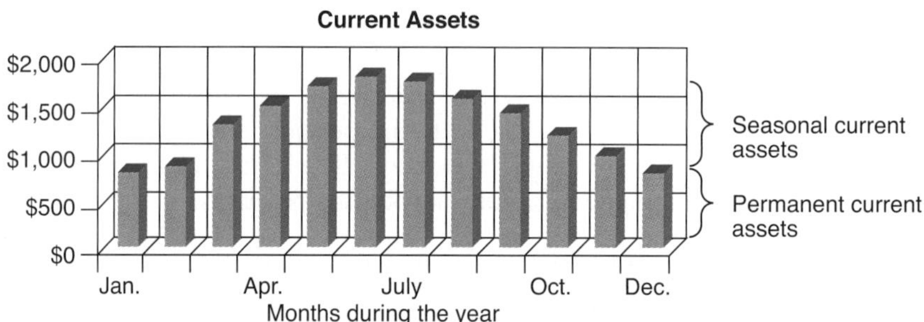

This particular company does most of its selling in the summer months. More inventory is purchased and manufactured in the early spring than at any other time of the year. Sales of the company's manufactured goods are also greater during the summer months, giving rise to accounts receivable that are higher than normal during the summer and fall. The peak working capital level is reached at the height of the selling season and is lowest when the business slows in the off-season. There is a permanent level of working capital required for this business (about $750), and a seasonal component (maximum of about $1,000). Businesses differ in their working capital requirements, but many have permanent and seasonal components.

If a company's working capital needs fluctuate from one season to the next, then the financing needs of the company are also seasonal. Some assets can be financed with short-term operating liabilities. For example, seasonal increases in inventory balances are typically financed with increased levels of accounts payable. However, operating liabilities are unlikely to meet all of the financing needs of a company. Additional financing is provided by short-term interest-bearing debt.

This section focuses on short-term nonoperating liabilities. These include short-term debt and interest as well as current maturities of long-term liabilities.

Short-Term Interest-Bearing Debt Seasonal swings in working capital are often financed with a bank line of credit (short-term debt). In this case the bank provides a commitment to lend up to a given level with the understanding that the amounts borrowed are repaid in full sometime during the year. An interest-bearing note is evidence of such borrowing.

When these short-term funds are borrowed, the cash received is reported on the balance sheet together with an increase in liabilities (notes payable). The note is reported as a current liability because the expectation is that it will be paid within a year. This borrowing transaction has no effect on income or equity, but there will be a financing cash inflow on the statement of cash flows. The borrower incurs (and the lender earns) interest on the note as time passes. Hence, it is required to accrue the interest liability and the related interest expense each time financial statements are issued.

To illustrate, assume that Banff Corp. borrows $1,000 cash from 1st Bank on January 1. The note bears interest at a 12% annual (3% quarterly) rate, and the interest is payable on the first of each subsequent quarter (April 1, July 1, October 1, January 1). Assuming that Banff Corp. issues calendar-quarter financial statements, this borrowing results in the following financial statement effects for the period January 1 through April 1:

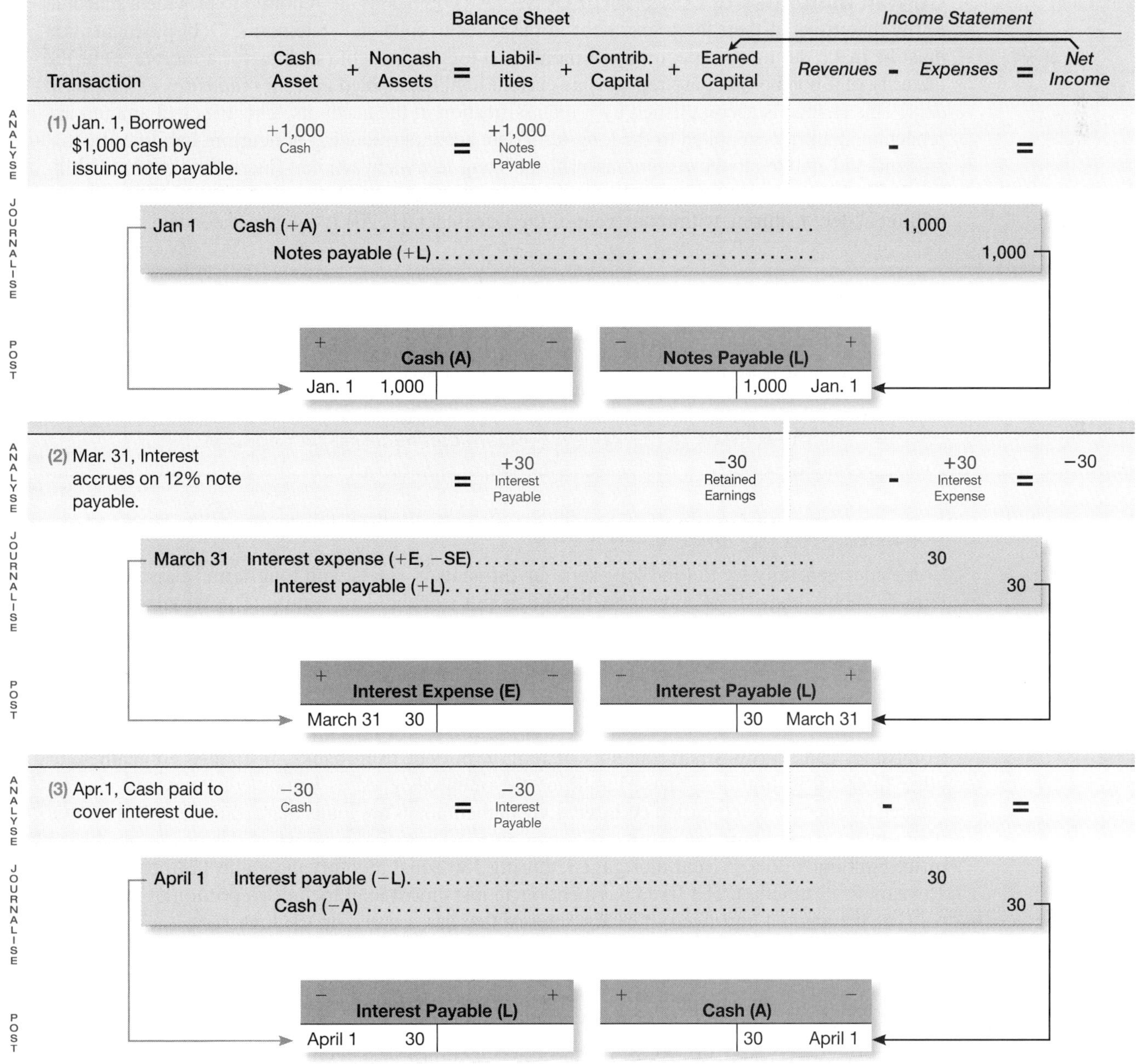

Transaction	Cash Asset	+ Noncash Assets	=	Liabilities	+ Contrib. Capital	+ Earned Capital	Revenues	− Expenses	=	Net Income
(1) Jan. 1, Borrowed $1,000 cash by issuing note payable.	+1,000 Cash		=	+1,000 Notes Payable				−	=	
(2) Mar. 31, Interest accrues on 12% note payable.			=	+30 Interest Payable		−30 Retained Earnings		− +30 Interest Expense	=	−30
(3) Apr. 1, Cash paid to cover interest due.	−30 Cash		=	−30 Interest Payable				−	=	

(1) Journalise:

Jan 1	Cash (+A)	1,000	
	Notes payable (+L)		1,000

Post:

+ Cash (A) −		− Notes Payable (L) +	
Jan. 1 1,000			1,000 Jan. 1

(2) Journalise:

March 31	Interest expense (+E, −SE)	30	
	Interest payable (+L)		30

Post:

+ Interest Expense (E) −		− Interest Payable (L) +	
March 31 30			30 March 31

(3) Journalise:

April 1	Interest payable (−L)	30	
	Cash (−A)		30

Post:

− Interest Payable (L) +		+ Cash (A) −	
April 1 30			30 April 1

The January 1 borrowing is reflected by an increase in cash and in notes payable. On March 31, this company issues its quarterly financial statements. Although interest is not paid until April 1, the company has incurred three months' interest obligation as of March 31. Failure to recognise this liability and the expense incurred would not fairly present the financial condition of the company. Accordingly, the quarterly accrued interest is computed as follows:

Interest Expense	=	**Principal**	×	**Annual Rate**	×	**Portion of Year Outstanding**
\$30	=	**\$1,000**	×	**12%**	×	**3/12**

The subsequent interest payment on April 1 is reflected in the financial statements as a reduction of cash and a reduction of the interest payable liability accrued on March 31. There is no expense reported on April 1, because it was recorded the previous day (March 31) when the financial statements were prepared. However, the payment of interest would be either an operating or a financing cash outflow in the statement of cash flows for the quarter beginning April 1. (For fixed-maturity borrowings specified in days, such as a 90-day note, we use a 365-day year for interest accrual computations, see Mid-Chapter Review 3 below.)

Current Maturities of Long-Term Debt All companies are required to provide a schedule of the maturities of their long-term debt in the notes to financial statements. Debt payments that must be made during the upcoming 12 months on long-term debt (such as for a mortgage) or the maturity of a bond or note are reported as current liabilities called *current maturities of long-term debt*. This change is accomplished by a reclassification in the accounts. The principal amount approaching maturity is debited to the long-term debt account (reducing noncurrent liabilities by that amount) and credited to the current maturities of long-term debt account (increasing current liabilities by that amount). In Samsung's balance sheet, the current liability section shows ₩2,425,831 million in debt maturing within one year of the December 31, 2013, balance sheet date.

MID-CHAPTER REVIEW 3

Marylebone plc borrowed £10,000 on a 90-day, 6% note payable dated January 15. The bank accrues interest daily based on a 365-day year. Use journal entries, T-accounts, and the financial statement effects template to show the implications (amounts and accounts) of the January 31 month-end interest accrual.

The solution to this review problem can be found on page 444.

LONG-TERM LIABILITIES

Companies generally try to fund long-term investments in assets with long-term financing. Long-term financing consists of long-term liabilities and stockholders' equity. The remainder of this chapter focuses on long-term debt liabilities. Other long-term liabilities are discussed in Chapter 10 and stockholders' equity is the focus of Chapter 11.

Instalment Loans

Companies can borrow small amounts of long-term debt from banks, insurance companies, or other financial institutions. These liabilities are often designed as instalment loans and may be secured by specific assets called **collateral**. Instalment loans are loans that require a fixed periodic payment for a fixed duration of time. For example, assume that a company decides to finance an office building with a 15-year mortgage requiring 180 equal monthly payments (180 payments = 15 years × 12 months). The fixed payment on an instalment loan includes a portion of the principal (i.e., the amount borrowed) plus any interest that has accrued on the loan.

To illustrate the accounting for instalment loans, assume that Shevlin Company borrowed \$40,000 from 1st Bank on July 1, 2012. The terms of the loan require that Shevlin repay the loan in 12 equal quarterly payments over a three-year period and charges 8% interest per year. The quarterly payment is \$3,782 and can be calculated using the present value factor for 12 periods (3 years × 4 quarters) and 2% interest (8% per year ÷ 4 quarters) as follows:

$$\text{Present Value} = \text{Payment} \times \text{Present Value Factor}$$

$$\frac{\text{Present Value}}{\text{Present Value Factor}} = \text{Payment}$$

$$\frac{\$40{,}000}{10.57534} = \$3{,}782$$

Using a financial calculator, we can compute the payment by letting N be the number of quarters and setting I/Yr equal to the interest rate per quarter. The payment can then be calculated as follows: N = 12; I/Yr = 2; PV = 40,000; FV = 0:

Calculator				
N	I/Yr	PV	PMT	FV
12	2	40,000	3,782	0

When Shevlin Company agrees to the loan terms, it receives the loan amount, $40,000 in cash, and incurs a $40,000 liability (instalment loan payable). The loan is recorded on July 1 as follows:

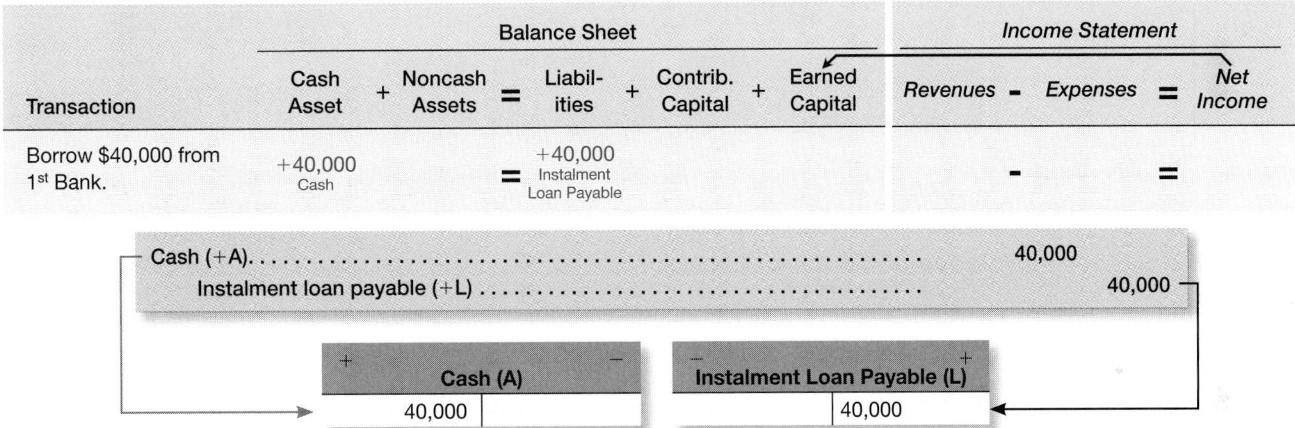

On October 1, 2012, the first payment of $3,782 is due. The payment includes both interest for the three months from July 1 through September 30, and some portion of the original loan amount (the **principal**). The division of the payment between interest and principal is best illustrated using a **loan amortisation table**, like the one in Exhibit 9.1.

EXHIBIT 9.1 Loan Amortisation Table

Date	[A] Beginning Balance	[B] Cash Payment	[C] ([A] x interest %) Interest	[D] ([B] – [C]) Principal	[E] ([A] – [D]) Balance
07/01/12					40,000
10/01/12	40,000	3,782	800	2,982	37,018
01/01/13	37,018	3,782	740	3,042	33,976
04/01/13	33,976	3,782	679	3,103	30,873
07/01/13	30,873	3,782	617	3,165	27,708
10/01/13	27,708	3,782	554	3,228	24,480
01/01/14	24,480	3,782	489	3,293	21,187
04/01/14	21,187	3,782	423	3,359	17,828
07/01/14	17,828	3,782	356	3,426	14,402
10/01/14	14,402	3,782	288	3,494	10,908
01/01/15	10,908	3,782	218	3,564	7,344
04/01/15	7,344	3,782	146	3,636	3,708
07/01/15	3,708	3,782	74	3,708	0

Each payment includes interest and principal. The first loan payment, due on October 1, 2012, is summarised in the second row of the table. Column [B] is the quarterly loan payment. Column [C] is the interest expense, computed by multiplying column [A] by the interest rate (2 percent per quarter). Column [D] is the principal portion of the payment, which is the cash payment (column [B]) less the interest (column [C]). The remaining balance on the loan is in column [E], which is equal to the beginning balance in column [A] less the principal payment from column [D]. The loan balance decreases with each payment until the loan is paid off on July 1, 2015.

The first payment is recorded as follows:

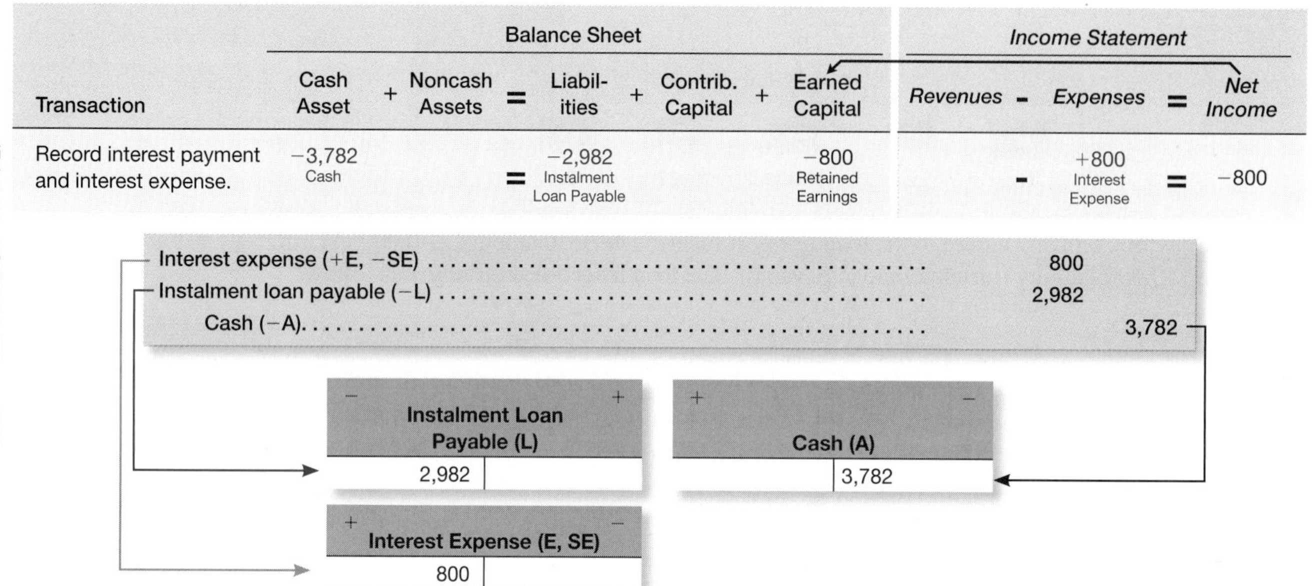

Subsequent payments are recorded similarly. Each loan payment is the same amount, quarter after quarter. And each period's interest expense is equal to the beginning loan balance times the periodic interest rate. Any difference between the payment and the interest expense affects the loan balance. In Exhibit 9.2, each payment contains some portion of interest expense and some portion of principal repayment, and the amounts change over time. As principal is repaid, the loan balance decreases, reducing the subsequent periods' interest expense and increasing the subsequent periods' principal repayment.

Bonds

Sometimes the amount of financing required by a company is greater than the amount that a bank or insurance company can provide. Companies can borrow larger amounts of money by issuing bonds (or notes) in the capital markets. Bonds and notes are debt securities issued by companies and traded in the bond markets. When a company issues bonds, it is borrowing money. The investors who buy the bonds are lending money to the issuing company. That is, the bondholders are the company's creditors. Because the bond markets provide companies with access to large amounts of capital, bonds represent a very common, cost-effective source of long-term debt financing.

Bonds and notes are structured like any other borrowing. The borrower receives cash and agrees to pay it back with interest. Generally, the entire **face amount** (principal) of the bond or note is repaid at maturity and interest payments are made (usually semiannually) in the interim.

Companies wishing to raise funds in the bond market normally work with an underwriter (e.g., **Credit Suisse**) to set the terms of the bond issue. The underwriter sells individual bonds (usually in $1,000 denominations) from this general bond issue to its retail clients and professional portfolio managers (e.g., **Allianz Global Investors**), and it receives a fee for underwriting the bond issue.

Once issued, the bonds can be traded in the secondary market between investors just like stocks. Market prices of bonds fluctuate daily despite the fact that the company's obligation for payment of principal and interest remains fixed throughout the life of the bond. This occurs because of fluctuations in the general level of interest rates and changes in the financial condition of the borrowing company.

The following sections analyse and interpret the reporting for bonds. We first examine the mechanics of bond pricing. In a subsequent section, we address the accounting for and reporting of bonds.

Pricing of Bonds

LO3 Explain and illustrate the pricing of long-term nonoperating liabilities.

Two different interest rates are crucial for understanding how a bond is priced.

- **Coupon (contract** or **stated) rate** The coupon rate of interest is stated in the bond contract. It is used to compute the dollar amount of (semiannual) interest payments that are paid to bondholders during the life of the bond issue.
- **Market (yield) rate** The market rate is the interest rate that investors expect to earn on the investment for this debt security. This rate is used to price the bond issue.

The coupon (contract) rate is used to compute interest payments and the market (yield) rate is used to price the bond. The coupon rate and the market rate are nearly always different (except for floating-rate bonds). The coupon rate is fixed prior to issuance of the bond and remains so throughout its life. Market rates of interest, on the other hand, fluctuate continually with the supply and demand for bonds in the marketplace, general macroeconomic conditions, and the financial condition of borrowers.

The bond price equals the **present value** of the expected cash flows to the bondholder. Specifically, bondholders normally expect to receive two different cash flows:

1. **Periodic interest payments** (usually semiannual) during the bond's life. These cash flows are typically in the form of equal payments at periodic intervals, called an **annuity**.
2. **Single payment** of the face (principal) amount of the bond at maturity.

The bond price equals the present value of the periodic interest payments plus the present value of the principal payment at maturity. We next illustrate the purchase of bonds at three different prices: at par, at a discount, and at a premium.

Bonds Issued at Par When a bond is issued at par, its coupon rate is identical to the market rate. Under this condition, a $1,000 bond sells for $1,000 in the market. To illustrate bond pricing, assume that investors wish to value a bond issue with a face amount of $100,000, a 6% annual coupon rate with interest payable semiannually (3% semiannual rate), and a maturity of 4 years.[5] Investors purchasing this issue receive the following cash flows:

	Number of Payments	Dollars per Payment	Total Cash Flows
Semiannual interest payments...............	4 years × 2 = 8	$100,000 × 3% = $ 3,000	$ 24,000
Principal payment at maturity	1	$100,000	100,000
			$124,000

Specifically, the bond agreement dictates that the borrower makes 8 semiannual payments of $3,000 each, computed as $100,000 × (6%/2), plus the $100,000 face amount at maturity, for a total of $124,000 in cash flows. Each of the 100 bonds in this bond issue provides the bondholder with an annuity of 8 payments of $30 and a principal payment of $1,000 at maturity. For an individual bond, the cash flows total $1,240 (= $30 × 8 + $1,000).

When pricing bonds, the number of periods used for computing the present value is the number of interest (coupon) payments required by the bond. In this case, there are 8 semiannual

[5] Semiannual interest payments are typical for bonds. With semiannual interest payments, the issuer pays bondholders two interest payments per year. The semiannual interest rate is the annual rate divided by two.

interest payments required, so we use 8, six-month periods to value the bond. The market interest rate (yield) is 6% per year, which is 3% per six-month period.

The bond price is the present value of the interest annuity plus the present value of the principal payment. Assuming that investors desire a 6% annual market rate (yield), the bond sells for exactly $100,000, which is computed as follows:

	Payment	Present Value Factor[a]	Present Value
Interest..................................	$ 3,000	7.01969[b]	$ 21,059
Principal..................................	$100,000	0.78941[c]	78,941
			$100,000

[a] Mechanics of using tables to compute present values are explained in Appendix A at the end of the text. Present value factors are taken from tables provided in Appendix A.

[b] Present value of ordinary annuity for 8 periods discounted at 3% per period.

[c] Present value of single payment in 8 periods hence discounted at 3% per period.

Because the bond contract pays investors a 6% annual rate when investors demand a 6% market rate, investors purchase these bonds at the **par (face) value** of $1,000 per bond, or $100,000 in total.[6] Using a financial calculator, we can compute the bond value as follows: N = 8; I/Yr = 3; PMT = 3,000; FV = 100,000:

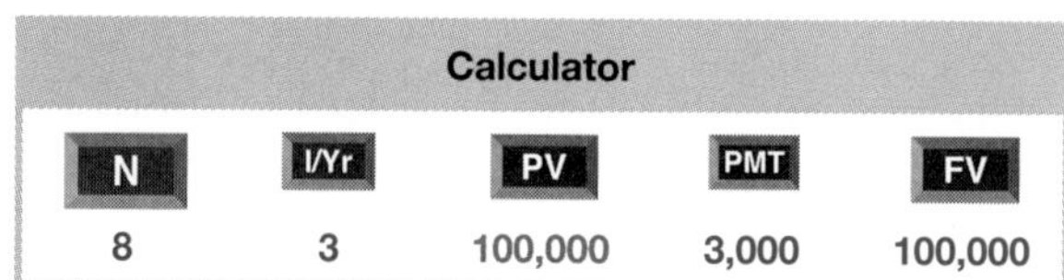

Bonds Issued at a Discount As a second illustration, assume that market conditions are such that investors demand an 8% annual yield (4% semiannual) for the 6% coupon bond, while all other details remain the same. The bond now sells for $93,267, computed as follows:

	Payment	Present Value Factor	Present Value
Interest..................................	$ 3,000	6.73274[a]	$20,198
Principal..................................	$100,000	0.73069[b]	73,069
			$93,267

[a] Present value of ordinary annuity for 8 periods discounted at 4% per period.

[b] Present value of single payment in 8 periods hence discounted at 4% per period.

Using a financial calculator, the bond is priced as follows: N = 8; I/Yr = 4; PMT = 3,000; FV = 100,000:

Calculator				
N	I/Yr	PV	PMT	FV
8	4	93,267	3,000	100,000

The market price of the bond issue is, therefore, $93,267. The price of each bond in the bond issue is $932.67 (= $93,267/100).

[6] If we purchase a bond after the semiannual interest date, we must pay accrued interest in addition to the purchase price. This interest is returned to us in the regular interest payment. (This procedure makes the bookkeeping easier for the issuer/underwriter.)

Because the bond carries a coupon rate *lower* than that which investors demand, the bond is less desirable and sells at a **discount**. In general, bonds sell at a discount whenever the coupon rate is less than the market rate.[7]

Bonds Issued at a Premium As a third illustration, assume that investors in the bond market demand a 4% annual yield (2% semiannual) for the 6% coupon bonds, while all other details remain the same. The bond now sells for $107,325, computed as follows:

	Payment	Present Value Factor	Present Value
Interest	$ 3,000	7.32548[a]	$ 21,976
Principal	$100,000	0.85349[b]	85,349
			$107,325

[a] Present value of ordinary annuity for 8 periods discounted at 2% per period.
[b] Present value of single payment in 8 periods hence discounted at 2% per period.

Using a financial calculator, the bond is priced as follows: N = 8; I/Yr = 2; PMT = 3,000; FV = 100,000:

Calculator				
N	I/Yr	PV	PMT	FV
8	2	107,325	3,000	100,000

The market price of the bond issue is, therefore, $107,325. The price of each bond in the bond issue is $1,073.25 (= $107,325/100).

Because the bond carries a coupon rate higher than that which investors demand, the bond is more desirable and sells at a **premium**. In general, bonds sell at a premium whenever the coupon rate is greater than the market rate. Exhibit 9.2 summarises this relation for bond pricing.

EXHIBIT 9.2 Coupon Rate, Market Rate, and Bond Pricing

Coupon rate > market rate	→	Bond sells at a **premium** (above face amount)
Coupon rate = market rate	→	Bond sells at **par** (at face amount)
Coupon rate < market rate	→	Bond sells at a **discount** (below face amount)

Effective Cost of Debt

When a bond sells for par, the cost to the issuing company is the cash interest paid. In our first illustration where the bond is issued at par, the *effective cost* of the bond is the 6% interest paid by the issuer.

When a bond sells at a discount, the issuer's effective cost consists of two parts: (1) the cash interest paid and (2) the discount incurred. The discount, which is the difference between par and the lower issue price, is a cost that must eventually be reflected in the issuer's income statement as an expense. This fact means that the effective cost of a discount bond is greater than if the bond had sold at par. A discount is a cost and, like any other cost, must eventually be transferred from the balance sheet to the income statement as an expense.

When a bond sells at a premium, the issuer's effective cost consists of (1) the cash interest paid and (2) a cost reduction due to the premium received. The premium is a benefit that must eventually find its way from the balance sheet to the income statement as a *reduction* of interest expense. As a result of the premium, the effective cost of a premium bond is less than if the bond had sold at par.

Bonds are priced to yield the return (market rate) demanded by investors in the bond market, which results in the effective interest rate of a bond *always* equaling the yield (market) rate,

[7] Bond prices are often stated in percent form. For example, a bond sold at par is said to be sold at 100 (that is, 100% of its face value, par). The bond sold at $932.67 is said to be sold at 93.267 (93.267% of par, computed as $932.67/$1,000).

regardless of the coupon (stated) rate of the bond. Bond prices are set by the market so as to always yield the rate required by investors based on the terms and qualities of the bond. Companies cannot influence the effective cost of debt by raising or lowering the coupon rate. We discuss the factors affecting the market yield later in the chapter.

The effective cost of debt is ultimately reflected in the amount reported in the issuer's income statement as interest expense. This amount can be, and usually is, different from the cash interest paid. The two are the same only for a bond issued at par. The next section discusses how management reports bonds on the balance sheet and interest expense on the income statement.

Reporting of Bond Financing

LO4 Analyse and account for financial statement effects of long-term nonoperating liabilities.

This section identifies and describes the financial statement effects of bond transactions.

Bonds Issued at Par When a bond sells at par, the issuing company receives the cash proceeds and accepts an obligation to make payments per the bond contract. Specifically, cash is increased and a liability (bonds payable) is increased by the same amount. Using the facts from our earlier illustration, the issuance of bonds at par has the following financial statement effects (there is no revenue or expense at the date the bond is issued):

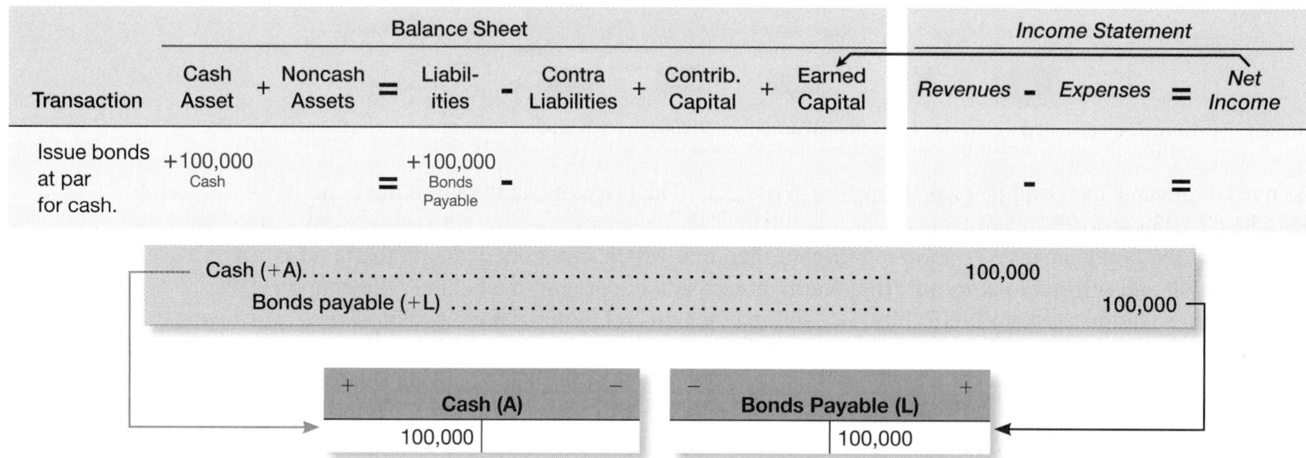

Bonds Issued at a Discount When a bond is sold at a discount, cash is increased by the proceeds from the sale of the bond (not the face amount of the bond), and the liability increases by the same amount. Again, using the facts above from our bond discount illustration, the financial statement effects follow:

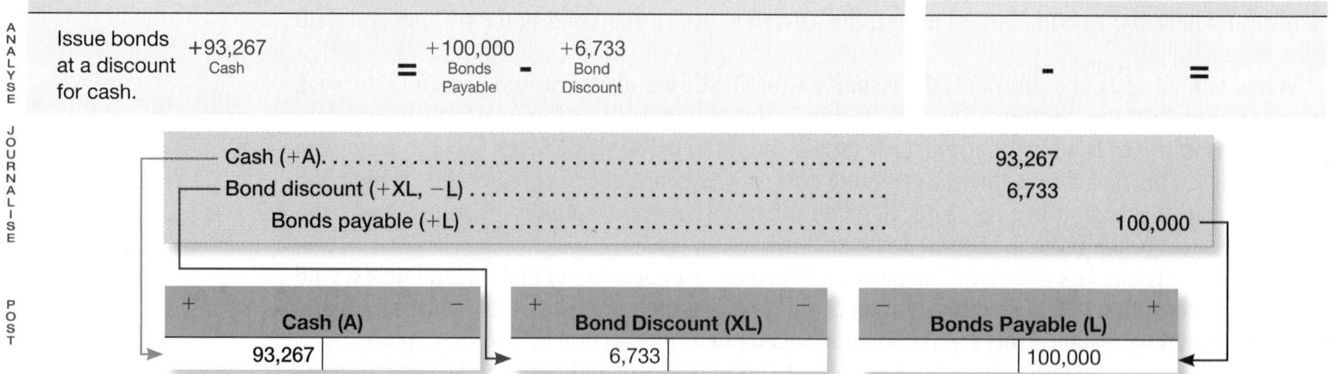

The bond liability amount reported on the balance sheet consists of two components (bond discount is a contra liability account).

Bonds payable, face	$100,000
Less bond discount	(6,733)
Bonds payable, net	$ 93,267

FYI "Bonds Payable, Net" is a common title reflecting the face value of the bond less the unamortised discount.

Discount bonds are reported on the balance sheet net of any discount. When the bond matures, however, the company is obligated to repay $100,000. Accordingly, at maturity, the bond liability must read $100,000, the amount that is owed. Therefore, between the bond issuance and its maturity, the discount must decline to zero. This reduction of the discount over the life of the bond is called **amortisation**. This amortisation causes the effective interest expense to be greater than the periodic cash interest payments based on the coupon rate.

BUSINESS INSIGHT

Zeros and Strips Zero coupon bonds and notes, called *zeros*, do not carry an explicit coupon rate. However, the pricing of these bonds and notes is done in the same manner as those with coupon rates—the exception is the absence of an interest annuity. This omission means that the price is the present value of just the principal payment at maturity; hence the bond is sold at a *deep discount*. For example, consider a 4-year, $100,000 zero coupon bond, priced to yield a market rate of 6%. The only payment would be the return of principal 4 years away. We already know that the present value of this single payment is $78,941. This "zero" would initially sell for $78,941 resulting in a substantial discount of $21,059.

Another interesting variation on traditional bonds is a *strip*, which is short for ***S****eparately* ***TR****aded* ***I****nterest and* ***P****rincipal*. Initially, a strip is priced and sold just like an ordinary bond. Subsequently, the two payment components—the periodic coupon payments and the *balloon* payment of principal which is due when the bond matures—are sold separately. A 4-year, $100,000 bond priced at $100,000 to yield 6% would be separated into two securities: 1) a zero, selling for $78,941, representing the present value of this single payment, and, 2) another security, priced at $21,059, representing the present value of the coupon payments.

Bonds Issued at a Premium When a bond is sold at a premium, the cash proceeds and net bond liability are recorded at the amount of the proceeds received (not the face amount of the bond). Again, using the facts above from our premium bond illustration, the financial statement effects are:

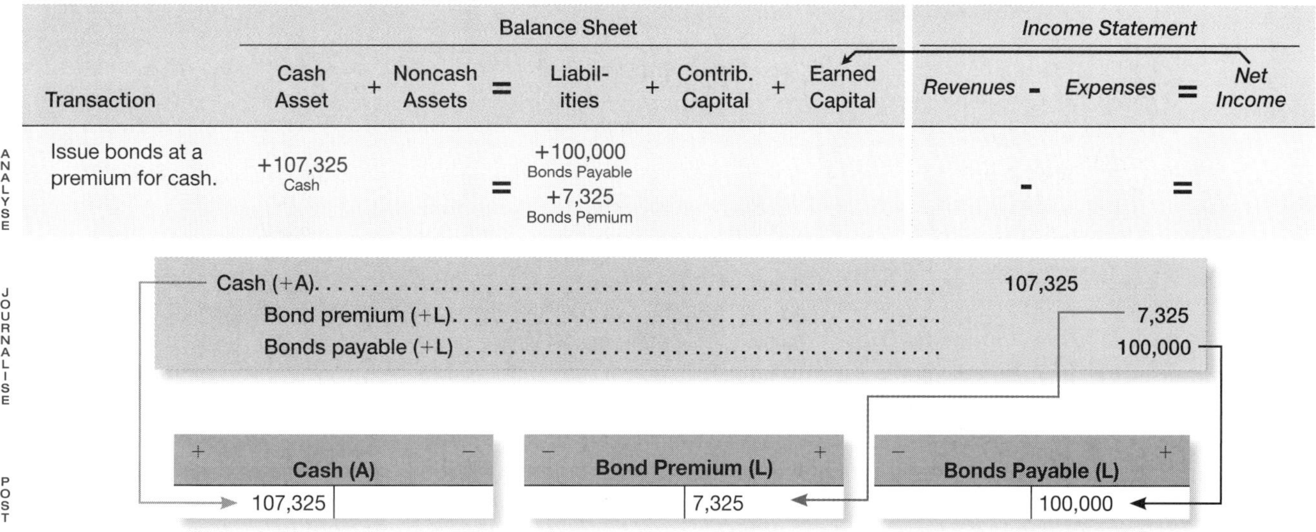

ANALYSE

	Balance Sheet									Income Statement				
Transaction	Cash Asset	+	Noncash Assets	=	Liabilities	+	Contrib. Capital	+	Earned Capital	Revenues	−	Expenses	=	Net Income
Issue bonds at a premium for cash.	+107,325 Cash			=	+100,000 Bonds Payable +7,325 Bonds Pemium						−		=	

JOURNALISE

Cash (+A)	107,325	
Bond premium (+L)		7,325
Bonds payable (+L)		100,000

POST

+ Cash (A) −		− Bond Premium (L) +		− Bonds Payable (L) +	
107,325			7,325		100,000

The bond liability amount reported on the balance sheet, again, consists of two parts (bond premium is a liability account):

Bonds payable, face	$100,000
Add bond premium	7,325
Bonds payable, net	$107,325

The $100,000 must be repaid at maturity, and the premium is amortised to zero over the life of the bond. The premium represents a *benefit,* which yields a *reduction* in interest expense on the income statement.

Effects of Discount and Premium Amortisation

The amount of interest expense that is reported on the income statement always equals the loan balance at the beginning of the period (bonds payable, net of discount or premium) multiplied by the market interest rate at the time of issue. For bonds issued at par, interest expense equals the cash interest payment. However, for bonds issued at a discount or premium, interest expense reported on the income statement equals interest paid adjusted for the amortisation of the discount or premium:

	Cash interest paid			Cash interest paid
+	Amortisation of discount	or	−	Amortisation of premium
	Interest expense			Interest expense

Specifically, periodic amortisation of a discount is added to the cash interest paid to get interest expense for a discount bond. Amortisation of the discount reflects the additional cost the issuer incurs from issuance of the bonds at a discount and its recognition, via amortisation, as an increase to interest expense. For a premium bond, the premium is a benefit the issuer receives at issuance. Amortisation of the premium reduces interest expense over the debt term. Consequently, interest expense on the income statement represents the *effective cost* of debt (the *nominal cost* of debt is the cash interest paid). This is true whether the bonds are issued at par, at a discount, or at a premium.

Companies amortise discounts and premiums using the effective interest method. To illustrate, recall the assumptions of the discount bond above—face amount of $100,000, a 6% annual coupon rate payable semiannually (3% semiannual rate), a maturity of 4 years, and a market (yield) rate of 8% annual (4% semiannual). These facts resulted in a bond issue price of $932.67 per bond or $93,267 for the entire bond issue. Exhibit 9.3 illustrates a bond discount amortisation table for this bond.

EXHIBIT 9.3 Bond Discount Amortisation Table

Semi-Annual Period	[A] Beginning Balance	[B] *(Face × coupon%)* Cash Interest Paid	[C] *([A] × market%)* Interest Expense	[D] *([C] − [B])* Discount Amortisation	[E] *(Prior bal − [D])* Discount Balance	[F] *(Face − [E])* Bond Payable Net
0					$6,733	$ 93,267
1	$93,267	$3,000	$3,731	$731	6,002	93,998
2	93,998	3,000	3,760	760	5,242	94,758
3	94,758	3,000	3,790	790	4,452	95,548
4	95,548	3,000	3,822	822	3,630	96,370
5	96,370	3,000	3,855	855	2,775	97,225
6	97,225	3,000	3,889	889	1,886	98,114
7	98,114	3,000	3,925	925	962	99,038
8	99,038	3,000	3,962	962	0	100,000

The interest period is denoted in the left-most column. Period 0 is the point in time at which the bond is issued. Periods 1–8 are successive six-month interest periods (recall, interest is paid semiannually). Column [B] is cash interest paid, which is a constant $3,000 per period (face amount × coupon rate). Column [C] is interest expense, which is reported in the income statement. This column is computed as the carrying amount of the bond at the beginning of the period (column [E] of the previous row) multiplied by the 8% yield rate (4% semiannual) used to compute the bond issue price. Column [D] is discount amortisation, which is the difference between interest expense and cash interest paid. Column [E] is the discount balance, which is the previous balance of the discount less the discount amortisation in column [D]. Column [F] is the net bond payable, which is the $100,000 face amount less the unamortised discount from column [E].

The amortisation process continues until period 8, at which time the discount balance is 0 and the net bond payable is $100,000 (the maturity value). An amortisation table reveals the financial statement effects of the bond for its duration. Specifically, we see the cash effects in column [B], the income statement effects in column [C], and the balance sheet effects in columns [D], [E], and [F].

To record the interest payment at the end of period 1, we use the values in row 1 of the amortisation table. The resulting entry is recorded as follows:

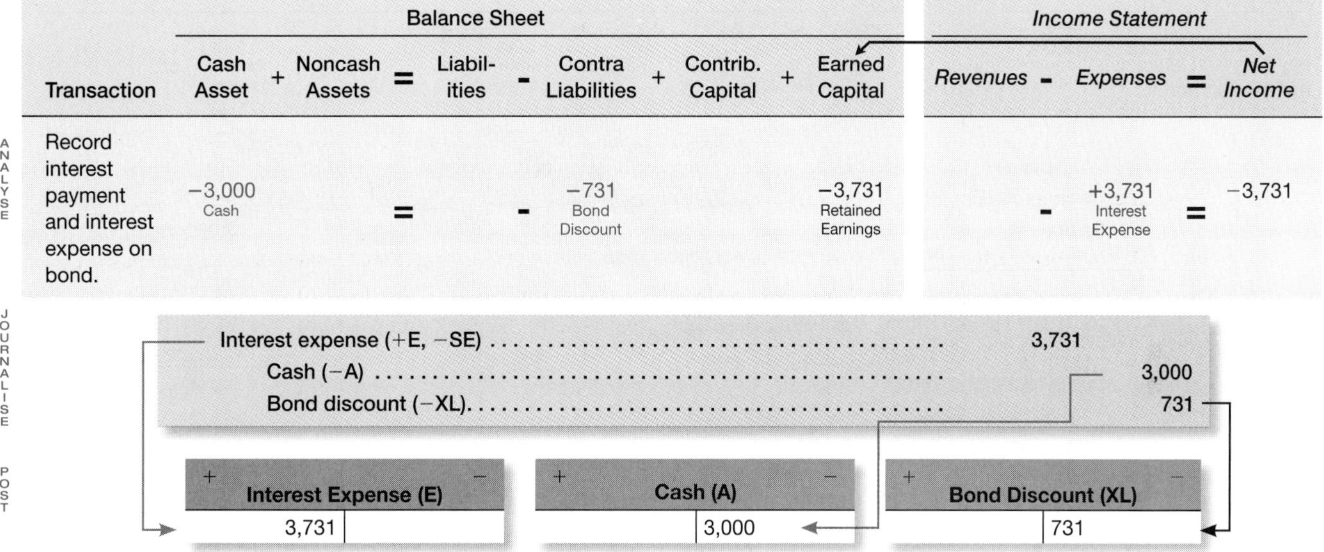

To illustrate amortisation of a premium bond, we use the assumptions of the premium bond above—$100,000 face value, a 6% annual coupon rate payable semiannually (3% semiannual rate), a maturity of 4 years, and a 4% annual market (yield) rate (2% semiannual). These parameters resulted in a bond issue price of $1,073.25 per bond or $107,325 for the entire bond issue. Exhibit 9.4 shows the bond premium amortisation table for this bond.

EXHIBIT 9.4 Bond Premium Amortisation Table

Semi-Annual Period	[A] Beginning Balance	[B] (Face × coupon%) Cash Interest Paid	[C] ([A] × market%) Interest Expense	[D] ([B] − [C]) Premium Amortisation	[E] (Prior bal − [D]) Premium Balance	[F] (Face + [E]) Bond Payable Net
0					$7,325	$107,325
1	$107,325	$3,000	$2,147	$853	6,472	106,472
2	106,472	3,000	2,129	871	5,601	105,601
3	105,601	3,000	2,112	888	4,713	104,713
4	104,713	3,000	2,094	906	3,807	103,807
5	103,807	3,000	2,076	924	2,883	102,883
6	102,883	3,000	2,058	942	1,941	101,941
7	101,941	3,000	2,039	961	980	100,980
8	100,980	3,000	2,020	980	0	100,000

Interest expense is computed using the same process that we used for discount bonds. The difference is that the yield rate is 4% (2% semiannual) in the premium case. Also, cash interest paid follows from the bond contract (face amount × coupon rate), and the other columns' computations reflect the premium amortisation. After period 8, the premium is fully amortised (equals zero) and the net bond payable balance is $100,000, the amount owed at maturity. Again, an amortisation table reveals the financial statement effects of the bond—the cash effects in column [B], the income statement effects in column [C], and the balance sheet effects in columns [D], [E], and [F].

To record the interest payment at the end of period 1, we, again, use the values in row 1 of the amortisation table. The resulting entry is recorded as follows:

	Balance Sheet									Income Statement				
Transaction	Cash Asset	+	Noncash Assets	=	Liabilities	+	Contrib. Capital	+	Earned Capital	Revenues	-	Expenses	=	Net Income
ANALYSE: Record interest payment and interest expense on bond.	−3,000 Cash			=	−853 Bond Premium				−2,147 Retained Earnings		-	+2,147 Interest Expense	=	−2,147

JOURNALISE

Interest expense (+E, −SE)	2,147	
Bond premium (−L)	853	
Cash (−A)		3,000

POST

+ Interest Expense (E) −		− Bond Premium (L) +		+ Cash (A) −	
2,147		853			3,000

The Fair Value Option

Thus far, we have described the reporting of liabilities at *historical cost*. This means that all financial statement relationships are established on the date that the liability is created and do not subsequently change. For example, the interest rate used to value a bond is the market rate of interest on the date that the bond is issued and the reported value of the bond is the face value plus the unamortised premium or minus the unamortised discount. Yet, once issued, bonds can be traded in secondary markets. Market interest rates fluctuate and, as a consequence, the market value of a bond is likely to change after the bond is issued.

Companies have an option to report some or all of their financial liabilities at fair value, to help reduce inconsistency (the so-called "accounting mismatch") attributed to measuring assets or liabilities, or recognising the gains and losses on them, on different bases. Companies must make this choice at the inception of the liability (e.g., at the time that a bond is issued) and cannot subsequently switch between fair value and historical cost for that liability. Gains and losses are split into the amount of change in fair value due to changes in credit risk, reported in other comprehensive income (discussed in Chapter 12), and the remaining amount reported in the income statement. However, the full amount of gains and losses can be reported in the income statement if doing so alleviates accounting mismatch in net income.

To illustrate how we report a liability at fair value, we refer to our example of a 4-year, 6% bond issued at a discount to yield 8%. The issue price of this bond is $93,267 and we assume that the bond is issued on June 30, 2012. Six months later, on December 31, the issuing company pays the first of eight coupon payments of $3,000. From Exhibit 9.3, we know that after this coupon payment, the bond payable, net of the discount, is equal to $93,998. Now assume that the market value of the bond has increased to $96,943. (This price increase is consistent with a market interest rate that has decreased to 7%.) The bond would now be reported on the balance sheet at a value of $96,943:

Bonds payable	$100,000
Less, unamortised discount	6,002
Bond payable, net (historical cost)	$ 93,998
Plus, fair value adjustment	2,945
Bond payable, net (fair value)	$ 96,943

The increase in the fair value of the bond must be added to an account that adjusts the bond payable liability. The balancing entry is included as a loss in the income statement, and ends up in retained earnings. The fair value adjustment is recorded as follows:

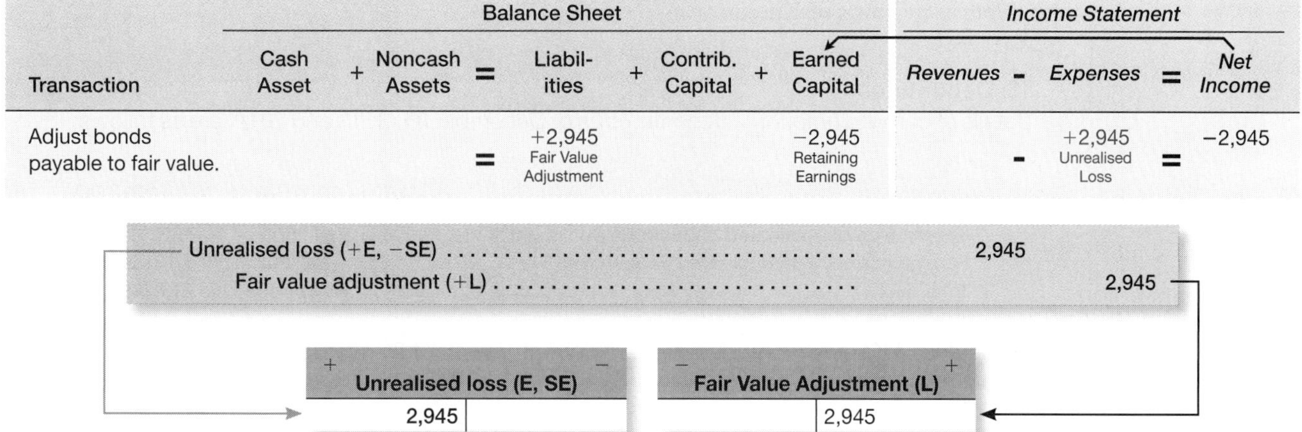

The fair value computation does not affect the calculation of interest expense or the amortisation of the bond discount in this or any subsequent period. The unrealised loss does have an effect on the income statement. For this illustration, the total effect on income for 2012 is $6,676, which is computed as:

Coupon payment, July 1—December 31	$3,000
Amortisation of the bond discount	731
Interest expense	$3,731
Unrealised loss	2,945
Total effect (decrease) on earnings	$6,676

If the fair value of this bond decreases (e.g., because interest rates increase), the fair value adjustment account would be debited and an unrealised gain would be credited and reported in the income statement. We discuss the fair value option further in Chapter 12.

Effects of Bond Repurchase

Companies can and sometimes do repurchase (also called *redeem*) their bonds prior to maturity. The bond indenture (contract agreement) often includes a **call provision** giving the company the right to repurchase its bond by paying a small premium above face value. Alternatively, the company can repurchase bonds in the open market. When a bond repurchase occurs, a gain or loss usually results, and is computed as follows:

Gain or loss on bond repurchase = Book value of the bond − Repurchase payment

The *book (carrying) value of the bond* is the net amount reported on the balance sheet. If the issuer pays more to retire the bonds than the amount carried on its balance sheet, a loss is reported on its income statement, usually called *loss on bond retirement*. The issuer reports a *gain on bond retirement* if the repurchase price is less than the book value of the bond. Any gains or losses on bond repurchases are reported as part of income from continuing operations.

The question arises as to how gains and losses on the redemption of bonds should affect our analysis of a company's profitability. Because bonds and notes payable represent nonoperating items, activities including the refunding of bonds and any gain or loss resulting from such activity should be omitted from our computation of net operating profit.

Financial Statement Footnotes

Companies are required to disclose details about their long-term liabilities, including the amounts borrowed under each debt issuance, the interest rates, maturity dates, and other key provisions. Following is Samsung's disclosure in note 16 to its 2013 annual report for its long-term debt (in millions of Korean won):

16. Debentures

Details of carrying amount of debentures as of December 31, 2013 and 2012, are as follows:

	2013	2012
Korean won denominated debentures (A)	₩198,566	₩697,822
Foreign currency denominated debentures (B)	1,112,502	1,131,552
Total	₩1,311,068	₩1,829,374

(A) Details of Korean won denominated debentures as of December 31, 2013 and 2012, are as follows:

	Issue Date	Due Date	Annual Interest Rates (%) as of December 31, 2013	2013	2012
Unsecured debentures	June 17, 2010	June 17, 2013	—	—	500,000
Unsecured debentures	Nov. 17, 2011	Nov. 17, 2014	4.1	500,000	500,000
Unsecured debentures	Nov. 17, 2011	Nov. 17, 2016	4.2	200,000	200,000
Less: Current portion				(500,000)	(500,000)
Less: Discounts				(1,434)	(2,178)
Total				198,566	697,822

(B) Details of foreign currency denominated debentures as of December 31, 2013 and 2012, are as follows:

	Issue Date	Due Date	Annual Interest Rates (%) as of December 31, 2013	2013	2012
US dollar denominated straight bonds	Oct. 2, 1997	Oct. 1, 2027	7.7	₩73,871 (US$70 million)	₩80,333 (US$75 million)
US dollar denominated unsecured bonds	Apr. 10, 2012	Apr. 10, 2017	1.8	₩1,055,300 (US$1,000 million)	₩1,071,100 (US$1,000 million)
Less: Current portion				(5,277)	(5,356)
Less: Discounts				(11,392)	(14,525)
Total				₩1,112,502	₩1,131,552

Samsung reports a book value for debentures (or long-term debt) of ₩1,311,068 million at year-end 2013. Of this amount, ₩198,566 million and ₩1,112,502 million are denominated in Korean wons and U.S. dollars, respectively. In total, ₩505,277 (500,000 + 5,277) million matures in the next year, hence its classification as a current liability (current portion of debentures) and the remainder matures after 2013. Samsung also reports ₩12,826 (1,434 + 11,392) million in unamortised discount on this debt.

In addition to amounts, rates, issue dates, and due dates on its debentures, Samsung also reports aggregate maturities for the 5 years subsequent to its balance sheet date:

(C) Maturities of debentures outstanding as of December 31, 2013, are as follows:

For the Years Ending December 31	Debentures
2014	₩ 505,277
2015	5,277
2016	205,277
2017	1,060,577
2018 and thereafter	52,763
Total	₩1,829,171

This reporting reveals that Samsung is required to make principal payments of ₩505,277 million in 2014 and ₩1,060,577 million in 2017. Such maturities are important as a company must meet its required payments, negotiate a rescheduling of the indebtedness, or refinance the debt to avoid default. The latter (default) usually has severe consequences as debt holders have legal remedies available to them, which can result in bankruptcy of the company.

If the fair value of long-term debt is higher than the book value, there will be an unrecognised liability (and loss if the debt is redeemed). The justification for not recognising unrealised gains and losses on the balance sheet and income statement is that such amounts can reverse with future fluctuations in interest rates. Further, because only the face amount of debt is repaid at maturity, unrealised gains and losses that arise during intervening years are not necessarily relevant. (This same logic is used to justify the nonrecognition of gains and losses on held-to-maturity investments in debt securities, a topic covered in Chapter 12.) At this time, Samsung, like most companies, has elected to report liabilities at historical (amortised) cost in the financial statements and disclose fair values in the footnotes.

Interest and the Cash Flows Statement

As discussed in Chapter 4, interest payments can be classified as either cash flows from operating activities or cash flow from financing activities. There are two issues with companies including interest payments in cash flows from operating activities. First, interest payments do not equal interest expense, which is included in the computation of net income. For companies using the indirect method to present cash flows from operating activities, the reconciliation of net income to operating cash flows should include an adjustment for any amortisation of bond discounts or premiums. Second, interest expense is typically related to nonoperating liabilities (interest-bearing bonds and notes). Hence, interest expense should be excluded from operating cash flow when analysing a company's operating performance.

ANALYSING FINANCIAL STATEMENTS

LO5 Explain how solvency ratios and debt ratings are determined and how they impact the cost of debt.

A major concern of managers and analysts is the solvency of the corporation. In this chapter we revisit one ratio and introduce a new ratio, both of which are designed to measure a firm's solvency. The first ratio is the debt-to-equity ratio (D/E), first introduced in Chapter 1. It measures the extent to which a company relies on debt financing, also known as financial leverage. The second ratio is times-interest-earned (TIE), which measures the ability of current operations to cover interest costs.

Analysis Objective

We want to gauge the ability of a company to satisfy its long-term debt obligations and remain solvent.

Analysis Tool Debt-to Equity Ratio

$$\textbf{Debt-to-equity ratio (D/E)} = \frac{\textbf{Total liabilities}}{\textbf{Total equity}}$$

Applying the Ratio to Samsung

2013	$\frac{64,059,008}{150,016,010}$	= 0.43 or 43%
2012	$\frac{59,591,364}{121,480,206}$	= 0.49 or 49%
2011	$\frac{54,486,633}{101,313,630}$	= 0.54 or 54%

Guidance A debt-to-equity ratio equal to 1.0 implies that the company is relying on debt and equity financing in equal amounts. As a company's reliance on debt increases and the company's long-term solvency becomes more of a concern, this ratio increases. A debt-to-equity ratio of about 1.5 is about average.

Samsung in Context

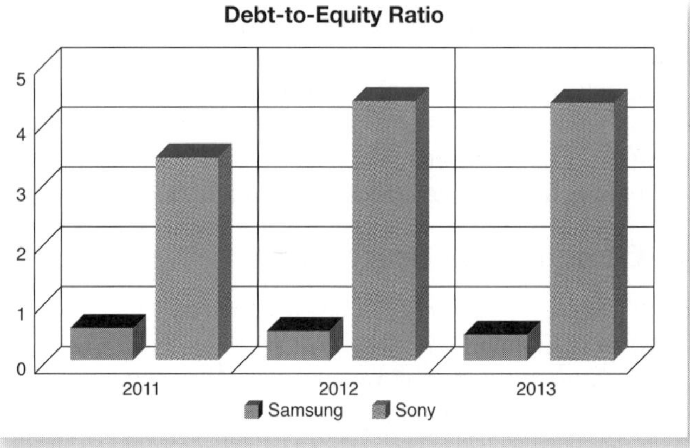

Analysis Tool Times Interest Earned

$$\textbf{Times interest earned (TIE)} = \frac{\textbf{Earnings before interest and taxes}}{\textbf{Interest expense}}$$

Applying the Ratio to Samsung

2013	$\frac{36,785,013}{7,754,972}$	= 4.74 times
2012	$\frac{29,049,338}{7,934,450}$	= 3.66 times
2011	$\frac{15,644,291}{7,893,421}$	= 1.98 times

Guidance When a company relies on debt financing, it assumes the burden of paying the interest on the debt. The times interest earned ratio measures the burden of interest costs by comparing earnings before interest and taxes (EBIT) to annual interest expense. A high TIE ratio indicates that a company is able to meet its interest costs without adversely affecting profitability.

Samsung in Context

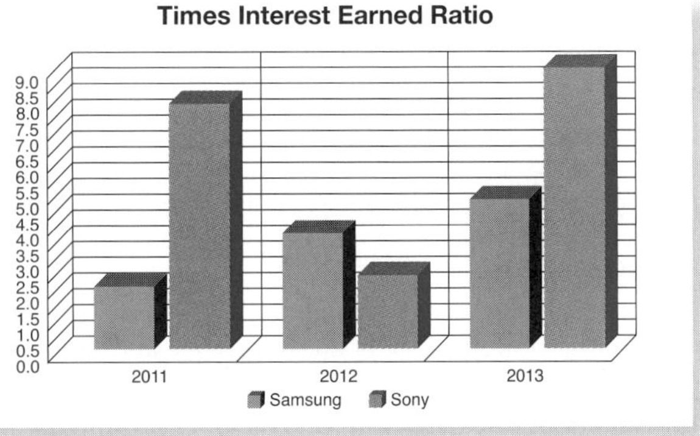

Takeaways Samsung's debt-to-equity ratio was below 1.0 over the 2011–2013 period, implying that it relied more on equity than debt to finance its investing and operating activities. In fact, its ratio decreased from 54% in 2011 to 43% in 2013. In contrast, Sony's debt-to-equity ratio was above 4.0 in 2012 and 2013, which was very high when compared to those of Samsung and other companies. On the other hand, Samsung's times interest earned ratio steadily increased from 1.98 times in 2011 to 4.74 times in 2013. The size of this ratio is driven by two factors—the amount of debt financing, which in turn determines interest expense, and profitability. The impact of profitability on the ratio can be seen from the above calculations, which show that the increasing trend in Samsung's ratio was attributed to a corresponding increase in the company's EBIT, while its interest expense remained stable over the 2011–2013 period. Except for 2012, Sony's times interest earned was very high, suggesting that it had strong earnings power to cover the high interest expenses as a result of its reliance on debt financing.

In sum, Samsung had a fairly low level of financial leverage, which was decreasing over the three-year period 2011–2013. Moreover, it had a reasonable times interest earned ratio, which increased to 4.74 times in 2013. Hence, Samsung was in good financial health, as indicated by these two measures of solvency.

Other Considerations In Chapter 5 we learned that debt financing is a double-edged sword. When used effectively, financial leverage increases return on equity because debt financing is generally less costly than equity financing. However, debt carries with it the risk of **default**, which is the risk that the company will be unable to pay its obligations when they come due (insolvency). To provide some protection against default risk, creditors usually require a company to execute a loan agreement that places restrictions on the company's activities. These restrictions, called covenants, impose indirect costs on a firm beyond the explicit cost of interest, and these indirect costs tend to increase as a company increases its reliance on debt financing. When a company's solvency ratios are close to the limits specified by its covenants, management is more likely to pass up profitable investment opportunities or engage in counterproductive earnings management activities to avoid violating these restrictions.

There are several variations on the ratios that we have discussed here and there is no single ratio that can be described as the best measure of company solvency. As with all ratios, solvency measures can be distorted by uncertain, inappropriate or inaccurate data. It is always helpful to analyse the footnotes to better understand the components of debt financing, their interest rates, when major payments are due, and what, if any, restrictive covenants exist. There is no substitute for diligence.

Debt Ratings and the Cost of Debt

Earlier in the chapter we learned that the effective cost of debt to the issuing company is the market (yield) rate of interest used to price the bond, regardless of the bond coupon rate. The rate of interest that a company must pay on its debt is a function of the maturity of that debt and the creditworthiness of the issuing company.

RESEARCH INSIGHT

Accounting Conservatism and Cost of Debt Research indicates that companies applying more conservative accounting methods incur a lower cost of debt. Research also suggests that while accounting conservatism can lead to lower-quality accounting income (because such income does not fully reflect economic reality), creditors are more confident in the numbers and view them as more credible. Evidence also implies that companies can lower the required return demanded by creditors (the risk premium) by issuing high-quality financial reports that include enhanced footnote disclosures and detailed supplemental reports.

A company's debt rating, also referred to as credit quality and creditworthiness, is related to default risk. Companies seeking to obtain bond financing from the capital markets, normally first seek a rating on their proposed debt issuance from one of several rating agencies such as **Standard & Poor's**, **Moody's Investors Service**, or **Fitch Ratings Inc**. The aim of rating agencies is to rate debt so that its default risk is more accurately determined and priced by the market. Such debt issuances carry debt ratings from one or more of the three large rating agencies as shown in Exhibit 9.5. This exhibit includes the general description attached to the debt for each rating class—for example, AAA is assigned to debt of prime maximum safety (maximum creditworthiness). Bonds with credit ratings below investment grade (Baa or BBB) are referred to as "high yield" bonds or, more pejoratively, "junk bonds." Many asset management companies and pension plans would not invest in junk bonds.

EXHIBIT 9.5 Corporate Debt Ratings and Descriptions

S&P	Moody's	Fitch	Description
AAA	Aaa	AAA	Prime Maximum Safety
AA+	Aa1	AA+	
AA	Aa2	AA	High Grade, High Quality
AA–	Aa3	AA–	
A+	A1	A+	
A	A2	A	Upper-Medium Grade
A–	A3	A–	
BBB+	Baa1	BBB+	
BBB	Baa2	BBB	Lower-Medium Grade
BBB–	Baa3	BBB–	
BB+	Ba1	BB+	
BB	Ba2	BB	Non-Investment Grade
BB–	Ba3	BB–	
B+	B1	B+	
B	B2	B	Speculative
B–	B3	B–	
CCC+	Caa1	CCC+	
CCC	Caa2	CCC	Substantial Risk
CCC–	Caa3	CCC–	
CC	Ca	CC	Extremely Speculative
C	C	C	May be in Default
D	—	D	Default

YOU MAKE THE CALL

You are the Vice President of Finance Your company is currently rated B by credit rating agencies. You are considering possible financial and other restructurings of the company to increase your credit rating. What types of restructurings might you consider? What benefits will your company receive from those restructurings? What costs will your company incur to implement such restructurings? [Answers on pages 428–429]

Samsung's unsecured bonds are rated A1 according to Moody's, as of July 2012. It is this rating that, in conjunction with the maturity of its bonds, establishes the market interest rate and consequent selling price. There are a number of considerations that affect the rating of a bond. Standard & Poor's lists the following factors among its credit rating criteria:

Business Risk
- Industry characteristics
- Competitive position (e.g., marketing, technology, efficiency, regulation)
- Management

Financial Risk
- Financial characteristics
- Financial policy
- Profitability
- Capital structure
- Cash flow protection
- Financial flexibility

Rating agencies use a number of accounting ratios to help establish creditworthiness, including measures of liquidity, solvency and profitability. These ratios are variants of the ratios we describe in Chapter 5 and in this chapter, especially those used to assess solvency.

There are other relevant factors in setting debt ratings including the following:

- **Collateral** Companies can provide security for debt in the form of mortgages on assets. To the extent debt is secured, the debt holder is in a preferred position vis-à-vis other creditors.
- **Covenants** Debt agreements (indentures) can contain restrictions on the issuing company to protect debt holders. Examples are restrictions on excessive dividend payment, on other company acquisitions, on further borrowing, and on maintaining minimum levels for key liquidity and solvency ratios. These covenants provide debt holders some means of control over the issuer's operations because, unlike equity investors, they do not have voting rights.
- **Options** Debt obligations involve contracts between the borrowing company and debt holders. Options are sometimes written into debt contracts. Examples are options to convert debt into stock (so that debt holders have a stake in value creation) and options allowing the issuing company to repurchase its debt before maturity (usually at a premium).

CHAPTER-END REVIEW

On January 1, 2015, Yorkville Company issues $300,000 of 15-year, 10% bonds payable for $351,876, yielding an effective interest rate of 8%. Interest is payable semiannually on June 30 and December 31. (1) Show computations to confirm the issue price of $351,876, and (2) provide Yorkville's journal entries, T-accounts, and complete financial statement effects template for (a) bond issuance, (b) semiannual interest payment and premium amortisation on June 30, 2015, and (c) semiannual interest payment and premium amortisation on December 31, 2015.

The solution to this review problem can be found on pages 444–445.

SUMMARY

Identify and account for current operating liabilities. (p. 402) LO1

- Current liabilities are short-term and generally non-interest-bearing; accordingly, firms try to maximise the financing of their assets using these sources of funds.
- ROE increases when firms make use of accounts payable increases to finance operating assets; a firm must avoid excessive "leaning on the trade" for short-term gains that can damage long-term supplier relationships.

- When cash discounts are offered by creditors, companies use the net of discount method to report accounts payable information.
- Accrued liabilities are identified at the end of an accounting period to reflect liabilities and expenses that have been incurred during the period but are not yet recognised in financial statements.
- While all accruals result in a liability on the balance sheet and an expense on the income statement, management has latitude in determining (in some cases, estimating) their amount and timing; this discretion offers the opportunity for managing earnings.

LO2 Describe and account for current nonoperating (financial) liabilities. (p. 408)

- Management will generally try to assure that the debt service on financial (nonoperating) liabilities coincides with the cash flows from the assets financed.
- When large amounts of financing are required for, say, plant and equipment, firms find that bonds, notes, and other forms of long-term financing provide a cost-efficient means of raising capital.

LO3 Explain and illustrate the pricing of long-term nonoperating liabilities. (p. 413)

- The coupon rate indicated on a bond contract determines the periodic interest payment. The required return on any bond called the market (yield or effective) rate is determined by market conditions and rarely equals the coupon (contract) rate. The market rate is used to price the bond and determines the effective cost of the debt to the issuer.
- If the market rate is below the coupon rate, the bond will sell at a premium to its face value, assuring that the owner of the bond earns only the market rate of interest. If the market rate exceeds the coupon rate, the bond will sell at a discount so that the bond is issued at less than its face value.

LO4 Analyse and account for financial statement effects of long-term nonoperating liabilities. (p. 416)

- A discount for a bond selling below its face value represents additional interest expense over time to the issuer because the issuer received less than face value upon issuance, but must pay the holder the face value at the bond's maturity; this discount represents additional interest beyond the coupon payment to the holder. The premium on a bond selling above its face value lowers the interest cost to the issuer and the interest revenue received by the holder.
- Companies may choose to report liabilities at fair value; if the fair value option is elected, changes in fair value are reported as gains or losses in the income statement.
- Gains and losses on bonds repurchased, equal to the difference between the book value and the cash paid, must be reported in operating income, unless extraordinary; they do not represent operating activities and should be removed from operating cash flows in our analysis.

LO5 Explain how solvency ratios and debt ratings are determined and how they affect the cost of debt. (p. 423)

- Two debt-related ratios that are particularly useful in evaluating a company's solvency include the debt-to-equity ratio (page 429) and the times interest earned ratio (page 429).
- The market rate of interest to a firm reflects the creditworthiness of the particular issuer. Credit agencies play an important role in this process by issuing debt ratings.
- Borrowing is typically secured by covenants that place the issuer in a superior position to other creditors and covenants that put restrictions on the borrower's activities; bonds can also contain options including those for conversion or repurchase.

GUIDANCE ANSWERS . . . YOU MAKE THE CALL

You are the Analyst Accrued liabilities must be probable and estimable before they can be reported in the balance sheet. If Dow's environmental costs turn out to be higher than management estimates, it may be understating its liabilities (and overstating equity). As an analyst, if you suspect that Dow's estimate is too low, you should add an additional estimated liability to the company's balance sheet.

You are the Vice President of Finance The types of restructurings you might consider are those yielding a strengthening of the financial ratios typically used to assess liquidity and solvency by the rating agencies. Such restructurings typically include inventory reduction to generate cash, the reallocation of cash outflows from investing activities (PPE) to debt reduction, and issuing stock for cash used to reduce debt (an equity-for-debt recapitalisation). These actions increase liquidity or reduce financial leverage and, thus, should yield an improved debt rating. An improved debt rating gives your company access to more debt holders, as your current debt rating is below investment grade and is not a suitable investment for many professionally managed portfolios. An improved debt rating also yields a lower interest rate on your debt. Offsetting these benefits are costs such as the following: (1) potential loss of sales from inventory stock-outs; (2) potential future cash flow reductions and loss of market power from reduced investing in PPE; and (3) costs of equity issuances (which is more than debt because investors demand a higher return to compensate for added risk and the lack of tax deductibility of dividends vis-à-vis interest payments), which can yield a net increase in the total cost of capital. All cost and benefits must be assessed before you pursue any restructurings.

KEY RATIOS

$$\text{Debt-to-equity ratio (D/E)} = \frac{\text{Total liabilities}}{\text{Total equity}} \qquad \text{Times interest earned} = \frac{\text{Earnings before interest and taxes}}{\text{Interest}}$$

KEY TERMS

Accounts payable (p. 401)
Accrued expenses (p. 401)
Accrued liabilities (p. 401)
Amortisation (p. 417)
Annuity (p. 413)
Call provision (p. 421)
Cash discounts (p. 402)
Collateral (p. 410, 427)
Contingent liabilities (p. 407)
Coupon (contract or stated) rate (p. 413)
Covenants (p. 427)
Current maturities of long-term debt (p. 402)
Default (p. 425)
Deferred performance liabilities (p. 402)
Discount (p. 415)
Face amount (p. 412)
Financial leverage (p. 400)
Leaning on the trade (p. 402)
Loan amortisation table (p. 411)
Market (yield) rate (p. 413)
Net-of-discount method (p. 402)
Options (p. 427)
Par (face) value (p. 414)
Periodic interest payments (p. 413)
Premium (p. 415)
Present value (p. 413)
Principal (p. 411)
Provisions (p. 407)
Reserves (p. 407)
Short-term debt (p. 402)
Single payment (p. 413)
Trade payable (p. 401)

MULTIPLE CHOICE

1. Which of the following statements is correct? A decrease in accrued wages liability:
   a. decreases cash flows from operations.
   b. decreases working capital.
   c. increases net income.
   d. increases net nonoperating (financial) assets.
2. On April 1, 2013, a firm borrows $12,000 at an annual interest rate of 10% with payments required semiannually on September 30 and March 31. How much interest payable and how much interest expense should appear on the firm's books at the end of the firm's fiscal year, December 31, 2014?
   a. $900 payable and $300 expense.
   b. $300 payable and $900 expense.
   c. $600 payable and $600 expense.
   d. $900 payable and $600 expense.
3. A firm issues $30,000,000 of 10-year bonds and receives $29.5 million in cash. Which of the following statements is correct?
   a. The bonds do not have a coupon rate because they are zeros.
   b. The market rate exceeds the coupon rate.
   c. The contract rate exceeds the market rate.
   d. The bonds were issued at par.

Multiple Choice Answers
1. a 2. b 3. b 4. c 5. d

4. A firm issues $5 million of 10-year 6% notes with interest paid semiannually. At issuance the firm received $5,817,565 cash reflecting a 4% yield. What is the amount of premium written off against interest expense in the first year the notes are outstanding?
   a. $48,318
   b. $24,527
   c. $67,971
   d. $33,649

5. On June 1, 2013, Wild Inc. repays long-term debt due maturing on June 1, 2013. Which of the following ratios for the year 2013 is (are) decreased by this repayment?
   a. Current Ratio
   b. Quick Ratio
   c. Times Interest Earned
   d. Debt-to-Equity

DISCUSSION QUESTIONS

Q9-1. What does the term *current liabilities* mean? What assets are usually used to settle current liabilities?

Q9-2. What is the justification for using the net-of-discount method to record inventory purchases when cash discounts are offered?

Q9-3. What is an accrual? How do accruals impact the balance sheet and the income statement?

Q9-4. What is the difference between a bond coupon rate and its market interest rate (yield)?

Q9-5. How does issuing a bond at a premium or discount affect the bond's *effective* interest rate vis-à-vis the coupon (stated) rate?

Q9-6. Why do companies report a gain or loss on the repurchase of their bonds (assuming the repurchase price is different from bond book value)?

Q9-7. How do debt ratings affect the cost of borrowing for a company?

Q9-8. How would you interpret a company's reported gain or loss on the repurchase of its bonds?

Q9-9. What do the following terms mean? (a) term loan, (b) bonds payable, (c) serial bonds, (d) call provision, (e) convertible bonds, (f) face value, (g) nominal rate, (h) bond discount, (i) bond premium, and (j) amortisation of bond premium or discount.

Q9-10. What are the advantages and disadvantages of issuing bonds rather than common stock?

Q9-11. A $3,000,000 issue of 10-year, 9% bonds was sold at 98 plus accrued interest three months after the bonds were dated. What net amount of cash is received?

Q9-12. How does issuing bonds at a premium or discount "adjust the contract rate to the applicable market rate of interest"?

Q9-13. Regardless of whether premium or discount is involved, what generalisation can be made about the change in the book value of bonds payable during the period in which they are outstanding?

Q9-14. If the effective interest amortisation method is used for bonds payable, how does the periodic interest expense change over the life of the bonds when they are issued (a) at a discount and (b) at a premium?

Q9-15. How should premium and discount on bonds payable be presented in the balance sheet?

Q9-16. On April 30, 2015, one year before maturity, Kowloon Tong Company retired $200,000 of 9% bonds payable at 101. The book value of the bonds on April 30 was $197,600. Bond interest was last paid on April 30, 2015. What is the gain or loss on the retirement of the bonds?

Q9-17. Pecs KFT borrowed money by issuing a 20-year mortgage note payable. The note will be repaid in equal monthly instalments. The interest expense component of each payment decreases with each payment. Why?

MINI EXERCISES

M9-18. Recording Cash Discounts LO1

On November 15, 2015, Giverny S.A. purchased inventory costing €6,200 on credit. The credit terms were 2/10, n/30.

a. Assume that Giverny S.A. paid the invoice on November 23, 2015. Prepare journal entries to record the purchase of this inventory and the cash payment to the supplier using the net-of-discount method.

b. Set up the necessary T-accounts and post the journal entries from question *a* to the accounts

c. Compute the cost of a lost discount as an annual percentage rate.

M9-19. Recording Cash Discounts LO1

Schrand Corporation purchases materials from a supplier that offers credit terms of 2/15, n/60. It purchased $12,500 of merchandise inventory from that supplier on January 20, 2014.

a. Assume that Schrand Corporation paid the invoice on February 15, 2014. Prepare journal entries to record the purchase of this inventory and the cash payment to the supplier using the net-of-discount method.

b. Set up the necessary T-accounts and post the journal entries from question *a* to the accounts.

c. Compute the cost of a lost discount as an annual percentage rate.

M9-20. Analysing and Computing Financial Statement Effects of Bond Interest LO4

Huddart Company gave a creditor a 90-day, 8% note payable for $7,200 on December 16.

a. Prepare the journal entry to record the year-end December 31st accounting adjustment Huddart must make.

b. Post the journal entries from part *a* to their respective T-accounts.

c. Record the transaction from part *a* in the financial statement effects template.

	Balance Sheet										*Income Statement*				
Transaction	Cash Asset	+	Noncash Assets	=	Liabil-ities	+	Contrib. Capital	+	Earned Capital		*Revenues*	-	*Expenses*	=	*Net Income*

M9-21. Analysing and Determining the Amount of a Liability LO1, 2

For each of the following situations, indicate the liability amount, if any, which is reported on the balance sheet of Otago Inc., at December 31, 2015.

a. Otago owes $110,000 at year-end 2015 for its inventory purchases.

b. Otago agreed to purchase a $28,000 drill press in January 2016.

c. During November and December of 2015, Otago sold products to a firm with a 90-day warranty against product failure. Estimated 2016 costs of honouring this warranty are $2,200.

d. Otago provides a profit-sharing bonus for its executives equal to 5% of its reported pretax annual income. The estimated pretax income for 2015 is $600,000. Bonuses are not paid until January of the following year.

M9-22. Interpreting Relations between Bond Price, Coupon, Yield, and Rating LO3

The information regarding a bond issuance by Barbizon S.A. follows:

Barbizon S.A.—€500 million of notes was priced with the following terms in two parts:

Amount: €250 million; Maturity: Jan. 12, 2021; Coupon: 4.25%; Price: 99.476; Yield: 4.349%; Ratings: Baa (Moody's), A (S&P), A (Fitch).

Amount: €250 million; Maturity: Jan. 12, 2027; Coupon: 5.125%; Price: 99.926; Yield: 5.134%; Ratings: Baa (Moody's), A (S&P), A (Fitch).

a. Discuss the relation between the coupon rate, issuance price, and yield for the 2021 issue.

b. Compare the yields on the two bond issues. Why are the yields different when the bond ratings are the same?

M9-23. Determining Gain or Loss on Bond Redemption LO4

On April 30, 2014, one year before maturity, Easton Company retires $200,000 of its 9% bonds payable at the current market price of 101 (101% of the bond face amount, or $200,000 × 1.01 = $202,000). The bond book value on April 30, 2014, is $197,600 reflecting an unamortised discount of $2,400. Bond interest is presently fully paid and recorded up to the date of retirement. What is the gain or loss on retirement of these bonds?

LO4 **M9-24. Interpreting Bond Disclosures**

PCCW LIMITED (HONG KONG)

PCCW Limited is a Hong Kong-based telecommunications and media company. The company reports the following maturities schedule for its long-term debt in its 2013 annual report (in millions of Hong Kong dollars).

26 Long-Term Borrowings	The Group	
In HK$ millions	2012	2013
Repayable within a period		
over one year, but not exceeding two years.	2,292	6,910
over two years, but not exceeding five years.	13,352	16,774
over five years	2,282	5,390
	17,926	29,074

a. What does the HK$6,910 million indicate for 2013?

b. What implications does this payment schedule have for your evaluation of PCCW's liquidity and solvency?

LO4 **M9-25. Classifying Debt Accounts into the Balance Sheet or Income Statement**

Indicate the proper financial statement classification (balance sheet or income statement) for each of the following accounts:

a. Gain on Bond Retirement
b. Discount on Bonds Payable
c. Mortgage Notes Payable
d. Bonds Payable
e. Bond Interest Expense
f. Bond Interest Payable (due next period)
g. Premium on Bonds Payable
h. Loss on Bond Retirement

LO4 **M9-26. Interpreting Bond Footnote Disclosures**

AIR CANADA (CANADA)

In its December 31, 2013 balance sheet, **Air Canada** reports $3,959 million of long-term debt and finance leases. According to the notes, aircraft financing is secured primarily by specific aircraft with a carrying value of $3,222 million and it is also supported by a loan guarantee by the Export-Import Bank of the United States ("EXIM").

The notes to Air Canada's financial statements include the following reference to restrictive covenants:

> Some of the financing and other major agreements to which Air Canada is a party contain... restrictive, financial (including in relation to asset valuations, liquidity, minimum EBITDA results, fixed charge coverage ratio and debt coverage ratios) and other covenants which affect and, in some cases, significantly limit or prohibit, among other things, the manner in which Air Canada may structure or operate its business, including by reducing Air Canada's liquidity, limiting Air Canada's ability to incur indebtedness, create liens, sell assets, pay dividends, make capital expenditures, and engage in acquisitions, mergers or restructurings or a change of control.
>
> A failure by Air Canada to comply with its contractual obligations... could result in a variety of material adverse consequences, including the acceleration of its indebtedness, the withholding of credit card proceeds by the credit card service providers and the exercise of remedies by its creditors, lessors or other co-contracting parties, and such defaults could trigger additional defaults under other indebtedness or agreements. Also, the lenders under the financing arrangements could foreclose upon all or substantially all of the assets of Air Canada, which secure Air Canada's obligations.

Required

a. Why do creditors impose restrictive covenants on borrowers?

b. How might restrictive covenants such as these affect management decisions?

c. What implications do these restrictions have on an analysis of the company and its solvency?

LO4 **M9-27. Analysing Financial Statement Effects of Bond Redemption**

Holthausen Corporation issued $400,000 of 11%, 20-year bonds at 108 on January 1, 2008. Interest is payable semiannually on June 30 and December 31. Through January 1, 2014, Holthausen amortised $4,191 of the bond premium. On January 1, 2014, Holthausen retires the bonds at 103.

a. Prepare journal entries to record the transactions.
b. Post the journal entries from part *a* to their respective T-accounts.
c. Record each of the transactions from part *a* in the financial statement effects template.

M9-28. Analysing Financial Statement Effects of Bond Redemption LO4

Dechow, Inc., issued $250,000 of 8%, 15-year bonds at 96 on July 1, 2007. Interest is payable semiannually on December 31 and June 30. Through June 30, 2014, Dechow amortised $3,186 of the bond discount. On July 1, 2014, Dechow retired the bonds at 101.

a. Prepare journal entries to record the issue and retirement of these bonds. (Assume the June interest expense has already been recorded.)
b. Post the journal entries from part *a* to their respective T-accounts.
c. Record each of the transactions from part *a* in the financial statement effects template.

M9-29. Analysing and Computing Accrued Interest on Notes LO4

Compute any interest accrued for each of the following notes payable owed by Penman, Inc., as of December 31, 2013 (use a 365-day year):

Lender	Issuance Date	Principal	Interest Rate (%)	Term
Nissim	11/21/13	$18,000	10%	120 days
Klein	12/13/13	14,000	9	90 days
Bildersee	12/19/13	16,000	12	60 days

M9-30. Interpreting Warranty Liability Disclosures LO1

SINGAPORE AIRLINES LIMITED (SINGAPORE)

Singapore Airlines Limited reports the following information in note 20 of its 2013 annual report:

20 Provisions (in $ millions)

Included are provisions for warranty claims, provisions made for upgrade costs and provisions for return costs for leased aircraft. It is expected that the return costs will be incurred by the end of the lease terms.

An analysis of the provisions is as follows:

	The Group March 31	
	2013	2012
Balance at April 1	$353.9	$264.5
Provision during the year	181.8	157.1
Provision utilised during the year	(28.5)	(44.0)
Provision written back during the year	(13.6)	(23.7)
Balance at March 31	493.6	353.9
Current	72.3	35.3
Non-current	421.3	318.6
	$493.6	$353.9

Required

a. Prepare a journal entry to record warranty expense for Singapore Airlines in 2013.
b. Post the entry from part a in the T-accounts.
c. What is meant by "utilised" in the table above?
d. What is meant by "written back" in the table?

M9-31. Computing Bond Issue Price LO3

Bushman, Inc., issues $500,000 of 9% bonds that pay interest semiannually and mature in 10 years. Compute the bond issue price assuming that the bonds' market rate is:

a. 8% per year compounded semiannually.
b. 10% per year compounded semiannually.

LO3 **M9-32. Computing Issue Price for Zero-Coupon Bonds**

Baiman, Inc., issues $500,000 of zero-coupon bonds that mature in 10 years. Compute the bond issue price assuming that the bonds' market rate is:

a. 8% per year compounded semiannually.
b. 10% per year compounded semiannually.
c. If prior to the debt issue at 10%, the firm had total assets of $3 million and total equity of $1 million, what would be the effect of the new borrowing on the financial leverage of the firm?

LO1 **M9-33. Financial Statement Effects of Accounts Payable Transactions**

Petroni Company had the following transactions relating to its accounts payable:

1. Purchases $300 of inventory on credit.
2. Sells $300 of inventory for $420 on credit (cost side recorded in part 3).
3. Records $300 cost of sales with transaction 2.
4. $300 cash paid to settle accounts payable from 1.
5. $420 cash received from accounts receivable in 2.

a. Prepare journal entries to record the transactions.
b. Post the journal entries from part *a* to their respective T-accounts.
c. Record each of the transactions from part *a* in the financial statement effects template.

LO3, 4 **M9-34. Computing Bond Issue Price and Preparing an Amortisation Table in Excel**

On January 1, 2013, Kaplan, Inc., issues $500,000 of 9% bonds that pay interest semiannually and mature in 10 years (December 31, 2022).

a. Using the Excel PV worksheet function, compute the issue price assuming that the bonds' market rate is 8% per year compounded semiannually.
b. Prepare an amortisation table in Excel to demonstrate the amortisation of the book (carrying) value to the $500,000 maturity value at the end of the 20th semiannual period.

LO4 **M9-35. Classifying Bond-Related Accounts**

Indicate the proper financial statement classification for each of the following accounts:

Gain on Bond Retirement (material amount)
Discount on Bonds Payable
Mortgage Notes Payable
Bonds Payable
Bond Interest Expense
Bond Interest Payable
Premium on Bonds Payable

LO3, 4 **M9-36. Recording and Assessing the Effects of Instalment Loans**

On December 31, 2013, Thomas, Inc., borrowed $700,000 on a 12%, 15-year mortgage note payable. The note is to be repaid in equal semiannual instalments of $50,854 (payable on June 30 and December 31).

a. Prepare journal entries to record (1) the issuance of the mortgage note payable, (2) the payment of the first instalment on June 30, 2014, and (3) the payment of the second instalment on December 31, 2014. Round amounts to the nearest dollar.
b. Post the journal entries from part *a* to their respective T-accounts.
c. Record each of the transactions from part *a* in the financial statement effects template.

LO3 **M9-37. Determining Bond Prices**

Guell S.A. plans to issue €900,000 of 10% bonds that will pay interest semiannually and mature in 5 years. Assume that the effective interest rate is 12% per year compounded semiannually. Compute the selling price of the bonds. Use Tables 2 and 3 in Appendix A near the end of the book.

EXERCISES

E9-38. Analysing and Computing Accrued Warranty Liability and Expense LO2, 5

Waymire Company sells a motor that carries a 60-day unconditional warranty against product failure. Waymire estimates that between the sale and lapse of the product warranty, 2% of the 69,000 units sold this period will require repair at an average cost of $50 per unit. A warranty liability of $10,000 is currently on the balance sheet.

a. How much warranty expense must Waymire report in its income statement and what amount of *additional* warranty liability must it report on its balance sheet for this year?

b. What analysis issues do we need to consider with respect to the amount of reported warranty liability?

c. What solvency ratios are increased if warranty liabilities rise?

E9-39. Analysing Contingencies and Assessing Liabilities LO1

The following independent situations represent various types of liabilities. Analyse each situation and indicate which of the following is the proper accounting treatment for each company: (1) record in accounts, (2) disclose in a financial statement footnote, or (3) neither record nor disclose.

a. A stockholder has filed a lawsuit against Clinch Corporation. Clinch's attorneys have reviewed the facts of the case. Their review revealed that similar lawsuits have never resulted in a cash award and it is highly unlikely that this lawsuit will either.

b. Foster Company signed a 60-day, 10% note when it purchased items from another company.

c. The state of New South Wales notifies Shevlin Company that it is filing a lawsuit for groundwater pollution against Shevlin and another company that has a plant adjacent to Shevlin's plant. Test results have not identified the exact source of the pollution. Shevlin's manufacturing process often produces by-products that can pollute groundwater.

d. Sloan Company manufactured and sold products to a retailer that sold the products to consumers. The Sloan Company warranty offers replacement of the product if it is found to be defective within 90 days of the sale to the consumer. Historically, 1.2% of the products are returned for replacement.

E9-40. Analysing and Computing Accrued Wages Liability and Expense LO1

Thames plc pays its employees on the 1st and 15th of each month. It is March 31 and Thames is preparing financial statements for this quarter. Its employees have earned £25,000 since the 15th of this month and have not yet been paid. How will Thames's balance sheet and income statement change to reflect the accrual of wages that must be made at March 31? What balance sheet and income statement accounts would be incorrectly reported if Thames failed to make this accrual (for each account indicate whether it would be overstated or understated)?

E9-41. Analysing and Reporting Financial Statement Effects of Bond Transactions LO4

On January 1, 2014, Hutton Corp. issued $300,000 of 15-year, 11% bonds payable for $377,814, yielding an effective interest rate of 8%. Interest is payable semiannually on June 30 and December 31.

a. Show computations to confirm the issue price of $377,814.

b. Prepare journal entries to record the bond issuance, semiannual interest payment and premium amortisation on June 30, 2014, and semiannual interest payment and premium amortisation on December 31, 2014. Use the effective interest rate.

c. Post the journal entries from part *b* to their respective T-accounts.

d. Record each of the transactions from part *b* in the financial statement effects template.

E9-42. Computing the Bond Issue Price LO3

Sakura Inc., issues ¥900,000 of 11% bonds that pay interest semiannually and mature in seven years. Assume that the market interest (yield) rate is 12% per year compounded semiannually. Compute the bond issue price.

E9-43. Interpreting Warranty Liability Disclosures LO1

FIAT S.P.A. (ITALY)

Fiat S.p.A. is a global automaker that designs, manufactures, distributes and sells vehicles for the mass market under the Fiat and Chrysler brands, as well as luxury cars under the Ferrari and Maserati brands. Fiat also operates in the components sector and in the production systems sector.

The following disclosure was provided by Fiat in its 2013 annual report:

At 31 December 2013 the Group had provisions for estimated expenses related to product warranties of €3,656 million (€3,617 million at 31 December 2012). Estimates of warranty costs are principally based on assumptions regarding the lifetime of warranty costs of each vehicle, as well as historical claims experience... Moreover, the Group makes provisions for estimated product liability costs arising from personal injuries alleged to be the result of product defects. The valuation of the reserve is actuarially determined on an annual basis based on, among other factors, the number of vehicles sold and product liability claims incurred.

The warranty provision represents the best estimate of commitments given by the Group for contractual, legal, or constructive obligations arising from product warranties given for a specified period of time beginning at the date of sale to the end customer. This estimate is principally based on assumptions regarding the lifetime warranty costs of each vehicle and each model year of that vehicle line, as well as historical claims experience for vehicles. The Group establishes provisions for product warranty obligations when the related sale is recognised. Warranty provisions also include management's best estimate of the costs that are expected to be incurred in connection with product defects that could result in a general recall of vehicles, which are estimated by making an assessment of the historical occurrence of defects on a case-by case basis and are accrued when a reliable estimate of the amount of the obligation can be made.

26. Other provisions
Changes in Other provisions are as follows:

(€ million)	At December 31, 2012	Charge	Utilisation	Release to income	Translation differences	Changes in the scope of consolidation and other changes	At December 31, 2013
Warranty provision	3,617	1,962	(1,720)	(13)	(194)	4	3,656
Restructuring provision...	261	41	(90)	(21)	(2)	2	191
Investment provision.....	13	—	—	—	(2)	1	12
Other risks.............	4,899	8,279	(7,507)	(217)	(222)	4	5,236
Total Other provisions....	8,790	10,282	(9,317)	(251)	(420)	11	9,095

Required

a. Prepare a journal entry to record warranty expense for Fiat in 2013.

b. Post the entry from part *a* in the T-accounts.

c. Fiat reported sales of €86,816 million in 2013. Calculate the ratio of warranty expense to sales for 2013.

LO4 **E9-44. Reporting Financial Statement Effects of Bond Transactions**
Lundholm, Inc., which reports financial statements each December 31, is authorised to issue $500,000 of 9%, 15-year bonds dated May 1, 2015, with interest payments on October 31 and April 30. Assume the bonds are issued at par on May 1, 2015.

a. Prepare journal entries to record the bond issuance, payment of the first semiannual period's interest, and retirement of $300,000 of the bonds at 101 on November 1, 2016.

b. Post the journal entries from part *a* to their respective T-accounts.

c. Record each of the transactions from part *a* in the financial statement effects template.

LO3, 4 **E9-45. Reporting Financial Statement Effects of Bond Transactions**
On January 1, 2013, McKeown, Inc., issued $250,000 of 8%, 9-year bonds for $220,776, yielding a market (yield) rate of 10%. Semiannual interest is payable on June 30 and December 31 of each year.

a. Show computations to confirm the bond issue price.

b. Prepare journal entries to record the bond issuance, semiannual interest payment and discount amortisation on June 30, 2013, and semiannual interest payment and discount amortisation on December 31, 2013. Use the effective interest rate.

c. Post the journal entries from part *b* to their respective T-accounts.

d. Record each of the transactions from part *b* in the financial statement effects template.

LO3, 4 **E9-46. Reporting Financial Statement Effects of Bond Transactions**
On January 1, 2014, Shields, Inc., issued $800,000 of 9%, 20-year bonds for $879,172, yielding a market (yield) rate of 8%. Semiannual interest is payable on June 30 and December 31 of each year.

a. Show computations to confirm the bond issue price.

b. Prepare journal entries to record the bond issuance, semiannual interest payment and premium amortisation on June 30, 2014, and semiannual interest payment and premium amortisation on December 31, 2014. Use the effective interest rate.

c. Post the journal entries from part *b* to their respective T-accounts.

d. Record each of the transactions from part *b* in the financial statement effects template.

E9-47. Analysing Bond Pricing, Interest Rates, and Financial Statement Effect of a Bond Issue LO3, 4

Following is a price quote for €200 million of 6.55% coupon bonds issued by Freiburg A.G. that mature in October 2028:

Ratings Industry	Issue Call Information	Coupon/Maturity	Price/YTM
A1/AA.	Freiburg A.G.	6.550	108.104
Industrial	Non Callable, NYBE, DE	10-01-2028	5.890

This quote indicates that Freiburg's bonds have a market price of 108.104 (108.104% of face value), resulting in a yield of 5.89%.

a. Assuming that these bonds were originally issued at or close to par value, what does the above market price reveal about the direction that interest rates have changed since Freiburg issued its bonds? (Assume that Freiburg's debt rating has remained the same.)

b. Does the change in interest rates since the issuance of these bonds affect the amount of interest expense that Freiburg is reporting in its income statement? Explain.

c. If Freiburg was to repurchase its bonds at the above market price of 108.104, how would the repurchase affect its current income?

d. Assuming that the bonds remain outstanding until their maturity, at what market price will the bonds sell on their due date of October 1, 2028?

E9-48. Analysing and Reporting Financial Statement Effects of Bond Transactions LO3, 4

On January 1, 2015, Lantau Corp. issued $600,000 of 20-year, 11% bonds for $554,860, yielding a market (yield) rate of 12%. Interest is payable semiannually on June 30 and December 31.

a. Confirm the bond issue price.

b. Prepare journal entries to record the bond issuance, semiannual interest payment and discount amortisation on June 30, 2015, and semiannual interest payment and discount amortisation on December 31, 2015. Use the effective interest rate.

c. Post the journal entries from part *b* to their respective T-accounts.

d. Lantau elected to report these bonds in its financial statements at fair value. On December 31, 2015, these bonds were listed in the bond market at a price of 101 (or 101% of par value). What entry is required to adjust the reported value of these bonds to fair value?

e. Prepare a table summarising the effect of these bonds on earnings for 2015, including interest expense and any unrealised gain or loss resulting from the fair value adjustment in requirement *d*.

E9-49. Reporting and Interpreting Bond Disclosures LO1, 2, 4

The adjusted trial balance for the HarbourFront Corporation at the end of 2015 contains the following accounts:

$ 25,000	Bond Interest Payable
600,000	9% Bonds Payable due 2017
500,000	10% Bonds Payable due 2016
19,000	Discount on 9% Bonds Payable
15,000	Premium on 10% Bonds Payable
170,500	Zero-Coupon Bonds Payable due 2018
100,000	8% Bonds Payable due 2020

Prepare the long-term liabilities section of the balance sheet. Indicate the proper balance sheet classification for accounts listed above that do not belong in the long-term liabilities section.

LO3, 4 **E9-50. Recording and Assessing the Effects of Instalment Loans**
On December 31, 2014, Montmartre S.A., borrowed €500,000 on an 8%, 10-year mortgage note payable. The note is to be repaid in equal quarterly instalments of €18,278 (beginning March 31, 2015).

a. Prepare journal entries to reflect (1) the issuance of the mortgage note payable, (2) the payment of the first instalment on March 31, 2015, and (3) the payment of the second instalment on June 30, 2015. Round amounts to the nearest dollar.

b. Post the journal entries from part *a* to their respective T-accounts.

c. Record each of the transactions from part *a* in the financial statement effects template.

PROBLEMS

LO1 **P9-51. Interpreting Warranty Liability Disclosures**

PHILIPS N.V. (THE NETHERLANDS)

Philips N.V. is a Dutch electronics and technology company that operates in three overlapping sectors: Healthcare, Lighting, and Consumer Lifestyle. The following information was extracted from the company's 2013 annual report (amounts in millions of euros).

Product warranty
The provision for product warranty reflects the estimated costs of replacement and free-of-charge services that will be incurred by the Company with respect to products sold. The Company expects the provision will be utilised mainly within the next year. The changes in the provision for product warranty are as follows:

	2011	2012	2013
Balance as of January 1	404	378	319
Changes:			
Additions	444	370	350
Utilisations	(470)	(427)	(363)
Transfer to assets classified as held for sale	—	—	(24)
Translation differences	1	(4)	(16)
Changes in consolidation	(1)	2	-
Balance as of December 31	378	319	266

Required

a. What was the amount of warranty expense included on the 2013 income statement?

b. What was the amount of product warranty reported on the 2013 balance sheet?

c. What was the amount of warranty costs incurred in 2013? (That is, what amount was spent for warranty repairs and settlements in 2013?)

LO3, 4 **P9-52. Recording and Assessing the Effects of Bond Financing (with Accrued Interest)**
Bled, d.d., which closes its books on December 31, is authorised to issue €500,000 of 9%, 15-year bonds dated May 1, 2015, with interest payments on November 1 and May 1.

Required
Assuming that the bonds were sold at 100 plus accrued interest on October 1, 2015, prepare the necessary journal entries, post the journal entries to their respective T-accounts, and record each transaction in the financial statement effects template.

a. The bond issuance.

b. Payment of the first semiannual period's interest on November 1, 2015.

c. Accrual of bond interest expense at December 31, 2015.

d. The adjustment to fair value on December 31, 2015 assuming that Bled, d.d. elected to use the fair value option. On that date, the bond traded at a price of 99 (99% of par value) in the bond market.

e. Payment of the semiannual interest on May 1, 2016. (The firm does not make reversing entries.)

f. Retirement of €300,000 of the bonds at 101 on May 1, 2020 (immediately after the interest payment on that date). Assume that the fair value adjustment account has a debit balance of €15,000 as of that date.

P9-53. Interpreting Debt Footnotes on Interest Rates and Expense

LO3, 4

METRO INC. (CANADA)

Metro Inc. operates a network of 566 food stores and 257 drugstores in Quebec and Ontario, Canada. It discloses the following note in its 2013 annual report relating to its debt (in millions of Canadian dollars):

20. DEBT

	2013	2012
Revolving Credit Facility, bearing interest at a weighted average rate of 2.47% (2.48% in 2012), repayable on November 3, 2017 or earlier	—	315.4
Series A Notes, bearing interest at a fixed nominal rate of 4.98%, maturing on October 15, 2015 and redeemable at the issuer's option at fair value at any time prior to maturity.	200.0	200.0
Series B Notes, bearing interest at a fixed nominal rate of 5.97%, maturing on October 15, 2035 and redeemable at the issuer's option at fair value at any time prior to maturity.	400.0	400.0
Loans, maturing on various dates through 2027, bearing interest at an average rate of 3.16% (3.06% in 2012).	28.1	32.6
Obligations under finance leases, bearing interest at an effective rate of 8.6% (8.6% in 2012)	39.0	43.2
Deferred financing costs.	(4.7)	(5.2)
	662.4	986.0
Current portion	12.4	12.1
	650.0	973.9

The revolving credit facility with a maximum of $600.0 bears interest at rates that fluctuate with changes in bankers' acceptance rates and is unsecured. As at September 28, 2013, the unused authorised revolving credit facility was $600.0 ($284.6 as at September 29, 2012). Given that the Corporation frequently increases and decreases this loan through bankers' acceptances with a minimum of 30 days and to simplify its presentation, the Corporation found that it is preferable for the understanding of its financing activities to present the consolidated statement of cash flows solely with net annual changes.

Minimum required payments on debt in the upcoming fiscal years will be as follows:

	Loans	Notes	Obligations under finance leases	Total
2014	8.6	—	6.8	15.4
2015	1.7	—	5.7	7.4
2016	1.1	200.0	6.0	207.1
2017	0.8	—	5.8	6.6
2018	0.4	—	5.4	5.8
2019 and thereafter.	15.5	400.0	30.1	445.6
	28.1	600.0	59.8	687.9

The minimum payments in respect of the obligations under finance leases included interest amounting to $20.8 on these obligations in 2013 ($24.1 in 2012).

On October 1, 2013, the maturity of the revolving credit facility was extended to November 3, 2018 and this change is not taken into consideration in the present note tables

Metro's income statement shows that its financing costs (i.e., interest expense) was $41.1 million in 2013 and its cash flow statement shows that it paid interest of $42.5 million in 2013.

Required

a. What were the average coupon rate and average interest rate on Metro's debt in 2013?

b. Does your computation in part *a* seem reasonable given the disclosure relating to specific bond issues? Explain.

c. Why can the amount of interest paid be different from the amount of interest expense recorded in the income statement?

d. What were the scheduled maturities for Metro's debt? Why is this information useful in analysing financial condition?

LO3, 4 P9-54. Recording and Assessing the Effects of Bond Financing (with Accrued Interest)

Sussex, Inc., which closes its books on December 31, is authorised to issue $800,000 of 9%, 20-year bonds dated March 1, 2015, with interest payments on September 1 and March 1.

Required

Assuming that the bonds were sold at 100 plus accrued interest on July 1, 2015, prepare the necessary journal entries, post the journal entries to their respective T-accounts, and record each transaction in the financial statement effects template.

a. The bond issuance.
b. Payment of the semiannual interest on September 1, 2015.
c. Accrual of bond interest expense at December 31, 2015.
d. Payment of the semiannual interest on March 1, 2016. (The firm does not make reversing entries.)
e. Retirement of $200,000 of the bonds at 101 on March 1, 2016 (immediately after the interest payment on that date).

LO3, 4 P9-55. Preparing an Amortisation Schedule and Recording the Effects of Bonds

On December 31, 2014, Pancras plc issued £720,000 of 11%, 10-year bonds for £678,708, yielding an effective interest rate of 12%. Semiannual interest is payable on June 30 and December 31 each year. The firm uses the effective interest method to amortise the discount.

Required

a. Prepare an amortisation schedule showing the necessary information for the first two interest periods. Round amounts to the nearest dollar.
b. Prepare the journal entries for (1) the bond issuance on December 31, 2014, (2) to record bond interest expense and discount amortisation at June 30, 2015, and (3) to record bond interest expense and discount amortisation at December 31, 2015.
c. Post the journal entries from part *b* to their respective T-accounts.
d. Record each of the transactions from part *b* in the financial statement effects template.

LO3, 4 P9-56. Preparing an Amortisation Schedule and Recording the Effects of Bonds (with Accrued Interest)

On April 30, 2015, Thuile S.p.A. issued €250,000 of 6%, 15-year bonds for €206,770, yielding an effective interest rate of 8%. Semiannual interest is payable on October 31 and April 30 each year. The firm uses the effective interest method to amortise the discount.

Required

a. Prepare an amortisation schedule showing the necessary information for the first two interest periods. Round amounts to the nearest dollar.
b. Prepare the journal entries (1) for the bond issuance on April 30, 2015, (2) to record the bond interest payment and discount amortisation at October 31, 2015, (3) the adjusting entry to record bond interest expense and discount amortisation at December 31, 2015, the close of the firm's accounting year, and (4) to record the bond interest payment and discount amortisation at April 30, 2016.
c. Post the journal entries from part *b* to their respective T-accounts.
d. Record each of the transactions from part *b* in the financial statement effects template.

LO3, 4 P9-57. Recording and Assessing the Effects of Instalment Loans: Semiannual Instalments

On December 31, 2013, Wasley Corporation borrowed $500,000 on a 10%, 10-year mortgage note payable. The note is to be repaid with equal semiannual instalments, beginning June 30, 2014.

Required

a. Compute the amount of the semiannual instalment payment. Use the appropriate table (in Appendix A near the end of the book) or a financial calculator, and round amount to the nearest dollar.
b. Prepare the journal entry (1) to record Wasley's borrowing of funds on December 31, 2013, (2) to record Wasley's instalment payment on June 30, 2014, and (3) to record Wasley's instalment payment on December 31, 2014. (Round amounts to the nearest dollar.)
c. Post the journal entries from part *b* to their respective T-accounts.
d. Record each of the transactions from part *b* in the financial statement effects template.

P9-58. Recording and Assessing the Effects of Instalment Loans: Quarterly Instalments LO3, 4

On December 31, 2014, Hung Hom Corporation borrowed $950,000 on an 8%, 5-year mortgage note payable. The note is to be repaid with equal quarterly instalments, beginning March 31, 2015.

Required

a. Compute the amount of the quarterly instalment payment. Use the appropriate table (in Appendix A near the end of the book) or a financial calculator, and round amount to the nearest dollar.

b. Prepare the journal entries (1) to record the borrowing of funds by Hung Hom Corporation on December 31, 2014, (2) to record the instalment payment by Hung Hom Corporation on March 31, 2015, and (3) to record the instalment payment by Hung Hom Corporation on June 30, 2015.

c. Post the journal entries from part *b* to their respective T-accounts.

d. Record each of the transactions from part *b* in the financial statement effects template.

P9-59. Reporting Provisions LO1, 2

BP PLC (UNITED KINGDOM)

BP operates off-shore oil drilling platforms including rigs in the Gulf of Mexico. In April 2010, explosions and a fire on the Deepwater Horizon rig led to the death of 11 crew members and a 200-million-gallon oil spill in the Gulf of Mexico. BP's 2010 annual report included the following description of its provision related to this accident:

> In estimating the amount of the provision, BP has determined a range of possible outcomes for Individual and Business Claims, and State and Local Claims.... BP has concluded that a reasonable range of possible outcomes for the amount of the provision at 31 December 2010 is $6 billion to $13 billion. BP believes that the provision recorded at 31 December 2010 of $9.2 billion represents a reliable best estimate from within this range of possible outcomes.

Required

How did BP report the $9.2 billion estimate in its 2010 financial statements?

CASES AND PROJECTS

C9-60. Analysing Debt Footnotes LO3, 4

ASTRAZENECA PLC (UNITED KINGDOM)

AstraZeneca Plc is a British biopharmaceutical company. It is involved in discovery, development to manufacturing and distribution, and the commercialisation of medicines. The company provides the following notes in its 2013 annual report relating to its loans and borrowings (amounts in millions of U.S. dollars):

14 Interest-bearing loans and borrowings		Repayment Dates	2013 $m	2012 $m
Current liabilities				
Bank overdrafts		On demand	222	105
Finance leases			30	22
5.4% Callable bond	US dollars	2012	—	—
5.4% Callable bond	US dollars	2014	766	—
Other loans		Within one year	770	774
Total			1,788	901
Non-current liabilities				
Finance leases			72	62
5.4% Callable bond	US dollars	2014	—	805
5.125% Non-callable bond	euros	2015	1,035	990
5.9% Callable bond	US dollars	2017	1,854	1,895
1.95% Callable bond	US dollars	2019	996	995
7% Guaranteed debentures	US dollars	2023	356	399
5.75% Non-callable bond	pounds sterling	2031	573	561
6.45% Callable bond	US dollars	2037	2,717	2,717
4% Callable bond	US dollars	2042	985	985
Total			8,588	9,409

The maturity profile of the anticipated future contractual cash flows including interest in relation to the Group's financial liabilities, on an undiscounted basis and which, therefore, differs from both the carrying value and fair value, is as follows:

	Bank Overdrafts and Other Loans $m	Bonds $m	Finance Leases $m	Trade and Other Payables %m	Total Non-Derivative Financial Instruments $m	Interest Rate Swaps $m	Cross-Currency Swaps $m	Total Derivative Financial Instruments $m	Total $m
Within one year	993	1,217	34	10,370	12,614	(70)	(16)	(86)	12,528
In one to two years	—	1,482	33	1,044	2,559	(70)	(16)	(86)	2,473
In two to three years	—	393	31	660	1,084	(51)	(16)	(67)	1,017
In three to four years. . . .	—	2,143	18	285	2,446	(51)	(16)	(67)	2,379
In four to five years	—	290	3	230	523	(51)	(15)	(66)	457
In more than five years . .	—	10,497	—	1,010	11,507	(77)	(229)	(306)	11,201
	993	16,022	119	13,599	30,733	(370)	(308)	(678)	30,055
Effect of interest	(1)	(6,872)	(71)	—	(6,890)	370	97	467	(6,423)
Effect of discounting, fair values and issue costs . .	—	132	—	(885)	(753)	(193)	24	(169)	(922)
December 31, 2013.	992	9,282	102	12,714	23,090	(193)	(187)	(380)	22,710

Required

a. How much long-term loans and borrowings did AstraZeneca report on its 2013 balance sheet?

b. What is the maturity profile of the expected future cash flows for these long-term loans and borrowings? Why is information on the maturity profile of debt useful in analysing a company's financial health?

c. AstraZeneca reported $495 million in interest expense in its 2013 income statement and $475 million in interest paid in its statement of cash flows. Why can the amount of interest paid be different from the amount of interest expense recorded in the income statement?

d. Consider the 4% callable bonds that mature in 2042: (i) Assuming that these bonds with a face value of $985 million were trading at 98 (98% of face value) as of December 2013, what does the 98 market price reveal about the direction that interest rates have changed since AstraZeneca sold these bonds? (Assume that AstraZeneca's debt rating has remained unchanged.) (ii) Does the change in interest rates since the issuance of these bonds affect the amount of interest expense that AstraZeneca is reporting in its income statement? Explain. (iii) If AstraZeneca was to repurchase these bonds at the above market price of 98 on December 31, 2013, how would the repurchase affect its financial statements? (iv) Assuming that the bonds remain outstanding until their maturity, at what market price will the bonds sell on their due date?

LO3, 4, 5 **C9-61. Assessing Debt Financing, Company Interests, and Managerial Ethics**

Foster Corporation is in the third quarter of the current year, and projections are that net income will be down about $600,000 from the previous year. Foster's return on assets is also projected to decline from its usual 15% to approximately 13%. If earnings do decline, this year will be the second consecutive year of decline. Foster's president is quite concerned about these projections (and his job) and has called a meeting of the firm's officers for next week to consider ways to "turn things around—and fast."

Margot Barth, treasurer of Foster Corporation, has received a memorandum from her assistant, Lorie McNichols. Barth had asked McNichols if she had any suggestions as to how Foster might improve its earnings performance for the current year. McNichols' memo reads as follows:

> As you know, we have $3,000,000 of 8%, 20-year bonds payable outstanding. We issued these bonds 10 years ago at face value. When they mature, we would probably replace them with other bonds. The economy right now is in a phase of high inflation, and interest rates for bonds have soared to about 16%. My proposal is to replace these bonds right now. More specifically, I propose:
>
> 1. Immediately issue $3,000,000 of 20-year, 16% bonds payable. These bonds will be issued at face value.
> 2. Use the proceeds from the new bonds to buy back and retire our outstanding 8% bonds. Because of the current high rates of interest, these bonds are trading in the market at $1,900,000.
> 3. The benefits to Foster are that (a) the retirement of the old bonds will generate a $1,100,000 gain for the income statement and (b) there will be an extra $1,100,000 of cash available for other uses.

Barth is intrigued by the possibility of generating a $1,100,000 gain for the income statement. However, she is not sure this proposal is in the best long-run interests of the firm and its stockholders.

Required

a. How is the $1,100,000 gain calculated from the retirement of the old bonds? Where would this gain be reported in Foster's income statement?
b. Why might this proposal not be in the best long-run interests of the firm and its stockholders?
c. What possible ethical conflict is present in this proposal?

SOLUTIONS TO REVIEW PROBLEMS

Mid-Chapter Review 1

Solution

a. The discount would be $580 ($29,000 × 0.02). Thus, Bugis would pay $28,420 ($29,000 − $580).
b. The cost of the lost discount is $29 per day ($580/20) or $10,585 per year (simple interest). The implicit financing cost of the lost discount is 37.24% ($10,585/$28,420).

Mid-Chapter Review 2

Solution

Keukenhof incurred €33,774,000 in warranty claims in 2015 (€000):

€56,934 + €39,570 − warranty claims = €62,730. Warranty claims = €33,774.

This cost would be recorded as follows:

ANALYSE

	Balance Sheet									Income Statement				
Transaction	Cash Asset	+	Noncash Assets	=	Liabilities	+	Contrib. Capital	+	Earned Capital	Revenues	−	Expenses	=	Net Income
Payment to satisfy warranty claims	−33,774 Cash			=	−33,774 Warranty Liability						−		=	

JOURNALISE

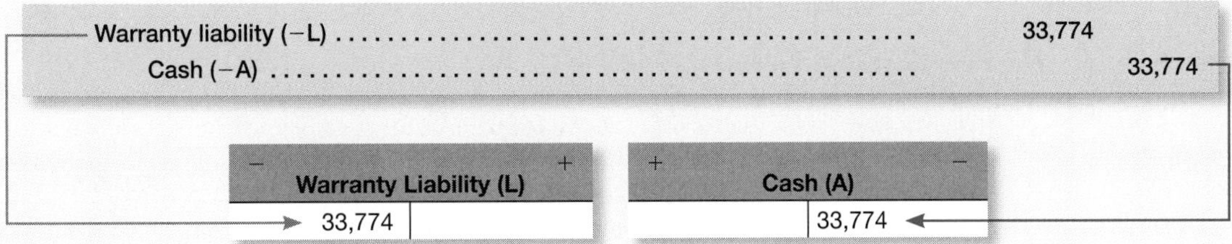

Warranty liability (−L)	33,774	
Cash (−A)		33,774

POST

− Warranty Liability (L) +	
33,774	

+ Cash (A) −	
	33,774

The credit entry to cash assumes that cash was paid to satisfy the warranty claims. Keukenhof could also have credited wages payable, or parts inventory as needed.

Mid-Chapter Review 3

Solution

The related journal entry to recognise the accrual of interest is:

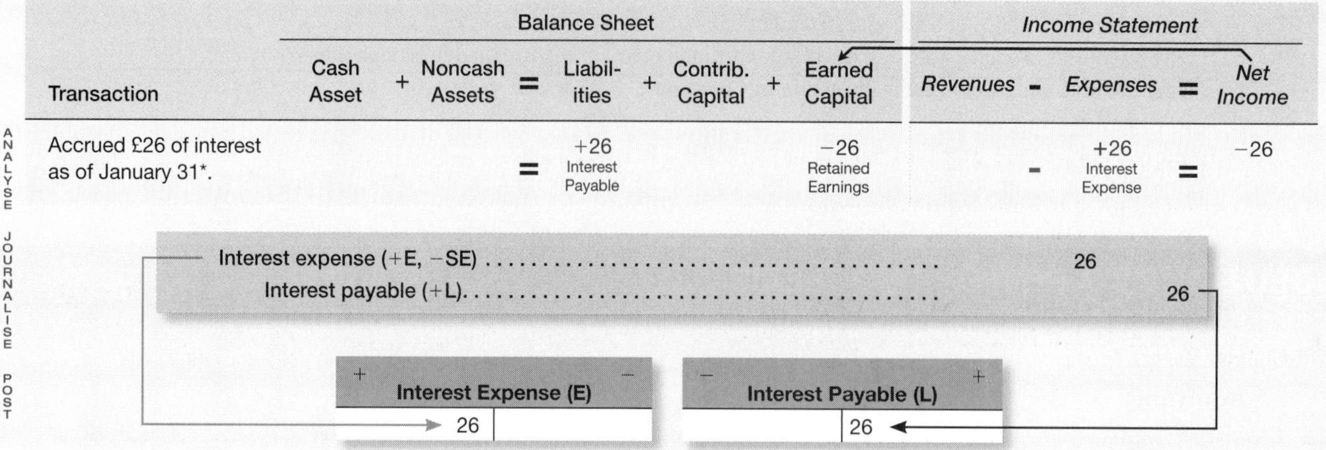

Transaction	Cash Asset	+	Noncash Assets	=	Liabilities	+	Contrib. Capital	+	Earned Capital	Revenues	−	Expenses	=	Net Income
Accrued £26 of interest as of January 31*.				=	+26 Interest Payable				−26 Retained Earnings		−	+26 Interest Expense	=	−26

	Dr.	Cr.
Interest expense (+E, −SE)	26	
Interest payable (+L)		26

+ Interest Expense (E) −	
26	

− Interest Payable (L) +	
	26

*Accrued interest for a 16-day period at January 31 = £10,000 × 0.06 × 16/365 = £26.

Chapter-End Review

Solution

1. Issue price for $300,000, 15-year, 10% semiannual bonds discounted at 8%:

Present value of principal payment ($300,000 × 0.30832)	$ 92,496
Present value of semiannual interest payments ($15,000 × 17.29203)	259,380
Issue price of bonds	$351,876

2.

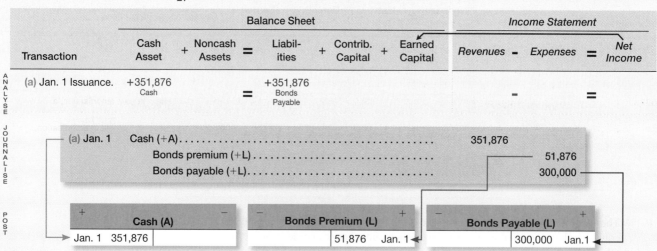

Transaction	Cash Asset	+	Noncash Assets	=	Liabilities	+	Contrib. Capital	+	Earned Capital	Revenues	−	Expenses	=	Net Income
(a) Jan. 1 Issuance.	+351,876 Cash			=	+351,876 Bonds Payable						−		=	

		Dr.	Cr.
(a) Jan. 1	Cash (+A)	351,876	
	Bonds premium (+L)		51,876
	Bonds payable (+L)		300,000

+ Cash (A) −	
Jan. 1 351,876	

− Bonds Premium (L) +	
	51,876 Jan. 1

− Bonds Payable (L) +	
	300,000 Jan.1

continued

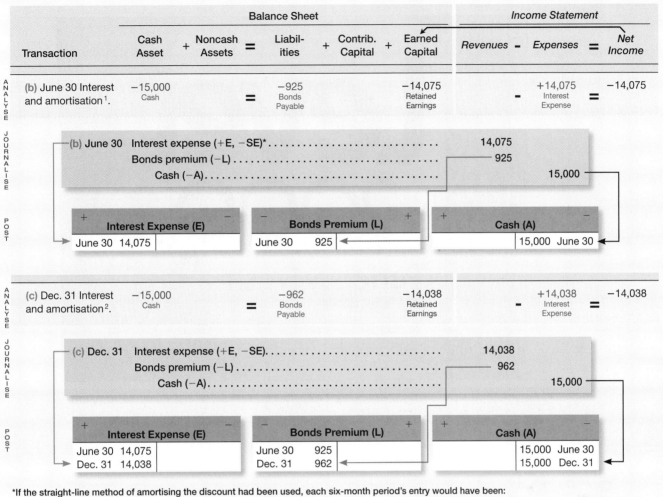

	Balance Sheet									Income Statement				
Transaction	Cash Asset	+	Noncash Assets	=	Liabil-ities	+	Contrib. Capital	+	Earned Capital	Revenues	-	Expenses	=	Net Income
ANALYSE (b) June 30 Interest and amortisation[1].	−15,000 Cash			=	−925 Bonds Payable				−14,075 Retained Earnings		-	+14,075 Interest Expense	=	−14,075

JOURNALISE

(b) June 30	Interest expense (+E, −SE)*	14,075	
	Bonds premium (−L)	925	
	Cash (−A)		15,000

POST

+ Interest Expense (E) −	
June 30 14,075	

− Bonds Premium (L) +	
June 30 925	

+ Cash (A) −	
	15,000 June 30

Transaction	Cash Asset	+	Noncash Assets	=	Liabil-ities	+	Contrib. Capital	+	Earned Capital	Revenues	-	Expenses	=	Net Income
ANALYSE (c) Dec. 31 Interest and amortisation[2].	−15,000 Cash			=	−962 Bonds Payable				−14,038 Retained Earnings		-	+14,038 Interest Expense	=	−14,038

JOURNALISE

(c) Dec. 31	Interest expense (+E, −SE)	14,038	
	Bonds premium (−L)	962	
	Cash (−A)		15,000

POST

+ Interest Expense (E) −	
June 30 14,075	
Dec. 31 14,038	

− Bonds Premium (L) +	
June 30 925	
Dec. 31 962	

+ Cash (A) −	
	15,000 June 30
	15,000 Dec. 31

*If the straight-line method of amortising the discount had been used, each six-month period's entry would have been:

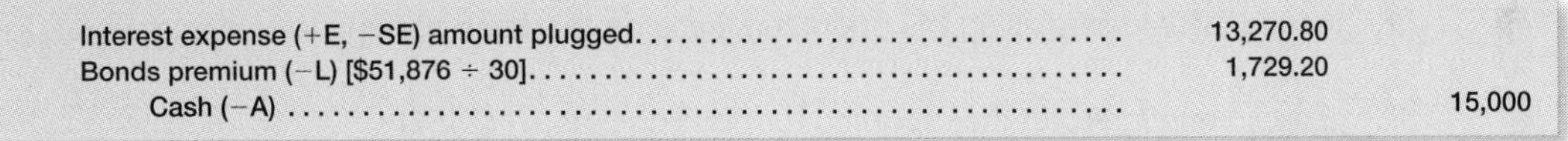

Interest expense (+E, −SE) amount plugged	13,270.80	
Bonds premium (−L) [$51,876 ÷ 30]	1,729.20	
Cash (−A)		15,000

1 $300,000 × 0.10 × 6/12 = $15,000 cash payment; 0.04 × $351,876 = $14,075 interest expense; the difference is the bond premium amortisation, a reduction of the net bond carrying amount.

2 0.04 × ($351,876 − $925) = $14,038 interest expense. The difference between this amount and the $15,000 cash payment is the premium amortisation, a reduction of the net bond carrying amount.

LEARNING OBJECTIVES

1. Define off-balance-sheet financing and explain its effects on financial analysis. (p. 448)
2. Account for leases using the operating lease method and the finance lease method. (p. 449)
3. Explain and interpret the reporting for pension plans. (p. 457)
4. Analyse and interpret pension footnote disclosures. (p. 460)
5. Describe and interpret accounting for income taxes. (p. 467)
6. Appendix 10A: Convert off-balance-sheet operating leases to the finance lease method. (p. 474)

CHAPTER

10

Reporting and Analysing Leases, Pensions, and Income Taxes

UNILEVER
www.unilever.com

Unilever Group is a global consumer products company. It owns more than 400 brands of personal care, home care, refreshment, and foods products that are sold to two billion consumers in over 190 countries. Its most well-known brands include Dove soap, VO5 shampoo, Surf detergent, Ben & Jerry's ice cream, Lipton tea, and Hellmann's mayonnaise. Unilever reported €49.8 billion revenue in 2013, making it the third largest consumer products company in the world by revenues. The major competitors of Unilever are Nestle (Switzerland) and Procter & Gamble (USA).

Unilever was formed in 1930 by the merger of Margarine Unie (Netherlands) and Lever Brothers (UK). After the merger, it maintains two separate legal parent companies: Unilever NV, headquartered in Rotterdam, and Unilever PLC, headquartered in London. However, it is operating as a single business entity through various agreements between the two parent companies and the same group of directors sitting on the boards of both companies. Unilever NV lists its ordinary shares on both Euronext Amsterdam (ticker: UNA) and the New York Stock Exchange (ticker: UN). Unilever PLC has shares listed on the London Stock Exchange (ticker: ULVR) and cross-listed on the New York Stock Exchange (ticker: UL).

Unilever confronts competing demands for its available cash flow as a result of a heavy debt load, which includes borrowed money, leases, pension and other postemployment obligations, and deferred income tax liabilities. Like many companies, Unilever leases some of the fixed assets that it uses. The magnitude of obligations arising from its leases is often larger than that shown on the balance sheet. In many cases, neither the leased properties (the assets) nor the lease obligations (the liabilities) would be on Unilever's balance sheet. That omission can alter investors' perceptions of the capital investment Unilever needs to operate its business, as well as the level of debt it carries. Methods that companies apply to avoid reporting potential liabilities (and related expenses) are commonly referred to as off-balance-sheet financing.

Pensions, other postemployment benefit obligations, and deferred income taxes are major liabilities reported in many firms' financial statements. These liabilities represent a substantial obligation for most companies, including Unilever. In this chapter, we will explore the reporting of leases, pensions, and income taxes, along with the various assumptions that underlie the reported figures. We also examine the impact that these obligations have on reported earnings and cash flows. Our task will be to explain how these obligations arise, and how they affect the company's financial position and performance. Understanding this information is essential if we are to assess the future potential of Unilever and other companies.

Sources: www.unilever.com; Unilever Annual Report and Accounts 2013; Investor Relation, 2013, "Introduction to Unilever," available on Unilever website.

CHAPTER ORGANISATION

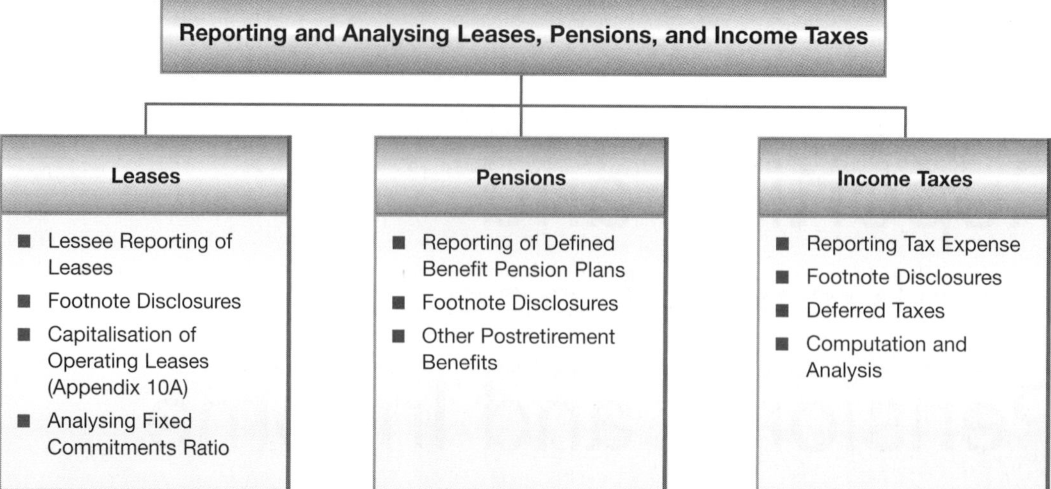

INTRODUCTION

LO1 Define off-balance-sheet financing and explain its effects on financial analysis.

Investors, creditors, and other users of financial statements assess the composition of a company's balance sheet and its relation to the income statement. Chapter 6 introduced the concept of earnings quality to refer to the extent to which reported income reflects the underlying economic performance of a company. Similarly, the quality of the balance sheet refers to the extent to which the assets and liabilities of a company are reported in a manner that accurately reflects its economic resources and obligations. For example, in Chapter 8, we highlighted the reporting of noncapitalised intangible assets to illustrate how some assets can be excluded from the balance sheet. This chapter focuses on the reporting of liabilities that can often only be found in the notes to the financial statements.

Financial managers are keenly aware of the importance that financial markets place on the quality of balance sheets. This importance creates pressure on companies to *window dress* their financial

BUSINESS INSIGHT

Nike's Off-Balance-Sheet Obligations Rafael Nadal, Rory McIlroy, Maria Sharapova, and Cristiano Ronaldo are just some of the marquee athletes who endorse **Nike, Inc.** products. These athletes sign long-term, multimillion dollar contracts to use and promote Nike shoes, apparel, and accessories. These long-term endorsement contracts are just one of Nike's off-balance-sheet obligations. Consider the following note from Nike's annual report.

Contractual Obligations

Our significant long-term contractual obligations as of May 31, 2011, and significant endorsement contracts entered into through the date of this report are as follows ($ millions):

	Cash Payments Due During the Year Ended May 31,						
Description of Commitment	**2012**	**2013**	**2014**	**2015**	**2016**	**Thereafter**	**Total**
Long-term debt	$ 200	$ 48	$ 58	$ 8	$109	$ 37	$ 460
Operating leases	374	310	253	198	174	535	1,844
Endorsement contracts	800	806	742	615	463	1,018	4,444
Product purchase obligations	3,175	—	—	—	—	—	3,175
Other	277	137	22	4	1	—	441
Total	$4,826	$1,301	$1,075	$825	$747	$1,590	$10,364

Of these obligations disclosed, only its long-term debt is included in the balance sheet. If the other obligations were presented in the balance sheet at their present values, Nike's debt-to-equity ratio would increase in 2011 by 163% from 0.52 to 1.37.

statements in order to report their financial condition and performance in the best possible light. One means of improving the perceived financial condition of the company is by keeping debt off the balance sheet. **Off-balance-sheet financing** refers to financial obligations of a company that are not reported as liabilities in the balance sheet.

Off-balance-sheet financing reduces the amount of debt reported in the balance sheet, thereby lowering the company's financial leverage ratios. Additionally, many off-balance-sheet financing techniques remove assets from the balance sheet, along with the liabilities, without reducing revenues or markedly affecting net income. Such techniques cause operation ratios, such as return on assets (ROA), to appear stronger than they are.

FYI Off-balance-sheet financing usually requires off-balance-sheet assets—this means the off-balance-sheet remains balanced!

This chapter focuses on three common financial obligations that companies report in their financial statements—leases, pensions, and income taxes. The liability section of Unilever's balance sheet is presented in Exhibit 10.1. The amounts reported on Unilever's balance sheet related to leases, pensions and income taxes are highlighted.

EXHIBIT 10.1 Unilever Balance Sheet (Liabilities Only)

As at December 31 (in € millions)	2013	2012
Current Liabilities:		
Financial liabilities (including finance leases)	€ 4,010	€ 2,656
Trade payables and other current liabilities	11,735	11,668
Current tax liabilities	1,254	1,129
Provisions	379	361
Liabilities associated with assets held for sale	4	1
	17,382	15,815
Noncurrent Liabilities:		
Financial liabilities (including finance leases)	7,491	7,565
Noncurrent tax liabilities	145	100
Pensions and post-retirement healthcare liabilities:		
Funded schemes in deficit	1,405	2,060
Unfunded schemes	1,563	2,040
Provisions	892	846
Deferred tax liabilities	1,524	1,414
Other noncurrent liabilities	296	400
	13,316	14,425
Total liabilities	€30,698	€30,240

In addition to the obligations presented in its balance sheet, Unilever reports most of its leases in its footnotes and not on its balance sheet. Whether they are reported in the footnotes or on the balance sheet, management enjoys considerable discretion in determining the value of these obligations and how they are presented. Understanding the information in these disclosures enables us to analyse the impact of these obligations on the financial condition of the company.

LEASES

LO2 Account for leases using the operating lease method and the finance lease method.

We begin the discussion of off-balance-sheet financing with leasing. A lease is a contract between the owner of an asset (the **lessor**) and the party desiring to use that asset (the **lessee**). Because this is a private contract between two willing parties, it is governed only by applicable commercial law, and can include whatever provisions are negotiated between the parties. The lessor and lessee can be any legal form of organisation, including private individuals, corporations, partnerships, and joint ventures.

Leases generally contain the following terms:

- The lessor allows the lessee the unrestricted right to use the asset during the lease term.
- The lessee agrees to make periodic payments to the lessor and to maintain the asset.

- The legal title to the asset remains with the lessor. At the end of the lease, either the lessor takes physical possession of the asset, or the lessee purchases the asset from the lessor at a price specified in the lease contract.

From the lessor's standpoint, lease payments are set at an amount that yields an acceptable return on investment, commensurate with the credit standing of the lessee. The lessor, thus, obtains a quality investment, and the lessee gains use of the asset.

From the lessee's perspective, the lease serves as a financing vehicle, similar to an intermediate-term secured bank loan. However, there are several advantages to leasing over bank financing:

- Leases often require less equity investment than bank financing. That is, banks often only lend a portion of the asset's cost and require the borrower to make up the difference from its available cash.
- Leases often require payments to be made at the beginning of the period (e.g., the first of the month). However, because leases are contracts between two parties, their terms can be structured in any way to meet their respective needs. For example, a lease can allow variable payments to match seasonal cash inflows of the lessee, or have graduated payments for companies in their start-up phase.
- If the lessee requires the use of the asset for only a part of its useful life, leasing avoids the need to sell a used asset.
- Because the lessor retains ownership of the asset, leases provide the lessor with tax benefits such as accelerated depreciation deductions. This fact can lead to lower payments for lessees.
- According to current IFRS, if the lease is properly structured, neither the leased asset nor the lease liability is reported on the lessee's balance sheet. Accordingly, leasing can be a form of off-balance-sheet financing.

FYI At the time of the writing of this text, the IASB plans to issue a new lease accounting standard, which will become effective from January 1, 2019. We discuss this new standard below.

Lessee Reporting of Leases

IFRS identifies two different approaches for the reporting of leases by the lessee:

- **Finance lease method**. This method requires that both the lease asset and the lease liability be reported on the balance sheet. The lease asset is depreciated like any other long-term asset. The lease liability is amortised like debt, where lease payments are separated into interest expense and principal repayment.
- **Operating lease method**. Under this method, neither the lease asset nor the lease liability is on the balance sheet. Lease payments are recorded as rent expense by the lessee when paid.

To illustrate the two approaches to lease accounting, assume that Richardson Electronics agrees to lease retail store space in a shopping center. The lease is a 5-year lease with annual payments of $10,000 due at each year-end. (Most leases require payments at the beginning of each period; we use year-end payments here for simplification.) Using a 7% interest rate, the present value of the five annual lease payments equals $41,002, computed as $10,000 × 4.10020 (Appendix A, Table A.3). This amount is used for valuing the lease under the finance lease method.

Using a calculator, the present value of the annual lease payments is computed as follows[1]:

Calculator

N	I/Yr	PV	PMT	FV
5	7	**41,002**	10,000	0

[1] The result produced by the financial calculator is actually −41,002. The present value will always have the opposite sign from the payment. So, if the payment is positive, the present value will be negative. Appendix A illustrates the use of a financial calculator to compute present values. In this calculation, it is important to set the payments per year (period) to 1 and make sure that the payments are set to occur at the end of each period.

Operating Leases When the operating lease method is used, lease assets and lease liabilities are not recorded in the balance sheet. No accounting entry is recorded when the lease agreement is signed. At each year-end, Richardson would record the rent payment as rent expense as follows.

Rent expense (+E, −SE)	10,000	
Cash (−A)		10,000

Because no asset or liability is reported, the only time an operating lease affects the balance sheet is if rent is prepaid (resulting in prepaid rent in current assets) or if unpaid rent is accrued (resulting in accrued rent payable, a current liability). The income statement reports the lease payment as rent expense. The existence and key details of the lease agreement are disclosed in a footnote.

Finance Leases When the finance lease method is applied, the lessee records an asset and a liability at the time that the lease agreement is signed. Both the asset and the liability are valued using the present value of the lease payments. The entry that would be recorded when Richardson Electronics signs its lease is:

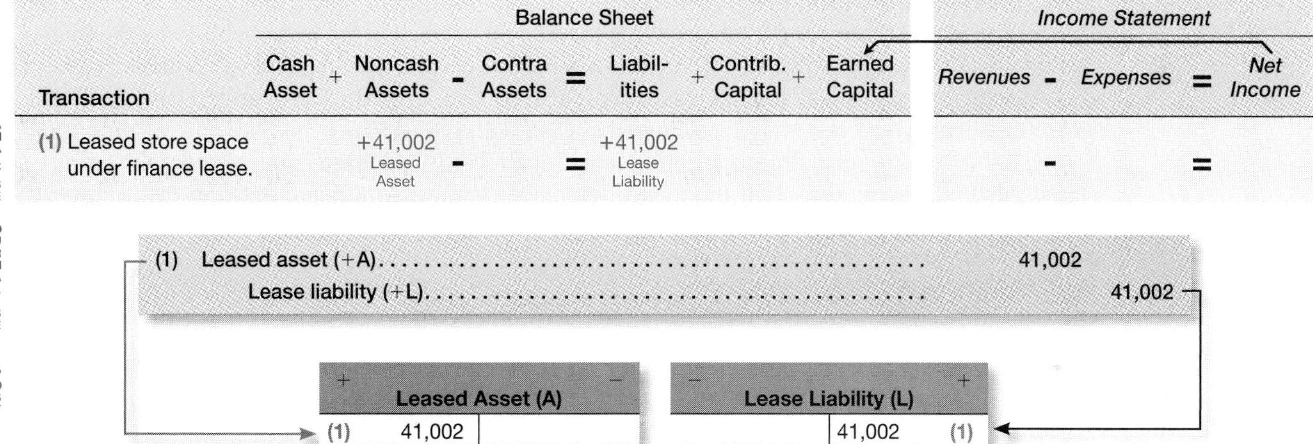

The asset is reported among long-term (PPE) assets in the balance sheet and the liability is reported in long-term debt.

At the end of the first year, two entries are required, one to account for the asset and the other to account for the lease payment. Like other long-term assets, the leased asset must be depreciated. The entry to depreciate Richardson's leased asset (assuming straight-line depreciation, a lease term of 5 years, and zero residual value [\$41,002/5 = \$8,200]) is:

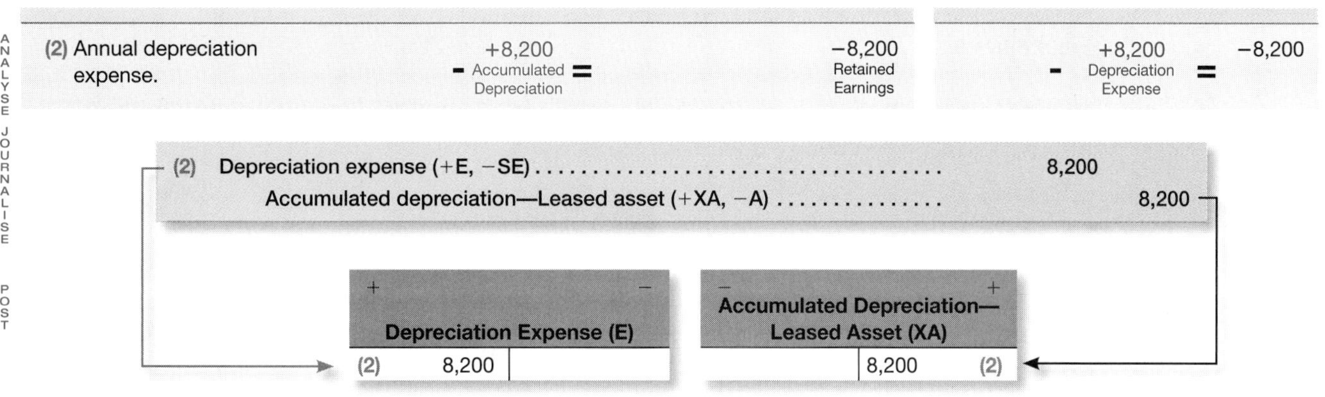

The financial statement effects and related entry to record the annual lease payment are:

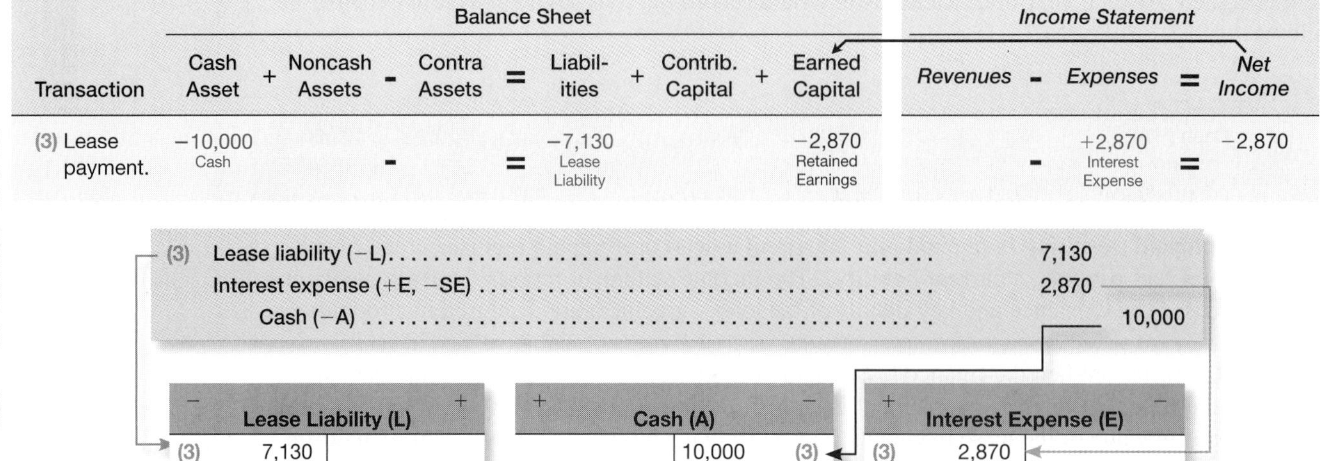

The $10,000 cash payment is split between interest expense and principal repayment. The $2,870 interest expense is computed by multiplying the unpaid balance in the lease liability by the interest rate ($41,002 × 7%). The $7,130 debit to lease liability (principal repayment) is the difference between the lease payment and interest expense ($10,000 − $2,870). The year-end balance in the lease liability account is $33,872, calculated as ($41,002 − $7,130).

Exhibit 10.2 presents the amortisation table for Richardson's lease liability under the finance lease method. The amortisation of finance leases is identical to the amortisation of instalment loans introduced in Chapter 9.

EXHIBIT 10.2 Amortisation Table for a Finance Lease Liability

A Year	B Beginning-year Lease Liability	C Interest Expense (B × 7%)	D Payment	E Principal Repayment (D − C)	F Ending-year Lease Liability (B − E)
1	$41,002	$2,870	$10,000	$7,130	$33,872
2	33,872	2,371	10,000	7,629	26,243
3	26,243	1,837	10,000	8,163	18,080
4	18,080	1,266	10,000	8,734	9,346
5	9,346	654	10,000	9,346	0

Comparing Operating Lease and Finance Lease Methods In Exhibit 10.2, the interest expense decreases each year as the lease liability decreases. Exhibit 10.3 compares total expenses for the operating lease and the finance lease methods over the 5-year life of the Richardson Electronics lease.

EXHIBIT 10.3 Comparison of Expenses under Alternative Lease Accounting Methods

	Finance Lease Method			Operating Lease Method
Year	Interest Expense	Depreciation Expense	Total Expense	Rent Expense
1	$2,870	$ 8,200	$11,070	$10,000
2	2,371	8,200	10,571	10,000
3	1,837	8,200	10,037	10,000
4	1,266	8,201	9,467	10,000
5	654	8,201	8,855	10,000
Total	$8,998	$41,002	$50,000	$50,000

Exhibit 10.3 shows how the finance lease method reports a higher total expense (depreciation plus interest) in the early years of the lease and a lower total expense in the later years. Total expense over the 5-year life of the lease is the same under both methods and is equal to the total of the lease payments ($50,000).

The effects of these two accounting methods on the lessee's financial statements are summarised in Exhibit 10.4.

EXHIBIT 10.4 Financial Statement Effects of Lease Methods for the Lessee

Lease Type	Assets	Liabilities	Expenses	Cash Flows
Finance	Lease asset reported	Lease liability reported	Depreciation and interest expense	Interest is operating cash flow; principal is financing
Operating......	Lease asset not reported	Lease liability not reported	Rent expense	Payment is operating cash flow

IFRS requires the lessee to capitalise a lease if the lease transfers substantially all the risks and rewards of the leased asset from the lessor to the lessee. In particular, the lease is classified as a finance lease if *one or more* of the following conditions are met:

1. The lease transfers ownership of the leased asset to the lessee by the end of the lease term;
2. The lessee has the option to purchase the leased asset at a bargain price at the end of the lease;
3. The lease covers a major part of the leased asset's useful life;
4. The present value of the minimum lease payments is equal to a major portion of the fair value of the leased asset;
5. The leased asset is specifically made for the lessee and has limited alternative uses.

Accounting for leases using the operating lease method offers several reporting benefits to the lessee:

- The lease asset is not reported on the balance sheet. This reporting means that asset turnover ratios are higher because reported operating assets are lower and revenues are unaffected.
- The lease liability is not reported on the balance sheet. This means that common balance sheet measures of leverage (such as liabilities divided by equity) are improved. Consequently, many managers believe the company would then command a better debt rating and a lower interest rate on borrowed funds.
- For the early years of the lease term, rent expense reported for an operating lease is less than the sum of depreciation and interest expense reported for a finance lease. This reporting means that net income is higher in those early years with an operating lease. (However, the corporation's net *operating* profit after taxes is *lower* for an operating lease because rent expense is an operating expense whereas only depreciation expense [not interest expense] is considered an operating expense for a finance lease.)

The benefits of using the operating method to account for leases are quite clear to managers, leading them to avoid lease capitalisation if possible. Furthermore, the lease accounting standard is structured around rigid requirements relating to capitalisation. Whenever accounting standards are rigidly defined, clever managers that are so inclined can structure lease contracts to meet the letter of the standard to achieve a desired accounting result even though the essence of the transaction would suggest a different accounting treatment.

Footnote Disclosures of Leases

Disclosures of expected payments for leases are required under both the finance and operating lease methods. Unilever provides a typical disclosure from its 2013 annual report:

20. COMMITMENTS...

Leases are classified as finance leases whenever the terms of the lease transfer substantially all the risks and rewards of ownership. All other leases are classified as operating leases.

Assets held under finance leases are initially recognised at the lower of fair value at the date of commencement of the lease and the present value of the minimum lease payments. Subsequent to initial recognition, these assets are accounted for in accordance with the accounting policy relating to that specific asset. The corresponding liability is included in the balance sheet as a finance lease obligation. Lease payments are apportioned between finance costs in the income statement and reduction of the lease obligation so as to achieve a constant rate of interest on the remaining balance of the liability.

Lease payments under operating leases are charged to the income statement on a straight-line basis over the term of the lease.

Long-term finance lease commitments (in € million)	Future minimum lease payments 2013	Finance cost 2013	Present value 2013	Future minimum lease payments 2012	Finance cost 2012	Present value 2012
Buildings(a)	€290	€103	€187	€324	€142	€182
Plant and machinery	22	5	17	26	6	20
	312	108	204	350	148	202
The commitments fall due as follows:						
Within 1 year	25	10	15	28	13	15
Later than 1 year but not later than 5 years	107	36	71	119	63	56
Later than 5 years	180	62	118	203	72	131
	€312	€108	€204	€350	€148	€202

(a) All leased land is classified as operating leases.

Long-term operating lease commitments (in € million)	2013	2012
Land and buildings	€1,328	€1,400
Plant and machinery	459	547
	1,787	1,947
Operating leases fall due as follows:		
Within 1 year	335	383
Later than 1 year but not later than 5 years	913	1,015
Later than 5 years	539	549
	€1,787	€1,947

Unilever's footnote disclosure reports the minimum contractual lease payment obligations that come due within one year, later than one year but not later than five years, and after five years. This presentation is similar to disclosures of future maturities for long-term debt. The company must also provide separate disclosures for finance leases and operating leases (Unilever has both finance and operating leases outstanding).

The purpose of this lease disclosure is to provide information concerning current and future payment obligations. These contractual obligations are similar to debt payments. While the obligations under finance leases are reported in long-term debt, the operating lease obligations are not reported in the balance sheet. However, the operating lease obligations must be considered in our evaluation of the company's financial condition (see Appendix 10A for details).

Finance Leases and the Cash Flow Statement A finance lease results in an increase to long-term operating assets and an increase in long-term liabilities. However, in many cases, there is no effect on cash flows at the inception of the lease—see entry (1) on page 451. As a consequence, the initial inception of the lease should be reported as a material noncash transaction and not presented in the cash flow statement under either investing or financing cash flows. Subsequently, the depreciation of the leased asset is added to cash flow from operations (an expense that does not require a cash outlay) and the principal portion of the lease payment is treated as debt repayment under cash flows from financing activities.

YOU MAKE THE CALL

You are the Division President You are the president of an operating division. Your CFO recommends operating lease treatment for asset acquisitions to reduce reported assets and liabilities on your balance sheet. To achieve this classification, you must negotiate leases with terms that you feel are not advantageous to your company. What is your response? [Answer on page 479]

BUSINESS INSIGHT

New Leases Standard On January 13, 2016, the IASB issued a new accounting standard for leases, which will become effective from January 1, 2019. The new standard defines a lease with respect to whether an identified asset exists and whether a customer has control over the use of the identified asset throughout the term of the contract. The standard requires all leases be recorded by the lessees as both an asset and a liability. Hence, the accounting method would be similar to the current method for finance leases. In future editions of this text, we will incorporate examples from company disclosures as the new standard is applied and will discuss any future updates and guidance from the IASB.

ANALYSING FINANCIAL STATEMENTS

Analysis Objective

We want to assess the effect of financial obligations, including off-balance-sheet commitments, on financial solvency and liquidity.

Analysis Tool Fixed Commitments Ratio

$$\textbf{Fixed commitments ratio} = \frac{\textbf{Operating cash flow before fixed commitments}}{\textbf{Fixed commitments}}$$

Applying the Fixed Commitments Ratio to Unilever Fixed commitments are contractual obligations that companies have to meet with cash outflows. Typical fixed commitments include repayment of long-term debt, interests on financial liabilities, operating lease payments, purchase obligations, finance lease obligations, pensions and similar commitments, and other long-term commitments. Some fixed commitments, such as operating lease payments and purchase commitments, are cash outflows that are classified as operating activities in the cash flow statement. Others (for example, payments due on long-term debt) are classified as financing cash flows, and some can be classified as investing cash flows (for example commitments to purchase plant assets). In 2013, Unilever reports total fixed commitments of €5,357 million, of which €872 million is classified as operating. To calculate operating cash flow before fixed commitments, we add back the fixed commitments that are classified as operating (€872) to operating cash flow (€6,294).

$$2013: \frac{6{,}294 + 872}{5{,}357} = 1.34$$

$$2012: \frac{6{,}836 + 927}{5{,}377} = 1.44$$

$$2011: \frac{5{,}452 + 992}{2{,}925} = 2.20$$

Guidance A fixed commitments ratio less than 1.0 indicates that a company is generating insufficient cash flows from operations to meet its contractual obligations. Some commitments may be met by selling assets, or by raising additional financing. For example, when long-term debt comes due, it can be refinanced with new debt if the company is otherwise in sound financial health.

Unilever in Context

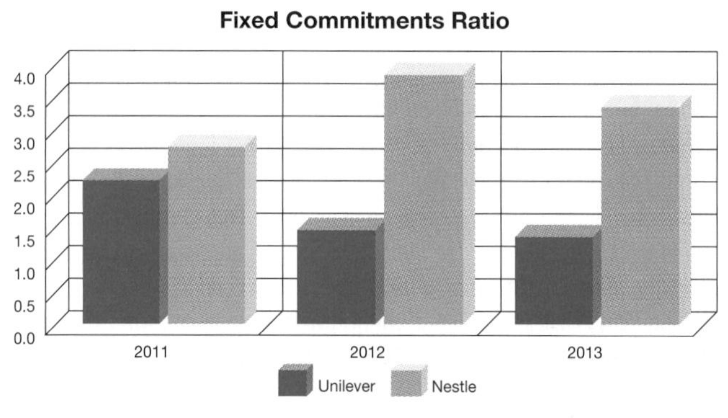

Takeaways Over the three-year period 2011–2013, Unilever exhibited a fixed commitments ratio higher than 1.0, suggesting that it had generated sufficient cash flows from its operations to cover its contractual obligations. Its fixed commitments ratio dropped from 2.20 in 2011 to 1.44 in 2012 and 1.34 in 2013, because the amount of its debt repayments increased in both 2012 and 2013. In comparison, the fixed commitments ratio of Nestle S.A., a Swiss multinational food and beverage company, was higher than that of Unilever. This is mainly because Nestle had relatively lower debt and lease obligations (both operating and finance) than Unilever had during those three years.

Other Considerations The fixed commitments ratio is but one measure of financial solvency and liquidity. It should be used in conjunction with other ratios, such as the debt-to-equity ratio and the current ratio in an effort to gauge the ability of the firm to meet its financial obligations.

MID-CHAPTER REVIEW 1

Assume that **Fast Retailing Co.**, the parent company of UNIQLO, leased a vacant retail space with the intention of opening another store. The lease calls for annual lease payments of $32,000, due at the end of each of the next ten years. The appropriate discount rate is 7%.

1. If the lease is treated as a finance lease, what journal entry(ies) would Fast Retailing make to record the initial signing of the lease agreement?
2. How would Fast Retailing record the first lease payment and depreciation expense at the end of the first year of the lease?
3. If this lease is accounted for as an operating lease, what entry(ies) would be necessary during the first year?

The solution to this review problem can be found on pages 498–499.

PENSIONS

LO3 Explain and interpret the reporting for pension plans.

Companies frequently offer retirement or pension plans as a benefit for their employees. There are two general types of pension plans:

1. **Defined contribution plan**. This plan requires the company to make periodic contributions to an employee's account (usually with a third-party trustee like a bank), and many plans require an employee matching contribution. Following retirement, the employee makes periodic withdrawals from that account. The amount that can be withdrawn is determined by how much is contributed to the plan and the rate of return earned on the investment. A tax-advantaged account is a typical example. Under such a plan, the employee makes contributions that are exempt from taxes until they are withdrawn after retirement.
2. **Defined benefit plan**. This plan also requires the company to make periodic payments to a third party, which then makes payments to an employee after retirement. Retirement benefits are usually based on years of service and the employee's salary, not on the amount invested or the rate of return. The company may not set aside sufficient funds to cover these obligations (local law may set minimum funding requirements). As a result, defined benefit plans can be in surplus or in deficit. All pension investments are retained by the third party until paid to the employee. In the event of bankruptcy, employees with underfunded pension plans have the standing of a general creditor, but usually have additional protection in the form of government pension benefit insurance.

For a defined contribution plan, the company contribution is recorded as an expense in the income statement when the cash is paid or the liability accrued. A defined benefit plan is more complex. Although the company contributes cash or securities to the pension investment account, the pension obligation is not satisfied until the employee receives pension benefits, which may be many years into the future. This section focuses on how a defined benefit plan is reported in the financial statements, and how we assess company performance and financial condition when such a plan exists.

Balance Sheet Effects of Defined Benefit Pension Plans

Pension plan assets are primarily investments in stocks and bonds (mostly of other companies, but it is not uncommon for companies to invest pension funds in their own stock). Pension liabilities (called the **projected benefit obligation** or **PBO**) are the company's obligations to pay current and former employees. The difference between the fair value of the pension plan assets and the projected benefit obligation is called the **funded status** of the pension plan. If the PBO exceeds the pension plan assets, the pension is **in deficit**. Conversely, if pension plan assets exceed the PBO, the pension plan is **in surplus**. Companies are required to recognise on their balance sheets net benefit liability for pension plans in deficit and net benefit asset for pension schemes in surplus.

Pension plan assets consist of stocks and bonds whose value changes each period in four ways. First, the pension plan assets increase by the interest income (i.e., "expected return") on pension assets. IFRS requires companies to calculate interest income using the same rate as the discount rate they used to determine their pension benefit obligations (discussed below). Second, the value of the investments increases or decreases because of actual returns (in the forms of interest, dividends, and gains or losses) on the stocks and bonds held. Third, the pension plan assets increase when the company or employees contribute additional cash or securities to the investment account. Fourth, the plan assets decrease by the amount of benefits paid to retirees during the period. These four changes in the pension plan assets are articulated below.

	Pension Plan Assets
	Pension plan assets, beginning balance
+	Interest income (computed using the discount rate for the period)
+	Actual returns on plan assets, excluding amounts in interest income
+	Company and employee contributions to pension plan
−	Benefits paid to retirees
=	Pension plan assets, ending balance

The pension liability, or PBO (projected benefit obligation), is computed as the present value of the expected future benefit payments to employees. The present value of these future payments depends on the number of years the employee is expected to work (years of service) and the employee's salary level at retirement. Consequently, companies must estimate future wage increases, as well as the number of employees expected to reach retirement age with the company and how long they are likely to receive pension benefits following retirement. Once the future retiree pool is determined, the expected future payments under the plan are discounted to arrive at the present value of the pension obligation. The discount rate is based on high quality corporate bonds or similar government bonds. This is the PBO. A reconciliation of the PBO from beginning balance to year-end balance follows.

	Pension Obligation
	Projected benefit obligation, beginning balance
+	Service cost
+	Interest cost
+/−	Actuarial losses (gains)
−	Benefits paid to retirees
=	Projected benefit obligation, ending balance

As this reconciliation shows, the balance in the PBO changes during the period for four reasons.

- First, **service cost** is comprised of current service cost, past service cost, and gain or loss on settlement. As employees continue to work for the company, their pension benefits increase. Current service cost represents the additional (future) pension benefits earned by employees during the current year. Past service cost results from the adoption of a new pension plan or from the amendment of an existing plan. Settlement or curtailment of a plan creates gain (or loss) if the company pays less (or more) to settle the plan's obligation or to transfer the obligation to a third party, such as an insurance company.
- Second, **interest cost** accrues on the outstanding pension liability, just as it would with any other long-term liability (see the accounting for bond liabilities in Chapter 9). Because there are no scheduled interest payments on the PBO, the interest cost accrues each year, that is, interest is added to the existing liability.
- Third, the PBO can increase (or decrease) due to **actuarial losses (and gains)**, which arise from differences in the actual versus the expected return on plan asset or when companies make *changes in actuarial assumptions* (including assumptions that are used to estimate the PBO, such as the rate of wage inflation, termination and mortality rates, and the discount rate used to compute the present value of future obligations). For example, if a company increases the discount rate used to compute the present value of future pension plan payments from, say, 8% to 9%, the present value of future benefit payments declines (just like bond prices) and the company records a gain. Conversely, if the discount rate is reduced to 7%, the present value of the PBO increases and a loss is recorded. Other assumptions used to estimate the pension liability (such as the expected wage inflation rate or the expected life span of current and former employees) can create similar actuarial losses or gains.
- Fourth, pension benefit payments to retirees reduce the PBO (just as the payments reduce the pension plan assets).

Finally, the net pension liability (or asset) that is reported in a company's balance sheet, then, is computed as follows:

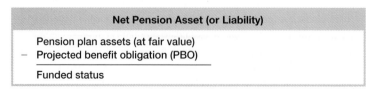

	Net Pension Asset (or Liability)
	Pension plan assets (at fair value)
−	Projected benefit obligation (PBO)
	Funded status

If the pension plan is in deficit (liabilities exceed assets), it is reported on the balance sheet as a liability. If the plan is in surplus (assets exceed liabilities), the overfunded plan is reported as an asset, but only up to a ceiling. The asset ceiling is the present value of either the refunds or reductions in future contributions, computed using the same discount rate used to value the PBO. Companies typically maintain many pension plans, with some in deficit and others in surplus. They are required to separately present net pension asset for benefit plans in surplus and net pension liability for plans in deficit (offsetting is generally not permitted, except when legal right exists).[2]

Income Statement Effects of Defined Benefit Pension Plans

In a defined benefit plan, pension expense is not determined by the company's contribution to the pension fund. Instead, net pension expense is computed as follows.

	Net Pension Expense (Reported in the Income Statement)
	Service cost
+	Interest cost on pension obligation
−	Interest income on pension asset
=	Net pension expense

Pension service cost is usually included with other forms of compensation expense in selling, general, and administrative (SG&A) expenses. Interest cost and interest income are included in or listed under net finance costs/income on the income statement. IFRS requires that the components of pension expense be disclosed separately in footnotes.

The net pension expense has three main components. The first component, service cost, includes current service cost, past service cost, and gain or loss from settlement (described in the PBO section above). The second component is the interest cost on pension obligation (also described in the PBO section). The third component is the interest income on pension plan assets, which reduces total pension expense. IFRS requires interest income be computed using the same rate as the discount rate applied to calculate the PBO. Use of interest income (as expected return) rather than actual return is an important distinction. IFRS believes that plan assets are long-term investments and, hence, short-term fluctuations in actual returns should be excluded from the computation of net income.

Any difference between the actual return and the interest income (i.e., expected return) on plan assets is reported in the Statement of Comprehensive Income. The gains and losses resulting from changes in actuarial assumptions and experience adjustments are also recognised immediately in other comprehensive income. Experience adjustment gains and losses arise when companies adjust their pension costs for the differences between the actuarial assumptions and the actual outcomes.

	Remeasurements of the Net Defined Benefit Liability or Asset (Reported in the Statement of Comprehensive Income)
	Actual return net of the interest income (i.e., expected return) on plan assets
+	Actuarial gains and losses
+	Gains and losses from experience adjustments
=	Total defined benefit costs recognised in other comprehensive income

Most analysts consider the service cost portion of pension expense to be an operating expense, similar to salaries and other benefits. However, the interest cost component is generally viewed as a financing cost.

[2] During the early 2000s, long-term interest rates declined drastically and many companies lowered their discount rate for computing the present value of future pension payments. Lower discount rates meant higher PBO values. This period also witnessed a bear market and pension plan assets declined in value. The combined effect of the increase in PBO and the decrease in asset values caused many pension funds to become severely underfunded.

YOU MAKE THE CALL

You are a Consultant to the IASB. The Board has asked your input on whether the assets in the pension fund should be netted against Pension Benefit Obligation (PBO) or whether the pension asset and the pension obligation should be reported separately. How would you advise the Board? [Answer on page 479]

Footnote Disclosures—Components of Plan Assets and PBO

LO4 Analyse and interpret pension footnote disclosures.

IFRS requires extensive footnote disclosures for pensions (and other postretirement benefits that we discuss later). These notes provide details relating to the net pension liability reported in the balance sheet and the components of pension expense reported as part of SG&A expense in the income statement.

Unilever indicates in footnote 4B to its 2013 annual report that the funded status of its pension plans and other post-employment benefits plans are €(1,445) million and €(532) million, respectively, on December 31, 2013. This means that Unilever's benefit plans are underfunded in aggregate. However, some of its benefit plans are in surplus and others are in deficit. Following are the disclosures Unilever makes in its footnote on pensions and similar obligations.

4B. PENSIONS AND SIMILAR OBLIGATIONS (Excerpt only)

DESCRIPTION OF PLANS

In many countries the Group operates defined benefit pension plans based on employee pensionable remuneration and length of service. The majority of plans are either final salary, career average or hybrid plans and are externally funded. Benefits are determined by the plan rules and are linked to inflation in some countries. The Group also provides other post-employment benefits, mainly post-employment healthcare plans in the United States. These plans are predominantly unfunded. The Group increasingly also operates a number of defined contribution plans, the assets of which are held in external funds.

BALANCE SHEET

The assets, liabilities and surplus/(deficit) position of the pension and other post-employment benefit plans at the balance sheet date were:

	2013		2012	
(in € million)	Pension plans	Other post-employment benefit plans	Pension plans	Other post-employment benefit plans
Fair value of assets	18,313	6	17,665	8
Present value of liabilities	(19,758)	(538)	(20,355)	(660)
Net liabilities	(1,445)	(532)	(2,690)	(652)
Pension liability net of assets	(1,445)	(532)	(2,690)	(652)
Of which in respect of:				
Funded plans in surplus:				
Liabilities	(6,068)	—	(4,967)	(1)
Assets	7,056	3	5,722	4
Aggregate surplus	988	3	755	3
Pension asset net of liabilities	988	3	755	3
Funded plans in deficit:				
Liabilities	(12,649)	(16)	(13,985)	(22)
Assets	11,257	3	11,943	4
Pension liability net of assets	(1,392)	(13)	(2,042)	(18)
Unfunded plans:				
Pension liability	(1,041)	(522)	(1,403)	(637)

RECONCILIATION OF CHANGE IN ASSETS AND LIABILITIES
Movements in assets and liabilities during the year:

(in € million)	Assets 2013	Assets 2012	Liabilities 2013	Liabilities 2012	Total 2013	Total 2012
January 1	€17,673	€16,044	€(21,015)	€(18,984)	€(3,342)	€(2,940)
Current service cost	—	—	(301)	(290)	(301)	(290)
Employee contributions	18	18	—	—	18	18
Special termination benefits	—	—	(18)	(17)	(18)	(17)
Past service costs including losses/(gains) on curtailments	—	—	89	47	89	47
Settlements	—	(6)	—	6	—	—
Actual return on plan assets (excluding amounts in net finance income/charge)	934	1,371	—	—	934	1,371
Interest cost	—	—	(793)	(892)	(793)	(892)
Interest income	660	747	—	—	660	747
Actuarial gain/(loss) arising from changes in demographic assumptions	—	—	(158)	(148)	(158)	(148)
Actuarial gain/(loss) arising from changes in financial assumptions	—	—	235	(1,678)	235	(1,678)
Actuarial gain/(loss) arising from experience adjustments	—	—	(69)	(156)	(69)	(156)
Employer contributions	593	605	—	—	593	605
Benefit payments	(1,196)	(1,227)	1,196	1,227	—	—
Reclassification of benefits [(b)]	23	17	(23)	(23)	—	(6)
Currency retranslation	(386)	104	561	(107)	175	(3)
December 31	€18,319	€17,673	€(20,296)	€(21,015)	€(1,977)	€(3,342)

(b) Certain liabilities have been reclassified as employee benefit liabilities.

The above reconciliation shows the changes in Unilever's net benefit plan assets and liabilities during 2013 (as well as 2012). In particular, Unilever's pension plan assets began the year with a fair value of €17,673 million, which increased by €18 million from employee contributions, by €1,594 million (= €934 million + €660 million) from actual investment return on plan assets, and by €593 million from company contributions. The company drew down its plan assets to make pension payments of €1,196 million to retirees, leaving the pension plan assets with a year-end balance of €18,319 million, after accounting for reclassification and currency translation loss.

Unilever's projected benefit obligation (PBO) and other post-employment benefit obligation (discussed later) began 2013 with a balance of $21,015 million. They increased by the accrual of €230 million (= €301 million + €18 million − €89 million) in service cost and €793 million in interest cost. During the year, Unilever also realised an actuarial net gain of €8 million (= −€158 million + €235 million − €69 million), which decreased the pension liability. The PBO decreased as a result of €1,196 million in benefits paid to retirees, which reduced the plan assets by the same amount, as mentioned above. The ending balance of PBO was €20,296 million.

The funded status of Unilever's benefit plans at year-end is €(1,977) million (= €18,319 million − €20,296 million). The negative balance indicates that its benefits plans are in deficit. The PBO and pension plan assets accounts cannot be separated into operating and nonoperating components; thus, most analysts treat the benefit plan surplus as an operating asset and a benefit plan deficit as an operating liability.

Footnote Disclosures—Components of Pension Expense

Unilever incurred €466 million in pension expense in 2013. While the €133 million in net finance cost is separately reported in its income statement, the rest is not broken out separately. Instead, it is included in SG&A expense. Details of this expense are found in its footnote on pensions and similar obligations, which follows:

INCOME STATEMENT
The charge to the income statement comprises:

(in € million)	2013	2012	2011
Charged to operating profit:			
Defined benefit pension and other benefit plans:			
Current service cost	(301)	(290)	(265)
Employee contributions	18	18	15
Special termination benefits	(18)	(17)	(31)
Past service cost including (losses)/gains on curtailments	89	47	338
Settlements	–	–	3
Defined contribution plans	(121)	(116)	(90)
Total operating cost	(333)	(358)	(30)
Finance income/(cost)	(133)	(145)	(95)
Net impact on the income statement (before tax)	(466)	(503)	(125)

Most analysts consider the service cost portion of pension expense to be an operating expense, similar to salaries and other benefits. However, the net finance cost component (= interest cost − interest income) is generally viewed as a financing cost. Unilever reported a total service cost in 2013 of €212 million (€301 − €18 + €18 − €89), which would be treated as an operating expense for analysis purposes. In addition, Unilever reported €121 million in pension cost related to defined contribution plans. This cost is considered an operating expense.

RESEARCH INSIGHT

Valuation of Pension Footnote Disclosures The IASB requires footnote disclosure of the major components of pension cost presumably because it is useful for investors. Pension-related research has examined whether investors assign different valuation multiples to the components of pension cost when assessing company market value. Research finds that the market does, indeed, attach different interpretation to pension components, reflecting differences in information about recurring vs. nonrecurring expenses.

Interest cost is the product of the PBO and the discount rate. This discount rate is set by the company. The expected dollar return on pension assets is the product of the pension plan asset balance and the expected long-run rate of return on the investment portfolio. This rate is set equal to the discount rate. Further, the PBO is affected by the expected rate of wage inflation, termination and mortality rates, all of which are estimated by the company.

IFRS requires disclosure of several rates used by the company in its estimation of PBO and the related pension expense. Unilever discloses the following table in its pension footnote:

ASSUMPTIONS

With the objective of presenting the assets and liabilities of the pensions and other post-employment benefit plans at their fair value on the balance sheet, assumptions under IAS 19 are set by reference to market conditions at the valuation date. The actuarial assumptions used to calculate the benefit liabilities vary according to the country in which the plan is situated. The following table shows the assumptions, weighted by liabilities, used to value the principal defined benefit plans (which cover approximately 97% of total pension liabilities) and the plans providing other post-employment benefits.

	December 31, 2013		December 31, 2012	
	Principal defined benefit pension plan	Other post-employment benefit plans	Principal defined benefit pension plans	Other post-employment benefit plans
Discount rate	4.2%	5.2%	3.9%	4.0%
Inflation	2.6%	n/a	2.3%	n/a
Rate of increase in salaries	3.1%	3.1%	3.2%	3.6%
Rate of increase for pensions in payment (where provided)	2.5%	n/a	2.1%	n/a
Rate of increase for pensions in deferment (where provided)	2.8%	n/a	2.3%	n/a
Long-term medical cost inflation	n/a	5.4%	n/a	5.0%

The valuations of other post-employment benefit plans generally assume a higher initial level of medical cost inflation, which falls from 8% to the long-term rate within the next five years. Assumed healthcare cost trend rates have a significant effect on the amounts reported for healthcare plans.

During 2013, Unilever increased its assumed discount rate, which is used to compute the present value of the PBO and to determine the interest cost on PBO, as well as the interest income (i.e., expected return) on plan assets. However, the discount rate increase appears to be justified by an equivalent 0.3% point increase in expected inflation rate.

Changes in these assumptions have the following general effects on pension expense and, thus, profitability. This table summarises the effects of increases in the various rates. Decreases have the exact opposite effects of increases.

Estimate change	Probable effect on pension expense	Reason for effect
Discount rate increase	Increases	While the higher discount rate reduces the PBO, the lower PBO is multiplied by a higher interest rate. The rate effect is generally larger than the discount effect, resulting in increased pension expense.
Investment return (the same as the discount rate) increase	Decreases	The dollar amount of expected return on plan assets is the product of the plan assets balance and the discount rate. Increasing the discount rate increases the expected return on plan assets, thus reducing pension expense.
Wage inflation increase	Increases	The expected rate of wage inflation affects future wage levels that determine expected pension payments. An increase, thus, increases PBO, which increases both the service and interest cost components of pension expense.

IFRS requires companies to disclose the sensitivities of the pension liabilities to changes in the key assumptions. Unilever reported the results of its sensitivity analyses in its pension footnote, which follows:

	Change in assumption	Change in liabilities
Discount rate	Increase by 0.5%	−7%
Inflation rate	Increase by 0.5%	+5%
Life expectancy	Increase by 1 year	+3%
Long-term medical cost inflation	Increase by 1.0%	+1%

An equivalent decrease in each assumption would have an equal and opposite impact on liabilities.

The sensitivity analyses above have been determined based on reasonably possible changes of the respective assumptions occurring at the end of the reporting period and may not be representative of the actual change. It is based on a change in the key assumption while holding all other assumptions constant. When calculating the sensitivity to the assumption, the same method used to calculate the liability recognised in the balance sheet has been applied. The methods and types of assumptions used in preparing the sensitivity analysis did not change compared with the previous period.

Footnote Disclosures and Future Cash Flows

Unilever contributed €593 million in cash to its defined benefit plans and paid €121 million into its defined contribution plans. Thus its cash contributions totaled €714 million (€593 million + €121 million). Hence, the net periodic pension cost (expense) of €466 million is considerably less than the cash that Unilever contributed to its benefit plans.

Companies use their pension plan assets to pay pension benefits to retirees. When markets are booming, as was true during the 1990s, pension plan assets can grow rapidly. However, when markets reverse, as in the bear market of the early 2000s and in 2008–2009, the value of pension plan assets can decline. The company's annual pension plan contribution is an investment decision influenced, in part, by market conditions and minimum required contributions specified by local law. Companies' cash contributions come from borrowed funds or operating cash flows.

RESEARCH INSIGHT

Why Do Companies Offer Pensions? Research examines why companies choose to offer pension benefits. It finds that deferred compensation plans and pensions help align the long-term interests of owners and employees. Research also examines the composition of pension investments. It finds that a large portion of pension fund assets are invested in fixed-income securities, which are of lower risk than other investment securities. This implies that pension assets are less risky than nonpension assets. However, in severe economic downturns, some corporations curtail their pension plan contributions in order to protect cash flow.

Unilever paid €1,196 million in pension benefits to retirees in 2013, yet it contributed only €714 million to pension assets that year. The remaining amount was paid out of available funds in the investment account. Cash contributions to the pension plan assets are the relevant amounts for an analysis of projected cash flows. Unilever disclosed the contribution payments made in the last three fiscal years 2011–2013 and the payment expected to be paid in fiscal 2014:

Group cash flow in respect of pensions and similar post-employment benefits comprises company contributions paid to funded plans and benefits paid by the company in respect of unfunded plans, as set out in the following table (including the current estimate of contributions for 2014):

(in € million)	2014 Estimate	2013	2012	2011
Company contributions to funded plans:				
Defined benefit	470	453	435	297
Defined contributions	130	121	116	90
Benefits paid by the company in respect of unfunded plans:				
Defined benefit	150	141	170	166
Group cash flow in respect of pensions and similar benefits	750	715	721	553

The Group's funding policy is to periodically review the contributions made to the plans while taking account of local legislation.

As of 2013, Unilever's plan assets account reported a balance of €18,319 million, as discussed above, and during the year the plan assets generated a gain of €1,594 million (= €934 million + €660 million). Hence, the plan asset account was generating sufficient investment returns to cover the benefit payments of €1,196 million for 2013. The €714 million contribution would help strengthen the funded status of Unilever's benefit plans.

One application of the pension footnote is to assess the likelihood that the company will be required to increase its cash contributions to the pension plan. This estimate is made by examining the funded status of the pension plan and the projected payments to retirees. For severely underfunded plans, the projected payments to retirees will not be covered by existing pension assets and current negative investment returns. When this occurs, the company will need to divert operating cash flow from other prospective projects to cover its pension plan. Alternatively, if operating cash flows will not be sufficient, it will likely need to borrow to fund those payments. This decision can be especially troublesome as the debt service payments include interest, thus, effectively increasing the effective cost of the pension contribution.

Other Post-Employment Benefits

In addition to pension benefits, many companies provide health care and insurance benefits to retired employees. These benefits are referred to as **other post-employment benefits (OPEB)**. These benefits present reporting challenges similar to pension accounting. However, companies most often provide these benefits on a "pay-as-you-go" basis and it is rare for companies to make contributions in advance for OPEB. As a result, this liability, known as the **accumulated post-employment benefit obligation (APBO)**, is largely, if not totally, unfunded. IFRS requires that the unfunded APBO liability, net of any unrecognised amounts, be reported in the balance sheet and the annual service costs and interest costs be accrued as expenses each year. This requirement is controversial for two reasons. First, future health care costs are especially difficult to estimate, so the value of the resulting APBO (the present value of the future benefits) is fraught with error. Second, these benefits are provided at the discretion of the employer and can be altered or terminated at any time. Consequently, employers argue that without a legal obligation to pay these benefits, the liability should not be reported in the balance sheet.

Other post-employment benefits can produce large liabilities. For example, Unilever reports an underfunded OPEB obligation of €532 million at the end of fiscal year 2013. Our analysis of cash flows related to pension obligations could be extended to OPEB obligations. For example, in addition to its pension payments, Unilever also discloses that it expects to make health care payments to retirees totaling €150 million in 2014. Because health care obligations are rarely funded until payment is required (most jurisdictions do not impose a minimum funding requirement on OPEB), there are no investment returns to fund the payments. Our analysis of projected cash flows must consider this potential cash outflow.

RESEARCH INSIGHT

Valuation of Nonpension Post-Employment Benefits The IFRS requires employers to accrue the costs of all nonpension post-employment benefits; known as *accumulated post-employment benefit obligation* (APBO). These benefits consist primarily of health care and insurance. This requirement is controversial due to concerns about the reliability of the liability estimate. Research finds that the APBO (alone) is associated with company value. However, when other pension-related variables are included in the research, the APBO liability is no longer useful in explaining company value. Research concludes that the pension-related variables do a better job at conveying value-relevant information than the APBO number alone, which implies that the APBO number is less reliable.

MID-CHAPTER REVIEW 2

LVMH Moët Hennessy • Louis Vuitton S.A. (LVMH) is a French luxury goods conglomerate. The following pension data are taken from note 29 of LVMH, 2013 annual report.

29.3. Breakdown of the change in net recognised commitment

(€ millions)	Defined benefit obligation	Market value of plan assets	Net recognised commitment
As of December 31, 2012	€1,163	€(650)	€513
Service cost	79	—	79
Net interest cost	33	(18)	15
Payments to beneficiaries	(87)	63	(24)
Contributions to plan assets	—	(68)	(68)
Contributions of employees	8	(8)	—
Changes in scope and reclassifications	18	—	18
Changes in regimes	(8)	—	(8)
Actuarial gains and losses: experience adjustments	1	(35)	(34)
Actuarial gains and losses: changes in demographic assumptions	(6)	—	(6)
Actuarial gains and losses: changes in financial assumptions	(37)	—	(37)
Translation adjustment	(41)	34	(7)
As of December 31, 2013	€1,123	€(682)	€441

Following is LVMH's note for its pension cost as reported in its 2013 income statement.

29.1. Expense for the fiscal year

The expense recognised in the fiscal years presented for retirement benefit obligations, contribution to medical costs, and other employee benefit commitments is as follows:

(€ millions)	2013	2012	2011
Service cost	€79	€64	€56
Net interest cost	15	11	9
Actuarial gains and losses	2	9	5
Past service cost	—	1	2
Changes in regimes	(8)	(2)	(5)
Total expense for the period for defined benefit plans	€88	€83	€67

Required

1. In general, what factors impact a company's pension benefit obligation during a period?
2. In general, what factors impact a company's pension plan investments during a period?
3. What amount is reported on the balance sheet relating to the LVMH pension plan?
4. How does the interest income (i.e., expected return) on plan assets affect pension cost?
5. How much net pension cost is reflected in LVMH's 2013 income statement?
6. Assess LVMH's ability to meet payment obligations to retirees.

The solution to this review problem can be found on page 499.

ACCOUNTING FOR INCOME TAXES

LO5 Describe and interpret accounting for income taxes.

Companies maintain two sets of books, one for reporting to their shareholders and creditors and one to report to tax authorities. This is not unethical or illegal. In fact, it is often required. Companies with publicly traded securities compute and report financial accounting income under the rules provided by the financial accounting standards setters. As we have discussed, this income computation is done on the accrual basis, and it is meant to provide information about firm performance to outside stakeholders, such as investors and creditors.[3] Companies must also compute taxable income and report the amount on their tax return(s) filed with the tax authorities in the jurisdictions in which they are required to file. Taxable income is determined under the rules promulgated by the government of the taxing jurisdiction. Tax authorities have different objectives from financial accounting standard setters. The tax rules are set in order to raise money to fund government activities, to encourage or discourage certain behaviors, and (hopefully) based on some sense of fairness and equity. In contrast, financial accounting income is meant to provide information about firm performance to investors, creditors, and other stakeholders so that these parties can make informed decisions about investments and loans. The rules and objectives are very different for the two income measures, and as a result, the two resulting income numbers for a company can be very different.

Our objective here is to learn how to determine a corporation's income tax expense that is reported on the income statement for financial accounting purposes. Financial accounting uses accrual accounting, thus, income tax expense is determined using accrual accounting just like all other expenses. As a result, income tax expense on the income statement is not the cash taxes paid for the reporting period. Instead, it is the accrual-based expense measure, meaning it is the total income tax expense related to the financial accounting income reported in the period regardless of whether those income taxes are paid in the current period or in the future. Furthermore, because it is accrual-based, there will be resulting assets and liabilities that need to be accounted for on the balance sheet. These include what are called deferred tax liabilities and deferred tax assets.

Book-Tax Differences

There are two general types of differences between taxable income and financial accounting income, also known as book-tax differences—permanent differences and temporary differences.

A permanent difference is an item of income or expense that is accounted for differently for book and tax purposes in the current year and never reverses in a future year. A simple example of a permanent difference is interest income on tax-exempt bonds. While this interest income is included in financial accounting income, it is not included in taxable income. Thus, if a company has tax-exempt bond interest income, its financial accounting income will be higher than its taxable income by the amount of tax-exempt interest. This difference will not reverse in the future because the tax-exempt interest is never included in taxable income. The accounting for income tax with respect to a permanent difference is straightforward; no deferred tax assets or liabilities are created. Income tax expense is lower (in this case) in the current year as a result of the taxes saved by investing in tax-exempt bonds.

A temporary difference is an item of income or expense that is different between book and taxable income in the current year, but will reverse in a future year such that the same amount is included in taxable income and book income over time. Temporary differences are:

1. created by using accrual accounting for book and cash accounting for tax, and/or
2. created by using different rules for determining the accrual amount for book than for tax.

FYI We use the term book income to refer to income before income taxes, as reported in financial statements. Taxable income refers to income reported in the income tax return.

A common example of a temporary difference is depreciation. For financial accounting purposes companies often use straight-line depreciation as discussed in Chapter 8. For tax purposes, however, companies use an accelerated method of depreciation. Thus, early in an asset's life, tax depreciation will be greater than book depreciation. However, over the life of the asset the same amount of depreciation will be recorded for book and tax (assuming zero salvage value). This is

[3] All companies have to report to tax authorities but many privately held companies do not have to comply with GAAP.

a temporary difference because tax depreciation is higher earlier on but will be equal to or less than book depreciation in later years in the asset's life. In other words, the book-tax difference will reverse. The computation of the income tax expense is more difficult in this case. We need to account for the taxes due on taxable income (the cash taxes) *and* an accrual of taxes that are known to be due in a future period when the depreciation difference reverses. In other words, our total income tax expense is the tax expense related to financial accounting income for the period regardless of whether the taxes are actually paid this year. The accrual for the portion not yet paid creates a **deferred tax liability**—the book-tax difference in this period will lead to higher taxable income relative to book income in the future. This higher relative taxable income means higher cash taxes to be paid in the future—that is, a liability.

Example Assume Clark Corporation is in its first year of business. It purchases a piece of equipment that costs $200,000 with a useful life of 4 years and no net salvage value. The firm uses straight-line depreciation for financial reporting purposes and accelerated depreciation for tax purposes (we will use double declining balance depreciation for our example). Comparing the depreciation schedules reveals the following information:

	Tax Reporting	Financial Reporting		
Year	DDB Depreciation	Straight-Line Depreciation	Tax vs. Book Difference	Cumulative Tax-Book Difference
1	$100,000	$50,000	$50,000	$50,000
2	50,000	50,000	0	50,000
3	25,000	50,000	(25,000)	25,000
4	25,000	50,000	(25,000)	0

Assume the corporate statutory tax rate is 40%, we expect the tax rate to stay at 40% for the entire 4 years, and that depreciation is the only book-tax difference for the Clark Corporation. The deferred tax liability at the end of each year is the cumulative book-tax difference times the tax rate. The tax rate to be used is the tax rate expected to be in effect when the book-tax difference reverses. The deferred tax expense each period is the current year book-tax difference (which is the change in the cumulative book-tax difference) times the tax rate. The deferred tax liability at the end of each year and the deferred tax expense for each year for Clark Corporation would be:

Year	Cumulative Tax-Book Difference	Tax Rate	Deferred Tax Liability, End of Year	Deferred Tax Expense
1	$50,000	40%	$20,000	$20,000
2	50,000	40%	20,000	0
3	25,000	40%	10,000	(10,000)
4	0	40%	0	(10,000)

Now assume for illustration that financial accounting earnings each year before depreciation and taxes are $125,000 and there are no other book-tax differences. The yearly calculation of financial reporting and taxable income along with the income tax expense is as follows:

	Tax			
Year	1	2	3	4
Earnings before depreciation	$125,000	$125,000	$125,000	$125,000
Depreciation deduction	(100,000)	(50,000)	(25,000)	(25,000)
Taxable income	25,000	75,000	100,000	100,000
Tax due on the tax return (@ 40%)	10,000	30,000	40,000	40,000

Year	1	2	3	4
	Financial Reporting			
Earnings before depreciation	$125,000	$125,000	$125,000	$125,000
Depreciation expense	(50,000)	(50,000)	(50,000)	(50,000)
Earnings before tax	75,000	75,000	75,000	75,000
Tax expense	30,000	30,000	30,000	30,000

The entry to record income tax expense in Year 1 follows using the financial statement effects template and journal entry form:

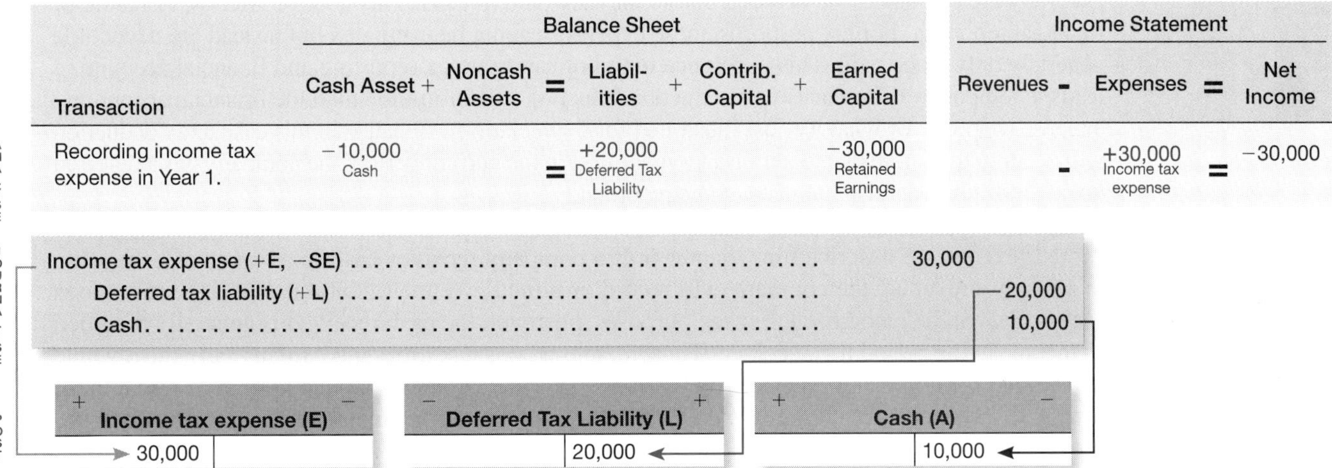

Transaction	Cash Asset +	Noncash Assets	=	Liabilities +	Contrib. Capital +	Earned Capital	Revenues –	Expenses	=	Net Income
Recording income tax expense in Year 1.	−10,000 Cash		=	+20,000 Deferred Tax Liability		−30,000 Retained Earnings	–	+30,000 Income tax expense	=	−30,000

	Dr.	Cr.
Income tax expense (+E, −SE)	30,000	
Deferred tax liability (+L)		20,000
Cash		10,000

+ Income tax expense (E) –	– Deferred Tax Liability (L) +	+ Cash (A) –
30,000 |	| 20,000	| 10,000

In Year 4, Clark Corporation records its income tax expense. The entry is recorded as follows:

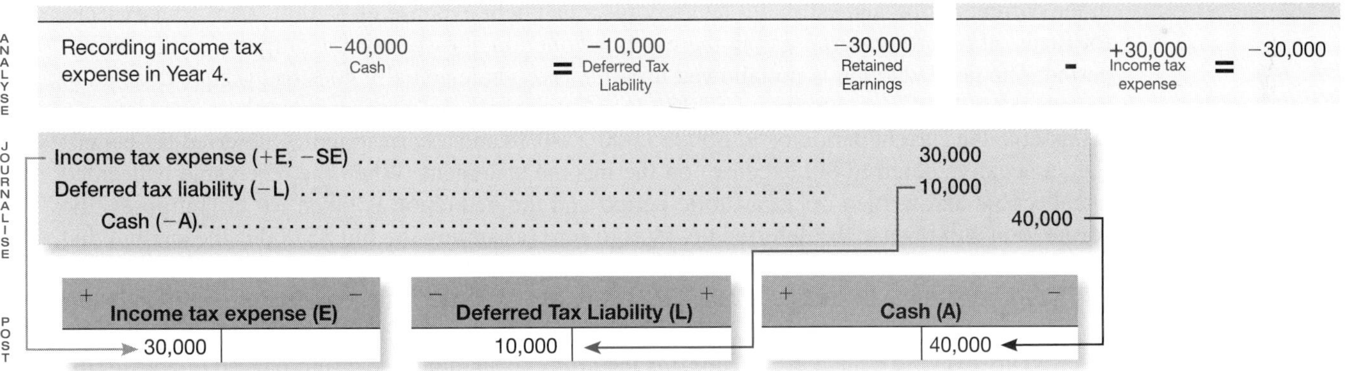

Transaction	Cash Asset +	Noncash Assets	=	Liabilities +	Contrib. Capital +	Earned Capital	Revenues –	Expenses	=	Net Income
Recording income tax expense in Year 4.	−40,000 Cash		=	−10,000 Deferred Tax Liability		−30,000 Retained Earnings	–	+30,000 Income tax expense	=	−30,000

	Dr.	Cr.
Income tax expense (+E, −SE)	30,000	
Deferred tax liability (−L)	10,000	
Cash (−A)		40,000

+ Income tax expense (E) –	– Deferred Tax Liability (L) +	+ Cash (A) –
30,000 |	10,000 |	| 40,000

The analysis highlights several facts:

1. Over the 4 years, tax payments to the tax authority total \$120,000 = \$10,000 + \$30,000 + \$40,000 + \$40,000. Total tax expense on the books for the 4 years also equals \$120,000 = 4 × \$30,000.
2. The timing of the tax payments differs from the tax expense recognised on the books.
3. The deferred tax liability created in the first year because the tax code allows a larger deduction for depreciation, is reduced to zero in the 4th year when the useful life of the asset is over and the timing of the depreciation deductions reverse.
4. The cash flow takes place consistent with the tax code. The accounting expense amount is an accrual-basis measure.
5. In year 1, the corporation's income tax expense consists of current income tax expense of \$10,000 and deferred income tax expense of \$20,000 for the total income tax expense of \$30,000. In year 4, the corporation has current income tax expense of \$40,000 and deferred

income tax expense of $(10,000) for a total income tax expense of $30,000. The total income tax expense is shown on the income statement and the more detailed breakout into current and deferred expense is disclosed in the notes to the financial statements.

Depreciation generally will lead to a deferred tax liability because tax depreciation is usually faster than book depreciation. There are also transactions that generate the necessity to record a **deferred tax asset**. For example, bad debts, warranty expense, and many other accrued expenses usually require an associated deferred tax asset to be recorded. For financial accounting purposes, bad debt expense and warranty expense are expensed using management estimates before the receivable actually goes bad and before the warranty costs are actually paid. Again, this is because financial accounting is done on the accrual method and expenses that are associated with the revenue recorded generally are estimated and accrued before they are paid in cash. This is the conservative nature of financial reporting. For tax purposes, these expenses cannot be estimated but instead are deductible generally only when paid. This difference in timing between tax reporting and financial accounting leads to temporary differences where the tax deduction is later in time than the financial accounting expense (opposite of what we just illustrated for depreciation). Because in this case a tax deduction will occur in the future due to a transaction or event in the current period, the company has a deferred tax asset (future benefit) that needs to be recorded.

Temporary book-tax differences also occur with items of revenue. Take for example, unearned revenue we described in Chapter 6. If a company receives cash in advance of being able to recognise revenue, the company will record unearned revenue (a liability) until the revenue is earned and can be recognised. For tax purposes, however, the cash received is generally recorded as income in the period it is received. Thus, there is a book-tax difference. In this case, the revenue is recorded for tax in an earlier period than for financial accounting, meaning that in some future year(s) taxable income will be less than financial accounting income when the revenue is recognised according to the financial accounting rules. That means the company has a deferred tax asset to record in the year the cash is received because in a future period taxable income will be lower than book income because of the unearned revenue recorded in the current year.

As a brief example, let's say that the corporation Josie's Jewelry, Inc. makes sales of $100,000 in the current period and estimates and records a bad debt expense of $5,000. This is an expense for financial reporting purposes but there is no deduction allowed for tax purposes in the current period. The tax deduction is not allowed until the receivable actually goes bad (i.e., is deemed to be uncollectible). Using a tax rate of 40%, Josie's Jewelry would report an increase in a deferred tax asset in the current period of $2,000 ($5,000 × 40%) and a corresponding deferred tax benefit (i.e., a negative deferred tax expense) on the income statement. When the receivable is deemed uncollectible and written off in a future period and the deduction is taken for tax purposes, the corporation will reverse the deferred tax asset to zero (assuming the full $5,000 is the amount that eventually is deducted for tax purposes) and record a $2,000 deferred tax expense. Notice that in this future period, the deduction is taken for tax purposes so the actual tax paid is lower and thus, current tax expense is lower by $2,000. In addition, because of the deferred tax asset reversal, deferred tax expense is increased. Thus, the net effect on income in the future period is zero. This is correct because the tax benefit was accrued in the first period when the revenue was earned, bad debt expense was recorded, and deferred tax asset was established.[4]

Net Operating Losses Another book-tax difference is a net operating loss carryover. For tax purposes, corporations can carryover operating losses to future years.[5] Financial accounting does not have such a rule; if a corporation has a loss for financial reporting, the loss is recorded and the

[4] When a company has both deferred tax assets and deferred tax liabilities, the assets and liabilities are first separated into current and non-current amounts. The current deferred tax assets and current deferred tax liabilities are then reported net in the balance sheet under current assets or current liabilities, whichever is greater. Non-current amounts are treated similarly. It is not uncommon, therefore to see a company report deferred tax assets under current assets in the balance sheet, while reporting deferred tax liabilities under non-current liabilities.

[5] In most jurisdictions, tax rules allow companies to carry net operating losses back and forward. In essence, allowing loss carryovers for tax purposes approximates an averaging of income over time so companies with volatile income are not required to pay high taxes in years with high income and then get no relief in years with losses. We ignore the carryback in our discussion for simplicity (and because it does not create a deferred tax asset).

corporation starts the next year with a clean slate and measures income for that next year only. Thus, the net operating loss carryover is a temporary book-tax difference. Because the loss carryover represents future deductions for tax purposes, the company has and must record an increase to deferred tax assets and a deferred tax benefit (i.e., negative deferred tax expense) in the amount of the loss carryover times the tax rate (the tax rate expected to be in effect when the loss carryover will be used to offset taxes). Thus, even though the corporation is not getting the cash benefits of the deduction yet, the accounting rules require the company to accrue the benefit to the current period.

Valuation Allowance After a corporation computes its income tax expense and records its deferred tax assets and liabilities, the corporation has yet another step to complete. The corporation must evaluate the realisability of the deferred tax assets. This means that management must estimate whether the company will have sufficient future taxable income to offset the future deductions represented by the deferred tax assets. If management does not think the company will have enough future taxable income to be able to use all the deferred tax assets (i.e., future deductions), then a reserve (i.e., a contra-asset) must be established against the deferred tax assets. Thus, the deferred tax assets on the balance sheet will not be overstated. As an analogy, recall that when a company has accounts receivables it must evaluate the collectability of those receivables and establish an allowance for doubtful accounts to ensure the accounts receivable asset is not overstated. In addition, inventory is valued at lower of cost or market (i.e., net realisable value) so that inventory is not overstated on the balance sheet. Again, this is the conservative nature of the financial accounting rules. Similarly, if a corporation has deferred tax assets (i.e., future tax deductions) that management does not expect to be able to use to offset future taxable income, then the company must record a **valuation allowance**. When the contra-asset is recorded, deferred tax expense is increased which decreases accounting income (and if a valuation allowance is reduced, deferred tax expense is reduced, increasing income). A more detailed discussion is beyond the scope of this text, but net operating losses and associated valuation allowances have been an important part of many companies' accounting for income taxes as we will see below.

Income Tax Disclosures

Unilever reported profit before taxation (i.e., income before income taxes) of €7,114 million in 2013. The difference between the profit reported in the income statement and the profit reported on the tax return is due to both temporary differences and permanent differences. Unilever reported an income tax expense of €1,851 million in 2013. In 2012, Unilever reported profit before taxation of €6,533 million and income tax expense of €1,697 million.

To fully understand how income tax expense (or benefit) is determined, we refer to the footnotes. Note 6 to Unilever's 2013 annual report contains the table shown below.

Tax charge in income statement (in € millions)	2013	2012 (Restated)	2011 (Restated)
Current tax			
Current year	(2,320)	(1,859)	(1,524)
Over/(under) provided in prior years	232	(135)	93
	(2,088)	(1,994)	(1,431)
Deferred tax			
Origination and reversal of temporary differences	177	164	(179)
Changes in tax rates	7	81	1
Recognition of previously unrecognised losses brought forward	53	52	34
	237	297	(144)
	(1,851)	(1,697)	(1,575)

The income tax expense or benefit reported in the income statement consists of two primary components:

Current tax expense—this is the amount that has been paid or is payable to tax authorities in the current period. It is usually based on the tax return.

Deferred tax expense—this is the effect on tax expense due to changes in deferred tax liabilities and assets. It is the result of temporary differences between the reported income statement and the tax return.

Based on this table, Unilever reported a tax expense of €2,320 million for current taxes in 2013. This tax expense suggests that Unilever reported a profit on its tax return in 2013. Since the company overpaid €232 million in tax in prior years, it expects a tax payment of €2,088 million in 2013. Unilever also reported a net deferred tax benefit (the opposite of a tax expense) of €237 million. A deferred tax benefit increases deferred tax assets and/or reduces deferred tax liabilities. The sum of current tax and deferred tax gives a total tax expense of €1,851 million in 2013.

Companies must also disclose the components of deferred tax assets and liabilities. Unilever reports deferred tax assets of €1,084 and deferred tax liabilities of €1,524 million in 2013. The components of Unilever's deferred tax assets and liabilities are also presented in Note 6, which follows:

Deferred income tax assets and liabilities are offset when there is a legally enforceable right to set off current tax assets against current tax liabilities and when the deferred income taxes relate to the same fiscal authority. The following amounts, determined after appropriate offsetting, are shown in the consolidated balance sheet:

Deferred tax assets and liabilities (in € million)	Assets 2013	Assets 2012	Liabilities 2013	Liabilities 2012	Total 2013	Total 2012
Pensions and similar obligations . . .	€ 368	€ 551	€ 72	€ 199	€ 440	€ 750
Provisions	532	561	140	58	672	619
Goodwill and intangible assets.	58	(111)	(1,221)	(1,325)	(1,163)	(1,436)
Accelerated tax depreciation	(176)	(175)	(521)	(448)	(697)	(623)
Tax losses	142	133	5	1	147	134
Fair value gains	10	7	(28)	(28)	(18)	(21)
Fair value losses	(11)	1	7	11	(4)	12
Share-based payments.	96	51	77	121	173	172
Other	65	32	(55)	(3)	10	29
	€ 1,084	€ 1,050	€(1,524)	€(1,414)	€ (440)	€ (364)
Of which deferred tax to be recovered/(settled) after more than 12 months	€ 896	€ 725	€(1,563)	€(1,378)	€ (667)	€ (653)

Unilever's deferred tax liabilities were greater than its deferred tax assets in both 2013 and 2012. The net deferred tax liabilities increased by €76 million in 2013, from €364 million to €440 million. The following table from the same footnote explains the changes in Unilever's net deferred tax liabilities:

Movements in 2013 and 2012 (in € million)	As at January 1, 2013	Income statement	Other	As at December 31, 2013	As at January 1, 2012 (Restated)	Income statement	Other (Restated)	As at December 31, 2012 (Restated)
Pensions and similar obligations . . .	€ 750	€ 5	€(315)	€ 440	€ 686	€ (39)	€103	€ 750
Provisions	619	96	(43)	672	661	105	(147)	619
Goodwill and intangible assets.	(1,436)	221	52	(1,163)	(1,721)	92	193	(1,436)
Accelerated tax depreciation	(623)	(66)	(8)	(697)	(668)	(45)	90	(623)
Tax losses	134	12	1	147	100	43	(9)	134
Fair value gains	(21)	(3)	7	(17)	(20)	6	(7)	(21)
Fair value losses	12	(17)	–	(5)	31	5	(24)	12
Share-based payments.	172	(8)	9	173	118	64	(10)	172
Other	29	(3)	(16)	10	47	66	(84)	29
	€ (364)	€237	€(313)	€ (440)	€ (766)	€297	€105	€ (364)

This table also ties €237 million of the changes in net deferred tax liabilities to the deferred tax component of the 2013 tax benefit mentioned above.

Companies also report in the footnotes a reconciliation of differences between the average statutory tax rate in the countries in which they operate, and the tax expense reported in the income statement. The **effective tax rate** is determined by dividing the income tax expense by the income before income taxes. Unilever provided the reconciliation in its tax footnote reproduced below:

The reconciliation between the computed weighted average rate of income tax expense, which is generally applicable to Unilever companies, and the actual rate of taxation charged is as follows:

Reconciliation of effective tax rate	2013	2012	2011
Computed rate of tax[(a)]	28%	26%	27%
Differences due to:			
Incentive tax credits	(4)	(5)	(5)
Withholding tax on dividends	2	2	2
Adjustments to previous years	(4)	—	(1)
Expenses not deductible for tax purposes	2	2	1
Other	2	1	2
Effective tax rate	26%	26%	26%

(a) The computed tax rate used is the average of the standard rate of tax applicable in the countries in which Unilever operates, weighted by the amount of profit before taxation generated in each of those countries. For this reason the rate may vary from year to year according to the mix of profit and related tax rates.

This footnote shows that Unilever's 2013 effective tax rate was 26% (€1,851 million/€7,114 million), while the weighted average statutory tax rate was 28%. Effective tax rates can vary considerably from one company to another due to permanent differences, tax credits, and other factors.

Deferred Taxes in the Cash Flow Statement

Income taxes, including deferred income taxes, are reported in the operating section of the cash flow statement. When the cash flow statement is prepared using the direct method, deferred income taxes are excluded from taxes paid in cash. When the indirect (or reconciliation) method is used, the deferred portion of the income tax expense must be added back to net income as an expense not requiring the use of cash. The amount of income taxes paid in cash is then reported at the bottom of the cash flow statement or in the footnotes.

Computation and Analysis of Taxes

The procedure that accountants use to compute income tax expense is to first calculate the tax obligation (from the company's tax return), then compute any changes in deferred tax liabilities or assets. From these two amounts, we can then calculate tax expense as follows.

$$\text{Tax expense} = \text{Tax obligation} - \text{Changes in deferred tax assets and liabilities}$$

An analysis of deferred taxes can yield useful insights. An increase in deferred tax liabilities indicates that a company is reporting higher profits in its income statement than in its tax return. The difference between reported corporate profits and taxable income increased substantially in the late 1990s, just prior to the stock market decline.

Although an increase in deferred tax liabilities can be the result of legitimate differences between financial reporting standards and tax rules, we must be aware of the possibility that such differences can also be caused by tax avoidance or by earnings management, improper revenue recognition, or other questionable accounting practices.

CHAPTER-END REVIEW

The following footnote is from the 2013 annual report of Cathay Pacific Airways Limited, the flag carrier of Hong Kong.

5. Taxation

(in Hong Kong $ million)	2013	2012
Current tax expenses		
Hong Kong profits tax	182	145
Overseas tax	182	218
Over provisions for prior years	(36)	(149)
Deferred tax		
Origination and reversal of temporary differences	347	195
	675	409

Required

1. (a) What is the amount of income tax expense reported on its income statement? (b) How much of its income tax expense is payable in cash? (c) Assuming that its deferred tax liability increased, identify an example that could account for such a change.
2. Prepare the entry, using both the financial statement effects template and in journal entry form, to record its income tax expense for 2013.

The solution to this review problem can be found on page 499.

APPENDIX 10A: Capitalisation of Operating Leases

LO6 Convert off-balance-sheet operating leases to the finance lease method.

When a company uses the operating lease method to report its leases, it can have significant resources that are not recognised as assets and significant obligations that are not recognised as liabilities on its balance sheet. As a result, there are distortions in many important measures of financial condition and performance.

- Return on assets (ROA) and asset turnover ratios are overstated due to nonreporting of lease assets.
- Financial leverage ratios are understated by the nonreporting of lease liabilities.
- Net operating profit margin (NOPM) is understated. Although, over the life of the lease, rent expense under operating leases equals depreciation plus interest expense under finance leases, only depreciation expense is included in net operating profit after tax (NOPAT)—interest is a nonoperating expense (see Appendix 5A for details).
- While cash payments are the same whether the lease is classified as operating or finance, cash flow from operations is higher for finance leases because part or all of the lease payment (the principal and interest) is treated as a financing cash outflow.

When operating leases are not capitalised, the balance sheet neither reflects all of the assets that are used in the business, nor the nonoperating obligations for which the company is liable. Such noncapitalisation of leases makes ROE appear to be higher. This result is, of course, an important reason why managers want to exclude leases from the balance sheet.

Despite structuring leases to achieve off-balance-sheet financing, required lease disclosures allow us to capitalise operating leases for analysis purposes. This capitalisation process involves four steps (these are the same steps that we would follow if the leases had been classified as finance leases):

1. Estimate the discount rate.
2. Estimate the future payments required under operating leases.

3. Compute the present value of future operating lease payments.
4. Adjust statements to include the present value from Step 3 as both a lease asset and a lease liability.

Step 1. To estimate the appropriate discount rate, we can use the rate that corresponds to the company's credit rating or the rate from any recent borrowings involving intermediate-term secured obligations. Companies typically disclose these details in their long-term debt footnote. To illustrate the capitalisation of operating leases, we use the Delta Company lease footnote given below. For this illustration, we assume a discount rate of 8%, which is approximately equal to the average rate of interest on Delta's debt.

The following tables summarise, as of December 31, 2011, our minimum rental commitments under finance leases and noncancelable operating leases with initial or remaining terms in excess of one year:

Year Ending December 31 ($ millions)	Operating Leases	Finance Leases
2012	$ 1,462	$ 221
2013	1,441	196
2014	1,380	168
2015	1,271	155
2016	1,126	163
Thereafter	7,588	323
Total minimum lease payments	$14,268	1,226
Less: amount representing interest		(489)
Present value of future minimum lease payments		737
Less: unamortised premium		(6)
Less: current obligations under finance leases		(117)
Long-term finance lease obligations		$ 614

Step 2. The future payments required under operating leases are detailed in Delta's footnotes. The leases footnote typically provides the required cash payment for each of the next five years and then an amount representing total payments for all years after that. In Delta's 2011 annual report, it reported cash payments for operating leases due each year from 2012 through 2016. In addition, it reports that scheduled lease payments after 2016 total $7,588 million.

One limitation of the footnote disclosure is that the information about the lease payments occurring after the next five years (in 2017 and later) is presented as a lump sum instead of specific payment amounts for each year. Unless we have detailed information about operating leases beyond that which is presented in the footnotes, we are limited to making an assumption about these cash payments. One approach is to assume that the lease payment that we know is due in 2016 ($1,126 million) is repeated in 2017 and each subsequent year until the total amount of lease payments is reached. This usually requires that we assume a smaller, residual lease payment in the last year to reach the total payments exactly. Using this assumption, Delta's operating lease payments would be $1,126 million each year from 2017 through 2022, and $832 million in 2023.[6]

Step 3. Once we have a discount rate from Step 1 and a series of cash flows from Step 2, we are ready to compute the present value of the cash flows. Because the lease payments vary from year to year, we cannot compute the present value as an ordinary annuity. One approach is to compute the present value of each payment and then total the present values. This approach is presented in Exhibit 10A.1 using present value factors from Table A.2 in Appendix A.

[6] There are other reasonable assumptions that we could make that would be consistent with the facts presented in the footnotes. As outsiders analysing the financial statements, we are limited to estimating the present value of a company's operating leases and to do that, some assumptions are unavoidable.

EXHIBIT 10A.1 Present Value of Delta Company Operating Lease Payments

	Year ($ millions)	Operating Lease Payment	Present Value Factor (Table A.2, 8%)	Present Value (Payment × PV Factor)
1	2012	$ 1,462	0.92593	$1,354
2	2013	1,441	0.85734	1,235
3	2014	1,380	0.79383	1,096
4	2015	1,271	0.73503	934
5	2016	1,126	0.68058	766
6	2017	1,126	0.63017	710
7	2018	1,126	0.58349	657
8	2019	1,126	0.54027	608
9	2020	1,126	0.50025	563
10	2021	1,126	0.46319	522
11	2022	1,126	0.42888	483
12	2023	832	0.39711	330
		$14,268		$9,258

As an alternative to using the present value tables from Appendix A, we can use the NPV function in Excel to compute the present value.[7] This approach is illustrated in the spreadsheet below:

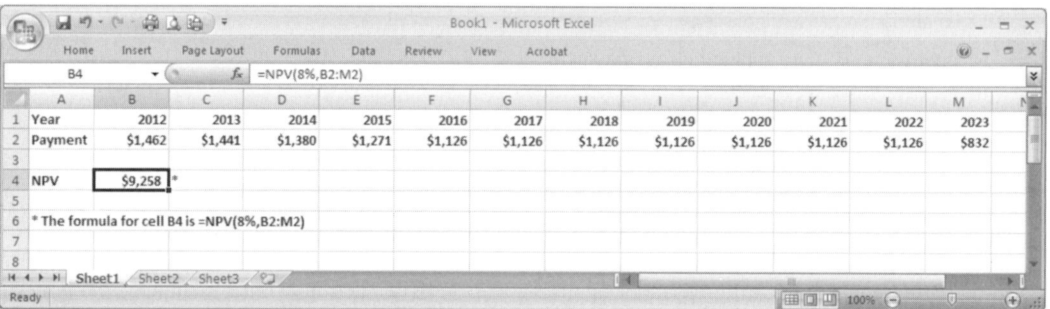

B4 =NPV(8%,B2:M2)

	A	B	C	D	E	F	G	H	I	J	K	L	M
1	Year	2012	2013	2014	2015	2016	2017	2018	2019	2020	2021	2022	2023
2	Payment	$1,462	$1,441	$1,380	$1,271	$1,126	$1,126	$1,126	$1,126	$1,126	$1,126	$1,126	$832
3													
4	NPV	$9,258 *											
5													
6	* The formula for cell B4 is =NPV(8%,B2:M2)												

Step 4. Once we've computed the present value of the operating lease payments, we can use the computed amount to adjust the balance sheet and income statement as we illustrate in Exhibit 10A.2.

EXHIBIT 10A.2 Analytical Adjustments from Capitalisation of Delta Company's Operating Leases

($ millions)	Reported	Adjustments	Adjusted	Percent Increase
Assets	$43,499	$9,258	$52,757	21.3%
Liabilities	44,895	9,258	54,153	20.6%
Equity	(1,396)		(1,396)	—

By adding the present value of the operating lease payments to both the assets and the liabilities in the balance sheet, we are, in effect, treating these leases as finance leases. If these operating leases had been recorded as finance leases all along, the initial entry to record the leases would have been as shown in the following financial statement effects template.

[7] The NPV function is also available on most financial calculators.

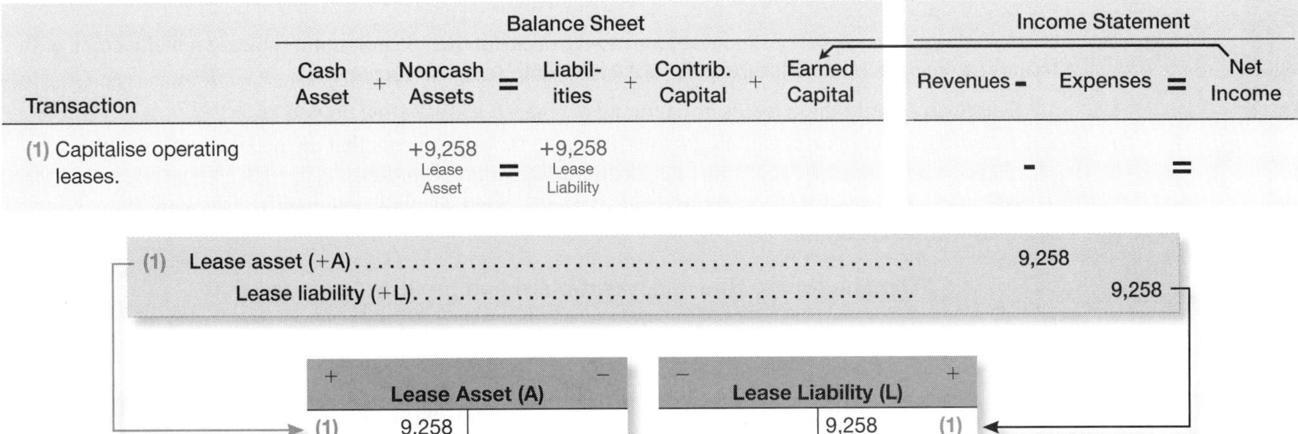

Operating Leases and Financial Ratios An asset acquired under an operating lease will not appear in the company balance sheet and the related liability will not appear among the liabilities. The omission also affects the income statement, although to a lesser extent. Depreciation is understated but the rent expense offsets the understatement. However, as we have seen, it is possible to estimate the capitalised value of the assets and the size of the associated obligation, which can then be considered in an analysis of the firm using the ratios we have previously introduced.

The capitalisation of operating leases has a marked impact on Delta's balance sheet. For the airline and retailing industries, for example, lease assets (airplanes and real estate) comprise a large portion of net operating assets and these leases are usually classified as operating.

Using the year-end data presented in Exhibit 10A.2 and given revenues of $35,115 million, asset turnover (using year-end figures) decreases from 0.81 ($35,115/$43,499) to 0.67 ($35,115/$52,757). In general for firms with operating leases, leverage (liabilities to equity) would be higher than we would infer from reported financial statements. The adjusted assets and liabilities arguably present a more realistic picture of the invested capital required to operate Delta as well as other firms with significant operating lease commitments.

It is important to consider operating lease commitments that do not appear on the balance sheet as payments that must be satisfied with cash, just as is the case with the other fixed commitments such as interest on outstanding debt. Other off-balance-sheet commitment items, such as purchase commitments, should also be included. The impact of these commitments can be gauged using the ratio of operating cash flow to fixed commitments.

APPENDIX-END REVIEW

Following is the leasing footnote disclosure from note 10 in The Gap Inc.'s 2011 annual report.

We lease most of our store premises and some of our corporate facilities and distribution centers. These operating leases expire at various dates through 2031. Most store leases are for a five-year base period and include options that allow us to extend the lease term beyond the initial base period, subject to terms agreed upon at lease inception. Some leases also include early termination options, which can be exercised under specific conditions. We also lease certain equipment under operating leases that expire at various dates through 2015. The aggregate minimum non-cancelable annual lease payments under leases in effect on January 28, 2012, are:

Fiscal Year	(In millions)
2012	$1,025
2013	917
2014	801
2015	677
2016	530
Thereafter	1,609
Total minimum lease commitment	$5,559

The total minimum lease commitment amount above does not include minimum sublease rental income of $46 million receivable in the future under non-cancelable sublease agreements.

1. Does Gap classify these leases as operating or finance leases? How do you know?
2. Assuming its leases are operating leases, compute the adjustments that are necessary for analysis of Gap's balance sheet. (Use Gap's recent intermediate term borrowing rate of 7%.)
3. Assuming the same facts as determined in part 2, what income statement adjustments should an analyst consider, if any?

The solution to this review problem can be found on page 500.

SUMMARY

LO1 Define off-balance-sheet financing and explain its effects on financial analysis. (p. 448)

- Off-balance-sheet financing refers to financial obligations of the company that are not recognised as liabilities in the balance sheet. Recognising these obligations often requires recognising off-balance-sheet assets.
- Off-balance-sheet financing improves financial leverage ratios and its corresponding unrecognised assets improve performance measures.

LO2 Account for leases using the operating lease method and the finance lease method. (p. 449)

- Operating lease payments are treated as ordinary rent expense. No asset or liability is recorded.
- A finance lease records an asset and a liability equal to the present value of the minimum lease payments. The income statement reports interest expense on the liability and depreciation on the asset.

LO3 Explain and interpret the reporting for pension plans. (p. 457)

- Pension and other postretirement obligations represent one of the largest obligations for most companies.
- The projected benefit obligation is the present value of the estimated future benefits that a company expects to pay retired employees.
- The net liability that a company reports on the balance sheet is the projected benefit obligation offset by the plan assets.

LO4 Analyse and interpret pension footnote disclosures. (p. 460)

- Pension footnotes provide detailed information about changes in pension obligations, changes in plan assets, and the determinants of pension expense.
- Pension footnotes provide information allowing us to interpret pension expenses and cash flows.

LO5 Describe and interpret accounting for income taxes. (p. 467)

- While income tax expense is reported below income from operations, it is an operating expense. The initial item in an indirect cash flow statement is net income, which reflects the deduction of the tax expense.
- Income tax expense is determined as the sum of the tax computed as due to the government and the net change in deferred taxes.
- Deferred taxes occur because of differences between IFRS reporting and the tax due based on the rules of the tax authority. The former are based on accrual accounting while the latter are often based on a cash-based accounting system.

LO6 Appendix 10A: Convert off-balance-sheet operating leases to the finance lease method. (p. 474)

- Compute the present value of future cash payments required under operating leases. These cash obligations are disclosed in footnotes.
- Add a lease asset and a lease liability to the balance sheet equal to the present value of the future cash payments.

GUIDANCE ANSWERS . . . YOU MAKE THE CALL

You are the Division President You must take care in accepting lease terms that are not advantageous to your company merely to achieve off-balance-sheet financing. Long-term shareholder value is created by managing your operation well, including negotiating leases with acceptable terms. Lease footnote disclosures also provide sufficient information for skilled analysts to undo the operating lease treatment. This means that you can end up with effective capitalisation of a lease with lease terms that are not in the best interests of your company and with few benefits from off-balance-sheet financing. There is also the potential for lost credibility with stakeholders.

You are a Consultant to the IASB Normally accountants do not favor offsetting liabilities against the related assets as is currently the reporting practice required under IFRS. However, because the pension fund is a separate legal entity, there is a problem with reporting the pension plan assets among the firm's assets. A company does not have unilateral control over a pension trust. It can put assets into the trust but can not easily get them out of the trust. For this reason, the pension assets do not meet the criteria we normally require for recognition. This is one of the reasons why IFRS puts a ceiling on how much net pension fund assets can be reported on the balance sheet.

KEY RATIOS

$$\text{Fixed commitments ratio} = \frac{\text{Operating cash flow before fixed commitments}}{\text{Fixed commitments}}$$

$$\text{Effective tax rate} = \frac{\text{Provision for income taxes (expense)}}{\text{Income before income taxes}}$$

KEY TERMS

Accumulated post-employment benefit obligation (APBO) (p. 465)
Actuarial losses and gains (p. 458)
Deferred tax asset (p. 470)
Deferred tax liability (p. 468)
Defined benefit plan (p. 457)
Defined contribution plan (p. 457)
Effective tax rate (p. 473)
Finance lease method (p. 450)
Funded status (p. 457)
In deficit (p. 457)
In surplus (p. 457)
Interest cost (p. 458)
Lessee (p. 449)
Lessor (p. 449)
Off-balance-sheet financing (p. 449)
Operating lease method (p. 450)
Other post-employment benefits (OPEB) (p. 465)
Pension plan assets (p. 457)
Projected benefit obligation (PBO) (p. 457)
Service cost (p. 458)
Valuation allowance (p. 471)

MULTIPLE CHOICE

1. IFRS requires that certain leases be accounted for as *finance leases*. The reason for this treatment is that this type of lease
   a. conveys all of the benefits and risks of ownership of the asset.
   b. is an example of form over substance.
   c. provides the use of the lease asset to the lessee for a limited period of time.
   d. is an example of off-balance-sheet financing.

2. For a lease that is accounted for as an operating lease by the lessee, the monthly rental payments should be
   a. allocated between interest expense and depreciation expense.
   b. allocated between a reduction in the liability for lease assets and interest expense.
   c. recorded as a reduction in the liability for lease assets.
   d. recorded as rent expense.

Multiple Choice Answers
1. a 2. d 3. d 4. b 5. d 6. c

3. The balance sheet liability for a finance lease would be reduced each period by the
   a. lease payment.
   b. lease payment plus the amortisation of the related asset.
   c. lease payment less the amortisation of the related asset.
   d. lease payment less the periodic interest expense.

4. Which of the following statements characterises defined benefit pension plans?
   a. The employer's obligation is satisfied by making the necessary periodic contribution.
   b. Retirement benefits are based on the plan's benefit formula.
   c. Retirement benefits depend on how well pension fund assets have been managed.
   d. Contributions are made in equal amounts by employer and employees.

5. When the value of pension plan assets is greater than the projected benefit obligation,
   a. the difference is added to pension expense.
   b. the difference is reported as deferred pension cost.
   c. the difference is reported as a contra equity adjustment.
   d. the pension plan is overfunded.

6. Which of the following is *not* a component of net pension expense?
   a. Interest cost
   b. Return on plan assets
   c. Benefits paid to retirees
   d. Amortisation of prior service cost

Superscript [A] denotes assignments based on Appendix 10A.

DISCUSSION QUESTIONS

Q10-1. What are the financial reporting differences between an operating lease and a finance lease? Explain.

Q10-2.[A] Are footnote disclosures sufficient to overcome nonrecognition on the balance sheet of assets and related liabilities for operating leases? Explain.

Q10-3. Is the expense of a lease over its entire life the same whether or not it is capitalised? Explain.

Q10-4. What are the economic and accounting differences between a defined contribution plan and a defined benefit plan?

Q10-5. Under what circumstances will a company report a net pension asset? A net pension liability?

Q10-6. What are the components of pension expense that is reported in the income statement?

Q10-7. What effect does the use of expected returns on pension investments and the deferral of unexpected gains and losses on those investments have on income?

Q10-8. How is the initial valuation determined for the asset and the liability with a finance lease?

Q10-9. Over what time period should the cost of providing retirement benefits to employees be expensed?

Q10-10. What accounting analysis is required when the accumulated retirement benefits under a firm's pension plan exceed the assets in its pension fund?

Q10-11. Under what circumstances should a tax payment be recorded as deferred taxes?

MINI EXERCISES

LO2 **M10-12. Accounting for Leases**

On January 3, 2015, Lascaux S.A. signed a lease on a machine for its manufacturing operation. The lease requires Lascaux S.A. to make six annual lease payments of €12,000 with the first payment due December 31, 2015. Lascaux S.A. could have financed the machine by borrowing the purchase price at an interest rate of 7%.

a. Prepare the journal entries that Lascaux S.A. would make on January 3 and December 31, 2015, to record this lease assuming
   i. the lease is reported as an operating lease.
   ii. the lease is reported as a finance lease.

b. Assuming that the lease is treated as a finance lease, post the journal entries of part *a* to the appropriate T-accounts.

c. Show how the entries posted in part *b* would affect the financial statements using the financial statement effects template.

M10-13. Accounting for Leases LO2

On July 1, 2015, Eyzies S.A. leased a warehouse building under a 10-year lease agreement. The lease requires quarterly lease payments of €4,500. The first lease payment is due on September 30, 2015. The lease was reported as a finance lease using an 8% annual interest rate.

a. Prepare the journal entry to record the initial signing of the lease on July 1, 2015.

b. Prepare the journal entries that would be necessary on September 30 and December 31, 2015.

c. Post the entries from parts *a* and *b* in their appropriate T-accounts.

d. Prepare a financial statement effects template to show the effects of the entries from parts *a* and *b* on the balance sheet and income statement.

e. Redo parts *a* and *b* assuming that the lease is reported as an operating lease. Is the expense recognised in 2015 under the operating lease method higher or lower than under the finance lease method? Explain.

M10-14. Accounting for Operating and Finance Leases LO2

On January 1, 2015, Whistler, Inc., entered into two lease contracts. The first lease contract was a six-year lease for computer equipment with $15,000 annual lease payments due at the end of each year. Whistler took possession of the equipment on January 1, 2015. The second lease contract was a six-month lease, beginning January 1, 2015, for warehouse storage space with $1,000 monthly lease payments due the first of each month. Whistler made the first month's payment on January 1, 2015. The present value of the lease payments under the first contract is $74,520. The present value of the lease payments under the second contract is $5,853.

Required

a. Assume that the first lease contract is a finance lease. Prepare the appropriate journal entry for this lease on January 1, 2015.

b. Assume the second lease contract is an operating lease. Prepare the proper journal entry for this lease on January 1, 2015.

M10-15.[A] Analysing and Interpreting Leasing Footnote Disclosures LO2, 6

Balatonlelle Kft reports the following information related to non-cancelable leases in its 2014 annual report.

At December 31, 2014, we operated more than 7,400 restaurants, leasing the underlying land and/or building in nearly 6,200 of those restaurants with the vast majority of our commitments expiring within 20 years from the inception of the lease. Our longest lease expires in 2151. We also lease office space for headquarters and support functions, as well as certain office and restaurant equipment. We do not consider any of these individual leases material to our operations. Most leases require us to pay related executory costs, which include property taxes, maintenance, and insurance.

a. Balatonlelle has both finance and operating leases. In general, what effects does each of these lease types have on Balatonlelle's balance sheet and its income statement?

b. What types of adjustments might you consider to Balatonlelle's balance sheet for analysis purposes?

M10-16.[A] Analysing and Capitalising Operating Lease Payments Disclosed in Footnotes LO6

Grenoble S.A. discloses the following in its 2014 annual report relating to its leasing activities:

(In millions)	Finance leases	Operating leases
2015	€ 65	€ 612
2016	27	578
2017	26	538
2018	26	494
2019	26	462
Thereafter	267	2,653
Total minimum lease payments	€437	€5,337

At December 31, 2014, the present value of minimum payments under finance leases was €279 million.

Operating leases are not reflected on-balance-sheet. In our analysis of a company, we often desire to capitalise these operating leases, that is, add the present value of these lease payments to both the reported assets and liabilities.

a. Compute the present value of Grenoble's operating lease payments assuming a 7% discount rate.

b. What effect does capitalisation of Grenoble's operating leases have on its total liabilities (it reported total liabilities of €6,918 million for 2014).

LO3 **M10-17. Accounting for Pension Benefits**

Butchart Corporation has a defined contribution pension plan for its employees. Each year, Butchart contributes to the plan an amount equal to 4% of the employee payroll for the year. Butchart's 2015 payroll was $400,000. Butchart also provides a life insurance benefit that pays a $50,000 death benefit to the beneficiaries of retired employees. At the end of 2015, Butchart estimates that its liability under the life insurance program is $625,000. Butchart has assets with a fair value of $175,000 in a trust fund that are available to meet the death benefit payments.

Required

a. Prepare the journal entry at December 31, 2015, to record Butchart's 2015 defined contribution to a pension trustee who will manage the pension funds for the firm's employees.

b. What amount of liability for death benefit payments must Butchart report in its December 31, 2015, balance sheet? Explain.

LO3, 4 **M10-18. Analysing and Interpreting Pension Disclosures—Expenses and Returns**

Canton Company discloses the following information in its annual report:

(In millions)	2014
Service cost	$ 22
Interest cost	126
Expected return on plan assets	(148)
Other	36
Settlement loss (gain)	15
Net periodic pension benefit cost	$ 51

a. How much pension expense does Canton report in its 2014 income statement?

b. What effect does its "expected return on plan assets" have on its reported pension expense? Explain.

c. Explain use of the word *expected* as it relates to results of pension plan investments.

LO3, 4 **M10-19. Analysing and Interpreting Pension Disclosures—Expenses and Returns**

Orchid, Inc., discloses the following pension footnote in its annual report:

	Pension Benefits	
(In millions)	2014	2013
Service cost	$24	$25
Interest cost	64	62
Amortisation of prior service cost	1	1
Expected return on plan assets	(71)	(70)
Other	31	23
Net periodic benefit cost	$49	$41

a. How much pension expense does Orchid report in its 2014 income statement?

b. What effect does its "expected return on plan assets" have on its reported pension expense? Explain.

c. Explain use of the word *expected* as it relates to results of pension plan investments.

LO3, 4 **M10-20. Analysing and Interpreting Retirement Benefit Footnote**

Paddington plc discloses the following footnote relating to its retirement plans in its 2014 annual report:

15. RETIREMENT BENEFITS The Company maintains the Paddington Savings & Retirement Plan, a qualified plan. In addition, the Company maintains the Paddington Nonqualified Savings and Supplemental Retirement Plan. The Company's contributions are based on a percentage of associates' eligible annual compensation. The cost of the Company's contributions to these plans was £19.4 million in Fiscal 2014 and £17.8 million in Fiscal 2013.

a. Does Paddington have a defined contribution or defined benefit pension plan? Explain.
b. How does Paddington account for its contributions to its retirement plan?
c. How is Paddington's obligation to its retirement plan reported on its balance sheet?

M10-21. Computing and Reporting Deferred Income Taxes **LO5**

Hung Hom Inc. paid $12,000 on December 31, 2013, for equipment with a two-year useful life. The equipment was depreciated for book purposes at $6,000 in 2014 and 2015. Hung Hom deducted the entire amount on its 2013 tax return. Assume this was the firm's only depreciable asset and that the firm's tax rate was 35% for 2013 and 2014 and 40% for 2015. Assume, further, that Hung Hom's income before depreciation and taxes was $320,000 in 2013, $400,000 in 2014, and $420,000 in 2015.

Required

a. Calculate the book value of the asset on 12/31 for 2013, 2014, and 2015.
b. Calculate the tax basis of the asset on 12/31 for 2013, 2014, and 2015.
c. What deferred tax liability should be reported for 2013, 2014, and 2015?
d. Prepare journal entries to record income taxes for 2013, 2014, and 2015.

M10-22. Computing and Reporting Deferred Income Taxes **LO5**

Sha Tin, Inc., purchased $600,000 of construction equipment on January 1, 2015. The equipment is being depreciated on a straight-line basis over six years with no expected salvage value. Accelerated depreciation is being used on the firm's tax returns. At December 31, 2017, the equipment's book value is $300,000 and its tax basis is $173,000 (this is Sha Tin's only temporary difference). Over the next three years, straight-line depreciation will exceed accerlerated depreciation by $31,000 in 2018, $31,000 in 2019, and $65,000 in 2020. Assume that the income tax rate in effect for all years is 40%.

a. What amount of deferred tax liability should appear in Sha Tin's December 31, 2017, balance sheet?
b. What amount of deferred tax liability should appear in Sha Tin's December 31, 2018, balance sheet?
c. What amount of deferred tax liability should appear in Sha Tin's December 31, 2019, balance sheet?
d. Where should the deferred tax liability accounts be classified in Sha Tin's 2017, 2018, and 2019 year-end balance sheets?

EXERCISES

E10-23.[A] Analysing and Interpreting Leasing Footnote **LO2, 6**

The 2011 annual report of Target Corporation, provides the following footnote ($ thousands).

21. Leases We lease certain retail locations, warehouses, distribution centers, office space, land, equipment, and software. Assets held under finance lease are included in property and equipment. Operating lease rentals are expensed on a straight-line basis over the life of the lease. . . . we determine the lease term by assuming the exercise of those renewal options that are reasonably assured. The exercise of lease renewal options is at our sole discretion. The expected lease term is used to determine whether a lease is finance or operating and is used to calculate straight-line rent expense. Additionally, the depreciable life of buildings and leasehold improvements is limited by the expected lease term.

Rent expense is included in SG&A. Some of our lease agreements include rental payments based on a percentage of retail sales over contractual levels . . . Certain leases require us to pay real estate taxes, insurance, maintenance, and other operating expenses associated with the leased premises. These expenses are classified in SG&A consistent with similar costs for owned locations.

Most long-term leases include one or more options to renew, with renewal terms that can extend the lease term from one to more than fifty years. Certain leases also include options to purchase the leased property.

Future Minimum Lease Payments (millions)	Operating Leases	Finance Leases
2012	$ 194	$ 122
2013	197	118
2014	157	123
2015	151	121
2016	144	120
After 2016	3,045	3,736
Total future minimum lease payments	$3,888	4,340
Less: Interest		(2,651)
Present value of future minimum finance lease payments		$1,689

a. Compute the present value of Target's operating leases. Assume a 6% discount rate.

b. If the operating leases are classified as finance leases, indicate how the amount in part *a* would be reported in Target's balance sheet using the financial statement effects template.

c. Would recognition of the operating leases affect the current ratio? Explain.

d. Prepare journal entries to record the capitalisation of Target's operating leases at the end of fiscal 2011. Enter them in the appropriate T-accounts.

e. Do these leases represent a substantial fixed commitment to Target given Target's operating cash flow of $5,434 million in 2011?

LO2, 6 E10-24.[A] **Analysing, Interpreting, and Capitalising Operating Leases**
Buona Vista, Inc. reports the following data concerning leases in its 2014 annual report.

Note 14—Commitments and Contingencies
The Company leases space for certain of its offices, warehouses and retail stores under leases expiring from one to twenty-four years after May 31, 2014. . . . Amounts of minimum future annual rental commitments under noncancelable operating leases in each of the five years ending May 31, 2015 through 2019 are $374 million, $310 million, $253 million, $198 million, $174 million, respectively, and $535 million in later years.

a. What adjustment(s) might you consider to Buona Vista's balance sheet given this information and assuming that Buona Vista's discount rate is 7%? Explain.

b. Show how the amount computed in part *a* would be reported in the balance sheet using the financial statement effects template.

c. Prepare journal entries to record the capitalisation of these operating leases at the end of fiscal 2014. What journal entries would be required to record lease payments and lease related expenses in 2015 if these leases were accounted for as finance leases? Assume straight-line depreciation and a ten-year life.

d. Post the journal entries from part *c* to the appropriate T-accounts.

LO2, 6 E10-25.[A] **Analysing and Interpreting Leasing Footnote**
Burnaby Inc. included the following footnote in its fiscal 2014 annual report:

The approximate future minimum lease payments under finance and all other leases at January 29, 2015 were as follows (amounts in millions):

Fiscal year	Finance Leases	Operating Leases
2015	$ 106	$ 800
2016	104	746
2017	100	682
2018	93	637
2019	90	557
Thereafter	766	4,577
Total minimum lease payments	1,259	$7,999
Less imputed interest	810	
Present value of minimum lease payments	449	
Amount included in current liabilities	29	
Long-term lease obligations excluding current instalments	$ 420	

The assets under finance leases recorded in Property and Equipment, net of amortisation, totaled $328 million and $336 million at January 29, 2015 and January 30, 2014, respectively.

Burnaby reported stockholders' equity of $17,898 million and total assets of $40,518 million in its fiscal 2014 balance sheet.

a. What was the total amount of finance lease obligations reported in Burnaby's fiscal 2014 balance sheet? Why is this amount not equal to the $328 million that it reported for assets under finance leases on that date?

b. Using an 8% discount rate, compute the present value of Burnaby's scheduled operating lease payments.

c. Estimate the effect that capitalising operating leases would have on Burnaby's debt-to-equity ratio.

E10-26.[A] Analysing and Interpreting Footnote on Both Operating and Finance Leases **LO2, 6**

Whampoa Communications Inc. provides the following footnote relating to its leasing activities in its annual report.

The aggregate minimum rental commitments under noncancelable leases for the periods shown at December 31, 2014, are:

Years (dollars in millions)	Finance Leases	Operating Leases
2015	$ 92	$ 2,004
2016	88	1,779
2017	66	1,558
2018	53	1,298
2019	47	1,004
Thereafter	130	4,746
Total minimum rental commitments	476	$12,389
Less interest and executory costs	124	
Present value of minimum lease payments	352	
Less current instalments	66	
Long-term obligation at December 31, 2014	$286	

a. Assuming that this is the only available information relating to its leasing activities, what amount does Whampoa report on its balance sheet for its lease obligations? Does this amount represent its total obligation to lessors? How do you know?

b. What effect has its lease classification as finance or operating had on Whampoa's balance sheet? Over the life of its leases, what effect does this lease classification have on its net income?

c. Based on the information provided by Whampoa in this footnote, what amount of interest expense will it report on finance leases in 2015? (*Hint:* prepare a journal entry to record the 2015 lease payment.)

d. Estimate the present value of Whampoa's operating leases using a 6% discount rate. What would be the effect on Whampoa's balance sheet if these leases were reported as finance leases?

E10-27.[A] Analysing, Interpreting, and Capitalising Operating Leases **LO6**

One-north Company provided the following information in its 2014 annual report ($ millions):

Future minimum rental payments under operating leases with remaining noncancelable terms in excess of one year are as follows:

(In millions)	Operating
2015	$ 223
2016	209
2017	176
2018	146
2019	126
Thereafter	1,269
Total	$2,149

a. Assuming a 5% discount rate, what adjustments to One-north's balance sheet would be necessary to convert these operating leases into finance leases?

b. If the leases were reported as finance leases instead of operating leases, what would be the effect on One-north's 2015 income statement?

LO3, 4 **E10-28. Analysing and Interpreting Pension Plan Benefit Footnote**

Kinderdijk N.V. provides the following footnote relating to its retirement plans in its 2014 annual report:

Defined Contribution Plans Team members who meet certain eligibility requirements can participate in a defined contribution plan by investing up to 80 percent of their compensation, as limited by statute or regulation. Generally, we match 100 percent of each team member's contribution up to 5 percent of total compensation. Company match contributions are made to funds designated by the participant. Benefits expense related to these matching contributions was €197 million, €190 million, and €178 million in 2014, 2013, and 2012, respectively.

a. Does Kinderdijk have a defined contribution or defined benefit pension plan? Explain.

b. How would Kinderdijk account for its contributions to its retirement plan?

c. How is Kinderdijk's obligation to its retirement plan reported on its balance sheet?

d. Do you see any problems for employees in Kinderdijk's plan?

LO4 **E10-29. Analysing and Interpreting Pension Footnote—Funded and Reported Amounts**

Cam River plc., reports the following pension footnote in its 2014 annual report.

December 31 (In £ millions)	Pension Plans 2014
Change in benefit obligation	
Benefit obligation at beginning of year	£1,108
Service cost	24
Interest cost	64
Curtailment gain	(7)
Special termination benefits	5
Benefits paid	(40)
Actuarial (gain) loss	227
Benefit obligation at end of year	£1,381
Change in plan assets	
Fair value of plan assets at beginning of year	£ 907
Actual return on plan assets (including interest income)	83
Employer contributions	53
Benefits paid	(40)
Administrative expenses	(5)
Fair value of plan assets at end of year	£ 998
Funded status	£ (383)

a. Describe what is meant by *service cost* and *interest cost*.

b. What is the source of funds to make payments to retirees?

c. Show the computation of the 2014 funded status for Cam River.

d. What net pension amount is reported on its 2014 balance sheet?

E10-30. Analysing and Interpreting Pension Footnote—Funded and Reported Amounts LO3, 4

Rothenburg GmbH reports the following pension data in its 2014 annual report.

At December 31 (€ millions)	Pension 2014
Change in Benefit Obligations	
Beginning of year	€29,217
Service cost	307
Interest cost	1,590
Plan amendments	(485)
Actuarial loss (gain), net	3,360
Benefits paid and settlements	(3,407)
End of year	30,582
Change in Plan Assets	
Beginning of year	25,814
Actual return on plan assets (including interest income)	1,191
Company contributions	512
Benefits paid and settlements	(3,407)
End of year	24,110
Funded Status	
End of year	€ (6,472)

a. Describe what is meant by service cost and interest cost.
b. What is the source of funds to make payments to retirees?
c. Show the computation of Rothenburg's 2014 funded status.
d. What net pension amount is reported on its 2014 balance sheet?

E10-31. Computing and Reporting Deferred Income Taxes LO5

Early in January 2015, Rideau, Inc., purchased equipment costing $16,000. The equipment had a 2-year useful life and was depreciated in the amount of $8,000 in 2015 and 2016. Rideau deducted the entire $16,000 on its tax return in 2015. This difference was the only one between its tax return and its financial statements. Rideau's income before depreciation expense and income taxes was $236,000 in 2015 and $245,000 in 2016. The tax rate in each year was 40%.

Required

a. What amount of deferred tax liability should Rideau report in 2015 and 2016?
b. Give the journal entries to record income taxes for 2015 and 2016.
c. Repeat requirement *b* if the tax rate in 2015 was only 35%.

E10-32. Calculating and Reporting Deferred Income Taxes LO5

Bens' Corporation paid $12,000 on December 31, 2013, for equipment with a three-year useful life. The equipment will be depreciated in the amount of $4,000 each year. Bens' took the entire $12,000 as an expense in its tax return in 2013. Assume this is the only timing difference between the firm's books and its tax return. Bens' tax rate is 40%.

Required

a. What amount of deferred tax liability should appear in Bens' 12/31/2013 balance sheet?
b. Where in the balance sheet should the deferred tax liability appear?
c. What amount of deferred tax liability should appear in Bens' 12/31/2014 balance sheet?

LO5 **E10-33. Recording Income Tax Expense**

BAYER A.G. (GERMANY)

Bayer A.G. is a global company with operations in the fields of health care, agriculture, and high-tech polymer materials. It is best known for its original brand of aspirin. The company reports the following tax information in Note 14 to its 2013 financial report:

14. Taxes

The breakdown of tax expenses by origin was as follows:

Tax Expense by Origin (€ million)	2012	2013
Taxes paid or accrued		
Income taxes		
Germany	€ (534)	€ (795)
Other countries	(1,026)	(849)
Deferred taxes	(1,560)	(1,644)
from temporary differences	782	569
from tax loss carryforwards and tax credits	55	54
	837	623
Total	€ (723)	€(1,021)

a. Record Bayer's income tax expense for 2013 using the FSET.
b. Record Bayer's income tax expense for 2013 using journal entries.
c. Explain how the income tax expense affects Bayer's financial statements.
d. Bayer reported income before income taxes of €4,207 million for 2013. Calculate Bayer's effective tax rate for 2013.

LO5 **E10-34. Recording Income Tax Expense**

LOBLAW COMPANY LIMITED (CANADA)

Loblaw Company Limited is Canada's largest grocery retailer, with 570 corporate stores and 496 franchise stores across British Columbia, Alberta, Ontario, and Quebec. The company reports the following tax information in Note 7 to its 2013 financial report:

Note 7. Income Taxes

Income taxes recognised in the consolidated statements of earnings were as follows:

(millions of Canadian dollars)	2013	2012
Current income taxes:		
Current period	$289	$257
Adjustment in respect of prior periods	(1)	(19)
	$288	$238
Deferred income taxes:		
Origination and reversal of temporary differences	(50)	(36)
Adjustment in respect of prior periods	(10)	8
	(60)	(28)
Income taxes	$228	$210

a. Record Loblaw's income tax expense for 2013 using the FSET.
b. Record Loblaw's income tax expense for 2013 using journal entries.
c. Explain how the income tax expense affects Loblaw's financial statements.
d. Loblaw reported earnings before income taxes of $858 million for 2013. Calculate Loblaw's effective tax rate for 2013.

PROBLEMS

LO2, 6 **P10-35.[A] Analysing, Interpreting, and Capitalising Operating Leases**

Staples, Inc., reports the following footnote relating to its finance and operating leases in its fiscal 2011 annual report ($ thousands).

Future minimum lease commitments due for retail and support facilities (including lease commitments for 37 retail stores not yet opened at January 28, 2012) and equipment leases under noncancellable operating leases are as follows (in thousands):

Fiscal Year	Total
2012	$ 867,147
2013	774,273
2014	664,264
2015	557,642
2016	454,235
Thereafter	1,269,073
	$4,586,634

Rent expense was approximately $839.6 million, $829.4 million, and $834.3 million for 2011, 2010, and 2009, respectively.

a. What dollar adjustment(s) might you consider to Staples' balance sheet given this information and assuming that Staples intermediate-term borrowing rate is 7%? Explain. (Staples reported total liabilities of $6,408 million for 2011.) Round the average life to the nearest year.

b. Show how the amount computed in part *a* would be reported in the balance sheet using the financial statement effects template.

c. Prepare journal entries to record the capitalisation of these operating leases at the end of fiscal 2011. What journal entries would be required to record lease payments and lease related expenses in 2012 if these leases were accounted for as finance leases? Assume leased assets are depreciated over a 9-year life using the straight-line method.

d. Post the journal entries from part *c* to the appropriate T-accounts.

P10-36.[A] **Capitalising Operating Leases** LO2, 6

The 2014 annual report of Pyrmont, Inc., included the following footnote.

OPERATING LEASES The Company leases restaurant and office facilities and certain equipment under operating leases having initial terms expiring between 2015 and 2024. Certain of these leases require the payment of contingent rentals based on a percentage of gross revenues, as defined by the terms of the applicable lease agreement. Total rental expense for the year ended December 31, 2014, 2013 and 2012, was approximately $209.0 million, $204.2 million and $207.4 million, respectively. Future minimum rental payments under non-cancelable operating leases (including leases for restaurants scheduled to open in 2015) are as follows (in thousands):

2015	$ 179,814
2016	174,888
2017	158,484
2018	140,767
2019	122,707
Thereafter	563,788
Total minimum lease payments	$1,340,448

Required

a. Prepare the journal entry to record Pyrmont's rent expense under operating leases on December 31, 2014. Assume that this expense was paid in cash and none of this expense was prepaid or accrued in other years.

b. Assume that Pyrmont reclassified its operating leases as finance leases and that the appropriate discount rate is 8%. What amount would Pyrmont report as a lease liability in its December 31, 2014, balance sheet?

c. If these leases are treated as finance leases instead of operating leases, what would be the effect on Pyrmont's 2014 income statement? Its 2015 income statement? The assets are depreciated on a straight-line basis over 10 years.

d. Show the results of capitalisation using the Financial Statement Effects Template.

e. If these leases had been treated as finance leases instead of operating leases, what would be the effect on Pyrmont's 2014 statement of cash flows?

LO6 **P10-37.**[A] **Analysing, Interpreting, and Capitalising Leasing Disclosures**

The Ultimo Co., Inc., annual report has the following footnote (11) related to its leasing activities.

The future minimum lease payments under our finance and operating leases by fiscal year (not including contingent rentals) at March 3, 2012, were as follows ($ millions):

Fiscal Year	Finance Leases	Operating Leases
2013	$21	$1,216
2014	21	1,154
2015	18	1,063
2016	10	940
2017	3	792
Thereafter	23	2,352
Subtotal	96	$7,517
Less: imputed interest	(15)	
Present value of lease obligations	$81	

Required

a. What does Ultimo report on its balance sheet in regard to its leases?

b. What is the general effect that capitalisation of Ultimo's operating leases would have on its balance sheet? Over the life of the lease, what effect does this classification have on its net income?

c. Using a 10% discount rate, estimate the assets and liabilities that it fails to report as a result of its off-balance-sheet lease financing.

d. Using the financial statement effects template, show how capitalising these operating leases would affect the balance sheet and income statement. Assume straight-line depreciation over a 10-year life.

e. Prepare journal entries to record the capitalisation of these operating leases at March 3, 2012. What journal entries would be required to record the operating lease and lease related expenses in fiscal year 2013 if these leases were accounted for as finance leases?

f. Post the journal entries from part *e* to the appropriate T-accounts.

g. What impact would capitalisation of the company's operating leases have on analysing Ultimo? What ratios might be affected?

LO3, 4 **P10-38.** **Analysing and Interpreting Pension Disclosures**

HYUNDAI MOTOR COMPANY (SOUTH KOREA)

Hyundai Motor Company (HMC) is a South Korean automaker, with headquarters in Seoul. HMC reported the following pension plan information in note 33 to its 2013 annual report:

(2) The significant actuarial assumptions used by the Group as of December 31, 2013 and 2012, are as follows:

Description	December 31, 2013	December 31, 2012
Discount rate	4.45%	3.74%
Rate of expected future salary increase	4.97%	4.74%

(3) The amounts recognised in the consolidated statements of financial position related to defined benefit plans as of December 31, 2013 and 2012, consist of the following:

Description (In millions of Korean won)	December 31, 2013	December 31, 2012
Present value of defined benefit obligations	₩3,131,966	₩2,975,771
Fair value of plan assets	(2,749,943)	(2,154,022)
	₩ 382,023	₩ 821,749
Net defined benefit liabilities	389,306	821,749
Net defined benefit assets	(7,283)	—

(4) Changes in net defined benefit assets and liabilities for the year ended December 31, 2013, are as follows:

Description (In millions of Korean won)	Present value of defined benefit obligations	Fair value of plan assets	Net defined benefit liabilities
Beginning of the year	₩2,975,771	₩(2,154,022)	₩ 821,749
Current service cost	473,463	—	473,463
Past service cost	21,337	—	21,337
Interest expenses (income)	115,713	(82,893)	32,820
	3,586,284	(2,236,915)	1,349,369
Remeasurements:			
Return on plan assets	—	(7,684)	(7,684)
Actuarial gains arising from changes in demographic assumptions	(85,942)	—	(85,942)
Actuarial gains arising from changes in financial assumptions	(230,175)	—	(230,175)
Actuarial gains arising from experience adjustments and others	(22,660)	—	(22,660)
	(338,777)	(7,684)	(346,461)
Contributions	—	(590,241)	(590,241)
Benefits paid	(120,090)	80,259	(39,831)
Transfers in (out)	1,105	1,080	2,185
Effect of foreign exchange differences and others	3,444	3,558	7,002
End of the year	₩3,131,966	₩(2,749,943)	₩ 382,023

(5) The sensitivity analyses below have been determined based on reasonably possible changes of the significant assumptions occurring as of December 31, 2013, while holding all other assumptions constant.

Description (In millions of Korean won)	Effect on the net defined benefit liabilities as of December 31, 2013	
	Increase by 1%	Decrease by 1%
Discount rate	(326,031)	385,624
Rate of expected future salary increase	313,430	(275,984)

Required

a. How much service cost does HMC report in its 2013 income statement?

b. HMC reports an 82,893 million Korean won interest income on plan assets. Approximately, how is this amount computed? What is the actual gain or loss realised on its plan assets in 2013? What is the purpose of using interest income on plan assets instead of the actual gain or loss?

c. What factors affected its 2013 pension liability? What factors affected its 2013 plan assets?

d. What does the term funded status mean? What is the funded status of the 2013 HMC retirement plans? What amount of asset or liability does HMC report on its 2013 balance sheet relating to its retirement plans?

e. HMC increased its discount rate from 3.74% to 4.45% in 2013. What effect(s) does this have on its balance sheet and its income statement?

f. HMC changed its estimate of expected annual wage increases used to determine its defined benefit obligation in 2013. What effect(s) does this change have on its financial statements? In general, how does such a change affect income?

LO3, 4 **P10-39. Analysing and Interpreting Pension Footnote—Funded and Reported Amounts**

TELUS CORPORATION (CANADA)

TELUS Corporation is a Canadian telecommunications company, headquartered in Burnaby, British Columbia. TELUS provides a wide range of products and services, including wireless, data, Internet, voice, television, entertainment, and video. The company reports the following pension plan information in note 14 to its 2013 annual report:

Information concerning our defined benefit plans, in aggregate, is as follows:

	Pension benefit plans		Other benefit plans	
(millions)	2013	2012	2013	2012
Accrued benefit obligation:				
Balance at beginning of year	$8,511	$ 7,748	$ 67	$ 75
Current service cost	131	124	—	—
Past service cost	1	3	—	—
Interest cost	329	345	2	2
Actuarial loss (gain) arising from:				
Demographic assumptions	299	(7)	1	(7)
Financial assumptions	(973)	667	(2)	2
Settlements	—	—	(21)	—
Benefits paid	(388)	(369)	(5)	(5)
Balance at end of year	7,910	8,511	42	67
Plan assets:				
Fair value at beginning of year	7,147	6,751	23	26
Return on plan assets				
Notional interest income on plan assets at discount rate	276	304	1	1
Actual return on plan assets greater (less) than discount rate	717	266	—	(1)
Settlements	—	—	(21)	—
Contributions				
Employer contributions	198	171	2	2
Employees' contributions	29	30	—	—
Benefits paid	(388)	(369)	(5)	(5)
Administrative fees	(5)	(6)	—	—
Fair value at end of year	7,974	7,147	—	23
Effect of asset ceiling limit				
Beginning of year	(5)	(5)	(2)	(2)
Change	(54)	—	2	—
End of year	(59)	(5)	—	(2)
Fair value of plan assets at end of year, net of asset ceiling limit	7,915	7,142	—	21
Funded status—plan surplus (deficit)	$ 5	$(1,369)	$(42)	$(46)

The plan surplus (deficit) is reflected in the Consolidated Statements of Financial Position as follows:

As at December 31 (millions)	2013	2012
Funded status—plan surplus (deficit)		
Pension benefit plans	$ 5	$(1,369)
Other benefit plans	(42)	(46)
	$(37)	$(1,415)
Presented in the Consolidated Statements of Financial Position as:		
Other long-term assets	$325	$ —
Other long-term liabilities	(362)	(1,415)
	$ (37)	$(1,415)

Expense

Our defined benefit pension plan expense (recovery) was as follows:

Years ended December 31 (millions)	2013				2012			
Recognised in	Employee benefits expense	Financing costs	Other comprehensive income	Total	Employee benefits expense	Financing costs	Other comprehensive income	Total
Current service cost	$102	$ —	$ —	$ 102	$ 94	$ —	$ —	$ 94
Past service cost.	1	—	—	1	3	—	—	3
Net interest; return on plan assets								
Interest expense arising from accrued benefit obligations.	—	329	—	329	—	345	—	345
Return, including interest income, on plan assets (1)	—	(276)	(717)	(993)	—	(304)	(266)	(570)
	—	53	(717)	(664)	—	41	(266)	(225)
Administrative fees	5	—	—	5	6	—	—	6
Re-measurements arising from:								
Demographic assumptions.	—	—	299	299	—	—	(7)	(7)
Financial assumptions.	—	—	(973)	(973)	—	—	667	667
	—	—	(674)	(674)	—	—	660	660
Changes in the effect of limiting net defined benefit assets to the asset ceiling.	—	—	54	54	—	—	—	—
	$108	$ 53	$(1,337)	$(1,176)	$103	$ 41	$394	$538

(1) The interest income on plan assets included in the employee defined benefit plans net interest amount included in Financing costs reflects a rate of return on plan assets equal to the discount rate used in determining the accrued benefit obligations.

Required

a. Describe what is meant by current service cost and interest cost.

b. What is the actual return on pension investments in 2013?

c. Provide an example under which an "actuarial loss," such as the $299 million loss that TELUS reports in 2013, might arise.

d. What is the source of funds to make payments to retirees?

e. How much cash did TELUS contribute to its pension plans in 2013?

f. How much cash did TELUS pay to retirees in 2013?

g. Show the computation of its 2013 funded status.

h. What net pension amount is reported on its 2013 balance sheet?

P10-40. Interpreting the Income Tax Expense Footnote (Difficult)

LO5

SINGAPORE TELECOMMUNICATIONS LIMITED (SINGAPORE)

Singapore Telecommunications Limited (SingTel) is the largest mobile network operator in Singapore. Together with its mobile associates in Australia and 25 countries across Asia and Africa, they serve over 500 million mobile customers. SingTel reports the following tax information in its 2014 financial report.

Tax Expense

	Group	
(S$ millions)	2014	2013
Current tax		
Singapore.	S$153.6	S$244.9
Overseas	440.7	406.8
	594.3	651.7
Deferred tax expense/(credit).	120.0	(12.0)
Tax expense attributable to current year's profit.	714.3	639.7

Required

a. What amount of tax expense is reported in SingTel's 2014 income statement? How much of this tax expense was paid or payable in cash at the end of fiscal year 2014?

b. SingTel reported profit before tax of S$4,347.9 million for 2014. Calculate SingTel's effective tax rate for 2014.

c. Assume that SingTel's deferred tax credit in 2013 is due to a decrease in deferred tax liabilities. Provide an example that would be consistent with this situation.

d. Assume that SingTel's deferred tax credit in 2013 is due to an increase in a deferred tax asset. Explain how temporary differences would create a deferred tax asset. What would cause this asset to decrease in value?

LO5 **P10-41. Calculating and Reporting Income Tax Expense**

Lynch Company began operations in 2013. The company reported $24,000 of depreciation expense on its income statement in 2013 and $26,000 in 2014. On its tax returns, Lynch deducted $32,000 for depreciation in 2013 and $37,000 in 2014. The 2014 tax return shows a tax obligation (liability) of $19,200 based on a 40% tax rate.

Required

a. Determine the temporary difference between the book value of depreciable assets and the tax basis of these assets at the end of 2013 and 2014.

b. Calculate the deferred tax liability for each year.

c. Calculate the income tax expense for 2014.

d. Prepare a journal entry to record income tax expense and post the entry to the appropriate T-accounts for 2014.

LO5 **P10-42. Calculating and Reporting Income Tax Expense**

Rialto S.p.A. began operations in 2013. The company reported €130,000 of depreciation expense on its 2013 income statement and €128,000 in 2014. Rialto S.p.A. deducted €140,000 for depreciation on its tax return in 2013 and €122,000 in 2014. The company reports a tax obligation of €45,150 for 2014 based on a tax rate of 35%.

Required

a. Determine the temporary difference between the book value of depreciable assets and the tax basis of these assets at the end of 2013 and 2014.

b. Calculate the deferred tax liability at the end of each year.

c. Calculate the income tax expense for 2014.

d. Prepare a journal entry to record income tax for 2014 and post the entry to the appropriate T-accounts.

CASES AND PROJECTS

LO3, 4 **C10-43. Analysing and Interpreting Pension Disclosures**

AIR NEW ZEALAND LIMITED (NEW ZEALAND)

Air New Zealand Limited is the national airline of New Zealand, headquartered in Auckland. The company's June 30, 2014 annual report has the following note related to its retirement plans.

28. PENSION OBLIGATIONS

Defined benefit plans

The Group operates two defined benefit plans for qualifying employees in New Zealand and overseas. The New Zealand plan is now closed to new members. The plans provide a benefit on retirement or resignation based upon the employee's length of membership and final average salary. Each year an actuarial calculation is undertaken using the Projected Unit Credit Method to calculate the present value of the defined benefit obligation and the related current service cost. The most recent actuarial valuations were provided for June 30, 2014.

Movement in net defined benefit obligation

The following table shows a reconciliation from the opening balances to the closing balances for the net defined obligation and its components.

	Group and Company Defined Benefit Obligations		Group and Company Fair Value of Plan Assets		Group and Company Net Defined Benefit Obligation	
($ millions)	**2014**	**2013**	**2014**	**2013**	**2014**	**2013**
Balance at the beginning of the year	(131)	(134)	126	114	(5)	(20)
Included in profit or loss						
Current service cost	(2)	(3)	—	—	(2)	(3)
Interest (expense)/income	(4)	(3)	4	3	—	—
	(6)	(6)	4	3	(2)	(3)
Included in OCI						
Remeasurements gain/(loss):						
Actuarial gain/(loss) arising from:						
- financial assumptions	7	(3)	—	—	7	(3)
- experience assumptions	(4)	—	—	—	(4)	—
Return on plan assets excluding interest income	—	—	4	12	4	12
Effect of movements in exchange rates	—	1	—	(1)	—	—
Other	1	4	—	—	1	4
	4	2	4	11	8	13
Other						
Contributions paid by employer	—	—	5	5	5	5
Contributions paid by members	(2)	(2)	2	2	—	—
Benefits paid	19	9	(19)	(9)	—	—
	17	7	(12)	(2)	5	5
Balance at the end of the year	(116)	(131)	122	126	6	(5)
Represented by:						
Defined benefit asset					7	—
Defined benefit liability					(1)	(5)

The Group expects to contribute approximately $5 million to its defined benefit plans in 2015.

Assumptions used

The following table provides the weighted average assumptions used by the actuaries to develop the net periodic pension cost and the actuarial present value of projected benefit obligations for the Group's plans:

	Group and Company	
	2014	**2013**
Gross discount rate	3.9%	3.1%
Future base salary increases	3.5%	3.3%

Required

a. How much pension expense (revenue) does Air New Zealand report in its 2014 income statement?

b. Air New Zealand reports a $4 million interest income (i.e., expected return) on plan assets as an offset to a $4 million interest expense. Approximately, how is interest income computed? What is the actual gain or loss realised on its 2014 plan assets?

c. What factors affected its 2014 pension liability? What factors affected its 2014 plan assets?

d. What does the term funded status mean? What is the funded status of the 2014 Air New Zealand retirement plans at the end of 2014? What amount of asset or liability should Air New Zealand report on its 2014 balance sheet relating to its retirement plans?

e. Air New Zealand changed its discount rate from 3.1% to 3.9% in 2014. What effect(s) does this change have on its balance sheet and its income statement?

f. How much cash did Air New Zealand contribute to its pension plans in 2014?

g. How much cash did Air New Zealand pay to retirees in 2014?

LO5 **C10-44. Interpreting Income Tax Disclosures**

TELSTRA CORPORATION LIMITED (AUSTRALIA)

Telstra Corporation Limited is a leading telecommunications and information services company in Australia, based in Melbourne. The company operates Australia's largest and fastest national mobile network. The following tax information is taken from Note 9 to Telstra's fiscal year 2014 annual report.

	Telstra Group As at June 30	
	2014 $m	Restated 2013 $m
Major components of income tax expense		
Current tax expense	$1,799	$1,588
Deferred tax resulting from the origination and reversal of temporary differences	(90)	(4)
Under provision of tax in prior years	6	1
	$1,715	$1,585
Notional income tax expense on profit differs from actual income tax expense recorded as follows:		
(Loss)/profit before income tax expense from discontinued operation	(168)	219
Profit before income tax expense from continuing operations	6,228	5,157
Profit before tax	6,060	5,376
Notional income tax expense calculated at the Australian tax rate of 30%	1,818	1,613
Which is adjusted by the tax effect of:		
Different rates of tax on overseas income	(44)	(24)
Non-assessable and non-deductible items (a)	(56)	(2)
Amended assessments	(9)	(3)
Under provision of tax in prior years	6	1
Income tax expense on profit	$1,715	$1,585
Comprising:		
Tax expense from continuing operations	1,679	1,517
Tax expense from discontinued operation	36	68
Income tax (benefit)/expense recognised directly in other comprehensive income or equity during the year	(16)	196

(Deferred tax liability)/deferred tax asset Deferred tax items recognised in the income statement (including impact of foreign exchange movements in deferred tax items recognised in the income statement)	Telstra Group As at June 30	
	2014 $m	Restated 2013 $m
Property, plant and equipment	$(1,110)	$(1,199)
Intangible assets	(881)	(883)
Borrowings and derivative financial instruments	(14)	(22)
Provision for employee entitlements	307	297
Revenue received in advance	103	139
Provision for workers' compensation	19	18
Allowance for doubtful debts	34	48
Defined benefit asset/liability (b)	105	97
Trade and other payables	95	153
Other provisions	28	31
Income tax losses	1	2
Other	13	(11)
	$(1,300)	$(1,330)

Required

a. What amount of income tax expense did Telstra report for the year ended June 30, 2014? How much of this tax expense was paid or payable at the end of fiscal year 2014?

b. Explain how the income tax expense affects Telstra's financial statements for the fiscal year ended June 30, 2014.

c. Calculate Telstra's effective tax rate for fiscal year 2014. Why was Telstra's effective tax rate lower than the Australian statutory tax rate of 30%?

d. Telstra reported income taxes payable of $296 million in its June 30, 2014 balance sheet, and $444 million at June 30, 2013. What amount of income taxes did Telstra pay in cash during the fiscal year 2014?

e. Explain how "Revenue received in advance" results in a deferred tax asset.

C10-45. Interpreting Income Tax Disclosures

Cheung Kong (Holdings) Limited is a Hong Kong-based multinational conglomerate. It is one of the largest real estate developers in Hong Kong. Cheung Kong reports the following tax information in its 2013 annual report.

CHEUNG KONG (HOLDINGS) LIMITED (HONG KONG)

5. Taxation

($ million)	2013	2012
Current tax		
Hong Kong profits tax	$1,026	$1,095
Tax outside Hong Kong	330	122
Deferred tax	166	17
	$1,522	$1,234

Hong Kong profits tax has been provided for at the rate of 16.5% (2012 – 16.5%) on the estimated assessable profits for the year and operating profit (after adjusting for share of taxation of joint ventures) is reconciled with taxation as follows:

($ million)	2013	2012
Adjusted operating profit at Hong Kong tax rate of 16.5% (2012 – 16.5%)	$4,047	$3,768
Effect of tax rate differences at locations outside Hong Kong	2,087	1,289
Effect of change of tax rate on deferred tax liabilities at location outside Hong Kong	(696)	(300)
Surplus on loss of control of indirect interest in joint ventures	–	(219)
Interest income from infrastructure business	(108)	(96)
Dividend income	(110)	(63)
Increase in fair value of investment properties	(297)	(751)
Profit on disposal of investment properties	(455)	–
Net effect of tax losses and deductible temporary differences utilised/not recognised	(55)	(58)
Net effect of non-assessable/deductible items	(203)	(116)
Others	(4)	(7)
	4,206	3,447
Less: Share of taxation of joint ventures	(2,684)	(2,213)
	$1,522	$1,234

Required

a. What amount of income tax expense did Cheung Kong report in its 2013 income statement? How much of this tax expense was paid or payable in cash at the end of fiscal year 2014?

b. Calculate Cheung Kong's adjusted operating profit for 2013. Calculate Cheung Kong's effective tax rate for 2013. In general, why is a company's effective tax rate different from the statutory tax rate?

c. Cheung Kong reported income taxes payable of $1,162 million in its December 31, 2013 balance sheet, and $661 million at December 31, 2012. What amount of income taxes did it pay in cash during the fiscal year ended December 31, 2013?

d. Prepare a journal entry to record income tax expense for the fiscal year ended December 31, 2013.

e. Explain how the use of accelerated tax depreciation on fixed assets results in a temporary difference between tax and financial reporting. Did the item create a deferred tax asset or a liability?

SOLUTIONS TO REVIEW PROBLEMS

Mid-Chapter Review 1

Solution

1. The present value of the lease payments is \$224,755, computed as \$32,000 × 7.02358.

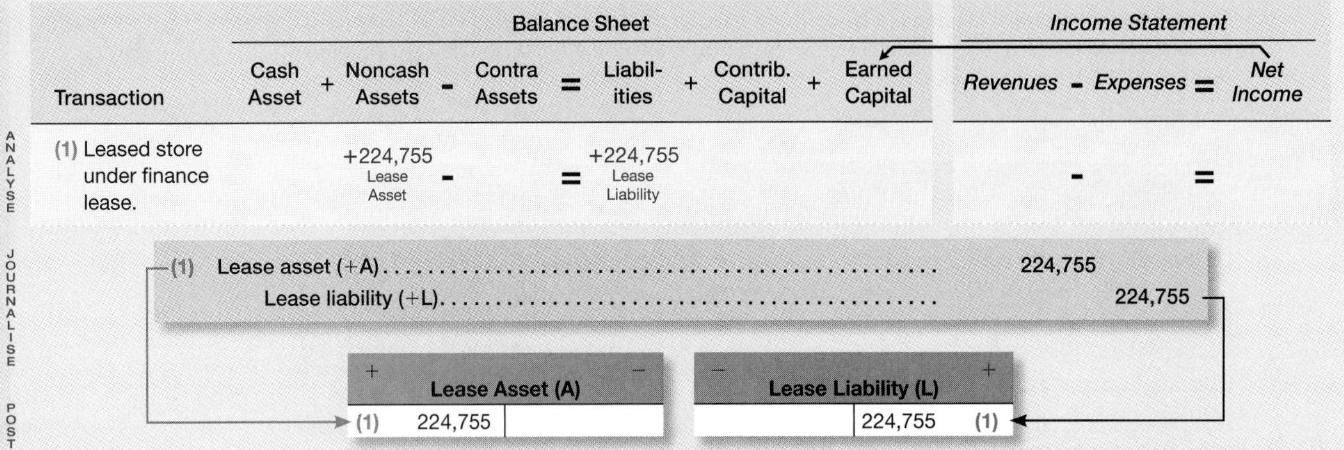

ANALYSE

Transaction	Cash Asset	+ Noncash Assets	− Contra Assets	= Liabilities	+ Contrib. Capital	+ Earned Capital	Revenues	− Expenses	= Net Income
(1) Leased store under finance lease.		+224,755 Lease Asset		+224,755 Lease Liability					

JOURNALISE

	Debit	Credit
(1) Lease asset (+A)	224,755	
Lease liability (+L)		224,755

POST

Lease Asset (A) +	−
(1) 224,755	

−	Lease Liability (L) +
	224,755 (1)

2, 3. At the first year-end, Fast Retailing would record depreciation expense of \$22,476 (\$224,755/10) and interest expense of \$15,733 (\$224,755 × 0.07).

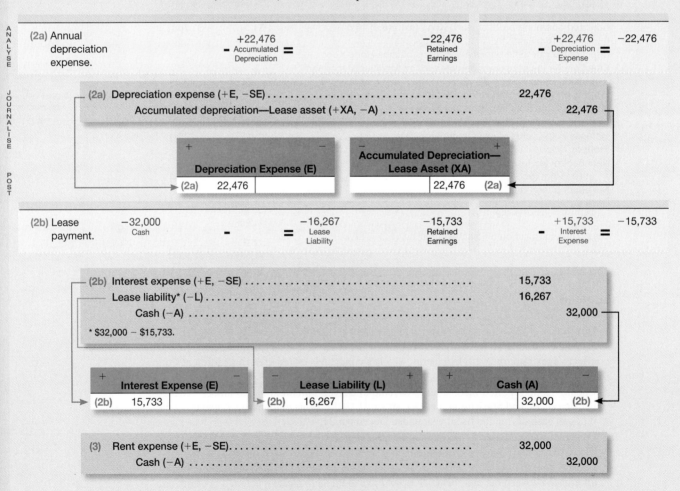

ANALYSE

Transaction	Cash Asset	+ Noncash Assets	− Contra Assets	= Liabilities	+ Contrib. Capital	+ Earned Capital	Revenues	− Expenses	= Net Income
(2a) Annual depreciation expense.			+22,476 Accumulated Depreciation			−22,476 Retained Earnings		+22,476 Depreciation Expense	−22,476

JOURNALISE

	Debit	Credit
(2a) Depreciation expense (+E, −SE)	22,476	
Accumulated depreciation—Lease asset (+XA, −A)		22,476

POST

Depreciation Expense (E) +	−
(2a) 22,476	

−	Accumulated Depreciation—Lease Asset (XA) +
	22,476 (2a)

Transaction	Cash Asset	+ Noncash Assets	− Contra Assets	= Liabilities	+ Contrib. Capital	+ Earned Capital	Revenues	− Expenses	= Net Income
(2b) Lease payment.	−32,000 Cash			−16,267 Lease Liability		−15,733 Retained Earnings		+15,733 Interest Expense	−15,733

	Debit	Credit
(2b) Interest expense (+E, −SE)	15,733	
Lease liability* (−L)	16,267	
Cash (−A)		32,000

* \$32,000 − \$15,733.

Interest Expense (E) +	−
(2b) 15,733	

−	Lease Liability (L) +
(2b) 16,267	

Cash (A) +	−
	32,000 (2b)

	Debit	Credit
(3) Rent expense (+E, −SE)	32,000	
Cash (−A)		32,000

No journal entry is required at lease signing. At the end of the first year, Fast Retailing would record the lease payment as rent expense.

Mid-Chaper Review 2

Solution

1. A pension benefit obligation increases primarily by service cost, interest cost, and actuarial losses. The latter are increases in the pension liability as a result of changes in actuarial assumptions. It is decreased by the payment of benefits to retirees and by actuarial gains.
2. Pension investments increase through positive investment returns for the period and by cash contributions made by the company. Investments decrease by payments made to retirees and investment losses.
3. LVMH's funded status is €(441) million (€1,123 million PBO − €682 million pension assets) as of 2013. The negative amount indicates that the plan is underfunded. Therefore, this amount is reported as a liability on the company's balance sheet.
4. Interest income on plan assets acts as an offset to service cost and interest cost in computing the net pension cost. As the interest income increases (decreases), net pension cost decreases (increases).
5. LVMH reports net pension expense of €88 million in 2013.
6. LVMH's funded status is negative, indicating an underfunded plan. The company contributed €68 million to the pension plan in 2013. It is likely that the company will need to increase its future funding levels to cover the plan's requirements. This action is likely to have negative consequences for its ability to fund other operating needs, and could damage its competitive position in the future.

Chapter-End Review

Solution

1. *a.* HK$675 million..
   b. HK$328 = $182 + $182 − $36 is currently payable or has already been paid in 2013
   c. The most obvious example would be depreciation allowed in 2013 by the tax code exceeded that calculated by the straight-line method.

ANALYSE

	Balance Sheet									Income Statement				
Transaction	Cash Asset	+	Noncash Assets	=	Liabilities	+	Contrib. Capital	+	Earned Capital	Revenues	-	Expenses	=	Net Income
Entry to record income tax expense.	−328 Cash			=	+337 Deferred Tax Liability				−675 Retained Earnings		-	+675 Income Tax Expense	=	−675

JOURNALISE

POST

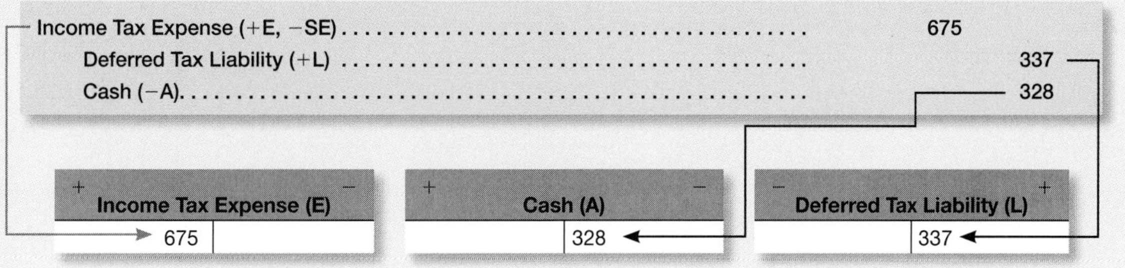

Income Tax Expense (+E, −SE) 675
Deferred Tax Liability (+L) 337
Cash (−A) 328
Income Tax Expense (E)
675
Cash (A)
328
Deferred Tax Liability (L)
337

Appendix-End Review

Solution

1. Gap's leases are classified as operating leases—see footnote. Also, since there are no disclosures in the leasing footnote related to finance leases, we know that all of the leases are classified as operating.
2. Using a 7% discount rate, the present value of its operating leases follows ($ millions):

	Year	Operating Lease Payment	Present Value Factor (Table A.2, 7%)	Present Value (Payment × PV Factor)
1	2012	$1,025	0.93458	$ 958
2	2013	917	0.87344	801
3	2014	801	0.81630	654
4	2015	677	0.76290	516
5	2016	530	0.71299	378
6	2017	530	0.66634	353
7	2018	530	0.62275	330
8	2019	530	0.58201	308
9	2020	19	0.54393	10
Total		$5,559		$4,309

Gap's operating leases represent $4,309 million of unreported operating assets and unreported nonoperating liabilities. These amounts should be added to the balance sheet for analysis purposes.

3. Potential income statement adjustments would include elimination of the rent expense currently reported in Gap's SG&A expenses and replacing it with the depreciation of the capitalised lease asset and the interest on the capitalised lease liability. Whereas rent expense is considered as an operating expense, only the depreciation expense is similarly classified. The interest is, of course, a nonoperating expense. NOPAT, as a result, is increased following the financial statement adjustment for operating lease capitalisation.

LEARNING OBJECTIVES

1. Describe business financing through share issuances. (p. 504)
2. Explain and account for the issuance and repurchase of shares. (p. 507)
3. Describe how operations increase the equity of a business. (p. 512)
4. Explain and account for dividends and share splits. (p. 512)
5. Define and illustrate comprehensive income. (p. 517)
6. Describe and illustrate the basic and diluted earnings per share computations. (p. 520)
7. Appendix 11A: Analyse the accounting for convertible securities, share rights, and share options. (p. 524)

CHAPTER

11

Reporting and Analysing Shareholders' Equity

Thomson Reuters Corporation is a leading provider of intelligent information for businesses and professionals worldwide. The company was created in April 2008 with the merger of the Thomson Corporation, a Canadian information company, and Reuters Group PLC, a British media and financial information company. The ordinary shares of Thomson Reuters are listed on the Toronto and New York Stock Exchanges (ticker: TRI). The company adopted IFRS in 2009.

THOMSON REUTERS CORPORATION
ThomsonReuters.com

Thomson Reuters organises its business in four distinct core customer groups: Financial & Risk, Legal, Tax & Accounting, and Intellectual Property & Science. Its business model involves delivering data, electronic content, software, and tools to customers to help them make better decisions. The company's major brands and products include Elkon, ONE, Datastream, DataScope, FindLaw, ONESOURCE, IP Manager, and Web of Science. The company also owns and operates Reuters, a global provider of real-time news and information services. In fiscal year 2013, the Financial & Risk division accounted for slightly over half of the company's revenues and the Legal division accounted for almost 30%. Thomson Reuters is competing with many world-class companies, such as Bloomberg, S&P Capital IQ, Dow Jones, Wolters Kluwer, Reed Elsevier, LexisNexis, and ProQuest. However, the company ranks first or second in most of the market segments that it operates.

To expand its global presence, Thomson Reuters has invested in rapidly growing international markets. In 2011, the company completed 39 acquisitions, including the Brazilian tax company Masterstaf, and in 2012 it acquired another 29 companies, including a large number in Asia, the Middle East, and Latin America. In 2013, Thomson Reuters added to its legal product business by acquiring the London-based Practical Law Company.

Jim Smith became Thomson Reuters's new CEO in 2012. Thomson Reuters's strategy for 2013 and beyond has been to accelerate innovation and increase efficiencies by simplifying its corporate structure and taking advantage of its scale. The company has also shifted its growth focus from acquisitions toward organic initiatives, especially investing in high-growth opportunities.

The capital needed to support Thomson Reuters's growth strategy and its commitment to research and innovation exceeds the funds generated directly from its operating activities. Besides borrowing, the company also raises additional capital, in part, from equity investors through the issuance of ordinary shares. Like many companies, Thomson Reuters also engages in equity transactions for other reasons, including share-based compensation plans and share repurchase programs. This chapter describes the reporting and analysis of equity transactions, including share issuances, share repurchases, dividends, comprehensive income, and convertible securities.

Sources: ThomsonReuters.com; Thomson Reuters 2013 Annual Report.

CHAPTER ORGANISATION

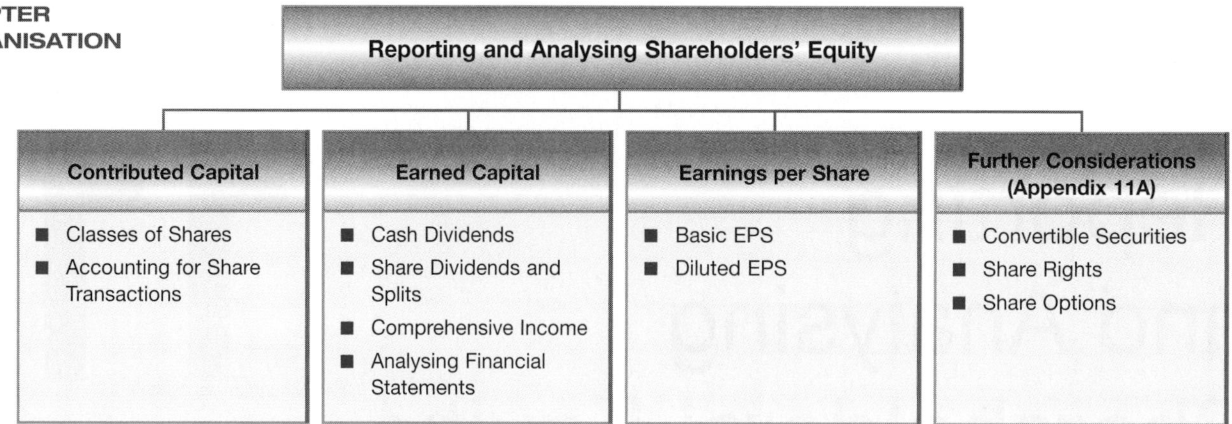

INTRODUCTION

LO1 Describe business financing through share issuances.

A company finances its assets from one of three sources: either it borrows funds from creditors, it obtains funds from shareholders or it reinvests excess cash flow from operations. On average, companies obtain about half of their external financing from borrowed sources and the other half from shareholder investment. This chapter describes the issues relating to shareholders' equity, including the accounting for share transactions (issues and repurchases of shares, and dividends), the accounting for share options, and the computation of earnings per share. Finally, we discuss the accounting for convertible securities, an increasingly prevalent financing vehicle.

When a company issues shares to the investing public, it records the receipt of cash (or other assets) and an increase in contributed capital, a part of shareholders' equity, representing investment in the company by shareholders. The increase in cash and equity is equal to the issue price of the shares on the issue date multiplied by the number of shares sold.

Contributed capital is accounted for at *historical cost*. Consequently, fluctuations in the market price of the issuer's shares subsequent to the initial public offering do not directly affect the financial statements of the issuing company. These fluctuations are the result of transactions between outside parties not involving the issuer. When and if shares are repurchased and subsequently resold, the issuer's contributed capital decreases (increases) by the purchase (sales) price of the shares.

FYI Corporations never record gains or losses resulting from transactions between the company and its owners.

There is an important difference between accounting for shareholders' equity and accounting for transactions involving assets and liabilities: *there is never any gain or loss reported on the purchase and sale of shares or the payment of dividends*. Instead, these "gains and losses" are reflected as increases and decreases in the contributed capital component of the issuing company's shareholders' equity.

This chapter focuses on the two broad categories of shareholder investment: contributed capital and earned capital. Exhibit 11.1 provides an illustration of this breakdown using **Thomson Reuters**'s shareholders' equity as of December 31, 2013.

EXHIBIT 11.1 Thomson Reuters's Shareholders' Equity

	Equity (millions of dollars)	Dec. 31, 2013
Contributed capital	Share capital:	
	Ordinary shares, no par value; unlimited shares authorised; 820,155,832 outstanding	$10,060
	Preference shares, Series II, no par value; 6,000,000 shares authorised; 6,000,000 issued	110
	Contributed surplus	177
Earned capital	Retained earnings	7,303
	Accumulated other comprehensive income (loss)	(1,614)
	Total shareholders' equity	16,036
	Non-controlling interests*	394
	Total equity	$16,430

* Non-controlling interests arise from the company's consolidation of non-wholly-owned subsidiaries. They will be discussed in Chapter 12.

Thomson Reuters, like other companies, has two broad categories of shareholders' equity:

1. **Contributed capital** This section reports the proceeds received by the issuing company from original share issuances. Contributed capital often includes share capital (or capital stock), preference share, and contributed surplus (or share premium). Netted against these capital accounts is treasury shares, the amounts paid to repurchase the issuer's shares from its investors less the proceeds from the resale of such shares. Collectively, these accounts are generically referred to as contributed capital (or *paid-in capital*).
2. **Earned capital** This section consists of (a) retained earnings, which represent the cumulative income and losses of the company less any dividends to shareholders, and (b) accumulated other comprehensive income (AOCI), which includes changes to equity that are not included in income and are, therefore, not reflected in retained earnings. The typical items in AOCI are foreign currency translation adjustments, changes in market values of derivatives, unrecognised gains and losses on available-for-sale securities, and pension adjustments.

Before turning to a discussion of contributed capital and earned capital, we note one other item in Exhibit 11.1—**Non-controlling interests**. This amount results from the practice of consolidating subsidiaries that are controlled, but not wholly owned, and it represents neither capital contributed to Thomson Reuters nor capital earned by Thomson Reuters's shareholders. Chapter 12 provides a brief introduction to this topic. Total equity is the sum of non-controlling interests and total shareholders' equity, which is defined as contributed capital plus earned capital.

CONTRIBUTED CAPITAL

We begin our discussion with contributed capital. Contributed capital represents the cumulative cash inflow that the company has received from the sale of various classes of shares, less the net cash that it has paid out to repurchase its shares from the market.

Thomson Reuters's contributed capital consists of share capital, preference shares, and contributed surplus.

Classes of Shares

There are two general classes of shares: ordinary and preference. The difference between the two lies in the respective legal rights conferred upon each class.

Ordinary Shares **Ordinary (or common) shares** represent the primary ownership unit in a corporation. Ordinary shareholders have voting rights that allow them to participate in the governance of the corporation. The total number of ordinary shares is usually presented on the face of the balance sheet. There are three numbers of shares to be aware of:

- The number of **shares authorised** represents the upper limit on the number of shares that the corporation can issue. This number is established in the *articles of incorporation* and can only be increased by an affirmative shareholder vote.
- The number of **shares issued** is the actual number of shares that have been sold to shareholders by the corporation.
- The number of **shares outstanding** is the number of issued shares less the number of shares repurchased as treasury shares.

Thomson Reuters's ordinary (or common) shares are described as follows in its 2013 annual report:

> Common shares of the Company have no par value and the authorised common share capital is an unlimited number of shares.

The Thomson Reuters ordinary shares have the following important characteristics:

- Thomson Reuters has authorised the issuance of an unlimited number of shares. When shares are first issued, the number of shares outstanding equals those issued. Any shares subsequently repurchased as treasury shares are subtracted from issued shares to derive outstanding shares. As of December 31, 2013, Thomson Reuters had 820,155,832 shares outstanding, yielding a value of $10,060 million.
- Thomson Reuters's ordinary shares have no par value. The **par value** is an arbitrary amount set by company organisers at the time of formation. Generally, par value has no substance from a financial reporting or statement analysis perspective, although it has some legal implications, which are usually minor. Its main impact is in specifying the allocation of proceeds from share issuances between the two contributed capital accounts on the balance sheet: share capital and contributed surplus. For shares with no par value, the entire proceeds from share issuances go to share capital (the $177 million of contributed surplus must be generated from other equity transactions, which are discussed later in this chapter).

Some corporations issue multiple classes of shares with differential voting rights (e.g., Class A ordinary shares with one vote per share, Class B ordinary shares with ten votes per share, etc.). This structure allows the founders to raise capital while retaining voting control over the corporation.

Preference Shares **Preference (or preferred) shares** generally have some preference, or priority, with respect to ordinary shares. Two typical preferences are:

1. **Dividend preference** Preference shareholders receive dividends on their shares before ordinary shareholders do. If dividends are not paid in a given year, those dividends are normally forgone. However, some preference share contracts include a cumulative provision stipulating that any forgone dividends must first be paid to preference shareholders, together with the current year's dividends, before any dividends are paid to ordinary shareholders.
2. **Liquidation preference** If a company fails, its assets are sold (liquidated) and the proceeds are paid to the creditors and shareholders, in that order. Shareholders, therefore, have a greater risk of loss than do creditors. Among shareholders, the preference shareholders receive payment in full before any proceeds are paid to ordinary shareholders. This liquidation preference makes preference shares less risky than ordinary shares. Any liquidation payment to preference shares is normally at its par value, although it is sometimes specified in excess of par, called a **liquidating value**.

The preference shares of Thomson Reuters are described in Note 24 to its 2013 annual report:

Series II, Cumulative Redeemable Preference Shares

The authorised preference share capital of the Company is an unlimited number of preference shares without par value. The directors are authorised to issue preference shares without par value in one or more series, and to determine the number of shares in, and terms attaching to, each such series. As of December 31, 2013 and 2012, 6,000,000 Series II, cumulative redeemable preference shares were authorised, issued and outstanding. The Series II preference shares are non-voting and are redeemable at the option of the Company for C$25.00 per share, together with accrued dividends. Dividends are payable quarterly at an annual rate of 70% of the Canadian bank prime rate applied to the stated capital of such shares.

Following are several important features of the Thomson Reuters preference shares:

- The directors of Thomson Reuters are authorised to issue an unlimited number of preference shares without par value in one or more series.
- As of December 31, 2013, six million Series II preference shares were authorised, issued and outstanding.
- Thomson Reuters preference shares are non-voting, which is generally true for preference shares.

- Thomson Reuters preference shares pay a dividend at an annual rate of 70% of the Canadian Bank prime rate of its par (stated) value, payable quarterly.
- Thomson Reuters preference shares are cumulative. This feature provides preference shareholders with protection that unpaid dividends (called dividends in arrears) must be paid to them before any dividends are paid to ordinary shareholders.
- Thomson Reuters can redeem (repurchase) its preference shares at any time for $25 per share. There are three additional features sometimes seen in preference share agreements:

1. **Call feature** The call feature provides the issuer with the right, but not the obligation, to repurchase the preference shares at a specified price. This price can vary according to a specified time. A decline in the market rate of interest is one event that can lead to the firm exercising the call provision. While of value to the issuer of the preference shares, the call provision makes the issue less attractive to potential investors. The result is a lower offering price per share.
2. **Conversion feature** The yield on preference shares, especially when coupled with a cumulative feature, is similar to the interest rate on a bond or note. Further limited protection is offered because preference shareholders receive the par value at liquidation like debtholders receive face value. The fixed yield and liquidation value for the preference shares limit the upside potential return of preference shareholders. This constraint can be overcome by inclusion of a conversion feature that allows preference shareholders to convert their shares into ordinary shares at their option at a predetermined conversion ratio. Some preference share contracts give the company an option to force conversion.

   The conversion feature causes the shares to be more attractive to potential investors because the preference shareholders now have the opportunity to share in the fruits of a successful company with the ordinary shareholders. Indeed, the market price of preference shares tends to reflect the added value of the conversion feature.
3. **Participation feature** Preference shares sometimes carry a participation feature that allows preference shareholders to share ratably with ordinary shareholders in dividends. The dividend preference over ordinary shares can be a benefit when dividend payments are meager, but a fixed dividend yield limits upside potential if the company performs exceptionally well. This limitation can be overcome with a participation feature.

Accounting for Share Transactions

We cover the accounting for share transactions in this section, including the accounting for share issuances and for share repurchases.

LO2 Explain and account for the issuance and repurchase of shares.

Share Issuance Share issuances, whether ordinary or preference, yield an increase in both assets and shareholders' equity. Companies use share issuances to obtain cash and other assets for use in their business.

BUSINESS INSIGHT

Alibaba's IPO In September of 2014, Alibaba Group offered its shares to the general public for the first time. The first public sale of common shares by a corporation is called an initial public offering, or IPO for short. After the IPO, any offering of shares to the public is called a seasoned equity offering.

At the time, Alibaba's IPO was the largest in history, raising approximately US$25 billion. The common shares had a par value of US$0.000025, but was offered to the public for US$68 per share. Within a couple of months after the shares opened for trade on the New York Stock Exchange, the price increased to almost $120 per share, but then began to fall. By the company's fiscal year end in March 2015, Alibaba's shares were trading for just over $83 per share, about 20% greater than their original offer price and almost 50 times their earnings per share.

Share issuances increase assets (cash) by the number of shares sold multiplied by the issuance price of the share on the issue date. Equity increases by the same amount, which is reflected in contributed capital accounts. Specifically, assuming the issuance of ordinary shares, the share capital account increases by the number of shares sold multiplied by its par value and the contributed surplus (or share premium) account is increased for the remainder of the purchase price.[1]

To illustrate, assume that Sancere Company issues 10,000 shares of $1 par value ordinary shares at a market price of $43 cash per share. The financial statement effects and entries for this share issuance follow.

ANALYSE

	Balance Sheet									Income Statement				
Transaction	Cash Asset	+	Noncash Assets	=	Liabil-ities	+	Contrib. Capital	+	Earned Capital	*Revenues*	−	*Expenses*	=	*Net Income*
Issue 10,000 ordinary shares with $1 par value for $43 cash per share.	+430,000 Cash			=			+10,000 Share Capital +420,000 Contributed Surplus				−		=	

JOURNALISE

POST

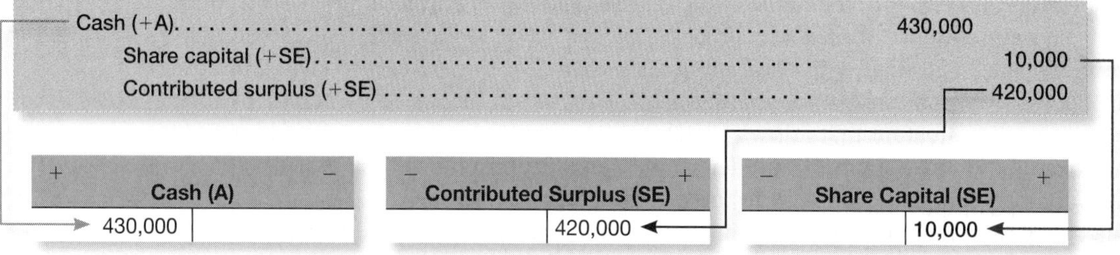

Specifically, the following financial statement effects of the share issuance are:

1. Cash increases by $430,000 (10,000 shares × $43 per share).
2. Share capital increases by the $10,000 par value of shares sold (10,000 shares × $1 par value).[2]
3. Contributed surplus increases by the $420,000 difference between the issue price and par value ($430,000 − $10,000).

FYI Share issuance affects the balance sheet, the statement of cash flows and the statement of changes in equity. There is never any revenue or gain from share issuance reported in the income statement.

Once shares are issued, they are freely traded in the market among investors. The proceeds of those sales and any gains and losses on those sales do not affect the issuing company and are not recorded in its accounting records. Further, fluctuations in the issuing company's share price subsequent to issuance do not directly affect its financial statements. Hence, the equity section of the balance sheet cannot be used to determine the current market value of the company. The market value is given by the product of the number of ordinary shares outstanding and the price per share.

For example, **INDITEX S.A.**, the Spanish multinational clothing company, describes its outstanding ordinary shares in its 2013 annual report, as follows:

> **Share capital**
>
> At January 31, 2014, the Parent's share capital amounted to euros 93,499,560 and was represented by 623,330,400 registered shares of euros 0.15 par value each. . . . The Parent's share premium at January 31, 2014 amounted to euros 20,379 thousand. . .

[1] Companies who offer their shares for sale to the general public are called *public corporations*. In a *private company*, ownership is limited to a smaller number of investors and the shares are not available to the general public. The distinction between public and private corporations should not be confused with media references to the public sector and the private sector. The *public sector* refers to government entities. Virtually all business entities, including public corporations, are considered part of the *private sector*.

[2] Ordinary shares can also be issued as "no par" or as "no par with a stated value." For no par shares, the share capital account is increased by the entire proceeds of the issuance and no amount is assigned to contributed surplus. For no par shares with a stated value, the stated value is treated just like par value; that is, share capital is increased by the number of shares multiplied by the stated value, and the remainder is assigned to the contributed surplus account.

INDITEX's share capital is equal to the number of shares outstanding multiplied by the ordinary share's par value: €93,499,560 = 623,330,400 × €0.15. The share premium (i.e., contributed surplus) of €20,379,000 is the remaining proceed from share issuance. Therefore, total proceeds from share issuances are €113,878,560 (€93,499,560 + €20,379,000), or €0.18 per share (€113,878,560/623,330,400).

RESEARCH INSIGHT

Share Issuance and Stock Returns Seasoned equity offerings are issuances of common shares by firms that already have outstanding shares. On average, share price declines when a company announces that it will issue additional shares. Investors infer that issuing common shares rather than debt is an indication that management believes the shares are overvalued in the market, making it a more attractive form of financing. In addition, research has found that companies engage in earnings management around seasoned equity offerings, using both accrual estimates (e.g., underestimating bad debt expense or warranty expense) and real transactions (e.g., cutting R&D or accelerating sales). As a result, both earnings and share returns decline in subsequent periods.

Share Repurchase Thomson Reuters provides the following description of its share repurchase program in its 2013 annual report.

Share Repurchases

The Company may buy back shares (and subsequently cancel them) from time to time as part of its capital strategy. Under its current normal course issuer bid ("NCIB"), the Company may repurchase up to 30 million common shares between May 22, 2013 and May 21, 2014 in open market transactions on the TSX, the NYSE and/or other exchanges and alternative trading systems, if eligible, or by such other means as may be permitted by the TSX.

In 2013, the Company repurchased approximately 10.9 million common shares for approximately $400 million at an average price per share of $36.79. In 2012, the Company repurchased approximately 5.9 million common shares for approximately $168 million at an average price per share of $28.26.

Decisions regarding any future repurchases will be based on market conditions, share price and other factors including opportunities to invest capital for growth.

Thomson Reuters bought back some of its ordinary shares in 2012 and 2013. One reason a company will repurchase shares is if it feels that the market undervalues them. Management reasons that the repurchase sends a positive signal to the market about the company's financial condition that favorably affects its share price and, thus, allows the company to resell those shares for a "gain." Recent research provides evidence that share prices generally increase following the announcement of a share repurchase program. Any such gain on resale is *never* reflected in the income statement. Instead, the excess of the resale price over the repurchase price is added to contributed surplus. IFRS prohibits companies from reporting gains via share transactions with their own shareholders.

Another reason shares are repurchased is to offset the dilutive effects of an employee share option program. When an employee exercises share options, the number of shares outstanding increases. These additional shares reduce earnings per share and are, therefore, viewed as *dilutive*. In response, many companies repurchase an equivalent number of shares in a desire to keep outstanding shares constant. Corporations also buy back their own shares in order to concentrate ownership to avoid an unwelcome takeover action.

A share repurchase has the opposite financial statement effects from a share issuance. That is, cash is reduced by the price of the shares repurchased (number of shares repurchased multiplied by the purchase price per share) and shareholders' equity is reduced by the same amount. The reduction in equity is achieved by increasing a contra equity account called **treasury shares**. *A contra equity account is a negative equity account with a debit balance,* which reduces shareholders' equity. Thus, when a contra equity account increases, total equity decreases.

Any subsequent reissuance of treasury shares does not yield a gain or loss. Instead, the difference between the proceeds received and the repurchase price of the treasury shares is reflected as an increase or decease to contributed surplus.

To illustrate, assume that 3,000 Sancere Company ordinary shares previously issued for $43 are later repurchased for $40. The financial statement effects and entries for this share repurchase follow.

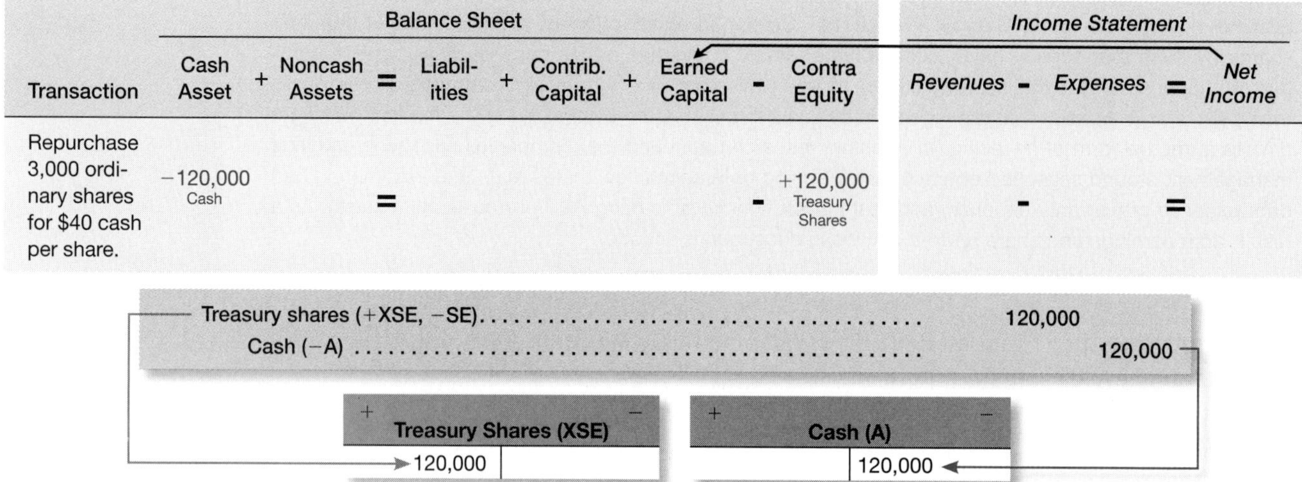

Transaction	Cash Asset	+ Noncash Assets	= Liabil-ities	+ Contrib. Capital	+ Earned Capital	- Contra Equity	Revenues	- Expenses	= Net Income
Repurchase 3,000 ordinary shares for $40 cash per share.	−120,000 Cash		=			- +120,000 Treasury Shares		-	=

ANALYSE / JOURNALISE / POST

Treasury shares (+XSE, −SE) 120,000
Cash (−A) 120,000

Treasury Shares (XSE): + 120,000 | −
Cash (A): + | 120,000 −

Assets (cash) and equity both decrease. Treasury shares (a contra equity account) increases by $120,000, which reduces shareholders' equity by that same amount.

Assume that these 3,000 shares are then subsequently resold for $42 cash per share. The financial statement effects and entries for this treasury share sale follow.

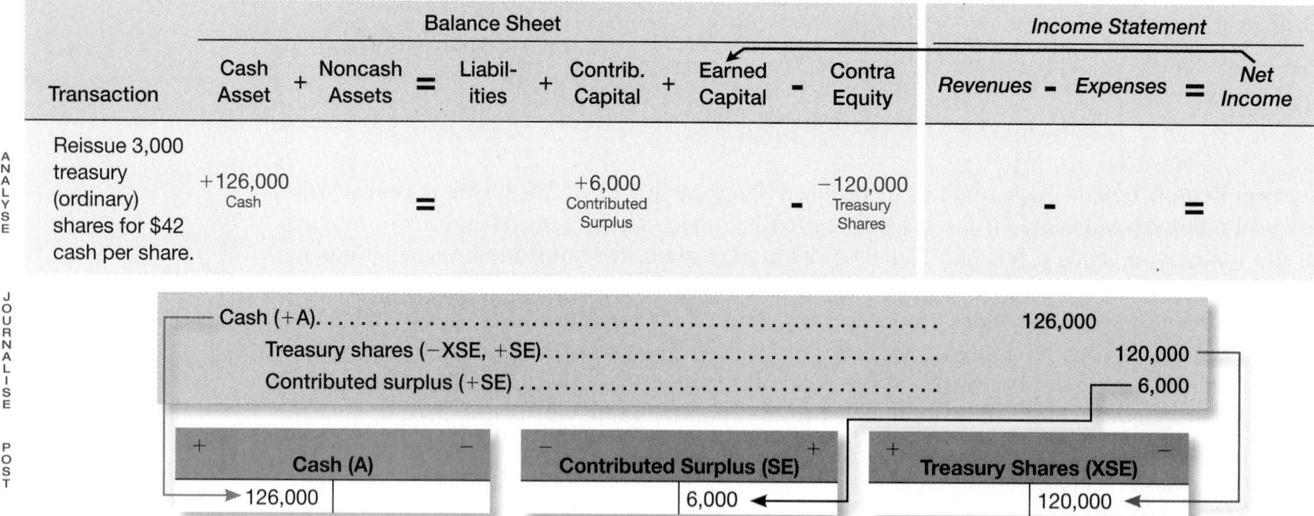

Transaction	Cash Asset	+ Noncash Assets	= Liabil-ities	+ Contrib. Capital	+ Earned Capital	- Contra Equity	Revenues	- Expenses	= Net Income
Reissue 3,000 treasury (ordinary) shares for $42 cash per share.	+126,000 Cash		=	+6,000 Contributed Surplus		- −120,000 Treasury Shares		-	=

ANALYSE / JOURNALISE / POST

Cash (+A) 126,000
Treasury shares (−XSE, +SE) 120,000
Contributed surplus (+SE) 6,000

Cash (A): + 126,000 | −
Contributed Surplus (SE): − | 6,000 +
Treasury Shares (XSE): + | 120,000 −

Cash assets increase by $126,000 (3,000 shares × $42 per share), the treasury share account is reduced by the $120,000 cost of the treasury shares issued, and the $6,000 excess (3,000 shares × $2 per share) is reported as an increase in contributed surplus.[3] Again, there is no effect on the income statement—companies are prohibited from reporting gains and losses from repurchases and reissuances of their own shares. When there have been several repurchases and sales

[3] If the reissue price is below the repurchase price, then the contributed surplus account associated with treasury shares is reduced until it reaches a zero balance, after which retained earnings is reduced.

of treasury shares, a question arises as to which shares were sold. Typically the solution is to assume a flow such as the first shares repurchased are the first ones assumed to be sold (first-in, first-out).

Instead of reselling the treasury shares, a company may retire or cancel them (as Thomson Reuters does). To illustrate, assume that Sancere Company retires 3,000 treasury shares (recall that the $1 par value shares were originally issued for $43 per share and later repurchased for $40 per share). The financial statement effects and entries for the retirement of these treasury shares are as follows.

ANALYSE

	Balance Sheet													Income Statement				
Transaction	Cash Asset	+	Noncash Assets	=	Liabil-ities	+	Contrib. Capital	+	Earned Capital	-	Contra Equity			Revenues	-	Expenses	=	Net Income
Retire 3,000 treasury (ordinary) shares.				=			−3,000 Share Capital −126,000 Contributed Surplus		+9,000 Retained Earnings	-	−120,000 Treasury Shares				-		=	

JOURNALISE

POST

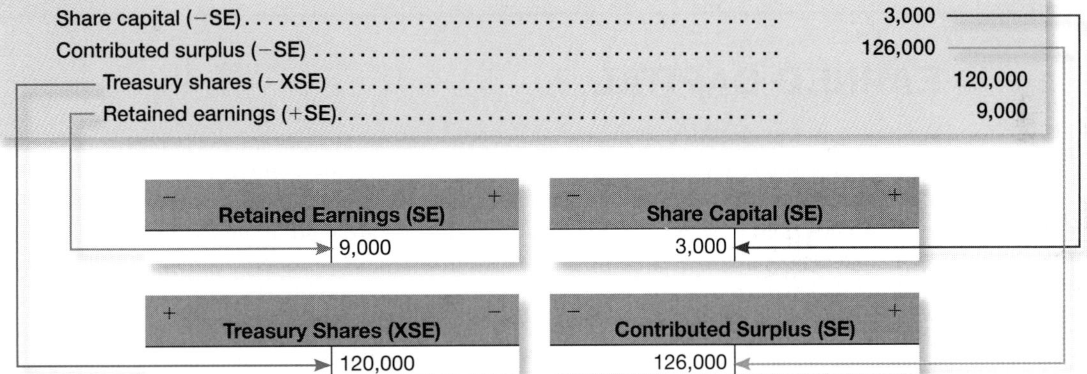

The treasury shares account is reduced by the $120,000 cost of the shares retired, share capital decreases by the $3,000 par value of shares retired (3,000 shares × $1 par value), contributed surplus decreases by the $126,000 difference between the original $43 issue price and par value ($129,000 − $3,000), and the $9,000 difference between the original issue price and the $40 repurchase price ($129,000 − $120,000) is reported as an increase in retained earnings.[4] Similar to resale of treasury shares, the retirement of treasury shares has no income statement effect.

Since Thomson Reuters has no treasury shares outstanding, we use INDITEX's description of its treasury shares from its 2013 annual report as an illustration.

> **Treasury shares**
>
> The annual general shareholders' meeting held on July 16, 2013 approved a long-term share-based incentive plan (see note 27) and authorised the board of directors to acquire treasury shares to cater for that plan. . .
>
> As a result, in 2013 450,000 treasury shares were acquired with an average acquisition cost of euros 103.32 per share. . . for a total of euros 46,494 thousand.

INDITEX has repurchased a cumulative total of 450,000 ordinary shares for €46,494,000, an average repurchase price of €103.32 per share. This compares with other contributed capital of €113,878,560 (€93,499,560 + €20,379,000). INDITEX indicates that the reason for the repurchases is to have shares available to give to employees under the new share-based incentive plan.

[4] Local securities laws may require a specific accounting treatment. For example, United Kingdom securities regulation requires a company purchasing its own shares to transfer the par value of the shares purchased from retained earnings to a "capital redemption reserve" account to maintain the company's capital.

YOU MAKE THE CALL

You are the Chief Financial Officer You believe that your company's share price is lower than its real value. You are considering various alternatives to increase that price, including the repurchase of company shares in the market. What are some considerations relating to this decision? [Answer on page 530]

MID-CHAPTER REVIEW 1

Capilano Corporation reported the following transactions relating to its share accounts in 2015.

Jan. 15 Issued 10,000 shares of $5 par value ordinary shares at $17 cash per share.
Mar. 31 Purchased 2,000 shares of its own ordinary shares at $15 cash per share.
June 25 Reissued 1,000 shares of its treasury shares at $20 cash per share.

Show the financial impact of each transaction using the financial statement effects template, provide the appropriate journal entry for each transaction, and post the journal entries to the related T-accounts.

The solution to this review problem can be found on page 548.

EARNED CAPITAL

LO3 Describe how operations increase the equity of a business.

We now turn our attention to the earned capital portion of shareholders' equity. Earned capital represents the cumulative profit that has been retained by the company. Recall that earned capital is increased by income earned and decreased by any losses incurred. Earned capital is also decreased by dividends paid to shareholders. Not all dividends are paid in the form of cash, however. In fact, companies can pay dividends in many forms, including property (such as land, for example) or additional shares. We cover both cash and share dividends in this section. Earned capital also includes the positive or negative effects of accumulated other comprehensive income (AOCI). The earned capital of Thomson Reuters is highlighted in the following graphic:

Shareholders' Equity (millions of dollars)	Dec. 31, 2013
Share capital:	
Ordinary shares, no par value; unlimited shares authorised; 820,155,832 outstanding.	$10,060
Preference shares, Series II, no par value; 6,000,000 shares authorised; 6,000,000 issued. . .	110
Contributed surplus.	177
Retained earnings	7,303
Accumulated other comprehensive income (loss).	(1,614)
Total shareholders' equity.	16,036
Non-controlling interests.	394
Total equity	$16,430

Cash Dividends

LO4 Explain and account for dividends and share splits.

Many companies, but not all, pay dividends. Their reasons for dividend payments are varied. Most dividends are paid in cash on a quarterly basis. The following is a description of Thomson Reuters's dividend policy from its 2013 annual report.

Dividends

Our company (and our predecessor companies) have paid dividends for over 30 years and we view dividends as a critical component of shareholder return.

Any dividends that we declare on our shares take into account all factors that our board considers relevant, including our available cash flow, financial condition and capital requirements. Our target dividend payout ratio is 40% to 50% of annual free cash flow over the long term.

Our board reviews our dividend policy in the first quarter of each fiscal year. In February 2014, our board approved an increase in our annualised dividend rate to $1.32 per share (or $0.33 per share on a quarterly basis), effective with our dividend payable on March 17, 2014 to holders of record as of February 24, 2014. This was the 21st consecutive annual dividend increase for our company. The declaration of dividends by our board and the amount of those dividends is at the discretion of the board.

We pay dividends on our Series II preference shares quarterly at an annual rate of 70% of the Canadian bank prime rate applied to the stated capital of these shares.

The table below sets forth the dividends declared on our common shares and Series II preference shares in the last three years and the first quarter of 2014.

	Common shares (US$)	Series II preference shares (C$)
2011		
Q1	$0.310000	C$0.129452
Q2	$0.310000	C$0.130890
Q3	$0.310000	C$0.132329
Q4	$0.310000	C$0.132329
2012		
Q1	$0.320000	C$0.130533
Q2	$0.320000	C$0.130533
Q3	$0.320000	C$0.131967
Q4	$0.320000	C$0.131967
2013		
Q1	$0.325000	C$0.129452
Q2	$0.325000	C$0.13089
Q3	$0.325000	C$0.132329
Q4	$0.325000	C$0.132329
2014		
Q1	$0.330000	C$ *

* The first quarter 2014 dividend on our Series II preference shares had not yet been declared by our company as of the date of this annual report.

Outsiders closely monitor dividend payments. It is generally perceived that the level of dividend payments is related to the expected long-term core income. Accordingly, dividend increases are usually accompanied by share price increases, and companies rarely reduce their dividends unless absolutely necessary. Dividend reductions are, therefore, met with substantial share-price declines.

Financial Effects of Cash Dividends Cash dividends reduce both cash and retained earnings by the amount of the cash dividends paid. To illustrate, Thomson Reuters paid $1,028 million in 2013 cash dividends on its ordinary and preference shares. The financial statement effects of this cash dividend payment are reflected as a reduction in assets (cash) and a reduction in retained earnings as follows.

($ Billions) Transaction	Cash Asset	+	Noncash Assets	=	Liabilities	+	Contrib. Capital	+	Earned Capital	*Revenues*	−	*Expenses*	=	*Net Income*
	Balance Sheet									*Income Statement*				
Paid $1,028 million cash dividends on ordinary and preference shares.	−1.028 Cash			=					−1.028 Retained Earnings		−		=	

ANALYSE

JOURNALISE

	Dr	Cr
Retained earnings (−SE)	1.028	
Cash (−A)		1.028

POST

− Retained Earnings (SE) +		+ Cash (A) −	
1.028			1.028

Dividend payments have no effect on profitability. They are a direct reduction to retained earnings and bypass the income statement.

BUSINESS INSIGHT

Importance of Dividends Dividends are traditionally viewed as an indicator of the health of the paying corporation. Dividend-paying companies are typically reluctant to reduce dividends, let alone eliminate their periodic dividend payment. But as Anne Mulcahy, the former CEO of Xerox, has pointed out (*WSJ*. 11/28/2007), such behaviour can be shortsighted if not downright foolish. Mulcahy suggests, "Heed outsiders' key warnings of a looming cash squeeze. Prioritise spending needs and accept that dividends might not top the list. Get ready for a new set of shareholders once the [dividend] payout goes. And don't rush to reinstate the dividend payout until . . . recovery is rock solid." She goes on to advise not to dispense with essential activities or to sell subsidiaries at bargain prices to assure the dividend payment.

Preference share dividends have priority over those for ordinary shares, including unpaid prior years' preference dividends (dividends in arrears) when preference shares are cumulative. To illustrate, assume that Brisbane Company has 15,000 shares of $50 par value, 8% preference shares outstanding and 50,000 shares of $5 par value ordinary shares outstanding. During its first three years in business, assume that Brisbane declares $20,000 dividends in the first year, $260,000 of dividends in the second year, and $60,000 of dividends in the third year. If the preference shares are cumulative, the total amount of dividends paid to each class of share in each of the three years will be:

	Preference Shares	Ordinary Shares
Year 1		
Current-year dividend ($750,000 × 8%; but only $20,000 is paid, leaving $40,000 in arrears)	$20,000	
Balance to ordinary		$ 0
Year 2		
Arrearage from Year 1 [($750,000 × 8%) − $20,000]	40,000	
Current-year dividend ($750,000 × 8%)	60,000	
Balance to ordinary [$260,000 − ($40,000 + $60,000)]		160,000
Year 3		
Current-year dividend ($750,000 × 8%)	60,000	
Balance to ordinary		0

MID-CHAPTER REVIEW 2

North Point Corporation has outstanding 10,000 shares of $100 par value, 5% preference shares and 50,000 shares of $5 par value ordinary shares. During its first three years in business, North Point declared no dividends in the first year, $300,000 of cash dividends in the second year, and $80,000 of cash dividends in the third year.

a. If the preference shares are cumulative, determine the total amount of dividends paid to each class of shares for each of the three years.

b. If the preference shares are not cumulative, determine the total amount of dividends paid to each class of shares for each of the three years.

The solution to this review problem can be found on page 549.

Share Dividends and Splits

Dividends need not be paid in cash. Many companies pay **share dividends**, that is dividends in the form of additional shares. Companies can also distribute additional shares to their shareholders with a share split. We cover both of these distributions in this section.

Share Dividends When dividends are paid in the form of the company's shares, retained earnings are reduced and contributed capital is increased. However, the amount by which retained earnings are reduced depends on how the share dividends are valued on the issue date. Currently, IASB does not have an accounting standard for share dividends. We discuss two possible approaches to value a share dividend: fair value and par value. Exhibit 11.2 illustrates the effects of these two approaches.

EXHIBIT 11.2 Analysis of Share Dividend Effects

Valuation of Share Dividend	Retained Earnings	Contributed Capital
Fair value approach	Reduce by **market value** of shares distributed	Share capital increased by par value of shares distributed; contributed surplus increased for the balance
Par value approach	Reduce by **par value** of shares distributed	Share capital increased by par value of shares distributed; contributed surplus remained unchanged

Under the fair value approach, retained earnings are reduced by the *market* value of the shares distributed (dividend shares × market price per share) and contributed capital is increased by the same amount. For the contributed capital increase, the share capital is increased by the par value of the shares distributed and the remainder [dividend shares × (market value per share − par value per share)] increases contributed surplus. Under the par value approach, retained earnings are reduced by the *par* value of the shares distributed (dividend shares × par value per share), and share capital is increased by the same amount (no change to contributed surplus).

To illustrate the financial statement effects of dividends, assume that a company has 1 million shares of $5 par, ordinary shares outstanding. It then declares a share dividend of 15% of the outstanding shares (1,000,000 shares × 15% = 150,000 shares) when the market price of the shares is $30 per share. Under the fair value approach, this share dividend has the following financial statement effects:

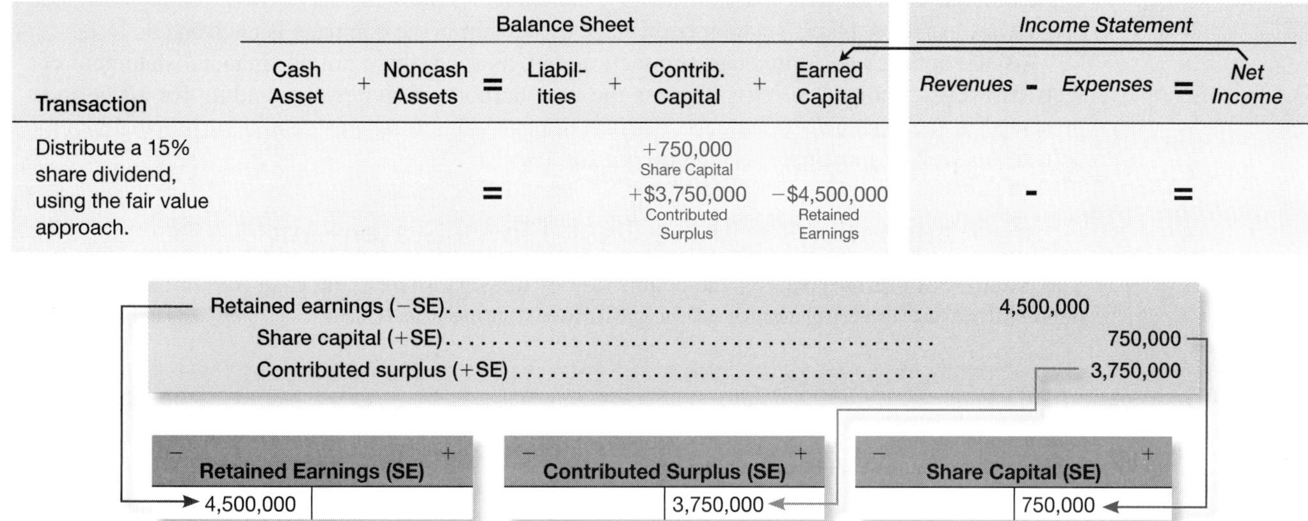

Retained earnings are reduced by $4,500,000, which equals the market value of the share dividend (150,000 shares × $30 market price per share). The increase in contributed capital is treated as follows: share capital is increased by the par value of $750,000 (150,000 shares × $5 par value), and the remainder of $3,750,000 increases contributed surplus. Similar to cash dividend payments, the share dividends never impact income. But unlike cash dividends, share dividends do not affect the cash flows from financing activities.

Under the par value approach, the share dividend has the following financial statement effects and related entries:

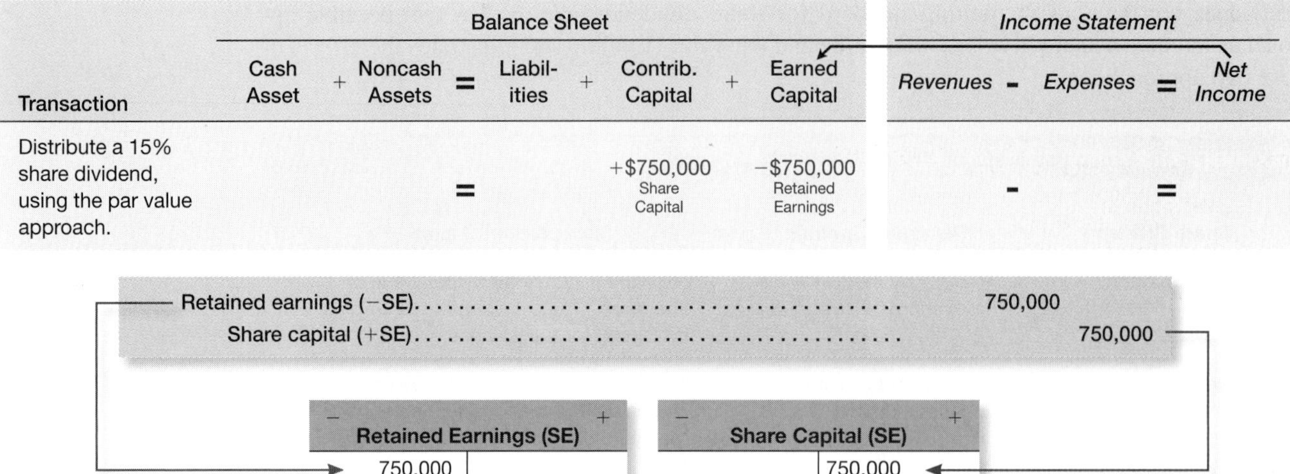

Retained earnings are reduced by $750,000, which equals the par value of the share dividend (150,000 shares × $5 par value per share). Share capital is increased by the par value of $750,000. There is no effect on contributed surplus because the dividend is reported at par value.

Since a share dividend does not involve cash, total equity remains unchanged regardless of whether the share dividend is valued at fair value or par value. Moreover, companies should show comparable shares outstanding for all prior periods for which earnings per share (EPS) is reported in the statements. The reasoning is that a share dividend has no effect on the ownership percentage of each ordinary shareholder. As such, to show a dilution in reported EPS would erroneously suggest a decline in profitability when it is simply due to an increase in shares outstanding.

Share Splits A **share split** is a proportionate distribution of shares and, as such, is similar in substance to a share dividend. A typical share split is 2-for-1, which means that the company distributes one additional share for each share owned by a shareholder. Following the distribution, each investor owns twice as many shares, yet their percentage ownership in the company is unchanged.

A share split is not a monetary transaction and, as such, there are no financial statement effects. However, companies must disclose the new number of shares outstanding for all periods presented in the financial statements. Further, the par value of shares should be proportionately adjusted as well (for example, halved for a 2-for-1 split).[5]

Share Transactions and the Cash Flows Statement

The issuance of ordinary shares, the acquisition of treasury shares, and cash (but not share) dividends affect the financing section of the cash flow statement as follows:

Transaction	Effect on Cash Flow
Issuance of ordinary shares	Increase
Acquisition of treasury shares	Decrease
Sale of treasury shares	Increase
Cash dividends paid	Decrease

Share splits and share dividends do not influence the cash flows statement and are often used when cash is short.

[5] If local law requires that par value not be reduced for a share split, this event should be described and recorded as a *share split effected in the form of a dividend*.

MID-CHAPTER REVIEW 3

The shareholders' equity of Merino Corporation, a New Zealand clothing company, at December 31, 2014, follows.

Share capital:	
5% preference shares, $100 par value, 10,000 shares authorised; 4,000 shares issued and outstanding	$ 400,000
Ordinary shares, $5 par value, 200,000 shares authorised; 50,000 shares issued and outstanding	250,000
Contributed surplus:	
Preference shares	40,000
Ordinary shares	300,000
Retained earnings	656,000
Total shareholders' equity.	$1,646,000

The following transactions occurred during 2015. Show the financial impact of each transaction using the financial statement effects template, provide the appropriate journal entry for each transaction, and post the journal entries to the related T-accounts.

Apr. 1 Declared and issued a 100% share dividend on all outstanding ordinary shares when the market value of the shares was $11 per share. Assume that Merino used the par value approach to value this share dividend.

Dec. 7 Declared and issued a 3% share dividend on all outstanding ordinary shares when the market value of the shares was $7 per share. Assume that Merino used the fair value approach to value this share dividend.

Dec. 31 Declared and paid a cash dividend of $1.20 per share on all outstanding ordinary shares.

The solution to this review problem can be found on pages 549–550.

Comprehensive Income

LO5 Define and illustrate comprehensive income.

Comprehensive income is a more inclusive notion of company performance than net income. It includes all recognised changes in equity that occur during a period except those resulting from transactions with owners in their capacity as owners.

Specifically, comprehensive income includes net income *plus* additional gains and losses not included in the income statement. These additional gains and losses are called *other comprehensive income* and include, for example, foreign currency adjustments, unrealised gains or losses on available-for-sale securities and derivatives (Chapter 12), adjustments to pension and other benefit plans (Chapter 10), and revaluation surplus on PPE assets (Chapter 8). Comprehensive income includes the effects on a company of some economic events that are often outside of management's control. Accordingly, some observers assert that net income is a measure of management's performance, while comprehensive income is a measure of company performance.

Comprehensive income can be reported by firms in one of two ways. The first reporting method is to present a statement of comprehensive income that combines net income and other comprehensive income in one statement. Such a statement begins much like any income statement, with revenues, cost of goods sold, operating expenses and so forth. However, in the statement of comprehensive income, net income is a subtotal, followed by the gains and losses that are classified as other comprehensive income. The second reporting approach presents other comprehensive income in a separate statement immediately following the income statement. Thomson Reuters follows the second reporting approach. Its statement of comprehensive income is presented in Exhibit 11.3.

Unlike net income, other comprehensive income is not closed to retained earnings at the end of each accounting period. Instead, other comprehensive income is closed to a separate earned capital account called **accumulated other comprehensive income** (abbreviated AOCI).

In its 2013 balance sheet, Thomson Reuters reports accumulated other comprehensive income of −$1,614 million, compared to −$1,537 million in 2012. The change from 2012 to 2013 of

−$77 was part of the $202 other comprehensive income for 2013 that Thomson Reuters reported in its statement of comprehensive income (Exhibit 11.3).

EXHIBIT 11.3 Thomson Reuters's 2013 Statement of Comprehensive Income

(millions of U.S. dollars)	2013
Net earnings	$185
Other comprehensive income (loss):	
Cash flow hedges adjustments to earnings	160
Foreign currency translation adjustments to earnings	(4)
Items that may be subsequently reclassified to net earnings:	
Cash flow hedges adjustments to equity	(121)
Foreign currency translation adjustments to equity	(112)
Items that will not be reclassified to net earnings:	(233)
Net remeasurement gains (losses) on defined benefit pension plans	279
Other comprehensive income (loss)	202
Total comprehensive income	387
Comprehensive income for the period attributable to:	
Common shareholders	339
Non-controlling interests	$ 48

Summary of Equity

A summary of transactions that affect equity is included in the statement of changes in equity. This statement reports a reconciliation of the beginning and ending balances of important equity accounts. Thomson Reuters's statement of changes in equity is shown in Exhibit 11.4.

Thomson Reuters's statement of changes in equity reveals the following key transactions for 2013:

- Total comprehensive income increased equity by $387 million (net income of $185 million plus other comprehensive income of $202 million, as shown in Exhibit 11.3).
- Dividend payments to preference and ordinary shareholders decreased equity by $1,080 million ($3 million + $1,077 million).
- Repurchases of ordinary shares decreased equity by $500 million.
- Employee stock compensation plans increased equity by $103 million.
- Other transactions (change in ownership interest of subsidiaries, payments to non-controlling interests, and shares issued under dividend reinvestment plan) also altered equity.

EXHIBIT 11.4 Thomson Reuters's 2013 Statement of Changes in Equity

(millions of U.S. dollars)	Stated share capital	Contributed surplus	Total capital	Retained earnings	Unrecognised (loss) gain on cash flow hedges	Foreign currency translation adjustments	Total accumulated other comprehensive loss ("AOCL")	Non-controlling interests	Total
Balance, December 31, 2012	$10,201	$170	$10,371	$8,311	$(56)	$(1,481)	$(1,537)	$353	$17,498
Comprehensive income (loss)[1]	—	—	—	416	39	(116)	(77)	48	387
Change in ownership interest of subsidiary[2]	—	—	—	(10)	—	—	—	34	24
Distributions to non-controlling interest	—	—	—	—	—	—	—	(41)	(41)
Dividends declared on preference shares	—	—	—	(3)	—	—	—	—	(3)
Dividends declared on common shares	—	—	—	(1,077)	—	—	—	—	(1,077)
Shares issued under Dividend Reinvestment Plan ("DRIP")	39	—	39	—	—	—	—	—	39
Repurchases of common shares[3]	(166)	—	(166)	(334)	—	—	—	—	(500)
Stock compensation plans	96	7	103	—	—	—	—	—	103
Balance, December 31, 2013	$10,170	$177	$10,347	$7,303	$(17)	$(1,597)	$(1,614)	$394	$16,430

(1) Retained earnings for the year ended December 31, 2013 includes net remeasurement gains on defined benefit pension plans of $279 million, net of tax (2012 - losses of $153 million, net of tax).

(2) Includes cash contribution of $24 million by the non-controlling interests.

(3) Includes stated share capital of $32 million and retained earnings of $68 million related to the Company's pre-defined share repurchase plan. See note 24.

ANALYSING FINANCIAL STATEMENTS

Analysis Objective

We want to measure the return on investment by ordinary (or common) shareholders.

Before getting to the specifics of the performance ratio, we must address a complexity introduced when a company (like Thomson Reuters) has a subsidiary that is not 100% owned. Suppose Company A owns 85% of the common shares of Company B. The remaining 15% of B's shareholders are called a "noncontrolling interest." Company A would be required to incorporate the assets, liabilities, revenues and expenses of Company B in its "consolidated" financial statements. As a result, Company A's consolidated net income would include all the income from both A and B. However, companies are required to separately report "net income attributable to common shareholders" and "net income attributable to noncontrolling interests" in their consolidated income statements. We use this information to develop the following measure of profit that can be attributed to common shareholders of the reporting company.

$$\textbf{Net income available for common shareholders} \\ = \textbf{Net income attributable to common shareholders} - \textbf{Preference dividends}$$

A similar adjustment is required on the consolidated balance sheet, where total equity consists of "common shareholders' equity" plus "equity attributable to noncontrolling interests" (as can be seen in Exhibit 11.1).

Analysis Tool Return on Common Equity (ROCE)

$$\textbf{Return on Common Equity (ROCE)} = \frac{\textbf{Net income available for common shareholders}}{\textbf{Average common shareholders' equity}}$$

Applying the Ratio to Thomson Reuters

$$\textbf{2013 ROCE} = \frac{\$137 - \$3}{(\$16{,}036 + \$17{,}145)/2} = \textbf{0.008 or 0.8\%}$$

$$\textbf{2012 ROCE} = \frac{\$1{,}989 - \$3}{(\$17{,}145 + \$16{,}405)/2} = \textbf{0.118 or 11.8\%}$$

Guidance ROCE is similar to ROE except that when we compute ROCE, we remove the effect of noncontrolling interests and preference shares from both the numerator and denominator.

Thomson Reuters in Context

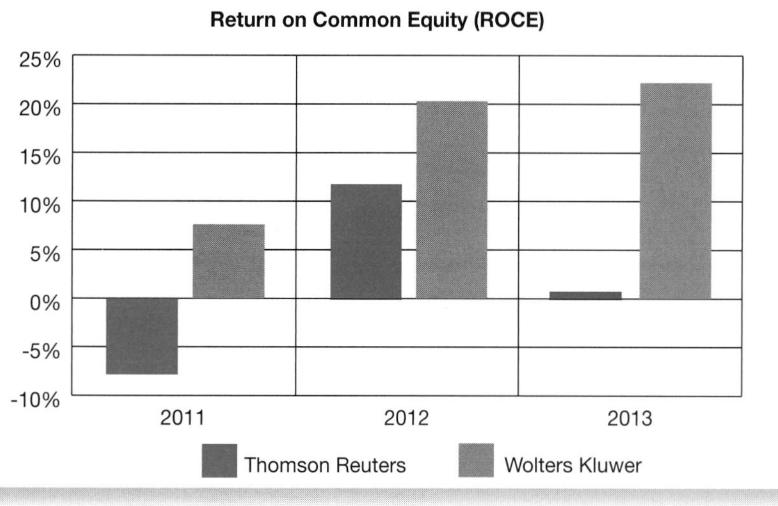

Takeaways Over the 2011–2013 period, Thomson Reuters's ROCE has been volatile and weak compared to that of its competitor, Wolters Kluwer N.V. In particular, Thomson Reuters exhibited a negative ROCE in 2011, and recovered in 2012 to report a ROCE of 11.8%, but its performance dropped below 1.0% in 2013. In contrast, Wolters Kluwer provided its ordinary shareholders a strong return on their investment. The ROCE of Wolters Kluwer increased from 7.6% in 2011 to over 20% in both 2012 and 2013.

Many companies have little or no preference shares and non-controlling interests, so the difference between return on common equity (ROCE) and return on equity (ROE = Net income / Average total equity) will be immaterial for these firms. When preference shares or non-controlling interests are present, ROCE is a more accurate measure of return to ordinary shareholders than ROE.

Other Considerations In Chapter 5 we learned that ROE can be decomposed into two components: return on assets and return on financial leverage. Differences between firms may reflect a difference in performance, or a difference in the reliance on debt financing. A similar division can be done with ROCE with the caveat that ROCE essentially treats preference shares as debt rather than equity.

One final point: the financial press sometimes refers to a measure called **book value per share**. This amount is the net book value of the company that is available to ordinary shareholders, defined as: shareholders' equity (i.e., total equity less noncontrolling interests) less preference shares, divided by the number of ordinary shares outstanding (issued ordinary shares less treasury shares). Thomson Reuters's book value per share is computed as: ($16,036 million − $110 million)/(820,155,832 shares) = $19.42 book value per ordinary share.

MID-CHAPTER REVIEW 4

The shareholders' equity of Aosta S.p.A. at December 31, 2014, follows.

Share capital, €5 par value, 400,000 shares authorised; 160,000 shares issued and outstanding	€800,000
Contributed surplus	920,000
Retained earnings	513,000

During 2014, the following transactions occurred:

June 28	Declared and issued a 10% ordinary share dividend when the market value is €11 per share. Aosta uses the fair value approach to value this share dividend.
Dec. 5	Declared and paid a cash dividend of €1.25 per share.
Dec. 31	Updated retained earnings for net income of €412,000.

Compute the year-ending balance of retained earnings for 2015.

The solution to this review problem can be found on page 550.

EARNINGS PER SHARE

LO6 Describe and illustrate the basic and diluted earnings per share computations.

The income statement reports at least one, and potentially two, earnings per share (EPS) numbers: basic and diluted. The difference between the two measures is illustrated as follows:

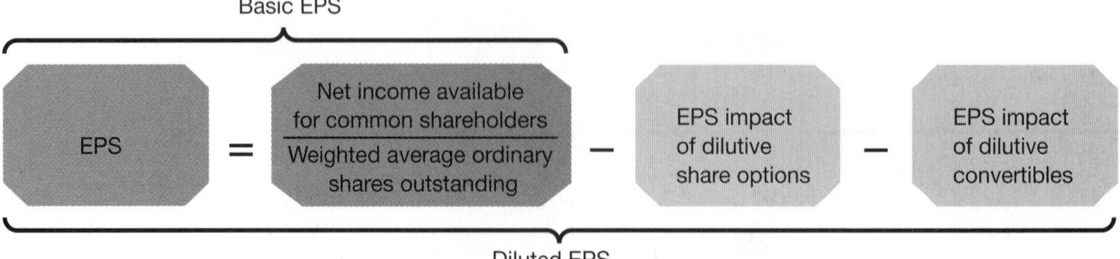

All public companies are required to report basic EPS. If the company has a complex capital structure, it is also required to report diluted EPS. A company is said to have a **complex capital structure** if it has certain *dilutive securities* outstanding. **Dilutive securities** are securities that can be converted into ordinary shares and would therefore reduce (or dilute) the earnings per share upon conversion. The three primary types of dilutive securities are:

- Stock (or share) options
- Convertible debt
- Convertible preference shares

The Appendix at the end of this chapter details the accounting for these securities. A company with none of these dilutive securities outstanding is said to have a **simple capital structure**.

Basic EPS (BEPS) is computed as earnings available for ordinary shareholders (net income less preference dividends) divided by the weighted average number of ordinary shares outstanding for the year. (The number of shares is "weighted" by the amount of time each share was outstanding during the year.) The subtraction of preference share dividends yields the income per ordinary share available for dividend payments to ordinary shareholders. The preference dividends are subtracted because this portion of net income does not accrue to the ordinary shareholders.

Computation of **diluted EPS (DEPS)** reflects the added shares that would have been issued if all share options and other convertible securities had been exercised at the beginning of the year. When DEPS is calculated, the corporation needs to consider the maximum potential reduction (dilution) of its BEPS that could occur if the conversion of these securities took place. To do so means that any of these securities that do not reduce BEPS upon conversion are not to be considered converted. The result must be a figure that is lower than BEPS. The actual calculation can be quite complex. This does not detract from the importance of the DEPS value. The diluted earnings per share figure is favored by analysts as a better indicator of performance compared to basic earnings per share. Because reported DEPS never exceeds reported BEPS, the calculation is considered conservative.

Computation and Analysis of EPS

The computation of basic EPS is relatively straightforward, particularly when the firm neither issues nor buys any of its shares during the year. The formula is:

$$\text{Basic EPS (BEPS)} = \frac{\text{Net income available for common shareholders}}{\text{Weighted average number of ordinary shares outstanding}}$$

To illustrate this calculation, assume that Kai Tak Company reported net income attributable to common shareholders of $200,000 in 2014 and paid $24,000 in preference dividends. At the beginning of the year, the company had 44,000 ordinary shares outstanding. On June 30 (exactly the midpoint of the year) it purchased 8,000 ordinary shares as treasury shares. Thus, the number of shares outstanding for the first six months of 2014 was 44,000 and, for the second half of the year, the company had 36,000 shares outstanding. The weighted average number of shares outstanding was, therefore, 40,000 [(44,000 + 36,000)/2]. Basic EPS would be calculated as follows:

$$\text{Basic EPS} = \frac{\$200{,}000 - \$24{,}000}{40{,}000 \text{ shares}} = \$4.40 \text{ per share}$$

The computation of diluted EPS is more complex in that it requires adjusting the basic EPS calculation for the effect of dilutive securities. This will typically require adjusting both the numerator and denominator of the calculation.

$$\text{Diluted EPS (DEPS)} = \frac{\text{Net income available for common shareholders} + \text{Add-backs}}{\begin{matrix}\text{Weighted average number} \\ \text{of common shares}\end{matrix} + \begin{matrix}\text{Shares of convertible securities and} \\ \text{share options assumed to be converted}\end{matrix}}$$

To illustrate, assume that Kai Tak Company's preference shares are convertible into 8,000 ordinary shares. To calculate diluted EPS, we must assume that the convertible preference shares were converted at the beginning of the year. If this had occurred, two things would have been different for the company. First, the weighted average number of shares outstanding would be higher by 8,000 shares. Second, the company would not have paid preference dividends of $24,000. The resulting calculation would be:

$$\text{Diluted EPS} = \frac{(\$200{,}000 - \$24{,}000) + \$24{,}000}{(40{,}000 + 8{,}000)\text{ shares}} = \$4.17 \text{ per share}$$

A full description of the procedures for calculating diluted EPS is beyond the scope of this text. However, as the calculation above illustrates, diluted EPS adjusts basic EPS for the effect of dilutive securities. Reported DEPS must be no larger than BEPS to reflect its conservative message.

Thomson Reuters reports both basic and diluted EPS. The table below, drawn from Thomson Reuters's 2013 consolidated income statement, presents its basic and diluted EPS figures.

(millions of U.S. dollars, except per share amounts)	Notes	Year Ended December 31 2013	2012
Earnings per share:	10		
Basic earning per share:			
From continuing operations		$0.15	$2.40
From discontinued operations		0.01	—
Basic earnings per share		$0.16	$2.40
Diluted earnings per share:			
From continuing operations		$0.15	$2.39
From discontinued operations		0.01	—
Diluted earnings per share		$0.16	$2.39

In Note 10 to Thomson Reuters's 2013 financial statement, the company presents the weighted average number of shares outstanding used in the basic EPS calculation and that used in the diluted EPS computation, as well as the corresponding reconciliation.

The weighted average number of shares outstanding, as well as a reconciliation of the weighted average number of shares outstanding used in the basic earnings per share computation to the weighted average number of shares outstanding used in the diluted earnings per share computation, is presented below:

Weighted average number of shares outstanding	Year ended December 31, 2013	2012
Basic	828,235,931	827,640,398
Effect of stock options	2,748,746	1,963,382
Diluted	830,984,677	829,603,780

There were 5,463,033 and 3,746,760 share-based compensation awards at December 31, 2013 and 2012, respectively, where the exercise price was greater than the average market price. Accordingly, these awards were anti-dilutive, and therefore excluded from the diluted earnings per share computation.

Several observations should be made regarding Thomson Reuters's EPS disclosures:

1. Thomson Reuters reports basic EPS of $0.16 in 2013 and $2.40 in 2012. Diluted EPS is the same as basic EPS in 2013 and $0.01 lower in 2012. The difference between basic and diluted EPS is caused by the effect of dilutive securities. Specifically, Thomson Reuters has outstanding stock options. Most publicly traded companies have at least one type of dilutive security outstanding. However, the dilutive effect of stock options on Thomson Reuters's EPS is negligible.
2. The income statement further separates these EPS figures into EPS from continuing operations and EPS from discontinued operations. In 2013, discontinued operations increased Thomson Reuters's EPS by $0.01 per share. IFRS requires separate reporting of the effects of nonrecurring items on EPS, including discontinued operations (see Chapter 6).
3. Thomson Reuters used weighted average shares outstanding of 828,235,931 shares to calculate basic EPS. This number is not the same as the number of shares outstanding at December 31, 2013. Nor is it the simple average of the beginning and ending numbers of shares outstanding. The precise number of shares used in the EPS calculations requires knowing exactly when ordinary share and treasury share transactions occurred during the year so that the weighted average number of shares outstanding can be calculated. This information is not always available in a company's annual report.

EPS figures are sometimes used as a method of comparing operating results for companies of different sizes under the assumption that the number of shares outstanding is proportional to the income level (that is, a company twice the size of another will report double the income and will have double the ordinary shares outstanding, leaving EPS approximately equal for the two companies). This assumption is erroneous. Management controls the number of ordinary shares outstanding. Different companies also have different philosophies regarding share issuance and repurchase. For example, consider that most companies report annual EPS of less than $5, while **Berkshire Hathaway Inc.** reported EPS of $12,092 for 2014! The large amount occurs because Berkshire Hathaway has so few common shares outstanding, not necessarily because it has stellar profits.

Most analysts prefer to concentrate their attention on diluted EPS versus basic EPS as the more important measure, but the value of the EPS number is influenced by a number of factors including the number of ordinary shares outstanding. For this reason, comparisons are more useful over time than across firms, but a careful reader should differentiate between EPS growth that comes from increases in the numerator and EPS growth that comes from decreases in the denominator. For these reasons, EPS may be of limited use in evaluating a firm's operational performance.

RESEARCH INSIGHT

Employee stock options (ESOs) give the holders the right, but not the obligation, to acquire a specified number of common shares at a specified price and within a stated period. As dilutive securities, ESOs reduce diluted EPS when newly granted ESOs move into the money and existing ESOs move further into the money. Research finds that executives increase the level of their companies' share repurchases to mitigate the effect ESOs have on diluted EPS. Evidence also shows that executives buy back more shares when their companies' net earnings are falling short of the level required to meet certain EPS growth targets. Source: Bens, Daniel, Venky Nagar, Douglas Skinner, and Franco Wong, "Employee stock options, EPS dilution, and stock repurchases," Journal of Accounting and Economics, 2003.

CHAPTER-END REVIEW

Heathrow plc reported net income of £1,750 million in fiscal 2015. The weighted average number of ordinary shares outstanding during 2015 was 760 million shares. Heathrow paid £40 million in dividends on preference shares, which were convertible into 10 million ordinary shares.

1. Calculate Heathrow's basic earnings per share for 2015.
2. Calculate Heathrow's diluted earnings per share for 2015.
3. What EPS numbers should Heathrow report on its 2015 income statement?

The solution to this review problem can be found on page 551.

APPENDIX 11A: Dilutive Securities: Further Considerations

Convertible Securities

LO7 Analyse the accounting for convertible securities, share rights, and share options.

Convertible securities are debt and equity securities that provide the holder with an option to convert those securities into other securities (usually ordinary shares). Convertible bonds and convertible preference shares, for example, give the holders the option to convert the securities into a predetermined number of ordinary shares at a predetermined conversion price.

Conversion privileges offer an additional benefit to the holder of a security. That is, debt holders and preference shareholders carry senior positions as claimants in bankruptcy, and have a fixed-interest or dividend yield. With a conversion privilege, the holders can enjoy the residual benefits of ordinary shareholders should the company perform well.

A conversion option is valuable and yields a higher price for the securities than they would otherwise command. However, conversion privileges impose a cost on ordinary shareholders. That is, the higher market price received for convertible securities is offset by the cost imposed on the subordinate ordinary shares. Conversion of these securities into ordinary shares dilutes the ownership percentage of existing ordinary shareholders.

Convertible preference shares give holders the right to convert their preference shares into a predetermined number of ordinary shares. To illustrate, assume 5,000 convertible preference shares of $10 par value were issued at $100 per share, with each share convertible into 12 ordinary shares that have a $5 par value. The financial statement effects and appropriate journal entries would be:

ANALYSE

	Balance Sheet						Income Statement		
Transaction	Cash Asset +	Noncash Assets =	Liabil-ities +	Contrib. Capital +	Earned Capital −	Contra Equity	Revenues −	Expenses =	Net Income
Issue 5,000 convertible preference shares of $10 par value for $100 per share.	+500,000 Cash		=	+50,000 Share Capital—Preference +450,000 Contributed Surplus—Convertible Preference		−	−	=	

JOURNALISE

POST

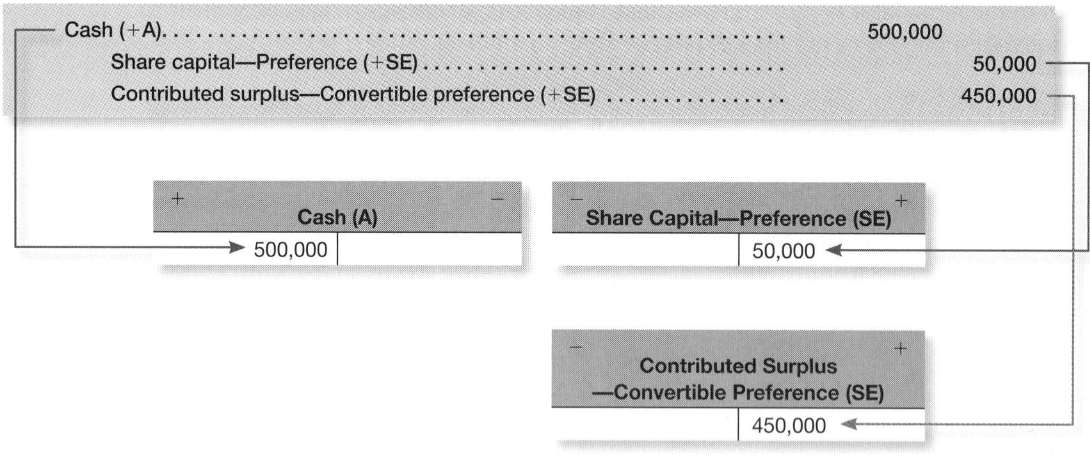

Now assume that 2,000 of these preference shares are converted to 24,000 (= 2,000 × 12) ordinary shares. The financial statement effects and appropriate journal entries follow:

	Balance Sheet							Income Statement		
Transaction	Cash Asset	+ Noncash Assets	= Liabilities	+ Contrib. Capital	+ Earned Capital	- Contra Equity		Revenues	- Expenses	= Net Income
ANALYSE: Convert 2,000 convertible preference shares to 24,000 ordinary shares.			=	+10,000 Share Capital—Ordinary; +190,000 Contributed Surplus—Ordinary; −20,000 Share Capital—Preference; −180,000 Contributed Surplus—Convertible Preference		-			-	=

JOURNALISE

	Dr.	Cr.
Share capital—Preference (−SE)	20,000	
Contributed surplus—Convertible preference (−SE)	180,000	
Share capital—Ordinary (+SE)		10,000
Contributed surplus—Ordinary (+SE)		190,000

POST

− Share Capital—Ordinary (SE) +	
	10,000

− Contributed Surplus—Ordinary (SE) +	
	190,000

− Share Capital—Preference (SE) +	
20,000	

− Contributed Surplus—Convertible Preference (SE) +	
180,000	

Convertible debt gives holders the option to convert the debt into ordinary shares at a predetermined conversion price. Convertible bonds are a compound financial instrument, because they have both equity and liability components. For reporting purposes, the value of the convertible bonds is divided into their separate debt and equity values.

To illustrate, assume that a company sells 10 convertible bonds at face value for $10,000. Each bond can be converted into 10 ordinary shares of $1 par value. Similar straight bonds would be selling for $9,000. Hence, the conversion equity component is $1,000. At the issuance of the convertible bonds, the accounting and financial statement effects would be:

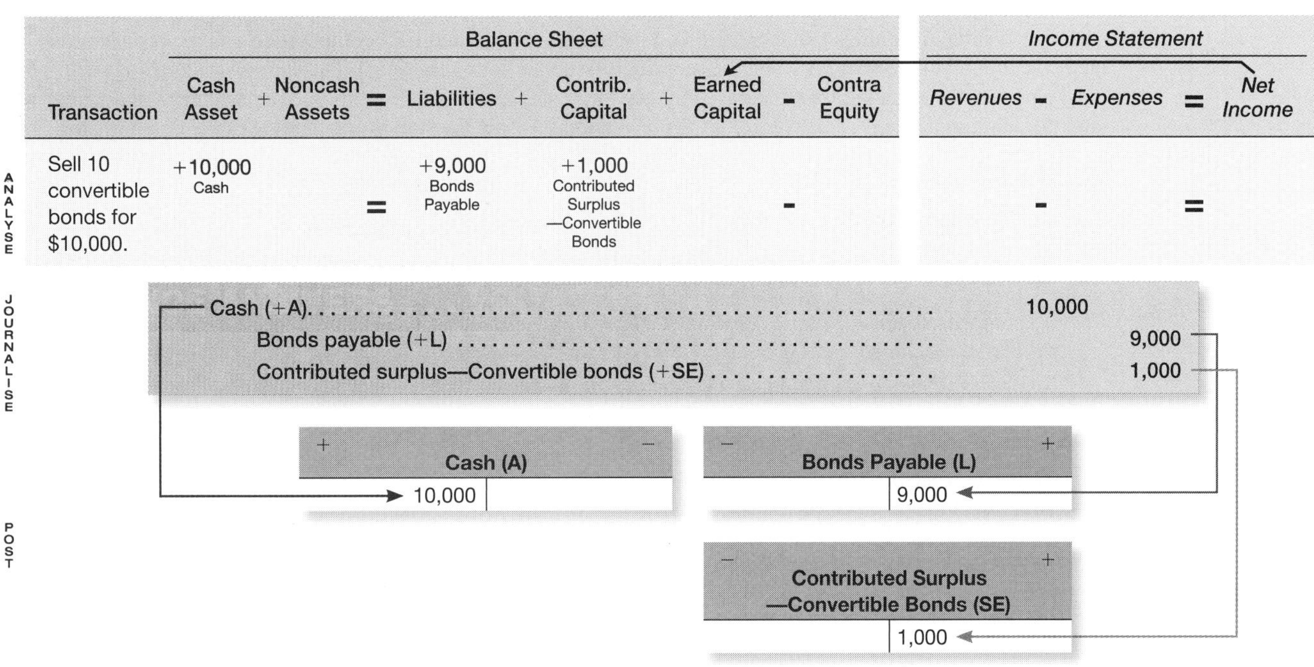

	Balance Sheet							Income Statement		
Transaction	Cash Asset	+ Noncash Assets	= Liabilities	+ Contrib. Capital	+ Earned Capital	- Contra Equity		Revenues	- Expenses	= Net Income
ANALYSE: Sell 10 convertible bonds for $10,000.	+10,000 Cash		= +9,000 Bonds Payable	+1,000 Contributed Surplus—Convertible Bonds		-			-	=

JOURNALISE

	Dr.	Cr.
Cash (+A)	10,000	
Bonds payable (+L)		9,000
Contributed surplus—Convertible bonds (+SE)		1,000

POST

+ Cash (A) −	
10,000	

− Bonds Payable (L) +	
	9,000

− Contributed Surplus—Convertible Bonds (SE) +	
	1,000

Note that the values of the debt and equity components of the convertible bonds are recorded separately. If all 10 bonds are converted to 100 (= 10 × 10) ordinary shares, the appropriate journal entry will be as follows:

ANALYSE

	Balance Sheet						Income Statement		
Transaction	Cash Asset +	Noncash Assets =	Liabilities +	Contrib. Capital +	Earned Capital −	Contra Equity	Revenues −	Expenses =	Net Income
Convert 10 convertible bonds to 100 ordinary shares of $1 par value.		=	−9,000 Bonds Payable	−1,000 Contributed Surplus—Convertible Bonds +100 Share Capital—Ordinary +9,900 Contributed Surplus—Ordinary	−		−	=	

JOURNALISE

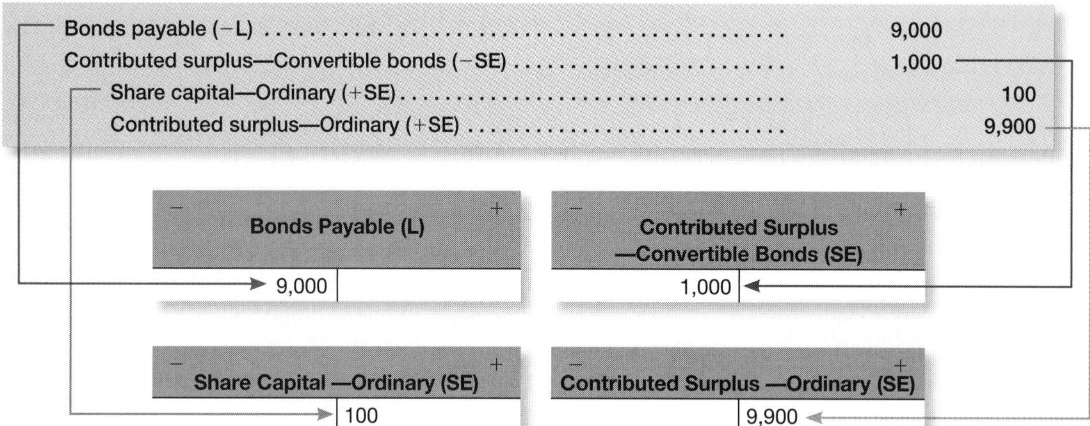

Bonds payable (−L)	9,000	
Contributed surplus—Convertible bonds (−SE)	1,000	
Share capital—Ordinary (+SE)		100
Contributed surplus—Ordinary (+SE)		9,900

POST

The key financial statement effects of the conversion are:

- The bond's fair value ($9,000) and the conversion equity component ($100) are removed from the balance sheet.
- Share capital increases by the par value of the shares issued (100 shares × $1 par = $100) and contributed surplus increases for the balance ($9,900).
- There is no effect on income from this conversion.

One final note: the potentially dilutive effect of convertible securities is taken into account in the computation of diluted earnings per share (EPS). Specifically, the diluted EPS computation assumes conversion at the beginning of the year (or when the security is issued if during the year). The earnings available to ordinary shares in the numerator are increased by any forgone after-tax interest expense or preference dividends, and the additional shares to be issued in the conversion increase the shares outstanding in the denominator.

Share Rights

Corporations often issue **share rights** that give the holder an option to acquire a specified number of ordinary shares under prescribed conditions and within a stated period. The evidence of share rights is a certificate called a **share warrant**. Share rights are issued for several reasons, which include the following:

- To compensate outside parties (such as underwriters, promoters, board members, and other professionals) for services provided to the company;
- To provide existing shareholders with the preemptive right, that is, the first opportunity, to buy additional shares when the corporation decides to raise additional equity capital through share issuances;
- To compensate officers and other employees of the corporation (rights in this form are referred to as **share options** or **share-based payments**);
- To enhance the marketability of other securities issued by the company (for example, by issuing rights to purchase ordinary shares with convertible bonds).

Share rights or warrants specify the:

- Number of rights represented by the warrant
- Option price per share (which can be zero)
- Number of rights needed to obtain a share of the issuer
- Expiration date of the rights
- Instructions for the exercise of rights

Accounting for share rights is complex. The goals of this discussion are to understand the essence of (1) share rights issued to current shareholders and (2) share options issued to employees and others.

Share rights issued to current shareholders have three important dates: (1) Announcement date of the rights offering; (2) Issuance date of the rights; and (3) Expiration date of the rights. Between the announcement date and the issuance date, the price of the share will reflect the value of the rights. After the issuance date, the shares and the rights trade separately. Shareholders can exercise their rights, sell their shares, or allow the rights to lapse.

To illustrate, assume on December 10, 2013, a company announces the issue of rights to purchase one additional share of its $5 par value common for every 10 shares currently held on January 1, 2014. The exercise price per share is $20 and the rights expire September 1, 2014. Assume further that 7,000 of the rights are exercised.

- No recognition is required at the announcement date and at the issuance date.
- The first entry is made when the first share right is exercised. We give only the summary entry that would be appropriate after September 1, 2014.

Sept 1: To record the issuance of 7,000 ordinary shares on exercise of share rights.
The financial statement effects and related entries would be (amounts in millions).

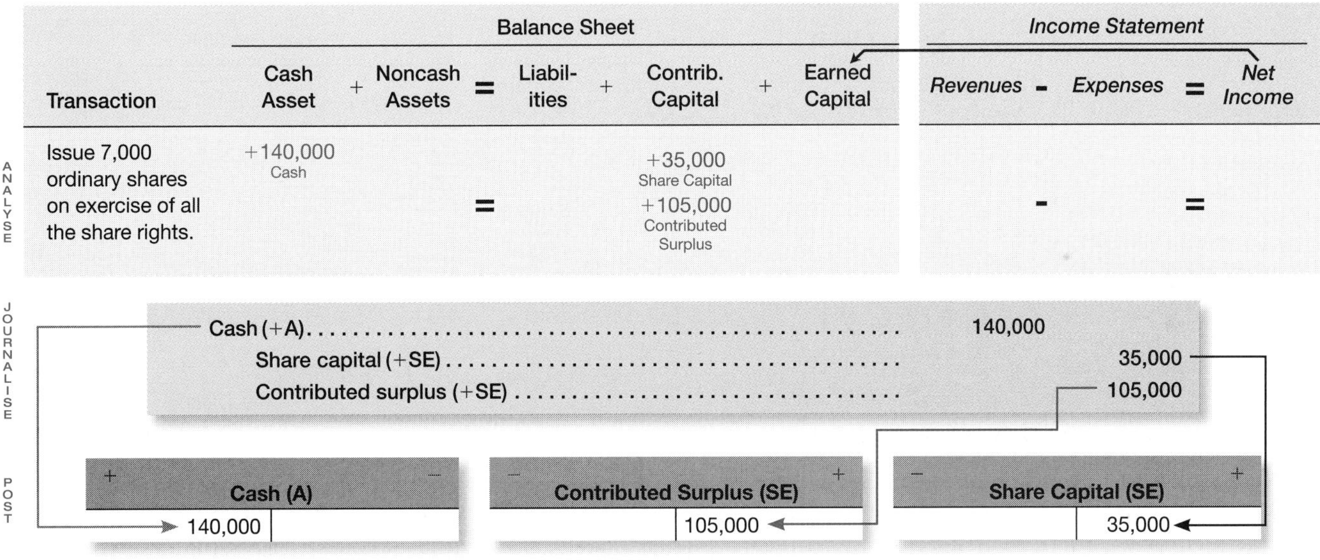

Share Options

Share or stock options are a form of share-based payments, in which a company receives goods or services in exchange for its equity securities. Share option grants normally require a vesting period. The **vesting period** is a period of time during which the employee is not allowed to exercise the option. For example, an option may expire in 5 years and vest over a period of 3 years. Such an option would be exercisable in the fourth or fifth year of its life. Rather than recognising the entire option value as compensation expense at the time that the option grant is awarded, IFRS requires that the fair value of the option be recorded ratably over the vesting period.

To illustrate share option accounting, suppose that on January 1, 2013, a company grants options to purchase 200,000 shares to senior management as part of its performance bonus plan. The options are granted with an exercise price of $30 (the current price), and can be exercised after vesting in 2 years. The firm uses an accepted valuation method (not discussed here) to obtain a value of $10 per share. The accounting and financial statement effects and related entries for 2013 would be:

	Balance Sheet						Income Statement		
Transaction	Cash Asset +	Noncash Assets =	Liabil-ities +	Contrib. Capital +	Earned Capital −	Contra Equity	Revenues −	Expenses =	Net Income
ANALYSE: 200,000 options granted at $30, valued at $10 per share, 50% vested.		=		+$1,000,000 Contributed Surplus	−$1,000,000 Retained Earnings	−	−	+$1,000,000 Compensaton Expense	= −$1,000,000

JOURNALISE

Jan 1	Compensation expense (+E, −SE)	1,000,000	
	Contributed surplus (+SE)		1,000,000

POST

+ Compensation Expense (E) −	
Jan 1 1,000,000	

− Contributed Surplus (SE) +	
	1,000,000 Jan 1

A similar entry is required in 2014, bringing the total share-based compensation expense to $2 million. Next, suppose that its share price rises and all options are exercised on November 15, 2015, with the shares being issued from treasury shares purchased previously at $25. The accounting and financial statement effects follow. In effect, senior management has purchased these shares by contributing $2 million in employment services and $6 million in cash.

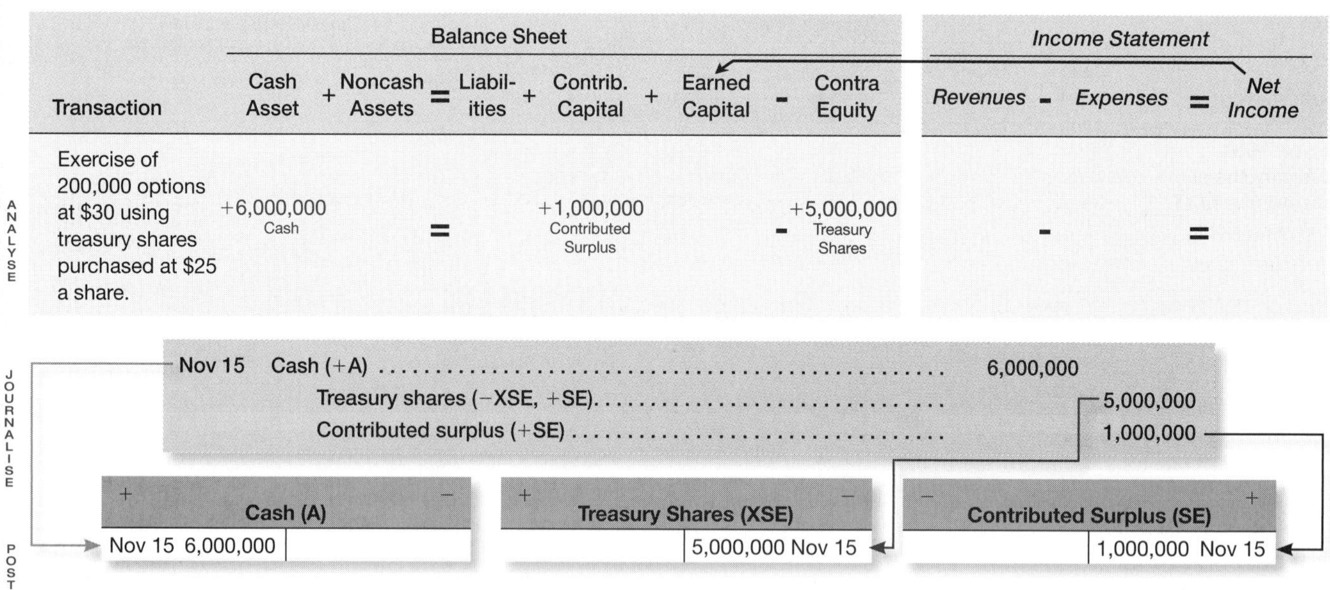

	Balance Sheet						Income Statement		
Transaction	Cash Asset +	Noncash Assets =	Liabil-ities +	Contrib. Capital +	Earned Capital −	Contra Equity	Revenues −	Expenses =	Net Income
ANALYSE: Exercise of 200,000 options at $30 using treasury shares purchased at $25 a share.	+6,000,000 Cash	=		+1,000,000 Contributed Surplus	−	+5,000,000 Treasury Shares	−	=	

JOURNALISE

Nov 15	Cash (+A)	6,000,000	
	Treasury shares (−XSE, +SE)		5,000,000
	Contributed surplus (+SE)		1,000,000

POST

+ Cash (A) −	
Nov 15 6,000,000	

+ Treasury Shares (XSE) −	
	5,000,000 Nov 15

− Contributed Surplus (SE) +	
	1,000,000 Nov 15

APPENDIX 11A REVIEW

Kallapur, Inc. has issued convertible debentures: each $1,000 bond is convertible into 200 ordinary shares of $1 par value. Assume that the bonds were sold at a discount, and that each bond has a current unamortised discount equal to $150.

Required

1. Prepare journal entries for the transaction assuming conversion of one bond.
2. Post the journal entries to the related T-accounts.
3. Using the financial statement effects template, illustrate the effects of the conversion of one of its bonds.

The solution to this review problem can be found on page 551.

SUMMARY

Describe business financing through share issuances. (p. 504) LO1

- Contributed capital represents the cumulative cash inflow that the company has received from the sale of various classes of shares, ordinary and preference.
- Preference shares receive preference in terms of dividends before ordinary shares and if cumulative receive all dividends not paid in the past before ordinary dividends can be paid. Preference shares can also be designated as convertible into ordinary shares at the holder's option and at a predetermined conversion ratio. Voting privileges reside only with the ordinary shares.

Explain and account for the issuance and repurchase of shares. (p. 507) LO2

- Ordinary shares are often repurchased by the firm for use in share award programs or to signal management confidence in the company. Repurchased shares are either held for reissue or cancelled. The repurchase is debited to a contra equity account titled treasury shares.

Describe how operations increase the equity of a business. (p. 512) LO3

- Earned capital, called retained earnings, represents the cumulative profit that has been retained by the company. Earned capital is increased by income earned and decreased by losses and dividends declared by the firm. Earned capital also includes the effects of items included in other comprehensive income.

Explain and account for dividends and share splits. (p. 512) LO4

- Dividends in the form of shares decrease retained earnings and increase contributed capital by an equivalent amount.
- A share split is a proportionate distribution similar in substance to a share dividend. The new number of shares outstanding must be disclosed. Otherwise, no further accounting is required unless local law requires that the par value be proportionally adjusted.

Define and illustrate comprehensive income. (p. 517) LO5

- Comprehensive income includes several additional items not recognised in net income including: adjustments for changes in foreign exchange rates, unrealised changes in available-for-sale securities, pension liability adjustments. The concept is designed to highlight impacts on equity that are beyond management's control.

Describe and illustrate the basic and diluted earnings per share computations. (p. 520) LO6

- Earnings per share is a closely watched number reported for all publicly traded firms. Basic EPS is computed as the ratio of net income (less preference dividends) to the average number of outstanding shares for the period. The value of this performance metric is subject to all the difficulties in measuring net income including the fact that net income can increase due to an acquisition that can have no impact on the number of outstanding shares.
- Most analysts are more interested in what is termed diluted earnings per share. This conservative calculation, which, if reported, never exceeds basic EPS, reflects the maximum reduction in basic EPS possible assuming conversion of the convertible securities.
- Share options that are "in the money" are always dilutive.
- Convertible securities that would be antidilutive are treated as if they were not converted.

Appendix 11A: Analyse the accounting for convertible securities, share rights, and share options. (p. 524) LO7

- Convertible securities are debt and equity instruments, including share rights, that allow these securities to be exchanged for other securities, typically ordinary shares. The convertible feature adds value to the security to which it is attached.
- Share options, one form of share right, allow the holders to exchange them at a specified (strike) price for ordinary shares. This right is valuable and should create an expense when granted to an employee or other individual. Expense recognition is appropriate, using the value obtained by applying an options-pricing model, even though the calculation is not precise. The option will not be exercised unless the market price of the ordinary shares exceeds the strike price.
- Convertible preference shares and convertible debt securities need to be considered in the calculation of DEPS to the extent conversion reduces reported BEPS.

GUIDANCE ANSWERS . . . YOU MAKE THE CALL

You are the Chief Financial Officer Several points must be considered. (1) Treasury shares are likely to prop up earnings per share (EPS). While the numerator (earnings) is likely dampened by the use of cash for the share repurchase, EPS is likely to increase because of the reduced shares in the denominator. (2) If the shares are sufficiently undervalued (in management's opinion), the share repurchase and subsequent resale can provide a better return than some alternative investments. (3) Share repurchases send a strong signal to the market that management feels its share are undervalued. This is more credible than merely making that argument with analysts. On the other hand, company cash is diverted from other investments. This is bothersome if such investments are mutually exclusive either now or in the future.

KEY RATIOS

$$\text{Return on Common Equity (ROCE)} = \frac{\text{Net income available for common shareholders}}{\text{Average common shareholders' equity}}$$

$$\text{Basic earnings per share (BEPS)} = \frac{\text{Net income available for common shareholders}}{\text{Weighted average number of ordinary shares outstanding}}$$

$$\text{Diluted earnings per share (DEPS)} = \frac{\text{Net income available for common shareholders} + \text{Add-backs}}{\text{Average number of ordinary shares} + \text{Shares of convertible securities and share options assumed to be converted}}$$

$$\text{Net income available for common shareholders} = \text{Net income attributable to common shareholders} - \text{Preference dividends}$$

KEY TERMS

Accumulated other comprehensive income (p. 517)
Basic EPS (p. 521)
Book value per share (p. 520)
Call feature (p. 507)
Common shares (p. 505)
Complex capital structure (p. 521)
Comprehensive income (p. 517)
Contributed capital (p. 505)
Conversion feature (p. 507)
Convertible debt (p. 525)
Convertible preference shares (p. 524)
Convertible securities (p. 524)
Diluted EPS (p. 521)
Dilutive securities (p. 521)
Dividend preference (p. 506)
Earned capital (p. 505)
Liquidating value (p. 506)
Liquidation preference (p. 506)
Non-controlling interests (p. 505)
Ordinary (or common) shares (p. 505)
Participation feature (p. 507)
Par value (p. 506)
Preference (or preferred) shares (p. 506)
Preferred shares (p. 506)
Share-based payments (p. 526)
Share dividends (p. 514)
Share options (p. 526)
Share rights (p. 526)
Shares authorised (p. 505)
Shares issued (p. 505)
Shares outstanding (p. 505)
Share split (p. 516)
Share warrant (p. 526)
Simple capital structure (p. 521)
Treasury shares (p. 509)
Vesting period (p. 527)

MULTIPLE CHOICE

1. Suppose Thomson Reuters issues 100,000 ordinary shares, $0.05 par value, to obtain a warehouse and the accompanying land when the share price is $22.00. Which one of the following statements is not true?
   a. The newly acquired assets will increase total assets by $2.2 million.
   b. Retained earnings are unaffected.
   c. The share capital account increases by $5,000.
   d. Total shareholders' equity increases by $2,195,000.

2. Assume Thomson Reuters resells 10,000 of its shares that were purchased when the market price of the shares was $25. If the shares are resold for $22, which one of the following statements holds?
   a. Contributed surplus decreases by $30,000.
   b. The treasury share account increases by $30,000.
   c. Contributed surplus increases by $30,000.
   d. The treasury share account decreases by $30,000.

3. Suppose Thomson Reuters declares a 200,000 ordinary share dividend (par $0.05) when the market value of a share is $20.00. Which one of the following statements is true?
   a. The share capital account increases by $10,000.
   b. Contributed surplus decreases by $3.99 million.
   c. Retained earnings increases by $4 million.
   d. Contributed surplus increases by $4 million.

4. Which of the following statements is true?
   a. When a *large share dividend* is paid, retained earnings are reduced by the market value of the shares distributed.
   b. Neither share dividends nor share splits affect basic earnings per share calculations.
   c. A three-for-one share split increases the total outstanding shares by 300%.
   d. A share split has no financial statement effects because it is not a monetary transaction.

5. Which of the following statements is not true in relation to diluted EPS (DEPS)?
   a. Share options that are in the money will always cause DEPS to be less than basic EPS.
   b. Convertible bonds, if dilutive, will cause changes in both the numerator and the denominator of DEPS.
   c. Share analysts tend to concentrate their attention on DEPS instead of basic EPS.
   d. Thomson Reuters's only equity contract that can lead to dilution is stock options.

Multiple Choice Answers
1. d 2. a 3. a 4. d 5. d

Superscript A denotes assignments based on Appendix 11A.

DISCUSSION QUESTIONS

Q11-1. Define *par value share*. What is the significance of a share's par value from an accounting and analysis perspective?

Q11-2. What are the basic differences between preference shares and ordinary shares? What are the typical features of preference shares?

Q11-3. What features make preference shares similar to debt? Similar to ordinary shares?

Q11-4. What is meant by dividend arrearage on preference shares? If dividends are two years in arrears on $500,000 of 6% preference shares, and dividends are declared at the end of this year, what amount of total dividends must preference shareholders receive before any distributions are made to ordinary shareholders?

Q11-5. Distinguish between authorised shares and issued shares. Why might the number of shares issued be more than the number of shares outstanding?

Q11-6. Describe the difference between contributed capital and earned capital. Specifically, how can earned capital be considered as an investment by the company's shareholders?

Q11-7. How does the account contributed surplus arise? What inferences, if any, can you draw from the amount of contributed surplus as reported on the balance sheet relative to the ordinary share amount in relation to the financial condition of the company?

Q11-8. Define *share split*. What are the major reasons for a share split?

Q11-9. Define *treasury share*. Why might a corporation acquire treasury shares? How are treasury shares reported in the balance sheet?

Q11-10. If a corporation purchases 600 shares of its own ordinary shares at $10 per share and resells them at $14 per share, where would the $2,400 increase in capital be reported in the financial statements? Why is no gain reported?

Q11-11. A corporation has total shareholders' equity of $4,628,000 and one class of $2 par value ordinary shares. The corporation has 500,000 shares authorised; 300,000 shares issued; 260,000 shares outstanding; and 40,000 treasury shares. What is its book value per share?

Q11-12. What is a share dividend? How does an ordinary share dividend distributed to ordinary shareholders affect their respective ownership interests?

Q11-13. What is the difference between the accounting for a share dividend using the fair value approach and the accounting for a share dividend using the par value approach?

Q11-14. Employee share options have a potentially dilutive effect on earnings per share (EPS) that is recognised in the diluted EPS computation. What can companies do to offset these dilutive effects and how might this action affect the balance sheet?

Q11-15. What information is reported in a statement of changes in equity?

Q11-16. What items are typically reported under equity category of other comprehensive income (OCI)?

Q11-17. What is a share option vesting period? How does the vesting period affect the recognition of compensation expense for share options?

Q11-18.[A] Describe the accounting for a convertible bond. Can the conversion ever result in the recognition of a gain in the income statement?

MINI EXERCISES

LO2 **M11-19. Analysing and Identifying Financial Statement Effects of Share Issuances**

On June 1, Beatty Corp. issues (*a*) 8,000 shares of $50 par value preference shares at $68 cash per share and it issues (*b*) 12,000 shares of $1 par value ordinary shares at $10 cash per share. Indicate the financial statement effects of these two issuances using the financial statement effects template.

LO2 **M11-20. Analysing and Identifying Financial Statement Effects of Share Issuances**

On September 1, Magliolo, Inc., (*a*) issues 18,000 shares of $10 par value preference shares at $48 cash per share and (*b*) issues 120,000 shares of $2 par value ordinary shares at $37 cash per share.

a. Prepare the journal entries for the two issuances.
b. Post the journal entries from *a* to the related T-accounts.
c. Using the financial statement effects template, illustrate the effects of these two issuances.

LO2 **M11-21. Analysing Share Capital and Share Premium**

CATHAY PACIFIC AIRWAYS LIMITED (HONG KONG)

Following is the equity section from the **Cathay Pacific Airways Limited**, balance sheet (in millions of Hong Kong dollars, except par value).

Equity	December 31, 2013
Share capital, HK$0.20 par value:	
5,000,000,000 shares authorised; 3,933,844,572 shares issued	$ 787
Retained profit	40,342
Share premium	16,295
Investment revaluation reserve	984
Cash flow hedge reserve	2,340
Capital redemption reserve and others	2,140
Funds attributable to the owners of Cathay Pacific	62,888
Non-controlling interests	125
Total equity	$63,013

a. Show the computation to derive $787 million for the share capital account.
b. At what average price were the Cathay Pacific shares issued?
c. How many shares of Cathay Pacific ordinary shares are outstanding as of December 31, 2013?

M11-22. Identifying and Analysing Financial Statement Effects of Share Issuance and Repurchase LO2

On January 1, 2014, Esplanade Company issues 5,000 shares of $100 par value preference shares at $250 cash per share. On March 1, the company repurchases 5,000 shares of previously issued $1 par value ordinary shares at $83 cash per share.

a. Prepare the journal entries for the two transactions.
b. Post the journal entries from *a* to the related T-accounts.
c. Using the financial statement effects template, illustrate the effects of these two transactions.

M11-23. Assessing the Financial Statement Effects of a Share Split LO4, 6

Avignon S.A.
On April 25, 2015, the Company's Board of Directors approved a three-for-one share split (in the form of a share dividend) of the Company's ordinary shares. The share split was effective on June 4, 2015, for shareholders of record on May 21, 2015. All weighted average shares, per share amounts, and references to share compensation data for all periods have been adjusted to reflect the effect of the share split

This note to its 2015 balance sheet further indicates that amounts have been "restated for three-for-one share split effective June 4, 2015." What restatements has Avignon made to its balance sheet as a result of this action?

M11-24. Computing Basic and Diluted Earnings per Share LO6

YVR Corporation began 2015 with 120,000 shares of ordinary shares and 16,000 shares of convertible preference shares outstanding. On March 1 an additional 10,000 shares of ordinary shares were issued. On August 1, another 16,000 shares of ordinary shares were issued. On November 1, 6,000 shares of ordinary shares were acquired for the treasury. The preference shares have a $2 per-share dividend rate, and each share may be converted into one ordinary share. YVR Corporation's 2015 net income is $501,000.

a. Compute basic earnings per share for 2015.
b. Compute diluted earnings per share for 2015.
c. If the preference shares were not convertible, YVR Corporation would have a simple capital structure. How would this change YVR's earnings per share presentation?

M11-25. Assessing Share Capital and Treasury Share Balances LO2, 6

Following is the equity section from the SFU Company balance sheet ($ thousands).

Shareholders' Equity	January 28, 2015
Share capital—$.01 par value: 150,000,000 shares authorised, 103,300,000 shares issued	$ 1,033
Share premium	369,171
Retained earnings	2,320,571
Accumulated other comprehensive (loss) income, net of tax	6,455
Treasury shares, at average cost 17,662,000 shares	(834,774)
Total shareholders' equity	$1,862,456

a. SFU has repurchased 17,662,000 shares that comprise its January 28, 2015, treasury shares account. Compute the number of outstanding shares as of January 28, 2015.
b. If this repurchase took place March 31, 2014, what would have been the effect on the denominator of the basic EPS calculation?

M11-26. Identifying and Analysing Financial Statement Effects of Cash Dividends LO4

Hastings Corp. has outstanding 6,000 shares of $50 par value, 6% preference shares, and 40,000 shares of $1 par value ordinary shares. The company has $328,000 of retained earnings. At year-end, the company declares and pays the regular $3 per share cash dividend on preference shares and a $2.20 per share cash dividend on ordinary shares.

a. Prepare the journal entries for the two dividend payments.
b. Post the journal entries from *a* to the related T-accounts.
c. Using the financial statement effects template, illustrate the effects of these two dividend payments.

LO4 M11-27. **Analysing and Identifying Financial Statement Effects of Share Dividends**
Quarry Bay Corp. has outstanding 70,000 shares of $5 par value ordinary shares. At year-end, the company declares and issues a 4% share dividend when the market share price is $21 per share.

a. Prepare the journal entries for the share dividend declaration and payment. The company values this share dividend at fair value.
b. Post the journal entries from *a* to the related T-accounts.
c. Using the financial statement effects template, illustrate the effects of this dividend declaration and payment.

LO4 M11-28. **Analysing, Identifying, and Explaining the Effects of a Share Split**
On September 1, Macquarie Company has 250,000 shares of $15 par value ($165 market value) ordinary shares that are issued and outstanding. Its balance sheet on that date shows the following account balances relating to the ordinary shares.

Share capital	$3,750,000
Share premium	2,250,000

On September 2, Macquarie splits its shares 3-for-2 and reduces the par value to $10 per share.

a. How many ordinary shares are issued and outstanding immediately after the share split?
b. What is the dollar balance of the share capital account immediately after the share split?
c. What is the likely reason that Macquarie Company split its shares?

LO4 M11-29. **Distributing Cash Dividends to Preference and Ordinary Shareholders**
Clarke Quay Company has outstanding 20,000 shares of $50 par value, 6% cumulative preference shares, and 80,000 shares of $10 par value ordinary shares. The company declares and pays cash dividends amounting to $160,000.

a. If no arrearage on the preference shares exists, how much in total dividends, and in dividends per share, is paid to each class of share?
b. If one year's dividend arrearage on the preference shares exists, how much in total dividends, and in dividends per share, is paid to each class of share?

LO3, 4 M11-30. **Analysing and Preparing a Retained Earnings Reconciliation**
Use the following data to prepare the 2014 retained earnings reconciliation for Bakerloo Plc.

Total retained earnings, December 31, 2013	£347,000
Share dividends declared and paid in 2014	28,000
Cash dividends declared and paid in 2014	35,000
Net income for 2014	94,000

LO4 M11-31. **Accounting for Share Dividend and Share Split**
Pyrmont Corporation has 40,000 shares of $10 par value ordinary shares outstanding and retained earnings of $820,000. The company declares a 100% share dividend. The market price at the declaration is $17 per share. The company values this share dividend at par value.

a. Prepare the general journal entry for the share dividend.
b. Assume that the company splits its shares two for one and reduces the par value from $10 to $5 rather than declaring a 100% share dividend. How does the accounting for the share split differ from the accounting for the 100% share dividend?

LO6 M11-32. **Computing Basic and Diluted Earnings per Share**
During 2013, Kowloon Corporation had 50,000 shares of $10 par value ordinary shares and 10,000 shares of 8%, $50 par value convertible preference shares outstanding. Each preference share may be converted into three ordinary shares. Kowloon Corporation's 2013 net income was $440,000.

a. Compute the basic earnings per share for 2013.
b. Compute the diluted earnings per share for 2013.

LO6 M11-33. **Computing Earnings per Share**
Bayeux SA began the year with a simple structure consisting of 38,000 ordinary shares outstanding. On May 1, 10,000 additional shares were issued, and another 1,000 shares were issued on September 1. The company had a net income for the year of €234,000.

a. Compute the earnings per share of ordinary shares.

b. Assume that the company also had 6,000 shares of 6%, €50 par value cumulative preference shares outstanding throughout the year. Compute the earnings per share of ordinary shares.

M11-34. Computing Earnings per Share

LO6

BURBERRY GROUP PLC (UNITED KINGDOM)

The British luxury goods company Burberry Group Plc reports the following information regarding its earnings per share in its 2012/2013 annual report.

9. Earnings per share

The calculation of basic earnings per share is based on profit or loss attributable to owners of the Company for the year divided by the weighted average number of ordinary shares in issue during the year. Basic and diluted earnings per share based on adjusted profit before taxation are also disclosed to indicate the underlying profitability of the Group.

	Year to 31 March 2013 £m	Year to 31 March 2012 £m
Attributable profit for the year before exceptional items(1) and discontinued operations	£312.4	£273.8
Effect of exceptional items(1) (after taxation)	(58.1)	(10.2)
Attributable profit for the year from continuing operations	254.3	263.6
Attributable loss from discontinued operations	—	(0.3)
Attributable profit for the year	£254.3	£263.3

(1) Refer to note 6 for details of exceptional items.

The weighted average number of ordinary shares represents the weighted average number of Burberry Group plc ordinary shares in issue throughout the year, excluding ordinary shares held in the Group's employee share option plan trusts (ESOP trusts).

Diluted earnings per share is based on the weighted average number of ordinary shares in issue during the year. In addition, account is taken of any options and awards made under the employee share incentive schemes, which will have a dilutive effect when exercised. Refer to note 26 for additional information on the terms and conditions of the employee share incentive schemes.

	Year to 31 March 2013 Millions	Year to 31 March 2012 Millions
Weighted average number of ordinary shares in issue during the year	436.2	435.9
Dilutive effect of the employee share incentive schemes	10.3	8.4
Diluted weighted average number of ordinary shares in issue during the year	446.5	444.3

a. Compute basic and diluted earnings per share for the year ended March 31, 2013.

b. What is the reason that basic and diluted earnings per share differ in 2013?

M11-35.[A] Analysing Share Option Expense for Income

LO7

Granville & Co., Inc., reported net income of $6,272 million for the 2014 fiscal year. Its 2014 annual report contained the following information regarding its share options.

Employee share options are granted to purchase Company ordinary shares at the fair market value at the time of grant. These awards generally vest one-third each year over a three-year period, with a contractual term of 7-10 years. The weighted average exercise price of options granted in 2014 was $36.47 and the weighted average fair value of options granted was $5.39 per option.

a. Granville granted 8,209,000 options to employees in 2014. Using a journal entry, show how the share option grants would be recorded in 2014 (assume all grants took place on January 1, 2014).

b. How does the granting of share options affect EPS?

c. Granville employees exercised 12,435,000 options in 2014, paying a total of $321 million in cash to the company. Using a summary journal entry, show how these option exercises would be recorded in 2014.

d. How does the exercise of share options affect EPS?

LO2, 4, 6 M11-36. **Examining the Effect of Share Transactions**

Year 1: Gaglardi Company sells 10,000 no-par ordinary shares for $30/share. Year 2: Gaglardi Company buys 1,000 no-par ordinary shares for $28/share. Year 3: Gaglardi Company declares but has not yet paid a dividend on its no-par ordinary shares of $2 per share. The company's basic earnings per share were $10 in the third year.

Indicate the effect (increase, decrease, no effect) of each of these share decisions for each year on the items listed.

Year	Total Assets	Total Liabilities	Total Equity	EPS	Operating Income
1.					
2.					
3.					

LO1, 2, 6 M11-37. **Reporting Equity**

Lougheed Company began business this year and immediately sold 600,000 common shares for $18,000,000 and paid $1,000,000 in common dividends. In midyear, the firm bought back some of its own shares. The company reports the following additional information at year-end:

Net income.	$5,000,000
Share capital	$6,000,000
Retained earnings beginning of year	$ 0
Common shares authorised:	1,000,000
Outstanding at year's end:	550,000

a. What was the average sales price of a common share?

b. What is the par value of the common?

c. How much is in the Contributed Surplus account at the end of the year?

d. Determine the retained earnings amount at the end of the year.

e. How many shares are in the treasury at the end of the year?

f. Compute basic EPS.

LO1, 2, 4 M11-38. **Analysing Earnings Per Share Effects of Convertible Securities**

Epernay SA reports the following data in its 2014 annual report. The data relate to the corporation's computation of its earnings per share calculations.

Numerator:	
Net income (€millions)	€86
Adjustment for dilutive securities:	
Interest on convertible debt, net of tax.	12
Income available to common shareholders after adjustment for assumed conversions . . .	€98
Denominator:	
Weighted average shares outstanding used for Basic EPS (thousands)	278,689
Adjustment for dilutive securities:	
Employee share options	1,660
Convertible debt	66,118
Weighted average shares outstanding used for diluted EPS	346,467

Required

a. What is the objective behind the calculation of diluted EPS?

b. Calculate Epernay's basic EPS.

c. Calculate Epernay's diluted EPS.

d. Epernay excluded 22,300 share options from the computation of diluted EPS. Under what circumstances would this be appropriate?

EXERCISES

E11-39. Identifying and Analysing Financial Statement Effects of Share Transactions **LO2**

Kingsway Company reports the following transactions relating to its share accounts.

Feb	20	Issued 10,000 shares of $1 par value ordinary shares at $25 cash per share.
Feb	21	Issued 15,000 shares of $100 par value, 8% preference shares at $275 cash per share.
June	30	Purchased 2,000 shares of its own ordinary shares at $15 cash per share.
Sep	25	Sold 1,000 shares of the treasury share at $21 cash per share.

a. Prepare the journal entries for these transactions.
b. Post the journal entries from *a* to the related T-accounts.
c. Using the financial statement effects template, illustrate the effects of these transactions.

E11-40. Analysing and Identifying Financial Statement Effects of Share Transactions **LO2**

AKL Corp. reports the following transactions relating to its share accounts.

Jan	15	Issued 25,000 shares of $5 par value ordinary shares at $17 cash per share.
Jan	20	Issued 6,000 shares of $50 par value, 8% preference shares at $78 cash per share.
Mar	31	Purchased 3,000 shares of its own ordinary shares at $20 cash per share.
June	25	Sold 2,000 shares of the treasury share at $26 cash per share.
July	15	Sold the remaining 1,000 shares of treasury share at $19 cash per share.

a. Prepare the journal entries for these transactions.
b. Post the journal entries from *a* to the related T-accounts.
c. Using the financial statement effects template, illustrate the effects of these transactions.

E11-41. Analysing and Identifying Share Capital **LO1, 2**

RIO-TINTO GROUP (AUSTRALIA AND UNITED KINGDOM)

Rio Tinto Group is a British-Australian mining company. It is a dual-listed company, traded on the London Stock Exchange under Rio Tinto plc and the Australian Securities Exchange under Rio Tinto Limited. The following note about Rio Tinto plc's share capital is taken from the company's 2013 annual report.

27 Share capital – Rio Tinto plc

	2013 Number (million)	2012 Number (million)
Issued and fully paid up share capital of 10p each		
At January 1	1,425.376	1,453.400
Ordinary shares issued	0.001	—
Ordinary shares purchased but uncancelled on January 1	—	(1.800)
Own shares purchased and cancelled	—	(26.224)
At December 31	1,425.377	1,425.376
Shares repurchased and held in treasury	12.682	14.119
Shares repurchased and awaiting cancellation	—	—
Shares held by public	1,412.695	1,411.257
Total share capital	1,425.377	1,425.376

a. How many shares are issued at December 31, 2013?
b. How many shares are purchased by the company and held in treasury at December 31, 2013?
c. How many shares are outstanding at December 31, 2013?
d. How should Treasury Shares be treated in calculating earnings per share?
e. What is the dollar balance of the share capital account at December 31, 2013?

E11-42. Analysing and Distributing Cash Dividends to Preference and Ordinary Shares **LO4**

BNE Company began business on March 1, 2013. At that time, it issued 20,000 shares of $60 par value, 7% cumulative preference shares and 100,000 shares of $5 par value ordinary shares.

Through the end of 2015, there has been no change in the number of preference and ordinary shares outstanding.

a. Assume that BNE declared and paid cash dividends of $0 in 2013, $183,000 in 2014, and $200,000 in 2015. Compute the total cash dividends and the dividends per share paid to each class of shares in 2013, 2014, and 2015.

b. Assume that BNE declared and paid cash dividends of $0 in 2013, $84,000 in 2014, and $150,000 in 2015. Compute the total cash dividends and the dividends per share paid to each class of shares in 2013, 2014, and 2015.

LO6 E11-43. **Computing Basic and Diluted Earnings per Share**

Devonshire Corporation began the year 2014 with 25,000 shares of ordinary shares and 5,000 convertible preference shares outstanding. On May 1, an additional 9,000 shares of ordinary shares were issued. On July 1, 6,000 ordinary shares were acquired for the treasury. On September 1, the 6,000 treasury shares were reissued. The preference shares have a $4 per-share dividend rate, and each share may be converted into two ordinary shares. Devonshire Corporation's 2014 net income is $230,000.

a. Compute earnings per share for 2014.

b. Compute diluted earnings per share for 2014.

c. If the preference shares were not convertible, Devonshire Corporation would have a simple capital structure. How would this change Devonshire's earnings per share presentation?

LO4, 6 E11-44. **Analysing and Distributing Cash Dividends to Preference and Ordinary Shares**

Hoskin Company has outstanding 15,000 shares of $50 par value, 8% preference shares and 50,000 shares of $5 par value ordinary shares. During its first three years in business, it declared and paid no cash dividends in the first year, $280,000 in the second year, and $60,000 in the third year.

a. If the preference shares are cumulative, determine the total amount of cash dividends paid to each class of shares in each of the three years.

b. If the preference shares are noncumulative, determine the total amount of cash dividends paid to each class of shares in each of the three years.

c. How should each type of preferred dividends be treated in calculating EPS?

LO2 E11-45. **Analysing and Computing Issue Price, Treasury Share Cost, and Shares Outstanding**

FIAT S.p.A. (ITALY)

Following are the statement of changes in equity and note 23 from the 2013 annual report of Fiat S.p.A., a Spanish automotive manufacturer.

Statement of Changes in Equity

(€ thousand)	Share capital	Share premium reserve	Legal reserve	Reserve available for the purchase of own shares	Reserve for own shares	Retained profit/ (loss)	Gains/ (losses) recognised directly in equity	Stock option reserve	Other reserves (1)	Own shares (2)	Profit/ (loss) for the year	Total equity
Amount at December 31, 2012 (as reported)	4,476,442	1,071,403	528,577	941,043	258,957	1,910,973	(17,375)	53,562	89,829	(258,957)	(152,350)	8,902,104
Effect of IAS 19 amendments						4,043	(5,151)				48	(1,060)
Amount at January 1, 2013	4,476,442	1,071,403	528,577	941,043	258,957	1,915,016	(22,526)	53,562	89,829	(258,957)	(152,302)	8,901,044
Allocation of prior year loss:												
To retained profit/(loss)						(152,302)					152,302	—
Effect of exercise of stock options under the November 2006 stock option plan	1,020	2,363										3,383
Purchase of own shares relating to payment of fractions of shares resulting from conversion of preference and savings shares				(1)	1					(1)		(1)
Valuation of stock option/stock grant plans						1,069		9,069				10,138
Total comprehensive income for the period							5,590				(226,698)	(221,108)
Amount at December 31, 2013	4,477,462	1,073,766	528,577	941,042	258,958	1,763,783	(16,936)	62,631	89,829	(258,958)	(226,698)	8,693,456

Share capital

At December 31, 2013, fully paid-up share capital amounts to €4,477 million (€4,476 million at December 31, 2012) and consists of 1,250,687,773 ordinary shares (1,250,402,773 ordinary shares at December 31, 2012), with a par value of €3.58 each. The capital increase from the previous year is due to the issue of 285,000 new shares in relation to the exercise of stock options.

The following table provides a reconciliation between the number of Fiat S.p.A. shares outstanding at December 31, 2011 and the number outstanding at December 31, 2013:

(number of shares in thousands)	At December 31, 2011	Conversion of preferences and saving shares	Share based payments	At December 31, 2012	Exercise of Stock Options	Al December 31, 2013
Ordinary shares issued	1,092,681	157,722	—	1,250,403	285	1,250,688
Less: Ordinary treasury shares	(38,568)	(10)	4,000	(34,578)	—	(34,578)
Ordinary shares outstanding	1,054,113	157,712	4,000	1,215,825	285	1,216,110
Preference shares issued	103,292	(103,292)	—	—	—	—
Savings shares issued	79,913	(79,913)	—	—	—	—
Total Shares issued by Fiat S.p.A.	1,275,886	(25,483)	—	1,250,403	285	1,250,688
Less: Treasury shares	(38,568)	(10)	4,000	(34,578)	—	(34,578)
Total Fiat S.p.A. outstanding shares	1,237,318	(25,493)	4,000	1,215,825	285	1,216,110

The mandatory conversion of all 103,292,310 Fiat S.p.A. preference shares and 79,912,800 Fiat S.p.A. savings shares into 157,722,163 Fiat S.p.A. ordinary shares, approved by the extraordinary Shareholders' Meeting of April 4, 2012, took place (at a conversion ratio of 0.850 ordinary shares for every preference share and 0.875 ordinary shares for every savings share). From May 21, 2012 only Fiat S.p.A. ordinary shares are traded on the Borsa Italiana electronic exchange ("MTA").

a. How many ordinary shares are issued as of December 31, 2013?
b. How many ordinary shares are outstanding as of December 31, 2013?
c. Explain the derivation of the €4,477,462 (thousand) in the share capital account.
d. Using balances at December 31, 2013, compute the average issue price of Fiat's ordinary shares.
e. At what average cost were the Fiat treasury shares as of December 31, 2013?
f. Why would a company such as Fiat want to buy back its own shares?

E11-46. Analysing and Distributing Cash Dividends to Preference and Ordinary Shares LO4

Changi Company began business on June 30, 2013. At that time, it issued 18,000 shares of $50 par value, 6% cumulative preference shares and 90,000 shares of $10 par value ordinary shares. Through the end of 2015, there has been no change in the number of preference and ordinary shares outstanding.

a. Assume that Changi declared and paid cash dividends of $63,000 in 2013, $0 in 2014, and $378,000 in 2015. Compute the total cash dividends and the dividends per share paid to each class of shares in 2013, 2014, and 2015.
b. Assume that Changi declared and paid cash dividends of $0 in 2013, $108,000 in 2014, and $189,000 in 2015. Compute the total cash dividends and the dividends per share paid to each class of shares in 2013, 2014, and 2015.

E11-47. Analysing and Identifying Financial Statement Effects of Dividends LO4

Downing Plc has outstanding 25,000 shares of £10 par value ordinary shares. It also has £405,000 of retained earnings. Near the current year-end, the company declares and pays a cash dividend of £1.90 per share and declares and issues a 4% share dividend. The market price of the shares at the declaration date is £35 per share. The company values this share dividend at fair value.

a. Prepare the journal entries for these two separate dividend transactions.
b. Post the journal entries from *a* to the related T-accounts.
c. Using the financial statement effects template, illustrate the effects of these two separate dividends.

E11-48. Identifying and Analysing Financial Statement Effects of Dividends LO4

The equity of Choi Hung Company at December 31, 2013, appears below.

Share capital, $10 par value, 200,000 shares authorised; 80,000 shares issued and outstanding	$800,000
Share premium	480,000
Retained earnings	305,000

During 2014, the following transactions occurred:

May 12 Declared and issued a 7% share dividend; the market value of the ordinary shares was $18 per share. The company values this share dividend at fair value.

Dec. 31 Declared and paid a cash dividend of 75 cents per share.

a. Prepare the journal entries for these transactions.
b. Post the journal entries from *a* to the related T-accounts.
c. Using the financial statement effects template, illustrate the effects of these transactions.
d. Prepare a retained earnings reconciliation for 2014 assuming that the company reports 2014 net income of $283,000.

LO4 E11-49. **Analysing and Identifying Financial Statement Effects of Dividends**
The equity of YEG Company at December 31, 2013, is shown below:

5% preference shares, $100 par value, 10,000 shares authorised; 4,000 shares issued and outstanding	$ 400,000
Ordinary shares, $5 par value, 200,000 shares authorised; 50,000 shares issued and outstanding	250,000
Contributed surplus—preference shares	40,000
Contributed surplus—ordinary shares	300,000
Retained earnings	656,000
Total equity	$1,646,000

The following transactions, among others, occurred during 2014.

Apr. 1 Declared and issued a 100% share dividend on all outstanding ordinary shares. The market value of the shares was $11 per share. YEG values this share dividend at par value.

Dec. 7 Declared and issued a 3% share dividend on all outstanding ordinary shares. The market value of the shares was $14 per share. YEG values this share dividend at par value.

Dec. 20 Declared and paid (1) the annual cash dividend on the preference shares and (2) a cash dividend of 80 cents per ordinary share.

a. Prepare the journal entries for these transactions.
b. Post the journal entries from *a* to the related T-accounts.
c. Using the financial statement effects template, illustrate the effects of these transactions.
d. Prepare a 2014 retained earnings reconciliation assuming that the company reports 2014 net income of $253,000.

LO4, 6 E11-50. **Analysing, Identifying, and Explaining the Effects of a Share Split**
On March 1 of the current year, Sussex Company has 400,000 shares of $20 par value ordinary shares that are issued and outstanding. Its balance sheet shows the following account balances relating to ordinary shares.

Share capital	$8,000,000
Share premium	3,400,000

On March 2, Sussex Company splits its ordinary shares 2-for-1 and reduces the par value to $10 per share.

a. How many ordinary shares are issued and outstanding immediately after the share split?
b. What is the dollar balance in its share capital account immediately after the share split?
c. What is the dollar balance in its share premium account immediately after the share split?
d. What is the effect of a share split on the calculation of EPS?

LO4, 6 E11-51. **Assessing the Financial Statement Effects of a Share Split**

TELUS CORPORATION (CANADA)

TELUS Corporation is a Canadian national telecommunications company based in Vancouver, British Columbia. TELUS reports a share split in the following note taken from its 2013 annual report.

(b) Stock split
A subdivision of our Common Shares on a two-for-one basis was effected April 16, 2013. All references, unless otherwise indicated, to the number of shares outstanding, per share amounts and share-based compensation information in these consolidated financial statements have been retrospectively restated to reflect the impact of the subdivision.

a. What are the reasons for a share split?
b. What restatements has TELUS made to its balance sheet as a result of this action?
c. What is the effect of a share split on the calculation of TELUS's earnings per share?
d. What are the differences between a share split and a share dividend?

E11-52. Computing Earnings per Share LO6

PCCW LIMITED (HONG KONG)

PCCW Limited is a Hong Kong-based telecommunications company. The company provides the data for computing its earnings per share in the following note from its 2013 annual report.

14 EARNINGS PER SHARE
The calculations of basic and diluted earnings per share are based on the following data:

	2012 (Restated)	2013
Earnings (in HK$ million)		
Earnings for the purpose of basic and diluted earnings per share	1,661	1,885
Number of shares		
Weighted average number of ordinary shares	7,272,294,654	7,272,294,654
Effect of PCCW Shares purchased from the market under the Company's share award schemes	(9,092,300)	(18,985,730)
Effect of PCCW Shares vested under the Company's share award schemes	—	2,226,513
Weighted average number of ordinary shares for the purpose of basic earnings per share	7,263,202,354	7,255,535,437
Effect of PCCW Shares awarded under the Company's share award schemes	—	9,811,488
Weighted average number of ordinary shares for the purpose of diluted earnings per share	7,263,202,354	7,265,346,925

a. Compute basic and diluted earnings per share in 2013.
b. What are the reasons that basic and diluted earnings per share differ in 2013?

E11-53. Analysing and Computing Issue Price, Treasury Share Cost, and Shares Outstanding LO4, 6

PHILIPS NV (THE NETHERLANDS)

Philips N.V. is a multinational electronics and technology company, with headquarters in Amsterdam, Netherlands. The equity section of the company's 2013 balance sheet is given below (€ millions).

Equity	2012	2013
Shareholders' equity:		
Preference shares, par value EUR 0.20 per share:		
Authorised: 2,000,000,000 shares (2012: 2,000,000,000 shares)		
Issued: none		
Common shares, par value EUR 0.20 per share:		
Authorised: 2,000,000,000 shares (2012: 2,000,000,000 shares)		
Issued and fully paid: 937,845,789 shares (2012: 957,132,962 shares)	191	188
Capital in excess of par value	1,304	1,796
Retained earnings	10,724	10,415
Revaluation reserve	54	23
Currency translation differences	(93)	(569)
Available-for-sale financial assets	54	55
Cash flow hedges	20	24
Treasury shares, at cost: 24,508,022 shares (2012: 42,541,687 shares)	(1,103)	(718)
	11,151	11,214
Non-controlling interests	34	13
Group equity	11,185	11,227

a. How many preference shares are authorised and issued at year-end 2013?
b. How many common shares are authorised and issued at year-end 2013?
c. How many common shares are outstanding at year-end 2013?
d. Show the computation to derive €188 million for the share capital account at year-end 2013.
e. At what average price were the common shares issued at year-end 2013?
f. At what average cost has Philips repurchased its shares as of year-end 2013?
g. Why would a company such as Philips want to repurchase its shares?
h. Explain how the repurchase of shares affects the computation of EPS.

LO2, 4, 6 **E11-54.** **Interpreting Information in the Statement of Changes in Equity**

HENKEL AG & CO. KGaA (GERMANY)

Henkel AG & Co. KGaA is a German manufacturer of laundry and home cleaning products, personal care products, and adhesives. Its top three brands are Persil detergent, Schwarzkopf shampoo, and Loctite adhesive. Henkel's 2013 and 2014 statements of changes in equity are presented below.

Consolidated statement of changes in equity

In million euros	Issued capital					Other components of equity					
	Ordinary shares	Preferred shares	Capital reserve	Treasury shares	Retained earnings	Currency translation	Hedge reserve per IAS 39	Available-for-sale reserve	Shareholders of Henkel AG & Co. KGaA	Non-controlling interests	Total
At January 1, 2013	260	178	652	(91)	9,381	(806)	(199)	1	9,376	135	9,511
Net income	—	—	—	—	1,589	—	—	—	1,589	36	1,625
Other comprehensive income	—	—	—	—	95	(530)	17	1	(417)	(14)	(431)
Total comprehensive income for the period	—	—	—	—	1,684	(530)	17	1	1,172	22	1,194
Dividends	—	—	—	—	–407	—	—	—	(407)	(25)	(432)
Sale of treasury shares	—	—	—	—	—	—	—	—	—	—	—
Changes in ownership interest with no change in control	—	—	—	—	–95	—	—	—	(95)	(18)	(113)
Other changes in equity	—	—	—	—	–2	—	—	—	(2)	-	(2)
At December 31, 2013/January 1, 2014	260	178	652	(91)	10,561	(1,336)	(182)	2	10,044	114	10,158
Net income	—	—	—	—	1,628	—	—	—	1,628	34	1,662
Other comprehensive income	—	—	—	—	–266	613	15	1	363	14	377
Total comprehensive income for the period	—	—	—	—	1,362	613	15	1	1,991	48	2,039
Dividends	—	—	—	—	–525	—	—	—	(525)	(23)	(548)
Sale of treasury shares	—	—	—	—	—	—	—	—	—	—	—
Changes in ownership interest with no change in control	—	—	—	—	–2	—	—	—	(2)	(2)	(4)
Other changes in equity	—	—	—	—	—	—	—	—	—	(1)	(1)
At December 31, 2014	260	178	652	(91)	11,396	(723)	(167)	3	11,508	136	11,644

Required

a. Did Henkel issue any additional ordinary or preference shares in 2014?
b. What were Henkel's net income and total comprehensive income in 2014?
c. What are the major components in Henkel's other comprehensive income?
d. Why does the treasury shares account have a negative balance?
e. Did Henkel buy or sell any treasury shares in 2014?
f. How much in dividends did Henkel pay in 2014?

PROBLEMS

LO2, 6 **P11-55.** **Analysing and Identifying Financial Statement Effects of Share Transactions**

The equity section of Circular Quay Company at December 31, 2013, follows.

8% preference shares, $25 par value, 50,000 shares authorised; 6,800 shares issued and outstanding	$170,000
Ordinary shares, $10 par value, 200,000 shares authorised; 50,000 shares issued and outstanding	500,000
Contributed surplus—preference shares	68,000
Contributed surplus—ordinary shares	200,000
Retained earnings	270,000

During 2014, the following transactions occurred:

Jan. 10 Issued 28,000 ordinary shares for $17 cash per share.
Jan. 23 Purchased 8,000 ordinary shares for the treasury at $19 cash per share.
Mar. 14 Sold one-half of the treasury shares acquired January 23 for $21 cash per share.
July 15 Issued 3,200 preference shares for $128,000 cash.
Nov. 15 Sold 1,000 of the treasury shares acquired January 23 for $24 cash per share.

Required

a. Prepare the journal entries for these transactions.
b. Post the journal entries from *a* to the related T-accounts.

c. Using the financial statement effects template, illustrate the effects of each transaction.
d. Indicate the impact of each transaction on the calculation of basic EPS.
e. Prepare the December 31, 2014, equity section of the balance sheet assuming the company reports 2014 net income of $59,000.

P11-56. Analysing and Identifying Financial Statement Effects of Share Transactions LO2, 6

The equity of Shek O Company at December 31, 2013, follows.

7% preference shares, $100 par value, 20,000 shares authorised; 5,000 shares issued and outstanding	$ 500,000
Ordinary shares, $15 par value, 100,000 shares authorised; 40,000 shares issued and outstanding	600,000
Share premium—preference shares	24,000
Share premium—ordinary shares	360,000
Retained earnings	325,000
Total equity	$1,809,000

The following transactions, among others, occurred during 2014.

Jan. 12	Announced a 3-for-1 share split, reducing the par value of the ordinary shares to $5 per share. The authorised shares were increased to 300,000 shares.
Sept. 1	Acquired 10,000 ordinary shares for the treasury at $10 cash per share.
Oct. 12	Sold 1,500 treasury shares acquired September 1 at $12 cash per share.
Nov. 21	Issued 5,000 ordinary shares at $11 cash per share.
Dec. 28	Sold 1,200 treasury shares acquired September 1 at $9 cash per share.

Required

a. Prepare the journal entries for these transactions.
b. Post the journal entries from *a* to the related T-accounts.
c. Using the financial statement effects template, illustrate the effects of each transaction.
d. Indicate the impact of each transaction on the calculation of basic EPS.
e. Prepare the December 31, 2014, equity section of the balance sheet assuming that the company reports 2014 net income of $83,000.
f. Compute return on common equity for 2014.

P11-57. Identifying and Analysing Financial Statement Effects of Share Transactions LO2, 6

The equity of Bras Basah Company at December 31, 2013, follows.

Ordinary shares, $5 par value, 350,000 shares authorised; 150,000 shares issued and outstanding	$750,000
Contributed surplus	600,000
Retained earnings	346,000

During 2014, the following transactions occurred.

Jan. 5	Issued 10,000 ordinary shares for $12 cash per share.
Jan. 18	Purchased 4,000 ordinary shares for the treasury at $14 cash per share.
Mar 12	Sold one-fourth of the treasury shares acquired January 18 for $17 cash per share.
July 17	Sold 500 shares of the remaining treasury shares for $13 cash per share.
Oct. 1	Issued 5,000 shares of 8%, $25 par value preference shares for $35 cash per share. This is the first issuance of preference shares from 50,000 authorised shares.

Required

a. Prepare the journal entries for these transactions.
b. Post the journal entries from *a* to the related T-accounts.
c. Using the financial statement effects template, illustrate the effects of each transaction.
d. Prepare the December 31, 2014, equity section of the balance sheet assuming that the company reports net income of $72,500 for the year.
e. How will each transaction affect the calculation of basic EPS?

LO2, 4 P11-58. Identifying and Analysing Financial Statement Effects of Share Transactions
Following is the equity of Cockle Bay Corporation at December 31, 2013.

8% preference shares, $50 par value, 10,000 shares authorised; 7,000 shares issued and outstanding ...	$ 350,000
Ordinary shares, $20 par value, 50,000 shares authorised; 25,000 shares issued and outstanding.	500,000
Share premium—preference shares. ...	70,000
Share premium—ordinary shares. ...	385,000
Retained earnings ...	238,000
Total equity ...	$1,543,000

The following transactions, among others, occurred during 2014.

Jan. 15 Issued 1,000 preference shares for $62 cash per share.
Jan. 20 Issued 4,000 ordinary shares at $36 cash per share.
May 18 Announced a 2-for-1 ordinary shares split, reducing the par value of the ordinary shares to $10 per share. The authorisation was increased to 100,000 shares.
June 1 Issued 2,000 ordinary shares for $60,000 cash.
Sept. 1 Purchased 2,500 ordinary shares for the treasury at $18 cash per share.
Oct. 12 Sold 900 treasury shares at $21 cash per share.
Dec. 22 Issued 500 preference shares for $59 cash per share.

Required

a. Prepare the journal entries for these transactions.
b. Post the journal entries from *a* to the related T-accounts.
c. Using the financial statement effects template, illustrate the effects of each transaction.

LO2, 5 P11-59. Analysing and Interpreting the Statement of Changes in Equity

SINGAPORE AIRLINES LIMITED (SINGAPORE)

Singapore Airlines Limited is the flag carrier of Singapore. Following is the company's statement of changes in equity for the fiscal year ended March 31, 2013.

STATEMENTS OF CHANGES IN EQUITY

		Attributable to Owners of the Parent									
For The Financial Year Ended 31 March 2013 (in $ million)	Notes	Share capital	Treasury shares	Capital reserve	Foreign currency translation reserve	Share-based compensation reserve	Fair value reserve	General reserve	Total	Non-controlling interests	Total equity
Balance at April 1, 2012 ...		1,856.1	(258.4)	99.1	(186.3)	165.9	(47.6)	11,264.6	12,893.4	294.0	13,187.4
Comprehensive income											
Currency translation differences. ...	16(b)	—	—	—	(5.5)	—	—	—	(5.5)	(1.1)	(6.6)
Net fair value changes on available-for-sale assets ...	16(d)	—	—	—	—	—	4.2	—	4.2	—	4.2
Net fair value changes on cash flow hedges. ...		—	—	—	—	—	17.3	—	17.3	—	17.3
Surplus on dilution of interest in an associated company due to share options exercised ...		—	—	—	—	—	—	0.1	0.1	—	0.1
Share of other comprehensive income of associated and joint venture companies ...		—	—	12.5	—	—	(1.0)	—	11.5	0.2	11.7
Other comprehensive income for the financial year ...		—	—	12.5	(5.5)	—	20.5	0.1	27.6	(0.9)	26.7
Profit for the financial year ...		—	—	—	—	—	—	378.9	378.9	62.7	441.6
Total comprehensive income for the financial year, net of tax ...		—	—	12.5	(5.5)	—	20.5	379.0	406.5	61.8	468.3
Transactions with owners, recorded directly in equity											
Surplus on dilution of interest in subsidiary companies due to share options exercised ...		—	—	—	—	(6.8)	—	16.3	9.5	13.2	22.7
Share-based compensation expense. ...	5	—	—	—	—	5.4	—	—	5.4	—	5.4
Share options and share awards lapsed ...		—	—	—	—	(3.4)	—	3.4	—	—	—
Purchase of treasury shares. ...	15	—	(37.7)	—	—	—	—	—	(37.7)	—	(37.7)
Treasury shares reissued pursuant to equity compensation plans. ...	15	—	26.3	(1.3)	—	(9.4)	—	—	15.6	—	15.6
Dividends. ...	13	—	—	—	—	—	—	(188.0)	(188.0)	(56.4)	(244.4)
Total transactions with owners. ...		—	(11.4)	(1.3)	—	(14.2)	—	(168.3)	(195.2)	(43.2)	(238.4)
Balance at March 31, 2013. ...		1,856.1	(269.8)	110.3	(191.8)	151.7	(27.1)	11,475.3	13,104.7	312.6	13,417.3

Required

a. Did Singapore Airlines issue any new ordinary shares in 2013?
b. Did Singapore Airlines buy back any ordinary shares in 2013?
c. What were Singapore Airlines's net income, other comprehensive income, and comprehensive income in 2013? What is the difference between net income and comprehensive income?
d. As of March 1, 2013, the company has 1,199,851,018 ordinary shares outstanding. At what average price were these shares issued?

P11-60. Analysing and Interpreting Financial Statement Effects of Share Repurchase

LO5, 6

SINGAPORE AIRLINES LIMITED (SINGAPORE)

The following is note 15 from the fiscal 2013 annual report of **Singapore Airlines Limited**. The note provides information on the company's treasury share transactions during 2012 and 2013.

15 Treasury Shares (in $ million)

	The Group and the Company March 31	
	2013	**2012**
Balance at April 1	(258.4)	(43.0)
Purchase of treasury shares.	(37.7)	(272.1)
Treasury shares reissued pursuant to equity compensation plans:		
For cash on exercise of employee share options	15.6	32.2
Transferred from share-based compensation reserve.	9.4	13.9
Loss on reissuance of treasury shares.	1.3	10.6
	26.3	56.7
Balance at March 31	(269.8)	(258.4)

Treasury shares relate to ordinary shares of the Company that are held by the Company.

During the financial year, the Company purchased 3,655,000 (2011–12: 24,213,000) of its ordinary shares by way of on-market purchases at share prices ranging from $10.20 to $10.77 (2011–12: $10.16 to $14.23). The total amount paid to purchase the shares was $37.7 million (2011–12: $272.1 million) and this is presented as a component within equity attributable to owners of the Parent.

The Company reissued 1,712,015 (2011–12: 3,291,677) treasury shares pursuant to its employee share option plans at a weighted average exercise price of $9.14 (2012: $9.84) each. In addition, 471,915 (2011–12: 550,777) shares, 189,880 (2011–12: 292,230) shares and 5,295 (2011–12: 58,570) shares were reissued pursuant to the RSP, PSP and time-based RSP respectively. The number of treasury shares as at March 31, 2013 was 24,355,389 (2012: 23,079,494).

Where the consideration paid by the Company for the purchase or acquisition of treasury shares is made out of revenue reserves, such consideration will correspondingly reduce the amount available for the distribution of cash dividends by the Company.

Required

a. Calculate the average cost of the shares the company repurchased during fiscal 2013.
b. Calculate the average cost of the shares held as treasury shares at March 31, 2013.
c. Why did Singapore Airlines repurchase its own shares?
d. How are treasury shares treated in calculating earnings per share?
e. As pointed out by Singapore Airlines, what is the potential negative consequence of share repurchase?

CASES AND PROJECTS

C11-61. Interpreting Disclosure on Preferred Shares

LO1, 2

BOMBARDIER INC. (CANADA)

Bombardier Inc. is a Canadian Aerospace and transportation company, with headquarters in Montreal, Quebec. The company reports the following in footnote 29 to its 2013 financial report related to its preferred shares.

The preferred shares issued and fully paid were as follows, as at:

	December 31, 2013	December 31, 2012	January 1, 2012
Series 2 Cumulative Redeemable Preferred Shares	9,692,521	9,692,521[(1)]	9,464,920
Series 3 Cumulative Redeemable Preferred Shares	2,307,479	2,307,479[(1)]	2,535,080
Series 4 Cumulative Redeemable Preferred Shares	9,400,000	9,400,000	9,400,000

Series 4 Cumulative Redeemable Preferred Shares

Redemption: The Corporation may, subject to certain provisions, on not less than 30 nor more than 60 days' notice, redeem for cash the Series 4 Cumulative Redeemable Preferred Shares at $25.00 Cdn.

Conversion: The Corporation may, subject to the approval of the Toronto Stock Exchange and such other stock exchanges on which the Series 4 Cumulative Redeemable Preferred Shares are then listed, at any time convert all or any of the outstanding Series 4 Cumulative Redeemable Preferred Shares into fully paid and non-assessable Class B Shares (Subordinate Voting) of the Corporation. The number of Class B Shares (Subordinate Voting) into which each Series 4 Cumulative Redeemable Preferred Shares may be so converted will be determined by dividing the then applicable redemption price together with all accrued and unpaid dividends to, but excluding the date of conversion, by the greater of $2.00 Cdn and 95% of the weighted average trading price of such Class B Shares (Subordinate Voting) on the Toronto Stock Exchange for the period of 20 consecutive trading days, which ends on the fourth day prior to the date specified for conversion or, if that fourth day is not a trading day, on the trading day immediately preceding such fourth day. The Corporation may, at its option, at any time, create one or more further series of Preferred Shares of the Corporation, into which the holders of Series 4 Cumulative Redeemable Preferred Shares could have the right, but not the obligation, to convert their shares on a share-for-share basis.

Dividend: The holders of Series 4 Cumulative Redeemable Preferred Shares are entitled to fixed cumulative preferential cash dividends, if declared, at a rate of 6.25% or $1.5625 Cdn per share per annum, payable quarterly on the last day of January, April, July and October of each year at a rate of $0.390625 Cdn per share.

Required

a. Explain the cumulative feature of the Series 4 preferred shares.

b. Explain the redeemable feature of the Series 4 preferred shares.

c. Explain the conversion feature of the Series 4 preferred shares.

d. Explain how the conversion of these preferred shares would affect Bombardier's balance sheet.

e. How should preference shares be treated in an analysis of a company?

LO1, 2, 3 C11-62. **Identifying Corporate Takeover, Share Ownership, and Managerial Ethics**

Ron King, chairperson of the board of directors and chief executive officer of Image, Inc., is pondering a recommendation to make to the firm's board of directors in response to actions taken by Jack Hatcher. Hatcher recently informed King and other board members that he (Hatcher) had purchased 15% of the voting shares of Image at $12 per share and is considering an attempt to take control of the company. His effort to take control would include offering $16 per share to shareholders to induce them to sell shares to him. Hatcher also indicated that he would abandon his takeover plans if the company would buy back his shares at a price 50% over its current market price of $13 per share.

King views the proposed takeover by Hatcher as a hostile maneuver. Hatcher has a reputation of identifying companies that are undervalued (that is, their underlying net assets are worth more than the price of the outstanding share), buying enough shares to take control of such a company, replacing top management, and, on occasion, breaking up the company (that is, selling off the various divisions to the highest bidder). The process has proven profitable to Hatcher and his financial backers. Shareholders of the companies taken over also benefited because Hatcher paid them attractive prices to buy their shares.

King recognises that Image is currently undervalued by the market but believes that eventually the company will significantly improve its financial performance to the long-run benefit of its shareholders.

Required

What are the ethical issues that King should consider in arriving at a recommendation to make to the board of directors regarding Hatcher's offer to be "bought out" of his takeover plans?

LO1, 2, 3 C11-63. **Understanding Shareholders' Meeting, Managerial Communications, and Financial Interpretations**

The shareholders' equity section of Pillar Corporation's comparative balance sheet at the end of 2013 and 2014 is presented below. It is part of the financial data just reviewed at a shareholders' meeting.

	December 31, 2014	December 31, 2013
Ordinary shares, $10 par value, 600,000 shares authorised; issued at December 31, 2014, 275,000 shares; 2013, 250,000 shares.	$ 2,750,000	$2,500,000
Paid-in capital in excess of par	4,575,000	4,125,000
Retained Earnings (see Note)	2,960,000	2,825,000
Total shareholders' equity.	$10,285,000	$9,450,000

Note: Availability of retained earnings for cash dividends is restricted by $2,000,000 due to a planned plant expansion.

The following items were also disclosed at the shareholders' meeting: net income for 2014 was $1,220,000; a 10% share dividend was issued December 14, 2014; when the share dividend was declared, the market value was $28 per share; the market value per share at December 31, 2014, was $26; management plans to borrow $500,000 to help finance a new plant addition, which is expected to cost a total of $2,300,000; and the customary $1.54 per share cash dividend had been revised to $1.40 when declared and issued the last week of December 2014. As part of its investor relations program, during the shareholders' meeting management asked shareholders to write any questions they might have concerning the firm's operations or finances. As assistant controller, you are given the shareholders' questions.

Required

Prepare brief but reasonably complete answers to the following questions:

a. What did Pillar do with the cash proceeds from the share dividend issued in December?
b. What was my book value per share at the end of 2013 and 2014?
c. I owned 7,500 shares of Pillar in 2013 and have not sold any shares. How much more or less of the corporation do I own at December 31, 2014, and what happened to the market value of my interest in the company?
d. I heard someone say that share dividends don't give me anything I didn't already have. Why did you issue one? Are you trying to fool us?
e. Instead of a share dividend, why didn't you declare a cash dividend and let us buy the new shares that were issued?
f. Why are you cutting back on the dividends I receive?
g. If you have $2,000,000 put aside in retained earnings for the new plant addition, which will cost $2,300,000, why are you borrowing $500,000 instead of just the $300,000 needed?

C11-64. Assessing Share Buybacks, Corporate Accountability, and Managerial Ethics LO2, 3

Liz Plummer, vice president and general counsel, chairs the Executive Compensation Committee for Sunlight Corporation. Four and one-half years ago, the compensation committee designed a performance bonus plan for top management that was approved by the board of directors. The plan provides an attractive bonus for top management if the firm's earnings per share grows each year over a five-year period. The plan is now in its fifth year; for the past four years, earnings per share has grown each year. Last year, earnings per share was $1.95 (net income was $7,800,000 and the weighted average common shares outstanding was 4,000,000). Sunlight Corporation has no preference shares and has had 4,000,000 common shares outstanding for several years. Plummer has recently seen an estimate that Sunlight's net income this year will decrease about 5% from last year because of a slight recession in the economy.

Plummer is disturbed by an item on the agenda for the board of directors meeting on June 20 and an accompanying note from Rob Lundy. Lundy is vice president and chief financial officer for Sunlight. Lundy is proposing to the board that Sunlight buy back 600,000 shares of its own ordinary shares on July 1. Lundy's explanation is that the firm's share is undervalued now and that Sunlight has excess cash available. When the share subsequently recovers in value, Lundy notes, Sunlight will reissue the shares and generate a nice increase in contributed capital.

Lundy's note to Plummer merely states, "Look forward to your support of my proposal at the board meeting."

Required

Why is Plummer disturbed by Lundy's proposal and note? What possible ethical problem does Plummer face when Lundy's proposal is up for a vote at the board meeting?

SOLUTIONS TO REVIEW PROBLEMS

Mid-Chapter Review 1

Solution

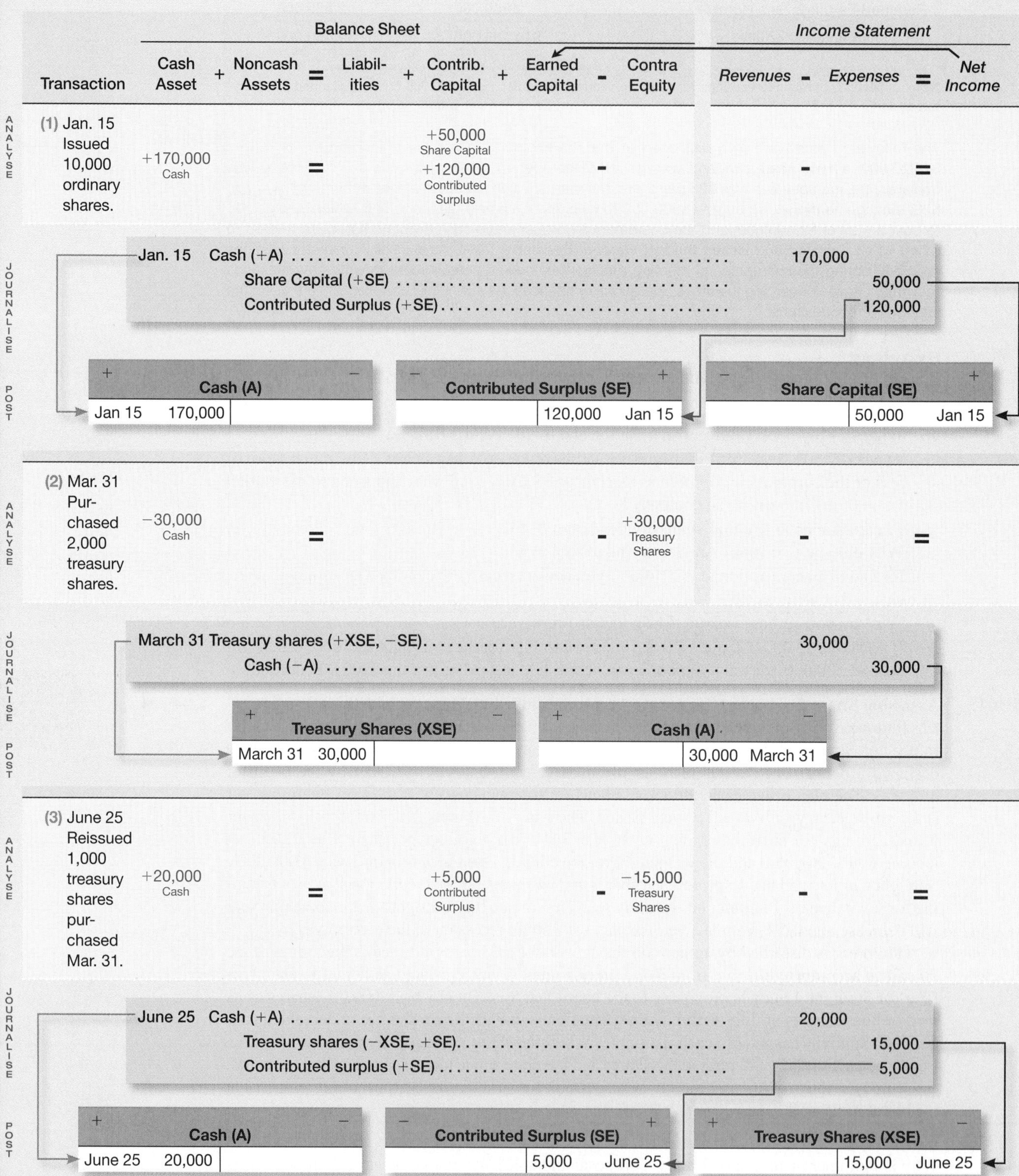

Mid-Chapter Review 2

Solution

a.

	Preference Shares	Ordinary Shares
Year 1	$ 0	$ 0
Year 2		
Arrearage from Year 1 ($1,000,000 × 5%)	50,000	
Current-year dividend ($1,000,000 × 5%)	50,000	
Balance to ordinary		200,000
Year 3		
Current-year dividend ($1,000,000 × 5%)	50,000	
Balance to ordinary		30,000

b.

	Preference Shares	Ordinary Shares
Year 1	$ 0	$ 0
Year 2		
Current-year dividend ($1,000,000 × 5%)	50,000	
Balance to ordinary		250,000
Year 3		
Current-year dividend ($1,000,000 × 5%)	50,000	
Balance to ordinary		30,000

Mid-Chapter Review 3

Solution

	Balance Sheet									Income Statement				
Transaction	Cash Asset	+	Noncash Assets	=	Liabil-ities	+	Contrib. Capital	+	Earned Capital	Revenues	-	Expenses	=	Net Income
(1) Apr. 1 Declared a 100% share dividend (valued at par value).				=			+250,000 Share Capital		−250,000[1] Retained Earnings		-		=	

ANALYSE JOURNALISE POST

(1) April 1	Retained earnings (−SE)	250,000	
	Share capital (+SE)		250,000

− Retained Earnings (SE) +	
April 1 250,000	

− Share Capital (SE) +	
	250,000 April 1

1 This share dividend reduces retained earnings at the par value of shares distributed (50,000 shares × 100% × $5 par value = $250,000). Contributed capital increases by the same amount ($250,000 to share capital).

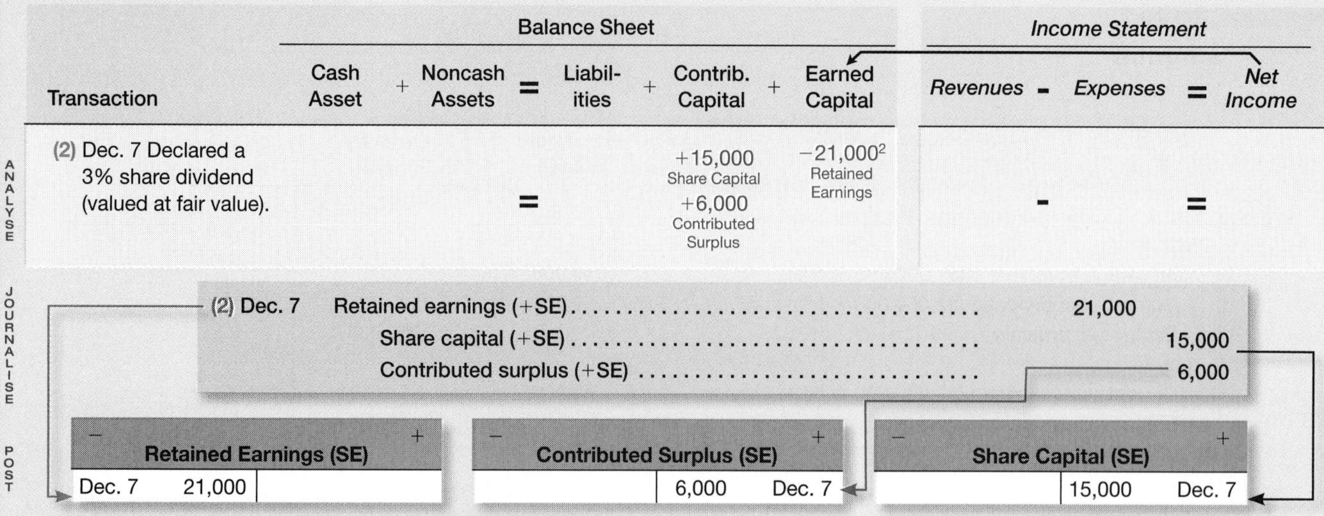

Balance Sheet
Income Statement
Transaction
Cash Asset + Noncash Assets = Liabilities + Contrib. Capital + Earned Capital
Revenues - Expenses = Net Income
ANALYSE
(2) Dec. 7 Declared a 3% share dividend (valued at fair value).
+15,000 Share Capital
+6,000 Contributed Surplus
−21,000[2] Retained Earnings
JOURNALISE
(2) Dec. 7 Retained earnings (+SE) 21,000
Share capital (+SE) 15,000
Contributed surplus (+SE) 6,000
POST
Retained Earnings (SE)
Dec. 7 21,000
Contributed Surplus (SE)
6,000 Dec. 7
Share Capital (SE)
15,000 Dec. 7

2 This small share dividend reduces retained earnings at the market value of shares distributed (3% × 100,000 shares × $7 per share = $21,000). Contributed capital increases by the same amount ($15,000 to share capital and $6,000 to contributed surplus).

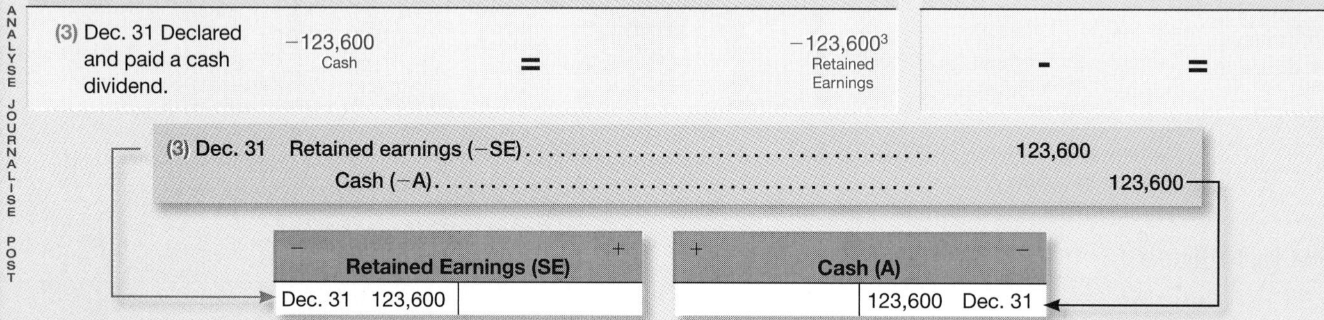

3 At the time of the cash dividend, there are 103,000 shares outstanding. The cash paid is, therefore, 103,000 shares × $1.20 per share = $123,600.

Mid-Chapter Review 4

Solution

Retained Earnings Reconciliation
For Year Ended December 31, 2015

Retained earnings, December 31, 2014		€513,000
Add: Net income		412,000
		925,000
Less: Cash dividends declared [160,000 + .10(160,000)][€1.25]	€220,000	
Share dividends declared (160,000)(.10)(€11)	176,000	396,000
Retained earnings, December 31, 2015		€529,000

Chapter-End Review

Solution

1. Basic EPS would be calculated as follows (millions, except per share amount):

$$\text{Basic EPS} = \frac{£1{,}750 - £40}{760 \text{ shares}} = £2.25 \text{ per share}$$

2. Diluted EPS is calculated as follows (millions, except per share amounts):

$$\text{Diluted EPS} = \frac{£1{,}750}{770 \text{ shares}} = £2.27 \text{ per share}$$

3. Heathrow would only report basic EPS on its income statement. Diluted EPS, as calculated in requirement 2, is actually higher than basic EPS because the convertible preference shares are anti-dilutive. IFRS requires that reported diluted EPS must be lower than basic EPS. Consequently, Heathrow would not report the diluted EPS number.

Appendix 11A Review

Solution

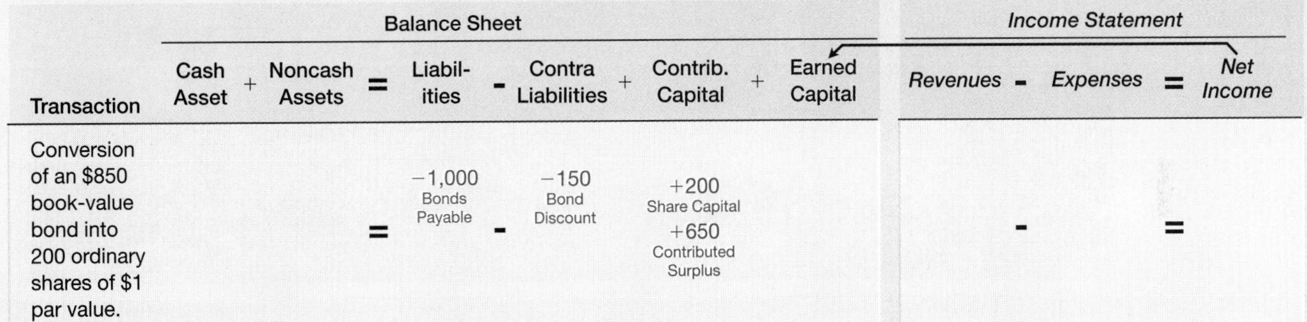

	Transaction	Cash Asset	+	Noncash Assets	=	Liabilities	-	Contra Liabilities	+	Contrib. Capital	+	Earned Capital	Revenues	-	Expenses	=	Net Income
ANALYSE	Conversion of an $850 book-value bond into 200 ordinary shares of $1 par value.				=	−1,000 Bonds Payable	-	−150 Bond Discount		+200 Share Capital +650 Contributed Surplus				-		=	

Balance Sheet: Cash Asset through Earned Capital. *Income Statement*: Revenues through Net Income.

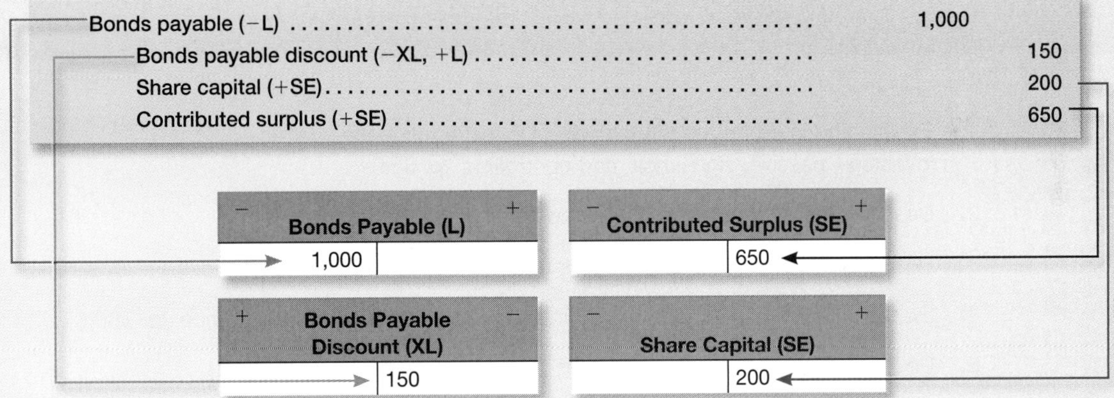

JOURNALISE

	Dr.	Cr.
Bonds payable (−L)	1,000	
Bonds payable discount (−XL, +L)		150
Share capital (+SE)		200
Contributed surplus (+SE)		650

POST

LEARNING OBJECTIVES

1. Explain and interpret the three levels of investor influence over an investee—passive, significant, and controlling. (p. 554)
2. Describe the term "fair value" and the fair value hierarchy. (p. 556)
3. Describe and analyse accounting for passive investments. (p. 557)
4. Explain and analyse accounting for investments with significant influence. (p. 566)
5. Describe and analyse accounting for investments with control. (p. 571)
6. Appendix 12A: Illustrate and analyse accounting mechanics for equity method investments. (p. 583)
7. Appendix 12B: Apply consolidation accounting mechanics. (p. 584)
8. Appendix 12C: Discuss the reporting of derivative securities. (p. 586)

CHAPTER

Reporting and Analysing Financial Investments

12

SMRT Corporation Ltd (SMRT) and its subsidiaries are a public transport operator in Singapore. The company operates the Mass Rapid Transit (MRT) and Light Rail Transit (LRT) systems, as well as a fleet of over 1,200 buses and 3,300 taxis. Moreover, SMRT manages about 36,800 square meters of commercial space around its train stations and leases advertising space within its transport network. Finally, it also offers engineering, maintenance, and project management services in Singapore and abroad.

SMRT Corporation Ltd
www.smrt.com.sg

SMRT faces competition at home from **ComfortDelGro Corporation**, Singapore's largest multimodal public transport company, and other licenced taxi and car service companies. It also competes overseas with ComfortDelGro and **MTR Corporation**, a Hong Kong-based rail and property development company, as all three companies expand their transport and property development businesses to other countries, including Australia, China, Indonesia, Sweden, and the United Kingdom.

SMRT Revenue by ($ millions) Business Segments, fiscal year 2014

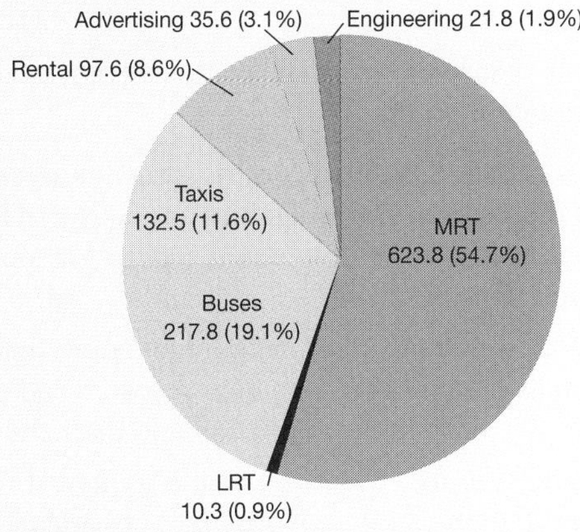

The ordinary shares of SMRT have been publicly traded on Singapore Exchange since July 2000 (ticker: S53). As of January 31, 2014, **Temasek Holdings Private Ltd**, an investment company owned by the Singapore government, was SMRT's largest shareholder, with a 54.2% ownership. While SMRT reports under the Singapore Financial Reporting Standards (SFRS), the Singapore Accounting Standards Council has adopted substantially all IFRSs into the SFRS.

(continued on next page)

(continued from previous page)

SMRT started in 1987, when the predecessor of SMRT Trains Ltd was formed to operate the new MRT system. Similarly, SMRT Light Rail Pte Ltd was established in 1997 to manage the LRT system that came on line in 1999. SMRT Trains and SMRT Light Rail became wholly owned subsidiaries of SMRT, when it was incorporated in March 2000. In 2001, SMRT acquired a licensed bus and taxi company in Singapore to create two wholly owned subsidiaries: SMRT Buses Ltd and SMRT Taxis Pte Ltd. In 2008, SMRT acquired a 49% equity stake in Shenzhen Zona Transportation Group, making the Chinese transport company an associate of SMRT. In 2012, SMRT and Alphaplus Investments Ltd formed SMRT Alpha Pte Ltd to operate the mall at the Singapore Sports Hub. With a 70% equity interest in the joint venture, SMRT has control over SMRT Alpha. At the end of fiscal 2014, SMRT had a total of 17 wholly owned subsidiaries, one non-wholly owned subsidiary (SMRT Alpha), and an associate (Shenzhen Zona). Besides its investments in these companies, SMRT also has invested in other equity and debt securities, but it has little influence or control over these investee companies.

As we discuss in this chapter, the accounting method used to report investments depends on the investor company's purpose in making the investment and on the degree of influence or control that the investor company can exert over the investee company. One consequence of these accounting methods is that small changes in the amount invested can produce significant changes in the investor's financial statements.

Sources: www.smrt.com.sg; SMRT Corporation Ltd 2014 Annual Report.

CHAPTER ORGANISATION

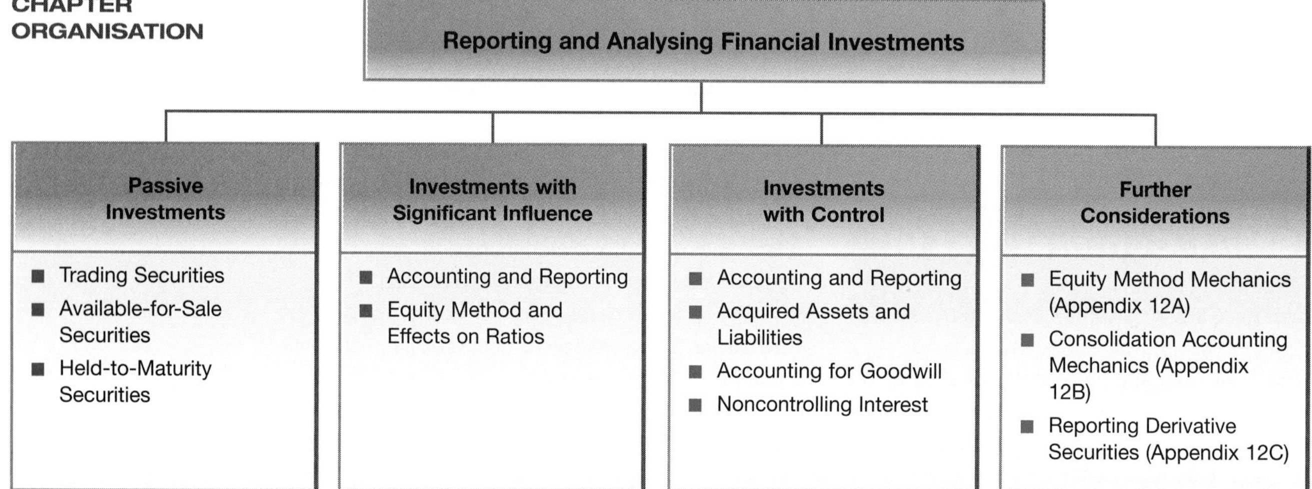

INTRODUCTION

LO1 Explain and interpret the three levels of investor influence over an investee—passive, significant, and controlling.

Most companies invest in government securities or the securities of other companies. These investments often have the following strategic goals:

- **Short-term investment of excess cash.** Companies often generate excess cash for investment either during slow times of the year (after receivables are collected and before seasonal production begins) or for liquidity needs (such as to counter strategic moves by competitors or to quickly respond to acquisition opportunities).
- **Alliances for strategic purposes.** Companies often acquire an equity interest in other companies for strategic purposes, such as gaining access to their research and development activities, to supply or distribution markets, or to their production and marketing expertise.
- **Market penetration or expansion.** Acquisitions of controlling interests in other companies can achieve vertical or horizontal integration in existing markets or can be avenues to penetrate new and growing markets.

Investments in government securities and in the securities of other companies are usually referred to as **financial investments**. Firms make these investments for different purposes, so accounting for the investments can follow one of five different methods, each of which affects the balance sheet and the income statement differently. To help assimilate the materials in this chapter, Exhibit 12.1 provides a graphical depiction of accounting for financial investments as we will explore it.

EXHIBIT 12.1 Financial Investment Diagram

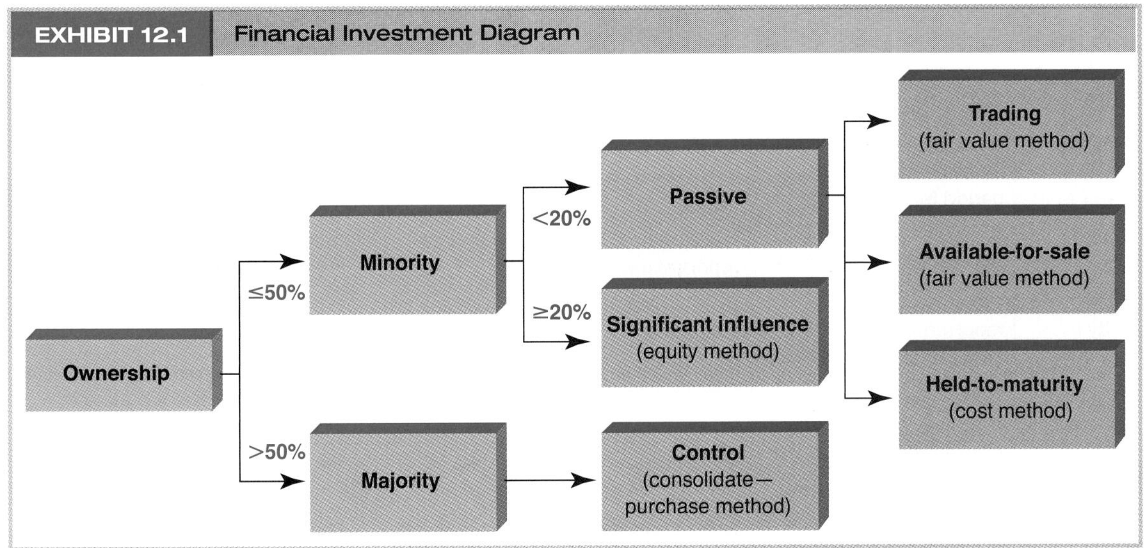

The degree of influence or control that the investor company (purchaser) can exert over the investee organisation (the company or government whose securities are being purchased) determines the accounting method. IFRS identifies three levels of influence/control:

1. **Passive influence**. In this case, the purchasing company is merely an investor and cannot exert influence over the investee organisation. The purchaser's goal for this investment is to realise dividends and capital gains. Generally, passive investor status is presumed if the investor company owns less than 20% of the outstanding voting shares of the investee. Investments in debt securities, such as bonds or notes of other organisations, are also classified as passive investments.

2. **Significant influence**. An investor company can sometimes exert significant influence over, but not control, the activities of an investee company. This level of influence can result from the percentage of voting shares owned. It also can result from legal agreements, such as a license to use technology, a formula, or a trade secret like production know-how. It also can occur when the investor company is the sole supplier or customer of the investee. Generally, significant influence is presumed if the investor company owns 20% to 50% of the voting shares of the investee.

3. **Controlling influence**. When a company has control over another, it has the ability to elect a majority of the board of directors and, as a result, the ability to determine its strategic direction and hiring of executive management. Control is generally presumed if the investor company owns more than 50% of the outstanding voting shares of the investee company. Control can sometimes occur at less than 50% share ownership by virtue of legal agreements, technology licensing, or other contractual means.

Once the level of influence/control is determined, the appropriate accounting method is applied as outlined in Exhibit 12.2.

There are two basic reporting issues with investments: (1) how investment income should be recognised and (2) at what amount (cost or fair value) the investment should be reported on the balance sheet. We next discuss both of these issues under each of the three investment types.

EXHIBIT 12.2 Investment Type, Accounting Treatment, and Financial Statement Effects

	Accounting	Balance Sheet Effects	Income Statement Effects	Cash Flow Effects
Passive	Trading	Investment balance reported as end-of-period fair value	Dividend payments from investee are included in income Capital gain/loss recognised in the period in which it occurs	Purchase/sale of investee yields investing cash flows Dividend payments received from investee are operating or investing cash inflows
	Available-for-Sale	Investment balance reported as end-of-period fair value	Dividend payments from investee are included in income Capital gain/loss recognised when investment sold; interim gain/loss reported as AOCI*	Purchase/sale of investee yields investing cash flows Dividend payments received from investee are operating or investing cash inflows
	Held-to-Maturity	Investment balance reported at acquisition cost (net of amortisation)	Dividend payments from investee are included in income Capital gain/loss recognised when investment sold	Purchase/sale of investee yields investing cash flows Dividend payments received from investee are operating or investing cash inflows
Significant Influence	Equity Method	Investment balance reflects purchase price and subsequent changes in proportion owned of investee's equity	Investor reports income equal to percent owned of investee income Sale of investee yields gains/losses	Purchase/sale of investee yields investing cash flows Dividend payments received from investee are operating or investing cash inflows
Control	Consolidation	Balance sheets of investor and investee are presented as if one entity	Income statements of investor and investee are presented as if one entity Sale of investee yields gains/losses	Purchase/sale of investee yields investing cash flows Cash flows of investor and investee are presented as if one entity

*AOCI is defined on page 517 and discussed further in the following pages.

FAIR VALUE: AN INTRODUCTION

LO2 Describe the term "fair value" and the fair value hierarchy.

The term **fair value** is finding increasing use in the language of accounting, but it is particularly prevalent in the accounting for financial investments. When an investor purchases a security for $100, the relevance of that acquisition cost fades rather quickly. If the investor considers selling the security a year later, the original $100 cost is much less meaningful than the current price for the security in the markets. Or, if we were to look at the balance sheet of a company, it would be useful to know how much its investments are worth today, rather than what was paid for them at various points in the past.

When accounting requires the use of fair value, IFRS defines fair value as the amount that an independent buyer would be willing to pay for an asset (or the amount that would need to be paid to discharge a liability) in an orderly transaction. For an asset that is actively traded on financial markets, fair value is the amount that we would receive by selling that asset at the balance sheet date. But fair value is also used when there is no active market for the asset. When SMRT accounts for its acquisition of another company, it must report the fair value of the patent portfolio that it obtained in that transaction. In such cases, fair value is not "mark-to-market," but rather "mark-to-model." For instance, fair value might be determined by a discounted cash flow analysis as in Chapter 9. IFRS allows various methods to be used in determining the "most representative" fair value at the appropriate date.

While fair values are often deemed to be more relevant than historical cost, they are also viewed as more subjective—particularly when fair value is determined by reference to a model rather than a liquid market. For this reason, IFRS requires that firms disclose the methods used to determine fair value for their assets using a **fair value hierarchy**.

Level 1: Values based on quoted prices in active markets for identical assets/liabilities. An example would be an ordinary share of a company traded on an active exchange.

Level 2: Values based on observable inputs other than Level 1 (e.g., quoted prices for similar assets/liabilities or interest rates or yield curves). An example would be a bond that is infrequently traded, but that is similar to bonds that are actively traded.

Level 3: Values based on inputs observable only to the reporting entity (e.g., management estimates or assumptions). An example would be an operating asset that is judged to be impaired.

SMRT's use of fair value to report its investments is presented in the coming pages. The purpose of the classification is to provide an assessment of the subjectivity that underlies the numbers in the balance sheet (and sometimes, the income statement), with Level 1 being the most reliable and Level 3 being the most subjective.

In addition, companies have a **fair value option** that provides them with the *option* of using fair value to measure the value of most financial assets and liabilities. This option extends the use of fair value to a wide range of financial assets and liabilities, including accounts and notes receivable, accounts and notes payable, and bonds payable. This standard is optional, however, and thus far its application has been limited mostly to financial institutions such as banks and insurance companies.[1]

PASSIVE INVESTMENTS

LO3 Describe and analyse accounting for passive investments.

The term "passive" refers to the investor's role in trying to influence the operations of the investee organisation. So, short-term investments of excess cash are typically passive investments, usually in liquid securities. In addition, investors seeking trading profits from short-term capital gains would be considered passive investors, even though their trading style may be active. Passive investments can involve either equity or debt securities. Debt securities have no ownership interest, so they are always passive. Equity investments are passive when the ownership level is not sufficient to influence or control the investee. Passive investments can be broadly grouped into two categories: those reported at cost and those reported at fair value. Furthermore, there are two methods for reporting investments at fair value. These alternative treatments are discussed below.

Acquisition and Sale

When an investment is acquired, regardless of the amount of shares purchased or the percentage of outstanding shares acquired, the investment is initially recorded on the balance sheet at its fair value, that is, its price on the date of purchase. This accounting is the same as that for the acquisition of other assets such as inventories or plant assets. Subsequent to acquisition, investments are carried on the balance sheet as current or noncurrent assets, depending on management's expectations about their ultimate holding period (the assets are reported as current assets if management expects to dispose of them within one year).

When investments are sold, any recognised gain or loss on sale usually is equal to the difference between the proceeds received and the book (carrying) value of the investment on the balance sheet. However, there is one passive investment method where that is not true.

To illustrate the simplest acquisition and sale of a passive investment, assume that QEW Company purchases an investment in King Company consisting of 1,000 shares for $20 cash per share (the acquisition price includes transaction costs such as brokerage fees). Later in the same reporting period, QEW sells 400 of the 1,000 shares for $30 cash per share. The financial statement effects of these transactions and their related entries for QEW follow:

[1] Other assets that *must* be reported at fair value include (1) derivative securities, such as options, futures and forward contracts, that are purchased to hedge price, interest rate, or foreign exchange rate fluctuations, (2) long-term assets that are impaired, and (3) inventories that have been written down to fair value based on the lower-of-cost-or-market rule. In addition, IFRS provides companies with the *option* of using fair value to measure the value of most financial assets and liabilities, as well as the revaluation model for reporting the value of noncurrent operating assets (discussed in Chapter 8).

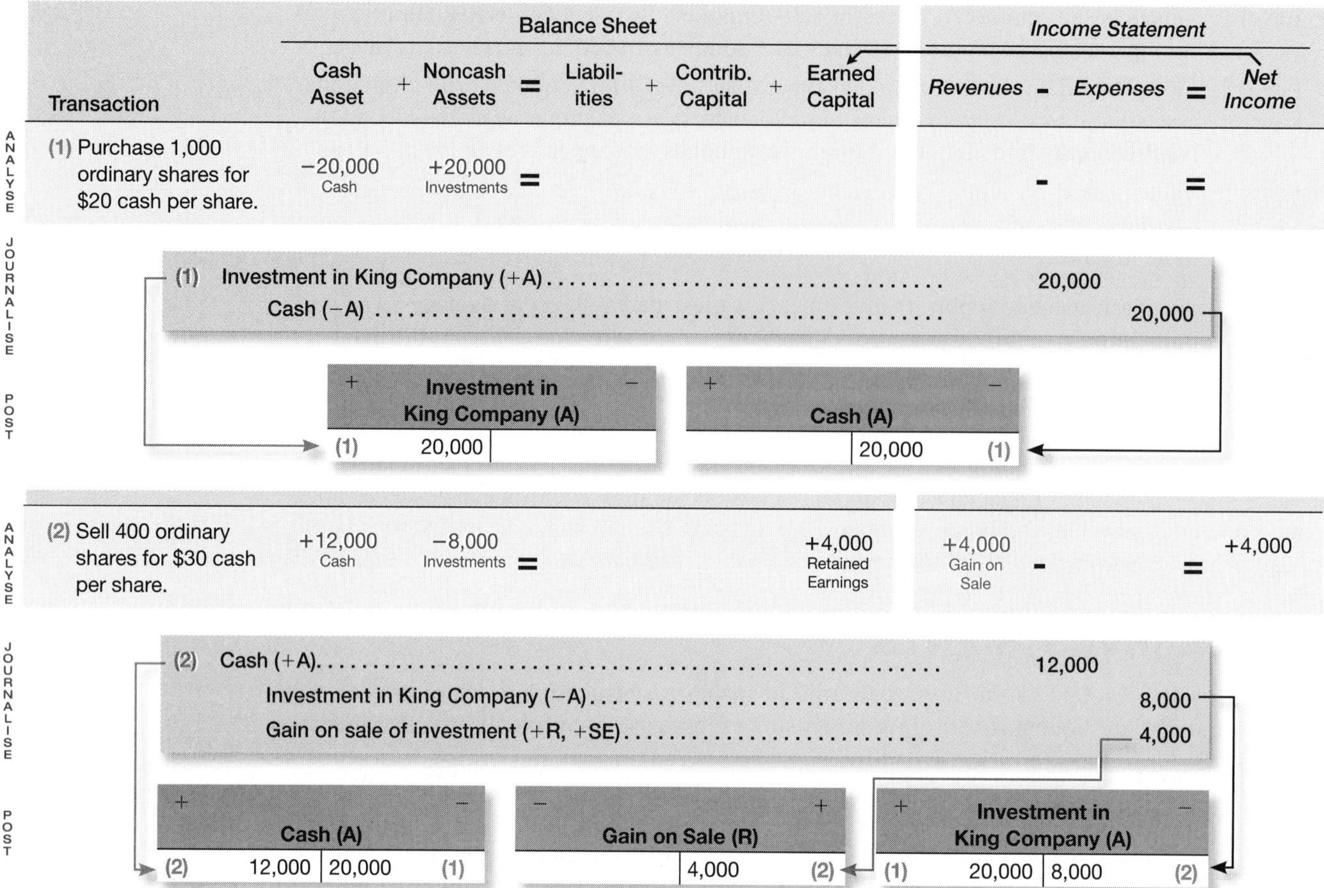

The gain or loss on sale is reported as a component of *other income,* which is commonly commingled with interest and dividend revenue in the income statement.

On the statement of cash flows, the $20,000 purchase (transaction 1) would be an investing cash outflow, and the $12,000 proceeds (transaction 2) would be an investing cash inflow. If QEW Company presents its cash flows from operating activities using the indirect method, we would see a subtraction of the $4,000 gain on sale among the adjustments from net income to cash from operations.

Accounting for the purchase and sale of investments is similar to any other asset. There is no difference in accounting for purchases and sales across the different types of passive investments when those purchases and sales occur in the same reporting period.

However, as QEW Company reaches the end of its fiscal reporting period (a quarter- or year-end), we can see that there are different ways in which we might determine the balance sheet value of the 600 shares of King Company that QEW Company still owns. And, that balance sheet value will be the asset's book value going forward, affecting gains and losses now and when the shares are ultimately sold.

Investments Marked to Fair Value

FYI Investments in both equity and debt securities are classified as fair value through profit or loss (FVTPL) if they are held for trading, or if they are designated by management under the fair value option.

The following two classifications of marketable securities require the investment to be reported on the balance sheet at current fair value:

1. **Trading (T) securities.** These are investments in securities that management intends to actively buy and sell for trading profits as market prices fluctuate.
2. **Available-for-sale (AFS) securities.** These are investments in securities that management intends to hold for capital gains and dividend revenue; although it may sell them if the price is right or if the organisation needs cash.

Investments in both equity and debt securities qualify for these classifications. Management's assignment of securities between these two classifications depends on the degree of turnover (transaction volume) it expects in the investment portfolio, which reflects its intent to actively trade the securities or not. Available-for-sale portfolios exhibit less turnover than do trading portfolios. Once that classification is established, reporting for a portfolio follows procedures detailed in Exhibit 12.3.

EXHIBIT 12.3 Accounting Treatment for Trading and Available-for-Sale Investments

Investment Classification	Reporting of Fair Value Changes	Reporting Gains and Losses on Sale	Reporting Dividends Received
Trading (T)	Balance sheet values are updated to reflect fair value changes; unrealised gains and losses are reported as investment income; affects equity via retained earnings	Gain or loss on sale equals proceeds minus the most recent book (fair) value	Reported as investment income in income statement
Available-for-Sale (AFS)	Balance sheet values are updated to reflect fair value changes; unrealised gains and losses bypass the income statement and are reported directly in accumulated other comprehensive income (AOCI), a component of equity; these changes are reported in the statement of changes in equity	Gain or loss on sale equals proceeds minus the original acquisition cost of the investment; any unrealised gains or losses in accumulated other comprehensive income must be eliminated	Reported as investment income in income statement

FYI IFRS permits companies to have multiple portfolios, each with a different classification. Management can change portfolio classification provided it adheres to strict disclosure and reporting requirements if its expectations of turnover change.

Both trading (T) and available-for-sale (AFS) investments are reported at fair values on the statement date. Whether the change in fair value affects current income depends on the investment classification: available-for-sale securities have no immediate income effect; trading securities have an income effect. The impact on equity is similar for both classifications, with the only difference being whether the change is reflected in retained earnings or in accumulated other comprehensive income (AOCI) in equity. Dividends and any gains or losses on security sales are reported in the investment income section of the income statement for both classifications.

FYI When trading securities are marked-to-fair value, the unrealised gain is recorded as income and reported in the income statement. For available-for-sale investments, unrealised gains are reported as other comprehensive income.

Fair Value Adjustments To illustrate the accounting for changes in fair value subsequent to purchase (and before sale), assume that QEW's investment in King Co. (600 remaining shares purchased for $20 per share) could be sold for $25 per share at year-end. The investment must be marked to fair value in an adjusting entry to reflect the $3,000 unrealised gain ($5 per share increase for 600 shares).

If the investment is classified as trading securities (T) the entry would be:

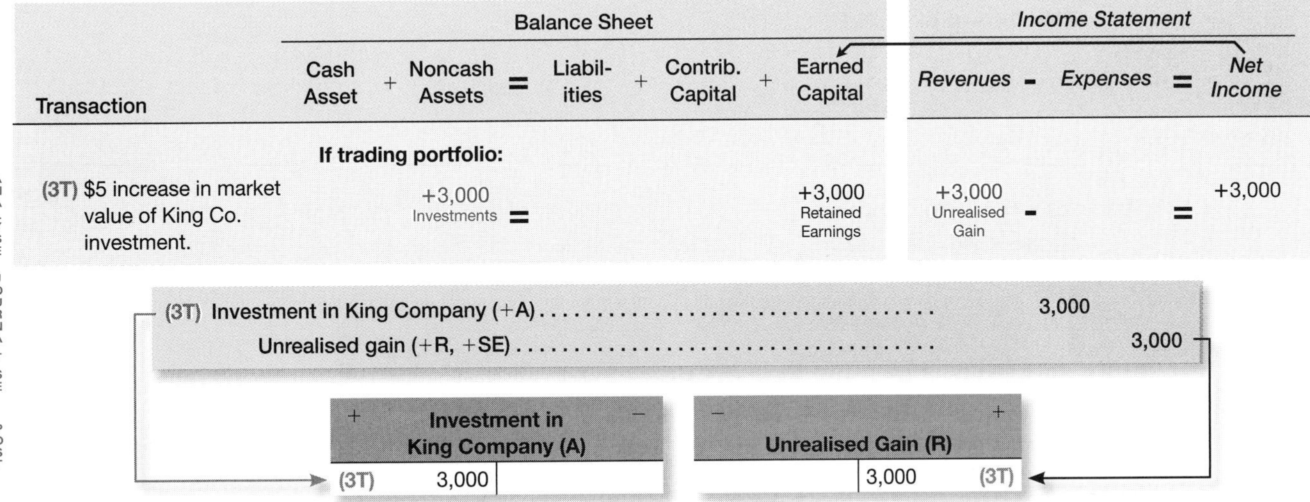

The investment account is increased by $3,000, making the end-of-year book value of QEW's investment equal to $15,000, its fair value. Total investment income reported on QEW's income statement would be $7,000, consisting of $4,000 in realised holding gains and $3,000 in unrealised holding gains. If QEW is actively trading to achieve capital gains, then this approach seems like the correct way to keep track of its trading performance.

This entry to adjust the balance sheet to reflect the fair value of the securities is an adjusting entry. It would need to be made at the end of every fiscal period as financial reports are being prepared.

What happens when the securities are subsequently sold? Assume that QEW Company sells its 600 shares of King Company for $23 per share shortly after the end of the last reporting period. QEW receives $13,800 in cash, and it no longer owns the shares of King Company. When the trading method is used, the accounting for the sale of shares is relatively simple:

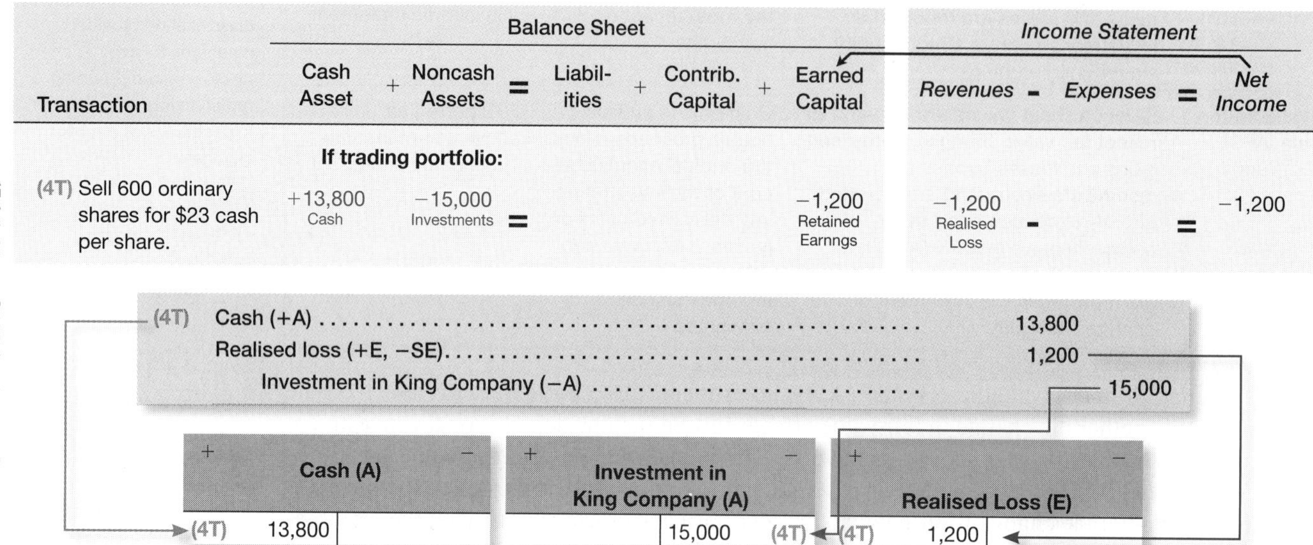

Under the trading securities method, holding gains and losses (both realised and unrealised) are recognised in income in the period in which they occur. Holding these 600 shares caused a gain of $3,000 in the prior period and a loss of $1,200 in the current period. Again, if QEW Company is actively seeking capital gains, we would say that they were not as successful in the current period as they had been in the previous period.

If QEW Company had classified its investment in King Company as available-for-sale (AFS) securities, the end-of-year adjusting entry would be the following:

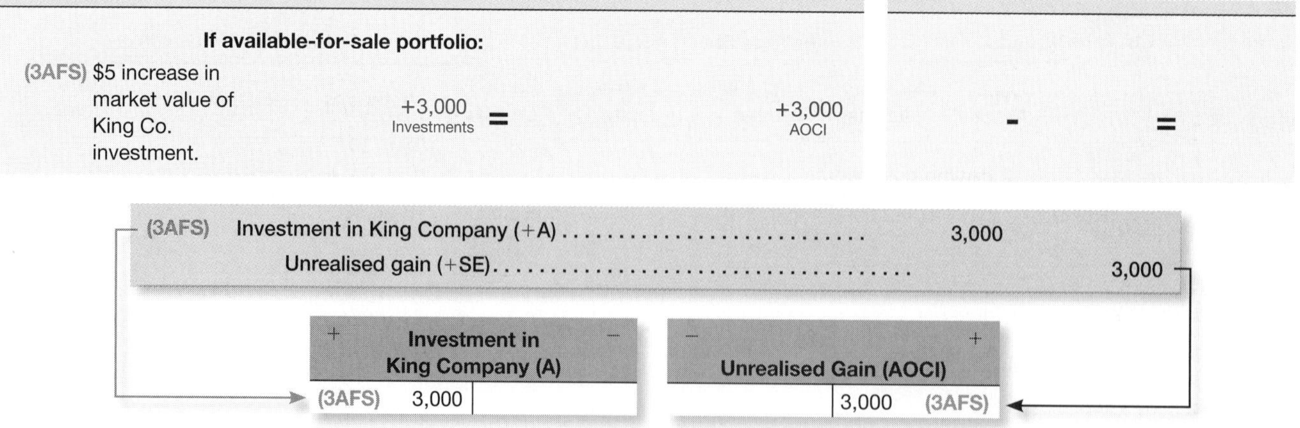

As under the trading method, the investment account is increased by $3,000 to reflect the increase in fair value of the shares owned. However, when accounted for as an AFS security, the unrealised gain (or loss) is reflected as an increase in accumulated other comprehensive income (AOCI), a separate component of equity. Therefore, the increase in the investment does not result in an immediate income statement effect. Under AFS, QEW Company's investment income for this period would reflect only the $4,000 realised gain from the sale of 400 shares. The $3,000 unrealised gain is reflected in equity, but not reported on the income statement. In a sense, the balance sheet has been updated to reflect the current values, but the income statement has been left out of the picture for the time being.

When QEW Company sells the 600 shares for $13,800 in the subsequent period, the entry under AFS would be the following:

Transaction	Cash Asset	+	Noncash Assets	=	Liabil-ities	+	Contrib. Capital	+	Earned Capital	Revenues	-	Expenses	=	Net Income
If available-for-sale portfolio:														
(4AFS) Sell 600 ordinary shares for $23 cash per share.	+13,800 Cash		−15,000 Investments	=					−3,000 AOCI +1,800 Retained Earnings	+1,800 Realised Gain	-		=	+1,800

ANALYSE

JOURNALISE

	Dr.	Cr.
(4AFS) Cash (+A)	13,800	
Accumulated other comprehensive income—AOCI (−SE)	3,000	
Investment in King Company (−A)		15,000
Realised gain (+R, +SE)		1,800

POST

+ Cash (A) −		+ Investment in King Company (A) −		− AOCI (SE) +		− Realised Gain (R) +	
(4AFS) 13,800			15,000 (4AFS)	(4AFS) 3,000			1,800 (4AFS)

Under AFS, the realised gain (loss) goes into income when the security is sold, and the amount is determined by comparing the amount received when the shares are sold ($23 per share) to the amount paid for the shares when originally purchased ($20 per share). When the investment is sold, the entry must delete the investment (which was valued at $25 per share at the end of last period) *and* the unrealised holding gain ($5 per share) that was put into accumulated other comprehensive income when those shares were revalued. Both the Investment in King Company account and the AOCI for King Company have zero balances after this transaction.

The principal difference between trading and available-for-sale accounting is in the income statement. Under the trading security method, QEW Company records income of $7,000 in the first period and a loss of $1,200 in the second period. Under available-for-sale, QEW Company records income of $4,000 in the first period and income of $1,800 in the second period. The total income from the investment in King Company is the same ($5,800 = $7,000 − $1,200 = $4,000 + $1,800), but the timing is different. These differences are summarised in the following table:

	Income reported in income statement from investment in 1,000 shares at a cost of $20 per share	
	Trading	**Available-for-sale**
Period 1:		
Sell 400 shares at $30 per share	$4,000	$4,000
Adjust remaining 600 shares to fair value of $25 per share	3,000	—
Total period 1 income	$7,000	$4,000
Period 2:		
Sell 600 shares at $23 per share	($1,200)	$1,800
Total period 2 income (loss)	($1,200)	$1,800
Total income – period 1 plus period 2	$5,800	$5,800

Because of the difference in the way unrealised gains and losses are reported, the classification of investments as either trading or available-for-sale will have an effect on key ratios that might be used to evaluate the performance of a company. Ratios that use net income in the calculation are affected. Return on equity (ROE), return on assets (ROA) and profit margin (PM) are among the ratios affected. Return on net operating assets (RNOA), which is discussed in Appendix A at the end of Chapter 5, would not be affected by this classification because passive investments would be considered nonoperating assets and excluded from the calculation of net operating assets and the gains and losses would be excluded from net operating profit after taxes (NOPAT).

Investments Reported at Cost

Investments for which no current fair values exist must be accounted for using the cost method. Under the **cost method**, the investment is continually reported at its historical cost, and any cash dividends and interest received are recognised in current income.

Debt securities that management intends to hold to maturity are also reported using the cost method (adjusted for amortisation). These debt securities are classified as **held-to-maturity (HTM)**. Exhibit 12.4 identifies the reporting of these securities.

EXHIBIT 12.4 Accounting Treatment for Held-to-Maturity Investments

Investment Classification	Reporting of Fair Value Changes	Reporting Interest Received and Gains and Losses on Sale
Held-to-Maturity (HTM)	Fair value changes are not reported in either the balance sheet or income statement	Reported as finance income in income statement

Fluctuations in fair value are not reflected on either the balance sheet or the income statement. The presumption is that these investments are held to maturity, at which time they are settled at their face value. Fluctuations in fair value, as a result, are less relevant for this investment classification. Any interest received, and gains and losses on the sale of these investments, are recorded in current income.

Financial Statement Disclosures

Companies are required to disclose detailed information on their investment portfolios in notes to financial statements. SMRT reports its accounting policies for its investments in the following note to its 2014 annual report:

3.7 Non-derivative financial instruments

Available-for-sale financial assets

Equity and debt securities held by the Group are classified as being available-for-sale and are stated at fair value, determined as the quoted bid price at the balance sheet date. Any resultant gain or loss is recognised in other comprehensive income and presented within equity in the fair value reserve. The exceptions are impairment losses and foreign exchange gains and losses on monetary items such as debt securities, which are recognised in the income statement. When these investments are derecognised, the cumulative gain or loss previously recognised directly in other comprehensive income is recognised in the income statement. Where these investments are interest-bearing, interest calculated using the effective interest method is recognised in the income statement.

Unquoted equity and other investments are measured at cost less accumulated impairment losses. It is not practicable to reliably estimate the fair value of unquoted available-for-sale financial assets due to the lack of market prices in an active market, significant range of fair value estimates, and the inability to reasonably assess the probabilities of the various estimates.

Financial assets classified as available-for-sale are recognised by the Group on the date it commits to purchase the investments, and derecognised on the date a sale is committed.

Held-to-maturity investments

If the Group has the positive intent and ability to hold debt securities to maturity, they are classified as held-to-maturity. Held-to-maturity investments are recognised initially at fair value plus any directly attributable transaction costs. Subsequent to initial recognition, held-to-maturity investments are measured at amortised cost using the effective interest method, less any impairment losses.

Financial assets classified as held-to-maturity are recognised by the Group on the date it commits to purchase the investments, and derecognised on the date a sale is committed.

This note indicates that SMRT has both available-for-sale and held-to-maturity investments.

SMRT's available-for-sale portfolio is carried at fair value, which is determined as the quoted bid price. Unrealised gains and losses on its available-for-sale investments are recognised in other comprehensive income (they do not affect current net income), and are reported as the component of equity generally called "accumulated other comprehensive income" (or "fair value reserve"). Gains and losses on the sale of investments, however, are reported in current net income. SMRT's held-to-maturity securities are carried at amortised cost.

SMRT also indicates that the reported values of its investments are net of accumulated impairment losses. As the company explains in Note 3.12 (reproduced below), if there is any objective evidence that the value of the investments is impaired, they are written down to current fair value and that loss is reported in current income.

Impairment of financial assets

A financial asset is assessed at each balance sheet date to determine whether there is any objective evidence that it is impaired. A financial asset is considered to be impaired if objective evidence indicates that one or more events have a negative effect on the estimated future cash flows of that asset.

An impairment loss in respect of a financial asset measured at amortised cost is calculated as the difference between its carrying amount, and the present value of the estimated future cash flows discounted at the original effective interest rate (i.e., the effective interest rate computed at initial recognition of these financial assets). Receivables with a short duration are not discounted.When a decline in the fair value of an available-for-sale financial asset has been recognised directly in equity and there is objective evidence that the value of the asset is impaired, the cumulative loss that has been recognised directly in equity is recognised in the income statement even though the financial asset has not been derecognised. The amount of the cumulative loss that is recognised in the income statement is the difference between the acquisition cost and current fair value, less any impairment loss on that financial asset previously recognised in the income statement.

Individually significant financial assets are tested for impairment on an individual basis. The remaining financial assets are assessed collectively in groups that share similar credit risk characteristics.

All impairment losses are recognised in the income statement.

Following is the investments line items from the asset section of SMRT's balance sheet ($ thousands):

As at March 31	Note	2014	2013
Non-current assets			
Other investments	8	$20,713	$32,171
Current assets			
Other investments	8	5,000	—

Note 8 to SMRT's financial statement provides further information about the composition of its investment portfolio:

8 Other Investments

($ thousands)	Group 2014	Group 2013
Non-current		
Quoted available-for-sale equity security	$ 4,226	$ 5,257
Quoted held-to-maturity debt securities	16,487	26,914
	20,713	32,171
Current		
Quoted held-to-maturity debt securities	5,000	—
Total	$25,713	$32,171

Held-to-maturity debt securities bear interest at rates ranging from 2.81% to 3.60% (2013: 2.81% to 5.45%) per annum and will mature in 0.92 years to 8.46 years (2013: 1.92 years to 9.45 years).

The maximum exposure to credit risk of the debt securities at the balance sheet date is the carrying amount. Debt securities are neither past due nor impaired.

This note reveals that SMRT's available-for-sale portfolio is carried as a noncurrent asset with a fair value of $4,226 (all dollar amounts are in thousands). Moreover, its held-to-maturity securities are carried at amortised cost, $16,487 as a noncurrent asset and $5,000 as a current asset.

Following is the fair value reserve line items from SMRT's statement of changes in equity ($ thousands):

Fair value reserve	
At April 1, 2013	$1,547
Other comprehensive income	(1,031)
At March 31, 2014	$ 516

Fair value reserve (or unrealised gains and losses on available-for-sale securities) reflects the difference between the acquisition cost and the current fair value of the AFS securities. Hence, the cost of SMRT's AFS investments is $3,710 ($4,226—$516). Finally, the change in fair value reserve is −$1,031, which is also reported in SMRT's statement of comprehensive income.

Because held-to-maturity investment is carried at amortised cost, SMRT discloses the carrying cost, fair value, and unrecognised gain/loss of the investment in the following note:

Fair values

The fair values of financial assets and liabilities which are not carried at fair value in the balance sheet as at March 31, 2014 are represented in the following table:

Group ($ thousands)	Note	2014 Carrying amount	2014 Fair value	2013 Carrying amount	2013 Fair value
Financial assets					
Held-to-maturity debt securities	8	$16,487	$16,349	$26,914	$26,963
Unrecognised gain/(loss)			(138)		49

This note indicates that the carrying cost and fair value of SMRT's held-to-maturity investment portfolio are $16,487 and $16,349, respectively. Hence, this investment has an unrealised loss of $138, which is not recognised in SMRT's financial statements. The reason why unrealised gain/loss on HTM securities is not recognised in the financial statements is due to the fact that it is the intention of the management to hold these securities to maturity. Hence, any interim fluctuations in the value of these securities are irrelevant for the company. Nonetheless, investors can find the unrealised gain/loss information from the note to the financial statements.

Finally, SMRT provides required information about the determination of fair values for its marketable securities in the note below:

Fair value hierarchy

The table below analyses financial instruments carried at fair value by valuation method. The different levels have been defined as follows:

- Level 1: quoted prices (unadjusted) in active markets for identical assets or liabilities;
- Level 2: inputs other than quoted prices included within Level 1 that are observable for the asset or liability, either directly (i.e., as prices) or indirectly (i.e., derived from prices);
- Level 3: inputs for the asset or liability that are not based on observable market data (unobservable inputs).

Group ($ thousands)	Level 1	Level 2	Level 3	Total
2014				
Quoted available-for-sale equity security	$4,226	—	—	$4,226
2013				
Quoted available-for-sale equity security	5,257	—	—	5,257

The disclosures show that the fair values of SMRT's available-for-sale securities are Level 1, that is they are determined by looking at quoted prices in active markets for identical assets. SMRT holds neither Level 2 nor Level 3 financial instruments.

Potential for Earnings Management

The difference between available-for-sale investments and trading securities—as far as the way changes in fair value are reported—creates the potential for earnings management. For example, if management wishes to report higher net income, investments that have increased in value could be classified as trading securities while investments that have declined in value could be classified as available-for-sale securities. This classification would mean that the unrealised gains on the trading securities would be reported on the income statement, while the unrealised losses on available-for-sale securities would bypass the income statement (they are reported in the statement of comprehensive income) and be subtracted from accumulated other comprehensive income (AOCI). In addition, management is free to reclassify investments if it sees fit to do so.

Because of the potential for earnings management, the IFRS requires that investments be measured at fair value at the time that a security is reclassified from one category to another. If trading securities are reclassified as available-for-sale securities, for example, any unrealised gain or loss must be recognised as income at the time of the reclassification. This prevents management from moving investments between categories to hide a loss in AOCI.

Nevertheless, available-for-sale securities offer the opportunity for earnings management, because management can decide when to recognise the unrealised gain (or loss) in the income statement. When investments are classified as available-for-sale securities, any unrealised gain or loss is recorded directly in equity as AOCI until one of two things happens: (1) management decides to sell the securities, or (2) management decides to reclassify the investment as trading securities. In either case, the unrealised gain or loss is immediately recognised in the income statement and thus transferred from AOCI to retained earnings.

SMRT's footnote allows us to observe how a firm might use its investments in marketable securities to manage its net income for the year. Suppose, for example, that SMRT wanted to increase net income for the 2014 reporting year. SMRT's available-for-sale securities show gross unrealised gains of $516 (thousand). These gains have not been reported previously in SMRT's income statement. So, if SMRT decided to reclassify these available-for-sale securities as trading securities, it could immediately recognise the $516 (thousand) unrealised gain and report it on its 2014 income statement.

Instead of reclassifying the investments, SMRT could sell the securities and recognise the gain. (The unrealised gain would now be realised.) In fact, SMRT could sell the investment to record the gain and then immediately buy back similar securities at the same price (or very near to it). The company would incur some transaction costs, but it would be able to increase its income without changing its portfolio or reclassifying its investments.

One way to determine whether a company is selling and buying available-for-sale securities to manage earnings is to examine the cash flow statement. Under the heading of investing activities, companies are required to report cash flows from buying and selling investments separately. Of course, we cannot automatically conclude that these transactions were the result of earnings management. Moreover, realised gains and losses on available-for-sale investments are disclosed in a company's financial statement notes. Hence, we can assess the extent in which the sales of available-for-sale securities boost net income. Finally, we could look at the adjustments to net income in the indirect method cash from operations to identify gains and losses from investing activities.

MID-CHAPTER REVIEW 1

Part 1: Available-for-sale securities

Show the effects (amount and account) of the following four transactions involving investments in marketable securities classified as available-for-sale in the financial statement effects template, prepare the journal entries, and post the journal entries to the appropriate T-accounts.

1. Purchased 1,000 Lytton ordinary shares for $15 cash per share.
2. Received cash dividend of $2 per share on Lytton ordinary shares.
3. Year-end market price of Lytton ordinary shares is $18 per share.
4. Sold all 1,000 Lytton ordinary shares for $19,000 cash.

Part 2: Trading securities

Using the same transaction information 1 through 4 from part 1, prepare the journal entries, post the journal entries to the related T-accounts, and enter the effects (amount and account) relating to these transactions in the financial statement effects template assuming that the investments are classified as trading securities.

The solution to this review problem can be found on pages 610–612.

INVESTMENTS WITH SIGNIFICANT INFLUENCE

LO4 Explain and analyse accounting for investments with significant influence.

Many companies make investments in other companies that yield them significant influence over those other companies. These intercorporate investments are usually made for strategic reasons including:

- **Prelude to acquisition.** Significant ownership can allow the investor company to gain a seat on the board of directors from which it can learn much about the investee company, its products, and its industry.
- **Strategic alliance.** One example of a strategic alliance is an investment in a company that provides inputs for the investor's production process. This relationship is closer than the usual supplier–buyer relationship, often because the investor company provides trade secrets or technical know-how of its production process.
- **Pursuit of research and development.** Many research activities in the pharmaceutical, software, and oil and gas industries are conducted jointly. The common motivation is to reduce risk or the amount of capital invested by the investor. The investor company's equity investment often carries an option to purchase additional shares or the entire company, which it can exercise if the research activities are fruitful.

A crucial feature in each of these investments is that the investor company has ownership sufficient to exert *significant influence* over the investee company. IFRS requires that such investments be accounted for using the *equity method*.

Significant influence is the ability of the investor to affect the financing or operating policies of the investee. Ownership levels of 20% to 50% of the outstanding ordinary shares of the investee presume significant influence. Significant influence can also exist when ownership is less than 20%. Evidence of such influence can be that the investor company is able to gain a seat on the board of directors of the investee by virtue of its equity investment, or the investor controls technical know-how or patents that are used by the investee, or the investor is able to exert significant influence by virtue of legal contracts between it and the investee. There is growing pressure for determining significant influence by the facts and circumstances of the investment instead of the strict ownership percentage rule reflected in current corporate reporting.

Accounting for Investments with Significant Influence

Investments with significant influence must be accounted for using the **equity method**. The equity method of accounting for investments reports the investment on the balance sheet at an amount equal to the proportion of the investee's equity owned by the investor; hence the name equity method. (This accounting assumes acquisition at book value. Acquisition at an amount greater than book value is covered in Appendix 12A.) Contrary to passive investments that are reported at fair value, equity method investments increase (decrease) with increases (decreases) in the equity of the investee.

Equity method accounting is summarised as follows:

- Investments are initially recorded at their purchase cost.
- Dividends received are treated as a recovery of the investment and, thus, reduce the investment balance (dividends are *not* reported as income as is the case with passive investments).
- The investor reports income equal to its proportionate share of the reported income of the investee; the investment account is increased by that income or decreased by its share of any loss.
- The investment is *not* reported at fair value as is the case with most passive investments.

To illustrate the accounting for investments using the equity method, consider the following scenario: Assume that Cyberport acquires a 30% interest in Mitel Networks, a company seeking to develop a new technology in a strategic alliance with Cyberport. At acquisition, Mitel reports $1,000 of equity, and Cyberport purchases its 30% stake for $300. At the first year-end, Mitel reports profits of $100 and pays $20 in cash dividends to its shareholders ($6 to Cyberport). Following are the financial statement effects for Cyberport (the investor company) for this investment using the equity method:

	Balance Sheet									Income Statement				
Transaction	Cash Asset	+	Noncash Assets	=	Liabil-ities	+	Contrib. Capital	+	Earned Capital	*Revenues*	–	*Expenses*	=	*Net Income*
(1) Purchased 30% investment in Mitel for $300 cash.	−300 Cash		+300 Investment in Mitel	=							–		=	
(2) Mitel reports $100 income.			+30 Investment in Mitel	=					+30 Retained Earnings	+30 Investment Income	–		=	+30
(3) Mitel pays $20 cash dividends, $6 to Cyberport.	+6 Cash		−6 Investment in Mitel	=							–		=	
Ending balance of Cyberport's investment account.			324											

The related journal entries and T-accounts are:

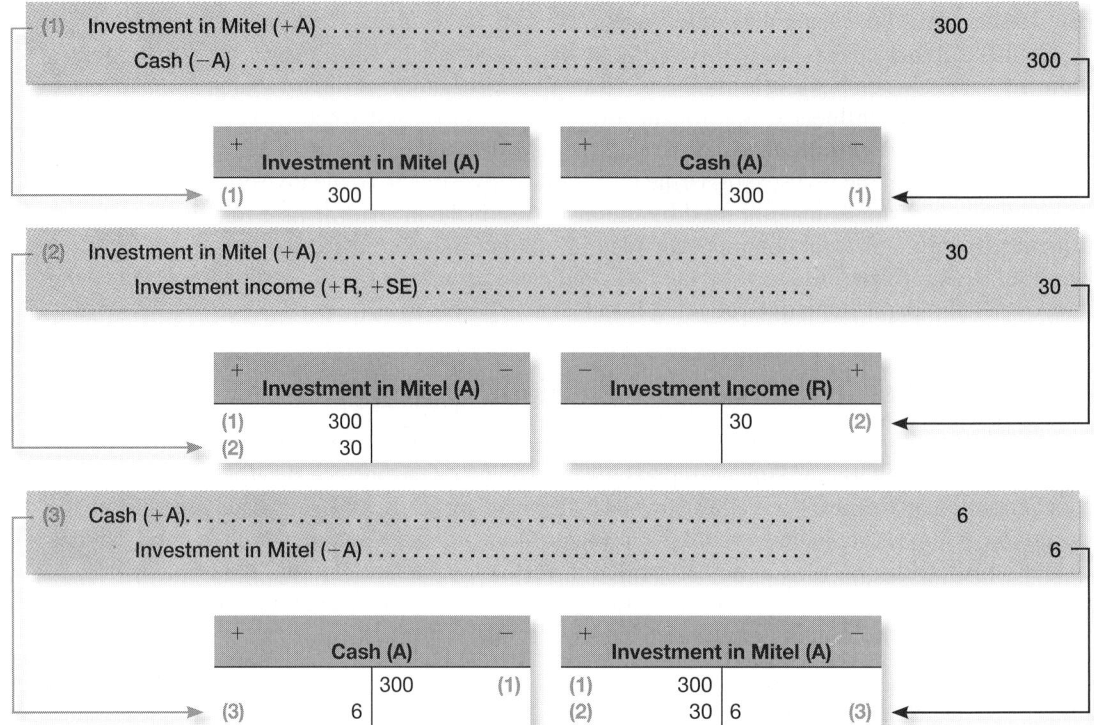

The investment is initially reported on Cyberport's balance sheet at its purchase price of $300, representing a 30% interest in Mitel's equity of $1,000. During the year, Mitel's equity increases to $1,080 ($1,000 plus $100 income and less $20 dividends). Likewise, Cyberport's investment increases by $30 to reflect its 30% share of Mitel's $100 income and decreases by $6 from Mitel's $20 of dividends (30% × $20). After these transactions, Cyberport's investment in Mitel is reported on Cyberport's balance sheet at 30% of $1,080, or $324. Appendix 12A covers the case in which Cyberport might have paid a premium over 30% of the fair value of Mitel's net assets.

On the statement of cash flows, the original investment in Mitel would be seen as a $300 investing cash outflow. The $6 dividend received would be an investing or operating cash inflow. If the dividend is classified as an operating cash inflow, the indirect method presentation would start with net income, which includes $30 in income from Mitel, and a negative $24 adjustment would be necessary (entitled something like "excess of equity income over dividends received") to arrive at the correct operating cash inflow of $6.

Two final points about equity method accounting: First, just as the equity of a company is different from its fair value, so is the balance of the equity investment account different from its fair value. Indeed, there can be a substantial difference between the book value of an investment and its fair value. Second, if the investee company reports income, the investor company also reports income. Recognition of equity income by the investor, however, does not mean that it has received that income in cash. Cash is only received if the investee's directors declare a dividend payment.

FYI Investee dividend-paying ability can be (a) restricted by regulatory agencies or foreign governments, (b) prohibited under debt agreements for highly leveraged borrowers, and/or (c) influenced by directors that the investor does not control.

RESEARCH INSIGHT

Equity Income and Stock Prices The equity method of accounting for investments does not recognise any dividends received from the investee or any fair value changes for the investee in the investor's income until the investment is sold. However, research has found a positive relation between investors' and investees' share prices at the time of investees' earnings and dividend announcements. This relation suggests that the share market includes information regarding investees' earnings and dividends when assessing the share prices of investor companies. This finding implies the market looks beyond the book value of the investment account in determining share prices of investor companies. The finding also reflects the fact that the earnings from the operations of subsidiaries are considered earnings of the parent corporation.

Financial Statement Disclosures

Consider the Swiss food and beverage company Nestlé S.A., which reports associates and joint ventures using the equity method as indicated in the following note from its 2013 annual report.

Associates

Companies where the Group has the power to exercise a significant influence but does not exercise control are accounted for using the equity method. The net assets and results are adjusted to comply with the Group's accounting policies. The carrying amount of goodwill arising from the acquisition of associates is included in the carrying amount of investments in associates.

Joint ventures

Joint arrangements whereby the parties have rights to the net assets of the arrangement are joint ventures and are accounted for using the equity method.

The balance sheet amount for an equity method investment is equal to the proportion owned of the equity of the investee company when the investment is acquired at book value. Following is the investments line item from the asset section of Nestlé's balance sheet:

As at December 31, (in millions of CHF)	Note	2013	2012
Non-current assets			
Investments in associates and joint ventures	16	CHF 12,315	CHF 11,586

In Note 16, reproduced below, Nestlé provides additional details on its investments in associates and joint ventures.

16. Associates and joint ventures

	2013				2012			
(In millions of CHF)	L'Oréal	Other associates	Joint ventures	Total	L'Oréal	Other associates	Joint ventures	Total
At January 1	CHF 8,785	CHF 1,068	CHF 1,733	CHF 11,586	CHF 7,708	CHF 921	CHF 1,688	CHF 10,317
Currency retranslations	137	(3)	(45)	89	(58)	(2)	(7)	(67)
Investments	—	106	(78)	28	—	86	(7)	79
Share of results	1,083	(9)	190	1,264	1,031	29	193	1,253
Share of other comprehensive income	115	—	(28)	87	497	—	5	502
Dividends and interest received	(506)	(12)	(139)	(657)	(431)	(15)	(139)	(585)
Modification of the scope of consolidation[(a)]	—	—	—	—	—	7	—	7
Other	(89)	6	1	(82)	38	42	—	80
At December 31	CHF 9,525	CHF 1,156	CHF 1,634	CHF 12,315	CHF 8,785	CHF 1,068	CHF 1,733	CHF 11,586

(a) 2012 comparatives have been adjusted following the final valuation of the Wyeth Nutrition acquisition (see Note 2)

At the end of fiscal year 2013, Nestlé reports on its balance sheet a total "investments in associates and joint ventures" of CHF 12,315 million, of which CHF 9,525 million is its investments in the French cosmetics company L'Oréal. The major changes since 2012 in the balance of this investment account include an increase of CHF 1,264 million from Nestlé's share of reported income of its associates and joint ventures (it is also reported in Nestlé's income statement) and a reduction of CHF 657 million because of dividends received from the investees.

Nestlé also provide key financial statement information on its principal associate, L'Oréal, in the note below:

16.1 L'Oréal

The Group holds 178,381,021 shares in L'Oréal, the world leader in cosmetics, representing a 29.7% participation in its equity after consideration of its own shares (2012: 178,381,021 shares representing a 29.8% participation). At December 31, 2013, the market value of the shares held amounts to CHF 27.9 billion (2012: CHF 22.6 billion).

Summarised financial information

(In billions of CHF)	2013	2012
Total current assets	CHF 11.4	CHF 9.9
Total non-current assets	26.9	25.7
Total assets	38.3	35.6
Total current liabilities	8.1	7.7
Total non-current liabilities	2.5	2.6
Total liabilities	10.6	10.3
Total equity	27.7	25.3
Total sales	28.2	27.1
Profit from continuing operations	3.6	3.5
Other comprehensive income	0.4	1.7
Total comprehensive income	4.0	5.2

Reconciliation of the carrying amount

(In billions of CHF)	2013	2012
Share held by the Group in the equity of L'Oréal	CHF 8.2	CHF 7.5
Goodwill and other adjustments	1.3	1.3
Carrying amount	9.5	8.8

16.2 Other associates

The Group holds a number of other associates that are individually not material for the Group.

16.3 Joint ventures

The Group holds 50% of a number of joint ventures operating in the food and beverages and in pharmaceutical activities. These joint ventures are individually not material for the Group, the main ones being Galderma and Cereal Partners Worldwide.

The note indicates that L'Oréal's assets totaled CHF 38.3 billion at the end of fiscal 2013, and its liabilities totaled CHF 10.6 billion. The note information also reveals that L'Oréal had total sales of CHF 28.2 billion and profit from continuing operations of CHF 3.6 billion. Since Nestlé owns less than 50% of L'Oréal, it reports only the net amount of its equity investment among its assets. The carrying value of Nestlé's investment in L'Oréal is CHF 9.5 billion, which is substantially lower than the market value of CHF 27.9 billion.

Equity Method Accounting and Effects on Ratios

Under equity method accounting, only the net equity owned is reported on the balance sheet (not the assets and liabilities to which the investment relates), and only the net equity in earnings is reported in the income statement (not the investee's sales and expenses). Both the balance sheet and income statements are, therefore, markedly affected. Further, because the assets and liabilities are left off the balance sheet, and because the sales and expenses are omitted from the income statement, several financial ratios are also affected.

- **Profit margin (PM = Earnings without interest expense [EWI]/Sales revenue).** Most analysts include equity income (sales less expenses) in EWI because it relates to operating investments. (These subsidiaries are performing operating activities, for example, producing processed materials, for Nestlé.) However, the investee's sales are omitted from the investor's sales. The reported PM is, thus, *overstated*.

- **Asset turnover ratios (Sales revenue/Average assets).** Because the investee's sales and its assets are omitted from the investor's financial statements, asset turnover ratios such as inventory turnover, receivables turnover, and PPE turnover are affected. The direction of the effect is, however, *indeterminable*.
- **Financial leverage (Debt-to-equity = Total liabilities/Total equity).** Financial leverage is *understated* because the liabilities of the investee are omitted from the numerator of the debt-to-equity ratio.

Profitability ratios like ROE and ROA are also affected by the use of equity method investments, though the exact direction would require a careful analysis of the noncontrolling interests described in the following section. Analysts frequently adjust reported financial statements for equity investments before conducting their analysis. One approach to adjusting the reported financial statements would be to consolidate the equity method investee with the investor company.

YOU MAKE THE CALL

You are the Chief Financial Officer A substantial percentage of your company's sales are made through a key downstream producer, who combines your product with other materials to make the product that is ultimately purchased by consumers. In the last two years, this downstream producer has been branching out into other products that limit the capacity that can be devoted to your product. As a result, the growth prospects for your company have been diminished. What potential courses of action can you consider? Explain. (Answer on page 589.)

MID-CHAPTER REVIEW 2

Show the effects (amount and account) relating to the following four transactions involving investments in marketable securities accounted for using the equity method in the financial statement effects template, prepare the journal entries, and post the journal entries to the related T-accounts.

1. Purchased 5,000 Piccadilly ordinary shares at £10 cash per share. These shares reflect 30% ownership of Piccadilly.
2. Received a £2 per share cash dividend on Piccadilly ordinary shares.
3. Made an adjustment to reflect £100,000 income reported by Piccadilly.
4. Sold all 5,000 Piccadilly ordinary shares for £90,000.

The solution to this review problem can be found on pages 613–614.

INVESTMENTS WITH CONTROL

LO5 Describe and analyse accounting for investments with control.

If the investor company owns enough of the voting shares of the investee company such that it can exercise control over the investee, it must report **consolidated financial statements**. For example, in notes to its annual report describing its accounting policies, SMRT reports:

> The consolidated financial statements relate to the Company and its subsidiaries (together referred to as the "Group") and the Group's interest in associate.
>
> **Subsidiaries**
>
> Subsidiaries are entities in which the Group has the power, directly or indirectly, to govern the financial and operating policies so as to obtain benefits from its activities, generally accompanied by a shareholding giving rise to a majority of the voting rights. The existence and effect of potential voting rights that are currently exercisable or convertible are considered when assessing whether the Group controls another entity.

continued

continued from previous page

Investments in subsidiaries are stated in the Company's balance sheet at cost less impairment losses. Subsidiaries are consolidated from the date on which control is transferred to the Group. They are de-consolidated from the date in which control ceases...

Transactions eliminated on consolidation

All significant intra-group transactions, balances and unrealised gains are eliminated on consolidation...

This statement means that SMRT's financial statements are an aggregation of those of the parent company and all its subsidiary companies to create the financial statements of the total economic entity. This process involves adding up the separate financial statements, while being careful to remove items between the separate entities.

Accounting for Investments with Control

Accounting for business combinations (acquisitions) involves one additional step to equity method accounting. Under the equity method, the investment balance represents the proportion of the investee's equity owned by the investor, and the investor company income statement includes its proportionate share of the investee's income. **Consolidation accounting** (1) replaces the investment balance with the investee's assets and liabilities to which it relates, and (2) replaces the equity income reported by the investor with the investee's sales and expenses to which it relates. Specifically, the consolidated balance sheet includes the gross assets and liabilities of the investee company, and the income statement includes the gross sales and expenses of the investee.

To illustrate, consider the following scenario. Penman Company acquires all of the ordinary shares of Nissim Company by exchanging $3,000 cash for all of Nissim's ordinary shares. In this case, the $3,000 purchase price is equal to the book value of Nissim's equity (contributed capital of $2,000 and retained earnings of $1,000), and we assume that the fair values of Nissim's assets and liabilities are the same as their book values. On Penman's balance sheet, the investment in Nissim Co. appears as a financial investment (IFRS only requires consolidation for financial statements issued to the public, not for the internal financial records of the separate companies). Penman records an initial balance in the investment account of $3,000, which equals the purchase price. The balance sheets for Penman and Nissim immediately after the acquisition, together with the required consolidating adjustments (or eliminations), and the consolidated balance sheet that the two companies report are shown in Exhibit 12.5.

EXHIBIT 12.5 Mechanics of Consolidation Accounting (Purchased at Book Value, where Book Values = Fair Values)

	Penman Company	Nissim Company	Consolidating Adjustments*	Consolidated
Current assets	$ 5,000	$1,000		$ 6,000
Investment in Nissim	3,000	0	(3,000)	0
PPE, net	10,000	4,000		14,000
Total assets	$18,000	$5,000		$20,000
Liabilities	$ 5,000	$2,000		$ 7,000
Contributed capital	10,000	2,000	(2,000)	10,000
Retained earnings	3,000	1,000	(1,000)	3,000
Total liabilities and equity	$18,000	$5,000		$20,000

*The accounting equation remains in balance with these adjustments.

Penman controls the activities of Nissim, so IFRS requires consolidation of the two balance sheets. That is, Penman must report a balance sheet as if the two companies were one economic entity. For the most part, this process involves adding together the companies' resources and obligations. However, if one company has a claim on the other (e.g., a receivable) and the other company has an obligation to the first (e.g., a payable), the consolidation process must eliminate both the claim and the obligation. In the case of Penman Company and Nissim Company, the consolidated balances for current assets, PPE, and liabilities are the sum of those accounts on each balance sheet. Penman's asset Investment in Nissim represents a claim on Nissim Company, and Nissim's equity accounts represent an obligation that is held by Penman, and this intercompany claim/obligation must be eliminated to complete the consolidation. This elimination is accomplished by removing the financial investment of $3,000, and removing Nissim's equity to which that investment relates.

The consolidated balance sheet is shown in the far right column of Exhibit 12.5. It shows total assets of $20,000, total liabilities of $7,000, and equity of $13,000 ($10,000 + $3,000). Consolidated equity equals that of the parent company—this is always the case when the parent owns 100% of the subsidiary's shares.

Comparing the left and right columns of Exhibit 12.5 demonstrates the difference between the equity method and consolidation. In the left column, it appears that Penman spent $3,000 to acquire a financial asset. However, in the right column, it appears that Penman spent $3,000 to acquire a "bundle" of assets and liabilities consisting of $1,000 in cash plus $4,000 in PPE minus $2,000 in liabilities. The purchase of the financial asset was the means by which this bundle was acquired. The net value of this bundle is $3,000, so the net assets don't change. But the financial statement reader gets more information about what was acquired.

Penman Company's statement of cash flows would show an investing cash outflow for the acquisition of Nissim Company. However, the outflow is shown net of the cash received in the acquisition, which was $1,000. Therefore, the investing section would have a line item showing something like "Cash paid for acquisitions, net of cash acquired" with an outflow of $2,000.

In addition, the changes in Penman's operating assets and liabilities on this year's balance sheet from last year's balance sheet will no longer match the adjustments for operating assets and liabilities on the indirect method statement of cash flows from operations. For instance, the change in Penman's receivables will be changes due to its own operations (Including Nissim after the acquisition) plus any receivables acquired in the Nissim acquisition.

The illustration above assumes that the purchase price of the acquisition equals book value and the fair values of the acquired company's assets and liabilities are equal to their book values. What changes, if any, occur when the purchase price and book value are different? To explore this case, consider an acquisition where purchase price exceeds book value (the typical scenario). This situation might arise, for example, if an investor company believes it is acquiring something of value that is not reported on the investee's balance sheet—such as tangible assets whose fair values have risen above book value, or unrecorded intangible assets like patents or corporate synergies. If an acquisition is made at a price in excess of book value, all net assets acquired (both tangible and intangible) must be recognised on the consolidated balance sheet.

To illustrate an acquisition where purchase price exceeds book value, assume that Penman Company acquires Nissim Company for $4,000 instead of the $3,000 purchase price we used in the previous illustration. Also assume that in determining its purchase price, Penman feels that the additional $1,000 ($4,000 vs. $3,000) is justified because (1) Nissim's PPE is worth $300 more than its book value, and (2) Penman expects to realise $700 in additional value from corporate synergies.

The $4,000 investment account reflects two components: the book value acquired of $3,000 (as before) and an additional $1,000 of newly acquired assets. The post-acquisition balance sheets of the two companies, together with the consolidating adjustments and the consolidated balance sheet, are shown in Exhibit 12.6.

EXHIBIT 12.6 Mechanics of Consolidation Accounting (Purchased above Book Value)

	Penman Company	Nissim Company	Consolidating Adjustments	Consolidated
Current assets	$ 4,000	$1,000		$ 5,000
Investment in Nissim	4,000	0	(4,000)	0
PPE, net	10,000	4,000	300	14,300
Goodwill			700	700
Total assets	$18,000	$5,000		$20,000
Liabilities	$ 5,000	$2,000		$ 7,000
Contributed capital	10,000	2,000	(2,000)	10,000
Retained earnings	3,000	1,000	(1,000)	3,000
Total liabilities and equity	$18,000	$5,000		$20,000

The consolidated balances for current assets, PPE, and liabilities are the sum of those accounts on each company's balance sheet. The investment account, however, includes newly acquired assets that must be reported on the consolidated balance sheet. The consolidation process in this case has two steps. First, the $3,000 equity of Nissim Company is eliminated against the investment account as before. Then, the remaining $1,000 of the investment account is eliminated through the adjustments for newly acquired assets on the consolidated balance sheet ($300 of PPE and $700 of goodwill not reported on Nissim's balance sheet). Thus, the consolidated balance sheet reflects the book value of Penman and the *fair value* (book value plus the excess of Nissim's fair value over book value) for Nissim Company at the acquisition date.

To illustrate consolidation mechanics, consider the balance sheets of the Group (consolidated) and the Company (parent) that SMRT reports in its annual report as shown in Exhibit 12.7. Note 6 (not reproduced here) indicates that SMRT has 17 wholly owned subsidiaries and a 70% ownership of SMRT Alpha Pte Ltd. The investment in these 18 subsidiaries is reported at $325,823 (all dollar amounts are in thousands) on the balance sheet of SMRT (Company). This investment account is subsequently eliminated in the consolidation process (Group), together with the equity of these subsidiaries to which it relates.

As discussed above, the general process of consolidation is an adding up of the resources and obligations of the various entities controlled by the parent company. For example, SMRT (Company) reports Property, plant and equipment of $11,537 in fiscal year 2014, while the Group reports consolidated Property, plant and equipment of $1,641,769.

The consolidation process also requires the elimination of any intercompany transactions, such as sales and loans, between the parent and its subsidiaries. Hence, the consolidated accounts payable, accounts receivable, sales, and expenses are less than the sum of the respective accounts of the parent and subsidiary companies.

EXHIBIT 12.7 SMRT'S Consolidated Balance Sheet

BALANCE SHEETS
As at March 31, 2014

($ thousands)	Note	Group 2014	Group 2013	Company 2014	Company 2013
Non-current assets					
Property, plant and equipment	4	$1,641,769	$1,435,797	$ 11,537	$ 9,555
Intangible asset	5	13,614	13,614	—	—
Investments in subsidiaries	6	—	—	325,823	344,169
Interest in associate	7	52,629	50,554	—	—
Other investments	8	20,713	32,171	—	—
		1,728,725	1,532,136	337,360	353,724
Current assets					
Inventories	9	84,325	59,901	—	—
Trade and other receivables	10	98,938	86,074	78,965	64,459
Other investments	8	5,000	—	—	—
Fixed deposits with banks and financial institutions		8,615	213,782	—	—
Cash at banks and in hand		146,909	332,512	5,682	4,967
		343,787	692,269	84,647	69,426
Total assets		$2,072,512	$2,224,405	$422,007	$423,150
Equity attributable to equity holders of SMRT					
Share capital	11	$168,240	$167,496	$168,240	$167,496
Reserves	12	2,229	946	1,977	2,560
Accumulated profits		631,283	599,806	227,759	235,207
		801,752	768,248	397,976	405,263
Non-controlling interest		(92)	312	—	—
Total equity		801,660	768,560	397,976	405,263
Non-current liabilities					
Interest-bearing borrowings	14	480,017	607,125	—	—
Provisions	15	25	55	—	—
Deferred tax liabilities	16	155,808	142,867	1,435	1,377
Fuel equalisation account	17	20,312	20,312	—	—
Deferred grants	18	48,949	52,489	42	87
		705,111	822,848	1,477	1,464
Current liabilities					
Interest-bearing borrowings	14	156,393	2,347	—	—
Trade and other payables	19	355,183	577,138	22,302	15,536
Provisions	15	50,263	45,321	252	261
Current tax payable		3,902	8,191	—	626
		565,741	632,997	22,554	16,423
Total liabilities		1,270,852	1,455,845	24,031	17,887
Total equity and liabilities		$2,072,512	$2,224,405	$422,007	$423,150

Noncontrolling Interest

Noncontrolling interest represents the equity of shareholders who own a minority of the shares of one or more of the subsidiaries in a consolidated entity. When a company acquires a controlling interest in a company, it must consolidate the subsidiary when preparing its financial statements by reporting all of the subsidiary's assets and liabilities in the consolidated balance sheet and all of the subsidiary's revenues and expenses in the consolidated income statement. This is true even when the controlling parent company acquires less than 100% of the subsidiary. When less than 100% of the subsidiary's shares are acquired, there are two groups of shareholders: the parent company's shareholders and the noncontrolling shareholders who own a minority of the subsidiary's shares. These noncontrolling shareholders have a claim on the net assets and the earnings of the subsidiary company.

To illustrate the reporting of noncontrolling interest, assume that Penman Company acquires 80% of Nissim Company for $2,400 (80% of $3,000). Because Penman must consolidate 100% of the assets and liabilities of Nissim, Penman's equity must increase to maintain the accounting equation. A new equity account titled noncontrolling interests is added to Penman's shareholders' equity. The consolidation worksheet is presented in Exhibit 12.8.

EXHIBIT 12.8 Mechanics of Consolidation Accounting (Less than 100% of Subsidiary Shares Purchased at Book Value)

	Penman Company	Nissim Company	Consolidating Adjustments	Consolidated
Current assets	$ 5,600	$1,000		$ 6,600
Investment in Nissim	2,400	0	$(2,400)	0
PPE, net	10,000	4,000		14,000
Total assets	$18,000	$5,000		$20,600
Liabilities	$ 5,000	$2,000		$ 7,000
Contributed capital	10,000	2,000	(2,000)	10,000
Retained earnings	3,000	1,000	(1,000)	3,000
Penman shareholders' equity	13,000			13,000
Noncontrolling interests			600	600
Total equity	13,000			13,600
Total liabilities and equity	$18,000	$5,000		$20,600

The contributed capital of the consolidated entity (share capital, contributed surplus, treasury shares, etc.) refers to the parent company's shareholders' equity (in this example, Penman Company). The net assets owned by the noncontrolling shareholders are represented in one account, labeled noncontrolling interests. Each period, the noncontrolling interests equity account is increased by the noncontrolling shareholders' share of the subsidiary's net income, and decreased by any dividends paid to those shareholders.

The consolidated income statement lists total consolidated revenues and expenses and consolidated net income. After net income is computed, the portion of net income that is attributed to noncontrolling interests is subtracted. If the noncontrolling shareholders own 20% of the subsidiary's shares, then 20% of the earnings of the subsidiary are subtracted from the consolidated entity's income statement. (This is not 20% of the consolidated company's earnings, only 20% of the subsidiary's earnings.)

As an illustration of the presentation of noncontrolling interests in the balance sheet, refer to the equity section of **SMRT**'s consolidated balance sheet (Group) in Exhibit 12.7. SMRT's total equity is listed at $801,752. This is the equity claim of those investors who own shares in SMRT. Next, the -$92 of noncontrolling interests is listed. This amount represents the share of SMRT subsidiaries' net assets that is owned by minority shareholders. The final line lists the total equity of $801,660, which is the sum of SMRT's shareholders' equity and the noncontrolling interests.

SMRT's consolidated income statement presents noncontrolling interests as follows:

SMRT Corporation Consolidated Income Statement (excerpts) Year ended March 31, 2014 ($ thousands)	2014	2013
Revenue	1,163,893	1,119,469
Profit from operations	84,234	110,205
Finance costs	(10,431)	(7,065)
Interest and investment income	1,270	2,305
Share of results of associate (net of tax)	(418)	(381)
Profit before income tax	74,655	105,064
Income tax expense	(13,157)	(21,864)
Profit after income tax	61,498	83,200
Attributable to:		
Equity holders of SMRT	61,902	83,338
Non-controlling interest	(404)	(138)

SMRT presents profit after income tax of $61,498, which is income for the consolidated entity. Next, SMRT divides the consolidated income into the income attributable to SMRT's shareholders ($61,902) and the income attributable to noncontrolling interests (−$404).

Reporting of Acquired Assets and Liabilities

Acquisitions are often made at a purchase price in excess of the book value of the investee company's equity. The excess purchase price must be allocated to all of the assets and liabilities acquired, including those that do not currently appear on the balance sheet of the investee. This allocation can be done in three steps:

Step 1: Adjust the book value of all tangible assets acquired and all liabilities assumed to fair value. This adjustment addresses the issue of misvalued assets and liabilities on the investee firm's balance sheet.

Step 2: Assign a fair value to any identifiable intangible assets. Recall from Chapter 8 that intangible assets are only reported on the balance sheet if they are purchased; internally created intangible assets are not capitalised. This step allows the acquiring firm to assign a value to the investee's intangible assets, even if those assets are not reported on the investee firm's balance sheet.

Step 3: Assign the residual amount to goodwill. Goodwill is the excess of the acquisition price over the fair value of identifiable net assets acquired. That is, whatever value cannot be assigned to identifiable tangible and intangible assets is considered goodwill.[2]

The acquiring company is required to disclose relevant information about the allocation of the purchase price in its footnotes.

For example, consider the British healthcare company **GlaxoSmithKline Plc** (GSK), which reported the allocation of its £255 million purchase price in May 2013 for **Okairos AG** and two other businesses in excerpts from Note 38 to its 2013 annual report:

38 Acquisitions and disposals

Details of the acquisition and disposal of significant subsidiaries and associates, joint ventures and other businesses are given below:

2013

Acquisitions

[2] What happens if goodwill is negative? Such a "bargain purchase" is uncommon, because it implies that the "whole" of the acquired company is worth less than the sum of its parts. Therefore, when an acquirer believes that it has made a bargain purchase, it must carefully check its valuation of all the components of the goodwill calculation. If that review confirms that the acquirer has made a bargain purchase, then it recognises a gain in its income from continuing operations.

During the year GSK completed the acquisition of three businesses for cash, including Okairos AG, a European based biopharmaceutical company focused on the development of a specific vaccine technology in the prophylactic and therapeutic fields, which was acquired in May. The total purchase price for these businesses of £255 million included £7 million of cash acquired and £1 million of contingent consideration.

(In £ millions)	Book value	Fair value adjustments	Fair value
Net assets acquired			
Intangibles	£—	£198	£198
Property, plant and equipment	20	3	23
Inventory	6	—	6
Trade and other receivables	16	—	16
Other assets including cash and cash equivalents	8	—	8
Deferred tax provision	—	(23)	(23)
Trade and other payables	(26)	—	(26)
	24	178	202
Goodwill	—	53	53
	£24	£231	£255
Cash consideration paid			254
Contingent consideration			1
Total consideration			£255

If the acquisitions had been made at the beginning of the year, it is estimated that Group turnover would have increased by approximately £50 million for the year. Okairos has been fully integrated into the GSK business and it is not practicable to separately identify the impact on the Group profit for the year. The other acquisitions occurred shortly before the end of the year and had no material impact on the Group profit for the year.

The goodwill arising on the acquisitions reflects potential for business synergies and the value of workforce acquired. The majority of this goodwill is not expected to be deductible for income tax purposes.

The results of the acquisitions are reported within the US, Europe, EMAP, Japan, Other trading and unallocated Pharmaceuticals and Vaccines and Consumer Healthcare operating segments. The transactions were accounted for using the acquisition accounting method.

The above note reveals that GSK paid £255 million for three businesses that have a total book value of £24 million. The allocation of the £255 million purchase price is shown in the last column of the table in the note. In particular, GSK assigned a fair value of £198 million to intangible assets, adjusted the book value of property, plant and equipment from £20 million to £23 million, booked a £23 million deferred tax liability, and assumed the inventory, receivables, other assets, and payables at their book values. The fair value of identifiable net assets acquired totals £202 million, which is £53 million below the £255 million purchase price. GSK assigned the £53 million residual value to goodwill. Goodwill can only be recognised as an asset in an acquisition and only then in the amount by which the purchase price exceeds the fair value of the net assets acquired, including all identifiable intangible assets.

Reporting of Goodwill Goodwill is not subject to amortisation, but IFRS requires companies to test goodwill annually for impairment or whenever there is evidence that it may be impaired. Impairment losses on goodwill are reported in the income statement and are not reversible in subsequent reporting periods.

For the purpose of conducting an impairment test, assets are grouped at the lowest levels for which there are separately identifiable cash flows, known as cash-generating units (CGUs). Goodwill is allocated to a company's CGUs or groups of CGUs that are expected to benefit from the acquisition in which the goodwill arose. The impairment test is a two-step process:

1. The recoverable amount of a CGU is compared with the carrying amount of the CGU. By definition, the recoverable amount is the higher of a CGU's fair value less costs of disposal or its value in use. The fair value of the CGU can be estimated using valuation methods such as market comparables, discounted cash flow model, and so on. Value in use is the present value of the estimated future cash flows based on current management plans for the CGU's operations.[3]
2. If the recoverable amount is below the carrying amount, the CGU is deemed impaired. The impairment loss is first allocated to reduce the carrying amount of any goodwill allocated to the CGU and then to the other assets of the CGU.

To illustrate the impairment computation, assume that a CGU of Ouchy S.A. has a fair value less disposal costs of €800,000, value in use of €775,000, and carrying amount of €900,000. Further assume that the carrying value of the CGU's goodwill is €140,000. Given this information, the recoverable amount of the CGU is €800,000 (higher of €800,000 or €775,000). Because the recoverable amount of €800,000 is lower than the carrying value of €900,000, the CGU is impaired by €100,000. The €100,000 impairment loss is allocated to reduce the carrying value of the CGU's goodwill from €140,000 to €40,000.

The financial statement effects and related journal entry and T-accounts are:

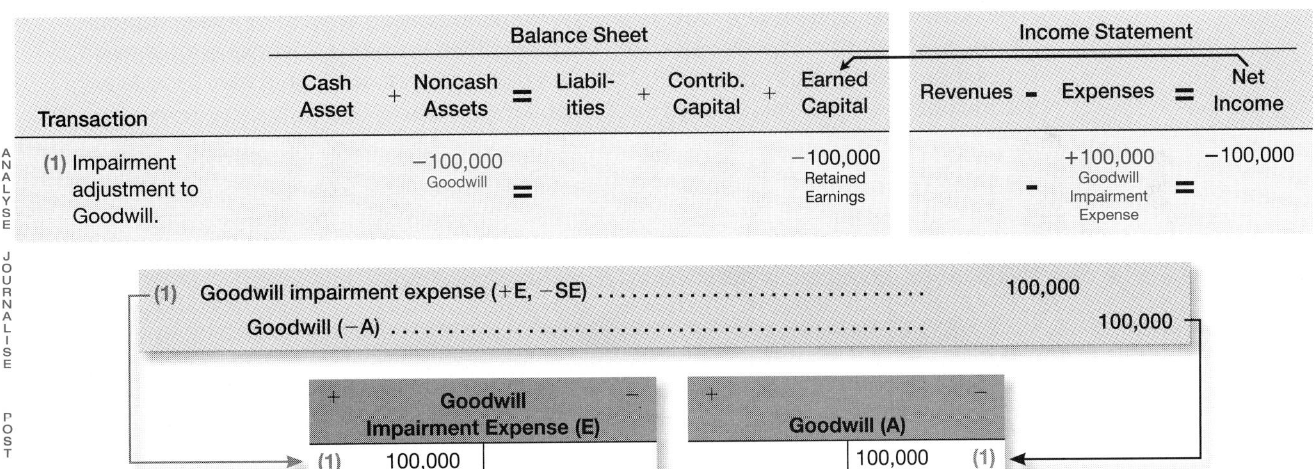

	Balance Sheet					Income Statement		
Transaction	Cash Asset +	Noncash Assets =	Liabil-ities +	Contrib. Capital +	Earned Capital	Revenues −	Expenses =	Net Income
(1) Impairment adjustment to Goodwill.		−100,000 Goodwill			−100,000 Retained Earnings		+100,000 Goodwill Impairment Expense	−100,000

ANALYSE

JOURNALISE

(1) Goodwill impairment expense (+E, −SE) 100,000
Goodwill (−A) 100,000

POST

+ Goodwill Impairment Expense (E) −	
(1) 100,000	

+ Goodwill (A) −	
	100,000 (1)

This analysis of investee company implies that goodwill must be written down by $100,000. The impairment loss is reported as a separate line item in the consolidated income statement. The related footnote disclosure describes the reasons for the write-down.

Billabong International Limited, an Australian sporting goods company, reports the following goodwill impairment in excerpts from note 18 of its 2013 annual report (all dollar amounts are in thousands):

[3] The fair value of the investee company can be determined using market comparables or another valuation method (such as the discounted cash flow model, residual operating income model, or P/E multiples).

Note 18. Non-current assets—Intangible assets

($ thousands)	Indefinite life Goodwill	Brands	Other*	Finite life	Total
Year ended June 30, 2013					
Opening net book amount	$388,478	$383,418	$6,991	$17,013	$ 795,900
Additions **	753	—	—	16,545	17,298
Adjustment to contingent consideration (note 28)	(13,007)	—	—	—	(13,007)
Disposals	—	—	(643)	(11)	(654)
Amortisation charge	—	—	—	(7,037)	(7,037)
Impairment charge (note (a) and (e))	(292,934)	(300,572)	(297)	(10,513)	(604,316)
Exchange differences	11,973	7,408	691	4,430	24,502
Closing net book amount	$95,263	$90,254	$6,742	$20,427	$ 212,686
At June 30, 2013					
Cost	$553,520	$573,524	$9,332	$51,706	$1,188,082
Accumulated amortisation and impairment	(458,257)	(483,270)	(2,590)	(31,279)	(975,396)
Net book amount	$95,263	$90,254	$6,742	$20,427	$ 212,686

(a) Impairment tests for goodwill and brands

Goodwill is allocated to the Group's cash-generating units (CGU) identified according to brands acquired or geographical regions where operations existed at the time goodwill arose. Brands are allocated to the Group's cash-generating units (CGUs) identified according to individual brands.

The recoverable amount of a CGU is firstly determined based on value-in-use (VIU) calculations. These calculations use cash flow projections based on financial budgets with anticipated growth rates approved by the Board of Directors covering a four-year period and include a terminal value based upon maintainable cash flows.

If the VIU of a CGU is lower than its carrying amount, then the CGU's fair value less costs to sell (FVLCTS) is determined as AASB 136 requires the recoverable amount of a CGU to be the higher of VIU and FVLCTS. In applying the FVLCTS approach, the recoverable amount of a CGU is assessed using market based valuation techniques such as discounted cash flow analysis, comparable transactions and observable trading multiples.

Carrying value ($ thousands)	Goodwill 2013	Goodwill 2012	Brands 2013	Brands 2012
Billabong	$ —	$ —	$ —	$252,116
Element	—	850	—	28,630
Von Zipper	—	—	1,187	1,187
Kustom	1,763	3,746	10,540	10,540
Palmers	—	—	—	5,113
Honolua	7,090	6,453	4,385	4,385
Beachculture	—	—	—	853
Amazon	—	—	—	1,074
Xcel	3,504	10,920	3,666	3,336
Tigerlily	—	1,889	2,470	3,600
Sector 9	13,663	26,613	9,704	8,831
DaKine	—	77,719	36,739	44,128
RVCA	62,554	73,943	21,563	19,625
Australia	—	57,473	—	—
New Zealand	6,689	8,232	—	—
North America	—	114,619	—	—
Europe	—	6,021	—	—
	$95,263	$388,478	$90,254	$383,418

As at June 30, 2013, all of the above CGUs were tested for impairment in accordance with AASB 136. Due to the deterioration in trading conditions in the global retail sector, the Group has experienced significant declines in sales and profitability across a number of regions and brands and as a result impairment charges were recognised for the CGUs set out in the table below.

Impairment charge	Goodwill		Brands	
($ thousands)	2013	2012	2013	2012
Billabong	$ —	$ 55,083	$252,116	$182,417
Element	850	—	28,630	—
Kustom	1,983	—	—	—
Palmers	—	—	5,113	—
Beachculture	—	—	853	—
Amazon	—	—	1,158	—
Xcel	8,027	—	—	—
Tigerlily	1,889	—	1,130	—
DaKine	69,736	—	11,572	—
Sector 9	12,958	—	—	—
RVCA	18,416	—	—	—
Australia	57,473	17,410	—	—
New Zealand	2,178	—	—	—
South Africa	—	32,347	—	—
North America	113,359	39,500	—	—
Europe	6,065	—	—	—
	$292,934	$144,340	$300,572	$182,417

Billabong recognised $292,934 and $144,340 in goodwill impairment charges in fiscal years 2013 and 2012, respectively. The company explains in the above note that the impairments are attributed to declines in sales and profitability. At the end of June 30, 2013 (fiscal year 2013), Billabong had a goodwill balance of $95,263, made up of $553,520 in original cost net of $458,257 in accumulated impairment. Billabong's computations described in the note above are complex and illustrate the difficulties in determining impairment charges.

BUSINESS INSIGHT

In competitive bidding situations, the winning bidder is likely to be the one who most overvalued the item, a phenomenon known as the "winner's curse." Therefore, acquisition goodwill is viewed with some skepticism by financial analysts. Does the goodwill represent synergies like future cost savings or business opportunities that are available only to the combined companies? Or, does it represent an overpayment?

A *Wall Street Journal* article described multi-billion dollar goodwill impairment charges by Hewlett-Packard, Microsoft and Boston Scientific and ascribes these charges to acquisitions that did not "pan out." The article identified more companies whose goodwill assets exceeded their total market value.

When companies record a goodwill impairment charge, they often emphasise that the impairment was a "non-cash charge," implying that it is therefore less important. That statement is true as far as the current period is concerned, but acquisitions involve cash or some other item of value. In Hewlett-Packard's case, its $8 billion goodwill impairment in the third quarter of 2012 was primarily related to its acquisition of EDS, which required a cash outflow of more than $13 billion when the deal closed in 2008 and resulted in about $10.4 billion in goodwill. Goodwill impairment requires no *current* cash outflows, but it does reflect on the wisdom of *past* cash outflows.

Source: Scott Thurm, "Buyers Beware: The Goodwill Games," *Wall Street Journal*, August 14, 2012.

Limitations of Consolidation Reporting Consolidation of financial statements is meant to present a financial picture of the entire set of companies under control of the parent. Because investors typically purchase shares in the parent company and not in the subsidiaries, the view is more relevant than would be one of the parent company's own balance sheet with subsidiaries reported as equity investments. Still, we must be aware of certain limitations that the consolidation process entails:

1. Consolidated income does not imply that cash is received by the parent company and is available for subsidiaries. The parent can only receive cash via dividend payments, and dividend payments may trigger tax obligations. It is readily possible, therefore, for an individual subsidiary to experience cash flow problems even though the consolidated group has strong cash flows. Likewise, debts of a subsidiary are not obligations of the consolidated group. Thus, even if the consolidated balance sheet is strong, creditors of a failing subsidiary are often unable to sue the parent or other subsidiaries to recoup losses.
2. Consolidated balance sheets and income statements are a mix of the subsidiaries, often from different industries. Comparisons across companies, even if in similar industries, are often complicated by the different mix of subsidiary companies. Companies are required to report some financial results for their business segments. For instance, SMRT reports revenue, operating expenses, depreciation and amortisation, operating profits, operating asset, operating liabilities, and capital expenditure for each of its eight operating segments: rail operations, bus operations, taxi operations, commercial rental, advertising, engineering services, other services, and investment holding and support services.
3. Segment disclosures on individual subsidiaries are affected by intercorporate transfer-pricing policies that can artificially inflate the profitability of one segment at the expense of another. Companies also have considerable discretion in the allocation of corporate overhead to subsidiaries, which can markedly affect segment and subsidiary profitability.

FINANCIAL STATEMENT ANALYSIS

This section introduces no new ratios, but the topics covered in Chapter 12 do have implications for ratios covered in other chapters. For instance, gains and losses on available-for-sale securities are not recognised in income until those securities are sold. Therefore, management can increase net income by selling securities on which it has gains or decrease net income by selling securities on which it has losses. As a result, management may have a means to smooth the variations in income over time, using gains and losses from previous periods that have nothing to do with current performance. As careful financial statement users, we can read the footnotes to find the realised gains and losses included in income for the period.

Financial ratio comparisons are also affected by the percentage ownership of associate companies. For instance, suppose Naughton Group has 50% ownership in the company that distributes its products. Chapman Enterprises, a competitor of Naughton, owns 55% of the shares of the company that distributes its products. While the difference between 50% and 55% ownership probably has little economic significance, the accounting reports for Naughton and Chapman will look very different. Naughton's income statement will report only its own revenues and expenses, while Chapman's income statement will report its own revenues and expenses *and* the revenues and expenses of the distribution company (less any intercompany adjustments). Naughton's balance sheet will report its own assets, including its 50% equity in the distributor, while Chapman's balance sheet will report its own assets *plus* the assets of the distribution company. Financial statement readers should interpret comparisons of ratios like PPE Turnover in light of these effects.

A similar "quantum" change in accounting occurs at 20% ownership. There may appear to be little economic difference between owning 19% of a company's shares and owning 20% of those shares. But there is a significant difference in the accounting for those two alternatives, and this difference sometimes affects the choice between a 19% investment and a 20% investment. If the investee is a start-up earning losses, a 20% investment would require the investor to recognise 20% of those losses in its own income. A 19% investment would not recognise any share of the losses.

Finally, acquisitions disrupt the usual relationships between income statement and balance sheet items. When one company acquires another, the acquirer consolidates the acquired company as of the date that the deal closes. At that point, it includes the acquired company's assets and liabilities on the consolidated balance sheet, and it begins to report the acquired company's revenues and expenses from that time forward. So, if Hoskin Corp. acquires 100% of Lynch, Inc. on December 31, 2014, how will the inventory turnover ratio be affected? The 2014 cost of goods sold for Hoskin will reflect a year of Hoskin's COGS plus one day of Lynch's COGS. The beginning-of-year inventory will be 100% of Hoskin's inventory at that time, but the end-of-year inventory will be 100% of Hoskin's inventory *plus* 100% of Lynch's inventory. The inventory turnover ratio is likely to decrease significantly, but that decrease is due to the acquisition, not necessarily a decline in Hoskin's performance. A careful reader of the financial statements should try to separate out the effects of the acquisition from the ongoing performance of the company.

CHAPTER-END REVIEW

On January 1 of the current year, Kensington Company purchased all of the ordinary shares of Lawrence Company for $600,000 cash—this is $200,000 in excess of Lawrence's book value of its equity. The balance sheets of the two firms immediately after the acquisition follow:

	Kensington (Parent)	Lawrence (Subsidiary)	Consolidating Adjustments	Consolidated
Current assets	$1,000,000	$100,000		
Investment in Lawrence	600,000	—		
PPE, net	3,000,000	400,000		
Goodwill	—	—		
Total assets	$4,600,000	$500,000		
Liabilities	$1,000,000	$100,000		
Contributed capital	2,000,000	200,000		
Retained earnings	1,600,000	200,000		
Total liabilities and equity	$4,600,000	$500,000		

During purchase negotiations, Lawrence's PPE was appraised at $500,000, and all of Lawrence's remaining assets and liabilities were appraised at values approximating their book values. Also, Kensington concluded that payment of an additional $100,000 was warranted because of anticipated corporate synergies. Show the impact of the transaction in the financial statement effects template, prepare the appropriate journal entry, post the journal entry to the related T-accounts, and prepare the consolidated balance sheet at acquisition.

The solution to this review problem can be found on pages 614–615.

APPENDIX 12A: Equity Method Mechanics

LO6 Illustrate and analyse accounting mechanics for equity method investments.

The appendix provides a comprehensive example of accounting for an equity method investment. Assume that Petroni Company acquires a 30% interest in the outstanding voting shares of Wahlen Company on January 1, 2015, for $234,000 in cash. On that date, Wahlen's book value of equity is $560,000. Petroni agrees to pay $234,000 for a company with a book value of equity equivalent to $168,000 ($560,000 × 30%) because it feels that (1) Wahlen's balance sheet is undervalued by $140,000 (Petroni estimates PPE is undervalued by $50,000 and that Wahlen has unrecorded patents valued at $90,000) and (2) the investment is expected to yield intangible benefits valued at $24,000. (The $140,000 by which the balance sheet is undervalued translates into an investment equivalent of $42,000 [$140,000 × 30%]. This, plus the intangible benefits valued at $24,000, comprises the $66,000 difference between the purchase price [$234,000] and the book value equivalent [$168,000].)

The effect of the investment on Petroni's books is to reduce cash by $234,000 and to report the investment in Wahlen for $234,000. The investment is reported at its fair value at acquisition, just like all other asset acquisitions, and it is reported as a noncurrent asset because the expected holding period of equity method investments is in excess of one year. Subsequent to this purchase there are three main aspects of equity method accounting:

1. Dividends received from the investee are treated as a return *of* the investment rather than a return *on* the investment (investor company records an increase in cash received and a decrease in the investment account).
2. When the investee company reports net income for a period, the investor company reports its proportionate ownership of that income. This amount is usually reported in the investment income section of its income statement. Thus, both income and the investment account increase from equity method income. If the investee company reports a net *loss* for the period, income of the investor company is reduced as well as its investment account by its proportionate share.
3. The investment balance is not marked-to-fair value (market) as with passive investments. Instead, it is recorded at its historical cost and is increased (decreased) by the investor company's proportionate share of investee income (loss) and decreased by any cash dividends received. Unrecognised gains (losses) can, therefore, occur if the fair value of the investment differs from this adjusted cost. (If a decline in value is deemed "other than temporary," then the investment would be written down.)

To illustrate these mechanics, let's return to our illustration and assume that subsequent to acquisition, Wahlen reports net income of $50,000 and pays $10,000 cash dividends. Petroni would reflect these events in the FSET as follows:

Transaction	Balance Sheet: Cash Asset	+ Noncash Assets	= Liabil-ities	+ Contrib. Capital	+ Earned Capital	Income Statement: Revenues	− Expenses	= Net Income
(1) Purchase 30% of Wahlen Co. stock.	−234,000 Cash	+234,000 Invesment in Wahlen	=				−	=
(2) Recognise 30% of Wahlen Net Income		+15,000 Invesment in Wahlen			+15,000 Retained Earnings	+15,000 Invesment Income		+15,000
(3) Receive 30% of Wahlen Dividends	+3,000 Cash	−3,000 Invesment in Wahlen						

After these entries, the investment balance is $246,000. Petroni has an investing cash outflow of $234,000 and an operating cash inflow of $3,000. Retained earnings increase by $15,000 from recognising the 15% share of Wahlen's net income.

However, Petroni must also account for the differential values that accounted for the purchase premium. If Wahlen's PPE is undervalued by $50,000 and has an expected remaining life of twenty years, Petroni must amortise $750 (=30%*$50,000/20 years) in value for each of the next twenty years. And, if the unrecorded patents have an expected useful life of nine years, Petroni must amortise $3,000 (=30%*$90,000/9 years) of the investment's value for each of the coming nine years. These amortisations are deducted from the investment income recognised by Petroni. The entries are the following:

Transaction	Cash Asset	+ Noncash Assets	= Liabil-ities	+ Contrib. Capital	+ Earned Capital	Revenues	− Expenses	= Net Income
(4) Depreciate additional PPE value.		−750 Investment in Wahlen	=		−750 Retained Earnings	−750 Investment Income	−	= −750
(5) Amortise additional patent assets.		−3,000 Investment in Wahlen			−3,000 Retained Earnings	−3,000 Investment Income		−3,000

A part of the premium paid by Petroni is attributed to items that have definite lives (PPE and patents), and we must account for those amounts in judging the investment's performance. In this case, Petroni records income of $11,250 on its $234,000 investment—$15,000 for its share of Wahlen's income, minus the $3,750 amortisation of the premiium paid for PPE and patents. The Investment in Wahlen asset has a value of $242,250 ($234,000 + 15,000 − 3,000 − 750 − 3,000) after all entries.

The amount attributed to goodwill is tested for impairment annually, but it is not subject to periodic amortisation.

LO7 Apply consolidation accounting mechanics.

APPENDIX 12B: Consolidation Accounting Mechanics

This appendix is a continuation of the example we introduced in Appendix 12A, extended to the consolidation of a parent company and one wholly owned subsidiary. Assume that Petroni Company acquires 100% (rather than 30% as in Appendix 12A) of the outstanding voting shares of Wahlen Company on January 1, 2015.

To obtain these shares, Petroni pays $420,000 cash and issues 20,000 shares of its $10 par value ordinary shares. On this date, Petroni has a fair value of $18 per share, and Wahlen's book value of equity is $560,000. Petroni is willing to pay $780,000 ($420,000 plus 20,000 shares at $18 per share) for this company with a book value of equity of $560,000 because it believes Wahlen's balance sheet is understated by $140,000 (its PPE is undervalued by $50,000 and it has unrecorded patents valued at $90,000). The remaining $80,000 of the purchase price excess over book value is ascribed to corporate synergies and other unidentifiable intangible assets (goodwill). Thus, the purchase price consists of the following three components:

Investment ($780,000)	
	Book value of Wahlen ($560,000)
	Excess fair value over book ($140,000)
	Goodwill ($80,000)

The investment in Wahlen appears as a financial asset on Petroni's books. This means that at acquisition, Petroni's assets increase by $360,000 (cash decreases by $420,000 and the investments account increases by $780,000) and its equity (contributed capital) increases by the same amount.

The balance sheets of Petroni and Wahlen at acquisition follow, including the adjustments that occur in the consolidation process and the ultimate consolidated balance sheet.

Accounts	Petroni Company	Wahlen Company	Consolidation Adjustments* Entry S	Entry A	Consolidated Balance Sheet
Cash	$ 168,000	$ 80,000			$ 248,000
Receivables, net	320,000	180,000			500,000
Inventory	440,000	260,000			700,000
Investment in Wahlen	780,000	0	(560,000)	(220,000)	0
Land	200,000	120,000			320,000
PPE, net	1,040,000	320,000		50,000	1,410,000
Patent	0	0		90,000	90,000
Goodwill	0	0		80,000	80,000
Totals	$2,948,000	$960,000			$3,348,000
Accounts payable	$ 320,000	$ 60,000			$ 380,000
Long-term liabilities	760,000	340,000			1,100,000
Contributed capital	1,148,000	80,000	(80,000)		1,148,000
Retained earnings	720,000	480,000	(480,000)		720,000
Totals	$2,948,000	$960,000			$3,348,000

*Entry S refers to elimination of subsidiary equity, and Entry A refers to adjustment of assets and liabilities acquired.

The initial balance of the investment account at acquisition ($780,000) reflects the $700,000 fair value of Wahlen's net tangible assets and patents ($560,000 book value + $140,000 undervaluation of assets) plus the goodwill ($80,000) acquired. Goodwill is the excess of the purchase price over the fair value of the net assets acquired. It does not appear on Petroni's balance sheet as an explicit asset at this point. It is, however, included in the investment balance and will emerge as a separate asset during consolidation.

The process of completing the initial consolidated balance sheet involves eliminating Petroni's investment account and replacing it with the assets and liabilities of Wahlen Company to which it relates. Recall the investment account consists of three items: the book value of Wahlen ($560,000), the excess of net asset fair value over book value ($140,000), and goodwill ($80,000). The consolidation process eliminates each item as follows:

Entry S: Elimination of Wahlen's book value of equity: Investment account is reduced by the $560,000 book value of Wahlen, and each of the components of Wahlen's equity ($80,000 share capital and $480,000 retained earnings) are eliminated.

Entry A: Elimination of the excess of purchase price over book value: Investment account is reduced by $220,000 to zero. The remaining adjustments increase assets (A) by the additional purchase price paid. PPE is written up by $50,000, and a $90,000 patent asset and an $80,000 goodwill asset are reported.

Stepping back from the consolidation process, we can see its effects by comparing the Petroni Company (parent) balance sheet to the consolidated balance sheet. The Petroni Company balance sheet shows a financial asset valued at $780,000. Consolidation gives us a different perspective. Rather than viewing this as a financial investment, consolidation views the financial investment as the *means* by which Petroni Company acquired a bundle of assets and liabilities. That is, the financial asset of $780,000 has been replaced by Cash ($80,000), Receivables ($180,000), Inventory ($260,000), Land ($120,000), PPE—net ($370,000), Patent ($90,000), Goodwill ($80,000), Payables ($60,000), and Long-term liabilities ($340,000). This bundle has a net value equal to the $780,000, but it provides much more detail about the transaction that Petroni engaged in.

The one part of the balance sheet that is not changed by the consolidation is the shareholders' equity section. The consolidated shareholders' equity accounts are the same as the parent company shareholders' equity accounts when the parent owns 100% of the subsidiary.

Consolidation is similar in successive periods. To the extent that the excess purchase price has been assigned to depreciable assets, or identifiable intangible assets that are amortised over their useful lives, the new assets recognised initially are depreciated. If the PPE value adjustment has an estimated life of 20 years, then the consolidated income statement would include depreciation of 1/20 of this $50,000 each year. Amortisation of the $90,000 patent would also appear in the consolidated income statement. Finally, because goodwill is not amortised under IFRS, it remains at its carrying amount of $80,000 on the consolidated balance sheet unless and until it is impaired and written down.

APPENDIX 12C: Accounting for Investments in Derivatives

LO8 Discuss the reporting of derivative securities.

Derivatives refer to financial instruments that are utilised by companies to reduce various kinds of risks. Some examples follow:

- A company expects to purchase raw materials for its production process and wants to reduce the risk that the purchase price increases prior to the purchase.
- A company has an accounts receivable on its books that is payable in a foreign currency and wants to reduce the risk that exchange rates move unfavorably prior to collection.
- A company borrows funds on a floating rate of interest (such as linked to the prime rate) and wants to convert the loan to a fixed rate of interest.

Companies are commonly exposed to these and many similar types of risk. Although companies are generally willing to assume the normal market risks that are inherent in their business, many of these financial-type risks can add variability to income and are uncontrollable. Fortunately, commodities, currencies, and interest rates are all traded on various markets and, further, securities have been developed to manage all of these risks. These securities fall under the label of derivatives. They include forward contracts, futures contracts, option contracts, and swap agreements.

Companies use derivatives to manage many of these financial risks. The reduction of risk comes at a price: the fee that another party (called the counterparty) is charging to assume that risk. Most counterparties are financial institutions, and managing financial risk is their business and a source of their profits. Although derivatives can be used effectively to manage financial risk, they can also be used for speculation with potentially disastrous results. It is for this reason that regulators passed standards regarding their disclosure in financial statements.

Reporting of Derivatives Derivatives work by offsetting the gain or loss for the asset or liability to which they relate. Derivatives thus shelter the company from such fluctuations. For example, if a hedged receivable denominated in a foreign currency declines in value (due to a strengthening of the $US), the derivative security will increase in value by an offsetting amount, at least in theory. As a result, net equity remains unaffected and no gain or loss arises, nor is a loss reported in income.[4]

Although accounting for derivatives is complex, it essentially boils down to this: the derivative contract, and the asset or liability to which it relates, are both reported on the balance sheet at fair value. The asset and liability are offsetting *if* the hedge is effective and, thus, net equity is unaffected. Likewise, the related gains

[4] Unrealised gains and losses on derivatives classified as effective *cash flow hedges* (such as those relating to planned purchases of commodities) are accumulated in other comprehensive income (OCI) and are not recognised in current income until the transaction is complete (such as when both the purchase and sale of inventory occurs). Unrealised gains and losses on derivatives classified as *fair value hedges* (such as those relating to interest rate hedges and swaps, and the hedging of asset values such as relating to securities) as well as the changes in value of the hedged asset (liability) are recorded in current income.

and losses are largely offsetting, leaving income unaffected. Income is impacted only to the extent that the hedging activities are ineffective or result from speculative activities. It is this latter activity, in particular, that regulators were concerned about in formulating accounting standards for derivatives.

Disclosure of Derivatives Companies are required to disclose both qualitative and quantitative information about derivatives in notes to their financial statements and elsewhere (usually in Management's Discussion and Analysis section). The aim of these disclosures is to inform outsiders about potential risks underlying derivative securities.

Following are excerpts from Air Canada's note 17 to its 2013 annual report relating to its use of derivatives.

Risk Management

Under its risk management policy, Air Canada manages its interest rate risk, foreign exchange risk, share based compensation risk and market risk through the use of various interest rates, foreign exchange, fuel and other derivative financial instruments. Air Canada uses derivative financial instruments only for risk management purposes, not for generating trading profit. As such, any change in cash flows associated with derivative instruments is designed to be offset by changes in cash flows related to the risk being hedged. . .

Fuel Price Risk

Fuel price risk is the risk that future cash flows will fluctuate because of changes in jet fuel prices. In order to manage its exposure to jet fuel prices and to help mitigate volatility in operating cash flows, the Corporation. . . uses derivative contracts based on jet fuel, heating oil and crude-oil based contracts. The Corporation's policy permits hedging of up to 75% of the projected jet fuel purchases for the next 12 months, 50% for the next 13 to 24 months and 25% for the next 25 to 36 months. These are maximum (but not mandated) limits. There is no minimum monthly hedging requirement. . .

As of December 31, 2013, approximately 20% of the Corporation's anticipated purchases of jet fuel for 2014 are hedged at an average West Texas Intermediate ("WTI") equivalent capped price of US$100 per barrel. The Corporation's contracts to hedge anticipated jet fuel purchases over the 2014 period are comprised of call options with notional volumes of 5,136,000 barrels. The fair value of the fuel derivatives portfolio at December 31, 2013 is $20 in favour of the Corporation ($16 in favour of the Corporation in 2012) and is recorded within Prepaid expenses and other current assets.

Foreign Exchange Risk

The Corporation's financial results are reported in Canadian dollars, while a large portion of its revenues, expenses, debt obligations and capital commitments are in foreign currencies, primarily in US dollars. Foreign exchange risk is the risk that fluctuations in foreign exchange rates will adversely impact operating results and cash flows. . .

As at December 31, 2013, the Corporation had outstanding foreign currency options and swap agreements to purchase US dollars and Euros against Canadian dollars on $1,645 (US$1,547) and $72 (EUR $34, GBP $16) which mature in 2014 and 2015 at a weighted average rate of $1.0341 per $1.00 US dollar (2012—$1,289 (US$1,296) which matured in 2013). The fair value of these foreign currency contracts as at December 31, 2013 was $13 in favour of the Corporation (2012—less than $1 in favour of the Corporation). These derivative instruments have not been designated as hedges for accounting purposes and are recorded at fair value. During 2013, a gain of $68 was recorded in Foreign exchange gain (loss) related to these derivatives (2012—$20 gain).

Air Canada indicates that it uses various types of derivatives for risk management purposes only. For example, it entered into call option contracts to hedge about 20% of its projected jet fuel purchases for 2014, capping its fuel cost at US$100 per barrel. Under hedge accounting treatment, unrealised gains and losses on these option contracts are accumulated in the Accumulated Other Comprehensive Income (AOCI) portion of its shareholders' equity until the fuel is purchased. Once that fuel is purchased, those unrealised gains and losses are removed from AOCI and the gain (loss) on the option is used to offset the loss (gain) on fuel.

Moreover, Air Canada hedged its foreign exchange exposure using options and swaps. However, these derivative transactions did not qualify for hedge accounting treatment. As a result, the gains and losses on these derivative contracts are reported immediately in the income statement. The accounting for derivatives is complex and restrictive. Companies have voiced concerns about the type of hedging transactions that would qualify for special hedge accounting treatment. In this case, Air Canada decided to enter into a derivatives position that it believed is more effective in hedging its foreign exchange exposure, even though the derivatives did not qualify for hedge accounting treatment.

Although the fair value of derivatives and their related assets or liabilities can be substantial, the net effect on earnings and equity is usually minor because companies are mainly using them as hedges and not as speculative securities. The accounting standards for derivative instruments were enacted in response to a concern that speculative activities were not adequately disclosed. Subsequent to its passage, the financial effects have often appeared modest (with occasional exceptions such as JP Morgan Chase's "London Whale"). Either these companies were not speculating to the extent expected, or they have since reduced their level of speculation in response to increased scrutiny from better disclosures.

SUMMARY

LO1 Explain and interpret the three levels of investor influence over an investee–passive, significant, and controlling. (p. 554)

- Ownership of 20% or less in another corporation is treated as a passive investment by the investor.
- Significant influence is assumed to be available to the investor corporation if it owns more than 20% but not over 50% of the outstanding voting shares of the investee corporation.
- Control is generally presumed if the investing firm owns more than 50% of the outstanding voting shares of the investee corporation.

LO2 Describe the term "fair value" and the fair value hierarchy. (p. 556)

- Fair value is the amount that an independent buyer would be willing to pay for an asset (or the amount that would need to be paid to discharge a liability) in an orderly transaction.
- Fair value can be determined by reference to a market price when available, but it may also be determined by other methods (discounted cash flow analysis, pricing of comparable assets, etc.). IFRS defines three levels of fair value determination:
  - ❑ Level 1: Values based on quoted prices in active markets for identical assets/liabilities
  - ❑ Level 2: Values based on observable inputs other than Level 1 (e.g., quoted prices for similar assets/liabilities or interest rates or yield curves)
  - ❑ Level 3: Values based on inputs observable only to the reporting entity (e.g., management estimates or assumptions).
- IFRS requires that companies disclose their fair value determinations in the footnotes of their financial statements.

LO3 Describe and analyse accounting for passive investments. (p. 557)

- Ownership of 20% or less in another corporation is treated as a passive investment by the investor. Investing for returns is the objective rather than influencing another corporation's decisions. The investment is reported as a long-term asset only if the intention is to retain the asset for longer than a year. Passive investments are segregated into two types, called trading securities or securities available for sale.
- Trading securities are securities that will be converted into cash in a very short period of time. Any trading securities held at the end of an accounting period are marked to their fair value. The value change is recognised as an unrealised gain (or loss) in the income statement.
- Available-for-sale securities are held for long-term capital gains or dividends. Any securities held at the end of an accounting period are also marked to their fair value. However, the value change bypasses the income statement to become part of equity called other comprehensive income.
- Gains, losses realised on sale, and dividends on passive investments are reported as finance income in the income statement.
- Debt securities that management intends to hold to maturity are carried at amortised cost unless their value is considered impaired in which case the security is written down. Otherwise changes in fair value are not recognised on the balance sheet or the income statement.

LO4 Explain and analyse accounting for investments with significant influence. (p. 566)

- Significant influence is assumed to be available to the investor corporation if it owns more than 20% but not over 50% of the outstanding voting shares of the investee corporation. Typically, the investment is initially recorded as a long-term asset at the purchase price.
- In the case of significant influence, the equity method of reporting is followed.

- Under the equity method, the investor corporation reports the investment as a, typically, long-term asset. The investor recognises its proportionate share of the investee's net income as income and an increase in the investment account. Any dividends received by the investor are treated as a recovery of the investment and reduce the investment balance.

Describe and analyse accounting for investments with control. (p. 571) LO5

- If a corporation is considered to have control of another corporation, the financial statements of both firms are consolidated and reported as though they were a single entity.
- Control is generally presumed if the investing firm owns more than 50% of the outstanding voting shares of the investee corporation.
- Control can exist in special cases with less than 50% of the outstanding voting shares of the investee. Control means that the investor has the ability to affect the strategic direction of the investee.
- At the time of the acquisition, acquired assets and liabilities are restated at fair value in the consolidated balance sheet.
- If the purchase price exceeds the fair value of acquired assets, the remainder is labeled "goodwill." Goodwill is not amortised, but tested for impairment annually.

Appendix 12A: Illustrate and analyse accounting mechanics for equity method investments. (p. 583) LO6

- Under the equity method of accounting, neither the investee's assets nor its liabilities are reported on the investor's balance sheet. Only the proportionate investment is reported. Further, only the investor's proportionate share of investee's income is reported in income; and the investee's sales and expenses are omitted.
- The result is that revenues and expenses, but not NOPAT, are understated; NOPM (NOPAT/Sales) is overstated; and net operating assets (NOA) are understated. Also, financial leverage is understated. ROE remains unaffected.

Appendix 12B: Apply consolidation accounting mechanics. (p. 584) LO7

- Identifiable intangible assets (such as patents, trademarks, customer lists) often result from the acquisition of one corporation by another. This is a situation in which the acquirer will have control and consolidation accounting is required.
- Intangibles are valued at the purchase date and then amortised over their economic life. Any remaining purchase price not allocated to tangible or identifiable intangible assets is treated as goodwill.
- Goodwill is not amortised but is written down when and if considered impaired. The write-down is an expense of the period.
- Reports of consolidated corporations are often difficult to understand because they commingle the assets, liabilities, revenues, expenses, and cash flows of several businesses that can be very different. SMRT and its 18 subsidiaries provide an example.

Appendix 12C: Discuss the reporting of derivative securities. (p. 586) LO8

- Derivatives refer to financial instruments that are utilised by companies to reduce various kinds of risks.
- Derivatives work by offsetting the gain or loss for the asset or liability to which they relate.
- The accounting for derivatives boils down to this: the derivative contract and the asset or liability to which it relates are both reported on the balance sheet at fair value. The asset and liability are offsetting if the hedge is effective. Likewise, the related gains and losses are largely offsetting, leaving income unaffected.

GUIDANCE ANSWERS . . . YOU MAKE THE CALL

You are the Chief Financial Officer When a key component of a company's distribution process begins to turn its attention to other products, it can have a detrimental effect on the prospects for future growth. For instance, the soft-drink companies depend heavily on their bottling companies to get the product to the consumer. In these circumstances, companies may purchase enough shares in the distribution company to exert significant influence (or even control) over the key distributor.

KEY TERMS

Asset turnover ratios (Sales revenue/Average assets) (p. 571)
Available-for-sale (AFS) securities (p. 558)
Consolidated financial statements (p. 571)
Consolidation accounting (p. 572)
Controlling influence (p. 555)
Cost method (p. 562)
Derivatives (p. 586)
Equity method (p. 567)
Fair value (p. 556)
Fair value hierarchy (p. 556)
Fair value option (p. 557)
Financial investments (p. 554)
Financial leverage (Debt-to-equity = Total liabilities/Total equity) (p. 571)
Held-to-maturity (HTM) (p. 562)
Noncontrolling interest (p. 575)
Passive influence (p. 555)
Profit margin (PM = Earnings without interest expense [EWI]/Sales revenue) (p. 570)
Significant influence (p. 555)
Trading (T) securities (p. 558)

MULTIPLE CHOICE

Multiple Choice Answers
1. c 2. e 3. a 4. b

1. Corporation A owns 50% of corporation B. This is a case where:
a. Corporation A controls corporation B.
b. Corporation A does not control corporation B.
c. Corporation A has significant influence on corporation B.
d. Corporation A does not have a significant influence on corporation B.
e. Both *a* and *c* are correct.

2. In accounting for available-for-sale securities, the:
a. Securities are reported at their fair value, along with their fair value adjustment from cost.
b. Securities are reported at cost.
c. Increases in fair value are reported in income.
d. Increases in fair value are not reported in income.
e. Both *a* and *d* are correct.

3. Which of the following statements is true of investments accounted for under the equity method?
a. Investor reports its percentage share of the investee's income in its operating income.
b. Investor reports dividends received from the investee in its operating income.
c. Investment is reported at its fair value.
d. Investment is reported at cost plus any dividends received from the investee.
e. Investment is reported at fair value less any dividends received from the investee.

4. Which of the following statements is true about goodwill?
a. Current reporting standards require that goodwill be amortised over its economic life.
b. Goodwill is written down when the fair value of the investee implies a goodwill value below the investor's goodwill account.
c. Goodwill can be recognised only when the acquisition price does not exceed the value of the tangible and identifiable intangible assets acquired.
d. The recording of goodwill can be based on the acquisition of assets such as patents and trademarks.
e. Goodwill equals retained earnings.

Superscript A (B, C) denotes assignments based on Appendix 12A (12B, 12C).

DISCUSSION QUESTIONS

Q12-1. What measure (fair value or amortised cost) is used for the balance sheet to report (a) trading securities, (b) available-for-sale securities, and (c) held-to-maturity securities?

Q12-2. What is an unrealised holding gain (loss)? Explain.

Q12-3. Where are unrealised holding gains and losses related to trading securities reported in the financial statements? Where are unrealised holding gains and losses related to available-for-sale securities reported in the financial statements?

Q12-4. What does *significant influence* imply regarding financial investments? Describe the accounting procedures used for such investments.

Q12-5. On January 1 of the current year, YUL Company purchases 40% of the ordinary shares of CDG Company for $250,000 cash. During the year, CDG reports $80,000 of net income and pays $60,000 in cash dividends. At year-end, what amount should appear in YUL's balance sheet for its investment in CDG?

Q12-6. What accounting method is used when a stock investment represents more than 50% of the investee company's voting shares? Explain.

Q12-7. What is the underlying objective of consolidated financial statements?

Q12-8. Figolu Company purchases all of the ordinary shares of Gamby Company for $750,000 when Gamby Company has $300,000 of share capital and $450,000 of retained earnings. If a consolidated balance sheet is prepared immediately after the acquisition, what amounts are eliminated in preparing it? Explain.

Q12-9.[B] Bradshaw Company owns 100% of Dee Company. At year-end, Dee owes Bradshaw $75,000. If a consolidated balance sheet is prepared at year-end, how is the $75,000 handled? Explain.

Q12-10. What are some limitations of consolidated financial statements?

MINI EXERCISES

M12-11. Interpreting Disclosures of Available-for-Sale Securities LO1, 3

Use the following year-end footnote information from LHR Plc's annual report to answer parts *a* and *b*.

(£ millions)	2014
Cost of available-for-sale investments securities	£36,135
Gross unrealised gains	810
Gross unrealised losses	(22)
Fair value of available-for-sale investments securities	£36,923

a. At what amount is its available-for-sale investments reported on LHR's 2014 balance sheet? Explain.

b. How is its net unrealised gain of £788 million (£810 million − £22 million) reported by LHR in its financial statements?

M12-12. Accounting for Available-for-Sale and Trading Securities LO3

Assume that Wasley Company purchases 6,000 common shares of Pincus Company for $12 cash per share. During the year, Wasley receives a cash dividend of $1.10 per common share from Pincus, and the year-end market price of Pincus common shares is $13 per share. How much income does Wasley report relating to this investment for the year if it accounts for the investment as:

a. Available-for-sale investment?

b. Trading investment?

M12-13. Analysing Disclosures of Investment Securities LO1, 2

On its July 30, 2015 balance sheet, Hallstatt AG reports available-for-sale investments with a value of €36,923 million. As available-for-sale securities, these investments are reported at their fair value, and Hallstatt provides the following information in its footnotes.

	July 30, 2015 Fair Value Measurements			
	Level 1	Level 2	Level 3	Total Balance
Available-for-sale investments:				
Government securities	€ —	€19,139	€ —	€19,139
Government agency securities	—	8,776	—	8,776
Non-government and agency securities	—	3,132	—	3,132
Corporate debt securities	—	4,394	—	4,394
Asset-backed securities	—	—	121	121
Publicly traded equity securities	€1,361	€ —	€ —	€ 1,361

a. Explain the differences between the three columns labeled Level 1, Level 2 and Level 3.

b. Are all of these investments "marked-to-fair value?" If not, which ones are not marked-to-fair value? Which investment values do you regard as most subjective? Least subjective?

c. If Hallstatt needed to raise cash to take advantage of an investment opportunity, which of these investments do you regard as most liquid (i.e., most easily turned into cash)? Least liquid?

LO1, 4 M12-14. **Analysing and Interpreting Equity Method Investments**

Stober Company purchases an investment in Lang Company at a purchase price of $1 million cash, representing 30% of the book value of Lang. During the year, Lang reports net income of $100,000 and pays cash dividends of $40,000. At the end of the year, the fair value of Stober's investment is $1.2 million.

a. At what amount is the investment reported on Stober's balance sheet at year-end?

b. What amount of income from investments does Stober report? Explain.

c. Stober's $200,000 unrealised gain in investment fair value (choose one and explain):

1. Is not reflected on either its income statement or balance sheet.
2. Is reported in its current income.
3. Is reported on its balance sheet only.
4. Is reported in its other comprehensive income.

d. Prepare journal entries to record the transactions and events above.

e. Post the journal entries from *d* to their respective T-accounts.

f. Record each of the transactions from *d* in the financial statement effects template.

LO1, 4 M12-15. **Calculating Income for Equity Method Investments**

Kross Company purchases an equity investment in Penno Company at a purchase price of $5 million, representing 40% of the book value of Penno. During the current year, Penno reports net income of $600,000 and pays cash dividends of $200,000. At the end of the year, the market value of Kross's investment is $5.3 million. What amount of income does Kross report relating to this investment in Penno for the year? Explain.

LO1, 4 M12-16. **Interpreting Disclosures on Investments in Joint Ventures (Equity Method)**

Aberdeen H.K. Ltd. has a 50 percent equity interest in two joint ventures—Central Partners and Admiralty Inc.—and uses the equity method to account for these investments. The company's annual report for the fiscal year ending May 29, 2015 states that Aberdeen has the ability to exert significant influence over these joint venture companies, and their investment balances "are stated at cost plus our share of undistributed earnings or losses. . . In addition, we make advances to our joint ventures in the form of loans or capital investments." At May 30, 2014, Aberdeen's balance in "Investments in and advances to joint ventures" was $398.1 million.

How do the following items affect the financial statements of Aberdeen?

a. Aberdeen's share of joint venture income was $96.4 million for the fiscal year ending May 29, 2015.

b. Aberdeen's cash received from "distributions of earnings from joint ventures" was $72.7 million for the fiscal year ending May 29, 2015.

c. The balance in "Investments in and advances to joint ventures" was $519.1 million on May 29, 2015. Suppose that the only other event affecting this account was due to advances made by Aberdeen or advances repaid by the joint ventures. Did Aberdeen's advances to joint ventures increase or decrease during the year? By how much?

LO1, 5 M12-17. **Computing Consolidating Adjustments and Noncontrolling Interest**

Sussex Company purchases 80% of Hirst Company's ordinary shares for $600,000 cash when Hirst Company has $300,000 of share capital and $450,000 of retained earnings. If a consolidated balance sheet is prepared immediately after the acquisition, what amounts are eliminated when preparing that statement? What amount of noncontrolling interest appears in the consolidated balance sheet?

LO1, 5 M12-18. **Computing Consolidated Net Income**

Benartzi Company purchased a 90% interest in Liang Company on January 1 of the current year. Benartzi Company had $600,000 net income for the current year *before* recognising its share of Liang Company's net income. If Liang Company had net income of $150,000 for the year, what is the consolidated net income for the year?

M12-19. Effect of Investing on Ratios LO4, 5

DeFond Company wishes to secure a reliable supply of a key component for its production processes, and its management is considering two alternative investments. Verduzco Company produces exactly the supply that DeFond needs, so DeFond could use cash to purchase 100% of the ordinary shares of Verduzco. Lin Company produces twice as much of the component that DeFond needs, but DeFond could form a joint venture with another company where each would purchase 50% of Lin Company's ordinary shares and each take 50% of Lin Company's output.

The table that follows gives the balance sheet information for all three companies prior to any investment by DeFond. For the questions below, assume that DeFond would be able to purchase shares at the investee companies' book value and that the investee companies' assets and liabilities have fair values equal to their book values.

	DeFond Company	Verduzco Company	Lin Company
Cash	$ 800	$ 100	$ 200
Investment	—	—	—
Noncash assets	2,000	900	1,800
Liabilities	2,200	700	1,400
Shareholders' Equity	600	300	600

a. Suppose that DeFond purchases 100% of Verduzco's ordinary shares for $300. Produce the consolidated balance sheet for DeFond immediately after the acquisition.

b. Suppose that DeFond purchases 50% of Lin's ordinary shares for $300. Produce the balance sheet for DeFond immediately after the investment (using the equity method).

c. From a business perspective, either of these investments will accomplish the objective of obtaining a reliable supply of components. How will the financial ratios differ between the two alternatives?

M12-20. Reporting of and Analysing Financial Effects of Trading (Debt) Securities LO1, 3

Hartgraves Company had the following transactions and adjustments related to a bond investment that is a trading security.

2013

Oct. 1 Purchased $500,000 face value of Skyline, Inc.'s 7% bonds at 97 plus a brokerage commission of $1,000. The bonds pay interest on September 30 and March 31 and mature in 20 years. Hartgraves Company expects to sell the bonds in the near future.

Dec. 31 Made the adjusting entry to record interest earned on investment in the Skyline bonds.

31 Made the adjusting entry to record the current fair value of the Skyline bonds. At December 31, 2013, the fair value of the Skyline bonds was $490,000.

2014

Mar. 31 Received the semiannual interest payment on investment in the Skyline bonds.

Apr. 1 Sold the Skyline bond investment for $492,300 cash.

a. Prepare journal entries to record these transactions.

b. Post the journal entries from *a* to their respective T-accounts.

c. Record each of the transactions in the financial statement effects template.

M12-21. Reporting of and Analysing Financial Effects of Trading (Equity) Securities LO1, 3

Blouin Company had the following transactions and adjustment related to a stock investment that is a trading security.

2013

Nov. 15 Purchased 10,000 shares of Lane, Inc.'s ordinary shares at $17 per share plus a brokerage commission of $1,200. Blouin expects to sell the shares in the near future.

Dec. 22 Received a cash dividend of $1.00 per ordinary share from Lane.

31 Made the adjusting entry to reflect year-end fair value of the equity investment in Lane. The year-end fair value of the Lane ordinary shares is $15.50 per share.

2014

Jan. 20 Sold all 10,000 Lane ordinary shares for $150,000.

a. Prepare journal entries to record these transactions.

b. Post the journal entries from *a* to their respective T-accounts.

c. Record each of the transactions in the financial statement effects template.

LO1, 3 M12-22. **Reporting of and Analysing Financial Effects of Available-for-Sale (Equity) Securities**
Refer to the data for Blouin Company in Mini Exercise 12-21. Assume that when the shares were purchased, management did not intend to sell the shares in the near future. Record the transactions and adjustments for Blouin Company as an available-for-sale security.

LO1, 5 M12-23. **Computing Equity in Consolidation**
On January 1 of the current year, Hugo SA purchased all of the common shares of Carnot SA for €575,000 cash. On this date, the equity of Hugo SA consisted of €600,000 in share capital and €310,000 in retained earnings. Carnot SA had €350,000 in share capital and €225,000 in retained earnings. What amount of total equity appears on the consolidated balance sheet?

EXERCISES

LO1, 3 E12-24. **Assessing Financial Statement Effects of Trading and Available-for-Sale Securities**
Four transactions involving investments in marketable securities classified as trading follow.

(1) Purchased 6,000 common shares of Liu, Inc., for $12 cash per share.
(2) Received a cash dividend of $1.10 per common share from Liu.
(3) Year-end market price of Liu common shares is $11.25 per share.
(4) Sold all 6,000 common shares of Liu for $66,900.

a. Prepare journal entries to record the four transactions.
b. Post the journal entries from *a* to their respective T-accounts.
c. Record each of the transactions from *a* in the financial statement effects template.
d. Using the same transaction information as above and assuming the investments in marketable securities are classified as available-for-sale, (i) prepare journal entries to record the transactions, (ii) post the journal entries to their respective T-accounts, and (iii) record each of the transactions in the financial statement effects template.

LO1, 3 E12-25. **Assessing Financial Statement Effects of Trading and Available-for-Sale Securities**
For the following transactions involving investments in marketable securities, assume that:

a. Investments are classified as trading.
1. Ohlson Co. purchases 5,000 common shares of Freeman Co. at $16 cash per share.
2. Ohlson Co. receives a cash dividend of $1.25 per common share from Freeman.
3. Year-end market price of Freeman common shares is $17.50 per share.
4. Ohlson Co. sells all 5,000 common shares of Freeman for $86,400 cash.
(i) prepare journal entries to record the four transactions, (ii) post the journal entries to their respective T-accounts, and (iii) record each of the transactions in the financial statement effects template.

b. Investments are classified as available-for-sale (for same four transactions from *a*).
(i) prepare journal entries to record the transactions, (ii) post the journal entries to their respective T-accounts, and (iii) record each of the transactions in the financial statement effects template.

LO1, 3 E12-26. **Interpreting Note Disclosures on Security Investments**
WESTPAC BANKING CORPORATION (AUSTRALIA)
Founded in 1817, Westpac Banking Corporation was the first bank established in Australia. Westpac has branches and controlled entities throughout Australia, New Zealand, and the Pacific region. It also has offices in London, New York, Hong Kong, and Singapore. The following is the asset section of Westpac's balance sheet as of September 30, 2014:

(in $ million)	Note	2014	2013
Assets			
Cash and balances with central banks	43	$ 25,760	$ 11,699
Receivables due from other financial institutions	8	7,424	11,210
Trading securities and other financial assets designated at fair value	9	45,909	49,089
Derivative financial instruments	29	41,404	28,356
Available-for-sale securities	10	36,024	30,011
Loans	11	580,343	536,164
Life insurance assets		11,007	13,149
Regulatory deposits with central banks overseas		1,528	1,571
Due from subsidiaries		—	—
Investments in subsidiaries		—	—
Property, plant and equipment	13	1,452	1,174
Deferred tax assets	14	1,397	1,773
Goodwill and other intangible assets	15	12,606	12,341
Other assets	16	5,988	4,560
Total assets		$770,842	$701,097

The available-for-sale securities reserve section of Westpac's statement of changes in equity, as of September 30, 2014, is provided below:

Available-for-sale securities reserve	
Balance as at beginning of the year	12
Current period movement due to changes in other comprehensive income:	
Net gains/(losses) from changes in fair value	263
Exchange differences	—
Income tax effect	(79)
Transferred to income statements	(94)
Income tax effect	27
Balance as at end of the year	129

a. What are the differences between trading securities and available-for-sale securities?

b. What are the fair value of Westpac's trading securities and available-for-sale securities at September 30, 2014?

c. Assume that the acquisition cost of the trading securities was $44,700 at September 30, 2014. Did Westpac have an unrealised gain or loss on these securities?

d. How did the unrealised gain or loss on trading securities affect Westpac's 2014 balance sheet and income statement?

e. Did Westpac have an unrealised gain or loss on its available-for-sale securities?

f. How did the unrealised gain or loss on available-for-sale securities affect Westpac's 2014 balance sheet and income statement?

g. Did Westpac sell any available-for-sale securities in fiscal year 2014? If yes, did it recognise any gain or loss on the sale?

E12-27. Reporting of and Analysing Financial Effects of Trading (Debt) Securities LO1, 3

Ghent N.V., Inc., had the following transactions and adjustments related to a bond investment that is classified as a trading security.

2014

Nov. 1 Purchased €300,000 face value of Joos, Inc.'s 9% bonds at 102 plus a brokerage commission of €900. The bonds pay interest on October 31 and April 30 and mature in 15 years. Ghent N.V. expects to sell the bonds in the near future.

Dec. 31 Made the adjusting entry to record interest earned on investment in the Joos bonds.

31 Made the adjusting entry to record the current fair value of the Joos bonds. At December 31, 2014, the fair value of the Joos bonds was €301,500.

2015

Apr. 30 Received the semiannual interest payment on investment in the Joos bonds.
May 1 Sold the Joos bond investment for €300,900 cash.

a. Prepare journal entries to record these transactions.
b. Post the journal entries from *a* to their respective T-accounts.
c. Record each of the transactions in the financial statement effects template.

LO1, 5 E12-28. **Reporting of Equity in Consolidation**

SYD Company purchased 75% of the ordinary shares of Milsons Company for $600,000 in cash when the equity of Milsons Company consisted of $500,000 in share capital and $300,000 in retained earnings. On the acquisition date, the equity of SYD Company consisted of $900,000 in share capital and $440,000 in retained earnings. Prepare the equity section in the consolidated balance sheet as of the acquisition date.

LO1, 3 E12-29. **Interpreting Note Disclosures on Available-for-Sale Securities**

HYUNDAI MOTOR COMPANY (SOUTH KOREA)

Headquartered in Seoul, South Korea, **Hyundai Motor Company** (HMC) is a one of the largest automotive manufacturers in the world. HMC's 2013 annual report provides the following information for available-for-sale (AFS) securities:

(7) Financial assets

The Group classifies financial assets into the following specified categories: financial assets at fair value through profit or loss ("FVTPL "), held-to-maturity ("HTM") financial assets, loans and receivables and available-for-sale ("AFS") financial assets. The classification depends on the nature and purpose of the financial assets and is determined at the time of initial recognition. . .

4) AFS financial assets

AFS financial assets are those non-derivative financial assets that are designated as AFS or are not classified as loans and receivables, HTM financial assets nor financial assets at FVTPL. AFS financial assets are measured at fair value. However, investments in equity instruments that do not have a quoted market price in an active market and whose fair value cannot be reliably measured are measured at cost.

A gain or loss on changes in fair value of AFS financial assets is recognised in other comprehensive income, except for impairment loss, interest calculated using the effective interest method and foreign exchange gains and losses on monetary assets. Accumulated other comprehensive income is reclassified to profit or loss from equity at the time of impairment recognition or elimination of related financial assets. Dividends on an AFS equity instrument are recognised in profit or loss when the Group's right to receive payment is established.

(2) AFS financial assets that are measured at fair value as of December 31, 2013 and 2012, consist of the following:

	December 31, 2013			December 31, 2012
Description (In millions of Korean Won)	**Acquisition Cost**	**Valuation difference**	**Book value**	**Book value**
Debt instruments.	₩ 123,906	₩ 334	₩ 124,240	₩ 15,074
Equity instruments	1,445,018	946,138	2,391,156	1,541,461
	₩1,568,924	₩946,472	₩2,515,396	₩1,556,535

a. At what amount is HMC's AFS investment portfolio reflected on its balance sheet? In your answer identify its fair value, cost, and any unrealised gains and losses.
b. How are its unrealised gains and/or losses reflected in HMC's balance sheet and income statement?
c. How are any impairment losses and the gains and losses realised from the sale of AFS securities reflected in HMC's balance sheet and income statement?

E12-30. Assessing Financial Statement Effects of Equity Method Securities LO1, 4

The following transactions involve investments in marketable securities and are accounted for using the equity method.

(1) Purchased 12,000 common shares of Barth Co. at $9 cash per share; the shares represent 30% ownership in Barth.
(2) Received a cash dividend of $1.25 per common share from Barth.
(3) Recorded income from Barth stock investment when Barth's net income is $80,000.
(4) Sold all 12,000 common shares of Barth for $120,500.

a. Prepare journal entries to record these four transactions.
b. Post the journal entries from *a* to their respective T-accounts.
c. Record each of the transactions in the financial statement effects template.

E12-31. Assessing Financial Statement Effects of Equity Method Securities LO1, 4

The following transactions involve investments in marketable securities and are accounted for using the equity method.

(1) Healy Co. purchases 15,000 common shares of Palepu Co. at $8 cash per share; the shares represent 25% ownership of Palepu.
(2) Healy receives a cash dividend of $0.80 per common share from Palepu.
(3) Palepu reports annual net income of $120,000.
(4) Healy sells all 15,000 common shares of Palepu for $140,000 cash.

a. Prepare journal entries to record these four transactions.
b. Post the journal entries from *a* to their respective T-accounts.
c. Record each of the transactions in the financial statement effects template.

E12-32. Assessing Financial Statement Effects of Passive and Equity Method Investments LO1, 3, 4

On January 1, 2013, Ball Corporation purchased, as a stock investment, 10,000 common shares of Leftwich Company for $15 cash per share. On December 31, 2013, Leftwich announced net income of $80,000 for the year and paid a cash dividend of $1.10 per share. At December 31, 2013, the market value of Leftwich's shares was $19 per share.

a. Assume that the shares acquired by Ball represent 15% of Leftwich's voting shares and that Ball classifies the shares as available-for-sale. For the following transactions, (1) prepare journal entries, (2) post those journal entries to their respective T-accounts, and (3) record each of the transactions in the financial statement effects template.
   1. Ball purchased 10,000 common shares of Leftwich at $15 cash per share; the shares represent a 15% ownership in Leftwich.
   2. Leftwich reported annual net income of $80,000.
   3. Received a cash dividend of $1.10 per common share from Leftwich.
   4. Year-end market price of Leftwich common shares is $19 per share.

b. Assume that the shares acquired by Ball represent 30% of Leftwich's voting shares and that Ball accounts for this investment using the equity method since it is able to exert significant influence. For the same four transactions as above, (1) prepare journal entries, (2) post those journal entries to their respective T-accounts, and (3) record each of the transactions in the financial statement effects template.

E12-33. Interpreting Disclosures on Investments in Joint Ventures and Associates LO1, 4

TESCO PLC (UNITED KINGDOM)

Tesco Plc is a British multinational retailer, with operations in the United Kingdom, Asia, and Europe. The company reports its investments in joint ventures and associates in the following note from its 2013 annual report.

Interests in joint ventures and associates

The Group uses the equity method of accounting for its interest in joint ventures and associates. The following table shows the aggregate movement in the Group's investment in joint ventures and associates:

(in £ millions)	Joint ventures	Associates	Total
At February 25, 2012	£308	£115	£423
Additions*	11	87	98
Disposals	(1)	(43)	(44)
Foreign currency translation	10	6	16
Share of post-tax profits of joint ventures and associates	35	19	54
Other movements in reserves	–	(2)	(2)
Dividends received from joint ventures and associates	(46)	(5)	(51)
At February 23, 2013	317	177	494
Additions*	3	2	5
Disposals	(1)	—	(1)
Foreign currency translation	(2)	(16)	(18)
Share of post-tax profits of joint ventures and associates	43	8	51
Other movements in reserves	—	(5)	(5)
Dividends received from joint ventures and associates	(39)	(23)	(62)
Transferred to assets of the disposal group	(178)	—	(178)
At February 22, 2014	£143	£143	£286

*Additions are net of £5m deferred gain (2013: £60m).

Share of post-tax profits of joint ventures includes £(9)m loss attributable to joint venture operations of China for the first six months of the year ended February 22, 2014.

a. What amount does Tesco report on its balance sheet for investments in associates at February 22, 2014?

b. How does Tesco's share of income of its associates affect its fiscal 2013 income statement and balance sheet?

c. Why does cash dividends received from joint ventures and associates reduce Tesco's investments in these companies?

d. How do changes in the market value of the associate companies affect Tesco's balance sheet?

LO2, 5, 7 **E12-34. Allocation of Acquisition Purchase Price**

DEUTSCHE TELEKOM AG (GERMANY)

On May 1, 2013, Deutsche Telekom AG completed its acquisition of MetroPCS Communications Inc. for €1,640 million. In its 2013 annual report, Deutsche Telekom reported the allocation of this purchase price to the various assets and liabilities that it acquired in this transaction.

The fair values of MetroPCS's acquired assets and liabilities recognised at the acquisition date are presented in table T060 below. Following the original determination of fair values at the date of the transaction, the measurement basis for derivative financial instruments were adjusted within non-current financial assets and liabilities as of September 30, 2013. As a result, the carrying amounts of both items increased by €90 million each. The purchase price allocation was completed on December 31, 2013.

T060 millions of €	Fair value at the acquisition date
Assets	
Current Assets	**€1,980**
Cash and cash equivalents	1,639
Trade and other receivables	65
Other financial assets	10
Inventories	131
Other assets	135
Non-current assets	**5,349 + GW**
Intangible assets	4,097 + GW
Of which: FCC licenses	2,920
Of which: goodwill	GW
Of which: customer base	845
Of which: brand name	178
Of which: other	154
Property, plant and equipment	1,033
Other financial assets	216
Deferred tax assets	3
Assets	**7,329 + GW**
Liabilities and shareholders' equity	
Current liabilities	**521**
Financial liabilities	43
Trade and other payables	205
Income tax liabilities	1
Other provisions	68
Other liabilities	204
Non-current liabilities	**5,823**
Financial liabilities	5,037
Other provisions	161
Deferred tax liabilities	518
Other liabilities	107
Liabilities	**€6,344**

a. How are the values in the above table determined?

b. How much Goodwill (GW) would Deutsche Telekom recognise from this acquisition? How will that goodwill be treated in subsequent periods?

c. Do you think Deutsche Telekom's shareholders would prefer to see an allocation that gives a lot of value to separately identifiable assets or an allocation where most of the acquisition price goes to goodwill? Why?

E12-35. Reporting of and Analysing Financial Effects of Trading (Equity) Securities LO1, 3

IFC Company had the following transactions and adjustment related to a stock investment classified as a trading security.

2013

Nov. 15 Purchased 5,000 shares of ICC, Inc.'s common shares at $16 per share plus a brokerage commission of $900. IFC Company expects to sell the shares in the near future.

Dec. 22 Received a cash dividend of $1.25 per share of common shares from ICC.

31 Made the adjusting entry to reflect year-end fair value of the stock investment in ICC. The year-end market price of the ICC common shares is $17.50 per share.

2014

Jan. 20 Sold all 5,000 ICC common shares for $86,400.

a. Prepare journal entries to record these transactions.

b. Post the journal entries from *a* to their respective T-accounts.

c. Record each of the transactions in the financial statement effects template.

E12-36. Reporting of and Analysing Financial Effects of Available-for-Sale (Equity) Securities LO1, 3

Refer to the data for IFC Company in Exercise 12-35. Assume that when the shares were purchased, management did not intend to sell the shares in the near future. Record the transactions and adjustments for IFC Company under this assumption.

LO1, 3, 4 E12-37. **Reporting and Interpreting Stock Investment Performance**

Kasznik Company began operations in 2014 and, by year-end (December 31), had made six equity investments. Year-end information on these equity investments follows.

Company	Cost or Equity Basis (as appropriate)	Year-End Fair Value	Investment Classification
Barth, Inc.	$ 68,000	$ 65,300	Trading
Foster, Inc.	162,500	160,000	Trading
McNichols, Inc.	197,000	192,000	Available-for-sale
Patell, Inc.	157,000	154,700	Available-for-sale
Ertimur, Inc.	100,000	102,400	Equity method
Soliman, Inc.	136,000	133,200	Equity method

a. At what total amount are the trading equity investments reported at in the December 31, 2014, balance sheet?

b. At what total amount are the available-for-sale equity investments reported at in the December 31, 2014, balance sheet?

c. At what total amount are the equity method equity investments reported at in the December 31, 2014, balance sheet?

d. What total amount of unrealised holding gains or unrealised holding losses related to equity investments appears in the 2014 income statement?

e. What total amount of unrealised holding gains or unrealised holding losses related to equity investments appears in the equity section of the December 31, 2014, balance sheet?

f. What total amount of fair value adjustment to equity investments appears in the December 31, 2014, balance sheet? Which category of shares investments does the fair value adjustment relate to? Does the fair value adjustment increase or decrease the financial statement presentation of these equity investments?

LO1, 4 E12-38. **Analysing Equity Method Investment Footnotes**

Wellesley & Co., Inc. reports a December 31, 2013 balance of $494 million in "Investments in associates accounted for using the equity method" ("Investments in associates"). Provide the entries for the following events for fiscal year 2014:

a. Wellesley's share of income from its associates was $610 million.

b. Wellesley received dividends and distributions from its associates of $216 million during fiscal year 2014.

c. During fiscal year 2014, Wellesley divested its joint venture TTC. The proceeds from this divestiture were $175 million, and Wellesley reported a gain on the divestiture of $136 million.

d. After these events, what should be the balance in Wellesley's Investments in associates account at December 31, 2014? The actual balance was $886 million. What might explain any differences between these two values?

LO1, 7 E12-39. **Constructing the Consolidated Balance Sheet at Acquisition**

On January 1 of the current year, Healy Company purchased all of the common shares of Miller Company for $500,000 cash. Balance sheets of the two firms at acquisition follow.

	Healy Company	Miller Company	Consolidating Adjustments	Consolidated
Current assets	$1,700,000	$120,000		
Investment in Miller	500,000	—		
Plant assets, net	3,000,000	410,000		
Goodwill	—	—		
Total assets	$5,200,000	$530,000		
Liabilities	$ 700,000	$ 90,000		
Contributed capital	3,500,000	400,000		
Retained earnings	1,000,000	40,000		
Total liabilities and equity	$5,200,000	$530,000		

During purchase negotiations, Miller's plant assets were appraised at $425,000; and, all of its remaining assets and liabilities were appraised at values approximating their book values. Healy also concluded that an additional $45,000 (in goodwill) demanded by Miller's shareholders was warranted because Miller's earning power was better than the industry average. (1) Prepare the consolidating adjustments, (2) Prepare the consolidated balance sheet at acquisition, (3) Prepare journal entries to record the transactions, (4) Post the journal entries to their respective T-accounts, and (5) Record each of the transactions in the financial statement effects template.

E12-40. Constructing the Consolidated Balance Sheet at Acquisition **LO1, 7**

Rayburn Company purchased all of Kanodia Company's common shares for cash on January 1, at which time the separate balance sheets of the two corporations appeared as follows:

	Rayburn Company	Kanodia Company	Consolidating Adjustments	Consolidated
Investment in Kanodia	$ 600,000	—		
Other assets	2,300,000	$700,000		
Goodwill	—	—		
Total assets	$2,900,000	$700,000		
Liabilities	$ 900,000	$160,000		
Contributed capital	1,400,000	300,000		
Retained earnings	600,000	240,000		
Total liabilities and equity	$2,900,000	$700,000		

During purchase negotiations, Rayburn determined that the appraised value of Kanodia's Other Assets was $720,000; and, all of its remaining assets and liabilities were appraised at values approximating their book values. The remaining $40,000 of the purchase price was ascribed to goodwill. (1) Prepare the consolidating adjustments, (2) Prepare the consolidated balance sheet at acquisition, (3) Prepare journal entries to record the transactions, (4) Post the journal entries to their respective T-accounts, and (5) Record each of the transactions in the financial statement effects template.

E12-41. Assessing Goodwill Impairment **LO1, 5**

On January 1, 2013, Perigord SA purchases 100% of Nimes SA for €16.8 million. At the time of acquisition, Nimes's equity is reported at €16.2 million. Perigord ascribes the excess of €600,000 to goodwill. Assume that the fair value of Nimes less costs of disposal is €16.6 million and the value in use of Nimes is €16.5 million as of December 31, 2013. Perigord treats Nimes as a cash-generating unit for the purpose of conducting a goodwill impairment test.

a. Provide computations to determine if the goodwill has become impaired and, if so, the amount of the impairment.

b. What impact does the impairment of goodwill have on Perigord's financial statements?

E12-42.[B] Constructing the Consolidated Balance Sheet at Acquisition **LO1, 5, 7**

Easton Company acquires 100 percent of the outstanding voting shares of Harris Company on January 1, 2013. To obtain these shares, Easton pays $210,000 in cash and issues 5,000 of its $10 par value common shares. On this date, Easton's shares have a fair value of $36 per share, and Harris's book value of equity is $280,000. Easton is willing to pay $390,000 for a company with a book value for equity of $280,000 because it believes that (1) Harris's buildings are undervalued by $40,000, and (2) Harris has an unrecorded patent that Easton values at $30,000. Easton considers the remaining balance sheet items to be fairly valued (no book-to-fair value difference). The remaining $40,000 of the purchase price excess over book value is ascribed to corporate synergies and other general unidentifiable intangible assets (goodwill). The January 1, 2013, balance sheets at the acquisition date follow:

	Easton Company	Harris Company	Consolidating Adjustments	Consolidated
Cash	$ 84,000	$ 40,000		
Receivables	160,000	90,000		
Inventory	220,000	130,000		
Investment in Harris	390,000	—		
Land	100,000	60,000		
Buildings, net	400,000	110,000		
Equipment, net	120,000	50,000		
Total assets	$1,474,000	$480,000		
Accounts payable	$ 160,000	$ 30,000		
Long-term liabilities	380,000	170,000		
Common stock	500,000	40,000		
Additional paid-in capital	74,000	—		
Retained earnings	360,000	240,000		
Total liabilities & equity	$1,474,000	$480,000		

a. Show the breakdown of the investment into the book value acquired, the excess of fair value over book value, and the portion of the investment representing goodwill.

b. Prepare the consolidating adjustments and the consolidated balance sheet. Identify the adjustments by whether they relate to the elimination of equity [S] or the excess of purchase price over book value [A].

c. How will the excess of the purchase price over book value acquired be treated in years subsequent to the acquisition?

LO1, 4 **E12-43. Interpreting Disclosures on Investments in Joint Ventures and Associates**

ROGERS COMMUNICATIONS INC. (CANADA)

Rogers Communications Inc. is a Canadian communications and media company, based in Toronto. The following information is taken from Note 17 of the company's 2014 annual report:

INVESTMENTS, ASSOCIATES AND JOINT VENTURES

We have interests in a number of associates and joint ventures, some of which include:

Maple Leaf Sports and Entertainment Limited (MLSE)

MLSE, a sports and entertainment company, owns and operates the Air Canada Centre, the NHL's Toronto Maple Leafs, the NBA's Toronto Raptors, the MLS' Toronto FC, the AHL's Toronto Marlies and other assets. We, along with BCE Inc., jointly own an indirect net 75% equity interest in MLSE with our portion representing a 37.5% equity interest in MLSE. Our investment in MLSE is a joint venture and is accounted for using the equity method.

shomi

In 2014, we entered into a joint venture equally owned by Rogers and Shaw Communications Inc. to develop, launch and operate a premium subscription video-on-demand service offering movies and television series for viewing on-line and through cable set-top boxes. Our investment in shomi is a joint venture and is accounted for using the equity method.

The following table provide summary financial information on all our material associates and joint ventures and our portions thereof. We record our investments in joint ventures and associates using the equity method.

(In millions of dollars)	2014	2013
Current assets	$ 261	$ 153
Long-term assets	2,577	2,434
Current liabilities	432	334
Long-term liabilities	1,247	1,146
Total net assets	1,159	1,108
Our share of net assets	580	554
Revenues	714	648
Expenses	736	644
Total net (loss) income	(22)	4
Our share of net (loss) income	$ (11)	$ 2

a. What amount does Rogers report on its balance sheet for investments in joint ventures and associates at the end of fiscal 2014?

b. How does Rogers's share of income of its joint ventures and associates affect its fiscal 2014 income statement and balance sheet?

c. How do changes in the market value of the joint ventures and associate companies affect Rogers's balance sheet?

d. What journal entry would Rogers make to record cash dividends received from its joint ventures and associates?

PROBLEMS

P12-44. Analysing and Interpreting Available-for-Sale Securities Disclosures LO3, 4, 5

L'ORÉAL SA (FRANCE)

L'Oréal SA is the world's largest cosmetics company, with headquarters in Clichy, France. The following notes in excerpts are taken from the company's 2013 annual report.

NOTE 15 Non-current financial assets

(€ millions)	December 31, 2013		December 31, 2012		December 31, 2011	
	Carrying amount	Acquisition cost	Carrying amount	Acquisition cost	Carrying amount	Acquisition cost
Financial assets available-for-sale						
Sanofi(1)	€9,117.7	€4,033.5	€8,440.2	€4,033.5	€6,709.4	€4,033.5
Unlisted securities(2)	6.8	8.7	5.1	7.3	6.0	7.1
Financial assets at amortised cost						
Non-current loans and receivables	83.8	88.7	86.0	90.8	185.6	190.6
TOTAL	€9,208.3	€4,130.8	€8,531.3	€4,131.6	€6,900.9	€4,231.2

(1) L'Oréal's stake in Sanofi was 8.93% at December 31, 2013. The carrying amount at December 31, 2011, December 31, 2012 and December 31, 2013 (€6,709.4 million, €8,440.2 million and €9,117.7 million respectively) corresponds to the market value of the shares based on the closing price at each of these dates (€56.75, €71.39 and €77.12 respectively). The acquisition cost of €4,033.5 million corresponds to an entry cost of €34.12.

(2) As the fair value of unlisted securities cannot be reliably determined, they are stated at cost less any impairment losses.

20.4. Other comprehensive income

The following table indicates movements in these items:

(€ millions)	December 31, 2013	December 31, 2012	December 31, 2011
Financial assets available-for-sale			
Reserve at beginning of period	€4,406.7	€2,675.8	€1,624.1
Changes in fair value over period	677.5	1,730.9	1,052.2
Impairment loss recorded in profit and loss	—	—	—
Changes in fair value recorded in profit and loss	—	—	(0.5)
Reserve at the end of period	€5,084.2	€4,406.7	€2,675.8

Required

a. At what amount does L'Oréal report its available-for-sale investments on its balance sheets for 2013?

b. What are its net unrealised gains (losses) for 2013? By what amount did these unrealised gains (losses) affect its reported income in 2013?

c. What is the difference between realised and unrealised gains and losses? Are realised gains and losses treated differently in the income statement than unrealised gains and losses?

d. L'Oréal's 2013 pre-tax income was €4,024.4 million. What is the maximum amount L'Oréal could have increased pre-tax income by selling available-for-sale securities on the last day of 2013?

LO1, 5, 7 **P12-45. Preparing the Consolidated Balance Sheet**

On January 1, 2013, Rosti Company purchased for €392,000 cash a 70% equity interest in Alpine, Inc., which then had share capital of €420,000 and retained earnings of €140,000. Balance sheets of the two companies immediately after the acquisition were as follows:

	Rosti	Alpine
Current assets	€258,000	€160,000
Equity investment—Controlling (Alpine)	392,000	—
Plant and equipment (net)	265,000	460,000
Total assets	€915,000	€620,000
Liabilities	€ 50,000	€ 60,000
Share capital	700,000	420,000
Retained earnings	165,000	140,000
Total liabilities and equity	€915,000	€620,000

At the time of Rosti's investment, the fair values of Alpine's assets and liabilities were equal to their book values.

Required

Prepare the consolidated balance sheet on the acquisition date; include a column for consolidating adjustments (see Exhibits 12.5 and 12.8 for guidance).

LO1, 5, 7 **P12-46. Analysing Price Allocation**

SANOFI SA (FRANCE)

In its 2011 annual report, **Sanofi SA**, reported on its acquisition of Genzyme Corporation in April 2011. The purchase price was €14,814 million. This acquisition price was allocated to the separate assets and liabilities acquired as follows:

(€ million)	Fair Value at Acquisition Date
Property, plant and equipment	€ 1,933
Other intangible assets	10,063
Noncurrent financial assets	102
Inventories	925
Accounts receivable	764
Cash and cash equivalents	1,267
Long-term and short-term debt	(835)
Liability related to the "Bayer" contingent consideration	(585)
Accounts payable	(313)
Deferred taxes	(2,422)
Other assets and liabilities	(171)
Net assets of Genzyme as of April 4, 2011	**10,728**
Goodwill	**4,086**
Purchase price	**€14,814**

Required

a. Of the total assets acquired, what portion is allocated to tangible and financial assets and what portion to intangible assets?

b. Are the assets (both tangible and intangible) of the acquired company reported on the consolidated balance sheet at the book value as reported on the acquired company's balance sheet immediately prior to the acquisition, or at the fair value on the date of the acquisition? Explain.

c. How are the tangible and intangible assets accounted for subsequent to the acquisition?

LO1, 3, 4, 5 **P12-47. Analysing and Reporting Debt Investment Performance**

Columbia Company began operations in 2013 and by year-end (December 31) had made six bond investments. Year-end information on these bond investments follows.

Company	Face Value	Cost or Amortised Cost	Year-End Fair Value	Classification
Ling, Inc.	$100,000	$102,400	$105,300	Trading
Wren, Inc.	$250,000	$262,500	$270,000	Trading
Olanamic, Inc.	$200,000	$197,000	$199,000	Available for sale
Fossil, Inc.	$150,000	$154,000	$160,000	Available for sale
Meander, Inc.	$100,000	$101,200	$102,400	Held to maturity
Resin, Inc.	$140,000	$136,000	$137,000	Held to maturity

Required

a. At what total amount will the trading bond investments be reported in the December 31, 2013, balance sheet?

b. At what total amount will the available-for-sale bond investments be reported in the December 31, 2013, balance sheet?

c. At what total amount will the held-to-maturity bond investments be reported in the December 31, 2013, balance sheet?

d. What total amount of unrealised holding gains or unrealised holding losses related to bond investments will appear in the 2013 income statement?

e. What total amount of unrealised holding gains or unrealised holding losses related to bond investments will appear in the equity section of the December 31, 2013, balance sheet?

f. What total amount of fair value adjustment to bond investments will appear in the December 31, 2013, balance sheet? Which category of bond investments does the fair value adjustment relate to? Does the fair value adjustment increase or decrease the financial statement presentation of these bond investments?

P12-48. Analysing and Interpreting Disclosures on Consolidations **LO1, 4, 6**

Dundas Inc. consists of two business units: the manufacturing company (parent corporation) and a wholly owned finance subsidiary. These two units are consolidated in Dundas's 2014 annual report. Following is a supplemental disclosure that Dundas includes in its annual report that shows the separate balance sheets of the parent and its subsidiary, as well as consolidating adjustments and the consolidated balance sheet presented to shareholders. This supplemental disclosure is not mandated under IFRS, but is voluntarily reported by Dundas as useful information for investors and creditors. Using this disclosure, answer the following requirements:

Required

a. Does each individual company (unit) maintain its own financial statements? Explain. Why does IFRS require consolidation instead of providing the financial statements of individual companies (units)?

b. What is the balance of Investments in Financial Products Subsidiaries as of December 31, 2014, on the parent's balance sheet (Machinery and Engines)? What is the equity balance of the Financial Products subsidiary to which this relates as of December 31, 2014? Do you see a relation? Will this relation always exist? Explain the consolidating adjustment shown on the line labeled Investments in unconsolidated associate companies.

c. Refer to your answer for *a*. How does the equity method of accounting for the investment in the subsidiary company obscure the actual financial condition of the parent company that is revealed in the consolidated financial statements?

d. Refer to the Consolidating Adjustments column reported—it is used to prepare the consolidated balance sheet. Generally, what do these adjustments accomplish?

e. Compare the consolidated balance of equity with the equity of the parent company (Machinery and Engines). Will the relation that is evident always hold? Explain.

f. Recall that the parent company uses the equity method of accounting for its investment in the subsidiary, and that this account is eliminated in the consolidation process. What is the relation between consolidated net income and the net income of the parent company? Explain.

g. What do you believe is the implication for the consolidated balance sheet if the fair value of the Financial Products subsidiary is greater than the book value of its equity?

		Supplemental Consolidating Data		
December 31, 2014 ($ millions)	Consolidated	Machinery and Engines	Financial Products	Consolidating Adjustments
Assets				
Current assets				
Cash and short-term investments	$ 3,057	$ 1,829	$ 1,228	$ —
Receivables—trade and other	10,285	5,497	430	4,358
Receivables—finance	7,668	—	12,202	(4,534)
Deferred and refundable income taxes	1,580	1,515	65	—
Prepaid expenses and other current assets	994	525	481	(12)
Inventories	14,544	14,544	—	—
Total current assets	38,128	23,910	14,406	(188)
Property, plant and equipment—net	14,395	11,492	2,903	—
Long-term receivables—trade and other	1,130	281	271	578
Long-term receivables—finance	11,948	—	12,556	(608)
Investments in unconsolidated associate companies	133	133	—	—
Investments in Financial Products subsidiaries	—	4,035	—	(4,035)
Noncurrent deferred and refundable income taxes	2,157	2,593	97	(533)
Intangible assets	4,368	4,359	9	—
Goodwill	7,080	7,063	17	—
Other assets	2,107	813	1,294	—
Total assets	$81,446	$54,679	$31,553	$(4,786)
Liabilities				
Current liabilities				
Short-term borrowings	$ 3,988	$ 157	$ 3,895	$ (64)
Accounts payable	8,161	8,106	165	(110)
Accrued expenses	3,386	2,957	443	(14)
Accrued wages, salaries and employee benefits	2,410	2,373	37	—
Customer advances	2,691	2,691	—	—
Dividends payable	298	298	—	—
Other current liabilities	1,967	1,590	382	(5)
Long-term debt due within one year	5,660	558	5,102	—
Total current liabilities	28,561	18,730	10,024	(193)
Long-term debt due after one year	24,944	8,446	16,529	(31)
Liability for postemployment benefits	10,956	10,956	—	—
Other liabilities	3,583	3,145	965	(527)
Total liabilities	68,044	41,277	27,518	(751)
Commitments and contingencies				
Redeemable noncontrolling interest	473	473	—	—
Equity attributable to shareholders of Dundas				
Share capital	4,273	4,273	906	(906)
Treasury shares	(10,281)	(10,281)	—	—
Profit employed in the business	25,219	25,219	2,880	(2,880)
Accumulated other comprehensive income	(6,328)	(6,328)	154	(154)
	12,883	12,883	3,940	(3,940)
Noncontrolling interests	46	46	95	(95)
Total equity	12,929	12,929	4,035	(4,035)
Total liabilities, redeemable noncontrolling interest and equity	$81,466	$54,679	$31,553	$(4,786)

CASES AND PROJECTS

C12-49. Analysing and Interpreting Disclosures on Equity Method Investments LO1, 4, 5, 6

VODAFONE GROUP PLC (UNITED KINGDOM)

In the footnotes to its annual report for the fiscal year ended March 31, 2011, Vodafone Group Plc reported the following concerning its investments in associates using the equity method.

14. Investments in associates

At March 31, 2011 the Company had the following principal associates carrying on businesses which affect the profits and assets of the Group. The Company's principal associates all have share capital consisting solely of ordinary shares, unless otherwise stated, and are all indirectly held. The country of incorporation or registration of all associates is also their principal place of operation.

Name	Principal Activity	Country of Incorporation or Registration	Percentage[1] Shareholdings
Cellco Partnership[2]	Network operator	US	45.0
Société Française du Radiotéléphone S.A. ('SFR')[3]	Network operator	France	44.0
Safaricom Limited[4,5]	Network operator	Kenya	40.0

Notes:

[1] Rounded to nearest tenth of one percent.

[2] Cellco Partnership trades under the name Verizon Wireless.

[3] On April 3, 2011 the Group announced an agreement to sell its entire 44% interest in SFR. See note 32 for further information.

[4] The Group also holds two non-voting shares.

[5] At March 31, 2011 the fair value of Safaricom Limited was KES 61 billion (£456 million) based on the closing quoted share price on the Nairobi Stock Exchange.

32. Subsequent events

SFR

On April 3, 2011 the Group announced an agreement to sell its entire 44% shareholding in SFR to Vivendi for cash consideration of €7.75 billion (£6.8 billion). The Group will also receive a final dividend from SFR of €200 million (£176 million) on completion of the transaction.

Subject to customary competition authority and regulatory approvals, the transaction is expected to complete during the second calendar quarter of 2011.

At March 31, 2011 the SFR investment had a carrying value of £4.2 billion and was reported within the Non-Controlled Investments and Common Functions segment.

In Vodafone's annual report for the following year, it provided the following information in its footnotes:

14. Investments in associates

At March 31, 2012 the Company had the following principal associates carrying on businesses which affect the profits and assets of the Group. The Company's principal associates all have share capital consisting solely of ordinary shares, unless otherwise stated, and are all indirectly held. The country of incorporation or registration of all associates is also their principal place of operation.

Name	Principal Activity	Country of Incorporation or Registration	Percentage[1] Shareholdings
Cellco Partnership[2]	Network operator	US	45.0
Safaricom Limited[3,4]	Network operator	Kenya	40.0

Notes:

[1] Effective ownership percentages of Vodafone Group Plc at March 31, 2012, rounded to the nearest tenth of one percent.

[2] Cellco Partnership trades under the name Verizon Wireless.

[3] The Group also holds two non-voting shares.

[4] At March 31, 2012 the fair value of Safaricom Limited was KES 51 billion (£386 million) based on the closing quoted share price on the Nairobi Stock Exchange.

The Group's share of the aggregated financial information of equity accounted associates is set out below.

	2012 £m	2011 £m	2010 £m
Share of revenue in associates	20,601	24,213	23,288
Share of result in associates	4,963	5,059	4,742
Share of discontinued operations in associates	—	18	93

	2012 £m	2011 £m
Non-current assets	38,788	45,446
Current assets	3,764	5,588
Share of total assets	**42,552**	**51,034**
Non-current liabilities	3,990	5,719
Current liabilities	2,888	6,656
Non-controlling interests	566	554
Share of total liabilities and non-controlling interests	**7,444**	**12,929**
Share of equity shareholders' funds in associates	**35,108**	**38,105**

Finally, the cash flows from investing activities for this year were reported as follows:

	2012 €m	2011 €m	2010 €m
Cash flows from investing activities			
Purchase of interests in subsidiaries and joint ventures, net of cash acquired	(149)	(46)	(1,777)
Other investing activities in relation to purchase of subsidiaries	310	(356)	—
Purchase of interests in associates	(5)	—	—
Purchase of intangible assets	(3,090)	(4,290)	(2,134)
Purchase of property, plant and equipment	(4,762)	(4,350)	(4,841)
Purchase of investments	(417)	(318)	(522)
Disposal of interests in subsidiaries and joint ventures, net of cash disposed	832	—	—
Disposal of interests in associates	6,799	—	—
Disposal of property, plant and equipment	117	51	48
Disposal of investments	66	4,467	17
Dividends received from associates	4,023	1,424	1,436
Dividends received from investments	3	85	141
Interest received	322	1,659	195
Taxation on investing activities	(206)	(208)	—
Net cash flow from investing activities	**3,843**	**(1,882)**	**(7,437)**

Required

a. What is the opening balance in Vodafone's asset for investments in associates for the fiscal year ended March 31, 2012? What entry did Vodafone make to recognise income from these associates during the fiscal year ended March 31, 2012?

b. What entry did Vodafone make to record dividends from associates for the fiscal year ended March 31, 2012? (Vodafone reports dividends received as an investing cash inflow.)

c. What other entries affected the asset for investments in associates during the fiscal year ended March 31, 2012?

LO1, 3, 4 C12-50. **Analysing Financial Statement Effects of Passive and Equity Investments**

On January 2, 2013, Magee, Inc., purchased, as an equity investment, 20,000 shares of Dye, Inc.'s common shares for $21 per share, including commissions and taxes. On December 31, 2013, Dye announced a net income of $280,000 for the year and declared a dividend of 80 cents per share, payable January 15, 2014, to shareholders of record on January 5, 2014. At December 31, 2013, the market value of Dye's shares was $18 per share. Magee received its dividend on January 18, 2014.

Required

a. Assume that the shares acquired by Magee represent 10% of Dye's voting shares and are classified in the trading category. Prepare all journal entries appropriate for this investment, beginning with the purchase on January 2, 2013, and ending with the receipt of the dividend on January 18, 2014. (Magee recognises dividend income when received.)

b. Post the journal entries from part *a* to their respective T-accounts.

c. Record each of the transactions from part *a* in the financial statement effects template.

d. Assume that the shares acquired by Magee represent 40% of Dye's voting shares. Prepare all journal entries appropriate for this investment, beginning with the purchase on January 2, 2013, and ending with the receipt of the dividend on January 18, 2014.

e. Post the journal entries from part *d* to their respective T-accounts.

f. Record each of the transactions from part *d* in the financial statement effects template.

C12-51. Assessing Management Interpretation of Consolidated Financial Statements LO1, 2, 3, 4

Demski, Inc., manufactures heating and cooling systems. It has a 75% interest in Asare Company, which manufactures thermostats, switches, and other controls for heating and cooling products. It also has a 100% interest in Demski Finance Company, created by the parent company to finance sales of its products to contractors and other consumers. The parent company's only other investment is a 25% interest in the common shares of Knechel, Inc., which produces certain circuits used by Demski, Inc. A condensed consolidated balance sheet of the entity for the current year follows.

DEMSKI, INC., AND SUBSIDIARIES
Consolidated Balance Sheet
December 31, 2013

Assets		
Current assets		$19,300,000
Equity investment—Influential (Knechel)		2,600,000
Other assets		71,400,000
Excess of cost over equity acquired in net assets of Asare Company		1,700,000
Total assets		$95,000,000
Liabilities and equity		
Current liabilities		$10,300,000
Long-term liabilities		14,200,000
Equity		
Share capital	$50,000,000	
Retained earnings	16,700,000	
Demski, Inc. shareholders' equity	66,700,000	
Noncontrolling interests	3,800,000	
Total equity		70,500,000
Total liabilities and equity		$95,000,000

This balance sheet, along with other financial statements, was furnished to shareholders before their annual meeting, and all shareholders were invited to submit questions to be answered at the meeting. As chief financial officer of Demski, you have been appointed to respond to the questions at the meeting.

Required

Answer the following shareholder questions.

a. What is meant by *consolidated* financial statements?

b. Why is the investment in Knechel shown on the consolidated balance sheet, but the investments in Asare and Demski Finance are omitted?

c. Explain the meaning of the asset Excess of Cost over Equity Acquired in Net Assets of Asare Company.

d. What is meant by *noncontrolling interest* and to what company is this account related?

LO1, 2, 3 C12-52. Understanding Intercorporate Investments, Accounting Practices, and Managerial Ethics

Doug Stevens, controller of Nexgen, Inc., has asked his assistant, Gayle Sayres, for suggestions as to how the company can improve its financial performance for the year. The company is in the last quarter of the year and projections to the end of the year show the company will have a net loss of about $400,000.

"My suggestion," said Sayres, "is that we sell 1,000 of the 200,000 common shares of Heflin Company that we own. The 200,000 shares give us a 20% ownership of Heflin, and we have been using the equity method to account for this investment. We have owned this stock a long time and the current market value of the 200,000 shares is about $750,000 above our book value for the stock."

"That sale will only generate a gain of about $3,750," replied Stevens.

"The rest of the story," continued Sayres, "is that once we sell the 1,000 shares, we will own less than 20% of Heflin. We can then reclassify the remaining 199,000 shares from the influential category to the trading category. Once in the trading category, we value the shares at their current fair value, include the rest of the $750,000 gain in this year's income statement, and finish the year with a healthy net income."

"But," responded Stevens, "we aren't going to sell all the Heflin shares; 1,000 shares maybe, but certainly not any more. We own those shares because they are a long-term supplier of ours. Indeed, we even have representation on their board of directors. The 199,000 shares do not belong in the trading category."

Sayres rolled her eyes and continued, "The classification of an investment as trading or not depends on management's intent. This year-end we claim it was our intent to sell the shares. Next year we change our minds and take the shares out of the trading category. Generally accepted accounting principles can't legislate management intent, nor can our outside auditors read our minds. Besides, why shouldn't we take advantage of the flexibility in GAAP to avoid reporting a net loss for this year?"

Required

a. Should generally accepted accounting principles permit management's intent to influence accounting classifications and measurements?

b. Is it ethical for Doug Stevens to implement the recommendation of Gayle Sayres?

SOLUTIONS TO REVIEW PROBLEMS

Mid-Chapter Review 1

Solution to Part 1

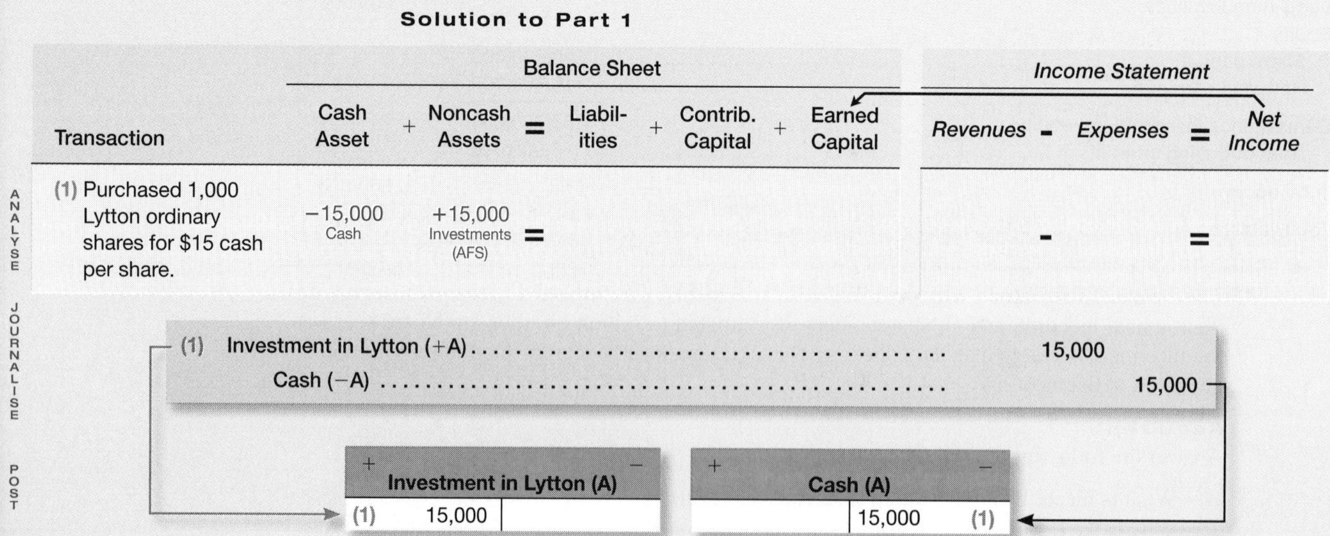

	Balance Sheet									Income Statement				
Transaction	Cash Asset	+	Noncash Assets	=	Liabil-ities	+	Contrib. Capital	+	Earned Capital	Revenues	−	Expenses	=	Net Income
(1) Purchased 1,000 Lytton ordinary shares for $15 cash per share.	−15,000 Cash		+15,000 Investments (AFS)	=							−		=	

ANALYSE / JOURNALISE / POST

(1) Investment in Lytton (+A) 15,000
  Cash (−A) 15,000

+ Investment in Lytton (A) −	
(1) 15,000	

+ Cash (A) −	
	15,000 (1)

continued

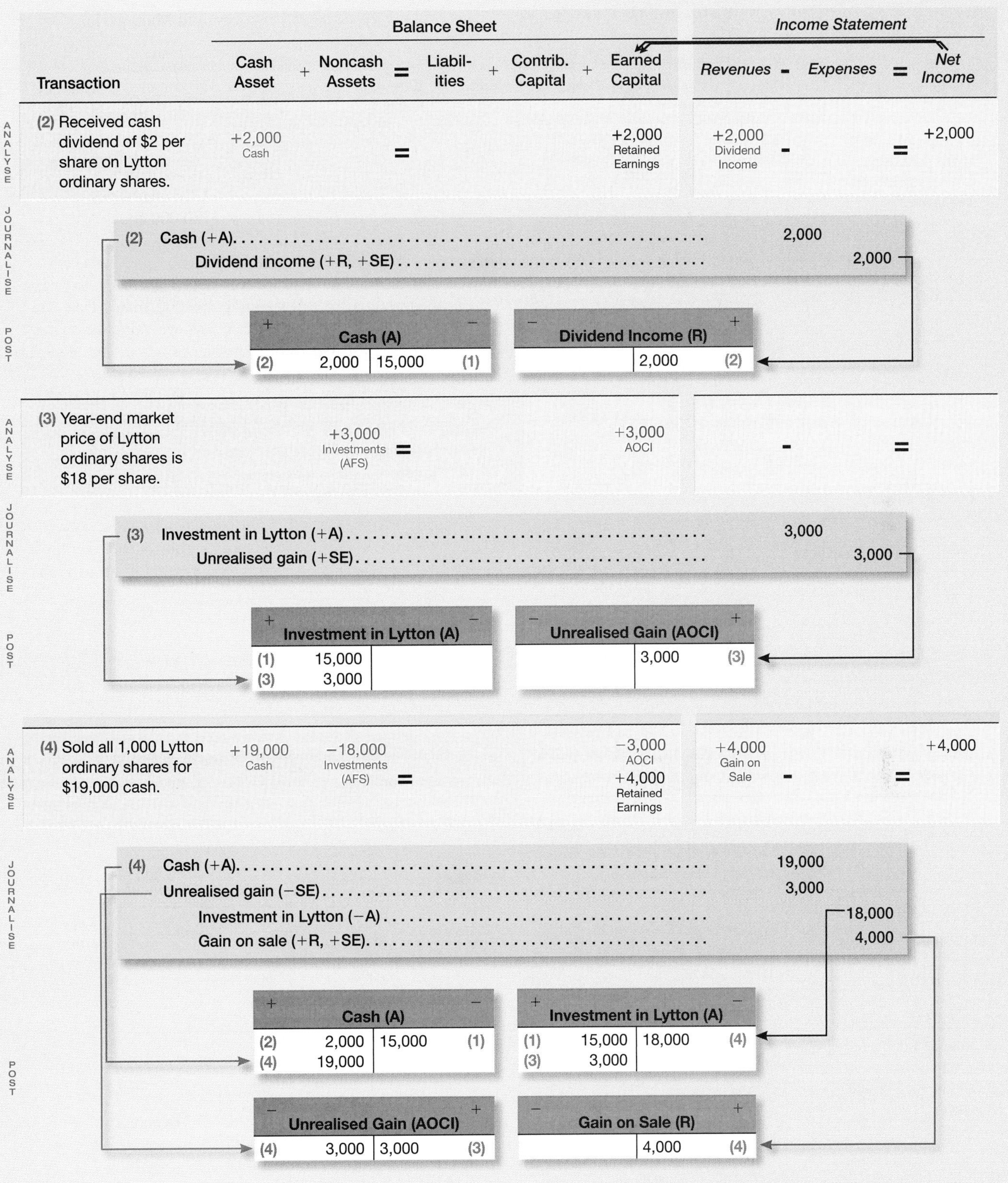
Balance Sheet
Income Statement
Transaction
Cash Asset
+ Noncash Assets
= Liabil-ities
+ Contrib. Capital
+ Earned Capital
Revenues - Expenses = Net Income
ANALYSE
(2) Received cash dividend of $2 per share on Lytton ordinary shares.
+2,000 Cash
=
+2,000 Retained Earnings
+2,000 Dividend Income
-
=
+2,000
JOURNALISE
(2) Cash (+A). 2,000
Dividend income (+R, +SE) 2,000
POST
Cash (A)
(2) 2,000 | 15,000 (1)
Dividend Income (R)
2,000 (2)
ANALYSE
(3) Year-end market price of Lytton ordinary shares is $18 per share.
+3,000 Investments (AFS)
=
+3,000 AOCI
-
=
JOURNALISE
(3) Investment in Lytton (+A) 3,000
Unrealised gain (+SE). 3,000
POST
Investment in Lytton (A)
(1) 15,000
(3) 3,000
Unrealised Gain (AOCI)
3,000 (3)
ANALYSE
(4) Sold all 1,000 Lytton ordinary shares for $19,000 cash.
+19,000 Cash
−18,000 Investments (AFS)
=
−3,000 AOCI
+4,000 Retained Earnings
+4,000 Gain on Sale
-
=
+4,000
JOURNALISE
(4) Cash (+A). 19,000
Unrealised gain (−SE). 3,000
Investment in Lytton (−A) 18,000
Gain on sale (+R, +SE). 4,000
POST
Cash (A)
(2) 2,000 | 15,000 (1)
(4) 19,000
Investment in Lytton (A)
(1) 15,000 | 18,000 (4)
(3) 3,000
Unrealised Gain (AOCI)
(4) 3,000 | 3,000 (3)
Gain on Sale (R)
4,000 (4)

Solution to Part 2

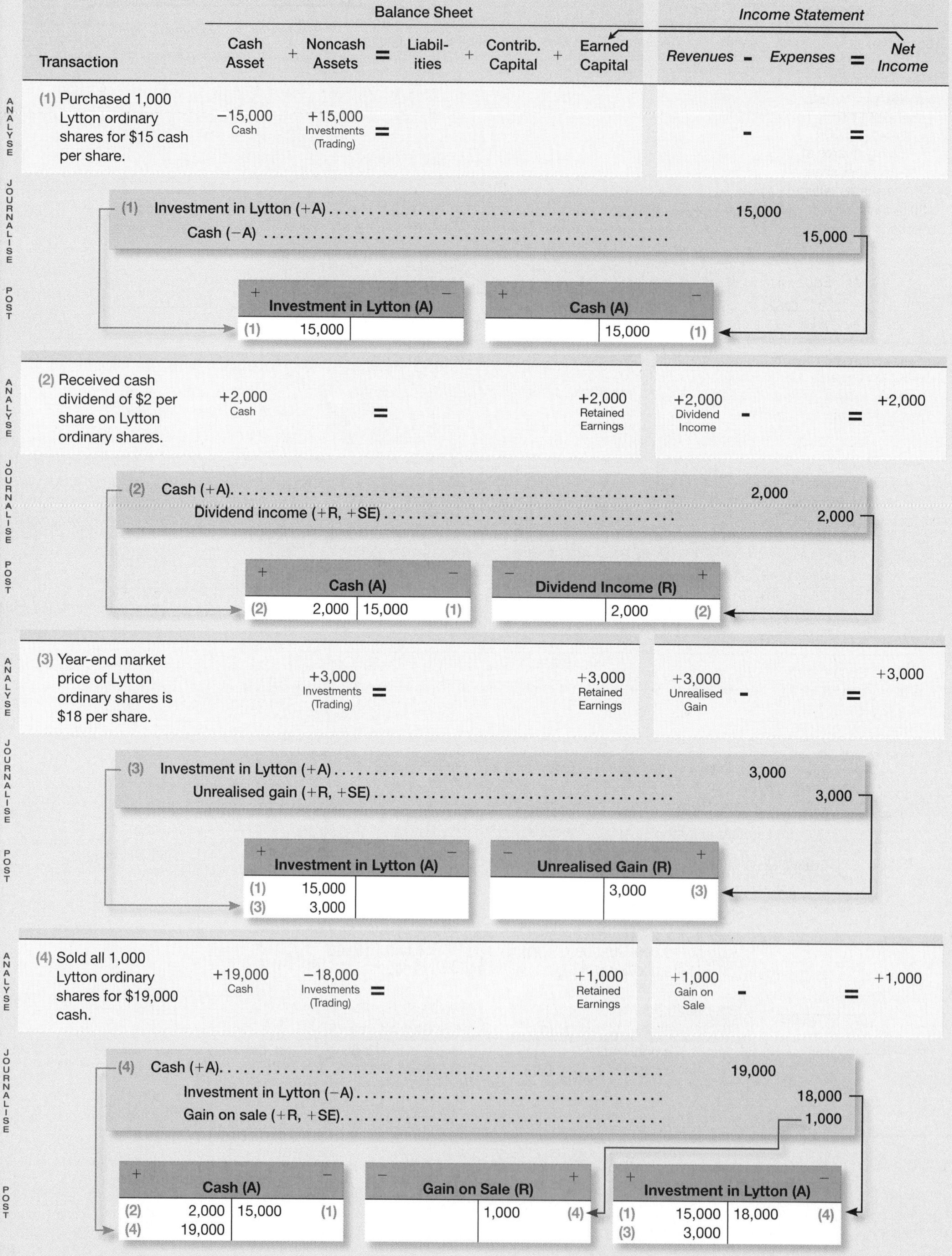

Mid-Chapter Review 2

Solution

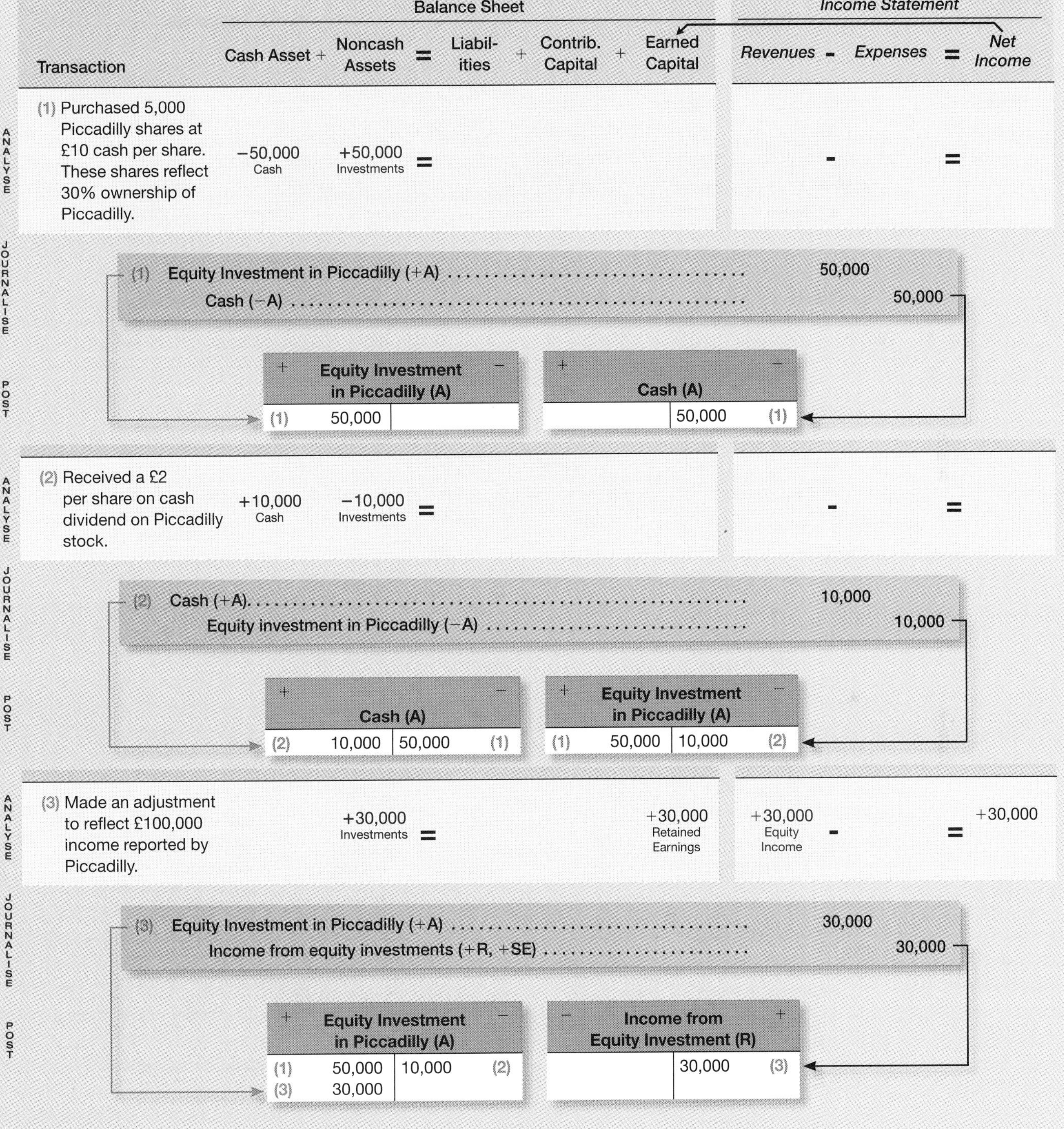

continued

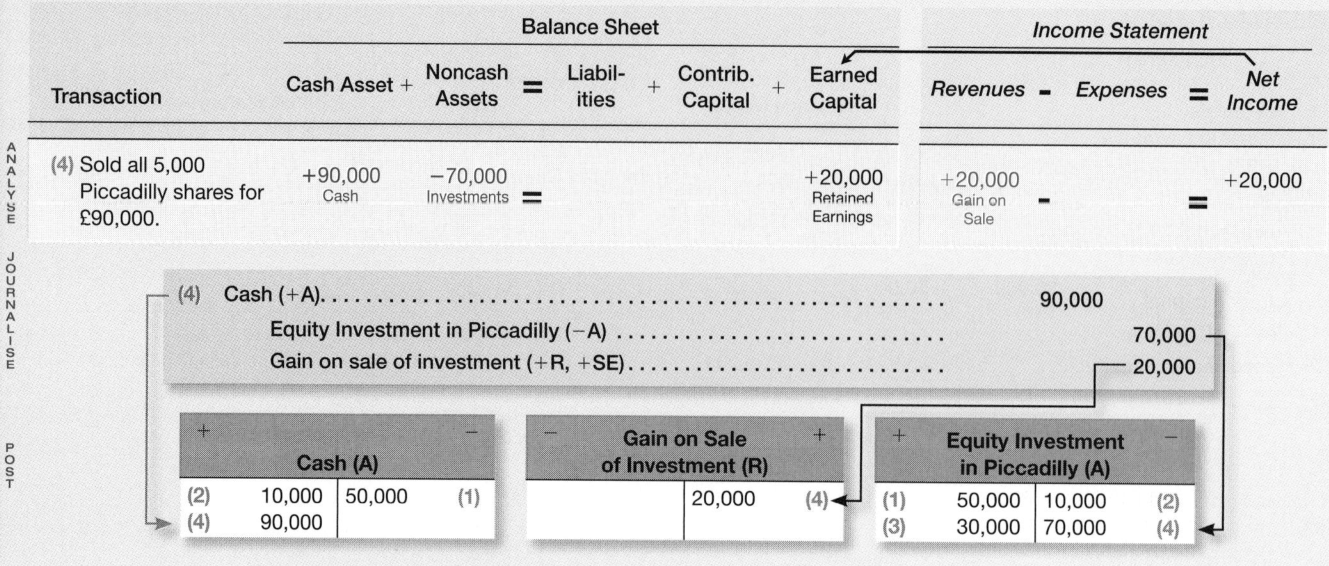

	Balance Sheet					Income Statement		
Transaction	Cash Asset +	Noncash Assets =	Liabil-ities +	Contrib. Capital +	Earned Capital	Revenues −	Expenses =	Net Income
(4) Sold all 5,000 Piccadilly shares for £90,000.	+90,000 Cash	−70,000 Investments			+20,000 Retained Earnings	+20,000 Gain on Sale		+20,000

	Debit	Credit
(4) Cash (+A)	90,000	
Equity Investment in Piccadilly (−A)		70,000
Gain on sale of investment (+R, +SE)		20,000

Cash (A) (+ / −): (2) 10,000; (4) 90,000 | 50,000 (1)

Gain on Sale of Investment (R) (− / +): | 20,000 (4)

Equity Investment in Piccadilly (A) (+ / −): (1) 50,000; (3) 30,000 | 10,000 (2); 70,000 (4)

Chapter-End Review

Solution

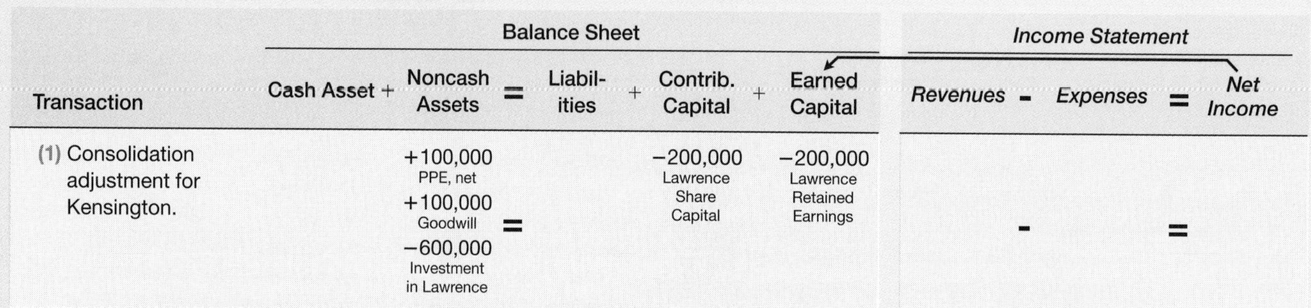

	Balance Sheet					Income Statement		
Transaction	Cash Asset +	Noncash Assets =	Liabil-ities +	Contrib. Capital +	Earned Capital	Revenues −	Expenses =	Net Income
(1) Consolidation adjustment for Kensington.		+100,000 PPE, net +100,000 Goodwill −600,000 Investment in Lawrence		−200,000 Lawrence Share Capital	−200,000 Lawrence Retained Earnings			

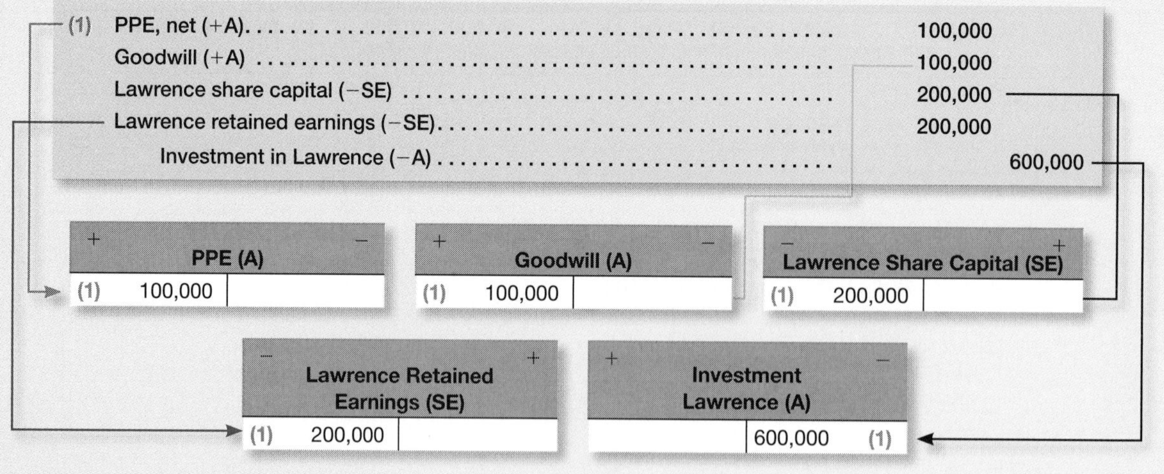

	Debit	Credit
(1) PPE, net (+A)	100,000	
Goodwill (+A)	100,000	
Lawrence share capital (−SE)	200,000	
Lawrence retained earnings (−SE)	200,000	
Investment in Lawrence (−A)		600,000

PPE (A) (+ / −): (1) 100,000 |

Goodwill (A) (+ / −): (1) 100,000 |

Lawrence Share Capital (SE) (− / +): (1) 200,000 |

Lawrence Retained Earnings (SE) (− / +): (1) 200,000 |

Investment Lawrence (A) (+ / −): | 600,000 (1)

	Kensington (Parent)	Lawrence (Subsidiary)	Consolidating Adjustments	Consolidated
Current assets	$1,000,000	$100,000		$1,100,000
Investment in Lawrence	600,000	—	$(600,000)	
PPE, net	3,000,000	400,000	100,000	3,500,000
Goodwill	—	—	100,000	100,000
Total assets	$4,600,000	$500,000		$4,700,000
Liabilities	$1,000,000	$100,000		$1,100,000
Contributed capital	2,000,000	200,000	(200,000)	2,000,000
Retained earnings	1,600,000	200,000	(200,000)	1,600,000
Total liabilities and equity	$4,600,000	$500,000		$4,700,000

Notes: The $600,000 investment account is eliminated together with the $400,000 book value of Lawrence's equity to which it mainly relates. The remaining $200,000 consists of the additional $100,000 in PPE assets and the $100,000 in goodwill from expected corporate synergies. Following these adjustments, the balance sheet items are summed to yield the consolidated balance sheet.

APPENDIX

A Compound Interest and the Time-Value of Money

Suppose you were lucky enough to hold a winning lottery ticket that allowed you to choose when you would receive your prize. Most of us would answer: Now! But let's say this ticket gave you the option of receiving \$20,000 now, or \$24,000 two years from now. Which would you choose?

Of course, \$24,000 is better than \$20,000. But the choice is not that simple. If you take the \$20,000 today, you can buy a new car, pay next semester's tuition, or invest the money in the stock market. If you wait, you'll receive the larger prize, but you may have to take the bus for the next two years, postpone your college studies, or pass up on a great investment opportunity.

This is the essence of what is called the **time-value of money**. A dollar received today is worth more than a dollar received two years in the future. Having cash in our possession, gives us the opportunity to spend or invest that cash today. Cash received in the future cannot be spent or invested today.[1]

The easiest way to illustrate the time-value of money is to assume that we collect the \$20,000 cash prize today and invest it in a money-market account that guarantees a 10% return on your investment. In one year, the investment would be worth \$22,000—which is the original \$20,000 investment plus \$2,000 interest (\$20,000 × 10%). At the end of two years, the investment would be worth \$24,200 [= \$22,000 + (\$22,000 × 10%) = \$22,000 × 1.10].

In the second year, the investment earns a return of \$2,200, which is \$22,000 × 10%. The interest earned in the second year is greater than the interest earned in year one because the interest earned in the first year earns interest in year two. This interest earned on interest is called **compound interest**. As interest accumulates on an investment, both the original investment and the accumulated interest will earn a return in subsequent periods. Interest calculated on the original investment, but not on interest accrued in prior periods, is called **simple interest**.

This Appendix explains and illustrates the concepts of time-value of money and compound interest. It is divided into three sections. The first two address future value concepts and present value concepts, respectively. In the last section, we illustrate the use of spreadsheet software to compute present and future values.

FUTURE VALUE CONCEPTS

As illustrated above, \$20,000 invested today to earn a return of 10% per year will accumulate interest and be worth \$24,200 in two years. The \$24,200 is referred to as the *future value* of \$20,000 because it represents what \$20,000 invested today at 10% would be worth two years in the future. The **future value** of any amount is the amount that an investment is worth at a future date if invested at a given rate of compound interest.

[1] The time value of money is primarily due to lost opportunities. However, the risk associated with some future cash flows will influence our assessment of their time value. That is, there may be some uncertainty associated with a future payment. For instance, in our lottery ticket example, there may be a possibility that the payer could default on the \$24,000 payment. Risk is reflected in time value calculations by using higher interest rates for risky cash flows.

Assume that we allow our $20,000 investment to continue to earn interest for three years. The interest will continue to compound and the future value will continue to grow. This is illustrated in Exhibit A.1.

EXHIBIT A.1 Future Value of $20,000

Initial investment.	$20,000
Interest earned in year 1 (initial investment × 10%)	2,000
Investment plus accumulated interest (future value) in 1 year.	22,000
Interest earned in year 2 (year 1 amount × 10%)	2,200
Investment plus accumulated interest (future value) in 2 years	24,200
Interest earned in year 3 (year 2 amount × 10%)	2,420
Investment plus accumulated interest (future value) in 3 years	$26,620

As Exhibit A.1 illustrates, the future value of $20,000 invested for three years at 10% per year is $26,620. This can be calculated as $\$26{,}620 = \$20{,}000 \times 1.10 \times 1.10 \times 1.10 = \$20{,}000 \times (1.10)^3$. Similarly, if the interest rate is 8%, the future value is $\$25{,}194 = \$20{,}000 \times (1.08)^3$. That is, to determine the future value of an amount n periods in the future, we multiply the present value by one plus the interest rate, raised to the nth power:

$$\textbf{Future Value} = \textbf{Present Value} \times (1 + \textbf{interest rate})^n$$

The future value of any amount depends on two factors: time and rate. That is, how many periods (e.g., years or months) into the future do we want to project the future value and what rate of return (or interest rate) do we use? There are two simple methods that we can use to obtain future values. The first method uses tables presented at the end of this Appendix. Table 1 presents the future value of a single amount. To use the table, move across the top of the table to choose the appropriate interest rate and then move down the column to choose the number of periods in the future.

For example, if we move across the top to the 10% column and the down to period 3, Table 1 provides a value of 1.33100. This is the future value of $1 in three periods at 10% interest per period and is called the **future value factor**. If we want to calculate the future value of $20,000, we multiply the *future value factor* from Table 1 by $20,000:

Initial Amount	×	**Future Value Factor**	=	**Future Value**
$20,000	×	**1.33100**	=	**$26,620**

The future value can also be calculated using a financial calculator. Financial calculators require four inputs to calculate a fifth value, which is the solution. We illustrate the use of a calculator with the following graphic:

Calculator

N	I/Yr	PV	PMT	FV
3	10	20,000	0	26,620

On the financial calculator, N is the number of periods (3), I/Yr is the interest rate per period (10), PV is the current, or present, value ($20,000), PMT refers to a periodic payment (0 in our example) and FV is the future value. Because we are calculating the future value in this illustration, that value is highlighted in red as the solution.[2]

Whether we use the tables at the end of the Appendix or a financial calculator, it is important to recognise that these computations are based on an interest rate *per period*. Most interest rates are stated on an annual, or *per year*, basis. However, for compound interest calculations, a period need not be equal to a year. Therefore, we must always be careful to adjust our interest rate *per year* to the appropriate interest rate *per period* and use the corresponding number of time periods in our calculations.

To illustrate, assume that our $20,000 investment paid 8% annual interest, *compounded quarterly*. Although the interest rate is quoted as 8% *per year*, the rate is actually 2% every three-month *period* (=8%/4).

[2] Actually, most calculators return a solution of −26,620. The calculator interprets the PV as an investment (cash out) and FV as the return (cash in). So, if PV is entered as a positive amount, then FV will come back negative, and vice versa.

Hence, in three years, we would have twelve periods. To determine the future value, we would go down the 2% column in Table 1 to the 12-period row to get a future value factor of 1.26824.

Initial Amount	×	Future Value Factor	=	Future Value
$20,000	×	**1.26824**	=	**$25,365**

Alternatively, using the financial calculator:

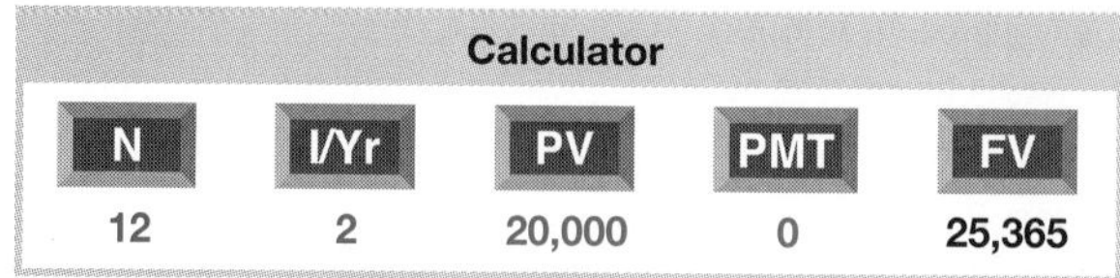

Calculator				
N	I/Yr	PV	PMT	FV
12	2	20,000	0	**25,365**

That is, the future value of $20,000 invested for three years at 8%, compounded quarterly, is $25,365.

PRESENT VALUE CONCEPTS

The concept of *present value* is the inverse of future value. Rather than determining how much an amount today is worth in the future, present value determines how much a future amount is worth today. The **present value** of an amount is the value *today* of a cash flow occurring at a future date given a rate of compound interest. As was the case with future value, present values depend on two factors: time and rate.

Present value is a particularly useful concept because it allows us to compare cash flows occurring at different times in the future. We can do this because we can calculate the value of each cash flow at a common point in time—today. For example, let's say we want to compare two investments. Investment A pays $15,000 in two years. Investment B pays $16,000 in three years. We cannot compare these two investments directly, because the payoffs occur at different times in the future.[3] However, we can determine how much each payoff is worth today. If the appropriate interest rate is 8%, the present value of Investment A is $12,860 and the present value of Investment B is $12,701. (We demonstrate how to compute these amounts below.) Hence, Investment A is worth more today than investment B. By determining the value of each cash payoff at the same point in time (today) we can easily compare the alternatives.

Present Value of a Single Amount

To determine the present value of a single cash payment occurring one period in the future, we simply divide the future cash flow by one plus the interest rate (the interest rate is also called the **discount rate**):[4]

$$\text{Present Value} = \frac{\text{Future Value}}{(1 + \text{discount rate})}$$

If the cash flow occurs *n* periods in the future, we divide by one plus the discount rate raised to the nth power:

$$\text{Present Value} = \frac{\text{Future Value}}{(1 + \text{discount rate})^n}$$

There are two simple methods for obtaining the present value of a single cash flow occurring at any date in the future. The first method relies on Table 2 at the end of this Appendix. We use Table 2 in the same way we used Table 1 to calculate future values. First, we choose the column representing the appropriate discount rate, and then we move down the column to select the number of periods in the future. The value in the table is the **present value factor**. We then multiply the future amount by the *present value factor* to get the present value.

---

[3] The reason that this comparison is difficult is that Investment A pays a return in two years while Investment B doesn't pay a return until year 3. One way to understand this complexity is to ask: What will happen to the cash earned on Investment A during the third year? Or, alternatively, if we invest the return on Investment A for an additional year, how much would we earn after three years? By comparing present values, we are implicitly assuming that any cash payoffs from either investment could be reinvested at the rate of return used to calculate the present value.

[4] The term "discount rate" is often used when referring to present values. This is because when future cash flows are valued using present value calculations, the present value is always less than the future cash amount. Hence, we say that the future value is "discounted" to the present value using the "discount rate."

For example, consider Investment A. From Table 2, the present value factor for 8% and two periods is 0.85734. The present value of $15,000 received in two years, discounted at 8% per year is calculated as follows:

Future Amount	×	**Present Value Factor**	=	**Present Value**
$15,000	×	**0.85734**	=	**$12,860**

The present value can also be computed using a financial calculator. In this case, N=2; I/Yr = 8; PMT = 0; FV = 15,000 and PV is our answer (highlighted in red).

Calculator				
N	I/Yr	PV	PMT	FV
2	8	12,860	0	15,000

By similar means we can compute the present value of Investment B. The present value factor for 8%, and three periods is 0.79383. The present value of $16,000 received in three years, discounted at 8% per year is:

Future Amount	×	**Present Value Factor**	=	**Present Value**
$16,000	×	**0.79383**	=	**$12,701**

Or, using the financial calculator, we get the same answer as follows:

Calculator				
N	I/Yr	PV	PMT	FV
3	8	12,701	0	16,000

Present Value of an Annuity Sometimes, we are faced with determining the present value of a series of regular, equal payments, called an **annuity**. For example, let's say we have an investment that pays $7,000 each year for the next three years. We can calculate the present value of each payment and then sum the results to get the present value of the entire annuity. Assume the appropriate discount rate is 6% per year. From Table 2, the present value factors for a 6% discount rate are 0.94340 for one period, 0.89000 for two periods, and 0.83962 for three periods. The calculation of the present value is presented in Exhibit A.2 (rounded to the nearest whole dollar):

EXHIBIT A.2 Present Value of an Annuity of 3 Payments of $7,000 Discounted at 6%

	Future Payment	×	Present Value Factor	=	Present Value
1	$7,000		0.94340		6,604
2	7,000		0.89000		6,230
3	7,000		0.83962		5,877
					$18,711

While this method of computing the present value of an annuity is accurate, it can be tedious for annuities with many cash payments. Table 3 at the end of this Appendix presents present value factors for annuities of various lengths. This table is used in the same way as Table 2: first we choose the column reflecting our discount rate, and then we choose the row representing the number of payments. From Table 3, the present value factor for an annuity of three payments discounted at 6% is 2.67301. To calculate the present value of an annuity, we multiply the periodic payment by the present value factor:

Payment	×	**Present Value Factor**	=	**Present Value**
$7,000	×	**2.67301**	=	**$18,711**

Or alternatively, using a financial calculator, we enter N=3, I/Yr=6, PMT=7,000, FV=0, and the solution is the PV, highlighted in red:

Calculator				
N	I/Yr	PV	PMT	FV
3	6	18,711	7,000	0

Instalment Loans One useful application of the present value of an annuity is to value an *instalment loan*. An **instalment loan** is a loan that requires a series of equal payments, or instalments, each of which includes interest and some of the original principal. Assume that we take out a bank loan requiring 12 quarterly payments of $2,000 and an annual interest rate of 8%. When working with annuities, a period is the time between payments and the number of payments is the number of periods we use in our calculations. Because the payments are made quarterly, the 8% annual rate is compounded quarterly. That is, the effective interest rate is 2% per quarter. To calculate the loan amount, we use Table 3 to get the present value factor for 12 payments discounted at 2%, and then multiply the factor by our $2,000 payment, as follows:

Payment	×	**Present Value Factor**	=	**Present Value**
$2,000	×	**10.57534**	=	**$21,151**

Calculator				
N	I/Yr	PV	PMT	FV
12	2	21,151	2,000	0

That is, if we agreed to make 12 quarterly payments of $2,000, including an interest charge of 2% per quarter, we could borrow $21,151.

A more common calculation would be to determine the loan payment given the amount borrowed. For example, if we borrow $30,000 and agree to repay the loan in 24 equal monthly payments at a 12% annual interest rate (1% per month), what monthly payment would we need to make to repay the loan plus interest? To compute the payment, we divide the present value (the loan amount) by the present value factor from Table 3 (1%, 24 periods) as follows:

Present Value	÷	**Present Value Factor**	=	**Payment**
$30,000	÷	**21.24339**	=	**$1,412.20**

Using a financial calculator, we can calculate the payment (PMT) directly, given the other inputs:

Calculator				
N	I/Yr	PV	PMT	FV
24	1	30,000	1,412.20	0

Bond Valuation From Chapter 9, we know that a typical corporate bond has a face value of $1,000 and pays periodic interest payments every six months based on the stated (or coupon) interest rate. That is, the face value and the stated rate of a bond allow us to lay out the cash flows that will be paid to the bondholder. We also know that bonds are valued using the market interest rate, which may be different from the stated rate.

Bonds represent a combination of an annuity of the periodic interest payments and a single future payment of the face value, or principal payment, sometimes called a **balloon payment**. In order to value a bond, we must calculate the present value of each of these two components. Let's assume that we wish to value a $1,000, 5-year, 7% bond that pays a semi-annual coupon payment. The face value is $1,000 and the semi-annual payment is $35 (= $1,000 × 7%/2). Let's assume a market interest rate (yield) of 8% (which is 4% every six months). The bond is valued as the sum of two parts:

1. Use Table 2 to compute the value of the principal (balloon) payment.
2. Use Table 3 to compute the value of the annuity of interest (coupon) payments.

This calculation is illustrated in Exhibit A.3:

EXHIBIT A.3 Calculating a Bond Value Using Present Value Tables (4%, 10 periods)

	Cash Flow	×	Present Value Factor	=	Present Value
Face value: 1 payment of $1,000 at the end of 5 years (Table 2—4%, 10 periods)	$1,000	×	0.67556	=	675.56
Semi-annual coupon payments: 10-payment annuity of $35 every six months (Table 3—4%, 10 periods)	$35	×	8.11090	=	283.88
					$959.44

The bond value can also be calculated using a financial calculator, with the following inputs: N=10; I/Yr=4; PMT=35; FV=1,000. The solution is the PV:

Calculator

N	I/Yr	PV	PMT	FV
10	4	959.45	35	1,000

The calculator automatically adds the present value of the annuity (10 payments of $35) to the present value of the single amount ($1,000 principal value) to get the bond value.

Calculating Bond Yields Sometimes we know the future cash payments and the present value of those payments, but not the discount rate used to compute the present value. This would be useful, for example, if we knew the price of a bond but wanted to determine the yield.

To illustrate the calculation of a bond yield, assume that we have a $1,000, 8-year, 5% bond that is currently priced at 104 (104% of par value or $1,040). The semiannual interest payment is $25 (= $1,000 × 5%/2) and the principal amount of $1,000 is due in 8 years (16 semiannual periods). We input the following values: N=16; PV=1,040; PMT=25; FV=1,000. The solution is returned by pressing the I/Yr button:

Calculator

N	I/Yr	PV	PMT	FV
16	2.20	1,040	25	1,000

In this case, the calculator returns a solution of 2.20%. This is the interest rate *per period* that discounts the future payments on the bond to the present value of $1,040. Because each period is six months, we must double this rate to get the bond yield (or market rate of interest), which is always quoted on an annual basis. Thus the yield on this bond is 4.4% (= 2.2% × 2).[5]

USING EXCEL TO COMPUTE TIME VALUE

Spreadsheet software, such as Microsoft Excel© is extremely useful for performing a variety of time-value calculations. In this section, we illustrate a few of the features of Excel.

Future Value Calculations Calculating future value in Excel is straight forward by using the formula for future value or using the function wizard feature. Assume we wish to compute the future value of $12,000 invested today at 6% interest for four years. The formula for this calculation is:

=12000*1.06^4

[5] Technically, in order to obtain the result illustrated here, the amounts for PMT and FV must be entered with the same sign, but the PV amount must be entered with the opposite sign. For example, if we enter PV = −1,040, PMT = 25 and FV = 1,000, we would get the result above.

Excel returns the value 15149.72. An alternative method of making this calculation is by using the function wizard. The function wizard is accessed by clicking on the *fx* icon in the formula bar at the top of the spreadsheet.

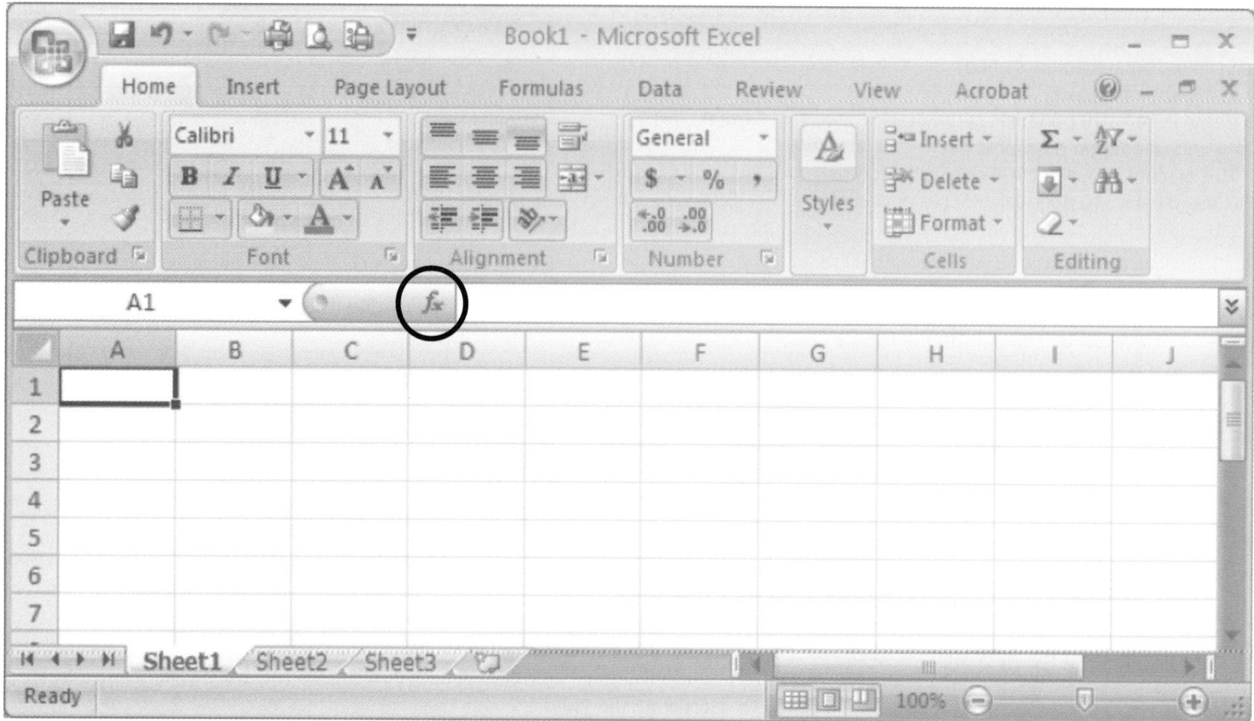

Clicking on this icon opens a dialog box that offers a variety of built-in functions. The dialog box appears as follows:

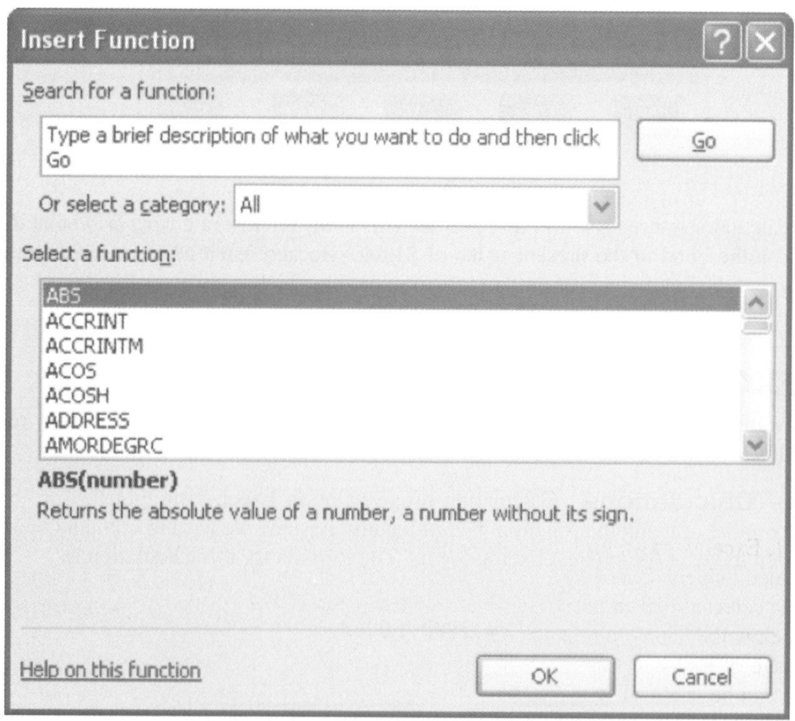

Now, the user can scroll through the long list of built-in Excel functions or customise the search by selecting a category of functions. In the screen shot below, the category of functions described as "Financial" is selected:

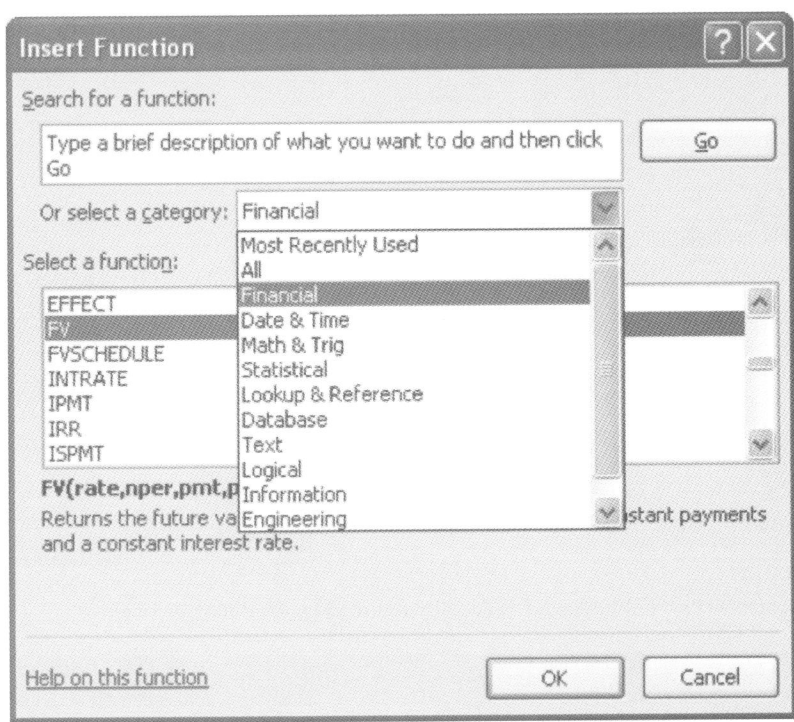

Scrolling through the list of financial functions, we select the FV function (for future value). A new dialog box appears:

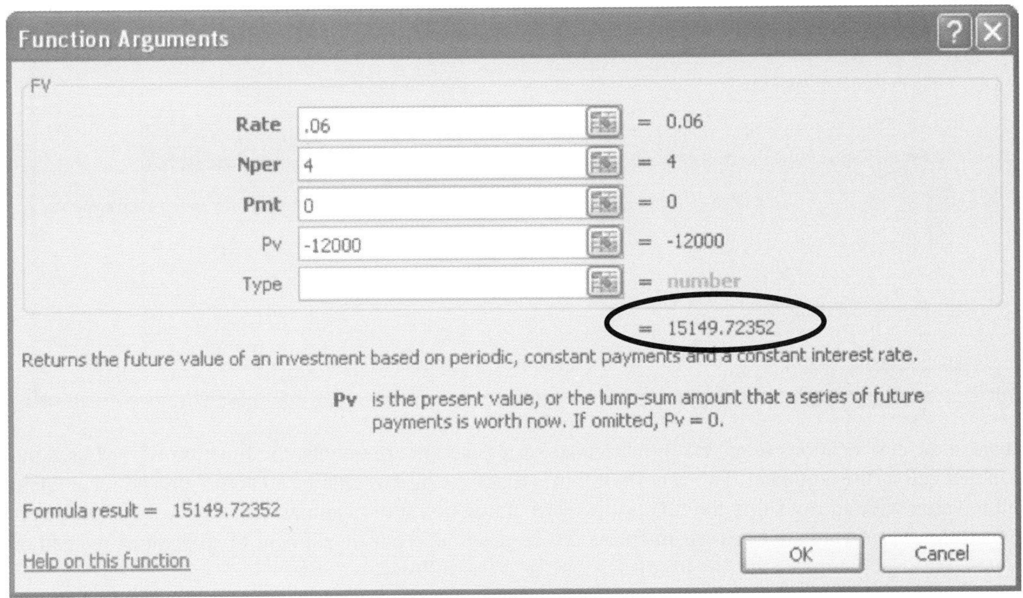

At this point, Excel works a lot like a financial calculator. We enter 0.06 into the box labeled "Rate," 4 in the box labeled "Nper," 0 in the "Pmt" box and -12,000 in the "PV" box. Excel returns the value of $15,149.72 in the selected cell in the spreadsheet. The solution to the calculation is also presented in the dialog box just below the inputs (circled in red above).

One advantage of Excel, is that it allows the user to enter cell locations as function arguments in the dialog box. This can be useful if we wish to gauge the impact of changing an argument. For instance, we could enter the following in a spreadsheet:

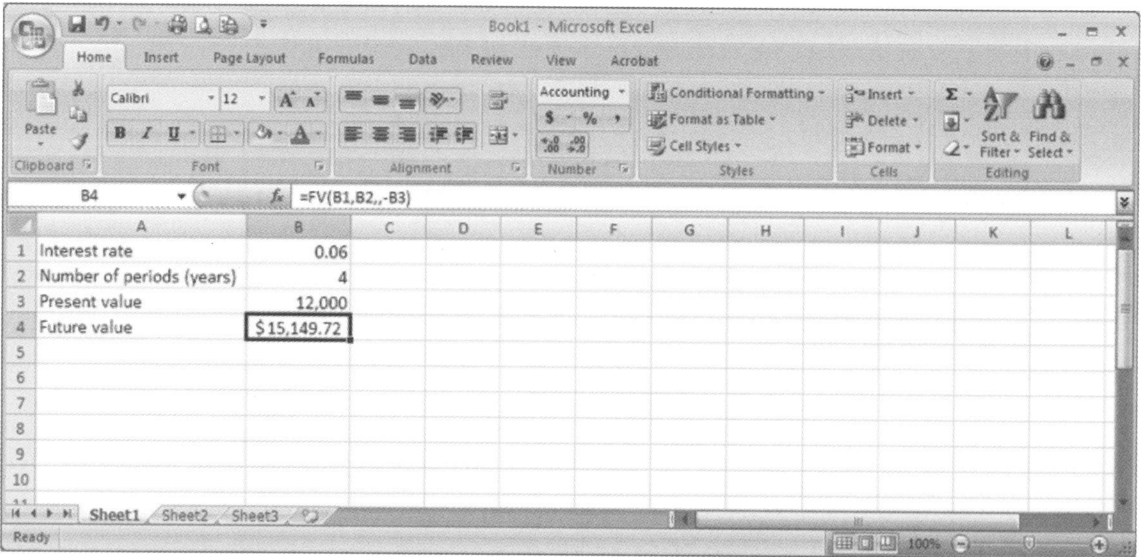

The amount presented as the "Future value" is actually returned by the dialog box below:

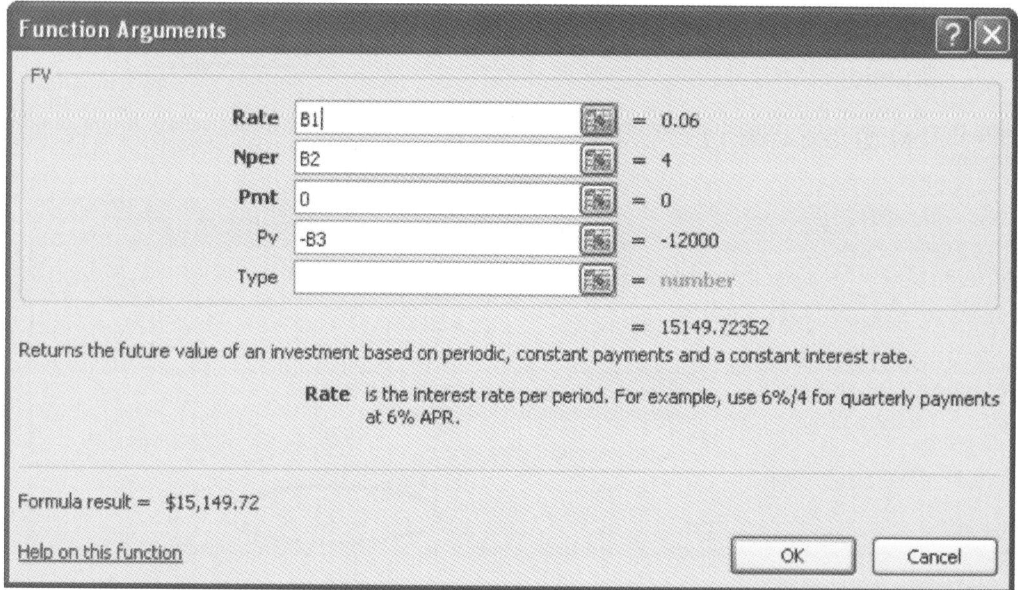

When we enter cell locations (e.g. "B1") in the boxes for function arguments, the function wizard uses the value in that cell as the argument. The benefit of this is that we can now change an argument and recalculate the future value without revisiting the function wizard dialog box. For example, let's say we wish to determine what the future value of our investment would be if we held our investment for five years instead of four years. We simply replace the "4" in cell B2 with a "5" as follows:

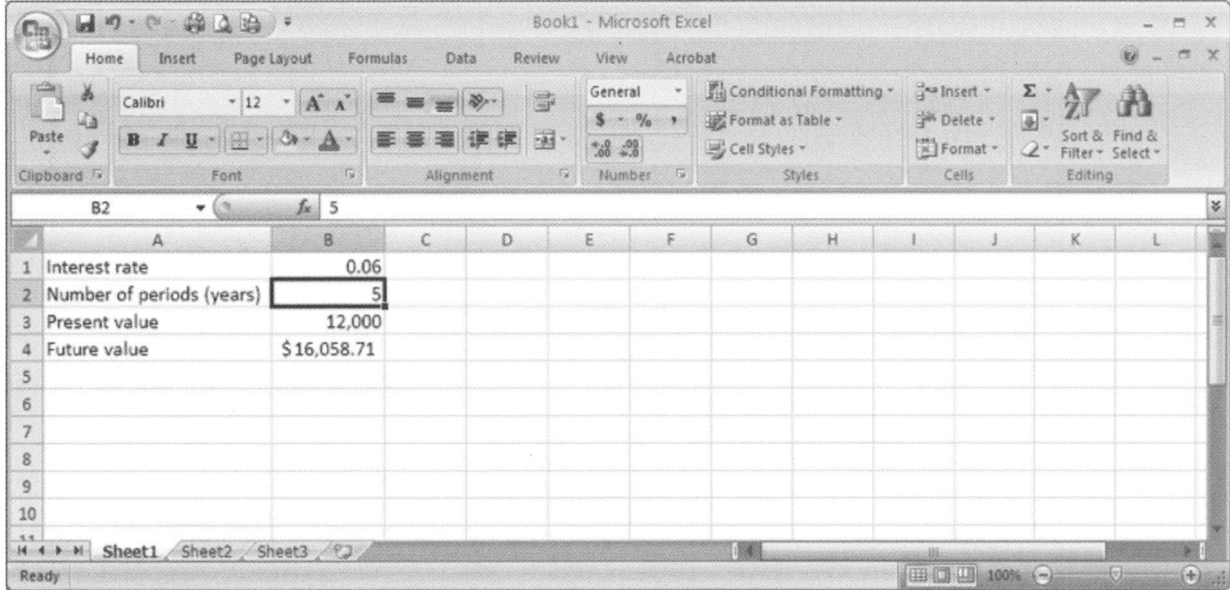

Excel automatically returns the value of $16,058.71 as the future value (cell B4).

Present Value Calculations Computing present value is as straight-forward as future value. The function to use is "PV" for present value. Let's assume we wish to calculate the present value of $15,000 that we expect to receive in two years discounted at 8% per year. Earlier, we determined that the present value is $12,860. To make this calculation using Excel, we enter each of the arguments in the spreadsheet as follows:

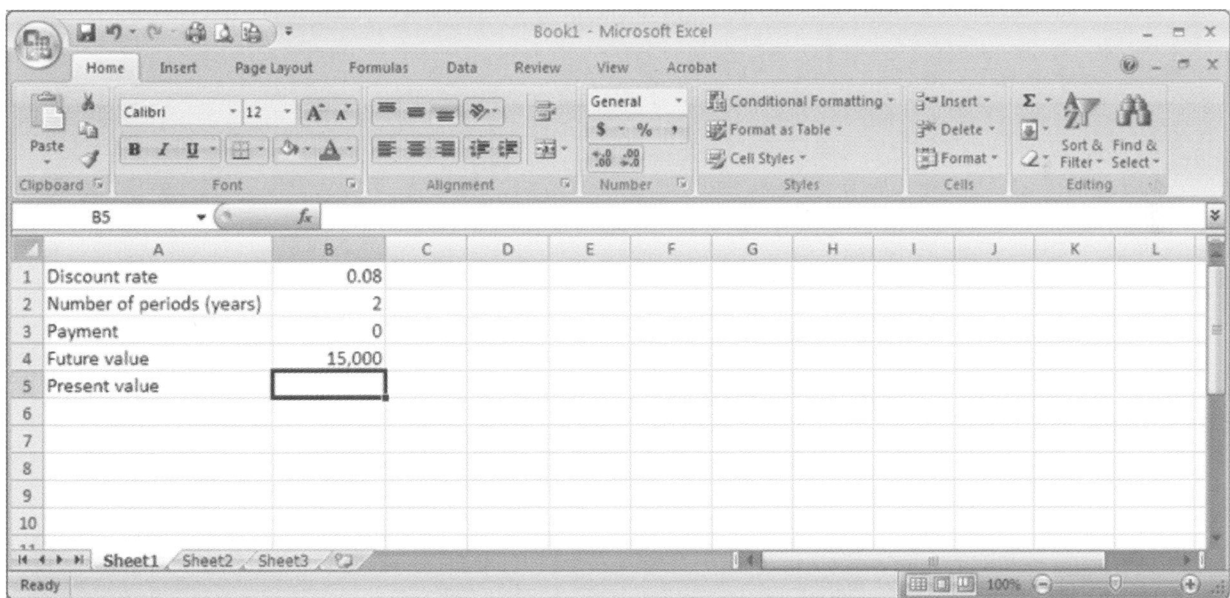

We then use the function wizard to access the "PV" function:

Function Arguments

PV

Rate	B1	=	0.08
Nper	B2	=	2
Pmt	-B3	=	0
Fv	-B4	=	-15000
Type		=	number

= 12860.0823

Returns the present value of an investment: the total amount that a series of future payments is worth now.

Rate is the interest rate per period. For example, use 6%/4 for quarterly payments at 6% APR.

Formula result = $12,860.08

Help on this function

OK Cancel

The PV function is similar to the FV function. The amount returned is the present value of $12,860.08. The "Pmt" argument in the PV function is used for annuity payments. In this example, we wanted the present value of a lump-sum amount paid in two years, so the payment was set to 0. However, we can use the same function to compute the present value of an annuity by entering the annuity payment as a negative amount in the "Pmt" argument or in the payment cell of our spreadsheet. Earlier, we determined that the present value of a series of $7,000 payments received annually for three years and discounted at 6% is $18,711. To compute this amount using Excel, we list the payment (Pmt) as 7,000 and the future value (FV) as 0:

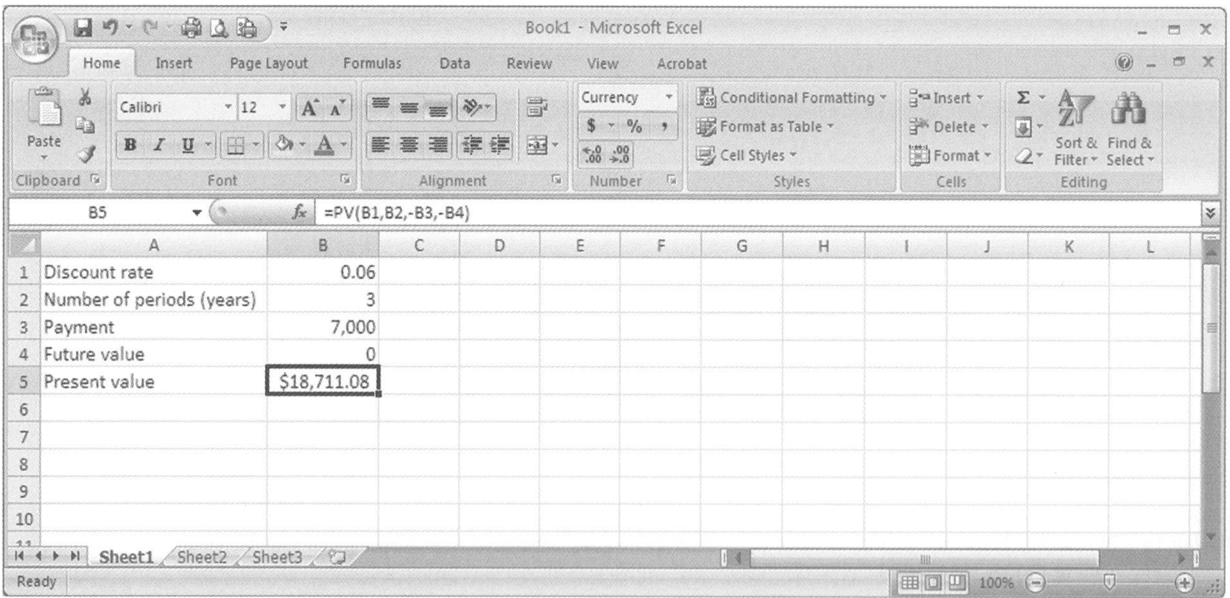

B5 =PV(B1,B2,-B3,-B4)

	A	B
1	Discount rate	0.06
2	Number of periods (years)	3
3	Payment	7,000
4	Future value	0
5	Present value	$18,711.08

Similarly, our instalment loan that requires 12 quarterly payments of $2,000 at 8% interest per year (2% per quarter) would have a present value of $21,150.68, which is computed as follows:

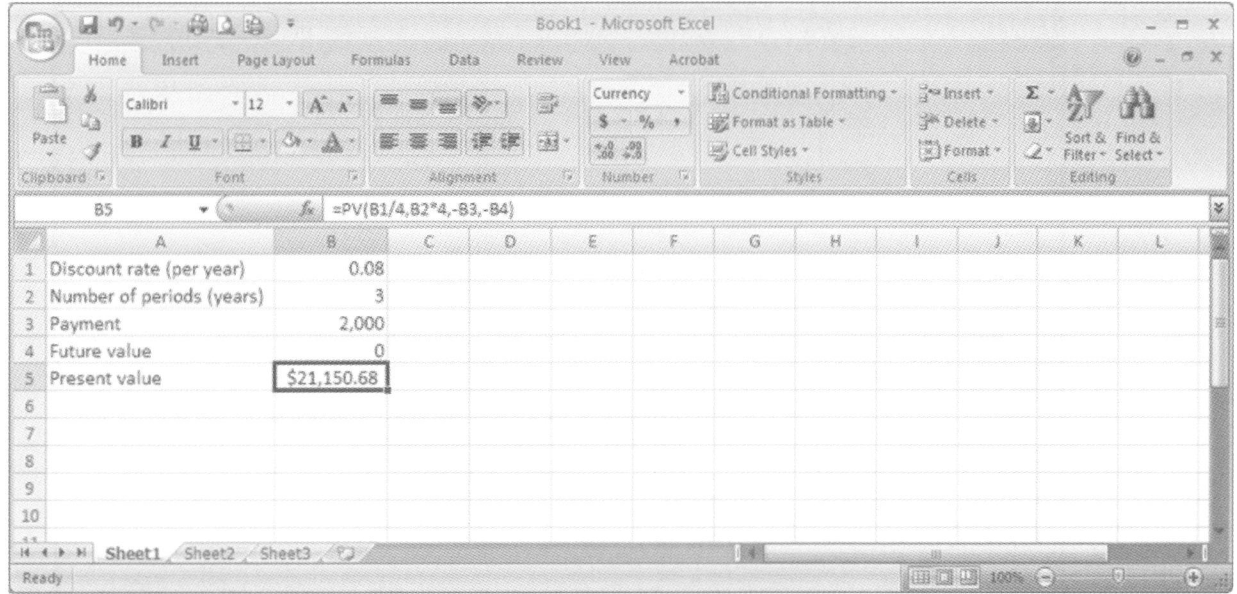

Because the payments are made quarterly, we need to adjust the 8% annual discount rate to 2% per quarter (8%/4) and the 3 year period to 12 quarterly payments (3x4). This is done in the function wizard as illustrated below:

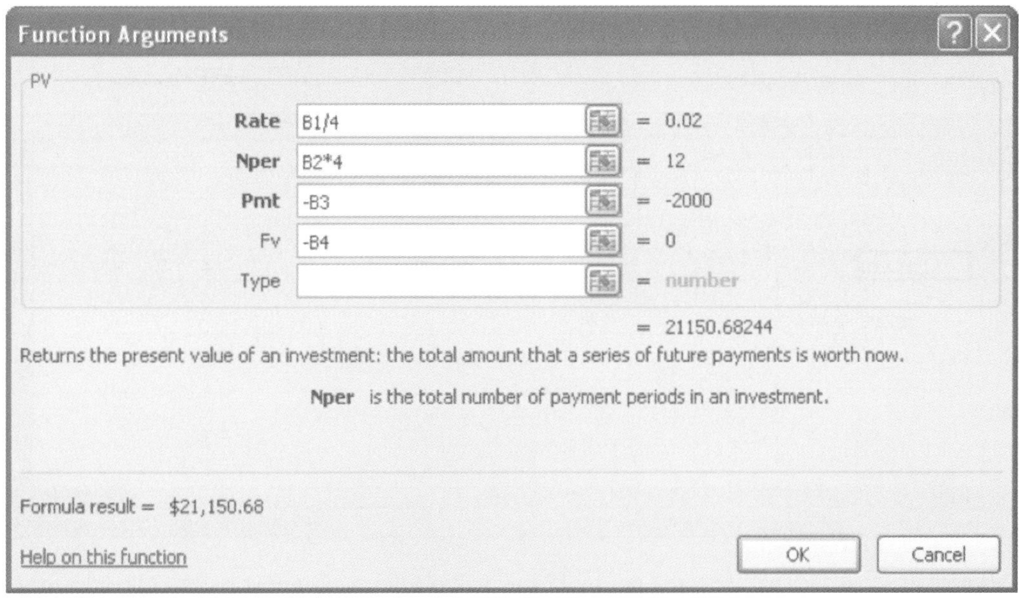

Another function that is very useful for instalment loans is the "PMT" function. This function calculates the payment required to pay off an instalment loan. Earlier, we calculated the payment on a $30,000 loan requiring 24 monthly payments at an annual interest rate of 12% (1% per month) to be $1,412.20 per month. Using the PMT function in Excel, we get the same result:

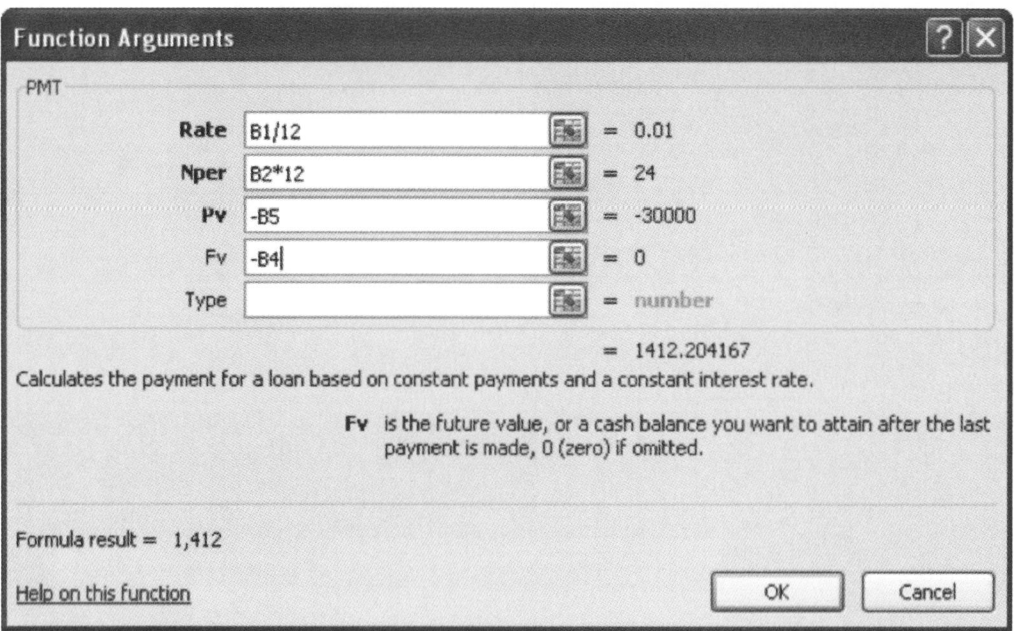

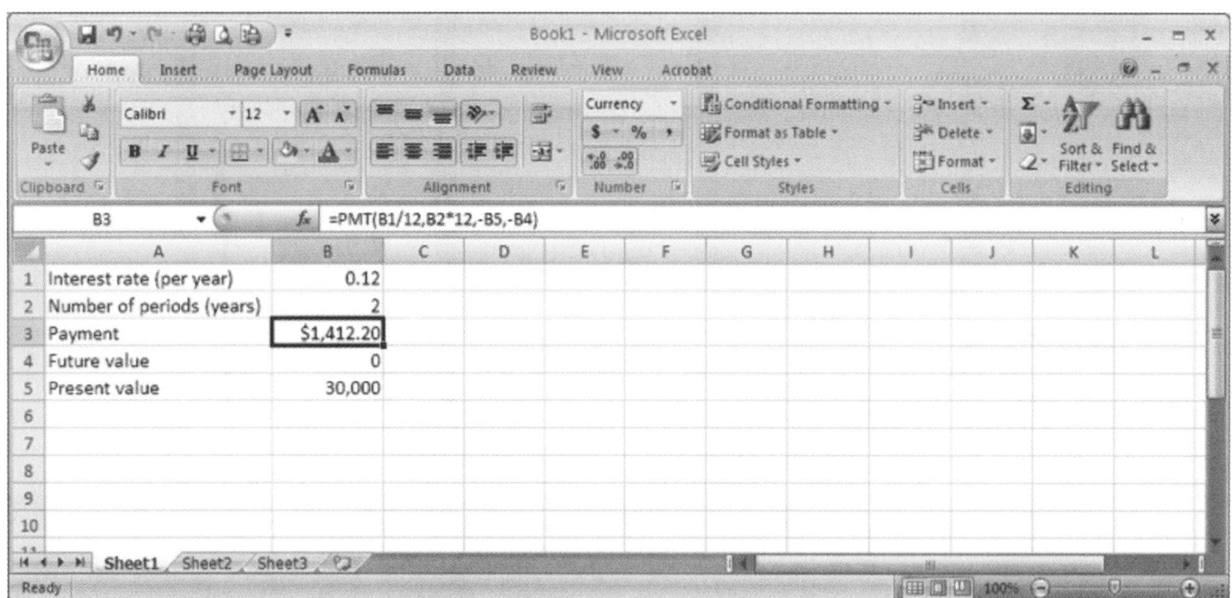

Here we need to divide the annual interest rate by 12 and multiply the number of years by 12 in order to allow for monthly compounding.

Excel is very useful for setting up loan amortisation tables. These tables lay out the loan payments and calculate the interest and principal included in each payment. To illustrate, assume we borrow $5,000 at 4% annual interest, and agree to repay the loan in 8 quarterly payments (four payments per year for two years). The quarterly payment is $653.45 calculated as follows:

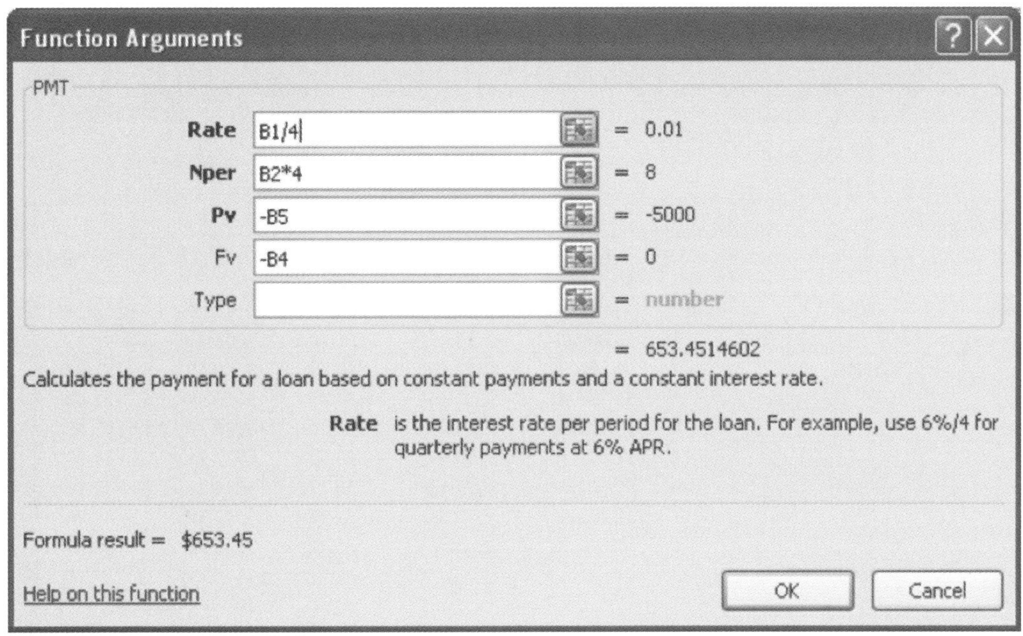

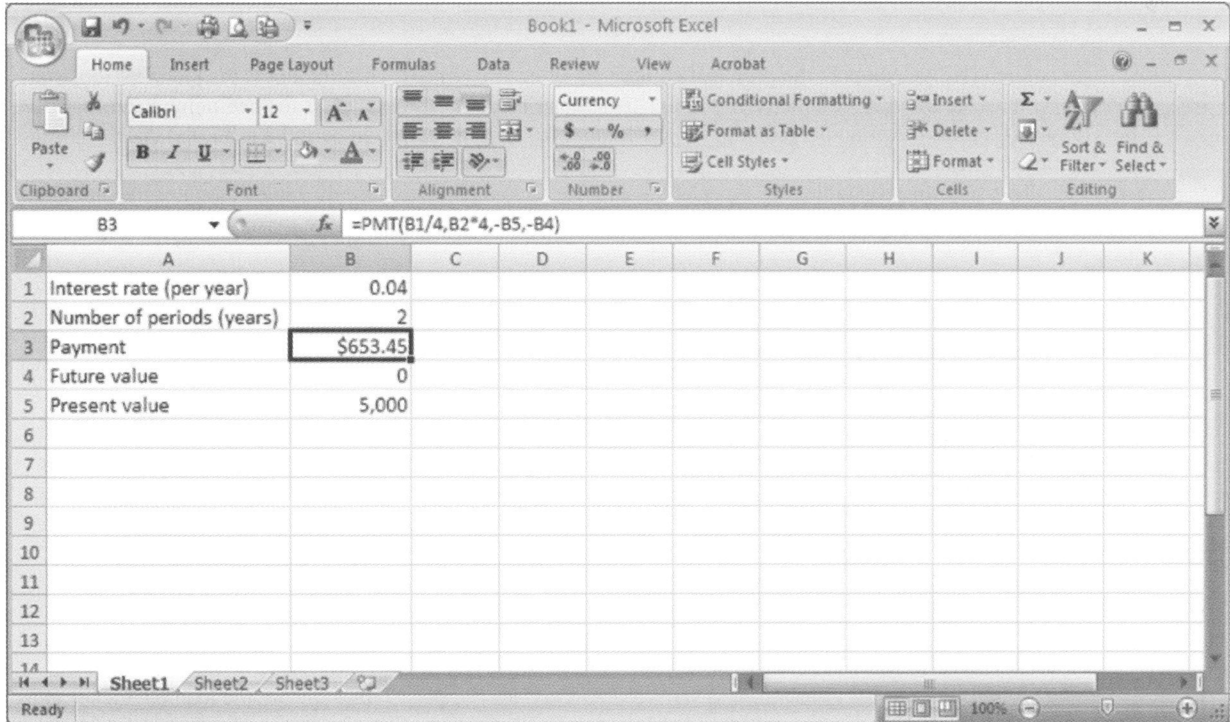

The loan amortisation table can be set up on the same worksheet or in a separate sheet linked to the payment calculation. Here we use the same worksheet.

The first column [D] lists the period (1 through 8). In the second column [E], we list the loan balance at the beginning of each period. For the first period, the beginning balance is the loan amount of $5,000. Thereafter, the beginning balance is set equal to the ending balance from the previous period, which is in column [I]. Column [F] lists the quarterly payment of $653.45. In column [G], we compute the interest each quarter. This amount is equal to the loan balance at the beginning of the period (Column [E]) times the interest rate (cell B1) divided by 4.

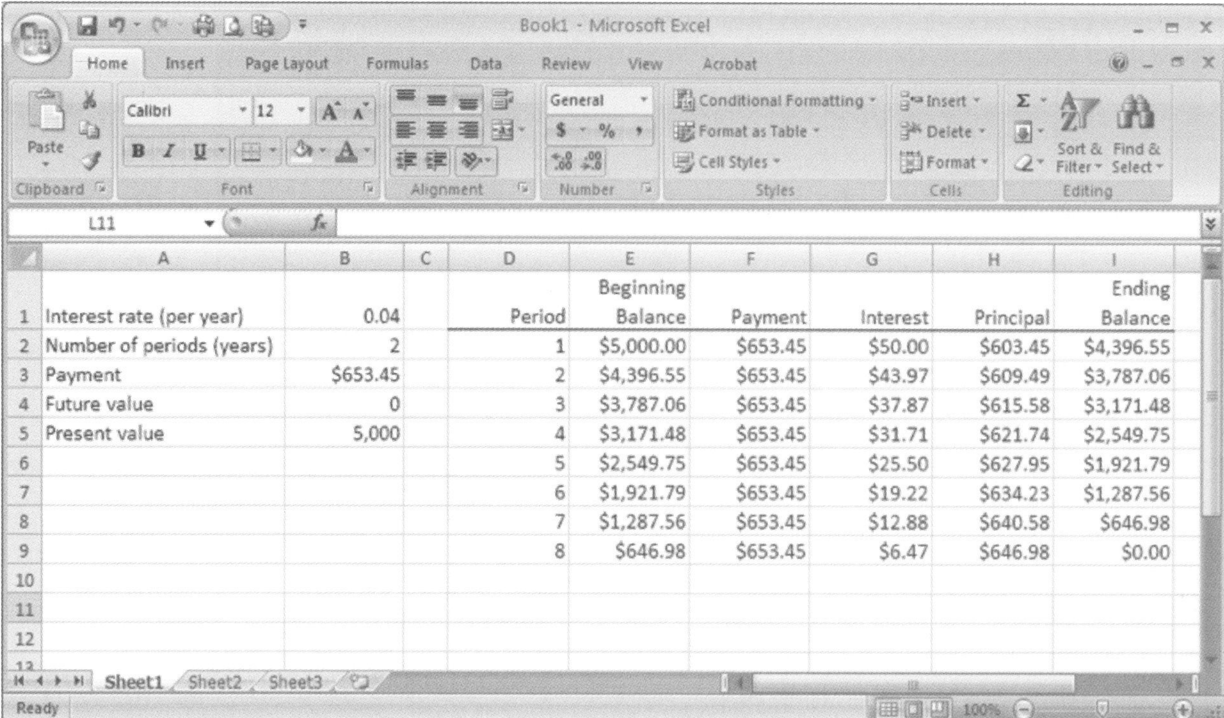

	A	B	C	D	E	F	G	H	I
1	Interest rate (per year)	0.04		Period	Beginning Balance	Payment	Interest	Principal	Ending Balance
2	Number of periods (years)	2		1	$5,000.00	$653.45	$50.00	$603.45	$4,396.55
3	Payment	$653.45		2	$4,396.55	$653.45	$43.97	$609.49	$3,787.06
4	Future value	0		3	$3,787.06	$653.45	$37.87	$615.58	$3,171.48
5	Present value	5,000		4	$3,171.48	$653.45	$31.71	$621.74	$2,549.75
6				5	$2,549.75	$653.45	$25.50	$627.95	$1,921.79
7				6	$1,921.79	$653.45	$19.22	$634.23	$1,287.56
8				7	$1,287.56	$653.45	$12.88	$640.58	$646.98
9				8	$646.98	$653.45	$6.47	$646.98	$0.00

In column [H] we compute the principal component of each payment. This amount is the payment (column [F]) minus the interest (column [G]). Finally, the ending balance (column [I]) is the beginning balance (column [E]) minus the principal (column [H]). Note that the ending balance in period 8 is $0 (the loan has been completely paid off).

Loan amortisation tables are especially useful for accountants because the table computes the amounts we enter for each payment. To illustrate, to record the original $5,000 loan, we make the following journal entry:

Cash (+A)	5,000.00	
Loan payable (+L)		5,000.00

Now, each period, we make a loan payment of $653.45 and that payment is part interest expense and part loan principal. To determine the split between interest and principal, we consult the loan amortisation table. For instance, in period 1, the payment is split as $50.00 of interest and $603.45 of principal. To record this payment, we would make the following journal entry:

Interest expense (+E, −SE)	50.00	
Loan payable (−L)	603.45	
Cash (−A)		653.45

Finally, Excel allows us to easily compute the present value of a series of irregular cash flows. To do this we use the NPV function. (NPV stands for *Net Present Value*). To compute NPV we need a series of cash flows at regular time intervals, such as one payment per year. If we skip a period, we must enter a 0 for that period. The cash flows can be a mixture of positive and negative cash flows (for instance receipts and payments). In the following spreadsheet, we present a series of seven cash flows and calculate the present value of these payments discounted at 5% using the NPV function.

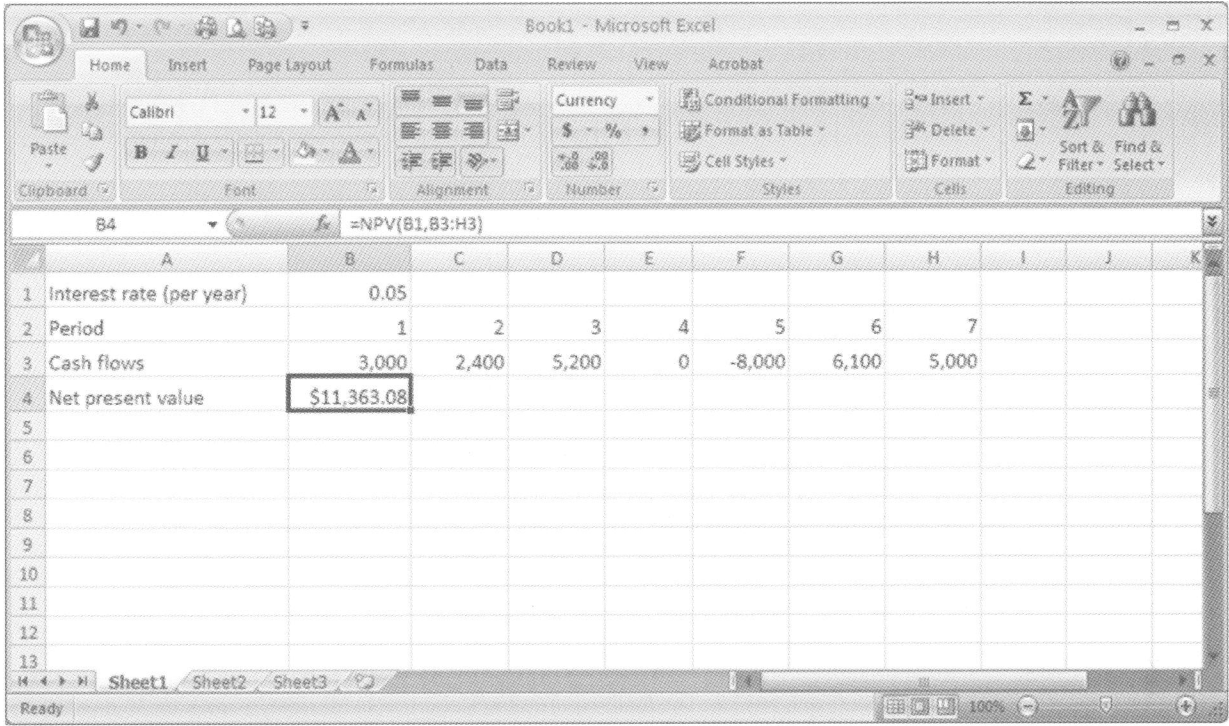

	A	B	C	D	E	F	G	H
1	Interest rate (per year)	0.05						
2	Period	1	2	3	4	5	6	7
3	Cash flows	3,000	2,400	5,200	0	-8,000	6,100	5,000
4	Net present value	$11,363.08						

The spreadsheet shows a net present value of $11,363.08. The function wizard dialog box for the NPV function is presented below:

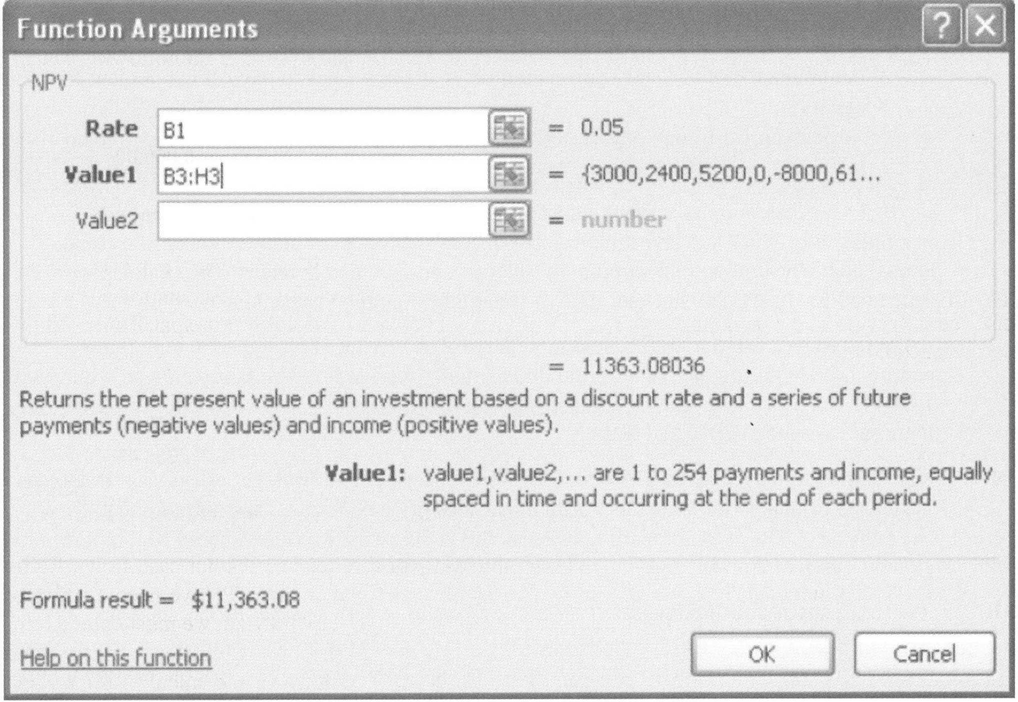

KEY TERMS

Annuity (p. 619)
Balloon payment (p. 620)
Compound interest (p. 616)
Discount rate (p. 618)
Future value (p. 616)
Future value factor (p. 617)
Instalment loan (p. 620)
Present value (p. 618)
Present value factor (p. 618)
Simple interest (p. 616)
Time-value of money (p. 616)

EXERCISES

EA-1. Dawn Riley deposited $4,000 in a money market account on January 2, 2014. How much will her savings be worth on January 2, 2020 if the money market account earns a return of

a. 4%?
b. 6%?
c. 8%?

EA-2. Jason Shields invested $7,500 in an account that pays a 12% return. How much will the account be worth in four years if the interest is compounded

a. annually?
b. quarterly?
c. monthly?

EA-3. Leslie Porter is planning a trip to Europe upon graduation in two years. She anticipates that her trip will cost $14,000. She would like to set aside an amount now to save for the trip. How much should she set aside if her savings earns 4% interest compounded quarterly?

EA-4. Matt Wilson has an investment opportunity that promises to pay him $24,000 in four years. He could earn 6% if he invested his money elsewhere. What is the maximum amount that he should be willing to invest in this opportunity?

EA-5. Robert Smith purchased a used car for $14,000. To pay for his purchase, he borrowed $12,500 from a local bank at 12%. The loan requires that Robert repay the loan by making 36 monthly payments. How much will Robert have to pay each month to repay the loan?

EA-6. Refer to Exercise EA-5. How much interest will Robert Smith pay as part of his first monthly payment?

EA-7. Sandy Nguyen just graduated from college and has $40,000 in student loans. The loans bear interest at a rate of 8% and require quarterly payments.

a. What amount should Sandy pay each quarter if she wishes to pay off her student loans in six years?
b. Sandy can only afford to pay $1,500 per quarter. How long will it take Sandy to repay these loans ?

EA-8. In 2013, Cart Inc. adopted a plan to accumulate funds for environmental remediation beginning July 2, 2018 at an estimated cost of $20 million. Cart plans to make five equal annual payments into a fund earning 6% interest compounded annually. The first deposit is scheduled for July 1, 2013. Determine the amount of the required annual deposit.

EA-9.On May 1, 2013, Ott, Inc. sold merchandise to Fox Inc. Fox signed a noninterest bearing note requiring payment of $60,000 annually for 7 years. The first payment is due May 1, 2014. The prevailing rate for similar notes on that date is 9%. What amount should Ott, Inc. report as revenue in 2013 and 2014?

EA-10. Rex Corporation accepted a $10,000, 5% interest bearing note from Brooks Inc. on December 1, 2013 in exchange for machinery with a list sales price of $9,500. The note is payable on December 1, 2016. If the prevailing interest rate is 8%, what revenues should Rex report in its income statement for the year ended December 31, 2013?

EA-11. Rye Company is considering purchasing a new machine with a useful life of ten years, at which time its salvage value is estimated to be $50,000. Management estimates a net increase in operating cash inflow due to the new machine at $200,000 per year. What is the maximum amount the company should be willing to pay for the machine if the relevant cost of capital associated with this type of investment is 12%.

EA-12. Debra Wilcox won $7 million in the California lottery. She must choose how she wants the prize to be paid to her. First, Debra can elect to receive 26 annual payments, with the first payment due immediately. Second, she can elect to receive a single payment immediately for the entire amount. However, if she elects the single payment option, the winning prize is reduced to one-half the winnings ($3.5 million). Which option should Debra choose if her cost of capital (discount rate) is

a. 8%?
b. 4%?
c. What rate would make Debra indifferent between these two options?

EA-13. Linda Reed, an executive at VIP Inc. has earned a performance bonus. She has the option of accepting $60,000 now or $100,000 5 years from now. What would you advise her to do? Explain and support with calculations.

EA-14. On September 1, 2013, Luft, Inc deposited $400,000 in a debt retirement fund. The company needs $955,000 cash to settle a maturing debt September 1, 2021. What is the minimal rate of compound interest required to assure the debt will be paid when due?

EA-15. Wolf Inc. establishes a construction fund on July 1, 2013, by making a single deposit of $360,000. At the end of each year, Wolf will deposit an additional $60,000. The fund guarantees a 12% return each year. How much will be in the fund on June 30, 2017?

EA-16. Sylvia Owen, owner of I-Haul Trucking is considering expanding operations from Seattle to the Portland area. Expansion is estimated to cost $10 million including the required new facilities and additional trucks. Owen has elected to finance the expansion by borrowing from her local bank at a yearly interest rate of 10%. She has agreed to repay the loan in twenty equal payments over a 10-year period to begin in one year.

a. What will Ms. Owen's periodic payments be?
b. How much of her first payment will be interest expense?
c. Assume that after ten years, Ms. Owen decided to pay off the loan early. How much would she owe at that time?

EA-17. On November 1, 2013, Ybarra Construction Company issued $200,000 of 5-year bonds that pay interest at an annual rate of 5%. The interest payments are due every six months (that is, the interest is compounded semi-annually). At the end of the five year period, Ybarra must pay the bond holders a balloon payment of $200,000.

a. What would the issue price of the bonds be if the prevailing interest rate is (i) 4%? (ii) 6%?
b. Compute the market price of these bonds on November 1, 2015 assuming that the prevailing market interest rate at that time is 8%.

EA-18. On August 1, 2013, Paradise Airlines agreed to lease a passenger jet from Boeing Corporation. The 20-year lease requires an annual payment of $450,000. If Paradise were to purchase the jet, it could borrow the necessary funds at a 9% interest rate.

a. What is the present value of the lease payments if the first payment is due on August 1, 2014?
b. What is the present value of the lease payments if the first payment is due on August 1, 2013?

EA-19. Burnham Corporation is comparing two alternatives for leasing a machine.

Alternative A is a lease that requires six annual payments of $8,000 with the first payment due immediately.

Alternative B is a lease that requires two payments of $11,000 and three payments of $9,000 with the first payment due one year from now.

a. Which alternative should Burnham choose if the relevant discount rate is 5%?
b. Which alternative should Burnham choose if the relevant interest rate is 7%?

EA-20. On January 2, 2014, DeSantis Company is comparing two alternatives for leasing a machine.

Alternative A is a lease that requires 24 quarterly payments $3,000 with the first payment due on March 31, 2014.

Alternative B is a lease that requires five annual payments of $14,300 with the first payment due on December 31, 2014.

Which alternative should DeSantis choose if the appropriate discount rate is 8% compounded quarterly?

TABLE A.1 Future Value of Single Amount $f = (1 + i)^t$

	Interest Rate											
Period	**0.01**	**0.02**	**0.03**	**0.04**	**0.05**	**0.06**	**0.07**	**0.08**	**0.09**	**0.10**	**0.11**	**0.12**
1	1.01000	1.02000	1.03000	1.04000	1.05000	1.06000	1.07000	1.08000	1.09000	1.10000	1.11000	1.12000
2	1.02010	1.04040	1.06090	1.08160	1.10250	1.12360	1.14490	1.16640	1.18810	1.21000	1.23210	1.25440
3	1.03030	1.06121	1.09273	1.12486	1.15763	1.19102	1.22504	1.25971	1.29503	1.33100	1.36763	1.40493
4	1.04060	1.08243	1.12551	1.16986	1.21551	1.26248	1.31080	1.36049	1.41158	1.46410	1.51807	1.57352
5	1.05101	1.10408	1.15927	1.21665	1.27628	1.33823	1.40255	1.46933	1.53862	1.61051	1.68506	1.76234
6	1.06152	1.12616	1.19405	1.26532	1.34010	1.41852	1.50073	1.58687	1.67710	1.77156	1.87041	1.97382
7	1.07214	1.14869	1.22987	1.31593	1.40710	1.50363	1.60578	1.71382	1.82804	1.94872	2.07616	2.21068
8	1.08286	1.17166	1.26677	1.36857	1.47746	1.59385	1.71819	1.85093	1.99256	2.14359	2.30454	2.47596
9	1.09369	1.19509	1.30477	1.42331	1.55133	1.68948	1.83846	1.99900	2.17189	2.35795	2.55804	2.77308
10	1.10462	1.21899	1.34392	1.48024	1.62889	1.79085	1.96715	2.15892	2.36736	2.59374	2.83942	3.10585
11	1.11567	1.24337	1.38423	1.53945	1.71034	1.89830	2.10485	2.33164	2.58043	2.85312	3.15176	3.47855
12	1.12683	1.26824	1.42576	1.60103	1.79586	2.01220	2.25219	2.51817	2.81266	3.13843	3.49845	3.89598
13	1.13809	1.29361	1.46853	1.66507	1.88565	2.13293	2.40985	2.71962	3.06580	3.45227	3.88328	4.36349
14	1.14947	1.31948	1.51259	1.73168	1.97993	2.26090	2.57853	2.93719	3.34173	3.79750	4.31044	4.88711
15	1.16097	1.34587	1.55797	1.80094	2.07893	2.39656	2.75903	3.17217	3.64248	4.17725	4.78459	5.47357
16	1.17258	1.37279	1.60471	1.87298	2.18287	2.54035	2.95216	3.42594	3.97031	4.59497	5.31089	6.13039
17	1.18430	1.40024	1.65285	1.94790	2.29202	2.69277	3.15882	3.70002	4.32763	5.05447	5.89509	6.86604
18	1.19615	1.42825	1.70243	2.02582	2.40662	2.85434	3.37993	3.99602	4.71712	5.55992	6.54355	7.68997
19	1.20811	1.45681	1.75351	2.10685	2.52695	3.02560	3.61653	4.31570	5.14166	6.11591	7.26334	8.61276
20	1.22019	1.48595	1.80611	2.19112	2.65330	3.20714	3.86968	4.66096	5.60441	6.72750	8.06231	9.64629
21	1.23239	1.51567	1.86029	2.27877	2.78596	3.39956	4.14056	5.03383	6.10881	7.40025	8.94917	10.80385
22	1.24472	1.54598	1.91610	2.36992	2.92526	3.60354	4.43040	5.43654	6.65860	8.14027	9.93357	12.10031
23	1.25716	1.57690	1.97359	2.46472	3.07152	3.81975	4.74053	5.87146	7.25787	8.95430	11.02627	13.55235
24	1.26973	1.60844	2.03279	2.56330	3.22510	4.04893	5.07237	6.34118	7.91108	9.84973	12.23916	15.17863
25	1.28243	1.64061	2.09378	2.66584	3.38635	4.29187	5.42743	6.84848	8.62308	10.83471	13.58546	17.00006
26	1.29526	1.67342	2.15659	2.77247	3.55567	4.54938	5.80735	7.39635	9.39916	11.91818	15.07986	19.04007
27	1.30821	1.70689	2.22129	2.88337	3.73346	4.82235	6.21387	7.98806	10.24508	13.10999	16.73865	21.32488
28	1.32129	1.74102	2.28793	2.99870	3.92013	5.11169	6.64884	8.62711	11.16714	14.42099	18.57990	23.88387
29	1.33450	1.77584	2.35657	3.11865	4.11614	5.41839	7.11426	9.31727	12.17218	15.86309	20.62369	26.74993
30	1.34785	1.81136	2.42726	3.24340	4.32194	5.74349	7.61226	10.06266	13.26768	17.44940	22.89230	29.95992
31	1.36133	1.84759	2.50008	3.37313	4.53804	6.08810	8.14511	10.86767	14.46177	19.19434	25.41045	33.55511
32	1.37494	1.88454	2.57508	3.50806	4.76494	6.45339	8.71527	11.73708	15.76333	21.11378	28.20560	37.58173
33	1.38869	1.92223	2.65234	3.64838	5.00319	6.84059	9.32534	12.67605	17.18203	23.22515	31.30821	42.09153
34	1.40258	1.96068	2.73191	3.79432	5.25335	7.25103	9.97811	13.69013	18.72841	25.54767	34.75212	47.14252
35	1.41660	1.99989	2.81386	3.94609	5.51602	7.68609	10.67658	14.78534	20.41397	28.10244	38.57485	52.79962
36	1.43077	2.03989	2.89828	4.10393	5.79182	8.14725	11.42394	15.96817	22.25123	30.91268	42.81808	59.13557
37	1.44508	2.08069	2.98523	4.26809	6.08141	8.63609	12.22362	17.24563	24.25384	34.00395	47.52807	66.23184
38	1.45953	2.12230	3.07478	4.43881	6.38548	9.15425	13.07927	18.62528	26.43668	37.40434	52.75616	74.17966
39	1.47412	2.16474	3.16703	4.61637	6.70475	9.70351	13.99482	20.11530	28.81598	41.14478	58.55934	83.08122
40	1.48886	2.20804	3.26204	4.80102	7.03999	10.28572	14.97446	21.72452	31.40942	45.25926	65.00087	93.05097

TABLE A.2 Present Value of Single Amount $p = 1/(1 + i)^t$

	Interest Rate											
Period	**0.01**	**0.02**	**0.03**	**0.04**	**0.05**	**0.06**	**0.07**	**0.08**	**0.09**	**0.10**	**0.11**	**0.12**
1	0.99010	0.98039	0.97087	0.96154	0.95238	0.94340	0.93458	0.92593	0.91743	0.90909	0.90090	0.89286
2	0.98030	0.96117	0.94260	0.92456	0.90703	0.89000	0.87344	0.85734	0.84168	0.82645	0.81162	0.79719
3	0.97059	0.94232	0.91514	0.88900	0.86384	0.83962	0.81630	0.79383	0.77218	0.75131	0.73119	0.71178
4	0.96098	0.92385	0.88849	0.85480	0.82270	0.79209	0.76290	0.73503	0.70843	0.68301	0.65873	0.63552
5	0.95147	0.90573	0.86261	0.82193	0.78353	0.74726	0.71299	0.68058	0.64993	0.62092	0.59345	0.56743
6	0.94205	0.88797	0.83748	0.79031	0.74622	0.70496	0.66634	0.63017	0.59627	0.56447	0.53464	0.50663
7	0.93272	0.87056	0.81309	0.75992	0.71068	0.66506	0.62275	0.58349	0.54703	0.51316	0.48166	0.45235
8	0.92348	0.85349	0.78941	0.73069	0.67684	0.62741	0.58201	0.54027	0.50187	0.46651	0.43393	0.40388
9	0.91434	0.83676	0.76642	0.70259	0.64461	0.59190	0.54393	0.50025	0.46043	0.42410	0.39092	0.36061
10	0.90529	0.82035	0.74409	0.67556	0.61391	0.55839	0.50835	0.46319	0.42241	0.38554	0.35218	0.32197
11	0.89632	0.80426	0.72242	0.64958	0.58468	0.52679	0.47509	0.42888	0.38753	0.35049	0.31728	0.28748
12	0.88745	0.78849	0.70138	0.62460	0.55684	0.49697	0.44401	0.39711	0.35553	0.31863	0.28584	0.25668
13	0.87866	0.77303	0.68095	0.60057	0.53032	0.46884	0.41496	0.36770	0.32618	0.28966	0.25751	0.22917
14	0.86996	0.75788	0.66112	0.57748	0.50507	0.44230	0.38782	0.34046	0.29925	0.26333	0.23199	0.20462
15	0.86135	0.74301	0.64186	0.55526	0.48102	0.41727	0.36245	0.31524	0.27454	0.23939	0.20900	0.18270
16	0.85282	0.72845	0.62317	0.53391	0.45811	0.39365	0.33873	0.29189	0.25187	0.21763	0.18829	0.16312
17	0.84438	0.71416	0.60502	0.51337	0.43630	0.37136	0.31657	0.27027	0.23107	0.19784	0.16963	0.14564
18	0.83602	0.70016	0.58739	0.49363	0.41552	0.35034	0.29586	0.25025	0.21199	0.17986	0.15282	0.13004
19	0.82774	0.68643	0.57029	0.47464	0.39573	0.33051	0.27651	0.23171	0.19449	0.16351	0.13768	0.11611
20	0.81954	0.67297	0.55368	0.45639	0.37689	0.31180	0.25842	0.21455	0.17843	0.14864	0.12403	0.10367
21	0.81143	0.65978	0.53755	0.43883	0.35894	0.29416	0.24151	0.19866	0.16370	0.13513	0.11174	0.09256
22	0.80340	0.64684	0.52189	0.42196	0.34185	0.27751	0.22571	0.18394	0.15018	0.12285	0.10067	0.08264
23	0.79544	0.63416	0.50669	0.40573	0.32557	0.26180	0.21095	0.17032	0.13778	0.11168	0.09069	0.07379
24	0.78757	0.62172	0.49193	0.39012	0.31007	0.24698	0.19715	0.15770	0.12640	0.10153	0.08170	0.06588
25	0.77977	0.60953	0.47761	0.37512	0.29530	0.23300	0.18425	0.14602	0.11597	0.09230	0.07361	0.05882
26	0.77205	0.59758	0.46369	0.36069	0.28124	0.21981	0.17220	0.13520	0.10639	0.08391	0.06631	0.05252
27	0.76440	0.58586	0.45019	0.34682	0.26785	0.20737	0.16093	0.12519	0.09761	0.07628	0.05974	0.04689
28	0.75684	0.57437	0.43708	0.33348	0.25509	0.19563	0.15040	0.11591	0.08955	0.06934	0.05382	0.04187
29	0.74934	0.56311	0.42435	0.32065	0.24295	0.18456	0.14056	0.10733	0.08215	0.06304	0.04849	0.03738
30	0.74192	0.55207	0.41199	0.30832	0.23138	0.17411	0.13137	0.09938	0.07537	0.05731	0.04368	0.03338
31	0.73458	0.54125	0.39999	0.29646	0.22036	0.16425	0.12277	0.09202	0.06915	0.05210	0.03935	0.02980
32	0.72730	0.53063	0.38834	0.28506	0.20987	0.15496	0.11474	0.08520	0.06344	0.04736	0.03545	0.02661
33	0.72010	0.52023	0.37703	0.27409	0.19987	0.14619	0.10723	0.07889	0.05820	0.04306	0.03194	0.02376
34	0.71297	0.51003	0.36604	0.26355	0.19035	0.13791	0.10022	0.07305	0.05339	0.03914	0.02878	0.02121
35	0.70591	0.50003	0.35538	0.25342	0.18129	0.13011	0.09366	0.06763	0.04899	0.03558	0.02592	0.01894
36	0.69892	0.49022	0.34503	0.24367	0.17266	0.12274	0.08754	0.06262	0.04494	0.03235	0.02335	0.01691
37	0.69200	0.48061	0.33498	0.23430	0.16444	0.11579	0.08181	0.05799	0.04123	0.02941	0.02104	0.01510
38	0.68515	0.47119	0.32523	0.22529	0.15661	0.10924	0.07646	0.05369	0.03783	0.02673	0.01896	0.01348
39	0.67837	0.46195	0.31575	0.21662	0.14915	0.10306	0.07146	0.04971	0.03470	0.02430	0.01708	0.01204
40	0.67165	0.45289	0.30656	0.20829	0.14205	0.09722	0.06678	0.04603	0.03184	0.02209	0.01538	0.01075

TABLE A.3 Present Value of Ordinary Annuity $p = \{1 - [1/(1 + i)^t]\}/i$

	Interest Rate											
Period	**0.01**	**0.02**	**0.03**	**0.04**	**0.05**	**0.06**	**0.07**	**0.08**	**0.09**	**0.10**	**0.11**	**0.12**
1	0.99010	0.98039	0.97087	0.96154	0.95238	0.94340	0.93458	0.92593	0.91743	0.90909	0.90090	0.89286
2	1.97040	1.94156	1.91347	1.88609	1.85941	1.83339	1.80802	1.78326	1.75911	1.73554	1.71252	1.69005
3	2.94099	2.88388	2.82861	2.77509	2.72325	2.67301	2.62432	2.57710	2.53129	2.48685	2.44371	2.40183
4	3.90197	3.80773	3.71710	3.62990	3.54595	3.46511	3.38721	3.31213	3.23972	3.16987	3.10245	3.03735
5	4.85343	4.71346	4.57971	4.45182	4.32948	4.21236	4.10020	3.99271	3.88965	3.79079	3.69590	3.60478
6	5.79548	5.60143	5.41719	5.24214	5.07569	4.91732	4.76654	4.62288	4.48592	4.35526	4.23054	4.11141
7	6.72819	6.47199	6.23028	6.00205	5.78637	5.58238	5.38929	5.20637	5.03295	4.86842	4.71220	4.56376
8	7.65168	7.32548	7.01969	6.73274	6.46321	6.20979	5.97130	5.74664	5.53482	5.33493	5.14612	4.96764
9	8.56602	8.16224	7.78611	7.43533	7.10782	6.80169	6.51523	6.24689	5.99525	5.75902	5.53705	5.32825
10	9.47130	8.98259	8.53020	8.11090	7.72173	7.36009	7.02358	6.71008	6.41766	6.14457	5.88923	5.65022
11	10.36763	9.78685	9.25262	8.76048	8.30641	7.88687	7.49867	7.13896	6.80519	6.49506	6.20652	5.93770
12	11.25508	10.57534	9.95400	9.38507	8.86325	8.38384	7.94269	7.53608	7.16073	6.81369	6.49236	6.19437
13	12.13374	11.34837	10.63496	9.98565	9.39357	8.85268	8.35765	7.90378	7.48690	7.10336	6.74987	6.42355
14	13.00370	12.10625	11.29607	10.56312	9.89864	9.29498	8.74547	8.24424	7.78615	7.36669	6.98187	6.62817
15	13.86505	12.84926	11.93794	11.11839	10.37966	9.71225	9.10791	8.55948	8.06069	7.60608	7.19087	6.81086
16	14.71787	13.57771	12.56110	11.65230	10.83777	10.10590	9.44665	8.85137	8.31256	7.82371	7.37916	6.97399
17	15.56225	14.29187	13.16612	12.16567	11.27407	10.47726	9.76322	9.12164	8.54363	8.02155	7.54879	7.11963
18	16.39827	14.99203	13.75351	12.65930	11.68959	10.82760	10.05909	9.37189	8.75563	8.20141	7.70162	7.24967
19	17.22601	15.67846	14.32380	13.13394	12.08532	11.15812	10.33560	9.60360	8.95011	8.36492	7.83929	7.36578
20	18.04555	16.35143	14.87747	13.59033	12.46221	11.46992	10.59401	9.81815	9.12855	8.51356	7.96333	7.46944
21	18.85698	17.01121	15.41502	14.02916	12.82115	11.76408	10.83553	10.01680	9.29224	8.64869	8.07507	7.56200
22	19.66038	17.65805	15.93692	14.45112	13.16300	12.04158	11.06124	10.20074	9.44243	8.77154	8.17574	7.64465
23	20.45582	18.29220	16.44361	14.85684	13.48857	12.30338	11.27219	10.37106	9.58021	8.88322	8.26643	7.71843
24	21.24339	18.91393	16.93554	15.24696	13.79864	12.55036	11.46933	10.52876	9.70661	8.98474	8.34814	7.78432
25	22.02316	19.52346	17.41315	15.62208	14.09394	12.78336	11.65358	10.67478	9.82258	9.07704	8.42174	7.84314
26	22.79520	20.12104	17.87684	15.98277	14.37519	13.00317	11.82578	10.80998	9.92897	9.16095	8.48806	7.89566
27	23.55961	20.70690	18.32703	16.32959	14.64303	13.21053	11.98671	10.93516	10.02658	9.23722	8.54780	7.94255
28	24.31644	21.28127	18.76411	16.66306	14.89813	13.40616	12.13711	11.05108	10.11613	9.30657	8.60162	7.98442
29	25.06579	21.84438	19.18845	16.98371	15.14107	13.59072	12.27767	11.15841	10.19828	9.36961	8.65011	8.02181
30	25.80771	22.39646	19.60044	17.29203	15.37245	13.76483	12.40904	11.25778	10.27365	9.42691	8.69379	8.05518
31	26.54229	22.93770	20.00043	17.58849	15.59281	13.92909	12.53181	11.34980	10.34280	9.47901	8.73315	8.08499
32	27.26959	23.46833	20.38877	17.87355	15.80268	14.08404	12.64656	11.43500	10.40624	9.52638	8.76860	8.11159
33	27.98969	23.98856	20.76579	18.14765	16.00255	14.23023	12.75379	11.51389	10.46444	9.56943	8.80054	8.13535
34	28.70267	24.49859	21.13184	18.41120	16.19290	14.36814	12.85401	11.58693	10.51784	9.60857	8.82932	8.15656
35	29.40858	24.99862	21.48722	18.66461	16.37419	14.49825	12.94767	11.65457	10.56682	9.64416	8.85524	8.17550
36	30.10751	25.48884	21.83225	18.90828	16.54685	14.62099	13.03521	11.71719	10.61176	9.67651	8.87859	8.19241
37	30.79951	25.96945	22.16724	19.14258	16.71129	14.73678	13.11702	11.77518	10.65299	9.70592	8.89963	8.20751
38	31.48466	26.44064	22.49246	19.36786	16.86789	14.84602	13.19347	11.82887	10.69082	9.73265	8.91859	8.22099
39	32.16303	26.90259	22.80822	19.58448	17.01704	14.94907	13.26493	11.87858	10.72552	9.75696	8.93567	8.23303
40	32.83469	27.35548	23.11477	19.79277	17.15909	15.04630	13.33171	11.92461	10.75736	9.77905	8.95105	8.24378

Glossary

A

absorption costing An approach to product costing that treats both variable and fixed manufacturing costs as product costs.

accelerated cost recovery system (ACRS, MACRS) A system of accelerated depreciation for tax purposes introduced in 1981 (ACRS) and modified starting in 1987 (MACRS); it prescribes depreciation rates by asset classification for assets acquired after 1980

accelerated depreciation (method) Depreciation method in which more depreciation expense is recorded early in an asset's useful life and less in its later life

access control matrix A computerised file that lists the type of access that each computer user is entitled to have to each file and program in the computer system

account An individual record of increases and decreases for an item in the accounting system

accounting The process of identifying, measuring, and communicating financial information to help people make economic decisions

accounting cycle The sequence of activities used to accumulate and report financial statements during a fiscal year

accounting entity An economic unit that has identifiable boundaries and that is the focus for the accumulation and reporting of financial information

accounting equation The basic financial relationship that investing equals financing, commonly expressed as assets = liabilities + equity

accounting period The time period, typically one year (or quarter), to which periodic accounting reports are related

accounting rate of return The average annual increase in net income that results from acceptance of a capital expenditure proposal divided by either the initial investment or the average investment in the project.

accounting system The structured collection of people, policies, procedures, equipment, files, and records that a company uses to collect, record, classify, process, store, report, and interpret financial data

accounts payable Amounts owed to suppliers for goods and services purchased on credit

accounts payable turnover Ratio defined as cost of goods sold divided by average accounts payable

accounts receivable Amounts due to a company from customers arising from the sale of products on credit

accounts receivable aging method A procedure that uses an aging schedule to determine the year-end balance needed in the allowance for uncollectible accounts account

accounts receivable turnover (ART) Annual net sales divided by average accounts receivable (net)

accrual accounting The recognition of revenue when earned and the matching of expenses when incurred

accruals Adjustments that reflect revenues earned but not received or recorded and expenses incurred but not paid or recorded

accrued expense An expense incurred before payment is made, such as wages, utilities, and taxes; recognised with an adjusting entry

accrued income Any revenues or income for an accounting period that have been earned and realised, but are not received or billed

accrued liabilities Obligations for expenses that have been recognised and recorded but not yet paid

accrued revenue The value of services provided that have not as yet been billed or paid for by a client

accumulated depreciation A contra asset reported in the balance sheet; reflects the total depreciation recorded for an asset up to the balance sheet date

accumulated other comprehensive income or loss Accumulated changes in equity that are not reported in the income statement

accumulated postretirement obligation (APBO) A liability for benefits, such as health care benefits, to be paid after an employee retires

acid test ratio More specific than the current ratio as a test of short-term solvency, the acid test ratio (also known as the quick ratio) measures the availability of cash and other current monetary assets that can be quickly generated into cash to pay current liabilities. The general equation for the acid test ratio is: (Cash + Marketable securities + Current receivables)/Current liabilities.

activities list *see* operations list.

activity A unit of work.

activity-based budgeting An approach to budgeting that uses an activity cost hierarchy to budget physical inputs and costs as a function of planned activity. It is mechanically similar to the output/input approach to budgeting where physical inputs and costs are budgeted as a function of planned activity.

activity-based costing (ABC) Used to develop cost information by determining the cost of activities and tracing their costs to cost objectives on the basis of the cost objective's utilisation of units of activity.

activity-based management (ABM) The identification and selection of activities to maximise the value of the activities while minimising their cost from the perspective of the final consumer.

activity cost drivers Specific units of work (activities) performed to serve customer needs that consume costly resources.

activity costing The determination of the cost of specific activities performed to fill customer needs.

activity dictionary A standardised list of processes and related activities.

additional paid-in capital Amounts received from the primary owners of a company in addition to the par or stated value of common stock

adjusted trial balance A listing of all general ledger account balances prepared after adjustments are recorded and posted

adjusting The process of adjusting the historical financial statements prior to the projection of future results; also called recasting and reformulating

adjusting entries Journal entries made at the end of an accounting period to reflect accrual accounting; rarely involve cash; usually affect a balance sheet account (an asset or liability account) and an income statement account (an expense or revenue account)

aging analysis Estimate of expected uncollectible accounts based on the number of days past invoices are outstanding

aging schedule An analysis that shows how long customers' accounts receivable balances have remained unpaid

allowance for uncollectible accounts An estimate of the receivables that a company will be unable to collect; reported as a contra-asset

allowance method An accounting procedure whereby the amount of uncollectible accounts expense is estimated and recorded in the period in which the related credit sales occur

Altman's Z-score A predictor of potential bankruptcy based on multiple ratios

American Institute of Certified Public Accountants (AICPA) Professional organisation of CPAs in the United States

amortisation The systematic allocation of an account balance to expense; usually refers to the periodic writing off of an intangible asset

annuity A pattern of cash flows in which equal amounts are spaced equally over a number of periods

appraisal costs Quality costs incurred to identify nonconforming products or services before they are delivered to customers.

arm's length Any transaction between two unrelated parties

articles of incorporation A document prepared by persons organising a corporation that sets forth the structure and purpose of the corporation and specifics regarding the classes of shares to be issued

articulation The linkage of financial statements within and across accounting periods

assembly efficiency variance The difference between the standard cost of actual assembly inputs and the flexible budget cost for assembly.

assembly rate variance The difference between the actual cost and the standard cost of actual assembly inputs.

asset a resource owned by the company that is expected to provide the company future economic benefits

asset turnover The sales to average assets ratio, which reflects effectiveness in generating sales from assets; also called total asset turnover

asset utilisation The efficiency a company has in turning over assets

asset write-downs Restructuring activity where long-term assets or unsalable inventory is reduced in value in the company financial reports; also called write-offs or charge-offs

audit An examination of a company's financial statements by a firm of independent certified public accountants

audited Financial statements that have been reviewed by an independent party (such as an audit firm); financial statements that present fairly and in all material respects the company's financial condition and the results of its operations

audit report A report issued by independent auditors that includes the final version of the financial statements, accompanying notes, and the auditor's opinion on the financial statements

authorised shares The maximum number of shares that a corporation may issue

automatic identification systems (AIS) The use of bar coding of products and production processes that allows inventory and production information to be entered into a computer without writing or keying.

available-for-sale (AFS) securities Investments in securities that management intends to hold for capital gains and dividend revenue

average cash cycle (ACC) The average period of time from when cash is invested in inventories until they are sold; the addition of the average collection period and modified average inventory days outstanding less the modified average payable days outstanding

average collection period (ACP) A measure related to accounts receivable turnover, which is defined as average accounts receivable divided by average daily sales

average cost (AC) Inventory costing method that views cost of goods sold as an average of the cost to purchase all inventories available for sale during a particular period

average inventory days outstanding (AIDO) A companion measure to inventory turnover computed as average inventory divided by average daily cost of goods sold; also called days inventory outstanding

average payable days outstanding A ratio defined as average accounts payable divided by average daily cost of goods sold

B

backflush costing An inventory accounting system used in conjunction with JIT in which costs are assigned initially to cost of goods sold. At the end of the period, costs are backed out of cost of goods sold and assigned to appropriate inventory accounts for any inventories that may exist.

bad debt expense The cost of uncollectible accounts; also called provision for uncollectible accounts

balanced scorecard A performance measurement system that includes financial and operational measures which are related to the organisational goals. The basic premise is to establish a set of indicators that can be used to monitor performance progress and then compare the goals that are established with the results.

balance sheet A financial report based on the accounting equation that lists a company's assets, liabilities, and equity at a certain point in time

balloon payment A lump sum payment due when a bond or other loan matures

bank reconciliation A schedule that accounts for all differences between the ending balance on the bank statement and the ending balance of the general ledger's cash account, as well as determining the reconciled cash balance at the end of the month

basic EPS Earnings per share, defined as net income less dividends on preferred shares divided by weighted average of common shares outstanding for the year

batch level activity An activity performed for each batch of product produced.

bearer One of the terms that may be used to designate the payee on a promissory note; means the note is payable to whoever holds the note

benchmarking A systematic approach to identifying the best practices to help an organisation take action to improve performance.

big bath Situation where a company recognises large write-offs in a period of already depressed income

bill of materials A document that specifies the kinds and quantities of raw materials required to produce one unit of product.

board of directors Governing body of a corporation; elected by the shareholders to represent shareholder interests and oversee management

bond A long-term debt instrument that promises to pay interest periodically and a principal amount at maturity, usually issued by the borrower to a group of lenders; bonds may incorporate a wide variety of provisions relating to security for the debt involved, methods of paying the periodic interest, retirement provisions, and conversion options

book value The dollar amount carried in the accounts of a particular item; the value of an item less its accumulated depreciation; also called net book value or carrying value

book value per share The net book value of a company available to common shareholders, defined as shareholders' equity less preferred shares divided by the number of common shares outstanding

borrows at a discount When the face amount of the note is reduced by a calculated cash discount to determine the cash proceeds

bottom-up budget A budget where managers at all levels—and in some cases even non-managers—become involved in the budget preparation.

break-even point The unit or dollar sales volume where total revenues equal total costs.

budget A formal plan of action expressed in monetary terms.

budget committee A committee responsible for supervising budget preparation. It serves as a review board for evaluating requests for discretionary cost items and new projects.

budget office An organisational unit responsible for the preparation, distribution, and processing of forms used in gathering budget data. It handles most of the work of actually formulating the budget schedules and reports.

budgetary slack Occurs when managers intentionally understate revenues or overstate expenses in order to produce favorable variances for the department.

budgeted financial statements Hypothetical statements that reflect the "as if" effects of the budgeted activities on the actual financial position of the organisation. They reflect what the results of operations will be if all the predictions in the budget are correct.

budgeting Projecting the operations of an organisation and their financial impact on the future.

bundled sales Two or more products sold together under one lump-sum price

C

calendar year A fiscal year that runs from January 1 to December 31

call provision A company's right to repurchase its own bond

capacity costs Operating expenses related to providing the ability to produce and sell products and provide services to customers; includes costs such as depreciation, rent, utilities, insurance and other related costs; *see* committed fixed costs

capital The assets that provide value to the company

capital budgeting A process that involves the identification of potentially desirable projects for capital expenditures, the subsequent evaluation of capital expenditure proposals, and the selection of proposals that meet certain criteria.

capital expenditures Financial outlays to acquire property, plant, and equipment; sometimes abbreviated as CAPEX

capital lease A lease that transfers to the lessee substantially all of the benefits and risks related to ownership of the property; the lessee records the leased property as an asset and establishes a liability for the lease obligation

capital lease method Method of reporting leases that requires both the lease asset and lease liability to be reported on the balance sheet

capital markets Financing sources that often involve a company's issuance of securities (shares, bonds, and notes)

capitalisation The recording of an asset's cost as an asset on the balance sheet rather than as an expense on the income statement; these costs are transferred to expense as the asset is used up

capitalisation of interest A process that adds interest to an asset's initial cost if a period of time is required to prepare the asset for use

capitalised To include a portion of an asset's cost on the balance sheet

capitalised interest Interest incurred during construction that is recorded as a part of the cost of a self-constructed (rather than purchased) asset

cash Currency, bank deposits, certificates of deposit, and other cash equivalents

cash accounting Accounting method where revenues are only recognised when received in cash and expenses are only recognised when paid in cash; sometimes referred to as cash-basis accounting

cash and cash equivalents A balance sheet account that combines cash with certain short-term, highly liquid investments

cash budget Summarises all cash receipts and disbursements expected to occur during the budget period.

cash (operating) cycle The period of time from when cash is invested in inventories until inventory is sold and receivables are collected

cash discounts A price reduction offered by suppliers to buyers if payment is made within a specified time period; usually established as part of the credit terms and stated as a percentage of the purchase price

cash equivalents Short-term, highly liquid investments that are easily convertible into a known cash amount and are relatively unaffected by interest rate changes

cash flow from operations divided by net income An objective performance measure; the higher this ratio, the higher the quality of income

centralisation When top management controls the major functions of an organisation (such as manufacturing, sales, accounting, computer operations, marketing, research and development, and management control).

certificate of deposit (CD) An investment security available at financial institutions generally offering a fixed rate of return for a specified period of time

chained target costing Bringing in suppliers as part of the coordination process to attain a competitively priced product that is delivered to the customer in a timely manner.

change in accounting estimate Modification to a previous estimate of an uncertain future event, such as the useful life of a depreciable asset, uncollectible accounts receivable, and warranty expenses; applied currently and prospectively only

change in accounting principle Adoption of a generally accepted accounting principle that differs from one previously used for reporting purposes. Accounting changes require full disclosure in the footnotes of the financial statements describing justification and the effect on cumulative income or loss of the change.

channel stuffing When a company uses its market power over customers or distributors to induce them to purchase more goods than necessary to meet their normal needs

chart of accounts Form that facilitates transaction analysis and the preparation of general ledger entries

check A written order directing a particular bank to pay a specified amount of money to a person named on the check

clean surplus accounting Income that explains successive equity balances

closing procedures Part of the accounting cycle in which the balances of temporary accounts are transferred into permanent accounts

coefficient of determination (R2) A measure of the percent of variation in the dependent variable that is explained by variations in the independent variable when the least-squares estimation equation is used.

collateral Mortgages on assets a company owns as security for debt financing

collectibility risk The chance that items sold on credit will not be paid in full

commitments A contractual arrangement by which both parties to the contract still have acts to perform

committed fixed costs (capacity costs) Costs required to maintain the current service or production capacity or to fill a previous legal commitment.

common-size comparative financial statement A financial statement in which each item is presented as a percentage of a key figure such as sales or total assets

common cost A cost incurred for the benefit of two or more cost objectives—an indirect cost.

common segment costs Costs related to more than one segment and not directly traceable to a particular segment. These costs are referred to as common costs because they are incurred at one level for the benefit of two or more segments at a lower level.

common size statement A financial statement that has had all its accounts converted into percentages. As such, a common size statement is very useful for detecting items that are out of line, that deviate from some present amount, or that may be indications of other problems.

common shares/stock The basic ownership class of shares carrying the rights to vote, share in earnings, participate in future share issues, and share in any liquidation proceeds after prior claims have been settled

comparative balance sheet Financial statement that compares the assets, liabilities, and equity of a company over several distinct periods

comparative financial statements A frequently encountered form of horizontal analysis that compares dollar and percentage changes for important items and classification totals

comparative income statement Financial statement that compares the revenues and expenses of a company over several distinct periods

compensating balance A minimum amount that a bank requires a firm to maintain in a bank account as part of a borrowing arrangement

competitor analysis The comparison of a firm's financial measures to similar measures or other firms in the industry or to industry averages

completed contract method Revenue recognition method in which revenue is deferred until the contract is complete

complex capital structure Shareholders' equity that includes dilutive securities outstanding; required to report diluted EPS (earnings per share)

compound interest Interest that accrues on outstanding interest

compound journal entry A journal entry that involves more than two accounts

comprehensive income The total income reported by the company, including net profit and all other changes to equity other than those arising from capital (share) transactions; typical components of other comprehensive income (OCI) are unrealised gains (losses) on available-for-sale securities and derivatives, minimum pension liability adjustment, and foreign currency translation adjustments

computer-aided design (CAD) A method of design that involves the use of computers to design products.

computer-aided manufacturing (CAM) A manufacturing method that involves the use of computers to control the operation of machines.

computer-integrated manufacturing (CIM) The ultimate extension of the CAD, CAM, and FMS concepts to a completely automated and computer-controlled factory where production is self-operating once a product is designed and the decision to produce is made.

conceptual framework Guidelines developed by the FASB to provide a structure for considering future standards, as well as to guide accountants in areas where standards do not currently exist

conservatism An accounting principle stating that judgmental determinations should tend toward understatement rather than overstatement of net assets and income

consignment A type of sale in which a consignor delivers product to a consignee, but retains ownership until the consignee sells the product to the ultimate customer

consistency An accounting principle stating that, unless otherwise disclosed, accounting reports should be prepared on a basis consistent with the preceding period

consolidated financial statements An aggregation (an adding up) of financial statements of the parent company and all its subsidiary companies, less any intercompany activities

contingency A possible future event; significant contingent liabilities must be disclosed in the notes to the financial statements

contingent liability A potential obligation, the eventual occurrence of which usually depends on some future event beyond the control of the firm; contingent liabilities may originate with such events as lawsuits, credit guarantees, and environmental damages

continuous budgeting Budgeting based on a moving time frame that extends over a fixed period. The budget system adds an identical time period to the budget at the end of each period of operations, thereby always maintaining a budget of exactly the same time length.

continuous improvement (Kaizen) budgeting An approach to budgeting that incorporates a targeted improvement (reduction) in costs; management requests that a given process will be improved during the budgeting process. This may be applied to every budget category or to specific areas selected by management. Kaizen budgeting is based upon prior performance and anticipated operating conditions during the upcoming period.

continuous improvement (Kaizen) costing Establishing cost reduction targets for products or services that an organisation is currently providing to customers.

continuous improvement An approach to activity-based management where the employees constantly evaluate products, services, and processes, seeking ways to do better.

contra-asset account A means to offset an asset account without directly reducing that account

contra accounts Accounts used to record reductions in or offsets to a related account

contract rate The rate of interest stated on a bond certificate

contributed capital The net funding that a company receives from issuing and reacquiring its equity shares; the difference between what the company receives from issuing shares and the cost it takes to buy them back

contributed surplus Amounts received from the primary owners of a company in addition to the par or stated value of common shares.

contribution income statement An income statement format in which variable costs are subtracted from revenues to figure contribution margin, and fixed costs are then subtracted from contribution margin to calculate net income.

contribution margin ratio The portion of each dollar of sales revenue contributed toward covering fixed costs and earning a profit.

contribution margin The difference between total revenues and total variable costs; this amount goes toward covering fixed costs and providing a profit.

controlling The process of ensuring that results agree with plans.

controlling influence When a company owns a majority of another company's voting shares, such that it has the ability to elect a majority of the board of directors and, as a result, the ability to affect its strategic direction and hiring of executive management

conversion cost The combined costs of direct labour and manufacturing overhead incurred to convert raw materials into finished goods.

conversion feature Contract provision that allows bondholders or preferred shareholders to convert their shares into common shares at a predetermined conversion ratio

convertible bond A bond incorporating the holder's right to convert the bond to common shares under prescribed terms

convertible securities Debt and equity securities that provide the holder with an option to convert those securities into other securities

cookie jar reserve Accounting method in which income is shifted from the current period to a future period

copyright An exclusive right that protects an owner against the unauthorised reproduction of a specific written work or artwork

core (persistent) components Elements of income that are most likely to persist and are most relevant for projecting future financial performance

core income A company's income from its usual business activities that is expected to continue (persist) into the future

corporation A form of business organisation that is a separate legal entity from its owners; characterised by a large number of owners who own shares of equity and who are not involved in managing the day-to-day operations of the company

cost allocation base A measure of volume of activity, such as direct labour hours or machine hours, that determines how much of a cost pool is assigned to each cost objective.

cost behavior How costs respond to changes in an activity cost driver.

cost center A responsibility center whose manager is responsible only for managing costs.

cost driver A factor that causes or influences costs.

cost driver analysis The study of factors that influence costs.

cost estimation The determination of the relationship between activity and cost.

cost flow assumption One of several alternative methods used to account for inventory and cost of goods sold when input prices change

cost method Accounting method in which investment is continually reported at its historical cost, and cash dividends and interest are recognised in current income

cost objective An object to which costs are assigned. Examples include departments, products, and services.

cost of capital The average cost of obtaining the resources necessary to make investments.

cost of goods sold An expense reflecting the cost of merchandise or manufactured products sold to customers

cost of goods sold percentage The ratio of cost of goods sold divided by net sales

cost of production report Used in a process costing system; summarises unit and cost data for each department or process for each period.

cost pool A collection of related costs, such as departmental manufacturing overhead, that is assigned to one or more cost objectives, such as products.

cost prediction The forecasting of future costs.

cost prediction error The difference between a predicted future cost and the actual amount of the cost when, or if, it is incurred.

cost principle An accounting principle stating that asset measures are based on the prices paid to acquire the assets

cost reduction proposal A proposed action or investment intended to reduce the cost of an activity that the organisation is committed to keeping.

cost-volume-profit (CVP) analysis A technique used to examine the relationships among total volume of some independent variable, total costs, total revenues, and profits during a time period (typically a month or a year).

cost-volume-profit graph An illustration of the relationships among activity volume, total revenues, total costs, and profits.

coupon bond A bond with coupons for interest payable to bearer attached to the bond for each interest period; whenever interest is due, the bondholder detaches a coupon and deposits it with his or her bank for collection

coupon (contract or stated) rate The interest rate stated in the bond contract; used to compute interest payments during the bond's life

covenants Contractual requirements that the loan recipient maintain minimum levels of capital to safeguard lenders

credit card fee A fee charged retailers for credit card services provided by financial institutions; the fee is usually stated as a percentage of credit card sales

credit (entry) An entry on the right-hand side of an account; used to record decreases in assets and increases in liabilities and shareholders' equity

credit guarantee A guarantee of another company's debt by cosigning a note payable; a guarantor's contingent liability that is usually disclosed in a balance sheet footnote

credit memo A document prepared by a seller to inform the purchaser that the seller has reduced the amount owed by the purchaser due to a return or an allowance

creditors Those to whom a company owes money; those who provide debt financing

credit period The maximum amount of time, usually stated in days, that the purchaser of merchandise has to pay the seller

credit sales A business transaction between companies where no cash immediately changes hands; also called sales on account

credit terms The prescribed payment period for purchases on credit with discount specified for early payment

cumulative (preferred shares) A feature associated with preferred shares whereby any dividends in arrears must be paid before dividends may be paid on common shares

cumulative effect of a change in principle The cumulative effect on net income to the date of a change in accounting principle

currency translation adjustment The unrecognised gain or loss on assets and liabilities denominated in foreign currencies

current assets The most liquid assets, which can be converted into cash within one year or one operating cycle

current liabilities Obligations such as accounts payable, accrued liabilities, unearned revenues, short-term notes payable, and current maturities of long-term debt that are due within one year

current maturities of long-term debt Long-term borrowings that are scheduled to mature in whole or in part during the upcoming year, including accrued interest

current rate method Method of translating foreign currency transactions under which balance sheet amounts are translated using exchange rates in effect at the period-end consolidation date and income statement amounts using the average exchange rate for the period

current ratio Measure of liquidity defined as current assets divided by current liabilities; a ratio greater than 1.0 implies positive net working capital

customer level activity An activity performed to obtain or maintain each customer.

customer profitability analysis A presentation showing the profits of individual or categories of customers net of the cost of serving and supporting those customers.

customer profitability profile A graphical presentation showing the cumulative profits from the most profitable to the least profitable customer

cycle efficiency The ratio of value-added to nonvalue-added manufacturing activities.

cycle time The total time required to complete a process. It is composed of the times needed for setup, processing, movement, waiting, and inspection.

D

dashboards Software programs that tabulate and display scorecard results using graphics that mimic the instrument displays on an automobile dashboard

days sales in inventory Inventories divided by average cost of goods sold

days sales in receivables A measure of both solvency and performance, the days receivable outstanding tells how long it takes to convert accounts receivable into cash or how well the firm is managing the credit extended to customers. The general equation for days receivable outstanding is: Ending receivables/Average daily sales.

debenture bond A bond that has no specific property pledged as security for the repayment of funds borrowed

debit (entry) An entry on the left-hand side of an account; used to record increases in assets and decreases in liabilities and shareholders' equity

debt-to-equity (DE) A common measure of financial leverage, defined as total liabilities divided by total equity

debt-to-equity ratio A measure of long-term solvency, the debt-to-equity ratio indicates the balance between the amounts of capital that creditors and owners provide. The general equation for the debt-to-equity ratio is: Total liabilities/Total equity.

decentralisation The delegation of decision-making authority to successively lower management levels in an organisation. The lower in the organisation the authority is delegated, the greater the decentralisation.

declining-balance method An accelerated depreciation method that allocates depreciation expense to each year by applying a constant percentage to the declining book value of the asset

default The nonpayment of interest and principal or the failure to adhere to various terms and conditions of an investment

deferral An accounting adjustment in which assets and revenues received in advance of a certain accounting period are allocated as expenses and revenues during that period

deferred income taxes The difference between income tax expense as reported in the income statement and income taxes due to taxing authorities; reported in the balance sheet as either an asset or liability

deferred performance liabilities Obligations that will be satisfied, not by paying cash, but instead, by providing products or services to customers

deferred revenue A liability representing revenues received in advance; also called unearned revenue

deferred revenue *see* unearned revenue

deferred tax asset Situation when tax reporting income is less than financial reporting income; the deferred tax asset expires when the temporary difference reverses

deferred tax liability Taxes to be paid in the future when taxable income is higher than financial reporting income; also called deferred taxes

deferred tax valuation allowance Reduction in a reported deferred tax asset to adjust for the amount that is not likely to be realised

defined benefit plan Pension plan in which the company makes periodic payments to an employee after retirement, generally based on years of service and employee's age

defined contribution plan Pension plan in which a company makes periodic contributions to a current employee's account, which the employee may drawn upon following retirement; many plans require an employee matching contribution

definite life A determinable period of time that an intangible asset, such as a patent or franchise right, exists

degree of operating leverage A measure of operating leverage, often computed as the contribution margin divided by income before taxes.

denominator variance see fixed overhead volume variance.

depletion The process of transferring costs from the resource account into inventory as resources are used up

deposits in transit Deposits not yet recorded by the bank

depreciation The decline in value of equipment and assets due to wear, deterioration, and obsolescence; process of allocating costs of equipment, vehicles, and buildings to the periods benefiting from their use

depreciation accounting The process of allocating the cost of equipment, vehicles, and buildings (not land) to expense over the time period benefiting from their use

depreciation and amortisation expenses Write-offs of previously recorded assets added to net income as it is converted to net operating cash flow

depreciation base The capitalised cost of an asset less the estimated residual value

depreciation method Means of calculating the reduction in an asset's value over its useful life

depreciation rate Method of depreciation equal to one divided by the item's useful life

depreciation tax shield The reduction in taxes due to the deductibility of depreciation from taxable revenues.

derivatives Financial instruments that are utilised by companies to reduce various kinds of risk

descriptive model A model that merely specifies the relationships between a series of independent and dependent variables.

design for manufacture Explicitly considering the costs of manufacturing and servicing a product while it is being designed.

detection control An internal control a company adopts to discover problems soon after they arise

differential cost analysis An approach to the analysis of relevant costs that focuses on the costs that differ under alternative actions.

diluted earnings per share (EPS) Earnings per share that includes share options and convertible securities in the calculations

dilutive securities Securities that can be converted into common shares and would therefore reduce (or dilute) the earnings per share upon conversion

direct association Recognising a cost directly associated with a specific source of revenue at the same time the related revenue is recognised

direct costing *see* variable costing.

direct department cost A cost directly traceable to a department upon its incurrence.

direct labour Wages earned by production employees for the time they spend working on the conversion of raw materials into finished goods.

direct materials The costs of primary raw materials that are converted into finished goods.

direct method (for cost allocation) A method of allocating service department costs to producing departments based only on the amount of services provided to the producing departments; it does not recognise any interdepartmental services.

direct method (for statement of cash flow) Accounting method that presents net cash flow from operating activities by showing the major categories of operating cash receipts and payments

direct segment fixed costs Costs that would not be incurred if the segment being evaluated were discontinued. They are specifically identifiable with a particular segment.

disclosure The act of providing financial and nonfinancial information to external users

discontinued operations Any separately identifiable component of a company that management abandons, sells or intends to sell

discount Situation where a bond's coupon rate is less than market rate

discount bond A bond that is sold for less than its par (face) value

discount on notes payable A contra account that is subtracted from the Notes Payable amount on the balance sheet; as the life of the note elapses, the discount is reduced and charged to interest expense

discount period The maximum amount of time, usually stated in days, that the purchaser of merchandise has to pay the seller if the purchaser wants to claim the cash discount

discount rate The interest rate used in present value calculations

discounted cash flow (DCF) model The value of a security is equal to the present value of the expected free cash flows to the firm, discounted at the weighted average cost of capital (WACC)

discounting The exchanging of notes receivable for cash at a financial institution at an amount that is less than the face value of the notes

discretionary cost center A cost center that does not have clearly defined relationships between effort and accomplishment.

discretionary fixed costs Costs set at a fixed amount each period at the discretion of management.

dividend discount model The value of a security today is equal to the present value of that security's expected dividends, discounted at the weighted average cost of capital

dividend payout ratio Dividend payments divided by net income

dividend preference The order in which shareholders receive dividends; preferred shareholders take precedence over common shareholders

dividends account A temporary equity account used to accumulate owner dividends from the business

dividend yield Annual dividends per share divided by the market price per share

division margin The amount each division contributes toward covering common corporate expenses and generating corporate profits. It is computed by subtracting all direct fixed expenses identifiable with each division from the contribution margin.

double declining balance (DDB) method An accelerated depreciation method that computes the depreciation rate as twice the straight-line rate times the remaining balance of the asset

double entry accounting system The dual effects where, in order to maintain the equality of the accounting equation, each transaction must affect at least two accounts

E

earned When referring to revenue, the seller's execution of its duties under the terms of the agreement, with the resultant passing of title to the buyer with no right of return or other contingencies

earned capital The cumulative net income (losses) retained by the company; income not paid to shareholders as dividends

earned income Income in which the seller has executed its duties under the terms of the sales agreement and the title has passed to the buyer

earnings before interest (EBI) Measures the income generated by a firm before taking into account any of its financing costs; computed as Net income + [Interest expense × (1 − Statutory tax rate)]

earnings before interest and taxes (EBIT) Measures the income generated by a firm before interest expense and income taxes

earnings management Discretionary choices management makes that mask the underlying economic performance of a company

earnings per share A measure of performance, earnings per share are disclosed on the income statement. The general equation for basic earnings per share is: Net income less preferred share dividends/ Weighted average number of common shares outstanding for the period.

earnings quality A measure of earnings in terms of sustainability, the ability for income to persist in future periods

earnings smoothing Earnings management with a goal to provide an earnings stream with less variability

economic consequences Issues resulting from accounting changes

economic profit The number of inventory units sold multiplied by the difference between the sales price and the replacement cost of the inventories (approximated by the cost of the most recently purchased inventories)

economic value added (EVA) Net operating profits after tax less a charge for the use of capital equal to beginning capital utilised in the business multiplied by the weighted average cost of capital

EDGAR Database maintained by the SEC where financial statements are available for download

effective cost The cost to a bond's issuing company for offering the bond, generally as cash interest paid plus the discount or premium incurred

effective interest method A method of amortising bond premium or discount that results in a constant rate of interest each period and varying amounts of premium or discount amortised each period

effective interest rate The rate determined by dividing the total discount amount by the cash proceeds on a note payable when the borrower borrowed at a discount

effective rate The current rate of interest in the market for a bond or other debt instrument; when issued, a bond is priced to yield the market (effective) rate of interest at the date of issuance

effective tax rate The average tax rate applied to pretax earnings; computed by dividing reported income tax expense by reported pretax earnings

efficient markets hypothesis Capital markets are said to be efficient if at any given time, current equity (share) prices reflect all relevant information that determines those equity prices

electronic data interchange (EDI) The electronic communication of data between organisations.

employee severance costs Accrued (estimated) costs for termination of employees as part of a restructuring program

employee share options A form of compensation that grants a select group of employees the right to purchase a fixed number of company shares at a fixed price for a predetermined time period

enterprise resource planning (ERP) Enterprise management information systems that provide organisations an integrated set of operating, financial, and management systems.

equity Capital provided by the company's owners, including shares, retained earnings, and contributed surplus; the owners' claim in the company

equity carve outs Corporate divestitures that are generally motivated by the belief that consolidated financial statements obscure the performance of individual business units

equity method Accounting method that reports investment on the balance sheet at an amount equal to the percentage of the investee's equity owned by the investor

equity valuation model A means of defining the value of an equity security in terms of the present value of future forecasted amounts

equivalent completed units The number of completed units that is equal, in terms of production effort, to a given number of partially completed units.

ethics The moral quality, fitness, or propriety of a course of action that can injure or benefit people; also, the values, rules, and justifications that governs one's way of life.

executory contract Situation such as a purchase order where a future sacrifice is probable and the amount of the sacrifice can be reasonably estimated, but the transaction that caused the obligation has not yet occurred

expense Outflow or use of assets, including costs of products and services sold, operating costs, and interest on debt, to generate revenue

expense to sales (ETS) A ratio measuring the percentage of each sales dollar that goes to cover a specific expense item; computed by dividing the expense by sales revenue

expensed Situation when a cost is recorded in the income statement and labeled as an expense

external failure costs Quality costs incurred when nonconforming products or services are delivered to customers.

extraordinary items Material gains or losses that are not related to normal business operations; must be both unusual in nature and infrequent in occurrence

F

face amount The principal amount of a bond, which is repaid at maturity

facility level activity An activity performed to maintain general manufacturing or marketing capabilities.

factoring Selling an account receivable to another company, typically a finance company or a financial institution, for less than its face value

fair value The value of an asset based on current rates in the general public

fair value option Provides companies with the option of using fair value to measure the value of most financial assets and liabilities

feedback value A characteristic of information that enables users to confirm or correct prior expectations

file A collection of related records.

finance lease see capital lease

financial accounting The process of recording, summarising, and analysing financial transactions designed primarily for decision makers outside of the company

Financial Accounting Standards Board (FASB) Standard-setting organisation which publishes accounting standards governing the preparation of financial reports

financial assets Normally consist of excess resources held for future expansion or unexpected needs; they are usually invested in the form of other companies' shares, corporate or government bonds, and real estate

financial leverage The proportionate use of borrowed funds in the capital structure, computed as net financial obligations (NFO) divided by average equity; financial leverage is considered favorable if the return on assets is higher than the fixed rate on borrowed funds and unfavorable if the fixed rate is greater than the return it generates.

financial reporting The process of preparing financial statements (income statement, balance sheet, and statement of cash flows) for a firm in accordance with generally accepted accounting principles

financial reporting objectives A component of the conceptual framework that specifies that financial statements should provide information (1) useful for investment and credit decisions, (2) helpful in assessing an entity's ability to generate future cash flows, and (3) about an entity's resources, claims to those resources, and the effects of events causing changes in these items

financial statement analysis Identifying and examining relationships between numbers within the financial statements and trends in these relationships from one period to the next

financial statement effects template Form that captures each transaction and its financial statement effects on the balance sheet and income statement

financial statement elements A part of the conceptual framework that identifies the significant components—such as assets, liabilities, shareholders' equity, revenues, and expenses—used to put financial statements together

financing activities Methods companies use to fund investment resources

finished goods Inventory account that records completed manufactured items waiting to be sold

finished goods inventory The dollar amount of inventory that has completed the production process and is awaiting sale to customers

first-in, first-out (FIFO) method One of the prescribed methods of inventory costing; FIFO assumes that the first costs incurred for the purchase or production of inventory are the first costs relieved from inventory when goods are sold

fiscal year The annual (one year) accounting period adopted by a company for its financial activities

five forces of competitive intensity Industry competition, bargaining power of buyers, bargaining power of suppliers, threat of substitution, threat of entry

fixed assets An alternate label for long-term assets; may also be called property, plant, and equipment (PPE)

fixed commitments ratio The ratio of operating cash flow to fixed commitments; computed as operating cash flow divided by fixed commitments

fixed costs Expenses that do not change with changes in sales volume (over a reasonable range)

fixed manufacturing overhead All fixed costs associated with converting raw materials into finished goods.

fixed overhead budget variance The difference between budgeted and actual fixed overhead.

fixed overhead volume variance The difference between total budgeted fixed overhead and total standard fixed overhead assigned to production.

fixed selling and administrative costs All fixed costs other than those directly associated with converting raw materials into finished goods.

flexible budgets Budgets that are drawn up for a series of possible production and sales volumes or adjusted to a particular level of production after the fact. These budgets, based on cost-volume or cost-activity relationships, are used to determine what costs should have been for an attained level of activity.

flexible budget variance Computed for each cost as the difference between the actual cost and the flexible budget cost of producing a given quantity of product or service.

flexible manufacturing systems (FMS) An extension of computer-aided manufacturing techniques through a series of manufacturing operations. These operations include the automatic movement of units between operations and the automatic and rapid setup of machines to produce each product.

for-profit organisation An organisation that has profit as a primary mission.

forecast The projection of financial results over the forecast horizon and terminal periods

forecast error Differences between amounts reported in the financial statements and amounts forecasted in pro forma financial statements

foreign currency transaction The $US equivalent of an asset or liability denominated in a foreign currency

foreign exchange gain or loss The gain (loss) recognised in the income statement relating to the change in the $US equivalent of an asset or liability denominated in a foreign currency

franchise A contractual agreement that gives a company the right to operate a particular business in an area for a particular period of time

free cash flow The net cash flow from operations less capital expenditures and dividends

full absorption cost *see* absorption costing.

full costing *see* absorption costing.

full costs Include all costs, regardless of their behavior patterns (variable or fixed) or activity level.

full disclosure principle An accounting principle stipulating the disclosure of all facts necessary to make financial statements useful to readers

fully diluted earnings per share *see* diluted earnings per share

functional currency The currency representing the primary currency in which a business unit conducts its operations

functional income statement A type of income statement where costs are classified according to function, rather than behavior. It is typically included in external financial reports.

fundamental analysis Method of using a company's financial information to estimate its value, which is used in buy-sell strategies

funded status The difference between a company's pension plan assets and the projected benefit obligation

future benefits Revenues or some other compensation a company expects to receive in a later period

future value The amount that a specific investment is worth at a future date if invested at a given rate of compound interest

future value factor A value that is multiplied by a current amount to obtain its equivalent value at a future date; the value of $1 invested for a number of periods at a specified interest rate

G

gain on bond retirement Situation where the repurchase price of a bond is less than the net bonds payable

general and administrative expense budget Presents the expenses the organisation plans to incur in connection with the general administration of the organisation. Included are expenses for such things as the accounting department, the computer center, and the president's office.

general journal A flexible journal that allows any type of business transaction to be included

general ledger A grouping of all of an entity's accounts that are used to prepare the basic financial statements

generally accepted accounting principles (GAAP) An overall set of standards and procedures accountants have developed that apply to the preparation of financial statements

goal A definable, measurable objective.

going concern concept An accounting principle that assumes that, in the absence of evidence to the contrary, a business entity will have an indefinite life

goodwill An intangible asset recorded when a company acquires another company, consisting of the value of a company above and beyond the fair value of its specific assets

gross margin The difference between net sales and cost of goods sold; also called gross profit

gross profit The difference between revenues (at selling prices) and cost of goods sold (at purchasing price or manufacturing cost)

gross profit margin (GPM) (percentage) A measure that reflects the net impact of sales on profitability, defined as gross profit divided by net sales

gross profit on sales The difference between net sales and cost of goods sold; also called gross margin

H

held-to-maturity (HTM) securities Debt securities that management holds on to for their full term

high-low method of cost estimation Utilises data from two time periods, a representative high activity period and a representative low activity period, to estimate fixed and variable costs.

historical cost The original acquisition cost, less the portion that that has expired or been transferred to the income statement

holding company The parent company of a subsidiary

holding gain The increase in replacement cost since the inventories were acquired, which equals the number of units sold multiplied by the difference between the current replacement cost and the original acquisition cost

horizon period The forecast period for which detailed estimates are made, typically 5–10 years

horizontal analysis An examination of data across two or more consecutive time periods, which assists in analysing company performance and predicting future performance

I

IASB see International Accounting Standards Board

IFRS see International Financial Reporting Standards

immediate recognition Costs recognised as expenses in a period when they were incurred, even though they cannot be directly linked to specific revenues

impairment Loss of property, plant, and equipment value determined by comparing the sum of expected future cash flows to the asset's net book value

imposed budget *see* top-down budget.

in-process research and development An intangible asset whose cost must be written off immediately upon purchase

income Also called net income, equals revenue minus expense, and is the increase in net assets (equity) resulting from the company's operations

income smoothing The discretionary management practice of choosing the timing of transactions in order to minimise fluctuations and maintain steady improvements in net income

income statement A financial report on operating activities that lists revenues less expenses over a period of time, yielding a company's net income

incremental budgeting An approach to budgeting where costs for a coming period are budgeted as a dollar or percentage change from the amount budgeted for (or spent during) some previous period.

indefinite lives Situation where an intangible asset's expected useful life extends far enough into the future that it is practically impossible to accurately determine

indirect department cost A cost reassigned, or allocated, to a department from another cost objective.

indirect method Accounting method for preparing the statement of cash flows in which the operating section begins with net income and converts it to cash flows from operations

indirect segment costs *see* common segment costs.

inspection time The amount of time it takes units to be inspected.

instalment loan Loan that requires a fixed periodic payment for a fixed duration of time

insufficient write-down Impairment of assets to a larger degree than is recognised

intangible assets Assets such as trademarks and patents that supply the owner rights rather than physical objects

integer programming A variation of linear programming that determines the solution in whole numbers.

intercorporate investments Investments in the securities of other companies

interdepartmental services Services provided by one service department to other service departments.

interest cost Interest accrued on outstanding pension liability, which is added to the liability each year

internal auditing A company function that provides independent appraisals of the company's financial statements, its internal controls, and its operations

internal controls Policies and procedures used to protect assets, ensure reliable accounting, promote efficient operations, and urge adherence to company policies

internal failure costs Quality costs incurred when materials, components, products, or services are identified as defective before delivery to customers.

internal rate of return (IRR) Often called the time-adjusted rate of return, the discount rate that equates the present value of a project's cash inflows with the present value of the project's cash outflows.

International Accounting Standards Board (IASB) The governing body established to develop acceptable accounting standards on a worldwide basis

International Financial Reporting Standards (IFRS) Guidelines developed by the IASB with the intention of unifying all public companies under one global set of reporting standards

inventory Goods purchased or produced for sale to customers

inventory carrying costs Costs of holding inventories, including warehousing, logistics, insurance, financing, and the risk of loss due to theft, damage, or technological or fashion change

inventory quality The rate at which inventory is turned over; the faster the turnover, the higher the quality

inventory shrinkage The cost associated with an inventory shortage; the amount by which the perpetual inventory exceeds the physical inventory

inventory turnover (in dollars) Often regarded as a measure of both solvency and performance, inventory turnover tells how long it takes to convert inventory into current monetary assets and how well the firm is managing investments in inventory. The general equation for inventory turnover is: Cost of goods sold/Average inventory cost.

inventory turnover (in units) The annual demand in units divided by the average inventory in units.

inventory turnover (INVT) Measure of inventory management computed as cost of goods sold divided by average inventory

investing activities Methods companies use to acquire and dispose of assets in the course of production and sales

investing creditors Those who primarily finance investing activities

investment center A responsibility center whose manager is responsible for the relationship between its profits and the total assets invested in the center. In general, the management of an investment center is expected to earn a target profit per dollar invested.

investment returns The increase in pension investments resulting from interest, dividends, and capital gains on the investment portfolio

investment tax credit A reduction in income taxes of a percent of the cost of a new asset in the year the new asset is placed in service.

invoice A document that the seller sends to the purchaser to request payment for items that the seller shipped to the purchaser

invoice price The price that a seller charges the purchaser for merchandise

IOU A slang term for a receivable

irrelevant costs Costs that do not differ among competing decision alternatives.

issued shares Common shares that have been sold and issued to shareholders; issued shares may be either outstanding or in the treasury

J

job cost sheet A document used to track the status of and accumulate the costs for a specific job in a job cost system.

job order production The manufacturing of products in single units or in batches of identical units.

job production *see* job order production.

joint costs All materials and conversion costs of joint products incurred prior to the split-off point.

joint products Two or more products simultaneously produced by a single process from a common set of inputs.

journal A tabular record in which business activities are analysed in terms of debits and credits and recorded in chronological order before they are entered in the general ledger; also called book of original entry

journal entries An accounting entry in a company's financial records that accountants use to represent individual transactions

just-in-time (JIT) inventory management A comprehensive inventory management philosophy that stresses policies, procedures, and attitudes by managers and other workers that result in the efficient production of high-quality goods while maintaining the minimum level of inventories.

just-in-time (JIT) inventory philosophy Receive inventory from suppliers into the production process just at the point it is needed

K

Kaizen costing *see* continuous improvement costing.

kanban system *see* materials pull system.

L

labour efficiency variance The difference between the standard cost of actual labour inputs and the flexible budget cost for labour.

labour rate (spending) variance The difference between the actual cost and the standard cost of actual labour inputs.

land improvements Improvements with limited lives made to land sites, such as paved parking lots and driveways

last-in, first-out (LIFO) method One of the prescribed methods of inventory costing; LIFO assumes that the last costs incurred for the purchase or production of inventory are the first costs relieved form inventory when goods are sold

lean accounting A system of product cost assignment where costs are assigned to value streams of multiple products rather than to individual products

leaning on the trade An increase in accounts payable, which results in an increase in net cash flows from operating activities

lean production A philosophy of inventory production and management that emphasises increased coordination throughout the value chain, reduced inventory, reduced production times, increased product quality, and increased employee involvement and empowerment

lease A contract between a lessor (owner) and lessee (tenant) for the rental of property

lease asset The value of a leased item

leasehold improvements Expenditures made by a lessee to alter or improve leased property

leasehold The rights transferred from the lessor to the lessee by a lease

lease liability The payments required to lease an item

least-squares regression analysis Uses a mathematical technique to fit a cost estimating equation to the observed data in a manner that minimises the sum of the vertical squared estimating errors between the estimated and actual costs at each observation.

lessee A party to a lease who wishes to use the asset

lessor The owner of property who transfers the right to use the property to another party by a lease

leveraging The use of borrowed funds in the capital structure of a firm; the expectation is that the funds will earn a return higher than the rate of interest on the borrowed funds

liability A probable future economic sacrifice resulting from a past or current event

licenses *see* operating rights

life-cycle budgeting An approach to budgeting when the entire life of the project represents a more useful planning horizon than an artificial period of one year.

life-cycle costs From the seller's perspective, all costs associated with a product or service ranging from those incurred with initial conception through design, pre-production, production, and after-production support. From the buyer's perspective, all costs associated with a purchased product or service, including initial acquisition costs and subsequent costs of operation, maintenance, repair, and disposal.

LIFO conformity rule IRS requirement to cost inventories using LIFO for tax purposes if they are costed using LIFO for financial reporting purposes

LIFO layer New layer added to inventory at an updated price each time inventory is purchased in companies using LIFO inventory costing; the most recent costs are transferred to cost of goods sold

LIFO liquidation Situation when, in companies using LIFO inventory costing, quantity of inventory sold exceeds that purchased, in which case the costs of older inventory is transferred to cost of good sold

LIFO reserve The difference between the cost of inventories using FIFO and the cost using LIFO

linear algebra method (reciprocal) method A method of allocating service department costs using a series of linear algebraic equations, which are solved simultaneously, to allocate service department costs both interdepartmentally among service departments and to the producing departments.

linear programming An optimising model used to assist managers in making decisions under constrained conditions when linear relationships exist between all variables.

liquidation preference In the event of a company's failure, preferred shareholders are reimbursed in full before common shareholders are paid

liquidation value per share The amount that would be received by a holder of a common share if the corporation liquidated

liquidity The ease of converting noncash assets into cash

list price The suggested price or reference price of merchandise in a catalog or price list

long-term debt Amounts borrowed from creditors that are scheduled to be repaid more than one year into the future

long-term debt-to-equity A common measure of leverage that focuses on long-term financing, defined as long-term debt divided by total equity

long-term investments Investments that the company does not intend to sell in the near future

long-term liabilities Debt obligations not due to be settled within the normal operating cycle or one year, whichever is longer

long-term operating asset turnover The rate that reflects capital intensity relative to sales, defined as net sales divided by average long-term operating assets

loss on bond retirement Situation if a bond's issuer pays more to retire the bonds than the amount carried on its balance sheet

lower of cost or market (LCM) GAAP requirement to write down the carrying amount of inventories on the balance sheet if the reported cost (using FIFO, for example) exceeds market value (determined by current replacement cost)

lower of cost or market (LCM) Process of reporting inventories at the lower of its cost or its current market value

M

maker Owner of a checking account

managed fixed costs *see* discretionary fixed costs.

management accounting A discipline concerned with financial and related information used by managers and other persons inside specific organisations to make strategic, organisational, and operational decisions.

management by exception An approach to performance assessment whereby management directs attention only to those activities not proceeding according to plan.

management discussion and analysis (MD&A) The section of the 10-K report in which a company provides a detailed discussion of its business activities

managerial accounting The process of recording, summarising, and analysing financial transactions designed primarily for decision makers within the company

manufacturers Companies that convert raw materials and components into finished products through the application of skilled labour and machine operations

manufacturing cost budget A budget detailing the direct materials, direct labour, and manufacturing overhead costs that should be incurred by manufacturing operations to produce the number of units called for in the production budget.

manufacturing costs Expenses associated with product production, including materials, labour, and overhead

manufacturing margin The result when direct manufacturing costs (variable costs) are deducted from product sales.

manufacturing organisations Organisations that process raw materials into finished products for sale to others.

manufacturing overhead All manufacturing costs other than direct materials and direct labour.

margin of safety The amount by which actual or planned sales exceed the break-even point.

marginal cost The varying increment in total cost required to produce and sell an additional unit of product.

marginal revenue The varying increment in total revenue derived from the sale of an additional unit.

marginal tax rate The tax rate that applies to the marginal dollar of income; the tax rate generally applied to nonoperating revenues and expenses

mark-to-market Method of valuing assets that results in an adjustment of an asset's carrying amount to its fair value

market method accounting Securities are reported at current market values (marked-to-market) on the statement date

market (yield) rate This is the interest rate that investors expect to earn on the investment in this debt security; this rate is used to price the bond issue

market segment level activity Performed to obtain or maintain operations in a market segment.

market value per share The current price at which a common share may be bought or sold

market value The published price (as listed on a stock exchange) multiplied by the number of shares owned

marketable securities Short-term investments that can be quickly sold to raise cash

markup The difference between an item's selling price and the cost incurred to produce it

master budget The grouping together of all budgets and supporting schedules. This budget coordinates all the financial and operational activities and places them into an organisation wide set of budgets for a given time period.

matching Recognising expenses in the same period that the associated revenue is recognised

matching principle An accounting guideline that states that income is determined by relating expenses, to the extent feasible, with revenues that have been recorded

materiality An accounting guideline that states that transactions so insignificant that they would not affect a user's actions or perception of the company may be recorded in the most expedient manner

materials inventory The physical component of inventory; the other components of manufactured inventory are labour costs and overhead costs

materials price variance The difference between the actual materials cost and the standard cost of actual materials inputs.

materials pull system An inventory production flow system in which employees at each station work to replenish the inventory used by employees at subsequent stations. The building of excess inventories is strictly prohibited. When the number of units in inventory reaches a specified limit, work at the station stops until workers at a subsequent station pull a unit from the in-process storage area.

materials push system An inventory production flow system in which employees work to reduce the pile of inventory building up at their work stations. Workers at each station remove materials from an in-process storage area, complete their operation, and place the output in another in-process storage area. Hence, they push the work to the next work station.

materials quantity variance The difference between the standard cost of actual materials inputs and the flexible budget cost for materials.

materials requisition form A document used to record the type and quantity of each raw material issued to the factory.

maturity date The date on which a note or bond matures

measuring unit concept An accounting guideline noting that the accounting unit of measure is the basic unit of money

merchandise inventory A stock of products that a company buys from another company and makes available for sale to its customers

merchandising firm A company that buys finished products, stores the products for varying periods of time, and then resells the products

merchandising organisations Organisations that buy and sell goods without performing manufacturing operations.

method of comparables model Equity valuation or share values are predicted using price multiples, which are defined as share price divided by some key financial statement number such as net income, net sales, book value of equity, total assets, or cash flow; companies are then compared with their competitors

minimum level budgeting An approach to budgeting that establishes a base amount for all budget items and requires explanation or justification for any budgeted amount above the minimum (base).

minority interest An ownership in a company that is less than a majority or controlling interest

minority interest The equity claim of a shareholder owning less than a majority or controlling interest in the company

mission The basic purpose toward which an organisation's activities are directed.

mixed costs Costs that contain a fixed and a variable cost element.

model A simplified representation of some real-world phenomenon.

modified accelerated cost recovery system (MACRS) *see* accelerated cost recovery system

movement time The time units spend moving between work or inspection stations.

mutually exclusive investments Two or more capital expenditure proposals where the acceptance of one investment automatically causes the rejection of the other(s).

N

natural resources Assets occurring in a natural state, such as timber, petroleum, natural gas, coal, and other mineral deposits

net-of-discount method Inventory capitalised at the net cost, assuming that a cash discount will be taken by the buyer

net asset based valuation model Equity is valued as reported assets less reported liabilities

net assets Assets minus liabilities

net book value (NBV) The cost of the asset less accumulated depreciation; also called carrying value

net financial expense Net operating profit after tax less net income

net financial obligations (NFO) The difference between financial (nonoperating) obligations and financial (nonoperating) assets; positive if obligations exceed assets

net financial rate Net financial expense divided by average net financial obligations

net income The difference between revenues and expenses when revenues exceed expenses

net interest rate (NIR) The average interest rate after taxes on total liabilities; calculated as [Interest expense × (1 − Statutory tax rate)]/Average total liabilities

net loss The difference between revenues and expenses when expenses exceed revenues

net operating assets (NOA) Current and long-term operating assets less current and long-term operating liabilities

net operating assets turnover (NOAT) A measure of turnover defined as sales divided by average net operating assets

net operating profit after tax (NOPAT) Sales less operating expenses (including taxes)

net operating profit margin (NOPM) The amount of operating profit produced as a percentage of each sales dollar; excludes all nonoperating revenues and expenses; calculated as Net operating profit after tax (NOPAT) divided by Sales revenue

net operating working capital (NOWC) Operating current assets less operating current liabilities

net operating working capital turnover (NOWCT) Management's effectiveness in using operating working capital, defined as net sales divided by average net operating working capital

net present value The present value of a project's net cash inflows from operations and disinvestment less the amount of the initial investment.

net profit margin The income to sales ratio, which reflects the profitability of sales; also called simply profit margin

net realisable value The value of a company's receivables, less an allowance for uncollectible accounts

net sales The total revenue generated by a company through merchandise sales less the revenue given up through sales returns and allowances and sales discounts

net sales volume variance Indicates the impact of a change in sales volume on the contribution margin, given the budgeted selling price and the standard variable costs. It is computed as the difference between the actual and the budgeted sales volumes times the budgeted unit contribution margin.

net working capital The difference between current assets and current liabilities; also called working capital

neutrality A characteristic of information that is free of any bias intended to attain a predetermined result or to induce a particular mode of behavior

no-par share Share that does not have a par value

nominal cost Cash interest paid on a debt

nominal rate The rate of interest stated on a bond certificate or other debt instrument

non-controlling interest see minority interest

non-operating revenues and expenses Costs related to the company's financing and investing activities, including interest revenue and interest expense

non-value-added activity An activity that does not add value to a product or service from the viewpoint of the customer.

noncash investing and financing activities Significant financial events that do not affect current cash flows, such as issuance of shares and bonds in exchange for property, plant, and equipment

noncurrent assets Assets not used up or converted to cash in one year; include Long-term financial investments, Property, plant, and equipment (PPE), and Intangible and other assets

noncurrent liabilities Obligations such as long-term debt and other long-term liabilities that are to be paid after one year

nonoperating expenses Expenses that relate to the company's financing activities and include interest income and interest expense, gains and losses on sales of securities, and income or loss on discontinued operations

non pro rata distribution A case where shareholder can accept or reject the distribution of shares

nonrecurring Revenues and expenses that are unlikely to arise in the future and are largely irrelevant to predictions of future performance

NOPAT Net operating profit after tax

normal operating cycle For a particular business, the average period of time between the use of cash in its typical operating activity and the subsequent collection of cash from customers

not-for-profit organisation An organisation that does not have profit as a primary goal.

not-sufficient-funds check A check from an individual or company that had an insufficient cash balance in the bank when the holder of the check presented it to the bank for payment

notes payable Account assigned to a company's financial borrowings

notes receivable Receivables that are based on a formal written promise to pay a specified amount and a predetermined date

notes to financial statements Footnotes in which companies discuss their accounting policies and estimates used in preparing the statements

O

objective function In linear programming models, the goal to be minimised or maximised.

objectivity principle An accounting principle requiring that, whenever possible, accounting entries are based on objectively determined evidence

off-balance-sheet financing A company's financial obligations that are not reported as liabilities in the balance sheet

on-balance-sheet financing The reporting of financing effects, namely current and noncurrent liabilities, on the balance sheet

operating activities Methods companies use to produce, promote, and sell its products and services

operating asset turnover The ratio obtained by dividing sales by average net operating assets

operating budget Detailed plans to guide operations throughout the budget period.

operating cash flow to capital expenditures ratio A measure that helps assess a firm's ability to replace its property, plant, and equipment, or expand as needed; calculated as operating cash flows from operating activities divided by annual capital expenditures

operating cash flow to current liabilities ratio A measure of the ability to liquidate current liabilities, calculated as net cash flow from operating activities divided by average current liabilities

operating cash flow to liabilities (OCFL) A method to compare operating flows to liabilities, defined as net cash flow from operations divided by total liabilities

operating creditors Those who primarily finance operating activities

operating cycle The time between paying cash for goods or employee services and receiving cash from customers

operating expense The usual and customary costs a company incurs to support its main business activities, including cost of goods sold, selling expenses, depreciation expenses, amortisation expenses, and research and development expenses

operating expense margin (OEM) The ratio obtained by dividing any operating expense item or category by sales

operating lease A lease by which the lessor retains the usual risks and rewards of owning the property

operating lease method Method of reporting leases where neither the lease asset nor the lease liability is on the balance sheet

operating leverage A measure of the extent that an organisation's costs are fixed.

operating profit margin The ratio obtained by dividing NOPAT by sales

operating rights A contractual agreement similar to franchise rights, but typically granted by government agencies

operational audit An evaluation of activities, systems, and internal controls within a company to determine their efficiency, effectiveness, and economy

operations list A document that specifies the manufacturing operations and related times required to produce one unit or batch of product.

opportunity cost The net cash inflow that could be obtained if the resources committed to one action were used in the most desirable other alternative.

optimal solution In linear programming models, the feasible solution than maximises or minimises the value of the objective function, depending on the decision maker's goal.

optimising model A model that suggests a specific choice between decision alternatives.

options *see* share options

order-filling costs Costs incurred to place finished goods in the hands of purchasers (for example, storing, packaging, and transportation).

order-getting costs Costs incurred to obtain customers' orders (for example, advertising, salespersons' salaries and commissions, travel, telephone, and entertainment).

order level activity An activity performed for each sales order.

ordinary annuity A series of fixed payments made at the end of each period over a specified time period

ordinary shares see common shares

organisation chart An illustration of the formal relationships existing between the elements of an organisation.

organisation costs Expenditures incurred in launching a business (usually a corporation), including attorney's fees and various fees paid to the state

organisation structure The arrangement of lines of responsibility within the organisation.

organisational-based cost systems Used for financial reporting, these systems focus on organisational units such as a company, plant, or department rather than on processes and activities.

organisational cost drivers Choices concerning the organisation of activities and the involvement of persons inside and outside the organisation in decision making.

organising The process of making the organisation into a well-ordered whole.

other long-term liabilities Various obligations, such as pension liabilities and long-term tax liabilities, that will be satisfied at least one year in the future

other post-employment benefits (OPEB) Benefits, other than pension benefits, such as health care and insurance benefits, provided by a company to retired employees

other postretirement benefits Items such as health care and insurance benefits offered to retired employees

outcomes assessment *see* performance measurement.

outlay costs Costs that require future expenditures of cash or other resources.

output/input budgeting An approach to budgeting where physical inputs and costs are budgeted as a function of planned unit level activities. The budgeted inputs are a function of the planned outputs.

outsourcing The external acquisition of services or components.

outstanding checks Checks not yet recorded by the bank

outstanding shares Common shares that are currently owned by shareholders (excludes treasury shares)

overfunded Situation where pension plan assets exceed pension liabilities

owners' equity The interest of owners in the assets of an entity; equal to the difference between the entity's assets and liabilities; also called shareholders' equity

P

packing list A document that lists the items of merchandise contained in a carton and the quantity of each item; the packing list is usually attached to the outside of the carton

paid-in capital The amount of capital contributed to a corporation by various transactions; the primary source of paid-in capital is from the issuance of shares

par (bonds) Face value of the bond

parent company A company owning one or more subsidiary companies

parsimonious method to multiyear forecasting Forecasting multiple years using only sales growth, net operating profit margin (NOPM), and the turnover of net operating assets (NOAT)

participation budget *see* bottom-up budget.

participation feature Contract provision that allows preferred shareholders to share ratably with common shareholders in dividends

partnership A form of business entity characterised by two or more owners who are also usually involved in managing the business

par value Face value of a bond; in ordinary shares, an arbitrary amount set by company organisers at the time of formation

passive influence Indicating lack of control of, or active participation in, the affairs of an investee company.

password A string of characters that a computer user enters into a computer terminal to prove to the computer that the person using the computer is truly the person named in the user identification code

patent An exclusive right to produce a product or use a technology

payback period The time required to recover the initial investment in a project from operations.

payee The person named on a check who will receive compensation

payer The bank that will compensate the recipient of a check

payment approval form A document that authorises the payment of an invoice

pension plan A plan to pay benefits to employees after they retire from the company; the plan may be a defined contribution plan or a defined benefit plan

percentage-of-completion method Revenue recognition method which recognises revenue by determining the costs incurred under the contract relative to its total expected costs

percentage of net sales method A procedure that determines the uncollectible accounts expense for the year by multiplying net credit sales by the estimated uncollectible percentage

percentage of sales A means to estimate uncollectible accounts that computes bad debts expense as a percentage of total sales

percent change Financial statement adjustment computed by dollar change (analysis period amount less base period amount) divided by base period amount, with the result multiplied by 100

performance measurement The determination of the extent to which actual outcomes correspond to planned outcomes.

period costs Expired costs not related to manufacturing inventory; they are recognised as expenses when incurred.

periodic interest payment Interest payments made in the form of equal cash flows at periodic intervals

period statement A financial statement accumulating information for a specific period of time; examples are the income statement, the statement of changes in equity, and the statement of cash flows

permanent account An account used to prepare the balance sheet; that is, asset, liability, and equity capital (contributed capital and retained earnings) accounts; any balance in a permanent account at the end of an accounting period is carried forward to the next period

permanent difference A difference in amount between two financial statements that does not reverse in time

persistent An amount that is expected to be maintained in future periods; see also recurring

physical inventory A year-end procedure that involves counting the quantity of each inventory item, determining the unit cost of each item, multiplying the unit cost times quantity, and summing the costs of all the items to determine the total inventory at cost

physical model A scaled-down version or replica of physical reality.

plan assets The assets of a pension plan that involve investments in shares and bonds

planning The process of selecting goals and strategies to achieve those goals.

planning activities The process of identifying a company's goals, and the strategies adopted to reach those goals

plant assets Land, buildings, equipment, vehicles, furniture, and fixtures that a firm uses in its operations; sometimes referred to by the acronym PPE

pooling of interests method A method of accounting for business combinations under which the acquired company is recorded on the acquirer's balance sheet at its book value, rather than market value; this method is no longer acceptable under GAAP for acquisitions occurring after 2001

position statement A financial statement, such as the balance sheet, that presents information as of a particular date

post-closing trial balance Accounting balance prepared after closing entries are recorded and posted to verify the equality between debits and credits in the general ledger after the adjusting and closing process

postdated check A check from another person or company with a date that is later than the current date; a postdated check does not become cash until the date of the check

posting The transfer of debit and credit entries from the journal to their related general ledger accounts

practical capacity The maximum possible activity, allowing for normal repairs and maintenance.

predetermined manufacturing overhead rate An overhead rate established at the start of each year by dividing the predicted overhead costs for the year by the predicted volume of activity in the overhead base for the year.

predictive value A characteristic of information referring to its ability to increase the accuracy of a forecast

preemptive right The right of a shareholder to maintain his or her proportionate interest in a corporation by having the right to purchase an appropriate share of any new share issue

preference or preferred shares Shares that possesses priority over common shares, such as first right to dividends or liquidation payout

premium When a bond's coupon rate is greater than the market rate

premium bond A bond that is sold for more than its par (face) value

prepaid expenses Costs paid in advance for rent, insurance, or other services

present value The amount of money a share or bond is worth at the current time

present value factor A value that is multiplied by a future amount to obtain its equivalent value at the current date; the value of $1 received in the future discounted for a number of periods at a specified discount rate

present value index The present value of the project's subsequent cash flows divided by the initial investment.

prevention control An internal control companies adopt to deter problems before they arise

prevention costs Quality costs incurred to prevent nonconforming products from being produced or nonconforming services from being performed.

price discrimination Illegally charging different purchasers different prices.

price earnings ratio A measure of performance, price earnings ratio compares the current market price with earnings per share of a company and arrives at a multiple of earnings represented by the selling price. Calculated as: Current market price per common share divided by Earnings per share

price fixing The organised setting of prices by competitors.

process A collection of related activities intended to achieve a common purpose.

process manufacturing A manufacturing environment where production is on a continuous basis.

process map (or process flowchart) A schematic overview of all the activities required to complete a process. Each major activity is represented by a rectangle on the map.

process reengineering The fundamental redesign of a process to serve internal or external customers.

processing time The time spent working on units.

product costs All costs incurred in the manufacturing of products; they are carried in the accounts as an asset (inventory) until the product is sold, at which time they are recognised as an expense (cost of goods sold).

production order A document that contains a job's unique identification number and specifies details for the job such as the quantity to be produced, the total raw materials requirements, the manufacturing operations and other activities to be performed, and perhaps even the time when each manufacturing operation should be performed.

product level activity An activity performed to support the production of each different type of product.

product margin Computed as product sales less direct product costs.

productivity The relationship between outputs and inputs.

profit center A responsibility center whose manager is responsible for revenues, costs, and resulting profits. It may be an entire organisation, but it is more frequently a segment of an organisation such as a product line, marketing territory, or store.

profit margin (PM) A ratio measuring profit, before interest expense, that is generated from each dollar of sales revenue; calculated as Earnings before interest (EBI) divided by Sales revenue

profit-volume graph Illustrates the relationship between volume and profits; it does not show revenues and costs.

profitability The ability of a company to generate net income

profitability analysis An examination of the relationships between revenues, costs, and profits.

pro forma financial statements Hypothetical statements prepared to reflect specific assumptions about a company and its transactions; often referring to forecasted financial statements

pro forma income GAAP income from continuing operations (excluding discontinued operations and extraordinary items), less transitory items

pro rata distribution Shares distributed to shareholders on a pro rata basis

project-level activity An activity performed to support the completion of each project.

projected benefit obligation (PBO) Pension liabilities that represent future obligations to current and former employees

promissory note A written promise to pay a certain sum of money on demand or at a determinable future time

property, plant, and equipment (PPE) Tangible assets recorded on a balance sheet, including land, factory buildings, warehouses, office buildings, office equipment, and other items used in the operation of a business

provision A potential obligation that is probable (i.e., at least 50% chance) that an outflow of future economic benefits will occur and the amount is reasonably estimable. A provision is recongised at the most likely amount, calculated as the expected value of all the possible amounts.

provision for income tax Income tax expense

Public Company Accounting Oversight Board (PCAOB) Board established by the Sarbanes-Oxley Act to approve auditing standards and monitor the quality of financial statements and audits

purchase method The prescribed method of accounting for business combinations; under the purchase method, assets and liabilities of the acquired company are recorded at fair value, together with identifiable intangible assets; the balance is ascribed to goodwill

purchase order A document that formally requests a supplier to sell and deliver specific quantities of particular items of merchandise at specified prices

purchase requisition An internal document that requests that the purchasing department order particular items of merchandise

purchases budget Indicates the merchandise or materials that must be acquired to meet current needs and ending inventory requirements.

Q

qualitative characteristics of accounting information The characteristics of accounting information that contribute to decision usefulness; the primary qualities are relevance and reliability

quality circles Groups of employees involved in the production of products who have the authority, within certain parameters, to address and resolve quality problems as they occur, without seeking management approval.

quality Conformance to customer expectations.

quality costs Costs incurred because poor quality of conformance does (or may) exist.

quality of conformance The degree of conformance between a product and its design specifications.

quality of design The degree of conformance between customer expectations for a product or service and the design specifications of the product or service.

quality of earnings The extent to which reported income reflects the underlying economic performance of a company

quantitative model A set of mathematical relationships.

quarterly data Selected quarterly financial information that is reported in annual reports to shareholders

quick ratio (QR) A ratio that reflects a company's ability to meet its current liabilities without liquidating inventories

R

raw materials and supplies Inventory account that records items used in production processes

raw materials inventories The physical ingredients and components that will be converted by machines and/or human labour into a finished product.

realised (or realisable) When referring to revenue, the receipt of an asset or satisfaction of a liability as a result of a transaction or event

realised or realisable income Income in which the company's net assets increase

receivables quality The likelihood of collecting on a receivables account, which a company can change by extending credit terms, taking on longer-paying customers, and increasing the allowance provision

recognition criteria The criteria that must be met before a financial statement element may be recorded in the accounts; essentially, the item must meet the definition of an element and must be measurable

reconciled cash balance A company's cash balance after accounting for deposits in transit and outstanding checks

record A related set of alphabetic and/or numeric data items.

recurring An amount that is expected to be reported again in future periods; *see* also persistent

redeem Company repurchasing their bonds prior to maturity

registered bond A bond for which the issuer (or the trustee) maintains a record of owners and, at the appropriate times, mails out interest payments

relational (cause-and-effect) cost center A cost center that has clearly defined relationships between effort and accomplishment (cause and effect).

relevance The usefulness of information to those who use financial statements in decision making

relevant costs Future costs that differ between competing decision alternatives.

relevant range The range of activity within which a linear cost function is valid.

reliability The ability to objectively determine and accurately measure a value, such as historical cost

remeasurement The computation of gain or loss in the translation of subsidiaries denominated in a foreign currency into $US when the temporal method is used

representational faithfulness A characteristic of accounting information referring to the degree with which it reflects the underlying economic events it purports to measure

residual (or salvage) value The expected realisable value of an asset at the end of its useful life

residual income for investment center Excess of investment center income over the minimum rate of return set by top management. The minimum dollar return is computed as a percentage of the investment center's asset base.

residual net operating income (ROPI) model An equity valuation approach that equates the firm's value to the sum of its net operating assets (NOA) and the present value of its residual operating income (ROPI)

residual operating income Net operating profits after tax (NOPAT) less the product of net operating assets (NOA) at the beginning of the period multiplied by the weighted average cost of capital (WACC)

responsibility accounting The structuring of performance reports addressed to individual (or group) members of an organisation in a manner that emphasises the factors they are able to control. The focus is on specific units within the organisation that are responsible for the accomplishment of specific activities or objectives.

restructuring costs Expenses typically associated with activities such as consolidating production facilities, reorganising sales operations, outsourcing activities, or discontinuing product lines

retailers Companies that buy products from wholesale distributors and sell the products to individual customers, the general public

retained earnings Earned capital, the cumulative net income and loss, of the company (from its inception) that has not been paid to shareholders as dividends

retained earnings reconciliation The reconciliation of retained earnings from the beginning to the end of the year; the change in retained earnings includes, at a minimum, the net income (loss) for the period and dividends paid, if any, but may include other components as well; also called statement of retained earnings

return The amount of money earned on an investment, often expressed as investment income divided by the amount invested; also called yield

return on assets (ROA) A computation of net income divided by average total assets; also called return on invested capital

return on common shareholders' equity A financial ratio computed as net income less preferred share dividends divided by average common shareholders' equity; sometimes referred to by the acronym ROCE

return on equity (ROE) The ultimate measure of performance from the shareholders' perspective, computed as net income divided by average equity

return on financial leverage (ROFL) A measure of the effect that financial leverage has on Return on equity (ROE); calculated as Return on equity (ROE) minus Return on assets (ROA)

return on investment The ratio obtained by dividing income by average investment; sometimes referred to by the acronym ROI

return on investment for investment center A measure of the earnings per dollar of investment. The return on investment of an investment center is computed by dividing the income of the center by its asset base (usually average total assets). It can also be computed as investment turnover times the return-on-sales ratio.

return on net operating assets (RNOA) A measure of operating returns; calculated as Net operating profit after taxes (NOPAT) divided by Average net operating assets (NOA)

return on sales An overall test of operating efficiency defined as net income divided by net sales revenue; Increase in net assets (assets less liabilities) as a result of business activities

revenue The increase in equity resulting from the sale of goods and services to customers

revenue center A responsibility center whose manager is responsible for the generation of sales revenues.

revenue recognition The timing and amount of revenue reported by a company

revenue recognition criteria Requirements that must be met for income to be recognised on the income statement; according to GAAP, revenue must be realised/realisable and earned

revenue recognition principle An accounting principle requiring that revenue be recognised when earned and realised (or realisable)

revenue variance The difference between the budgeted sales volume at the budgeted selling price and the actual sales volume at the actual selling price.

right of return The allowance for a customer to return a product within a specified period of time

risk-free rate The market rate of interest defined as the yield on U.S. Government borrowings, computed as yield rate less spread

risk The uncertainty of expected return, which is an intrinsic part of each investment

Robinson-Patman Act Prohibits price discrimination when purchasers compete with one another in the sale of their products or services to third parties.

rolling budget *see* continuous budgeting.

S

sale on account A sale of merchandise made on a credit basis

sales budget A forecast of sales revenue for a future period. It may also contain a forecast of sales collections.

sales mix The relative portion of unit or dollar sales derived from each product or service.

sales price variance The impact on revenues of a change in selling price, given the actual sales volume. It is computed as the change in selling price times the actual sales volume.

sales volume variance Indicates the impact on revenues of change in sales volume, assuming there was no change in selling price. It is computed as the difference between the actual and the budgeted sales volumes times the budgeted selling price.

salvage value The expected net recovery when a plant asset is sold or removed from service; also called residual value

Sarbanes-Oxley Act Act passed in 2002 which requires a company's CEO and CFO to personally sign a statement attesting to the accuracy and completeness of financial statements

scatter diagram A graph of past activity and cost data, with individual observations represented by dots.

secured bond A bond that pledges specific property as security for meeting the terms of the bond agreement

Securities and Exchange Commision (SEC) Commision created by the 1934 Securities Act to regulate the issuance and trading of securities

security valuation A determination of the value of equity securities

segment income All revenues of a segment minus all costs directly or indirectly charged to it.

segment margin The amount that a segment contributes toward the common (indirect) costs of the organisation and toward profits. It is computed as segment sales less direct segment costs.

segment reports Income statements that show operating results for portions or segments of a business. Segment reporting is used primarily for internal purposes, although generally accepted accounting principles also require disclosure of segment information for some public corporations.

segments Subdivisions of a firm for which supplemental financial information is disclosed

sell-off The outright sale of a business unit

selling expense budget Presents the expenses the organisation plans to incur in connection with sales and distribution.

semi-variable costs *see* mixed costs.

sensitivity analysis The process of examining the effect of alternative assumptions on the pro forma statements; helps to identify these effects before a decision is made so that costly mistakes can be avoided

serial bond A bond issue that staggers the bond maturity dates over a series of years

service cost The additional pension benefits earned by employees each year

service cost (pensions) The increase in the pension obligation due to employees working another year for the employer

service costing The process of assigning costs to services performed.

service department A department that provides support services to production and/or other support departments.

service organisations Nonmanufacturing organisations that perform work for others, including banks, hospitals, and real estate agencies.

setup time The time required to prepare equipment to produce a specific product.

share dividends The payment of dividends in common shares

shareholders Owners of a corporation; holders of common shares in a corporation

shareholders' equity *see* equity

share option A share right giving the holder the right to acquire a common share at a preset price within a specified period of time; used to compensate officers and other employees

share rights A shareholder's option to acquire a specified number of common shares under prescribed conditions and within a stated period

share split A distribution (or increase in the number) of common shares accompanied by a proportionate decrease in the par value

share warrant A certificate that provides the holder with stock rights

shares authorised The number of shares that a corporation can issue without amending its corporate charter

shares issued The actual number of shares that have been sold to shareholders by a corporation

shares outstanding The number of issued shares less the number of shares repurchased as treasury shares

Sherman Antitrust Act Prohibits price fixing.

short-term interest-bearing debt Short-term bank borrowings and notes expected to mature in whole or in part during the upcoming year

short-term notes payable Short-term debt payable to banks or other creditors

short term borrowings Debt payable to banks or other creditors that is due within one year or within one operating cycle

significant influence The ability of an investor to affect an investee's financing or operating policies

simple capital structure Shareholders' equity with no dilutive securities outstanding

simplex method A mathematical approach to solving linear programming models containing three or more variables.

sinking fund provision A bond feature that requires the borrower to retire a portion of the bonds each year or, in some cases, to make payments each year to a trustee who is responsible for managing the resources needed to retire the bonds at maturity

sole proprietorship A form of business characterised by a single owner who typically manages the daily operations

solvency Refers to the firm's ability to pay its debts as they become due.

solvency analysis A review of a company's ability to meet its financial obligations, which is aided by financial leverage ratios

source document Any written document or computer record evidencing an accounting transaction, such as a bank check or deposit slip, sales invoice, or cash register tape

special purpose entity *see* variable interest entity

spin-off A form of equity carve out in which a company distributes subsidiary shares it owns as dividends to its shareholders, making shareholders owners of the subsidiary

split-off A form of equity carve out in which divestiture is accomplished by the parent company's exchange of shares in the subsidiary in return for shares in the parent owned by its shareholders

split-off point The point in the process where joint products become separately identifiable.

spread The difference between the net financial return (NFR) and the return on net operating activities (RNOA); also called risk premium

standard cost A budget that indicates what it should cost to provide an activity or produce one batch or unit of product under efficient operating conditions.

standard cost variance analysis A system for examining the flexible budget variance, which is the difference between the actual cost and flexible budget cost of producing a given quantity of product or service.

stated value A nominal amount that may be assigned to each no-par common share and accounted for much as if it were a par value

statement of cash flows A financial report that identifies net cash flows into and out of a company from operating, investing, and financing activities over a period of time

statement of changes in equity A financial statement presenting information on the events causing a change in equity during a period; the statement presents the beginning balance, additions to, deductions from, and the ending balance of equity for the period

statement of cost of goods manufactured A report that summarises the cost of goods completed and transferred into finished goods inventory during the period.

statement of financial position A financial statement showing a firm's assets, liabilities, and shareholders' equity at a specific date; also called a balance sheet

statement of responsibility Form included with each financial statement of a publicly traded company assuring management is responsible for the statements, they have been prepared using GAAP, and they are audited by an outside organisation

static budget A budget based on a prior prediction of expected sales and production.

step costs Costs that are constant within a narrow range of activity but shift to a higher level with an increased range of activity. Total step costs increase in a step-like fashion as activity increases.

step method A method of allocating service department costs that gives partial recognition to interdepartmental services by using a methodology that allocates service department costs sequentially to both the remaining service departments and the producing departments.

storyboard A process map developed by employees who perform the component activities within a process.

straight-line depreciation Determination of annual depreciation expense by dividing the asset's cost by its estimated useful life

strategic business segment A segment that has its own mission and set of goals to be achieved. The mission of the segment influences the decisions that its top managers make in both short-run and long-run situations.

strategic cost management Making decisions concerning specific cost drivers within the context of an organisation's business strategy, its internal value chain, and its place in a larger value chain stretching from the development and use of resources to the final consumers.

strategic plan A guideline or framework for making specific medium-range or short-run decisions.

strategic position How an organisation wants to place itself in comparison to the competition.

strategic position analysis An organisation's basic way of competing to sell products or services.

strategy A course of action that will assist in achieving one or more goals.

structural cost drivers Fundamental choices about the size and scope of operations and technologies employed in delivering products or services to customers. These choices affect the types of activities and the costs of activities performed to satisfy customer needs.

suboptimisation When managers or operating units, acting in their own best interests, make decisions that are not in the best interest of the organisation as a whole.

subsequent events Events occurring shortly after a fiscal year-end that will be reported as supplemental information to the financial statements of the year just ended

subsidiaries Companies that are owned by the parent company

subsidiary ledger A set of accounts or records that contains detailed information about the items included in the balance of one general ledger account

sum-of-the-years'-digits method An accelerated depreciation method that allocates depreciation expense to each year in a fractional proportion, the denominator of which is the sum of the years' digits in the useful life of the asset and the numerator of which is the remaining useful life of the asset at the beginning of the current depreciation period

summary of significant accounting policies A financial statement disclosure, usually the initial note to the statements, which identifies the major accounting policies and procedures used by the firm

sunk costs Costs resulting from past decisions that cannot be changed.

suppliers Providers of merchandise for resale or materials needed for operating activities

systematic allocation Costs that benefit more than one accounting period and cannot be associated with specific revenues

T

T-account A graphic representation of an account, shaped like a large T, which uses one side to record increases to the account and the other side to record decreases

tangible assets Assets that have physical substance, such as property, plant, and equipment

target costing Establishes the allowable cost of a product or service by starting with determining what customers are willing to pay for the product or service and then subtracting a desired profit on sales.

temporary account An account used to gather information for an accounting period; at the end of the period, the balance is transferred to a permanent equity account; revenue, expense, and dividends accounts are temporary accounts

temporary difference A difference in amount between two financial statements that reverses in time

terminal period The forecast period following the horizon period

term loan A long-term borrowing, evidenced by a note payable, which is contracted with a single lender

theory of constraints Every process has a bottleneck (constraining resource), and production cannot take place faster than it is processed through the bottleneck. The theory's goal is to maximise throughput in a constrained environment.

throughput Sales revenue minus direct materials costs; *see also* theory of constraints.

time-adjusted rate of return *see* internal rate of return.

timeliness A characteristic of information that is received by decision makers before it loses its capacity to influence decisions

times interest earned (TIE) A determination of how much income is available to service debt, defined as earnings before interest and taxes divided by interest expense

times interest earned ratio A measure of long-term solvency and interest-paying ability; measured as income before interest expense and income taxes divided by interest expense

time value of money The recognition that the value of an amount of money depends on when the money is received;

tombstone An announcement of debt offered to the public

top-down budget A budget where top management decides on the primary goals and objectives for the organisation and communicates them to lower management levels.

total compensation cost The sum of gross pay, payroll taxes, and fringe benefits paid by the employer

trade credit The financing used to purchase inventories on credit from other companies

trade discount An amount, usually based on quantity of merchandise purchased, that the seller subtracts from the list price of merchandise to determine the invoice price

trademark A registered name, logo, package design, image, jingle, or slogan associated with a product

trade name An exclusive and continuing right to use a certain term or name to identify a brand or family of products

trading on the equity The use of borrowed funds in the capital structure of a firm; the expectation is that the funds will earn a return higher than the rate of interest on the borrowed funds

trading securities Investments in securities that management intends to actively buy and sell for trading profits as market prices fluctuate

transfer price The internal value assigned a product or service that one division provides to another.

transitory components Elements of income that are not recurring; financial projections are improved if these are excluded from them

transitory items Transactions or events that are not likely to recur

translation adjustment The change in the value of the net assets of a subsidiary whose assets and liabilities are denominated in a foreign currency

treasury shares Common shares that have been acquired by the issuing corporation; a contra equity account

trend analysis A type of horizontal analysis in which a base period is chosen and all subsequent period amounts are defined relative to the base

trend percentages A comparison of the same financial item over two or more years, stated as a percentage of a base-year amount

trial balance A list of the account titles in the general ledger, their respective debit or credit balances, and the totals of the debit and credit amounts

U

unadjusted trial balance Account balances before any adjustments are made

uncollectible accounts expense The expense stemming from the inability of a business to collect an amount previously recorded as a receivable; sometimes called bad debts expense; normally classified as a selling or administrative expense

underfunded Situation where pension liabilities exceed pension plan assets

unearned revenue Cash received for products or services to be provided at a later time

unit contribution margin The difference between the unit selling price and the unit variable costs.

unit level activity An activity performed for each unit of product produced or sold.

unit level approach An approach to analysing cost behavior that assumes changes in costs are best explained by changes in the number of units or sales dollars of products or services provided for customers.

units-of-production method A common depreciation method in which the useful life of the asset is defined in terms of the number of units of service provided by the asset

unrealised holding gain A gain resulting from holding an asset such as inventory as prices are rising

unrecognised prior service cost An accounting adjustment to a pension that represents the portion of the liability earned by employees prior to the plan's inception or a plan amendment

useful life The period of time over which the asset in expected to provide economic benefits to the company

V

value The worth in usefulness or importance of a product or service to the customer.

value-added activity An activity that adds value to a product or service from the viewpoint of the customer.

value chain The set of value-producing activities stretching from basic raw materials to the final consumer.

value chain analysis The study of value-producing activities, stretching from basic raw materials to the final consumer of a product or service.

value stream Consists of the production processes for similar products. Each value stream in a lean company not only has lean processes; it also has a lean accounting system because most costs should be directly traceable to one of the value streams.

variable costs Expenses that change in proportion to changes in sales volume

variable costing An approach to product costing that treats variable manufacturing costs as product costs and fixed manufacturing costs as period costs.

variable cost ratio Variable costs as a portion of sales revenue.

variable interest entity (VIE) Any form of business organisation (such as corporation, partnership, trust) that is established by a sponsoring company and provides benefits to that company in the form of asset securitisation or project financing; VIEs were formerly known as special purpose entities (SPEs)

variable manufacturing overhead All variable costs, except direct labour and direct materials, associated with converting raw materials into finished goods.

variable overhead effectiveness variance The difference between the standard variable overhead cost for the actual inputs and the flexible budget cost for variable overhead based on outputs.

variable overhead spending variance The difference between the actual variable overhead cost and the standard variable overhead cost for the actual inputs.

variable selling and administrative costs All variable costs other than those directly associated with converting raw materials into finished goods.

variance A comparison of actual and budgeted (or allowed) costs or revenues which are usually identified in financial performance reports.

verifiability A characteristic of accounting information referring to the ability of an independent auditor to reproduce the accounting information by examining the underlying economic events and transactions

vertical analysis A means of overcoming size differences among companies by expressing income statement items as a percentage of net sales and all balance sheet items as a percentage of total assets

vesting period A period of time during which the employee is not allowed to exercise a share option; also refers to a period after which an employee retains his or her pension benefits even if employment is terminated

virtual integration The use of information technology and partnership concepts to allow two or more entities along a value chain to act as if they were a single economic entity.

voucher Another name for the payment approval form

W

waiting time The time units spend in temporary storage waiting to be processed, moved, or inspected.

warranties Guarantees against product defects for a designated period of time after sale

wasting assets Assets consumed as they are used, including natural resources such as oil reserves, mineral deposits, or timberland; *see* natural resources

weighted average cost of capital (WACC) The discount rate where the weights are the relative percentages of debt and equity in the capital structure and are applied to the expected returns on debt and equity, respectively

weighted average method In process costing, a costing method that spreads the combined beginning inventory cost and current manufacturing costs (for materials, labour, and overhead) over the units completed and those in ending inventory on an average basis.

work-in-process inventories Partially completed goods consisting of raw materials that are in the process of being converted into a finished product.

working capital A measure of solvency, working capital is the difference between current assets and current liabilities and is the net amount of working funds available in the short run. The general equation for working capital is: Current assets minus Current liabilities.

work in process Inventory account that tracks the value of items currently being produced

work in process inventory The cost of inventories that are in the manufacturing process and have not yet reached completion

work ticket A document used to record the time a job spends in a specific manufacturing operation.

Z

z-score The outcome of the Altman Z-score bankruptcy prediction model

zero-based budgeting A variation of the minimum level approach to budgeting where every dollar of expenditure must be justified.

zero coupon bond A bond that offers no periodic interest payments but that is issued at a substantial discount from its face value

Index

D

E

I

J

K

L

T

U